Microsoft®
Windows® 98
ResourceKit

Microsoft Press

PUBLISHED BY
Microsoft Press
A Division of Microsoft Corporation
One Microsoft Way
Redmond, Washington 98052-6399

Library of Congress Cataloging-in-Publication Data
Microsoft Windows 98 Resource Kit / Microsoft Corporation.

      p.   cm.
   Includes index.
   ISBN 1-57231-644-6
    1. Microsoft Windows (Computer file)   2. Operating systems
(Computers) I. Microsoft Corporation.
QA76.76.063M5244   1998
005.4'469--dc21   98-2768
                                                  CIP

Printed and bound in the United States of America.

1 2 3 4 5 6 7 8 9 WCWC 3 2 1 0 9 8

Distributed in Canada by ITP Nelson, a division of Thomson Canada Limited.

A CIP catalogue record for this book is available from the British Library.

Microsoft Press books are available through booksellers and distributors worldwide. For further information about international editions, contact your local Microsoft Corporation office or contact Microsoft Press International directly at fax (425) 936-7329. Visit our Web site at mspress.microsoft.com.

Acquisitions Editors: Casey D. Doyle, David Clark, Anne Hamilton
Project Editor: Maureen Williams Zimmerman

Contributors to this book include the following:

Project Managers

Andrew McGehee, Ryan Marshall, Laura Burris

Lead Technical Writer

Abram Spiegelman

Technical Writers

Cheryl Jenkins, Kristin King, Pilar Ackerman, Shira Paul,
Darryl Mondrow, Dixie Crockford, Mark Wilkinson

CD Program Management

Martin Holladay, Chris Hallum

CD Online Author

Jay French

CD Development Team

Joseph Hughes, Kyle Sparks, Michelle Hofland

Editorial Team

Susan F. Serafin, Avon Murphy, Mike Scannell, Phyllis Collier, Brian Roberts

Graphic Design

Shelley Greer, Chris Blanton

Production Team

Shelley Greer, Nancy Jacobs, Sandy Dean, Candace Gearhart

Indexing

Julie Kawabata, Julie Miller, Patricia Masserman

Technical Consultants

Adam Sandford, Andy Glass, Bernie McIlroy, Bill Krueger, Bill Veghte, Billy Brackenridge, Bruce Johnson, Chris Merritt, Chuck Archer, Cliff Strom , Dan Spinazzola, Dave Alles, David Eitelbach, Eric Berman, Eric Stadter, Eugene Lin, George Allen, George Moore, Jeff Clark, Jeff Larsson, John Gray, Joseph Adamson, Karl Tussy, Lisa Halston, Michael Short, Michael Sisson, Mike Glass, Mike Laverty, Nancy Buchanan, Nick Dimmitt, Pasquale DeMaio, Paul Beane, Paul Clapman, Raja Abburi, Richard Barker, Rob McKaughan, Rob Young, Scott Harrison, Simon Smith, Tony Ka, Troy Shaw, Yuen Leung

Technical Contributors

Aaron Higgins, Aaron Reynolds, Adam Hecktman, Adrian Oney, Alan Page, Alex Hall, Alex Sutton, Alireza Dabagh, Amol Deshpande, Amy Peck, Andrew Rosen, Andy Raffman, Andy Seres, Andy Shamblin, Anne Gardiner, Annie Pearson, Anthony Leibovitz, Art Shelest, Arthur Guerra, Arvind Murching, Azfar Moazzam, Bambo Sofola, Bei-Jing Guo, Bill Parry, Brad Benefield, Brad Carpenter, Brent Ethington, Brent Ponto, Brian Hanna, Brian Lysak, Brian Schmidt, Bruce Green, Bryan Thompson, Bryan Young, Castedo Ellerman, Chad Petersen, Chee Chew, Chien-Her Ho Chin, Chris Brown , Chris Forehand, Chris Golden, Chris Steck, Christine Chang, Chuck Guy, Clark Sealls, Clay Muller,

Craig Beilinson, Crystal Webb, Cynthia Dominguez, Dan Perry, Dan Shapiro, Dave Gonsalves, Dave Parsons, Dave Sawyer, David Flenniken, David Hennessey, David S. Loudon, David Schott, Deborah Jay, Derek Jacoby, Diana Trickey, Don Martin, Dontin Wang, Douglas Dobbins, Drew Leaumont, Ed Stubbs, Eric Rockey, Ervin Peretz, Fletcher Bonds , Forrest Foltz, Frank Yerrace, Gary Mock, Gary Syck, George Hatoun, George J Rickle II, Giana Christofferson, Greg Hitchcock, Greg Jones, Greg Lowney, Günter Born, Harish Naidu, Hazel Lloyd, Henry Hammingh, Hitoshi Sekine, Isaac Heizer, James Blackwell, James Boldman, Jane Dailey, Janet Carey, Jason Cobb, Jason Garms, Jason Leznek, Jason Taylor, Jawad Khaki, Jay Arnold, Jay Borseth, Jay Stokes, Jean Saylor, Jeff Norris, Jeff Sherwin, Jeff Spencer, Jeff Taylor, Jeff Weisman, Jeff Willoughby, Jeff Witt, Jeffrey Nemecek, Jennifer Harrison, Jim Geist, Jim Hood, Jim Knowles, Jim McNelis, Jim Spoltman, Jim Taylor , Jody Lockridge, Joe Decuir, Joel Baxter, John Dunn, John Haskin, John Lee, John Paccagnan, Johnny Lee, Joseph Cheek, Josh Rice, Joshua Williams, Juan Flowers, Judy Sturholm, Julian Jiggins, Julie Sigsworth, Karl Knarr, Keith Loeber, Kennith Guajardo, Kevin Alewine, Kevin Douglas, Kevin Hinsey, Kim Akers, Kingston Wall, Klaas Langhout, Kory Ball, Larry Leach, Lee Coward, Len Smale, Leonard Severt, Linda Jeffries, Lon Barnes, Lonnie Ferguson, Loren Kohnfelder, Louise Rudnicki, Marcus Courtney, Margaret Schultz, Mario Goertzel, Mario Goertzel, Marius Bulau, Mark Kieffer, Mark Meyers, Mark Newell, Mark Patterson, Mark Schreffler, Martin Puryear, Marwan Batrouni, Mary Kirtland, MaryAnn Snyder, Matt Squires, Matthew Anderson, Maureen Sullivan, Michael Bernard, Michael Coleman, Michael Dennis, Michael Leo, Michael Shomaker, Michael Tinker, Michael Winser, Mike Flora, Mike Zintel, Mitchell Rundle, Mohammad (Shabbir) Alam, Munil Shah, Nigel Haslock, Nk Srinivas, Noel Cross, Noland Angara, Patty Andrade, Paul Midgen, Peggy Foerch, Peter Ford, Peter Hong, Peter Sankiewicz , Peter Stewart, Peter Zeng, Pierre-Yves Santerre, Pradeep Bahl, Ramesh Vyaghrapuri, Randy Grandle, Raymond Chen, Rena Utterstrom , Renee Ford, Rhonda Marshall, Rich Hagemeyer, Richard Gerschwiler, Richard Saunders, Rob Greenwell, Rob Wickham , Robert Corrington, Robert Gross, Robert Ingman, Robert Simpkins, Robert Tucker, Ross Speiran, Russ Kemsley, Russell Borland, Sabrina Ford, Sachin Kukreja, Saji Abraham, Samantha O'Hanlon, Sandeep Sahasrabudhe, Sankar Ramasubramanian, Santosh Jodh, Scott Brown, Sean Edmison, Shaun Pierce, Simon Maddock, Stephanie Selden, Stephen Toulouse, Steve Mitchell, Steve Powers, Stuart Higgins, Stuart Kwan, Tami Beutel Fosmark, Tammi McQueen-Smith, Terence Spies, Tim Moore, Tim Schreck, Timothy Johnson, Todd Emond, Tom Adams, Tom Lennon, Tom Yaryan, Trudy Culbreth, Vadim Eydelman, Vicki Milton, Vishal Jain, Vlad Sadovsky, Wassef Haroun, Wayne Cook, Wayne Schroll, Wes Keetch, Willem van der Hoeven, Zoe Emmanuel

Third-Party Contributors

Andre Kutz (Artisoft), Corey Plett (Novell), Ed Herlihy (Sun Microsystems), Jeff Curless (Digital Equipment Corp.), Nick Adler (Banyan)

Advanced Micro Devices (hardware contributor)

Contents

Part 3   Networking and Intranets

Part 4   Internet and Communication Tools

Introduction

Welcome to the *Microsoft® Windows® 98 Resource Kit*.

The *Microsoft Windows 98 Resource Kit* consists of this comprehensive volume and a single compact disc containing the Resource Kit tools and utilities that make it easier for you to get the most out of Windows 98.

The *Microsoft Windows 98 Resource Kit* presents detailed information on the Windows 98 operating system, plus topics that are either new for this release or reflect issues that our Technical Support people consider timely and important. You should consider this information to be an in-depth, technical supplement to the online documentation included as part of the Windows 98 product. It does not replace that information as the source for learning how to use the product features and programs.

About the Microsoft Windows 98 Resource Kit

This book, written in cooperation with the Windows 98 development team, includes the following major parts:

Part 1, "Deployment and Installation," provides an overview of the strategies for deploying Windows 98 throughout an organization. The chapters in this section describe the steps involved in setup, and provide details on the different methods for deploying Windows 98.

Part 2, "System Configuration," describes the options for configuring machines running Windows 98, including configuring and deploying the Active Desktop and Active Channels, using Profiles and System Policies, configuring security, and using the new FAT32 file system. In addition, chapters in this section cover printing, multimedia, and WebTV.

Part 3, "Networking and Intranets," covers networking with Windows 98, including using Windows 98 on Microsoft networks, Novell® NetWare® networks, and other networks. This section also covers remote networking and mobile computing.

Part 4, "Internet and Communication Tools," discusses the new suite of tools that let you share information on your intranet or over the Internet. Chapters in this section cover the new Internet Explorer 4 browsing software, tools such as NetMeeting™ and NetShow™, modems, and the new Outlook™ Express electronic mail client.

Part 5, "System Management," provides important information for administering Windows 98 both locally and remotely. Chapters in this section discuss device management, applications support, performance tuning, and troubleshooting.

Part 6, "Architecture," provides a detailed look at the inner workings of Windows 98. Topics covered include general Windows 98 architecture, Windows 98 network architecture, the new hardware management model, and the registry.

Part 7, "Appendixes," contains a glossary and useful reference information, and provides detailed information on Windows 98 system files and INF files.

Resource Kit Support

There is now a source for ongoing technical information on the Microsoft Press ResourceLink Web site. ResourceLink is the essential extension to the Resource Kits and offers the most up-to-date technical information, tools, and utilities for the support professional. You can access ResourceLink at:

http://mspress.microsoft.com/reslink.

The text and utilities that come with the *Microsoft Windows 98 Resource Kit* are not supported under any Microsoft standard support program or service. However, Microsoft Press provides corrections and updates for the *Microsoft Windows 98 Resource Kit* through the support area on the ResourceLink Web site.

Please refer to the license agreement printed on the last paper pages of this book for the conditions that apply to your use of the software on the included compact disc.

Resource Kit Feedback

If you have any comments or ideas regarding this book or the companion compact disc that are not addressed by the ResourceLink Web site, please send us your feedback via electronic mail to:

Rkinput@Microsoft.com

Microsoft will, at its sole discretion, address issues and bugs reported in this manner relating to the *Microsoft Windows 98 Resource Kit* text and utilities. This electronic mail address is only for issues relating to the *Microsoft Windows 98 Resource Kit* text and utilities—not for the Windows 98 operating system software.

Note Rkinput@Microsoft.com will ignore all e-mail regarding Windows 98 that is not directly related to the *Microsoft Windows 98 Resource Kit.*

Resource Kit Compact Disc

The compact disc that accompanies the *Microsoft Windows 98 Resource Kit* contains tools and utilities that apply to information in the *Microsoft Windows 98 Resource Kit*. This includes a collection of information resources, tools, and utilities that can make networking and working with the Windows 98 platform even easier.

Please refer to the license agreement printed on the last paper pages of this book for the conditions that apply to your use of the software on the included compact disc.

Installing the Resource Kit Tools and Utilities

The *Microsoft Windows 98 Resource Kit* compact disc includes a wide variety of tools and utilities to help you work more efficiently with Windows 98, including:

- Deployment tools
- Desktop and file tools
- Troubleshooting and support tools
- Administration tools
- Registry tools
- Scripting tools

▶ **To install the Resource Kit tools and utilities**

1. Insert the *Microsoft Windows 98 Resource Kit* compact disc into your CD-ROM drive.

   Your CD-ROM drive should automatically detect the compact disc and start the Setup program. If it does not, follow the steps below.

2. Click **Start**, and then click **Run**.

3. In the **Run** dialog box, type the following command and then click **OK**:

   D:\SETUP.EXE

   (where D: is your CD-ROM drive letter).

▶ **To access the Resource Kit tools, utilities, and online Help**

1. Click **Start,** and then click **Programs**.

2. From the **Programs** submenu, click **Windows 98 Resource Kit**. The
   following options are available on **Windows 98 Resource Kit** submenu.

Option	Description
Release Notes	Contains important current information regarding the Windows 98 Resource Kit compact disc.
Resource Kit Online Book	An online, fully searchable version of this book.
Resource Kit Tools Help	This online help file contains descriptions of and instructions for using the Resource Kit tools.
Tools Management Console	Provides a graphical interface for accessing all the tools, utilities, and documentation on the compact disc.

PART 1

Deployment and Installation

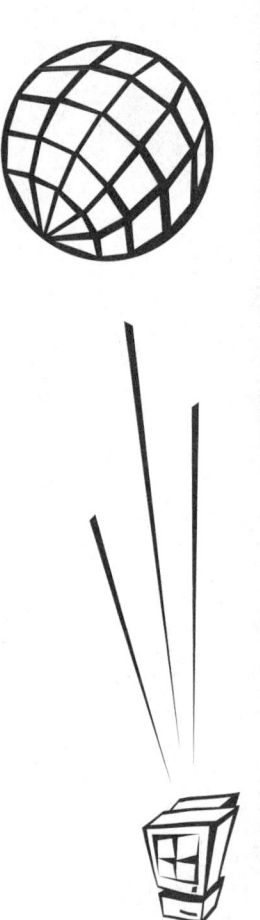

C H A P T E R   1

Deployment Strategy

1

This chapter provides information to help you define the best deployment strategy and plans for your organization. Because every organization is unique, not all of the information presented here may apply to you. We strongly recommend that you thoroughly test these guidelines in a pilot test environment before rolling out Microsoft® Windows® 98. If you are comfortable with the early planning phases of deployment, you can skip ahead to "Deciding on the Preferred Client Configuration" later in this chapter.

In This Chapter

See Also

- For information about preparing a Windows 98 installation, see Chapter 2, "Setting Up Windows 98."

- For more information on customizing an installation, see Chapter 3, "Custom Installations."

- For more information on automating an installation, see Chapter 4, "Automated Installations."

Overview of a Deployment Process

There is more than one way to deploy Windows 98 in an organization. This chapter describes the following deployment process for Windows 98:

- Reviewing Windows 98
- Preparing the Planning and Support teams
- Identifying the preferred network-client configuration
- Performing lab tests of the client configuration
- Planning the pilot rollout
- Conducting the pilot rollout
- Finalizing the rollout plan
- Rolling out Windows 98

For the purpose of illustrating this deployment process, this chapter uses five teams: Executive, Planning, Installation, Support, and Training. Your organization may or may not have teams that resemble the ones presented here, but the information presented here should help you come up with your own deployment process and teams.

- The Executive team includes the deployment project manager (usually the head of the Information Systems department) and members of the executive committee of the corporation. This team must include one or more individuals with decision-making authority over company policies and procedures.

- The Planning team includes the deployment project manager, key Installation team members, and a representative from each of the Support and Training teams.

- The Installation team includes technicians and individuals who will be conducting the installation. This team must include a specialist in 32-bit applications who can evaluate the proposed Windows 98 configuration for compatibility.

- The Support team includes staff of the help desk or Support department, and select individuals from the Planning team. This team develops a plan for supporting Windows 98 during and after deployment, integrating new methods and processes as needed into the existing support scheme.

- The Training team includes individuals responsible for user training.

Reviewing Windows 98 Features

In the first phase of the deployment process, the Executive and Planning teams learn about Windows 98 features and benefits. Those responsible for planning and conducting the rollout learn how Windows 98 helps reduce support costs and increase business profitability. Publications available from Microsoft Press® and from independent industry analysts provide the information you need.

Preparing the Teams

The team preparation phase involves gathering the resources, including equipment, software, and staff, to properly plan for testing and evaluating Windows 98. Members of the Support team should receive training during this phase.

Acquiring Staff and Software

The deployment project manager participates in the Executive team and leads the Planning team. Although this individual is usually the head of the Information Systems department, the executive committee may find a more appropriate individual, depending on the organization.

When setting up the Planning team, it is important to include a set of individuals representing the groups involved in the deployment process. This includes people from the Corporate Support and Employee Training departments, the Corporate Standards Committee, and key Installation team members. Individuals from the Finance and Accounting group will need to take part in planning and evaluation later on, but need not be assigned to the team for the full duration of the deployment process.

Your Installation team should include an applications expert who can evaluate 32-bit applications run with Windows 98.

Obtain Windows 98 during this phase. Microsoft recommends that you purchase the compact-disc version, so that you can use the administrative software tools not provided on the floppy disks.

Conducting a Sample Inventory

You must survey a representative sample of your network to identify the hardware and software typically used on client and server computers. By doing this sample inventory of your company's active equipment, you can accurately simulate the organizational environment in the lab. Such a simulation helps you make broad decisions about your company's computing infrastructure, such as choice of protocol or the default desktop configuration as it pertains to applications.

Software management tools are available to query computers on the network for hardware and software configurations. For detailed information about a large number of computers on a network, use a system management program, such as Microsoft Systems Management Server, to conduct the inventory.

Testing Lab Setup and Equipment

To evaluate and test the Windows 98 installation process effectively, set aside enough physical space and assemble a sufficient number of computers to test everything from automated Setup to hand-tuning options for the local computer. In addition, if your network environment includes the use of portable computers that dial in to the company, or if you use additional servers or mainframe computers for business data, make sure that the lab computers have full access to the network and an analog phone line.

It is important that you test and implement all Windows 98 features comprehensively in the lab with all mission-critical and non-critical business applications before moving to the pilot installation.

Training the Teams

By reviewing specific portions of the *Microsoft Windows 98 Resource Kit*, the Installation and Planning teams can gain an extensive understanding of Microsoft Windows 98 features and functionality. A review of the *Getting Started* guide included in the box and of the chapters contained in Part 1, "Deployment and Installation" of the *Microsoft Windows 98 Resource Kit*, can provide the teams with the information necessary to evaluate product features for system configuration.

Support team members must become familiar with all information in the *Microsoft Windows 98 Resource Kit* to prepare for their role in the deployment process. For extensive training, team members can receive instruction at a Microsoft Authorized Technical Education Center (ATEC) and participate in the Certified Professional program. Call (800) SOLPROV or (800) 765-7768 for information about authorized training offered for Windows 98 and the Certified Professional program, and for referral to a local Microsoft Solution Provider ATEC.

For additional information about Windows 98, particularly the background of its design and the history of its development, team members can read *Inside Windows 98* from Microsoft Press. This book contains guidelines and tips for applications developers working with Windows 98.

For other training information, see Appendix I, "Windows 98 Resource Directory."

Deciding on the Preferred Client Configuration

Detailed analysis is required to determine your preferred client-computer configuration. Starting with the ideal configuration, which uses the most functional and best-performing client software, evaluate each feature against your organization's needs and environment to determine whether the feature is appropriate and compatible. If you are considering different configuration alternatives, repeat this evaluation for each configuration.

The following sections describe feature options and decisions to evaluate in specifying the network client configuration.

Configuration Layout

When deciding where to place Windows 98 files, consider how the computers will be used, and evaluate the benefits of each placement option. Determine whether the computers are personal workstations, portable computers that occasionally connect to the network, or computers that are shared by more than one person.

Key Features of the Ideal Configuration

This section provides detailed discussions of the features that might be included in an ideal network client configuration.

Using a 32-bit, Protected-mode Network Client

For best performance, select a network client that uses a 32-bit redirector for network access. Windows 98 includes the 32-bit Microsoft Client for NetWare Networks and the Client for Microsoft Networks; each of these has a 32-bit redirector. The benefits of using a 32-bit, protected-mode client include the following:

- Provides for easy installation and configuration using built-in Windows 98 tools.
- Uses no real-mode memory.
- Provides faster data I/O across the network.
- Offers greater stability than real-mode redirectors.

- Allows more than one redirector to be run at a time, and thereby enables access to servers for multiple networks without having to reload the operating system for a new network client.

- Makes networking seamless in the Windows 98 user interface; users can browse the server for multiple networks in Network Neighborhood, all within the same name space—they do not need to know which type of network they are browsing.

If you are using another type of network, contact your network vendor regarding the availability of a 32-bit, protected-mode network client.

Using a 32-bit, Protected-mode Protocol

If you select a 32-bit, protected-mode network client, by default Windows 98 also sets up a 32-bit, protected-mode protocol. Even if you are running a real-mode client such as the Novell 3.*x* workstation shell (NETX) with a real-mode implementation of Internet Packet Exchange/Sequenced Packet Exchange (IPX/SPX) to access NetWare servers, you can still load the 32-bit version of the Microsoft IPX/SPX-compatible protocol. The benefits of adding the protected-mode protocol are better performance and better stability for network communications to servers that are not running NetWare (for example, computers running Windows 98 or Microsoft Windows NT®).

In addition, for protocols, such as Transmission Control Protocol/Internet Protocol (TCP/IP), the Microsoft 32-bit version enables additional functionality (such as the ability to use Dynamic Host Configuration Protocol [DHCP] and Windows Internet Naming Service [WINS] servers) that dynamically set the Internet Protocol (IP) addresses and resolve computer names for client computers on the network. Each protocol has a number of benefits, as discussed in Chapter 15, "Network Adapters and Protocols."

Using the Latest Network Adapter Drivers

For best performance, use the latest network adapter drivers available. These should be network driver interface specification (NDIS) 5.0–compatible drivers that provide Plug and Play capabilities. Such drivers take up no real-mode memory and can be loaded or unloaded dynamically as required.

The only instances in which you would not use the latest drivers are:

- The newest driver is not available for your network adapter.
- Your site requires Open Datalink Interface (ODI) cards and drivers.

Recommended Features for Network Clients

The following optional features are recommended for your preferred configuration. These features define how Windows 98 will be installed and administered in your organization. Some features that enable centralized and remote management of Windows 98 are much easier to install initially, than they are to roll out after Windows 98 has been installed. Microsoft recommends that you include these remote management features, whether you intend to use them or not. By doing this, the potential benefits of having them installed outweighs the cost of including them in your initial installation.

Using Group Policies

For centralized administration of client computers, you must enable Group policies. Group policies allow you to centrally edit and control individual user and computer configurations. For example, if you want to place a custom **Start** menu on user desktops or limit access to Control Panel options, Group policies make it easy to do so for a large number of users from a central location.

For information on the types of restrictions available and for details on how to implement system policies, see Chapter 8, "System Policies."

Using User Profiles

There are two reasons for enabling User Profiles. First, User Profiles must be enabled for Group Policies to work. Second, with user profiles, users can use personalized desktop settings each time they log on to a computer. This is especially useful for multiple users sharing a single computer who want to customize their desktops and have those custom settings loaded at logon. Conversely, a single user can move between computers using the same profile if the administrator stores that profile on the server. An administrator can also take advantage of profiles to require that a mandatory desktop configuration be loaded each time a user logs on. The ability to change profile settings can be controlled by the administrator. For information on how to use user profiles, see Chapter 7, "User Profiles."

Using the Windows Scripting Host

The Windows Scripting Host provides a low-memory scripting host that is ideal for non-interactive scripting needs, such as logon scripting or administrative scripting. In combination with Group Policies the Windows Scripting Host enables comprehensive configuration management of the Windows 98 desktop.

Enabling Remote Administration

To administer a computer's registry remotely, first install the network service called Microsoft Remote Registry Service, enable user-level security, and enable the Remote Administration feature. Remote administration capabilities allow you to conduct a variety of tasks remotely over the network such as administering the file system, sharing or restricting directories, and querying and making changes to the registry. If you plan to do any of these tasks, be sure to enable this feature during Windows 98 installation. For information on adding the Microsoft Remote Registry Service and other network services using Microsoft Batch 98 and INF Installer (Infinst.exe), see Chapter 3, "Custom Installations."

You should not enable Remote Administration if you do not need these services, because doing so causes unnecessary, extra processes to run on the client computer and on the network. These extra remote services could theoretically be used by individuals on the network—provided they knew the appropriate password—to access information on client computers. However, Windows 98 comes with security capabilities to protect against unauthorized use of the Remote Registry Service. For more information, see Chapter 23, "System and Remote Administration Tools."

Using User-level Security

User-level security is based on user account lists stored on Windows NT or Novell NetWare servers. The user accounts specify which users have access rights on the network. Windows 98 passes a user's request for access to the servers for validation. Pass-through user-level security protects shared network resources by requiring that a security provider authenticate a user's request to access resources.

User-level security is required for remote administration of the registry and for network access to full user profiles. For more information about implementing security in Windows 98, see Chapter 9, "Security."

Performing the Lab Test

This phase involves four significant efforts: preparing the site, conducting the installation, testing the installation, and restoring the system.

Preparing the Test Site and Equipment

Preparing the site involves ensuring that the location of each computer, the computer itself, and the hard disk in particular are all ready for Windows 98 to be installed. In terms of the physical site, make sure that you have the appropriate jacks for connecting to the network.

For the computer itself, make sure that it has the appropriate hard disk space, RAM (16 MB minimum), and processor (486DX/66 MHz minimum) to run Windows 98.

In addition, run virus detection, disk scanning, and defragmentation programs on the computer to correct any problems before installation. Although the computer may appear to be operating properly, software upgrades often uncover hardware or software problems because of the way they read and write data to the hard disk. Correct any such problems before installing Windows 98.

When preparing the site, be sure to back up critical data, the registry, and configuration files for the system, in case the installation fails or you need to revert to the previous operating system for some reason. This includes backing up INI files (such as System.ini), GRP files, Autoexec.bat, Config.sys, and all key data files. As an added precaution, create a system startup disk and back up the Windows and MS-DOS® directories and all the files in the root directory.

If you need to automate the restoration, consider using a commercial backup program instead of copying the files by hand.

Caution   Replacing configuration files alone, such as INI files, is not sufficient to restore your system.

For more information on system requirements, backup procedures, and other preparation steps for installing Windows 98, see Chapter 2, "Setting Up Windows 98."

Installing Windows 98 on Test Computers

Before setting up Windows 98 for the first time, verify that the computer's existing network is working properly. Then use Part 1, "Deployment and Installation," in the *Microsoft Windows 98 Resource Kit* to help you install and configure Windows 98 correctly Chapter 3, "Custom Installations," includes instructions on how to customize the installations using setup scripts. Take note of which options you want to predefine as entries for the Msbatch.inf file used for the setup script.

Testing the Installation

After you have set up a computer with Windows 98, you must run a variety of tests to make sure that it runs correctly on your network and that you can still perform all your usual tasks. Use your own testing methodology, or test the following to verify correct system operation:

- Connect to and browse the network.

- Set up a printer and test printing to local and network printers.

- Open, run, and close applications on both the client computer and the server.
- Shut down completely.

Make sure to test all mission-critical applications for proper function. If you encounter problems, try removing related features from the proposed configuration as a solution. Document any changes made to the original configuration.

If the preferred client configuration works as expected, you may also want to conduct additional testing of the optional software features and components in Windows 98. This can help you determine whether you are running Windows 98 optimally. For this kind of testing, conduct side-by-side evaluations on two computers, changing individual features on each one, to determine the following:

- Performance in terms of responsiveness and throughput
- Ease of use
- Stability
- Compatibility
- Functionality

To evaluate network client software for Novell NetWare, run your network performance tests in the following configurations:

- Windows 98 as a new installation using all protected-mode components, Microsoft Client for NetWare Networks (included with Windows 98), and the Microsoft Service for NetWare Directory Services client, if you are connecting to Novell 4.*x* servers that do not have bindery-emulation enabled.
- Windows 98 added to an existing installation of Windows 3.*x* and NetWare, using Client for NetWare Networks and protected-mode networking support components (NDIS adapter drivers).
- Windows 98 using Novell Client for Windows 95/98 and protected-mode drivers.

Perform several common tasks such as connecting to the network, administering a remote NetWare server, and so on, to test for ease of use. Similarly, run any business-specific NetWare applications under Microsoft Client for NetWare Networks to make sure that they are compatible. Any stability issues should become apparent during this testing.

When you have identified a configuration that performs well during testing, test the same configuration using other hardware from your company.

See Part 3, "Networking and Intranets," in the *Microsoft Windows 98 Resource Kit* to understand the differences in functionality between network clients.

Testing the Restoration Process

After thorough testing of the preferred client configuration, completely restore one of the test computers to the previous client configuration, and document the process. The degree to which you need to test and restore the computer depends on the tools available. Chapter 5, "Setup Technical Discussion," documents how to remove Windows 98 and restore the previous operating system manually.

Planning the Pilot Rollout

This phase involves three major efforts: automating the installation, documenting the logistics of the pilot installation, and preparing the user training plan. These efforts are a combination of planning and lab-testing work.

Installing the Source Files for Setup

Designate a network server that will be used as the source file for installing Windows 98 over the network using custom setup scripts, and install the Windows 98 source files on a server.

For more information on installing Windows 98 over the network using custom scripts, see Chapter 3, "Custom Installations." Document any changes to this process.

Automating the Installation

Automating the installation is a key step in reducing the cost of migration. By creating a setup script with predetermined answers for installation questions, the installation process can run from start to finish without user intervention. It is also possible to "push" the installation from the server, so that you can install Windows 98 on an individual personal computer without ever touching the computer. This automation work is done in the lab, prior to conducting the pilot rollout.

Automating the installation consists of creating a setup script, setting up Windows 98 on the server, and creating a push installation process. With a setup script you can perform a hands-free installation, so that the user need not respond to any prompts or even touch the computer during Windows 98 Setup.

Installing Windows 98 over the network requires that you install the Windows 98 source files on an installation point in a network server. Installing Windows 98 source files on the server is the simple process of copying the Windows 98 folder from your Windows 98 compact disk to an installation point in a network server.

Depending on the common network configuration at your site, you may determine that you need to remove a line from one or more configuration files as a global procedure before starting Windows 98 Setup. For example, you may want to use a protected-mode protocol such as Microsoft TCP/IP during Setup instead of the real-mode version of TCP/IP currently used on the target computers. In addition, users may be running certain terminate-and-stay-resident (TSR) programs or applications that should be closed before running Windows 98 Setup. In these cases, you can modify Netdet.ini on NetWare networks as described in Chapter 17, "Windows 98 on Third-Party Networks." On other networks, including Microsoft networks, modify the [Install] section of your setup script to automate these changes. For more information, see Appendix D, "Msbatch.inf Parameters for Setup Scripts."

In addition, you may want to manually add other files to the installation point on the server, such as custom bitmaps for screens or a predefined Wrkgrp.ini file for workgroup organization, so that client computers are fully configured when Windows 98 is installed.

Creating a push installation process involves doing some final work on the server, such as editing the logon script for the user. System management software such as Microsoft Systems Management Server can also be used to start the installation centrally. If you plan to use system management software in automating the installation, make sure it has been acquired and tested.

For more information on customizing and automating installations, see Chapter 3, "Custom Installations" and Chapter 4, "Automated Installations."

Documenting Rollout Logistics

To document your rollout logistics, determine the timing and the process for pilot installation, and choose the pilot user group.

Although it is a test, the first pilot rollout sets the tone for and presents an example of the final rollout, so it is important to be completely prepared in all aspects of the rollout. This requires that you determine the time it will take for installation, the personnel and tools needed to facilitate the process, and the overall schedule.

Start by identifying the target computers and their location. Then use the following list as the basis of your checklist for rollout logistics:

- Has a verified backup been performed for each of the target computers?

- Have passwords been reset for CMOS, the network, and applications?

- Have virus checking and disk defragmentation been performed?

- How many systems will be installed per day? Start with a conservative estimate and then increase or decrease the number, based on your experiences with the initial installations.

- At what time of day should the installations occur? You may want to schedule installations to occur on weekdays after normal business hours or on weekends.

- Who are the pilot users? Choose a pilot user group or department that is willing and able to accommodate the rollout. This group, ranging from 15 to 50 persons, should be representative of your overall user base. Try not to select a department that is attempting to meet a schedule deadline during the rollout or a group that is traditionally slow in adopting new technology.

- What is the schedule for pilot installations? When determining the installation time for the pilot rollout, base the projections on how long it takes for installation of an individual computer; remember to schedule the downtime for each user.

- Who will participate in the installations? In addition to the Installation team members, be sure to assign a system administrator with full rights on the server, including the right to administer mail or database server passwords.

- Is the deployment methodology as automated as possible?

As you develop the checklist of logistics, consider your goals for the pilot rollout and the factors that define its success. For example, you might set a percentage for successful upgrades or for automated installations that, if achieved, would indicate that the rollout had been successful. Document these goals and criteria, so that teams can monitor performance against them during the rollout.

Notifying Users of the Rollout

Another step at this stage is informing users about the pilot rollout plan. You can use a videotape presentation, an interoffice memo, or a company meeting as the means for communicating with users about the rollout. Regardless of the form used, the message must explain to users the benefits of moving to Windows 98 and describe the overall plan and process by which each group or department will make the move. This makes it easier for your users to plan for and accept the migration to Windows 98 as part of their schedules.

Developing User Training

The first steps in developing a training plan are to acquire a training lab, set up computers in the lab, and appoint a team member as instructor. (If in-house resources are not available, use a vendor to develop and conduct the training.) The instructor will be responsible for creating and testing the training program.

There are a number of training approaches and a variety of tools you can use. A recommended approach is to divide the training into sessions corresponding to three distinct topics: The Basics, Corporate-Specific Applications, and Customization.

The session entitled "The Basics" includes the top eight functions any user needs to know to accomplish daily work. Table 1.1 lists these functions.

Table 1.1   Top eight basic functions in using Windows 98

Function	To perform the function, use this
Run programs, load documents, find a file	**Start** button
Change settings	Control Panel
Get help on a specific topic	F1 or Help command
Switch between applications	Taskbar
Minimize, maximize, and close windows	Window buttons
Browse your hard disk	My Computer and Windows Explorer
Connect to a network drive	Network Neighborhood
Print a document	Point and Print

Windows 98 Help and the *Getting Started* book provide the information you need to train users in the basics. You can access the online version of the *Getting Started* book by clicking **Start**, pointing to **Help**, clicking the **Contents** tab, and selecting the **Getting Started Book**. Schedule training sessions of no more than 30 minutes each; in each session, users receive *just enough* information to be productive using Windows 98.

The "Corporate-Specific Applications" session varies by the environment and the types of applications run on the network. This session should focus on the top five to ten functions that will change because of the upgrade to Windows 98.

The "Customization" session is intended for more experienced users. The purpose of this session is to provide information and guidance that will help these users learn on their own after the training, and teach them how to work more productively with Windows 98. These topics could include:

- Adding items to the **Start** button.
- Adding items to the desktop (move, copy, shortcut).
- Using options controlled by the right mouse button.
- Adding a new device (for example, a printer).
- Changing the desktop (for example, screen saver settings).

After creating and testing the program, schedule training sessions to occur immediately before the rollout so that the instruction is *just in time,* ensuring that users retain most of what they learn by putting it to use right away.

Developing the Support Plan

Similar to the training plan, the support plan must be ready to go online the first day you begin performing Windows 98 installations. Because the quality of support available during the pilot rollout will be seen as an indicator of the quality of the rollout as a whole, it is important that you plan carefully to make sure effective support is available.

Staff the Support team for your pilot rollout with some of your best technicians dedicated solely to the pilot group for the first few weeks. The assigned technicians should carry pagers or be available by telephone at all times, to give immediate assistance to users. Help users help themselves by editing Windows 98 Help with company-specific information on applications or features. Doing so requires placing an Oem.cnt file and your custom Help file in the user's \Windows directory. For more information about Oem.cnt and the format of Windows 98 Help files, see the *Microsoft Windows Platform Software Development Kit*.

Conducting the Pilot Rollout

In conducting the pilot rollout, you simulate the final installation process, test the capabilities and performance of the system, survey user feedback, and make adjustments as needed. Repeat this process for 32-bit applications.

Simulating the Installation Process

The schedule for the pilot rollout should simulate—on a smaller scale—the schedule of the final rollout. As you conduct the pilot rollout, you may find that certain tasks take more or less time than expected, that some tasks need to be added, or that some tasks can be left out. Modify the pilot rollout schedule to account for such changes, and use the pilot schedule for projecting the final rollout timetable.

Testing Windows 98 Performance and Capabilities

In addition to the technicians responsible for conducting the pilot installation, extra technicians should be assigned to measure, observe, and test the installation. By tracking the time per installation, handling problems that arise, and identifying areas for improvement or automation, these individuals help ensure the success of both the pilot and final rollouts by making the installation more efficient.

In addition, after Windows 98 has been installed, these technicians test system capabilities, such as remote administration, for proper operation and monitor the client computers for performance, stability, and functionality, highlighting any inconsistencies with the lab configuration.

Surveying Users for Feedback

The final part of the pilot rollout involves surveying the users to gauge their satisfaction and proficiency with the new installation and to evaluate the level of training and support provided. Test users' proficiency by having them perform a few common tasks or use several of the new features in Windows 98; for example, have them register their survey results on the server.

When the survey results have been collected, combine them with the ideas for improvements identified during the pilot rollout. Use this information to prepare a checklist of open issues that must be resolved prior to the final rollout. Then assign team members to take the actions necessary to solve problems or make improvements. Indicate on the checklist how and when each item was resolved, adjusting the deployment plan if appropriate.

Finalizing the Rollout Plan

The final rollout plan is an extension of the pilot planning process, with the added steps of documenting, budgeting, and carrying out the final logistics. As you perform these steps, you should also update the policies and practices guidelines governing network and computer use in your company, and create a template for a central database that tracks specific configurations and uses of each network computer.

Completing the Rollout Logistics and Budget

As you prepare for final rollout, estimate the length and scope of the overall installation process. Also plan for all tools needed to complete the process within the stated time frame. If necessary, propose a formal budget for the company-wide implementation and present it to management for approval. Your budget should include the costs for personnel and resources, such as system management software.

After obtaining any necessary approval, purchase the resources required to facilitate the installation. If you need additional staff, be sure to hire experienced and qualified individuals for the team, and train them extensively before starting.

Complete your training, communication, and staffing plans for the final rollout at this time.

Updating the Policies and Practices Guidelines

Prior to final rollout, update all company policies regarding employees' use of the network and computer. Make sure to cover items such as password length and expiration requirements, and the level of approval needed to obtain remote dial-up privileges.

In addition, update the corporate standards lists for hardware and software usage; use these as a reference for bringing all computers into compliance during the rollout process.

Because Windows 98 makes possible the use of many new 32-bit applications and of Plug and Play–compliant hardware, these new products should be added to the list, and their older counterparts should be deleted.

Creating a Template for the Rollout Database

Use a template to create a central database for monitoring the progress of the rollout and to document any areas requiring further action. During preparations for the final rollout, create the template, using appropriate database management software. Complete the template with configuration information for every computer and user in the company, and place the template on the server. Then, during company-wide installation, the Installation team fills in the template for each computer and user, indicating whether any additional upgrading is needed. The team can then use the template to track open items following the rollout and to measure actual progress against original objectives.

Rolling Out Windows 98

Following the weeks of planning, organization, testing, communication, and training, the deployment teams and your organization as a whole should be ready for a full-scale rollout of Windows 98. The extensive preparation for this event may make deployment seem almost routine for the teams involved; however, that is exactly the kind of uncomplicated rollout a systems administrator dreams of. After completing the installations, users may not know how they got their work done without Windows 98.

C H A P T E R 2

Setting Up Windows 98

## 2

This chapter provides an overview of the new features of the Microsoft Windows 98 Setup program. It also provides a guide to the installation process with detailed information for preparing to run and running Windows 98 Setup.

If you want to install Windows 98 on more than one computer, or want to deploy it in a large organization, you can use this chapter for installing Windows 98 on a test computer in a pilot lab. You can then test the configuration and features that are most suitable for your organization without affecting your production environment. When you are satisfied with your test configuration, you can customize and automate your installations as explained in Chapter 3, "Custom Installations" and Chapter 4, "Automated Installations," respectively.

In This Chapter

See Also

- For information about customizing Microsoft Windows 98 installations with setup scripts, see Chapter 3, "Custom Installations."

- For information about automating Microsoft Windows 98 installations, see Chapter 4, "Automated Installations."

- For information about the parameters that can be used in setup scripts, see Appendix D, "Msbatch.inf Parameters for Setup Scripts."

Overview

This section provides an overview of the new features in Windows 98 Setup, what is different between Windows 98 and Windows 95 Setup, and an overview of the installation process you need to follow for a successful Windows 98 installation.

What Is New in Setup

Over the past two years, Windows 95 has had two supplemental releases, called OEM Services Releases (OSR-1 and OSR-2) to support new hardware and provide the latest Internet software. Windows 98 is both a retail and an original equipment manufacturer (OEM) release that incorporates all of the OSR-1, OSR-2, and Universal Serial Bus (USB) updates combined with new features and functionality, including the Internet Explorer 4 browsing software.

Windows 98 Setup makes the installation process faster and reduces the amount of user input. It provides the following enhancements:

- A more efficient Setup reduces the number of steps in the Setup process and uses the existing computer configuration for identifying legacy hardware.

- A Setup Wizard information bar that makes it easier for you to track installation progress.

- A mandatory Windows 98 Startup Disk allows you to start your computer in the event you cannot start your computer from its hard disk.

- A new cabinet file (CAB file) structure makes Setup faster. (A *cabinet* is a file that contains pieces of one or more files, usually compressed.)

- Enumeration of Plug and Play hardware occurs during the first boot portion of Setup. Enumeration is performed before detection to reduce hardware detection problems and errors. Existing devices are also verified during Setup. If verification fails, Setup performs full hardware detection.

- Anti-virus check.

The following sections explain these enhancements in detail.

A More Efficient Setup

The amount of user input required to set up Windows 98 is greatly reduced, making Windows 98 Setup more efficient than Windows 95 Setup. The most important enhancements that make Windows 98 Setup more efficient include the following:

Minimum User Input and Fewer Steps. The number of Setup steps has been reduced from twelve to five. All input required for installing Windows 98 is requested at the beginning of Setup. Once you provide the required information and have removed the Startup Disk, you can leave your computer unattended and come back to a computer that is ready to use.

Faster Legacy Hardware Detection. Windows 98 uses the current system configuration for identifying the legacy components. When running Setup from inside Windows 95, Setup verifies settings; if these are not accurate, it performs full legacy hardware detection. If you start Setup from MS-DOS, legacy hardware detection is performed after your computer is restarted for the first time.

Automatic Restart After Setup. Restarting the computer is now automatic, eliminating the need for user input. There is a 15 second delay to notify users that a reboot is going to take place.

Setup Wizard Information Bar

It is now easier to watch how Setup is progressing with the new Setup Wizard information bar located on the left side of the Setup screen, as shown in the following figure.

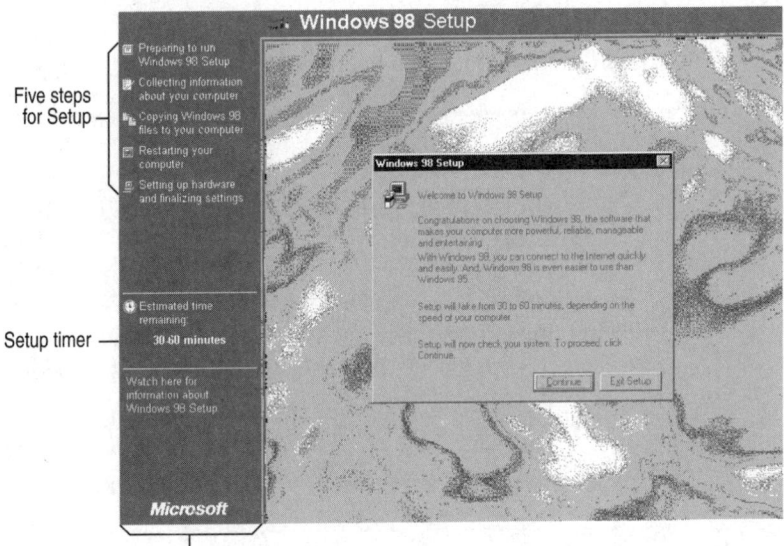

Five steps for Setup —

Setup timer —

Setup Wizard information bar

Windows 98 has a timer near the bottom of the Setup Wizard information bar that identifies the estimated time remaining to complete the installation. While Setup extracts the Precopy CAB files, it performs a throughput calculation to determine the time remaining to complete setup.

Note The timer is not a good indicator for the actual time remaining if Setup stops responding.

Startup Disk

The Startup Disk now contains generic, real-mode ATAPI CD-ROM and small computer system interface (SCSI) drivers. This allows CD-ROM devices to function when the protected-mode of the user interface is not available.

New Cabinet File Structure

The cabinet (CAB) file structure introduced in Windows 95 has changed in Windows 98 to make Setup faster. Windows 98 groups CAB files by function, for example, all related CAB files for network installation are in the same CAB file (Net#.cab). Also, if certain files are not needed for a particular type of installation, they are not copied.

In Windows 95 most of the files were contained in a Win95#.cab structure. The rest of the files were included in the Mini.cab and Precopy#.cab files.

About Cabinet Files

The Windows 98 files are stored as cabinet files (*.cab). A cabinet is a normal file that contains pieces of one or more files, usually compressed. When the Windows 98 compact discs (or the optional floppy disks) are created, files are compressed into folders. The Windows 98 files are read, then written as one continuous byte-stream, which is then divided into folders as appropriate. Folders can fill one or more cabinets.

The Windows 98 cabinet structure has changed slightly from that introduced in Windows 95. For more information on the Windows 98 cabinet structure, see Appendix B, "Windows 98 System File Details."

Enumeration of Plug and Play on First Boot

The enumeration of Plug and Play hardware is moved to the first boot portion of Setup. Enumeration is performed before detection to reduce hardware detection problems and errors.

Anti-Virus Check

When you start Setup, it checks if any anti-virus programs are running. If there are, Setup displays a dialog box informing you to disable the software.

Comparison of Windows 95 Setup and Windows 98 Setup

This section summarizes the difference between the Windows 95 and Windows 98 Setup programs. It applies whether you run Setup from Windows 95 or from MS-DOS.

Fewer Setup Steps. In Windows 98, the number of Setup steps is reduced from twelve to five.

Table 2.1   Comparison of Windows 95 Setup and Windows 98 Setup

Windows 95 Setup steps	Windows 98 Setup steps
1. Initializing Setup.	1. Preparing to run Windows 98 Setup.
2. Preparing for smart recovery.	2. Collecting information about your computer.
3. Reading the Setuplog.txt file.	3. Copying files to your computer.
4. Gathering information.	4. Restarting your computer.
5. Analyzing the computer (hardware detection).	5. Setting up hardware and finalizing settings.
6. Finding Windows components.	
7. Preparing to copy files.	
8. Copying files to your computer.	
9. Finishing Setup.	
10. Configuring hardware.	
11. Completing configuration options (Run Once options).	
12. Restarting your computer (second restart).	

CD-ROM Drivers in the Startup Disk. The Windows 98 Startup Disk contains generic, real-mode ATAPI CD-ROM and SCSI drivers that allow CD-ROM devices to become available when running Windows 98 from the Startup Disk. The CD-ROM driver is not guaranteed to work with all CD-ROM devices; it is offered as a replacement if the real-mode drivers that came with your CD-ROM are unavailable.

Windows 95 and Windows 98 Startup Disks. Due to changes in the real-mode and protected-mode kernels to support the file allocation table 32 (FAT32) file system, Windows 95 Startup Disks are not compatible with Windows 98. When setting up Windows 98 for the first time, it is mandatory that you make a new Startup Disk and keep it in a safe place.

Version Conflicts. When setting up Windows 95, if Setup encountered a file that was newer than the one being copied, it displayed a message identifying the file. You then had to decided whether to keep the existing one or replace it with the older version. Windows 98 has a new component called *Version Conflict Manager* (VCM). VCM manages version conflicts by keeping the existing file and storing the older file provided by Setup in the %WinDir%\VCM folder. %WinDir% refers to the directory that is specified during Setup for installing the Windows 98 files. No dialog box is displayed to the user during this process.

Quick Guide for a Smooth Installation Process

This section provides a recommended sequence of tasks to help you perform a smooth installation. It is a guide to preparing, installing, and troubleshooting Windows 98.

Note The steps in this guide do not correspond to the steps that Setup uses to install Windows 98. The Setup steps are listed in "Comparison of Windows 95 Setup and Windows 98 Setup" earlier in this chapter and described in detail in "Running Setup: Step-by-Step" later in this chapter.

To help you perform a smooth Windows 98 installation	See section or chapter
Assess your current configuration Check that your computer's hardware and software configuration is supported and meets the minimum requirements for Windows 98. You can find the minimum system requirements on the side of the Windows 98 product box. If you want Windows 98 to co-exist with your current operating system, consider the issues involved. Based on your user needs and existing configuration, choose Typical, Portable, Compact, or Custom Setup options.	"Preparing to Run Setup" in this chapter "Deciding Whether to Dual Boot Windows 98" in this chapter "Choosing Typical, Portable, Compact, or Custom Setup Options" in this chapter
Choose a method to run Setup • Run Setup from the Windows interface to upgrade to Windows 98 (preserving your current settings) from any of the supported Windows operating systems (Windows 95, Windows 3.1x, or Windows for Workgroups 3.1x). • Run Setup from MS-DOS. Choose this option to change current settings (such as your computer's name) on any of the supported Windows operating systems; to install Windows 98 on a computer not running Windows, a new computer, or a reformatted disk drive; or to restart Setup if it fails when running it from Windows.	"Choosing a Method to Run Setup" in this chapter
Start Windows 98 Setup Start Setup from the distribution media of your choice: compact disc, floppy disks, or an installation point on the network. Decide if you want to start Setup from a script.	"Choosing a Distribution Media" in this chapter
Run Windows 98 Setup Run Windows 98 Setup from Windows 95, Windows 3.1x, Windows for Workgroups 3.1x, or from MS-DOS.	"Running Setup: Step-by-Step" in this chapter
Add, remove, and configure Windows 98 components Windows 98 provides a variety of maintenance tools for adding, removing, and configuring Windows 98 components.	Chapter 20 "Internet Access and Tools" Chapter 23 "System and Remote Administration Tools"
Customize and automate your installation If you want to deploy Windows 98 on more than one computer, you can use several tools and methods to customize and automate your installation.	Chapter 3 "Custom Installations" Chapter 4 "Automated Installations"
Troubleshoot Setup If you run into problems, follow the troubleshooting guidelines to recover from a Setup failure. If necessary, you can uninstall Windows 98 to return your computer to its previous configuration.	"Troubleshooting Setup" in Chapter 5, "Setup Technical Discussion"

Preparing to Run Setup

To make the installation process as smooth as possible, follow these preparatory steps, as described in this section:

- Check that your computer meets the minimum system requirements.
- Based on your current installation and the needs of your users, make the appropriate installation configuration decisions: decide whether or not to dual boot Windows 98 and whether to set up a Typical, Portable, Compact, or Custom installation.
- Disable any software that could cause problems during Setup.
- Back up your existing configuration and data files.

Checking Requirements

This section lists the requirements for installing and running Windows 98.

Disk Space Requirements

Table 2.2 lists the amount of disk space required for installing Windows 98. This amount varies, depending on the types of hardware on the computer, the required drivers, and the optional components you choose.

Table 2.2 Approximate disk space requirements for running Windows 98 Setup

Installation method	Required disk space	Typical disk space
Windows 95 upgrade	120–295 MB	195 MB
Windows 3.1x or Windows for Workgroups 3.1x upgrade	120–295 MB	195 MB
New installation (FAT32 file system)	140–255 MB	175 MB
New installation (FAT16 file system)	165–355 MB	225 MB
Installation over the network:	165–355 MB	225 MB
On the server	170 MB	170 MB
On the client	175–225 MB	175–225 MB

Note If you are installing Windows 98 to a drive other than C, Setup can require up to 25 MB of free disk space on drive C for the system and log files created during Setup.

System Requirements

This section lists the hardware, software, and partition requirements for Microsoft Windows 98.

Hardware Requirements

Table 2.3 describes the basic hardware requirements for running Windows 98 from the hard disk of a local computer. Windows 98 is designed for computers that use Intel *x*86–based processors and compatibles. It cannot be installed on any other processor. Windows 98 does not have symmetric multiprocessing (SMP) support and, therefore, cannot take advantage of multiple processors (as Windows NT does).

Table 2.3   Hardware requirements

Component	Minimum requirement	Recommended
Disk space[1]	120 MB of free hard-disk space. A new installation can require up to 355 MB. For more information, see Table 2.2. You also need a certain amount of free disk space for a swap file, depending on how much RAM the computer has.	
Processor	486DX/66 MHz processor	Pentium or higher
Memory	16 MB	More improves performance
Monitor	VGA (16-color)	Super VGA (16- or 24-bit color)
Drive		One 3.5-inch high-density disk drive

[1] The amount of disk space you need depends on the type of installation you choose (Typical, Portable, Compact, or Custom). If you choose to set up a Custom installation, you can determine how much disk space you need by using Tables 2.7 through 2.16 in "Choosing Typical, Portable, Compact, or Custom Installation" later in this chapter.

Table 2.4 describes optional hardware components for Windows 98.

Table 2.4   Requirements for optional hardware components

Optional component	Minimum requirement	Recommended[1]
Mouse	Windows 98–compatible pointing device	Microsoft Mouse or Microsoft pointing device
Modem	14.4 baud modem for Microsoft Network (MSN™), Messaging, and Internet access	28.8 baud modem or higher

Table 2.4   Requirements for optional hardware components (*continued*)

Optional component	Minimum requirement	Recommended[1]
CD-ROM drive (if installing from compact disc)	1x speed or faster. You need to have the correct driver for your CD-ROM. Refer to the documentation for your CD-ROM drive.	8x speed or faster
Network adapter (if installing from the network)	NDIS 2.0 or MAC driver support	NDIS 4.0 or 5.0 with OnNow power management support
Audio card and speakers	Sound Blaster–compatible	Full-duplex sound card or external digital audio using universal serial bus (USB) or IEEE1394
DVD-ROM and decoder card (if you want to view full-size motion pictures)	Supports industry standards	Supports DVD-video and MPEG-2 playback
Scanner or digital camera (if you want to scan/import digital images or pictures)	Plug and Play–compatible	Use IEEE 1394 port connections
Second monitor and video card (if you want to use the multimonitor feature)	Optional	PCI, AGP or other non-1SA bus
IEEE 1394 bus (Firewire) (if you want high-speed digital sound and video transfer)	Optional	Device and controller support IEEE 1394 standards, Plug and Play, and OnNow power management
USB bus and HID hardware	Optional	Hardware complies with Universal Bus specifications and supports OnNow power management
ATI All-in-Wonder-Card	Optional	Required for watching television using WebTV for Windows

[1]   Microsoft strongly recommends that you choose hardware components that carry the "Designed for Microsoft Windows" logo because these products have been stringently tested to ensure that the hardware and its driver provide the optimal user experience when used with Microsoft Windows operating systems.

Tips for Required Disk Space with Compressed Disks

If you have disk compression software installed, the required amount of uncompressed disk space on the host drive before installing Windows 98 depends on several factors:

- The type of compression used such as Microsoft DriveSpace® or DoubleSpace®.
- The available free space on other drives.
- The existence of a permanent swap file (if any), and its location.
- The amount of available free space on other drives.

If the computer does not have a swap file already, you might have to resize the host drive to accommodate the swap file requirements. For more information, consult your compression software documentation; see also Chapter 10, "Disks and File Systems."

Software Requirements

You can install Windows 98 in a dualboot configuration with other operating systems. In these configurations, the minimum operating system software required to install Windows 98 will vary. You can install Windows 98 on a computer that is running any of the following operating systems:

- MS-DOS version 5.0 or later
- Windows 3.1*x*
- Windows for Workgroups 3.1*x*
- Dual boot OS/2 (with MS-DOS)
- Dual boot Windows NT (with MS-DOS)

For more information on installing Windows 98 with other operating systems, see Chapter 5, "Setup Technical Discussion."

MS-DOS Versions and Windows 98 Setup

To install Windows 98, your computer must have MS-DOS version 5.0 or later. To check the MS-DOS version, type **ver** at the command prompt.

Partition Requirements

Windows 98 can be installed on any drive that has enough free space and is a FAT partition. However, if you want to set up Windows 98 to dual boot with another Microsoft operating system, drive C must be FAT16.

Windows 98 cannot be installed on a computer that has only high-performance file system (HPFS) or Windows NT file system (NTFS) partitions. Also, you cannot set up a computer to dual boot Windows 98 and Windows 95.

Table 2.5 describes how Windows 98 Setup handles different types of disk partitions. For more information, consult the documentation for the related operating system.

Table 2. 5   Disk partition comparison

Partition type	How Windows 98 Setup handles such partitions
MS-DOS 5.0 or later (Fdisk and other vendors' partitioning software)	To install Windows 98, your computer's startup drive must be an MS-DOS startup partition. If your startup drive is formatted as HPFS or NTFS, you must create an MS-DOS startup partition before running Windows 98 Setup. For more information about creating an MS-DOS startup partition, see your computer documentation.
	Windows 98 Setup recognizes and begins installation on existing MS-DOS FAT partitions, if the partition is large enough to accommodate Windows 98 files (including swap files).
	Windows 98 supports MS-DOS Fdisk partitions on removable media drives such as the Iomega Bernoulli Box drives.
	Windows 98 recognizes and translates disk partitioning schemes created by other vendors' partitioning software, including Disk Manager Dmdrvr.bin and Storage Dimensions SpeedStor Sstor.sys.
Windows NT 4.x or earlier	Windows 98 cannot recognize information on an NTFS partition on the local computer. Windows 98 can be installed on Windows NT multiple-boot systems if enough disk space is available and the drive is a FAT16 partition. On a Windows NT multiple-boot system, Windows 98 Setup can either install Windows 98 on an existing FAT16 partition with MS-DOS and, optionally, Windows 3.1x, or you must partition and format free space on the hard disk in a FAT16 partition, then perform a new installation onto this new FAT16 partition. Windows NT cannot access local FAT32 partitions.
	For more information on installing Windows 98 on a computer running Windows NT, see "Installing Windows 98 on a Computer with Windows NT" later in this chapter.

Table 2.5   Disk partition comparison (*continued*)

Partition type	How Windows 98 Setup handles such partitions
OS/2	You must run Windows 98 Setup from MS-DOS. If it is not already present on the computer, you must first install MS-DOS and configure the computer for dual booting with OS/2. Then you need to boot to MS-DOS and run Setup from the MS-DOS prompt.
	For more information on installing Windows 98 on a computer running OS/2, see "Installing Windows 98 on a Computer with OS/2" later in this chapter.

Windows 98 works with disk compression drivers, such as Microsoft DriveSpace and DoubleSpace.

If you use other disk compression software, see the Readme.htm file, or contact your product support representative to determine compatibility. For more information, see Chapter 10, "Disks and File Systems."

Making Installation Configuration Decisions

You can choose from several installation configuration options:

- Install Windows 98 with another operating system (dual booting).
- Setting up a Typical, Portable, Compact, or Custom installation.
- Customizing or automating Windows 98 installations.

These installation configurations are described in the following sections.

Deciding Whether to Dual Boot Windows 98

You can configure your computer to dual boot with Windows 98 if it is running any of the following operating systems:

- MS-DOS 5.*x* or later
- Windows 3.1*x*
- Windows NT

You cannot dual boot Windows 98 and Windows 95.

Note Dual booting Windows 98 with or installing Windows 98 over third-party operating systems such as DR DOS has not been tested by Microsoft. Contact your operating system vendor for more information.

This section covers the considerations you must make when deciding whether or not to dual boot an existing operating system with Windows 98.

Tips for Dual-Boot Configurations

- Windows 98 can be installed on any drive that has enough free space and is a FAT16 partition.

- If Windows NT is already running on your computer, you must set up any programs you want to run on Windows NT again.

For more information on installing Windows 98 with other operating systems, see Chapter 5, "Setup Technical Discussion."

Can You Dual Boot Windows 98 and Windows NT 4.*x* or earlier?

You cannot install Windows 98 on a computer running any version of Windows NT. However, you can configure your computer to dual boot Windows 98 and Windows NT 4.*x* or earlier provided you follow these guidelines:

- Windows 98 must be set up in a different hard disk or partition from Windows NT.

- Drive C must be a FAT16 partition and must meet the minimum disk space requirements for a Windows 98 installation (195 MB of free hard-disk space for a typical installation).

- Run Windows 98 Setup by selecting Windows 95 from the **Boot Loader Operating System Selection** menu that appears at system startup. If Windows 95 does not appear on this menu, select MS-DOS instead.

If Windows NT is already installed, Windows 98 Setup adds itself as an entry to the Windows NT boot menu to allow the user to select between Windows 98 or Windows NT when starting the computer.

For more information on how to install Windows 98 on a computer running Windows NT, see "Installing Windows 98 on a Computer with Windows NT" later in this chapter. See also "Installing Windows 98 on a System Running Windows NT" and "Setting Up a Dual-Boot Configuration with Windows NT" in \Win98\Setup.txt on your Windows 98 compact disc.

**Data Access Restrictions for Windows 98/Windows NT Dual-Boot
Configurations**

- Dual boot Windows 98/Windows NT configurations are not
  recommended because Windows 98 and Windows NT do not use the
  same registry settings or hardware device drivers. Therefore, you must
  set up your programs twice, once under each operating system.
  However, you can set up your programs to the same directory under
  each operating system.

- Windows 98 cannot access Windows NT file system (NTFS) partitions.

- Windows NT cannot access FAT32 drives. FAT32 is a file system that
  was first implemented in Windows 95 OEM Service Release 2 (OSR-2).
  For more information on FAT32, see Chapter 10, "Disks and File
  Systems."

Can You Dual Boot Windows 98 and Windows 3.1x or MS-DOS 5.x?

You can configure your computer to dual boot with Windows 3.1x, as well as
other versions of Windows as long as they have MS-DOS 5.0 or later, by using
the F4 boot-to-previous-operating-system feature. To dual boot Windows 98
with these operating systems, your computer's drive C must be FAT16.

For information about how Windows 98 Setup treats disk partitions created under
other operating systems, see "Partition Requirements" earlier in this chapter. For
information about how Windows 98 Setup deals with the boot sector and installs
files for dual boot operation with other operating systems, see Chapter 5, "Setup
Technical Discussion."

Can You Dual Boot Windows 98 and Windows 95?

You cannot set up a computer to dual boot Windows 98 and Windows 95 because
Windows 98 is intended as an upgrade to Windows 95, and a such both versions
would try to use the same boot file. This configuration is therefore not supported.

Choosing Typical, Portable, Compact, or Custom Setup Options

You can choose from four different types of Windows 98 installations. The choice
you make dictates the size of the Windows 98 installation on the computer, the
number of features installed, and the amount of control the user has in
customizing the installation.

Choosing the Windows 98 Setup Options

If you run Windows 98 Setup from Windows 95, Setup identifies and uses the current configuration settings and installed component information to upgrade your existing configuration to Windows 98. If you want to add or remove the components or configuration you have now, you must use the **Windows Setup** tab in Add/Remove Programs. The **Setup Options** dialog box, where you can use the four Setup options (Typical, Portable, Compact, or Custom), only appears when you run Windows 98 Setup on a new installation.

Table 2.6 describes each of the Setup options and the components included with each option. The amount of disk space you need depends on the Setup option you choose (Typical, Portable, Compact, or Custom). This table uses the following conventions:

Symbol	Meaning
☑	The entire component set is installed by default.
✓	Only part of the component set is installed by default.
☒	This component set is not installed by default.

Table 2.6   Components installed and not installed by default for Typical, Portable, Compact, or Custom Setup options

Setup option	Component sets		Description
Typical	Accessibility	✓	The default option, recommended for most users. Performs most installation steps automatically for a standard Windows 98 installation with minimal user action. You need to confirm only the directory where Windows 98 files are to be installed, provide user and computer identification information, and specify whether to create a Startup Disk.
	Accessories	✓	
	Communications	✓	
	Desktop Themes	☒	
	Internet Tools	✓	
	Multilanguage Support	☒	
	Microsoft Outlook™ Express	☑	The total space needed by Setup for this option is 202.3 MB.
	Multimedia	✓	
	Online Services	☑	
	System Tools	✓	
	WebTV for Windows	☒	

Table 2.6   Components installed and not installed by default for Typical, Portable, Compact, or Custom Setup options (*continued*)

Setup option	Component sets		Description
Portable	Accessibility	✓	The recommended option for mobile users with portable computers. Installs the appropriate set of files for a portable computer. This includes installing Briefcase for file synchronization and the supporting software for direct cable connections to exchange files.
	Accessories	✓	
	Communications	✓	
	Desktop Themes	☒	
	Internet Tools	✓	
	Multilanguage Support	☒	The total space needed by Setup for this option is 176.3 MB.
	Microsoft Outlook Express	☑	
	Multimedia	✓	
	Online Services	☑	
	System Tools	✓	
	WebTV for Windows	☒	
Compact	Accessibility	✓	The option for users who have extremely limited disk space. Installs the minimum files required to run Windows 98. None of the optional components are installed.
	Accessories	☒	
	Communications	✓	
	Desktop Themes	☒	
	Internet Tools	☒	The total space needed by Setup for this option is 163.7 MB.
	Multilanguage Support	☒	
	Microsoft Outlook Express	☒	
	Multimedia	✓	
	Online Services	☑	
	System Tools	☒	
	WebTV for Windows	☒	

Table 2.6 Components installed and not installed by default for Typical, Portable, Compact, or Custom Setup options (*continued*)

Setup option	Component sets		Description
Custom	Accessibility	✓	The option for advanced users who want to customize all available Setup options. Installs the appropriate files based on the components selected.
	Accessories	✓	
	Communications	✓	
	Desktop Themes	☒	
	Internet Tools	✓	The total space needed by Setup for this option depends on the components you choose. The default Custom Setup option requires 204.3 MB
	Multilanguage Support	☒	
	Microsoft Outlook Express	☑	
	Multimedia	✓	
	Online Services	☑	
	System Tools	✓	
	WebTV for Windows	☒	

If you choose to set up a Custom installation, you can determine how much disk space you need by adding up the space each of the components you want to install uses.

Tables 2.7 through 2.16 show which components are installed or not installed by default for each Setup option. They also list the size for each component. When you select either the Typical, Portable, or Compact option, Windows 98 Setup selects the appropriate components (and sub-components). Setup also lets you either accept the default selection or change it.

Note These tables only list the component sets that have sub-components, therefore, Microsoft Outlook Express is not listed because it is only one component and its size is 3.8 MB.

Desktop Themes, Multilanguage Support, and WebTV for Windows are not included in any of the Setup options by default.

These tables use the following conventions:

Symbol	Meaning
☑	The entire component is installed by default for the Setup option selected.
✓	Only part of the component is installed by default for the Setup option selected.
☒	This component is not installed by default for the Setup option selected.

Table 2.7   Accessibility

Component	Size [MB]	Typical	Portable	Compact	Custom
Accessibility Options	0.5	☑	☑	☑	☑
Accessibility Tools	2.3	☒	☒	☒	☒

Table 2.8   Accessories

Component	Size [MB]	Typical	Portable	Compact	Custom
Briefcase	0.0	☒	☑	☒	☒
Calculator	0.2	☑	☒	☒	☑
Desktop Wallpaper	0.6	☒	☒	☒	☒
Document Templates	0.2	☑	☒	☒	☑
Games	0.6	☒	☒	☒	☒
Imaging	4.0	☑	☒	☒	☑
Mouse Pointers	0.0	☒	☒	☒	☒
Paint	1.0	☑	☒	☒	☑
Quick View	4.2	☒	☒	☒	☒
Screen Savers [1]	1.2	✓	☒	☒	✓
Additional Screen Savers	0.2	☒	☒	☒	☒
Flying Windows	0.1	☑	☒	☒	☑
OpenGL Screen Savers	1.1	☑	☒	☒	☑
Windows Scripting Host	0.9	☑	☑	☒	☑
WordPad	1.9	☑	☑	☒	☑

[1] Size with only the default components selected.

Table 2.9   Communications

Component	Size [MB]	Typical	Portable	Compact	Custom
Dial-Up Networking	0.8	☑	☑	☑	☑
Dial-Up Server	0.1	☒	☒	☒	☒
Direct Cable Connection	0.4	☒	☑	☒	☒
HyperTerminal	0.6	☒	☑	☒	☒
Microsoft Chat 2.1	4.5	☒	☒	☒	☒
Microsoft NetMeeting™	4.2	☑	☒	☒	☑
Phone Dialer	0.1	☑	☑	☒	☑
Virtual Private Networking	0.1	☒	☑	☒	☒

Table 2.10   Desktop Themes

Component	Size [MB]	Typical	Portable	Compact	Custom
Baseball	2.1	☒	☒	☒	☒
Dangerous Creatures	1.1	☒	☒	☒	☒
Desktop Themes Support	2.6	☒	☒	☒	☒
Inside Your Computer	1.1	☒	☒	☒	☒
Jungle	1.6	☒	☒	☒	☒
Leonardo da Vinci	1.8	☒	☒	☒	☒
More Windows	0.5	☒	☒	☒	☒
Mystery	1.4	☒	☒	☒	☒
Nature	1.2	☒	☒	☒	☒
Science	0.9	☒	☒	☒	☒
Space	1.7	☒	☒	☒	☒
Sports	1.1	☒	☒	☒	☒
The 60's USA	1.0	☒	☒	☒	☒
The Golden Era	1.1	☒	☒	☒	☒
Travel	1.0	☒	☒	☒	☒
Underwater	2.3	☒	☒	☒	☒
Windows 98	1.1	☒	☒	☒	☒

Table 2.11   Internet Tools

Component	Size [MB]	Typical	Portable	Compact	Custom
Microsoft FrontPage® Express	4.1	☑	☑	☒	☑
Microsoft VRML 2.0 Viewer	3.2	☒	☒	☒	☒
Microsoft Wallet	0.9	☒	☒	☒	☒
Personal Web Server	0.1	☑	☑	☒	☑
Real Audio Player 4.0	2.3	☒	☒	☒	☒
Web Publishing Wizard	1.0	☒	☒	☒	☒
Web-Based Enterprise Mgmt	3.2	☒	☒	☒	☒

Table 2.12   Multilanguage Support

Component	Size [MB]	Typical	Portable	Compact	Custom
Baltic	3.0	☒	☒	☒	☒
Central European	3.1	☒	☒	☒	☒
Cyrillic	3.0	☒	☒	☒	☒
Greek	3.0	☒	☒	☒	☒
Turkish	2.9	☒	☒	☒	☒

Table 2.13   Multimedia

Component	Size [MB]	Typical	Portable	Compact	Custom
Audio Compression	0.2	☑	☑	☑	☑
CD Player	0.2	☑	☑	☑	☑
Macromedia Shockwave Director	0.5	☑	☒	☒	☑
Macromedia Shockwave Flash	0.2	☑	☒	☒	☑
Media Player	0.2	☑	☑	☒	☑
Microsoft NetShow™ Player 2.0	3.9	☒	☒	☒	☒
Multimedia Sound Schemes	5.8	☒	☒	☒	☒
Sample Sounds	0.5	☒	☒	☒	☒
Sound Recorder	0.2	☑	☑	☒	☑
Video Compression	0.5	☑	☑	☒	☑
Volume Control	0.2	☑	☑	☒	☑

Table 2.14   Online Services

Component	Size [MB]	Typical	Portable	Compact	Custom
America Online	0.1	☑	☑	☑	☑
AT&T WorldNet Service	0.2	☑	☑	☑	☑
CompuServe	0.1	☑	☑	☑	☑
Prodigy Internet	0.4	☑	☑	☑	☑
The Microsoft Network	0.1	☑	☑	☑	☑

Table 2.15   System Tools

Component	Size [MB]	Typical	Portable	Compact	Custom
Backup	4.2	☒	☒	☒	☒
Character Map	0.1	☒	☒	☒	☒
Clipboard Viewer	0.1	☒	☒	☒	☒
Disk Compression Tools	2.0	☒	☑	☑	☑
Drive Converter (FAT32)	0.4	☑	☑	☒	☑
Group Policies	0.1	☒	☒	☒	☒
Net Watcher	0.2	☒	☒	☒	☒
System Monitor	0.2	☒	☒	☒	☒
System Resource Meter	0.1	☒	☒	☒	☒

Table 2.16   WebTV for Windows

Component	Size [MB]	Typical	Portable	Compact	Custom
WaveTop Data Broadcasting	10.3	☒	☒	☒	☒
WebTV for Windows	23.8	☒	☒	☒	☒

Deciding to Set up a Customized and/or Automated Installation

You can choose any combination of methods for configuring custom versions of Windows 98:

- Create custom setup scripts based on the Msbatch.inf format. Custom setup scripts contain predefined settings for all Setup options, and they can contain instructions for installing additional software.

- Define Wrkgrp.ini files to control users' choices for workgroups to join on the network.

- Enable user profiles and create system policies to specify and maintain the system configuration.

You can use setup scripts to create an automated mandatory installation scheme for installing Windows 98 on multiple computers from Windows 98 source files on servers. A *setup script* is a text file that contains predefined settings for all the options specified during Setup, and can contain instructions for installing other software. The setup script file requires an .inf extension, for example, Myscript.inf.

A setup script allows you to create an automated mandatory installation scheme for installing Windows 98 on multiple computers from Windows 98 source files on a network server. Once a setup script has been created or edited, Windows 98 can be installed automatically by running Setup at each client computer, using the name of the setup script as a command-line parameter. The following methods are possible:

- Use a logon script to run Setup from a custom setup script, automatically installing Windows 98 when each user logs on.

- Use Microsoft Systems Management Server to run Windows 98 Setup with a custom setup script as a mandatory action.

- Use network management software from another vendor to install Windows 98 automatically, based on custom setup scripts.

- Use a batch file that contains appropriate Setup command-line information and distribute it on disk or by electronic mail.

When to Use Setup Scripts

As a rule of thumb, it is recommended that you use setup scripts if you need to conduct a standardized installation on more than five computers.

Even though it is possible to use setup scripts to install Windows 98 in new computers or computers with newly formatted hard disks, the scripts required to perform this type for installation can be complicated. If you need to use a setup script to install Windows 98 on newly formatted disks, install Windows 98 on one computer first (as a model computer) and then run Microsoft Batch 98 on the model computer (using the **Gather now** button) to create a setup script with the model computer's settings.

For more information on custom installations, Chapter 3, "Custom Installations" and Appendix D, "Msbatch.inf Parameters for Setup Scripts."

Disabling Problematic Software

Before you install Windows 98, you should disable any software that can cause problems during setup. Problematic software includes anti-virus software, third-party utilities and drivers, and MS-DOS-based programs.

Disabling Anti-Virus Software

Windows 98 Setup makes changes to the boot sector of all hard disks in the computer. Because virus protection software is designed to prevent changes to the boot sector, it can often cause Setup to fail. Therefore, ensure that anti-virus software and BIOS level anti-virus protection are disabled.

Disabling Third-Party Display Utilities

Windows 98 Setup fails if it detects incompatible video drivers or display utilities. To ensure a successful Setup, disable all third-party video drivers and display utilities.

For more information, see "General Setup Issues" in \Win98\Setup.txt on your Windows 98 compact disc.

Note If Setup detects problematic software, it tries to provide instructions to correct the problem. If Setup is unable to diagnose the cause of the failure, it may present a message that states that Setup has failed. If this occurs, you must restart the computer and then restart Setup.

Disabling MS-DOS-based Programs

You cannot run Setup while other MS-DOS-based programs are running on your computer. Use ALT+TAB to find out which programs are running. Quit all programs except Setup, and then click **OK** to continue. If you do not do this, you will get error message SU0358. For information on this error message and other Setup error messages, see "Setup Error Messages" in \Win98\Setup.txt on your Windows 98 compact disc.

Backing Up Your Existing Configuration

One of the most important preparatory steps before installing Windows 98 is backing up your current system configuration (if you have an existing operating system installed on your computer) and any critical business and personal data. The following sections provide some guidelines for backing up an existing Windows 95 configuration and business and personal data.

Backing Up Windows 95

If for any reason you need to uninstall Windows 98, you can return to your previous Windows 95 installation as long as you backed up the Windows 95 system files during Windows 98 Setup.

To uninstall Windows 98 and return to your previous configuration, the following conditions must be met:

- Have clicked **Yes (recommended)** on the **Save System Files?** dialog box that appeared when you installed Windows 98 for the first time. If you clicked **Yes**, two files containing the saved Windows 95 system files, Winundo.dat and Winundo.ini, were created in the root directory of the partition that you designated during Setup.

- Have not compressed your system or boot partition after installing Windows 98, or any partition in the same physical drive where Winundo.dat is located.

- Have not converted any file systems to FAT32, unless your Windows 95 version is OSR-2.

For more information on how to uninstall Windows 98, see "Uninstalling Windows 98" in Chapter 5, "Setup Technical Discussion."

Checklist for Preparing to Run Setup

This section provides a checklist to help you verify that you completed all the necessary preparatory steps described in "Preparing to Run Setup" earlier in this chapter.

☐   **Have you decided which installation configuration suits your needs best?**

Decide whether you want to upgrade your existing Windows 95 configuration (keeping existing settings), set up Windows 98 to a newly formatted hard disk, or use a setup script to install Windows 98 on multiple computers. Decide if you want to dual boot Windows 98 with another operating system. Decide if you want to install components for a Typical, Portable, Compact, or Custom installation. Decide if you want to run Setup locally or from the network.

☐   **Is the hardware supported?**

Read the Windows 98 Readme file and Setup.txt on the installation disks for any notes related to your computer hardware. If any specific computer component is not supported, Windows 98 selects a generic driver or uses the existing driver installed on the computer. If you install support manually for a hardware component that does not appear in the installation dialog boxes, select the model that your hardware can emulate or that is of the closest type. (All supported hardware components are listed when you run the Add New Hardware Wizard, as described in Chapter 30, "Hardware Management.") For late-breaking information on hardware compatibility, see the Windows 98 Hardware Compatibility List from the Microsoft Web site, **http://www.microsoft.com**.

☐   **Do the computer components meet the minimum requirements?**

Verify that your computer meets the minimum requirements as described in "Checking Requirements" earlier in this chapter. You can also find the minimum system requirements on the side of your Windows 98 product box.

☐   **Are all unnecessary TSR programs and time-out features disabled?**

Disable all terminate-and-stay resident (TSR) programs and device drivers loaded in Config.sys or Autoexec.bat (or in any batch files called from Autoexec.bat), except those required for partition or hard disk control, network drivers, or any driver required for operation of a device such as video, CD-ROM, and so on.

Some portable computers (such as the IBM ThinkPad) automatically suspend operation after a specified time-out interval, or when the cover is closed. You should disable this feature while Windows 98 Setup is running.

For more information on using TSR programs and drivers with Windows 98, see "Using Terminate-and-Stay-Resident (TSR) Programs and Drivers" in \Win98\Setup.txt on your Windows 98 compact disc.

❏ **Is the installation drive checked and defragmented?**

Windows 98 Setup runs ScanDisk to check the integrity of the drive where Windows 98 will be installed only when you start it from MS-DOS. If you start Setup.exe from Windows 95 and you also want to check the integrity of the drive where Windows 98 will be installed, you should either start Setup from MS-DOS or run ScanDisk manually.

If, in addition to the integrity check performed by ScanDisk, you also want to check and defragment the entire hard disk drive thoroughly (not just the drive where Windows 98 will be installed), you can use a third-party defragmentation software. Be sure to defragment all compressed drives, because a highly fragmented compressed drive reports more available hard-disk space than is actually available. If you use disk compression software other than DriveSpace or DoubleSpace, be sure to run the disk-checking utility provided with your compression software. For information, see the documentation provided with the compression software.

❏ **Are all key system files backed up?**

Make sure you backed up the following:

- All critical business and personal data.
- All initialization (INI) files in the Windows directory.
- All registry data (DAT) files in the Windows directory.
- All password (PWL) files in the Windows directory.
- All Program Manager group (GRP) files in the Windows directory.
- All critical real-mode drivers specified in Config.sys and Autoexec.bat.
- Config.sys and Autoexec.bat in the root directory.
- Proprietary network configuration files and logon scripts.

❏ **Does the networking software work correctly?**

Make sure that the network software is running correctly before you start Windows 98 Setup. If you run Windows 98 Setup from MS-DOS, it uses the settings from the existing network configuration to set up the new configuration. Check the Windows 98 Readme file for additional notes related to your networking software.

If you are running Setup from a Windows 3.1*x* or Windows for Workgroups 3.1*x*–based computer that has Novell Client for Windows 95/98 or real-mode Artisoft LANtastic, Setup will fail. You must remove these components before running Setup.

❏ **Have you disabled any anti-virus protection software?**

Any bootable, anti-virus software can cause problems with Windows 98 Setup. Before you run Setup, remove them from memory and reboot your computer.

❏ **Have you disabled third-party display utilities?**

Windows 98 Setup fails if it detects incompatible video drivers or display utilities. For more information, see "General Setup Issues" in \Win98\Setup.txt on your Windows 98 compact disc.

❏   **Have you disabled any MS-DOS-based programs?**

Disable any MS-DOS-based programs running on your computer. Use ALT+TAB to find out which programs are running. Quit all programs except Setup, and then click **OK** to continue.

❏   **If your computer has Windows 95 installed, do you have the Windows 95 boot disk available?**

To recover in case of a Windows 98 Setup failure, make sure you have the Windows 95 boot disk available during Setup.

❏   **Did you check the MS-DOS SYS file?**

To recover in case of a Windows 98 Setup failure, check the MS-DOS SYS file to ensure you can boot your computer from MS-DOS.

Choosing a Method to Run Setup

You can run the Windows 98 Setup program (Setup.exe) from the:

- Windows 95 user interface.
- Windows 3.1x or Windows for Workgroups 3.1x user interface.
- MS-DOS command prompt.

The method you choose for running Setup depends on your current configuration. Table 2.17 is a guide to help you choose the appropriate method. You can find the sections listed in this table later in this chapter.

Table 2.17   Choosing a method to run Setup

If you are	Start Setup following the steps in	Read
Upgrading from Windows 95, keeping current configuration settings, such as the installation directory.	"Upgrading Windows 95 Keeping Current Settings"	"Running Setup from the Windows 95 Interface"
Upgrading from Windows 95, changing the current installation directory.	"Upgrading Windows 95 Changing Current Settings"	"Running Setup from MS-DOS"
Upgrading from Window 3.1x or Window for Workgroups 3.1x.	"Upgrading Windows 3.1x or Windows for Workgroups 3.1x"	"Running Setup from the Windows 3.1x Interface"
Installing Windows 98 on a new computer or a reformatted hard disk.	"Performing a New Installation"	"Running Setup on a New Installation"

Table 2.17   Choosing a method to run Setup (*continued*)

If you are	Start Setup following the steps in	Read
Installing Windows 98 on a computer running Windows NT	"Installing Windows 98 on a Computer with Windows NT"	"Running Setup on a New Installation"
Standardizing and customizing Windows 98 on several computers.	"Standardizing Windows 98 on Multiple Computers"	"Running Setup from MS-DOS"

The following sections provide more details on these methods of running Setup.

Choosing a Distribution Media

The Windows 98 files are distributed on compact disc. However, you can optionally request Windows 98 floppy disks from Microsoft or you can store these files on an installation point on a network server. Therefore you can start Windows 98 Setup from the following media:

- The Windows 98 compact disc.
- The Windows 98 floppy disks.
- From a Windows 98 *installation point*. You create an installation point by copying the Windows 98 installation files from the Windows 98 compact disc (or floppy disks) to a shared directory with write permissions on a network server.

Points to Remember Before Starting Setup

- Starting Setup from an installation point requires approximately 170 MB of free disk space on the server, and typically 175–225 MB on the client computer where Windows 98 will be installed.

- If you use a compact disc to set up Windows 98, the CD-ROM must be connected to the motherboard so that the CD-ROM drivers included in the Windows 98 Startup Disk work. CD-ROM drives connected to a sound card are not recognized during startup.

- Except for TSRs required for partition or hard disk control, network drivers, or device drivers such as CD-ROM, no TSRs or Windows-based applications should be running when you start Windows 98 Setup. Close any such applications before continuing with Setup.

Upgrading Windows 95 Keeping Current Settings

If your computer is running Windows 95 and you want to keep its current configuration settings, such as the directory where Windows 95 installed, the computer name, its network settings, and so on, start Setup from within the Windows 95 user interface.

This is the recommended method because it requires minimum user interaction and it is the easiest method. With this method, Windows 98 is automatically installed in the same directory where Windows 95 is installed. Furthermore, most of the information needed for upgrading is automatically taken from your current Windows 95 installation. Windows 98 automatically identifies and transfers the current configuration programs and installed programs. With this method, you cannot change the installation directory or choose the Setup options as described in "Choosing Typical, Portable, Compact, or Custom Setup Options" earlier in this chapter.

Note If you do not have enough hard-disk space to install Windows 98, try emptying your Recycle Bin.

▶ **To start Windows 98 Setup from the Windows 95 user interface**

1. Start Windows 95.

2. Close all programs, including any anti-virus programs.

   For information about closing an anti-virus program, see the program documentation and Setup.txt on your Windows 98 compact disc or Setup Disk 1 floppy disk.

3. If you are installing Windows 98 from a compact disc, insert the Windows 98 compact disc into your CD-ROM drive and make it the active drive.

   – Or –

   If you are installing Windows 98 from floppy disks, insert Setup Disk 1 into the floppy disk drive and make it the active drive. For example, type **a:** if the disk is in the A drive.

   – Or –

   If you are installing Windows 98 from source files on a network server, connect to that server and switch to the shared network directory that contains the Windows 98 source files.

4. If a message appears asking if you want to upgrade, click **Yes**. The Windows 98 Setup Wizard starts. Follow the instructions that appear on your screen as described in "Running Setup from the Windows 95 Interface" later in this chapter.

   If a message does not appear, click **Start**, and then click **Run**.

   The **Run** dialog box appears.

5. In **Open**, enter the path and name of the Setup file. (Type the drive letter, followed by a colon (:), a backslash (\), and the word **setup**.) For example:

d:\setup

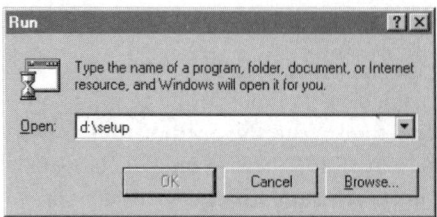

6. Click **OK**.

   The Windows 98 Setup Wizard starts.

7. Follow the instructions on the screen, as described in "Running Setup from the Windows 95 Interface" later in this chapter.

Upgrading Windows 95 Changing Current Settings

If your computer is running Windows 95 but you want to change its current settings, start Setup from MS-DOS. With this method, Setup displays dialog boxes that let you change or choose the following settings:

- Installation directory (**Select Directory** dialog box)
- Components you want to install (**Setup Options** dialog box)
- User name and company (**User Information** dialog box)
- Computer name, description, and workgroup (**Identification** dialog box)
- Computer settings such as keyboard layout and language support (**Computer Settings** dialog box)

▶ **To start Windows 98 Setup from MS-DOS**

1. Shut down Windows 95 and restart your computer in MS-DOS mode.

2. If you are installing Windows 98 from compact disc, insert the Windows 98 compact disc into your CD-ROM drive and make it the active drive.

   – Or –

   If you are installing Windows 98 from floppy disks, insert Setup Disk 1 into the floppy disk drive and make it the active drive. For example, type **a:** if the disk is in the A drive.

   – Or –

   If you are installing Windows 98 from source files on a network server, connect to that server and switch to the shared network directory that contains the Windows 98 source files.

3. At the command prompt, type the drive letter, followed by a colon (:), a backslash (\), and the word **setup**. For example,

    d:\setup

4. Press ENTER.

    Setup quickly scans your computer, and then the Windows 98 Setup Wizard starts.

5. Follow the instructions on the screen, as described in "Running Setup from MS-DOS" later in this chapter.

Upgrading Windows 3.1x or Windows for Workgroups 3.1x

If you want to upgrade a computer that is running Windows 3.1x or Windows for Workgroups 3.1x, start Setup from within its Windows user interface. Windows 98 Setup migrates most of the information it needs from your current Windows installation. It automatically identifies and transfers the current configuration programs and installed programs.

Note If you are running Setup from a Windows 3.1x or Windows for Workgroups 3.1x–based computer that has Novell Client for Windows 95/98 or real-mode Artisoft LANtastic, Setup will fail. You must remove these components before running Setup.

▶   **To start Windows 98 Setup from Windows 3.1x or Windows for Workgroups 3.1x**

1. Start Windows 3.1x or Windows for Workgroups 3.1x.

2. Close all programs, including any anti-virus programs.

    For information about closing an anti-virus program, see the program documentation and Setup.txt on your Windows 98 compact disc or Setup Disk 1 floppy disk.

3. If you are installing Windows 98 from a compact disc, insert the Windows 98 compact disc into your CD-ROM drive and make it the active drive.

    – Or –

    If you are installing Windows 98 from floppy disks, insert Setup Disk 1 into the floppy disk drive and make it the active drive. For example, type **a:** if the disk is in the A drive.

    – Or –

    If you are installing Windows 98 from source files on a network server, connect to that server and switch to the shared network directory that contains the Windows 98 source files.

4. Open Program Manager.

5. On the **File** menu, click **Run**.

   The **Run** dialog box appears.

6. In **Open**, enter the path and name of the Setup file. (Type the drive letter, followed by a colon [:], a backslash [\], and the word **setup**.) For example:

   d:\setup

7. Click **OK**.

   The Windows 98 Setup Wizard starts.

8. Follow the instructions on the screen, as described in "Running Setup from the Windows 3.1x Interface" later in this chapter.

If you do not want to migrate your current settings, run Setup from MS-DOS as explained in the procedure "To start Windows 98 Setup from MS-DOS" earlier in this chapter and read the step-by-step information in "Running Setup on a New Installation" later in this chapter.

Performing a New Installation

If you want to install Windows 98 on a computer with a new hard disk drive or a computer with a reformatted hard disk drive you start Setup from MS-DOS using the Windows 98 compact disc, the Windows 98 floppy disks, or an installation point on a network server.

When starting Setup from MS-DOS using either a network server or local CD-ROM drive, the real-mode network or CD-ROM drivers must be loaded. If the real-mode network drivers are running when you start Windows 98 Setup, the appropriate network client is installed automatically. Setup detects existing network components. installs the appropriate supporting software automatically, and adds the necessary network setting in the registry.

When you perform a new installation, Setup installs Windows 98 in a new folder and does not transfer any existing system settings. Windows 98 becomes your default operating system and uses standard system settings. You need to reinstall any existing programs you want to use because this is an entirely new installation of Windows.

Caution If you follow this procedure, you may no longer be able to use some of the software currently on your computer, including your applications and your current operating system. After you install Windows 98, you may need to reinstall the applications you want to use.

Before you begin, you should be prepared to provide the following information:

- Name of the installation directory (for example, **c:\Windows**).

  If you do not know the directory in which to install Windows 98, you can use Setup to create a new one. When prompted, type a new directory name.

- Network information, such as your computer name, workgroup, and computer description (if your computer is on a network).

▶ **To perform a new installation from the Windows 98 compact disc**

1. Insert a Windows 98 Startup Disk in the CD-ROM drive.

   Note For information about creating a Startup Disk, see Chapter 5, "Setup Technical Discussion." If you have purchased a full version of Windows 98, use the Startup (boot) floppy disk provided in the box.

2. Restart your computer.

   The Microsoft Windows 98 **Startup** menu appears.

3. Insert the Windows 98 compact disc into your CD-ROM drive.

4. Type the number **1** and press ENTER.

   A series of scans is performed, and then the MS-DOS prompt appears.

5. At the MS-DOS prompt, type the word **setup** and press ENTER.

   A message informs you that Setup is going to perform a check. If this message does not appear, then your computer cannot locate your CD-ROM drive. For information about installing the correct CD-ROM driver, consult your drive's documentation or contact your hardware manufacturer.

6. Press ENTER.

   Microsoft ScanDisk checks your disk drives for errors.

7. When ScanDisk finishes, press the **X** key.

   After Setup initializes, Windows 98 Setup begins.

8. Follow the instructions on the screen, as described in "Running Setup on a New Installation" later in this chapter.

   Note If you are using the upgrade version of Windows 98, Setup may ask you to insert your original Windows 95 or Windows 3.1*x* disks.

▶ **To perform a new installation using the Windows 98 floppy disk**

1. Insert Setup Disk 1 into your floppy-disk drive.

2. Restart your computer.

3. At the MS-DOS prompt, type the word **setup** and press ENTER.

   The Windows 98 Setup Wizard starts.

   Note If you are using the full, floppy-disk version of Windows 98, skip this step because Setup automatically starts.

   ---

4. Follow the instructions on the screen, as described in "Running Setup on a New Installation" later in this chapter.

After starting Setup, Setup initializes and checks your system:

- It runs real-mode ScanDisk to check the hard disk for errors. (You will not see it run, unless an error occurs.) Unlike the protected-mode version of ScanDisk, the real-mode counterpart cannot fix errors in long file names. ScanDisk does not perform a surface scan; therefore the disk is not checked for physical errors.

   Note If you get file system errors during Setup, you should run ScanDisk and perform a surface scan before running Setup again.

- It initializes the registry and checks it for corruption.

Tip When you run Windows 98 Setup, ScanDisk performs a quick check of the hard disk. You can skip this quick check (for example, if the computer uses disk compression software from another vendor) by using the **/iq** or **/is** switch with the **setup** command, as described in "Using the Setup Command-Line Switches" later in this chapter. If you choose to skip automatically running ScanDisk, be sure to use another utility to check the integrity of the hard disk before running Setup.

▶ **To perform a new installation from an installation point on a network server**

1. Insert a boot disk in the floppy-disk drive.

   You must use a boot disk with the appropriate network files and drivers that will allow you to connect to your network.

2. Restart your computer.

3. Connect to the network server that contains the Windows 98 installation point.

4. At the command prompt, type the path and the file name of the setup file and press ENTER. For example

   e:\InsPoint\setup

A message informs you that Setup is going to perform a check. If this message does not appear, then your computer cannot locate your CD-ROM drive. For information about installing the correct CD-ROM driver, consult your drive's documentation or contact your hardware manufacturer.

5. Press ENTER.

Microsoft ScanDisk checks your disk drives for errors.

6. When ScanDisk finishes, press the **X** key.

After Setup initializes, Windows 98 Setup begins.

7. Follow the instructions on the screen, as described in "Running Setup on a New Installation" later in this chapter.

Installing Windows 98 on a Computer with Windows NT

You cannot install Windows 98 on a computer running any version of Windows NT. However, you can configure your computer to dual boot Windows 98 and Windows NT 4.*x* or earlier provided you follow these guidelines:

- Windows 98 must be set up in a different hard disk or partition than Windows NT.

- Drive C must be a FAT16 partition and must meet the minimum disk space requirements for a Windows 98 installation (195 MB of free hard-disk space for a typical installation).

- Run Windows 98 Setup by selecting Windows 95 from the **Boot Loader Operating System Selection** menu that appears at system startup. If Windows 95 does not appear on this menu, select MS-DOS instead.

  If the Windows NT Loader (NTLDR) stops responding, you can use the Windows NT recovery disks to restore the Windows NT boot sector.

- You cannot install Windows 98 to a directory with a shared Windows 3.1*x*/ Windows NT configuration. You need to install Windows 98 in a different directory.

- If your computer is not configured to dual boot MS-DOS and Windows NT, and you want that configuration, configure it to dual boot MS-DOS and Windows NT before you start Windows 98 Setup.

If Windows NT is already installed, Windows 98 Setup adds itself as an entry to the Windows NT boot menu to allow the user to select between Windows 98 or Windows NT when starting the computer.

For more information on how to install Windows 98 on a computer running Windows NT, see "Installing Windows 98 on a System Running Windows NT" and "Setting Up a Dual-Boot Configuration with Windows NT" in \Win98 \Setup.txt on your Windows 98 compact disc.

▶ **To start Windows 98 Setup from Windows NT**

1. Start your computer in the usual way.

2. Select **Windows 95** from the **Boot Loader Operating System Selection** menu that appears at system startup. If Windows 95 does not appear on this menu, select MS-DOS instead.

3. If you were able to start Windows 95, follow the instructions in "Upgrading Windows 95 Keeping Current Settings" or "Upgrading Windows 95 Changing Current Settings" earlier in this chapter.

   – Or –

   If you started MS-DOS instead, follow the instructions in "Performing a New Installation" earlier in this chapter.

4. Edit the Boot.ini file as explained in the following procedure "To edit the Boot.ini file."

▶ **To edit the Boot.ini file**

1. In Windows Explorer, click **View**, click **Options**, and then click **Show all files**.

2. Make sure **Hide file extensions for known file types** is not checked, and then click **OK**.

3. Right-click the **Boot.ini** file, and then click **Properties**.

4. Clear the **Read-only** check box, and then click **OK**.

5. Right-click the **Boot.ini** file, click **Copy**, right-click a blank area of the Windows Explorer dialog box, and then click **Paste**.

   A backup copy with the file name Copy of Boot.ini is created.

6. Double-click the **Boot.ini** file to open it.

7. Add the name and location of Windows NT in the [Operating Systems] section of the file. For example:

```
[Operating Systems]
C:\Winnt="Windows NT 4.0"
C:\"Microsoft Windows"
```

8. Save and close the Boot.ini file.

9. Right-click the Boot.ini file, and then click **Properties**.

10. Select the **Read-only** check box, and then click **OK**.

Installing Windows 98 on a Computer with OS/2

You cannot install Windows 98 on a computer running OS/2. To run Windows 98 Setup, you need to start MS-DOS and run Setup from MS-DOS as explained in "Running Setup from MS-DOS" later in this chapter.

Note If you are upgrading over OS/2 on an HPFS partition, you must have your OS/2 Disk 1 available when running Windows 98 Setup.

If you start MS-DOS from a floppy disk and then run Setup, you will no longer be able to start OS/2 after Windows 98 has been installed. You must delete the Autoexec.bat and Config.sys files that OS/2 uses before running Windows 98 Setup.

▶ **To remove OS/2 after installing Windows 98**

1. Back up the data files you want to keep.
2. Delete the files in each of your OS/2 directories and subdirectories, and then delete the OS/2 directories.
3. In My Computer or Windows Explorer, click **View**, click **Options**, and then click **Show All Files**. Delete the following OS/2 files:
   - Ea data.sf
   - OS21dr.msg
   - OS2krnl
   - OS2boot
   - Wp data.sf

Standardizing Windows 98 on Multiple Computers

If you intend to standardize Windows 98 on multiple computers, the most efficient way to install Windows 98 is by using setup scripts. Setup scripts allow you to customize and automate your installations. You can run Windows 98 Setup using a script that is located on a local computer or on a network server.

For information about creating and customizing setup scripts, see Chapter 3, "Custom Installations." For information on automated installations, see Chapter 4 "Automated Installations."

Tip for Accessibility Needs and Windows 98 Setup

Users who require accessibility aids with Windows might find it difficult to install Windows 98 in the usual way because accessibility aids cannot run with Windows 98 Setup.

To solve this problem, a setup script can be created with predefined answers for those users. Then the user can run Setup from the command prompt using this setup script. Windows 98 Setup will run without requiring additional user input. For more information, see Chapter 3, "Custom Installations" and Appendix H, "Accessibility."

Windows 98 Files Located on a Local Computer

You can automate Setup when both the Windows 98 files and the setup script are located locally on the same computer.

Note Windows 98 Setup uses Msbatch.inf if it is located in the installation directory whether or not it is specified on the command line.

▶ **To automate Windows 98 Setup when files are located on a local computer**

- At the command prompt, run Windows 98 Setup by specifying the batch file that contains the setup script, using the following syntax:

    D:**_Windows_directory_\Setup.exe a:**_script.inf_

    Where _Windows_directory_ is the directory that contains the Windows 98 files and _script.inf_ is the name of your setup script.

Windows 98 Files Located on a Network Server

You can also automate Setup when both the Windows 98 files and the setup script are located on a server that can be accessed by the local computer.

Note Windows 98 Setup uses Msbatch.inf if it is located in the installation directory whether or not it is specified on the command line.

▶ **To automate Windows 98 Setup when files are located on a server**

- At the command prompt, run Windows 98 Setup by specifying the batch file that contains the setup script, using the following syntax:

    _server_name__Windows_directory_**\Setup.exe** _script.inf_

Where *server_name* is the name of the sever, *Windows_directory* is the directory that contains the Windows 98 files, and *script.inf* is the name of your setup script.

Note If Windows 98 is installed from a server, the location of that network directory is stored in the registry. When you add a device or require additional support files to run Windows 98, Setup automatically attempts to retrieve the files from the same location on the server. This eliminates the need to maintain a permanent network connection on the computer and makes it easier to modify the configuration of a computer in a networked environment.

Using the Setup Command-Line Switches

Windows 98 Setup provides options to control the installation process. These options, or switches, are specified on the command line as arguments for the **setup** command (such as **setup /d**). Similar to MS-DOS command arguments, the specific option is preceded by a forward slash (/) character (not the backslash used to specify directory arguments).

Windows 98 Setup can be run with the **setup** command switches listed in Table 2.18.

Table 2.18   Setup command switches

Switch	Meaning
/?	Provides help for syntax and use of **setup** command-line switches.
/C	Do not load the SmartDrive disk cache.
/D	Do not use the existing version of Windows for the early phases of Setup. Use this switch if you have problems starting Setup that might be due to missing or damaged supporting files for Windows.
/DOMAIN: *domain_name*	Set the Windows NT Logon Validation domain used by Client for Microsoft Networks to *domain _name*.
/F	Do not look in the local cache for file names. Setup runs a little slower and saves a small amount of memory.
/IA	Turn off the "after providers" listed in the [AfterProvider] section of the Setupc.inf file.
/IB	Turn off the "before providers" listed in the [BeforeProvider] section of the Setupc.inf file.
/IC	Do a clean boot. If this is set and KeepRMDrivers=1 is not in the registry, drivers are commented out from the Config.sys/Autoexec.bat file.
/ID	Do not check for the minimum disk space required to install Windows 98.
/IE	Skip the Startup Disk screen.

Table 2.18   Setup command switches (*continued*)

Switch	Meaning
/IF	Do a "fast" setup. Do not notify setupx DOS FindFirst to not look up file names in the cache.
/IH	Run ScanDisk in the foreground so that you can see the results. Use this switch if the system stalls during the ScanDisk check or if an error results.
/IL	Load the Logitech mouse driver. Use this option if you have a Logitech Series C mouse.
/IM	Skip the check for low conventional memory.
/IN	Do not call the networking Setup software. Neither the networking software nor the Networking Wizard screens will be used.
/IQ	Do not check for cross-linked files.
/IR	Do not update the master boot record (MBR).
/IS	Do not run ScanDisk.
/NOSTART	Copy a minimal installation of the required dynamic-link libraries (DLLs) used by Windows 98 Setup, then exit to MS-DOS without installing Windows 98.
/NA#	Do not notify the user when other applications are running. **#** = **1** Do not display the warning message. **#** = **2** Do not display the error message for running MS-DOS-based applications. **#** = **3** Do not display either of the above messages. If you do not specify a number for #, (that is, if you just use **/NA**), Setup will not display either of the messages.
/NF	Do not prompt to remove the floppy disk from drive A at the end of the **Copying Windows 98 Files to Your Computer** Setup step (step three). Use this switch when installing Windows 98 from a bootable compact disc.
/NH	Do not run Hwinfo.exe when running Setup from the Windows 95 user interface.
/NR	Skips the registry check.
/PI	Keep forced configured hardware settings (hardware not using default settings). Some BIOS require hardware to have a forced configuration to work. By default, Setup removes the forced configuration and some hardware does not work properly after this is done.
/PJ	Load Advanced Configuration and Power Interface (ACPI) by default.

Table 2.18   Setup command switches (*continued*)

Switch	Meaning
script_filename	Use settings in the specified script to install Windows 98 automatically; for example, **setup msbatch.inf** specifies that Setup should use the settings in Msbatch.inf. You must specify the full file name. The setup script file name must be eight characters long with a three-character extension (8.3 file name).
	For more information about script file names, see Chapter 4, "Automated Installations."
/SRCDIR	Specifies the source directory where the Windows 98 Setup files are located.
/S *filename*	Load the specified Setup.inf file when starting setup.
/T:*tempdir*	Specifies the directory where Setup is to copy its temporary files. This directory must already exist, but any existing files in the directory will be deleted.
/U:*UPI*	Specifies the UPI.
/IV	Do not display billboards.
/IW	Do not dispay the **License Agreement** dialog box.
/IX	Do not perform a character set check.

In localized versions of Windows 98, Setup can also be run with the following switches.

Switch	Meaning
/A	Use AT drive mode (Japanese NEC version only).
/IF	Do not perform a bootable setup. It prevents BootMulti=1 from being put into the Msdos.sys file if a clean install is being performed and the drive is not an AT drive (Japanese NEC version only).
/IJ	Do not prompt user for boot drive (Japanese NEC version only).
/IO	Call the exit Windows executable (Japanese NEC version only).
/IY	Ignore language mismatches.

Running Setup: Step-by-Step

You can run the Windows 98 Setup program (Setup.exe) from the:

- Windows 95 user interface.
- Windows 3.1x user interface.
- MS-DOS command prompt.

Depending on the method you chose to run Setup, as explained in "Choosing a Method to Run Setup" earlier in this chapter, the Setup dialog boxes that appear and the information they request vary. This section provides step-by-step information on the installation process when running Setup from:

- MS-DOS when installing Windows 98 on a computer with a new or reformatted hard disk.
- The Windows 95 user interface when upgrading Windows 95 keeping current settings.
- MS-DOS when upgrading Windows 95 changing current settings.
- The Windows 3.1x user interface when upgrading Windows 3.1x.

Note Each of the following sections provide step-by-step information on the installation process; however, only the first section, "Running Setup on a New Installation," shows every screen shot of the process. Subsequent sections show only screen shots that are unique to that setup process.

Remove Conflicting Managers
In order for detection to run properly, you must remove conflicting managers from the Config.sys file, otherwise you will be asked to remove it during first boot. You must remove the following configuration managers:

- EMM386 (only if using the highscan option)
- EMM
- 386MAX

Note Windows 98 Setup always restarts your computer at least once during the installation process, but it can restart your computer more times. It restarts your computer twice if it can access the source path in real-mode for the hardware detection phase; it restarts your computer three times if a driver must be loaded to access it in protected mode.

Running Setup on a New Installation

To install Windows 98 on a computer with a new or reformatted hard disk, you start Setup from MS-DOS.

Important If you run Setup from MS-DOS using a network server or local CD-ROM drive, either the real-mode network or CD-ROM drivers must be loaded respectively.

After starting Setup from MS-DOS, it performs a routine check on your computer. It:

- Runs the real-mode version of ScanDisk. It creates the Scandisk.log file and checks for errors in the directory structure, file allocation table, and file system. A surface scan is not performed, the disk is not checked for physical errors, and long file name errors are not fixed. These errors are fixed only when you run ScanDisk in protected-mode (from Windows). If ScanDisk finds errors, it will let you know. You can view the log file by selecting **View Log** from the ScanDisk screen; otherwise, select **Exit**.

- Initializes your system and copies the necessary files for installing Windows 98.

- Displays the Windows 98 Setup screen. This screen has an information bar o n the left-hand side that displays the five steps that Setup will perform and a timer that shows the estimated time remaining to complete the installation. To begin the Setup process, click **Continue**.

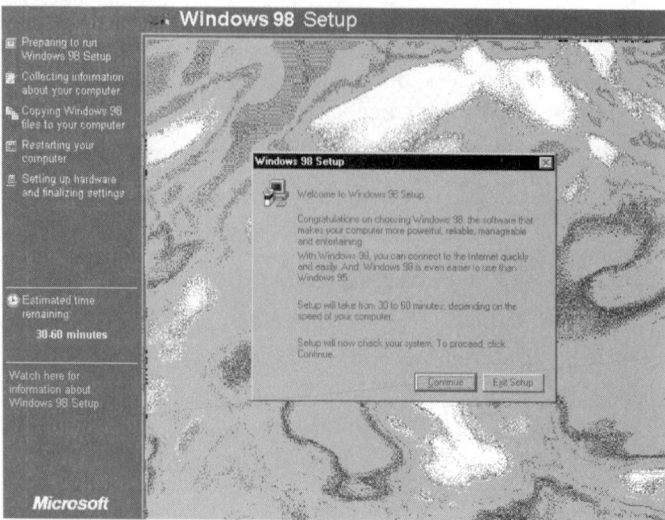

Setup prepares the Windows 98 Setup Wizard. Then, Setup starts its five-step installation process:

1. Preparing to run Windows 98 Setup.

2. Collecting information about your computer.

3. Copying Windows 98 files to your computer.

4. Restarting your computer.

5. Setting up hardware and finalizing settings.

The following sections describe each of these steps.

Step One: Preparing to Run Windows 98 Setup

During this step, Setup prepares the Windows 98 Setup Wizard, which guides you through the installation process. Setup:

- Displays the **Windows 98 Setup** dialog box.

- Creates the Setuplog.txt file in the root directory (C:\).
- Identifies the drive where Windows 98 is being installed and the source drive where the Windows 98 installation files are located (drive assignment).
- Creates the C:\Wininst0.400 temporary directory and copies Mini.cab to it. Mini.cab contains the mini-Windows program files required by Setup.
- Extracts all files in Precopy1.cab and Precopy2.cab to C:\Wininst0.400. These are the files necessary to run Setup Wizard.

Step Two: Collecting Information About Your Computer

During this step, Setup collects information about your computer and prepares it for copying the Windows 98 files through the following phases, where Setup:

- Presents the License Agreement (**License Agreement** dialog box).
- Prompts you to enter the Product Key (**Product Key** dialog box).
- Prompts you to select a directory for installing Windows 98 (**Select Directory** dialog box).
- Informs you that it is preparing the directory where it will install Windows 98 and verifying that there is enough space to install it (**Preparing Directory** dialog box).

- Lets you choose the type of Setup you want—Typical, Portable, Compact, or Custom (**Setup Options** dialog box).

- Prompts you to enter your name and company name (**User Information** dialog box).

- Lets you install the most common components or customize your selection (**Windows Components** dialog box).

- Lets you add or remove components (**Select Components** dialog box).

- Prompts you to identify your computer on the network (**Identification** dialog box).

- Lets you select the location for getting region-specific information from the Internet (**Establishing Your Location** dialog box).

- Prompts you to create the Startup Disk (**Startup Disk** dialog box).

- Starts copying files (**Start Copying Files** dialog box).

The License Agreement

After Setup Wizard is loaded, the License Agreement is displayed. You must accept the License Agreement to continue.

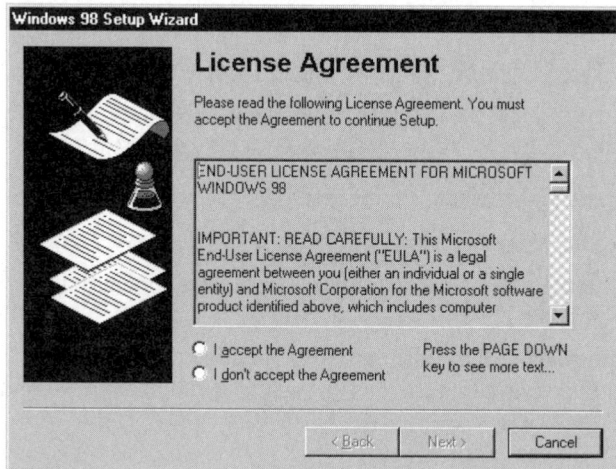

Product Key

Setup prompts you to enter the Product Key.

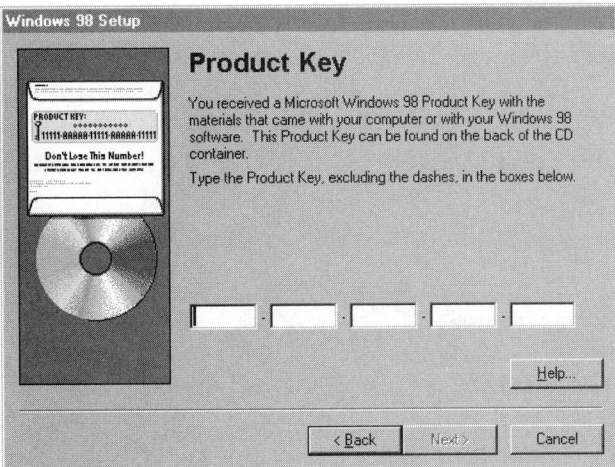

Type the Product Key in the spaces provided. The Product Key is located either on the Certificate of Authenticity (COA) or on the backliner of your Windows 98 compact disc. If the number you type is not accepted, check the following:

- Make sure the **Caps Lock** key is not on.

- If you are using the keypad to the right of your keyboard, make sure the **Num Lock** key is on.

The **Product Key** dialog box might not appear if you are installing Windows 98 from the network, depending on the requirements at your site.

Select Directory

After you enter your Product Key, the **Select Directory** dialog box appears.

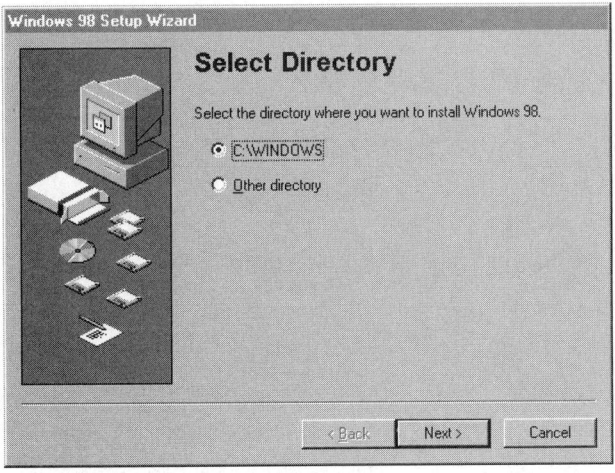

The default directory is C:\Windows. If you want to install Windows in a directory other than C:\Windows, follow these steps.

▶ **To install Windows 98 in a new directory**

1. In the **Select Directory** dialog box, click **Other directory**, and then click **Next**.

   The **Change Directory** dialog box appears.

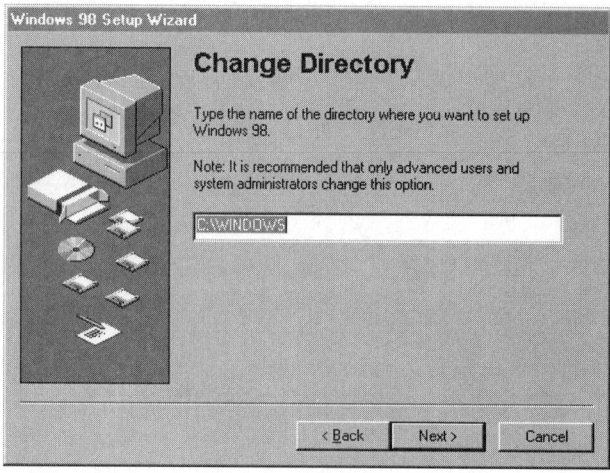

2. Type a new directory name, and then click **Next**. If you specify a directory that does not exist, Setup creates one for you.

Preparing Directory

After you select a directory, the **Preparing Directory** dialog box appears.

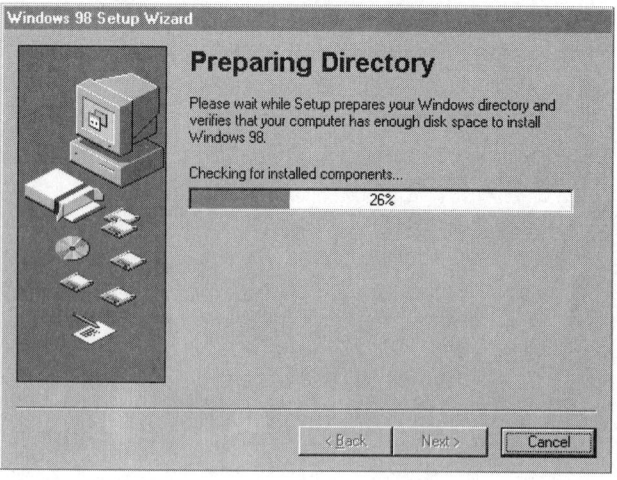

Setup checks for installed components and then checks whether there is adequate disk space for the files. It creates the Windows 98 directory structure, including all required folders under the \Windows (or *Your_InstallDirectory*) and \Program Files folders.

Note If there is not enough disk space, Setup Wizard prompts you to free some hard-disk space and then restart Setup.

Setup Options

Once Setup finishes setting up the directory structure, it prompts you to select the type of Setup you want through the **Setup Options** dialog box.

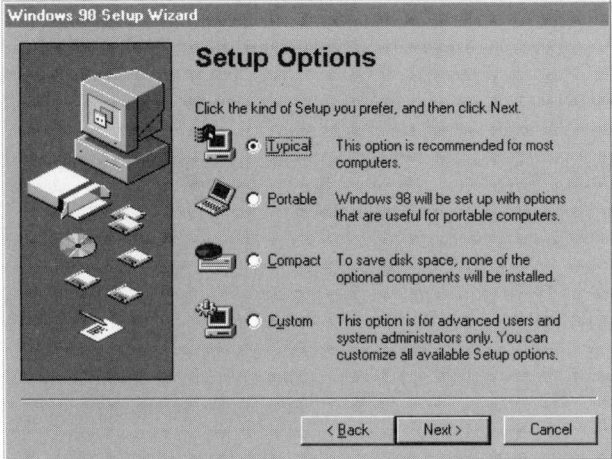

Each Setup option contains a specific set of components to install. When you choose a Setup option, Setup selects by default a set of appropriate components based on your choice. Later, through the **Select Components** dialog box, Setup gives you the choice to either accept the default selection or select your own components.

▶ **To choose a Setup option**

- In the **Setup Options** dialog box, click the Setup option you want, then click **Next**. The **Typical** Setup option is selected as the default.

Click this option	If you want
Typical	All of the components that are usually installed with Windows 98. Most users should select this Setup option.
Portable	To install the options generally required for portable computers.

Click this option	If you want
Compact	The smallest possible installation of Windows 98. For example, you may want to perform a Compact installation if your hard disk does not have much free space. Setup then installs no optional components. If you later want to use an optional component, such as Games or WebTV for Windows, then you have to install it. To install an optional component after Setup is completed, use Add/Remove Programs in Control Panel.
Custom	To choose which optional components are installed. If you do not select a Custom installation, then Setup installs only the optional components that are selected by *default*. If you know you are going to need certain Windows components, you may want to select a Custom installation and ensure that those components are included during Setup. Pan European users should choose this option in order to select the required regional settings and keyboard layout for their locale. Pan European users should choose this option in order to select the required regional setting and keyboard layout for their locale.

For a list of all Windows 98 components included in each Setup option, see Table 2.6 in "Choosing Typical, Portable, Compact, or Custom Setup Options" earlier in this chapter.

User Information

After the Setup Options phase, Windows 98 Setup asks you to type your name and company name, which Windows 98 uses to identify you for various operations. You must enter this information for Setup to continue.

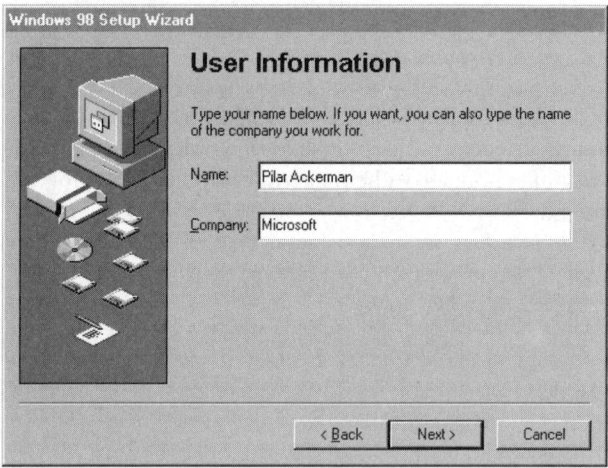

Windows Components

After you provide the user information, Setup displays the **Windows Components** dialog box.

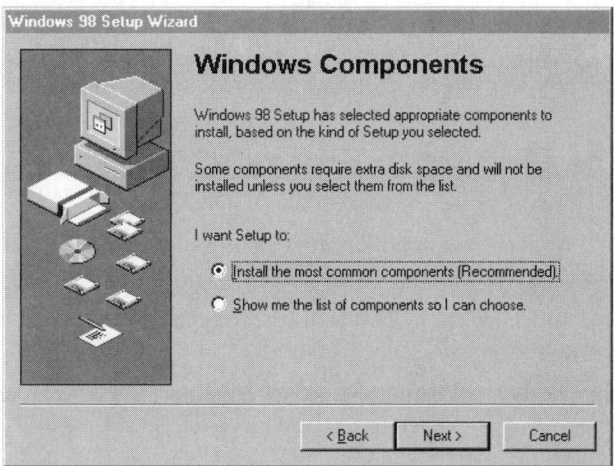

If you select **Install the most common components**, Setup continues the installation. If you select **Show me the list of components so I can choose**, the **Select Components** dialog box appears.

Select Components

The **Select Components** dialog box lets you customize your installation by choosing the components you want to install. For more information on which components are installed by default and the size of each component, see Tables 2.7 through 2.16 in "Choosing Typical, Portable, Compact, or Custom Setup Options" earlier in this chapter.

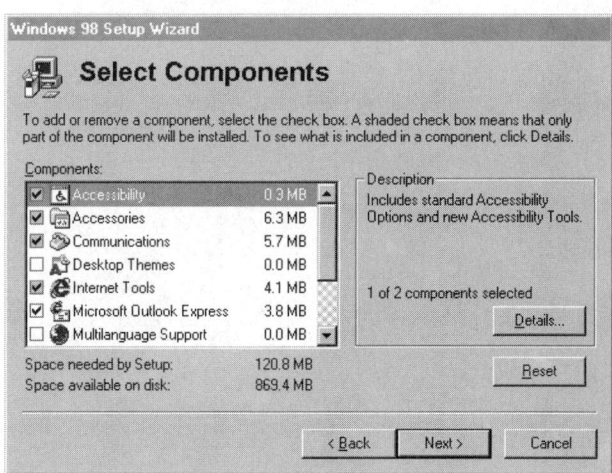

▶ **To select which components are installed**

1. In the **Components** list, click a component set (for example, **Communications**), and then click **Details**. A shaded box means that only part of the component will be installed.

   A dialog box appears, listing the components in the category.

2. Select or deselect the component you want to add or remove, and then click **OK**.

   - To add a component, make sure the component is checked.

   - To remove a component, clear its check box.

   - To prevent a component from being installed, make sure the component is not checked.

3. Repeat this procedure for each category in the **Components** list in the **Select Components** dialog box.

4. When you are satisfied with your selections, click **Next**. If you want to reset the list of components to the default, click **Reset**.

Note You can install or remove any of these components after Windows 98 is installed by using Add/Remove Programs in Control Panel.

Identification

After you have selected which components you want to install, Setup prompts you to identify how you want your computer to be identified on your network by displaying the **Identification** dialog box.

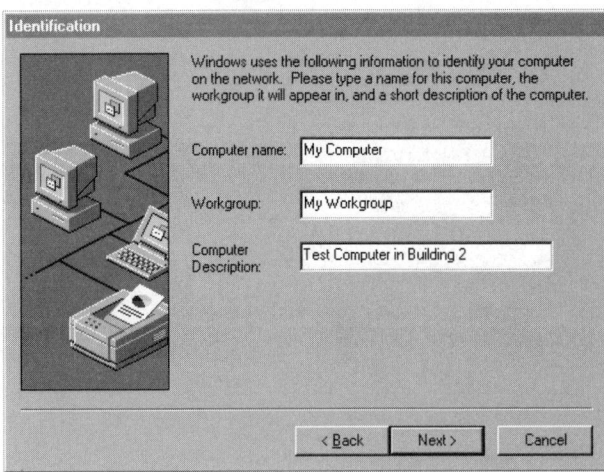

- The computer name must be unique on the network, and can be up to 15 characters long with no spaces (no blank characters). The name can contain only alphanumeric characters and the following special characters:

  ! @ # $ % ^ & ( ) - _ ' { } . ~

- The workgroup name can be up to 15 characters long and uses the same naming convention as the computer name. The workgroup is used to associate groups of computers together for more efficient browsing. The network administrator can provide guidelines for workgroup selection by using Wrkgrp.ini, as described in Chapter 3, "Custom Installations."

- The computer description can be up to 48 characters long, but it cannot contain any commas (,). This text appears as a comment next to the computer name when users are browsing the network, so you can use it to describe the department or location of the computer.

Establishing Your Location

Next, Setup prompts you to establish your location by displaying the **Establishing Your Location** dialog box.

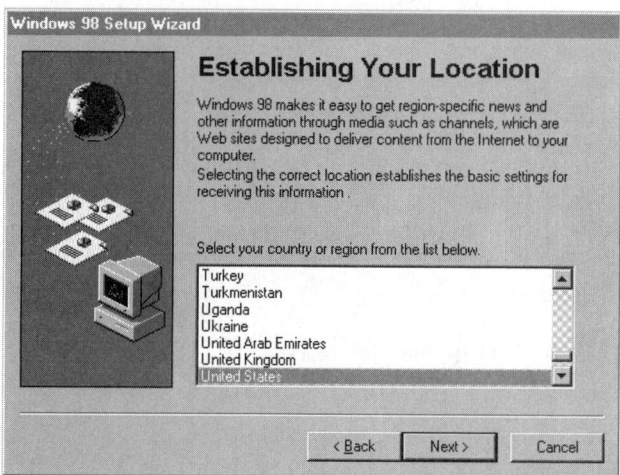

Select the location for getting region-specific news and other information through media such as *channels*—Web sites designed to deliver content from the Internet to your computer. Channels become available on your Windows 98 desktop Channel Bar after you install Windows 98 successfully.

▶ **To establish a location for receiving region-specific Internet information**

1. From the **Select your country or region from the list below** list, click the country or region you want. For example, **United States**.

2. Click **Next**.

Startup Disk

After establishing your location, Setup prompts you to create a Windows 98
Startup Disk by displaying the **Startup Disk** dialog box.

The Startup Disk is a bootable system disk with a collection of real-mode
Windows 98 commands and utilities that you can use to restart your computer
if you have trouble starting Windows 98 or to run diagnostic programs. It is
recommended that you create several Startup Disks. You can create a Startup
Disk during Setup and you can create extra copies by using Add/Remove
Programs in Control Panel.

To make a Startup Disk, you need one 1.44 MB floppy disk or two 1.2 MB
floppy disks.

▶ **To create a Startup Disk during Setup**

1. Click **Next** on the **Startup Disk** dialog box.

   Setup starts creating the Startup Disk.

2. Label a floppy disk "Windows 98 Startup Disk" and insert it into drive A.

3. Click **OK** to create the disk.

▶ **To create a Startup Disk using Add/Remove Programs in Control Panel**

1. In Control Panel, double-click Add/Remove Programs.

2. Click the **Startup Disk** tab.

3. Click **Create Disk**.

4. Follow the instructions on the screen.

For information about how to use a Startup Disk and its functionality, see "Using a Startup Disk" in Chapter 5, "Setup Technical Discussion." For information on the contents of the Startup Disk, see Appendix B, "Windows 98 System File Details."

Caution You cannot start Windows 98 if you try to start your computer with a Windows 95 Startup Disk or other existing startup disks (of any version of Microsoft Windows other than Windows 98).

The Startup Disk includes a real-mode generic ATAPI CD-ROM driver (Oakcdrom.sys) that allows the CD-ROM to function when the protected mode of the graphical user interface is not available. This driver is a generic IDE CD-ROM driver, and it does not work with SCSI CD-ROMs. Several third-party SCSI drivers are also included on the Startup Disk. In general, CD-ROM manufacturers include a floppy disk with the correct CD-ROM driver to use with their CD-ROM. However, if for some reason the specific driver for your CD-ROM is not available, you can use the generic ATAPI/SCSI CD-ROM driver included on the Startup Disk.

Note If your computer's CD-ROM is connected to a sound card, you need to copy the correct drivers for your CD-ROM drive and controller to the Startup Disk, and then edit the Config.sys file on the Startup Disk so that the correct drivers are loaded. Consult the documentation for your CD-ROM drive and controller to get the correct files and configuration settings.

Start Copying Files

After Setup finishes creating the Startup Disk, the **Start Copying Files** dialog box appears. Click **Next** to start copying files.

Step Three: Copying Windows 98 Files to Your Computer

After Setup has collected the information it needs from your computer, it begins copying the Windows 98 files to your computer. During this phase, Windows 98 Setup does not require your input.

Caution Do not interrupt file copying. If Setup is interrupted during the file-copying phase, Windows 98 may not run when you restart your computer because Windows 98 will not have all of the necessary files to start. If you interrupt Setup during this phase, you must run Setup again.

If you started Setup over a network, from a compact disc, or removable hard drive, Setup copies the appropriate Driver*x*.inf files that are necessary to access the installation media (installation point on a network server, compact disc, or removable hard drive) to continue Setup after your computer is restarted.

Step Four: Restarting Your Computer

After Setup finishes copying the Windows 98 files to your computer, you are prompted to restart your computer. You can click the **Restart Now** button to restart your computer immediately; if you do not click the button or wait more than 15 seconds to click it, Setup restarts your computer automatically.

After Setup restarts your computer, the following message appears on your screen:

`Getting ready to start Windows 98 for the first time.`

Step Five: Setting Up Hardware and Finalizing Settings

During this phase, Setup configures the following:

- Control Panel
- Programs on the **Start** menu
- Windows Help
- MS-DOS program settings
- Tuning Up Application Start
- Time zone
- System Configuration

When Setup finishes setting up hardware and configuring settings, Setup restarts your computer and asks you to log on. If your computer is connected to the network, you may be asked for a domain name and a network password. After you log on, Setup:

- Builds a driver information database.
- Updates system settings.
- Sets up personalized settings such as settings for the Internet Explorer 4 browsing software, **Start** menu, Online services, Volume Control, and Channels.

Then, Setup displays the **Welcome to Windows 98** dialog box.

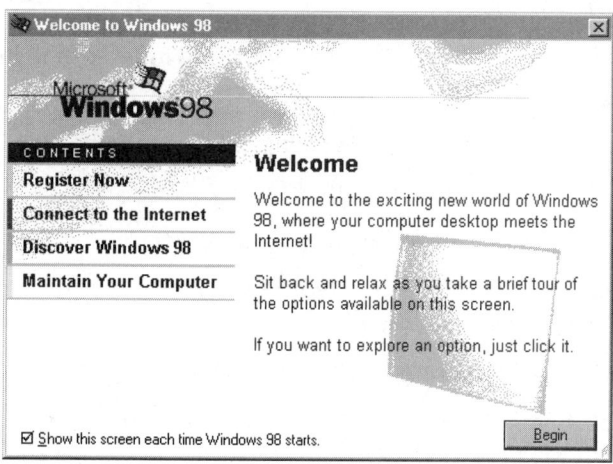

Running Setup from the Windows 95 Interface

To upgrade your Windows 95–based computer to Windows 98, keeping your computer's configuration settings, you start Setup from the Windows 95 user interface. If you want to install Windows 98 on a computer with Windows 95 but want to change current settings, start Setup from MS-DOS and read the step-by-step information in "Running Setup from MS-DOS" later in this chapter.

When upgrading from Windows 95, Windows 98 Setup:

- Uses the same settings as the current installation.
- No longer performs full hardware detection, although Setup verifies legacy hardware registry settings.
- Migrates the information on applications and utilities already installed to Windows 98.

When running Windows 98 Setup from the Windows 95 user interface, it skips some of the tasks that were performed by Windows 95 Setup, including the following:

- Performing full hardware detection.
- Allowing you to choose Setup options (Custom, Typical, Portable, and Compact).
- Configuring hardware.

These tasks were removed in Windows 98 Setup to help speed the installation process and minimize user interaction. You can still add or remove components after setting up Windows 98 by using the **Windows Setup** tab from Add/Remove Programs in Control Panel, or by running Setup from MS-DOS (through the **Setup Options** dialog box, which is displayed when running Setup from MS-DOS).

After starting Setup from Windows 95, the **Windows 98 Setup** screen appears. To begin the Setup process, click **Continue**.

Following are the five steps that Setup performs during the installation process:

1. Preparing to run Windows 98 Setup.
2. Collecting information about your computer.
3. Copying Windows 98 files to your computer.
4. Restarting your computer.
5. Setting up hardware and finalizing settings.

The following sections describe each of these steps.

Step One: Preparing to Run Windows 98 Setup

During this step, Setup checks your system and prepares Setup Wizard.

Checking Your System

During this phase, Setup performs the following tasks:

- Creates the Setuplog.txt file in the root directory (C:\).

- Checks for anti-virus software. If CMOS anti-virus is enabled, Setup may fail or stop. Setup writes the following lines in Setuplog.txt:

```
fsCmosAVCheck: Attempting CMOS Anti Virus Test
fs CmosAVCheck: CMOS Anti Virus Test SUCCEEDED
```

The last line is added only if the anti-virus test succeeds. If your computer is running anti-virus software that is protecting the master boot record, Setup asks you to disable the anti-virus software before proceeding. Setup modifies the Autoexec.bat file to call Suwarn.bat. If Setup fails or stops, Suwarn.bat runs at next reboot and displays a message explaining why Setup failed and asking you to disable all anti-virus software or contact your hardware vendor.

Preparing the Setup Wizard

Setup prepares the Windows 98 Setup Wizard, which guides you through the rest of the installation process. After you click **Continue**, Setup:

- Creates the C:\Wininst0.400 temporary directory and copies Mini.cab to it. Mini.cab contains the mini-Windows program files required by Setup.
- Extracts all files in Precopy1.cab and Precopy2.cab to C:\Wininst0.400. These are the files necessary to run Setup Wizard.

Note If Setup fails, and Recovery was not selected, additional directories may be created: \Wininst1.400, \Wininst2.400, and so on.

Step Two: Collecting Information About Your Computer

During this step, Setup collects information about your computer and prepares it for copying the Windows 98 files through the following phases, where Setup:

- Presents the License Agreement (**License Agreement** dialog box).
- Prompts you to enter the Product Key (**Product Key** dialog box).
- Checks your system by running protected-mode ScanDisk (**Checking Your System** dialog box).
- Initializes your system by checking the registry for corruption (**Initializing Your System** dialog box).
- Informs you that it is preparing the directory where it will install Windows 98 and verifying that there is enough space to install it (**Preparing Directory** dialog box).
- Gives you the option to save system files (**Save System Files** and **Saving System Files** dialog boxes).
- Lets you select the location for getting region-specific information from the Internet (**Establishing Your Location** dialog box).

- Prompts you to create the Startup Disk (**Startup Disk** dialog box).
- Starts copying files (**Start Copying Files** dialog box).

The License Agreement

After Setup Wizard is loaded, the License Agreement is displayed. You must accept the License Agreement to continue.

Product Key

Setup prompts you to enter the Product Key through the **Product Key** dialog box. Type the Product Key in the spaces provided. The Product Key is located either on the Certificate of Authenticity (COA) or on the backliner of your Windows 98 compact disc. If the number you type is not accepted, check the following:

- Make sure the **Caps Lock** key is not on.
- If you are using the keypad to the right of your keyboard, make sure the **Num Lock** key is on.

The **Product Key** dialog box might not appear if you are installing Windows 98 from the network, depending on the requirements at your site.

Checking Your System

After you accept the License Agreement and enter your Product Key, Setup checks your system by running protected-mode ScanDisk and initializes your computer's registry.

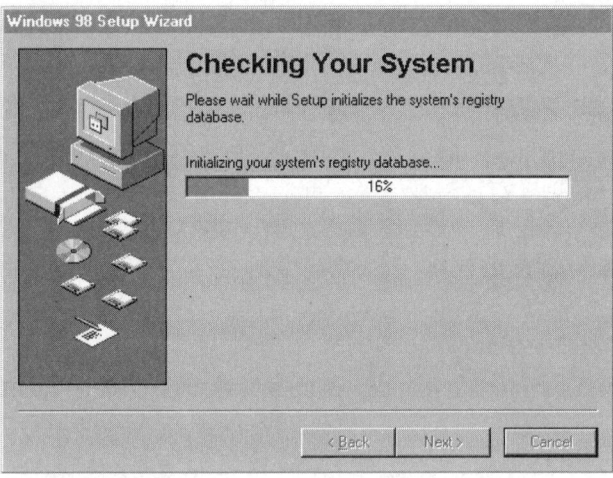

You will not see it run, unless an error occurs. If ScanDisk encounters an error in long file names, it fixes them. ScanDisk does not perform a surface scan, therefore, the disk is not checked for physical errors.

Initializing Your System

After running ScanDisk, Setup checks the registry for corruption by running the ScanRegW.exe utility, with the switch **/w** in protected mode. This verifies the integrity of the registry. If an error is found, Setup prompts you to reboot your computer and run ScanRegW in real-mode from the command prompt.

ScanRegW does not fix nor restore corrupted registries—it just detects corruption and prompts the user to try real-mode ScanReg. ScanRegW also backs up the registry, up to five different versions. This gives users the ability to restore a specific backup of the registry that they know was error free.

Note Typical registries are larger than 2 MB. Having up to five backups plus a working version of the registry requires a lot of disk space. To free up space, delete older backups that you no longer need.

Preparing Directory

After you select a directory, the **Preparing Directory** dialog box appears. Setup checks for installed components and then checks whether there is adequate disk space for the files. It creates the Windows 98 directory structure, including all required folders under the \Windows (or *Your_InstallDirectory*) and \Program Files folders.

Note If there is not enough disk space, Setup Wizard prompts you to free some hard-disk space and then restart Setup.

Save System Files

Setup displays the **Save System Files** dialog box. It gives you the option to save your existing MS-DOS and Windows system files so you can uninstall Windows 98 if necessary. This requires up to 50 MB of extra disk space.

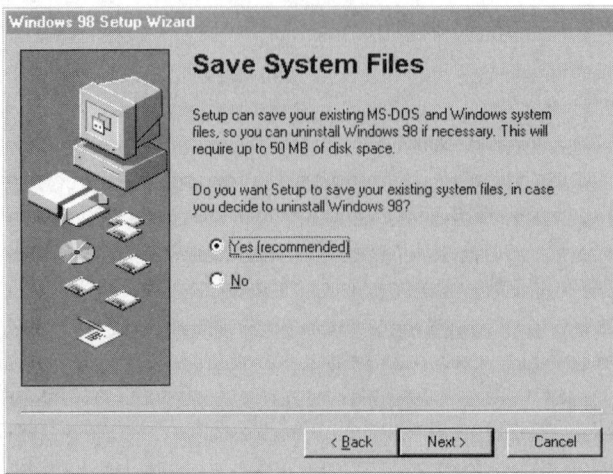

Yes (recommended). It is highly recommended that you choose this option. If you experience problems with Windows 98, you will be able to restore your Windows 95 configuration by uninstalling Windows 98. If you choose this option, Setup displays the **Saving System Files** dialog box.

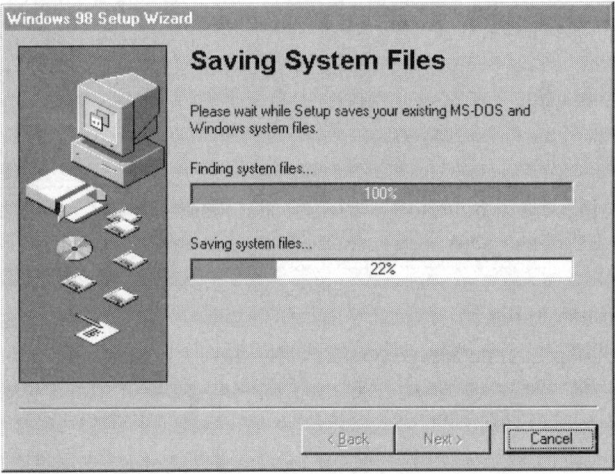

It finds the system files and it saves them in the following files:

- **Winundo.dat**. This file contains all the files required to restore Windows 95. It can be up to 50 MB in size.

- **Winundo.ini**. This file contains information about the original location of the files stored in Winundo.dat.

Setup saves the current system files to the root directory. However, it lets you choose the location if you have more than one logical drive.

No. If you select **No**, you will not be able to uninstall Windows 98. To remove Windows 98, you have to delete the Windows 98 directory and reinstall the previous operating system. Any Windows-based programs installed after Windows 98, have to be reinstalled.

Caution   If you converted your drive to FAT32 or compressed it with DriveSpace, you cannot uninstall Windows 98, even if you saved your system files.

Establishing Your Location

Next, Setup prompts you to establish your location by displaying the **Establishing Your Location** dialog box. Select the location for getting region-specific news and other information through media such as *channels*—Web sites designed to deliver content from the Internet to your computer. Channels become available on your Windows 98 desktop Channel Bar after you install Windows 98 successfully.

▶ **To establish a location for receiving region-specific Internet information**

1. From the **Select your country or region from the list below** list, click the country or region you want. For example, **United States**.

2. Click **Next**.

Startup Disk

After establishing your location, Setup prompts you to create a Windows 98 Startup Disk by displaying the **Startup Disk** dialog box. The Startup Disk is a bootable system disk with a collection of real-mode Windows 98 commands and utilities that you can use to restart your computer if you have trouble starting Windows 98 or to run diagnostic programs. It is recommended that you create several Startup Disks. You can create a Startup Disk during Setup and you can create extra copies by using Add/Remove Programs in Control Panel.

To make a Startup Disk, you need one 1.44 MB floppy disk or two 1.2 MB floppy disks.

▶ **To create a Startup Disk during Setup**

1. Click **Next** on the **Startup Disk** dialog box.

   Setup starts creating the Startup Disk.

2. Label a floppy disk "Windows 98 Startup Disk" and insert it into drive A.

3. Click **OK** to create the disk.

▶ **To create a Startup Disk using Add/Remove Programs in Control Panel**

1. In Control Panel, double-click Add/Remove Programs.

2. Click the **Startup Disk** tab.

3. Click **Create Disk**.

4. Follow the instructions on the screen.

For information about how to use a Startup Disk and its functionality, see "Using a Startup Disk" in Chapter 5, "Setup Technical Discussion." For information on the contents of the Startup Disk, see Appendix B, "Windows 98 System File Details."

Caution You cannot start Windows 98 if you try to start your computer with a Windows 95 Startup Disk or other existing startup disks (of any version of Microsoft Windows other than Windows 98).

The Startup Disk includes a real-mode generic ATAPI CD-ROM driver (Oakcdrom.sys) that allows the CD-ROM to function when the protected mode of the graphical user interface is not available. This driver is a generic IDE CD-ROM driver, and it does not work with SCSI CD-ROMs. Several third-party SCSI drivers are also included on the Startup Disk. In general, CD-ROM manufacturers include a floppy disk with the correct CD-ROM driver to use with their CD-ROM. However, if for some reason the specific driver for your CD-ROM is not available, you can use the generic ATAPI/SCSI CD-ROM driver included on the Startup Disk.

Note If your computer's CD-ROM is connected to a sound card, you need to copy the correct drivers for your CD-ROM drive and controller to the Startup Disk, and then edit the Config.sys file on the Startup Disk so that the correct drivers are loaded. Consult the documentation for your CD-ROM drive and controller to get the correct files and configuration settings.

Start Copying Files

After Setup finishes creating the Startup Disk, the **Start Copying Files** dialog box appears. Click **Next** to start copying files.

Step Three: Copying Windows 98 Files to Your Computer

After Setup has collected the information it needs from your computer, it begins copying the Windows 98 files to your computer. During this phase, Windows 98 Setup does not require your input.

Caution Do not interrupt file copying. If Setup is interrupted during the file-copying phase, Windows 98 may not run when you restart your computer because Windows 98 will not have all of the necessary files to start. If you interrupt Setup during this phase, you must run Setup again.

If you started Setup over a network, from a compact disc, or removable hard drive, Setup copies the appropriate Driver*x*.inf files that are necessary to access the installation media (installation point on a network server, compact disc, or removable hard drive) to continue Setup after your computer is restarted.

Step Four: Restarting Your Computer

After Setup finishes copying the Windows 98 files to your computer, you are prompted to restart your computer. You can click the **Restart Now** button to restart your computer immediately; if you do not click the button or wait more than 15 seconds to click it, Setup restarts your computer automatically.

After Setup restarts your computer, the following message appears on your screen:

```
Getting ready to start Windows 98 for the first time.
```

Setup also performs the following actions:

- It modifies the Win.ini, System.ini, and registry files to add the Windows 98–specific settings.

- It examines the Autoexec.bat and Config.sys files (if they exist) for incompatible device drivers and terminate-and-stay-resident (TSR) programs as specified by entries in the Setupc.inf file. This file is located in the \Windows\Inf folder, which is a hidden folder. Setup comments out, using the REM command, any incompatible or unnecessary entries from this files.

Note If you determine that any of your programs or hardware do not run correctly after setting up Windows 98, and the programs require specific entries in either the Config.sys or the Autoexec.bat file, you can restore them by removing the REM comments from their entries. For example, Setup comments out any real-mode mouse drivers entries in either file. It is possible that if you restore these files, this could interfere with the functionality of Windows 98. If this is the case, contact the manufacturer of the hardware or software to check whether there is a Windows 98–compatible version.

Step Five: Setting Up Hardware and Finalizing Settings

After Setup restarts your computer for the first time, Setup detects the hardware you have installed on your computer. This is different from Windows 95 Setup, where hardware detection occurred prior to the file-copy phase. Performing hardware detection after restarting your computer once is more reliable and less likely to create problems that cause the computer to stop responding.

During this phase, Setup configures the following:

- Control Panel
- Programs on the **Start** menu
- Windows Help
- MS-DOS program settings
- Tuning Up Application Start
- Time zone
- System Configuration

When starting Windows 98 Setup from Windows 95, Setup detects only Plug and Play devices. Setup retains the Windows 95 non–Plug and Play settings, as well as the existing printer and Microsoft Windows Messaging settings.

If you need to add a non–Plug and Play device, you must do so either before upgrading to Windows 98 or after upgrading. If you choose to install the new non–Plug and Play device after upgrading to Windows 98, you need to use Add New Hardware from Control Panel.

When Setup finishes setting up hardware and configuring settings, Setup restarts your computer and asks you to log on. If your computer is connected to the network, you may be asked for a domain name and a network password. After you log on, Setup:

- Builds a driver information database.
- Updates system settings.
- Sets up personalized settings such as settings for the Internet Explorer 4 browsing software, **Start** menu, Online services, Volume Control, and Channels.

Then, Setup displays the **Welcome to Windows 98** dialog box.

Running Setup from MS-DOS

If you want to upgrade your Windows 95–based computer to Windows 98 but want to change the installation directory, you must start Setup from MS-DOS. You also run Setup from MS-DOS if you tried to upgrade Windows 95 keeping current settings (starting Setup from Windows 95) but Setup failed.

Important If you run Setup from MS-DOS using a network server or local CD-ROM drive, either the real-mode network or CD-ROM drivers must be loaded respectively.

After starting Setup from MS-DOS, it performs a routine check on your computer. It:

- Runs the real-mode version of ScanDisk. It creates the Scandisk.log file and checks for errors in the directory structure, file allocation table, and file system. A surface scan is not performed, the disk is not checked for physical errors, and long file name errors are not fixed. These errors are fixed only when you run ScanDisk in protected-mode (from Windows). If ScanDisk finds errors, it will let you know. You can view the log file by selecting **View Log** from the ScanDisk screen; otherwise, select **Exit**.

- Initializes your system and copies the necessary files for installing Windows 98.

- Displays the Windows 98 Setup screen. This screen has an information bar on the left-hand side that displays the five steps that Setup will perform and a timer that shows the estimated time remaining to complete the installation.

Setup prepares the Windows 98 Setup Wizard. Then, Setup starts its five-step installation process:

1. Preparing to run Windows 98 Setup.
2. Collecting information about your computer.
3. Copying Windows 98 files to your computer.
4. Restarting your computer.
5. Setting up hardware and finalizing settings.

The following sections describe each of these steps.

Step One: Preparing to Run Windows 98 Setup

During this step, Setup prepares the Windows 98 Setup Wizard, which guides you through the installation process. Setup:

- Displays the **Windows 98 Setup** dialog box.

- Creates the Setuplog.txt file in the root directory (C:\).

- Identifies the drive where Windows 98 is being installed and the source drive where the Windows 98 installation files are located (drive assignment).

- Creates the C:\Wininst0.400 temporary directory and copies Mini.cab to it. Mini.cab contains the mini-Windows program files required by Setup.

- Extracts all files in Precopy1.cab and Precopy2.cab to C:\Wininst0.400. These are the files necessary to run Setup Wizard.

Step Two: Collecting Information About Your Computer

During this step, Setup collects information about your computer and prepares it for copying the Windows 98 files through the following phases, where Setup:

- Presents the License Agreement (**License Agreement** dialog box).
- Prompts you to enter the Product Key (**Product Key** dialog box).
- Prompts you to select a directory for installing Windows 98 (**Select Directory** dialog box).
- Checks your system (**Checking Your System** dialog box).
- Informs you that it is preparing the directory where it will install Windows 98 and verifying that there is enough space to install it (**Preparing Directory** dialog box).
- Gives you the option to save system files (**Save System Files** dialog box).
- Lets you select the location for getting region-specific information from the Internet (**Establishing Your Location** dialog box).
- Prompts you to create the Startup Disk (**Startup Disk** dialog box).
- Starts copying files (**Start Copying Files** dialog box).

The License Agreement

After Setup Wizard is loaded, the License Agreement is displayed. You must accept the License Agreement to continue.

Product Key

Setup prompts you to enter the Product Key through the **Product Key** dialog box. Type the Product Key in the spaces provided. The Product Key is located either on the Certificate of Authenticity (COA) or on the backliner of your Windows 98 compact disc. If the number you type is not accepted, check the following:

- Make sure the **Caps Lock** key is not on.
- If you are using the keypad to the right of your keyboard, make sure the **Num Lock** key is on.

The **Product Key** dialog box might not appear if you are installing Windows 98 from the network, depending on the requirements at your site.

Select Directory

After you enter your Product Key, the **Select Directory** dialog box appears. The default directory is C:\Windows. If you want to install Windows in a directory other than C:\Windows, follow these steps.

▶ **To install Windows 98 in a new directory**

1. In the **Select Directory** dialog box, click **Other directory**, and then click **Next**. The **Change Directory** dialog box appears.

2. Type a new directory name, and then click **Next**. If you specify a directory that does not exist, Setup creates one for you.

Checking Your System

Setup checks your system and initializes your computer's registry.

Preparing Directory

After you select a directory, the **Preparing Directory** dialog box appears. Setup checks for installed components and then checks whether there is adequate disk space for the files. It creates the Windows 98 directory structure, including all required folders under the \Windows (or *Your_InstallDirectory*) and \Program Files folders.

Note If there is not enough disk space, Setup Wizard prompts you to free some hard-disk space and then restart Setup.

Save System Files

Setup displays the **Save System Files** dialog box. It gives you the option to save your existing MS-DOS and Windows system files so you can uninstall Windows 98 if necessary. This requires up to 50 MB of extra disk space.

Yes (recommended). It is highly recommended that you choose this option. If you experience problems with Windows 98, you will be able to restore your Windows 95 configuration by uninstalling Windows 98. If you choose this option, Setup displays the **Saving System Files** dialog box. It then finds the system files and saves them in the following files:

- **Winundo.dat**. This file contains all the files required to restore Windows 95. It can be up to 50 MB in size.

- **Winundo.ini**. This file contains information about the original location of the files stored in Winundo.dat.

Setup saves the current system files to the root directory. However, it lets you choose the location if you have more than one logical drive.

No. If you select **No**, you will not be able to uninstall Windows 98. To remove Windows 98, you have to delete the Windows 98 directory and reinstall the previous operating system. Any Windows-based programs installed after Windows 98, have to be reinstalled.

Caution If you converted your drive to FAT32 or compressed it with DriveSpace, you cannot uninstall Windows 98, even if you saved your system files.

Establishing Your Location

Next, Setup prompts you to establish your location by displaying the **Establishing Your Location** dialog box. Select the location for getting region-specific news and other information through media such as *channels*—Web sites designed to deliver content from the Internet to your computer. Channels become available on your Windows 98 desktop Channel Bar after you install Windows 98 successfully.

▶ **To establish a location for receiving region-specific Internet information**

1. From the **Select your country or region from the list below** list, click the country or region you want. For example, **United States**.

2. Click **Next**.

Startup Disk

After establishing your location, Setup prompts you to create a Windows 98 Startup Disk by displaying the **Startup Disk** dialog box. The Startup Disk is a bootable system disk with a collection of real-mode Windows 98 commands and utilities that you can use to restart your computer if you have trouble starting Windows 98 or to run diagnostic programs. It is recommended that you create several Startup Disks. You can create a Startup Disk during Setup and you can create extra copies by using Add/Remove Programs in Control Panel.

To make a Startup Disk, you need one 1.44 MB floppy disk or two 1.2 MB floppy disks.

▶ **To create a Startup Disk during Setup**

1. Click **Next** on the **Startup Disk** dialog box.

    Setup starts creating the Startup Disk.

2. Label a floppy disk "Windows 98 Startup Disk" and insert it into drive A.

3. Click **OK** to create the disk.

▶ **To create a Startup Disk using Add/Remove Programs in Control Panel**

1. In Control Panel, double-click Add/Remove Programs.

2. Click the **Startup Disk** tab.

3. Click **Create Disk**.

4. Follow the instructions on the screen.

For information about how to use a Startup Disk and its functionality, see "Using a Startup Disk" in Chapter 5, "Setup Technical Discussion." For information on the contents of the Startup Disk, see Appendix B, "Windows 98 System File Details."

Caution You cannot start Windows 98 if you try to start your computer with a Windows 95 Startup Disk or other existing Startup Disks (of any version of Microsoft Windows other than Windows 98).

The Startup Disk includes a real-mode generic ATAPI CD-ROM driver (Oakcdrom.sys) that allows the CD-ROM to function when the protected mode of the graphical user interface is not available. This driver is a generic IDE CD-ROM driver, and it does not work with SCSI CD-ROMs. Several third-party SCSI drivers are also included on the Startup Disk. In general, CD-ROM manufacturers include a floppy disk with the correct CD-ROM driver to use with their CD-ROM. However, if for some reason the specific driver for your CD-ROM is not available, you can use the generic ATAPI/SCSI CD-ROM driver included on the Startup Disk.

Note If your computer's CD-ROM is connected to a sound card, you need to copy the correct drivers for your CD-ROM drive and controller to the Startup Disk, and then edit the Config.sys file on the Startup Disk so that the correct drivers are loaded. Consult the documentation for your CD-ROM drive and controller to get the correct files and configuration settings.

Start Copying Files

After Setup finishes creating the Startup Disk, the **Start Copying Files** dialog box appears. Click **Next** to start copying files.

Step Three: Copying Windows 98 Files to Your Computer

After Setup has collected the information it needs from your computer, it begins copying the Windows 98 files to your computer. During this phase, Windows 98 Setup does not require your input.

Caution Do not interrupt file copying. If Setup is interrupted during the file-copying phase, Windows 98 may not run when you restart your computer because Windows 98 will not have all of the necessary files to start. If you interrupt Setup during this phase, you must run Setup again.

If you started Setup over a network, from a compact disc, or removable hard drive, Setup copies the appropriate Driver*x*.inf files that are necessary to access the installation media (installation point on a network server, compact disc, or removable hard drive) to continue Setup after your computer is restarted.

Step Four: Restarting Your Computer

After Setup finishes copying the Windows 98 files to your computer, you are prompted to restart your computer. You can click the **Restart Now** button to restart your computer immediately; if you do not click the button or wait more than 15 seconds to click it, Setup restarts your computer automatically.

After Setup restarts your computer, the following message appears on your screen:

```
Getting ready to start Windows 98 for the first time.
```

Step Five: Setting Up Hardware and Finalizing Settings

During this phase, Setup configures the following:

- Control Panel
- Programs on the **Start** menu
- Windows Help
- MS-DOS program settings
- Tuning Up Application Start
- Time zone
- System Configuration

When Setup finishes setting up hardware and configuring settings, Setup restarts your computer and asks you to log on. If your computer is connected to the network, you may be asked for a domain name and a network password. After you log on, Setup:

- Builds a driver information database.
- Updates system settings.
- Sets up personalized settings such as settings for the Internet Explorer 4 browsing software, **Start** menu, Online services, Volume Control, and Channels.

Then, Setup displays the **Welcome to Windows 98** dialog box.

Running Setup from the Windows 3.1x Interface

You can upgrade your Windows 3.1x computer by starting Setup from the Windows 3.1x user interface.

After starting Setup from Windows 3.1*x*, the **Windows 98 Setup** screen appears and Setup starts its five-step installation process:

1. Preparing to run Windows 98 Setup.

2. Collecting information about your computer.

3. Copying Windows 98 files to your computer.

4. Restarting your computer.

5. Setting up hardware and finalizing settings.

The following sections describe each of these steps.

Step One: Preparing to Run Windows 98 Setup

During this step, Setup checks your system and prepares the Windows 98 Setup Wizard, which guides you through the installation process. Setup:

- Creates the Setuplog.txt file in the root directory (C:\).

- Identifies the drive where Windows 98 is being installed and the source drive where the Windows 98 installation files are located (drive assignment).

- Creates the C:\Wininst0.400 temporary directory and copies Mini.cab to it. Mini.cab contains the mini-Windows program files required by Setup.

- Extracts all files in Precopy1.cab and Precopy2.cab to C:\Wininst0.400. These are the files necessary to run Setup Wizard.

Step Two: Collecting Information About Your Computer

During this step, Setup collects information about your computer and prepares it for copying the Windows 98 files through the following phases, where Setup:

- Presents the License Agreement (**License Agreement** dialog box).

- Prompts you to enter the Product Key (**Product Key** dialog box).

- Prompts you to select a directory for installing Windows 98 (**Select Directory** dialog box).

- Checks your system (**Checking Your System** dialog box).

- Informs you that it is preparing the directory where it will install Windows 98 and verifying that there is enough space to install it (**Preparing Directory** dialog box).

- Gives you the option to save system files (**Save System Files** dialog box).

- Lets you choose the type of Setup you want—Typical, Portable, Compact, or Custom (**Setup Options** dialog box).

- Lets you install the most common components or customize your selection (**Windows Components** dialog box).

- Lets you add or remove components (**Select Components** dialog box).

- Lets you select the location for getting region-specific information from the Internet (**Establishing Your Location** dialog box).

- Prompts you to create the Startup Disk (**Startup Disk** dialog box).

- Starts copying files (**Start Copying Files** dialog box).

The License Agreement

After Setup Wizard is loaded, the License Agreement is displayed. You must accept the License Agreement to continue.

Product Key

Setup prompts you to enter your product key through the **Product Key** dialog box. Type the product key in the spaces provided. The Product Key is located either on the Certificate of Authenticity (COA) or on the backliner of your Windows 98 compact disc. If the number you type is not accepted, check the following:

- Make sure the **Caps Lock** key is not on.

- If you are using the keypad to the right of your keyboard, make sure the **Num Lock** key is on.

The **Product Key** dialog box might not appear if you are installing Windows 98 from the network, depending on the requirements at your site.

Select Directory

After you enter your product key, the **Select Directory** dialog box appears. The default directory is C:\Windows. If you want to install Windows in a directory other than C:\Windows, follow these steps.

▶ **To install Windows 98 in a new directory**

1. In the **Select Directory** dialog box, click **Other directory**, and then click **Next**. The **Change Directory** dialog box appears.

2. Type a new directory name, and then click **Next**. If you specify a directory that does not exist, Setup creates one for you.

Migrating Your Existing Applications and System Settings

If you choose to install Windows 98 in a new directory, you need to reinstall your Windows-based applications to make them work properly under Windows 98 because Windows 98 because application support files such as DLLs will be missing from the Windows 98 directory. Windows 98 Setup cannot transfer this information automatically.

You cannot migrate your existing system settings and groups by copying all the GRP and INI files from your previous Windows directory into the new installation directory. This does not work with Windows 98, because GRP files and INI file entries cannot be used by Windows 98 unless Windows 98 Setup migrates this information to the registry. You must run Windows 98 Setup and install Windows 98 in the existing Windows directory to migrate GRP and INI file information from your existing configuration.

Checking Your System

Setup checks your system and initializes your computer's registry.

Preparing Directory

After you select a directory, the **Preparing Directory** dialog box appears. Setup checks for installed components and then checks whether there is adequate disk space for the files. It creates the Windows 98 directory structure, including all required folders under the \Windows (or *Your_InstallDirectory*) and \Program Files folders.

Note If there is not enough disk space, Setup Wizard prompts you to free some hard-disk space and then restart Setup.

Save System Files

Setup displays the **Save System Files** dialog box. It gives you the option to save your existing MS-DOS and Windows system files so you can uninstall Windows 98 if necessary. This requires up to 50 MB of extra disk space.

Yes (recommended). It is highly recommended that you choose this option. If you experience problems with Windows 98, you will be able to restore your Windows 95 configuration by uninstalling Windows 98. If you choose this option, Setup displays the **Save System Files** dialog box. It finds the system files and saves them in the following files:

- **Winundo.dat**. This file contains all the files required to restore Windows 95. It can be up to 50 MB in size.

- **Winundo.ini**. This file contains information about the original location of the files stored in Winundo.dat.

Setup saves the current system files to the root directory. However, it lets you choose the location if you have more than one logical drive.

No. If you select **No**, you will not be able to uninstall Windows 98. To remove Windows 98, you have to delete the Windows 98 directory and reinstall the previous operating system. Any Windows-based programs installed after Windows 98, have to be reinstalled.

Caution If you converted your drive to FAT32 or compressed it with DriveSpace, you cannot uninstall Windows 98, even if you saved your system files.

Setup Options

Once Setup finishes setting up the directory structure, it prompts you to select the type of Setup you want through the **Setup Options** dialog box. Each Setup option contains a specific set of components to install. When you choose a Setup option, Setup selects by default a set of appropriate components based on your choice. Later, through the **Select Components** dialog box, Setup gives you the choice to either accept the default selection or select your own components.

▶ **To choose a Setup option**

- In the **Setup Options** dialog box, click the Setup option you want, then click **Next**. The **Typical** Setup option is selected as the default.

Click this option	If you want
Typical	All of the components that are usually installed with Windows 98. Most users should select this Setup option.
Portable	To install the options generally required for portable computers.
Compact	The smallest possible installation of Windows 98. For example, you may want to perform a Compact installation if your hard disk does not have much free space. Setup then installs no optional components. If you later want to use an optional component, such as Games or WebTV for Windows, then you have to install it. To install an optional component after Setup is completed, use Add/Remove Programs in Control Panel.

Click this option	If you want
Custom	To choose which optional components are installed. If you do not select a Custom installation, then Setup installs only the optional components that are selected by *default*. If you know you are going to need certain Windows components, you may want to select a Custom installation and ensure that those components are included during Setup. Pan European users should choose this option in order to select the required regional settings and keyboard layout for their locale. Pan European users should choose this option in order to select the required regional setting and keyboard layout for their locale.

For a list of all Windows 98 components included in each Setup option, see Table 2.6 in "Choosing Typical, Portable, Compact, or Custom Setup Options" earlier in this chapter.

Windows Components

If you choose the Typical Setup option, Setup displays the **Windows Components** dialog box. If you select **Install the most common components**, Setup continues the installation. If you select **Show me the list of components so I can choose**, the **Select Components** dialog box appears.

Select Components

The **Select Components** dialog box lets you customize your installation by choosing the components you want to install. For more information on which components are installed by default and the size of each component, see Tables 2.7 through 2.16 in "Choosing Typical, Portable, Compact, or Custom Setup Options" earlier in this chapter.

▶ **To select which components are installed**

1. In the **Components** list, click a component set (for example, **Communications**), and then click **Details**. A shaded box means that only part of the component will be installed.

   A dialog box appears, listing the components in the category.

2. Select or deselect the component you want to add or remove, and then click **OK**.

   - To add a component, make sure the component is checked.

   - To remove a component, clear its check box.

   - To prevent a component from being installed, make sure the component is not checked.

3. Repeat this procedure for each category in the **Components** list in the **Select Components** dialog box.

4. When you are satisfied with your selections, click **Next**. If you want to reset the list of components to the default, click **Reset**.

Note You can install or remove any of these components after Windows 98 is installed by using Add/Remove Programs in Control Panel.

Establishing Your Location

Next, Setup prompts you to establish your location by displaying the **Establishing Your Location** dialog box. Select the location for getting region-specific news and other information through media such as *channels*—Web sites designed to deliver content from the Internet to your computer. Channels become available on your Windows 98 desktop Channel Bar after you install Windows 98 successfully.

▶ **To establish a location for receiving region-specific Internet information**

1. From the **Select your country or region from the list below** list, click the country or region you want. For example, **United States**.

2. Click **Next**.

Startup Disk

After establishing your location, Setup prompts you to create a Windows 98 Startup Disk by displaying the **Startup Disk** dialog box. The Startup Disk is a bootable system disk with a collection of real-mode Windows 98 commands and utilities that you can use to restart your computer if you have trouble starting Windows 98 or to run diagnostic programs. It is recommended that you create several Startup Disks. You can create a Startup Disk during Setup and you can create extra copies by using Add/Remove Programs in Control Panel.

To make a Startup Disk, you need one 1.44 MB floppy disk or two 1.2 MB floppy disks.

▶ **To create a Startup Disk during Setup**

1. Click **Next** on the **Startup Disk** dialog box.

   Setup starts creating the Startup Disk.

2. Label a floppy disk "Windows 98 Startup Disk" and insert it into drive A.

3. Click **OK** to create the disk.

▶ **To create a Startup Disk using Add/Remove Programs in Control Panel**

1. In Control Panel, double-click Add/Remove Programs.

2. Click the **Startup Disk** tab.

3. Click **Create Disk**.

4. Follow the instructions on the screen.

For information about how to use a Startup Disk and its functionality, see "Using a Startup Disk" in Chapter 5, "Setup Technical Discussion." For information on the contents of the Startup Disk, see Appendix B, "Windows 98 System File Details."

Caution You cannot start Windows 98 if you try to start your computer with a Windows 95 Startup Disk or other existing Startup Disks (of any version of Microsoft Windows other than Windows 98).

The Startup Disk includes a real-mode generic ATAPI CD-ROM driver (Oakcdrom.sys) that allows the CD-ROM to function when the protected mode of the graphical user interface is not available. This driver is a generic IDE CD-ROM driver, and it does not work with SCSI CD-ROMs. Several third-party SCSI drivers are also included on the Startup Disk. In general, CD-ROM manufacturers include a floppy disk with the correct CD-ROM driver to use with their CD-ROM. However, if for some reason the specific driver for your CD-ROM is not available, you can use the generic ATAPI/SCSI CD-ROM driver included on the Startup Disk.

Note If your computer's CD-ROM is connected to a sound card, you need to copy the correct drivers for your CD-ROM drive and controller to the Startup Disk, and then edit the Config.sys file on the Startup Disk so that the correct drivers are loaded. Consult the documentation for your CD-ROM drive and controller to get the correct files and configuration settings.

Start Copying Files

After Setup finishes creating the Startup Disk, the **Start Copying Files** dialog box appears. Click **Next** to start copying files.

Step Three: Copying Windows 98 Files to Your Computer

After Setup has collected the information it needs from your computer, it begins copying the Windows 98 files to your computer. During this phase, Windows 98 Setup does not require your input.

Caution Do not interrupt file copying. If Setup is interrupted during the file-copying phase, Windows 98 may not run when you restart your computer because Windows 98 will not have all of the necessary files to start. If you interrupt Setup during this phase, you must run Setup again.

If you started Setup over a network, from a compact disc, or removable hard drive, Setup copies the appropriate Driver*x*.inf files that are necessary to access the installation media (installation point on a network server, compact disc, or removable hard drive) to continue Setup after your computer is restarted.

Step Four: Restarting Your Computer

After Setup finishes copying the Windows 98 files to your computer, you are prompted to restart your computer. You can click the **Restart Now** button to restart your computer immediately; if you do not click the button or wait more than 15 seconds to click it, Setup restarts your computer automatically.

After Setup restarts your computer, the following message appears on your screen:

```
Getting ready to start Windows 98 for the first time.
```

Step Five: Setting Up Hardware and Finalizing Settings

During this phase, Setup configures the following:

- Control Panel
- Programs on the **Start** menu
- Windows Help
- MS-DOS program settings
- Tuning Up Application Start
- Time zone
- System Configuration

When Setup finishes setting up hardware and configuring settings, Setup restarts your computer and asks you to log on. If your computer is connected to the network, you may be asked for a domain name and a network password. After you log on, Setup:

- Builds a driver information database.
- Updates system settings.
- Sets up personalized settings such as settings for the Internet Explorer 4 browsing software, **Start** menu, Online services, Volume Control, and Channels.

Then, Setup displays the **Welcome to Windows 98** dialog box.

C H A P T E R   3

Custom Installations

3

This chapter provides information about customizing Microsoft Windows 98 installations with the new Windows 98 tools: Microsoft Batch 98 (Batch.exe), INF Installer (Infinst.exe), and Dbset.exe. It also describes how to customize your installation for automating Setup, specifying workgroup memberships, and restricting users' abilities to change their configuration.

In This Chapter

See Also

- For information about automating Microsoft Windows 98 Installations, see Chapter 4, "Automated Installations."

- For information about using user profiles and system policies to customize desktop and system settings, see Chapter 8, "System Policies."

- For information about how to restrict user's abilities to change configurations, see Chapter 7, "User Profiles."

- For information about the parameters that can be used in setup scripts, see Appendix D, "Msbatch.inf Parameters for Setup Scripts."

Overview of Custom Installations

In Windows 98, you cannot modify the default INF files to customize the Setup steps or the final Windows 98 installation. Instead, Windows 98 provides more flexible, easier to use tools that rely mainly on setup scripts in Msbatch.inf format.

This chapter describes the following methods for customizing your installation:

- Using the new Windows 98 tools—Microsoft Batch 98 (Batch.exe), INF Installer (Infinst.exe), and Dbset.exe —to create and edit custom setup scripts and to add custom drivers.
- Customizing the Netdet.ini file for detecting components on NetWare networks.
- Customizing the Wrkgrp.ini file to specify a list of workgroups that users can choose to join.
- Creating user profiles and system policies to customize the desktop and system settings, or to restrict users' abilities to change the configuration. Additional information for using user profiles and system policies are described in Chapter 7, "User Profiles," and Chapter 8, "System Policies."

Introduction to Custom Setup Scripts

A custom setup script is a file in Msbatch.inf format that contains predefined settings for all the options that can be specified during Setup and many additional settings. Custom setup scripts can contain instructions for installing additional software.

Windows 98 provides Setup scripting capabilities to make an organization-wide rollout easier and less time consuming. Because Windows 98 is an upgrade to Windows 95, it automatically analyzes the Windows 95 installation and identifies the installed components and upgrades accordingly. However, by using a custom setup script it is possible to install any number of these components to suit the needs of your organization and users.

Also, if you need to upgrade more than 50 computers, you will probably want to use an automated installation, which also requires that you create or customize an existing setup script. For more information on creating automated installations, see Chapter 4, "Automated Installations."

You can specify custom settings for Windows 98 installations by creating a custom setup script with Microsoft Batch 98 (Batch.exe in the *Microsoft Windows 98 Resource Kit* utilities) and using this setup script when installing Windows 98. The default setup script is stored with the source files on the server. Custom setup scripts can be stored in users' home directories or in an installation point on a network server.

Creating a Custom Setup Scripts

The easiest way to create a custom setup script is a two-step process. First, you install Windows 98 on a model computer with all the optional components needed for other similar computers in your organization. To select optional components during Setup, you use the **Custom** option in the **Setup Options** dialog box, as explained in "Running Setup from MS-DOS" in Chapter 2, "Setting Up Windows 98."

Second, you run Microsoft Batch 98 (Batch.exe) as explained in "Using Microsoft Batch 98 (Batch.exe)" later in this chapter. You can find Batch.exe in the *Microsoft Windows 98 Resource Kit* utilities.

Tip The *Microsoft Windows 98 Resource Kit* utilities include generic setup scripts for a variety of cases. These scripts can be used as is or modified to automate Windows 98 Setup.

A setup script contains *sections* that are identified by *headings* and it contains at least the following two sections:

```
[Setup]
```

```
[OptionalComponents]
```

[Setup] Section

In the [Setup] section of the script file it is possible to control how much, if any, user interaction is required during the Setup procedure. In an environment where a large number of computers must be upgraded with a minimum amount of time and user input, proper use of this section can make a big difference in the cost of upgrading in terms of time spent.

The following sample [Setup] section lists some common settings for an unattended setup:

```
[Setup]
EBD=0; Do not create the Windows 98 Startup Disk.
ShowEula=0; Do not display the license agreement.
UNINSTAL=0; Do not prompt to save uninstall information.
```

[Optional Components] Section

The [Optional Components] section controls what components of Windows 98 are installed on the system. In the upgrade scenario this section is most valuable for adding new components to the existing installation during the upgrade procedure. Any item followed by "=1" will be installed. Conversely, if the item if followed by "=0" it will not be installed.

The following is a sample list of optional components new to Windows 98 that can be installed, or not installed, depending on the settings in this section:

```
[OptionalComponents]
"Accessories"=1
"Communications"=1
"Accessibility"=1
"Accessibility Options"=1
"Accessibility Tools"=1
"Personal Web Server"=1
"Dial-Up Networking"=1
"Dial-Up Server"=1
"Internet Tools"=1
"Microsoft Outlook Express"=0
"Microsoft Chat 2.1"=1
"Web TV for Windows"=1
"WaveTop Data Broadcasting"=1
"Imaging"=1
"Microsoft NetMeeting"=1
"Microsoft NetShow Player 2.0"=1
"Online Services"=1
"America Online"=1
"AT&T WorldNet Service"=0
"Web Publishing Wizard"=1
"Windows Scripting Host"=1
"Microsoft VRML 2.0 Viewer"=1
```

For a complete list of all components, see Appendix D, "Msbatch.inf Parameters for Setup Scripts."

Tip for Defining Custom Entries in Setup Scripts

Use the Custom Setup option to install Windows 98 on a single computer. You can define all the optional components and other items you want installed for other similar computers at your site.

After Windows 98 is completely installed on this single computer, you can use any text editor to copy the [OptionalComponents], [Setup], [NameAndOrg], and [System] sections from Setuplog.txt in the computer's root directory. Add this information to define settings for the same sections in the custom setup script.

This is especially useful for defining entries for [OptionalComponents] or when many computers require the same [System] settings. Some settings for the [Network] section can also be copied from Setuplog.txt.

Editing an Existing Setup Script

You can modify existing setup scripts with a text editor to create alternate or more detailed setup scripts.

▶ **To edit Msbatch.inf**

1. Use a text editor, such as Notepad, to open the Msbatch.inf file.

2. Edit the file, and save it in text-only format.

The following are the editing guidelines for setup scripts:

- Each section starts with a unique section name enclosed in brackets ([ ]).

- Only sections and key words defined in Appendix D, "Msbatch.inf Parameters for Setup Scripts," are evaluated by Windows 98 Setup.

- Each section can contain one or more entries. The typical entry consists of a key word and a value separated by an equal sign (=).

- Key words within a section do not have to be unique, but each key word and its value should follow the guidelines for that key word.

- A comment can be included anywhere on a line by starting the comment with a semicolon (;).

Automating Installations with Custom Setup Scripts

After a setup script and other customization files are created, Windows 98 can be installed automatically by running Setup on each client computer, using the name of the setup script as a command-line parameter. Setup can be run from any of the following:

- From a logon script.

- From server-based system management software.

- From a batch file that contains the appropriate setup command line, distributed on floppy disk or by electronic mail.

For more information on automating installations with logon scripts, system management software, and distribution of batch files through e-mail, see Chapter 4, "Automated Installations."

Setup Components that Cannot Be Customized

Some Windows 98 Setup dialog boxes cannot be customized. Table 3.1 summarizes the items that cannot be customized or the screens that cannot be skipped when running Windows 98 Setup with a custom script. Error messages cause Setup to stop and wait for user input.

For example, messages that cannot be skipped include "**Looking for a Previous Version of Windows**" and warnings about disk space and conflicting network components.

Table 3.1   Setup components that cannot be skipped or customized

Dialog box or message	Comment
MS-DOS Uninstall	This message appears if Setup detects MS-DOS Uninstall information on the computer. You cannot turn off this display or automate a response.
OS/2 Detected	This message appears if Setup detects that a version of OS/2 is installed on the system. You cannot turn off this display or automate a response.
Boot Manager Partition	This message appears if Setup detects Boot Manager has been installed. You cannot use Boot Manager once you set up Windows 98. You cannot turn off this message or automate a response.
Quit All Windows Programs	This message appears if Setup detects that other programs are running. You cannot turn off this display or automate a response. This message always appears if Setup is run using a Windows-based network management tool, such as Microsoft Systems Management Server.
Not Enough Disk Space	This message appears if there is not enough hard disk space to support the specified installation type. You cannot turn off this display from a setup script. However, to avoid this message, start Windows 98 Setup using the **setup /id** switch.

Caution Setup will fail during installation if it runs out of disk space.

Looking for a Previous Version of Windows	This message appears when Setup detects a previous version of Windows.
Checking Your System	This information message always appears. You cannot turn off this display, but no response is required.
Preparing Directory	This information message always appears. You cannot turn off this display, but no response is required.
Analyzing Your Computer	This information message always appears. You cannot turn off this display, but no response is required.
ScanDisk	Before Setup starts its five-step installation process, it runs ScanDisk. To prevent ScanDisk from running, run setup with the **/is** switch.

Comparison of Customization Methods

This section compares the customization methods used for Windows 95 and Windows for Workgroups versus the new ones prescribed for Windows 98.

Windows 95 Versus Windows 98

If you are upgrading from Windows 95, you can refer to Table 3.2 to compare the customization methods used for Windows 95 versus the ones prescribed for Windows 98. This table does not include all of the new tools available to customize Windows 98. These tools are described in "Using the New Windows 98 Tools to Customize Installations" later in this chapter.

Table 3.2   Comparison of customization methods for Windows 95 and Windows 98

Windows 95	Windows 98
Msbatch.inf to customize system settings, force Setup options, and copy additional files.	Msbatch.inf (same format).
NetSetup to prepare a network server to run Setup.exe on client computers.	Simple drag-and-drop solution: copy the Windows 98 CAB files to an installation point on a network server.
NetSetup to create setup scripts.	Microsoft Batch 98.
NetSetup for creating and managing machine directories, which contain specific configuration information for client computers on a shared installation.	Shared installations are not supported in Windows 98.
Adding device drivers by using a trial and error process.	INF Installer (Infinst.exe).
Automate.inf for creating setup scripts that include the Windows 98 Accessibility Options.	Microsoft Batch 98 to generate a script with the Windows 98 Accessibility Options.
Netdet.ini for detecting components on NetWare networks.	Netdet.ini (same format).
Wrkgrp.ini to specify a list of workgroups that users can join.	Wrkgrp.ini (same format).
System policies and user profiles to customize the desktop contents and restrict users' abilities to change configurations.	System policies and user profiles.
Apps.inf to create program information files (PIFs) for applications.	Apps.inf (same format).

Windows for Workgroups Versus Windows 98

If you are upgrading from Windows for Workgroups, you can refer to Table 3.3 to compare the customization methods used for Windows for Workgroups versus the methods prescribed for Windows 98.

Table 3.3   Comparison of customization methods for Windows for Workgroups and Windows 98

Windows for Workgroups	Windows 98
Setup.shh to customize system settings.	Msbatch.inf settings.
Setup.inf to copy additional files or to force Setup options.	Msbatch.inf settings.
Control.inf to list incompatible terminate-and-stay-resident (TSR) programs or force selection of devices or network clients.	Netdet.ini for NetWare TSRs; built into Setup for all others.
Apps.inf to create program information files (PIFs) for applications.	Apps.inf (same format).
Wrkgrp.ini to control workgroup membership.	Wrkgrp.ini (similar format, with a new entry for Windows 98 features).
[New.Groups] in Setup.inf for custom program groups.	System policies to customize the desktop contents.
setup /p to restore program groups; manually copying GRP files to restore desktop contents.	Grpconv.exe to convert program groups or restore default menus, as described in Chapter 5, "Setup Technical Discussion."
System.ini, Win.ini, or Control.ini to modify system or desktop settings.	For upgrades from Windows 3.*x*, custom settings are migrated; for the rare cases in which there are no equivalents in the user interface or in system policies, you can still modify INI files.

Using the New Windows 98 Tools to Customize Installations

Windows 98 includes new and improved tools that make it easier to customize and automate Windows 98 installations. The following figure compares the tools and processes used in Windows 95 versus the new ones used in Windows 98.

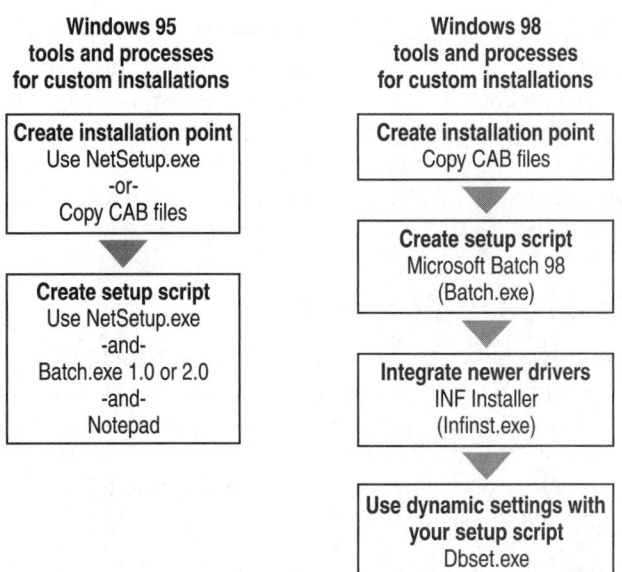

The new Windows 98 tools for customizing Setup provide the following enhancements.

Custom Setup improved with Microsoft Batch 98 (Batch.exe).   The new Microsoft Batch 98 (Batch.exe) provides a single, comprehensive, and easy-to-use solution for custom installation. You can customize Setup to accept the end user license agreement; to remove desktop icons and turn off the Registration Wizard; enable user profiles; add group policies; customize setup for the Internet Explorer 4 browsing software, and all the new shell and desktop options. Batch.exe now offers a more intuitive, Windows 98–like user interface and provides error checking.

Adding device drivers simplified with INF Installer (Infinst.exe).   Infinst.exe allows you to add device drivers automatically. It works on all classes of devices, eliminates the need to manually edit driver and custom INF files, and eliminates driver conflicts. You can use INF Installer in conjunction with Microsoft Batch 98 to integrate third-party network clients into your Windows 98 installation.

Using Dbset.exe to customize setup scripts and other text files.   With Dbset.exe you can easily individualize setup scripts and other types of text files. For example, you can create a template setup script with settings that you want to use for all users in your organization or workgroup. Then, you create a database file with specific data for each user, for example, user_name, computer name, and so on. From the template and database file Dbset.exe creates an individualized setup script by replacing the variable names (for example user_name) with the actual name of the user (for example, Maria). With Dbset.exe, you can also customize other types of files, such as registry files and write environment variables.

NetSetup is replaced with Microsoft Batch 98. The Windows 95 server-based Setup (Netsetup.exe) has been eliminated to avoid Layout.inf disparity and large footprint problems. Its functionality has been replaced by Microsoft Batch 98 and a simple method for distribution share creation: drag-and-drop. With this drag-and-drop method, you simply create an installation point on a network server and copy the Windows 98 CAB files to that point. Windows 98 does not support either remote-boot (with RIPL software) or shared installations.

Using Microsoft Batch 98 (Batch.exe)

Microsoft Batch 98 (Batch.exe) is a Windows-based program that makes it easy to create setup scripts that can be used to automate Windows 98 installation. With Batch.exe, you can create unattended installations because when you install Windows 98 using a setup script, Setup consults this file instead of prompting the user for each piece of information. However, there are some circumstances when user intervention is still required.

Even though Batch.exe runs on Windows 95 and Windows NT, it is best to run it on a Windows 98 model computer to take full advantage of its configuration scanning functionality. This functionality is available through the **Gather now** button as explained in "Batch.exe Features" later in this chapter.

Batch.exe Features

Microsoft Batch 98 is an improved version of the Batch.exe utility available in Windows 95. Batch.exe now offers a more intuitive, Windows 98–like user interface as shown in the following figure.

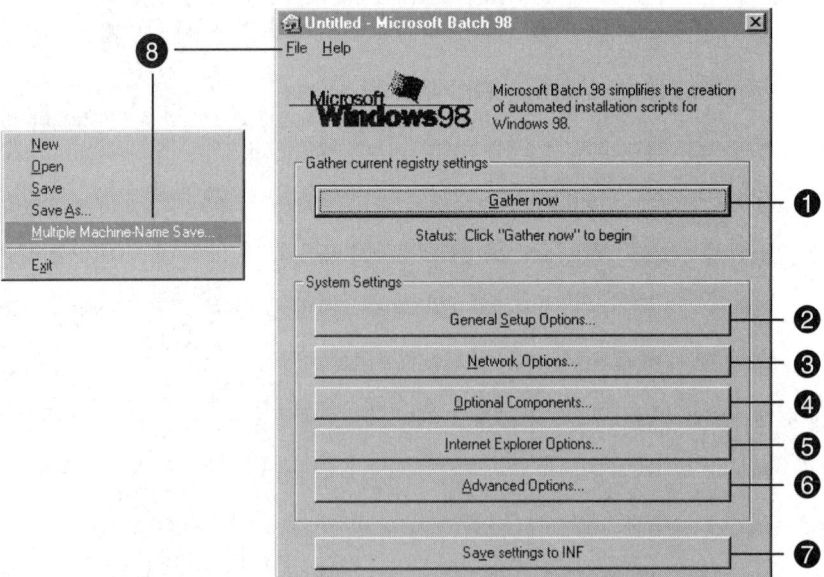

Some of the new functionality and enhancements in Microsoft Batch 98 include the following.

Create a custom script based on current registry settings. You can use Batch.exe to scan an existing Windows 98 model computer's configuration by using **Gather now** (❶) and create a setup script in Msbatch.inf format based on that information with **Save settings to INF** (❼).

Accept the end-user license agreement automatically. You can customize Setup to not display either the **License Agreement** or the **Product Key** dialog boxes and accept their terms automatically using the **Install Info** and **Setup Prompts** tabs in **General Setup Options** (❷).

Customize computer and user information. You can specify the user's name, company name, computer name, workgroup, and computer description using the **User Info** tab in **General Setup Options** (❷). If you are upgrading from an existing Windows installation and want to preserve current user settings, do not enter this information.

Control user input. You can control how much input a user has while setting up Windows 98. The administrator can choose which options (if any) setup will provide for user input and which defaults to provide. Use the **Install Info**, **Desktop**, and **Setup Prompts** tabs in **General Setup Options** (❷).

Disable or enable uninstall information support. You can instruct Setup to automatically create Uninstall information, to automatically skip the Installation Directory warning, or to prompt the user with the choice to do so during setup. Use the **Install Info** tab in **General Setup Options** (❷).

Allow each user to customize the computer's configuration. You can maintain separate desktop and **Start** menu settings for each user who logs on to the computer. Use the **User Profiles** tab in **General Setup Options** (❷).

Automatically install local or network printers. You can install printers, network or local, or skip the Printer Setup Wizard altogether. Use the **Printers** tab in **General Setup Options** (❷).

Automatically install and customize network clients. You can automatically install the Client for Microsoft Networks and the Client for NetWare versions 3.*x* and 4.*x*, and you can enable support for other third-party networks. You can also set options for each client, including validated logon, preferred server, default logon, and the first network drive. Use the **Clients** and **Additional Clients** tabs in **Network Options** (❸).

Automatically install network protocols. You can automatically install protected-mode stacks for NetBEUI, IPX/SPX, TCP/IP, and 32-bit DLC, and define settings for IPX/SPX and TCP/IP. Use the **Protocols** tab in **Network Options** (❸).

Enable support for network services. You can install file and printer sharing services for either Microsoft networks or NetWare 3.*x*/4.*x* networks using the **Services** tab in **Network Options** (❸). You can also enable support for additional network services, clients, and protocols using the **Additional Clients** tab in **Network Options** (❸).

Preselect optional components. You can use **Optional Components** (❹) to choose which Optional Components to include and exclude during Windows 98 Setup. You can edit the Optional.ini file provided with Batch.exe to control what Optional Components are presented in Batch 98. This is useful to limit the choices available and to include components not provided with Windows 98.

Customize Internet Explorer 4.0 Setup. You can customize Setup for Internet Explorer 4.0 as well as many of the new shell and desktop options. For example, you can specify the Internet security and proxy settings using the **Security** and **Proxy Settings** tabs in **Internet Explorer Options** (❺).

Enable or disable software and driver upgrades from the Internet. You can enable or disable upgrading software and drivers from the Internet. You can also specify which local or remote intranet page to use for upgrading drivers and software. Use the **Windows Update** tab in **Advanced Options** (❻).

Add registry files to the Windows 98 Setup installation point. You can add registry files to the installation point from which you will install Window 98. If they are specified in your setup script, Window 98 Setup adds them automatically during the Run Once portion of Setup. Use the **Additional Files** tab in **Advanced Options** (❻).

Simultaneously create setup scripts for multiple computers. Batch.exe can save up to 9,999 separate setup scripts simultaneously. By supplying a text file listing each computer's name (and IP address, if desired), you can save multiple setup scripts created from the same template. Use the **Multiple Machine-Name Save** option on the **File** menu (❽).

Creating Custom Scripts with Batch.exe

By using Microsoft Batch 98 (Batch.exe) and completing the options, you create a custom script in Msbatch.inf format that can be used in unattended installations— running Windows 98 Setup with minimal user intervention.

Batch.exe is especially useful when you are testing alternate configurations and need to run Setup repeatedly. Batch.exe can be used to define all options in a setup script.

▶ **To create a custom script with Microsoft Batch 98**

1. Install Windows 98 on a model computer with the configuration you want to use for your setup script.

2. Install Microsoft Batch 98 (Batch.exe) by running Setup.exe from the \Tools\Reskit\Batch directory on your Windows 98 compact disc.

3. On the **Start** menu, point to **Programs**, and then click **Microsoft Batch 98**.

   The Microsoft Batch 98 screen appears.

4. Click **Gather now** to retrieve the registry information from your model computer.

   Once Batch.exe gathers the registry information, the status below the **Gather now** button will display **Complete**.

5. Use the System Settings (**General Setup Options**, **Network Options**, **Optional Components**, **Internet Explorer Options**, and **Advanced Options**) to customize the settings you want to use for your setup script.

   For more information on these settings, see "Understanding the Microsoft Batch 98 Options" later in this chapter.

6. Click **Save settings to INF** to save your settings to a setup script.

   Batch.exe creates a setup script in Msbatch.inf format (with the default name of Msbatch.inf) based on the current registry settings it gathered from your computer. By default, Batch.exe saves the script file in the directory where Microsoft Batch 98 was installed.

After you create the setup script, you can run Windows 98 Setup by specifying the name of the script as a command-line parameter, as described in "Running Custom Setup Scripts" later in this chapter. Depending on how many options you completed in Batch Setup, you might not have to provide any additional input while installing Windows 98.

For more information on using Batch.exe, see "Understanding the Microsoft Batch 98 Options" later in this chapter. For a description of the parameters in the file created by Batch Setup, see Appendix D, "Msbatch.inf Parameters for Setup Scripts." If you want to modify the file that is created, follow the guidelines for editing setup scripts, as described in "Editing an Existing Setup Script" earlier in this chapter.

Tip for Ensuring User Logon Capabilities in Setup Scripts

By default, Windows 98 Setup preserves the network identification information from the user's previous networking configuration, including the logon domain or preferred server. However, in cases where this information is not already defined, you must specify settings in the setup script. If you want to preserve existing settings, do not specify any network settings in the Msbatch.inf file. If users are installing Windows 98 from a server that requires logon validation, make sure the script defines the correct logon server. For a computer that will run Client for Microsoft Networks and use the Windows NT network for network logon validation, you should define values for **LogonDomain=** and **ValidatedLogon=** in the [VRedir] section. For a computer that will run Client for NetWare Networks, define a correct value for **PreferredServer=** in the [NWRedir] section. If the appropriate values are not defined in a setup script, the user might not have the validated access required to complete the final Setup steps for installing printers and other actions.

Understanding the Microsoft Batch 98 Options

Microsoft 98 Batch groups the system settings you can customize into five options: **General Setup Options** ❶, **Network Options** ❷, **Optional Components** ❸, **Internet Explorer Options** ❹, and **Advanced Options** ❺ as shown in the following figure.

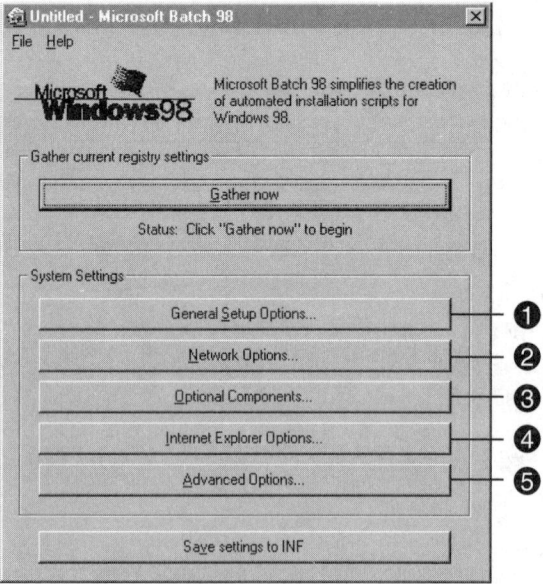

The following sections describe these options providing information that maps the information you enter in the Microsoft 98 Batch dialog boxes to the appropriate sections in your INF setup script. For information on the format that INF setup scripts use, see Appendix D, "Msbatch.inf Parameters for Setup Scripts."

General Setup Options

With the **General Setup Options** dialog box you customize many of the Windows 98 general settings, such as the installation directory, user name, and computer name. You can also use this dialog box to prevent Setup from prompting you for information, allowing you to create a fully automated setup script.

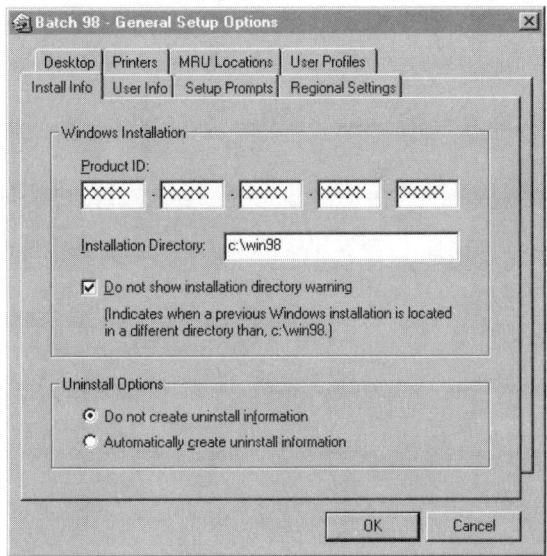

The following sections describe each of the property pages in the **General Options** dialog box.

Install Info

In the **Install Info** property page, you set parameters that will be defined in the [Setup] section of your setup script. Table 3.4 maps the elements (fields, check boxes, and options) in **Install Info** where you enter or select information to the corresponding parameters in your setup script.

Table 3.4   Install Info elements

Property Page Element	Description
Product ID [Setup] ProductKey="MyProductID"	Type the product key located either on the Certificate of Authenticity or on the back of your Windows 98 compact disc.
Installation Directory [Setup] InstallDir="MyWin98Dir"	Type the directory path where Windows 98 is to be installed. If you are upgrading from Windows 95 or Windows 3.1*x*, the default is the current Windows installation directory. If you are creating a template script for other computers, you might have to change this default.
Do not show installation directory warning [Setup] NoDirWarn=1 (checkbox selected)	Select this check box to instruct Setup not to display the installation directory warning. Use this setting when upgrading from Windows 95 or Windows 3.1*x*.
NoDirWarn=0 (checkbox cleared)	Clear this check box to instruct Setup to display the **Installation Directory Warning** dialog box.
Do not create uninstall information [Setup] Uninstall=0	Click this option to instruct Setup not to create the backup files for uninstalling Windows 98 and not to display the **Uninstall Options** dialog box.
Automatically create uninstall information [Setup] Uninstall=1	Click this option to instruct Setup to write all the backup files for uninstalling Windows 98 in the directory specified by the user during installation, through the **Uninstall Options** dialog box.

User Info

In the **User Info** property page, you can provide the information Setup needs for determining who will use the computer. Table 3.5 maps the elements in **User Info** that you enter or select to the corresponding parameters in your setup script.

Table 3.5   User Info elements

Property Page Element	Description
User Name[1] [NameAndOrg] Name=	Type the name of the registered user of this copy of Windows 98.
Company Name[1] [NameAndOrg] Org=	Type the name of the organization that is the registered owner of this copy of Windows 98.
Computer Name[1, 2] [Network] ComputerName=	Type the name you want to use to identify your computer on the network. The computer name must be unique.

Table 3.5   User Info elements (*continued*)

Property Page Element	Description
Workgroup[1, 2] [Network] Workgroup=	Type the name of the workgroup that your computer belongs to.
Description[1, 2] [Network] Description=	Type the name you want to use to describe your computer to other users, for example the location of the computer or your department. On many networks, you can use a computer's description to search for it on the network.

[1] On a new installation, Setup prompts for this information if it is not provided on a script. On a Windows upgrade, Setup reads this information from the previous Windows version.

[2] For more information on naming conventions, see "Computer Identification Parameters in [Network]" in Appendix D, "Msbatch.inf Parameters for Setup Scripts."

Setup Prompts

In the **Setup Prompts** property page, you can enter settings to eliminate many of the prompts Setup generates. The **Setup Prompts** settings are necessary to generate a fully automated Setup script. These settings cannot be gathered from a model computer using **Gather now**. Table 3.6 maps the elements in **Setup Prompts** that you enter or select to the corresponding parameters in your setup script.

Table 3.6   Setup Prompts elements

Property Page Element	Description
Auto-accept end-user license agreement [Setup] ShowEula=	Check this box to prevent Setup from displaying the **License Agreement**.
Do not prompt for emergency startup disk [Setup] EBD	Check this box to prevent being prompted to create a Windows 98 Startup Disk.
Automatically reboot PCI and PnP machines during setup [Setup] VRC	Check this box to automatically reboot during Setup.
Do not search source folder for new devices [Setup] DevicePath	Clear this box to allow Setup to search for new drivers in the Windows 98 installation point if Setup detects new hardware. Clearing this box does not cause Setup to prompt you for a source folder for new drivers, however, it can slow down the installation of new hardware.

Table 3.6   Setup Prompts elements (*continued*)

Property Page Element	Description
Skip the PC Card (PCMCIA) wizard	Check this box to prevent Setup from displaying the **PC Card (PCMCIA) Wizard** dialog box when Setup detects a PC Card controller. This is necessary only when you run Setup on computers with PC Card slots.
	Clear this box if real-mode PC Card drivers will be loaded after Setup restarts your computer for the first time; otherwise, Setup will fail.
	Using a real-mode PC Card network boot diskette to initially gain network access and launch Setup will not cause Setup to fail with this box checked.

Regional Settings

In the **Regional Settings** property page, you can set the time zone, keyboard layout, and regional settings.

Desktop

In the **Desktop** property page, you can configure which desktop icons, such as My Documents and Internet Explorer, will be available on the desktop. When upgrading from an existing Windows installation, some icons that were already present on the desktop will be migrated to the new Windows 98 desktop. You can also prevent the **Welcome to Windows 98** and the **Windows Registration Wizard** screens from being displayed. Table 3.7 maps the elements in **Desktop** that you enter or select to the corresponding parameters in your setup script.

Table 3.7   Desktop elements

Property Page Element	Description
My Documents	Check this box to include **My Documents** on the desktop.
Connect to the Internet	Check this box to include **Connect to the Internet** on the desktop. This is a shortcut to a wizard that guides you through the steps for connecting to the Internet. If you plan to use a setup script that specifies all the necessary settings for connecting to the Internet or if you do not plan to use the Internet Explorer browsing software, you may want to clear this box. If you check the **Internet Explorer & Outlook Express** box, the **Connect to the Internet** check box will be grayed-out and the **Connect to the Internet** icon will not appear on the desktop.

Table 3.7   Desktop elements (*continued*)

Property Page Element	Description
Network Neighborhood	Check this box to include **Network Neighborhood** on the desktop. This icon appears only if your computer is on a network. Clearing this check box prevents users from easily accessing other computers in their workgroup or adjusting their network settings through their desktop.
Internet Explorer & Outlook Express	Check this box to include **Internet Explorer** and **Outlook Express** on the desktop. When you check this box, the **Connect to the Internet** shortcut is removed from the desktop. If you check this box, it is recommended that you specify the proxy settings in the **Proxy Settings** property page (**Internet Explorer Options**).
Recycle Bin	Check this box to include **Recycle Bin** on the desktop.
Setup the Microsoft Network	Check this box to include **Set Up The Microsoft Network** on the desktop.
Delete online service from desktop after setup	Check this box to remove **Online Services** from the desktop when starting Windows 98 for the first time.
Do not show the Windows 98 welcome screen	Check this box not to display the **Welcome to Windows 98** screen.
Do not show the Windows registration wizard	Check this box to disable the **Register Now** option on the **Welcome to Windows 98** screen.

Printers

You can use the **Printers** property page, to install network or local printers. Enter the printer information exactly as you enter it in the Add Printer Wizard. After you have entered the printer name, type, and port, click **Add** to add that printer to the list of printers to be installed during setup. These settings are saved to the [Printers] section of your setup script. To add more printers, repeat this procedure for each printer you want to add. To install printers successfully, you must have access to them after Setup finishes its installation process. Table 3.8 maps the elements in **Printers** that you enter or select to the corresponding parameters in your setup script.

Table 3.8   Printers elements

Property Page Element	Description
Printer Name	Type a name for your printer, for example **Marketing Printer**.
Printer Type	Enter the type of printer you want to install, for example **HP LaserJet 5Si/5Si MX PS.** You must enter the printer type exactly as you do in the Windows 98 Add Printer Wizard.
Printer Port	Type the network path or the queue name of your printer. For example, the printer port for a local printer could be **LPT1**. For a network printer it could be **\\Server1\print8**.

MRU Locations

In the **MRU Locations** property page, you specify the locations—most recently used (MRU) paths—where Setup searches for drivers that will appear in the drop down menus when Setup detects new hardware. These locations can be either local or network locations specified by a UNC path. These settings are saved to the [InstallLocationsMRU] section of your setup script.

User Profiles

In the **User Profiles** property page, you can specify user profile settings. You can also specify if all users of a computer will use the same preferences and desktop settings or if they can customize their own preferences and settings. For more information on user profiles, see Chapter 7, "User Profiles."

Network Options

With the **Network Options** dialog box, you customize network settings.

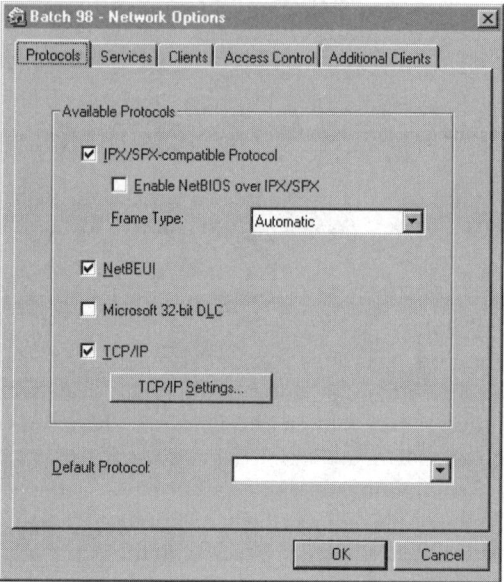

If you enter any information in this dialog box, Setup removes all previous network components that are not specified here. If you do not provide any network information, Setup adds the default Windows 98 network components.

For more information on how to configure network settings, see Chapter 14, "Introduction to Networking Configuration." For information on how to specify parameters in a setup script for installing networking components, see "[Network]" in Appendix D, "Msbatch.inf Parameters for Setup Scripts."

Certain network settings are not compatible with each other and Microsoft Batch 98 prevents these options from being selected together. When you select a particular network setting, Microsoft Batch 98 automatically disables (grays-out) any incompatible settings or prompts you to choose which network setting you want to select.

Optional Components

With the **Optional Components** dialog box, you can customize your installation by choosing the components you want to install.

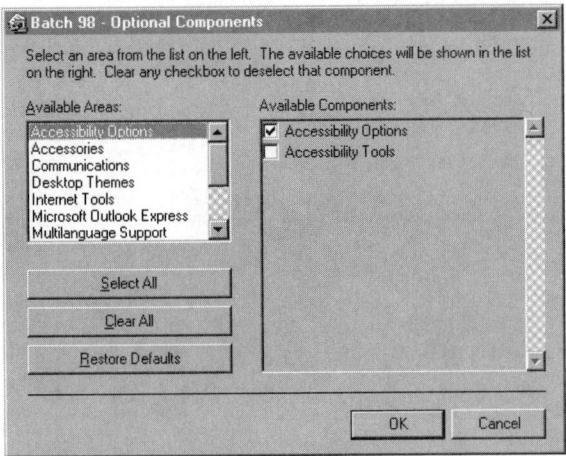

Microsoft Batch 98 uses the Optional.ini file to determine the available optional components. This is the location for specifying accessibility options.

Certain optional components depend on others to be installed to function. If a component depends on another component that has not been selected to be installed, the dependent component will be disabled (grayed out). For more information on optional component dependencies, see "[OptionalComponents]" in Appendix D, "Msbatch.inf Parameters for Setup Scripts."

For more information on which components are installed by default and the sizes of each component, see "Choosing Typical, Portable, Compact, or Custom Setup Options" in Chapter 2, "Setting Up Windows 98."

Internet Explorer Options

With the **Internet Explorer Options** dialog box, you can customize the browser and shell settings for Windows 98. This allows a high level of customization of the Windows 98 user interface.

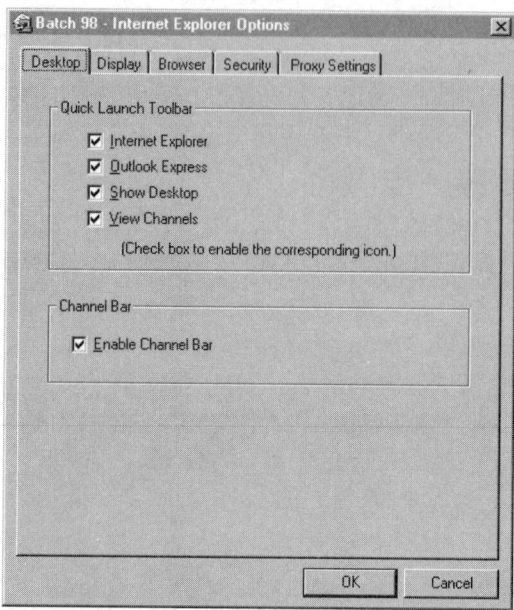

The following sections describe each of the property pages in the **Internet Explorer Options** dialog box.

Desktop

In the Desktop property page, you can specify which **Quick Launch** toolbar icons will be available and if you want to enable the channel bar. Table 3.9 maps the elements in **Desktop** that you enter or select to the corresponding parameters in your setup script.

Table 3.9   Desktop elements

Property Page Element	Description
Internet Explorer	Check this box to have the Internet Explorer link available in the **Quick Launch** toolbar.
Outlook Express	Check this box to have the Outlook Express link available in the **Quick Launch** toolbar. This box will be unavailable if Outlook Express is not selected in optional components.
Show Desktop	Check this box to have the Show Desktop link available in the **Quick Launch** toolbar. This allows users to have easy access to their desktop when applications are open.

Table 3.9   Desktop elements (*continued*)

Property Page Element	Description
View Channels	Check this box to have the View Channels link available in the **Quick Launch** toolbar. This allows users to launch the Channel Bar.
Channel Bar	Check this box to have the channel bar present on the Desktop. This does not require active desktop to be enabled.

Display

In the **Display** property page, you can specify whether active desktop is enabled, whether to open each folder in the same or separate windows and the method of clicking to select and open items. If single click is selected, items will be selected and opened consistently with your settings for using the Internet Explorer browsing software.

Browser

In the **Browser** property page, you can specify default Web pages for Home Page, Post Setup Page and Online Support Page. The post setup page is only seen the first time Internet Explorer is used to browse.

Security

In the **Security** property page, you can specify levels for security for various zones of Web content. The available zones are Local Intranet, Trusted, Internet and Restricted site. First select the Zone you wish to set the security level for and then click High, Medium, or Low depending on the level of security desired. High will prevent potentially dangerous content from being download. Medium will warn when content is potentially dangerous before it is downloaded. Low will allow all content to be downloaded.

Proxy Settings

In the **Proxy Settings** property page, you can specify how Internet Explorer should gain access to various locations. This allows you to preconfigure Internet Explorer to have access through your proxy server(s). In the **Exceptions** box, you can specify to bypass using a proxy for certain addresses.

Advanced Options

With the **Advanced Options** dialog box you can add registry files, specify policy locations and disable or redirect Windows Update.

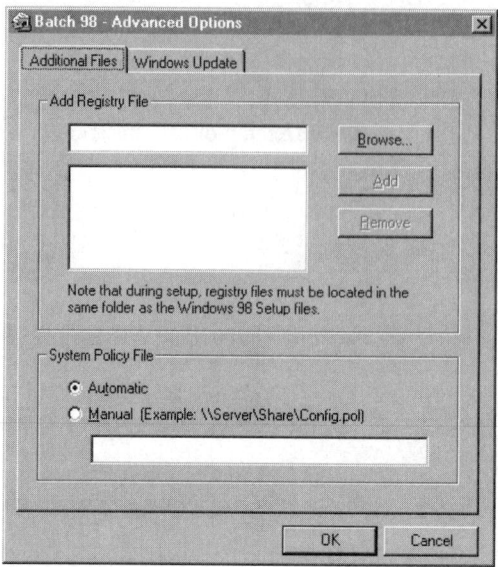

Additional Files

In the **Additional Files** dialog box, you can specify registry files to be imported and the location of a system policy file. Table 3.10 maps the elements in **Additional Files** that you enter or select to the corresponding parameters in your setup script.

Table 3.10   Additional Files elements

Property Page Element	Description
Add Registry File	Enter the name of a registry file to be merged into the registry during setup. The registry file must be manually copied to the setup share before setup is launched. The file will automatically be copied by setup to the %WinDir% directory during the Copying Files phase of Setup and merged during the Hardware Detection phase of Setup.
System Policy File	You can specify the location or a policy file if it is not in the default policy location. Specify the UNC path and name of the system policy file to be used. For more information on system policies see Chapter 8, "System Policies."

Windows Update

In the **Windows Update** property page, you can specify if drivers and software can be upgraded across the Internet through Windows Update. You can also redirect Windows Update to a Web page other than Microsoft's. This is useful if you would like to create your own internal Web page for disseminating drivers to multiple computers. Table 3.11 maps the elements in **Windows Update** that you enter or select to the corresponding parameters in your setup script.

Table 3.11   Windows Update elements

Property Page Element	Description
Enable upgrade of drivers via the internet	Check this box to allow upgrade of device drivers for hardware to be installed via Windows Update across the Internet.
Enable upgrade of software via the internet	Check this box to allow upgrade of software to be installed via Windows Update across the Internet.
Default Windows Update local page	Enter a local URL in this box to change the URL Windows Update opens if the user has never connected to the Internet before.
Default Windows Update remote page	Enter a URL in this box to change the URL that Windows Update uses to download drivers and software.

Retrieving Settings from a Model Computer

When you run Batch.exe in a Windows 98 computer and you click **Gather now**, Batch.exe scans the model computer in the following areas:

- All known Microsoft 32-bit networking clients and their settings
- All known Microsoft 32-bit networking services and their settings
- All known Microsoft 32-bit networking protocols and their settings
- Currently installed printers
- Current time zone
- User-level security settings
- Current Windows directory
- Current user and machine name and description information
- MRU (Most Recently Used) locations
- Optional components
- Network card settings

Batch.exe cannot determine the following:

- Uninstall options
- 16-bit networking (clients, services, and protocols)
- Some installation options pertaining to batch setup only (for instance, the **Auto-Accept the End-User License Agreement** option)

Modifying the Optional.ini File

This section describes the specifications for creating or modifying the Optional.ini file that Batch.exe uses to determine the available optional components. The syntax for the Optional.ini uses standard INI conventions:

Section Names

Section names must be unique within the entire file and must be enclosed in brackets ([ ]):

[Section_Name]

For example:

```
[Networks].
```

[Areas] Section

The main section in an Optional.ini file is [Areas]. This section defines the available subareas for all Optional Components. Within this section, create a *key* in this format:

Key#=Area_Name

where each area's number (#) is one greater than the preceding entry. The order of these entries is unimportant. Do not enclose the *Area_Name* in quotes, unless you want the quotes to be part of its name.

An Optional.ini file can contain up to 20 unique areas, for example:

```
[Areas]
Entry1=Accessories
Entry3=Screen Savers
Entry2=Communications
Entry4=The Microsoft Network
```

Keys

For each area listed in the [Areas] section, there should be a corresponding section. Within each of these sections, you specify keys with the following syntax:

Key#=Component_Name,**0** | **1**

After the component name, include a comma and then either a **0** (do not install component by default) or a **1** (install this component by default). Keys must be unique within each section. Leading spaces are ignored, and they cannot contain semicolons (;).

An Optional.ini file can contain up to 50 unique keys within each [Area]. Batch.exe processes the section until it finds an entry number that does not exist. If Batch.exe reads an entry that does not contain a default value, it assumes a default of 0 (do not install). For example:

```
[Accessories]
Entry1=Cardfile,1
Entry2=Clipboard Viewer
;Clipboard Viewer will automatically be assigned a value of 0.
Entry3=Object Packager,1
Entry4=Sound Recorder,0
Entry6=Calculator,1
;Calculator won't be read because Setup will stop reading the file when
it cannot find Entry5, which does not exist.
```

Three special categories can also be listed in the Optional.ini file: [Dependencies], [Defunct], and [NoChoice].

[Dependencies]

For optional components that have dependencies (one component must be installed in order to install another), create a section named [Dependencies].

To create a dependency, create a key using a key name that is the name of the component that requires the second component. The value of that key is the required component. Each component can have only one dependency; however, there is no limit to how deeply nested dependent components can be. (Component A can require component B, which requires component C, and so on.) Make sure you don't create a circular dependency loop (A → B → C → A).

There is no limit to the number of different dependencies, other than a one thousand character limit for the entire section. The following is an example of a [Dependencies] section:

```
[Dependencies]
Direct Cable Connection=Dial-Up Networking
;(DCC requires Dial-Up Networking.)
```

[Defunct]

The [Defunct] section can be used to list optional components whose names might have changed. Currently, if a user opens an existing INF file that contains optional components that are not listed in the Optional.ini file, the entries are discarded. However, before discarding them, Setup checks the [Defunct] section to see if the component has been given a new name.

Within the [Defunct] section, create a key whose name is the name of the old component name. The value of this key should be its new name. There is no limit to the number of defunct entries other than a one thousand character limit for the entire section. The following is an example of a [Defunct] section:

```
[Defunct]
Extra Cursors=Mouse Pointers
(Extra Cursors new name is Mouse Pointers.)
Nature Sound Scheme=Jungle Sound Scheme
(Nature has been changed to Jungle.)
```

[NoChoice]

The [NoChoice] section is used to list options that cannot be changed by the user through the Windows 98 Setup user interface, even if that option appears there.

To include a [NoChoice] section, include an entry similar to the keys for normal optional components, as described earlier, plus a value for the choice: **0** (for do not install), or **1** (for install). An option listed in this section does not need to be listed anywhere else in the INI file. The following is an example of a [NoChoice] section:

```
[NoChoice]
Entry1=The Microsoft Network,1
(MSN will always be installed.)
Entry2=Calculator,0
(Calculator will never be installed.)
Entry3=Custom Component,1
(A third-party component that Windows Setup is aware of will be
installed.)
```

Sample Optional.ini File

This section shows a sample Optional.ini file. You can add a [NoChoice] section anywhere in the file, but there can be only one [NoChoice] section.

```
[Areas]
Area1=Accessibility Options
Area2=Accessories
Area3=Communications
Area4=Disk Tools
Area5=Microsoft Fax
Area6=Multimedia
Area7=Screen Savers
Area8=The Microsoft Network
Area9=Windows Messaging


[Accessibility Options]
Entry1=Accessibility Options,0


[Accessories]
Entry1=Briefcase,0
Entry2=Calculator,1
Entry3=Character Map,0
Entry4=Clipboard Viewer,0
Entry5=Desktop Wallpaper,0
Entry6=DMI Mgmt Service Layer,0
Entry7=Document Templates,1
Entry8=Games,0
Entry9=Imaging,1
Entry10=Mouse Pointers,0
Entry11=Net Watcher,0
Entry12=Object Packager,1
Entry13=Online User's Guide,0
Entry14=Paint,1
Entry15=Quick View,0
Entry16=System Mgmt Infrastructure,0
Entry17=System Monitor,0
Entry18=System Resource Meter,0
Entry19=TWAIN 1.6,1
Entry20=Windows 98 Tour,0
Entry21=WordPad,1

[Communications]
Entry1=Dial-Up Networking,0
Entry2=Direct Cable Connection,0
Entry3=HyperTerminal,1
Entry4=Microsoft NetMeeting,1
Entry5=Phone Dialer,1
```

```
[Disk Tools]
Entry1=Backup,0
Entry2=Defrag,1
Entry3=Disk compression tools,1

[Microsoft Fax]
Entry1=Microsoft Fax Services,0
Entry2=Microsoft Fax Viewer,0

[Multimedia]
Entry1=Audio Compression,1
Entry2=CD Player,1
Entry3=Media Player,1
Entry4=Multimedia Sound Schemes,0
Entry5=Sample Sounds,0
Entry6=Sound Recorder,1
Entry7=Video Compression,1
Entry8=Volume Control,1

[Screen Savers]
Entry1=Additional Screen Savers,0
Entry2=Flying Windows,1
Entry3=OpenGL Screen Savers,1

[The Microsoft Network]
Entry1=The Microsoft Network,0
```

Creating Setup Scripts Simultaneously for Multiple Computers

You can use Microsoft Batch 98 to create up to 9,999 setup scripts simultaneously by using the **Multiple Machine-Name Save** command from the **File** menu. Using a text editor, you create a text file listing, line-by-line, the name of each of the computers for which you want to create setup scripts. Optionally, you can provide their IP addresses, which must be unique. Then, you designate the destination directory where you want to save the setup scripts.

▶ **To create multiple setup scripts at once**

1. From the **File** menu on the main Batch setup screen, click **Multiple Machine-Name Save**.

2. Create a computer-name file (text file with all the computer names for which you want to create setup scripts.)

Using a text editor, such as Notepad, open a text file, enter a single computer name on each line, and terminate the line with a carriage return/line feed (press **ENTER** after typing each name). On Microsoft networks, computer names can contain only alphanumeric characters and these characters:

! @ $ % ^ ( ) { } _ ~.

The following shows an example of a text file that can be used for **Multiple Machine-Name Save**:

```
Chaos@
Super_Computer_5, 172.30.5.4
Print_Server_1
Mail_Server_1
Luna, 172.32.54.5
Saturn
Pluto
```

Note that you can include an IP address for any particular computer (on the same line as the machine name, separated by a comma) without having to include addresses for all computers. In this example, 'Super_Computer_5' and 'Luna' will be set up with listed IP addresses.

3. After you create and select the computer name file to be used, Batch.exe reads and saves all names and addresses.

Batch.exe displays a message indicating how many computer names it read.

4. Select a directory where all the setup script files will be saved. In the **Destination of Save** dialog box, find the directory you want to use. The directory must already exist. The name of the file in the **File Name** box is not important.

5. After the target directory has been selected, click **Save**.

Batch setup will create one INF file per name containing all the settings currently defined, using a series of files named Bstp0001.inf through Bstp9999.inf, written in the order that the names are listed in the machine name file. The only unique information in each file will be the computer name and any IP address provided. Using the previous example, the file Bstp0001.inf will contain the setup information for the computer named 'Chaos@' and file Bstp0007.inf will contain the setup information for the computer named 'Pluto.'

6. Click **Close** to close the **Multiple Machine-Name Save** dialog box.

Tips for Creating a Computer-Name File

When creating a computer-name file (text file with all the computer names for which the **Multiple Machine-Name Save** command creates a setup script), consider the following:

- Do not use all periods for computer names. Other networks may have different requirements.

- If you want to include an IP address for a given computer, put a single comma after the computer name and then type the IP address.

- A single blank line signifies the end of the computer-name file. The batch-mode save process does not check for errors in these values.

- If you enter incorrect information in the computer-name file, then Windows 98 Setup might stop and prompt you to enter the correct information.

Using Dbset.exe to Customize Setup Scripts and Other Files

You can use Dbset if your installation requires more customization flexibility than just being able to set the computer name or IP address. Dbset.exe is a configuration utility that allows you to individualize setup scripts and other types of text files. Dbset.exe searches and reads data from a text file (called *database file* in this section) and uses the data to either set environment variables or to write to an output file using a format specified by a template file. The template file can be a text file in Msbatch.inf format, a registry file, or any other type of text file.

For example, you can create a template setup script (in Msbatch.inf format) with settings that you want to use for all users in your organization or workgroup. Then, you create a database file with specific data for each user, for example, user_name, computer_name, and so on. From the template and database file, Dbset.exe creates an individualized setup script by replacing the variable names (for example user_name) with the actual name of the user (Maria).

The following examples show the syntax of the command, how to use it, and the results you obtain. In this section parameters enclosed in brackets [ ] indicate that the parameter is optional. If a value is not specified, Dbset.exe uses the default value. All the examples use the same database and template file introduced in the first two examples.

Using the Dbset.exe Command-Line Switches

Dbset.exe provides switches (some times called options) to control how it searches and reads data from a database file and how it uses the data to either set environment variables or how it writes the data in an output file.

These switches are specified on the command line as arguments for the **dbset** command (such as **dbset /r**). The specific option is preceded by a forward slash (/) character (not the backslash used to specify directory arguments).

Action

Writes data from an input text file, such as a database file, to either set MS-DOS environment variables or to write data to an output text file. If a text file is specified as the output, the data is formatted based on a template text file.

Syntax

dbset [/d [*database_file*]] [/f [*field_name*]] [/s:*delimiter*] [/i [*template_file*]]
   [/r [*output_file*]] [/m] [/o *record_overlay*] [/y] [*data*]

Parameters

delimiter
   Specifies the character used to separate one field from another in a record in the database file.

field_name
   Specifies the name of the field to be searched.

database_file
   Specifies the name and location of the database text file.

record_overlay
   Specifies a record with delimiters separating each of its fields.

template_file
   Specifies the text file you want to use as a template for formatting data written to the output file.

output_file
   Specifies the name of the output file where the data will be written.

Data
   Specifies the data item to search for in a database file. The default is to search for the match of "data" in the first field of each record in the database file. To specify another field to search, use the /f switch.

Switches

/d *database_file*

Specifies the name and location of database file. The default is Dbset.db. The database file contains records or structures of information separated into fields by delimiters. Each record has the same format as the first record in the file. The first record in the file also assigns the name, or data element, of each field. The field names are the same in every record in the file and are the logical definitions of the fields. In each record following the first the fields hold data items or the actual data. For each field name there can be many fields in the database file that hold data items. At a minimum, a database must contain one record which contains the field names. A one-record database is useful only when using the **/m** switch.

/f [*field*]

Specifies a field (by name) to search for a data match in. The default is the field that makes up the first column. A field is a unit of data in a record. A collection of fields, separated by delimiters, make up a record. A data item is the actual data stored in the field.

/s:*delimiter*

A character used to separate one field from another in a record. The default is a comma (,). Only one character may be specified as the delimiter.

/i *template_file*

Specifies the name and location of the template file. The default is Template.txt. The template file will be used as the basis for the output file. Variable names in the template file are denoted in %variable% format. Actual % characters are denoted by %%. The variable names will be matched with field names in the database file and replace with the values from the appropriate record. Variable names in the template file must match field names in the database file. If the **/i** switch is specified, the output is always a text file.

/r [*output_file*]

Specifies the name and location of the file to write to. The default is Dbset.txt. Text written to the output file will be in the format of the Template.txt file with the variable names replaced by data items from the database file.

/m [*data*]

Specifies to prompt for each variable or field. A "data" argument may be used to specify the record to search for in the database file. The specified data from the record will be used as the prompts. When using the **/m** switch, your database can contain only the record that contains all the field names you want to use.

/o [*record_overlay*]

Overwrites the data item of the field specified. The "record_overlay" is a record with delimiters separating each field. Each field should be empty except the field to be overwritten which should contain the new data item. Only the data in the output is changed, data in the database file is not. The new data item may not contain spaces.

/y

Answers yes to all warning messages. This allows for full automation for use in scripts, such as MS-DOS.bat files

/?

Show the help screen.

Input Files: Database or Template Files

Dbset.exe accepts two types of files as input: database and template files, both in text format.

A *database file* is made up of records. Each record consists of a collection of fields, separated by delimiters. (A *field* is a unit of data.) The first record in the file specifies the field names. The actual data, stored in the fields differ, while the field names are logical definitions of the fields and are the same for each record in the file. Field names need to match with variable names in the template file.

The following shows an example of a database file.

```
name,machine,staticip,mailsvr
Dan,dev_02,172.30.5.1,mail-svr-70
Sam,dev_01,172.31.55.5,mail-svr-59
Pasquale,dev_03,172.25.25.1,mail-svr-40
```

A *template file*, whose default name is Template.txt, contains the format used to write to an output file with variable names denoted as follows:

%variable_name%

If the percent sign (%) is part of any text in the template file, other than where variables are specified, the percent sign should be denoted by %%. Dbset.exe replaces %% by % in the output file, when the output file is created.

A template file does not need to contain all the variables in the database, but the database must contain all the variables in the template file. If the template file contains variables that are not represented in the database file the following error appears:

```
Error! Wrong template file
```

Creating a Template File

You can create template files from a variety of text files. For example, from the following registry file:

```
[HKEY_CURRENT_USER\Dbsetexample\Profile\Sam]
"User"="Sam"
"MachineName"="dev_01"
"IP"=172.31.55.5
"Server"="mail-svr-59"
```

Note All the examples that follow use these sample files as input files.

Example

You can create a template file that looks like this:

```
[HKEY_CURRENT_USER\Dbsetexample\Profile\%name%]
"User"="%name%"
"MachineName"="%machine%"
"IP"=%staticip%
"Server"="%mailsvr%"
```

Changing the Default Database File Name

The following example demonstrate how to use a file name other than the default name for a database file (Dbset.txt is the default database file name).

▶ **To change the default name for the database file**

- Use the following syntax:

   Dbset /d *database_file data*

Example

If you type:

Dbset /d MyDatabs.dbs /r Dan

Dbset.exe searches the file MyDatabs.dbs for the item Dan in the Name field and writes the data it found to the default output file, Dbset.txt, using the format of the default template file, Template.txt.

Example

If you type:

Dbset /d MyDatabs.dbs Dan

Dbset.exe finds the same data as in the previous example but it writes it to environment variables instead of an output file because neither the **/r** or **/i** switch were specified.

Changing the Default Search

The default Dbset.exe behavior is to search for the match of the data specified, in the first field of each record in the database file. In the sample output file described earlier, the data searched for was Sam in the Name field, which is the first field of each record. To specify another field to search for the data in, use the **/f** switch.

▶ **To search a field other than the default**

- Use the following syntax:

   Dbset /f *field data*

Example

If you type:

Dbset /f machine dev_02

Dbset.exe searches for dev_02 in the Machine field in each record in the file. Then Dbset.exe writes the data found in the record to environment variables.

Using Delimiters

A delimiter is a character used to separate one field from another in a record. You can specify only one character as the delimiter. The default is a comma (,).

▶ **To use a delimiter other than the default**

- Use the following syntax:

   Dbset /s:[*delimiter*]

Example

The following two examples show how to specify a character as the delimiter in the database file. When you execute:

Dbset /s:; Sam

Dbset.exe accesses the default database file and use the semicolon (;) as the delimiter. It then finds the data Sam in the Name field of a record and uses the data to write environment variables.

Changing the Default Template File Name

The following example demonstrate how to use a file name other than the default name for a template file (Template.txt is the default template file name).

▶ **To use a template file other than the default**

- Use the following syntax:

  Dbset /i *template_file data*

Example

If you type:

Dbset /r /i Temp.txt Sam

Dbset.exe uses Temp.txt as the template file instead of the default template name, Template.txt.

Creating Globally Unique Identifiers (GUIDs)

The database file can contain the variable $guid8$ and $guid10$. These entries in the database create a globally unique identifier (GUID), with either 8 or 10 characters, which is guaranteed to contain one or more of each of the following: capital letter, lower-case letter, number, or symbol.

Example

If you use the following database file, which contains GUID entries:

```
Name,machine,machine2,ID
johnd,jdoe,jdoe2,$guid8$
sohanl,v-samano,v-samano2,$guid10$
dspinn,dansp,dansp2,$guid10$
```

And you type:

Dbset johnd

Dbset.exe writes to environment variables the data found in the record, of the default database file, with "johnd" in the Name field. The environment variables might look like:

```
name=johnd
machine=jdoe
machine=jdoe2
mailsvr=sD8P9x,e
```

Output: Environment Variables or Output File

Dbset.exe supports two types of output: environment variables or a text output file.

Using Environment Variables as Output

When the specified output is writing to environment variables, Dbset.exe sets the environment variables specified by the field names of the database

---

Note To check the environment variable settings, type **set** at the command prompt.

▶ **To use environment variables as output**

- Use the following syntax:

  Dbset *data*

Example

If you type

Dbset Dan

Dbset.exe writes the data from the record called **dan** to environment variables as follows:

```
name=dan
machine=dev_02
staticip=172.30.5.1
server=mail-svr-70
```

Using a Text File as Output

Dbset.exe can also write to an output text file. To generate an output file, you must provide a template file. Text written to the output file will be in the same format as the template file, with the variable names replaced by data items from the database file. The default output file name is Dbset.txt.

▶ **To specify a text file as output**

- Use the following syntax:

  Dbset /r [*output_file*] *data*

Example

If you type:

Dbset /r Sam

Dbset.exe writes the data from the **Sam** record to the default output file (Dbset.txt) in the following format.

```
[HKEY_CURRENT_USER\Dbsetexample\Profile\Sam]
    "User"="Sam"
    "MachineName"="dev_01"
    "IP"=172.31.55.5
    "Server"="mail-svr-59"
```

If a template file is specified, the output will automatically be a file based on the template.

Example

If you type:

Dbset /r /i Temp.txt Sam

Dbset.exe writes the information it found in the record with the data Sam in the Name field, to the default output file in the format specified by Temp.txt.

Example

If you type:

Dbset /r MyOutput.txt Sam

Dbset.exe creates the file MyOutput.txt (if the file exists a prompt to overwrite the file will appear) and writes to it the information from the record that contains the data item Sam in the Name field. The data is written to MyOutput.txt in the same format as the default template file. If the default template file, Template.txt, does not exist, the following error message is displayed:

```
Error! Wrong template file!
```

Prompting

You can use Dbset.exe to prompt you to enter the data for each field of a record in the database file. You can specify a record that Dbset.exe will use to prompt you, or if you do not specify a record, Dbset.exe prompts you to enter the data. The database file is not modified.

▶ **To cause Dbset to prompt you for the data for each field**

- Use the following syntax:

    Dbset /m [*data*]

Example

If you type:

Dbset /m Sam

Dbset.exe accesses the default database file and displays the data in each of the fields of the record that contains Sam in the Name field. The user is prompted with each field one at a time, and has the option to edit the data. After Dbset.exe displays each field, it writes the data to environment variables.

For this example the data that Dbset.exe prompts to the user and the environment variable settings are as follows:

```
name=Sam
machine=dev_01
staticip=172.31.55.5
server=mail-svr-59
```

Example

If you type:

Dbset /m

Dbset.exe prompts the user to enter data for each of the fields in a record in the default database file. Then, it writes the data the user entered to environment variables.

Example

If you type:

Dbset /m /r

Dbset.exe prompts the users in the same way described in the preceding example but it writes the new data to the default output file (Dbset.exe) using the format of the default template (Template.txt).

Important   When the **/m** switch is followed with other switches, Dbset.exe assumes that the last parameter belongs to the switch specified last.

Example

If you type:

Dbset /m /r Output.txt

Dbset.exe prompts the users in the same way described in the preceding example but it writes the new data to Output.txt, using the format of the default template (Template.txt).

Overwriting Data in a Field in a Database File

You can use the **/o** switch to overwrite a data item in a field of the database file. To specify which field to overwrite, type the **/o** switch followed with as many delimiters as there are in the record of the database file. Leave each field empty except for the field you want to overwrite. In that field, type the new data. Using this **/o** switch does not change the data in the database file, only the data in the output is changed. The field and the new data item can not contain spaces.

▶ **To change the default name for the database file**

- Use the following syntax:

  Dbset /o *record data*

If you type:

Dbset /o ,dev_06,, Dan

Dbset.exe overwrites the data that exists in the second field (the Machine field) of the record that contains Dan in the first field (the Name field) with the new data dev_06.

The following example combines several of the switches used in the previous examples in the following syntax:

Dbset /d [*database_file*] **/r** [*output_file*] **/f** [*field*] **/i** [*template_file*] *data*

Using:

database_file = Database.db
output_file = Output.txt
field = machine
template_file = Temp.txt
data = dev_03

When you execute:

Dbset /d Database.db /r Output.txt /f machine /i Temp.txt dev_03

Dbset.exe accesses Database.db and the data **dev_03** in the **machine** field of a record. It overwrites the variables of Temp.txt with the data it found. It writes this information to the output file Output.txt using the format of Temp.txt.

Adding Custom Drivers with INF Installer (Infinst.exe)

With INF Installer (Infinst.exe), you can add device drivers or network drivers to a Windows 98 installation point. When you install Windows 98 from this installation point, the added drivers will be installed as if they were part of the original Windows 98 Setup program.

To use Infinst.exe, the Windows 98 installation point must be created with write permissions.

▶ **To run INF Installer**

1. Double-click the **Infinst.exe** icon

   The Inf Installer window appears.

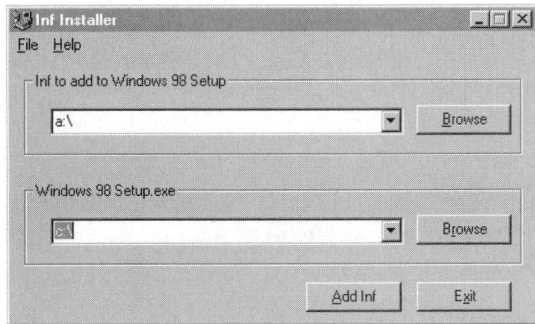

2. In **Inf to add to Windows 98 Setup**, type the path and file name of the INF file you want to add to the Windows 98 installation point. For example:

    A:\Drivers\Driver1.INF

3. In Windows 98 Setup.exe, type the path of the installation point followed by **Setup.exe** (the name of the Windows 98 Setup program). For example:

    \\Server1\ShareA\Setup.exe

4. Click **Add Inf**.

After you performed these tasks, Infinst.exe adds the drivers and associated INF files, which are listed in the [COPYFILES=] sections of the INF files, to the Windows 98 installation point you specified. It modifies all INF files that were already located in the installation point that had matching *Plug-and-Play IDs* (PnP IDs), as well the Custom.inf and Infist.log files, which were also located in the installation point.

The following list provides more details on how Infinst.exe works:

- Creates two directories in the Windows 98 installation point. One is for INF files that get overwritten by new INF files of the same name (Oldinf) and one is for storing the INF files included in the Windows 98 cabinet files (Wininf).

- Searches the INF file to be added for PnP IDs.

- Checks the INF files versioning (only INF files with version $CHICAGO$ should be added although Infinst.exe corrects certain versions to $CHICAGO$ automatically).

- Compares the PnP IDs it found when it searched the new INF file with the PnP IDs contained in all the INF files that are in the Wininf directory.

- If it finds an INF file with a matching PnP ID, it copies it to the Windows 98 installation point (the directory where the Windows 98 Setup files are located) as long as an INF file with the same name does not already exist in the installation point.

- Compares the PnP IDs it found on the new INF file with the PnP IDs in all the INF files that are in the Windows 98 installation point.

- If it finds an INF file with a matching PnP ID, it comments out the matching PnP IDs.

- Copies the new INF file and all necessary driver files to the directory where the Windows 98 Setup files reside.

- Edits the Custom.inf file. INF files and drivers of install media classes (such as net) are added to more section of the Custom.inf file than those of other classes because they may be needed earlier in the setup process.

- Appends to the Infinst.log.

Infinst.exe can add multiple INF files for single or multiple PnP devices, even if Windows 98 did not previously support them. The INF files must be compatible with Windows 98.

You can add any drivers you want with Infinst.exe and you can install or upgrade to Windows 98 following any of the methods described in Chapter 2, "Setting Up Windows 98." The drivers you added will be properly installed, regardless of what installation method you use.

Infinst.exe has the following design limitations:

- Adding an INF file with the same name as one included with Windows 98 or one previously added eliminates all the functionality of the previous INF file, regardless of PnP IDs.

- You must have write permission to the location of the Windows 98 Setup files are located, otherwise, Infinst.exe will not work. For example, Infinst.exe does not add drivers to a Windows 98 compact disc.

- Adding two INF files with the same PnP IDs eliminates the functionality of the INF file that was added first.

The following is a typical example of adding an INF file to Windows 98 and automating setup. The steps in this example show how to install remote registry services automatically during Windows 98 Setup. This allows you to automate the installation of network clients, services, protocols, and all types of hardware devices with properly written INF files. When adding hardware INF files, it is not necessary to make changes to your custom script.

▶ **To customize Windows 98 to support remote registry services**

1. Create a Windows 98 installation point. (A share with write permissions on a network server where the Windows 98 Setup files are located.) For example:

   \\Server1\Windows98

2. Create a custom script with Microsoft Batch 98 following the steps outlined in "Creating Custom Scripts with Batch.exe" earlier in this chapter.

   ▪ On **Network Options**, click the **Additional Clients** tab. In **Other Clients**, under **Protocols**, type **Remotereg**.

   ▪ On the **File** menu, click **Save As**. In **File Name**, enter the path for your installation point and the name of your setup script. For example:

     \\Server1\Windows98\Msbatch.inf

3. Following the steps outlined in "Adding Custom Drivers with INF Installer (Infinst.exe)" earlier in this chapter, add the following INF file for remote registry services:

   Regsvr.inf

   You can find this file in the \Tools\Reskit\Netadmin\Remotereg directory of the Microsoft Windows 98 compact disc.

4. Connect to your installation point, for example **\\Server1\Windows98** and then start Windows 98 Setup by typing:

   Setup.exe Msbatch.inf at the command prompt.

   – Or –

   \\Server1\Windows98\Setup.exe Msbatch.inf in the **Run** dialog box from the **Start** menu.

Running Custom Setup Scripts

After creating your custom script, you can run Setup with minimal user interaction.

▶ **To run Windows 98 Setup using a setup script with minimal user action**

1. Change to the directory where the Windows 98 Setup files are located.

2. At the command line, run Windows 98 Setup by specifying the batch file that contains the setup script, using this syntax:

   ```
   setup msbatch.inf
   ```

Note   You must specify a complete path and name for the INF file; otherwise, Setup returns an error.

If Msbatch.inf exists in the Windows directory on the server containing the Windows 98 source files, Setup uses it by default. Otherwise, for example, you would type **setup e:\Mybatch.inf** to run Setup using a setup script named Mybatch.inf on drive E.

To use a script in the Scripts directory on a server named NTSVR1, you would type **setup \\ntsvr1\scripts\Mybatch.inf** (provided, of course, that your operating system software can interpret UNC path names).

– Or –

Include the entire statement for running Windows 98 Setup in the logon script, so that the user does not have to type anything at the command prompt.

You can run Windows 98 Setup using a script that is located on a local computer or on a network server, as explained in the following sections.

Windows 98 Files Located on a Local Computer

You can automate Setup when both the Windows 98 files and the script are located locally on the same computer.

▶   **To automate Windows 98 Setup when files are located on a local computer**

- At the command prompt, run Windows 98 Setup by specifying the batch file that contains the setup script, using the following syntax:

  D:*Windows_directory***\\Setup.exe a:***script.inf*

  Where *Windows_directory* is the directory that contains the Windows 98 files and *script.inf* is the name of your setup script.

Windows 98 Files Located on a Network Server

You can also automate Setup when both the Windows 98 files and the script are located on a server that can be accessed by the local computer.

▶   **To automate Windows 98 Setup when files are located on a server**

1. Start the computer running the existing network client software.

2. Connect to the server or drive that contains the Windows 98 source files.

   The network administrator can include this step in the logon script to avoid user action.

3. At the command prompt, run Windows 98 Setup by specifying the batch file that contains the setup script, using the following syntax:

   *server_name**Windows_directory***Setup.exe** *script.inf*

   Where *server_name* is the name of the sever, *Windows_directory* is the directory that contains the Windows 98 files, and *script.inf* is the name of your setup script.

Note If Windows 98 is installed from a server, the location of that network directory is stored in the registry. When you add a device or require additional support files to run Windows 98, Setup automatically attempts to retrieve the files from the same location on the server. This eliminates the need to maintain a permanent network connection on the computer and makes it easier to modify the configuration of a computer in a networked environment.

When you run Windows 98 Setup in this way, Setup takes all settings from the custom script. For information not defined in the setup script, Windows 98 Setup migrates settings from an earlier version of Windows on the computer, uses built-in defaults, or prompts the user to provide information.

After copying files, Windows 98 Setup restarts the computer and begins the Run Once setup operations (printer setup, program group conversions, and so on). When these operations are finished, Windows 98 is completely installed.

When the user quits Windows 98 Setup at this point, Setup writes all changes to the registry. The user can restart the computer and log on with the usual logon name and password.

The network administrator can automate this process by providing each user with a floppy disk that contains the necessary files for starting the computer, connecting to the network, and running Windows 98 Setup with a custom setup script.

Note Setting up Windows 98 from a network server requires the user to logon to the network to access the Windows 98 Setup files to complete the installation. This means that the completion of Setup cannot be fully automated; however, the majority of Setup can still be automated.

Customizing Windows 98 in NetWare Networks

This section describes how to customize Windows 98 to use Novell's Novell Client for Windows 95/98 and to detect NetWare components and TSRs during Setup.

Customizing Windows 98 to Use the Novell Client for Windows 95/98

This section describes how to customize your Windows 98 installation to use Novell's Novell Client for Windows 95/98. For more information on configuring Novell NetWare clients, including the Novell Client for Windows 95/98, see Chapter 17, "Windows 98 on Third-Party Networks."

▶ **To automate a Windows 98 installation with the Novell Client for Windows 95/98**

1. Get the Novell Client for Windows 95/98 setup files from Novell's Web site at **http://www.novell.com/**.

   Novell provides special setup files for automating Windows installations using an Msbatch.inf custom setup script. You must use these files for your customized installation to work properly.

2. Create a Windows 98 installation point. (A share with write permissions on a network server where the Windows 98 Setup files are located.) For example:

   \\Server1\Windows98

3. Create a custom script with Microsoft Batch 98 following the steps outlined in "Creating Custom Scripts with Batch.exe" earlier in this chapter:

   ▪ Use the following settings:

For the following Batch.exe option	Do the following
Protocols tab in **Network Options**	Select the **IPX/SPX-compatible Protocol**
Additional Clients tab in **Network Options**	In **Other Clients**, under:
	Protocols, type **NovellIPX32**
	Clients, type **Novell32**

   ▪ On the **File** menu, click **Save As**. In **File name**, enter the path for your installation point and the name of your setup script. For example:

   \\Server1\Windows98\Msbatch.inf

4. Manually copy or add the [Novell32] section from the INF files and documentation supplied by Novell to your setup script (\\Server1\Windows98\Msbatch.inf).

5. Following the steps outlined in "Adding Custom Drivers with INF Installer (Infinst.exe)" earlier in this chapter, add the following Novell-supplied drivers for Novell Client for Windows 95/98:

   Nwclient.inf
   Nwtrans.inf

   Click **Yes** when Infinst.exe warns you about overwriting an existing Nwtrans.inf file.

6. Connect to your installation point, for example **\\Server1\Windows98** and then start Windows 98 Setup by typing:

Setup.exe Msbatch.inf at the command prompt.

– Or –

\\Server1\Windows98\Setup.exe Msbatch.inf in the **Run** dialog box from the **Start** menu.

Customizing Detection for NetWare Networks

This section describes the format of Netdet.ini, which is used to detect NetWare components and TSRs during Windows 98 Setup. You can use this information to add custom entries for detecting components on NetWare networks and defining actions to be taken during Setup based on detection results.

Note If you do not need to modify the default detection behavior for setting up Windows 98 on NetWare networks, you can skip this section.

The Netdet.ini and related Netos.dll files are stored in the Precopy2.cab file on the Windows 98 floppy disks or compact disc. The version used by Windows 98 Setup is stored in the %WinDir% directory (Windows 98 installation directory) on the local computer. If you modify this file, you can place the revised version of Netdet.ini in the share on the server that contains the Windows 98 source files.

Each component section in Netdet.ini consists of one or more *detection* entries, and one or more *event* entries. A detection entry has the following format:

detectionN=method1[*,method2...*]

Alternate *detection* entries can be used to define different actions to be taken, depending on how a component is detected. For example, a TSR detected in memory but not in a batch file might require different actions from the actions required when an entry for the TSR is found in Autoexec.bat. For example:

```
detection0=mcb
detection1=autoexec.bat
full_install0=migrate
full_install1=prevent
```

Each *method#* parameter in the *detection* statement defines a detection method, as listed in Table 3.12. Setup assumes that the component has been detected if one method detects it.

Table 3.12   Detection methods

Detection method	Meaning
assumed	Always detected; used to force an action unconditionally
autoexec.bat	Detected in an uncommented line in Autoexec.bat
config.sys	Detected in an uncommented line in Config.sys
custom_dll	Detected by calling external dynamic-link library (DLL) detection code
mcb	Detected by checking the list of TSRs maintained by MS-DOS in the memory control blocks (MCBs)
mcb_nobat	Detected in the MCB chain but not in Autoexec.bat
system.ini	Detected in an uncommented line in System.ini

The special detection method **custom_dll** requires two additional entries: **detection_dll**, which contains the file name of the DLL to be loaded, and **detection_call**, which contains the name of the entry point consistent with the following **typedef**:

```
typedef BOOL (WINAPI *LPDCALL)(LPSTR)
```

Adding custom entries based on this detection method requires that you have sufficient programmatic understanding of the calls made in the relevant DLLs. For an example of required entries for **custom_dll**, see the example entry for VLM later in this section.

The Netdet.ini file includes one or more *event* entries grouped by numerical suffixes that match the suffixes in *detection* entries (that is, *N* must be 0 or 1). Each *event* entry contains a list of actions to be performed if the associated *detection* action was successful. The following shows the form of *event* entries:

eventN=action1[(*parameter*)][,*action2*[(*parameter*)]...]

The *event* name is the name of the Setup code for handling installation of components related to the detected TSR or NetWare component. The following list shows the defined events.

Event	Meaning
Protstack_install*N*	The protected-mode protocol will be installed.
Nwredir_install*N*	The protected-mode network client will be installed.
Full_install*N*	The protected-mode protocol and network client will be installed.

Table 3.13 lists the defined action codes related to events in Netdet.ini.

Table 3.13   Netdet.ini action codes

Action code	Meaning
None	Do not do anything (NOP).
Prevent	Recommend against using during recommendation phase.
Remove	Comment out using REM in Autoexec.bat or a batch file called from Autoexec.bat.
Unremove	Remove REM comment from Autoexec.bat or a batch file called from Autoexec.bat.
Migrate	Comment out using REM in Autoexec.bat, and add to Winstart.bat.
Unmigrate	Remove REM comment in Autoexec.bat, and remove from Winstart.bat.
Install_devnode(*devnode*)	Cause specified device node to be installed.
Uninstall_devnode(*devnode*)	Cause specified device node to be removed.
Gen_install(*section*)	Cause action in an Install section to run (see the example for Source Routing for NetWare later in this section).

Notice that the event named **prevent** is a special case that is used during the recommendation phase when Setup is determining which new Windows 98 components can be installed without interfering with TSR dependencies defined in Netdet.ini. If a component is detected by the defined method and the **prevent** action is associated with the related event, then Setup will recommend against the usual Setup action for the event.

The following shows some examples of entries in Netdet.ini:

```
;;;;;; NOVELL Directory Services VLM 4.x ;;;;;;;;
; Prevents installation of Client for NetWare Networks
; if Novell NDS is used.
[VLM]
detection0=custom_dll
detection_dll=NETOS.DLL
detection_call=NW_IsNDSinUse
full_install0=prevent

;;;;;; IPX MONO Detection ;;;;;;;;
[IPXMONO]
detection0=custom_dll
detection_dll=NETDI.DLL
detection_call=NW_IsIpxMonoOnlyCard
full_install0=prevent
```

```
;;;;;;;;;;; SOURCE ROUTING FOR NETWARE ;;;;;;;;;
; Adds cache size for Source Routing.
[ROUTE]
detection0=mcb
full_install0=remove,gen_install(NWSRCR)

[NWSRCR]
AddReg=NWSRCR.reg
UpdateInis=NWSRCR_INI

[NWSRCR.reg]
HKLM,System\CurrentControlSet\Services\VxD\NWLINK,cachesize,,"16"
HKLM,System\CurrentControlSet\Services\VxD\NWLINK\Ndi\params\cachesize,"
",,"16"

[NWSRCR_INI]
%26%\protocol.ini,NWLINK$,,"cachesize=16"

;;;;;;;; NOVELL Named-Pipes Support ;;;;;;;;;;;;;;;;
[DOSNP.EXE]
detection0=mcb,mcb_nobat
protstack_install0=prevent
detection1=mcb_nobat
full_install1=prevent

;;;;;;; NOVELL NETBIOS ;;;;;;;;;;;;;;;;;;
; Installs NETBIOS over IPX if Novell NETBIOS is present.
[NETBIOS]
detection0=mcb
full_install0=remove,install_devnode(NWNBLINK)

;;;;;;; Btrieve ;;;;;;;;;;;
[Brequest.exe]
detection0=mcb,mcb_nobat
full_install0=migrate
detection1=mcb_nobat
full_install1=prevent
```

Customizing Windows 98 with Wrkgrp.ini Files

You can use a file named Wrkgrp.ini to specify a list of workgroups that users
can choose to join. You can use Wrkgrp.ini in these ways:

- To help reduce the proliferation of workgroup names on the network.

- To control the workgroup choices that users can make.

- To specify defaults for the NetWare preferred server or Windows NT domain
  on a per-workgroup basis.

The Wrkgrp.ini file is stored in the Windows directory on the server that contains the Windows 98 source files.

Windows 98 Setup uses the values defined in Wrkgrp.ini to set registry values in the workgroup, logon domain, preferred server, and other values. The same values are used to control options available for users to select in the Network option in Control Panel. The Wrkgrp.ini file contains the following sections:

- [Options] specifies the recognized options for workgroups.

- [Workgroups] contains a list of workgroups from which the user can choose.

In Windows 98, for each workgroup, you can specify the domain, preferred server, and so on, that everyone in a workgroup will use, depending on the network providers used.

Table 3.14 describes the format of the Windows 98 Wrkgrp.ini file.

Table 3.14   Wrkgrp.ini settings

Section or entry	Description
[Options] section:	
**ANSI=true	false**	Specifies whether the workgroups need to be converted from an original equipment manufacturer (OEM) character set to American National Standards Institute (ANSI). Default is **false**.
**Required=true	false**	Specifies whether users can type their own workgroup name or forces them to choose from those listed.
**ForceMapping=true	false**	Specifies whether users can change the workgroup, logon domain, or preferred server that are set by a mapping.
Mapping=_NP1_, _NP2_, _NP3_,... (comma-separated list of network providers)	Specifies a comma-separated list of the network providers to which workgroups can be mapped. Also specifies the order in which values will be listed in the [Workgroups] section. Implicitly, this specifies where in the registry to store settings. This parameter is optional. By default, workgroups map to _domain, preferred server_.
Default=_NP1 default,NP2 default, NP3 default,..._	Specifies the default mapping for workgroups listed in the [Workgroups] section that do not have a mapping defined. This allows you to add a single entry to an existing Windows for Workgroups Wrkgrp.ini file to get minimal mapping functionality. The format is the same as for specifying a mapping in [Workgroups].

Table 3.14 Wrkgrp.ini settings *(continued)*

Section or entry	Description
[Workgroups] section:	
workgroup=*optional_mapping*	Specifies a workgroup that users can choose and its mappings will automatically be defined in the order specified in **Mapping=**. There can be a *workgroup=* entry in the file for every workgroup that users can choose. Each name of a workgroup must be followed by an equal sign (=) for the workgroup name to be interpreted correctly.

The entry that defines the network providers for each workgroup has the following format in the [Workgroups] section:

workgroup_name=mapping1,mapping2,mapping3,...

By default in Windows 98, workgroups can be mapped to both Windows NT domains and NetWare preferred servers. (This is because Windows 98 includes network providers for these two networks.) For example:

```
MktMain=MktDom1,master1
```

This example specifies that the workgroup named MktMain has these two mappings: MktDom1 is the logon domain for the Windows NT network, and Master1 is the preferred server for the NetWare network.

Administrators can specify the 32-bit, protected-mode network providers that can be mapped for a workgroup by setting the **Mapping=** parameter in the [Options] section of Wrkgrp.ini. For example, if the network uses two network providers (MSNP32 for Microsoft networks and NWNP32 for NetWare networks), the following is defined in Wrkgrp.ini:

```
[options]
mapping=msnp32,nwnp32
```

The order specified in the **Mapping=** entry also specifies the order of items in the [Workgroups] section.

You can also use the **Default=** entry to specify a default mapping for workgroups that do not have an explicit mapping. This allows you to use an existing Wrkgrp.ini created for Windows for Workgroups 3.11, and add one entry to take advantage of Windows 98 functionality. For example, add the entry **Default=MktDom1,Master1** to use the servers described in the previous example as the default mapping.

If a Wrkgrp.ini exists, the Workgroup field in Windows 98 Setup and the Network option in Control Panel both show all the workgroups listed in Wrkgrp.ini. Users can choose a workgroup from the list or type a workgroup name. If **Required=true** in Wrkgrp.ini, the user must choose from the list.

In Wrkgrp.ini, **ForceMapping=** controls whether mapped values can be changed in the Windows 98 user interface. For example, if **ForceMapping=true** and the user selects a workgroup that is mapped to a domain, the user cannot change the value in the **Access Control** tab in the Network option in Control Panel, and in the **Enter Network Password** dialog box.

Note If Windows 98 Setup finds the Wrkgrp.ini file in the Windows 98 source files, it copies the file to the shared Windows directory.

Customizing Windows 98 with Profiles and Policy Files

You can predefine settings in user profiles and system policy files to control user actions. For example:

- You can enforce a mandatory desktop configuration by installing a mandatory user profile (User.man) in users' home directory.
- You can control the user's security privileges, network access, and desktop configuration if you install system policy files on the logon server. This is the Public directory on a NetWare server or the \Netlogon directory on the primary domain controller for a Windows NT domain.

To take advantage of these features in Windows 98, you must define the user profile and system policy settings to be used. Then place these files in the appropriate directories before users run Windows 98 Setup. When users log on to Windows 98, the profiles and policies will be used automatically.

For information about creating and using user profiles and system policy files, see Chapter 7, "User Profiles" and Chapter 8, "System Policies." You can enable user profiles and policies using a setup script created with Microsoft Batch 98. For an example of setup script statements that enable user profiles, group policies, and remote administration, see Appendix D, "Msbatch.inf Parameters for Setup Scripts."

C H A P T E R   4

Automated Installations

4

This chapter provides information about automating Microsoft Windows 98 installations. If you intend to roll out Windows 98 on multiple computers, you can read this chapter for information on what you need to do to automate Microsoft Windows 98 Setup.

In This Chapter

See Also

- For information on automating Windows 98 installations with Microsoft Systems Management Server, see Appendix E, "Microsoft Systems Management Server."

- For information on how to define statements in setup scripts see Appendix D, "Msbatch.inf Parameters for Setup Scripts."

Overview of Automated Installations

In an environment where you need to upgrade more than a handful of computers to Windows 98, you must automate the Setup process. Automating the Setup process eliminates user interaction, standardizes the Windows 98 configuration on every desktop, and makes an organization-wide rollout easier and less time consuming. You will probably want to use an automated installation if you are responsible for installing Windows 98 on more than 50 computers.

An automated installation can be either a pull installation or a push installation. In a *pull installation* the user performs the upgrade, using tools provided by the administrator. In a *push installation* the administrator performs the upgrade, either directly or through system management software, such as Microsoft Systems Management Server.

Automating an installation is a three-step process:

1. Create a custom setup script with the desired configuration for your users as described in Chapter 3, "Custom Installations."
2. Set up an installation point on the network with the Windows 98 source files.
3. Use one of the following methods to upgrade the client computers in your organization to Windows 98:

   - Use a logon script that includes a statement to run Setup with a setup script, automatically installing Windows 98 when each user logs on.
   - Create an Apps.ini file that lets users upgrade from Windows 95 to Windows 98 simply by clicking a button.
   - Create a system policy that includes a statement to run Setup with a setup script, automatically upgrading from Windows 95 to Windows 98 when each user logs on.
   - Use Microsoft Systems Management Server to run Windows 98 Setup with a setup script as a mandatory job, as described in Appendix E, "Microsoft Systems Management Server."
   - Use network management software from other vendors to install Microsoft Windows 98 based on the setup scripts you create. Refer to the documentation for your network management software for information about performing remote installation of software.

For some types of automated installation, you should also implement version checking before running Setup to ensure that Windows 98 is not installed over itself or on an incompatible operating system.

The following sections provide details about automating installations with logon scripts, Apps.ini, and system policies, and then describes how to implement version checking.

Note The examples in this chapter direct you to add the Msbatch.inf command to setup scripts. This is good practice, but it is not necessary if the Msbatch.inf file is located in the same directory as your installation files.

Using Apps.ini for Pull Installations

By creating an Apps.ini file, you can let users upgrade from Windows 95 to Windows 98 simply by clicking a button. Using an Apps.ini file provides the benefit of simplicity and the benefit that users can choose when to upgrade their operating systems.

The general process is as follows:

1. Create a batch file that includes the Setup command, any switches you need, and any other commands you might need, such as version-checking commands.
2. Create a PIF file for that batch file.
3. Create an Apps.ini file that contains a reference to the PIF file.
4. Create a system policy to activate the **Network Install** tab in the Add/Remove Programs option in Control Panel.

Creating the Batch File and PIF File

First, create a batch file that you can use to perform pull installations. The batch file should contain, at minimum, the following:

```
\\Server\Share\Setup.exe
```

You could also add switches to the Setup command, and you could use the Msbatch.inf parameter. Additionally, you could add other commands, such as a section that checks the version of your operating system so users cannot run Windows 98 Setup from a Windows 98–based computer. For more information, see "Implementing Version Checking for Automated Installations," later in this chapter.

Next, create a PIF file for the batch file. For information about creating PIF files, see Chapter 25, "Application Support." Make sure to select the check box **Close on exit**, so the batch program window will close after it runs. Otherwise, you will have problems with Setup.

Creating the Apps.ini file

Next, create an Apps.ini file (or an entry in an existing Apps.ini file) that refers to the PIF file. For information about how to create an Apps.ini file, see Chapter 25, "Application Support." The following example shows a basic Apps.ini file:

```
[AppInstallList]
ProgramName = * \\Server\Share\Directory\Filename.pif
```

You could also use Apps.ini to set up different computers with different configurations. For example, you could use Apps.ini to set up Windows 98 with Windows NT on some computers, and Novell Client for Windows 95/98 on others. You could even control which users get which client by giving different users different levels of access to the share that contains the Setup.exe command. The following example shows this configuration:

```
[AppInstallList]

********************** Marketing **********************=
Windows 98 Upgrade - Windows NT=
*\\Server\Marketing_Share\Directory\WinNT.pif
-=*
*********************** Sales ***********************=
Windows 98 Upgrade - Novell Client=
*\\Server\Sales_Share\Directory\Client32.pif
```

In this example, WinNT.pif refers to a batch file that includes an Msbatch.inf statement. The Msbatch.inf file directs Windows 98 Setup to install Windows NT when performing the upgrade. Thus, when a user clicks the Windows NT entry, Windows 98 is installed with Windows NT. Likewise, when a user clicks the Novell Client entry, Windows 98 is installed with Novell Client for Windows 95/98.

Now, suppose you have given the users in Marketing network access to Marketing_Share but no access to Sales_Share, and you have given the users in Sales network access to Sales_Share but no access to Marketing_Share. The Marketing users can run Setup and get the Windows NT, and the Sales users can run Setup and get Novell Client for Windows 95/98.

Giving Users Access to the Apps.ini File

Finally, you must set a system policy so users can access the Apps.ini file. After you set the policy, a **Network Install** tab appears on the Add/Remove Programs option in Control Panel. The tab shows all the applications the user can install, and the user simply clicks on the application to install. To set the policy, you must first add the Appsini.adm template, then set the policy named **Network path to APPS.INI**.

▶ **To add the Appsini.adm template**

1. In System Policy Editor, click the **Options** menu, and then click the **Policy Template**.

2. Click **Add**, and then select the **Appsini.adm** file. This file is located in your \Windows\INF directory.

3. Click **Open**, and then click **OK**.

▶ **To set a system policy to give users access to Apps.ini**

1. In System Policy Editor, click the **File** menu, and then click **New Policy** if you have no existing policy file, or **Open Policy** if you have an existing policy file.

2. Double-click **Default Computer**.

3. Click the plus sign to expand the **Network Install** section, and then click the plus sign to expand the **Use APPS.INI for Network Installs** section.

4. Select the check box for the policy named **Enable Add/Remove Programs, Network Install tab**.

5. In the **Network path to APPS.INI** box, specify the full network path and file name for the Apps.ini file, and then click **OK**.

6. In the **File** menu, click **Save**, enter a name for your policy file, and then click **Save** again.

This policy adds the registry value **AppInstallPath** (string type) with the value of the universal naming convention (UNC) path to the following registry key:

HKEY_LOCAL_MACHINE\Software
\Microsoft\Windows\CurrentVersion

Using System Policies for Push Installations

You can create a push installation by using system policies. A push installation using system policies has the benefit of being simple to implement. You can install Windows 98 from a central location, without actually going to the computer being upgraded. However, consider the following issues if you are implementing a push installation using system policies:

- The user can stop Setup while it is in progress.

- Unless you make sure to check for the operating system version in a batch file, Windows 98 Setup will run every time the user logs onto the computer, even if the computer is already running Windows 98. You cannot prevent this by creating a special user account for upgrades, as you can with logon scripts, because the policy is computer-based rather than user-based.

The general steps for a push installation using system policies are as follows:

1. Create a batch file that checks to see your operating system version and conditionally runs Setup. For a sample batch file, see "Implementing Version Checking for Automated Installations," later in this chapter.

   At minimum, the batch file you create must include the UNC path for Setup, and it must check your operating system version before running Setup. You can also add Setup switches and other commands to the batch file.

2. Set the Run Once system policy and add a path to the batch file.

▶ **To set the Run Once system policy**

1. In System Policy Editor, click the **File** menu, click **New Policy** if you have no existing policy file, or **Open Policy** if you have an existing policy file.

2. Double-click **Default Computer**.

3. Click the plus sign to expand the **Windows 98 System** section, and then click the plus sign to expand the **Programs** section.

4. Select the check box for the policy named **Run Once**, and then click **Show**.

5. In the **Show Contents** dialog box, click **Add**.

6. In **Type the name of the item to be added**, type a name for your batch file (not the file name).

7. In **Type the value of the item to be added**, type the UNC path for the batch file that installs Windows 98 only if it is running the proper operating system. For example:

   \\Server\Share\Directory\Batch_file.bat

8. Click **Enter**, click **OK**, and then click **OK** again.

9. In the **File** menu, click **Save**, enter a name for your policy file, and then click **Save** again.

After you have set this policy, Windows 98 Setup runs automatically when the user logs on, as long as they are not already using Windows 98.

Using Logon Scripts for Push Installations

You can use logon scripts to create an automated, mandatory installation scheme for installing Windows 98 on multiple computers. This allows you to install Windows 98 from a central location, without actually going to the computer being upgraded.

You can use logon script push installations on Windows 95 computers and on computers running MS-DOS or Windows 3.x with the following real-mode network clients:

- Microsoft Workgroup Add-on for MS-DOS
- LAN Manager 2.x real-mode network client
- Novell NetWare real-mode network client (NETX or VLM)
- Windows for Workgroups real-mode and protected-mode clients

---

Note This method is only viable for smaller local area networks (LANs). If undue stress is placed on the network from hundreds of concurrent upgrades, the entire network can fail. However, it is a useful alternative in some situations, as when Systems Management Server is not available, staffing resources for deployment are limited, or only a few users typically log on at any one time.

This section describes logon scripts for several different configurations and explains how to set up servers for logon scripts and how to run logon scripts. For more information on logon scripts, see "Using Logon Scripts" in Chapter 18, "Logon, Browsing, and Resource Sharing."

To use logon scripts for push installations, you must do the following:

- Install the Windows 98 source files on an installation point.
- Create a setup script that includes the **Setup** command.
- Create the logon scripts that will be used to start the installation process.
- Create the special user accounts that will be used to run the logon scripts.
- For Windows for Workgroups computers, create a Startup.grp file that contains the command line for starting Windows 98 Setup, as described in "Preparing a Startup.grp File" later in this chapter.

A push installation actually begins when the user logs onto the client computer.

Because logon scripts run every time the user logs on, and the setup script includes the Windows 98 Setup command, you need to be careful so that Windows 98 Setup is run only once on each computer. The easiest way to do so is to create a special Upgrade account, which all users log onto in order to install Windows 98. This method avoids activating the Setup process again after Windows 98 has been installed. However, using a common Upgrade account might not work in some corporate environments, where INI files are copied to users' directories based on the user name specified at logon. In such cases, if Windows 98 is installed using an Upgrade account, each user's application settings will not be migrated to Windows 98. Furthermore, you can add statements to setup scripts to copy the related INI files to C:\Windows as part of the installation process.

Another method you can use with logon scripts to avoid the problem of running Setup a second time is to add a statement to the logon scripts to check the MS-DOS version with alternate actions defined when the version is Windows 98. For more information, see "Implementing Version Checking for Automated Installations," later in this chapter.

Important If the logon script processor stays in memory after you start Windows 98, and if the computer is not correctly configured to use extended memory, then there might not be sufficient memory available to run Setup. To solve this problem, you can increase the available memory before Setup begins by removing unnecessary terminate-and-stay-resident (TSR) programs and device drivers. For information about how to define statements in a setup script for changing the system configuration as part of installation, see Appendix D, "Msbatch.inf Parameters for Setup Scripts."

For login scripts on NetWare networks, you can use an exit command that runs Windows 98 Setup after the login script is complete. For Windows for Workgroups, you can use a Startup.grp file, as described in "Preparing a Startup.grp File," later in this chapter.

Preparing Logon Scripts for Push Installations for Windows 95 Clients

This section presents information about creating logon scripts that use the Upgrade account for installing Windows 98 on Windows 95 client computers.

Tip Avoid using relative path names in logon scripts and setup scripts so that you can ensure the commands are run from the correct directory.

Logon Scripts for Windows NT Servers

For client computers running Windows 95 on a Windows NT network where the Upgrade account is to be used to install Windows 98, the logon script must contain the following entry:

```
\\ntserver\distshare\setup.exe \\ntserver\distshare\msbatch.inf
```

If items being installed through the Msbatch.inf file require a mapped drive, the logon script must contain the following entries:

```
net use source_drive \\ntserver\distshare
source_drive\:setup source_drive\:msbatch.inf
```

Table 4.1 shows the syntax for the entries in the previous example.

Table 4.1   Logon script values for Windows 95 clients on a Windows NT network

Value	Description
Source_Drive	Maps a drive letter for the server containing the source files. Check the **lastdrive=** setting in Config.sys to make sure that the drive letter specified on the preceding command line is a valid logical drive letter. If it is not, the network connection will not be made, and the Setup process will fail.
\\Wtserver\DistShare	Specifies the Windows NT server that contains the Windows 98 source files.

For example, the logon script could be similar to the following:

```
net use k: \\ntserver\distshare
k:\setup.exe k:\msbatch.inf
```

Login Scripts for Protected-Mode NetWare Clients

Microsoft Client for NetWare Networks and Novell Client for Windows 95/98 (sometimes called Client 32) do not need to map a drive to the network distribution share, because both clients understand universal naming convention (UNC) syntax. You cannot call Windows 98 Setup directly as an external program, however, because the login script processor remains open in the background while Windows 98 Setup runs. This produces the error message **"One or more MS-DOS-based programs running"** (SU 0358). The following example will cause the error message:

```
#\\nwserver\install\Win98\setup \\nwserver\Win98\msbatch.inf
```

Therefore, you should have the login script call the program Start.exe (included with Windows 95) with the Windows 98 Setup as a parameter. For example:

```
#start \\nwserver\install\win98\setup \\nwserver\Win98\msbatch.inf
```

Start opens Windows 98 Setup as a separate process and then terminates, returning control to the login script processor. This allows Start to close normally and allows Windows to finish loading normally in the background.

Login Scripts for Real-Mode NetWare Clients

The login script for client computers running the real-mode NETX or VLM NetWare clients must contain the following kinds of entries:

```
map source_drive:nwserver/DistShare
source_drive:setup source_drive:msbatch.inf
```

Table 4.2 shows the syntax for the entries in the previous example.

Table 4.2   Login script values for real-mode NetWare clients

Value	Description
Source_Drive	Specifies the same drive letter as specified in the Startup group.
Nwserver/DistShare	Specifies the NetWare server that contains the Windows 98 source files.

For example, for a computer running Windows 95 with a real-mode network client, the login script could be similar to the following:

```
map k:=nwserver1/win98
#k:setup k:msbatch.inf
```

In the previous example, the "#" syntax informs the login script processor that the setup command is an external command, (separate from the login script processor itself).

For more information, consult your NetWare documentation.

Using Login Script Variables on NetWare Networks

For NetWare networks, you can use login script variables to control when Setup is run and who runs it. The most common form of login script variables is a Boolean logic test that compares actual values against target values. This section provides a few example of login script variables. For more information about using variables to control login script execution, consult your NetWare documentation.

The following examples use the operating system version and the platform type to determine whether the computer should run Windows 98 Setup.

Example 1 (Client for NetWare Networks):

```
If "%OS_VERSION"="v7.00"
and "%PLATFORM"="W95"
then #start \\dist\install\Win98\setup
```

Example 2 (Novell Client for Windows 95/98):

```
If "%OS_VERSION"="v4.00"
and "%PLATFORM"="W95"
then #start \\dist\install\Win98\setup
```

In these examples, Setup runs only if both logic tests are true. Once Windows 98 Setup runs, the operating system version variable will have a different value and the client will not attempt to run Setup again. If the user is on a different platform, such as a Macintosh system, Setup will never run.

Logon Scripts for Other Third-Party Networks

It might be possible for computers running Windows 95 on networks other than Windows NT or NetWare to use logon scripts for a push installation of Windows 98. The logon scripts must contain the following two elements:

- The network path to the setup files. (The path can use either UNC syntax or syntax specific to the networking software.)
- The proper execution of the setup command for Windows 98.

The following examples show logon scripts for OS/2 and Banyan VINES:

OS/2 Server example:

```
\\ntserver\distshare\setup.exe \\ntserver\distshare\msbatch.inf
```

Banyan VINES example:

```
Server@Context@share\setup.exe Server@Context@share\msbatch.inf
```

The setup process might require that a drive be mapped. If so, you must add a line that maps a drive to the server and network share where the setup files are installed. The following examples show logon scripts for OS/2 and Banyan VINES in which the drives are mapped:

OS/2 Server example:

```
net use source_drive: \\ntserver\distshare
source_drive:setup source_drive:msbatch.inf
```

Banyan VINES example:

```
setdrive source_drive share@group@org
source_drive:setup.exe source_drive: msbatch.inf
```

Note that with the Banyan VINES Setdrive statement, there is no colon after the source drive.

Preparing Logon Scripts for Push Installations for Windows 3.1, Windows for Workgroups, and MS-DOS Clients

This section presents information about creating logon scripts that use an Upgrade account for installing Windows 98 on client computers running Windows 3.1, Windows for Workgroups, or MS-DOS. Some of the logon script statements described in this section are related to using the Startup.grp file for Windows for Workgroups, as described in "Preparing a Startup.grp File" later in this chapter.

Tip Avoid using relative path names in logon scripts and setup scripts so that you can ensure the commands are run from the correct directory.

Logon Scripts for Windows 3.x or MS-DOS Clients with Windows NT Server

For a computer running Windows 3.x or MS-DOS real-mode network client, the logon script should be similar to the following:

```
net start full
net use drive_letter: \\server\distshare
drive_letter:setup drive_letter:msbatch.inf
```

If the client computer is running on a LAN Manager or Windows for Workgroups network, the logon script must contain the **net start full** statement. On a Windows for Workgroups network, the real-mode network client for Windows for Workgroups or Windows 3.1 also requires the entry **lmlogon=1** in the [Network] section of System.ini. This ensures that the full network redirector is loaded and the user is validated for network logon. Other logon script topics are discussed in the following section.

Logon Scripts for Windows for Workgroups Clients with Windows NT Server

For client computers running Windows for Workgroups on a Windows NT network where an Upgrade account is used to install Windows 98, the logon script must contain the following entries to use a Startup.grp file:

```
net use source_drive \\ntserver\distshare
rename windowsdir\startup.grp *.sav
copy path\startup.grp windowsdir\startup.grp
```

Table 4.3 shows the values for the entries in the previous example.

Table 4.3   Logon script values for Windows for Workgroups clients on a Windows NT network

Value	Description
Source_Drive	Maps a drive letter for the server containing the source files. This must be the same drive letter as specified in the Startup.grp file. Check the **lastdrive=** setting in Config.sys to make sure that the drive letter specified on the preceding command line is a valid logical drive letter. If it is not, the network connection will not be made and the Setup process will fail.
Wtserver\Distshare	Specifies the Windows NT server that contains the Windows 98 source files.
Windowsdir	Specifies the relative path to the user's \Windows directory.
Path	Specifies the path to the Startup group file.

For example, for a computer running Windows for Workgroups, the logon script could be similar to the following:

```
net use k: \\ntserver\distshare
rename .\startup.grp *.sav
copy \winnt\system32\repl\import\scripts\startup.grp .\startup.grp
exit
```

Preparing a Startup.grp File

If you are upgrading computers that run Windows for Workgroups, you can create a special Startup group that is used just once to run the logon script.

The use of the Startup group is mandatory only for computers running Windows for Workgroups 3.11 with logon validation performed by Windows NT Server. In this case, the user starts Windows for Workgroups, which loads the protected-mode protocols and processes the logon script. The logon script runs on a virtual machine (VM); although Windows 98 Setup cannot be run on a VM, the logon script can be used to create a modified Startup.grp file that causes Setup to run as a Windows-based application after the logon script finishes running.

Note For computers that use a real-mode network client, logon scripts can run Windows 98 Setup directly, without using a special Startup.grp file. Only computers that use a protected-mode network client need to use the Startup.grp method to run Setup from within Windows for Workgroups.

▶ **To prepare for push installations to upgrade earlier versions of Windows**

1. Run Windows for Workgroups on a computer.

2. If the Startup group is not present, use the **File New** command in Program
   Manager to create a Startup group.

3. In the Startup group, use the **File New** command to create an **Upgrade** option
   that contains the following command line:

   source_drive:setup [*source_drive*:*msbatch_format*.inf]

   If the setup script is named Msbatch.inf and is in the \Windows directory
   in the source files, you do not need to specify the script name on the command
   line. Otherwise, specify the drive and script name. For example:

   k:\setup k:\myscript.inf

   Specify the same source drive used in the logon script statements, as described
   in the following sections on setting up the server for push installations.

4. Copy the Startup.grp file to the installation point on the server that contains the
   Windows 98 source files.

5. Delete the group or option that you just created so that it is no longer stored on
   the computer where you are working.

6. In the Msbatch.inf file, add the following statements to make sure that
   Startup.grp is replaced after Setup:

   ```
   [install]
   renfiles=replace.startup.grp

   [replace.startup.grp]
   startup.grp, startup.sav

   [destinationdirs]
   replace.startup.grp=10
   ```

Login Scripts for Windows 3.1, Windows for Workgroups, and MS-DOS Clients on NetWare Networks

For information about using login scripts for real-mode NetWare clients if you are
using Windows 3.1, Windows for Workgroups, and MS-DOS, see "Login Scripts
for Real-Mode NetWare Clients," earlier in this chapter.

Setting Up Windows NT Server for Push Installations

This section summarizes the procedures for running logon scripts from Windows NT Server for push installations on Windows 95, Windows 3.1, Windows for Workgroups, and MS-DOS-based computers.

▶ **To prepare the server for push installations on a Windows NT network**

1. Install the Windows 98 source files in an installation point on a network server.

2. Create an Msbatch.inf file to meet your installation requirements, and copy this file into the installation point that contains the Windows 98 source files.

3. Using **User Manager for Domains** on a computer running Windows NT Server, create a user account named **Upgrade**, and specify **upgrade** as the password. Also, make sure the following options are selected for the Upgrade user account:

   - **User Cannot Change Password**

   - **Password Never Expires**

   By default, the user account is created in the domain where you logged onto the network. To create the user account in another domain, you must select that domain before creating the account. If your users log onto multiple domains, create the Upgrade user account in each domain.

4. Create the logon scripts that run Windows 98 Setup. For an example of a logon script for Windows NT networks, see "Logon Scripts for Windows NT Servers" earlier in this chapter.

5. Assign the logon script to the Upgrade user account. The logon script must be placed in the *Winnt*\System32\Repl\Export\Scripts directory on the computer running Windows NT Server.

   The replication service replicates this from the export server to the import server, so the file is copied to *Winnt*\System32\Repl\Import\Scripts on the server.

Setting Up a NetWare Server for Push Installations

This section summarizes the procedures for running login scripts from a NetWare server for push installations on Windows 95, Windows for Workgroups, Windows 3.1, and MS-DOS-based computers.

▶ **To prepare the server for push installations on a NetWare network**

1. Install the Windows 98 source files in an installation point on a network server.

2. Create an Msbatch.inf file to meet your installation requirements, and copy this file into the installation point that contains the Windows 98 source files.

3. On the NetWare server, create a user account named **Upgrade,** and specify **upgrade1** as the password. Also, set the types of options for this account as described in the following list.

   - **Allow User To Change Password = No**

   - **Force Periodic Password Changes = No**

4. Assign the **Upgrade** user account to the preferred server to which users have access.

5. Create a login script and assign it to the Upgrade user. The login script must be placed in the appropriate directory on the server where users will log on. For an example of a login script for NetWare networks, see "Login Scripts for Protected-Mode NetWare Clients" and "Login Scripts for Real-Mode NetWare Clients" earlier in this chapter.

Running Logon Scripts for Push Installations

This section describes running logon scripts for push installations on Windows 95, Windows 3.1, Windows for Workgroups, and MS-DOS.

The following lists the requirements for using an Upgrade account to upgrade from Windows 95:

- The Upgrade account must be created on the Windows NT domain, NetWare server or other network server, with a corresponding Upgrade logon script, as described in the sections "Setting Up Windows NT Server for Push Installations" and "Setting Up a NetWare Server for Push Installations" earlier in this chapter.

- The Upgrade logon script must contain statements to start Windows 98 Setup from a shared directory.

▶ **To run a logon script for a push installation**

- Tell users to log onto the network using the Upgrade user account and the relevant password.

  When a user logs on, the Windows 98 installation process begins automatically, using the settings in the Msbatch.inf file specified in the logon script.

After copying files, Windows 98 restarts the computer, runs hardware detection, and then begins the Run Once operations (group conversions, and so on). When the Run Once operations are finished, Windows 98 is completely installed. Note that this stage requires the user to log onto the network, so all configuration values must be specified in the setup script to support correct logon and to allow Windows 98 Setup to connect to the shared resources containing Windows 98 source files.

When the user quits Windows 98 at this point, Setup writes all changes to the registry. The user can restart the computer and log on using the usual logon name and password.

Implementing Version Checking for Automated Installations

No matter which method of automated installation you use, it is a good idea to check the operating system version before running Windows 98 Setup. That way you can ensure that Windows 98 is never installed over itself, or on a computer running an incompatible operating system, such as Windows NT. You can do so from a batch file.

The following is an example of a simple batch file, VerCheck.bat, that checks your operating system version and runs Setup only if the computer is running Windows 95. You can tailor this batch file to your own needs.

```
@echo off
ver > ver.txt

find "95" ver.txt > nul
if errorlevel 2 goto broken
if errorlevel 1 goto not95
if errorlevel 0 goto found95
echo Broke while looking for 95.  Please contact your network
echo administrator for help.
goto end

:not95
find "98" ver.txt > nul
if errorlevel 2 goto broken
if errorlevel 1 goto not98
if errorlevel 0 goto found98
echo Broke while looking for 98.  Please contact your network
echo administrator for help.
goto end
```

```
:not98
echo Could not identify operating system. Please contact your network
echo administrator.
goto end

:found98
echo Found Windows 98 and will not install Windows 98.
goto end

:found 95
REM This procedure runs Setup if Windows 95 is found. If desired, you
REM could instead run another batch file.
echo Found Windows 95. Will now upgrade this computer to Windows 98.
Map S: \\Server\Share
S:\Directory\Setup
goto end

:broken
echo Could not upgrade this computer to Windows 98. Please contact your
echo network administrator.
goto end

:end
```

You can refine this sample batch file in many different ways. For example, note that this batch file runs Setup immediately after discovering that the computer is running Windows 95. By using two batch files, you could ensure that Setup waits until the next boot.

▶ **To ensure that Setup waits until the next boot**

1. Create a batch file named Winstart.bat that runs Setup, and place it on a network server.

2. Create a second batch file that checks for Windows 95, and if it finds Windows 95, copies a second batch file named Winstart.bat from the network server to the user's \Windows directory.

Note This step will not work if users have renamed their Windows directories.

CHAPTER 5

Setup Technical Discussion

5

This chapter provides technical details about Microsoft Windows 98 Setup, including background information about Safe Recovery and detailed descriptions of the Setup and system startup processes.

In This Chapter

Overview of Setup Technical Discussion

You must know certain technical details when using Microsoft Windows 98 Setup within your particular computing environment. This chapter presents technical information about how to ensure the safe detection of hardware, recovery from problems, and verification of configurations. It goes on with detailed information about the startup process, system startup files, Windows 98 Setup with non-Windows 98 operating systems, removing Windows 98, and troubleshooting Windows 98 Setup.

Safe Detection, Safe Recovery, and Verification

This section provides technical details about the features that ensure safe hardware detection, recovery from Setup problems, and configuration verification in Windows 98 Setup.

Safe Detection in Windows 98 Setup

Devices and buses are grouped as classes in Windows 98 for purposes of detecting and installing device drivers and managing system resources. Windows 98 differentiates between devices and drivers that comply with the Plug and Play specification and earlier versions of devices and drivers (referred to in the *Microsoft Windows 98 Resource Kit* as *legacy devices*). Because of this differentiation, Windows 98 Setup detects hardware components and devices in two ways:

- Using Plug and Play, an interactive query process, to identify Plug and Play–compliant devices and peripherals.
- Using a Plug and Play detection process for legacy devices and peripherals.

After Setup detects a device, it adds configuration information to the registry and installs the appropriate device drivers. The same procedures used during Setup for detecting Plug and Play or legacy hardware devices are also used to detect or configure new devices after Windows 98 has been installed.

Windows 98 supports detection of base computer components, such as communications ports and processor type, and provides more robust detection of computer devices, such as display adapters, pointing devices, hard disk controllers, floppy-disk controllers, and network adapters.

Windows 98 Setup also tries to detect any hardware resource conflicts early in the installation process. This helps to avoid the problems that occur when such hardware resources as Interrupt Requests (IRQs), I/O addresses, and direct memory access (DMA) are used by more than one device.

To avoid computer failure during the detection process, Windows 98 uses a safe detection method to search for hints from configuration files, read-only memory (ROM) strings, or drivers loaded in memory to determine whether the computer contains each class of hardware. If no such hints are found, the detection process skips detection of the entire class. If hints are found, the detection process seeks information from specific I/O ports.

Windows 98 automatically reads the command lines in Config.sys to find hints for device class detection. Then Windows 98 loads detection modules based on information in the Msdet.inf file, which lists the hardware to be detected and points to specific INF files for each device class (for example, Scsi.inf for SCSI host adapters). Device information from the INF files is written to the registry.

For more information about the format of these files, see Appendix C, "Windows 98 INF Files."

Windows 98 can also read a particular Config.sys **device=** line for resource information to be avoided (that is, protected) during the detection process. This is useful if Windows 98 Setup cannot detect or support a certain device when it is known that the detection process can cause such a device to fail. For example, the detection process could render a fax modem inoperative because scanning the I/O port might confuse the device driver. Windows 98 can read the **device=** line in Config.sys for this model and protect the associated I/O region from other detection modules.

Windows 98 Setup asks you to confirm which classes should be skipped in the detection process. If you know that the computer has a device in one of those classes, you can force Setup to detect that device class.

Safe detection exists for four classes of devices: network adapters, SCSI controllers, proprietary CD-ROM adapters, and sound cards.

Safe Detection of Network Adapters

Windows 98 Setup performs the following kinds of steps for safe detection of network adapters:

- Find Lsl.com in memory; if present, inquire for network adapter settings.
- Find Ipx.com in memory; if present, inquire for network adapter settings.
- Search the Windows, Windows for Workgroups, and LAN Manager directories for Protocol.ini; if present, read the file to find network adapter settings.

Safe Detection of SCSI Controllers

When trying to detect SCSI adapters, Windows 98 Setup checks for device drivers in Config.sys and then scans ROM strings from the SCSI adapter for manufacturers' names. If known drivers or known strings are found, the corresponding detection procedure for that class is used; otherwise, the entire class is skipped. A list of the known strings and drivers that Windows 98 Setup checks is stored internally in a detection dynamic-link library (DLL). (For more information about the SCSI devices and drivers that Windows 98 supports, see the **Manufacturers** and **Models** lists in the Add New Hardware option in Control Panel.)

Different SCSI devices require different methods for safe detection. For example, a SCSI card is typically used with a combination of hard disks, CD-ROM drives, tape backup drives, scanners, and similar devices. For everything to work (except the hard disk), some sort of device driver must be loaded in Config.sys.

For hard disk drives, however, the driver usually is not loaded in Config.sys, but INT 13 ROM is enabled. Therefore, safe detection for SCSI class devices looks for a ROM string with a manufacturer's name.

Safe Detection of Proprietary Adapters for CD-ROM

Windows 98 supports Mitsumi, SONY, and Panasonic proprietary adapters for CD-ROM. Because drivers for these devices are loaded in Config.sys, safe detection first scans Config.sys for the drivers that are present. If a **device=** line for such a driver is found, the corresponding detection module is loaded for that type of device.

Safe Detection of Sound Cards

Safe detection scans Config.sys and reads System.ini for hints about sound cards. If known drivers are not found, the entire class is skipped.

If Windows 98 does not have detection code for certain hardware, the equipment manufacturer can force a device to be detected by adding information about it in the Msdet.inf file. Windows 98 detection behaves as if it has detected the device and installs the device according to the INF information provided by the equipment manufacturer.

Windows 98 Setup does not detect sound cards by scanning I/O ports; instead, it checks only Config.sys and System.ini and performs detection as prescribed in Msdet.inf. Detection of sound cards by scanning I/O ports can cause the computer to stall. This is because detection calls a driver specific to a device class to send a signal to an I/O port. The driver expects a predetermined response, such as a signature from the adapter's ROM. If the wrong driver sends a signal to an I/O port address occupied by a different device class, the computer can stall.

Safe Recovery with Setup Log Files

Windows 98 Setup creates several log files: Bootlog.txt, Detlog.txt, Netlog.txt, and Setuplog.txt, as well as Detcrash.log, should Setup fail. The following sections describe these files.

Basically, the computer might stop or stall at three points during Windows 98 Setup: before, during, or after hardware detection.

- If Setup fails before hardware detection, Windows 98 Setup recovers by reading Setuplog.txt to determine where the system stalled, what to redo, and what to skip.

- If Setup fails during hardware detection, the Detcrash.log file is created, containing information about the detection module that was running and the I/O port or memory resources it was accessing when the failure occurred.

When the detection process finds this file, it automatically runs in Safe Recovery mode to verify all the devices already in the registry and then skips all detection modules up to the failed module. Safe Recovery then skips detection and any attempts to configure the failed module, in effect skipping the action that caused the failure. Then, Safe Recovery continues the detection process, starting with the next module. If the detection process is completed successfully, Detcrash.log is deleted.

Detcrash.log can be read only by Setup. For information about the text equivalent of this information, see "Detlog.txt: The Hardware Detection Log File" later in this chapter.

- Sometimes the detection process causes some devices (such as a CD-ROM drive or a network connection) to quit working. If you rerun Setup, Safe Recovery recognizes that the detection process has already been completed successfully and assumes that all the necessary hardware information is in the registry. Therefore, it skips the detection process completely at this point and continues the installation process.

Setuplog.txt: The Setup Log File

The Setuplog.txt file is an ASCII text file that contains Windows 98 Setup information created during the installation process. While Windows 98 is being installed, corresponding entries are written to Setuplog.txt, listing information about the specific steps, their sequence, and the error conditions encountered. This file is used by Setup for recovery in case of setup failure, and it can also be used for troubleshooting errors that occur during the installation process.

Setup uses the information in Setuplog.txt to ensure that the installation does not fail twice because of the same problem. If you restart Windows 98 Setup after a setup process fails, Setup reviews the contents of Setuplog.txt to determine which steps completed successfully. If Setuplog.txt indicates that a process started but does not indicate that the process completed, that part of the installation process is skipped, and the next part is processed. Even if Setup encounters devices that cause several installation attempts, the installation process will always progress and skip the modules that failed.

Setuplog.txt is stored on the computer's root directory. Information is added to the file according to the order of the steps of the installation process. If an error occurs during installation, you can determine the probable cause of the error by examining the entries at the end of Setuplog.txt.

Information in Setuplog.txt is divided into the following basic categories:

- Selected Setup sections, including [OptionalComponents], [System], [NameAndOrg], [Setup], [Network], [Started], [Dialogs], [Windows 98 CD-ROM], [Reinstall], and [*batch_settings*].
- Setting up system startup parameters.

- Selecting the directory.
- Beginning the installation process.
- Queuing needed files in [FileQueue].
- Copying needed files in [FileCopy].
- Preparing to restart the system in [Restart].

Tip The [OptionalComponents], [System], and [NameAndOrg] sections can be copied from Setuplog.txt on a computer with a complete installation of Windows 98 and then added to equivalent sections in Msbatch.inf, as described in Chapter 3, "Custom Installations." Notice, however, that these sections in Setuplog.txt do not include networking information.

Table 5.1 shows entries in the Setuplog.txt file to check for information about the Setup process. Because entries are added to Setuplog.txt in the order that the related actions occur during Setup, you might be able to find a probable cause of any error by examining the entries at the end of the file.

Table 5.1   Summary of Setuplog.txt entries

Setuplog.txt entry	Description
InstallType	Type of installation
InstallDir	Directory where Windows 98 is installed
detection	Detection status
RunningApp	Applications running during installation
RootFilesRenamed	Files renamed in the root directory
error	Errors logged during installation
failed	Failures that occurred during installation
[OptionalComponents]	Optional components installed
[System]	System hardware configuration
batch settings	Installation parameters (Msbatch.inf settings)
Registry	Registry initialization status
filename	Verification that a specific file was loaded during Setup
[Choose Directory]	Location and type of Windows files
[FileCopy]	Files copied during Setup
[Restart]	Issues to be completed after the computer is restarted

Detlog.txt: The Hardware Detection Log File

The Detlog.txt file contains a record of whether a specific hardware device was detected and identifies the parameters for the detected device.

During Windows 98 Setup, after Setup restarts your computer for the first time, it begins hardware detection, which can also occur when you use the Add New Hardware option in Control Panel to add a new device. Both Windows 98 Setup and Device Manager use Sysdetmg.dll, which contains all the detection modules for each device class and specific devices.

Windows 98 loads detection modules based on information in Msdet.inf that points to specific INF files for each device class, from which information is retrieved and written to the registry. The device class installers are DLLs that work with Device Manager to install, configure, and remove devices or classes of devices in the system. Device Manager generates a list of compatible drivers for the device from the appropriate INF file. For information about using Device Manager to configure device drivers, and for information about the device classes used to identify logical device types, such as display, keyboard, and network adapters, see Chapter 24, "Device Management."

By creating an updated Detlog.txt file every time the detection process runs, the detection module tracks the detected devices and the I/O port addresses used. Any existing Detlog.txt is renamed Detlog.old. If the detection process causes Setup to stall or the computer to lock up, a binary file named Detcrash.log is created. Detlog.txt is an ASCII text file created only for users to read; Windows 98 Setup reads the binary information in Detcrash.log. Any changes made to Detlog.txt are not passed to Detcrash.log.

The Detlog.txt file can be found in the root directory of the startup drive after Windows 98 is installed. The entries in Detlog.txt are placed in the order of the hardware information discovered as each step of the detection process is carried out. Table 5.2 briefly describes entries that appear in Detlog.txt.

Table 5.2   Summary of Detlog.txt entries

Detlog.txt Entry	Description
Beginning of Detlog.txt:	
Parameters="xxxxxx"	Shows the switches specified in the Setup command line (that is, **setup** /p xxxxxx). For example: `Parameters "", Flags=01002233`
WinVer = ########	Shows that environment detection is run. The MS-DOS version is in the high word, and the Windows version is in the low word. For example: `WinVer=0614030b,`
AvoidMem = #####h-#####h	If present, indicates the address range specified as upper memory blocks (UMBs), which detection avoids. For example: `AvoidMem=cd4a0-cd50f`
DetectClass: Skip Class Media	Indicates that detection found no hints that the computer might have a particular device, so it skipped that class. For example, **DetectClass: Skip Class Media** indicates that no sound entries appear in the configuration files, so detection skips all the sound card detection modules. For **DetectClass: Skip Class Adapter**, detection skips searching for proprietary CD-ROM adapters such as SONY, Mitsumi, and Panasonic. **DetectClass: Skip Class Net** indicates that detection was skipped for network adapters.
DetectClass Override:	If one or more **skip class** entries appear in Detlog.txt, the Analyzing Your Computer screen appears in Setup to confirm skipping those classes, so you can override the decision. Related **DetectClass Override** lines appear in Detlog.txt for the classes checked.
Custom Mode:	Describes your selection for the devices you tell Windows 98 not to detect. For example: `CustomMode: resetting class ADAPTER ; Don't detect EtherLinkIII CustomMode: DETECTELNK3=0`
Devices verified =	Indicates the number of devices verified from the registry. If the number is 0, it usually means there was no existing registry, or the registry was empty.

Table 5.2   Summary of Detlog.txt entries *(continued)*

Detlog.txt Entry	Description

Detecting system devices:

Checking for:

Specifies that detection began looking for that device. The entry is followed by a description of the device or class being sought. When detection is checking for such a device as the Programmable Interrupt Controller, the **Checking for:** entry is followed by a **QueryIOMem:** entry specifying the Caller, rcQuery, and I/O range checked. If a device is detected, a **Detected:** entry is added specifying the device resource information. For example:

```
Checking for: Programmable Interrupt Controller
QueryIOMem: Caller=DETECTPIC, rcQuery=0
    IO=20-21,a0-a1
Detected: *PNP0000\0000 =
    [1] Programmable Interrupt Controller
    IO=20-21,a0-a1
    IRQ=2
```

Detecting network adapters:

Checking for:

This section lists the attempts to detect network adapters. For example:

```
Checking for: Network Cards using Novell
        ODI Driver
Checking for: EISA Network Cards
```

Protocol.ini Section

If detection finds Protocol.ini, it saves the [*net_card*] section in Detlog.txt. For example:

```
Checking for: Network Cards using
        Microsoft Windows For Workgroups
; path to WFW protocol.INI
WFW: path=d:\w311\protocol.ini
; protocol.ini mac driver section
Protocol.ini: [MS$EE16]
Protocol.ini: DriverName=EXP16$
```

NCD: detecting network adapter

Indicates that detection has found a network adapter using safe detection (usually Protocol.ini), but the system has information for verifying this adapter. If this adapter is verified, a **Detected** line follows. For example:

```
NCD: detecting network adapter *pnp812d
QueryIOMem: Caller=DETECTWFW, rcQuery=0
IO=300-30f
```

The hardware detection process continues examining computer hardware. The "|" symbol in the **IO=** line (for example, **IO=200-201 | 3e0-3e1**) indicates a range of I/O entries that are checked during the detection process. In the Detlog.txt file, you will find a **QueryIOMem:** and an **IO=** line for each I/O address checked.

For most devices, multiple I/O addresses are checked, which can result in a detailed and redundant device detection list. The I/O address ranges checked during detection are grouped on one I/O line. Multiple addresses on an IO= line are separated by commas. For example:

```
Checking for: ATI Ultra Pro/Plus (Mach 32) Display Adapter
QueryIOMem: Caller=DETECTMACH32, rcQuery=0
    IO=3b0-3bb,3c0-3df
QueryIOMem: Caller=DETECTMACH32, rcQuery=0
    Mem=a0000-afffff
```

If the system stalls during hardware detection, you can determine the probable cause of the error by examining the last entries in Detlog.txt. You can use the information in this file to determine specific error conditions occurring in the hardware detection and reconfigure or replace the specific adapter or device. Table 5.3 shows specific kinds of entries to check in Detlog.txt for information about the results of the hardware detection process.

Table 5.3   Detlog.txt entries to check for troubleshooting

Detlog.txt Entry	Description
detected	Detected devices
AvoidMem	Address ranges of UMBs avoided during detection
error	Errors logged during system detection
WinFlags	Setup mode used
Protocol.ini	Protocol.ini information that was saved during system upgrade
CustomMode	Hardware that was removed from detection in the custom **Analyzing Your Computer** dialog box
Devices verified	Devices found in the registry (if the value is 0, there was no existing registry, or the registry was empty)

Some additional notes on Detlog.txt and hardware detection:

- Detection does not detect enumerated devices such as Industry Standard Architecture (ISA) Plug and Play devices, peripheral component interconnect (PCI) devices, and Personal Computer Memory Card International Association (PCMCIA) devices. For information about these devices, see Chapter 14, "Introduction to Networking Configuration."

- If the computer stalls during detection, and you rerun Windows 98 Setup and choose Safe Recovery, new detection information is appended to the previous Detlog.txt file. The previous version of Detlog.txt is saved as Detlog.old, overwriting any previous Detlog.old files.

The hardware that has been tested and shown to be compatible with Windows 98 appears in the Manufacturers and Models lists in the Add New Hardware option in Control Panel.

Netlog.txt: The Network Setup Log File

Netlog.txt describes the detection results for network components during Windows 98 Setup. For information about Netdet.ini, the file that Setup uses to determine how to install networking components on computers running NetWare clients, see Chapter 17, "Windows 98 on Third-Party Networks."

Table 5.4 describes typical entries in a Netlog.txt file after you run Windows 98 Setup the first time. In this example, Client for Microsoft Networks is installed with the Internet Packet Exchange/Sequenced Packet Exchange (IPX/SPX)-compatible protocol, and both are bound to an Intel EtherExpress network adapter.

Table 5.4   Summary of Netlog.txt entries

Netlog.txt entry	Description
ClassInstall (0x6) on Intel EtherExpress 16 or 16TP at Enum\Root*PNP812D\0000	Network installation begins.
Examining class NET	Network detection is searching for network software of four class types: NET (network adapters), NETTRANS (protocols), NETCLIENT (clients), and NETSERVICES (such services as file and printer sharing).
Upgrade 2.00025000=VREDIR	A network client was found on the computer.
Upgrade to: VREDIR	The version of the network client was upgraded to the version included in Windows 98.
NdiCreate (Client for Microsoft Networks) OK	Setup successfully created an internal object representing the network client.
NdiCreate (Intel EtherExpress 16 or 16TP)	Setup successfully created an internal object representing the network adapter.
CreateNetwork, Batch=0	Setup referenced a batch file.
NdiCreate (IPX/SPX-compatible Protocol)	Setup successfully created an internal object representing the IPX/SPX-compatible protocol.
ClassInstall (0x6) end	

Table 5.4   Summary of Netlog.txt entries *(continued)*

Netlog.txt entry	Description
ClassInstall (0x9) on Intel EtherExpress 16 or 16TP at Enum\Root*PNP812D\0000	Protocols are about to be bound to the network adapter.
Validating IPX/SPX-compatible Protocol at Enum\Network\NWLINK \0000, rc=0x0	The IPX/SPX-compatible protocol is added to the registry and bound to the network adapter.
ClassInstall (0x9) on Intel EtherExpress 16 or 16TP at Enum\Root*PNP812D\0000	Clients are about to be bound to the network adapter.
Validating Client for Microsoft Networks at Enum\Network\VREDIR \0000, rc=0x0	Client for Microsoft Networks is added to the registry and bound to the network adapter.
ClassInstall (0x9) end	Setup has finished binding the protocol to the network adapter.
ClassInstall (0xa) on Intel EtherExpress 16 or 16TP at Enum\Root*PNP812D\0000	The network setup process is concluded.
ClassInstall (0xa) end	
ClassInstall (0xc) on Intel EtherExpress 16 or 16TP at Enum\Root*PNP812D\0000	
ClassInstall (0xc) end	

Windows 98 Startup Process

Windows 98 includes system files, Plug and Play mechanisms, and various options for starting the operating system. This section describes the Windows 98 system startup sequence.

During the real-mode startup process, devices use only static configurations; that is, no dynamic resource allocation or arbitration is provided. When the system startup process switches to protected mode, Configuration Manager ensures all devices are configured properly, as described in Chapter 28, "Windows 98 Architecture."

The system startup includes four phases:

- Bootstrapping the system with basic input/output system (BIOS) in control.
- Loading MS-DOS drivers and terminate-and-stay-resident (TSR) Programs for compatibility.
- Initializing static VxDs in real mode.
- Putting the protected-mode operating system in control and loading the remaining VxDs.

Bootstrapping in the BIOS Phase

Microsoft worked with several hardware manufacturers to define a new Plug and Play BIOS specification, which defines the interactions among a Plug and Play BIOS, Plug and Play devices, and option ROMs (sometimes called adapter ROMs). The Plug and Play BIOS enables and configures Plug and Play boot devices. The Plug and Play BIOS also passes configuration information to Configuration Manager in Windows 98 for configuring the remaining adapters and devices.

Booting with a Legacy BIOS

For legacy computers that do not have Plug and Play BIOS, the BIOS enables all devices on the ISA bus. A Plug and Play ISA card that has an option ROM must start up when the computer is turned on with the option ROM enabled.

Booting with a Plug and Play BIOS

A Plug and Play BIOS accesses nonvolatile random access memory (RAM) to determine which Plug and Play ISA cards should be enabled, where their option ROMs should be mapped, and what I/O, DMA, and other assignments are to be given to the cards.

The BIOS then programs the Plug and Play cards before the power-on self-test (POST). All cards that do not have configurations stored in the BIOS are disabled completely, reducing the chance of a conflict.

The Plug and Play BIOS also configures all devices on the motherboard. Some devices might have been disabled or assigned to different I/O addresses, IRQ settings, and so on, by Configuration Manager.

Loading Hardware Profiles and Real-mode Drivers

After BIOS initialization, the operating system attempts to determine the current configuration, including whether the computer is a docking station. This is done by using a hardware profile that Windows 98 selects before Config.sys is processed. The hardware profile is built by a detection process that collects information about interrupt usage, BIOS serial and parallel ports, BIOS computer identification, Plug and Play BIOS docking station data, and, if possible, docking station data that is unique to each original equipment manufacturer (OEM). Then the detection process builds a 2-byte value known as the *current hardware profile* (or the current configuration).

Each hardware profile has a name that matches a top-level menu item in a multiconfigured Config.sys file (that is, the long text in the menu, not the section name enclosed in square brackets). Windows 98 automatically selects that multiconfiguration menu item and processes the corresponding section of Config.sys.

Config.sys and Autoexec.bat are processed at this point. Although these files are not required for Windows 98, they are used for backward compatibility with applications created for MS-DOS or Windows 3.1*x*. In Windows 98, Config.sys and Autoexec.bat are processed much as they are processed under MS-DOS 6.*x*. Drivers and TSRs specified in these files are loaded in real mode.

For more information, see "System Startup Files" later in this chapter.

Note The real-mode MS-DOS errors are standard, as documented in the *MS-DOS 6.0 Programmer's Reference.*

Initializing Static VxDs at Startup

Windows 98 supports static VxDs that load during system startup in the same way as Windows 3.*x* VxDs, and it also supports dynamically loaded VxDs. Vmm32.vxd includes the real-mode loader, the executable Virtual Machine Manager, and common static VxDs. Notice, however, that if a VxD file is in the \Windows\System\Vmm32 directory, Windows 98 loads it in addition to the combined VxDs in Vmm32.vxd.

Note If you want to update a VxD that has been bound into the monolithic Vmm32.vxd, place the VxD file in the System\Vmm32 directory. Windows 98 always checks that directory and uses any individual VxDs it finds instead of loading those bound in Vmm32.vxd.

The following list shows the VxDs typically combined to create Vmm32.vxd. (A custom list is built for each computer.) These drivers used to be specified in the [386enh] section of System.ini.

*biosxlat	*ios	*vdd	*vmouse
*configmg	*parity	*vdef	*vmpoll
*dynapage	*reboot	*vfat	*vpd
*ebios	*vcache	*vfbackup	*vsd
*enable	*vcd	*vflatd	*vtdapi
*ifsmgr	*vcomm	*vkd	*vwin32
*int13	*vcond	*vmcpd	*vxdldr

VMM32 loads VxDs in three steps:

- VMM32 loads base drivers specified in the registry, which contains entries for every VxD not directly associated with any hardware. VxDs are located in the following branch of the registry:

  Hkey_Local_Machine\System\CurrentControlSet\Services\VxD

- If VMM32 finds a value **StaticVxD=** in any registry key, it loads that VxD and runs its real-mode initialization. For example, the following entry loads *V86MMGR:

```
SYSTEM\CurrentControlSet\Services\VxD\V86MemoryManger
    Description=MS-DOS Virtual 8086 Memory Manager
    Manufacturer=Microsoft
    StaticVxD=*V86MMGR
    EMMEXCLUDE=E000-EFFF
```

- VMM32 loads the static VxDs specified in the **device=***VxD lines in the [386enh] section of System.ini. These VxDs are actually loaded from VMM32, and appear in System.ini only for backward compatibility.

If a specific device conflicts with a device loaded from the registry, the device specified in System.ini takes precedence. However, if the device specified in System.ini cannot be found, an error occurs.

Many Windows 98 driver models, such as integrated office system (IOS) (for disk drivers) and the network, support dynamically loaded device drivers. These VxDs are not loaded by the VMM32 real-mode loader, but are loaded by a device loader that is responsible for loading and initializing the drivers at the correct time and in the correct order.

For example, for SCSI adapter miniport drivers, the device loader is *Ios. The entries for a SCSI adapter are found in the following registry key:

Hkey_Local_Machine\System\CurrentControlSet\Services\Class

Because there is no **StaticVxD=**xxx line in this registry entry, the VMM32 real-mode loader does nothing when Windows 98 identifies this device.

Configuration Manager attempts to find any device node that has a **DevLoader=** entry in the registry. The device loader (in the previous example, *Ios) examines the registry, finds the **PortDriver=** entry, loads the driver and any associated support drivers, and initializes the adapter.

Loading the Protected-Mode Operating System at Startup

In the previous phase, the following elements of the operating system were loaded:

- Win.com, which controls the initial checks and loading of the core Windows 98 components.
- Vmm32.vxd, which creates virtual machines and initiates VxD loading.
- System.ini, which is read for entries that differ from registry entries.

After all static VxDs have been loaded, Vmm32.vxd switches the processor to operate in protected mode, and the last phase of the boot process begins. This phase involves loading the protected-mode components of the operating system.

Loading Protected-Mode VxDs at Startup

The protected-mode Configuration Manager is initialized for importing configuration information from a Plug and Play BIOS (if available); otherwise, it develops the Plug and Play hardware tree by enumerating devices and loading dynamically loadable device drivers. These device drivers are identified by loading drivers from a specific directory.

The next phase resolves device resource conflicts for every device in the tree and then informs the devices of their configuration. When all devices have been enumerated, all conflicts have been resolved, and all devices have been initialized, Windows 98 is ready to be used.

Loading the Final System Components at Startup

The remaining Windows 98 system components are loaded in the following sequence:

- Kernel32.dll provides the main Windows components, and Krnl386.exe loads the Windows device drivers.
- Gdi.exe and Gdi32.exe provide the graphical device interface code.
- User.exe and User32.exe provide the user interface code.

- Associated resources, such as fonts, are loaded.
- Win.ini values are checked.
- The shell and desktop components are loaded.

At this point, a prompt appears so that you can log on by typing a user name and a password. After you log on, Windows 98 can process user-specific configuration information. If you do not log on, default settings are used. If Windows 98 is configured for network logon, the unified Windows 98 logon can be used to log on to the network during this process.

After Windows 98 is loaded and you log on, the Startup directory is processed.

System Startup Files

This section describes the following files involved in Windows 98 system startup:

- Io.sys, the real-mode operating system that replaces the MS-DOS version; VMM32 and Windows 98 device drivers take control from Io.sys.
- Msdos.sys, which contains special information for Windows 98, is also created. This gives compatibility with applications that require Msdos.sys to be present before they can be installed.
- Config.sys and Autoexec.bat.
- System.ini and Win.ini.
- Bootlog.txt, the log file that describes the system startup processes.

Table 5.5 summarizes how Setup renames the system files from the previous operating system when Windows 98 is installed. (The Windows 98 files are renamed with .W40 file name extensions when you start the computer with the other operating system.)

Table 5.5   Setup system file naming

Original MS-DOS file name	Renamed file under Windows 98
Autoexec.bat	Autoexec.dos
Command.com	Command.dos
Config.sys	Config.dos
Io.sys (or Ibmbio.com)	Io.dos
Mode.com	Mode_dos.com
Msdos.sys (or Ibmdos.com)	Msdos.dos

Io.sys: The Real-mode Operating System

In Windows 98, the Io.sys system file replaces the MS-DOS system files Io.sys and Msdos.sys. This real-mode operating system file contains the information needed to start the computer. Your computer no longer needs Config.sys and Autoexec.bat to start the Windows 98 operating system (although these files are preserved for backward compatibility with certain applications and drivers).

Note The Windows 98 Io.sys file is automatically renamed to Winboot.sys if you start the computer using your previous operating system.

The drivers loaded by default in Io.sys include the following files, if they are found on the hard disk:

- Himem.sys
- Ifshlp.sys
- Setver.exe
- Dblspace.bin or Drvspace.bin if Dlbspace.ini or Drvspace.ini exists in the root of the boot drive.

Most of the common functionality provided by the various Config.sys file entries in older operating systems is provided in Io.sys. Table 5.6 lists the common entries from Config.sys that are incorporated into Io.sys for Windows 98.

Table 5.6   Config.sys settings incorporated into Windows 98 Io.sys

Entry	Description
dos=high	Specifies that MS-DOS should be loaded in the high-memory area (HMA). Also, the **umb** value is included if EMM386 is loaded from Config.sys. (Io.sys does not load EMM386.)
himem.sys	Enables access to the HMA. This line loads and runs the real-mode Memory Manager. Himem.sys is loaded by default in Windows 98.
ifshlp.sys	The 32-bit Installable File System Manager uses the services provided by this driver to assist in trapping real-mode file system and network-related APIs.
setver.exe	Optional TSR-type device. It is included for compatibility. Some MS-DOS-based applications require a specific version of MS-DOS to be running. This file responds to applications that query for the version number and sets the version number required.
files=	Specifies the number of file handle buffers to create. This is specifically for files opened using MS-DOS calls and is not required by Windows 98. It is included for compatibility with older applications. The default value is 60.

Table 5.6   Config.sys settings incorporated into Windows 98 Io.sys *(continued)*

Entry	Description
lastdrive=	Specifies the last drive letter available for assignment. This is not required for Windows 98 but is included for compatibility with older applications. If Windows 98 Setup finds this entry, it is moved to the registry. The default value is z.
buffers=	Specifies the number of file buffers to create. This is specifically for applications using Io.sys calls and is not required by Windows 98. The default value is 30.
stacks=	Specifies the number and size of stack frames. This is not required for Windows 98 but is included for compatibility with older applications. The default value is 9,256.
shell=Command.com	Indicates what command process to use. By default, the **/p** switch is included to indicate that the command process is permanent and should not be unloaded. If the **/p** switch is not specified, Autoexec.bat is not processed and the command process can be unloaded when quitting the operating system.
fcbs=	Specifies the number of file control blocks that can be open at the same time. You should use a **fcbs=** line in Config.sys only if you have an older program that requires such a setting. The default value is 4.

▶ **To override default values in Windows 98 Io.sys**

- Place an entry in Config.sys with the value you want.

The values in Io.sys cannot be edited. If Config.sys contains switches or other parameters for any of the drivers or settings created by Io.sys, the Config.sys entries override the Io.sys defaults. Entries for **files=**, **buffers=**, and **stacks=** must be set in Config.sys to at least the default values in Io.sys.

Note   Io.sys does not load Emm386.exe. If any of your applications requires expanded memory or loads data into the high memory area, EMM386 must be loaded in Config.sys.

Msdos.sys: Special Startup Values

Windows 98 Setup creates a hidden, read-only system file named Msdos.sys in the root of the computer's boot drive. This file contains important paths used to locate other Windows files, including the registry. Msdos.sys also supports an [Options] section, which you can add to tailor the startup process.

The following example shows a typical file with default values:

```
[Options]
BootGUI=1

[Paths]
WinDir=C:\WINDOWS
WinBootDir=C:\WINDOWS
HostWinBootDrv=C
```

Most values in the [Options] section are *Boolean*—that is, the value can be 1 (enabled) or 0 (disabled). Table 5.7 describes entries in Msdos.sys, using the typical default values.   .

Table 5.7   Msdos.sys entries

Entry	Description
[Paths] section	
HostWinBootDrv=c	Defines the location of the boot drive root directory.
WinBootDir=	Defines the location of the necessary startup files. The default is the directory specified during Setup; for example, C:\Windows.
WinDir=	Defines the location of the Windows 98Windows 98 directory as specified during Setup.
[Options] section	
AutoScan=	Enables ScanDisk to run automatically when your computer restarts. The default is 1. When this value is set to 1, ScanDisk will run automatically., you will be prompted if you want to run ScanDisk; if you do not respond after one minute, ScanDisk runs automatically. Setting this value to 0 disables this feature. Setting it to 2 launches ScanDisk automatically (if needed), without prompting you.
BootDelay=*n*	Sets the initial startup delay to *n* seconds. The default is 0is 2. **BootKeys=0** disables the delay. The only purpose of the delay is to give the user sufficient time to press F8press ctrl after the Starting Windows message appears.
BootFailSafe=	Enables Safe Mode for system startup. The default is 0. (tThis setting is typically enabled typically by equipment manufacturers for installation.).
BootGUI=	Enables automatic graphical startup into Windows 98Windows 98. This is equivalent to putting the **win** statement in Autoexec.bat. The default is 1.

Table 5.7   **Msdos.sys entries** *(continued)*

Entry	Description
BootKeys=	Enables the startup option keys (that is, F5, F6, and F8). The default is 1. Setting this value to 0 overrides the value of **BootDelay=**n and prevents any startup keys from functioning. This setting allows system administrators to configure more secure systems. (These startup keys are described in Chapter 27, "General Troubleshooting.").
BootMenu=	Enables automatic display of the Windows 98Windows 98 Startup menu, so that the user must press CTRL to see the menu. The default is 0. Setting this value to 1 eliminates the need to press CTRL to see the menu.
BootMenuDefault=#	Sets the default menu item on the Windows Startup menu; the default is 3 for a computer with no networking components and 4 for a networked computer.
BootMenuDelay=#	Sets the number of seconds to display the Windows Startup menu before running the default menu item. The default is 30.
BootMulti=	Enables dual-boot capabilities. The default is 0. Setting this value to 1 enables the ability to start MS-DOS by pressing F4 or by pressing F8 to use the Windows Startup menu.
BootWarn=	Enables the Safe Mode startup warning. The default is 1.
BootWin=	Enables Windows 98Windows 98 as the default operating system. Setting this value to 0 disables Windows 98Windows 98 as the default; this is useful only with MS-DOS version 5 or 6.x on the computer. The default is 1.
DblSpace=	Enables automatic loading of Dblspace.bin. The default is 1.
DoubleBuffer=	Enables loading of a double-buffering driver for a SCSI controller. The default is 0. Setting this value to 1 enables double-bufferingdouble buffering, if required by the SCSI controller.
DrvSpace=	Enables automatic loading of Drvspace.bin. The default is 1.
LoadTop=	Enables loading of Command.com or Drvspace.bin at the top of 640K memory. The default is 1. Set this value to 0 with Novell NetWare or any software that makes assumptions about what is used in specific memory areas.
Logo=	Enables display of the animated logo. The default is 1. Setting this value to 0 also avoids hooking a variety of interrupts that can create incompatibilities with certain memory managers from other vendors.
Network=	Safe Mode With Networking is no longer supported in Windows 98Windows 98. This value should be set to 0 or left blank to disable this feature.

Tip for Starting an Earlier Version of MS-DOS

If you installed Windows 98 in its own directory, the earlier version of MS-DOS is preserved on your hard disk. If you set **BootMulti=1** in the [Options] section in the Windows 98 version of Msdos.sys, you can start the earlier version of MS-DOS by pressing F4 when the Starting Windows message appears during system startup.

Config.sys and Autoexec.bat

For Windows 95 and Windows 98, the content and method for handling Config.sys and Autoexec.bat during system startup have changed. Windows 98 automatically loads drivers and sets defaults by using Io.sys, the registry, and other mechanisms, rather than Config.sys and Autoexec.bat.

Computers that require certain real-mode drivers or TSRs, however, will continue to require that software be loaded from these configuration files. Also, Config.sys and Autoexec.bat might be required to enable certain software options. Some options, such as long command lines, can also be enabled by using the Command.com program properties, as shown in the following illustration.

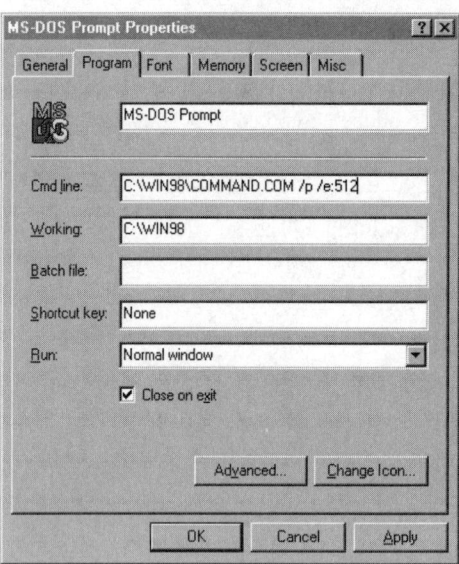

Config.sys Processing

Config.sys defaults are implemented by Io.sys, as described in the previous section. However, Config.sys can contain application-specific entries in addition to information stored in Io.sys. These are processed in the sequence they are listed. After the base Config.sys file has been read, all devices are loaded, and Command.com is started.

Windows 98 loads memory managers supplied by other vendors if they are present in Config.sys; however, some might cause errors. Similarly, Windows 98 allows the use of command shells from other vendors, but there are some differences. For example, long file names are disabled, which might also indicate that other problems could occur using these command shells.

Config.sys Changes for Windows 98

Windows 98 has predefined settings built in for most common Config.sys settings, so Windows 98 Setup removes many of these lines (such as settings for **files**, **buffers**, and **stacks**) if they are equivalent to the default values, by using **rem** to comment out the line.

Tips for Editing Config.sys in Windows 98

If you edit Config.sys in Windows 98, observe the following basic guidelines:

- Do not include the **smartdrv** command. Windows 98 includes built-in disk caching, and double-buffering is now provided by Dblbuff.sys.

- Remove any **device=mouse.sys** lines or similar lines. Windows 98 includes built-in mouse support.

Autoexec.bat Processing

Autoexec.bat is not required for Windows 95 or Windows 98, but it is included for compatibility purposes. If the computer has an Autoexec.bat file, each line is processed in sequence during system startup. Autoexec.bat can contain additional application-specific entries that are run in the sequence they are listed.

Windows 98 passes the initial environment to Command.com with the correct Windows and Windows Command directories already in the path and with the environment variables PROMPT, TMP, and TEMP already set. (**TEMP=** and **TMP=** indicate locations for temporary directories; both are specified for compatibility reasons.)

Table 5.8 describes the Autoexec.bat commands that have equivalent default settings created in Io.sys for Windows 98.

Table 5.8   Autoexec.bat equivalents for Windows 98 Io.sys default settings

Command	Meaning
net start	Loads the real-mode network components and validates the binding. Any errors received are placed in the Ndislog.txt file. (SYSINIT or Command.com performs the necessary **net start** command.)
set path	Sets the path as specified.

The default Windows 98 environment includes the following:

```
tmp=c:\windows\temp
temp=c:\windows\temp
prompt=$p$g
path=c:\windows;c:\windows\command
comspec=c:\windows\command\Command.com
```

Autoexec.bat Changes for Windows 98

Windows 98 Setup makes the following basic changes to Autoexec.bat:

- Updates the **path=** line statement.
- Uses **rem** to comment out incompatible TSRs.
- Deletes any **win** statement (or equivalent) and Share.exe.
- Copies the original Autoexec.bat to Autoexec.dos.
- Sets the Temp directory.

Tips for Editing Autoexec.bat in Windows 98

If you edit Autoexec.bat in Windows 98, observe the following basic guidelines:

- Do not include other versions of Windows in your path.

- Start the path with C:\Windows;C:\Windows\Command (using the name for the Windows 98 directory on your hard disk if it is not \Windows).

- Windows 98 Setup leaves your previous MS-DOS directory in the path. Do not change this.

- Do not add SMARTDrive or other disk caches. Windows 98 includes built-in caching.

- Do not include any statements for loading mouse support software. Windows 98 includes built-in mouse support.

- If it is necessary to connect to a network server when you start Windows 98, create a batch file, and run it from the STARTUP directory, rather than placing an entry in Autoexec.bat.

System.ini and Win.ini

This section describes changes related to system startup made by Windows 98 Setup to System.ini and Win.ini. Mappings for other changes between Windows 3.1x and Windows 98 are described in Chapter 31, "Windows 98 Registry."

System.ini Changes for Windows 98

Table 5.9 lists configuration options that have been added to System.ini, deleted, or moved to the registry. Most of these options for Windows 98 are now stored in the registry and are no longer required in System.ini.

Table 5.9   Changes made to System.ini entries in Windows 98

Change	Affected entries	
Added to the [Boot] section	comm.drv=comm.drv dibeng.drv=dibeng.dll gdi.exe=gdi.exe	sound.drv=sound.drv user.exe=user.exe
Added to the [386Enh] section	device=*int13 device=*dynapage	device=*vshare device=*vcd

Table 5.9   Changes made to System.ini entries in Windows 98 (*continued*)

Change	Affected entries	
Deleted in the [386Enh] section	device=*configmg device=*vfd device=isapnp.386 device=lpt.386 device=pagefile.386	device=serial.386 device=wshell.386 maxbps= timercriticalsection=
Moved from the [386Enh] section to the registry	Network= Network3= SecondNet=	Transport= V86ModeLANAs=
Moved from the [Network] section to the registry	AuditEnabled= AuditEvents= AuditLogSize= AutoLogon= Comment= ComputerName= DirectHost= EnableSharing= FileSharing= LANAs= LMAnnounce=	LMLogon= LogonDisconnected= LogonDomain= LogonValidated= Multinet= PasswordCaching= PrintSharing= Reshare= SlowLanas= Winnet= Workgroup=
Moved from the [Network drivers] section to the registry	All parameters	
Moved from the [nwnblink] section to the registry	lanabase=	

Set the related parameters using Windows 98 tools as follows:

- Set all memory-related parameters by using the System option in Control Panel. For information, see Chapter 26, "Performance Tuning."

- Set parameters for hardware devices by using Device Manager in the System option in Control Panel. For information, see Chapter 24, "Device Management."

Win.ini Changes for Windows 98

Table 5.10 shows how the font and desktop information in Win.ini is transferred to the registry in Windows 98.

Table 5.10   Changes made to Win.ini entries in Windows 98

Change	Affected entries	
Moved from the [Windows] section to the registry	Beep BorderWidth CursorBlinkRate DoubleClickSpeed KeyboardDelay KeyboardSpeed	MouseThreshold1 MouseThreshold2 MouseSpeed ScreenSaveActive ScreenSaveTimeOut SwapMouseButtons
Moved from the [Windows Metrics] section to the registry	BorderWidth CaptionHeight CaptionWidth MenuHeight MenuWidth MinArrange MinHorzGap	MinVertGap MinWidth ScrollHeight ScrollWidth SmCaptionHeight SmCaptionWidth

In addition, Setup always adds **ATMWorkaround=1** to the [Pscript.Drv] section in Win.ini.

Set the related parameters using Windows 98 tools as follows:

- Set all mouse parameters by using the Mouse option in Control Panel. For information, see Chapter 24, "Device Management."

- Set parameters for the keyboard by using the Keyboard option in Control Panel. For information, see Help.

- Set all screen and window display parameters by using the Display option in Control Panel. For information, see Chapter 24, "Device Management."

Bootlog.txt: The Startup Process Log

The Bootlog.txt file contains a record of the current startup process for starting Windows 98. This file is created during Setup when the Windows 98 operating system is first started from Windows 98 Setup. This file shows the Windows 98 components and drivers loaded and initialized, and the status of each.

When you use the F8 option for interactive system startup, you can choose to create a boot log during system startup. You can also use the **/b** switch to create a boot log when running Win.com from the command line to isolate configuration problems. For information, see Chapter 27, "General Troubleshooting."

The information in Bootlog.txt is written in sequence during startup, in roughly five major sections. Depending upon a specific error condition, you might need to examine multiple sections. Notice, however, that a **loadfailed=** entry means only that the related VxD refused to load. For example, **loadfailed=ebios** indicates that the EBIOS driver did not detect EBIOS in the computer and so reported that it should not be loaded. Table 5.11 shows the sections to examine and describes the possible errors and methods for correcting those errors.

Table 5.11   Bootlog.txt sections for determining errors

Section and errors	Corrective action
Loading real-mode drivers:	
No extended memory specification (XMS) memory	Verify that the section contains this entry: `loadsuccess=c:\windows\himem.sys` If not, verify the file and entry in Config.sys
Incorrect MS-DOS version (message appears when driver loads)	If this error appears when loading drivers or programs that worked before, verify that the section contains this entry: `loadsuccess=c:\windows\setver.exe.`
Windows 98 does not start on a SCSI hard drive	Verify that the section contains this entry: `loadsuccess=c:\windows\dblbuff.sys`
Ifshlp.sys message occurs	Verify that the section contains this entry: `loadsuccess=c:\windows\ifshlp.sys`
Loading VxDs:	

	Verify the loading, system, and device initialization of all VxDs by checking the section for these entries:
	`loading vxd = ios`
	`loadsuccess = ios`

Cannot access D??SPACE drives	Verify that the section contains this entry: `loadsuccess = c:\dblspace.bin`
Sharing violations occur	Might be due to failure of the Vshare VxD to load. The section might contain an entry such as: `loadfailed  = vshare`
System-critical initialization of VxDs:	

System-critical initialization error occurs	Verify that the section contains entries such as:
	`syscritinit=ios`
	`syscritinitsuccess=ios`

Table 5.11   Bootlog.txt sections for determining errors *(continued)*

Section and errors	Corrective action
Device initialization of VxDs:	
	Verify that the section contains entries such as:
	`deviceinit=ios` `deviceinitsuccess=ios`
Successful VxD initialization:	
	Verify that the section contains entries such as:
	`initcomplete=ios` `initcompletesuccess=ios`

Table 5.12 shows the kinds of entries in Bootlog.txt to examine for information about the system startup process.

Table 5.12   Bootlog.txt entries to examine for system startup

Bootlog.txt entry	Description
Error	Errors that were logged during startup
Fail	Failures that occurred during startup
Dynamic load success	Dynamically loaded VxDs
INITCOMPLETESUCCESS	Loaded VxDs
LoadStart, LoadSuccess, Loading Device, Loading Vxd	Indication of loading processes
LoadFailed	Indication that component failed to load
SYSCRITINIT, SYSCRITINITSUCCESS	System initialization actions
DEVICEINIT, DEVICEINITSUCCESS	Device initialization actions
Dynamic load device, Dynamic init device	Dynamic loading and initialization of devices
Initing, Init Success, INITCOMPLETE, Init, InitDone	Initialization actions
Status	Current status indicator

For example, if you see an entry such as **DynamicInitDevice=PPPMAC** but there is no matching entry such as **DynamicInitSuccess=PPPMAC**, that VxD failed to load. If a driver in the Windows System\Iosubsys directory stalls when it is being initialized, you can sometimes successfully start the system by renaming that file.

The following shows a sample Bootlog.txt file:

```
Loading Device = C:\WINDOWS\HIMEM.SYS
LoadSuccess   = C:\WINDOWS\HIMEM.SYS
Loading Device = C:\WINDOWS\EMM386.EXE
LoadSuccess   = C:\WINDOWS\EMM386.EXE
Loading Device = C:\WINDOWS\SETVER.EXE
LoadSuccess   = C:\WINDOWS\SETVER.EXE
Loading Device = C:\WINDOWS\COMMAND\ANSI.SYS
LoadSuccess   = C:\WINDOWS\COMMAND\ANSI.SYS
Loading Device = C:\WINDOWS\IFSHLP.SYS
LoadSuccess   = C:\WINDOWS\IFSHLP.SYS
Loading Vxd = VMM
LoadSuccess = VMM
Loading Vxd = nwlink.vxd
LoadSuccess = nwlink.vxd
Loading Vxd = vnetsup.vxd
LoadSuccess = vnetsup.vxd
```

Windows 98 Setup with Other Operating Systems

This section presents details related to installing Windows 98 over an existing operating system, including changes made to system files by Windows 98 Setup and configuring for dual-booting with the previous operating system.

Microsoft Windows 98 dual-boot is supported with Microsoft Windows NT, Windows 95 and MS DOS 5.*x*. Dual-boot with third-party operating systems, such as Novell DR DOS and IBM OS/2, is not supported. For more information on dual booting Windows 98 with a third-party operating system, you should contact your operating system vendor.

Table 5.13 summarizes some of the available options for upgrading with Windows 3.1*x*, MS-DOS, and Windows NT, and how you should install Windows 98 to take advantage of these options.

Table 5.13   Upgrade versus clean installations

Desired configuration	Install Windows 98 in a new directory	Upgrade existing Windows 3.1x/95 installation with Windows 98
Migrate existing Windows application settings and files		✓
Dual boot Windows 98 and MS-DOS	✓	
Dual boot Windows 98 and Windows NT[1]	✓	

[1] Windows 98 and Windows NT can work together properly if the computer is configured for dual booting between MS-DOS and Windows NT. However, you must install Windows 98 in a new directory.

The topics discussed in this section include the following:

- Upgrading Windows 95 to Windows 98 keeping your current configuration settings
- Upgrading Windows 95 to Windows 98 changing your current configuration settings
- Upgrading Windows 3.1x
- Dual booting Windows 98 with Windows 3.1x and MS-DOS
- Dual booting Windows 98 with Windows NT

Upgrading from Windows 95 to Windows 98

There are two methods for upgrading from Windows 95 to Windows 98. The method you choose depends on whether you want to retain the existing configuration settings (such as computer name, installation directory, and network settings) on your computer.

Keeping Current Configuration Settings

If you have a computer running Windows 95 and you want to upgrade it to Windows 98, keeping its current configuration settings (such as computer name, user name, and installation directory), run the Windows 98 Setup program from within Windows 95. This is the recommended method for upgrading Windows 95 to Windows 98, because it requires minimum user interaction and is the easiest method.

With this method, Windows 98 is installed in the same directory where Windows 95 was installed. Furthermore, Windows 98 Setup uses the existing configuration information to set installation defaults and to set other configuration options. Windows 98 Setup migrates all Windows 95 folders and programs to Windows 98, so they appear on the Windows 98 Start menu. Windows 98 automatically migrates all the shortcuts you had under Windows 95.

▶ **To upgrade Windows 95 to Windows 98 keeping current settings**

1. Start Windows 95.

2. Close all programs, including any anti-virus programs.

   For information about closing an anti-virus program, see the program documentation and Setup.txt on your Windows 98 disk.

3. If you are installing Windows 98 from a compact disc, insert the Windows 98 compact disc into your CD-ROM drive.

   – Or –

   If you are installing Windows 98 from floppy disks, insert Setup Disk 1 into the floppy disk drive.

– Or –

If you are installing Windows 98 from source files on a network server, connect to that server and switch to the shared network directory that contains the Windows 98 source files.

4. On the **Start** menu, click **Run**.

   The **Run** dialog box appears.

5. In the **Open** box, enter the location of the Windows 98 disc. For example, type the drive letter, followed by a colon (**:**), a backslash (****), and the word **setup**. For example: **d:\setup**.

6. Click **OK**.

   The Windows 98 Setup Wizard starts.

7. Follow the on-screen instructions, as described in "Running Setup from the Windows 95 Interface" in Chapter 2, "Setting Up Windows 98."

Changing Current Configuration Settings

If you want to upgrade your Windows 95 computer to Windows 98 but you want to change its current configuration settings (such as computer name and workgroup) or you want to install Windows 98 in a new directory, you run the Windows 98 Setup program from within MS-DOS.

Before you begin, you should be prepared to provide the following information:

- Name of the installation directory (for example, **c:\Win98**).

  If you do not know the directory in which to install Windows 98, you can use Setup to create a new one. When prompted, type a new directory name.

- Network information, such as your computer name, workgroup, and computer description (if your computer is on a network).

When starting Setup from MS-DOS using either a network server or local CD-ROM drive, the real-mode network or CD-ROM drivers must be loaded. If the real-mode network drivers are running when you start Windows 98 Setup, the appropriate network client is installed automatically. Setup detects existing network components, installs the appropriate supporting software automatically, and adds the necessary network settings in the registry.

▶ **To upgrade Windows 95 to Windows 98 changing current settings**

1. Start your computer up and press F8 when the message, **Starting Windows 95** appears. Then select **Command Prompt Only.**

   -Or-

   From Windows 95, click on **Start**, and click **Shut Down**. Then select **Restart in MS-DOS mode**.

2. If you are installing Windows 98 from a compact disc, insert the Windows 98 compact disc into the CD-ROM drive, and make it the active drive.

– Or –

If you are installing Windows 98 from floppy disks, insert Setup Disk 1 into the floppy disk drive and make it the active drive. For example, type **a:** if the disk is in the A drive.

– Or –

If you are installing Windows 98 from source files on a network server, connect to that server and switch to the shared network directory that contains the Windows 98 source files.

3. At the command prompt, type the drive letter, followed by a colon (**:**), a backslash (****), and the word **setup**. For example:

d:\setup

4. Press ENTER.

Setup quickly scans your computer, and then the Windows 98 Setup Wizard starts.

5. Follow the on-screen instructions, as described in "Running Setup from MS-DOS" in Chapter 2, "Setting Up Windows 98."

After starting Setup from MS-DOS, Setup initializes and checks your system:

- It runs real-mode ScanDisk to check the hard disk for errors. Unlike the protected-mode version of ScanDisk, the real-mode counterpart cannot fix errors in long file names. ScanDisk does not perform a surface scan; therefore, the disk is not checked for physical errors.

Note If you get file system errors during setup, you should run ScanDisk and perform a surface scan before running Setup again.

- It initializes the registry and checks it for corruption.

Tip When you run Windows 98 Setup, ScanDisk performs a quick check of the hard disk. You can skip this quick check (for example, if the computer uses disk compression software from another vendor) by using the **/iq** or **/is** switch with the **setup** command, as described in "Using the Setup Command-Line Switches" in Chapter 2, "Setting Up Windows 98." If you choose to skip automatically running ScanDisk, be sure to use another utility to check the integrity of the hard disk before running Setup.

Upgrading Windows 3.1x or Windows for Workgroups to Windows 98

If you have a computer running Windows 3.1x or Windows for Workgroups, you can upgrade it to Windows 98 by running the Windows 98 Setup program from within Windows 3.1x or Windows for Workgroups.

Most of the information needed for upgrading is automatically taken from your current installation of Windows 3.1x. Setup automatically identifies and transfers your current system settings and installed programs. Windows 98 Setup also saves settings so that you can continue to use the network configuration that you had previously.

▶ **To upgrade from Windows 3.1x or Windows for Workgroups to Windows 98**

1. Start Windows 3.1 or Windows for Workgroups.

2. Close all programs, including any anti-virus programs.

   For information about closing an anti-virus program, see the program documentation and Setup.txt on your Windows 98 compact disc.

3. If you are installing Windows 98 from a compact disc, insert the Windows 98 compact disc into the CD-ROM drive and make it the active drive.

   – Or –

   If you are installing Windows 98 from floppy disks, insert Setup Disk 1 into the floppy disk drive and make it the active drive. For example, type **a:** if the disk is in the A drive.

   – Or –

   If you are installing Windows 98 from source files on a network server, connect to that server and switch to the shared network directory that contains the Windows 98 source files.

4. In File Manager, select the disk drive you used in step 3.

5. On the **File** menu, click **Run**.

   The **Run** dialog box appears.

6. In the **Open** box, enter the location of the Windows 98 compact disc. For example, type the drive letter, followed by a colon (**:**), a backslash (\), and the word **setup** (or, you can click **Browse** and browse to the Setup.exe file).

7. Click **OK**.

   The Windows 98 Setup Wizard starts.

8. Follow the instructions on your screen.

Dual Booting Windows 98 with Windows 3.1x and MS-DOS

You can configure your computer to dual boot with Windows 3.1x as long as the computer has MS-DOS 5.0 or later by using the F4 boot-to-previous operating system feature. To dual boot Windows 98 with these operating systems, your computer's C drive must be FAT 16.

For more information about how Windows 98 Setup treats disk partitions created under other operating systems, see "Partition Requirements" in Chapter 2, "Setting Up Windows 98."

Important   To take advantage of the Windows 98 dual-boot capabilities, the entry **BootMulti=1** must be set in the Windows 98 Msdos.sys file in the root directory. For more information, see "Msdos.sys: Special Startup Values" earlier in this chapter.

▶ **To set up dual-boot capabilities for a new installation of Windows 98**

- During Windows 98 Setup, when you are installing Windows 98 for the first time, make sure you specify a new directory that does not already have another version of Windows in it.

Windows 98 Setup makes all of the necessary changes to preserve your existing version of MS-DOS, Windows 3.1x, or Windows for Workgroups 3.1x, and your current Autoexec.bat and Config.sys files.

If you have already installed Windows 98 without dual-boot capabilities, you can follow these steps to allow MS-DOS to dual boot with Windows 98. However, you will not be able to dual boot with your previous version of Windows.

▶ **To set up dual-boot capabilities after Windows 98 has been installed**

1. On a bootable floppy disk that starts MS-DOS 5.0 or later, rename the Io.sys, Msdos.sys, and Command.com files on the disk to Io.dos, Msdos.dos, and Command.dos.

2. Create two empty text files named Config.dos and Autoexec.dos. You can customize these now or later to be appropriate for the MS-DOS version you will be adding.

Caution   You must rename the MS-DOS versions of these files before copying them to the root directory. Otherwise, you will destroy your Windows 98 installation.

---

3. Copy all the .dos files to the root directory of the boot drive. This is usually drive C. Make duplicates of these files on your host drive if you want to use disk compression.

4. Mark the .dos files in the root directory of the boot drive with the hidden, system, and read-only attributes (**attrib -r -s -h *.dos**).

5. Change the Msdos.sys on the boot drive to include the line **bootmulti=1**. Instructions for making changes to Msdos.sys can be found earlier in this chapter.

Installing Windows 98 over MS-DOS

The versions of MS-DOS supported for installing Windows 98 are versions 5.0 or later.

Tip for Running MS-DOS After Windows 98 Is Installed

If you install Windows 98 in a different directory from the one containing your previous Windows 3.1*x* version, you can start the computer by using the previous version of MS-DOS. To do this, make sure the entry **BootMulti=1** is in the Windows 98 Msdos.sys file, and then press CTRL during system startup and choose the related option.

Files Deleted by Windows 98 Setup

This section lists MS-DOS and other files that are deleted by Windows 98 Setup. Notice, however, that these files are deleted from the old MS-DOS directory only if you install Windows 98 in the existing Windows 3.1*x* directory. Otherwise, the old MS-DOS files are all preserved so that you can start the computer using the older version of MS-DOS.

The Windows 98 command-line commands are stored in the Command subdirectory of the Windows directory. Deleting the related MS-DOS command file will not affect your ability to use the command under Windows 98. The versions that are deleted by Setup are known to be incompatible with Windows 98; for example, many of these MS-DOS commands do not support long file names. Table 5.14 shows files removed by Windows 98 Setup.

Table 5.14   Files removed by Windows 98 Setup

MS-DOS and Windows 3.1x files

Ansi.sys	D??space.exe[1]	Keyb.com	Ramdrive.sys
Attrib.exe	D??space.sys[1]	Keyboard.sys	Readme.txt
Chkdsk.exe	Edit.com	Label.exe	Scandisk.exe
Choice.exe	Edit.hlp	Mem.exe	Scandisk.ini
Country.sys	Ega.cpi	Mode.exe	Setver.exe
Debug.exe	Emm386.exe	More.com	Share.exe
Defrag.exe	Fc.exe	Move.com	Smartdrv.exe
Deltree.exe	Fdisk.exe	Mscdex.exe	Sort.exe
Diskcopy.exe	Find.exe	Msd.exe	Start.exe
Display.sys	Format.com	Networks.txt	Subst.exe
Doskey.com	Help.com	Nlsfunc.exe	Sys.com
D??space.bin[1]	Help.hlp	Os2.txt	Xcopy.exe

COMPAQ DOS 5.0 files

Cache.exe	Dos5help.chd	Fsedit.exe	Tu.exe
Cemm.exe	Fastart.exe	Help.exe	Upcu.exe
Cemmp.exe			

Non-MS-DOS operating system files

Delpurge.exe	Hidos.sys	Rendir.exe	Touch.exe
Delwatch.exe	Lock.exe	Setup.exe	Uninstal.exe
Diskmap.exe	Login.exe	Sys.com	Xdel.exe
Diskopt.exe	Memmax.exe	Taskmax.exe	Xdir.exe
Dosbook.exe	Password.exe	Taskmax.ini	

Table 5.14   Files removed by Windows 98 Setup *(continued)*

Pre-MS-DOS 5.0 files

Append.com	Enhdisk.sys	Keybfr.exe	Print.exe
Asgnpart.com	Fastopen.exe	Keybgk.com	Recover.exe
Backup.exe	Fastart.exe	Keybgr.com	Restore.exe
Bootf.com	Fdisk.com	Keybgr.exe	Select.com
Cache.sys	Filesys.exe	Keybit.com	Select.dat
Cemm.exe	For150.exe	Keybit.exe	Select.exe
Cemmp.exe	Format.exe	Keybno.com	Select.hlp
Chkdsk.exe	Gdu.exe	Keybsp.com	Select.prt
Cmpqadap.com	Graftabl.exe	Keybsv.exe	Select1.dat
Compact.exe	Graphics.exe	Keybsw.com	Select2.dat
Configur.com	Hardrive.sys	Keybuk.com	Setup.exe
Debug.exe	Hpcache.com	Keybuk.exe	Shell.clr
Detect.com	Hpdcache.com	Keybus.com	Shell.hlp
Diskcomp.exe	ifsfunc.exe	Label.exe	Shell.meu
Diskcopy.exe	IndskbIo.sys	Mode.exe	Shellb.com
Diskinit.com	Install.exe	Mvbuild.exe	Shellc.exe
Diskinit.exe	Keyb32.com	Pamcode.com	Tree.exe
Dosutil.meu	Keybchf.com	Paminstl.com	Vdisk.sys
Dskscan.exe	Keybchg.com	Part.exe	Xmaem.sys
Dsksetup.com	Keybda.com	Password.exe	Zcache.sys
Edlin.exe	Keybfr.com	Prep.exe	Zspool.com
Emm386.sys			

1 Drvspace.* or Dblspace.*

System Startup with MS-DOS Multiple Configurations

Windows 98 supports multiple configurations for the same computer, and it dynamically determines which configuration is being used. If Windows 98 cannot determine the specific configuration used during system startup before processing Config.sys, it presents a menu of available configurations as listed in the registry, and it prompts you to select the configuration you want.

If you have a multiple configuration established in Config.sys, that menu is presented next. However, if you use a multiple configuration to switch between different versions of Windows, you must edit Config.sys manually to repair this configuration after Windows 98 is installed. For information about how to create multiple configurations for the same computer under Windows 98, see Chapter 24, "Device Management."

Dual Booting Windows 98 with Windows NT

If you install Windows 98 to dual boot with Windows NT, boot to MS-DOS, and then run Setup from either MS-DOS or Windows 3.1*x*. You will not be able to install Windows 98 to a directory with a shared Windows 3.1*x*/Windows NT configuration; you will need to install Windows 98 in a different directory.

You can install Windows 98 to dual boot with Windows NT on a computer. This section provides some notes for installing Windows 98 with Windows NT.

Important In order to take advantage of the Windows 98 dual-boot capabilities, the entry **BootMulti=1** must be set in the Windows 98 Msdos.sys file in the root directory. For more information, see "Msdos.sys: Special Startup Values" earlier in this chapter.

▶ **To install Windows 98 to dual boot with Windows NT**

1. Ensure that the computer is configured to dual boot between Windows NT and MS-DOS. Check your Windows NT documentation for details.

2. Start the computer by using the MS-DOS operating system.

3. Run Windows 98 Setup as described in Chapter 2, "Setting Up Windows 98."

Remember that if your computer has any Windows NT file system (NTFS) partitions, they are not available locally from within Windows 98.

If you run MS-DOS from a floppy disk in order to install Windows 98, you will not be able to start Windows NT afterward. You can restore the multiboot configuration by starting the computer with your Windows NT Boot Disks and selecting the Repair option. You will then be prompted for your Windows NT Repair Disk.

To run MS-DOS after Windows 98 has been installed, you must select the MS-DOS option from the Windows NT multiboot menu. Then, from the Windows 98 Startup menu, select **Previous Version of MS-DOS**.

▶ **To install Windows NT on a computer where Windows 98 is installed**

• At the command prompt, switch to the directory that contains the Windows NT source files, and then type **winnt /w**.

The WINNT program is an MS-DOS-based application that creates the Windows NT Setup startup files and copies the system files to the hard disk from the source files. The **/w** switch allows WINNT to run under Windows. Using this switch also causes Windows NT Setup to skip the CPU detection process and the automatic restart at the end of Setup. You can also include the **/b** switch to copy the required startup files for Setup so that you do not have to create floppy disks for Setup.

For more information about the Windows NT operating system and about running computers with Windows 98 on a Windows NT network, see Chapter 16, "Windows 98 on Microsoft Networks."

Using a Windows 98 Startup Disk

This section describes the Windows 98 Startup Disk. You should make a Startup Disk and keep it on hand to help you boot your computer when you are having problems.

What Is New in the Startup Disk

The Startup Disk has changed significantly for Windows 98. The following items have been added:

- The Microsoft Windows 98 Startup Menu
- Real-Mode IDE CD-ROM support
- Real-Mode SCSI CD-ROM support
- Edb.cab file
- RAMDrive
- New extract command: Ext.exe

For a complete list of the contents of the Windows 98 Startup Disk, see "Contents of the Windows 98 Startup Disk" in Appendix B, "Windows 98 System File Details."

The Microsoft Windows 98 Startup Menu

If you boot the computer using the Startup Disk, a boot menu appears allowing you to start the computer with or without CD-ROM support. The drivers on the Startup Disk support a variety of ATAPI CD-ROM drives. An example of the menu is shown below.

```
Microsoft Windows 98 Startup Menu

1.  Start the computer with CD-ROM support.
2.  Start the computer without CD-ROM support.
3.  View the Help file.

Enter a choice: 1              Time remaining: 30
```

If you use the Startup Disk to boot the computer and choose to load the real-mode CD-ROM drivers, but cannot access a compact disc in the drive, it is likely that the CD-ROM is connected to a sound card. The CD-ROM must be connected to the controller on the motherboard.

After you make your selection, the Config.sys file loads the CD-ROM driver (if selected) and then loads a 2-MB RAMDrive.

The Autoexec.bat file calls a second batch file, Setram.bat, to find a drive letter for the RAMDrive. The temp variables, *path* and *comspec*, are set to the RAMDrive. The files Command.com, Mode.com, Keybrd?.sys, and Keyb.com are copied to the RAMDrive root directory.

The following line in the Autoexec.bat file expands the files to the RAMDrive:

```
%RAMD%\extract /y /e /l %RAMD% edb.cab > NUL
```

Finally, if a CD-ROM driver is loaded, MSCDEX is launched.

CD-ROM Support

Real-Mode IDE CD-ROM Support

The Windows 98 Startup Disk includes a real-mode generic ATAPI CD-ROM driver (Oakcdrom.sys) that allows the CD-ROM to function when the protected mode of the GUI interface is not available. This occurs when booting into either MS-DOS or Windows fails to boot into the GUI. Although CD-ROM manufacturers accompany CD-ROM drives with a floppy disk with the specific drivers to use, they may or may not be available when needed most.

Real-Mode SCSI CD-ROM Support

Real-mode generic SCSI CD-ROM drivers are also supported (Mylex Btdcrom.sys and Adaptec Aspicd.sys) to allow a SCSI CD-ROM to function when booting into MS-DOS.

RAMDrive

The RAMDrive created from the Config.sys file is 2 MB in size. Keep in mind that the tmp path points to this location. After the files are expanded and placed here, there is only about 1.384 MB of space available.

Warning The RAMDrive is created during the processing of the Config.sys file. Drive letter assignment for a CD-ROM is not performed until MSCDEX is loaded in the Autoexec.bat file. Therefore, customers who normally boot without a RAMDrive will find their CD-ROM drive moved one letter back.

Extract Command (Ext)

The Ext.exe command is a new and simple extract command designed to work with Extract.exe. You type **ext** at a command prompt. Ext.exe detects if the Win98 CDROM is in the drive and defaults to that directory for its source location. If it is not available, it defaults to A:\. Otherwise, you are asked to enter the path to the Windows CAB files.

You then enter the name(s) of the file(s) you want to extract and enter the path to the directory to extract the files to. The CAB files scroll up the screen until the file is found. A sample of the display is shown below.

```
Microsoft (R) Extract Command Line Helper
------------------------------------------------------------------
Please enter the path to the Windows CAB files (a:) : d:\Win98
Please enter the name(s) of the file(s) you want to extract:
explorer.exe
Please enter the path to extract to ("Enter" for current directory)
C:\Windows

The Options you entered were:
--------------------------------------------------
Source Path              : d:\Win98
File(s) to extract       : explorer.exe
Destination Path         : C:\Windows

Is this okay? (y/n)      :
```

Note It takes a long time to expand the file (a 60-KB file expands in 77 seconds on an Intel 266MMX Pentium machine).

Ext Error Messages

You might have to reset the TMP variable for large files, because it points to the RAMDrive and there is a limited amount of free space available. Use the command **Set TMP=C:**. Because EXT uses TMP, resetting the TEMP variable does not work. If you do not reset the TMP variable, you may get the following error message:

```
"Error: Out of memory while processing cabinet file Win98_41.cab"
```

Tip If you receive an error "Unable to write to disk" or "Disk initialization error" when creating a Startup Disk, the disk may be defective. Insert a different disk and start again.

Starting Your Computer with the Startup Disk

Follow the following procedure to start your computer with the Startup Disk.

▶   **To start your computer with the Startup Disk**

1. Insert the disk in the floppy drive of your computer and turn the computer on.

2. After a few moments, you see the "Microsoft Windows 98 Startup Menu" screen. Three menu items are offered.

3. If you need to access the CD-ROM, for example, to restart Setup or to use the troubleshooting tools, select **Start the computer with CD-ROM support**.

4. If you do not want to access the CD-ROM (for example, if you need to save memory or you are running Setup from the hard drive of the machine) select **Start the computer without CD-ROM support**.

5. You can also select **View the Help file** for more information about the Startup Disk.

For more information on setup problems and the Windows 98 Startup Disk, see "Troubleshooting Setup" later in this chapter.

Note   The generic CD-ROM drivers may not work with all CD-ROM hardware. If these drivers do not function with your hardware, you will have to use the drivers that shipped with your CD-ROM.

Removing Windows 98 from a Computer

You can uninstall Windows 98 as long as your current configuration satisfies the following conditions:

- You clicked **Yes (recommended)** on the **Save System Files?** dialog box that appeared when you installed Windows 98 the first time. If you clicked **Yes**, two files containing the saved Windows 95 system files, Winundo.dat and Winundo.ini, were created in the root directory of the partition that you designated during Setup.

- The system boot partition or any partition on the same physical drive where Winundo.dat is located was not compressed when you installed, and you did not compress it after installing Windows 98.

- You did not convert any file systems to FAT32, unless your Windows 95 version is OSR2.

Note   The retail and OSR1 versions of Windows 95 cannot read FAT32 drives.

Windows 98 can be removed from a computer by using the procedures described below. If the computer is configured for dual booting, you will be left with the previous versions of MS-DOS and Windows 3.1x intact. The recommended method for removing Windows 98 is to start the computer and use the F8 key to go to a command line, as described in the following procedure. When you do this, real-mode Windows 98 operating system files start the computer. If you encounter problems starting Windows 98 in this way, start your computer from the previous operating system (which might require using a floppy disk).

During the installation of Windows 98, you have the option of saving your Windows 95 system files. If you save your system files, you can uninstall Windows 98 and restore your Windows 95 environment. If you created shortcuts after you saved your system files, you have to delete them manually, because information about these shortcuts does not exist in the system files you saved.

Important This recovery capability is available only if you do not compress your primary partition after you upgrade to Windows 98.

▶   **To uninstall Windows 98**

1. In Control Panel, double-click Add/Remove Programs.

2. On the **Install/Uninstall** tab, click **Uninstall Windows 98**, and then click **Add/Remove**.

   The **Windows 98 Uninstall** dialog box appears explaining that you are about to remove Windows 98 from your computer and restore Windows 95.

3. Click **Yes** to continue with the uninstall procedure.

   A dialog box appears informing you that your disk(s) will be checked for errors.

4. Click **Yes**.

   The ScanDisk program scans all non-removable hard disks, and another dialog box appears asking if you want to continue.

5. Click **Yes**.

The computer restarts in MS-DOS mode, and the program Uninstal.exe runs automatically. This program is located in the \Windows\Command directory. The MS-DOS program restores the Windows 95 files and the settings contained in Winundo.dat; it then prompts you to restart the computer. Once the computer restarts, Windows 95 is restored.

Important Any programs that you have installed after installing Windows 98 must be reinstalled in the restored Windows 95 configuration.

Removing the Windows 95 System Files

To remove the Windows 95 system files, you can delete the Winundo.dat and Winundo.ini files manually. However, after doing this, the **Uninstall Windows 98** and **Delete Windows 98 uninstall information** items (Windows 98 uninstall information) will still be displayed in the **Install/Uninstall** tab on the **Add/Remove Programs Properties** dialog box. If you want to remove the Windows 95 system files and remove the Windows 98 uninstall information, use the following procedure.

▶ **To remove the Windows 95 system files and the Windows 98 uninstall information**

1. In Control panel, double-click Add/Remove Programs.

2. On the **Install/Uninstall** tab, click **Delete Windows 98 uninstall information**, and then click **Add/Remove**.

   The **Windows 98 Uninstall** dialog box appears explaining that if you remove these files, you can no longer uninstall Windows 98.

3. Click **Yes** to continue with the uninstall procedure.

   A dialog box appears informing you that the files have been successfully deleted.

4. Click **OK**.

   The **Delete Windows 98 uninstall information** and **Uninstall Windows 98** items no longer appear on the **Install/Uninstall** tab.

Removing Windows 98 with Command-Line Startup

Before you begin this process, make sure you have a system startup disk that contains an earlier version of MS-DOS and the Sys.com file. You need this startup disk because the Windows 98 startup files (real-mode operating system files) must be deleted, so the process for removing Windows 98 makes your hard disk temporarily unbootable.

Note The MS-DOS 6.*x* disk #1 is bootable, but the retail MS-DOS 5.0 disk #1 is not, and OEM versions may vary. To make a startup disk with MS-DOS 6.*x*, run **setup /f** from disk #1.

▶ **To remove Windows 98 when the computer is started to the command line**

1. Start the computer, and press CTRL when the "Starting Windows" message appears.

   If you have problems starting the computer in this way, you can use the "Removing Windows 98 with Your Previous Operating System" procedure later in this chapter.

2. Select **Command Prompt Only**.

3. To make it easier to delete files and directories, copy the Windows 98 version of Deltree.exe to the boot drive. At the command prompt, type:

   copy \windows\command\deltree.exe c:

4. To use the Windows 98 version of ScanDisk to clear invalid entries and long file names, copy the ScanDisk files from the Windows Command directory to the root directory. At the command prompt, type:

   copy \windows\command\scandisk.* c:

5. Use Notepad or a similar text editor to edit Scandisk.ini in the \Windows directory. Change the entries controlling whether ScanDisk looks for invalid characters in file names and volume labels:

   - Set **labelcheck=on** to specify that ScanDisk should check volume labels for invalid characters.

   - Set **spacecheck= on** to specify that ScanDisk should check for invalid spaces in file names.

   For information about the entries in Scandisk.ini, see that file in the Windows directory.

6. To remove all entries that your earlier version of MS-DOS might see as invalid, type **scandisk** followed by the letter identifying the drive containing the Windows 98 installation at the command prompt. For example:

   scandisk c:

   If you receive error messages during the ScanDisk process, refer to Help for information to help you resolve the error.

7. To delete the Windows 98 directory, type in the root directory of the drive containing the Windows 98 installation:

   deltree *windows*

   In this command, *windows* is the name of the directory containing the Windows 98 files.

Caution This command deletes all subdirectories of the Windows 98 directory. Before performing this step, make sure that the Windows 98 directory tree does not contain any critical data that has not been backed up.

This step also requires that you reinstall all Windows-based programs at the end of this procedure, so the correct drivers and settings are available in the restored Windows directory.

---

8. To delete the Windows 98 Config.sys and Autoexec.bat files, type in the root directory of the boot drive:

   deltree Config.sys
   deltree Autoexec.bat

9. To delete the Winboot.ini file and the Winboot directory, if present, type:

   deltree winboot.*

10. To delete the setup, boot, and detection log files, type:

    deltree setuplog.*
    deltree bootlog.*
    deltree detlog.*

11. To delete the real-mode operating system files Io.sys and Msdos.sys, in the root directory of the boot drive (or from the root directory of the host drive, if the boot drive is compressed), type:

    deltree Io.sys
    deltree Msdos.sys

12. To delete the Windows 98 compression drivers (Dblspace.bin and Drvspace.bin), if present, type in the root directory of the boot drive (or from the root directory of the host drive, if the boot drive is compressed):

    deltree d??space.bin

13. To delete the Windows 98 command processor (Command.com), type in the root directory of the boot drive (or both from the C drive and from the root of the host drive, if the boot drive is compressed):

    deltree Command.com

14. Put a bootable floppy disk with your earlier version of MS-DOS into drive A, and then restart the computer. After the computer starts from the floppy disk, put your earlier version of MS-DOS back on the boot drive (or the host drive, if the C drive is compressed) by typing **sys** followed by the letter identifying the boot or host drive and a colon. For example:

    sys c:

15. If you have MS-DOS version 6.0 and are using compression, copy Dblspace.bin from the DOS directory to the root directory of the boot drive. Also, for all versions of MS-DOS, if you have a **shell=** statement referencing Command.com from a different directory, copy Command.com to the root directory. Then remove the floppy disk, and restart the computer from the hard disk.

To start the system with previous configuration files, copy Config.dos to Config.sys and Autoexec.dos to Autoexec.bat.

If you remove Windows 98 from a dual-boot installation, Windows 98 will be removed completely, and the computer will start the same way it did before installing Windows 98.

If you removed Windows 98 from an upgraded Windows 3.1x installation, drivers that were located in the Windows directory (such as Himem.sys, Ifslhlp.sys, and Emm386.exe) will be missing until you reinstall Windows 3.1x. After this, the computer will start the same way it did before Windows 98 was installed.

You might need to reinstall the previous version of MS-DOS, if needed files were removed by Windows 98 Setup.

Removing Windows 98 with Your Previous Operating System

Use this procedure if you cannot start a computer in Windows 98 real mode as described in the preceding section.

Before you begin this process, make sure you have a bootable floppy disk that contains an earlier version of MS-DOS and the Sys.com file. The process for removing Windows 98 makes your hard disk temporarily unbootable, and the Windows 98 startup files (real-mode operating system files) must also be deleted.

Note The MS-DOS 6.x disk #1 is bootable, but the retail MS-DOS 5.0 disk #1 is not, and OEM versions may vary. To make a startup disk with MS-DOS 6.x, run **setup /f** from disk #1.

▶ **To remove Windows 98 when the computer is started with the previous operating system**

1. Start the computer, and press CTRL when the "Starting Windows" message appears.

2. Select **Previous Version of MS-DOS**.

3. To make it easier to delete files and directories, copy the Windows 98 version of Deltree.exe to the boot drive. At the command prompt, type:

   copy \windows\command\deltree.exe c:

4. To copy the Windows 98 version of ScanDisk files from the Windows Command directory to the root directory, type:

   copy \windows\command\scandisk.* c:

5. Use Notepad or a similar text editor to edit Scandisk.ini. Change the entries controlling whether ScanDisk looks for invalid characters in file names and volume labels:

   - Set **labelcheck=on** to specify that ScanDisk should check volume labels for invalid characters.

   - Set **spacecheck=on** to specify that ScanDisk should check for invalid spaces in file names.

6. To remove all entries that your earlier version of MS-DOS might see as invalid, type **scandisk** followed by the letter identifying the drive containing the Windows 98 installation at the command prompt. For example:

   scandisk c:

   If you receive error messages during the ScanDisk process, refer to online Help for information to help you resolve the error.

7. To delete the Windows 98 directory, type in the root directory of the drive containing the Windows 98 installation, type:

   deltree *windows*

   In this command, *windows* is the name of the directory containing the Windows 98 files.

Caution   This command deletes all subdirectories of the Windows 98 directory. Before performing this step, make sure that the Windows 98 directory tree does not contain any critical data that has not been backed up.

---

8. To delete the Windows 98 real-mode operating system file named Winboot.sys, which was renamed from Io.sys when you started the computer with your previous operating system, type the following command from the boot drive (or from the root directory of the host drive, if the boot drive is compressed):

   deltree winboot.*

9. Delete the Windows 98 files Msdos.w40, Command.w40, Config.w40, and Autoexec.w40 files. (The renaming of these operating system files occurred when you used F8 to start the previous operating system.) To do this, type the following command at the command prompt (if the boot drive is not compressed):

   deltree *.w40

   If the boot drive is compressed, you must delete Msdos.w40 from the root directory of the host drive and Command.w40 from the root directories of both the host drive and the boot drive.

10. To delete the setup, boot, and detection log files, type:

    deltree setuplog.*
    deltree bootlog.*
    deltree detlog.*

11. If you are using Stacker version 3.1, either skip this step or back up the STAC Dblspace.bin file before completing this step. To delete the Windows 98 compression drivers (Dblspace.bin and Drvspace.bin), in the root directory of the boot drive (or from the root directory of the host drive, if the boot drive is compressed), type:

    deltree d??space.bin

12. Put a bootable floppy disk with the earlier version of MS-DOS into drive A, and then restart the computer. After the computer starts from the floppy disk, put your earlier version of MS-DOS back on the boot drive (or the host drive, if the C drive is compressed) by typing **sys** followed by the letter identifying the boot or test drive and a colon. For example:

    sys c:

13. If you have MS-DOS version 6.0 and are using compression, copy Dblspace.bin to the root directory of the boot drive. Also, for all versions of MS-DOS, if you have a **shell=** statement referencing Command.com from a different directory, copy Command.com to the root directory. Then remove the floppy disk, and restart the computer from the hard disk.

If you remove Windows 98 from a dual-boot installation, Windows 98 will be removed completely, and the computer will start the same way it did before installing Windows 98.

If you removed Windows 98 from an upgraded Windows 3.1x installation, you might need to reinstall your previous version of MS-DOS if some of the necessary files were removed by Windows 98 Setup. Drivers that were located in the Windows directory (such as Himem.sys, Ifslhlp.sys, and Emm386.exe) will be missing until you reinstall Windows 3.1x into the Windows directory. After you reinstall Windows 3.1x, the computer will start the same way it did before Windows 98 was installed.

▶ **To remove Windows 98 from a computer with Windows NT installed**

1. Follow the procedure "To remove Windows 98 when the computer is started with the previous operating system" earlier in this section.

2. Use the Windows NT Setup disk #1 to restart your computer.

3. When prompted, choose **Repair**, then insert the Windows NT Emergency Repair Disk and choose the option to repair the boot files.

4. Restore your original MS-DOS and Windows 3.1*x* configuration.

The next section provides information about solving problems that might occur during Setup or system startup. For specific information about troubleshooting procedures and the tools provided with Windows 98 (including details about using the Startup menu and Safe Mode for troubleshooting), see Chapter 27, "General Troubleshooting."

Note If you have MS-DOS-based applications that require complete access to system resources, see the information about using MS-DOS Mode in Chapter 25, "Application Support."

Troubleshooting Setup

Setup uses different procedures to recover from a setup failure, depending on when the failure occurred in the setup process. Furthermore, other hardware and software issues may cause Setup to fail.

If necessary, you can uninstall Windows 98 and return to your previous Windows 95 configuration, as described later in this section. Once you have thoroughly tested all your programs, you can also remove the saved system files to free up the disk space they occupy.

If Setup fails, attempt to restart it using the following procedure.

▶ **To restart Setup after a failure**

1. Press F3 or click the **Exit** button.

   If the system does not respond, restart the computer by pressing CTRL+ALT+DEL. If this fails, turn off the computer, wait 10 seconds, and then turn it on again.

2. Start Setup again. Setup prompts you to use Safe Recovery to recover the failed installation. Choose the **Safe Recovery** option, and click the **Continue** button. Setup will skip the portion that caused the initial failure.

3. If Setup fails while copying files, the user may be required to manually load their Real Mode CD-ROM. The previous version of Windows 95 may no longer boot, and access to the CD-ROM is required.

Tips for Installing Real-mode CD-ROM Drivers

This section presents tips that will make installing real-mode CD-ROM drivers easier.

Using Drivers on a Windows 98 Startup Disk

If you have a Windows 98 Startup Disk from another installation, you can use the CD-ROM drivers included on that disk.

Using Drivers from Windows 95

If you are currently running Windows 95, chances are you already have a portion of the CD-ROM drivers loaded.

▶ **To use existing CD-ROM drivers when running Windows 95**

1. On the **Start** menu, click **Shut Down**, and then select **Restart in MS-DOS mode**.

2. Windows 98 starts up; press F8 when you see "Starting Windows 95."

3. Choose Command Prompt Only.

4. At the C:\ prompt, type **dosStart.bat**.

Using Drivers from Windows 3.1x or MS-DOS

If you lose access to your CD-ROM during the Windows 98 Setup process, and you are currently running Windows 3.1x, you can gain access to your CD-ROM again.

▶ **To use existing CD-ROM drivers while running Windows 3.1x**

1. Reboot the computer, and press F8 when you see "Starting Windows95." Select **Command Prompt Only**. If you are running MS-DOS, simply boot directly to the command prompt.

2. Edit Autoexec.bat by typing **Edit Autoexec.bat**.

3. Delete the text **Rem by Windows 98 Setup** in front of the line that includes the reference to Mscdex.exe.

4. Exit **Edit** by pressing ALT+F, typing **x**, and saying **Yes** to save the file.

5. Reboot. If Setup does not continue on its own, you should run it again, choosing **Smart Recovery** if prompted.

6. If the computer stops again during the hardware detection process, turn your machine off, wait 10 seconds, and then turn it back on. Setup should then continue and skip the offending detection module that caused Setup to hang. This process may be required more than once on some systems.

> **Tip** Whenever you encounter a Setup problem you cannot fix easily, restart your computer and wait 15 to 20 seconds before starting Setup again.

You can use the information in Setuplog.txt and Detlog.txt to check for the device or devices that caused the problems. Also review any messages added by Setup in the Autoexec.bat file for instructions on correcting setup problems.

The following sections describe specific setup problems and how to resolve them.

Starting Your Computer with the Windows 98 Startup Disk

If you have problems with Setup or have trouble starting Windows 98, you can use the Windows 98 Startup Disk to start your computer and gain access to your system files. You are prompted to create a Startup Disk during Windows 98 Setup. We recommend that you create extra Startup Disks after you install Windows 98 with Add/Remove Programs in Control Panel.

The Windows 98 Startup Disk contains several system and diagnostic programs, such as ScanDisk and Uninstall. The disk also contains a generic CD-ROM driver in case your computer has difficulty communicating with your CD-ROM drive.

> **Tip** To help you troubleshoot, you can create several Startup Disks with different configurations on each disk; for example, you can save a disk with the specific drivers for your hardware.

> **Important** Startup disks created with previous versions of Windows are not compatible with Windows 98. When you install Windows 98, you must create a new Startup Disk, either during Setup or using Control Panel.

▶ **To create a Startup Disk after installing Windows 98**

1. In Control Panel, double-click Add/Remove Programs.

2. The Add/Remove Programs Properties dialog box appears.

3. Click the **Startup Disk** tab, and then click **Create Disk**.

4. Label a floppy disk "Windows 98 Startup Disk," insert the disk in your floppy disk drive, and then click **OK**. Click **OK** again, and then follow the instructions on your screen.

5. Setup also creates a Windows\Command\EBD directory for emergency purposes when you can not boot your system and do not have a Startup Disk. This is created at the same time Setup prompts for the Startup Disk. To create an EBD from the MS-DOS prompt, run the Bootdisk.bat program located in the Windows\Command directory.

Important Any files currently on the floppy disk are erased when you create a Windows 98 Startup Disk.

For more information about the Windows 98 Startup Disk, and using it to start the computer, see "Using a Windows 98 Startup Disk" earlier in this chapter.

Using the Windows 98 Setup Built-In Troubleshooting Aids

Windows 98 contains log files and includes utilities that can assist you in correcting problems that occur during the setup or startup processes. This section describes the following built-in troubleshooting aids:

- Safe Recovery with Windows 98 Setup
- Installed components verification
- Startup diskto use ex
- Startup Menu options
- Win.com switches

Using Safe Recovery with Setup

Setup uses Safe Recovery to determine what caused an installation to fail. Safe Recovery uses the information available in Detchrash.log, for example, to avoid performing detection on the same device that caused Setup to fail before.

▶ **To use Safe Recovery if Setup fails**

1. Run Setup again.
2. When the **Safe Recovery** dialog box appears, click **Safe Recovery**.

You can also use the Setuplog.txt, Detlog.txt, and Bootlog.txt files in the root directory of the boot drive to determine why Setup failed. These text files contain, respectively, the Safe Recovery and hardware detection information in a readable form, plus a log of system startup actions. Setuplog.txt, for example, will show the point at which Setup failed.

To automatically scan these log files for installation or detection errors, you can use the following commands in a setup script. Create a batch file containing the following text and run it from the root directory of the boot drive (C:\) after an unsuccessful Setup attempt.

```
@echo off
echo "Entries found in Setuplog.txt" > log.txt
find /i /n "installtype" setuplog.txt >> log.txt
find /i /n "installdir" setuplog.txt >> log.txt
find /i /n "detection" setuplog.txt >> log.txt
find /i /n "runningapp" setuplog.txt >> log.txt
find /i /n "rootfilesrenamed" setuplog.txt >> log.txt
find /i /n "error" setuplog.txt >> log.txt
find /i /n "failed" setuplog.txt >> log.txt
echo "Entries found in Bootlog.txt" >> log.txt
find /i /n "fail" bootlog.txt >> log.txt
find /i /n "error" bootlog.txt >> log.txt
find /i /n "dynamic load success" bootlog.txt >> log.txt
find /i /n "initcomplete success" bootlog.txt >> log.txt
echo "Entries found in Detlog.txt" >> log.txt
find /i /n "avoidmem" Detlog.txt >> log.txt
find /i /n "detected" Detlog.txt >> log.txt
find /i /n "error" Detlog.txt >> log.txt
cls
type log.txt |more
other helpful info from Setuplog.txt…
    fsCmosAVCheck: Attempting CMOS Anti Virus Test
    fsCmosAVCheck: CMOS Anti Virus Test SUCCEEDED
```

Using a Startup Disk

You can use a Windows 98 Startup Disk to load the operating system and display an MS-DOS command prompt. The Startup Disk also contains utilities for troubleshooting a malfunctioning operating system. You can create a Startup Disk during Windows 98 Setup or afterward in Control Panel.

Caution It is strongly recommended that you create a Windows 98 Startup Disk as part of Windows 98 Setup, and that you maintain an updated copy of the Startup Disk each time you change the system configuration after installing Windows 98.

If you did not create a Startup Disk during Setup, you can create one using a single floppy disk.

▶ **To create a Windows 98 Startup Disk after Windows 98 is installed**

- In Add/Remove Programs in Control Panel, click the **Startup Disk** tab. Then click **Create Disk**, and follow the instructions on-screen.

    – Or –

    Run the Bootdisk.bat utility from the Windows\Command directory to create a Startup disk from MS-DOS.

Using Startup Menu Options

If the system fails to start, Windows 98 displays a **Startup** menu that contains troubleshooting options. You can also manually prompt Windows 98 to display the **Startup** menu.

▶ **To display the Windows 98 Startup menu**

- Restart the computer. Hold CTRL while the system is booting. This will take you to the boot menu. You no longer see the "Starting Windows 98" prompt. The F8 key is still functional, but the 2-second boot delay has been removed. If CTRL is mapped to other system functionality, you can use MSCONFIG and the **Advanced** option to enable the boot menu by default.

Table 5.15 describes **Startup** menu options. The contents of this menu can vary, depending on the options specified in the Msdos.sys, and the configuration of the computer.

Table 5.15   Startup menu options

Start menu option	Description
Normal	Starts Windows, loading all normal startup files and registry values.
Logged (Bootlog.txt)	Runs system startup creating a startup log file.
Safe Mode	Starts Windows, bypassing startup files and using only basic system drivers. You can also start this option by pressing F5 or typing **win /d:m** at the command prompt.
Step-by-Step Confirmation	Starts Windows, confirming startup files line-by-line. You can also start this option by pressing F8 when the **Startup** menu is displayed.
Command Prompt Only[1]	Starts the operating system with startup files and registry, displaying only the command prompt.

Table 5.15   Startup menu options *(continued)*

Start menu option	Description
Safe Mode Command Prompt Only[1]	Starts the operating system in Safe Mode and displays only the command prompt, bypassing startup files. Same as pressing SHIFT+F5.
Previous version of MS-DOS	Starts the version of MS-DOS previously installed on this computer. You can also start this option by pressing F4. This option is available only if **BootMulti=1** in Msdos.sys.

[1] When you start the computer at the command prompt, you can use switches with the **win** command to control Windows 98 startup for troubleshooting purposes, as described in Chapter 27, "General Troubleshooting."

The following sections describe when to use these **Startup** menu options to troubleshoot system problems.

Tip   Windows 98 uses entries in the Msdos.sys file to control **Startup** menu options, automatic loading of certain drivers, and path statements for system files. If Windows 98 does not start as expected, check the entries in Msdos.sys.

Safe Mode

If Windows 98 fails to start normally, select Safe Mode from the **Startup** menu to begin troubleshooting. Windows 98 automatically initiates Safe Mode if it detects that system startup failed (for example, if a Wnbbotng.sts signature file still exists in the Windows directory), or if the registry is corrupted (for example, if an important key such as System is missing), or if an application requests Safe Mode.

Safe Mode bypasses startup files, including the registry, Config.sys, Autoexec.bat, and the [Boot] and [386Enh] sections of System.ini, and provides you with access to the Windows 98 configuration files. You can make any necessary configuration changes, and then restart Windows 98 normally. Use Safe Mode for system startup in situations such as the following:

- If Windows 98 seems to stall for an extended period of time.
- If Windows 98 does not work correctly or has unexpected results.
- If you cannot print to a local printer after attempting other troubleshooting steps.
- If your video display does not work correctly.
- If your computer suddenly slows down.
- If you need to test an intermittent error condition.

When starting Windows 98 in Safe Mode, only the mouse, keyboard, and standard VGA device drivers are loaded. This makes Safe Mode useful for isolating and resolving error conditions caused by both real-mode and Windows drivers. The **Startup** menu can include three to four Safe Mode options, depending on whether the computer's hard disk is compressed or not. Each Safe Mode option disables a different portion of the startup process, as shown in Table 5.16.

Table 5.16 Startup actions disabled by Safe Mode

Action	Safe Mode	Command Prompt Only[1]
Process Config.sys and Autoexec.bat		
Load Himem.sys and Ifshlp.sys	✓	
Process registry information		
Load Command.com		✓
Load DoubleSpace or DriveSpace if present	✓	
Run Windows 98 Win.com	✓	
Load all Windows drivers		

[1] The Safe Mode Command Prompt Only option also loads DoubleSpace or DriveSpace if present.

Note Safe Mode With Networking is not supported in Windows 98.

Safe Mode Command Prompt Only

Safe Mode Command Prompt Only loads the Command.com and DoubleSpace or DriveSpace files (if present). It does not load Himem.sys, Ifshlp.sys, or Windows 98. The following are examples of when to use Safe Mode Command Prompt Only:

- If Windows 98 fails to start, even with the Safe Mode option.
- If you want to use command line tools (such as when editing Config.sys).
- If you want to avoid loading Himem.sys or Ifshlp.sys.

Step-by-Step Confirmation

Step-by-Step Confirmation allows you to specify which commands and drivers the system should process by confirming each line of the startup files. The following are examples of when to use Step-by-Step Confirmation:

- If the startup process fails during loading of the startup files.
- If any real-mode drivers must be loaded to run Windows 98 successfully.
- If you need to check for registry failure messages.

- If you need to verify that the expected drivers are being loaded.
- If you need to temporarily disable a specific driver or set of drivers.
- If you need to check for errors in startup files.

When you choose to confirm system startup line-by-line, the following prompts appear. (You can press ENTER to confirm or ESC to skip that part of system startup.)

- Load DoubleSpace (or DriveSpace) driver?
- Process the system registry?
- Create a startup log file (Bootlog.txt)?
- Process your startup device drivers (Config.sys)?

  Each line from Config.sys is displayed with the [Enter=Y,Esc=N] prompt. You can press TAB when the first Config.sys prompt appears to accept all options automatically.

- Process your startup command file (Autoexec.bat)?

  Each line from Autoexec.bat is displayed with the [Enter=Y,Esc=N] prompt. You can press TAB when the first Autoexec.bat prompt appears to accept all options automatically.

- Run win.com to start Windows 98?
- Load all Windows drivers?

If you press ENTER to answer **Yes** to each prompt, the result is the same as starting Windows 98 normally, except that the logo does not appear. Answering **No** to "Load All Windows Drivers?" runs Windows 98 in Safe Mode.

Using Win.com Switches

The following switches are available to start Windows 98 from the command prompt when you need to isolate an error condition:

win [/d:[f] [m] [n] [s] [v] [x]]

The **/d:** switch is used for troubleshooting when Windows 98 does not start correctly. The switches in Table 5.17can be used with the **/d:** switch.

Table 5.17   Switches used with the /d: switch

Switch	Meaning
f	Turns off 32-bit disk access. Try this if the computer appears to have disk problems, or if Windows 98 stalls. This is equivalent to **32BitDiskAccess=FALSE** in System.ini.
m	Starts Windows 98 in Safe Mode.

Table 5.17   Switches used with the /d: switch *(continued)*

Switch	Meaning
s	Specifies that Windows 98 not use ROM address space between F000:0000 and 1 MB for a break point. Try this if Windows 98 stalls during system startup. This is equivalent to **SystemROMBreakPoint=FALSE** in System.ini.
v	Specifies that the ROM routine should handle interrupts from the hard disk controller. Try this if Windows 98 stalls during system startup or disk operations. This is equivalent to **VirtualHDIRQ=FALSE** in System.ini.
x	Excludes all of the adapter area from the memory that Windows 98 scans to find unused space. This is equivalent to **EMMExclude=A000-FFFF** in System.ini.

Recovering from Common Setup Failures

This section covers how to diagnose and correct some of the most common Setup errors.

Recovering Before Your Computer Is Restarted for the First Time (First Restart)

If Setup encounters an error or stops before your computer is restarted for the first time during Setup, you must turn the computer off, turn it back on, and then run Setup again.

After the Setup Wizard has started again, Setup determines that a failure occurred, and the Safe Recovery screen appears:

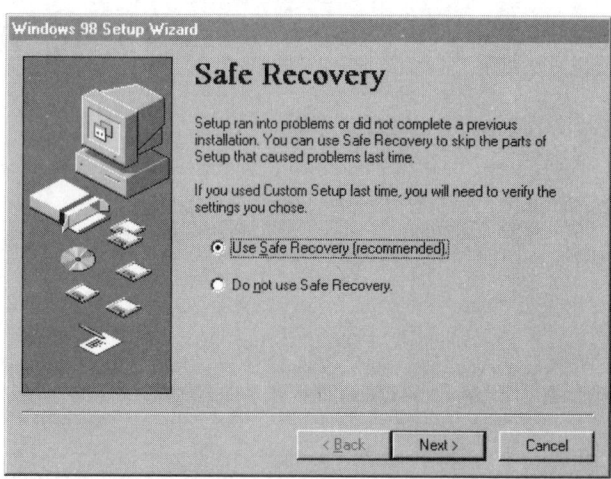

If you click **Use Safe Recovery (recommended),** Setup examines the Setuplog.txt file to determine where the failure occurred. Setup then resumes from the point where the failure occurred. If you click **Do not use Safe Recovery,** the Setup process will restart from the beginning.

The Safe Recovery option in Setup automatically skips previous problems so that Setup can be completed. You can also use Safe Recovery to repair damaged or corrupt installations.

Recovering During Hardware Detection

During Setup, the hardware detection phase is the most likely to cause Setup to fail. Figure 5.1 summarizes the cause, event, and solution for hardware detection problems.

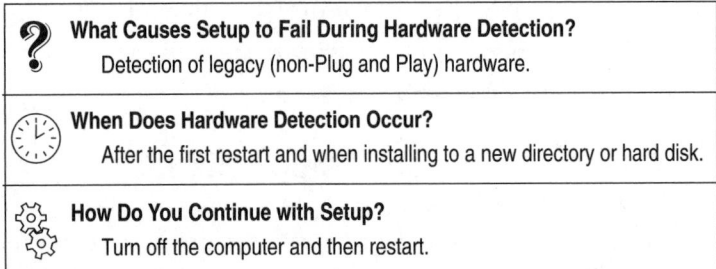

What Causes Setup to Fail During Hardware Detection?	
Detection of legacy (non-Plug and Play) hardware.	
When Does Hardware Detection Occur?	
After the first restart and when installing to a new directory or hard disk.	
How Do You Continue with Setup?	
Turn off the computer and then restart.	

Figure 5.1   Cause, event, and solution for hardware problems

Hardware detection of legacy devices, which takes place after the first restart, will only occur if Windows 98 is being set up in a new directory or into a newly formatted hard disk or when running Setup from Windows 95 and verification fails. During this phase, Setup writes data to and reads data from various hardware addresses, including I/O ports, IRQs, and memory address ranges.

During Setup, logs are maintained, which record Setup progress and store information that can be used for recovery. Table 5.18 describes the log files.

Table 5.18   Setup log files

Log file name	Purpose	Details
Detlog.txt	Records the start of a detection test and the test outcome. Keeps a record of devices Setup finds during the detection process.	A hidden file located in the root directory of the C drive.
Detcrash.log	Records which detection steps were successfully completed so that Setup will not fail on the same problem.	A hidden file created only if a detection step caused the computer to stop responding. Located in the root directory of the C drive.
Setuplog.txt	Records what took place during Setup, including successes and failures. Used by Safe Recovery to determine where Setup will resume.	Located in the root directory of the C drive.

If a failure occurs after the first restart, hardware detection recovery uses the log files to skip the module that caused the failure so that Setup can proceed.

Caution You should not delete any of the log files described in this table; otherwise, Setup will not be able to detect failures. For example, deleting the Detcrash.log file prevents Setup from recognizing and failure and skipping it to proceed.

▶ **To restart Setup after a hardware detection failure**

1. Turn the computer off for 10 to 15 seconds.
2. Turn the computer back on again.

Bypassing Previous Setup Failures

When a failure occurs, Setup reloads the detection modules, checks the log files, and resumes after the point where the failure occurred, as shown in Figure 5.2.

Figure 5.2 shows an example of how Setup handles failures. In the first attempt at running Setup, there is a failure, and Setup logs it in the Detcrash.log file and restarts again. In the second attempt, it skips the point where the first failure occurred and continues with the setup process, but it encounters a second failure. It logs the second failure and restarts again. On the third attempt, it skips the points where the two previous failures occurred and then continues, this time successfully until Setup is complete.

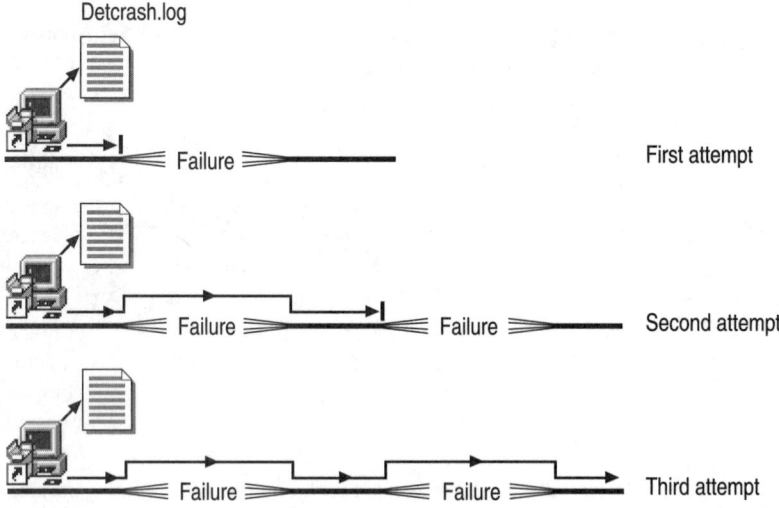

Figure 5.2   How Setup handles failures

Because detection can determine where a failure occurred, the installation process keeps moving forward by recognizing and bypassing the addresses where the previous attempts failed. Setup proceeds to the module where the failure occurred, checks Detcrash.log, verifies that the module caused the problem, skips the module, and then continues.

Even if the system fails several times, Setup continues to progress because it does not fail repeatedly on the same point of failure.

Tip You can easily find hardware that is not working by looking at the **Device Manager** tab in the **System Properties** dialog box accessed through the System icon in Control panel. Hardware that is not working appears with its tree expanded.

Verifying Installed Hardware

If your computer stops responding during hardware detection and you restart the computer, Windows 98 Setup may not detect some of your hardware. To verify that the computer's hardware has been detected, do the following:

▶ **To verify hardware detection**

1. In Control Panel, click System.

2. In the **System Properties** dialog box, click the **Device Manager** tab.

    Expand each item in Device Manager to verify that all your hardware is listed.

If the computer's hardware is not listed in Device Manager, then click Add New Hardware in Control Panel. If the Add New Hardware Wizard does not detect any new hardware, follow the on-screen directions and select the specific hardware from the Windows 98 hardware.

Recovering from Errors Due to Problematic Software

If Setup detects problematic software, it tries to provide instructions to correct the problem. If Setup is unable to diagnose the cause of the failure, it may present a message that states that Setup has failed. If this occurs, you must restart the computer and then restart Setup.

Troubleshooting Hard Disk Problems Using ScanDisk

Windows 98 Setup automatically runs ScanDisk to check for problems on your hard disk(s). If there are problems, Setup cannot continue until they are fixed.

Note The MS-DOS-based version of ScanDisk that Setup runs may detect long file name errors, but it cannot correct them. These errors will not prevent Setup from proceeding, but once it completes, you should run ScanDisk from within Windows 98 to correct these errors.

Fixing Hard Disk Problems

If you see a message during Setup that says you must run ScanDisk to fix problems on your hard disk and you are setting up Windows 98 over MS-DOS or a previous version of Windows, such as Windows 3.1, follow these steps.

▶ **To fix hard disk problems when setting up Windows 98 over MS-DOS or another version of Windows**

1. Exit Windows.

2. If you are setting up from floppy disks, insert Setup Disk 1 into the drive, and then type the following at the command prompt:

   ```
   a:scandisk.exe /all
   ```

   where "a" is the drive that contains the Windows disk.

   – Or –

   If you are setting up from a compact disc, insert the compact disc and then type the following:

   ```
   d:\win95\scandisk.exe /all
   ```

   where "d" is the drive that contains the compact disc.

3. Follow the instructions on your screen and fix any problems that ScanDisk finds.

4. Start Windows, and then run Setup again.

If you see a message during Setup that says you must run ScanDisk to fix problems on your hard disk and you are upgrading Windows 95 to Windows 98, follow these steps.

▶ **To fix hard disk problems when upgrading Windows 95 to Windows 98**

1. Exit Setup.

2. Click **Start**, point to **Programs**, point to **Accessories**, point to **System Tools**, and then click **ScanDisk**.

3. Check your hard disk(s) and any host drives you have for errors, and repair any problems found.

Note If you are running Setup from MS-DOS, ScanDisk will run and you will be able to fix most problems from within Setup.

Problems Running ScanDisk During Setup

If you get a message during Setup saying that there is not enough memory to run ScanDisk, free some conventional and/or upper memory, and then run Setup again. If you have MS-DOS 6.*x*, try running MemMaker to free memory.

If you still do not have enough memory, or if you have other problems while Setup is running ScanDisk, then you can bypass ScanDisk in Setup by running Setup with the **/is** option. To do this, type the following command:

setup /is

Note Bypassing ScanDisk during Setup is not recommended. If you do, there may be problems with your hard disk that could cause Windows 98 not to install or run correctly.

If you still have problems after running Setup with the **/is** option, try running Setup with the **/iq** option. To do this, type the following command:

setup /is /iq

Problems with Compressed Drives

If you have used compression software to compress your hard disk, you may get a message saying that there is not enough space on the host partition of the compressed drive. Setup may have to copy some files to your startup drive, the host for your startup drive, or the host for your Windows drive. If you get this message, you should free up some space on the specified drive, and then run Setup again. Try one of the following:

- Delete any unneeded files on your host partition.

- If you are running Windows 3.1 and have a permanent swap file, try making it smaller. In Control Panel, double-click 386 Enhanced, and then click **Virtual Memory**. Then modify the size of your swap file.

- Use your disk compression software to free up some space on the host drive for the compressed drive. If you compressed your drive by using DriveSpace or DoubleSpace, follow these steps:

  1. Quit Windows.

  2. Run Drvspace.exe or Dblspace.exe.

  3. Select the compressed drive on whose host you want to free space.

  4. On the **Drive** menu, click **Change Size**.

If you used other compression software, such as Stacker, consult the documentation that came with it.

Note If you notice a discrepancy in the amount of free space reported by Setup and the amount of space you think is available on your host drive, it may be because Windows uses some space for creating a swap file. This may not appear to take up any space when Windows is not running.

If you create a Startup Disk during Setup, make sure you do not use a compressed disk for the Startup Disk.

Problems with SuperStor Compression

If you have compressed your hard disk by using SuperStor, Setup may not be able to find your startup drive and install Windows 98. If you get a message about this during Setup, uncompress your disk and remove SuperStor, then run Setup again.

Problems with XtraDrive Compression

If you have compressed your hard disk with XtraDrive and you are upgrading a previous version of Windows, Setup will not be able to install Windows 98 unless you turn off the XtraDrive write cache. To turn this off, follow these steps:

▶ **To turn off the XtraDrive write cache**

1. Quit Windows.

2. Run Vmu.exe (XtraDrive's Volume Maintenance Utility).

3. Choose **Advanced Options**, and then press ENTER.

4. Set the EMS cache size to **0**.

5. Set the Conventional cache size to **1** (the minimum).

6. Set **Allow Write Caching** to **NO**.

7. At the confirmation prompt, choose **Yes**. You will see a message saying that you must restart your computer for the changes to take effect.

8. Quit **Volume Maintenance Utility**, and then restart your computer.

9. Start Windows, and then run Setup again.

Cannot Read Setup (CAB) Files

If you have Multimedia Cloaking and are installing Windows 98 from floppy disks, Setup may not run successfully. If you see messages about Setup not being able to read CAB files, then follow these steps.

▶ **To run Setup on computers with Multimedia Cloaking**

1. Remove the line referencing Cacheclk.exe from your Config.sys and Autoexec.bat files.

2. Restart your computer.

3. Run Setup again.

Installing from Your Local Hard Disk

One of the most common troubleshooting steps in Windows 98 Setup is installing from your local hard disk. By copying all the setup files to your hard disk, you can eliminate most of the problems associated with file copy and disk I/O issues. This also allows you to unload your CD-ROM drivers and free up conventional memory to assist with low memory errors.

▶ **To copy the setup files locally from within Windows 95**

1. Free an additional 120 MB of disk space beyond what Setup normally requires. Setup will typically require 195Mbytes for a Windows95 upgrade.

2. Create a temporary folder to store the Setup files on your hard drive.

3. Copy the contents of the Win98 folder on your Windows 98 CD-ROM to the temporary folder you just created (the subfolders underneath the Win98 folder are not required for Setup to complete successfully).

4. Reboot. Press F8 at the "Starting Windows95" screen, and choose "Safe Mode Command Prompt Only."

5. Now, switch to the temporary folder containing the Windows 98 Setup files and Type **setup**.

▶ **To copy the setup files locally from within MS-DOS**

1. Make sure you have access to your CD-ROM drive (see above for more information).

2. Free an additional 120 MB of disk space in addition to what Setup normally requires. Setup will typically require 195 MB for a Windows 95 upgrade.

3. Create a temporary folder on the drive with plenty of free space to store the Setup files. To create a temporary directory, switch to that drive letter and type **MD Win98tmp**.

4. Now, switch to the Windows 98 CD-ROM drive and the Win98 directory by typing**: d:\Win98** where "d:/" is the drive letter of your CD-ROM.

5. Copy the Windows 98 Setup files to the temporary directory you just created by typing: **Copy *.* C:\Win98tmp** where "C:\" is the drive you created the temporary folder and "win98tmp" is the temporary directory you created.

6. After all the files are copied, reboot your system and perform a clean boot by bypassing your startup files. (For more information, see "Performing a Clean Boot" later in this chapter.)

7. Switch to the temporary directory to which you just copied the Setup files and start setup by typing **setup**.

Performing a Clean Boot

If Windows 98 Setup is failing, it could be the result of third-party device drivers, utilities, or other programs running. Clean booting your system can fix many of these problems. There are several ways to perform a clean boot to install Windows 98.

▶ **To perform a clean boot using a floppy disk to start your computer**

1. If you have a Windows 98 Startup Disk, boot from that disk. This disk allows the option for loading with or without CD-ROM drivers and is a clean environment for running Setup. For more information see "Using a Windows 98 Startup Disk" in this chapter.

2. If you do not have a Windows 98 Startup Disk, boot from a previous Windows 95 or MS-DOS boot disk. This does not give access to your CD-ROM drivers, but this option can used if you copy the Setup files to your hard disk as described above.

▶ **To perform a clean boot using Windows95 Safe Mode Command Prompt Only**

1. Boot your system and hold F8 at the "Starting Windows 95" screen.

2. Choose **Safe Mode Command Prompt Only**. This does not provide access to your CD-ROM drive, but this option can be used if the Setup files are copied to your hard disk as described above.

Windows 98 Step by Step Boot

There are certain cases where you want load some drivers manually, for example, for troubleshooting purposes or when certain drivers are required by your system. You may also want to manually load your CD-ROM drivers if they were previously loaded by your system.

▶ **To perform a Windows 98 step by step boot**

1. Boot your system and hold the F8 key at the "Starting Windows95" prompt.

2. Choose the **Step by Step** option.

3. Now, say **YES** only to devices you need to. In most cases you always say **YES** to Himem.sys.

Setup Could Not Back Up Your System Files

If you see an error message while Setup is saving your system files, there may not be enough disk space, particularly on compressed disks. You should free up space on the drive you are saving your system files on (the default drive is C) by removing unnecessary files.

If you get a message saying "Setup cannot continue on this system configuration," you may have an older, incompatible disk partition. Before running Setup, you will need to back up your data and then repartition your disk.

Common Setup Errors

This section describes how to diagnose and correct other Setup errors.

For more information, see the Setuplog.txt log file that Setup creates in the root directory of your startup drive.

Setup fails to start.

If Setup fails to start, you should check memory, check for hardware detection conflicts, and check the access to the source for the Windows 98 installation files. Use the following checklist and procedures to find a solution.

- Check the computer for viruses.
- Check for sufficient conventional memory.

  Windows 98 requires 432 KB of conventional memory. If this is not available, check for unnecessary drivers or TSRs, remove them and then try again. You can also run the MS-DOS MemMaker utility to optimize conventional memory.

- Check the RAM configuration in Config.sys.

  For MS-DOS 4.x or earlier, settings should contain the following:

  ```
  device=himem.sys
  ```

  For MS-DOS 5 or later, settings should contain the following:

  ```
  device=himem.sys
  device=emm386.exe noems
  dos=high,umb
  ```

Note The path to these drivers is not specified in the preceding example. If you do not specify the path, you need to copy the drivers to the root of the startup drive. Using emm386 and dos=high,umb enables UMBs, but it is optional.

- Check for adequate XMS memory. Windows 98 requires at least 16 MB of XMS. If you are using MS-DOS 6.*x*, press F4 when you start the computer and the Starting MS-DOS message appears. Choose Step-by-Step Confirmation to verify that Himem.sys is loading. If not, make sure that verify the startup file syntax.

- At the command prompt, use **mem /c /p** to check for free conventional and XMS memory.

- If installing from a compact disc, check access to the drive.

- If installing from the network, check your network connection.

- Remove all extra entries in Config.sys and Autoexec.bat, except those required to start the system and, for a networked computer, to start the network. It is especially helpful to remove any entries related to non-Microsoft disk caching software.

Setup starts, but an error is reported during the installation process.

- Restart Windows 98 Setup and use Safe Recovery.

- Check the Setuplog.txt or Detlog.txt files.

- Verify that all system and networking components function normally. Run virus detection software and **scandisk** (specifying a Thorough Type of Test) to identify system problems that might cause errors.

- Check the content of the error message. Windows 98 Setup errors contain additional information about the condition causing Setup to fail. Examine the device or condition that the error describes.

- Verify that system hardware is compatible. If Setup repeatedly fails, or if you suspect hardware conflicts with the Setup process, verify that the system components are supported. You might want to skip hardware detection. To do this, see "Setup Stops During Hardware Detection" later in this chapter.

- Check for a missing or damaged file. If a driver or system component file is referenced in the error, check to see if the file exists, if it is in the expected location, and if it has the correct file size, date, and version. For more information, see Chapter 27, "General Troubleshooting."

Setup fails when run from floppy disks.

When Setup fails when it is being run from floppy disks, you might see a message asking you to insert a disk in the floppy drive when a disk is already in the drive. Or, you might use the **dir** command to examine a Setup floppy disk and find that it fails or that garbled characters appear on the screen.

To solve this problem, first disable any BIOS-enable virus checking routine. Then check your computer hardware documentation or check with the manufacturer to ensure that the computer's CMOS settings are correct. If changing settings as advised by the manufacturer does not solve the problem, you can use the Drivparm utility.

▶ **To use Drivparm to solve floppy-disk hardware problems**

1. Start the computer using the most basic configuration files possible, loading no additional hardware drivers or other software in Config.sys and Autoexec.bat.

2. Insert a standard disk in drive A or drive B. At the command prompt, switch to that drive and type **dir**.

3. If this works, insert a disk from the Windows 98 floppy disks in the same drive, and type **dir**.

4. If this fails, garbled characters appear on the screen, or subsequent attempts to read the floppy disk fail, insert one of the following statements at the end of Config.sys.

    For a 1.44 MB A drive, add:

    ```
    drivparm=/d:0 /f:7
    ```

    For a 1.44 MB B drive, add:

    ```
    drivparm=/d:1 /f:7
    ```

5. If Config.sys contains an entry for Driver.sys, disable it by adding **rem** before the related command line.

6. Save the Config.sys file, and restart the computer. Then repeat steps 2 and 3. If these steps are successful, leave the **Drivparm** statement in Config.sys so that you can run Windows 98 Setup.

    If this procedure is not successful, the problem is related to the CMOS settings on the computer. For information and assistance, contact your computer manufacturer.

You cannot access the server when installing from the network.

- Verify that the network domain is validating the user account.
- Check the user name, password, and access rights.
- Check basic network functionality.
- Check conventional and XMS memory.
- Check for and remove unnecessary drivers and TSRs.
- If using a login script, check that the login script runs properly.

You may also be installing from a Password Protected share. If this is the case, Setup may present you with a dialog that says there is a problem with your network settings. If you choose to continue (this is not recommended), you should then get the Enter Password dialog and setup should continue.

For more information, see Chapter 14, "Introduction to Networking Configuration."

The network connection fails when you are installing from the network.

- Try to reconnect to the network share.
- If you cannot reconnect, restart the computer, and try again.
- Use another computer on the network to verify the installation server is working.
- Check the basic network connection.

Setup stops during hardware detection.

When Setup stalls during hardware detection, you might need to disable hardware detection for a device or class of devices. Before you do this, wait until at least three minutes have passed with neither disk nor screen activity (that is, the mouse pointer cannot be moved). Some detection routines take long enough that the computer might appear to stop temporarily.

▶ **To skip hardware detection in order to avoid problems**

1. Run Windows 98 Setup from MS-DOS and, if this is not the first attempt to install, select **Safe Recovery**.

2. To disable the specific device detection during Setup, in the **Hardware Detection** dialog box, select the option to specify the hardware devices to detect. Then make sure the check box next to the device is not checked.

Setup cannot communicate with a device.

If Setup cannot communicate with a specific hardware device on the system during installation, a message states that Setup has found a hardware device on your computer that is not responding and prompts you to try this device again. For persistent problems, the message provides instructions on how to exit Setup and restart the computer.

This error message can be caused by one of the following:

- The network has stopped responding.
- A CD-ROM drive has stopped responding.
- A floppy disk drive has stopped responding.
- Setup can no longer access the hard drive to complete the installation process.

Follow the recommendation in the message to turn off the computer, turn it back on, and rerun Setup with Safe Recovery. If the problem persists, identify the problem from the preceding list and correct it.

Problems occur during the file-copying phase of Setup.

If this occurs, exit Setup, restart your computer, and rerun Setup. When prompted, select the **Safe Recovery** option and click **Continue**. The installation process should complete successfully.

If your computer stalls after all files have been copied, or if you receive an error at this point, it might be due to virus-protection software. Some computers have virus protection built into the ROM BIOS. You should disable the virus protection software or run your computer's configuration program to disable virus checking and then restart Setup. Select the **Safe Recovery** option, and the installation process should complete successfully.

An "Incorrect MS-DOS Version" error message appears.

This error can occur when starting Setup from MS-DOS if you are using the 386MAX software utility. If this error occurs, temporarily disable the 386MAX commands from the startup files, and then run Setup again.

A "Standard Mode: Fault in MS-DOS Extender" error message appears.

When running Windows 98 Setup from MS-DOS you might receive this error, indicating there might be a conflict in the upper memory region. To resolve this, either disable UMBs or remove EMM386 statements from Config.sys and rerun Setup.

A "Cannot Open File *.INF" error message appears.

If you receive an error that states that an INF file cannot be opened, you might need to free memory by disabling SMARTDrive in Autoexec.bat, or by closing any applications running in Windows.

Setup requests a new source path.

If this occurs, check the file source (the network drive or the CD-ROM drive).

❑   In My Computer, double-click the CD-ROM drive, and verify that the drive and files are accessible by viewing directories and loading readable text files.

– Or –

At the MS-DOS command prompt, use the **dir** and **type** commands to verify that the drive and files are accessible by viewing directories and loading readable text files.

❑   If the floppy disk drive is inaccessible, try reading a different disk. If that does not work, shut down and restart the computer. Check CMOS settings for the floppy disk drive using the hardware manufacturer's diagnostic routine (consult your hardware documentation).

❑   If installing from a compact disc, verify that MSCDEX and the CD-ROM drivers are loaded and configured properly.

Setup is unable to find a valid boot partition.

A valid MS-DOS partition must exist in order for Setup to install Windows 98. If Windows 98 Setup is unable to find a valid boot partition during installation, it displays an error message. If you receive an error message, there might be an actual partition error, but it is more likely that disk compression software or network components are mapping over the boot drive. This might occur if you are mapping a network drive to E, but E is the hidden host drive for your disk compression software, or you are using a LANtastic network and drive C is being mapped or shared.

▶ **To resolve the invalid partition error:**

- Verify the drive is not mapped over (or logically remapped).

- Verify a valid, active partition using Fdisk. If no valid partition exists, take appropriate drive or data recovery efforts. If no active partition exists, use Fdisk to mark an appropriate partition as active.

- Remove interfering drivers from the startup configuration files, and run Setup again.

- If you are using disk compression software, ensure that none of your mapped network drive letters conflict with the host drive for disk compression.

Setup finds insufficient disk space.

If Setup does not find sufficient space to install Windows 98, check for space on the destination and boot drives, and if you are using compression, check actual free space.

Setup fails automated installation from Msbatch.inf.

If the automated installation fails, check the following:

❏ Verify the network connection if source files are on the network.

❏ Check error messages, if any.

❏ Check the Msbatch.inf file contents and syntax.

❏ Check the network validation of user logon.

❏ Check for enough memory.

❏ Check for and remove unnecessary drivers and TSRs.

❏ If using a logon script, verify that the script ran properly.

Troubleshooting Startup Errors

This section describes specific conditions that might interfere with starting a Windows 98 computer and how to fix them.

In general, for system startup problems, the first problem-solving method is to start Windows 98 in Safe Mode. For information about how to start in Safe Mode and use Bootlog.txt for troubleshooting, see Chapter 27, "General Troubleshooting."

Windows 98 stalls during the first restart after installation.

Usually this occurs because of legacy hardware that was configured incorrectly before Windows 98 was installed. Remove settings for hardware services in Config.sys and Autoexec.bat. Also, ensure that any small computer system interface (SCSI) devices are terminated correctly. You might also need to disable the Industry Standard Architecture (ISA) enumerator. This software detects a new type of adapter that can be configured from the operating system. The detection sequence requires the ISA enumerator for I/O processes on some ports. Although every effort has been made to avoid ports commonly in use, you might have hardware that is also trying to use these I/O ports.

▶ **To disable the ISA enumerator**

- Remove the following line from the [386Enh] section of System.ini:

```
device = ISAPNP.386
```

A bad or missing file error occurs on startup.

If you receive a "Bad or missing *filename*" message when the system is starting (where *filename* might contain Himem.sys, Ifshlp.sys, and so on), do the following:

- Check the syntax of the entry in Config.sys or other startup file.
- Verify the existence, location, version, and integrity of the file.

If the file name to which the message refers is a device driver the computer needs for accessing the drive where Windows 98 is installed, move the **device=** line that contains the device driver to the beginning of Config.sys to allow access to the drive when Config.sys tries to load files from the Windows directory.

Windows 98 Has Damaged or Missing Core Files.

When Windows 98 loads, it counts on key files being available and undamaged. If a system file is damaged or missing, it might prevent loading or normal operation. If Vmm32.vxd or other core files are missing or damaged, you might need to run Windows 98 Setup and select the **Verify** option in **Safe Recovery** to replace the files.

BIOS or a BIOS setting is incompatible.

A ROM BIOS setting might prevent Windows 98 from installing or loading, because some computers have a feature that prevents applications from writing to the boot sector. This is usually in the form of anti-virus protection set through your computer's CMOS. If this is enabled, Windows 98 cannot complete the installation or cannot start properly.

If boot sector protection is enabled in the computer's BIOS, one of the following symptoms occurs:

- Windows 98 Setup stalls.

- Windows 98 stalls while starting.

- The anti-virus software prompts you to overwrite the boot sector. Choosing **Yes** might allow you to complete the Setup procedure, but Windows 98 stalls when it attempts to load.

To correct this problem, disable the Boot Sector protection feature through your computer's CMOS, then reinstall Windows 98. For information about disabling this feature, consult your hardware documentation or service center.

A VxD error returns you to the command prompt.

If a virtual device driver (VxD) is missing or damaged, Windows 98 displays an error message that indicates which VxD is involved. If the VxD is critical to the operation of Windows 98, then Windows 98 does not start and the screen displays the command prompt. You might need to run Windows 98 Setup and select Verify or Safe Recovery to replace the missing VxD.

You can selectively override a VxD that is included within Vmm32.vxd. If the same VxD is loaded twice, the second instance intercepts all the calls to that particular VxD. There are two ways to override this:

- Copy the related VXD file into the Windows System\Vmm32 directory.

- Edit System.ini to add the entry **device=** *filename*.**vxd** in the [386enh] section.

You cannot use dual boot to run a previous operating system.

To take advantage of the dual-boot support in Windows 98, you cannot install Windows 98 into an existing Windows 3.*x* directory, and the value **BootMulti=1** must be defined in the Windows 98 version of Msdos.sys.

Versions of MS-DOS earlier than 5.0 do not support Windows 98 dual-boot functionality. To return to your previous operating system, you have to remove Windows 98 and reinstall your previous operating system, as described earlier in this chapter.

You can *not* dual boot between Windows95 and Windows 98 (unless you have a third-party boot manager installed).

A "Previous MS-DOS Files Not Found" message appears.

When trying to dual-boot to the previous version of MS-DOS, you might receive an error message stating that your previous MS-DOS files were not found. It is probable that either the files are missing, or that your previous version of MS-DOS was not version 5.0 or later.

You must have MS-DOS 5.0 or later in order to start to a previous version of MS-DOS. Any version of MS-DOS earlier than 5.0 looks for the first three sectors of the Io.sys file in the first three sectors of the data area of the drive. In MS-DOS 5.0 or later, Io.sys is designed to be located outside the first three sectors of a drive's data area. In this situation, the only way to start to a version of MS-DOS prior to 5.0 is from a startup floppy disk.

Drivers, such as Dblspace.sys, that are loaded when you start the computer using the earlier version of MS-DOS might not be available.

Required real-mode drivers are missing or damaged.

The previous operating system might have required certain real-mode drivers (compression, partitioning, hard disk drivers, and so on), and does not start correctly without them.

- At system startup, press F8 and select **Step-by-Step Confirmation** to verify the correct loading of all specified drivers.

- Verify that any drivers required to support your hardware are all specified in the appropriate startup file.

Windows 98 does not recognize a device.

In some cases, Windows 98 is unable to recognize an installed device, and the device resources are unavailable to Windows 98. If Windows 98 does not recognize an installed device, remove it in Device Manager, and reinstall it by using the Add New Hardware option in Control Panel. You can also use Device Manager to check resource conflicts. For information, see Chapter 24, "Device Management." Or see the hardware conflict troubleshooting information in Help.

Installing drivers causes Windows 98 system startup to fail.

If you try to install drivers for Windows 3.x from other vendors over Windows 98 (such as sound or video drivers), running the provided installation program can cause Windows 98 to fail to start or operate correctly.

▶ **To recover, when using a device that is supported by Windows 98**

1. Remove all entries in System.ini that were added by the installation software from another vendor.

2. Delete the device in Device Manager in the **System** properties, as described in Chapter 24, "Device Management."

3. Shut down and restart Windows 98.

4. Use the Add New Hardware option in Control Panel to reinstall the device by using the Windows 98 drivers.

The wrong applications run after Windows 98 starts.

- In Windows Explorer, double-click the Windows Start Menu\Programs \StartUp directory, and then delete any items that you do not want to run when Windows 98 starts.

- If the programs that are running do not appear in the Start Menu folder in Windows Explorer, run Registry Editor and find this key:

```
HKey_Current_User\Software\Microsoft\Windows\CurrentVersion
\Explorer\Shell Folders
```

The value of **Startup=** should be *Windows***Start Menu\Program\StartUp**, where *Windows* is the drive and directory containing the Windows 98 files.

You experience interoperability problems with WinSock 2.0.

If you experience interoperability problems with Windows Sockets 2.0 (WinSock 2.0) and are unable to work around the problem, uninstall WinSock 2.0 to restore your WinSock 1.1 configuration. To uninstall WinSock 2.0, go to Control Panel and double-click Add/Remove Programs. On the **Install/Uninstall** tab, click **Restore WinSock 1.*x* configuration**, and then click **Add/Remove**. Click **Yes** when prompted if you want to restore your original configuration.

For more information about WinSock 2.0, WinSock 1.1, and third-party TCP/IP stack issues, see "Windows Sockets 2.0 and Third-Party TCP/IP Stack Installations" later in this chapter.

Solving interoperability problems with WinSock 2.0.

During setup, all WinSock 1.1 components are backed up. In the unlikely event that you experience interoperability problems with WinSock 2.0 and are unable to work around the problem, you can uninstall WinSock 2.0. This restores your WinSock 1.1 configuration.

When you uninstall WinSock 2.0 only the WinSock 2.0 related files are removed. The Windows 98 version of Microsoft TCP/IP and IPX/SPX stacks stay installed and will run with WinSock 1.1.

Note WinSock 1.1 is backed up only during the first time you install Windows 98. Subsequent installations of Windows 98 will not back up your WinSock configuration. If you uninstall WinSock 2.0 and want to restore it on your computer, you must reinstall Windows 98.

▶ **To uninstall WinSock 2.0 and restore WinSock 1.1**

1. In Control Panel, double-click Add/Remove Programs.

2. On the **Install/Uninstall** tab, click **Restore WinSock 1.x configuration**, then click **Add/Remove**.

3. Click **Yes** when prompted if you want to restore your original configuration.

Windows Sockets 2.0 and Third-Party TCP/IP Stack Installations

If you have a third-party TCP/IP stack installed, neither Windows Sockets 2.0 (WinSock 2.0) nor the Microsoft TCP/IP stack can be installed.

When Windows 98 Setup attempts to install the Microsoft TCP/IP stack. However, if your original Windows 95 configuration included a third-party WinSock 1.1 stack, the Microsoft TCP/IP stack will not install, nor will WinSock 2.0, which is implemented as part of the TCP/IP stack.

If you want WinSock 2.0, you must remove the third-party TCP/IP stack, then reinstall Microsoft TCP/IP (not Windows 98).

If you want to install Windows Sockets 2.0 you need to do the following:

1. Uninstall the third-party TCP/IP stack.

2. Reinstall Microsoft TCP/IP manually from the Network icon in Control Panel.

Some third-party TCP/IP stacks cannot be installed after Windows 98 Setup due to conflicts with Windows Sockets 2.0, which is installed with Microsoft TCP/IP. If you want to use a third-party TCP/IP stack with Windows 98, you should install it before running Windows 98 Setup. In almost all cases, this ensures that your third-party stack is successfully upgraded. If you do not do install the stack before running Setup, you can try restoring Windows Sockets 1.1, then installing the third-party TCP/IP stack, however, this method does not always work.

For more information about the WinSock 2.0 APIs and for information on how to install the drivers, see the *Microsoft Platform Developer's Kit*.

P A R T   2

System Configuration

C H A P T E R   6

Configuring the Active Desktop and Active Channels

6

This chapter describes how to effectively utilize the new Microsoft Windows 98 Active Desktop and Active Channel ("push") technologies in a corporate network or intranet environment. Network and workgroup administrators, and corporate intranet site authors and Webmasters, can tailor the Active Desktop toolbars, Active Desktop items, screen savers, and Channel bar to a workgroup's specific application and document needs. By effectively managing Favorites, Active Channels, and Webcasting, you can ensure that the most current information gets to the people who need it most.

In This Chapter

See Also

- For information about configuring the Microsoft Internet Explorer browsing software, see Chapter 20, "Internet Access and Tools."

Overview of Webcasting with the Active Desktop and Active Channels

This section presents an overview of Webcasting with the Active Desktop and Active Channels in a corporate network or intranet environment. It describes each of the elements that a network or workgroup administrator can configure, and compares how you might use each element to maximize your workgroup's access to the appropriate applications and information.

Webcasting on Corporate Intranets

Windows 98 extends the concept of Webcasting to the corporate intranet. *Webcasting* is a generic term referring to the automated delivery of personalized and up-to-date information via the Internet or a corporate intranet. By utilizing Webcasting through the Active Desktop and Active Channels, you can make it easier for users to find, receive, and organize the information and applications that they need. The Active Desktop provides a common, customizable user interface for organizing files, Web sites, and applications for individual users or workgroups. The integration of Windows 98 with the Internet Explorer 4 browsing software, coupled with the power of Active Channels to push and pull content from intranet or Web sites, provides true Web integration with desktops and a powerful and customizable information delivery architecture. Figure 6.1 illustrates the concept of Webcasting in a corporate intranet.

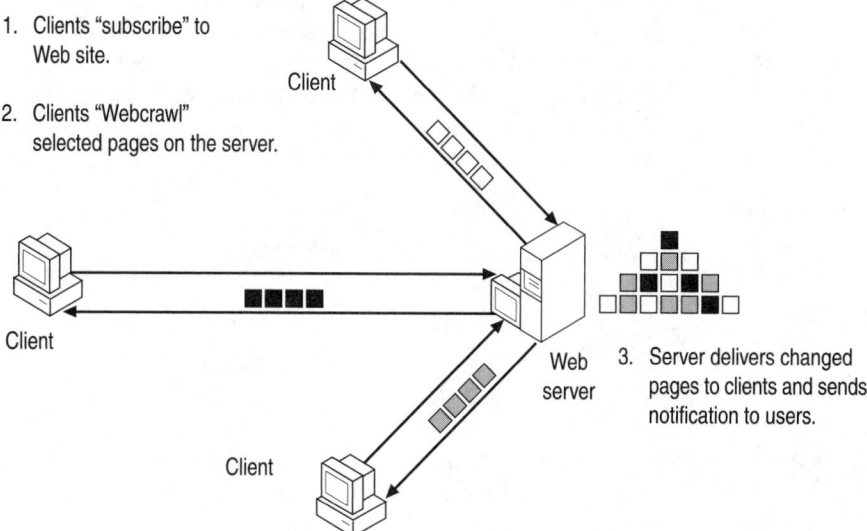

1. Clients "subscribe" to Web site.

2. Clients "Webcrawl" selected pages on the server.

Client

Client

Web server

3. Server delivers changed pages to clients and sends notification to users.

Client

Figure 6.1   Overview of Webcasting

You can Webcast Active Desktop configurations, as well as Active Channel content, applications and software updates, and content from other internal and external Web sites, to specific users or workgroups on an ongoing basis. This ensures that users and workgroups always have the latest configurations, applications, and information specific to their needs.

About the Active Desktop

The *Active Desktop* in Windows 98 integrates the Windows desktop with the Internet Explorer browsing software to provide a single metaphor for accessing content or applications, whether on a local computer, a corporate intranet, or the World Wide Web (WWW). The Active Desktop makes it easier for users to access favorite applications, files, folders, and Web sites. It also lets network and workgroup administrators create customized Active Desktop configurations specific to the needs of individuals or workgroups. Figure 6.2 shows an example of an Active Desktop.

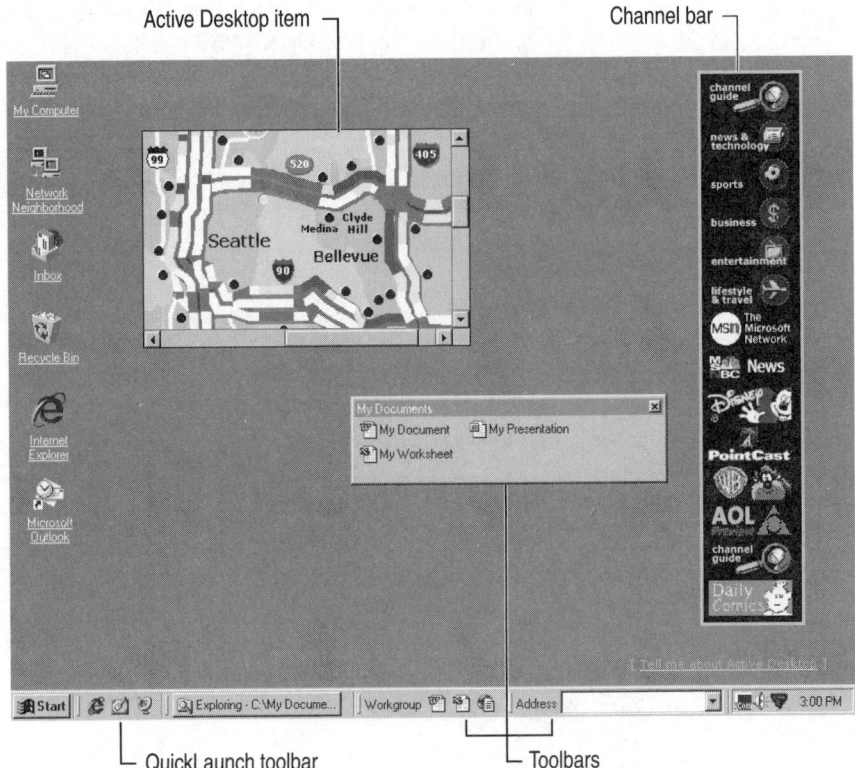

Figure 6.2   The Active Desktop

Using the Active Desktop, you can:

- Customize the **Start**, **Programs**, and **Favorites** menus.

- Create new toolbars and customize the default Windows 98 toolbars for accessing user-specific or workgroup-specific applications, files, and Web sites.

- Add HTML pages or graphics directly to the Active Desktop as wallpaper or Active Desktop items.
- Customize folders to be viewed as Web pages.

About Active Channels

An *Active Channel* is a Web site that automatically delivers content to a user's computer on a regular schedule. By effectively utilizing Active Channel technology, as well as Hypertext Markup Language (HTML)–based forms, Dynamic HTML, ActiveX™ controls, Distributed Component Object Model (DCOM) applications, and Java applets, you can vastly improve how your workgroup or company disseminates information and applications. You can also create software distribution channels and use automatic browser configuration to ensure that your users or workgroup always has the latest software updates and Active Desktop configurations.

Figure 6.3 provides an overview of how Active Channel content is delivered to users subscribed to an Active Channel Web site.

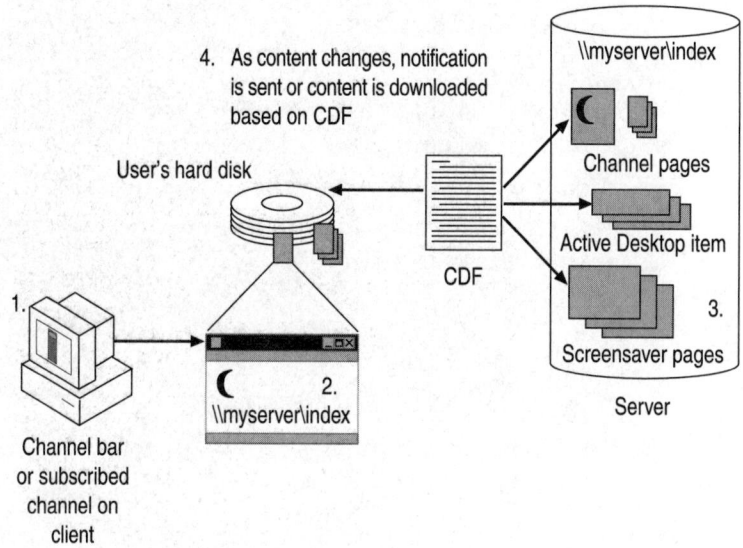

Figure 6.3   Overview of Active Channel delivery

A user "subscribes" to an Active Channel Web site by clicking a hyperlink to a *Channel Definition Format* (CDF) file, which contains subscription information about that channel. The CDF file is copied from the Active Channel server to the user's computer, and the channel is added to the user's Favorites and Channels in the Internet Explorer browsing software. The channel logo is also added to the Channel bar on the user's Active Desktop.

When users subscribe to a Web site as an Active Channel, they can browse the site offline, view an Active Channel Web page as an Active Desktop item, and display screen savers created by Active Channel authors. Whenever the content of the Active Channel is updated, subscribed users either receive e-mail notification that may include the changed pages, or download the changed pages automatically according to the subscription schedule. E-mail notification is delivered at the time of the subscription update. The subscription schedule is specified by the Active Channel Web site author in the CDF file but can be modified by users.

In a corporate intranet, an Active Channel Web site author or administrator creates a CDF file that specifies:

- What content should be delivered to subscribed users.
- How that content is to be used (for example, as a *channel item*, or "page" in the channel, as a screen saver, or as an Active Desktop item) and how updates are to be delivered (for example, by sending e-mail notification or by downloading the content directly to the user's computer).
- When and how often the user's computer should connect to the site to receive notification of updates or download updated content.

Network and workgroup administrators can then customize and deploy Active Channel subscriptions, Active Desktop items, Channel bars, and channel screen savers for specific users or workgroups. This ensures that your users or workgroups always have the latest information at their fingertips.

For information about configuring the Internet Explorer browsing software, see Chapter 20, "Internet Access and Tools."

For information about implementing distributed applications with DCOM, see Chapter 25, "Application Support."

Configuring the Active Desktop

This section describes each element of the Active Desktop that you can configure. It includes discussions of the possible uses in a workgroup environment for each element that you might want to customize, and presents procedures for doing so.

Once you have completed this section and created Active Desktop configurations for specific users or workgroups, you can deploy, maintain, and update them using the Internet Explorer 4 Administration Kit (IEAK) Profile Manager. You can also disable changes to Active Desktop configurations using system policies.

For information about installing, deploying, and updating customized Active Desktop and Active Channel configurations using the IEAK Profile Manager, see "Implementing Active Desktop and Active Channel Configurations" later in this chapter. For information about using system policies, see Chapter 8, "System Policies."

Considerations for Configuring the Active Desktop

By configuring a custom Active Desktop configuration for a workgroup and deploying it using the IEAK Profile Manager, you can ensure that each member of the team uses an identical desktop configuration. You can also control the extent to which specific users or workgroups can alter different elements of their Active Desktop configurations.

This means that, throughout the workgroup, each user has the same toolbars and taskbars, **Start** and **Programs** menus, wallpaper, and so on. Each user will access the same files, applications, and Web sites in the same way. This can substantially reduce the time and effort spent in training new team members. If you decide to use automatic deployment of Active Desktop configurations, you can also dramatically reduce the cost of setting up and configuring workgroup client computers.

Before you begin configuring and deploying Active Desktop configurations for your workgroup, you should consider the following:

Which files, applications, and Web sites (internal or external) does your workgroup need to access the most often?

Compile a list of these file names, paths to local or network applications, and Uniform Resource Locators (URLs). You will need this list when you are creating the default Active Desktop configuration for your workgroup.

Where should each of these elements live in your Active Desktop configuration?

Do you want to create custom **Start** and **Programs** menus for your workgroup? Do you want to add an application to the QuickLaunch toolbar, or would it be better to create a new toolbar containing all of your workgroup's most frequently used applications? Do you want to place most-visited URLs on the Favorites list, on a new toolbar, on the Channel bar, or on the Active Desktop as Active Desktop items or wallpaper?

For information about subscribing to Web sites using Favorites and Active Channels, see "Configuring Active Channels and Favorites" later in this chapter.

How will you deploy Active Desktop configurations?

If you want to deploy new Active Desktop configurations after setup, you can use the IEAK Profile Manager to deploy the latest configuration to each user at logon or through scheduled updates.

Do you want to let users customize their Active Desktop configurations?

Using the IEAK Profile Manager, you can control the extent to which individual users can customize their Active Desktops. For example, do you want to let users add their own URLs to a custom toolbar or as Active Desktop items? Consider the degree to which you want to permit users to customize their Active Desktops before you configure or deploy one.

Configuring the Start and Programs Menus

Windows 98 simplifies the process of customizing the contents of the **Start** menu (the menu that appears when a user clicks the **Start** button on the taskbar) and the **Programs** menu (the cascading menu of program groups and applications that appears when a user clicks the **Start** button and then points to **Programs**).

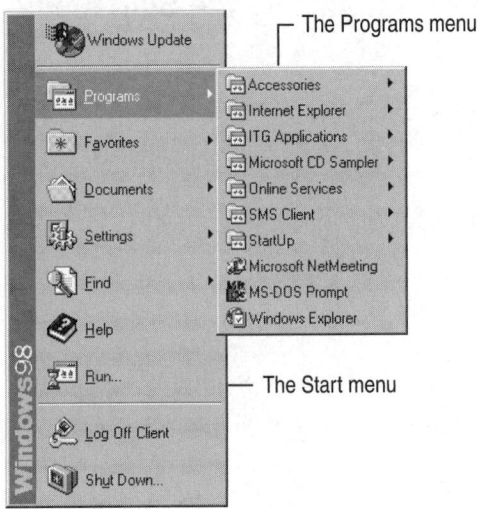

Considerations for Customizing the Start and Programs Menus

When customizing the **Start** and **Programs** menus, you should consider the following:

- Add the folders, documents, and applications that your workgroup uses most frequently to the **Start** menu. You also might want to add some of these items to the Windows taskbar, the QuickLaunch toolbar, or to new toolbars that you create.

- Add all of your workgroup's custom program groups and applications to the **Programs** menu. Whenever a Windows 95 or Windows 98–compatible application is installed on a computer, Windows creates a program group for that application on the **Programs** menu. However, you might want to reorganize the **Programs** menu and add custom program groups to suit the specific needs of your workgroup. For example, you might want to create a program group called "Inventory" that contains only the inventory applications specific to your workgroup.

- If your workgroup accesses distributed applications that use the Distributed Component Object Model (DCOM), you might want to customize application shortcuts to point to the appropriate local component or to a component on a network server.

Procedures for Customizing the Start Menu

In Windows 98, you can add and remove items from the top of the **Start** menu.

▶ **To add an item to the top section of the Start menu**

- Drag the item's icon to the **Start** button on the taskbar.

▶ **To remove an item from the top section of the Start menu**

- Click the **Start** button, right-click the item you want to remove, and then click **Delete** on the shortcut menu.

▶ **To reorder the items in the top section of the Start menu**

- Click the **Start** button, click the item that you want to move, and then drag it to the new location.

▶ **To rename an item in the top section of the Start menu**

1. Click the **Start** button, and then point to **Settings**.
2. Click **Taskbar & Start Menu**, and then click the **Start Menu Programs** tab.
3. Click **Advanced**.
4. Right-click the item you want to rename, and then click **Rename**.
5. Type the new name for the item.

Customizing the Programs Menu

The folders that appear on the **Programs** menu are arranged alphabetically by default. In Windows 98, you can add, remove, and reorder items.

▶ **To add or remove items from the Programs menu**

1. Click the **Start** button, point to **Settings**, and then click **Taskbar & Start Menu**.

2. Click the **Start Menu Programs** tab, and then do one of the following:

   ▪ To add an item, click **Add**, and then follow the wizard's instructions.

   ▪ To remove an item, click **Remove**, select the item you want to remove, and then click **Remove**.

▶ **To reorder items on the Programs menu**

1. Click the **Start** button, and then point to **Programs**.

2. On the **Programs** submenu, click the item you want to move, and then drag it to the new location.

Configuring the Taskbar and Toolbars

In Windows 98, you can simplify a user's or workgroup's access to files, applications, and URLs by:

▪ Customizing the QuickLaunch toolbar.

▪ Customizing the default Windows taskbar.

▪ Creating new toolbars.

▪ Adding floating toolbars to the Active Desktop.

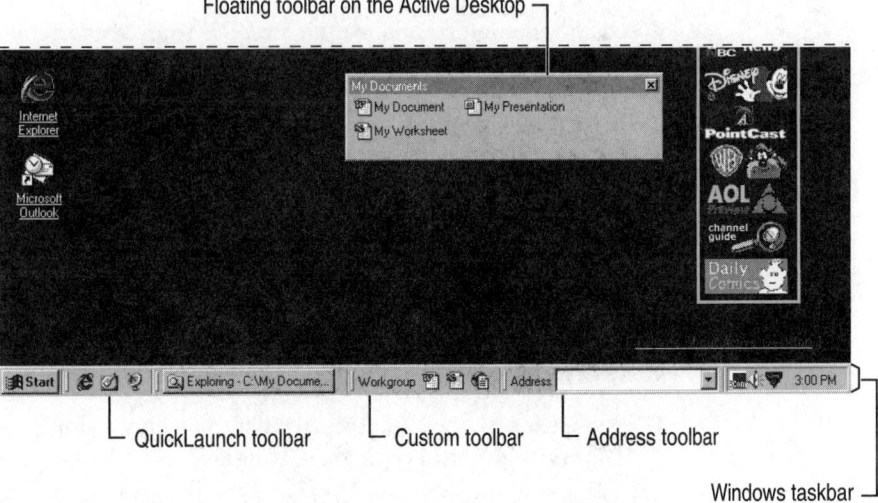

Considerations for Customizing the Taskbar and Toolbars

When customizing the Windows taskbar or QuickLaunch toolbar, or creating new custom toolbars, you should consider the following:

- Decide which files, folders, applications, and URLs your workgroup uses most frequently.

- Determine the best method of presentation for your workgroup. For example, if your workgroup consists of writers working on a specific Microsoft Word document, you might want to create a shortcut to Microsoft Word or to that document on the QuickLaunch toolbar. If your workgroup regularly accesses a folder of related files, applications, or URLs, you might want to create a toolbar containing the contents of that folder and place it on the Windows taskbar or as a floating toolbar on the Active Desktop.

- Before you create new toolbars, you should group the files, applications, and URLs that your workgroup uses most frequently into one or more appropriately-named folders. A new toolbar consists of the contents of a folder on a local or network drive; Windows 98 uses the folder name for the toolbar name.

Procedures for Customizing the Taskbar and Toolbars

Use the following procedures to customize the Windows taskbar and QuickLaunch toolbar, to create new toolbars, and to remove a folder or toolbar from the Windows taskbar.

▶ **To create a new toolbar on the default Windows taskbar**

- Drag a file, folder, application, or URL from My Computer or Windows Explorer to the taskbar to create a new toolbar.

▶ **To customize the Windows 98 QuickLaunch toolbar**

- Drag a file, folder, application, or URL from My Computer or Windows Explorer to the QuickLaunch toolbar.

▶ **To create a new toolbar**

You create a new toolbar using any existing folder. The new toolbar will contain icons representing the contents of that folder—files, subfolders, applications, and URLs. The name of the toolbar will be the same as the name of the folder.

1. Right-click on the Windows taskbar to display a shortcut menu, point to **Toolbars,** and then click **New Toolbar.**

2. In the **New Toolbar** dialog box, select the folder from which you want to create a toolbar, and then click **OK**. Windows 98 adds the folder as a new toolbar, named for that folder, to the Windows taskbar.

Tip The easiest way to create a new toolbar on the Windows taskbar is to drag a folder from My Computer or Windows Explorer onto the taskbar. If you want to add the new toolbar as a floating toolbar on the Active Desktop, drag the toolbar from the taskbar to the Active Desktop.

▶ **To add a floating toolbar to the Active Desktop**

- Drag the toolbar from the Windows taskbar to the background of the Active Desktop.

▶ **To add a toolbar to the edge of the Active Desktop**

- Drag a folder from My Computer or Windows Explorer to any edge of the Active Desktop.

▶ **To remove a folder or toolbar from the Windows taskbar**

- On the Windows taskbar, right-click the toolbar name to display the shortcut menu, and then click **Close**.

Using an HTML Page as Wallpaper

You can display an HTML page as the wallpaper on the Active Desktop. The HTML page can be on your local computer or on a network drive, but it cannot point to a URL on your intranet or on the World Wide Web.

For example, you might set the desktop wallpaper to your workgroup's home page, so that users can instantly access the latest information. If a user clicks a hyperlink on an HTML wallpaper page, the destination of the hyperlink opens in the Internet Explorer browsing window.

Note The Internet Explorer browsing software does not support the use of HTML pages that contain framesets as wallpaper.

▶ **To use an HTML page as the default Active Desktop wallpaper**

1. Right-click on the Active Desktop to display a shortcut menu, and then click **Properties**.

2. Click the **Web** tab, and then select the **View my Active Desktop as a web page** check box.

3. Click the **Background** tab, click **Browse**, and then browse to or type the path of the HTML page you want to use.

Setting Your Workgroup's Home Page in the Internet Explorer Browsing Software

In configuring your workgroup's Active Desktops, you probably want to specify the default Internet Explorer browsing software home page—the first page displayed when a user starts the Internet Explorer browsing software or clicks the **Home** button on a toolbar—that is the most appropriate for your workgroup. For example, you might want to use your workgroup's or company's intranet home page.

To specify the default home page in the Internet Explorer browsing software, browse to the appropriate home page for your workgroup, and then on the **View** menu, click **Internet Options**. On the **General** tab, click **Use Current**.

If you use the IEAK Profile Manager to deploy your Active Desktop configuration, you can import the default home page using the **Start and Search Page** item under **Wizard Settings**.

Using Graphics, HTML Pages, and Explorer Windows as Active Desktop Items

In Windows 98, you can add an HTML page, a Joint Photographic Experts Group (JPEG) or Graphics Interchange Format (GIF) graphic file, or an Explorer window to a local or network resource as an item on the Active Desktop. In a corporate intranet, for example, you might want to add a frequently-used HTML form, such as a sales order, for faster access by sales personnel. You might add an animated GIF file of your corporate logo to make it easier for users to copy and paste the logo into letters, spreadsheets, or Web pages. You might want to simplify access to a workgroup's share on a network server by adding it to their Active Desktops as an Explorer window.

The Microsoft Active Desktop Gallery on the World Wide Web contains unique Active Desktop items, such as the Microsoft Investor Ticker (shown in Figure 6.4) and Java clocks, that you can download for free. To use any of these items, visit the Active Desktop Gallery Web site at **http://www.microsoft.com/ie/ie40/gallery/**.

Figure 6.4   The Microsoft Investor Ticker Active Desktop item

You can also add Active Desktop items that display dynamic, regularly-updated content supplied by traditional and Active Channel Web sites. For information about using traditional or Active Channel Web sites as Active Desktop items, see "Using Active Channels and Web Sites as Active Desktop Items," later in this chapter.

For information about creating Active Channel Web sites on your intranet that deliver content as Active Desktop items, see "Creating and Managing Active Channels on Your Intranet" later in this chapter.

▶ **To add an Active Desktop item to the Active Desktop**

1. Right-click on the Active Desktop to display a shortcut menu, and then click **Properties**.

2. Click the **Web** tab, and then select the **View my Active Desktop as a web page** check box.

3. Click **New**.

4. If you want to select an item from the Microsoft Active Desktop Gallery, click **Yes**, and then select the item. Otherwise, click **No**, and then type or browse the path to the HTML page, graphic file, or directory that you want to display as an Active Desktop item.

Customizing Folders

Windows 98 gives you greater control over the appearance of folders. Using the new **Folder Options** dialog box, you can:

- Specify whether folders should be displayed in the classic Windows 95 style, in the new Windows 98 Web style (using a single-click to launch files and applications), or using a combination of custom settings. For example, you could define custom settings to use Web style and choose to disable the single-click option.

- Specify advanced settings, such as whether to show the **Map Network Drive** button on the toolbar, show file extensions, or show pop-up descriptions for folders.

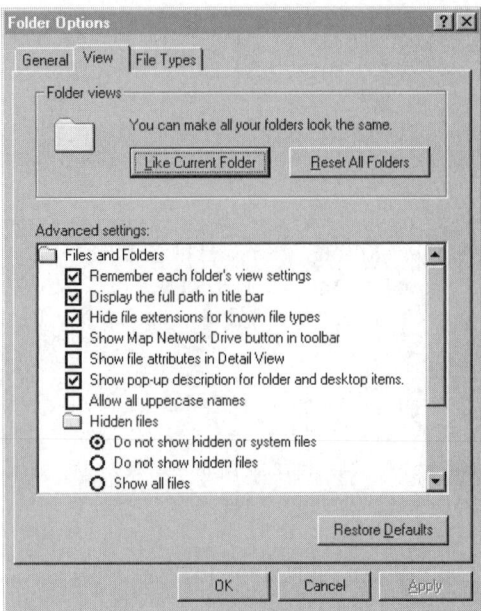

New to Windows 98, the Customize this Folder Wizard lets you display a background image for a folder, or create an HTML document to view the folder as a Web page.

Tip If you enable thumbnail views of folders in Web view of My Documents or Windows Explorer, your users can see thumbnail images of any Microsoft Office 97 files in those folders. To utilize thumbnail views for a folder, you must select the **Enable thumbnail view** check box on the **General** tab of that folder's **Properties** sheet. Users creating Office 97 documents should always select the **Save Preview Picture** check box on a document's **Properties** sheet.

▶ **To customize the display style of all folders**

1. In My Computer or Windows Explorer, click the **View** menu, and then click **Folder Options**.

2. Click the **General** tab of the **Folder Options** dialog box, and then select a display style for folders.

▶ **To customize advanced settings for viewing all folders**

1. In My Computer or Windows Explorer, click the **View** menu, and then click **Folder Options**.

2. Click the **View** tab of the **Folder Options** dialog box, and then select the options that you want for viewing folders.

▶ **To redirect the default folder for My Documents**

1. Right-click the My Documents folder on your Active Desktop, and then click **Properties**.

2. Type or browse to the target folder you want to use, and then click **OK**.

   When you initially save a new file in any Windows-based application, the specified target folder will be used as the default instead of the C:\My Documents folder, and when you open My Documents on your Active Desktop, it will open the new folder you have designated.

Maximizing Pop-up Descriptions with Microsoft Office 97

If your workgroup uses Microsoft Office 97, pop-up descriptions in Windows 98 can help your users find documents more quickly. When a user rests the mouse pointer over a file icon in Windows Explorer or My Computer, a pop-up description of that file appears. If the file was created using a Microsoft Office 97 application, such as Microsoft Word, the pop-up description is actually the content of the **Author** and **Subject** fields in the **Summary** tab of the file's **Properties**.

By recommending to your users that they always specify the author and subject of an Office 97 document, you can effectively utilize pop-up descriptions to make it faster and easier for users to find the files they need.

To enable pop-up descriptions for your users or workgroup, follow the procedure "To customize advanced settings for viewing all folders" (earlier in this chapter) and then select the **Show pop-up description for folder and desktop items** check box.

▶ **To display a background image or create an HTML page for a folder**

1. In My Computer or Windows Explorer, select the folder that you want to customize, and then on the **View** menu, click **Customize this Folder**.

2. Use the Customize this Folder Wizard to display a background image for the folder or to create an HTML document based on the standard template defined by Folder.htt. The HTML document will be displayed when the folder is viewed as a Web page.

   You can use this feature to customize the view your users have of a particular folder. For instance, you can display only certain files or none of them, and instead display informative text or even hyperlinks.

For more information about customizing folders, look up **folders** in the Windows 98 online Help index.

Configuring Active Channels and Favorites

This section describes the most effective methods of configuring your users' or workgroup's computers to receive information and updates from subscribed Web sites and Active Channel Web sites.

Once you have created custom Active Channel, subscriptions, and Favorites configurations for specific users or workgroups, you can deploy them using the IEAK Profile Manager.

For information about creating and deploying customized Active Desktop and Active Channel configurations in a corporate intranet, see "Implementing Active Desktop and Active Channel Configurations" later in this chapter.

For information about creating and managing Active Channels on your corporate intranet, see "Creating and Managing Active Channels on Your Intranet" later in this chapter.

Understanding Active Channels and Favorites

You can ensure that your users or workgroup consistently receive the latest information and applications from both internal and external Web sites by configuring Favorites and access to Active Channels.

About Active Channels

An Active Channel is an internal or external Web site that has been configured by the Web site author using a Channel Definition Format (CDF) file. The CDF file specifies the content of the Active Channel (the Active Channel pages) and when and how that content should be delivered to the user.

When a user subscribes to an Active Channel Web site, the CDF file and specified Active Channel content are downloaded to the user's computer. The user can customize the subscription options specified by the CDF file or accept the specifications set by the Active Channel Web site author. The Active Channel Web site is then added to the user's Favorites folder, and a channel logo is added to the Channel bar.

Active Channels on the Active Desktop

In Windows 98, the Active Desktop contains a Channel bar, which displays logos for each subscribed Active Channel.

When a user clicks an Active Channel logo on the Channel bar, that channel is displayed in a full-screen browsing window. The Active Channel Web pages are displayed in the right-hand portion of the window. The left-hand portion of the window displays the Channel bar, expanded to show a detailed map of the selected Active Channel Web site.

According to the subscription for the Active Channel, the user's computer regularly connects to the Active Channel Web site to check for, and optionally download, updated content.

The user may also receive notification of changes by e-mail. Once the user has manually or automatically downloaded the updated content, he or she can browse the Active Channel offline.

Depending on the contents of the CDF file and subscription options, an Active Channel Web page can also appear on the user's Active Desktop as an Active Desktop item or channel screen saver. An Active Desktop item is like having a live browsing window to an Active Channel Web page directly on the desktop. A channel screen saver is an Active Channel Web page that displays as a Windows screen saver.

For information about configuring Active Desktop items, see "Using Active Channels and Web Sites as Active Desktop Items" later in this chapter.

For information about configuring channel screen savers, see "Using Active Channel Screen Savers" later in this chapter.

For information about creating channels as Active Desktop items and channel screen savers for Active Channel Web sites, see "Creating and Managing Active Channels on Your Intranet" later in this chapter.

Subscription Options for Active Channels

The CDF file created by an Active Channel Web site author specifies the subscription options for that channel as follows:

- What content should be delivered to subscribed users.
- How that content is to be used (for example, as a *channel item*, or "page" in the channel, a screen saver, or as an Active Desktop item) and how updates are to be delivered (for example, by sending e-mail notification or by downloading the content directly to the user's computer).
- When and how often the user's computer should connect to the site to receive notification of updates or download updated content.

In a corporate intranet, a network or workgroup administrator most likely will accept the default subscription options specified by the Active Channel Web site author, in part because the download schedules are designed by the author and network administrators to minimize server loads. However, you can override the defaults specified by the CDF file to customize your workgroup's subscriptions. For example, if your server experiences delays due to heavy network traffic, you might configure your workgroup to receive e-mail notification of updated content in an Active Channel (as opposed to receiving automatic, scheduled download of that content).

For information about configuring subscriptions to Active Channels, see "Configuring Subscriptions" later in this chapter.

About Favorites

In Windows 98, Favorites let users subscribe to any internal or external Web site, and easily access any local or network resource. The Internet Explorer browsing software regularly checks Web sites subscribed to as Favorites for updated content according to the schedule and other options specified in the subscription. Depending on advanced subscription options, the user may also receive e-mail notification of the updates or automatically download the updated content.

You can configure your workgroup's Favorites to simplify access to the most frequently visited intranet or Web sites, and to files or folders they frequently access. By adding specific Web sites to Favorites and configuring their subscription options, you can ensure that your workgroup uses the most appropriate methods for receiving notification and downloading content whenever a Favorite Web site changes.

Considerations for Configuring Active Channels and Favorites

By effectively utilizing the power of Active Channel technology in Windows 98, you can coordinate a targeted flow of information to and from the users and workgroups that need that information the most. The key is deciding what information to Webcast, which users need that information, how often they need that information, and in what format you want the information to be Webcast or accessed.

What information do you want to Webcast?

Do your users or workgroups regularly access specific internal or external Web sites? What kinds of information do they need from these sites?

For example, if your workgroup's home page includes schedules and the names and e-mail addresses of team leads, you might want to subscribe your users to the workgroup's home page to receive updates automatically whenever schedule or team information changes. If your workgroup relies on the latest information from a white paper or product specification, you might want to notify your workgroup by e-mail of any changes to that document and include the document as an attachment to the e-mail. If your workgroup needs to follow a stock price or a count of inventory items minute-by-minute, you might subscribe your users to a stock or inventory ticker as an Active Desktop item or channel screen saver.

Which users need the information you plan to Webcast?

In some cases you will want to target the flow of broadband information—such as a change in team leadership or the location of a new intranet site—to an entire company or workgroup. In other cases, you will want to target information to specific users or workgroups—as when distributing a new template only to writers and editors, or distributing new employee evaluation guidelines only to managers.

How often do users need to receive updated information?

Do your users or workgroup need to receive updated information on a daily, weekly, or minute-to-minute basis, or should you simply notify them of the update and let them browse the new information at their leisure? A workgroup administrator or Active Channel Web site author can specify the appropriate format and frequency of the Webcast in the CDF file for each Active Channel. The urgency of the information can help you determine the best format for Webcasting it.

What format do you want the information to be Webcast or accessed?

For easy, frequent access, you might want to deliver your workgroup's intranet home page as an Active Desktop item, or place it on the Channel bar or a toolbar. If the information is time-critical, such as a stock ticker or inventory counter, you might want to deliver it as an Active Desktop item or channel screen saver. For information that is less time-critical, you might simply notify users of updates by sending e-mail notification, or specify regular, automatic Webcrawls to download new content.

Configuring the Channel Bar

As a workgroup administrator, you want to ensure that your workgroup has immediate access to the most relevant subscribed internal and external Active Channel Web sites. The simplest way to do this is to add these Active Channel Web sites to the default Windows 98 Channel bar deployed on each user's Active Desktop.

When you subscribe to an Active Channel Web site, the logo for that Active Channel is automatically added to the default Windows 98 Channel bar on the Active Desktop. You can also add Active Channel Web sites to the Channel bar without subscribing to them and remove any Active Channel Web sites that you do not want to appear on the Channel bar.

▶ **To add an Active Channel to the default Channel bar on the Active Desktop**

- Browse to the home or introductory page of the Active Channel Web site you want to add, and then click the **Add Active Channel** button.

  –Or–

  Drag the URL of the page you want to add onto the Channel bar or to the Favorites\Channels folder.

▶ **To delete an Active Channel from the default Channel bar on the Active Desktop**

- In the Channel bar, right-click the Active Channel you want to delete, and then click **Delete**.

Specifying a Custom Search Page

If you use the IEAK Profile Manager to deploy your Active Desktop configuration, you can specify the URL to a corporate or Internet search utility as the default for the Search explorer bar. This gives your workgroup immediate access to the most appropriate search engine.

For information about using the Profile Manager, see "Implementing Active Desktop and Active Channel Configurations" later in this chapter.

Using Active Channels and Web Sites as Active Desktop Items

Windows 98 lets you add any traditional or Active Channel Web page as an Active Desktop item on a user's or workgroup's Active Desktop.

Active Desktop items live alongside existing desktop shortcuts on the Windows 98 Active Desktop. An Active Desktop item lets you create dynamic links to your workgroup's favorite Web content. Active Desktop items are typically designed by Active Channel authors to provide summary information in a small amount of screen space. A user can click a hyperlink on an Active Desktop item to open a new browsing window; the user can then browse through the rest of the Web site.

Active Desktop items can be any size or shape and can display any HTML-based content. Like Active Channels, Active Desktop items update at regularly scheduled times specified by a CDF file or subscription, so their content is always up-to-date.

Practical Uses for Active Desktop Items

In a corporate intranet, you might want to add an Active Desktop item that displays your workgroup's home page, so that any changes to the home page would be displayed automatically on the user's desktop. You might add custom Active Desktop items created by Active Channel Web site authors for specific purposes or workgroups—for example, a "live" progress graph that shows the completion status of a project, or an "in" and "out" board showing each employee's in-office status.

When you add an Active Desktop item by subscribing a user to a traditional or Active Channel Web site, the URL for that Active Desktop item is automatically added to the user's Subscriptions folder. All content in the Active Desktop item is automatically cached offline in the user's cache. This makes content available for offline browsing if no Internet connection is available.

You can configure individual update schedules for each Active Desktop item you place on the Active Desktop. For example, a user's Active Desktop could display three different Active Desktop items: an inventory ticker that is updated once an hour, a workgroup home page that is updated once a day, and a newsletter that is updated once a week. Windows 98 automatically refreshes the Active Desktop item whenever the update occurs.

Note   You can also use an HTML page or graphic file on your computer as an Active Desktop item, or download items for free from the Microsoft Active Desktop Gallery. For information, see "Using Graphics, HTML Pages, and Explorer Windows as Active Desktop Items" earlier in this chapter.

For information about creating and deploying custom Active Desktop items for your workgroup, see "Creating and Managing Active Channels on Your Intranet" later in this chapter.

▶ **To add a traditional or Active Channel Web page as an Active Desktop item**

The simplest way to add an Active Desktop item from an Active Channel is to browse to the Active Channel and then click the **Add to Active Desktop** button on the channel's Web page. Otherwise, use the following procedure:

1. Right-click on the Active Desktop to display the shortcut menu, and then click **Properties**.

2. Click the **Web** tab, and then click **New**.

3. Click **No**, and then select or browse to the traditional or Active Channel Web page that you want to display as an Active Desktop item.

▶ **To customize the subscription for an Active Desktop item**

1. Right-click on the Active Desktop to display the shortcut menu, and then click **Properties**.

2. Click the **Web** tab, select the Active Desktop item you want to customize, and then click **Properties**.

3. Use the options on the **Subscription**, **Receiving**, and **Schedule** tabs to customize the subscription schedule, notification method, and so on.

Using Active Channel Screen Savers

In addition to the default screen savers, you can configure Windows 98 to use a screen saver provided by a subscribed Active Channel Web site. In a corporate intranet, you might want to use a channel screen saver that displays a stock ticker, broadcast bulletins, or an inventory counter. Windows 98 rotates between subscribed channel screen savers, displaying each for 30 seconds by default.

Optionally, a user can move the mouse and click objects on a channel screen saver without immediately dismissing the screen saver. Clicking a hyperlink on a screen saver opens a new browsing window and closes the screen saver. Clicking anything that is not an image, link, or object closes the screen saver. The user can also click the **Close** and **Properties** buttons in the screen saver toolbar to change the behavior of that screen saver.

For information about creating and deploying custom Active Channel screen savers for your workgroup, see "Creating and Managing Active Channels on Your Intranet" later in this chapter.

▶ **To select a channel screen saver**

1. Right-click on the Active Desktop to display the shortcut menu, and then click **Properties**.

2. Click the **Screen Saver** tab, and then in the **Screen Saver** box click **Channel Screen Saver**.

Setting an Online Support Page

If you use the IEAK Profile Manager to deploy your Active Desktop configuration, you can specify the URL to an online support page that users access by clicking **Online Support** on the Internet Explorer browsing software **Help** menu. This gives your users fast access to your technical support group's Web page.

For information about using the Profile Manager, see "Implementing Active Desktop and Active Channel Configurations" later in this chapter.

Configuring Subscriptions

You can optimize the targeted Webcasting of information to specific users or workgroups by effectively configuring their subscriptions to traditional Web sites and Active Channel Web sites, whether on your company's intranet or on the World Wide Web.

Considerations for Configuring Subscriptions

Before you begin configuring subscriptions, you should consider the following:

How do you want users to be notified of updates to a subscribed site? When the content of a subscribed Web site or Active Channel Web site changes, subscriptions can notify users by e-mail, or automatically download the changed content the next time the user connects to the intranet or World Wide Web. The user can then browse the changed content offline.

When and how often do you want users to receive downloads of updated content from subscribed sites? For Active Channel Web sites and Active Desktop items, the frequency and scheduling of downloads is specified by the CDF file created by the channel's author, but you can override those settings. For traditional internal and external Web sites, the default schedule for downloading is between 12:00 A.M. and 12:30 A.M. in the user's local time zone, but you can create custom schedules based on the needs of your users or the capacity of your network servers.

Note Before changing the download frequency or schedule for a subscribed Active Channel Web site or Active Desktop item on your company's intranet, you should consult with the appropriate Active Channel Web site authors or network administrators. They may have created optimal download schedules to minimize server loads and network traffic.

Procedures for Configuring Subscriptions to Web Sites

Use the following procedures to configure subscriptions to traditional Web sites on your corporate intranet or on the World Wide Web.

▶ **To subscribe to a Web site**

1. In the Internet Explorer browsing software, browse to the Web site to which you want to subscribe your users or workgroup.

2. On the **Favorites** menu, click **Add to Favorites**.

3. In the **Name** box on the **Add Favorite** dialog box, type the friendly name of the Web site as you want it to appear in the user's **Favorites** list, and then select the appropriate subscription option:

   ▪ Select **Yes, but only tell me when this page is updated** if you want users to be notified when content on the subscribed Web site changes.

   ▪ Select **Yes, notify me of updates and download the page for offline viewing** if you want users to be notified and receive downloaded content when content on the subscribed Web site changes.

   For either of these options, if you want your users to be notified of changes by e-mail, click the **Customize** button in the **Add Favorite** dialog box to start the Subscription Wizard. The wizard steps you through the process of specifying an e-mail address and server name, and allows you to modify the default subscription schedule.

▶ **To change subscription options for a subscribed Web site**

1. In the Internet Explorer browsing software, on the **Favorites** menu, click **Manage Subscriptions**.

2. Right-click the subscription that you want to change, and then on the shortcut menu, click **Properties**.

3. Use the options on the **Receiving** tab to change how notifications of updates are sent.

4. Use the options on the **Schedule** tab to change the frequency and schedule for downloading changed content from the subscribed Web site.

Procedures for Configuring Subscriptions to Active Channel Web Sites

▶ **To subscribe to an Active Channel Web site**

1. In the Internet Explorer browsing software, browse to the Active Channel Web site to which you want to subscribe your users or workgroup.

2. Click the **Add Active Channel** button on the Active Channel Web site's home or introductory page.

3. In the **Add Active Channel Content** dialog box, select an option for subscribing

   - If you want to be notified of updates to the site's content but do not want to automatically download the updated content when you connect to the site, click **Only tell me when updates occur**.

   - If you want to be notified and automatically download updates when you connect to the site, click **Notify me of updates and download the channel for offline viewing**.

     For either of these options, if you want your users to be notified of changes by e-mail, click the **Customize** button in the **Add Favorite** dialog box to start the Subscription Wizard. The wizard steps you through the process of specifying an e-mail address and server name, and allows you to modify the default subscription schedule specified by the CDF file for the Active Channel.

▶ **To change subscription options for a subscribed Active Channel Web site**

1. In the Internet Explorer browsing software, on the **Favorites** menu, click **Manage Subscriptions**.

2. Right-click the subscription that you want to change, and then on the shortcut menu, click **Properties**.

3. Use the options on the **Receiving** tab to change how notifications of updates are sent.

4. Use the options on the **Schedule** tab to change the frequency and schedule for downloading changed content from the subscribed Active Channel Web site.

Organizing Favorites

When a Web site is configured as a Favorite, a user can be notified of changed content on the Web site by e-mail. In addition, when the user rests the mouse pointer over the Favorite icon for that Web site, a pop-up description appears that provides information about that Web site or about the nature of the update to that Web site.

You can simplify your workgroup's access to the most frequently visited Web sites by effectively organizing their Favorites. You can place a Web site at the top level of the Favorites folder for faster access, or you can create subfolders to group Favorites. For example, you might want to group similar intranet Web sites into one folder and similar external Web sites into another, or you might want to create subfolders for each workgroup or division in your company.

Note You can also customize the Favorites folder under **Wizard Settings** in the IEAK Profile Manager. For more information, see "About the IEAK Profile Manager" later in this chapter.

▶ **To organize Favorites**

1. In the Internet Explorer browsing software, click the **Favorites** menu, and then click **Organize Favorites**.
2. Use the options in the **Organize Favorites** dialog box to move, rename, or delete Favorites, or to create, move, rename, or delete subfolders containing related Favorites.

Tip You can reorder the **Favorites** menu by clicking any item and dragging it to a new location.

Implementing Active Desktop and Active Channel Configurations

This section explains how to use the Internet Explorer Administration Kit (IEAK) Profile Manager to deploy your custom Active Channel and Active Desktop configurations. It also describes some of the additional features of the Profile Manager that you might want to use, such as automatic browser configuration and software distribution channels.

About the IEAK Profile Manager

The *IEAK Profile Manager* is a tool that network or workgroup administrators can use to create custom Active Desktop and Active Channel configurations and deploy them to users.

What You Can Do with the Profile Manager

Once you have created custom Active Desktop and Active Channel configurations on your computer as described in the previous sections of this chapter, you can use the IEAK Profile Manager to import those custom configurations and deploy them.

You can also use the Profile Manager to:

- Specify system policies and restrictions, such as whether users can close toolbars or modify their **Start** menus, and set additional options such as proxy settings.

- Customize additional components of the Internet Explorer browsing software, such as Outlook Express and Microsoft NetMeeting.

- Package these and additional applications that you want to distribute to users or workgroups into files that can be downloaded, distributed on floppy disk or compact disc, or installed by Active Setup.

- Deploy updates to Active Desktop and Active Channel configurations when a user starts the Internet Explorer browsing software, or at scheduled intervals, using automatic browser configuration.

- Set up and maintain software distribution channels, which you can use to distribute new applications or software updates.

How the Profile Manager Works

The Profile Manager lets you manage two categories of settings: **Wizard Settings** and **System Policies & Restrictions**.

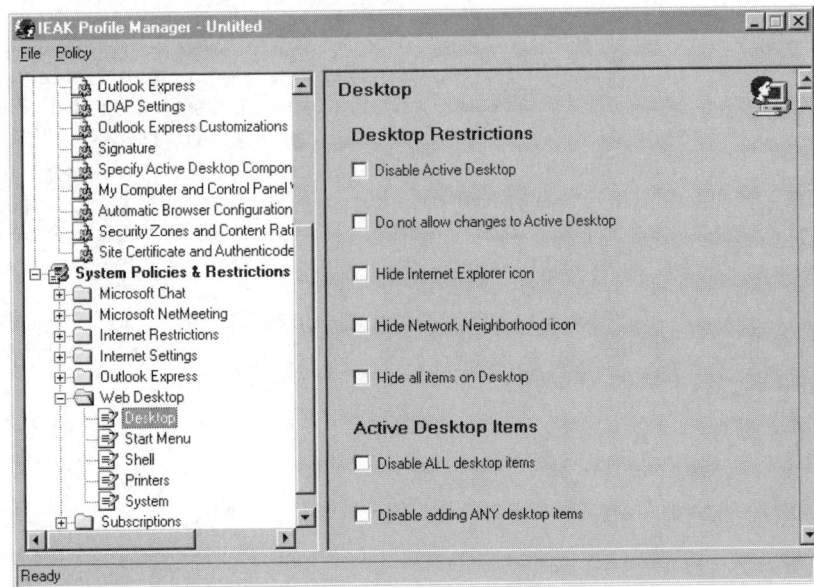

You click a category of settings (such as **Desktop**, in the Web Desktop folder) in the left pane, and then specify the individual options for that category (such as allowing users to alter their Active Desktops). For some categories, you can import custom Active Desktop configurations from your computer.

You then use the Profile Manager to create an auto-configuration file named *usergroup*.ins, where *usergroup* is the name of your workgroup. This file also contains information from policy template (ADM) files and INF files representing the Profile Manager settings, and any custom ADM files you may have imported.

The Profile Manager also creates companion cabinet (CAB) files used to configure users' computers. These files contain the installation information INF, INS, and ADM files and application updates or components that are automatically unpacked on users' computers. Windows 98 uses these unpacked INF files to change system policies and update desktop configurations.

Deploying Configurations

Once the Profile Manager has created the necessary files for your custom configurations, you can deploy them to users in the following ways:

- Whenever the Internet Explorer browsing software is restarted or updated.
- According to a schedule specified using automatic browser configuration.
- Using download sites on your corporate intranet.
- On compact discs or floppy disks.

If you have established software distribution channels, software updates will be deployed according to the channel specifications.

The *Microsoft Internet Explorer Resource Kit* provides extensive details, procedures, and technical discussions about planning, creating, and deploying custom configurations, creating software distribution channels, and much more. The *Microsoft Internet Explorer Resource Kit* (ISBN 1-57231-842-2) is available from Microsoft Press, or you can download a copy from the Internet Explorer Web site at **http://www.microsoft.com/ie/corp/**. To download the Internet Explorer 4.0 Administration Kit, visit the IEAK Web site at **http://ieak.microsoft.com/**.

For information about creating Active Channels and software distribution channels on your corporate intranet, see "Creating and Managing Active Channels on Your Intranet" later in this chapter.

Creating Active Desktop and Active Channel Configurations

Once you have created a custom Active Desktop and Active Channel configuration that you want to deploy to a specific workgroup, you can import those settings into the IEAK Profile Manager.

The IEAK Profile Manager can be installed on your computer from the Netadmin\Profmgr directory on the Microsoft Windows 98 Resource Kit compact disc.

▶ **To start the IEAK Profile Manager**

1. Click **Start**, point to **Programs**, point to **Windows 98 Resource Kit**, and then click **Tools Management Console**.

2. In the left pane, click the Tool Categories folder, and then click the Deployment Tools folder.

3. In the right pane, click **Profmgr.exe**.

Creating a Profile

You begin by creating or opening an INS file for your workgroup. Once you have created a new INS file, or opened an existing INS file, you can import your custom configuration and specify additional browsing software and security settings.

The Internet Explorer 4.0 Administration Kit includes several template INS files that can help you create your own INS files. Open one of these templates, located in the \IEAK\Reskit folder, save it under your workgroup's name, and then customize the settings.

Specifying Wizard Settings

The left pane of the Profile Manager contains two categories: **Wizard Settings** and **System Policies & Restrictions**. Click an item under **Wizard Settings**, and the right pane displays the options you can configure for that item. Table 6.1 describes the items you can use to configure the Active Desktop and Active Channel elements described in this chapter.

Table 6.1   Wizard Settings for Active Desktop and Active Channels

Item	Use to
Support Page	Specify the URL of your workgroup's or company's online support page, which opens in the browsing window when users click **Online Help** on the browsing window's **Help** menu.
Favorites	Specify your workgroup's favorite Web sites, which will be listed in the **Favorites** menu. You can import the default Favorites you created for your current Active Desktop and Active Channel configuration, or you can type any URL.
Desktop Wallpaper	Specify the path of a custom desktop wallpaper file.
Start and Search Page	Specify the home page for your workgroup when users click **Home**. You can use the default home page of your current Active Desktop configuration, or you can type any URL.

You can also set the search page that you want the users in your workgroup to see when they open the **Search** explorer bar. You can use the default Search explorer bar of your current Active Desktop configuration, or you can type any URL. |
Import Channels	Add or delete channels from the Channel bar and customize Subscriptions. You can import the Channel bar and Subscription configurations from your current Active Desktop configuration.
Import Software Updates	Import the Software Distribution Channels settings from your current configuration.
Specify Active Desktop Items	Import the Active Desktop items from your current configuration.
My Computer and Control Panel Webview Customization	Specify HTML files to display as Web views of My Computer and Control Panel.
Automatic Browser Configuration	Enable automatic browser configuration and specify URLs for auto-configure (INS) and auto-proxy (JS or PAC) files.

For information about configuring items for the Internet Explorer browsing software, such as Browser Title, or other components, such as Outlook Express, see Chapter 20, "Internet Tools and Accessories" and Chapter 22, "Electronic Mail with Outlook Express."

For detailed descriptions of these items, other items not described here, or information about using the Profile Manager, refer to the Profile Manager online Help system or the *Microsoft Internet Explorer Resource Kit.*

Specifying System Policies and Restrictions

The **System Policies & Restrictions** category contains folders of related items. Click a folder, and then click an item in the folder. The right pane displays the options you can configure for that item. Table 6.2 describes the items, organized by folder, that you can use to configure the Active Desktop and Active Channel elements described in this chapter.

Table 6.2   System Policies & Restrictions for Active Desktop and Active Channels

Folder	Item	Use to
Internet Restrictions	General	Restrict users from changing home page settings.
	Channels Settings	Restrict users from changing channel subscription, download schedules, and notification options.
Internet Settings	Advanced Settings	Enable or disable scheduled subscription updates, or launch channels in full-screen mode.
Web Desktop	Desktop	Restrict users from altering their Active Desktop configurations, wallpaper, Active Desktop items, and toolbars.
	Start Menu	Restrict users from altering the **Start** menu and Taskbar.
Subscriptions	Subscriptions	Restrict the amount of information downloaded from Subscriptions, the number of Subscriptions, Subscription update schedules, and Webcrawl levels.

The Profile Manager lets you specify many other Wizard Settings and System Policies & Restrictions than those described in this section. For more information about those options, refer to the Profile Manager online Help system, or see the *Microsoft Internet Explorer Resource Kit.* The *Microsoft Internet Explorer Resource Kit* can be purchased as a book and is also available online from the Internet Explorer Web site at **http://www.microsoft.com/ie/corp/.**

Deploying Active Desktop and Active Channel Configurations

After you have specified and saved the configuration options in the Profile Manager, the Profile Manager creates INS, INF, and ADM files, and packages those files (and any custom components you may have created) into CAB files. The CAB files can then be deployed to your users in a variety of ways. For information and guidance on designing and implementing your deployment strategy, see the *Microsoft Internet Explorer Resource Kit.*

Using Automatic Browser Configuration

You can also use the Profile Manager to set up automatic browser configuration. With *automatic browser configuration*, the Internet Explorer browsing software automatically checks the user's or workgroup's INS files, downloads any changes, and updates the configuration. You can specify scheduled intervals for these updates, or you can configure the Internet Explorer browsing software to check the INS files for updates every time the browser is launched.

For more information about automatic browser configuration, refer to the Profile Manager online Help system or the *Microsoft Internet Explorer Resource Kit.*

Using Software Distribution Channels

You can use software distribution channels to distribute new or updated application components to your users or workgroups. A *software distribution channel* is a type of Active Channel that uses an Open Software Distribution (OSD) file. The users' computers check the OSD file at scheduled intervals or at startup and automatically download and install any new or changed software components.

For information about creating software distribution channels on your company's intranet, see "Creating a Software Distribution Channel" later in this chapter.

For more information about implementing software distribution channels, refer to the Profile Manager online Help system or the *Microsoft Internet Explorer Resource Kit.*

Creating and Managing Active Channels on Your Intranet

This section is intended primarily for intranet Web site authors and administrators. It presents an overview of the new channel technology in Windows 98 and describes how to create and manage Active Channel Web sites on your corporate intranet.

Overview of Active Channels on an Intranet

An Active Channel Web site is simply a Web site that is enabled to take advantage of the new channel, or "push," technologies introduced in Windows 98. By effectively configuring your intranet Web sites as Active Channel Web sites, you can target the Webcasting of information, applications, content, bulletins, and updates to specific users or workgroups in your company. By effectively utilizing Active Channel technology, as well as HTML-based forms, Dynamic HTML, ActiveX controls, Distributed Component Object Model (DCOM) applications, and Java applets, you can vastly improve how your workgroup or company disseminates information and applications. Figure 6.5 illustrates Active Channels on an intranet.

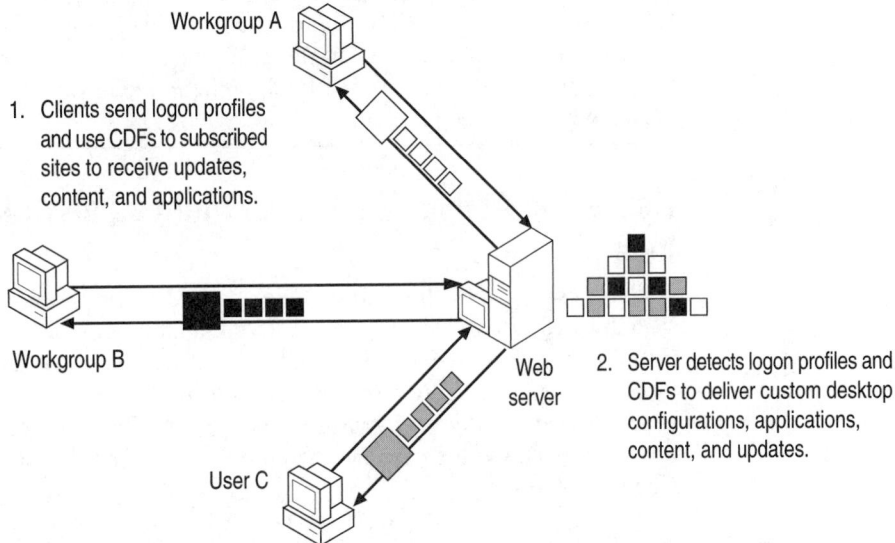

Figure 6.5   Active Channels on an intranet

You can transform any existing intranet Web site into an Active Channel Web site by creating a Channel Definition Format (CDF) file. The CDF file specifies:

- What content should be delivered to subscribed users.

- How that content is to be used (for example, as a *channel item*, or "page" in the channel, a screen saver, or as an Active Desktop item) and how updates are to be delivered (for example, by sending e-mail notification or by downloading the content directly to the user's computer).

- When and how often the user's computer should connect to the site to receive notification of updates or download updated content.

In the Channel bar, the Internet Explorer browsing software uses the CDF file to create a visual structure of the pages outlined in the Active Channel Web site. When a user clicks on the channel icon in the Channel bar, the channel expands to display a visual map of the pages in the Active Channel Web site. Pop-up descriptions display abstract text that describes the contents or nature of each site, page, or update.

You can create multiple CDF files for a single Active Channel Web site to target customized content for specific users or workgroups. For example, if your Web site contains information on different software products, you can create separate CDF files for each product to deliver information on that product only to the specific users or workgroups using or developing that software.

Note Create a separate CDF file for each Active Channel Web site, Active Desktop item, or channel screen saver. If your CDF file describes both an Active Channel Web site and an Active Desktop item, the information about the Active Desktop item will be ignored.

Delivering Active Channel Content as an Active Desktop Item

Active Desktop items live alongside existing desktop shortcuts on the Windows 98 Active Desktop. An Active Desktop item lets you create dynamic links to your workgroup's favorite Web content. Active Desktop items are typically designed to provide summary information in a small amount of screen space. A user can click a hyperlink on an Active Desktop item to open a new browsing window; the user can then browse through the rest of your Active Channel Web site.

Active Desktop items can be any size or shape and can display any HTML-based content. Like Active Channels, Active Desktop items update at regularly scheduled times specified by the CDF file, so their content is always up-to-date.

All content in an Active Desktop item is automatically cached offline in the user's cache. This makes content available for offline browsing if no Internet connection is available.

You should create individual CDF files and update schedules for each Active Desktop item that you create. For example, a user's Active Desktop could display three different Active Desktop items: an inventory ticker that is updated once an hour, a workgroup home page that is updated once a day, and a newsletter that is updated once a week. The Internet Explorer browsing software automatically refreshes the Active Desktop item whenever the update occurs.

You can download Active Desktop items from Microsoft's Active Desktop Gallery Web site at **http://www.microsoft.com/ie/ie40/gallery/**. For information about creating your own Active Desktop items, and for sample CDF code, visit the Internet Explorer Technologies page of Microsoft's Site Builder Network Web site at **http://www.microsoft.com/workshop/prog/ie4/**.

Delivering Active Channel Content as a Screen Saver

You can also deliver Active Channel content to users in the form of screen savers. With an Active Channel screen saver, a user can move the mouse and click objects on the screen saver without closing the screen saver. Clicking a link on a screen saver opens a new browser window and dismisses the screen saver.

Considerations for Creating and Maintaining Active Channels on Your Intranet

Channel technology in Windows 98 gives intranet site authors and administrators greater control in Webcasting content across the corporate intranet. However, it also leads to questions about what, when, and how to Webcast information so as to minimize server loads and target specific users.

What intranet sites should be configured as Active Channels?

Intranet site authors and administrators must work closely with workgroup and network administrators to determine which internal Web sites should be configured as Active Channels, and how and when these Active Channels should Webcast information across the corporate intranet. Web authors can then configure the appropriate sites as Active Channels by creating CDF files manually, or automatically using the Microsoft FrontPage 98 Channel Definition Wizard.

How do you want to deliver content and updates?

Do you want to notify users or workgroups by e-mail, or do you want to download updated content automatically according to the schedule you specify? Do you want to deliver content in the form of Active Channel Web pages, Active Desktop items, or channel screen savers? What abstracts do you want to appear as pop-up descriptions? What graphics do you want to use for the channel logo on the Channel bar and the channel icons displayed in the expanded Channel bar map of your site?

Will your Active Channel Web pages work when browsed offline?

If you want your Active Channel Web pages to work in offline browsing mode, you must make sure that all of the elements on your pages work offline. Many Java applets and ActiveX controls do not work offline.

How will Webcasting affect server loads?

One of the most crucial considerations for intranet site authors and administrators is the scheduling of Webcasting to minimize server loads. The CDF file for each Active Channel specifies when and how often updates from that Active Channel will be downloaded from the server to each subscribed user. By randomizing download schedules and efficiently distributing Active Channel content across network servers, you can minimize server loads and network traffic.

How can users be specifically targeted to receive Active Channel content?

You can utilize HTTP cookies, Active Server pages (ASP files), and the return of cached data from subscribed users' log files to target specific information and customized CDF files.

Considerations for Web Authors Creating Active Desktop Items or Screen Savers

Following are some considerations for Active Channel Web authors implementing Active Desktop items or channel screen savers:

The Active Desktop item or screen saver must work offline. Because many users will view Active Channel contents offline, an Active Desktop item or channel screen saver should display some reasonable content in the absence of an Internet or intranet connection. Any files the Active Desktop item uses should be cached on the user's computer. This can be particularly tricky for Java applets, because image objects typically sit in separate GIF or JPEG files on a Web server.

You can cache any object referenced by an Active Desktop item or channel screen saver. For example, if a component is built from an HTML document inside a floating frame, you can set the Active Desktop item or channel screen saver subscription to download any images, sounds, objects, or applets automatically, and to download any number of HTML links n levels deep. You can also specify individual subscriptions for any data files or objects that an Active Desktop item or channel screen saver might reference.

Note Java applets and ActiveX controls must be signed so they can access content from the offline cache. For further information on signing Java applets or ActiveX controls, see **http://www.microsoft.com/workshop/prog/** or **http://www.microsoft.com/java/**.

Avoid using navigation controls. Active Desktop items and channel screen savers have no navigation controls available for the user to move backward and forward. By default, clicking a link inside an Active Desktop item or channel screen saver creates a new browser window. You should not create in-place navigation controls in Active Desktop items or channel screen savers.

Size Active Desktop items carefully. An Active Desktop item needs to share the Active Desktop with any other icons or Active Desktop items the user or administrator has configured. You should create Active Desktop items as small as necessary to display their desired content. This gives Active Desktop users and administrators maximum flexibility in configuring Active Desktops. A good benchmark is to make sure that the Active Desktop item takes up no more than one-sixth the area of the screen.

Allow for component resizing and moving. Active Desktop items can be resized and moved. The Internet Explorer browsing software will set the size of the 2D HTML layer that contains the component, and will then try to reflow all HTML content within this space. You should design Active Desktop items with resizing in mind.

Creating Channel Definition Format Files

You create a Channel Definition Format (CDF) file manually using Windows Notepad, WordPad, or your favorite text editor. The CDF file is an XML-based document containing text-annotated tags that define your Active Channel Web site, Active Desktop item, or channel screen saver. You save the file using a .cdf file extension.

The following section describes the most significant elements of the CDF file that you might want to use in authoring your Active Channel content. For specifications and other information about creating CDF files and Active Channels, visit the Microsoft Internet Explorer 4 Authoring Web site at **http://www.microsoft.com/ie/authors/**.

Tip Microsoft FrontPage 98 includes the Channel Definition Wizard, which prompts you for the contents of your Active Channel and creates the CDF file for you. You can create an Active Channel Web site for both new Webs that you create in FrontPage 98 and existing Webs that you import into FrontPage 98. For more information, see Microsoft FrontPage 98 online Help, or visit the FrontPage 98 Web site at **http://www.microsoft.com/frontpage/**.

Specifying the Channel and Channel Items

A channel consists of a main HTML document to which you may add any number of subpages, or *channel items*. The main HTML document can be an existing page on your Web site or a new page that you create specifically for the channel.

The channel items are the Active Channel Web pages that appear in a hierarchical list that is displayed in full screen mode, when the user clicks the channel logo in the Channel bar.

Specifying the Main Page of the Channel

The main page of the channel is identified by the CHANNEL tag, and the information about the channel's subpages is contained within the <CHANNEL> </CHANNEL> block. In the opening CHANNEL tag, you identify the URL of the channel's main page with the HREF attribute:

```
<CHANNEL HREF="http://www.microsoft.com/ie/ie40/">
</CHANNEL>
```

Specifying the Channel Title

The TITLE tag specifies a short description of the channel that is displayed in the list of channels accessed from the **Favorites** menu. The TITLE also appears as a ToolTip when the user passes the mouse over the channel logo in the Channel bar on the Active Desktop:

```
<TITLE>My Channel</TITLE>
```

Specifying the Channel Items

The ITEM tag defines a subpage and its information. The HREF attribute specifies the URL of the subpage. TITLE gives a short definition of the page that appears in the Channel bar listing, and ABSTRACT provides a longer description that appears as a ToolTip when the user moves the mouse over the logo in the Channel bar:

```
<ITEM HREF="http://www.microsoft.com/workshop/author/dhtml/">
    <TITLE>Microsoft Dynamic HTML</TITLE>
    <ABSTRACT>Site Builder Network articles on Dynamic HTML</ABSTRACT>
</ITEM>
```

Supplying the Channel Logo and Item Icons

The LOGO tag specifies an 80 x 32-pixel logo and a 16 x 16-pixel icon. The logo appears in the Channel bar, which displays all the subscribed channels. The icon appears in the Channels submenu of the Internet Explorer browsing software **Favorites** menu.

The Channel logo

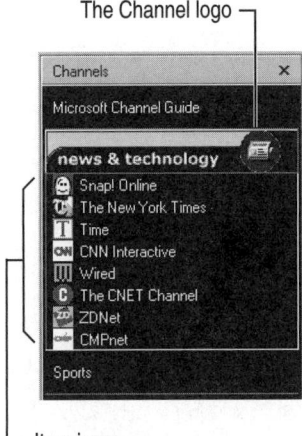

Item icons

The Internet Explorer browsing software uses the color in the top-left pixel as the background for the image when the user resizes the Channel bar beyond 80 pixels in width.

```
<LOGO
HREF="http://www.microsoft.com/workshop/prog/ie4/channels/dhtml.ico"
STYLE="icon" />
<LOGO
HREF="http://www.microsoft.com/workshop/prog/ie4/channels/dhtml1.gif"
STYLE="image" />
HREF="http://www.microsoft.com/workshop/prog/ie4/channels/dhtml2.gif"
STYLE="image-wide" />
```

There is also a wide channel logo (194 x 32 pixels) that can be specified by the LOGO tag. This is the logo displayed when the user opens a channel in full-screen mode for viewing, in the wide Channel bar that appears on the left side of the browser window and slides in and out.

Writing Abstracts for ToolTips

The ABSTRACT element of the ITEM tag provides a pop-up description of a channel item. The Abstract Description is displayed as a ToolTip when the user rests the cursor over the item. Use this feature to describe the content of an Active Channel Web page, to notify users that an update of that page is available, or to attract users' attention and encourage them to review that content immediately.

```
<ITEM HREF="http://www.microsoft.com/workshop/author/dhtml/">
  <TITLE>Microsoft Dynamic HTML</TITLE>
  <ABSTRACT>A new update of this page is available!</ABSTRACT>
</ITEM>
```

Specifying Usages for Channel Items

The USAGE VALUE tag specifies how a channel item should be used:

- **Channel** specifies that the item appears on the Channel bar on the Active Desktop. This is the default behavior when no USAGE element appears under an ITEM.

- **Email** specifies an item that is e-mailed to a subscribed user when the channel content is updated.

- **DesktopComponent** specifies that the item should be displayed as an Active Desktop item on the user's Active Desktop. Use an individual CDF file for each Active Desktop item that you create. If a CDF file defines a channel using the Channel value, the DesktopComponent value will be ignored.

- **ScreenSaver** specifies that the item should be displayed for 30 seconds during the rotation of Active Channel Screen Savers installed on the user's Active Desktop. Use an individual CDF file for each channel screen saver that you create. If a CDF file defines a channel using the Channel value, it can also include one ScreenSaver value.

The following example shows a CDF file for an Active Desktop item:

```
<ITEM HREF="http://www.microsoft.com/workshop/author/dhtml/">
  <TITLE>Microsoft Dynamic HTML</TITLE>
  <ABSTRACT>Site Builder Network articles on Dynamic HTML</ABSTRACT>
  <USAGE VALUE="DesktopComponent"></USAGE>
</ITEM>
```

Setting Levels of Crawling

The LEVEL value of the CHANNEL HREF or ITEM HREF tag specifies the number of levels deep the client should "site crawl" your channel (HTML content indexed by the HREF attribute), channel item, or Active Desktop item. The default is zero, which specifies only to pre-cache the cover page along with its images. Frames and their frame sets, as well as pages and their images, are considered part of the same level. Clients must follow hyperlinks with URLs within the same domain as the URL of the cover page.

The following example specifies a channel site crawl one level deep:

```
<CHANNEL HREF="http://www.microsoft.com/ie/ie40/"
    LEVEL="1">
</CHANNEL>
```

Setting Update Schedules to Minimize Server Load

The SCHEDULE tag defines the schedule used for updating your channel, Active Desktop item, or channel screen saver. Starting at midnight on STARTDATE, channel updating occurs once within each consecutive time interval of duration specified by the INTERVALTIME element. The EARLIESTTIME and LATESTTIME elements define the range of time within each interval in which a content update can occur.

The following example schedules a daily update sometime between noon and 6:00 P.M.:

```
<SCHEDULE>
    <INTERVALTIME DAY="1"/>
    <EARLIESTTIME HOUR="12"/>
    <LATESTTIME HOUR="18"/>
</SCHEDULE>
```

The following example schedules a weekly update at noon each Friday:

```
<SCHEDULE STARTDATE="1997-07-14">
<!-- 1997-07-14 is a Monday -->
    <INTERVALTIME DAY="7"/>
    <EARLIESTTIME DAY="4" HOUR="12"/>
    <LATESTTIME DAY="4" HOUR="12"/>
</SCHEDULE>
```

Active Channel Web site authors and administrators should work closely with network and workgroup administrators to schedule content downloads during periods of low network traffic. You can further minimize server loads by randomizing content update schedules, so that all subscribed users do not attempt downloads at the same time, and by distributing Active Channel Web sites between servers based on the number of hits, downloads, and server capacity.

Creating Add Active Channel and Add to Active Desktop Buttons

A user can subscribe to your Active Channel Web site or Active Desktop item by clicking a link on your channel's main page that points to the CDF file for the channel or Active Desktop item. Microsoft recommends that developers use standard GIF files for these buttons, which you can copy from the following code:

```
<A HREF=" http://www.microsoft.com/workshop/prog/ie4/channels/
  button.gif ">
    <img
src="http://www.microsoft.com/workshop/prog/ie4/channels/button.gif"
    width="110" height="24" border="0" alt="Subscribe to channel">
</A>
```

If you are using the Microsoft FrontPage 98 Channel Definition Wizard to create your Active Channel Web site, you can direct the wizard to create an **Add Active Channel** button and automatically place it on your home page. For more information, see Microsoft FrontPage 98 online Help.

Delivering Custom CDF Files Using HTTP Cookies

The HTTP cookie standard provides a powerful mechanism for personalizing Web content. You can create an Active Channel that uses regular HTTP cookies to dynamically generate custom CDF files based on individual user preferences. The CDF file enhances the existing cookie standard for personalized HTML by allowing personalized channels for individual users.

▶ **To create personalized channels for users or groups**

1. The first time users visit your Active Channel Web site, present them with a form asking for their preferences, as they relate to the channel. This page could be referenced by the **Add Active Channel** button or by a hyperlink. When the user submits the form data back to the server, the channel's CDF file can be referenced.

2. Store the user's preferences on the Web server hosting your Active Channel Web site, or within an HTTP cookie on the user's computer.

3. Whenever the Internet Explorer browsing software requests a CDF file for that user, dynamically generate a special CDF file or download an existing CDF file that matches that user's profile.

You can also use Active Server Pages (ASPs) with Microsoft Internet Information Server (IIS) to dynamically generate personalized CDF files. When using IIS, you must insert the following line at the top of the CDF file:

```
<% Response.ContentType = "application/x-cdf" %>
```

This ensures that the server will return the correct MIME/content type to the browser. Without this line, the browser will not perform the expected actions for CDF files. For example, the CDF file might be displayed as text in the browser window rather than launch the Subscription Wizard.

If you implement HTTP authentication in your Active Channel, make sure the Internet Explorer browsing software has the user name and password so it can update the channel content without user intervention. To accomplish this, you can force the Internet Explorer browsing software to ask the user for this information during the channel subscription setup process, by using the LOGIN element in the CDF file.

Creating a Software Distribution Channel

A software distribution channel is a mechanism for updating program files (such as Java class libraries, Java stand-alone applications, ActiveX controls, or platform native code) on a user's computer. A software distribution channel is based on a CDF file and the Open Software Description (OSD) format.

OSD lets you automatically download only the software that the user needs. By querying the users' computer about existing software and hardware, OSD can make more intelligent decisions about what the user needs and install the correct version.

You can also use OSD to simplify the computing experience by installing missing components on the fly. For example, if the user is missing a component that prevents another program from functioning, OSD can detect this and automatically download the missing component.

The IEAK Profile Manager comes with four CDF templates you can customize to create software distribution channels on your corporate intranet. For more information about using the Profile Manager to create software distribution channels, or to copy these templates, see "Templates for Software Distribution Channels" in the Profile Manager's online Help.

For more information about the Profile Manager, see "About the IEAK Profile Manager" earlier in this chapter.

Technical Notes

This section contains technical notes on the Active Desktop and Active Channels.

The Active Desktop

The Active Desktop in Windows 98 is built from two separate layers. The transparent icon layer exposes all the user's existing desktop shortcuts, and the background HTML layer hosts all Active Desktop items. The HTML layer is described by a single, local HTML file called Desktop.htm that is created and edited automatically by Windows 98. This file contains the following:

- HTML tags that represent each Active Desktop item. Each Active Desktop item consists of a single HTML tag with arbitrary x- and y-positions. The HTML tag for an Active Desktop item can be an image (<IMG>) tag, a floating frame (<IFRAME>) tag, or an object (<OBJECT>) tag, and is generated automatically by Windows 98. The floating frame is the most commonly used approach, because it neatly encapsulates an entire arbitrary HTML document that can contain anything the author desires. In either case, there is a single URL that points to the actual content.

- An ActiveX control that enables moving and resizing of the Active Desktop items and helps manage the list of items.

- Any other static HTML that the user wants to have in the background. By default, this is just a reference to the user's chosen wallpaper, which is exposed as the background watermark for the HTML page.

A Sample CDF File

The following is an example of a simple CDF file for a sub-channel (a channel within a channel):

```
<?XML version="1.0"?>

<CHANNEL
    HREF="http://www.microsoft.com/ie/ie40/">

    <TITLE>Dynamic HTML Channel</TITLE>
    <LOGO
HREF="http://www.microsoft.com/workshop/prog/ie4/channels/dhtml.ico"
STYLE="icon" />
    <LOGO
```

```
HREF="http://www.microsoft.com/workshop/prog/ie4/channels/dhtml.gif"
STYLE="image" />

    <ITEM HREF="http://www.microsoft.com/workshop/author/dhtml/">
        <TITLE>Microsoft Dynamic HTML</TITLE>
        <ABSTRACT>Site Builder Network articles on Dynamic HTML
        </ABSTRACT>
    </ITEM>

    <ITEM HREF="http://www.microsoft.com/workshop/prog/ie4/">
        <TITLE>Internet Explorer 4 Technologies</TITLE>
        <ABSTRACT>Site Builder Network articles on Internet Explorer 4
        </ABSTRACT>
    </ITEM>
    <CHANNEL HREF="http://www.microsoft.com/workshop/archives/">
        <TITLE>Site Builder Networks archives</TITLE>
        <ABSTRACT>Site Builder Network articles from the last 6
        months</ABSTRACT>

    <ITEM HREF="http://www.microsoft.com/workshop/archives/asp/">
        <TITLE>Active Server pages</TITLE>
        <ABSTRACT>Site Builder Network articles on Active Server
        Pages</ABSTRACT>
    </ITEM>

    <ITEM HREF="http://www.microsoft.com/workshop/archives/SQL/">
        <TITLE>Building a SQL backend for your Intranet</TITLE>
        <ABSTRACT>Site Builder Network articles on Intranets and SQL
        databases</ABSTRACT>
    </ITEM>
</CHANNEL>

</CHANNEL>
```

Additional Resources

For more information about	See this resource
Internet Explorer	*Microsoft Internet Explorer Resource Kit* **http://www.microsoft.com/ie/corp/** **http://ieak.microsoft.com/**
FrontPage 98	**http://www.microsoft.com/frontpage/**
Active Desktop Gallery	**http://www.microsoft.com/ie/ie40/gallery/**
Active Desktop items	**http://www.microsoft.com/workshop/prog/ie4/**
Java applets and ActiveX controls	**http://www.microsoft.com/java/** **http://www.microsoft.com/workshop/prog/**

C H A P T E R   7

User Profiles

7

This chapter describes how user profiles can help users maintain their own preferences, network settings, and application settings when logging on to a workstation. These features can help decrease the cost of managing numerous computers by allowing you to manage configurations remotely.

In This Chapter

See Also

- For more information about remote administration, see Chapter 23, "System and Remote Administration Tools."

- For more information about creating system policies, see Chapter 8, "System Policies."

Overview of User Profiles

A *user profile* consists of user-specific information contained in the User.dat file, which is one of the two files in the Microsoft Windows 98 registry. Optionally, a user profile can also contain special Windows 98 directories. The benefits of using user profiles are summarized in this section.

Multiple users on a computer can retain their personal settings. *Roaming users* can log on to the network from any computer and work with the same desktop settings as long as the computer is running a Windows 98 32-bit, protected-mode network client.

Windows 98 automatically maintains each user's profile. Whether profiles are stored locally or on the network, Windows 98 will maintain each individuals user settings automatically.

Mandatory profiles can be used to enforce consistent desktops. This is useful for novice users who cannot manage their own desktop settings. Mandatory profiles increase user productivity and ease the burden of training and support for system managers.

Choosing System Policies or Mandatory User Profiles

You can use either system policies or mandatory user profiles to enforce user settings. In certain situations, it may be desirable to use both system policies and mandatory user profiles. Table 7.1 illustrates how the two features differ.

Table 7.1   Differences between system policies and mandatory user profiles

Mandatory user profiles	System polices
Allow you to mandate only user-specific settings.	Allow you to mandate user-specific, computer-specific, and group-specific settings.
Control every user-specific setting.	Allow you to selectively determine a subset of user settings to control; users control their own remaining settings.

Note Family members or coworkers can also control their own individual settings on the same computer through the Users option in Control Panel. See online Help for more information.

Before implementing user profiles, consider the following issues:

- Do you want to use system policies for user settings? If so, you must enable user profiles on the computer.

- What do you want to include in user profiles? For example, you might choose to include the desktop, **Start** menu, or Network Neighborhood in the user profile.

- Do you want user profiles to work across the network so that they are available to roaming users? If so, the computers must be running a 32-bit, protected-mode network client. Also, you must make sure that each user has a home directory on the network.

- Should mandatory user profiles be used? If so, you must copy the necessary files to each user's home directory.

Important If you want to specify desktop, shell, and security settings for your organization as they relate to the Internet Explorer (IE) browsing software or any part of the IE suite, use the Internet Explorer 4.0 Administration Kit (IEAK) which is available at the IEAK Web site at **http://ieak.microsoft.com/**. The *IEAK Profile Manager* controls system policies, however, it does not control user profiles as discussed in this chapter. For more information about the IEAK Profile Manager, see Chapter 6, "Configuring the Active Desktop and Active Channels" and Chapter 20, "Internet Access and Tools."

How User Profiles Work

Each time the user logs on to a computer, Windows 98 searches the registry under the following key to determine whether the user has a local profile:

HKEY_LOCAL_MACHINE\Software\Microsoft\Windows\Current Version \Profile List

Windows 98 also checks for the user profile in the user's home directory on the server. If the user profile on the server is the most current, Windows 98 copies it to the local computer for use during the current session, and then it loads the settings in this local copy into the registry. If no local user profile exists, Windows 98 copies the server version to the local computer. If no profile is found, Windows 98 creates a new user profile on the local computer using default settings. If the user does not log on, Windows 98 automatically uses the Default User profile.

Both the local and the network copies of the user profile are automatically updated with current settings when the user logs off.

If the user is logged on at more than one computer at the same time, any changes made to the profile on the computer where the user first logs off will be overwritten when the user logs off the other computer. In other words, the last logoff is saved, and no merging of changes occurs.

In the \Profiles subdirectory of the \Windows directory, a folder is created for each user who has a profile on that computer. Each of these folders contains the following:

- A User.dat file that contains the user portion of the registry.

- An Application Data folder that contains the Address Book (User.wab), the QuickLaunch toolbar, Outlook Mail and News, and the Windows 98 Welcome.

- A Cookies folder that contains the contents of Cookies for IE.

- A Desktop folder that contains the contents of the Active Desktop. (Only if this has been enabled in the Personalized Items Settings in the Users option of Control Panel.)

- A Favorites folder that contains the channels for Internet Explorer. (Only if this has been enabled in the Personalized Items Settings in the Users option of Control Panel.)

- A History folder that contains the contents of the History option for IE.

- A My Documents folder that contains the contents of the My Documents folder on the user's desktop. (Only if this has been enabled in the Personalized Items Settings in the Users option of Control Panel.)

- A NetHood folder that contains additional shortcuts available while viewing Network Neighborhood items. (Only if this has been enabled by a system policy. For information about system policies, see Chapter 8, "System Policies.")

- A Recent folder that contains the contents of the Documents option on the **Start** menu.

- A Start Menu folder that contains the contents of the **Start** menu and includes the Programs folder. (Only if this has been enabled in the Personalized Items Settings in the Users option of Control Panel.)

- A Temporary Internet Files folder that contains the contents of the \Temporary Internet Files directory. (Only if this has been enabled in the Personalized Items Settings in the Users option of Control Panel.)

Enabling User Profiles

You can enable user profiles after Windows 98 has been installed, either locally on a single computer or for multiple computers. You can avoid having to go to each computer to enable user profiles by creating a system policy that can be downloaded automatically when the initial Windows 98 installation is complete. For information about enabling user profiles centrally on multiple computers, see Chapter 8, "System Policies."

Note Using Microsoft Batch 98 you can also enable user profiles during a clean install or an upgrade. For information about using Microsoft Batch 98, see Appendix D, "Msbatch.inf Parameters for Setup Scripts."

▶ **To enable user profiles on a local computer after setup**

1. In Control Panel, double-click Passwords, and then click the **User Profiles** tab.

2. Click **Users can customize their preferences and desktop settings**.

3. Select the options you want under **User profile settings**, and then click **OK**. These options describe what should be included as part of the user profile.

4. Shut down and restart the computer.

Tip If you include desktop icons in your user profile, only the shortcuts (icons that represent links) will be available when you log on to the network from another computer. Actual files on your desktop are part of your local user profile only.

▶ **To disable user profiles on a local computer**

- In Control Panel, double-click Passwords, and then click the **User Profiles** tab. Click **All users of this computer use the same preferences and desktop settings**.

Note If an application is installed after user profiles have been enabled with the option to include the **Start** menu and **Programs** in the profile, only the user who was logged on when the application was installed will have an entry for that application on the **Programs** menu. Other users will have to create shortcuts to the application on their **Programs** menus.

Preparing for User Profiles on a Network

If you want to make user profiles available on the network rather than on individual computers, you must perform the following preliminary steps:

- Install and run a 32-bit, protected-mode networking client (such as Microsoft Client for NetWare Networks or Client for Microsoft Networks) on the computers.

- Make sure that the server supports long file names for full user profile functionality. If the server does not support long file names, only User.dat will follow a user around the network. Users will not be able to download other folders, such as those that support the **Start** menu.

- For Microsoft networks, make sure that a network home directory exists for each user, because this is where user profiles are placed.

- For each computer, use the same names for the directory and the hard disk drive in which Windows 98 is installed. If Windows 98 is installed in C:\Windows on one computer and in C:\Win98 on another, some components of the user profile will not be transferred between the two computers. This is also true if Windows 98 is installed on different hard disks on different computers (for example, C:\Windows on one computer and D:\Windows on another).

Setting Up User Profiles on a Windows NT Network

You can use user profiles with Windows 98 on a Windows NT network if the computer is configured to use Client for Microsoft Networks.

Note Windows 98 does not use the Profiles directory on a Windows NT server; that directory is used only for Windows NT profiles.

▶ **To set up user profiles on a Windows NT network**

1. For each computer, make sure that user profiles are enabled, as described in "Enabling User Profiles" earlier in this chapter.

2. In Control Panel, double-click Network, and then select **Client for Microsoft Networks** as the Primary Network Logon client.

3. Select **Client for Microsoft Networks** in the list of installed network components, and then click **Properties**.

4. Select **Log on to Windows NT domain**, enter the domain name, and then click **OK**.

5. On the Windows NT server, make sure each user is properly set up and has an assigned home directory on a Windows NT network server. (You can use the Windows NT User Manager tool to create this directory.)

When the user logs off, Windows 98 automatically places an updated copy of the user profile in the user's assigned home directory on the Windows NT network, in the following path:

\\specified_server\user's home directory

For information about User Manager and home directories, see Microsoft Windows NT Server 4.0 online Help.

Setting Up User Profiles on a NetWare Network

You can use user profiles with Windows 98 on a NetWare network if the computer is configured to use Microsoft Client for NetWare Networks or another 32-bit NetWare client.

When a user account is created on a NetWare server, a subdirectory of the \Mail directory is automatically created for that user. Windows 98 uses this directory to store user profiles. Novell 4.x servers can specify where a user's home directory is located when using a client or service that supports Novell Directory Services (NDS).

▶ **To set up user profiles on a Novell NetWare network**

1. For each computer, make sure that user profiles are enabled, as described in "Enabling User Profiles" earlier in this chapter.

2. In Control Panel, double-click Network, and then select **Client for NetWare Networks** as the Primary Network Logon client.

3. Select **Client for NetWare Networks** in the list of installed network components, and then click **Properties**.

4. Enter the name of your preferred server, and then click **OK**.

5. On the NetWare server, make sure each user has an established \Mail directory.

When the user logs off, Windows 98 automatically places an updated copy of the user profile in the user's assigned \Mail directory on the NetWare network, as indicated in the following example. (The user's 8-digit ID can be determined by using the NetWare Syscon utility.)

\\preferred_server\sys\mail\user_id

Note On a network using Microsoft Service for Novell Directory Services, user profiles are stored in the home directory for each user object. Therefore, if your site has user profiles enabled, you must make sure that every user object in the directory tree has a home directory associated with it.

When you log on using bindery mode, your user profile is stored in the \Mail directory on your preferred server.

If a user alternates between bindery and Novell Directory Services when logging on, then user profiles will be stored in both the \Mail directory and the home directory. If the user always logs on from the same computer, both profiles will be updated properly. However, if the user logs on from several other computers, using both bindery and NDS modes, out-of-date user profiles could be copied.

Disabling Standard Roaming Profiles

You might want to have user profiles enabled on a computer but not allow the profiles to move between that computer and others.

▶ **To disable roaming profiles on a particular computer**

1. In Registry Editor, expand the **Hkey_Local_Machine\Network** key, and select the **Logon** subkey.

2. On the **Edit** menu, point to **New**, and then click **DWORD Value**.

3. Name the item **UseHomeDirectory**. The **Data** value should be set to zero.

Maintaining Roaming User Profiles on Other Networks

Windows 98 provides limited support for user profiles if the network does not have support for a 32-bit, protected-mode client or centralized network logon. This includes networks that provide only 16-bit network clients and peer networks such as Windows for Workgroups or Windows 98 without a Windows NT domain.

To enable roaming user profiles on such a network, you must first establish a network directory that can be accessed by all users. For security reasons, you should make sure that this directory has read-only permissions so that users cannot modify it. You must create in that directory a text file that lists the home directories for all users who can use roaming user profiles. For example, such a file might be named Profiles.ini on \\Bigserver\Profiles and have the following contents:

```
[Profiles]
Mary=\\bigserver\homedirs\mary\user.dat
John=\\bigserver\homedirs\john\user.dat
Pat=\\bigserver\homedirs\pat\user.dat
```

After you have created this file, you must configure each computer running Windows 98 to use it. First, disable roaming profiles. For more information about disabling roaming profiles, see "Disabling Standard Roaming Profiles" earlier in this chapter.

▶ **To configure a computer for roaming user profiles on other networks**

1. In Registry Editor, expand the **Hkey_Local_Machine\Network** key, and select the **Logon** subkey.

2. On the **Edit** menu, point to **New**, and then click **String Value**.

3. Type **SharedProfileList** and press ENTER. Then press ENTER again.

4. In the **Edit String** dialog box, type the universal naming convention (UNC) path and file name for the home directory list (for example, **\\Bigserver\Profiles\Profiles.ini**).

5. Click **OK**.

Thereafter, when a user logs on at this computer, Windows 98 will search in the specified text file to determine the user's home directory. The user's profile will be loaded from that home directory as it is from other networks. If the user is not listed in the text file, the user profile will be only local.

Defining Mandatory User Profiles

In Windows 98, you can create mandatory user profiles for use on Windows NT or NetWare networks. With this feature you can create a standard user profile for each computer and make sure it is implemented every time a user logs on. To do this, create a User.dat file with the settings you want, save it as User.man, and place it in the network directory for each user you want to use that profile. The network directory is either the user's home directory (on a Windows NT network) or \Mail directory (on a NetWare network).

If User.man is present when the user logs on, Windows 98 uses this mandatory copy to load settings into the registry rather than any previous local user profile. If the user manually makes changes to the desktop configuration during the work session, these changes are not saved to the master copy in the user's network directory when the user logs off.

▶ **To create a mandatory user profile**

1. Enable user profiles. For information about this procedure, see "Enabling User Profiles" earlier in this chapter.

2. On any computer running Windows 98, customize the desktop as you want it to appear for the mandatory user profile.

3. Copy the required files for the user profile to the home directory for Windows NT networks or to the \Mail directory for NetWare networks, as described in "Setting Up User Profiles on a Windows NT Network" and "Setting Up User Profiles on a NetWare Network" earlier in this chapter.

Note   Windows 98 copies these files automatically for normal user profiles, but not for mandatory user profiles.

---

4. Rename User.dat to User.man in the user's home directory and reset the file attributes to be read-only.

Customizing the Desktop

The User Profile folders are a subset of the shell Special folders. These folders contain links to various desktop items and, coupled with the user's registry, make up the user's profile.

One of the important things about the User Profile folders is how they affect the look and feel of the desktop when a user logs on. Table 7.2 shows some User Profile folders and their contents.

Table 7.2   User Profile folders and their contents

Folder name	Contents
Desktop	File system directory used to physically store file objects on the desktop.
NetHood	File system directory containing objects that appear in the Network Neighborhood.
Recent	File system directory that contains the user's most recently used documents.
Start Menu	File system directory containing Start menu items.
Programs	File system directory that contains the user's program groups (which are also file system directories).
StartUp	File system directory that corresponds to the user's Startup program group.

The User Profile folders can be located on the local hard drive or, for more centralized control and easier management, they can be located on a network server. The location of the Profile folders can be applied with system policies. For more information about system policies, see Chapter 8, "System Policies." To find out more about customizing the Active Desktop, see Chapter 6, "Configuring the Active Desktop and Active Channels."

CHAPTER 8

System Policies

This chapter describes how system administrators can use system policies to control what users can and cannot do on the Microsoft Windows 98 desktop and on the network. These features can help decrease the cost of managing numerous computers by allowing you to manage configurations remotely.

In This Chapter

See Also

- For more information about automated installation, see Chapter 4, "Automated Installations."

- For more information about remote administration, see Chapter 23, "System and Remote Administration Tools."

Overview of System Policies

System policies allow you to override local registry values for user or computer settings. Policies are defined in a policy (POL) file, usually called Config.pol. When a user logs on, system policy settings overwrite default settings in the local registry. You can also set system policies to contain additional custom settings specific to the network.

Unlike System.dat and User.dat (the two files that make up the registry), Config.pol is not a required component of Windows 98 Setup. The following list summarizes the benefits of system policies.

You can use system policies to enforce system configuration. You can restrict what users are allowed to do from the desktop and what they are allowed to configure using Control Panel. Also, you can use system policies to centrally configure network settings, such as the network client configuration options and the ability to install or configure file and printer sharing services. Finally, you can use policies to customize such parts of the desktop as Network Neighborhood and the Programs folder.

You can change registry settings with System Policy Editor. You can use System Policy Editor to change many common registry settings for an individual computer, either local or remote. You can use these settings in a system policy file to change registry values on multiple computers.

You can apply system policies individually or for a group. You can use group policies to define a set of policies to be applied on the basis of membership in the groups already defined on a Windows NT or Novell NetWare network. Group policies make computer management on the corporate network easier by using the current administrative organization of users.

Windows 98 provides a set of policies that you can use to specify settings for users. You can also add new registry settings to this set of policies, or you can modify policy templates to create new custom policies for any applications that use the Windows 98 registry.

Important If you want to specify desktop, shell, and security settings for your organization as they relate to the Internet Explorer 4 (IE) browsing software or any part of the IE browsing software suite, use the Internet Explorer Administration Kit (IEAK) Profile Manager. The Profile Manager is an administrative tool that is automatically installed on your computer when you install the *Windows 98 Resource Kit* from the compact disc. The Profile Manager controls system policies for the IE browsing software suite. See Chapter 6, "Configuring the Active Desktop and Active Channels," and Chapter 20, "Internet Access and Tools," for more information.

Choosing to Use System Policies or Mandatory User Profiles

You can use either system policies or mandatory user profiles to enforce user settings. In certain situations, it may be desirable to use both system policies and mandatory user profiles. The two features differ in the following ways:

- System policies let you mandate user-specific and computer-specific settings. Mandatory user profiles let you mandate only user-specific settings.

- System policies let you selectively determine a subset of user settings to control, and each user controls the remaining settings. Mandatory user profiles always control every user-specific setting.

Before deciding to implement system policies, you should consider the following issues:

- What types of restrictions and settings would you like to define and manage centrally? For example, do you want to limit access to the MS-DOS prompt and other applications, or to Control Panel options, or do you want to implement a standard desktop for all users?

- Do you want to use one set of standard settings for all users and computers, or do you want to customize settings by groups of users? Also, do you want to maintain individual settings for users and computers? Typically, you customize settings by groups, so that the majority of users are in groups (such as Accounting, Marketing, and so on), and a small group of individuals (such as administrators) have special privileges. If so, you must install special files to support group policies.

- Will you be using user system policies (as opposed to defining only computer policies)? If so, enable user profiles on the computers running Windows 98, and make sure that the computers use 32-bit, protected-mode network clients.

- Do system policies in Windows 98 meet your system administration needs, or do you need a more sophisticated system? If you need a high level of administrative control, you might want to consider using a more sophisticated management software tool, such as Microsoft Systems Management Server, rather than System Policy Editor. For information, see Appendix E, "Microsoft Systems Management Server."

Preparing to Use System Policies

System policies offer you a powerful mechanism for increasing control and manageability of computers across the network. With system policies, you can do the following:

- Restrict access to Control Panel options.
- Restrict what users can do from the desktop.
- Customize parts of the desktop.
- Configure network settings.

For example, you can preset a user's environment so that the MS-DOS prompt or unapproved applications are not available. You can choose from the set of system policies offered by Windows 98 or create custom system policies.

Important You need to make some decisions about the default set of system policies before installing Windows 98. For more information, see Part 1, "Deployment and Installation," of the *Microsoft Windows 98 Resource Kit*.

The system policy entries you set through System Policy Editor are reflected in the policy file (Config.pol), which overwrites default User.dat and System.dat settings in the registry when the user logs on. Policy entries change registry settings in the following ways:

- Desktop settings modify the **HKEY_CURRENT_USER** key in the registry, which defines the contents of User.dat. All policy settings affecting User.dat are defined for a specific user or for the default user.
- Logon and network access settings modify the **HKEY_LOCAL_MACHINE** key in the registry, which defines the contents of System.dat. All policy settings affecting System.dat are defined for a specific computer or for the default computer.

Figure 8.1 shows how these settings are interrelated.

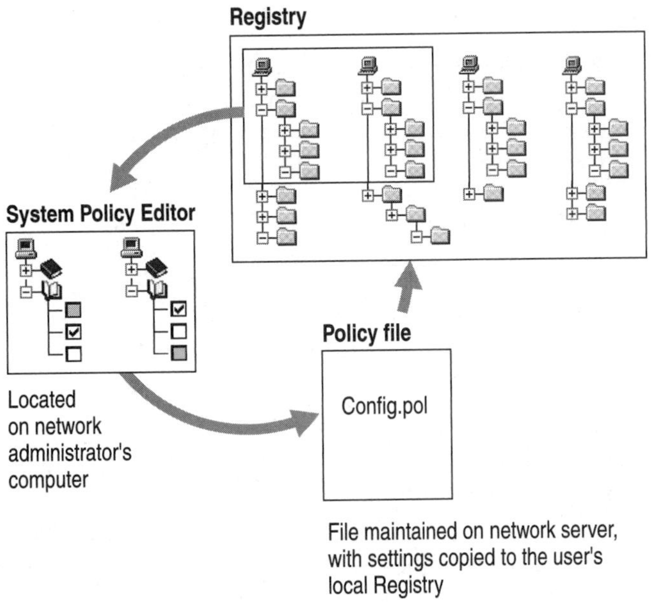

Figure 8.1   How policy settings are interrelated

To use System Policy Editor, first install it from the Windows 98 compact disc. The System Policy Editor consists of the following files. Poledit.exe, Poledit.inf, Windows.adm, and Common.adm. Other sample templates are provided but not required. Poledit.inf, Windows.adm, and Common.adm are placed in the Inf subdirectory of the Windows directory. Place Config.pol in a secure network location. Any custom templates you create use the ADM file name extension.

▶ **To install System Policy Editor**

1. In Control Panel, double-click Add/Remove Programs, click the **Windows Setup** tab, and then click **Have Disk**.

2. In the **Install From Disk** dialog box, click **Browse** and specify the Netadmin\Poledit directory on the Microsoft Windows 98 Resource Kit compact disc.

3. Click **OK**, and then click **OK** again in response to the dialog boxes.

4. In the **Have Disk** dialog box, select the **System Policy Editor** check box, and then click **Install**.

If you want to enable group policies support, place Grouppol.dll in the System subdirectory of the Windows directory on each client computer. In addition, you must make some changes to the registry on each computer to use Grouppol.dll.

You can install group policies during Setup using a batch install script or at any time using the Add/Remove Programs option of Control Panel. Once group policies have been enabled, they are no longer displayed as an option in Add/Remove Programs.

▶ **To install group policies**

1. In Control Panel, double-click Add/Remove Programs, click the **Windows Setup** tab, and then click **System Tools**.

2. Select the checkbox for **Group Policies**, click **OK**, and then click **OK** again.

Important System policies are based on the content of the registry and cannot be edited with a text editor. To define and manage system policies, use System Policy Editor and other supporting tools.

You can, however, use a text editor to edit the template files used by System Policy Editor, as described in "Using System Policy Templates" later in this chapter. If you want to use system policies, perform the following preliminary steps:

- On the administrator's computer, install System Policy Editor from the Netadmin\Poledit directory on the Microsoft Windows 98 Resource Kit compact disc. Decide which users can install and have access to this tool for modifying policies. You probably will not install System Policy Editor on most client computers.

- On the client computers, enable user profiles to ensure full support for system policies. If user profiles are not enabled, only the computer settings in any system policy will be written to the registry.

- Install support for group policies on the client computers if your site will use these. For more information, see "Using System Policy Editor" later in this chapter.

How System Policies Work

When the user logs on, Windows 98 checks the user's configuration information for the location of the policy file. Windows 98 then downloads the policies and copies the information into the registry by using the following process:

1. If user profiles are enabled, Windows 98 checks for the Config.pol file and parses it for the user and group names it contains. If it finds user information for this user, Windows 98 applies the user-specific policy. If it does not find the user in the Config.pol file, Windows 98 applies the Default User policy.

If support for group policies has been installed on the computer, Windows 98 checks whether the user is registered as a member of any groups. If so, group policies are downloaded starting with the lowest-priority group and ending with the highest-priority group. Group policies are processed for all groups the user belongs to. The group with the highest priority is processed last so that the settings in that group's policy file supersede those in lower-priority groups. Group policies are not applied if policies have been defined for a specific user. Then, all settings are copied into the User.dat portion of the registry.

2. Windows 98 checks for the Config.pol file that contains information for this computer. If one exists, Windows 98 applies the computer-specific policies to the user's desktop environment. If a policy for that computer does not exist, Windows 98 applies the default computer policy. This data is then copied into the System.dat portion of the registry.

By default, Windows 98 automatically attempts to download computer and user policies from the Netlogon directory on a Windows NT server or the Public directory on a NetWare server. This default location can be overridden in a policy file setting. If no server is present, Windows 98 uses the settings currently on the computer unless a manual update path for a policy is specified in the system registry.

System Policies for Users

You can manage user settings in system policies only if user profiles are enabled on the target computer. System Policy Editor uses the properties for Default User to define the default policies in the following areas:

Control Panel. Set policies to prevent the user from accessing such Control Panel features as network, password, or system settings.

Desktop. Set policies to use standard wallpaper and color schemes.

Network. Set policies to restrict peer resource sharing or to specify networking components and settings.

Shell. Set policies to customize folders on the desktop and to restrict changes to the user interface.

System. Set policies to restrict the use of registry editing tools, applications, and MS-DOS-based applications.

You can apply these policies to the default user, to specific named users, or to groups of users. For more information about the settings for each of these categories, see "System Policy Settings Summary" later in this chapter.

System Policies for Computers

You can use System Policy Editor to define settings for a default computer or for specific named computers. The default computer settings are used when no explicit computer specific policy has been configured.

Computer settings in system policies prevent users from modifying the hardware and environment settings for the operating system, ensuring that Windows 98 starts in a predictable way. You can set options to restrict access to computer-specific system and network features, as described in "System Policy Settings Summary" later in this chapter.

Internet Explorer Browsing Software System Policies

Windows 98 includes seven policy files, listed in Table 8.1, that contain settings for various components of the Internet Explorer browsing software. You can use these settings to control such things as the look of the Active Desktop and the Internet Explorer browsing software, and to specify the default security zone for Outlook Express HTML messages. For information about the Internet Explorer browsing software, see Chapter 20, "Internet Access and Tools" and Chapter 6, "Configuring the Active Desktop and Active Channels."

Table 8.1   Internet Explorer browsing software policy files

File Name	User Policy	Computer Policy
Chat.adm	Settings for Chat	
Conf.adm	Settings and restrictions for NetMeeting	Settings for NetMeeting protocols
Inetres.adm	Restrictions for Internet Explorer browsing software	Settings for Internet Explorer browsing software security and code download
Inetset.adm	Settings for Internet Explorer browsing software	Settings for Internet Explorer browsing software
Oe.adm	Settings for Outlook Express	
Shell.adm	Settings and restrictions for the Active Desktop	

Note You can also control Internet Explorer browsing software settings using the IEAK Profile Manager, which can be installed from the Microsoft Windows 98 Resource Kit compact disc. For information about the IEAK Profile Manager, see Chapter 6, "Configuring the Active Desktop and Active Channels" and Chapter 20, "Internet Access and Tools."

Preparing to Use System Policies on the Network

You can have Windows 98 copy system policies from the network either manually or automatically. If you want to copy system policies automatically, Windows 98 locates the system policy file (Config.pol) in the proper directory on the network and downloads its policy settings into the registry of the local computer when the user logs on. If you want to copy system policies manually, Windows 98 copies the system policy file from a location you specify. Automatic downloading works only if the file name for the system policy file is Config.pol.

Note Windows 98 supports automatic downloading for Windows NT and NetWare networks. The 32-bit, protected-mode network clients—subsequently made available for other networks—might also provide support for automatic downloading.

Setting Up for Automatic Downloading of System Policies

By default, Windows 98 downloads system policies automatically. However, if you have switched to manual downloading, the following procedures describe how to return to automatic downloading.

If you have created a POL file, Windows 98 automatically downloads it from the Netlogon directory on a Windows NT network or from the Public directory on a NetWare network.

▶ **To set up automatic downloading on Windows NT networks**

1. In Control Panel, double-click Network, and then make sure that **Client for Microsoft Networks** is specified as the Primary Network Logon client and that the domain is defined. For more information, see Chapter 18, "Logon, Browsing, and Resource Sharing."

2. Create the policy file to be downloaded, and save it in the following location:

   ```
   \\PDC\x$\WINNT\system32\Repl\Import\Scripts\Config.pol (where x =
   SystemDrive)
   ```

Important You must create the Config.pol file on a Windows 98 (or Windows 95) computer and then copy it to your Windows NT server in the location specified in the previous procedure. Because of the different registry formats in Windows 98/95 and Windows NT, creating the Config.pol file on the Windows NT server will prevent it from working on your Windows 98 client computers.

▶ **To set up automatic downloading on NetWare networks**

1. In Control Panel, double-click Network, and then make sure that **Microsoft Client for NetWare Networks** is specified as the Primary Network Logon client and that a preferred server is specified in properties for the network client. For more information, see Chapter 17, "Windows 98 on Third-Party Networks."

2. Create the policy file to be downloaded, and save it in the following location:

   \\preferred server\sys\public\Config.pol

For NetWare networks, the client computers must be running Microsoft Client for NetWare Networks. If the client computers are using NetWare 3.*x* workstation shell (NETX) or Virtual Loadable Module (VLM), policies must be downloaded manually.

Important Make sure you place system policy files on the user's preferred server. Policy files are not available if they are stored on other NetWare servers or on computers running File and Printer Sharing for NetWare Networks.

Setting Up for Manual Downloading of System Policies

If you use the Remote Update policy, you can configure Windows 98 to allow you to download policy files manually (even when they are stored locally) by indicating a separate network or local computer location. Manual downloading overrides automatic downloading and allows you to choose where a user's policies are stored.

You can set up each computer individually for manual downloading, but this can be time-consuming. If possible (that is, when the client computers use 32-bit, protected-mode network clients), you should set up each computer for automatic downloading and then use the Remote Update policy to point specific computers to other servers as appropriate for your environment and users.

However, for real-mode network clients, such as Novell NETX or VLM, you must enable manual downloading on each computer. After you configure the client computer, the system policy file will be downloaded the next time the user logs on.

▶ **To configure a computer for manual downloading of system policies**

1. In System Policy Editor, click the **File** menu, and then click **Open Registry**.

2. Double-click **Local Computer**.

3. Double-click **Windows 98 Network**, double-click **Update**, and the select the **Remote Update** check box.

Note The remote computer must be running the Microsoft Remote Registry service, Remote Administration must be enabled, and user-level security must be enabled.

Make sure to type the universal naming convention (UNC) path and the file name in the **Path for manual update** box.

On Windows NT or NetWare networks on which you are using automatic downloading of policies, you can set a system policy to allow manual downloading. This option works only after system policies have been downloaded automatically the first time after Windows 98 has been installed. The first automatic downloading includes information in the system policies that defines the location to be used for manual downloading.

▶ **To define the location of policies for manual downloading**

1. In System Policy Editor, open Config.pol, and then double-click the Default Computer icon.

2. Double-click **Windows 98 Network**, double-click **Update**, and then select the **Remote Update** check box.

3. In the **Update Mode** box, click **Manual**.

4. In the **Path for manual update** box, type the UNC path and file name for the system policy file you want to download. Make sure this file exists in the location you specify. (Otherwise, an error will result.)

Important On a Windows NT network, you must create the Config.pol file on a Windows 98 computer and then copy it to your Windows NT server. Because of the different registry formats in Windows 98 and Windows NT, creating the Config.pol file on the Windows NT server will prevent it from working on your Windows 98 client computers.

On large networks, when thousands of users log on at the same time, all gaining access to the same policy file, you might experience slow network performance. To avoid a bottleneck, Windows 98 offers load balancing on Windows NT networks. With load balancing enabled, policies are taken from the logon server (which can be a domain controller or a backup domain controller) rather than the primary domain controller. Although this spreads the load over many servers, it does require that you replicate the policy file on each server. For information about Windows NT replication, see the *Microsoft Windows NT Server Networking Guide* in the *Microsoft Windows NT Server Resource Kit* (for Windows NT version 4.0).

> **Note** Load-balancing works only when using a 32-bit protected mode client setup for automatic downloading of system policies.

▶ **To enable load balancing**

1. Perform the earlier procedure, "To define the location of policies for manual downloading."

2. Under **Settings for Remote Update**, make sure **Load-balance** is selected.

If you want to use load balancing, make sure it is enabled on each client computer. Also, make sure you have a current policy file on each server that will participate in load balancing, including all Windows NT domain controllers and servers. One convenient way to implement load balancing is to set this policy in the Config.pol file that is on the primary domain controller. As each client computer downloads this policy, it will subsequently look for Config.pol on the logon server.

Using System Policy Editor

You can use System Policy Editor to create system policies. More specifically, you can do the following with System Policy Editor:

- Set entries for the default computer and user policy entries. This creates a default policy file for all users and computers, which is downloaded when each user logs on.

- Create entries for individual users, individual computers, or groups of users. By default, these include the policy entries you defined for Default User and Default Computer.

- Specify whether and in what manner you want policies downloaded from a centralized server, or specify whether you want to have policies downloaded from other specific locations for all or some users.

> **Caution** System Policy Editor is a powerful tool; you should restrict its use to network administrators. To avoid unauthorized use, do not install this tool on users' computers, and restrict access to the source files so users cannot install it themselves.

Installing System Policy Editor

You can install and use System Policy Editor from the Netadmin\Poledit directory on the Microsoft Windows 98 Resource Kit compact disc.

▶ **To install System Policy Editor**

1. In Control Panel, double-click the Add/Remove Programs icon, click the **Windows Setup** tab, and then click **Have Disk**.

2. In the **Install From Disk** dialog box, click **Browse** and specify the Netadmin\Poledit directory on the Microsoft Windows 98 Resource Kit compact disc.

3. Click **OK**, and then click **OK** again in response to the dialog boxes.

4. In the **Have Disk** dialog box, select the **System Policy Editor** check box, and then click **Install**.

▶ **To run System Policy Editor**

- On the **Start** menu, click **Run**. Type **poledit**, and then click **OK**.

If you want to use group policies, you must install that capability on each computer running Windows 98 by either using a custom setup script when you install Windows 98 or using the Add/Remove Programs option in Control Panel.

▶ **To set up capabilities for group policies using Add/Remove Programs**

1. In Control Panel, double-click Add/Remove Programs, click the **Windows Setup** tab, and then click **Have Disk**.

2. In the **Install From Disk** dialog box, click **Browse** and specify the Netadmin\Poledit directory on the Microsoft Windows 98 Resource Kit compact disc.

3. Click **OK**, and then click **OK** again in response to the dialog boxes.

4. In the **Have Disk** dialog box, select the **Group Policies** check box, and then click **Install**.

Windows 98 Setup places Grouppol.dll in the Windows System directory on the client computer and makes the required registry changes.

For more information about adding the ability to use group policies when installing Windows 98 using custom setup scripts, see Chapter 4, "Automated Installations."

Modifying Policies and the Registry with System Policy Editor

You can use System Policy Editor in two different modes: Registry mode and Policy File mode:

- In *Registry mode*, you can directly edit the registry of the local or the remote computer, and changes are reflected immediately. For more information about editing the registry for a remote computer, see Chapter 23, "System and Remote Administration Tools."

- In *Policy File mode*, you can create and modify system policy (POL) files for use on other computers. In this mode, the registry is edited indirectly. Changes are reflected only after the policy is downloaded when the user logs on.

▶ **To use System Policy Editor in Registry mode**

- In System Policy Editor, on the **File** menu, click **Open Registry**. Then double-click the appropriate Local User or Local Computer icon, depending on what part of the registry you want to edit. After you make changes, you must shut down and restart the computer for the changes to take effect.

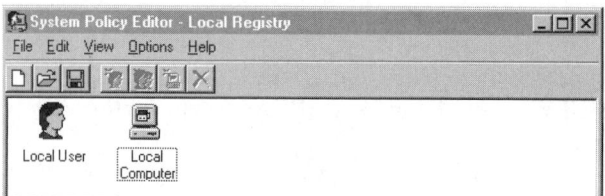

Important Use Registry mode only when you want to make direct changes to the registry. You should typically change system settings by using the Control Panel options and other tools provided with Windows 98.

▶ **To use System Policy Editor in Policy File mode**

- In System Policy Editor, on the **File** menu, click **New** or **Open** to open a policy file.

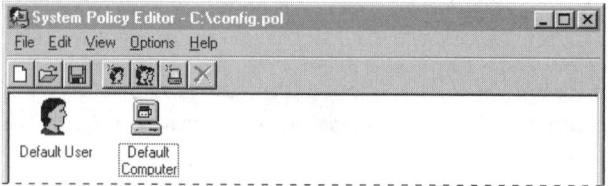

When you edit settings in Policy File mode, clicking a registry option sets one of three possible states:

- Selected
- Cleared
- Dimmed

Each time you select an option, the display cycles to show the next possible state. This is different from selecting a standard check box, which sets an option only to on or off. Table 8.2 summarizes the three possible states for options in a policy file.

Table 8.2   Option states in a policy file

Option state	Meaning
☑	Selected—this policy will be implemented, changing the state of the user's computer to conform to the policy when the user logs on. If the option was previously checked the last time the user logged on, Windows 98 makes no changes.
☐	Cleared— this generally forces the registry setting to the opposite of the on state. Depending on the specific policy, this has the effect of either implementing or not implementing the policy each time the user logs on.
▨	Dimmed—the setting is unchanged from the last time the user logged on, and Windows 98 will make no related modifications to the system configuration.

The dimmed state ensures that Windows 98 provides quick processing at system startup, because it does not need to process each entry each time a user logs on. |

Caution   When you define a policy option, make sure you have set the proper state for the option. If you set an option by selecting it but then change your mind and clear the option, you can inadvertently destroy the user's previous configuration. If you decide not to set a particular policy option, make sure that option is shaded so that the user can configure and retain the setting for that option.

For example, you might select the option to specify Microsoft Client for NetWare Networks and then click again to clear that option. When the user logs on and the policy is downloaded, this setting would wipe out the user's current configuration that specifies Client for NetWare Networks.

If a setting requires additional information, an edit control appears at the bottom of the **Default User Properties** dialog box. For example, if **Wallpaper** is selected in the **Desktop** settings, the following dialog box appears.

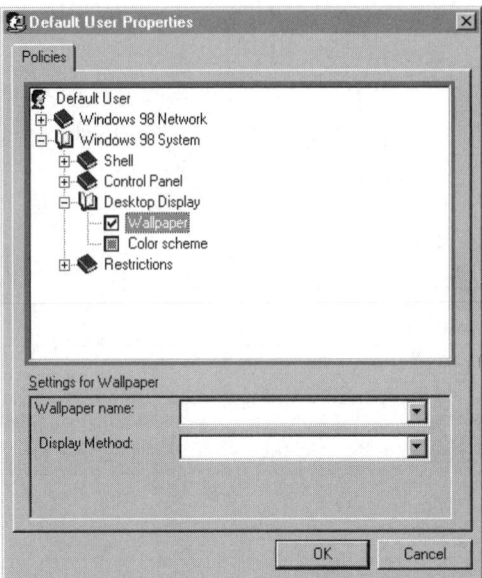

Usually, if a policy has been selected and you no longer want to enforce it, you should clear the box to cancel the policy. However, in the following cases, a few policies might behave differently than you might expect if the check box is cleared:

- The policy setting contains an edit box that must be completed (as opposed to a simple check box).

- The policy setting can also be set by users through Control Panel.

In these cases, you should consider making sure the check box is dimmed when you no longer want to enforce the policies. A user can then modify this information as needed.

Table 8.3 describes the results of different settings for such policies.

Table 8.3   Policy settings and their behavior

Policy	Behavior
Settings for Wallpaper	- Selecting it forces the specified wallpaper to be used.
	- Clearing it removes the wallpaper (the user will not have any wallpaper).
	- Leaving it dimmed means that the user can choose wallpaper after clicking Display in Control Panel.

Table 8.3   Policy settings and their behavior (*continued*)

Policy	Behavior
Client for NetWare Networks: Preferred Server	<ul><li>Selecting it sets the preferred server you specify.</li><li>Clearing it deletes the preferred server from the computer's registry. The user must specify the preferred server at every logon if set to primary logon.</li><li>Leaving it dimmed means the user can specify the preferred server after clicking Network in Control Panel.</li></ul>
Microsoft Client for Windows Networks: Domain	<ul><li>Selecting it sets the Windows NT Logon domain you specify.</li><li>Clearing it deletes the domain setting from the computer's registry. The user must specify the domain at every logon if set to primary logon.</li><li>Leaving it dimmed means the user can specify the domain after clicking Network in Control Panel.</li></ul>
Microsoft Client for Windows Networks: Workgroup	<ul><li>Selecting it sets the workgroup for that computer.</li><li>Clearing it deletes the workgroup setting from the computer's registry.</li><li>Leaving it dimmed means the user can specify the workgroup after clicking Network in Control Panel.</li></ul>

Creating System Policies

This section describes procedures for creating system policies.

To take advantage of automatic downloading, discussed earlier, create a policy file that contains user, computer, and group entries to reside in the Netlogon share of a Windows NT server or the Public directory of a NetWare server. Based on the client selected, Windows 98 automatically looks in one of these locations to download your newly created system policy.

▶ **To view or edit default system policies**

1. In System Policy Editor, click the **File** menu, and then click **New File**.

2. Double-click **Default User** to define the default settings for user-specific policies.

   –Or–

   Double-click **Default Computer** to define the settings for computer-specific policies.

3. Select the policies you want to put in place.

Creating Policies for Individual Users or Computers

This section describes how to create a system policy for a user or computer.

Tip To reduce the management load, minimize the number of user and computer entries in system policy files. Consider first creating one standard system policy for all users by editing default settings, and then creating settings for individuals on an exception basis.

▶ **To create system policies for a new user or computer**

1. In System Policy Editor, click the **Edit** menu, and then click **Add User** or **Add Computer**.

2. Type the name of the user or computer you want to add. System Policy Editor adds an icon for each user or computer you add.

Tip You can easily copy policy values to the new user or computer from an existing user or computer by copying and pasting them. Highlight an existing user or computer, and on the **Edit** menu, click **Copy**. Then highlight the new user or computer, and on the **Edit** menu, click **Paste**.

▶ **To edit existing system policies**

1. In System Policy Editor, double-click the icon for the user or computer policies you want to edit.

2. Select or clear individual policies by clicking the policy name.

Creating Policies for Groups

Group policies are supported for both Windows NT and NetWare networks. Creating policies for groups is similar to creating policies for users or computers.

You must first make sure that Grouppol.dll, which supports group policies, has been successfully installed on each client computer. For more information, see "Installing System Policy Editor" earlier in this chapter.

You cannot create new groups by using System Policy Editor; you can use only existing groups on the NetWare or Windows NT network. To create a new group, use the tools provided with your network administrative software.

► **To create system policies for groups**

1. In System Policy Editor, click the **Edit** menu, and then click **Add Group**.

2. Type the name of the group you want to add, and then click **OK**.

   –Or–

   If user-level security is enabled, click **Browse**, click the name of the group you want, and then click **OK**.

3. Select or clear policies by clicking the policy name.

Group policies are downloaded starting with the lowest-priority group and ending with the highest-priority group. All groups are processed. The group with the highest priority is processed last so that any of the settings in that group's policy file supersede those in lower-priority groups. You can use one policy file for each group, even if some of the client computers in the group do not have support installed for group policies. Client computers that are not configured for using group policies will ignore group policy files.

Important If a policy exists for a specific named user, group policies are not applied to that user.

► **To set priority levels for groups**

1. In System Policy Editor, click the **File** menu, and then click **Open File**.

2. Locate the Config.pol file, and then click **Open**.

3. On the **Options** menu, click **Group Priority**.

4. In the **Group Priority** dialog box, click on a group name, and then use **Move Up** and **Move Down** to move it into its relative priority.

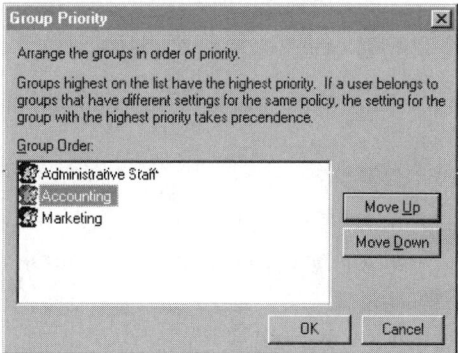

Creating NetWare Directory Services System Policies

Microsoft Service for NetWare Directory Services supports system policies on a Novell Directory Services (NDS) network. When your users log on, Windows looks for the policy file in the location you specify.

Note The first time system policies are implemented on an NDS tree, the tree's schema database, which defines the objects in the tree, is modified. This happens because the schema provides templates for each NDS object type, and adding system policies is a modification of some templates. To modify the schema, you must have Supervisor rights to the [Root] on the NDS tree. Subsequent implementations of system policies, however, can be done by administrators who do not have Supervisor rights to the [Root] on the NDS tree.

If you plan to implement user or group system policies, you must enable user profiles on your network. Also, for group policies, at least one NetWare version 4.1 server on the network must have bindery emulation enabled. Make sure the group and all the users in the group are in the bindery context for the server.

▶ **To set the system policies in a new or existing policy file**

1. In System Policy Editor, click the **Options** menu, and then click **Template**.

2. Click **Open Template**, and then type the path for *Filename*.adm.

3. If you have already implemented system policies on your network, open the current policy file.

    –Or–

    If you have not implemented system policies on your network, on the **File** menu, click **New**.

4. Set the policies, and then save them as Config.pol. (If a policy file with a different name already exists on your network, type the name of that policy file instead.) The new settings will be merged into the existing policy file.

▶ **To specify the location of the policy file**

1. In Network Neighborhood, find the organization or organizational unit object for which you have created the policy file.

2. Right-click the icon for the organization or organizational unit object, and then click **Properties**.

3. Click the **NDS Administration Settings** tab.

Note To gain access to the **NDS Administration Settings** tab, you must be a trustee for the volume object. You must also have the Supervisor object and Supervisor property correct for the volume.

---

4. Type the path and name of the system policy file.

Any container (Organization or Organizational Unit) can have its own policy file. When a user logs on to NDS, the Service for NetWare Directory Services looks in the parent container of the logon container, and so on up to the root.

The advantage of this is that you can put a policy file in the root and have it apply to every object in the tree, or you can have individual system policy files in any container below the root.

Managing Custom Folders for Use with System Policies

You can define five system policies to create a custom desktop. These policies use custom folders, created by the administrator, that contain the specific settings for the customized desktop. Table 8.4 summarizes the policies used to create a custom desktop.

Table 8.4   System policies used to create a custom desktop

Policy	Description
Custom Programs Folder	Shortcuts that appear in the **Programs** group on the **Start** menu.
Custom Network Neighborhood	Shortcuts to resources that appear in Network Neighborhood, including shortcuts to shared printers and files and to Dial-Up Networking connections.
Custom Desktop Icons	Shortcuts that appear on the desktop.
Custom Start Menu	Shortcuts and other options that appear on the **Start** menu, as defined by using the **Taskbar Properties** dialog box.
Custom Startup Folder	Programs or batch files that appear in the **Startup** group on the **Start** menu.

Before you create a custom desktop by using system policies, you must define custom folders.

▶   **To define custom folders for use with policy files**

1. Create and place the custom folders in a central location where users can gain access. You can use any valid folder names for the folders you create. Windows 98 uses the path defined for the related policy to find the folder.

Note   To prevent accidental removal or unauthorized changes, place custom folders in directories where users are restricted to read-only access.

---

2. Place the custom set of files and shortcuts you want in each folder.

- You can place any kind of files in the custom folders.

- For shortcuts, make sure that the path specified in the **Target** box in **Shortcut** properties is a UNC name, rather than a mapped directory. Otherwise, the users who will access resources using these shortcuts must have the same drives mapped in their logon scripts.

Caution Do not place folders in the custom Network Neighborhood. Windows 98 does not support this feature, and unpredictable results can occur.

▶ **To create a custom desktop using system policies**

1. In System Policy Editor, open the System Policy file.

2. In the System Policy file, set the related policies.

3. In the **Path to get Program items from** box, type the path to the folder's location.

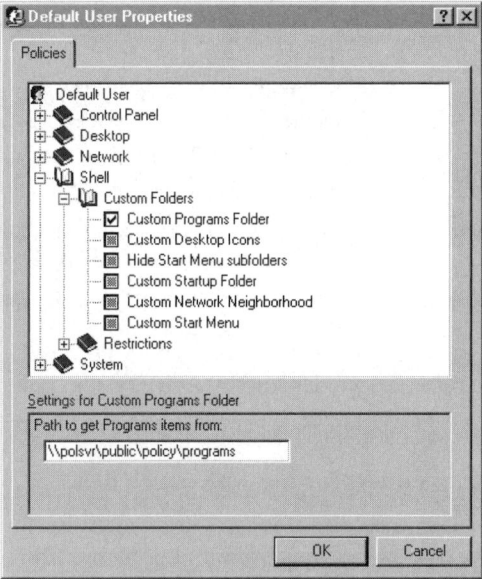

4. If you selected the **Custom Programs Folder** or **Custom Desktop Icons** policies, also select the **Hide Start Menu subfolders** policy check box to enable it. Otherwise, multiple **Programs** entries will appear on the user's **Start** menu—one for the location of the Custom Programs Folder and one for the default location.

If the custom folders will not be stored in the directories where Windows 98 automatically looks for them, you must specify another location when you specify the Custom Folders policies. For example, you might want to create these folders where the system policy files are located on the server.

The following list shows the default locations for custom folders.

- Custom Programs Folders:

  c:\windows\profiles\username\start menu\programs

- Custom Desktop Icons:

  c:\windows\profiles\username\desktop

- Custom Startup Folder:

  c:\windows\profiles\username\start menu\programs\startup

- Custom Network Neighborhood:

  c:\windows\profiles\username\nethood

- Custom Start Menu:

  c:\windows\profiles\username\start menu

NetWare Directory Services System Policies

Table 8.5 summarizes the new system policies provided by Microsoft Service for NetWare Directory Services.

Table 8.5   New system policies provided by Microsoft Service for NetWare Directory Services

Option	Description
Default Name Context	Sets the default context.
Preferred Tree	Sets the default NDS tree.
Disable automatic tree logon	Causes you to be prompted to log on to the NDS tree when starting Windows 98, even if your NDS password is the same as your Windows password.
Enable logon confirmation	Causes a confirmation dialog box to appear after you log on.
Default type of NetWare logon	Specifies whether you log on as a bindery user (for example, by using logon /b) or an NDS user by default.
Don't show Advanced logon button	Hides the **Advanced** button on the logon dialog box. The **Advanced** button enables you to choose a different tree or context when you log on.
Don't allow browsing outside the default context	Hides Directory Services containers outside the default context.
Don't show volume objects	Hides NDS volume objects from the directory tree in Network Neighborhood.

Table 8.5   New system policies provided by Microsoft Service for NetWare Directory Services (*continued*)

Option	Description
Don't show server objects	Hides NDS server objects from the directory tree in Network Neighborhood.
Don't show servers that aren't NDS objects	Hides all servers that are not objects in the Directory Tree (for example, bindery servers and peer servers).
Don't show printer objects	Hides NDS printer objects in Network Neighborhood.
Don't show print queue objects	Hides NDS queue objects in Network Neighborhood.
Don't show container objects	Hides NDS organizations and organizational units in Network Neighborhood.
Don't show peer workgroups	Hides Windows 98 workgroups within Network Neighborhood.
Load NetWare DLLs at startup	Automatically loads Novell-supplied NetWare dynamic-link libraries (DLLs) required by some NDS applications.

Restricting Access to Computer-Specific Settings

When you double-click the **Default Computer** icon in System Policy Editor, a list of system policy options for settings that apply to the computer appears. This section describes these options.

Restricting Access to Network Settings

Within this category of options, you can restrict the user's ability to share files and printers. Typically, you might want to set these policies to apply when file and printer sharing services are installed but when you do not want users to change which resources are shared on their computers. Table 8.6 describes the system policies you can apply to file and printer sharing.

Table 8.6   User policies restricting access to file and printer sharing

Option	Description
Sharing	
Disable file sharing controls	Removes the **Sharing** properties from directories in Windows Explorer.
Disable print sharing controls	Removes the **Sharing** properties from the Printer directory.

Restricting Access to Shell Settings

Table 8.7 describes the system policies you can apply to folders and user interface options.

Table 8.7   User policies restricting access to shell settings

Option	Description
Custom Folders	
Custom Programs Folder	Customizes the contents of the Programs directory. You must also type a path for the directory containing complete files or LNK files that define the Programs directory items.
Custom Desktop Icons	Customizes desktop icons. You must also type a path for the directory containing complete files or LNK files that define the desktop shortcuts.
Hide Start Menu subfolders	Check this when you use a custom Programs folder. Otherwise, two Programs entries will appear on the user's **Start** menu.
Custom Startup Folder	Customizes the contents of the Startup directory. You must also type a path for the directory containing complete files or LNK files that define the Startup directory items.
Custom Network Neighborhood	Customizes the contents of Network Neighborhood. You must also type a path for the directory containing complete files or LNK files that define the Network Neighborhood items.
Custom Start Menu	Customizes what is listed on the **Start** menu. You must also type a path for the directory containing complete files or LNK files that define the **Start** menu items.
Restrictions	
Remove 'Run' command	Prevents access to the **Run** command on the **Start** menu.
Remove Folders from 'Settings' on Start Menu	Prevents access to any item listed under **Settings** on the **Start** menu.
Remove Taskbar from 'Settings' on Start Menu	Prevents access to the **Taskbar** item listed under **Settings** on the **Start** menu.
Remove 'Find' command	Prevents access to any item listed under **Find** on the **Start** menu.
Hide Drives in 'My Computer'	Prevents display of drives in My Computer.
Hide Network Neighborhood	Prevents access to Network Neighborhood.
No 'Entire Network' in Network Neighborhood	Prevents access to the **Entire Network** icon in Network Neighborhood.
No workgroup contents in Network Neighborhood	Prevents workgroup contents from being displayed in Network Neighborhood.
Hide all items on Desktop	Prevents access to all items on the desktop.
Disable Shut Down command	Prevents access to the **Shut Down** command on the **Start** menu; displays explanation in a dialog box.
Don't save settings at exit	Prevents settings from being written to the file system.

Restricting Access to System Settings

The system policies in this category restrict the use of registry editing tools, applications, and MS-DOS-based applications. Table 8.8 describes the policies you can set within this category.

Table 8.8   User policies restricting access to system settings

Option	Description
Restrictions	
Disable registry editing tools	Prevents users from running registry editing tools.
Only run allowed Windows applications	Prevents users from running any Windows-based applications except those that are listed. Click **Show** to define the allowed applications.
Disable MS-DOS prompt	Prevents access to the MS-DOS prompt.
Disable single-mode MS-DOS applications	Prevents users from running MS-DOS-based applications in MS-DOS mode.

Restricting Access to Computer-Specific Network Settings

This category of options includes system policy settings for the following:

- Enabling user-level security.
- Logon dialog box settings.
- Microsoft Client for NetWare Networks settings.
- Microsoft Client for Windows Networks settings.
- Password settings.
- Dial-Up Networking settings.
- Sharing settings.
- Simple Network Management Protocol (SNMP) settings.
- Update settings for policy downloading.

These system policies are applied to the computer and are stored in System.dat. Table 8.9 describes the system policies you can set in this category.

Table 8.9   Computer policies restricting access to network settings

Option	Description
Access Control	
User-level access control	Enables user-level security on the local computer using pass-through logon validation by a Windows NT or a NetWare server. You must specify the server or domain, and the type of authenticator for validation.

Table 8.9   Computer policies restricting access to network settings (*continued*)

Option	Description
Logon	
Logon Banner	Allows you to specify text for a caption and other text to be displayed in a logon banner.
Require validation from network for Windows access	Each logging on must be validated by a server before access to Windows is allowed. This policy has no effect on a portable computer after it is undocked.
Don't show last user at logon	The user name field will be blank in the network logon screen.
Don't show logon progress	Disables the display of the logon progress dialog.
Password	
Hide share passwords with asterisks	Replaces characters with asterisks when users type passwords to access a shared resource. Applies to share-level security only; this setting is on by default.
Disable password caching	Prevents saving passwords. (Notice that the user cannot successfully use the Quick Logon feature for Microsoft networks if password caching is disabled.)
Require alphanumeric Windows password	Requires that the Windows password contain a combination of letters and numbers.
Minimum Windows password length	Requires that the Windows logon password has at least the specified number of characters.
Proxy Server	
Disable automatic location of proxy server	Prevents Windows 98 from checking with the Dynamic Host Configuration Protocol (DHCP) server for the presence of a proxy server.
Microsoft Client for NetWare Networks	
Preferred server	Allows you to specify the name of the NetWare network server this computer should log on to first.
Support long file names	Allows support for long file names. The values are 0 (no support for long file names on NetWare servers), 1 (support on NetWare servers version 3.12 and later), and 2 (support if the NetWare server supports long file names).
Disable automatic NetWare login	Specifies that Windows 98 should not first silently use the user's name and password to attempt to connect to a NetWare server, which is the default behavior.

Table 8.9   Computer policies restricting access to network settings (*continued*)

Option	Description
Microsoft Client for Windows Networks	
Log on to Windows NT	Specifies that this computer can participate in a Windows NT domain. Type the name of the domain. If this option is checked, the next two options are also available.
Display domain logon confirmation	Displays a message when the domain controller has validated user logon.
Disable caching of domain password	Specifies that no caching is used for the network password.
Workgroup	Specifies that this computer can participate in a workgroup. Type the name of the workgroup.
Alternate Workgroup	Specifies that an alternate workgroup must be defined to see Microsoft peer servers in other workgroups if your workgroup does not have any computers running File and Printer Sharing for Microsoft Networks (that is, they all run File and Printer Sharing for NetWare), but the computer runs a Microsoft network client. The workgroup specified should include at least one computer running File and Printer Sharing for Microsoft Networks.
File and Printer Sharing for NetWare Networks	
Disable SAP Advertising	Disables the Service Advertising Protocol (SAP). This computer will not advertise its presence, and NETX or VLM clients cannot see it or connect to it
File and Printer Sharing for Microsoft Networks	
Disable file sharing	Prevents file sharing over a network.
Disable print sharing	Prevents printer sharing over a network.
Dial-Up Networking	
Disable dial-in	Prevents dial-in connections to the computer.
Update	
Remote Update	Defines how system policies will be updated. If this option is selected, the next four options are also available.
Update Mode	Determines whether system policies are downloaded automatically (the default) or manually.
Path for manual update	Specifies the UNC path and file name for manual downloading of system policies.
Display error messages	When a user logs on, if the system policy file is not available, displays an error message.
Load-balance	For Windows NT networks, allows Windows 98 to look for policy files on the logon domain.

Restricting Access to Computer-Specific System Settings

This category of options includes system policy settings for the network path for setup and user profiles. Table 8.10 describes the system policies you can set within this category.

Table 8.10   Computer policies restricting access to system settings

Option	Description
Enable User Profiles	Enables basic user profiles functionality.
Network path for Windows Setup	Defines the network or local location of the Windows 98 Setup program and files. You must also type a UNC or local path for the setup directory.
Network path for Windows Tour	Defines the network location of the Windows 98 Tour program. You must also type a UNC path ending with Discover.exe.
Communities	Specifies one or more groups of hosts to which this computer belongs for purposes of SNMP administration. These are the communities that are allowed to query the SNMP agent.
Permitted managers	Specifies Internet protocol (IP) or Internetwork Packet Exchange (IPX) addresses allowed to obtain information from an SNMP agent. If this policy is not checked, any SNMP console can query the agent.
Traps For 'Public' community	Specifies trap destinations, or IP or IPX addresses of hosts in the public community to which you want the SNMP service to send traps. For more information about sending traps to other communities, see Chapter 23, "System and Remote Administration Tools."
Internet MIB (RFC 1156)	Allows you to specify the contact name and location if you are using Internet MIB.
Run	Defines applications and utilities to run when the user logs on. Click **Show** to specify items to run.
Run Once	Defines applications and utilities to run once when the user logs on. Click **Show** to specify items to run. (See comment below.)
Run Services	Defines services to run at system startup. Click **Show** to specify items to run.
Digital Signature Check	Allows you to specify how to handle installation of non-Microsoft signed drivers.
Disable Windows Update	Removes the Windows Update shortcut from the **Start** menu and prevents access to the Windows Update Web site
Override Local Web Page	Allows you to specify a path to a local Web page that is displayed when a user clicks on a Windows Update shortcut before connecting to the Internet with the Internet Connection Wizard.
Override Windows Update Site URL	Allows you to specify the URL of a site your users will access in place of the Windows Update Web site.

You can set the Run Once system policy to set values in the **Run Once** registry key, allowing any executable file to be run just once after a user logs on to the computer. After the related program is started, its name is removed automatically from the registry so it does not run again. However, if you leave this option selected in the policy file, every time the user logs on, that executable name will be placed in the **Run Once** registry key to be run again. To ensure that the executable runs only once, select the policy only long enough to be downloaded once into the user's registry. Then the policy must be cleared or changed so the same Run Once entry does not run the next time the user logs on.

System Policy Settings Summary

This section summarizes the policy options you can set by default in Windows 98. They are determined by a template (Windows.adm), which can be modified as discussed in "Using System Policy Templates" later in this chapter. You might find it helpful to run System Policy Editor as you study these options.

These policies are described in the order they appear in System Policy Editor. For each category, you must click the option that appears in bold type to display the related policies you can define for that category.

Restricting Access to User-Specific Settings

When you double-click **Default User** in System Policy Editor, a list of Control Panel, desktop, network, shell (user interface), and system settings appears so that you can predefine or restrict access to settings that apply when the user logs on to the system. These system policy settings are stored in User.dat.

Restricting Access to Control Panels

Table 8.11 describes the system policies you can apply to restrict access to settings in the Display, Network, Passwords, Printers, and System options of Control Panel.

Table 8.11   User policies restricting access to Control Panel options

Option	Description
Restrict Display settings	
Disable Display Control Panel	Prevents access to Display in Control Panel.
Hide Background page	Hides the **Background** properties of Display in Control Panel.
Hide Screen Saver page	Hides the **Screen Saver** properties of Display in Control Panel.
Hide Appearance page	Hides the **Appearance** properties of Display in Control Panel.
Hide Settings page	Hides the **Settings** properties of Display in Control Panel

Table 8.11   User policies restricting access to Control Panel options (*continued*)

Option	Description
Restrict Network settings	
Disable Network Control Panel	Prevents access to Network in Control Panel.
Hide Identification page	Hides the **Identification** properties of Network in Control Panel.
Hide Access Control page	Hides the **Access Control** (user-level versus share-level) properties of Network in Control Panel.
Restrict Passwords settings	
Disable Passwords Control Panel	Prevents access to Passwords in Control Panel.
Hide Change Passwords page	Hides the **Change Passwords** properties of Passwords in Control Panel.
Hide Remote Administration page	Hides the **Remote Administration** properties of Passwords in Control Panel.
Hide User Profiles page	Hides the **User Profiles** properties of Passwords in Control Panel.
Restrict Printers settings	
Hide General and Details pages	Hides the **General** and **Details** properties of Printers in Control Panel.
Disable Deletion of Printers	Prevents the deletion of installed printers.
Disable Addition of Printers	Prevents the installation of printers.
Restrict System settings	
Hide Device Manager page	Hides the **Device Manager** properties of System in Control Panel.
Hide Hardware Profiles page	Hides the **Hardware Profiles** properties of System in Control Panel.
Hide File System button	Hides the **File System** button from the **Performance** properties of System in Control Panel.
Hide Virtual Memory button	Hides the **Virtual Memory** button from the **Performance** properties of System in Control Panel.

Using System Policy Templates

When you run System Policy Editor, Windows 98 opens the default policy template, which contains existing policies you can enable or modify. A template is a listing of the possible policies you can use. By default, this template file is named Windows.adm and is stored in the Windows INF directory.

Creating a Custom System Policy Template

You can create custom system policy templates (ADM files) and switch between multiple templates in System Policy Editor. For example, it might be helpful to have system policy settings for corporate-specific applications, such as an in-house database, custom front end, or electronic mail package. After a template has been customized, you can load it and use it to set values in the registry.

Note If you want to define system policies for applications, the applications must be able to read the Windows 98 registry.

Creating your own template is helpful when you want to define a specific set of registry settings in your system policies, including settings not definable by default through System Policy Editor. As shown in Figure 8.2, the template defines the policies you can set through System Policy Editor. Changes you make there are reflected in the policy file (shown in the example as Config.pol), which in turn updates the registry when the user logs on.

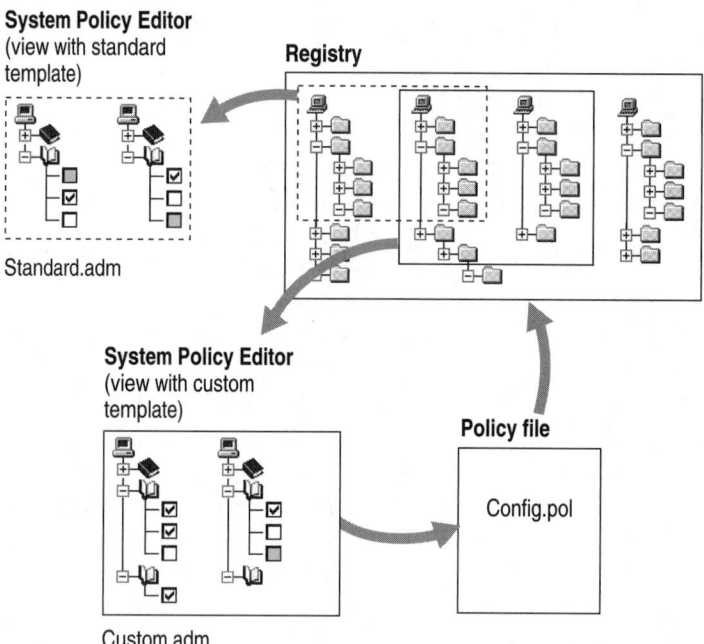

Figure 8.2   Using a custom system policy template to define policies

▶ **To use a template other than the default template**

1. In System Policy Editor, make sure all policy files are closed.

2. On the **Options** menu, click **Template**.

3. Click **Open Template**, and select an ADM file to be your template to begin setting system policies. Click **Open**.

4. Click **Close** to return to System Policy Editor.

You can create your own templates to be read by System Policy Editor. Users can then load a template and use it to set values in the registry. To create a template, use a text editor, such as WordPad, to edit or write an ADM file. You can open the default template named Windows.adm in the Windows INF directory to use as an example.

A template uses several key words, syntaxes, and symbols, as summarized in the following list.

- Class:

    CLASS *category_type*

- Category:

    CATEGORY *name*
        [KEYNAME *key_name*]
        [... *policy definition statements* ...]
    END CATEGORY

- Policy:

    POLICY *name*
        [KEYNAME *key_name*]
        [... *part definition statements* ...]
    END POLICY

- Part:

    PART *name part_type*
        type-dependent data
        [KEYNAME *key_name*]
        VALUENAME *value_name*
    END PART

Table 8.12 describes the keywords in system policy templates. Following this table are lists of the controls and values that can be defined in templates.

Table 8.12   System policy template keywords

Template keyword	Description
CLASS	Defines the registry key that can be edited; the value must be USER or MACHINE, corresponding to **HKEY_CURRENT_USER** or **HKEY_LOCAL_MACHINE**, respectively.
CATEGORY *name*	Defines a category in System Policy Editor. Category names that contain spaces must be enclosed in quotes. A category statement can appear only once for each category name.
END CATEGORY	Defines the end of a category and all its policies.
POLICY *name*	Defines a policy within a category. Policy names that contain spaces must be enclosed in quotes.
END POLICY	Defines the end of a policy and all its parts.
PART *name*	Defines one or more controls that can be used to set the values of a policy. Part names that contain spaces must be enclosed in quotes. Policy part types and type-dependent data are described in the following tables.
END PART	Defines the end of the control list.
VALUEON	Specifies the setting to assign to the value when the policy is selected.
VALUEOFF	Specifies the setting to assign to the value when the policy is cleared.
KEYNAME	Specifies the full path of the registry key. This is an optional registry key name to use for the category or policy. If there is a key name specified, it is used by all child categories, policies, and parts, unless they define a key name of their own.
VALUENAME	Defines the registry value entry name.
VALUE	Specifies the registry value to set to a *VALUENAME*.
!!	Indicates a string value.
[strings]	Defines a section containing string values.

A system policy template uses the part control indicators listed in Table 8.13.

Table 8.13   System policy template part control indicators

Part control indicator	Description
CHECKBOX	Displays a check box. The value is nonzero if checked by the user, and its value entry is deleted if it is unchecked.
NUMERIC	Displays an edit field with an optional spin control that accepts a numeric value.
EDITTEXT	Displays an edit field that accepts alphanumeric text.
COMBOBOX	Displays a combo box, which is an edit field plus a drop-down list for suggested values.

Table 8.13   System policy template part control indicators (*continued*)

Part control indicator	Description
TEXT	Displays a line of static (label) text. There is no registry value associated with this part type.
DROPDOWNLIST	Displays a drop-down list. The user can choose from only one of the entries supplied. The main advantage of a drop-down list is that, based on the user's selection, a number of extra registry edits can be performed.
LISTBOX	Displays a list box with **Add** and **Remove** buttons. This is the only part type that can be used to manage multiple values under one key.

A system policy template uses the type-specific information listed in Table 8.14.

Table 8.14   System policy template type-specific information

Type-specific modifier	Description
CHECKBOX	
DEFCHECKED	Causes the check box initially to be checked.
VALUEON	If specified, overrides the default "on" behavior of the check box. For example: **VALUEON "On"** writes "On" to the registry.
VALUEOFF	If specified, overrides the default "off" behavior of the check box. For example: **VALUEOFF "Off"** writes "Off" to the registry.
ACTIONLISTON	Specifies the optional actions to be taken if check box is "on."
ACTIONLISTOFF	Specifies the optional actions to be taken if check box is "off."
NUMERIC	
DEFAULT *value*	Specifies the initial numeric value for the edit field. If this statement is not specified, the edit field is initially empty.
MIN *value*	Specifies the minimum value for a number. Default value is 0.
MAX *value*	Specifies the maximum value for a number. Default value is 9999.
SPIN *value*	Specifies the increments to use for a spin control. Specifying **SPIN 0** removes the spin control; **SPIN 1** is the default.
REQUIRED	If specified, System Policy Editor will not allow a policy containing this part to be enabled unless a value has been entered.
TXTCONVERT	Writes values as strings rather than binary values.

Table 8.14   System policy template type-specific information (*continued*)

Type-specific modifier	Description
EDITTEXT	
DEFAULT *value*	Specifies the initial string for the edit field. If this statement is not specified, the edit field is initially empty.
EXPANDABLETEXT	Writes the value to the registry with the data type REG_EXPAND_SZ. This allows the use of environment variables.
MAXLEN *value*	Specifies the maximum length of the string in the edit field.
REQUIRED	If specified, System Policy Editor will not allow a policy containing this part to be enabled unless a value has been entered.
OEMCONVERT	Sets the ES_OEMCONVERT style in the edit field so that typed text is mapped from ANSI to OEM and back.
COMBOBOX	Accepts all the key words that EDITTEXT does, as well as NOSORT and SUGGESTIONS.
NOSORT	If specified, values in the combo box are not sorted alphabetically. This is useful when a sorted value list would cause them to be displayed in an illogical order.

SUGGESTIONS	Begins a list of suggestions to be placed in the drop-down list. Suggestions are separated with spaces and can be enclosed by quotes. The list is terminated with END SUGGESTIONS. For example:
	
	`SUGGESTIONS`
	`Alaska   Alabama   Mississippi   "New York"`
	`END SUGGESTIONS`

TEXT	Contains no type-specific data.
DROPDOWNLIST	
NOSORT	If specified, values in the drop-down list are not sorted. This is useful when a sorted value list would cause them to be displayed in an illogical order.
REQUIRED	If specified, System Policy Editor will not allow a policy containing this part to be enabled unless a value has bee4n entered.

Table 8.14   System policy template type-specific information (*continued*)

Type-specific modifier	Description
DROPDOWNLIST (*continued*)	
ITEMLIST	Begins a list of the items in the drop-down list. The list is terminated with END ITEMLIST. Each item in the list is specified as follows:

```
NAME name VALUE value
[ACTIONLIST actionlist]
```

. . .

name is the text to be displayed in the related drop-down list.

value is the value to be written for the part's value if this item is selected. Values are assumed to be strings, unless they are preceded by the key word NUMERIC. For example:

```
VALUE "Some value"
VALUE NUMERIC 1
```

If the VALUE key word is followed by the DELETE key word (that is, VALUE DELETE), this registry name/value pair will be deleted.

actionlist is an optional list to be used if this value is selected.

Type-specific modifier	Description
LISTBOX	
VALUENAME	Cannot be used with the list box type, because there is no single value name associated with this type. By default, only one column appears in the list box, and for each entry a value is created with an identical value name and value data. For instance, the **List Entry** value in the list box would create a value named "List Entry" containing "List Entry" as data.
VALUEPREFIX *prefix*	Defines the prefix to be used in determining value names. If a prefix is specified, this prefix plus "1," "2," and so on will be used instead of the default value naming scheme listed earlier in this table. The prefix can be empty (" "), which will cause the value names to be "1," "2," and so on. A prefix of **SomeName** will generate value names "SomeName1," "SomeName2," and so on.
EXPLICITVALUE	Causes the user to specify the value data and the value name. The list box shows two columns for each item, one for the name and one for the data. This key word cannot be used with the VALUEPREFIX key word.
ADDITIVE	If specified, values set in the list box are used in addition to whatever values exist in the target registry. Existing values are not deleted; by default, if ADDITIVE is not specified, the content of list boxes will "override" whatever values are set in the target registry.

Table 8.14   System policy template type-specific information (*continued*)

Type-specific modifier	Description
Strings	
!!	Indicates a string value. For example:
	`!!StrConst`
[*strings*]	Defines a section containing string values; the values are defined in the following format:
	var_name=string value
	For example:
	`StrConst="Control Name"`
Comments	Can be added by preceding the line with a semicolon (;).

Troubleshooting System Policies

This section discusses some common problems that you might encounter when implementing system policies and suggests some ways to fix these problems.

In general, when troubleshooting problems with system policies, verify the following:

- The related registry key is correct in the policy template (ADM) file.
- The related policy is set properly in the policy (POL) file.
- The related application actually uses the registry key being changed.
- The policy file is located in the correct network location, and the network location is accessible from the computer running Windows 98.
- For group policies, the user name, group name, and computer name are correct, and the user is a member of the specified group.

When troubleshooting system policies, you should turn on error messages. You can do this from the Remote Update policy, as explained in "Setting Up for Manual Downloading of System Policies" earlier in this chapter. This setting displays error messages when policies cannot be downloaded correctly; the error messages might help identify the problem.

The computer seems to be picking up some of the policies, but not all of them.

In this case, the computer might not be picking up any policies for Default User or for a particular user; it might be picking up only policies set for Default Computer or for a particular computer. In this case, make sure that user profiles are enabled on that computer. In Control Panel, double-click Passwords, click the **User Profiles** tab, and then set the desired options.

The computer does not seem to be picking up policies from a Config.pol file on the Windows NT domain.

- Make sure that there is a Config.pol file in the Netlogon share or folder on the primary domain controller on the Windows NT network. \\PDC\\x$\WINNT\system32\Repl\Import\Scripts\Config.pol (where x = SystemDrive).

- Make sure that the client computer has its domain set properly in the properties for Client for Microsoft Networks, in the Network option in Control Panel.

- Make sure that the client computer is successfully logging on to that domain.

- Make sure that the client computer is configured for automatic policy downloading. You can set this by using the Remote Update policy, as described in "Setting Up for Manual Downloading of System Policies" earlier in this chapter. Windows 98 is configured for automatic policy downloading by default.

- Enable error messages on the client computer, and see if an error message is displayed.

The computer running Microsoft Client for NetWare Networks does not seem to be picking up the policies from a Config.pol file on the NetWare server.

- Make sure that there is a Config.pol in the Public directory on the SYS: volume of a NetWare 3.x or 4.x server. You cannot put the Config.pol file on a computer running Windows 98 with File and Printer Sharing for NetWare Networks unless you are set up for manual downloading of system policies.

- Make sure that the client computer has its Preferred Server set to the NetWare server that contains Config.pol. This setting is located in the properties for Client for NetWare Networks, in the Network option in Control Panel.

- Make sure that the client computer is successfully logging on to that preferred server.

- Make sure that the client computer is configured for automatic policy downloading. You can set this by using the Remote Update policy, as described in "Setting Up for Manual Downloading of System Policies" earlier in this chapter.

- Enable error messages on the client computer, and see if an error message is displayed.

The computer running a Novell-supplied VLM or NETX client does not seem to be picking up the policies from the Config.pol on the NetWare server, even though the file is in SYS:PUBLIC.

Automatic downloading of system policies on a NetWare server works only when the client computer is running Microsoft Client for NetWare Networks. If the computer is running the Novell-supplied VLM or NETX client, you must use manual downloading from a mapped drive. For more information, see "Setting Up for Manual Downloading of System Policies" earlier in this chapter.

The client computer is set for manual downloading, but it is not picking up the policies.

- Make sure that the path specified for manual downloading includes the name of the policy file itself.

- Make sure that the directory in which you placed the policy file can be accessed by the user that is logging on to the computer running Windows 98.

You have implemented a policy and then cleared it, but it appears to still be in effect, or it does not do what you thought it would do.

Does the policy have an edit box that needs to be completed? For example, do you need to specify the wallpaper or workgroup name? If so, clearing the policy actually deletes the registry setting for that value. For example, by clearing the wallpaper policy, the wallpaper registry setting is made to be blank, and thus the user will have no wallpaper.

For all policies that involve settings that users can manipulate by using an option in Control Panel, the best way to stop enforcing that policy is to make sure that policy setting is unavailable, in order to allow the users to make their own choices. These policies are listed in "Using System Policy Editor" earlier in this chapter.

Does the user have the correct POL file? In automatic downloading of the policy file, the latest POL file may not yet have replicated to the other domain controllers at the time the user logs on. If this happens, and the user downloads an old copy of the POL file, ensure the policy has been replicated to the user's logon server, restart the Windows 98 machine, and then logon again to download the new POL file.

You set up group policies, but one or more of the users do not get these group policies when they log on.

- Is there a policy for that particular user? If so, group policies are ignored by design. This allows you to make exceptions to group policies for particular users.

- Make sure that the client computer is set up for group policy support.

- Make sure that the user or users are really members of that group.

- Make sure that the user or users are members of another group with higher priority.

- Make sure that user profiles are enabled on the client computer.

You used the policy named Only Run Allowed Windows Applications, but then you could not turn off this policy because you forgot to include Poledit.exe in the list.

- Did you set this policy for all users? If not, log on as another user, and run System Policy Editor to cancel this policy.

- If you can run Registry Editor, go to the following key and delete the RestrictRun entry:

   HKEY_CURRENT_USER\Software\Microsoft\Windows\CurrentVersion \Policies\Explore

- If you previously set this policy for the Default User, and as a result, no user can run System Policy Editor or Registry Editor, try the following:

   - If possible, disable user profiles in the Passwords option in Control Panel. You should be able to log on and run System Policy Editor. Then undo the policy and re-enable user profiles.

   - If you cannot disable user profiles because the Passwords option in Control Panel has been disabled, you must either rename the policy file on the server and logon as a user who has not logged on at the computer and change the policy, reinstall Windows 98 (so that user profiles will not be enabled), or use the Windows 98 startup disk and run the real-mode Registry Editor to disable user profiles.

You need to prevent users from modifying their computer configuration, including even more restrictions than are available through standard system policies.

Use one or more of the following methods for ensuring administrative control of the computer's configuration.

- In Msdos.sys for the user's computer, set **BootKeys=0 and BootSafe=0** so the user cannot press F8 to avoid starting Windows 98 and to prevent the computer from booting in Safe Mode. In addition, make sure that floppy disk startup is not enabled in the computer's complementary metal oxide semiconductor (CMOS) settings, and use password protection to prevent CMOS modifications. For more information about making these changes, see the documentation from your computer's manufacturer.

- For the registry on the user's computer, use System Policy Editor to enable the registry setting named Require Validation By Network For Windows Access.

- In the system policies that are downloaded when the user logs on, set the policy named Disable Registry Editing Tools.

CHAPTER 9

Security

This chapter presents an overview of security features provided in Microsoft Windows 98. It describes their use, together with security features of Internet Explorer version 4.0, in a networking environment. It is intended for system administrators and others who have authority to set security levels for network clients, and for those who need secure communication over the Internet.

In This Chapter

See Also

- For information about file and printer sharing services and user-level or share-level security, see Chapter 18, "Logon, Browsing, and Resource Sharing."

- For information about editing system policies, see Chapter 8, "System Policies."

- For information about security for Internet Explorer, see Chapter 20, "Internet Access and Tools."

- For information about Distributed Component Object Model (DCOM), see Chapter 29, "Windows 98 Network Architecture" and Chapter 25, "Application Support."

Overview of Security Features

Computer security refers to the protection of all components—hardware, software, and stored data—of a computer or a group of computers from damage, theft, or unauthorized use. A computer security plan that is well thought out, implemented, and monitored makes authorized computer use easy and unauthorized use or accidental damage difficult or impossible.

Personal computing depends increasingly on computers connected through networks, and more often through the Internet and intranets. You can use Windows 98 security to prevent unauthorized access to shared resources on computers in a network. The security features built into Windows 98 are described briefly in this section, and in more detail later in the chapter.

Logon Security

Windows 98 allows users to log on fully. In a networking environment, you can set your system up so that when a name and password pair have been validated against the security authority of a network server, the Windows 98 user interface is displayed.

Logon Password

A user can log on to all networks and Windows 98 at the same time. If a user's password for Windows 98 or for another network is the same as the password for the primary logon client, Windows 98 automatically logs the user on to Windows 98 and all networks using that password.

Note A unified password prompt does not enhance security, but eases logging on to the system. As the system administrator, you can require additional passwords for a more secure system.

For more information about the logon prompt, see "Using the Windows 98 Logon Password" later in this chapter. Once users log on to their machines, they have the option to cache their passwords. These passwords are cached in a file with a .pwl extension. The file name is the same as the user's name. See "Password Caching" later in this chapter.

Network Validation

With system policies, you can prevent users from logging on to Windows 98 if their Windows NT or Novell NetWare network logon is not validated. This causes the network logon dialog to appear before, or instead of, the Windows 98 logon prompt. Also, the user list may not be network wide, but specific to a server, and may be different for different servers.

For more information about logon security, see "Network Security" later in this chapter. For more information about system policies, see "Using System Policies to Enforce Password Security" later in this chapter, and Chapter 8, "System Policies."

Shared-Resource Security

When a computer is running Windows 98 with file and printer sharing services, other users can connect to shared printers, volumes, directories, and CD-ROM drives on that computer. To protect these shared resources, Windows 98 provides user-level and share-level security.

User-Level Security

With user-level security, a user's request to access a shared resource is passed through to a security provider, such as a Windows NT or NetWare server. The security provider grants or denies the request by checking the requestor's user name and password against a network-wide or server-wide stored list. User-level security does not require file and printer sharing services. These accounts must be created on the machine providing user-level authentication, such as a Windows NT or NetWare server. Windows 98 cannot act as an authentication server for user-level security.

This type of security allows fine-grained control over per-user access and allows individual accountability. The disadvantages are that you must create a user account for each user you want to grant access to, and you must grant that user the access.

Share-Level Security

With share-level security, users assign passwords to their shared resources. Any user who can provide the correct password is permitted to access the shared resource. The password is stored and checked by the computer where the resource resides. Share-level security requires file and printer sharing services.

Note Any subfolders of the shared folder, if they are also shared, must be set with the same level of security as the parent folder.

The advantage of this type of security paradigm is that it allows granting access to a broad range of people with very little effort. However, it is not as secure as user-level security, because the password is widely distributed and there is no notion of personal accountability.

Note You cannot use share-level security on NetWare networks, because the File and Printer Sharing for NetWare Networks utility does not support passwords. You can limit access, however, by defining a resource as read-only.

Password Controls

In addition to setting up passwords for security, Windows 98 also provides password caching, Password List Editor, and system policies.

Password Caching

Like unified logon, password caching provides a convenient and secure way to access protected resources. The first time a user connects to the resources and saves the password, Windows 98 caches the password in a PWL file. Whenever the user logs on again, the logon password unlocks the PWL file and the resource passwords it contains, and the user then has free access to those resources. If password caching is disabled, users must type the password each time they connect to a password-protected resource.

Password List Editor

Password List Editor lets you view resources on a password list. It also lets a user view or edit his or her own password file (PWL). You may then delete a password (you cannot view the actual password) so that it can be replaced.

System Policies

System policies let you enforce a password policy with some or all of these restrictions:

- Disable password caching.
- Require an alphanumeric Windows 98 logon password.
- Require a minimum Windows 98 logon password length.

You can also define system policies that prevent users from enabling peer resource sharing services and that enforce other security techniques, such as preventing users from configuring system components.

For more information, see "Using System Policies to Enforce Password Security" later in this chapter, and Chapter 8, "System Policies."

Internet and Intranet Security

The Internet is an effective way to communicate and share information with others, but with its use comes a greater need for security. The following security features make it easier for you to protect your computer and your privacy when using the Internet.

Internet Explorer

Internet Explorer 4.0 has new security options that let you configure a security level to a specific Web site according to how much you trust the content of that Web site. Four security zones are set up in Internet Explorer 4.0. They are:

- An Internet zone that by default contains all Internet sites.
- A Trusted sites zone to which you can assign Web sites you trust.
- A Restricted sites zone to which you can assign Web sites you do not trust.
- A Local intranet zone for computers connected to a local area network.

Outlook Express

Outlook Express includes tools to protect you from fraud, ensure your privacy, and prevent unauthorized access to your computer. These tools enable you to send and receive secure e-mail messages and to control potentially harmful e-mail messages through security zones.

Distributed Component Object Model

A distributed application consists of multiple processes that cooperate to accomplish a single task. The Distributed Component Object Model (DCOM) can be used to integrate distributed applications in a network, thus allowing specified users to have access to certain processes.

Firewalls

A firewall enforces a boundary between networks. The boundary prevents unauthorized access of private networks by preventing the passage of packets between networks.

Security Planning Checklist

You need to determine the type of exposure or risk you potentially have, and develop a security policy that reflects this level of risk. On the basis of that analysis, choose products, network technology, and business practices for the installation, integration, and management of your system.

Before you integrate Windows 98 security into your network security model, consider the following issues:

What kind of logon security do you need?   Do you allow users to log on to Windows 98 and the network with the same password? Do you want to require alphanumeric or minimum-length passwords for the Windows 98 logon password? Do you want to require that users be validated by the network security provider before being able to log on to Windows 98? For both Windows NT and NetWare networks, you can use system policies to require validation by a Windows NT or NetWare server before allowing access to Windows 98 and to specify other Windows 98 password restrictions.

What kind of resource protection do you need on Microsoft networks?   If you enable peer resource sharing, you must decide how to protect those resources with share-level or user-level security. User-level security provides greater security because the network security provider must authenticate the user name and password before access to the resource is granted. Share-level security is not available for NetWare networks.

For more information about NetWare networks, see Chapter 17, "Windows 98 on Third-Party Networks."

What kinds of access rights will users have to resources protected by user-level security?   You can specify the types of rights users or groups of users have to resources by setting Sharing properties for the shared resource (such as a folder or drive). For example, you can restrict other users to read-only access to files or give them read-access and write-access to files.

How do you want to enable user-level security?   You can enable security in a setup script or in system policies. If you enable user-level security in either a setup script or Control Panel, remote administration is enabled by default for domain administrators on a Windows NT network and for supervisors on a NetWare network.

Should password caching be allowed?   You can use system policies to disable password caching and thus require users to type a password each time they access a password-protected resource.

Should users be able to change Control Panel settings? You can use system policies to restrict users' ability to change the configuration of system components, their desktops, applications, or network connections in the Control Panel folder.

Does a particular hard disk need extra protection? Windows 98 security obstructs hacking over the network; but if a person has physical access to the computer, critical data could still be taken from the hard disk where it resides by using Safe Mode or a floppy disk to start the workstation. If specific data requires greater levels of security, you should store critical files on a secure server. If computers require greater levels of security, Windows NT Workstation is recommended, because it provides a means to protect resources on a hard disk based on a user's identity.

Are there applications that should not be run? You may need to restrict access to some applications while supplying access to other applications in your system. To implement this type of security, use system policies. You can also restrict access to parts of an application by using DCOM.

Do certain processes of an application need protection? If security is required for a distributed application—that is, one whose component processes are distributed over more than one computer in the network—use DCOM. DCOM provides the structure to share applications at the component level between a server and clients. The components can be shared over the Internet or an intranet. Using DCOM to set a security level for the application automatically applies that security level to each component, wherever located.

Should Internet or intranet access be limited? You may need to limit access to certain sites on the Internet and on your intranet. To implement this type of security, use Internet Explorer security features.

Network Security

Windows 98 allows users to log on fully. The first thing most users encounter after booting their Windows 98 systems is a logon dialog box, which varies depending on the type of network. Once the proper user name and password are validated against the security authority of the network server, the Windows 98 user interface is displayed.

System administrators can configure the Windows 98 system to allow entry into the operating system with no network access (this configuration is the default). As an alternative solution to this problem, system administrators can specify guest accounts that have limited network access.

The Windows 98 user logon should not be construed as a mechanism to fully secure personal computers. Because personal computers are still vulnerable to a floppy boot, all data stored on their disks is potentially available. The underlying file system in Windows 98 is the MS-DOS file allocation table (FAT) file system, which has no built-in encryption or other security mechanisms.

Network resources are secured under Windows 98 using the same security mechanisms employed by network servers on corporate networks. The user name and password in Windows 98 can be configured to be the same as those used by the network server. By doing this, the network manager can control network access, provide user-level security for access to shared resources on the local computer, control the various agents in Windows 98, and limit who has remote administration authority on this Windows 98 system. In this fashion, Windows 98 leverages the existing investment in network servers, management tools, utilities, and infrastructure. System administrators can manage user accounts centrally on the server, just as they always have. They can also use familiar tools for managing user accounts.

Implementing Network Security

Implementing security in a Windows 98 networking environment involves the following types of activity:

- Define user accounts on a network server or domain controller for user-level security. For more information, see the documentation for the software on the network security provider.

- Install file and printer sharing services, and then enable user-level or share-level security.

- Define access rights for resources protected by user-level security.

- Make the Windows 98 logon password and network logon password the same. Disable password caching if you do not want this feature. For more information, see "Using the Windows 98 Logon Password" and "Using the Windows 98 Password Cache" later in this chapter.

- Define system policies to restrict users' ability to configure the system or shared resources, and to enforce password policies.

- Define Internet and intranet security zones. For more information, see "Setting Up Security Zones" later in this chapter.

Sharing Resources

Windows 98 provides share-level or, alternatively, user-level security for protecting shared resources on computers running Windows 98 (the share level requires file and printer sharing services).

Share-level security protects shared network resources on the computer running Windows 98 with individually assigned passwords. For example, you can assign a password to a folder or a locally attached printer. If other users want to access it, they need to type in the appropriate password. If you do not assign a password to a shared resource, every user with access to the network can access that resource.

User-level security protects shared network resources by requiring that a security provider authenticate a user's request to access resources. The security provider, such as a Windows NT domain controller or a NetWare server, grants access to the shared resource by verifying that the user name and password are the same as those on the user account list stored on the network security provider. Because the security provider maintains a network-wide list of user accounts and passwords, each computer running Windows 98 does not have to store a list of accounts.

Note   For Microsoft networks, the security provider must be a Windows NT domain or workstation. For NetWare networks, it must be either a NetWare 4.*x* server running bindery emulation or a NetWare 3.*x* server.

Figure 9.1 shows how user-level security works for Microsoft networks. The reference numbers are explained after the illustration.

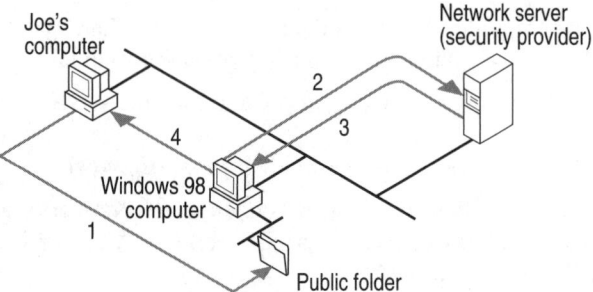

Figure 9.1   User-level security

1. Joe's computer is running Windows 98. Joe enters a password to access a shared resource protected by user-level security.

2. The Windows 98 computer passes a request to the server (security provider) to authenticate Joe's identity.

3. The security provider sends a verification to the computer if Joe's name and password combination are valid.

4. Windows 98 grants access to the shared resource according to rights assigned to Joe on the Sharing property sheet for that resource.

Joe's password is stored on his computer's PWL file to be used for authentication when he accesses that resource again. He will not be prompted for the password again during that session. When he logs off, the computer will erase his password from the file.

Setting Up Security for Shared Resources

Before a user can share a resource on a computer running Windows 98, the computer must be configured for share-level or user-level security, and file and printer sharing services must be installed by using the Network option in Control Panel. Configuring share-level or user-level security is described briefly in the following sections, and in Chapter 18, "Logon, Browsing, and Resource Sharing."

Note Share-level security is not available on NetWare networks.

▶ **To set up share-level security**

1. Install File and Printer Sharing for Microsoft Networks, as described in the "Installing Peer Resource Sharing" section of Chapter 18, "Logon, Browsing, and Resource Sharing."

2. On the computer that hosts the resource to be shared, in Control Panel, double-click Network, and then click the **Access Control** tab.

3. Click **Share-level access control**, and then click **OK**.

▶ **To set up user-level security on a Microsoft network**

1. Install File and Printer Sharing for Microsoft Networks, as described in the "Installing Peer Resource Sharing" section of Chapter 18, "Logon, Browsing, and Resource Sharing."

2. In Control Panel, double-click Network, and then click the **Access Control** tab.

3. Click **User-level access control**.

4. In the **User-level access control** box, type the name of the Windows NT domain or Windows NT workstation where the user accounts reside.

5. Click **OK**.

▶ **To set up user-level security on a NetWare network**

1. Install File and Printer Sharing for NetWare Networks, as described in the "Installing Peer Resource Sharing" section of Chapter 18, "Logon, Browsing, and Resource Sharing."

2. In Control Panel, double-click Network, and then click the **Access Control** tab.

3. Click **User-level access control**.

4. In the **User-level access control** box, type the name of the NetWare server.

5. Click **OK**.

For information about specifying values for security in custom setup scripts, see Appendix D, "Msbatch.inf Parameters for Setup Scripts." For information about using System Policy Editor to set user-level security and other security options, see Chapter 8, "System Policies."

Using Share-Level Security

You can restrict access to resources such as a shared folder or a printer by either defining it as read-only or assigning a password to it.

▶ **To share a folder or printer with share-level security**

1. In Windows Explorer, right-click the folder or printer to be shared, and then click **Properties**.

2. In the **Properties** menu, click the **Sharing** tab.

3. Click **Shared As**, and type the resource's share name.

   The shared resource name will be the computer name plus the share name. For example, in the following screen shot, if the computer name is mycomputer, this shared resource is \\mycomputer\mydocuments.

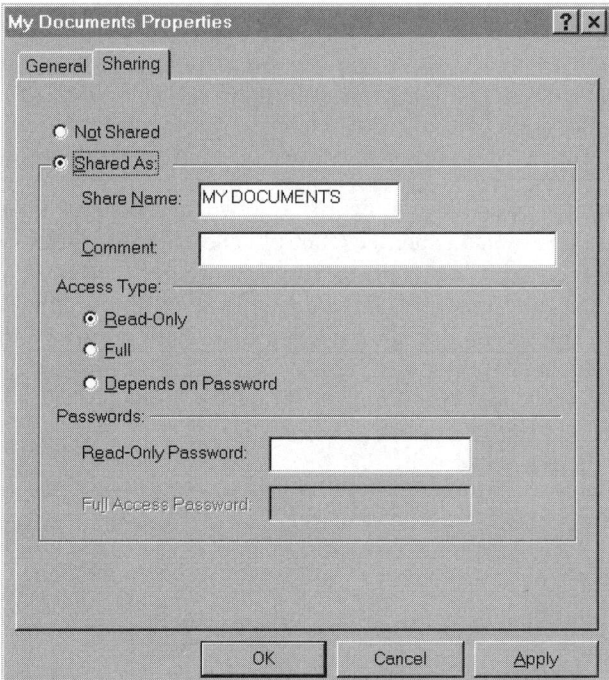

4. Specify whether you want users to have read-only or full access to this resource.

Note There is no read-only share-level access for a printer or remote administration.

---

5. Type the password for the specified access, and click **OK**.

Tip You can share a folder but hide it from the Network Neighborhood browsing list by adding a dollar sign ($) to the end of its share name (for example, PRIVATE$).

Using User-Level Security

Windows 98 uses the logon process to provide user-level security for a variety of services beyond network resource access, including the following services that are remotely accessible:

- File and printer sharing.
- Dial-up network access gateway control.
- Backup.
- Network and system management.

Pass-through security is implemented in Windows 98 as the mechanism to enable user-level security. *Pass-through* literally means that Windows 98 passes authentication requests through to a Windows NT or NetWare server. Windows 98 does not implement its own unique user-level security mechanism but instead uses the services of an existing server on the network.

Enabling pass-through security is a two-step process. First, user-level security must be enabled using the Control Panel. Second, the device must be shared, and users with access privileges must be specified. Right-clicking the drive C icon in My Computer and selecting **Properties** from the Shortcut menu displays a property sheet that shows which shares already exist and which users have access. It also allows new devices to be shared and new users to be added to specific shares. The Windows NT server or the NetWare bindery supplies the user names listed in this property sheet.

For more information about file and printer sharing, see Chapter 18, "Logon, Browsing, and Resource Sharing."

The Remote Administration function of a Windows 98 personal computer specifies the users or groups who have authority to manage the Windows 98 system, including the following:

- Dial-up network access gateway control.
- Backup.
- Remote access to the registry.
- Remote NetWatcher access.
- Remote system performance monitoring.

Remote Administration is controlled through the Passwords option in Control Panel. For more information about Remote Administration, see Chapter 23, "System and Remote Administration Tools."

For each network resource governed by user-level security, there is a list of users and groups that can access that resource.

▶ **To share a resource with user-level security**

1. In Windows Explorer or My Computer, right-click the icon for the resource to be shared, and then click **Properties**.
2. In the **Properties** menu, click the **Sharing** tab.
3. Click **Add**.
4. In the **Add Users** dialog box, click a user or group, and then assign access rights as described in the following paragraphs.

   Assign, for each user, a set of rights for the resource. The kinds of rights that you assign depend on the kind of resource you are securing:

   - For shared directories, you can let a user have read-only access, full access, or custom access. Within custom access, you can grant the user any or all of the following rights: read, write, create, list, delete, change file attributes, and change access rights.
   - For shared printers, a user either has the right to access the printer or not.
   - For remote administration, a user either has the right to be an administrator or not as defined in the Passwords option in Control Panel.

   Permissions are enforced for a resource as follows:

   - If the user has explicit rights to the resource, those rights are enforced.
   - If the user does not have explicit rights to the resource, the permissions are determined by taking all of the rights of each group to which the user belongs.
   - If none of the groups to which the user belongs has any rights to that resource, the user is not granted access to the resource.

When you do not explicitly assign access rights to a file or folder, Windows 98 uses implied rights. *Implied rights* are those assigned to the nearest parent folder of a file or folder. If none of the parent folders (up to and including the root directory of the drive) have explicit rights, no access is allowed.

Note Implied rights are displayed automatically on the property sheet for the shared file or folder.

Specifying Folder Access Rights in User-Level Security

Access rights specify what a user can do in a folder protected by user-level security. The access rights you define for a folder apply to all of its subfolders. You cannot, however, assign access rights to individual files in Windows 98. (Both Windows NT and NetWare let you assign access rights to files.)

Note Any subfolders of the shared folder, if they are also shared, must be set with the same level of security as the parent folder.

For each folder, you can assign read-only, full, or custom access. Custom access lets you further specify exactly what each user or group can do in the folder, as specified in Table 9.1.

Table 9.1   Custom access options

File operation	Required permissions
Read from a closed file	Read files
See a file name	List files
Search a folder for files	List files
Write to a closed file	Write, create, delete, change file attributes
Run an executable file	Read, list files
Create and write to a file	Create files
Copy files from a folder	Read, list files
Copy files to a folder	Write, create, list files
Make a new folder	Create files
Delete a file	Delete files
Remove a folder	Delete files
Change folder or file attributes	Change file attributes
Rename a file or folder	Change file attributes
Change access rights	Change access control

▶ **To define custom access**

1. Open the **Add Users** dialog box in a shared resource's properties (described in the procedure, "To share a resource with user-level security" earlier in this chapter).

2. In the **Add Users** dialog box, click a user or group, click **Custom**, and then click **OK**.

3. In the **Add Users** dialog box, click a user or group from the **Name** list, and then click **Custom**.

4. In the **Change Access Rights** dialog box, click the type of rights the user or group of users may have in the folder, and then click **OK**.

5. To remove a user or group of users, click that user or group, and then click **Remove**.

6. To edit the access rights for a user or group of users, click that user or group, and then click **Edit**.

Managing User Lists

Windows 98 user-level security depends on a list of accounts and groups located on a security provider. You cannot add or remove users and groups from the security provider list by using Windows 98 tools. However, you can do this by running User Manager for a Windows NT domain, SYSCON for NetWare 3.*x*, and NETADMIN for NetWare 4.*x* in a NetWare bindery environment. You can use these tools on a computer running Windows 98. These tools are provided by the respective vendors and not by Windows 98. Under Windows 98, you specify what rights users have to specific resources on the local computer as described in "Using Share-Level Security" earlier in this chapter. For more information about changing a user's access rights, see "Specifying Folder Access Rights in User-Level Security" earlier in this chapter.

Note Although Windows NT networks allow multiple domains, a computer running Windows 98 can specify only one domain for user-level security. However, you can set permissions for users or groups from any domain in the Sharing properties for the shared resource, as long as the two domains have a proper trust relationship. Also, rights may include user accounts from different trusted domains. To use a trust relationship to access multiple domains, you should consult the *Microsoft Windows NT Server 4.0 Concepts and Planning Guide*, part of the Windows NT Server documentation set.

Managing Security for Windows 98 in NetWare Bindery Environments

NetWare 3.*x* servers store all the information about users, groups, passwords, and rights in a database stored on the server called the *bindery*. NetWare 4.*x* servers can appear to have a bindery through bindery emulation, a feature that is enabled by default. There is a separate bindery for each NetWare server. Windows 98 can use the bindery of only one NetWare server as the security provider. It is common for a company to have one or more NetWare servers per department, where users log on to the server for their department. This scenario can pose a problem when the bindery differs from one NetWare server to another. For example, Sue and Bob log on to the Sales server, and Fred logs on to the R&D server. Because Sue is running Windows 98 and can specify only one server for pass-through validation, she specifies Sales (the server she uses for logon). She can now grant access to shared resources on her computer to Bob but cannot grant access to Fred.

The only way to solve this problem is to include all user accounts for all servers on one NetWare server. This server should be specified as the security provider for every computer running Windows 98 with File and Printer Sharing for NetWare Networks.

Note Windows 98 supports only bindery emulation to obtain user lists on NetWare 4.*x* servers. It does not support user lists obtained with NetWare Name Service (NNS) or other add-on services for that purpose.

Passwords

A good password policy helps users protect their passwords from other individuals. This helps to reduce the probability of someone logging on with another user's password and gaining unauthorized access to data.

The following guidelines should help you create a basic security policy:

- Tell users not to write down their passwords.

- Tell users not to use obvious passwords, such as their names, their spouses' names, their children's names, and so on.

- Do not distribute user accounts and passwords in the same communication. For example, if you are sending a new user's account name and password in writing, send the user name and the password at different times.

You can use the following Windows NT and NetWare security features to enhance Windows 98 security:

Enforce a reasonable minimum password length. This policy increases the number of permutations needed to guess someone's password randomly or programmatically. Additionally, you can enforce an alphanumeric password combination to achieve the same security.

Enforce maximum and minimum password age. This policy forces the user to change the password, preventing someone else from discovering it as a result of the password being in use for a long time. A minimum password age prevents a user from immediately reverting to a previous password after a change.

Enforce password uniqueness and maintain password history. This policy prevents users from toggling between their favorite passwords. You can specify the number of unique passwords that a user must have before that user can use a previously used password.

For more information about using Windows NT and NetWare security features, see the documentation for those products, or see the *Microsoft Windows NT Server Networking Guide* in the *Windows NT Server Resource Kit* (for Windows NT Server version 4.0) (ISBN 1-57231-343-9).

Using the Windows 98 Logon Password

With Windows 98, users can log on to all networks and Windows 98 at the same time. The first time a user starts Windows 98, logon dialog boxes appear for Windows 98 and for each network client on that computer. This is useful for you as a network administrator, because you can use existing user accounts on a network security provider to validate access to the network for users running Windows 98. For more information, see Chapter 18, "Logon, Browsing, and Resource Sharing."

If a user's password for Windows 98 or for another network is the same as the password for the primary logon client, Windows 98 logs the user on to Windows 98, and then the network automatically uses that password. When a user logs on to other networks with different passwords and chooses to save them, the passwords are stored in the password list file. The Windows 98 password unlocks this file. Thereafter, Windows 98 will use the passwords stored in the password list file to log a user on to other networks, so that no additional passwords need to be typed. This single logon provides a solution to the problem of password proliferation.

The Passwords option in Control Panel provides a way to synchronize logon passwords for different networks. This allows users to use the password for whatever logon dialog box appears first (the primary network logon client or Windows 98 logon) for logging on to all other network clients.

▶ **To change a password for a network resource to be the same as the Windows 98 logon password**

1. In Control Panel, double-click Passwords, and then click **Change Windows Password**.

2. In the **Change Windows Password** dialog box, select the other passwords you would like to change to use the same password as the Windows 98 password, and then click **OK**.

   To appear in this list, the related software must include a function that lets its password be changed.

3. In the second **Change Windows Password** dialog box, type the current (old) Windows 98 password, type a new password, and then, in the **Confirm new password** box, type the new password again. Click **OK**.

Note The Windows Screen Saver passwords option appears here only if the Windows screen saver has been turned on and the password-protected option has been selected.

You can maintain separate passwords for a network resource and require users to type a password each time they access it.

▶ **To change a password for a network resource**

1. In Control Panel, double-click Passwords, and then click **Change Other Passwords**.

2. In the **Select Password** dialog box, select the password you want to change, and then click **Change**.

3. In the **Change Password** dialog box, type the current (old) network password, type a new password, and then, in the **Confirm new password** box, type the new password again. Click **OK**.

   You must now type the new password to access the resource.

Note You can also use the Passwords option to change individual passwords to other network resources to be different from the Windows 98 logon password.

Using Windows 98 with NetWare Passwords

To log on to a NetWare network, you must type the name of the preferred server on which the related user account is stored. After the user name and password are validated by the network server, you can use resources shared on that server. If you are not validated, you will be prompted to enter a password whenever connecting to a NetWare server during this work session.

The first time you attempt to connect to a NetWare server other than the preferred server, Windows 98 searches for an appropriate user name and password in the PWL file. If no matching set of credentials is found, Windows 98 tries to log on using the Windows 98 password. If this fails, Windows 98 displays a NetWare logon prompt for you to enter a valid user name and password, which can then be stored in the PWL file.

▶ **To avoid use of automatic NetWare logon**

- Use system policies to enable the policy named **Disable Automatic NetWare Login**.

▶ **To change your password on a NetWare server**

1. At the command prompt, use the **net use** command to connect to the NetWare server's SYS volume. For example, for a server name NWSVR2, you would type:

   net use * \\nwsvr2\sys

2. At the command prompt, change to the drive for the NetWare server, and then make the Public folder the current folder. For example, if the drive is mapped to drive N, type:

   n:

   Then type:

   cd \public

   Note If you want to change your password on more than one server, connect to all affected servers before running the **setpass** command. Setpass is a utility provided by Novell and is not part of Windows 98.

   ---

3. At the command prompt, type **setpass**.

   If the server on which you want to change your password is different from the one on the current drive, type **setpass** and the name of the server.

   For example, to change your password on the server named NWSERVE1, type:

   setpass nwserve1

4. When you are prompted, type your old password, and then type and confirm the new password.

5. If you are connected to other NetWare servers that also use your old password, these servers are listed, and you are asked if you want to change your password on these servers also.

Using the Windows 98 Password Cache

Keeping track of multiple passwords can be a problem for users. Often, they either forget the passwords or write them down and post lists of passwords near their computers. When this happens, the security policy is no longer doing the job it was meant to do—to allow access to those who should have it and to deny access to those who should not.

Windows 98 solves this problem by storing passwords for resources in a password list file (PWL). This file stores passwords for the following network resources:

- Resources on a computer running Windows 98 that are protected by share-level security.
- Password-protected applications that have been specifically written to the password-caching application programming interface (API).
- Windows NT computers that do not participate in a domain.
- A Windows NT logon password that is not the Primary Network Logon.
- NetWare servers.

The password list file is stored in the Windows folder on the local computer by using an encryption algorithm. An unencrypted password is never sent across the network.

Caution If you delete PWL files, you will lose all previously stored passwords. You will need to retype each password.

Password caching is enabled by default when you install Windows 98. When you access a password-protected resource for the first time, make sure the **Save this password in your password list** option is selected (it should be selected by default) to save the password to the password list file.

Note If, during log on, you click **Cancel** to bypass the logon screen, the cache will not be opened, and you will be prompted for a password each time you attempt to use a protected resource.

You can disable password caching by using System Policy Editor, which is shipped on the Windows 98 compact disc but not automatically installed onto your system during Setup. Use the Add/Remove Programs option in Control Panel to install System Policy Editor.

▶ **To install System Policy Editor**

1. In Control Panel, double-click Add/Remove Programs, click the **Windows Setup** tab, and then click **Have Disk**.

2. In the **Install From Disk** dialog box, click **Browse** and specify the Tools\Admin\Poledit folder on the Windows 98 compact disc.

3. Click **OK**, and then click **OK** again in response to the dialog boxes.

4. In the **Have Disk** dialog box, click **System Policy Editor**, and then click **Install**.

▶ **To disable password caching by using system policies**

1. On the **Start** menu, click **Run**.

2. Type **poledit**, and then click **OK**.

3. In System Policy Editor, double-click the Local Computer icon.

4. In the Local Computer Properties, click **Network**.

5. Click **Passwords**.

6. Click the policy named **Disable Password Caching**.

For more information, see Chapter 8, "System Policies."

Note If you have any share-level security servers and you disable password caching and are running Client for Microsoft Networks, you should not use the **Quick Logon** feature in the Network option in Control Panel.

Using Password List Editor

If password caching is enabled, Windows 98 caches passwords in the password list file when you connect to a password-protected network resource. Password List Editor (Pwledit) lets you view the resources listed in a user's password list (PWL) file. It does not let you view the actual passwords, but lets you remove specific password entries if problems are encountered using a cached password.

Password List Editor works only if the password list file is unlocked, that is, if the user is logged on. It can be used to view only the contents of the logged-on user's password list file, so you should run it on the user's computer.

Note Only users themselves can view or edit their own PWL files.

Password List Editor can be found in the Netadmin\Pwledit folder on the Windows 98 compact disc.

▶ **To install Password List Editor**

1. In Control Panel, double-click Add/Remove Programs, click the **Windows Setup** tab, and then click **Have Disk**.

2. In the **Install From Disk** dialog box, click **Browse**.

3. Type the path name to Netadmin\Pwledit\Pwledit.inf, and then click **OK**.

4. In the **Have Disk** dialog box, click **Password List Editor**, and then click **Install**.

▶ **To run Password List Editor**

- On the **Start** menu, click **Run**. Type **pwledit**, and then click **OK**.

Using System Policies to Enforce Password Security

You can use system policies to increase security by requiring users to follow specific password guidelines. Using system policies, you can enforce password policies.

For information about restricting settings with system policies, see Chapter 8, "System Policies."

Internet Explorer Security

Internet Explorer 4.0 adds several security features to Windows 98, including support for security zones, Secure Socket Layer (SSL) versions 2.0/3.0 and Private Communication Technology (PCT) version 1.0 protocols, client and server authentication, and the Platform for Internet Content Selection (PICS) rating system. These security features make it easier for you to protect your computer and your privacy while using the Internet.

Security zones. You can divide the Web into zones and have Internet Explorer 4.0 provide different levels of security depending on which zone you have assigned to a Web site.

When you install Windows 98, you configure the following Internet Explorer settings:

- Internet zone
- Trusted sites zone
- Restricted sites zone
- Local intranet zone

A fifth zone, My Computer, is also created, but it is not configurable through the security options.

This system lets the administrator divide the Web content a browser can visit into groups, each of which can have a security level associated with it. The Web content can be anything from a Hypertext Markup Language (HTML) file to a graphic, an ActiveX control, a Java applet, or an executable file.

Authenticode technology. An Authenticode certificate identifies who published a piece of software and verifies that it has not been tampered with.

Certificate management. System administrators can control which Java applets, ActiveX controls, and other software can be run on their intranets, based on who published the software.

Capabilities-based Java security (sandboxing). The Internet Explorer 4.0 security model for Java makes it easy for you to control how Java applets interact with your computer system. You can decide what capabilities and levels of access to your computer or system you want to give Java applets. You can offer full access to applets from trusted sources while restricting applets from unknown sources to safe "sandboxes" where they cannot harm files.

Privacy protection. Internet Explorer 4.0 supports all standard Internet security protocols to ensure private communication over the Web. Internet Explorer prompts you before user names or passwords are sent to Web sites not designated as trusted. For trusted sites, you can choose not to be prompted before personal information is transmitted. Outlook Express—the Internet mail and news component of Internet Explorer 4.0—lets you encrypt messages and ensures that no one can falsely assume your identity on the Internet.

The following sections explain how to configure these settings.

Setting Up Security Zones

Internet Explorer 4.0 has security options that let you configure a security level to a specific Web site according to how much you trust the content of that Web site. Five predefined security zones, four of which have configurable security settings, are set up in Internet Explorer 4.0:

- Internet zone that by default contains all Internet sites.
- Trusted sites zone to which you can assign Web sites you trust.
- Restricted sites zone to which you can assign Web sites you do not trust.
- Local intranet zone for computers connected to a local area network.
- Local machine called My Computer, unsecured, providing full access to all aspects of the machine, not configurable.

Note Because security works differently in Internet Explorer 4.0, any existing Internet Explorer 3.0 settings are not preserved.

Using the **Internet Properties** dialog box in the Internet option in Control Panel, you can set the security options you want for Internet, Trusted sites, Restricted sites, and Local intranet, and then add or remove sites from the zones depending on your level of trust in each site.

In corporate environments, administrators can set up zones for users and can add or remove authentication certificates of software publishers that they do or do not trust so that users do not have to make security decisions while they are using the Internet.

For each security zone, you can choose a High, Medium, Low, or Custom security setting. Use the High setting for sites in a zone of untrustworthiness and Low in a trusted zone. The Custom option gives advanced users and administrators even more control over all security options, including the following:

- Access to files, ActiveX controls, and scripts.
- The level of capabilities given to Java applets.
- Whether sites must be identified with SSL authentication.

▶ **To set up security zones**

1. In Control Panel, double-click Internet.
2. Click the **Security** tab.
3. Configure the settings according to your security needs.

Setting Up the Internet Zone

By default, the Internet zone is set to the Medium security level. If you are concerned about security problems as users browse the Internet, change this setting to High. When this level is set to High, some Web pages may not be allowed to perform certain operations that can potentially compromise security.

For more advanced and detailed security control, use the Custom settings to configure each individual security setting for the zone.

▶ **To set up custom settings for the Internet zone**

1. In the **Security** tab, select **Custom**, and then click **Settings**.

2. Configure the settings according to your security needs.

Adding Sites to the Trusted and Restricted Zones

You can classify Web sites into two categories, according to how much you trust their contents:

- Trusted sites zone
- Restricted sites zone

By default, the Trusted sites zone is set to the Low security level. When you add a site to the Trusted sites zone, the site is allowed to perform more operations, and Internet Explorer will ask you to make fewer security decisions when you access the site. Add a site to this zone only if you trust all of its content never to do anything that may harm your computer. For the Trusted sites zone, it is strongly recommended that you use the HTTPS protocol so that you can securely connect to the site.

By default, the Restricted sites zone is set to the High security level. When you add a site to the Restricted sites zone, the site is allowed to perform only minimal, very safe operations. Add sites that you do not trust to this zone.

▶ **To add sites to the Trusted sites zone or Restricted sites zone**

1. In the **Security** tab, select either the **Trusted sites zone** or **Restricted sites zone** in the Zone list.

2. Click **Add Sites**, select the desired sites for that zone, and then click **OK**.

Setting Up the Local Intranet Zone

To be secure, the Local intranet zone must be set up in accordance with the proxy server and firewall configuration. All sites in the zone should be "inside the firewall," and proxy servers should be configured so that they do not allow an external Domain Name System (DNS) to be resolved in this zone.

By default, the Local intranet zone consists of local domain names and those set in proxy override in the **Connection** tab. Make sure that these settings are indeed secure for the installation; if they are not, adjust them as needed. You can check that the Local intranet zone is configured correctly by browsing various intranet and Internet pages and checking that the correct zone is shown in the status bar.

After you have checked that the Local intranet zone is secure, you can change the zone's security level to Low to allow a wider range of operations and make the Web pages more functional. You can also adjust individual security settings in the **Security Settings** dialog box as explained in "Setting Up the Internet Zone" earlier in this section.

If parts of your intranet are not secure or do not meet your security standards, you can exclude them from the Intranet zone by adding them to the Restricted sites zone.

The Local intranet zone is designed to be configured using the *Microsoft Internet Explorer Administration Kit*; however, you can also use the **Security** tab in the **Internet Properties** dialog box.

Summary of Authenticode Technology

When users download signed code to their computers, *Authenticode* verifies both its publisher and its integrity (that it has not been tampered with since the author published it). No software can be guaranteed to be 100 percent safe under all circumstances, but Authenticode uses public key technology to sign objects digitally and help you make informed decisions about blocking the execution of certain code. Authenticode works with all common types of downloadable code, including Java applets, ActiveX controls, and plug-ins.

Authenticode checks to see that a piece of software is digitally signed during the valid lifetime of the publisher's certificate.

Authenticode can also automatically check to make sure a software publisher's certificate has not been revoked. Publishers can have their certificates revoked if they abuse their code-signing agreement by, for example, creating malicious code that harms users' computers.

Summary of Certificate Management

Authentication certificates are a key tool in providing Internet security. Certificate management eases the administration of network security. The certificates, which are assigned to software publishers who meet defined levels of integrity and security in their code, give users a way to identify the origin of a piece of software on the Internet. This identification mechanism forms the basis of Authenticode. Certificate Management lets system administrators control which Java applets and ActiveX controls are allowed to run on their networks based on who published the applets or controls.

Example

Certificate Management

You can let users open and run all internally created controls, but keep all controls that originate from outside your corporate firewall from loading and running on company computers.

Site certificates verify that you are really connected to the Web sites that you believe you are connected to. Viewing information may not present a security risk, but sending information can. Security certificates are issued to particular organizations for specific periods of time. Before you send information, certificates are sent from the secure Web sites to Internet Explorer 4.0. These certificates provide certain information about security at those sites. Internet Explorer 4.0 verifies that the Internet address stored in the certificate is valid and that the current date precedes the expiration date.

Note   Site Certificates are active only for Uniform Resource Locators (URLs) using HTTPS. Communication to and from Web sites using HTTPS are kept private through encryption when this mode is active.

▶   **To see the site certificates stored in Internet Explorer 4.0**

1. Start Internet Explorer.

2. Click the **View** menu, and then click **Internet Options**.

3. Click the **Content** tab, and then click **Authorities**.

   By default, the **Certificate Authorities** dialog box contains a list of authorities that are allowed to issue certificates to sites.

If you are connected to a site with a certificate, a lock icon appears on the bottom right corner of the browser window.

Summary of Java Security (Sandboxing)

Support for *sandboxing*, the Java security model, was built into Internet Explorer 3.0 and has been enriched in Internet Explorer 4.0. Running a Java applet in a sandbox prevents it from accessing a computer or network resource and also greatly restricts what it can do. Internet Explorer lets you control access of applets to users' resources, such as their hard disks and network connections. It presents users with a range of security options, such as allowing a Java applet to access a specific amount of hard disk space on a client computer.

Summary of Privacy Protection

The following list describes the kinds of privacy protection built into Internet Explorer 4.0.

Secure channel services. Support for Secure Socket Layer (SSL) versions 2.0/3.0 and Private Communication Technology (PCT) version 1.0 ensures that personal or business communications using the Internet or an intranet are private. The SSL and PCT protocols create a secure channel so that no one can eavesdrop on communications. With secure communications guaranteed, users can buy consumer goods, reserve plane tickets, or conduct personal banking on the Internet.

Transport Layer Security. Transport Layer Security (TLS) is a new secure channel protocol under development by the Internet Engineering Task Force. TLS builds on existing protocols to create an improved Internet secure channel protocol.

Personal Information Exchange. The Personal Information Exchange (PFX) is a set of public key-based security technologies that is part of the Microsoft Internet security framework. PFX supports such Internet standards as X.509 and PKCS#12 certificate formats. Microsoft has submitted PFX for consideration as a new Public Key Cryptography Standard (PKCS).

Cookie privacy. Some Web sites use *cookie technology* to store information on client computers. These cookies are usually used to provide Web site personalization features. With Internet Explorer 4.0, you can choose whether or not to store a cookie.

Tip You can decline cookies from a site by selecting **Prompt before accepting cookies** on the **Advanced** tab in the **Internet Options** dialog box of the Internet Explorer **View** menu.

SOCKS firewall support. Many corporations provide their employees with access to the Internet through firewalls that protect the corporation from unwanted access. SOCKS is a standard protocol for traversing firewalls in a secure and controlled manner. Internet Explorer 4.0 is compatible with firewalls that use the SOCKS protocol.

Windows NT Server challenge/response. Corporations can take advantage of the Microsoft Windows NT LAN Manager challenge/response authentication that might already be in use on their Windows NT Server network. Users enjoy increased password protection and security while still able to use their existing Internet information servers.

CryptoAPI version 2.0. CryptoAPI provides the underlying security services for secure channels and code signing. Through CryptoAPI, developers can easily integrate strong cryptography into their applications. Cryptographic Service Provider (CSP) modules interface with CryptoAPI and perform functions, including key generation and exchange, data encryption and decryption, hashing, digital signatures, and signature verification. CryptoAPI is included as a core component of Windows 98 and Windows 95. Internet Explorer 4.0 automatically provides this support for earlier versions of Windows.

Microsoft Wallet. Microsoft Wallet supports securely storing important and private information, such as credit cards, electronic driver's licenses, ATM cards, and electronic cash. No application or person can view this information without a user's permission. In addition, a user decides where to store the information (on a computer, smart card, or floppy disk). Users have to enter password or account information only once and do not have to remember many different passwords. Users have complete control over who can see or use this information. Wallet allows information to be securely transferred to any computer and used with any application through the use of PFX technology. Designed for the future, Wallet supports additional payment methods (such as Internet cash) as well as other credentials and confidential information.

PICS standards for Internet content. Parents want the assurance that children can be blocked from visiting sites that display inappropriate information. Corporations have similar concerns, wanting to block the use of sites that offer no business value to their customers. Microsoft has been working closely with the Platform for Internet Content Selection (PICS) committee to help define standards for rating Internet content.

Forget your password? With Internet Explorer 4.0, you do not have to type your user name and password every time you want to access a subscription Web service. Instead, Internet Explorer 4.0 functions as your virtual wallet, flashing your personal certificate to Web servers that want to verify your identity. It works the other way, too. You can also store certificates of Web servers in Internet Explorer 4.0. This means you can verify the identity of any Web merchant or other Web server before you purchase goods or communicate with them.

Security Features in Outlook Express

As the use of e-mail and electronic commerce becomes more widely adopted, the amount of confidential information being exchanged over the Internet is growing rapidly. As a result, there is a need to make e-mail messages secure and private. In addition, with the growing popularity of ActiveX controls, scripts, and Java applets, there is an increased chance that the HTML content you receive in an e-mail message could damage or compromise files on your computer.

Outlook Express includes tools to protect you from fraud, ensure your privacy, and prevent unauthorized access to your computer. These tools enable you to send and receive secure e-mail messages and to control potentially harmful e-mail messages through security zones.

Using Security Zones for Outlook Express

Outlook Express enables you to choose which Internet Explorer security zone your incoming e-mail messages are in—either the Internet zone or the Restricted sites zone. Which zone you decide to select depends on how concerned you are about active content (e.g., ActiveX controls, scripts, and Java applets) weighed against the freedom to run that content on your computer. In addition, for each security zone, you can choose a High, Medium, Low, or Custom security level setting.

For more information about security zones, see "Setting Up Security Zones" earlier in this chapter.

Caution Changing the settings for the Internet zone or Restricted sites zone will also change this setting for Internet Explorer and vice versa.

▶ **To change the security zones settings for Outlook Express**

1. In Outlook Express, click the **Tools** menu.
2. Click **Options**, and then click the **Security** tab.
3. Configure the settings according to your security needs.

Using Digital IDs

To use secure e-mail in Outlook Express, you need a digital ID. Digital IDs (also called certificates) provide a means for proving your identity on the Internet, much as a driver's license or other ID cards identify you.

Digital IDs let you sign your e-mail messages, so that the intended recipients can make sure that the message actually came from you and has not been tampered with. Also, a digital ID allows other people to send you encrypted messages.

For more information, see Outlook Express Help.

Getting a Digital ID

You obtain your digital ID from a certifying authority, an organization responsible for issuing digital IDs and continuously verifying that digital IDs are still valid.

Using Your Digital ID

Before you can send signed e-mail messages, you must associate your digital ID with the e-mail account you want to use it with.

▶ **To associate your digital ID with an e-mail account**

1. In Outlook Express, click the **Tools** menu, and then click **Accounts**.
2. Select the account you want to use your ID with, click **Properties**, and then click the **Security** tab.
3. Select **Use a digital ID when sending secure messages from**.
4. Click **Digital ID**, and then select the digital ID you want to associate with this account.

Note Only the digital IDs with the same e-mail address as the e-mail address for the account will be shown.

Backing Up Your Digital ID

Part of your digital ID is an irreplaceable private key stored on your computer. If the private key is lost, you will no longer be able to send signed e-mail messages or read encrypted e-mail messages with that digital ID. You are strongly encouraged to make a backup of your digital ID in case the files containing it are damaged or made otherwise unreadable.

▶ **To back up your digital ID**

1. In Internet Explorer, click the **View** menu, and then click **Internet Options**.
2. Click the **Content** tab, and then click **Edit Profile**.
3. Click the **Digital IDs** tab.
4. The **Import** and **Export** buttons let you manage your digital IDs. Use **Export** to back up your digital ID.

Sending Secure E-mail Messages

Now that you have a digital ID, you can send secure e-mail messages. Secure e-mail messages in Outlook Express protects your Internet communications through both digital signatures and encryption. Using digital signatures, you can sign your e-mail message with a unique ID that assures the person receiving the message that you are the true sender of the message and that it was not tampered with in transit. Encrypting e-mail messages that you send can ensure that no one except the intended recipient can read the contents of the message while it is in transit.

Because Outlook Express uses the Secure/Multipurpose Internet Mail Extensions (S/MIME) standard, other people can read secure e-mail messages that you compose, using programs that support this technology. Likewise, you can read messages composed by other people by using e-mail programs that support S/MIME technology.

Sending and Receiving Signed E-mail Messages

Signed e-mail messages let recipients verify your identity. To send signed e-mail messages, you must have a digital ID of your own.

▶   **To digitally sign an e-mail message**

1. In Outlook Express, click the **Tools** menu.

2. Click **Options**, and then click the **Security** tab.

3. Select **Digitally sign all outgoing messages**.

    –Or–

    Use the **Digitally sign message** button on the message toolbar.

Signed e-mail messages from others lets you verify the authenticity of a message —that the message is from the supposed sender and the message has not been tampered with during transit. Signed e-mail messages are designated with special signed e-mail icons. Any problems with signed e-mail messages that you receive (described in Outlook Express security warnings) could indicate that the message has been tampered with or was not from the supposed sender.

Sending and Receiving Encrypted E-mail Messages

Encrypting an e-mail message prevents other people from reading it when it is in transit. To encrypt an e-mail message, you need the digital ID of the person you are sending the e-mail message to. The digital ID must be part of the person's entry in the Address Book.

▶ **To send encrypted e-mail messages**

1. In Outlook Express, click the **Tools** menu.

2. Click **Options**, and then click the **Security** tab.

3. Select **Encrypt contents and attachments for all outgoing messages**.

   –Or–

   Use the **Encrypt message** button on the message toolbar.

When you receive an encrypted e-mail message, you can be reasonably confident that the message has not been read by anyone else. Outlook Express automatically decrypts e-mail messages, provided that you have the correct digital ID installed on your computer.

Sending and Receiving Digital IDs

For others to be able to send you encrypted e-mail messages, they need your digital ID. To send it to them, simply send them a digitally signed e-mail message, and Outlook Express will automatically include your digital ID.

To send others encrypted e-mail messages, you need their digital ID. Outlook Express lets you retrieve digital IDs via directory services.

▶ **To find a digital ID**

1. In Outlook Express, click the **Edit** menu, and then click **Find People**.

2. Select a directory service that supports digital IDs (for example, the VeriSign directory service).

3. Enter the recipient's name or e-mail address in the appropriate search field, and then click **Find Now**.

4. Select a listing from the results pane, and then click **Add to Address Book**.

Changing Trust Status on Digital IDs

When you add someone's digital ID to your Address Book, it has a trust status associated with it that indicates whether you trust the individual, group, or corporation to whom the digital ID was issued. If a digital ID owner warns you that he or she suspects that the digital ID's private key has been compromised, you may want to change the trust status to "Explicitly Distrust."

▶ **To change the trust status of a digital ID**

1. In the Address Book, double-click the name of the contact.

2. Click the **Digital IDs** tab, select the digital ID whose trust level you want to change, and then click **Properties**.

3. Click the **Trust** tab, and then select an option in the Edit Trust area.

For more information, see Outlook Express Help.

Firewalls

An Internet firewall lets you take advantage of the services offered on the Internet, while limiting exposure to attack. A *firewall* may consist of a collection of hardware and software components that collectively provide a protected channel between networks with differing security. Potential paths to the private network are limited by configuring the firewall to accept only packets from Internet Protocol (IP) addresses and/or ports of the Transmission Control Protocol/Internet Protocol (TCP/IP) that have been designated by the system administrator.

For more information, see Chapter 20, "Internet Access and Tools."

Understanding Proxy Servers

The most critical component of your firewall is your proxy server. A *proxy server* listens to the computers on your internal network. When a client application makes a request, a proxy server responds by translating the request and passing it to the Internet. When a computer on the Internet responds, the proxy server passes that response back to the client application on the computer that made the request.

Proxy servers make a firewall safely permeable to users behind the secured entrance, while closing entryways in the private network to potential attacks. The proxy server must act as both a server and client. It serves proxy clients when accepting approved requests for external servers, and requests services from those servers on behalf of its clients. Proxy servers are commonly used by administrators of corporate networks connected to the Internet and by Internet Service Providers (ISPs).

Microsoft Proxy Server provides an easy, secure, and cost-effective way to bring Internet access to every desktop in an organization. Microsoft Proxy Server routes requests and responses between the Internet and client computers, acting as a liaison between them. In addition to routing requests, Microsoft Proxy Server provides a cache of frequently requested Internet sites, blocks access to specified sites, and provides secure access between your internal network and the Internet. It also offers firewall features.

Configuring Proxy Servers

Access to Web sites secured by Windows NT Challenge and Response requires that firewalls and proxy servers be configured to permit passage of Windows NT Challenge and Response.

If you want to use a proxy server or firewall to protect your local area network (LAN) from being accessed by others on the Internet, carry out the following steps, which set up your computer to gain access to the Internet through a firewall.

▶ **To set up a LAN proxy server or firewall**

1. Run the Internet Connection Wizard.

   Click **Start**, point to **Programs**, point to **Internet Explorer**, and then click **Connection Wizard**.

2. Configure your computer to connect to the Internet by using TCP/IP on your LAN.

3. When you are prompted for the gateway address, type an address only if your organization uses gateways for routing information over the network.

   Note The gateway computer is not the same as the proxy server or firewall computer that protects your LAN from the Internet, so do not type your proxy server or firewall address here.

4. In Control Panel, double-click Internet, and then click the **Connection** tab.

5. In the Proxy server area, select the **Access the Internet using a proxy server** check box.

6. Click **Advanced**.

7. In the first text box, type the Hypertext Transfer Protocol (HTTP) server address for the computer you want to use as the proxy server. In the second text box, type the port number. An example of a proxy server and port number is **http://myproxy.mycompany.com:80**.

   In this example, you would type **http://myproxy.mycompany.com** in the first text box, and **80** in the second text box.

   You can use a different proxy for different types of addresses. However, if you want to use the same proxy for all types of addresses, make sure you select the **Use the same proxy server for all protocols** check box.

8. In the Exceptions area, click the text box, and then type the names of the computers, domains, and ports on the Internet that, when accessed, will not go through the proxy server. Separate each item you type with a semicolon (;). Local addresses are defined as those in which the server name does not have a period (.) in it.

For example:

- http://internalweb/ is a local address.
- http://www.microsoft.com/ is not a local address.

For Help on these items, click the **?** in the title bar, and then click the item.

9. When you have finished changing settings, click **OK**.

10. Click **OK** to close the Internet properties in Control Panel.

If you are running Internet Explorer, restart your computer so that the new proxy settings can take effect.

Note If you are setting up Internet Explorer with a SOCKS proxy server, you must set it up separately from other proxy information (for example, HTTP, FTP, or Gopher). In most cases, this means that all other proxy fields should be left blank and the SOCKS field should contain the address of your SOCKS proxy server. The only exception is when you are using a SOCKS proxy server and a different proxy (for example, HTTP) on the same connection.

For more information about proxy servers and firewalls, see *Microsoft Proxy Servers Installation and Administration Guide*.

Distributed Component Object Model

The Component Object Model (COM) defines how components and their clients interact. The *Distributed Component Object Model* (DCOM) extends the COM infrastructure that underlies ActiveX, transparently and naturally adding support for reliable, secure, and efficient communication between ActiveX controls, scripts, and Java applets residing on different machines on a LAN, a wide area network (WAN), or the Internet. With DCOM, applications can be distributed across locations that make the most sense to your customer and to the application.

Because DCOM is a seamless evolution of COM, you can leverage your existing investment in all ActiveX applications, components, tools, and knowledge to move into standards-based distributed computing. As you do so, DCOM handles the low-level details of network protocols. DCOM enables component applications to operate across the Internet, because it works natively with such Internet technologies as TCP/IP and Java. It provides the "object glue" that allows business applications to work across the Web.

Figure 9.2 shows the overall DCOM architecture. The COM run-time provides object-oriented services to clients and components and uses the remote procedure call (RPC) and the security provider to generate standard network packets that conform to the DCOM wire protocol standard. COM provides sophisticated mechanisms for the marshaling and unmarshaling of method parameters that build on the RPC infrastructure defined as part of the distributed computing environment (DCE) standard. DCE RPC defines a standard data representation for all relevant data types, the Network Data Representation (NDR).

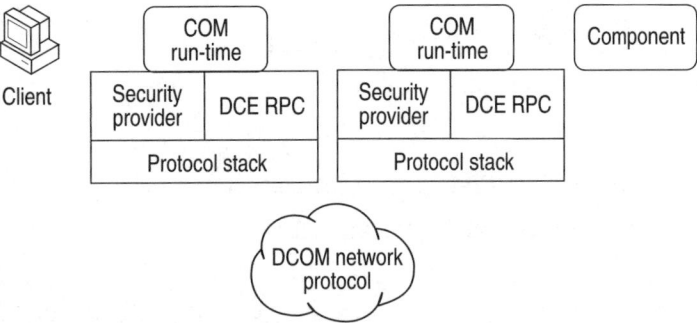

Figure 9.2   Overall DCOM architecture

A distributed application consists of multiple processes that cooperate to accomplish a single task. A distributed application can accommodate different clients with different capabilities by running components on the client side when possible and running them on the server side when necessary. A distributed application is also much more scalable than its monolithic counterparts, and easier to administer and deploy.

Designing a distributed application poses several challenges to the developer. One of the most difficult design issues is security: Who can access which objects? Which operations is an object allowed to perform? How can administrators manage secure access to objects? How secure does the content of a message need to be as it travels over the network?

Mechanisms to deal with security-related design issues have been built into DCOM from the ground up. DCOM provides an extensible and customizable security framework upon which developers can build when designing applications.

Different platforms use different security providers, and many platforms even support multiple security providers for different usage scenarios or for interoperability with other platforms. DCOM and RPC are built in such a way that they can simultaneously accommodate multiple security providers.

Common to all these security providers is their providing a means of identifying a security principal (typically a user account), a means of authenticating a security principal (typically through a password or private key), and a central authority that manages security principals and their keys. If a client wants to access a secured resource, it passes its security identity and some form of authenticating data to the resource, and then the resource asks the security provider to authenticate the client. Security providers typically use low-level custom protocols to interact with clients and protected resources.

Configuring Applications to Use DCOM

The DCOM Configuration tool can be used to configure 32-bit COM and DCOM applications.

▶ **To run the DCOM Configuration tool**

- Click **Start**, click **Run**, and then type **dcomcnfg**.

Note Before you can use an application with DCOM, you must use DCOM Configuration to set application properties, such as security and location.

Distributed Applications for the Internet or an Intranet

You can use DCOM to integrate client/server applications across multiple computers. DCOM provides the infrastructure that enables client/server applications to share components over the Internet or intranet.

▶ **To set default permissions for all DCOM applications**

1. Run dcomcnfg to open the DCOM Configuration tool.
2. Click the **Default Security** tab.
3. Click **Edit Default** for Default Access Permissions.
4. If necessary, click **Add** to add other user accounts to the **Name** box.

▶ **To set permissions for a DCOM application**

1. Run dcomcnfg to open the DCOM Configuration tool.
2. Click the application you want to configure, and then click **Properties**.
3. Click the **Security** tab.
4. Select **Use Custom Access Permissions** for launch, access, or configuration, and then click **Edit**.
5. If necessary, click **Add** to add other user or group accounts to the **Name** box.

▶ **To grant permissions that apply to all applications**

1. Run dcomcnfg to open the DCOM Configuration tool.

2. Click the **Default Security** tab.

▶ **To set the location of a DCOM application**

1. Run dcomcnfg to open the DCOM Configuration tool.

2. Click the application you want to configure, and then click **Properties**.

3. Click the **Location** tab, and specify the location of the application.

Troubleshooting Security

To make it easy for customers to contact Microsoft with any potential security issues, an e-mail address has been created: secure@microsoft.com. Please use this address to report security issues with a Microsoft product. Microsoft product teams respond to security issues you bring to their attention.

No Windows or Network logon dialog box appears at startup.

When you start Windows 98, you might not receive a Windows or a Network logon dialog box, or you might receive one of the following error messages:

```
No network provider accepted the given network path.
```

```
The operation being requested was not performed because the user has not
logged on to the network. The specified service does not exist.
```

Another symptom of this problem is the absence of the **Change Passwords** tab in the **Passwords Properties** dialog box.

This problem occurs if any of the following conditions are true:

- The primary network logon field is not set correctly.

- The following entry appears in the **HKEY_LOCAL_MACHINE\Software \Microsoft\Windows\CurrentVersion\Network\Real Mode Net** registry key:

  ```
  AutoLogon=<x>
  ```

  where <x> is a number.

- You are logging on to a Novell NetWare network, and the server you log on to is running multiple frame types.

- You are logging on to a Microsoft or NetWare network, and you have cached your network password.

- The network adapter is improperly configured.

Find Fast does not index password-protected files.

Because password-protected files are encrypted, they cannot be indexed. Find Fast does not index password-protected documents because they are not searchable files. Any references to file properties or content will not be addressed in the index. The behavior of Find Fast is, by design, to uphold the security and protection of your documents.

File and Printer Sharing for Microsoft Networks is unavailable.

When you use the right mouse button to click a drive, folder, or printer, there may be no Sharing command on the menu that appears even though File and Printer Sharing for Microsoft Networks is installed. The cause may be that Nwserver.vxd is loading even though File and Printer Sharing for NetWare Networks is not installed in network properties. If this service is installed and you do not use NetWare networks, you need to remove the Microsoft Client for NetWare Networks by clicking Network in Control Panel, clicking **Client for NetWare Networks**, and then clicking **Remove**. Click **OK**, and then restart your computer when you are prompted.

The user list with user-level security is incomplete.

Your Windows 98 system is configured for user-level security with a Windows NT system as the security provider, but when you try to add a user in a shared folder's properties, you may not see a full list of users. Or some users on the network who do not have an account in the user list from the security provider may be able to gain access to your shared Windows 98 computer.

This problem can occur when the security provider is a Windows NT Workstation that is a member of a Windows NT domain. The user list in the **Add Users** dialog box is the list of local user accounts defined on the Windows NT Workstation, but access to the Windows 98 computer is controlled by the accounts in the Windows NT domain.

Use the list of user and group accounts from the Windows NT domain. To do so, specify the name of the domain instead of the Windows NT Workstation on the **Access Control** tab of the Network option in Control Panel.

The selected security provider cannot be found.

When you select user-level security and enter the name of a server to use as a security provider, you may receive the following error message:

```
Window could not find the specified security provider on the network. Do
you wish to use the name you typed anyway?
```

This error message can occur for any of the following reasons:

- You specified an incorrect server name.

- The server type does not match the services selected for file and printer sharing. For example, you specified a NetWare server but File and Printer Sharing for Microsoft Networks is installed.

- The server is not operational.

- The network has not been started.

- You are not logged on to the Microsoft LAN Manager or the Windows NT domain.

▶ **To resolve this problem**

1. Verify that the server name you entered is correct.

2. Verify that the server type you specified matches the network services you are running. For example, if you are running File and Printer Sharing for NetWare Networks, make sure to specify a NetWare server.

3. Verify that the server is operational.

4. After you verify the previous items, if the network has not been started, restart the computer.

No logon servers are available.

When you attempt to connect to a share on a Windows 98 computer that is using a Microsoft Windows NT domain to provide user-level security, you may receive the following error message:

```
There are currently no logon servers available to service the logon
request.
```

This problem may occur regardless of which users have been given access to the share you are connecting to and which access rights each user has been given. It does not occur when the Windows 98 computer you are connecting to is configured for share-level security.

This problem can occur when your user account is configured so that you can log on only to certain computers in the domain. If your user account is configured in this manner and the Windows 98 computer you are attempting to connect to is not one of the specified computers, you are unable to connect to resources on that computer.

To work around the problem, configure the Windows 98 computer you are attempting to connect to for share-level security.

▶ **To configure Windows 98 for share-level security**

1. In Control Panel, double-click Network, and then click the **Access Control** tab.

2. Click **Share-level access control**, and then click **OK**.

3. Restart the computer when prompted.

Note After you change the type of access control a computer is using, any resources that were shared on that computer are no longer shared. You must share resources again to allow other people access to them.

Additional Resources

For more information about	See this resource
Windows NT	*Microsoft Windows NT Server Networking Guide* in the *Microsoft Windows NT Server Resource Kit* (for Microsoft Windows NT Server version 4.0)
	Microsoft Windows NT Server 4.0 Concepts and Planning Guide
Internet security	*Microsoft Internet Explorer Administration Kit*
Proxy servers	*Microsoft Proxy Servers Installation and Administrator's Guide*
	http://www.microsoft.com/security/

C H A P T E R   1 0

Disks and File Systems

This chapter is intended primarily for system administrators, network administrators, computer technicians, and anyone else interested in using utilities to partition and format hard disks, and using utilities, such as DriveSpace 3, Disk Defragmenter, and ScanDisk, to manage disks and data. It also describes the file allocation table (FAT) used by Microsoft Windows 98 and discusses how to manage long file names.

In This Chapter

See Also

- For more information about editing system policies, see Chapter 8, "System Policies."

- For more information about hard drives and other hardware devices, see Chapter 30, "Hardware Management."

Overview of Disks and File Systems

The 32-bit, protected-mode file system in Windows 98 allows optimal access to hard disks, CD-ROM drives, and network resources. The file system support means faster, better performance for all file I/O operations than was previously available.

You can use long file names and directory names in Windows 98 and in any applications that support long file names. The eight-character limit on file names that was imposed by the file system under MS-DOS no longer holds.

The file system in Windows 98 permits exclusive access to a disk device for file system utilities. For example, ScanDisk, a file system utility, requires exclusive access to the file system to ensure data integrity in a multitasking environment. Otherwise, if a file on the disk were to be saved while the utility was writing information to the disk at the same time, data corruption could occur.

The file system also detects when Windows 98 shuts down improperly. If Windows 98 is shut down without going through the standard shutdown sequence, real mode Scandisk will be executed at the next startup. The purpose of running Scandisk is to correct potential errors in the file allocation table (FAT) before continuing the boot process. In the event that a Disk read/write error is encountered during normal Windows 98 operation, a flag will also be set to run real mode Scandisk with Surface Scan.

Exclusive disk access means you can now run disk management and optimization utilities without quitting Windows. You can even complete tasks, such as disk defragmentation, without stopping work in other applications. The exclusive access support is used by the disk utilities provided with Windows 98 and can be used in Windows-based disk management utilities from any vendors that take advantage of the related application programming interface (API) in their utilities.

File Allocation Table

File allocation table (FAT) refers to a disk format, which is a way of organizing the storage space on a hard disk. The table organizes information about the files on the hard disk, representing each one as a chain of numbers that identifies where each part of a file is located. The FAT itself is similar to a table of contents in a book—the operating system uses it to look up a file and find which clusters that file is written to on the hard disk.

FAT is probably the most widely recognized disk format, being read by most operating systems. Microsoft originally devised FAT to manage files on floppy disks, and adapted it as a standard for file and disk management in MS-DOS. A 12-bit FAT was first used for managing floppy disks and logical drives smaller than 16 MB. MS-DOS version 3.0 introduced the 16-bit FAT for larger drives.

FAT32

FAT32 goes beyond the capabilities of FAT16. The most prominent feature is that it supports drives of up to 2 terabytes in size. In addition, FAT32 decreases the cluster size on large drives, thus reducing the amount of unused space. For example, with FAT16, a 2 GB drive has a 32 KB cluster size. The same drive under FAT32 has 4 KB clusters.

To maintain the greatest possible compatibility with existing programs, networks, and device drivers, FAT32 was implemented with as little change as possible to existing architecture, internal data structures APIs, and on-disk format for Windows 98.

However, because 4 bytes are now required to store cluster values, many internal and on-disk data structures and published APIs have been revised or expanded. In some cases, existing APIs have been prevented from working on FAT32 drives to prevent legacy disk utilities that use them from damaging the FAT32 drives. Most programs will be unaffected by these changes. Existing tools and drivers should continue to work on FAT32 drives. However, MS-DOS block device drivers (for example, Aspidisk.sys) and disk tools must be revised to support FAT32 drives.

All of Microsoft's bundled disk tools (Format, FDISK, Defrag, and MS-DOS-based and Windows-based ScanDisk) have been revised to work with FAT32. In addition, Microsoft is working with leading device driver and disk tool vendors to support them in revising their products to support FAT32.

Note A FAT32 volume cannot be compressed using Microsoft DriveSpace 3.

FAT16 vs. FAT32

FAT16 is still available because of its widespread compatibility with all other non-Microsoft operating systems. The major benefits of FAT32 are that it is more efficient than a 16-bit FAT on larger disks (sometimes by as much as 20–30 percent), and that it can support disk drives larger than 2 GB without having to use multiple partitions.

Note In real-mode MS-DOS or when running Windows 98 in safe mode, FAT32 is considerably slower than FAT16. If you need to run applications in MS-DOS mode, loading Smartdrv.exe in Autoexec.bat or your MS-DOS PIF file will be beneficial.

Some older applications that were written to FAT16 specifications may be unable to display free or total disk space over 2 GB correctly. Windows 98 provides new MS-DOS and Win32 APIs that applications can use to determine free or total disk space over 2 GB.

Table 10.1 shows a comparison of FAT16 and FAT32.

Table 10.1   FAT16 and FAT32 comparison

FAT16	FAT32
Most operating systems (MS-DOS, Windows 98, Windows NT, OS/2, and UNIX) are designed to implement and use it.	Currently, FAT32 can be used only in Windows 98 and Windows 95 OSR2.
It is efficient, both in speed and storage, on logical drives smaller than 256 MB.	Drives smaller that 512 MB are not supported by FAT32.
Disk compression, such as Drvspace, is supported.	Disk compression is not supported with FAT32.
FAT16 is limited in size to 65,525 clusters with each cluster being fixed in a size relative to the logical drive. If both the quantity of clusters and their maximum size (32 KB) is reached, the largest drive is limited to 2 GB.	FAT32 allows for (x) clusters, therefore, the largest drive can be up to 2 terabytes, based on the 32 KB cluster size limitation.
Storing files in a FAT16 system can be inefficient in larger drives as the size of the cluster increases. The space allocated for storing a file is based on the size of the Cluster Allocation Granularity, not the file size. A 10 KB file stored in a 32 KB cluster wastes 22 KB of disk space.	FAT32 cluster sizes are 4 KB (drives less than 800 MB).

Cluster Sizes of FAT16 and FAT32

The largest possible file for a FAT32 drive is 4 GB minus 2 bytes. Win32-based applications can open files this large without special handling. However, non-Win32-based applications must use Int 21h Function 716Ch (FAT32) with the EXTENDED_SIZE (1000h) open flag.

The FAT32 file system includes 4 bytes per cluster within the file allocation table. This differs from the FAT16 file system, which contains 2 bytes per cluster, and the FAT12 file system, which contains 1.5 bytes per cluster within the file allocation table.

Note that the high 4 bits of the 32-bit values in the file allocation table for FAT32 are reserved and are not part of the cluster number. Applications that directly read a FAT32 file allocation table must mask off these bits and preserve them when writing new values.

Table 10.2 provides a comparison of FAT16 and FAT32 cluster sizes according to drive size.

Table 10.2   Cluster sizes of FAT16 and FAT32

Drive size	FAT16 cluster size	FAT32 cluster size
256 MB–511 MB	8 KB	Not supported
512 MB–1023 MB	16 KB	4 KB
1024 MB–2 GB	32 KB	4 KB
2 GB–8 GB	Not supported	4 KB
8 GB–16 GB	Not supported	8 KB
16 GB–32 GB	Not supported	16 KB
>32 GB	Not supported	32 KB

Understanding FAT32

FAT32 provides the following enhancements over previous implementations of the FAT file system:

- Supports drives up to 2 terabytes in size.
- Uses space more efficiently. FAT32 uses smaller clusters (4 KB clusters for drives up to 8 GB in size), resulting in 10 to 15% more efficient use of disk space relative to large FAT drives, and reduces the resources necessary for the computer to operate.
- More robust. FAT32 has the ability to relocate the root directory and use the backup copy of the FAT instead of the default copy. In addition, the boot record on FAT32 drives has been expanded to include a backup of critical data structures. This means that FAT32 drives are less susceptible to a single point of failure than existing FAT volumes.
- Programs load up to 50% faster. FAT32's smaller cluster size enables the new and improved Disk Defragmenter to optimally locate the portions of an application and its supporting files needed at the time it is loaded.

All of Microsoft's bundled disk utilities (Format, FDISK, Defrag, MS-DOS and Windows ScanDisk, and DriveSpace) have been revised to work with FAT32.

Important   When the Drive Converter Wizard is done, the Disk Defragmenter utility runs. It is important that you let Disk Defragmenter run to completion after converting to FAT32. Not defragmenting the disk after converting to FAT32 will result in an even less efficient and slower computer than before the conversion.

You cannot dual boot Windows 98 and Windows NT 4.0 if you use FAT32. Windows NT 4.0 cannot access or boot from a FAT32 drive.

BIOS and Hibernate Issues for FAT32 File System

FAT32 allocates disk space much more efficiently than previous versions of the FAT file system. This results in tens and even hundreds of megabytes more free disk space on larger hard drives. When used with the new and improved Disk Defragmenter tool in Windows 98, FAT32 can significantly improve application load time.

You can easily convert a hard drive to FAT32 using the Converter Wizard, which is started by clicking Start, and pointing to **Programs**, **Accessories**, **System Tools**, and then clicking **Drive Converter (FAT32)**.

This conversion may impact the hibernate, or suspend-to-disk, features shipped with many systems. To support Windows 98, systems that implement hibernate through the APM BIOS or through the Advanced Configuration and Power Interface (ACPI) S4/BIOS state must support FAT32.

Important Various BIOS manufacturers include virus checkers, which look for changes to the Master Boot Record (MBR). In addition, older anti-virus utilities that are installed as real-mode drivers or TSRs may detect that the MBR has changed during an MS-DOS boot. Since a conversion to FAT32 will change the MBR, some virus checkers may erroneously detect the changes to the MBR as a software virus on your system. If a virus-checking utility detects an MBR change and offers to "fix" it, decline this option.

The easiest solution is to uninstall virus-checking software or disable BIOS level protection before converting to FAT32. After conversion, reinstall the software or re-enable the BIOS protection level.

Documentation on the disk structure of the FAT32 file system is available from the Microsoft Web site at **http://www.microsoft.com/hwdev/devdes/** and later in this chapter.

Checks Made by FAT32 Drive Converter Wizard in Protected Mode

The FAT32 Drive Converter Wizard performs a series of checks in protected mode during conversion. The checks are listed below:

1. The wizard checks for a list of hibernate files for APM and ACPI computers. If a hibernate file is found, the Drive Converter Wizard checks for the existence of a PC Card (PCMCIA) controller to see if the computer is a laptop.

2. If a hibernate file exists, the Drive Converter Wizard checks for ACPI and APM. If neither exist on the computer, the wizard converts FAT16 to FAT32.

   – Or –

If the hibernate partition size is greater than or equal to the maximum memory size, it is safe to convert.

3. The wizard checks for a list of known hibernate files:

- Amizvsus.pmf
- Save2dsk.bin
- PM_hiber.bin
- Hibrn8.dat
- Saveto.dsk
- Toshiber.dat

If any of these hibernate files exist on the computer, the wizard displays a message asking if it is okay to continue with the conversion. If you choose to continue the conversion, and you are working from a desktop computer, the hibernate file is deleted. If you are working from a laptop, the wizard recommends not converting to FAT32.

The series of checks is summarized in this table:

Check	Converter Wizard Action
No APM/ACPI	Converts FAT16 to FAT32.
APM/ACPI and hibernate file	Warns against conversion.
APM/ACPI and PC Card (PCMCIA) controller and no hibernate file	Strongly warns against conversion.
APM/ACPI and no hibernate file and no PC Card controller	Converts FAT16 to FAT32.

After the series of checks is made during the conversion, the wizard looks for applications that are incompatible with FAT32, and lists them. After the conversion is complete and Disk Defragmenter has run, use Add/Remove Programs from the Control Panel to uninstall the incompatible application (if found).

Check Made by FAT32 Drive Converter Wizard in Real Mode

The FAT32 Drive Converter Wizard also performs a check in real-mode conversion. The converter checks for the existence of hibernate files. Running the converter with the /hib switch (**cvt /hib**) automatically removes any hibernate files that are found.

Real-Mode Command Line Parameters

This section describes command line parameters available for the real-mode version of the Disk Converter (FAT32) utility. Only the first two parameters are required.

D: A drive letter followed by a colon specifies the drive letter of the volume to be converted to FAT32 format.

/CVT32 This parameter prevents a user from accidentally running the converter. Without this parameter, the utility will not run.

[/WIN] In normal operation, the converter is intended to be run under MS-DOS and not in an MS-DOS VM in Windows 98. Without this parameter, the converter will *not* run in an MS-DOS VM in Windows 98. Also, this parameter works only if the volume specified has no files open on it, meaning that a level-0 volume lock can be taken on the volume, preventing all possible file accesses by other system components and applications during the conversion. If a level-0 volume lock cannot be obtained on the volume to be converted, the conversion is cancelled. If a level-0 volume lock can be obtained on the volume to be converted and the **/WIN** parameter is present, the conversion proceeds.

[1 | 2 | 4 | 8 | 16 | 32] This parameter overrides the converter's internal cluster size selection logic. The default logic for cluster size selection is included below. *Overriding the cluster size is* **not** *recommended.* The cluster size selection logic that the converter uses provides the optimal balance between storage allocation efficiency and file system performance. Overriding the default will compromise either storage allocation efficiency, performance, or both. The cluster size overrides specify that the volume being converted should have a cluster size of 512 bytes or 1 KB or 2 KB or 4 KB or 8 KB or 16 KB. When a user overrides the optimal cluster size, the converter will warn you about the sub-optimal selection unless queries have been suppressed via the **/NOP** parameter.

```
if (((FAT16_clusters * sectors_per_cluster)/2) < 260*1024) {
    optimal cluster size = 512 bytes
}
else {
    optimal cluster size = 4k bytes
}
```

[/NOP] Suppress all warning dialogs, as well as user queries associated with the warning dialogs that the converter displays when it detects a problem. A warning dialog and associated user query informs the user of the condition and gives the opportunity to cancel the conversion.

[**/NOSCAN**] This parameter causes the converter to skip running MS-DOS SCANDISK prior to converting the volume.

Important Skipping ScanDisk before FAT32 conversion is *not* recommended.

[**/MIN**] This parameter overrides the minimum volume size logic that the converter uses to determine whether converting a volume to FAT32 is feasible. The conversion will take place even if the volume is too small to economically convert to FAT32. The logic the converter uses to determine if a volume is below the minimum size follows.

```
if (((FAT16_clusters * sectors_per_cluster)/2) < 512 * 1024) (
    do not convert volume)
```

[**/NT5**] If a FAT32-aware version of Windows NT is already installed on this system, this parameter causes the converter to convert the volume to FAT32 and provide for dual-boot capability between Windows NT and Windows 98. If there is no FAT32-aware version of Windows NT installed on the volume being converted, this switch is ignored.

[**/HIB**] The converter checks for any file in the following list of hibernate files present in the root directory of the volume to be converted to FAT32. If it detects any one of the files and the **/HIB** parameter is *not* present, the conversion is cancelled. If any of one of the files is present and the **/HIB** parameter is present, the file is deleted and the conversion proceeds. A warning dialog is displayed and the user is queried about whether to cancel the conversion unless warnings have been suppressed via the **/NOP** parameter.

- Amizvsus.pmf
- Save2dsk.bin
- PM_hiber.bin
- Hibrn8.dat
- Saveto.dsk
- Toshiber.dat

[**/ERRLOG filename**] Write the status code of the conversion to a file named "Filename." "Filename" may exist on the same volume being converted. The codes written to this file may be any of the following codes and their associated values.

Error	Value
CVT_ERR_NONE	0
CVT_ERR_USAGE	0x7000
CVT_ERR_INVALIDCMDLINEPARM	0x7001
CVT_ERR_INVALIDCLUSTSIZE	0x7002
CVT_ERR_RUN_CVT32	0x7003
CVT_ERR_INCOMPAT_BIOS	0x7004
CVT_ERR_BADDOSVER	0x7005
CVT_ERR_BADWINVER	0x7006
CVT_ERR_DOSMODEONLY	0x7007
CVT_ERR_NETWORK_DRIVE	0x7008
CVT_ERR_CDROM_DRIVE	0x7009
CVT_ERR_FLOPPY_DRIVE	0x700a
CVT_ERR_INVALIDDRIVE	0x700b
CVT_ERR_DRVSPACE	0x700c
CVT_ERR_DISKCOMPRESSION	0x700d
CVT_ERR_OUTOFMEMORY	0x700e
CVT_ERR_FAT32NOTSUPPORTED	0x700f
CVT_ERR_INT13NOTSUPPORTED	0x7010
CVT_ERR_GETDPBFAILED	0x7011
CVT_ERR_ALREADYFAT32	0x7012
CVT_ERR_DRIVETOOSMALL	0x7013
CVT_ERR_RUNSCANDISK	0x7014
CVT_ERR_BADMARK	0x7015
CVT_ERR_CANTUPDATEPART	0x7016
CVT_ERR_CANTLOCK	0x7017
CVT_ERR_DISKERROR	0x7018
CVT_ERR_UNKNOWNPARTTYPE	0x7019
CVT_ERR_DISKPROB_OR_DISKFULL	0x701a
CVT_ERR_USERABORTED	0x701b
CVT_ERR_SMALLCLUSTERS	0x701c
CVT_ERR_ANTIVIRUS	0x701d
CVT_ERR_ANTIVIRUSPOPUP	0x701e
CVT_ERR_EXTATTRIB	0x701f
CVT_ERR_UNINSTALL	0x7020
CVT_ERR_LOGFILE	0x7021

Error	Value
CVT_ERR_BOOTSECTFILE	0x7022
CVT_ERR_WIN9XNTBOOTCONFLICT	0x7023
CVT_ERR_HIB_FILE_EXIST	0x7024
CVT_ERR_MBR_HOOKER_EXIST	0x7025
CVT_ERR_PBRMBRBACKUPFILE	0x7026

[**/HELP**]   Use of this switch or the /? switch displays the following Help text. Does not perform a conversion.

```
Converts 16-bit FAT file system to 32-bit FAT file system.
Usage: CVT D: where D is the drive to convert.
```

Testing Hibernate with FAT32

Before converting a large number of computers in your organization, test hibernate with FAT32 using the following steps:

1. Start Windows 98.
2. Click **Start**, and point to **Programs**, **Accessories**, and **System Tools**, and click **Drive Converter (FAT32).** Follow the steps presented by the wizard.
3. After conversion is complete, point to **Start** and click **Shutdown**, using **Standby** to hibernate the computer.
4. Verify that the system correctly resumes from hibernate.
5. Run ScanDisk to verify that the file system is still intact.

Note This test should be performed on every brand of computer in your organization. Also, special consideration should be made on systems that may be similar, but purchased during different time frames.

The following scenarios should be tested:

- Start the computer in its shipping configuration with FAT16, convert to FAT32, and test as indicated above.
- On a computer that is already running FAT32 and hibernate, add the maximum amount of memory, and verify hibernate.
- If your BIOS uses a hibernate partition, boot the computer with the partition removed or reformatted (simulating users who upgrade their hard disk), and verify that the system handles the lack of hibernate partition and informs the user of what to do. If Windows shows a Start/Shutdown/Standby option, test it and make sure that the computer suspends to RAM instead of to disk.

System Commander and FAT32

System Commander replaces the Master Boot Record (MBR) in Windows 98. The Drive Converter (FAT32) checks for System Commander in both real mode and protected mode. If System Commander is found on the computer, the Converter Wizard does not convert FAT16 to FAT32.

To work around this problem, you must uninstall System Commander before converting to FAT32. If your version of System Commander supports FAT32, you can reinstall it after the conversion. You can also run the converter with the /mbr switch (**cvt /mbr**), which will stop the converter from replacing the Master Boot Record.

Overview of Disk Utilities

This section provides a brief description of disk utilities provided with Windows 98. All of the disk utilities, with the exception of DriveSpace 3, have been revised to include FAT32 support. The utilities are described in more detail later in this chapter.

Note In general, older disk utilities that perform low-level disk functions, such as defragmenters, disk repair tools, and disk compression utilities, do not function properly on FAT32 drives. In most cases, vendors have updated their utilities to be FAT32-aware. The older versions of these utilities should continue to work properly on Windows 98 FAT16 drives.

Drive Converter (FAT32)

This utility converts a hard drive from FAT16 to FAT32. After running the converter, Disk Defragmenter will run on that drive during your next boot. It is important to run Disk Defragmenter because system performance will be slow until you do. The entire process, including defragmentation, could take several hours.

Caution Windows 98 does not include a utility for converting a drive back to FAT16 once you have converted it to FAT32.

Fdisk and Format

These utilities, which you can use to partition and format disks, behave exactly as did their counterparts in MS-DOS versions 6.*x* and Windows 95. You can use a graphical version of Format in Windows Explorer.

Disk Defragmenter

The Disk Defragmenter (also called a disk optimizer) is used to defragment information on a disk. Windows 98 monitors applications that you launch and creates a log file for each application in the \Windows\Applog directory. Disk Defragmenter uses the log files to arrange program files in the order they are accessed when the program starts, causing the program to start more quickly.

DriveSpace 3

The built-in support for DriveSpace 3 disk compression is completely compatible with DoubleSpace® and DriveSpace 3 disk compression provided with MS-DOS 6.x and Windows 95 Plus Pack. Compression is performed by using a 32-bit virtual device driver that delivers improved performance over previously available real-mode compression drivers and frees conventional memory for use by MS-DOS-based applications when executed within Windows 98.

Note   The DriveSpace 3 program identifies FAT32 partitions but does not compress them.

ScanDisk

This graphical disk analysis and repair tool helps users check the integrity of disks and remedy problems it detects. Users can scan files and folders, or the disk surface for errors.

Disk Cleanup

Disk Cleanup offers users a list of ways to free disk space, including emptying the Recycle bin, removing old temporary files, and emptying the Internet cache. This disk space management utility is a wizard to help customers free up hard-disk space. The intent is to perform a series of typical disk space recovery tasks in a step-by-step fashion, in order to help novice users recover some disk space. The wizard is not intended to be a power-user tool and does not allow users the opportunity to delete or move system components, nor other files that could be dangerous to remove. The overriding criteria are safety and usability.

The following are the entry points for Disk Cleanup:

- **Low Disk Space** warning dialog box.
- Drive property page **Tools** tab.
- Published interface that third-party applications can call to provide entry to the wizard.

- The **System Tools** option in the **Accessories** program group on the **Start** menu.
- Online Help (this wizard replaces the Disk Space Troubleshooter in Help).

WinAlign

WinAlign is a tool designed to optimize the performance of executable code (binaries) on the Windows 98 platform. WinAlign aligns binary sections along 4 KB boundaries, aligning the executable sections with the memory pages. This allows the MapCache feature to map directly to sections in cache, resulting in a significant increase in performance through more available memory.

For more information about WinAlign, see the Windows 98 Resource Kit Tools Help.

Issues with Disks and File Systems

When installing Windows 98, be sure to create a new Windows 98 Startup Disk. Because of changes in the real mode and protected mode kernels to support FAT32, versions of Windows 95 and Windows 98 are not compatible with each other when booting to a floppy disk. A new Startup Disk is highly recommended.

Note You can also create a Startup Disk through Control Panel, Add/Remove Programs, Startup Disk.

To ensure disk integrity, have Task Scheduler run ScanDisk regularly. You can set this up with the Maintenance Wizard. Also, run Disk Defragmenter at regular intervals to optimize disk I/O performance.

For more information about Maintenance Wizard and Task Scheduler, see Chapter 27, "General Troubleshooting," and Chapter 23, "System and Remote Administration Tools."

You cannot dual boot Windows 98 and Windows NT 4.0 if you use FAT32. Windows NT 4.0 cannot access or boot from a FAT32 drive.

Be sure to use disk and file management utilities designed specifically for Windows 98. The disk and file management utilities for Windows 98 work with both FAT32 and FAT16 file systems. You also avoid losing long file names and data.

In some cases, the LFNBK utility lets you remove and later restore long file names on a disk. This makes it possible to run a utility not compatible with long file names.

For more information, see "Using the LFNBK Utility for Temporary
Compatibility" later in this chapter.

Caution   Stacker 4.0 from STAC Electronics and similar disk optimization
utilities are not compatible with long file names. If you use such software under
Windows 98, the long file names already on the computer will be destroyed, and
other critical errors could occur.

Contact the software manufacturer for information about Windows 98–
compatible upgrades for your disk utilities.

Windows 98 automatically provides long file name support. However,
Windows 98 file systems and OS/2 High Performance File System (HPFS)
each have slightly different ways of defining 8.3 file name aliases for long file
names. If you are using a mixed network environment, be sure to understand
the differences (as described in this chapter). Then to help minimize any naming
conflicts, define and publish a file-naming policy for users who share files.

Disk Management

Windows 98 provides utilities to partition and format a hard disk. Windows 98
also includes several utilities for managing disks, protecting data, and ensuring
good disk performance. To keep your computer in good working order, use these
programs on a regular basis. Table 10.3 outlines some tasks that are necessary to
manage your computer.

Table 10.3   Disk management tasks

To ensure that	Do this
Files are not lost if the hard disk fails	Run Microsoft Backup software. Back up your files at least once a week. See Chapter 27, "General Troubleshooting."
The computer can access files quickly and efficiently	Defragment the hard disk. See "Defragmenting Disks" later in this chapter.
Lost clusters do not take up space on a disk, or the hard disk is not damaged	Run ScanDisk. See "Using ScanDisk" later in this chapter.
System performs optimally	Run Maintenance Wizard. See Chapter 23, "System and Remote Administration Tools."
Space is available on the hard disk	Use Disk Cleanup and disk compression. See "Using Disk Cleanup" and "Using Disk Compression" later in this chapter.

A sample routine for managing a computer's hard disks might include the following tasks:

- Automatically running ScanDisk regularly to check the integrity of the hard disk.
- Occasionally using the Disk Defragmenter to optimize the hard disk.
- Use Disk Cleanup to remove unnecessary temporary files and to empty the Recycle bin and the Internet cache.

No matter what your computer management plan, carry it out at regular intervals using Task Scheduler. Task Scheduler is easy and automatic and performs tasks when you are not around or not using the computer.

Note For best results, do not run other programs while running either Disk Defragmenter or ScanDisk. Although you can use the computer for other tasks while running either of these utilities, each time you write to the disk, the utility automatically reinitiates itself to work with the current view of the disk.

Using Fdisk to Partition Hard Disks

This section describes how to use the Fdisk utility to configure a hard disk. For example, if you want to combine several partitions into one large partition, you must use Fdisk.

Fdisk is an extremely powerful program. If you delete a disk partition by using Fdisk, all the data in that partition will be permanently destroyed.

Caution Do not repartition the hard disk using Fdisk if the hard drive was partitioned using a third party program, such as those created by Disk Manager, EZ Drive, Storage Dimensions SpeedStor, Priam, or Everex partitioning programs. These programs provide drive translation between the hard disk drive and the BIOS, and are typically used on systems in which the BIOS does not support large drives. If the drive has been partitioned using one of these utilities, use that program to repartition the drive (as opposed to using Fdisk).

The above programs are not a complete list of utilities that provide disk partitioning. Other programs sold with various hard drives provide similar functionality, but have various names, depending on the manufacturer. Current partitioning software typically loads right after BIOS POST, but prior to the operating system. When these programs load, they usually display a banner page or text informing the customer to press a key sequence to boot to the floppy drive (generally the CTRL or SPACEBAR). Older versions of partitioning software load from a device=<driver> line in Config.sys. The following are examples of this type of driver: Dmdrvr.bin (Older Disk Manager), Sstor.sys (SpeedStor), Hardrive.sys (Priam), and Evdisk.sys (Everex).

If you are unsure which software is being used, consult your documentation, the computer manufacturer, or the hard disk drive manufacturer.

▶ **To configure a hard disk**

1. Create a Startup Disk using the Add/Remove Programs option in Control Panel.
2. Back up the files on the hard disk.

Note Step 2 is only necessary if there are files on the disk that you need or want to save.

3. Partition the hard disk using Fdisk.
4. Format the hard disk.
5. Restore the backed-up files.

Partitioning Drives

If you want to partition a hard disk into one drive, you must first use Fdisk to delete all existing partitions and logical drives, and then create a new primary partition and make it active. You can also partition a hard disk so that it has more than one logical drive.

Fdisk is an MS-DOS-based application that can be run from an MS-DOS command line or from within Windows 98 if partitioning an additional hard drive. The partitions that Fdisk creates are called MS-DOS partitions. The Startup Disk contains a copy of Fdisk, which you can use if a hard disk becomes corrupt or unreadable.

▶ **To start Fdisk**

1. If you are starting Fdisk from a Startup Disk, put the disk in drive a: and press CTRL+ALT+DEL to restart the computer. At the command prompt on the a: drive, type **fdisk**.

   – Or –

   At the command prompt, type **fdisk**.

2. If you have a hard disk smaller than 512 MB, the Fdisk Options screen appears.

   You can choose to do the following:

   ▪ Create a partition or logical drive.

   ▪ Set the active partition.

- Delete a partition or logical drive.

- Display partition information.

- If the computer has two or more hard disks, Fdisk displays a fifth option named **Change Current Fixed Disk Drive**, with which you can switch to another disk drive.

– Or –

If you have a hard disk larger than 512 MB, the following screen appears.

```
Your computer has a disk larger than 512 MB. This version of Windows
includes improved support for large disks, resulting in more efficient
use of disk space on large drives, and allowing disks over 2 GB to be
formatted as a single drive.

IMPORTANT: If you enable large disk support and create any new drives on this
disk, you will not be able to access the new drive(s) using other operating
systems, including some versions of Windows 95 and Windows NT, as well as
earlier versions of Windows and MS-DOS. In addition, disk utilites that
were not designed explicitly for the FAT32 file system will not be able
to work with this disk. If you need to access this disk with other operating
systems or older disk utilities, do not enable large drive support.

Do you wish to enable large disk support (Y/N)...........? [N]
```

Important If you enable large disk support, any drives created will be FAT32. As such, you will not be able to access the newly created drive if booting from a boot disk created by a previous version of Windows 95, Windows 95A, or MS-DOS. Windows 95B (OSR2) does support FAT32, however, it is recommended that you use your Windows 98 Emergency Boot Disk when booting from a floppy. In addition, legacy third-party disk utilities may not function on FAT32, so it is highly recommended you contact your software vendor to ensure FAT32 compatibility. Most third-party manufacturers already have FAT32 versions of disk utilities available. Utilities included with Windows 98 are compatible with FAT32.

Fdisk identified that you have a drive larger than 512 MB. It asks if you wish to enable large disk support, so that your system can use FAT32 as your file system. You can choose one of the following options:

- Answering "Y" means you will be using a 32-bit FAT. Fdisk can make the entire disk available as one partition (up to 2,047 GB).

- Answering "N" means you will be using a 16-bit FAT. Fdisk will only allow up to 2 GB for a partition even if the disk is larger.

  Windows 98 introduces many new performance enhancements, such as Application load acceleration, MapCaching, and idle time paging. Although these are features of the Windows 98 operating system, additional benefits are gained when running on FAT32 volumes.

Each Fdisk screen displays a Current Fixed Disk Drive line, followed by a number. If the computer has only one hard disk drive, this number is always 1. If the computer has more than one hard disk drive, the number shows the disk Fdisk is currently working on. The first hard disk drive on the computer is 1, the second is 2, and so on. The Current Fixed Disk Drive line refers only to physical disk drives.

Note If you installed a disk-compression program from Microsoft or another vendor, Fdisk displays the uncompressed, not the compressed, size of the drives. Also, Fdisk may not display information about all the drives used by a disk-compression program from another vendor.

▶ **To configure a hard disk using Fdisk**

1. Delete all MS-DOS partitions in the following order: logical drives, the extended MS-DOS partition, and then the primary MS-DOS partition.

2. Create a new primary MS-DOS partition.

3. (Optional) Create an extended partition and logical drives.

Caution If you use Fdisk to repartition a hard disk, all the files on the original partitions will be deleted. Be sure to back up all data files on the hard drive before using Fdisk.

Deleting Partitions and Logical Drives

You can use Fdisk to delete partitions before creating a new primary partition. You must delete partitions in the following order:

1. Any non-MS-DOS partitions.

2. Any logical drives in the extended MS-DOS partition.

3. Any extended MS-DOS partition.

4. The existing primary MS-DOS partition.

Important Back up your files on all partitions of the fixed disk prior to deletion. If the computer has a non-MS-DOS partition on a hard disk, you may have to boot to the operating system that created the partition in order to back up the data on the logical drive.

For more information, see the documentation that came with the non-MS-DOS operating system, or the disk-partitioning program from another vendor.

▶ **To delete a partition or logical drive**

1. In the Fdisk Options screen, press **3**, and then press ENTER. The Delete DOS Partition Or Logical DOS Drive screen appears.

2. Press the number for the kind of partition you want to delete, and then press ENTER.

3. Follow the directions on the screen, and repeat the steps for deleting any additional logical drives or partitions.

If Fdisk cannot delete a non-MS-DOS partition, quit Fdisk and delete the non-MS-DOS partition by using the software used to create it.

Creating a Primary MS-DOS Partition

On a new disk, or after you have deleted a primary MS-DOS partition, you can create a new primary MS-DOS partition.

▶ **To create a primary MS-DOS partition**

1. In the Fdisk Options screen, press **1**, and then press ENTER. The Create DOS Partition Or Logical DOS Drive screen appears.

2. Press **1**, and then press ENTER. The Create Primary DOS Partition screen appears.

3. If you want the partition to be the maximum size, press ENTER. Then insert a Startup Disk in drive a:, and press any key.

   – Or –

   If you do not want the partition to be the maximum size, press **n**, and then press ENTER. Another Create Primary DOS Partition screen appears.

4. To specify the partition size you want, follow the instructions on-screen, and then press ENTER.

   You can specify the partition size as a percentage of disk space or in megabytes of disk space. If you specify a percentage of disk space, include a percent sign (%) after the number.

5. If you create the Primary partition to use the entire hard drive, press ESC twice to exit FDISK, then reboot the computer to the floppy disk.

   If you chose not to use the entire drive for the Primary partition, you need to create the Extended DOS partition (unless you plan to use the remaining disk space for other reasons, such as a different operating system). To do this, select **Option 1** from the main FDISK options screen., then choose to create an **Extended DOS partition**. This will typically be set up for the remaining disk space on the drive. You will be prompted to create logical drives upon establishing the Extended DOS partition. Specify the partition size you want as a percentage or number of megabytes of disk space. Select logical drive sizes the same way.

Finally, if you created a Primary and an Extended partition, you need to set an active partition. From the main Fdisk options menu, select option 2, and then select the Primary partition to set active.

Verifying Drive Integrity

While using Fdisk, each time you create a partition or logical drive, Fdisk displays the following message on the bottom of the screen:

```
Verifying drive integrity,   ##% complete.
```

The percentage counts 0 to 100. When verifying the drive's integrity, Fdisk is checking the tracks where the system files and FAT will be stored. Fdisk displays this message since it has capabilities for setting up very large drives and the process may take some time.

The check initially verifies the number of tracks necessary to hold the system files and FAT as if the entire disk were partitioned as one primary partition. If you create an extended partition it will verify the number of tracks necessary to hold the system files and FAT as if the remaining portion were partitioned as one logical drive. Finally, with each logical drive created, Fdisk verifies the number of tracks necessary to hold the system files and FAT as if the remaining portion of the extended partition were defined as a logical drive. This repeats until you finish creating logical drives.

Formatting a Hard Disk

The Format command has changed to take into account 32-bit FAT and larger drives. The process for formatting a drive has not changed.

The hard disk on your computer must be formatted before you can run Windows 98 Setup. However, if Windows 98 is already installed and you need to reformat the hard disk, use the following procedure.

Note If the disk was compressed using DriveSpace, you must use the Format option in the DriveSpace program to format the compressed drive.

▶ **To format a hard disk drive with Windows 98 installed**

- In Windows Explorer, right-click the drive icon for that disk, and then click **Format**.

▶ **To format a hard disk drive using a Windows 98 Startup Disk**

1. Make sure a Startup Disk is in drive a:. Then, at the command prompt, type the following:

   format *drive:*

   For *drive*, type the letter of the drive you want to format.

   If you are formatting drive c:, copy system files to the hard disk by typing the following at the command prompt:

   format c: /s

   When the warning message appears, proceed with formatting by pressing Y. Then press ENTER.

2. When formatting is complete, type a volume label (if you want one), and then press ENTER.

3. If you want to format other drives, repeat steps 1 and 2.

4. Remove the floppy disks from all floppy disk drives, and restart the computer by pressing CTRL+ALT+DEL.

Assigning Drive Letters for Removable Media

Whenever a removable media device is present, the Windows 98 volume tracker ensures that the correct media is in the device and reports improper media removal or insertion.

The volume tracker keeps track of removable media in two ways:

- On non-write-protected disks, the volume tracker writes a unique ID in the disk's FAT header. This ID is different from the volume serial number.

- On write-protected disks, the volume tracker caches each disk's label, serial number, and basic input/output system (BIOS) parameter block.

Windows 98 supports existing removable media with MS-DOS-compatible partitions, which usually are created by using Fdisk utilities from other vendors. You can use Fdisk for Windows 98 to create partitions on removable media that are recognized by the BIOS. Drives that are recognized by the BIOS are also known as INT 13 drives.

Windows 98 does not perform volume tracking based on the volume serial number because all removable media do not have serial numbers or some might have duplicate serial numbers (as is the case with bulk-formatted floppy disks). Therefore, the file system driver must assign unique IDs to removable media the first time there is a request to mount the specific media, unless unique numbers have already been written to the media. These unique numbers identify the media for volume tracking.

You can control the number of drive letters to be reserved during system startup for each removable media drive.

▶ **To reserve drive letters for removable media**

1. In the System option in Control Panel, click the **Device Manager** tab.

2. In the hardware list, double-click the item that represents the removable device. Removable drives are typically found under CD-ROM or Disk drives.

3. In the **Properties** dialog box, click the **Settings** tab.

4. In the **Reserved Drive Letters** area, select a letter in the **Start Drive Letter** list to define the first drive to be assigned to this device.

   In the **End Drive Letter** list, select the last drive to be assigned to this device. Click **OK**.

5. To close the **System Properties** dialog box, click **OK**.

6. When prompted, restart the computer.

The MaxRemovableDrivePartition entry in the registry allocates the drive letters to be used by partitions on removable media. If this entry is not present in the registry, the number of drive letters to be assigned is based on the number of partitions present on the media when the system starts. If no media are present at startup, Windows 98 reserves one drive letter for each of the removable media.

To support variable-sized disks and partitions, Windows 98 recalculates the disk geometry every time a media change is detected. If you insert media with more partitions than specified by the MaxRemovableDrivePartition entry in the registry, a message warns you that some partitions on the media are not accessible in the current configuration and prompts you to increase the value of MaxRemovableDrivePartition.

Converting an Existing FAT16 Drive to a FAT32 Drive

Use the FAT32 Drive Converter to convert your drive to FAT32.

Caution Windows 98 does not include a utility for converting a drive back to FAT16 once you have converted it to FAT32.

Drive Converter (FAT32)

▶ **To convert to FAT32 using Drive Converter (FAT32)**

> **Caution** The Drive Converter (FAT32) makes changes to the boot record and file allocation tables of any hard disk that is converted.

1. Click **Start**, point to **Programs**, point to **Accessories**, and then click **System Tools**.
2. Click **Drive Converter (FAT32)**. This launches the Drive Converter (FAT32) Wizard. Follow the directions on the screen.

The Drive Converter (FAT32) named Cvt1.exe, by default is installed in the Windows folder. The Drive Converter (FAT32) program does the following:

1. Launches the Drive Converter (FAT32).
2. Scans your system for applications that may be incompatible with FAT32.

   The list of programs that the Drive Converter (FAT32) will search for are kept in the registry at:

   HKEY_LOCAL_MACHINE\SYSTEM\CurrentControlSet\Control \SessionManager\CheckBadApps400

3. Warns you that the system will be restarted and prompts you to save your work.
4. Prompts you to specify which drive to convert; only one drive at a time can be converted.
5. Prompts you to back up your files.

Managing the Recycle Bin to Free Disk Space

When you delete a file or directory, it is moved to the Recycle Bin, but it still takes up space on the hard disk. Use one or all of the following methods to ensure disk space is not being used by the contents of the Recycle Bin:

- Avoid moving items to the Recycle Bin by pressing SHIFT when you use the mouse or keyboard to delete items.
- Avoid moving items to the Recycle Bin by specifying that items are removed from the disk immediately when you delete them.
- Empty the Recycle Bin regularly.
- Use the Maintenance Wizard to schedule emptying the Recycle Bin on a regular basis. For more information, see Chapter 27, "General Troubleshooting."

You can also configure the Recycle Bin to use only a set amount of space so that you are prompted to empty the bin more often.

▶   **To configure the Recycle Bin**

1. Right-click the Recycle Bin icon, and then click **Properties**.

Note You can configure properties separately for each hard disk drive on the computer by clicking the option named Configure Drives Independently.

---

2. If you want deleted items to be removed from the Recycle Bin immediately, make sure **Do Not Move Files To The Recycle Bin** is checked.

3. If you want to specify the amount of hard disk space the Recycle Bin can use, drag the slider to the desired percentage.

For more information about the Recycle Bin, see Help.

Using Disk Cleanup

Disk Cleanup presents you with a list of ways that you can get more disk space, including emptying the recycle bin, removing temporary files, and emptying the Internet cache.

Note This utility also appears when a user is running out of hard disk space. If Windows attempts to allocate space on a hard drive (create a file or resize an existing file) and the free disk space drops below a set threshold, a low disk space notification will appear. This notification prompts the user to run Disk Cleanup. The threshold is 25–65 MB, depending on the volume size. The low disk space warning only appears once during a Windows session. The user will see a second warning only when they completely run out of disk space. The out of disk space warning will always appear when Windows attempts to allocate space on a drive that is completely full.

▶   **To start Disk Cleanup**

- In My Computer, right-click a drive, click **Properties**, and then click **Disk Cleanup**.

    – Or –

    Click **Start**, point to **Programs**, point to **Accessories**, point to **System Tools**, and then click **Disk Cleanup**.

Disk Cleanup automatically runs when it detects a low disk threshold. It will suggest several options to delete, depending on the disk drive, so that you can free up some disk space. Disk Cleanup will only run once if it detects a low disk threshold until you try to copy a file to the drive or until you restart your computer.

Using Microsoft Backup

Microsoft Backup, a Windows 98 utility for backing up data, provides options for backing up files to removable disks or tapes, restoring from disks or tapes, and comparing backup file sets to files on the hard disk. Microsoft Backup supports the QIC 113 backup tape specification, which includes support for long file names.

For users familiar with the Windows 3.1 Backup utility, the following list describes important differences in Backup under Windows 95 and Windows 98:

- The Windows 98 version of Microsoft Backup does not support restoring backup sets created by MS-DOS version 6.*x* Backup utilities.

- The recommended method for creating a complete backup file set for the computer is the **Full System Backup** option. This option automatically selects the files required for a system backup.

   If you decide to modify the default selections (by clearing the check boxes for some folders), be sure that you select at least the \Windows directory; otherwise, the registry will not be backed up.

- When using the **Backup** tab in the **Settings Options** dialog box, notice that selecting **Differential** under the **Type Of Backup** option causes the utility to back up only files that have changed since the last time Backup was run. With this setting, new files will not be added to the file set and deleted files will not be removed.

- Backup has support for parallel, IDE/ATAPI, and SCSI devices.

- Backup supports backups to local, removable, and network drives.

For more information about Microsoft Backup, see Chapter 27, "General Troubleshooting."

▶ **To make a Startup Disk**

- Double-click Add/Remove Programs in Control Panel, and then click the **Startup Disk** tab.

Defragmenting Disks

Over time, as programs read from and write to a hard disk, information stored on the disk can become fragmented—that is, files are stored in noncontiguous clusters. Fragmentation does not affect the validity of the information—the files are still complete when they are opened. But it takes much longer for the computer to read and write fragmented files than it does for unfragmented files.

To improve file access time, you can defragment uncompressed drives and compressed DriveSpace or DoubleSpace drives.

Disk Defragmenter has been enhanced to make programs start much faster. When a program starts (loads), it typically reads an EXE file and various DLL files. However, only portions of the EXE and DLL files are read during start. Furthermore, these reads are not sequential and jump back and forth, both within the same file and between files. Every one of these non sequential accesses translate to a disk seek and a performance penalty. Windows 98 Disk Defragmenter tries to place disk clusters in the order they are read, so these seeks are eliminated or greatly reduced, shortening the time needed to start the program.

To record the disk access patterns of programs during their startup, Windows 98 uses a process called Task Monitor. Task Monitor automatically monitors programs you use and record their disk access patterns during their start. These records, called log files, are stored in the \Windows\Applog directory. In addition to access patterns, Task Monitor also records the number of times you use programs. This usage information enables Disk Defragmenter to favor more frequently used programs in optimizing the disk.

The format of the log file name is *application.lgn*, where *application* is the name of the application and *n* is the drive letter where the application files reside. Table 10.4 outlines some log file name formats.

Table 10.4   Log file name formats

File name	Description
Notepad.lgc	Log file for Notepad, which is located on drive C
Word.lgd	Log file for Word, which is located on drive D
Excel.lgd	Log file for Microsoft Excel, which is located on drive D
MSinfo.lgc	Log file for MSInfo, which is located on drive C

When Disk Defragmenter (Defrag.exe) runs, it calls Cvtaplog.exe to gather information from all the lg*n* files and build an Applog.dt*n* file, one for each drive. The Applog.dt*n* file contains information about cluster placement optimization instructions which are read by Defrag.exe. Defrag.exe uses this information to place disk clusters in the optimized order so that programs start up faster.

Important Disk Defragmenter does not work with most third party compression utilities, nor will it work on read-only drives, locked drives, network drives, FFS drives, or drives created with ASSIGN, SUBST, or JOIN.

▶ **To defragment a disk drive**

1. Click **Start**, point to **Programs**, point to **Accessories**, point to **System Tools**, and then click **Disk Defragmenter**.

   – Or –

   Click the **Start** button, click **Run**, and then type **defrag**.

2. In the **Select Drive** dialog box, specify the drive that requires defragmentation.

3. Click the **Settings** button if you want to do any of the following:

   - Rearrange program files so they start faster.

   - Check the drive for errors.

   - Choose the above options for this session only or for all sessions.

4. Click **OK**.

Tip Showing details while the Disk Defragmenter is running causes it to take longer than it does when showing only summary information or running it minimized. For quickest performance, minimize the Disk Defragmenter window while the utility is running.

▶ **To see defragmentation information for a particular drive**

1. In My Computer, right-click the drive's icon.

2. Click **Properties**, and then click the **Tools** tab.

   The **Tools Properties** dialog box shows the number of days since the last complete defragmentation process ran on the drive. You can also run Disk Defragmenter from this dialog box.

Performance with Other Programs

Excessive disk activity by other programs can interfere with defragmentation, and may cause Disk Defragmenter to restart frequently and take an inordinate amount of time to complete. If this happens, close all programs while Disk Defragmenter is running.

Some screen savers cause excessive disk activity. To prevent screen savers from running during defragmentation, either change the screen saver to **None** from Display in the Control Panel or modify the registry.

Caution Only advanced users and system administrators should use Registry Editor to modify the registry. If you use Registry Editor to change values, you will not be warned if any entry is incorrect. Editing the registry directly by using registry Editor can cause errors in loading hardware and software, and can prevent users from being able to start the computer.

Before modifying registry values, *always* back up your system. See "Backing up and Recovering the Registry" in Chapter 31, "Windows 98 Registry".

▶ **To prevent screen savers from running during defragmentation**

1. Open Registry Editor.

2. Create a string named DisableScreenSaver under **HKEY_CURRENT_USER\Software\Microsoft\Windows \CurrentVersion\Applets\Defrag\Settings.**

3. Set its value to **yes**.

Some programs are always running in the background of Windows 98 and are difficult to close. If you closed all programs and Disk Defragmenter still restarts frequently and cannot complete, you may want to run Disk Defragmenter before Windows displays the logon prompt (at this point, most programs have not been started).

▶ **To run Disk Defragmenter before Windows displays the logon prompt**

1. Open Registry Editor.

2. Go to **HKEY_LOCAL_MACHINE\Software\Microsoft\Windows \CurrentVersion\RunServicesOnce**, and create a new string value named **Defrag**.

3. Set the value to **defrag.exe**

   – Or –

   Set the value to **defrag** with your choice of command line switches. See "Command Line Switches for Disk Utilities" later in this chapter.

4. Close Registry Editor and restart your computer.

Disk Defragmenter runs before the Windows logon prompt with minimal interruptions. Putting this command line under the **RunServiceOnce** key takes effect only once. Subsequent computer restarts will not cause Disk Defragmenter to run again.

Fine-Tuning Program Start

The Cvtaplog.exe file is called by Defrag.exe to determine the program optimization order and to build the optimization cluster list. The optimization order is recorded in Optlog.txt, which is located in the \Windows\Applog (hidden) folder on your system. The log file lists programs that were used and not optimized, and explains why (see "Flags for Ineligible Programs"). It also records values of various control parameters.

The following is a sample Optlog.txt file:

```
Program Launch Optimization Log - Created Sat Jan 17 01:00:02 1998

Programs Eligible for Optimization:
Ord Flag ProgName  Uses    LastExecDate Program Path
1         WINWORD   85      1998.01.15   C:\PROGRAM FILES\MSOFFICE\OFFICE\WINWORD.EXE
2         RUNDLL32  82      1998.01.16   C:\WINDOWS\RUNDLL32.EXE
3         MSPAINT   54      1997.11.22   C:\PROGRAM FILES\ACCESSORIES\MSPAINT.EXE
4         NSPLAYER  47      1998.01.12   C:\PROGRAM FILES\NETSHOW\PLAYER\NSPLAYER.EXE
5         EXCEL     41      1998.01.16   C:\PROGRAM FILES\MSOFFICE\OFFICE\EXCEL.EXE
6         BSHELF98  30      1998.01.16   C:\PROGRAM FILES\REFERENCE\BOOKSHELF 98\BSHELF98.EXE


Programs Ineligible for Optimization:
Ord Flag ProgName Uses    LastExecDate Program Path
7    S    NOTEPAD  54      1998.01.07   C:\WINDOWS\NOTEPAD.EXE
8    U    TAX      10      1997.04.15   C:\TAX96\TAX96.EXE

Control Parameters:
Use app profile    = Yes
Minimum log size   = 1000
Maximum no use days = 90
Maximum apps       = 50

Flags for Ineligible Programs:
S = Log size smaller than <Minimum log size>
U = Program not used for more than <Maximum no use days>
P = No profile for program
E = Associated program no longer exists
D = Log deleted (may be combined with one of the above)
```

Note that "Programs Eligible for Optimization" are optimized in the order of most used to least used. The program with the highest use is optimized first. A flag (reason) is given for each of the "Programs Ineligible for Optimization."

Control parameters are configurable in the registry.

Caution   Only advanced users and system administrators should use Registry Editor to modify the registry. If you use Registry Editor to change values, you will not be warned if any entry is incorrect. Editing the registry directly by using registry Editor can cause errors in loading hardware and software, and can prevent users from being able to start the computer.

Before modifying registry values, *always* back up your system. See "Backing up and Recovering the Registry" in Chapter 31, Windows 98 Registry.

All control parameters are DWORD values under the **HKLM\software \Microsoft\Windows\CurrentVersion\Applets\Defrag\AppStartParams** key. In the absence of control parameter settings in the registry, the default value for the parameter is used. The default value and the meaning of each parameter is as follows:

Value Name	UseProfile
Type	DWORD
Default	1
Meaning	0 means do not use task monitor's app profile. When profile is not used, programs are optimized in FindFirst/FindNext order of the Application.lgn files in the \Windows\Applog folder, and the following parameters are ignored.

Value Name	MinLogSize
Type	DWORD
Default	1000
Meaning	Minimum log file size in bytes to qualify for optimization. Programs with log files smaller than this value are not optimized. If UseProfile is 0, this parameter is ignored.

Value Name	MaxNoUseDays
Type	DWORD
Default	90
Meaning	Programs not used for longer this many days do not qualify for optimization. If UseProfile is 0, this parameter is ignored.

Value Name	MaxApps
Type	DWORD
Default	50
Meaning	Maximum number of apps to be optimized. Programs are optimized in descending order of usage counts, up to this max number. If UseProfile is 0, this parameter is ignored.

Value Name	ExcludeFiles
Type	SZ
Default	None. Already set up as System.dat\User.dat\System.ini\Win.ini.
Meaning	A list of files excluded from program start optimization. Certain files, such as System.dat, are better organized contiguously than fragmented for program start optimization. File names are separated by a backslash in this string.

Disk Region Optimized for Program Start

If program start optimization is performed, Disk Defragmenter notes in the registry the boundaries of the disk region optimized for program start. This region is the region of the disk used to store the clusters for the program start optimization and may look to other disk optimization programs as being heavily fragmented. Programs can query the registry for the boundaries of this region, and then will leave this region alone.

Under the **HKEY_LOCAL_MACHINE\software\Microsoft\Windows \CurrentVersion\Applets\Defrag\AppStartParams** key is an entry for each drive optimized for program start. The entry is written when Disk Defragmenter completes defragmenting the drive. The entry name is a single letter specifying the driver letter. Its value is a pair of DWORDs specifying the first cluster and the last cluster of the region respectively. For example, the following entry as displayed by Registry Editor says on drive C, the disk region optimized for program start is clusters 0x00000003 to 0x000033F5:

```
C    03 00 00 00 F5 33 00 00
```

Using ScanDisk

ScanDisk is a full-featured disk analysis and repair program. ScanDisk has been upgraded to recognize and fix issues with FAT32 drives. You can use ScanDisk on both uncompressed and compressed drives. ScanDisk will check compressed drives created with third-party compression software, but will do so as if they are uncompressed. ScanDisk cannot check the compression integrity of third party compression programs. ScanDisk can, however, provide a detailed analysis of compression structures on DoubleSpace and DriveSpace drives.

Windows 98 provides two versions of ScanDisk: a graphical Windows-based version (Scandskw.exe) that you can run from the **Start** menu or from Windows Explorer, and an MS-DOS-based version (Scandisk.exe) that is contained in the \Windows\Command folder. Running Scandisk.exe while in Windows will invoke Scandskw.exe.

Note ScanDisk cannot find or fix errors on CD-ROM drives, network drives, or drives created by using **assign**, **subst**, **join**, or **interlnk**.

ScanDisk checks and fixes problems in the following areas on hard disk drives, floppy disk drives, RAM drives, and memory cards:

- FAT16 and FAT32.
- Long file names.
- File system structure (lost clusters, cross-linked files).
- Directory tree structure.

- Physical surface of the drive (bad sectors).

- DriveSpace 3 or DoubleSpace volume header, volume file structure, compression structure, and volume signatures.

Tip You can add ScanDisk to the Windows Maintenance Wizard List. For more information, see Chapter 27, "General Troubleshooting."

You can place ScanDisk in Task Scheduler so that it is run at regularly scheduled times. You can also run ScanDisk from the **Tools Properties** dialog box for a drive. To do this, right-click that drive's icon, click **Properties**, and then click the **Tools** tab. Click the **Check Now** button to begin running ScanDisk.

ScanDisk can check and repair mounted DriveSpace 3 or DoubleSpace drives. You can run ScanDisk from the command prompt to check and repair unmounted compressed volume files (CVFs). When you run ScanDisk to check a compressed drive, by default, ScanDisk checks the host (physical) drive first. In general, you should allow it to do so because an error on the host drive could cause problems with the compressed drive.

▶ **To run ScanDisk**

1. Click **Start**, click **Run**, and type **scandisk**.

2. Click the drive you want to analyze or repair.

3. In the Type Of Test area, click **Standard** or **Thorough**.

   - Standard checks the files and folders on the selected drive for errors.

   - Thorough checks files and folders for errors, but it also checks the physical integrity of the disk's surface.

4. If you do not want ScanDisk to prompt you before repairing each error it finds, make sure **Automatically Fix Errors** is checked.

5. If you are running a thorough test, click the **Options** button to specify which areas of the disk to check or which type of processing to perform. Select the options you want to use, and then click **OK**.

6. Click **Advanced** to set advanced options as needed, and then click **OK**. For more information about each option, see Help.

7. To begin checking the disk, click **Start**.

▶ **To run ScanDisk on unmounted CVFs**

- Boot the computer to an MS-DOS command prompt, change to the drive that contains the unmounted CVF, and type the following command:

  scandisk drvspace.*nnn*

  – Or –

  scandisk dblspace.*nnn*

  where *nnn* is a number. This starts an MS-DOS session and runs ScanDisk on the corresponding DriveSpace 3 or DoubleSpace CVF.

Using Disk Compression

A compressed drive is not a real disk drive, although to most programs it appears to be. Instead, a compressed drive exists on the hard disk as a *compressed volume file* (CVF). A CVF is a file with read-only, hidden, and system attributes, and that contains a compressed drive. Each CVF is located on an uncompressed drive, which is referred to as the CVF's host drive. A CVF is stored in the root directory of its host drive and has a file name, such as Drvspace.000 or Dblspace.000.

Note DriveSpace 3 included with Windows 98 has been modified to recognize FAT32 drives, but it will not compress them.

CVFs can store more data than the space they use on their host drives; for example, a typical CVF might use 100 MB of space on its host drive but contain 200 MB of compressed data. DriveSpace 3 assigns a drive letter to the compressed volume so that you can use it as a disk drive and can access the files it contains. The host drive will have a separate drive letter (although it might be hidden).

Caution Do not tamper with a CVF. If you do, you might lose all the files on the compressed drive.

With Windows 98 DriveSpace 3, you can compress drives and manage drives compressed with DriveSpace 3 or DoubleSpace. (You can even have drives of both compression types on your computer.)

When Windows 98 is installed, Setup replaces the Dblspace.bin or Drvspace.bin file in the root directory of the boot drive with versions that can be unloaded during the system startup process and replaced with Drvspacx.vxd.

Using DriveSpace 3 for Disk Compression

Using DriveSpace 3, you can compress and uncompress data on floppy disks, removable media, or hard disk drives. DriveSpace 3 frees space on disks by compressing the data or space the disks contain. The first time you use DriveSpace to compress data or space on a drive, the disk will have 50 to 100 percent more free space than it did before.

DriveSpace 3 contains these enhancements over Windows 95 DriveSpace:

- Enhanced compression with support for compressed drives up to 2 GB using a 32 KB cluster size.

- Support for storing compressed data for a cluster in multiple fragments when there are not enough contiguous sectors on the disk to store the entire cluster.

- Compression of up to 20 percent faster on Pentium-based computers. Other *x*86-based computers should also run faster with DriveSpace 3 when the compression is configured for best performance.

- DriveSpace 3 settings for specifying whether to use compression, what type of compression to use, and how to use it.

- Support for compression enhancements on existing drives.

You can use a compressed drive just as you did before compressing it. In addition, DriveSpace 3 creates a new uncompressed drive, called the host drive, where it stores the CVF. If the host drive contains any free space in addition to the CVF, you can also use it to store files that must remain uncompressed.

As with earlier CVF versions, a DriveSpace 3 CVF has a name in the form: Drvspace.*nnn*, where *nnn* is the CVF sequence number in the range 000 through 254.

Windows 98 also places drive-specific compression information (and the tools to manipulate it) where you would expect to find it: in the drive's properties. (System-wide compression settings and functions are still available in the DriveSpace 3 programs.) To present this information, a **Compression** tab is added to the **Property** dialog boxes for all local hard and floppy disk drives, except compressed drives created by software from other vendors. Uncompressed drives that are hosts for one or more compressed volume files also have a **Compression** tab added to their properties. For hidden host drives, you must use the DriveSpace 3 program to view information about the drive.

Using Compression Agent

Compression Agent gives you the following compression choices:

- Whether specified files should be in UltraPack format, and whether to downgrade a file from UltraPack format.
- Whether individual files, folders, or file types should be compressed and, if so, with what method.
- Whether to use compression for the rest of your files and, if so, which type.

You can start Compression Agent manually or have Task Scheduler start it automatically. You can also use the Maintenance Wizard to schedule Compression Agent. Compression Agent uses the Windows 98 Last Access Date to determine which files have not been used within a defined time, but does not modify the Last Access Date for any files.

How Compression Works with DriveSpace 3

DriveSpace 3 compresses data in 32 KB blocks (instead of 8 KB blocks used for Dblspace or Drvspace), and supports two levels of compression: HiPack and UltraPack.

HiPack compression uses the same encoding format as standard compression.

UltraPack format offers better compression than standard or HiPack compression, but files compressed in UltraPack format are slower to decompress. UltraPack compression is available by running Compression Agent. You cannot configure DriveSpace to save files in UltraPack format automatically. And, because UltraPack encoding format uses DriveSpace 3 CVFs, Drvspace.bin and Drvspacx.vxd must be installed to read the CVFs.

DriveSpace 3 for Windows 98 can create a compressed drive of up to 2 GB. You can also create a new compressed drive from the free space on an uncompressed drive that is part of a unremovable FAT16 hard disk. After compression, you will notice that the uncompressed drive contains less free space than it did before. This space is now being used by the new compressed drive, which is stored in a hidden file with a file name, such as Drvspace.001.

Tip The registry can reside on compressed drives that were created by "preload" compression software such as Stacker 4.0, DoubleSpace, DriveSpace 3, and AddStor SuperStor/DS.

A swap file can reside on a compressed drive if a protected-mode driver (that is, Drvspace.vxd) controls the compressed drive. DriveSpace 3 marks the virtual memory as uncompressible.

If your swap file is on a compressed drive created by a real-mode compression drive, you should move the swap file to another drive, such as the host drive.

For more information about changing the location of your swap file, see Chapter 26, "Performance Tuning."

Example

Suppose you have a 200 MB hard disk with 100 MB of data on it. Uncompressed, this disk has 100 MB of free space. You can increase the amount of disk space in either of two ways:

Use DriveSpace 3 to compress both the data and the free space on the disk.
Because DriveSpace 3 reports file sizes of compressed files as though they were uncompressed, the disk is now a 400 MB disk with 100 MB of data and 300 MB of free space.

Create a new compressed drive from free space on the hard disk. DriveSpace 3 will report that you have two drives, one with 200 MB of free space and the other with 100 MB of data and no free space. (You can also create an empty drive using only part of the available free space.)

The compression policies specified in the **Compression Agent Settings** dialog box control the policy used to compress files. However, you can also force or prevent a particular compression type on a particular file, or set of files, or folders, based on the following exceptions to the default compression policy:

- Never compress.
- Always compress with UltraPack format.
- Always compress with HiPack format.

The following shows the Compression Agent command line syntax:

cmpagent [*drive*: | /**all**] [/**noprompt**]

The following list describes the parameters for this command:

Parameter	Description
drive:	Specifies drive to be recompressed.
/all	Specifies all local, fixed drives that are compressed.
/noprompt	Runs without waiting for the user to click **Start**, and without displaying a summary at the end. Errors are displayed. This switch can be shortened as /**nop**.

Fine-Tuning Compression

You typically use the default values for compression, which specify using standard or no compression when saving files. Set Task Scheduler to run Compression Agent when the computer is not busy. Compress seldom-used files into UltraPack format and all other files into HiPack format. While deciding which methods and formats to use, consider whether you want maximum disk space or maximum system performance.

Maximizing hard disk space on a computer

Specify that UltraPack format be used to compress most files. (UltraPack format is recommended for Pentium-based computers.) Specify that files be compressed as they are saved. If your computer is fast, specify that HiPack format be used.

Maximizing system performance

Files compressed in UltraPack format are slower to decompress—if you access a document or run an application that is compressed in UltraPack format, you must wait before you can begin to work again. For slower computers that require maximum performance, use Task Scheduler and Compression Agent to specify that all compression is done while the computer is idle instead of compressing files as they are saved.

Suggestions for defining maximum performance: Use DriveSpace 3 to specify that compression occurs only offline (when files are not being saved) or only when disk space is low. Specify a high threshold for UltraPack (for example, compress files not accessed for 30 days or more). Set exceptions for files that should not be compressed in UltraPack format (for example, do not compress executable files).

Note If you choose not to compress files as they are saved, or to compress files only when disk space is low (using Depends On Free Space), the system reports free space as though files will not be compressed. As a result, the computer appears to have less free space than when files are compressed as they are saved. However, if you use Compression Agent regularly, you will be able to store the same amount of data in this space.

Although the option to compress a drive provides more usable space, the process takes longer than creating a new compressed drive because DriveSpace 3 has to compress the data on the drive.

Important Before you use DriveSpace 3 to compress a drive, you should back up the files the drive contains.

▶ **To compress a drive**

1. Click **Start**, click **Run**, and then type **drvspace**.

2. In DriveSpace 3, click the drive you want to compress.

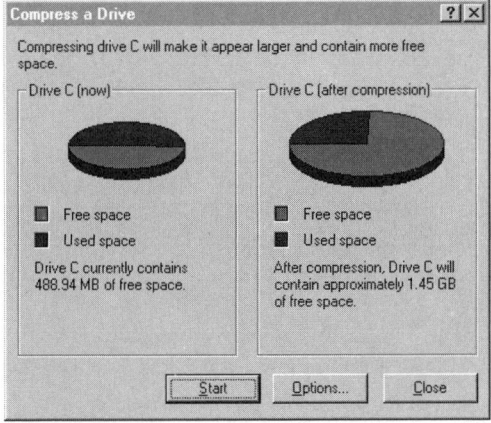

3. Click the **Drive** menu, and then click **Compress**.

   The **Compress a Drive** dialog box appears, listing the drive it is about to compress.

4. If you want to specify the drive letter or free space to leave available for the host drive, and whether the host will be hidden, click **Options**.

   Make modifications in the **Compression Options** dialog box as needed, and then click **OK**.

Note By default, DriveSpace 3 hides the host drive if the amount of free space is 2 MB or less.

---

5. Click **Start** to continue.

6. DriveSpace 3 prompts you to create a Startup Disk. Click **Yes** or **No**.

7. DriveSpace 3 prompts you to back up your files. If you want to back them up at this time, click **Back Up Files**.

8. To start compression, click **Compress Now**.

DriveSpace 3 checks the drive for disk errors, and then it compresses the drive. This process can take from several minutes to several hours, depending on the speed of the hard disk and processor and on the amount of data the hard disk contains. Because DriveSpace 3 checks and rechecks the validity of the data as it compresses files, the process is very safe. In fact, if the compression process is interrupted accidentally (for example, by a power outage), DriveSpace 3 recovers and continues without losing any data.

If any files are open on the drive, DriveSpace 3 will prompt you to close them. For drives that always have files opened (such as the drive containing Windows 98 or the drive containing a swap file), DriveSpace 3 will restart the computer and use a limited version of Windows in place of Windows 98 while it compresses the drive. To do this, a directory named Failsave.drv is created that contains the system files required for this operation. After compression, your computer will restart again, this time with Windows 98. When the compression is completed, DriveSpace 3 shows how much free space is available on the drive.

▶ **To create a new compressed drive**

1. In DriveSpace 3, click the drive that has free space you want to use to create the new compressed drive.

2. Click the **Advanced** menu, and then click **Create Empty**.

3. If you want to leave some free space on the original drive, decrease the value in the **Using** box.

4. To start compression, click **Start**.

▶ **To uncompress a drive**

1. In DriveSpace 3, click a drive to uncompress.

2. Click the **Drive** menu, and then click **Uncompress**.

3. To start uncompressing, click **Start**.

   If there is not enough space on the host drive to contain the uncompressed files, DriveSpace 3 displays a warning. Otherwise, DriveSpace 3 prompts you to back up files and shows the status of the process as it progresses.

Note If you try to change the size of a drive that was mounted with a real-mode DriveSpace 3 or DoubleSpace driver, you will be prompted to restart the computer so that the drive can be remounted under Windows 98. This will also occur for other operations using the real-mode DriveSpace 3 driver.

Fine-tuning Storage Space

On an uncompressed drive, free space indicates how much additional data you can store on that drive. For example, if a drive has 2 MB of free space, you can expect to fit 2 MB of data on it. However, the free space on a compressed drive is only an estimate of how much data you can fit on that drive.

When you store a file on a compressed drive, DriveSpace 3 compresses the file so that it takes up as little space as possible. Some files can be compressed more than others; for example, a text file can be compressed much more than a program file. DriveSpace 3 cannot detect the compressibility of files you have not stored yet, so it only estimates a compressed drive's free space.

DriveSpace 3 estimates a drive's free space by using the estimated compression ratio, which you can set to specify the compressibility of the files you plan to store. For example, if the estimated compression ratio is 3-to-1, DriveSpace 3 calculates the drive's free space based on the assumption that each file to be stored can be compressed to one-third its original size.

Usually, the best compression estimate to use is the actual compression ratio for the files already stored on the drive. Sometimes you might want to reset the estimated compression ratio of each drive to match that drive's actual compression ratio.

You might want to change the estimated compression ratio if it differs greatly from the actual compressibility of the files to be stored. For example, if you plan to store extremely compressible files, such as bitmap files, you might want to specify a higher estimated compression ratio.

Changing a drive's estimated compression ratio does not affect how much DriveSpace 3 actually compresses the files on that drive; it changes only the way DriveSpace 3 estimates the free space on the compressed drive.

▶ **To change the estimated compression ratio**

1. In DriveSpace 3, click the compressed drive you want to change.

2. Click the **Advanced** menu, and then click **Change Ratio**.

3. In the **Compression Ratios** area, type a new ratio box or drag the slider to the desired ratio. Click **OK**.

You can also adjust the amount of free space for a compressed drive or its host drive. This is equivalent to changing the size of the compressed drive and its CVF. When you increase free space on a compressed drive, you decrease it on its host, and vice versa.

▶   **To change the amount of free space on a drive**

1. In DriveSpace 3, click the drive on which you want to change the amount of free space.

2. Click the **Drive** menu, and then click **Adjust Free Space**.

3. In the **Adjust Free Space** dialog box, type a new value or use the slider to adjust the amount of free space available on the compressed and host drives. Click **OK**.

Using Task Scheduler

Task Scheduler is an application for scheduling programs to run at specific times. Programs can be scheduled to run based on several criteria, such as time and date, or a range of times, or whether the computer is idle or is not running on batteries. Task Scheduler supports options for specifying when Compression Agent, Disk Defragmenter, ScanDisk, and other programs will run.

Example

You might use Task Scheduler to do the following:

- Dial-in to an online service during off-peak hours, look for certain topics, download the results, and hang up.

- Run a spreadsheet application such as Microsoft Excel, and use one or more macros to perform extensive computations on worksheets.

- Designate that ScanDisk run a standard test nightly and a thorough test monthly.

For more information about using Task Scheduler, see Chapter 27, "General Troubleshooting."

Technical Notes on Disk Device Support

Win32 Driver Model (WDM) defines a device-driver architecture that provides a common set of I/O services understood by both Windows 98 and future versions of Windows NT. With WDM, developers can write a single bus driver or device driver for both operating systems.

The ability to have binary-compatible device drivers comes from the layered architecture. Each layer isolates portions of the services required of a device driver and lets hardware vendors contain all hardware-specific functionality into a single file. Before WDM, device drivers had to include hooks for a particular operating system in addition to the elements necessary to interact with a specific piece of hardware. The non-layered approach prevents device drivers from being supported across multiple operating systems.

The WDM layered architecture is based on the concept of driver classes. There are six layers to WDM.

- Device Class Drivers
- Device Minidrivers
- Bus Class Drivers
- Bus Minidrivers
- OS Services (Ntkern.vxd)
- Virtual Device Drivers (legacy .vxd's)

Windows 98 uses the layered block device drivers to manage input and output to block devices, such as disks and CD-ROM drives. A *block device* is a device such as a disk drive that moves information in groups of bytes (blocks) rather than one byte at a time. Layered block device drivers are 32-bit, flat-model device drivers that run in protected mode. These drivers support conventional and small computer system interface (SCSI) disk drives, plus partitioned and non-partitioned removable media. Windows 98 also uses layered block device drivers to manage Windows 3.*x* FastDisk drivers, MS-DOS-based real-mode device drivers, and Windows NT miniport drivers.

Each layered block device driver can be loaded dynamically, so the appropriate driver can be loaded or unloaded as needed without restarting the computer. Although the drivers are virtual device drivers (VxDs), they do not use the standard virtual device services and APIs. Instead, the I/O Supervisor provides the services and functions the device drivers need to complete their tasks.

Specifically, the block I/O subsystem in Windows 98 provides the following:

- Architecture to support all Plug and Play features.
- Support for miniport drivers that are compatible with Windows NT.

- Compatibility support for Windows 3.1 FastDisk drivers and MS-DOS-based real-mode device drivers.

- Protected-mode drivers that take over real-mode MS-DOS-based device drivers when it is safe to do so.

For more information about the block I/O subsystem, see Chapter 28, "Windows 98 Architecture." For more information about WDM, see Chapter 30, "Hardware Management."

Supported Disk Devices

Windows 98 provides better disk device support than Windows 95 and ensures compatibility with existing MS-DOS-based and Windows-based disk device drivers.

Windows 98 also provides enhanced support for large media using logical block addressing, including hard disks with more than 1024 cylinders. Extensions to the INT 13 disk controller support are provided in the protected-mode disk handler drivers for this support.

The following types of hard disk drives are supported under Windows 98:

IDE	IDE LBA
IDE DMA	SCSI

The following types of bus adapters are supported under Windows 98:

EISA	PCI	SCSI 2
ISA	PCMCIA	VL bus
MCA		

The following sections describe support in Windows 98 for IDE, SCSI, high-speed floppy disk, and removable media devices. Information about SCSI and non-SCSI port drivers is also included.

IDE Drives and Controllers

Windows 98 provides improved support for integrated device electronics (IDE) drive configurations, as summarized in this section.

Alternate IDE controllers. Windows 98 provides protected-mode support for the use of one or more IDE controllers in a computer, or the combination of an IDE controller in a portable computer and an alternate controller in a docking station (available, for example, in some Compaq docking station products). IDE controllers provide support for multiple disk drives.

IDE-based CD-ROM drives. Windows 98 supports CD-ROM drives that connect to IDE-compatible disk controllers.

Large IDE disk drives. IDE drives that support a logical block addressing (LBA) scheme are available, allowing them to exceed the 0.5 GB (528 MB) size limitation. Windows 98 provides protected-mode support for IDE disk drives larger than 504 MB.

Note The BIOS must also support LBA, otherwise third-party partitioning software is required.

The cluster size for a drive is defined by the Format program, depending on the size of the local drive as shown in Table 10.2.

Bus mastering chip sets. Windows 98 provides support for bus mastering chip sets, such as Intel Triton and Opti Viper M.

Note Bus mastering should only be enabled for specific hard drive models that are certified by their manufacturer to work properly with a Windows bus master driver. The drives must indicate that they support direct memory access (DMA) in the drive ID data. Check properties in the disk drive to see if a check box for DMA appears, which indicates that the controller supports DMA. However, it is a good idea to check with the hard disk manufacturer to see if the hard drive supports DMA.

Self-monitoring analysis and reporting technology (SMART). Windows 98 provides support for SMART hard-drive fault prediction systems, which have been developed by several hard drive vendors.

Tape backup units. Windows 98 provides support for IDE, floppy, and SCSI tape backup units.

ATAPI-CD changers. Windows 98 provides support for ATAPI-CD changers with up to seven CD slots.

CD-ROM Disk Driver

The file Ppa3.mpd for the parallel Zip drive is included on the Windows 98 compact disc, in the drivers section of \Storage\Iomega\PPA3 (you can update the driver manually). The drivers Cdfs.vxd and Cdvsd.vxd are updated to include support for the following:

- ISO-9660 format compact discs greater than 4 GB in size.
- CD-ROM file system (CDFS) read-ahead now supports slower hardware and applications that access the compact disc randomly.
- CDI disks with appropriate application software.

DVD Storage

DVD-ROM drives as storage media are supported by Windows 98. To use a DVD-ROM drive, it must be compliant to the Mt. Fuji specification (also called SFF8090). The CD-ROM class driver in Windows 98 has been updated to support DVD-ROM drives as well.

All DVD-ROM drives are required to support DMA. To enable support for DMA, go to the **Device Manager** tab, select **Properties** for the drive, select the **DMA** check box, and reboot to run on DMA.

Windows 98 has a new read-only Universal Disk Format (UDF) system, which supports reading media formatted according to UDF specification 1.02. Most DVD movie discs today are authored with UDF bridge format, which contains both the ISO-9660 and the UDF file system structures. You can tell if a disc is mounted by UDF or CDFS by checking the properties of a drive in Explorer. In My Computer, right-click on a drive, and then click **Properties**. The File System line in the properties page tells you whether the disc is mounted by UDF or CDFS.

Unlike CDFS, UDF is a generic file system, but it is primarily used by DVD discs. UDF uses the main file system cache (vcache) and there are no performance settings for end users to change.

Some legacy third-party DVD movie player software may require MSCDEX functions, which are supported by CDFS only and not UDF. Use the following procedure to disable UDF for troubleshooting.

▶ **To disable UDF for troubleshooting**

1. Click **Start**, click **Run**, type **MSConfig**, and then click **OK**.

2. Click **Advanced**, and then select the **Disable UDF file system** check box.

   When you are finished troubleshooting, clear the **Disable UDF file system** checkbox to enable UDF file system.

For more information about the System Configuration Utility (MSConfig), see Chapter 27, "General Troubleshooting."

Although most DVD discs contain both ISO 9660 and UDF file system structures, UDF takes precedence in mounting such discs. If UDF is disabled using the above registry key, CDFS will try to mount. However, Microsoft DVD playback software requires UDF be mounted on DVD discs.

SCSI Devices and Drivers

Windows 98 provides support for SCSI disk devices. SCSI support in Windows 98 includes disk SCSI translator drivers, the SCSI Port Manager, and SCSI miniport drivers.

- A disk SCSI translator driver (also called a SCSI'izer) is responsible for constructing SCSI command descriptor blocks for a specific device class and carrying out device-level error recovery and logging. There are two of these drivers (one for each class): one for SCSI hard disk devices and one for CD-ROM devices.

- SCSI Port Manager manages the interaction between the SCSI'izer and a SCSI miniport driver, initializes the miniport driver, converts the I/O request format, and provides other services for the miniport driver.

- The SCSI miniport driver is responsible for detecting and initializing a specific set of SCSI adapters. The driver also handles interrupts, transmits I/O requests to the device, and carries out adapter-level error recovery and logging. Windows 98 supports the use of Windows NT miniport SCSI drivers without modification or recompiling. Compatibility with Windows NT–based miniport drivers ensures broad device support for disk devices under Windows 98, while simplifying the driver development efforts for hardware manufacturers.

Windows 98 provides broad support for popular SCSI controllers. Windows 98 includes 32-bit disk device drivers for popular SCSI controllers from Adaptec, Future Domain, and other manufacturers. Windows 98 also provides compatibility support for the Advanced SCSI Programming Interface (ASPI) and Common Access Method (CAM), which allows application and driver developers to submit I/O requests to SCSI devices. This allows existing MS-DOS-based applications and drivers that use the ASPI or CAM specification to work properly under Windows 98. Windows 98 also includes 16-bit and 32-bit drivers to support Windows-based ASPI clients and applications.

Although Windows 98 can use Windows NT miniport drivers, the best choice for a SCSI driver is one that complies with Plug and Play. Most Windows NT miniport drivers ignore configuration information from the SCSI Manager and check I/O ports to identify hardware. Miniport drivers in Windows 98 must honor configuration information without scanning for other adapters if the configuration information is not the default configuration. This is because many adapters supported under Windows 98 have port ranges that conflict with other adapters and are affected adversely by scanning. For example, Artisoft LANtastic network adapters occupy a range of port addresses used by Adaptec 154X adapters, and accessing these ports will cause the system to lock up.

Windows 98 provides several .MPD files with Plug and Play capabilities, including the ability to transition from protected mode to real mode (to support MS-DOS-based applications that must run in MS-DOS Mode) and to accept configuration information from the SCSI Manager for dynamically loading and unloading drivers.

High-Speed Floppy Disk Driver

Windows 98 includes the Hsflop.pdr floppy disk driver. The driver provides significantly enhanced performance on many machines.

Windows 98 provides protected-mode support for communicating with floppy disk controllers. Windows 98 provides INT 13 hard disk controller support as 32-bit device drivers, which results in improved performance, stability, and system robustness.

Windows 98 provides floppy disk controller support as a 32-bit device driver, and offers improved performance for file I/O to floppy disk drives, plus improved reliability of the system. You can format a disk or copy files to and from a disk while performing other tasks.

Tip Windows 98 scans for floppy drives on each boot, which is helpful for laptops and other computers from which the floppy can be removed. If you are on a desktop with a floppy drive that is stationary, you can turn this option off to speed up boot time.

1. From Control Panel, click **System**, and then click the **Performance** tab.
2. Click **File System**, and then click the **Floppy Disk** tab.
3. Uncheck the box next to **Search for new floppy disk drives each time your computer starts**.
4. Click **OK**.

Removable Media and Docking Devices

Windows 98 provides protected-mode support for removable media devices with MS-DOS-compatible partitions, including floppy disk drives and controllers, Bernoulli drives, and CD-ROM, plus docking stations for portable computers. Windows 98 allows the system to lock or unlock the device to prevent the media from being removed prematurely.

Windows 98 also supports an eject mechanism for devices that support it, so that users can use software control to eject media from a device (for example, new floppy disk drives that support software-based media ejection).

Docking refers to the insertion or removal of a device in the system. Devices that can be docked include almost anything, depending on the hardware—monitors, network access, removable hard disk drives, or any removable resource. A *docking station* is a base unit into which you can insert the portable hardware and that includes drive bays, expansion slots, and additional ports. Port replicators can also be used as docking station substitutes that provide extra functionality not available in the portable docking device.

If a docking change occurs in the computer configuration during operation, such as the insertion of a portable computer into the docking station, the system is notified so that the new device can be configured and applications can be notified of the change.

Windows 98 supports "hot" docking, where the device can be docked or undocked while running at full power, and "cold" docking, where the device must be powered off or restarted before the device can be docked or undocked. Legacy portable computers use cold docking.

In addition, some devices require certain preliminary steps before they can be docked or undocked. For example, if you have a file open and decide to remove the hard disk, the file must be closed. To handle these situations, Windows 98 supports different undocking systems, depending on the type of hardware:

- Auto-ejection, which is a software interface that operates a VCR-type ejection mechanism, allowing Windows 98 to request user action to resolve any open resources. The user can save files, and so on, before the system ejects the dockable resource.

- Manual ejection, where the user undocks the resource without using any software interface. Because the system cannot be notified when this occurs, any closing of files or other actions must be performed manually to prevent loss of data.

Hardware Profiles are used to set up multiple hardware configurations. This is especially useful for laptops that have docking stations or workstations with removable storage media.

Hardware Profiles are automatically created for portable computers when the system is docked or undocked. Furthermore, a new Hardware Profile would be created if the portable computer is placed in a different docking station.

LS-120 Support

The real mode MS-DOS kernel, protected mode, file system components, and the various formatting utilities are updated to support the LS-120 (120 MB) floppy drives built into some computers.

Non-SCSI Port Drivers

A non-SCSI port driver usually works with a specific adapter, so the driver is retained in memory only if the related adapter is present in the system. Windows 98 includes, for example, port drivers for IDE, ESDI, or floppy disk drives.

A port driver provides the same functionality as the SCSI Manager and miniport driver, but these drivers are monolithic and are not portable to Windows NT. A port driver manages and controls the adapter for a given block device. The port driver detects and initializes the adapter, handles interrupts, transmits I/O requests to the device, and carries out adapter-level error recovery and logging.

Important Do not use a **device=** entry in System.ini to load a port driver. Windows 98 loads appropriate drivers from the System\Iosubsys subdirectory in the \Windows directory.

Master Boot Record

When the computer is powered on, a mechanism is required to manipulate interrupts, find the hard disk(s), and launch code necessary to load drivers located on the boot drive. This mechanism is contained in the Master Boot Record (MBR). The MBR of a hard disk resides at the first physical sector of the disk: track 0, side 0, sector 1.

The MBR is divided into five sections: Jump Code, Error Messages, Free Space, the Partition Tables, and Ending Signature. Table 10.5 outlines some of the more important components of the MBR.

Table 10.5   Important components of the MBR

Area	Functions or purpose
Jump Code: 139 bytes	Load MBR into memory Enable interrupts Scan disk characteristics Find C: drive Load boot sector from C: drive
Error Messages: 80 bytes	Invalid Partition Table Error loading operation system Missing operating system
Free Space: 227 bytes	
Partition Tables: 64 bytes	Active partition Starting head, sector, and cylinder Partition Type Ending head, sector, and cylinder Total number of sectors on this partition
Ending Signature: 2 bytes	Define the MBR boundary

If one of the values becomes corrupted, the system probably will not boot. Likewise, if a new value is introduced by an operating system and an existing software utility does not understand the new value, there is a possibility of data corruption.

The area of the MBR that has changed for FAT32 is the Partition Table. The Partition Table is divided into four 16-byte entries. Inside the Partition Table is the Partition Type. This entry is important for identifying the partition structure for the operating system. In order for FAT32 to accomplish its new capabilities, the MBR contains the following two new Partition Types:

DOS32. Defines primary 32-bit FAT partitions of up to 2,047 GB. It is used when the primary partition does not require logical block addressing (LBA) to access that partition. LBA is a method of accessing hard disk drives based on the extensions of INT 13.

DOS32X. Defines 32-bit FAT partitions of up to 2,047 GB. It is used when any portion of either the primary or extended partition is beyond 1,024 cylinders, 63 sectors per track, and 16 heads, and requires LBA to access. These new 32-bit FAT partition types cannot be accessed through MS-DOS 6.*x* or earlier.

The Legacy Boot Sector

The Boot Sector is the first sector on every logical drive. The Boot Sector contains a table of that drive's characteristics and the code that boots the operating system. When the system starts, this code is loaded into memory where it loads the operating system files from the disk. The remainder of the Boot Sector is boot code and error messages.

The following is the first 64 bytes of a typical Boot Sector on a logical drive. Table 10.6 details some of the more important entries. All values are in hex, not decimal.

```
EB 3E 90 4D 53 57 49 4E-34 2F 31 00 02 04 01 00    .>.MSWIN4.1.....
02 00 02 00 00 F8 CA 00-23 00 0C 00 23 00 00 00    ........#...#...
B1 28 03 00 80 00 29 88-98 24 1D 20 20 20 20 20    .(....)..$.
20 20 20 20 20 20 46 41-54 31 36 20 20 20 F1 7D         FAT16    .}
```

Table 10.6   Important characteristics of the Boot Sector

Length	Contents
3 bytes	Jump to boot code.
8 bytes	Windows name and version.
2 bytes	Bytes per sector.[1]
1 byte	Sectors per cluster (always a power of 2).[1]
2 bytes	Number of reserved sectors before the first FAT.[1]
1 byte	Number of FATs.[1]
2 bytes	Number of root directory entries (max limit).[1]
2 bytes	Total number of sectors (00 00 if the drive is greater than 32 MB).[1]

Table 10.6   Important characteristics of the Boot Sector *(continued)*

Length	Contents
1 byte	Media descriptor; here it is F8, which identifies this disk as a hard drive of any capacity.[1]
2 bytes	Number of sectors per FAT.[1]
2 bytes	Number of sectors per track.[1]
2 bytes	Number of heads.[1]
4 bytes	Number of hidden sectors.[1]
4 bytes	Number of sectors if drive is greater than 32 MB.[1]
1 byte	Drive number; here it is 80, which means primary partition.
1 byte	RESERVED.
1 byte	Extended boot signature (always 29h).
4 bytes	Volume ID number.
11 bytes	Volume label.
8 bytes	Type of file system (12-bit FAT or 16-bit FAT).

[1] This portion of the Boot Sector is known as the BIOS Parameter Block (BPB). It offers physical disk characteristics that MS-DOS/Windows use for finding specific disk locations. For example, by adding or multiplying values together, it gives details as to where the FAT, root directory, and data area begin and end.

For more information about the Boot Sector, see the Microsoft *Programmer's Reference*. It contains detailed information about each of the values previously mentioned.

Changes to the Boot Sector

The number of reserved sectors before the first FAT is 1. This is the Boot Sector itself. FAT32 drives usually contain 32, but can vary based on how the drive is set up.

New Boot Sector BIOS Parameter Block

A FAT32 BIOS Parameter Block (BPB) is larger than a standard BPB and is referred to as Big FAT BIOS Parameter Block (BF_BPB). With this additional information, the Boot Sector is now two sectors since it is not possible to fit the boot code into 512 bytes. This additional sector is located in one of the 32 reserved sectors.

The BF_BPB is an extended version of the 12-bit and 16-bit FAT BPB. It contains an identical structure to a standard BPB, but also includes several extra fields for FAT32-specific information. Changes in the BPB for FAT32 include the following:

Root Directory Field.   This entry contains the number of root directories. For hard drives this has always been 512 (00 02h). This field is changed to 00 00 and is ignored on FAT32 drives.

Sectors Per FAT.   The number of sectors per FAT entry in the original BPB is changed to zero. This acts as a pointer to the entry in the BF_BPB as the boot process moves to the BF_BPB.

Drive Description.   New to FAT32 is a 2 byte field called Drive Description that determines the number of FATs on a drive. These 2 bytes set the flags to determine whether there is one or two FATs on the drive. If set, there is only one FAT. If the flag is clear, there are two FATs. FAT32 created by the FORMAT command will always create two FATs.

First Root Directory Cluster.   The root directory size is now limited to 65,535 entries, can grow just like a sub-directory, and its location is flexible. This value points to the cluster number of the first cluster of the root directory of the FAT32 drive.

File Information Sector.   This entry points to the second sector of the Boot Sector that contains the total free and most recently allocated cluster on the drive. This allows a FAT32 volume to obtain the quantity of free clusters on a volume as well as the most recently allocated cluster without having to read the entire FAT.

Backup Copy of Boot Sector.   Another important change to Boot Sector processing is a backup copy of the Boot Sector. With previous versions of the FAT file system, users worked in a "single point of failure" scenario. That is, if the Boot Sector became corrupted or unreadable, the volume would stop working. FAT32 has made adjustments to offset this potential problem.

When Fdisk writes to the boot volume that has a change, and that volume is using a FAT32 partition ID, Fdisk will write a backup Boot Sector to sector 6 of that volume. If the new MBR receives a read error, or has a signature validation problem with reading the Boot Sector, it will search sector 6 and try reading the rest of the bootstrap loader.

32-bit File Allocation Table

The purpose of the FAT has not changed. It still acts as a table for linking the clusters of a file together. File/Directory entries point to the first cluster in the file which the operating system uses to find the first entry in the FAT. The FAT then tracks the location of the remaining clusters in the file. The entries are twice the size (4 bytes) and you can hold many more clusters on a FAT32 drive.

With the 16-bit FAT, the quantity of clusters on a drive is 65,525 (2^{16} with 10 reserved). With a 32-bit FAT, the highest 4 bits of the 32-bit values are reserved and are not part of the cluster number. Therefore, the maximum amount of clusters on a 32-bit FAT is: 268,435,445 (2^{28} with 10 reserved).

Stepping Through a FAT32 Entry

The starting cluster given in the file/directory entry tells the operating system where to find the first piece of that file. The starting cluster also tells the operating system where to look in FAT32 for the next cluster number. The entry for a starting cluster in a file entry is in bold below.

```
49 4F 20 20 20 20 20 20-44 4F 53 07 00 00 00 00    IO    SYS.....
00 00 00 00 00 00 80 32-3E 1B 02 00 46 9F 00 00    .......2....F...
```

Two additional entries are used in the 32-bit directory entry. These two entries are taken from a reserved area and in this example are shown above as 00 00. Together with the existing 2 byte entry (02 00), there is a four-byte entry (00 00 00 02) to search the FAT. The following is a sample tracing of the file in a 32-bit FAT:

```
F8 FF FF 0F FF FF FF 0F-03 00 00 00 04 00 00 00
05 00 00 00 06 00 00 00-07 00 00 00 08 00 00 00
09 00 00 00 0A 00 00 00-0B 00 00 00 0C 00 00 00
0D 00 00 00 0E 00 00 00-0F 00 00 00 10 00 00 00
11 00 00 00 12 00 00 00-13 00 00 00 14 00 00 00
15 00 00 00 16 00 00 00-17 00 00 00 18 00 00 00
19 00 00 00 1A 00 00 00-1B 00 00 00 FF FF FF F8
```

As with FAT16, F8 is the media descriptor byte. The next 7 bytes, FF FF 0F FF FF FF 0F, are reserved. The clusters are grouped in 4 byte numbers as:

```
03 00 00 00, 04 00 00 00, 05 00 00 00, 06 00 00 00
```

And so on. Invert the numbers to read:

```
00 00 00 03, 00 00 00 04, 00 00 00 05, 00 00 00 06
```

And so on, to trace the file through the FAT. (The contents in the second entry is 00 00 00 03. F8 FF FF FF, and FF FF FF 0F are grouped as entries 0 and 1 respectively.) The new end of file marker is FF FF FF F8.

How Win.com Determines Improper Shutdown

Of the first 112 bytes of the FAT32, the first 8 bytes are reserved. The eighth byte of the reserved area, by default, is 0F. The virtual file allocation table (VFAT) and the Windows 98 shutdown process manipulate the fourth bit of this byte to 1 or 0.

- 0 = VFAT has written to disk
- 1 = Windows has properly shutdown

When you write a file to the disk, VFAT handles the write. During the write, VFAT clears the fourth bit to 0 (07h). When Windows 98 exits properly, this bit is reset to 1. During reboot, Win.com reads that bit. If it is set to 0, it runs ScanDisk to check the drive for errors.

Hard Sector Error.   Windows 98 detects a hard sector error during startup. This process toggles the third bit to zero (0Bh). When detected during startup, Windows 98 automatically launches ScanDisk with a surface scan test.

Disabling ScanDisk at Boot.   There is a way to disable the improper shutdown check. It is in the Msdos.sys file under [OPTIONS]. The parameters for AutoScan are as follows:

Value	Definition
AUTOSCAN = 0	Ignore the bits in the reserved FAT entry
AUTOSCAN = 1	Default behavior, run ScanDisk

Mirroring

On all FAT drives, historically, there are two copies of the FAT. If an error occurs reading the primary copy, the file system will attempt to read from the backup copy. On 12-bit and 16-bit FAT drives, the first FAT is always the primary copy and a modification is automatically written to the second copy. When a second FAT is written to as a backup, the process is called mirroring.

On new FAT32 drives, mirroring a secondary FAT can be disabled. This means that a read/write is quicker using one FAT, or if the first FAT is sitting on corrupted sectors, the second FAT can be used as a primary with the first FAT ignored.

Note   On FAT32 drives, a FAT can be very large. Disabling duplicate FAT writes can make FAT access quicker. Windows 98 does not provide a mechanism for eliminating the use of a second FAT. Mirroring is always enabled. Third-party utilities, however, might include this ability as users with larger hard disks might want to disable a second FAT to speed disk access. Any issues about mirroring should be directed to that third-party utility.

Root Directory

With FAT32, the limitation is now 65,535 root directory entries.

There is a new entry in the Boot Sector that points to the first cluster of the root directory. The root directory is no longer forced to reside at a specific location after the second FAT and it can grow just like a subdirectory.

There is a trade off in performance when you have a large number of directory entries to pass across when searching for actual data. For this reason, it is recommended that you limit the number of root directory entries to a small, manageable number. There is no actual recommended size for the same reasons as there is no optimal cluster size to choose from.

Extensions Changed, Superseded, or No Longer Supported

The following list presents some areas where FAT32 may be incompatible with legacy software:

- Share services are a part of the installable file system (IFS) manager. VFAT uses them to provide full file sharing functionality. All MS-DOS-based, Win16-based, and Win32-based applications have full file sharing services available to them. As a consequence, the MS-DOS utility Share.exe is no longer necessary and is not provided in Windows 98.

- VFAT implements an enhanced version of FASTOPEN. As such, the MS-DOS FASTOPEN utility is no longer necessary, but can install without error.

- Windows 3.x File Manager is not supported since it may misreport free or total disk space.

- File Control Block (FCB) has limited support but this should not be a problem.

- Dealing with files larger than 2 GB (opening, creating, writing) may cause problems on non-FAT32-aware programs.

- Absolute disk reads and write utilities should be upgraded to recognize FAT32.

- Users should not dual-boot Windows 98 with FAT32 and Windows NT 4.0.

- Interlink does not work on FAT32.

VCACHE and CDFS Supplemental Cache

The 32-bit VFAT works in conjunction with a 32-bit, protected-mode cache driver (VCACHE), and replaces and improves on the 16-bit, real-mode SMARTDrive disk cache software provided with MS-DOS and Windows 3.1.

The VCACHE driver uses an improved caching algorithm over SMARTDrive to cache information read from or written to a disk drive, and results in improved performance for reading information from the cache. Also, the VCACHE driver is responsible for managing the cache pool for the Universal Disk Format (UDF) system, and the 32-bit network redirectors.

Another big improvement in VCACHE over SMARTDrive is that the memory pool used for the cache is dynamic and is based on the amount of available free system memory. Users no longer need to allocate a block of memory to set aside as a disk cache; the system automatically allocates or deallocates memory used for the cache based on system use. The performance of the system also scales better than earlier versions of Windows, due to the intelligent cache use.

The 32-bit, protected-mode CDFS implemented in Windows 98 provides improved CD-ROM access performance over the real-mode MSCDEX driver in Windows 3.1 and is a full 32-bit ISO 9660 CD file system. The CDFS driver replaces the 16-bit, real-mode MSCDEX driver, and it features 32-bit, protected-mode caching of CD-ROM data. If MSCDEX is specified in the user's Autoexec.bat when Windows 98 is installed, the 32-bit CDFS driver is used instead.

CDFS has a larger and smarter cache than MSCDEX, optimized just for CD-ROMs and separate from VCACHE. The CDFS driver cache is dynamic and requires no configuration or static allocation on the part of the user.

CDFS reads ahead in parallel with the application so that multimedia presentations play back more smoothly than with earlier versions of Windows. Because CDFS uses a separate cache, the cache memory can be swapped out to the hard disk when CD-ROM activity pauses. This gives applications more room to run and protects the main hard disk cache from being flushed out whenever a very large multimedia stream is played back.

The supplemental cache size for CDFS is used to hold path, table, directory, and file information. This particular cache is used to improve CD streaming and to reduce seek latency as effectively as possible with a moderately sized cache. This means that the cache is more complex, using smart priority-based caching schemes to achieve results optimized for CD-ROMs.

For more information about configuring the CD-ROM cache to match the characteristics of CD-ROM drive types, see Chapter 26, "Performance Tuning."

Command-Line Switches for Disk Utilities

This section describes the commands that can be used from the command line to run ScanDisk, DriveSpace, and Disk Defragmenter disk utilities. These commands are provided to allow these disk utilities to be run from batch files.

Note To provide compatibility with existing batch files, Windows 98 provides a **start** command to allow synchronous use of Windows-based programs from the command-line. To run a Windows-based program from the command-line and wait for it, use this syntax:

start /W "*program_name arguments*"

Defrag

This command controls Windows 98 Disk Defragmenter.

Syntax

defrag [*drive:* | **/all**] [**/F** | **/U** | **/Q**] [**/noprompt**] [**/concise** | **/detailed**]

Parameters

drive:
    Drive letter of the disk to be optimized.

/all
    Defragment all local, nonremovable drives.

/F
    Defragment files and free space.

/U
    Defragment files only.

/Q
    Defragment free space only.

/concise
    Display the Hide Details view (default).

/detailed
    Display the Show Details view.

/noprompt
    Unattended mode; do not stop and display confirmation messages.

DrvSpace

This command controls Windows DriveSpace at the command line, and can be used with either DblSpace or DrvSpace drives. These command switches are maintained for use in batch files and for compatibility with the compression utilities provided in MS-DOS version 6 and higher. Each switch performs the indicated operation, without asking for any additional input before beginning.

Additionally, the **/interactive** switch can be added to any command line to have DriveSpace ask for any missing parameters, and the **/noprompt** switch can be added to any syntax except the **/info** and **/settings** command-lines. The **/noprompt** switch prevents any confirmation dialog boxes from appearing (except for error messages). Notice that there is no way to prevent error messages from being displayed.

When you run DriveSpace without command-line arguments, the DriveSpace Manager appears, with menu commands for selecting the operations to perform.

Syntax

drvspace **/compress** *d:* [/**size**=*n*| /**reserve**=*n*] [/**new**=*e:*]
drvspace **/create** *d:* [/**size**=*n* | /**reserve**=*n*] [/**new**=*e:*] [/**cvf**=*nnn*]
drvspace **/delete** *d:*\d*??*space.*nnn*
drvspace **/format** *d:*\d*??*space.*nnn*
drvspace **/host**=*e: d:*
drvspace [/**info**] *d:*
drvspace **/mount** {[=*nnn*] *d:* | *d:*\d*??*space.*nnn*} [/**new**=*e:*]
drvspace **/move** *d:* /**new**=*e:*
drvspace **/ratio**[=*n*] *d:*
drvspace **/settings**
drvspace **/size**[=*n*| /**reserve**=*n*] *d:*
drvspace **/uncompress** *d:*
drvspace **/unmount** *d:*

Parameters

d*??*space.*nnn*
   The file name of the hidden compressed volume file on the host drive, which can be either Drvspace.*nnn* or Dblspace.*nnn*, where *nnn* represents the actual file name extension.

The following sections provide details about these parameters.

If you add switches or parameters to the **drvspace** command, the operating system carries out the requested task without starting the DriveSpace program. The command syntax differs from task to task, as summarized in the following list.

Action	Command
Compress a hard disk drive or floppy disk.	**drvspace /compress**
Create a new compressed drive in the free space on an existing drive.	**drvspace /create**
Delete a compressed drive.	**drvspace /delete**
Format a compressed drive.	**drvspace /format**
Display information about a compressed drive.	**drvspace /info**
Mount a compressed volume file (CVF). When DriveSpace mounts a CVF, it assigns it a drive letter; you can then use the files that CVF contains.	**drvspace /mount**

Action	Command
Change estimated compression ratio of a compressed drive.	**drvspace /ratio**
Change the size of a compressed drive.	**drvspace /size**
Uncompress a compressed drive.	**drvspace /uncompress**
Unmount a compressed drive.	**drvspace /unmount**

Dblspace.bin, Drvspace.bin, and Drvspace.sys

Dblspace.bin or Drvspace.bin is the part of the system that provides access to the compressed drives. When you start the computer, the operating system loads D??space.bin along with other operating system functions, before carrying out the commands in Config.sys and Autoexec.bat. D??space.bin initially loads in conventional memory, since it loads before device drivers that provide access to upper memory. Normally, if the hard disk drive has been compressed using DriveSpace, D??space.bin is loaded even if you press F8 and choose an alternate startup option.

Drvspacx.vxd is the protected-mode driver for DriveSpace. This driver takes over from the real-mode D??space.bin driver when Windows 98 switches to protected mode. The real-mode driver is required for starting the computer, but after the system switches to protected mode, DRVSPACX ensures that you have 32-bit, protected-mode performance, and the memory used by the real-mode driver is reclaimed.

The Dblspace.sys device driver does not provide access to compressed drives; instead it determines the final location of D??space.bin in memory. When loaded with a **device** command, the Dblspace.sys device driver moves D??space.bin from the top to the bottom of conventional memory. When loaded with a **devicehigh** command, Dblspace.sys moves D??space.bin from conventional to upper memory, if available. Whenever possible, Dblspace.sys moves a portion of D??space.bin into the HMA.

How DriveSpace Assigns Drive Letters

When you compress a drive using DriveSpace, it creates a new drive and assigns a drive letter to that drive. DriveSpace skips the first four available drive letters and assigns the next available drive letter to the new drive. For example, if the computer has only drives A, B, and C, DriveSpace skips letters D, E, F, and G, and assigns drive letter H to the new drive.

When assigning letters to additional drives (for example, if you compress another drive), DriveSpace works backwards from the first drive letter it assigned. In the example above, DriveSpace would next assign the letter G.

DriveSpace attempts to avoid drive-letter conflicts with drives created by **fdisk**, RAMDrive, networks, or other installable device drivers that assign drive letters. However, if a drive-letter conflict does occur, DriveSpace resolves the conflict by reassigning its drive letters.

Drvspace /Compress

Compresses the files and free space on an existing hard disk drive, floppy disk, or other removable media. Compressing an existing drive makes more space available on that drive.

Note DriveSpace cannot compress a drive that is completely full. To compress the startup hard disk drive, the drive must contain at least 2 MB of free space. Other hard disk drives and floppy disks must contain at least 768 KB of free space. (DriveSpace cannot compress 360 KB floppy disks.)

Syntax

drvspace /compress *drive1*: [**/new**=*drive2*:] [**/reserve**=*size*]

Parameters

drive1:
Specifies the existing drive you want to compress.

Switches

/compress
Compresses the hard disk drive or floppy disk specified by the drive parameter. This switch can be abbreviated to **/com**.

/new=*drive2*:
Specifies the drive letter for the uncompressed (host) drive. After DriveSpace compresses an existing drive, the system will include both the existing drive (now compressed) and a new uncompressed drive. If you omit the **/new** switch, DriveSpace assigns the next available drive letter to the new drive.

/reserve=*size*
Specifies how many megabytes of space to leave uncompressed. Because some files do not work properly when stored on a compressed drive, you may want to reserve some uncompressed space. The uncompressed space will be located on the new uncompressed drive. This switch can be abbreviated to **/reser**.

Drvspace /Compress Examples

To compress drive D, type the following command:

```
drvspace /compress d:
```

On drives larger than 256 MB, more space will be left on the host (because D??space drives cannot be larger than 512 MB). Because this command does not specify how much space to leave uncompressed, DriveSpace leaves 2 MB of uncompressed space (the default). Because the command does not specify a drive letter for the uncompressed drive, DriveSpace assigns the next available drive letter to the new uncompressed drive (the host drive).

To direct DriveSpace to compress drive E, assign the drive letter F to the new uncompressed drive (the host drive), and leave 4 MB of uncompressed space on drive F, type the following command:

```
drvspace /compress e: /new=f: /reserve=4
```

Drvspace /Create

Creates a new compressed drive by using free space on an uncompressed drive. The new compressed drive will provide more storage capacity than the amount of space it uses.

Syntax

drvspace /create *drive1*: [/**new**=*drive2*:] [/**size**=*size* | /**reserve**=*size*] [/**cvf**=*nnn*]

Parameters

drive1:

Specifies the uncompressed drive that contains the space you want to use to create the new drive.

Switches

/create

Creates a new compressed drive by using free space on the uncompressed drive specified by *drive1*. This switch can be abbreviated to **/cr**.

/new=*drive2*:

Specifies the drive letter for the new compressed drive. The **/new** switch is optional; if you omit it, DriveSpace assigns the next available drive letter to the new drive.

/reserve=*size*

Specifies how many megabytes of free space DriveSpace should leave on the uncompressed drive. To make the compressed drive as large as possible, specify a size of 0.

You can include either the **/reserve** switch or the **/size** switch, but not both. If you omit both switches, DriveSpace uses all but 2 MB of free space. The **/reserve** switch can be abbreviated as **/reser**.

/size=*size*

Specifies the total size, in megabytes, of the compressed volume file. (This is the amount of space on the uncompressed drive that you want to allocate to the compressed drive.) You can include either the **/reserve** switch or the **/size** switch, but not both.

/cvf=*nnn*

Reports extension of the CVF file.

Drvspace /Create Examples

To create a new compressed drive that uses all available space on uncompressed drive E, type the following command:

```
drvspace /create e: /reserve=0
```

To create a new compressed drive by using 10 MB of space on uncompressed drive E, type the following command:

```
drvspace /create e: /size=10
```

To create a new compressed drive by using space on uncompressed drive D, and to direct DriveSpace to leave 2.75 MB of free space on drive D, type the following command:

```
drvspace /create d: /reserve=2.75
```

The following command creates a new compressed drive by using all but 2 MB of the space on drive D:

```
drvspace /create d:
```

Because the command includes neither the **/reserve** switch nor the **/size** switch, DriveSpace uses the default value for the **/reserve** switch and leaves 2 MB of space on drive D.

Drvspace /Delete

Deletes the selected compressed drive and erases the associated compressed volume file.

Caution   Deleting a compressed drive erases the entire drive and all the files it contains.

Syntax   **drvspace /delete** *d*:**\d??space.*###***

Parameters   *d*:**\d??space.*###***
                    Specifies the drive you want to delete. (DriveSpace will not allow you to delete any drive containing open files, including the drive containing Windows 98.)

Switch   **/delete**
                    Deletes the specified drive. This switch can be abbreviated as **/del**.

**Drvspace /Delete The following command directs DriveSpace to delete the compressed volume
Example**   for drive C:

```
drvspace /delete h:\dblspace.###
```

DriveSpace then deletes the compressed volume file for drive C. This completely erases the compressed drive and all the files it contains.

Drvspace /Format

Formats the selected compressed drive.

Caution Formatting a compressed drive deletes all the files it contains. You cannot unformat a drive that has been formatted by using **drvspace /format**.

Syntax

drvspace /format *d*:**\d??space.###**

Parameters

d:**\d??space.###**

Specifies the drive you want to format. (DriveSpace will not allow you to format any drive containing open files, including the drive containing Windows 98.)

Switch

/format

Directs DriveSpace to format the specified compressed drive. This switch can be abbreviated as **/f**.

Drvspace /Format Example

The following command directs DriveSpace to format compressed drive E:

```
drvspace /format h:\dblspace.###
```

DriveSpace then formats compressed drive E, which completely erases all the files on it.

Drvspace /Info

Displays information about the selected drive's free and used space, the name of its compressed volume file, and its actual and estimated compression ratios. You can use this command while Windows is running.

Syntax

drvspace [**/info**] | [*drive*:]

Parameters

drive:

Specifies the compressed drive about which you want information. If you do not specify a drive letter, DriveSpace displays information about the current drive.

Switch

/info

Directs DriveSpace to display information about the selected drive. This switch is optional and can be omitted as long as you specify a drive letter.

Drvspace /Info Examples

The following command displays information about the current drive:

```
drvspace /info
```

The following command displays information about drive C:

```
drvspace /info c:
```

The following command displays information about drive E:

```
drvspace e:
```

Drvspace /Mount

Establishes a connection between a compressed volume file (CVF) and a drive letter so that you can use the files the CVF contains. DriveSpace usually mounts CVFs automatically. You need to mount a CVF only if you previously unmounted it.

Syntax

drvspace /mount[*=nnn*] *drive1*: [**/new**=*drive2*:]
drvspace /mount *d*:\d??space.### [**/new**=*drive2*:]

Parameters

drive1:
  Specifies the drive that contains the compressed volume file you want to mount. You must specify a drive letter.

Switches

/mount=*nnn*
  Directs DriveSpace to mount the compressed volume file with the file name extension specified by the *nnn* parameter. For example, to mount a CVF named DBLSPACE.001, you would specify **/mount**=001. If you omit the *nnn* parameter, DriveSpace attempts to mount the compressed volume file named DBLSPACE.000.

/new=*drive2*:
  Specifies the drive letter to assign to the new drive. This switch is optional; if you do not specify a drive letter, DriveSpace assigns the new drive the next available drive letter.

Drvspace /Mount Examples

To mount a compressed floppy disk in drive A, type the following:

```
drvspace /mount a:
```

To mount the compressed volume file DBLSPACE.001 located on uncompressed drive D, type the following:

```
drvspace /mount=001 d:
```

Drvspace /Ratio

Changes the estimated compression ratio of the selected drive. DriveSpace uses this ratio to estimate how much free space the drive contains. You might want to change the estimated compression ratio if you plan to store new files with a compression ratio that differs greatly from the current ratio.

Syntax

drvspace /ratio[*=r.r*] [*drive*:]

Parameters	*drive*:

Specifies the drive for which you want to change the estimated compression ratio. If you do not specify a drive, DriveSpace changes the estimated compression ratio for the current drive.

Switch   **/ratio**=*r.r*

Changes the estimated compression ratio of the specified drive. To change the ratio to a specific number, specify the ratio you want. You can specify a ratio from 1.0 to 16.0. However, not all drives can accept values in this entire range. If you do not specify a ratio, DriveSpace sets the drive's estimated compression ratio to the average actual compression ratio for all the files currently on the drive. This switch can be abbreviated as **/ra**.

Drvspace /Ratio Examples   To change the estimated compression ratio of the current drive to match that drive's actual compression ratio, type the following command:

```
drvspace /ratio
```

To change the estimated compression ratio for drive D so that it is 3.2 to 1, type the following:

```
drvspace /ratio=3.2 d:
```

To change the estimated compression ratio of the current drive to 6 to 1, type the following:

```
drvspace /ratio=6
```

Drvspace /Size

Enlarges or reduces the size of a compressed drive. You might want to enlarge a compressed drive if its host drive contains plenty of free space. You might want to reduce its size if you need more free space on the host drive.

Syntax   **drvspace /size**[=*size1* | **/reserve**=*size2*] *drive*:

Parameters   *drive*:

Specifies the drive you want to resize.

Switches   **/size**=*size1*

Changes the size of the specified drive. You can specify the new size of the drive by using the *size1* parameter. The size of the drive is the number of megabytes of space that the drive's compressed volume file uses on the uncompressed (host) drive.

You can specify the drive's new size by using either the *size1* parameter or the **/reserve** switch, but not both. If you include neither the *size1* parameter nor the **/reserve** switch, DriveSpace makes the drive as small as possible.

/**reserve**=*size2*

Specifies how many megabytes of free space you want the uncompressed (host) drive to contain after DriveSpace resizes the drive. The **/reserve** switch can be abbreviated as **/reser**.

You can specify the drive's new size by using either the **/reserve** switch or the *size1* parameter of the **/size** switch, but not both. If you include neither the **/reserve** switch nor the *size1* parameter, DriveSpace makes the drive as small as possible.

Drvspace /Size Examples

To change the size of drive C so that its compressed volume file uses 60.5 MB of space on drive D, type the following command:

```
drvspace /size=60.5 c:
```

To change the size of drive E so that its host drive, drive D, contains 20 MB of free uncompressed space, type the following command:

```
drvspace /size /reserve=20 e:
```

To change the size of drive C so that it is as large as possible, type the following command:

```
drvspace /size /reserve=0 c:
```

Drvspace /Uncompress

Uncompresses a drive that was compressed by using DriveSpace.

Syntax

drvspace /uncompress *drive*:

Parameter

drive:

Specifies the drive you want to uncompress.

Switch

/uncompress

Uncompresses the specified drive.

Notes on Drvspace /Uncompress

Backing up before uncompressing.   Before uncompressing the drive, you should back up the files it contains. If you include the **/interactive** switch, DriveSpace will prompt for this.

Invalid pathnames after uncompressing.   When you uncompress a drive, DriveSpace either changes that drive's letter or the letter of its host drive (depending on how the compressed drive was originally created). DriveSpace shows how the drive letters will change when it decompresses the drive. Some programs have settings that include explicit pathnames and drive letters. If a program's settings specify a drive that is no longer valid after uncompressing, the program will probably display an error message or be unable to find one of its components or data files. In that case, you need to correct the drive letter specified by that setting.

Disk space. You can uncompress a drive only if the data it contains will fit on the host drive. If you use the **drvspace /uncompress** command, and DriveSpace indicates the drive will not have enough free disk space, delete unnecessary files or move them to another drive.

Duplicate file names on compressed and host drives. If the root directories of the compressed and host drives contain files or directories with identical names, DriveSpace cannot uncompress the compressed drive. If this happens, DriveSpace displays an error message. Remove or rename one copy of each file, and then try uncompressing the drive again.

Uninstalling DriveSpace. When you uncompress the last mounted compressed drive, DriveSpace first decompresses the drive, and then prompts you to remove the DrvSpace driver from memory.

Drvspace /Uncompress Example

To uncompress drive E, type the following command:

```
drvspace /uncompress e:
```

Drvspace /Unmount

Breaks the connection between the selected drive's compressed volume file and its drive letter. Unmounting a drive makes it temporarily unavailable.

You cannot unmount a drive containing open files, including the drive containing Windows 98.

Syntax

drvspace /unmount [*drive***:**]

Parameters

*drive***:**
> Specifies the drive you want to unmount. This parameter is optional; if you omit it, DriveSpace unmounts the current drive.

Switch

/unmount
> Unmounts the specified compressed drive.

Drvspace /Unmount Example

To unmount compressed drive E, type the following command:

```
drvspace /unmount e:
```

ScanDisk

This command syntax controls Windows ScanDisk.

Note At the command prompt (for example, when you use F8 to start only the command prompt), you can use **scandisk** with the same switches to run the MS-DOS-based equivalent for this command. At the command prompt, type **scandisk /?** for more information.

Syntax	scandskw [*drive:*] [/A] [/N] [/P]
	scandisk *drive:*\dblspace.*nnn*
	scandisk *drive:*\drvspace.*nnn*

Parameters

drive:
Specifies one or more drives to be checked.

/A or **/All**
Checks all local, nonremovable hard disk drives.

/N or **/NonInteractive**
Starts and closes ScanDisk automatically. However, this switch does not prevent ScanDisk from stopping to report errors found on the drive.

/p or **/Preview**
Runs ScanDisk in Preview mode, where it reports and seems to correct errors that it finds, but it does not actually write changes to the disk.

Important When running **scandskw** in Preview mode, it appears as though ScanDisk is fixing errors, but it is not. Also, notice that unlike other settings in ScanDisk, the **/Preview** switch is not saved in the registry, so the next time you run ScanDisk, it is no longer in Preview mode.

To determine whether ScanDisk is running in Preview mode, look for the tag "(Preview)" in the caption of the main ScanDisk window.

Dblspace.*nnn* or **Drvspace.***nnn*
Checks the specified unmounted DoubleSpace or DriveSpace compressed volume file, where *nnn* is the file name extension for the hidden host file.

Table 10.7 describes the codes provided when ScanDisk finished running.

Table 10.7   Exit codes after ScanDisk has finished

Exit code	Description
0x00	Drive checked, no errors found.
0x01	Errors found, all fixed.
0xFA	Check could not start—cannot load or find Dskmaint.dll.
0xFB	Check could not start—insufficient memory.
0xFC	Errors found, but at least some were not fixed.
0xFD	At least one drive could not be checked.
0xFE	Check was canceled.
0xFF	Check was terminated because of an error.

You can capture the exit code in a batch file to define an action to take in the event of particular exit code. For example:

```
start /w scandksw c: d: /n
if errorlevel exitcode goto command
...
```

In this sample, **start /w** forces the batch file to stop and wait for **scandskw** to finish (otherwise, because it is a Windows-based program, the batch file would continue as soon as **scandskw** had been launched). Also in this example, if the actual exit code is greater than or equal to the exit code specified by *exitcode*, the batch file runs the specified *command*; otherwise, it continues to the next line in the batch file. The **goto** *command* entry could specify any command you want.

File System Management

With the Windows 98 installable file system, multiple file systems can coexist on the computer. Windows 98 includes the file systems described in Table 10.8.

Table 10.8   Windows 98 file systems

File System	Description
Virtual File Allocation Table	In Windows 98, the 32-bit *virtual file allocation table* (VFAT) file system is the primary file system and cannot be disabled. VFAT can use 32-bit, protected-mode drivers or 16-bit, real-mode drivers. Although VFAT will function correctly when 16-bit disk drivers are being used by IO Supervisor (IOS), its performance is compromised. Many new performance enhancements in VFAT are unavailable when using 16-bit disk drivers. Typically, a 16-bit disk driver is used when MS-DOS terminate-and-stay-resident programs (TSRs) have chained themselves into the MS-DOS kernel. For optimal performance, remove MS-DOS TSRs. Actual allocation on disk is still 12-, 16-, or 32-bit (depending on the size of the volume), so FAT on the disk uses the same structure as previous versions of this file system. VFAT handles all hard disk drive requests, using 32-bit code for all file access for hard-disk volumes.
Network Redirectors	A network redirector (such as Microsoft Client for NetWare Networks or Client for Microsoft Networks) is a file system driver that accesses the network file system. Windows 98 supports multiple network redirectors simultaneously, as described in Chapter 29, "Windows 98 Network Architecture."

Table 10.8   Windows 98 file systems (*continued*)

File System	Description
UDF	Universal Disk Format system. DVD disks use UDF.
CD-ROM File System	The virtual CD-ROM file system (CDFS) has the same responsibilities for a CD-ROM device as VFAT has for a standard hard disk. If a CD-ROM device is detected, the CDFS driver loads dynamically. When CDFS is installed, the standard disk type-specific device and Disk SCSI translator are replaced with CD-ROM versions. The CDFS driver is a protected-mode version of MSCDEX.EXE, providing the interface from the CD-ROM device to the operating system, as described in "VCACHE and CDFS Supplemental Cache" earlier in this chapter and in Chapter 28, "Windows 98 Architecture."
	If the CD-ROM drive and its drivers support the multisession command, CDFS can support multisession capabilities, which provide a method for adding data to a CD-ROM (this is most applicable to CD-recordable media). The multisession command returns a number that identifies the first sector of the last session on the media so that CDFS can recognize the media.

All these file systems support long file names and can use the protected-mode cache (VCACHE) for read-ahead (except CDFS). VFAT also supports lazy-write throughput, so applications can write immediately to the cache, and VFAT can write the information to disk later. For more information, see "VCACHE and CDFS Supplemental Cache" earlier in this chapter.

Other software vendors can also implement file systems. For example, a vendor might provide a file system that allows a computer running Windows 98 to connect to a different operating system (for example, Apple Macintosh or UNIX) to share files.

The Installable File System Manager (IFSMGR) receives all INT 21 calls and determines which file system driver should receive the call to process it. IFSMGR uses a real-mode stub named Ifshlp.sys to send INT 21 calls back to IFSMGR, as described in Chapter 28, "Windows 98 Architecture."

File system drivers manage the high-level I/O requests from applications. The file system driver processes requests from applications and initiates low-level I/O requests through the I/O Supervisor.

Protected-mode disk compression is not integrated into the file system, but is supported by a layer in the I/O subsystem.

System File Checker

System File Checker verifies the integrity of your operating system files and offers to restore missing, corrupted, or replaced files. System File Checker can be configured to back up existing files before restoring the originals. A log file (Sfclog.txt) is generated by default. Additional options include the ability to customize search criteria based on folder and/or file extension, choose a different verification data file, create a new verification file, or restore the default verification data file (Default.sfc).

For more information about System File Checker, see Chapter 27, "General Troubleshooting."

Using Long File Names

For MS-DOS version 6.22 and earlier, file names cannot exceed eight characters and file name extensions cannot exceed three characters in length (referred to as "8.3 file names"). The period character (.) is used only to separate the file name from the file name extension. With long file name support in Windows 98, these 8.3 file name constraints are gone.

For all Windows 98 file systems, users can specify file names that are up to 255 characters long and that can contain more than one period. These long file names are any names that exceed 8.3 characters in length or contain any lowercase character or most characters that are not valid in the 8.3 name space.

The following sections present information about long file name support in Windows 98, including information and recommendations for supporting long file names in a mixed network environment.

Long File Name Support in Windows 98

For every long file name, an alias entry is generated automatically that complies with the 8.3 file name rules for backward compatibility. Automatically generated aliases are composed of the first six characters of the file name plus ~n (where n is a number) and the first three characters after the last period. So the file name ThisIsALong.File.Name is associated with the automatically generated alias THISIS~1.NAM. If the alias name already exists, the algorithm will generate a unique value for n.

Note Neither the user nor an application can control the name created by the automatic alias process. Related issues are discussed in "Long File Names and Network Compatibility" later in this chapter.

For the file name to comply with the 8.3 file name rules, it must use only the valid characters for an alias and it must be all uppercase. Valid characters for 8.3 file names (and aliases) can be any combination of letters and numbers, a space (ASCII 20H), ASCII characters greater than 127, and the following special characters:

```
$ % ' - _ @ ~ ` ! ( ) ^ # &
```

The following additional characters are valid in long file names, but are not valid in alias names or 8.3 file names:

```
+ , ; = [ ]
```

The following rules also apply for Windows 98 file systems:

- Maximum file name component length is 255 characters, including NULL.
- Maximum path length is 260 characters, including NULL (compared to 80 characters for a short name).
- The OEM character set used by the installable file system (IFS) is determined by the registry and the contents of the file Unicode.bin.
- The long file name directory entries use the Unicode character set to store the names.

The file name and the alias are the same if the file name meets 8.3 file name rules (that is, if it contains only valid characters for an alias and it is all uppercase). This means that a file name using only valid characters for an alias and following the 8.3 file name format is still not the same as the alias name if it contains lowercase characters. However, in this case the alias is the uppercase version of the file name. For example, if the long file name is Examples.txt, its alias is EXAMPLES.TXT. The case is preserved in the long file name. (Note, though, that path-based APIs in the Windows 98 file system are not case-sensitive. So a search of the form "EXAMPLES.TXT" or "Examples.txt" will find the same files.)

Tip To see the alias for a file, right-click the file in any shell program such as Windows Explorer, and then select **Properties** from the context menu. The value for MS-DOS Name in the **General Properties** dialog box shows the alias assigned to this file. Also, the **dir** command at the command prompt shows the long file name.

Long File Names and Network Compatibility

By using a process called tunneling, Windows 98 preserves long file names for files that are opened and saved using an application that does not recognize long file names. Tunneling preserves long file names on the local computer as well as files accessed across the network.

Tunneling is supported for any file system that IFSMGR recognizes. The file system in turn must "authorize" tunneling to allow its use in that file system. Tunneling is authorized automatically with VFAT.

Correct network tunneling is the responsibility of the server—that is, the server must be configured to support long file names. A server running any edition of Windows NT 3.5 or Windows 98 file and printer sharing services will preserve long file names. For example, a user who is running Windows for Workgroups might open and save a file on a peer server that is running file and printer sharing services (for either Microsoft networks or NetWare networks). In this case, the long file name will be preserved by the file system on the peer server, because the peer server uses IFSMGR and VFAT to store the data.

- Windows NT file system (NTFS) supports long file names, but includes architecture for security that Windows 98 does not use. Windows NT 3.5 supports long file names on FAT drives and uses the same algorithm for aliases as used in Windows 98. However, Windows NT 3.1 does not recognize long file names on FAT drives and removes them.

- HPFS supports long file names with aliases similar to the method used in Windows 98.

- The UDF file system supports long file names.

- The CD-ROM file system (CDFS) also supports long file names.

The following sections provide details about long file name support on various networks.

Long File Names with Windows 98 Protected-Mode Clients

Windows 98 protected-mode network clients (Client for Microsoft Networks and Client for NetWare Networks) support long file names. If the network server that the computer is connected to supports long file names, then Windows 98 can read, create, and copy local long file name files on the network share. On some servers, the length of file names, restricted characters, and the algorithm for creating 8.3 file names from long file names might differ from those under Windows 98.

Client for Microsoft Networks does not authorize tunneling, so tunneling is not used to preserve long file names on down-level servers connected through the Windows 98 client (for example, a computer running Windows for Workgroups or LAN Manager Services). However, Microsoft Client for NetWare Networks does authorize tunneling, so tunneling can preserve long file names in connections to older NetWare servers when running Client for NetWare Networks.

Windows 98 can access files on HPFS or NTFS partitions on remote drives. However, there is no built-in support in the release of Windows 98 for adding either of these file systems as another installable file system under Windows 98. Therefore, Windows 98 cannot access either an HPFS or NTFS partition on a local disk drive by using the file system drivers provided with Windows 98. (Other vendors, however, can add HPFS support.)

Please note the following interoperability exceptions for other file systems:

Long file names can be used on computers running file and printer sharing services and can be viewed on computers using protected-mode Windows 98 network clients. Real-mode network clients running under Windows 98 can see only the 8.3 version file name aliases.

If Windows 98 has been configured with File and Printer Sharing for NetWare Networks, any MS-DOS-based NetWare clients using NETX or VLM will see 8.3 file names when browsing resources on the computer running Windows 98. Computers using Client for NetWare Networks can see long file names.

Long file names are supported for NetWare servers if the server is configured to use the OS/2 name space. For information, see Chapter 17, "Windows 98 on Third-Party Networks."

Note Older Microsoft or Microsoft-compatible clients (for example, LAN Manager, Workgroup Add-on for MS-DOS, Windows for Workgroups, and so on) cannot use shared folders that have long file names. These older network clients might have problems connecting to and using a shared directory with a long file name as the directory name. Defining a short share name does not correct this problem.

LAN Manager with HPFS and HPFS/386 Volumes

HPFS and HPFS/386 partitions on LAN Manager OS/2-based computers have a maximum file name length of 254 characters and use the 8.3 file name alias on the first instance. For example:

```
longfilenameold.tst --> LONGFILE.TST
longfilenamenew.tst --> LONGFIL0.TST
```

Long file names on a LAN Manager server with HPFS or HPFS/386 partitions are supported and viewable by Windows 98 protected-mode network clients. Real-mode network clients can see only the 8.3 file name aliases.

LAN Manager workstations with HPFS or HPFS/386 cannot see Windows 98 long file names. The LAN Manager workstation software has no awareness of the long file name-over-FAT file scheme used by Windows 98.

Windows NT 3.1 with HPFS or NTFS Volumes

Support for long file names on FAT volumes is identical in Windows NT 3.5 and Windows 98. Therefore, a computer with dual-boot capabilities for Windows NT 3.5 and Windows 98 can see long file names on local FAT volumes by using both operating systems.

HPFS partitions exist on Windows NT computers only in the case of an upgrade over OS/2. File names on Windows NT 3.1 HPFS partitions have a maximum file name length of 254 characters and use the 8.3 file name alias on the first instance. For example:

```
longfilenameold.tst --> LONGFILE.TST
longfilenamenew.tst --> LONGFIL0.TST
```

File names on Windows NT 3.1 NTFS partitions have a maximum file name length of 255 characters and use the 8.3 file name alias on the first instance. For example:

```
longfilenameold.tst --> LONGFI~1.TST
longfilenamenew.tst --> LONGFI~2.TST
```

Long file names on shared Windows NT 3.1 HPFS and NTFS partitions are supported and viewable by Windows 98 protected-mode network clients. Real-mode network clients can see only the 8.3 file name aliases.

Windows NT 3.1 computers cannot see Windows 98 long file names. Windows NT 3.1 has no awareness of the long file name-over-FAT file scheme used by Windows 98.

Administering Long File Names

If you are supporting long file names at a site with many users, consider the issues in this section.

If you back up files to a server that does not support Windows 98 long file names, use the LFNBK utility to save and restore long file names.

For information, see "Using the LFNBK Utility for Temporary Compatibility" later in this chapter.

Be aware of utilities that will not work with the Windows 98 directory entries for long file names. Some virus scanning programs, disk repair utilities, disk optimizers, and other programs depend on the FAT file system and might not work with long file names. If you are unsure whether a utility is compatible with the long file name system, check with the manufacturer. If you must use an incompatible program, be sure to turn off long file names by using the LFNBK utility before proceeding.

Do not use file names that are more than 50 to 75 characters long. Although file names can be up to 255 characters, the full path name cannot be more than 260 characters. To save room for moving a file from one directory to another, use file names shorter than the limit. Besides, file names that are too long can make browsing a list difficult.

Publish a naming convention for your site so that users are aware of naming considerations and can prevent problems with the long file names they use.

For example, your policy could recommend making the first three or four letters significant, so that the 8.3 file name aliases can be distinguished from each other. The following example shows the alias names for some long file names:

```
Status Report for Oct    ->   STATUS~1.TXT
Status Report for Nov    ->   STATUS~2.TXT
Status Report for Dec    ->   STATUS~3.TXT
```

Using the following alternate file names, you can distinguish between the 8.3 file names:

```
Oct Status Report    ->      OCTSTA~1.TXT
Nov Status Report    ->      NOVSTA~1.TXT
Dec Status Report    ->      DECSTA~1.TXT
```

You could also recommend that users give files a short file name as part of the long file name. For example:

```
Mktg_rpt-Marketing Report for our new project  ->  MKTG_R~1.TXT
```

As part of the naming convention, recommend that users check the properties for files to ensure that the alias (the MS-DOS Name in the **Properties** dialog box) is what they expect it to be.

Tip On FAT16 drives, it is usually best to store files in a directory beneath the root directory. This is especially true for files with long file names. Files with long file names use more directory entries than files with 8.3 file names. Because the number of entries in the root is limited to 512, the root directory can fill up with fewer files if long file names are used.

Notice that typing the command **mkdir Examples** creates a long file name directory entry that contains the name Examples to preserve the case, plus an 8.3 file name alias entry with the name EXAMPLES for compatibility. In this example, two directory entries are used.

Using the LFNBK Utility for Temporary Compatibility

Most hard disk utility programs released before Windows 98 require updating to work correctly with Windows 98. If you use a hard disk utility that was not created especially for use with Windows 98, you might lose long file names and you are at risk of losing data. Examples of such programs include the following:

- Older MS-DOS versions of Norton Utilities by Peter Norton Computing
- PC Tools by Central Point Software, Inc.
- Microsoft Defragmenter for MS-DOS version 6.0, 6.2, 6.21, or 6.22
- Stacker 4.0 by STAC Electronics

In special cases, you might need to run backup or disk management utilities created for older versions of Windows or MS-DOS that are not compatible with the extended file system capabilities of Windows 98. Or you might need occasionally to run an application that is not compatible with long file names. In such cases, you can use the LFNBK utility to remove (and later restore) long file names on a disk.

▶ **To install the LFNBK utility**

- From the Windows 98 compact disc, copy Lfnbk.exe to the \Windows directory on your computer.

> **Caution** The LFNBK utility is intended for use only by experienced Windows 98 users with special needs for compatibility with older disk utilities. It is not intended for everyday use by average users.
>
> Microsoft recommends that users rely on the disk management utilities included with Windows 98 or use Windows 98-compatible utilities from other vendors, rather than attempting to use older utilities that are not compatible with Windows 98.
>
> Notice also that the DriveSpace 3 utility included with Windows 98 is compatible with long file names and can be used without LFNBK to manage compressed disks created with older versions of DriveSpace 3 or DoubleSpace.

The following shows the syntax for LFNBK:

lfnbk [/v] [/b | /r | /pe] [/nt] [/force] [/p] [*drive*]

Table 10.9 lists and describes the parameters for this command.

Table 10.9   LFNBK parameters

Parameter	Description
/v	Reports actions on the screen.
/b	Backs up and removes long file names on the disk.
/r	Restores previously backed-up long file names.
/pe	Extracts errors from backup database.
/nt	Does not restore backup dates and times.
/force	Forces LFNBK to run, even in unsafe conditions.
/p	Finds long file names but does not convert them to 8.3 file name aliases. This reports the existing long file names, along with the associated dates for file creation, last access, and last modification of the file.

▶ **To preserve long file names with disk utilities that do not recognize them**

1. Turn off tunneling.

   In the System option in Control Panel, click the **Performance** tab, and then click **File System**. In the **File System Performance** dialog box, click the **Troubleshooting** tab, and check the option named **Disable Long Name Preservation for Old Programs**.

2. Close all other applications. LFNBK cannot rename open files.

3. At the command prompt, type **lfnbk /b** [drive] to back up and remove long file names.

4. Restart the computer, and then run the disk utility. If it is an MS-DOS-based utility, run it in MS-DOS Mode. For a Windows-based utility, run it in the usual way.

5. At the command prompt, type **lfnbk /r** [drive] to restore long file names.

6. Turn tunneling on again, and then restart the computer.

The LFNBK utility actually renames each file with a long file name to its associated alias. The file name changes are stored in the Lfnbk.dat file in the root of the drive where you are running LFNBK. This file is used to restore long file names (when you run LFNBK with the /r switch).

The following list provides some brief notes for using the LFNBK utility:

- You cannot use LFNBK to repair long file name problems.

- LFNBK might not be able to rename files with exact matches to long file name aliases, and the related alias is not guaranteed to be the same as before running LFNBK.

- After you run LFNBK and then restart Windows 98, the default **Start** menu will appear, rather than your custom **Start** menu. After you run lfnbk /r to restore long file names, your custom **Start** menu will also be restored.

- If the directory structure changes after you run lfnbk /b, then long file names cannot be restored with lfnbk /r. For example, if you run a disk utility that prunes or removes subdirectories, LFNBK cannot restore the long file names within those subdirectories.

Creating Long File Names at the MS-DOS Prompt

At an MS-DOS prompt or when Windows 98 is started only at the command prompt (from the F8 Startup menu), the keyboard buffer's ability to create long file names is limited to 127 characters. This is because the default command-line character limitation is 127 characters. In the default configuration, the MS-DOS environment will not allow more than 127 characters in a given command line. (However, in batch files, or for environment variables and other virtual machine (VM) elements, the long file name support is 244 characters.)

You can increase the global command-line character limit for the keyboard buffer to its maximum by placing the following line in Config.sys:

```
shell=c:\windows\command.com /u:255
```

If the shell command is already present with the /u switch, increase the value to 255.

This command will affect all VMs and the Windows 98 command line.

With the command-line character limit set to its maximum of 255 characters, file names are limited to 255 characters minus the contents of the command line. For example, the command line might contain the following:

```
copy con "long filename"
```

In this case, the maximum length of the long file name is 244 characters (255 minus the 11 characters of the command including spaces and quotation marks).

Note It is necessary to put the file name in quotation marks on the command line only if the file name contains special characters, such as spaces.

Notice, however, MS-DOS-based applications configured to run in MS-DOS Mode use only the real-mode FAT file system. Because of this, long file names created in a Windows environment are not visible when the system runs in MS-DOS Mode; only the 8.3 file name aliases are visible.

The same is true of files with long file names that are copied to a floppy disk subsequently used by a down-level FAT file system such as MS-DOS 6.0, Windows 3.1, OS/2 2.11, Windows NT 3.1, and so on.) On down-level file systems, only the 8.3 file name alias is visible on the floppy disk, even if it contains long file names created in Windows 98.

Technical Notes on Long File Names

This section summarizes some technical points with regard to long file names. This information will be helpful to you if you experience problems with long file names.

Using long file names on SUBST drives. Windows 98 supports long files names on SUBST drives.

File Names and Extensions. The following are valid file names for Windows 98 applications:

- 12345678.abc (MS-DOS name)
- 12345678.abcdef (no limit on extensions)
- 12345678901234567890123456789012345678.abc (long file name)
- 12345678901234567890123456789012345678.abcdef (long file name and long extension)
- This is a valid file name (long names with spaces that mean something)

To see the MS-DOS name associated with a long file name, use the right mouse button to click the file, and then click **Properties**.

Troubleshooting Disks and File Systems

This section provides information for troubleshooting disk and tape drive problems, FAT32 problems, and file system problems.

For more information about using the **Troubleshooting** dialog box for **File System Properties** in the System option in Control Panel, see Chapter 26, "Performance Tuning."

Disks and Tape Drives

The system did not shut down cleanly, or the disk suffers a hard error.

ScanDisk will be run automatically when your system restarts. By default, a message will be displayed before ScanDisk starts. You can override this behavior by setting the AutoScan variable in the [Options] section of the Msdos.sys file:

- AutoScan = 0 will disable this feature entirely.
- AutoScan = 1 is the default, ScanDisk will run automatically.

There are performance problems with the floppy disk drive.

You can try preventing the floppy disk device driver from attempting to use first-in, first-out (FIFO). To do this, add the value ForceFIFO=0 to the following registry key:

HKEY_LOCAL_MACHINE\System\CurrentControlSet \Services\Class\FDC \0000

Windows 98 cannot access the drive or reports 2 GB disk space on a larger drive.

Microsoft does not recommend using Windows 98 with a FAT16 volume larger than 2 GB created in Windows NT. On a dual-boot computer with both Windows 98 and Windows NT installed, you can read from and write to the drive, but you might experience strange results, such as programs reporting 0 bytes free space on the drive. However, you should not experience data loss when accessing a 4 GB drive.

Hard disk drive limited to 8 GB partition.

When you try to partition a drive that is larger than 8 GB in size, the maximum partition size may be 8 GB. This can occur if the hard disk controller does not fully support the interrupt 13 extensions. This information applies to both IDE and SCSI hard disk drives. For a hard disk that is larger than 8 GB and uses the FAT32 file system to be fully addressed, it must support interrupt 13 extensions. Io.sys tests for the presence of interrupt 13 extensions. If interrupt 13 extensions are not detected, the default CHS LBA limit of 7.9 GB is used.

To determine whether your BIOS supports interrupt 13 extensions, please refer to the drive's documentation or manufacturer. Contact the drive controller's manufacturer for information about a possible BIOS upgrade to a version of the BIOS that fully supports interrupt 13 extensions.

Disk utilities fail on a Windows 98 volume.

Disk utilities that were not designed for the Windows 98 VFAT file system can find unexpected values in fields that were once reserved for MS-DOS. Use disk utilities designed for Windows 98 instead. You might be able to use some earlier utilities by first running LFNBK, as described in "Using the LFNBK Utility for Temporary Compatibility" earlier in this chapter.

Problems occur after compressing the Windows 98 volume with Stacker.

Stacker version 4.0 and earlier does not recognize or accommodate long file names. If you compress your Windows 98 volume by using the Stacker DOS compression program, your desktop shortcuts will need to be repaired manually and you will also need to move User.dat from the host volume to your compressed volume. If you are using Stacker, do not run DriveSpace 3 or DoubleSpace.

Parameter value not in allowed range for Format.

If you specify a value that is not 1 or an exponent of 2, or if you specify a value that is larger than 64, Format returns this message:

```
Parameter value not in allowed range.
```

Specify a value in the correct range.

Backup does not detect your tape drive.

Microsoft Backup does not work with all tape drives. If you install Backup and get a message that your tape drive has not been detected, click the **Help** button and connect to Seagate's Web site using the provided URL to see a list of supported tape drives.

Tape drive detection.

Plug and Play software does not detect tape drives. This is a function of the drivers provided with the Windows 98 Backup program, or the software that came with the drive. As a result, the tape drive may appear as an unknown device in Device Manager. If your backup software does not detect your tape drive, contact the company that wrote the software.

Tape drive compatibility.

If your tape drive does not appear in the list of supported drives located on Seagate's Web site (click the **Help** button and connect to Seagate's Web site using the provided URL), contact your tape drive manufacturer for information about backup software that you can use with Windows 98.

Running Zip Tools on an Iomega Parallel Zip Disk.

From within My Computer or Windows Explorer, if you right-click the Zip disk and then click **Format**, the Format window displays an option for you to do a full format of the drive. If you select this option, the following blue-screen fatal-exception error might occur:

```
A fatal exception 0E has occurred at 0028:C3C64C51 in VXD IOMEGA (01) +
00000CB5. The current application will be terminated.
```

Pressing any key closes the Windows Explorer window.

To correct this problem, contact Iomega and obtain a new Iomega.vxd file. Using the **Find** command on the **Start** menu, find the old Iomega.vxd file and replace it with the newer version.

ScanDisk reports errors on files or folders made with different code pages.

If you have created or named files or folders while using different code pages, ScanDisk may report errors about these files or the folders they reside in. If you are affected by this, open ScanDisk's **Advanced** dialog box and make sure **Check Files For Invalid File Names** is not checked. Note that turning off this option may inhibit ScanDisk's ability to detect or repair seriously damaged folders.

The Drvspace or Dblspace /mount command in Autoexec.bat does not work.

This occurs because Windows 98 Setup deletes or renames the MS-DOS-based versions of Drvspace.exe and Dblspace.exe. To solve this problem, use scandisk /mount as the replacement command line in Autoexec.bat. The version of ScanDisk provided with Windows 98 has been enhanced for this purpose.

Installing program requiring specific drive letter.

Use the SUBST command to associate the required drive letter with the program's installation folder. For example:

```
subst <drive>: <C:\dir>
```

FAT32

This section discusses problems and potential support issues that exist with FAT32. The list below summarizes some points to remember about FAT32:

- You cannot boot to a previous operating system and access a FAT32 volume.
- Windows NT 4.0 cannot access a FAT32 volume.
- DriveSpace 3 is not supported on a FAT32 volume. However, you can have one drive FAT32 and the other a FAT16 and use DriveSpace 3 on the 16-bit FAT volume.
- Disk Manager users should upgrade to 7.04 or higher.

- CHKDSK will not fix errors on FAT32 drives; instead, use ScanDisk.
- Applications having problems with a program set up on a FAT32 drive should have their program upgraded.
- Legacy versions of ScanDisk will not work on FAT32.
- DrivParm has been updated to recognize FAT32.
- File Control Blocks (FCBs) has limited support.
- Dealing with files larger than 2 GB may cause problems on non-FAT32-aware programs.
- Absolute disk read and write utilities should be upgraded to recognize FAT32.
- Interlink will not work on FAT32.

Booting from a previous operating system.

The new file system is not backward compatible. You cannot access a FAT32 volume from any MS-DOS version before 7.1. Attempting to access a FAT32 volume with a previous version of MS-DOS will initiate a "Non-DOS Partition" error message. If you boot from a floppy with a previous version and all the drives are FAT32, you will not be able to access the drives. There is no problem accessing the C drive if the C drive is a 12-bit or 16-bit FAT.

You must have a Startup Disk from the new operating system.

Windows NT (version 4.0 or earlier) and FAT32.

Currently, Windows NT cannot access a FAT32 drive. You will get one of two messages.

If the capacity of the drive is greater than 4 GB:

```
The drive is not a valid partition.
```

If the capacity of the drive is less than 4 GB:

```
The drive is not formatted.
```

DriveSpace 3.

DriveSpace 3 and FAT32 are incompatible. DriveSpace 3 is included with Windows 98, and it has been modified to detect FAT32 drives, but it will not compress them. You can still compress FAT16 drives even if another drive is FAT32. DriveSpace 3 components are included in Windows 98.

DriveSpace 3 and Cluster Allocation Granularity.

Do not assume that since you reduce the amount of slack space at the end of the clusters, the capacity of a FAT32 drive should increase as much as if you were using DriveSpace 3. There are two components in DriveSpace 3 compression— tokenization and reduction of the cluster size.

There are no compression features in FAT32; just smaller clusters. Gained space is not a function of compression, but more a function of the files sizes on the drive and how many files are on that drive. If you do not have many files on the drive, there will not be a significant improvement in space. The point and advantage of FAT32 is efficiency.

Disk Manager.

Using Ontrack Systems Disk Manager product on a system that is booting from a FAT32 drive may result in a long pause at boot time and/or that the drive will be set to run in compatibility mode. With version 7.0x, you can use the /L=0 option with Disk Manager to avoid this pause.

If you are using an earlier version of Disk Manager, you should update to version 9.0 and use the /L=0 switch if you use FAT32. Contact Ontrack for an upgraded driver, or check their site on the World Wide Web.

Io.sys floppy disk support.

Io.sys floppy disk support had some problems that have been fixed. When Io.sys copied the BIOS Parameter Block (BPB) from a floppy disk into memory, some data structures were truncated and some fields were ignored based on assumptions that the media was a floppy disk. Also, initializing a drive as "other" (such as an external floppy) would always set up as a 12-bit FAT and discard bits identifying the total sectors or not examine the number of read/write heads.

The problems in building the BPB have all been fixed so that Io.sys now correctly copies all of the BPB fields out of the boot sector on the disk inserted in the drive. Also, Io.sys has increased less than 5 KB in size in conventional memory because of the changes in the real-mode kernel that accommodate FAT32 drives.

If a program was written to work around these problems on its own, you may need to obtain an update that recognizes FAT32. If you begin to experience external drive problems from an application or driver, test with Windows, not the application in question. You can obtain an update that recognizes FAT32 from the vendor.

Making sure a disk is formatted for a FAT32 system.

When you try to defragment a FAT32 file system drive, you may receive the following error message:

```
Windows cannot defragment this drive. Make sure the disk is formatted
and free of errors. Then try defragmenting the drive again.
ID No: DEFRAG0026
```

This can be caused by running an earlier version of Defrag.exe than the version included with Windows 98.

Invalid media error message when formatting a FAT32 partition.

When you try to format a FAT32 file system partition larger than 8,025 MB from within Windows 98, you may receive the following error message:

```
Verifying <xxx.xx>M
Invalid media or track 0 bad-disk unusable
Format terminated
```

where <xxx.xx> is the size of the partition.

This error occurs if there is a non-MS-DOS partition preceding the extended MS-DOS partition and the primary MS-DOS partition has been formatted using the real-mode Format.exe command. To resolve this issue, format the volume using the following steps.

▶ **To format the volume**

1. Click **Start**, click **Shut Down**, click **Restart in MS-DOS mode**, and then click **OK**.

2. Type the following command

   ```
   format <drive>:
   ```

   where *<drive>* is the drive letter for the partition you want to format.

3. Press ENTER.

4. When the partition is formatted, type **Exit** to restart Windows 98.

You must run CVT1 to convert a drive to FAT32.

When you attempt to convert a drive to the FAT32 file system, you may receive the following error message:

```
You must run CVT1 to convert a drive to FAT32. In Windows, click the
Start button, point to Accessories, point to System Tools, and then
click the Drive Converter (FAT32) icon. The conversion was canceled.
```

This error message can occur if you attempt the conversion when in an MS-DOS window. When the computer is booted to a command prompt, run Cvt.exe by typing the following command:

```
cvt <drive> /cvt32
```

where *<drive>* is the drive to be converted.

Windows 98 partition types not recognized by Windows NT.

When you set up Windows NT on a computer that has Windows 98 preinstalled, the FAT partitions may be shown as unknown.

Windows NT cannot recognize primary partitions using the FAT32 format. Backup any data that you might need to save and then delete the partition(s) using Fdisk from either MS-DOS or Windows 98.

Windows 98 supports four partition types for FAT file systems that Windows NT cannot recognize. The partition type can be identified by the System ID byte in the partition table. This byte is located at the following offsets:

```
0x1C2 = Partition 1
0x1D2 = Partition 2
0x1E2 = Partition 3
0x1F2 = Partition 4
```

The four values used by Windows 98 that Windows NT does not recognize are as follows:

```
0x0B       Primary  Fat32 Partitions up to 2047 GB
0x0C       Same as 0x0B, uses Logical Block Address Int 0x13 extensions
0x0E       Same as 0x06, uses Logical Block Address Int 0x13 extensions
0x0F       Same as 0x05, uses Logical Block Address Int 0x13 extensions
```

The FAT partition types that Windows NT version 3.*x* and 4.0 can recognize are:

```
0x01       Fat12 < 10 megabytes
0x04       Fat16 < 32 megabytes
0x06       Fat16 > 32 megabytes
0x05       Extended (may be FAT, HPFS or NTFS)
```

CHKDSK.

CHKDSK will not find or repair errors on FAT32. CHKDSK is not being updated to repair the new file system, but it will display the file system statistics. Use the real-mode ScanDisk if you cannot get into Windows 98.

Application setup.

The standard API for determining the free space on a drive is being intercepted by shell32.dll. When installing to a drive larger than 2 GB or with more than 2 GB free, shell32.dll readjusts the values for 16-bit programs to run properly.

All properly coded programs should call the correct API for determining free space and existing disk space. There should be no problem installing 16-bit applications on a FAT32 volume. If the program hangs during installation or displays an error message indicating not enough space to install, the application is using a different API and you should obtain an update from the vendor.

ScanDisk.

Legacy versions of ScanDisk will not work on FAT32. You can receive a variety of error messages, but the following is the most common on that Windows 98 displays:

```
This version of Microsoft ScanDisk will work only with MS-DOS versions
5.0 and later.
```

With an old version of Scandskw.exe, Scandisk.exe, or Dskmaint.dll on the drive, you will also receive errors.

In both cases, you should use the file versions that come with Windows 98.

DRIVPARM.

DRIVPARM is a Config.sys command. The numbers entered for the /f, /h, /s, and /t switches were not checked to see if they were too large, now they are. The /f number must be < 10; the /h number must be < 256; the /s number must be < 64; and the /t number must be <= 1024.

Check Help for assistance with these parameters. There are three new switches that allow the setting of other device parameters. If none of these new flags is present, the call continues to do exactly what it did in previous versions.

```
/a:# - sectors/cluster, must be 1, 2, 4, 8, 16, 32, or 64
/v:# - number of reserved sectors
/r:# - number of root directory entries, must be a multiple of 16
```

A value of 0 means use the default value.

The new switches allow media of any type to be set, including 12-bit, 16-bit, and 32-bit FAT.

Important It is strongly recommended that you specify /f:7 whenever using any of these new switches so that the media defined will have the 0F0h media byte value. /f:5 will give an error. The other /f:# are allowed, but may not work properly if their default media byte value is not 0F0h.

FAT32 Extension Changes

With the significant changes to the new file system, some previous extensions are no longer supported or have changed. The following list are extensions no longer supported.

SHARE.

SHARE is no longer supported in real mode under MS-DOS 7.1. Share services are a part of the IFS manager. VFAT uses them to provide full file sharing functionality. All MS-DOS-, Win16-, or Win32-based applications have full file sharing services available to it. As a consequence, the MS-DOS utility Share.exe is no longer necessary and is not provided in Windows 98.

FASTOPEN.

FASTOPEN support has been removed from the Io.sys. As with SHARE, it can be installed without error, but Io.sys never calls it.

Windows 3.1 File Manager.

Winfile.exe (the old Windows 3.1 File Manager) does not show accurate free drive space on FAT32 drives that are over 2 GB in size, nor will it display long file names.

Extensions Changed or Superseded

The following functions/extensions have new limitations on FAT32 media.

FCBs.

Support for File Control Blocks (FCBs) is reduced. The Open and Create functions only work for creating a volume label on a FAT32 drive. Programs still using FCBs for finding, deleting or renaming a file will still perform as expected.

Writing to a large file.

To increase a file to a size greater than 2 GB in size, the file must be opened with a new Extended Size flag. If such a file is not opened using this flag, write functions fail and you receive an "**Error Access Denied**" message.

Opening and creating a large file.

To open a file to a size greater than 2 GB in size, the file must be opened with a new Extended Size flag.

Errors arise from opening or changing files greater than 2 GB from non-FAT32 aware programs. You will need to obtain an upgrade from the application vendor.

Interrupts 25h/26h absolute disk read/write.

Many utilities use absolute disk reads and writes to function. Utilities include disk editors, backup programs, defragmenters, virus scanning software (especially Master Boot Record [MBR] and Boot Sector [BS] scanning), and repair utilities. These utilities can cause problems accessing a drive where the underlying foundation is unknown.

Int 25h/26h is superseded by Int 21h Function 7305h Ext ABSDiskReadWrite for FAT32 drives. As with Windows 95, Int 25h/26h is designed to fail by displaying a blue screen and informing the customer not to read/write to the disk. Programs designed for Windows 98 that invoke volume locking will need to be upgraded for FAT32. These utilities should continue to work properly on FAT16 drives. Also, Windows 95 utilities, including ScanDisk and Defrag, do not work on FAT32 volumes.

Free disk space.

If total or free disk space is greater than 2 GB, then 2 GB is returned. This function, GetDiskFreeSpace, is superseded by GetDiskFreeSpaceEx. GetDiskFreeSpace, for compatibility reasons, now never reports more than 1.999999 GB free under Windows 98.

The only time you might have a problem is if the program does not use GetDiskFreeSpace when determining free space on a volume. If a program has a problem with a drive larger than 2 GB, then it is probably using some other method to determine the free space. You should contact the manufacturer to update the program to FAT32.

Drive parameters.

MS-DOS and Windows keep track of drive characteristics in memory. For example, if you are copying a file to a floppy disk from Microsoft Excel, the application goes to this area to identify the media type. The information here is identical to the BIOS Parameter Block (BPB) in the Boot Sector. Properly written programs use this area of memory for that drive's information instead of going to the BPB. This area of memory is called the Drive Parameter Block (DPB).

When applications need to know about a drive, such as drive letter, or size of its sector, they access the DPB and use its information accordingly. The functions used to get that information have been superseded. The new DPB contains the FAT32 values by extending the existing DPB to include new 32-bit values while keeping the existing 16-bit fields for compatibility.

On drives larger than 2 GB (or if there is more than 2 GB free), if an application is displaying strange behavior anytime a drive or disk is accessed, it could be getting incomplete information from the old DPB. Also, some programs assume the size of internal Windows data structures. For example, some applications assume that a DPB is 33 bytes long and will never change in size. Programs like this will need to be upgraded to recognize the new ExtDPB. Also, third-party drivers that depend on the old DPB to load will hang if they do not have an error handler in place to terminate the driver.

Dual boot and FAT32.

You cannot use FAT32 on a machine that you need to dual boot to the original release of Windows 95, Windows NT 4.0 (or earlier), Windows 3.1, or MS-DOS 6.x. These operating systems are unable to access a FAT32 partition. However, it is still possible to use dual boot where there are multiple hard disks installed.

InterLink.

The InterLink networking product contained in MS-DOS 6.x will not function properly in MS-DOS mode if you are using FAT32. If you are running InterLink as a server on a FAT32 drive, all connections and inquiries (such as DIR) result in the following error message:

```
"File allocations table bad, Drive X"
```

Also, the InterLink Manager shows the incorrect total drive size. This problem does not occur on FAT16 drives. To see your FAT32 server, start your computer in protected mode with InterLink running.

You will need to use Direct Cable Connection to get connectivity.

Save to File (Hibernate) feature may be incompatible with FAT32.

On computers containing a BIOS made by Phoenix Technologies, you might not be able to use the Save to File feature if your primary (boot) drive is formatted using FAT32. If your PhDISK utility is earlier than version 5.0, you must obtain an updated version of the utility and an updated ROM BIOS from your computer manufacturer in order to use a Save to Disk file. With older versions of the ROM BIOS, your computer may be unable to start if it tries to read a Save to Disk file from a FAT32 drive. If this occurs, you must disable the Save to File feature in your ROM BIOS. This does not affect computers using a disk partition to store the Save to Disk data.

Ontrack Systems Disk Manager.

If you use the Ontrack Systems Disk Manager program on a computer with FAT32 drives, there might be a long pause when you start your computer and/or the drive will be set to run in compatibility mode. If you use version 9.0x, you can avoid this pause by using the /L=0 option with Disk Manager. To do this, carry out the following steps:

▶ **To use the /L=0 option with Disk Manager**

1. Start Disk Manager.

2. Click the **Maintenance** menu, and then click **Update Dynamic Drive Overlay**.

3. Add /L=0 to any other options that are already present.

4. Save the settings, and then restart your computer.

   If you are running an earlier version of Disk Manager and you want to use FAT32, you should update to version 7.04 or later and use the /L=0 switch.

V Communications System Commander.

Versions 2.28 and earlier of V Communications System Commander are incompatible with FAT32. If your primary (boot) hard disk uses FAT32 exclusively, you must obtain version 3.0 or later of System Commander.

Iomega Jaz tools may be incompatible with FAT32.

If you format an Iomega Jaz disk using FAT32, you may need to obtain updated versions of the Jaz tools. Older versions of the tools do not support FAT32 Jaz disks properly. As a result, the eject, write-protection, and password-protection options will be disabled. Updated versions of these tools that are compatible with FAT32 are available from Iomega, and from the Microsoft Windows Driver Library contained on the Windows CD-ROM disk and available for download from various online services.

Syquest Techology, Inc. device drivers.

Older versions of the Squatdvr.sys and Sqdriver.sys device drivers are incompatible with this version of Windows and will hang when your computer starts if your primary (boot) hard disk uses FAT32. You must remove the associated DEVICE= line from your Config.sys file in order to start your computer from a FAT32 drive. Updated versions of these drivers that are compatible with FAT32 are available from Syquest, and from the Microsoft Windows Driver Library contained on the Windows compact disc and available for download from various online services.

File Systems

Troubleshooting using the File System property sheet.

If you have programs that do not respond properly to the Windows 98 file system, there are settings you can use to isolate the problem areas.

Caution It is strongly recommended that only advanced users and system administrators change the settings in this procedure.

▶ **To change the settings of the File System Troubleshooting property sheet**

1. In the Control Panel, double-click System, and then click the **Performance** tab.

2. Click **Advanced**, and then click **File System**.

3. Click the **Troubleshooting** tab.

4. Click the setting you want to test. The switch settings are described in Table 10.10.

5. Click **OK** and test to determine whether the setting selected solves the problem.

If the problem is not solved, repeat the prior steps, choosing a different setting, until the problem is identified.

Table 10.10   Debugging switch settings for file systems

Switch	Description
Disable protected-mode hard disk interrupt handling	Windows 98 captures the Int13h interrupts and processes them with a 32-bit virtual driver. If your program is having intermittent disk access problems, you may want to turn off this functionality. The program may then handle the Intl3h interrupts. This usually results in slower hard disk access, but it may solve problems with certain programs.
Disable synchronous buffer commits	This setting changes the behavior of the Commit File call. This setting should only be used when requested by the vendor of a specific program. Using this setting may decrease system reliability.
Disable all 32-bit protected-mode drivers	If you have a hard drive that is not completely compatible with Windows 98 and you are having problems accessing that drive, consider disabling the protected-mode drivers. This setting turns off the protected-mode drivers and enables the real-mode drivers. Again, this may result in slower hard drive access times.

Table 10.10   Debugging switch settings for file systems (*continued*)

Switch	Description
Disable write-behind caching for all drives	This turns off the write caching functions. Caching is only performed on reads from the drives. Disabling the write-behind cache greatly slows down the processing of writing (saving) data to the drives, but it is safe. When a program indicates that data is written to the disk, the data is on the disk and not in a cache waiting to be written to the disk. If you are working in an environment where the quality of electrical power is questionable, for example, if there are frequent power spikes, brownouts, or power failures, and the data being written to the drive is critical, you may opt for this setting.

The 8.3 file name alias was changed.

This can happen when you use options such as Copy, Backup, or Restore. For example, if a file with the name LongFileName is associated with an alias LONGFI~2, and this file is copied to a different directory by using the following:

```
copy LongFileName \TMP\LongFileName
```

Then the alias associated with this file can become LONGFI~1, if such an alias is not already present in the target directory.

The long file name was destroyed.

This can happen when transferring files to or from file systems that do not support long file names, when running file searches, or when using certain disk utilities. The long file name cannot be restored.

A long file name was lost after the file was edited on another computer.

This occurs because down-level file systems are not aware of the long file name extensions to the FAT file system.

Hard disk device drivers cause the computer to stall.

The I/O Supervisor, which loads hard disk (block) device drivers, requires the driver's files (having file name extensions PDR, MPD, VXD, and .386) to be located in the System\Iosubsys subdirectory of the \Windows directory.

If the computer locks up during startup or hardware detection, try the following:

- Check for Windows NT miniport drivers (SYS files in the \Iosubsys directory). These drivers detect the I/O ports and might cause the computer to stop. Replace the Windows NT driver with either a Windows 98 miniport or a real-mode driver.

- Check the Ios.ini file for real-mode drivers not replaced by protected-mode drivers.

- When loading protected-mode drivers, the real-mode driver generally remains loaded in memory even though the protected-mode driver "takes over." If you suspect a conflict, type **rem** at the beginning of the line in Config.sys that calls the real-mode driver.

- Users might have problems with devices (such as tape backups) that use ASPI drivers. Try using only real-mode drivers, then try using only protected-mode drivers.

Long file names do not work correctly on DEC PATHWORKS servers.

Long file names do not work correctly on Digital Equipment Corporation (DEC) PATHWORKS servers up to and including version 5.0b. You will be able to create and delete long file name files and make and remove long file name folders, but the files and folders will not appear when you use the DIR command, or when you open an Explorer window to the PATHWORKS server. PATHWORKS server version 5.00 EC01 corrects this problem and is available from DEC.

Virus-detection utilities do not remove a virus.

In general, virus-detection utilities created from earlier versions of Windows can detect but not clean viruses from Windows 98. This is because virus-detection utilities use low-level writes to repair the disk. MS-DOS-based utilities can still be run using the **lock** command.

Tip Long file names can cause problems for some disk utilities. Be sure to use disk utilities that are long file name-aware. If you are not sure whether your utility is long file name-aware, consult your disk utility documentation. If long file names are not mentioned, then your utility probably does not support long file names.

Using a down-level file system command (such as copy or rename) rather than the Windows 98 equivalent will destroy a long file name.

Because the root directory is limited to 512 entries, you can fill the root directory with fewer files by using long file names because each long file name takes more than one entry in the directory.

CHAPTER 11

Printing, Imaging, and Fonts

This chapter describes support for printers, still imaging devices, and fonts in Microsoft Windows 98. It includes an overview of the printing subsystem and explains how to set up and administer printers and print servers. It also discusses acquiring and printing images, including new support in Windows 98 for TWAIN, Image Color Matching (ICM), scanners, and still image digital cameras. Finally, this chapter explains font matching and font support in Windows 98.

In This Chapter

See Also

- For information about support for imaging devices and drivers in the Win32® Driver Model (WDM), see Chapter 30, "Hardware Management."

Printing Support in Windows 98

Windows 98 adds the following enhancements to the printing support and subsystem introduced with Windows 95.

New printer drivers. Windows 98 has over 200 new printer drivers to support a broader range of the latest printer models and technologies.

Improved Web printing. The Microsoft Internet Explorer 4 browsing software has implemented the new cascading style sheet (CSS) extensions to HTML for printing Web pages. Cascading style sheets enable such enhancements as background printing of Web pages, recursive printing of hyperlinks on a Web page, and for frames pages, the ability to print a specific frame or all frames on a page.

Improved color management. Windows 98 supports the new Image Color Matching (ICM) version 2.0 standards. When you acquire an image from an input device, such as a scanner or still image digital camera, ICM 2.0 maintains the image's original color mapping, from display and editing in applications through printed or electronic output. In other words, ICM 2.0 ensures that the original image colors are accurately interpreted by an input device, displayed on a monitor, and output to a color printer or electronic format.

For detailed information about ICM 2.0, see "Image Color Matching 2.0 Support" later in this chapter.

New Hewlett-Packard JetAdmin 2.54 utility. The Windows 98 compact disc includes an updated version of the Hewlett Packard (HP) JetAdmin utility, which lets you install and configure HP printers connected to a network through an HP JetDirect print server (network interface). The update provides additional features and support for the latest printer models from Hewlett-Packard.

For more information about the JetAdmin utility, see "Using the Hewlett-Packard JetAdmin Utility" later in this chapter.

Overview of the Windows 98 Printing Subsystem

In Windows 98, the print spooler is implemented as a series of 32-bit virtual device drivers and dynamic-link libraries (DLLs), and consolidates the spooler functionality into a single architecture. The spooler provides smooth background printing by using background thread processing. This means that the spooler passes data to the printer only when the printer is ready to receive more information.

The spooler provides quick return-to-application time. It allows you to set printer properties for an individual printer instead of requiring global printing properties. For example, each printer can have a different separator page, and each can specify whether jobs will be printed directly or to a queue.

Figure 11.1 illustrates how Windows 98 prints documents.

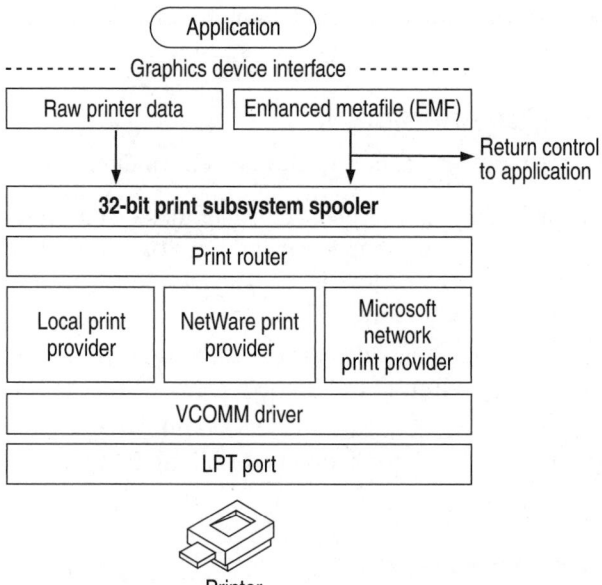

Figure 11.1   Overview of printing in Windows 98

During printer installation Windows 98 reads INF files to install the proper printer drivers. Although the previous OEMSetup.inf file format is still supported for compatibility with Windows 3.x, the new INF format offers added functionality, including support for installing printing subsystem components, such as the printer driver and port monitor, and for installing Plug and Play printers. All information about an installed printer is stored in the registry.

For information about enhanced metafiles (EMFs), printer drivers, and other components of the printing subsystem, see "How the Printing Subsystem Works" later in this chapter.

Considerations Before Installing Printers

Before configuring printers and installing fonts in Windows 98, you should consider the issues summarized in this section.

General Considerations

The following are general considerations for printing:

- When purchasing new printers, consider those with support for bidirectional communication and extended capabilities ports (ECPs). These features allow Plug and Play–compliant printers to send status messages to Windows 98 and utilize high-speed printing.

- ECPs are not automatically configured. For more information on ECPs, see "Extended Capabilities Port Support" later in this chapter.

- If your printer uses font cartridges, you will also need to install the fonts on your computer. For information on installing fonts, see "Installing Fonts" later in this chapter.

Network Considerations

The following are considerations for printing on a corporate network:

- To share a printer on either Microsoft or NetWare networks, the print server must be running a 32-bit, protected-mode client, and file and printer sharing services must be enabled. For information, see Chapter 18, "Logon, Browsing, and Resource Sharing."

- With *Point and Print*, users can install a network printer if the print server has been configured with the correct printer drivers. You need to designate which network servers will function as print servers and configure them to store Point and Print information. For information on Point and Print, see "Remote Installation Using Point and Print" later in this chapter.

The following are specific considerations for printing on NetWare networks:

- To use Point and Print with NetWare servers, you must decide which print servers will store printer driver files. You can store pointers in the NetWare bindery to the print servers that have printer drivers installed on them. For information, see "Remote Installation Using Point and Print" later in this chapter.

How the Printing Subsystem Works

This section presents detailed information about the Windows 98 printing subsystem.

Bidirectional Communication

Through *bidirectional parallel communication*, Windows 98 detects Plug and Play–compliant printers that return device ID values (as described in Institute of Electrical and Electronics Engineers [IEEE] specification 1284). This feature allows applications to directly query printers to determine their physical attributes.

Bidirectional communication provides the benefit of configuring printer driver settings on the print server without user intervention. The printer driver can automatically determine how much memory the printer has, what device fonts are available.

Bidirectional communication also allows printers to send unsolicited messages, such as "out of paper" or "printer offline," to Windows 98 and to applications. Bidirectional communication also makes possible much more detailed status reporting on a wider variety of information, such as low toner conditions, paper jams, maintenance needs, and so on.

To use bidirectional printing, you must have the following:

- A bidirectional printer.
- An IEEE 1284–compliant cable (a cable that has "1284" printed on it).

Extended Capabilities Port Support

An extended capabilities port (ECP) provides high-speed printing. Support for ECP and ECP devices is included in Windows 98. If you have an ECP, you can connect either ECP or non-ECP devices to the port. In either case, using an ECP improves I/O performance.

Enhanced Metafile Spooling

In Windows 98, all output to non-PostScript printers spools as enhanced metafiles (EMFs). By contrast, output to PostScript printers spools as PostScript-language raw printer data. Programs print using EMFs as much as twice as fast as raw printer data.

EMFs include instructions about how a document is to be printed. For example, if a document contains a solid black rectangle, the EMF contains a command to draw a rectangle with the given dimensions and then fill it in with a solid color, using the color black. Figure 11.2 shows how Windows 98 spools EMFs when printing from a Windows-based application.

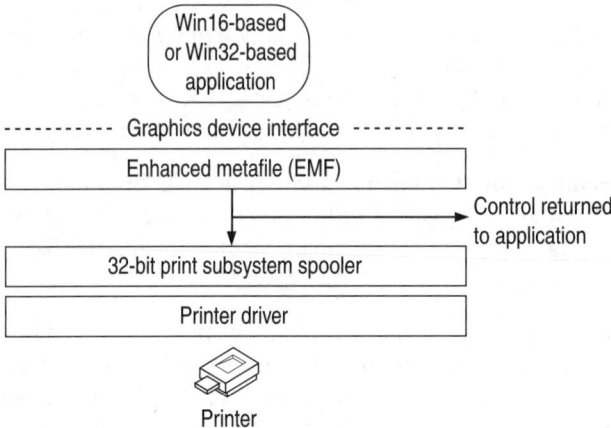

Figure 11.2   Enhanced metafile spooling in Windows 98

EMF information is generated by the Graphics Device Interface (GDI) before spooling. After the GDI creates the EMF, control is returned to the application. The 32-bit printing subsystem spooler interprets the EMF in a background thread and sends the information to the printer driver. This returns control to the application faster than waiting for the printer driver to interpret all printer calls directly.

Printing Support for MS-DOS-based Applications

In Windows 98, MS-DOS-based applications spool directly to the 32-bit Windows 98 print spooler. This support is integrated into a print spooler virtual device, which takes the output destined for a printer port and places it in the Windows 98 print spooler before sending the data to the printer. This functionality works with all existing MS-DOS-based applications and results in quicker return-to-application time.

Although MS-DOS-based applications do not benefit from EMF spooling, users will not encounter device contention issues, and will instead experience smoother background printing and improved printing performance.

Printer Drivers

The Windows 98 device driver model makes it easy for printer manufacturers to create drivers for their printers. The printer driver model is composed of two parts: a universal driver and a minidriver. The universal printer driver, supplied by Windows 98, communicates with the other parts of the operating system and includes information pertinent to all printers. Between the universal printer driver and the printers are minidrivers, written by printer manufacturers, that transmit information between the universal printer driver and a specific make and model of printer. These minidrivers are installed when you add a local or network printer. Figure 11.3 illustrates the Windows 98 printer driver model.

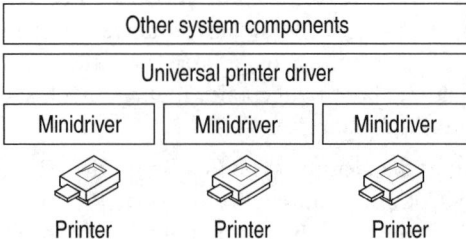

Figure 11.3   The Windows 98 printer driver model

Microsoft cooperates with printer manufacturers to ensure the compatibility of minidrivers. Microsoft worked closely with Adobe Systems, for example, to develop the PostScript driver. The following sections describe the universal printer driver and the PostScript driver included with Windows 98.

Universal Printer Driver

The Windows 98 universal printer driver supports mainstream page description languages, including HP page composition language (PCL), Epson ESC P/2, Canon CaPSL, Lexmark PPDS, monochrome HP GL/2, and most of the older dot-matrix technologies.

The universal printer driver fully supports device-resident Intellifont and TrueType scalable device fonts. It also supports downloading TrueType font outlines to HP PCL printers as bitmap soft fonts or as graphics, and supports character sets with more than 256 characters. For more information about fonts, see "Font Support in Windows 98" later in this chapter.

The universal printer driver includes the following:

- Full 600 dots per inch (dpi) support, with support for future expandability to higher resolutions.
- Monochrome HP GL/2 support, providing full LaserJet 4 functionality.

- Generic Text support using TTY.drv.

- Support for Epson ESC P/2 raster graphics directly through the universal driver, rather than through minidrivers.

- Easy-to-use **Properties** dialog boxes for configuring printer driver settings.

PostScript Driver

The PostScript driver included with Windows 98 offers the following features:

- PostScript Level 2 support. This feature is automatically enabled for printers reporting as Level 2 from their PostScript printer description (PPD) file.

- Support for ICM 2.0. The PostScript driver allows the server to offload ICM to the PostScript processor to improve performance. This flexibility allows you to take advantage of image color management on either the printer or the server. For more information about image color management, see "Imaging Support in Windows 98" later in this chapter.

- Control over output data format. The PostScript driver supports CTRL+D handling, Binary Communications Protocol (BCP), Tagged Binary Communications Protocol (TBCP), and pure binary (8-bit) channels (AppleTalk).

- Support for PPD version 4.2 files. These are ASCII files that contain printer model information that drivers and other software retrieve in order to control a PostScript printer. These files cannot be edited. For compatibility, Windows Printer Description (WPD) files are still supported.

- Support for Simplified Printer Description (SPD) files. When a printer is installed, Windows 98 reads the PPD file for each PostScript printer and creates an SPD file, which is a simplified version of the PPD file containing only information used by the Windows 98 PostScript driver.

Note Windows 98 does not support editing of PPD, SPD, or INF files. If you need to change these files, contact Adobe Systems.

- Tracking of PostScript virtual memory availability in the printer. This allows you to print more complex documents.

- Easy-to-use **Properties** dialog boxes for configuring printer driver settings.

- Support for installable device options, as described in the PPD file, through the user interface.

Installing and Configuring Printers

You can install printers in Windows 98 in the following ways:

- After Setup using the Add Printer Wizard.
- During Setup when using custom setup scripts, as described in Appendix D, "Msbatch.inf Parameters for Setup Scripts."
- With Point and Print.
- With Plug and Play.

If you are upgrading from an earlier version of Windows, Windows 98 Setup automatically migrates all previously installed printers.

Standard Installation Using the Add Printer Wizard

Windows 98 provides the Add Printer Wizard to simplify installing printers, and a central place—the Printers folder—for running the wizard and for managing printing processes. You can open the Printers folder in the following ways:

- From the **Start** menu, point to **Settings**, and then click **Printers**.
- In My Computer, double-click Printers.
- In Control Panel, double-click Printers.

▶ **To install a printer with the Add Printer Wizard**.

- In the Printers folder, double-click Add Printer. The Add Printer Wizard leads you though the process of setting up and configuring a printer.

  The only difference between installing a network printer and a local printer with the Add Printer Wizard is that you must specify the path to the network printer or browse to find its network location.

Printing from the Active Desktop

Once you have installed a printer, you can create a shortcut to it on your Active Desktop. This enables you to quickly print a document by simply dragging it onto the shortcut you create.

▶ **To print a document from the Active Desktop**

1. On the **Start** menu, point to **Settings**, and then click **Printers**.

2. Right-click the printer's icon and drag it onto the Active Desktop.

3. Click **Create Shortcut(s) Here**.

4. Drag a document from My Documents, Windows Explorer, or My Computer onto the printer shortcut on your Active Desktop.

Remote Installation Using Point and Print

Point and Print allows users to install a printer over a network by providing printer driver information. A user "points" to a print server in one of three ways:

- By using the Add Printer Wizard and browsing to or typing the path of the print server.

- By typing the path of the print server in the **Run** dialog box on the **Start** menu.

- By opening the print server's print queue using Network Neighborhood or Windows Explorer.

The type of information retrieved depends on the type of print server to which you connect and can include the following:

- Printer driver files.

- The name of the server on which printer driver files are stored.

- Printer model information, which specifies which printer driver to retrieve from the Windows directory on a local computer or on the network.

Configuring a Windows 98 Print Server for Point and Print

A computer running Windows 98 can function as a print server by providing printer drivers and settings (such as paper size, memory, and page orientation) to another computer running Windows 98. You must share the printer, enabling file and print sharing services for either Microsoft networks or NetWare networks. You can apply user-level security to the shared printer. For information, see Chapter 9, "Security," and Chapter 18, "Logon, Browsing, and Resource Sharing."

Configuring a Windows NT Print Server for Point and Print

A computer running Windows 98 can connect to a Windows NT print server to retrieve Point and Print information. The printer model name on the Windows NT print server must be the same as the printer model name in the Windows 98 INF files. If the printer model names are the same, Windows 98 installs the printer driver files from the directory on the local computer or network location from which Windows 98 was installed. If these names are not the same, Windows 98 prompts you for the printer model. Windows 98 cannot retrieve the printer settings from a Windows NT print server, so you need to adjust printer settings, such as paper size, on the computer running Windows 98.

A Microsoft Windows NT Client Access License is required if the computer running Windows 98 will be connecting to print servers running Windows NT Server. For information, see Chapter 16, "Windows 98 on Microsoft Networks," or contact your Microsoft reseller.

Configuring a NetWare Print Server for Point and Print

A client computer running Windows 98 can connect to an appropriately configured NetWare print server to retrieve printer driver files. You can configure a NetWare print server to store printer driver files in the NetWare bindery or the Novell Directory Services (NDS) directory tree, or to store references in the bindery or directory tree to other print servers that store the printer drivers. To configure the NetWare print server for the bindery, you must have Supervisor privileges on the server, and the client computer must be running Client for NetWare Networks. You must also have Supervisor privileges to the Root object on the NDS tree the first time you implement Point and Print on that NDS tree. However, you do not need Supervisor privileges for subsequent implementations of Point and Print on that NDS tree.

When requested, the NetWare print server automatically copies the printer drivers to the specified path on the client computer running Windows 98. You should specify the printer driver path before you specify a model name. Because printer settings cannot be retrieved from a NetWare print server, you need to adjust printer settings, such as paper size, on the computer running Windows 98.

▶ **To configure the NetWare 3.*x* server for Point and Print using the Microsoft Client for NetWare Networks**

1. Log on as Supervisor.

2. On the Desktop, right-click **Network Neighborhood**, and then click **Find Computer**.

3. In the **Find Computer** dialog box, type the name of the print server, and then click **Find Now**. Double-click its icon in the **Name** list box.

4. In the print server's dialog box, right-click the icon for the printer, and then click **Point and Print Setup**.

5. In the context menu, click **Set Driver Path**.

6. Type the universal naming convention (UNC) path (in the form *server**volume**directory*) for the driver files. For example:

   ```
   \\novsvr\sys\drivers\epson24
   ```

7. Right-click the **Printer** icon, and then click **Point and Print Setup**.

8. In the context menu, click **Set Printer Model**.

9. In the **Select** dialog box, click the printer manufacturer in the **Manufacturers** list and the printer in the **Models** list. Click **OK**.

▶ **To configure the NetWare 3.x server for Point and Print using the Microsoft Service for NDS**

1. On the Desktop, double click **Network Neighborhood**, and then right-click the printer you want to configure.

2. Click Properties, and then click the **Point and Print Setup** tab.

Note To use the **Point and Print Setup** tab, you must be a trustee for the printer object. You must also have the Supervisor Object and Supervisor Property rights for the printer.

---

3. Click **Enable Point and Print**.

4. In the text box, type the UNC path to a directory where the drivers are stored. Make sure you have Write access to this folder, and that your users have Read access to it.

5. Click **Set Printer Model**, and then select the appropriate driver from the list of manufacturers and models.

6. Click **OK** to apply the changes and copy the files to the server.

Installing a NetWare Printer with Point and Print

After you have configured the NetWare print server to store Point and Print information, you can connect to a printer on the NetWare print server using the following procedure.

▶ **To use Point and Print to connect to a NetWare printer**

1. In Network Neighborhood, double-click the NetWare server icon.

2. Drag the print queue from the NetWare server window to your Printers folder.

3. Follow the online instructions. The Add Printer Wizard prompts you to type a name for this printer.

   Windows 98 automatically copies the files for the printer driver (including DRV, DLL, HLP, and other files, as needed) to the Windows System directory.

Automatic Installation Using Plug and Play

For Plug and Play–compliant printers, all you need to do is plug the printer cable into a port, make sure the printer is turned on, and start Windows 98. The printer reports its device ID to Windows 98, which searches INF files to find the ID that matches the values reported by the printer, and then proceeds with installation in the following ways:

- If an exact match is found, Windows 98 automatically installs the correct printer support.

- If an exact match is not found, but a compatible printer driver is found, Windows 98 displays a dialog box showing that the printer was found and that a compatible printer driver is available. You can then provide a disk containing a Windows 98 printer driver that is an exact match or ask Windows 98 to install the compatible driver it has found.

If you do not want Windows 98 to install a driver at all, you still need to walk through the wizard, however you can tell it to look for an existing driver (related to a device other than your printer). When the wizard displays the final dialog box, you will get the message "Windows has not installed a driver for this device...Unknown Device." You can click **Finish** at this point to complete the wizard. Windows 98 automatically determines the best printer driver to use.

Additional Printer Support

This section describes additional software tools supplied with Windows 98 to support printing from several commonly used third-party network print servers.

Using the Hewlett-Packard JetAdmin Utility

Windows 98 includes the latest version (2.54) of the Hewlett-Packard JetAdmin utility, an administrative tool used to install and configure HP printers connected to a network using an HP JetDirect print server. This new version supports the latest printer models from HP. The HP JetAdmin utility lets you:

- Set up a new interface and printer or change an existing configuration.

- Modify printer settings.

- Configure the HP JetDirect interface and printer.

- Add or remove print queues.

- Select drivers to install and assign Windows 98 printer drivers to a network printer.

- Select the printer operating mode and set the printer description.

For more information about this product, see HP JetAdmin Help.

Installing JetAdmin 2.54 from the Compact Disc

You install JetAdmin 2.54 from the Windows 98 compact disc. It is located in the Drivers\Printers\Jetadmin directory. The installation instructions are in the Jareadme.txt file in the Disk1 folder of this directory.

Note Before installing this version of JetAdmin, you should remove any previous versions from your computer. To do so, in Control Panel, click Add/Remove Programs, and then select the previous version of JetAdmin that you want to remove.

Using the Microsoft Remote Procedure Call Print Provider

A Windows 98 client computer can obtain complete information about print jobs from a Windows NT print server by using the Microsoft Remote Procedure Call (RPC) Print Provider utility supplied with Windows 98. The Microsoft RPC Print Provider provides the full set of Win32 APIs required for a Windows 98 client computer to administer printer queues on a Windows NT server.

The Microsoft RPC Print Provider is located on the Microsoft Windows 98 Resource Kit compact disc in the Netadmin\Rpcpp folder. For instructions on installing and using this utility, right-click the Rpcpp.txt file in that folder, and then follow the instructions.

Printing Documents

In Windows 98, you can print documents in three ways.

▶ **To print a document**

- If the document is open, on the **File** menu, click **Print**.

  –Or–

  If the document is not open, right-click the document in Windows Explorer, and then click **Print**.

  –Or–

  Drag the document icon onto the printer icon in the Printers folder or on your Active Desktop.

Tip To create a printer icon on your Active Desktop, use the right mouse button to drag a printer's icon from the Printers folder to the Active Desktop, and then click **Create Shortcut(s) Here** on the pop-up menu.

With the Microsoft protected-mode network clients and networks from other vendors supporting UNC paths, you no longer need a physical redirection to a network printer in order to print.

Some 16-bit applications do not work with UNC printer names. If you use a network client that does not support UNC connections, or if you need to have a redirected LPT port to support printing from a particular application, you can still make a connection to a printer by using the appropriate network commands (such as **net use lpt1:** *server**printer* or **capture lpt1:**).

▶ **To change printer settings**

1. On the **Start** menu, point to **Settings**, and then click **Printers**.

    –Or–

    In Control Panel, double-click Printers.

2. Right-click the printer icon, and then in the context menu, click **Properties**.

Managing Printer Queues

You can use the **Print Queue** dialog box to manage printer queues and print jobs remotely. For example, if you have administrative privileges for a printer, you can pause and purge printer queues; users can pause or purge their own print jobs.

▶ **To view documents waiting to be printed**

*   In the Printers folder or on the Active Desktop, click the icon for the printer.

    This shows the print queue and the print jobs it contains.

Deferred Printing Support

Windows 98 supports deferred printing to network printers. If a network printer is not available, a user can still generate the print job, which is stored on the user's computer for later printing. This feature is useful when a portable computer has been removed from its docking station, when working at a remote site, or when a network printer connection is temporarily lost because of network or printer problems.

If a network printer is not available, or if a portable computer has been removed from its docking station, that printer icon will be dimmed, and that printer will be set to work offline. Any jobs printed to that printer are stored on the user's hard disk.

You can set any printer in the Printers folder to work offline using the following procedure.

▶ **To prepare for deferred print jobs**

1. On the **Start** menu, point to **Settings**, and then click **Printers**.

    –Or–

    In Control Panel, double-click Printers.

2. Right-click the printer icon, and then click **Use Printer Offline**. The printer will be dimmed.

Imaging Support in Windows 98

Windows 98 includes extensive new features for color management and still imaging.

Image Color Matching (ICM) 2.0 support. New ICM 2.0 standards ensure the integrity and consistency of colors, from source to display to output WYSIWYG. ICM 2.0 also has a faster default Color Management Module (CMM); supports up to eight channel color spaces, including RGB, sRGB, and CMYK; and provides flexible profile management APIs.

Images from TWAIN-compliant devices. You can now acquire images from TWAIN-compliant input devices, such as scanners or still image digital cameras, directly into TWAIN-compliant applications, such as Microsoft Picture It!™ The new architecture ensures communication between applications and input devices.

Still imaging architecture and device support. Windows 98 includes a new architecture for still image devices. The Windows 98 still imaging architecture (STI) enables device manufacturers to enhance the user's experience with still image devices. STI-compliant devices appear in Control Panel upon installation. The devices' Properties provide for device configuration and testing.

Image Color Matching 2.0 Support

Image Color Matching (ICM) 2.0 ensures the consistency and integrity of colors throughout the publishing process. Figure 11.4 outlines a typical publishing process.

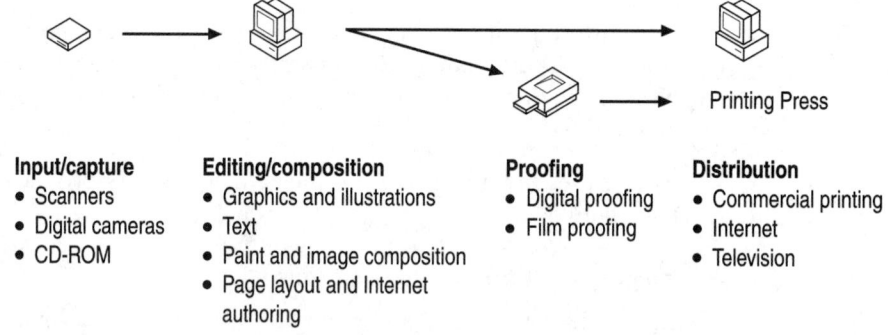

Printing Press

Input/capture	Editing/composition	Proofing	Distribution
• Scanners	• Graphics and illustrations	• Digital proofing	• Commercial printing
• Digital cameras	• Text	• Film proofing	• Internet
• CD-ROM	• Paint and image composition		• Television
	• Page layout and Internet authoring		

Figure 11.4   The publishing process

In this process, images captured from input devices, such as scanners and still image digital cameras, are brought together in editing and composition applications, such as Imaging for Windows by Eastman Kodak, and Microsoft Picture It! Graphic designers use a variety of tools and proofing systems to simulate the final output, which can take the form of film plates for delivery to commercial printing presses, output to a color printer, or graphics for the Internet or corporate intranet.

ICM 2.0 ensures the consistent reproduction of colors throughout this process. When you scan or otherwise acquire an image from an input device, ICM 2.0 maintains the image's original color mapping, from display and editing in applications through printed or electronic output. In other words, ICM 2.0 ensures that the original image colors are accurately interpreted by an input device, displayed on a monitor, and output to a printed or electronic format.

Input devices must either provide an International Color Consortium (ICC) color profile with an acquired image or output sRGB, using the sRGB profile provided by Windows 98. This ensures that display and output devices can properly interpret the color characteristics of the acquired image. Monitors must also include their own color profile, as must printer and other output devices. All components must have an associated color profile so that ICM can manage the color continuity throughout the entire image editing process.

For detailed information about ICM 2.0, see "Technical Notes on Imaging" later in this chapter.

TWAIN Support

TWAIN is an industry-standard software protocol and API that provides easy integration of image data between input devices, such as scanners and still image digital cameras, and software applications. Using TWAIN, Windows 98 and Windows NT 5.0 share the same APIs and architecture for supporting input devices.

Communicating with TWAIN

TWAIN enables users to acquire images directly from an input device while within a TWAIN-compliant application. Hardware vendors can write a single TWAIN-compliant driver for a device, which can then be used by all TWAIN-compliant applications to acquire images. Figure 11.5 presents a simple overview of the relationship between input devices and applications using TWAIN.

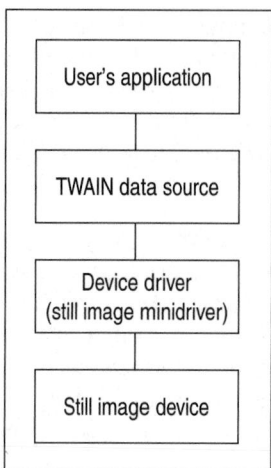

Figure 11.5   TWAIN architectural overview

Figure 11.5 uses a four-layer protocol to illustrate how applications and input devices communicate using TWAIN. Table 11.1 outlines the four-layer protocol and its function.

Table 11.1   TWAIN architectural layer functions

Architectural layer	Function
User's application	Represents the user's application, such as Microsoft Picture It!, used to scan or otherwise acquire an image from a TWAIN-compliant input device, such as a scanner or still image digital camera.. The application requesting an image sends the request to the TWAIN data source.
TWAIN data source	Implements instructions and communications required for transferring the image.
Device driver	Represents the input device.
	The software elements that control acquisitions, called data sources, reside in this layer. A data source is typically a TWAIN-compliant driver written by a hardware vendor to get data from a hardware device and pass it to a TWAIN-compliant application.
Still image device	Represents a physical input device, such as a scanner or still image digital camera.

For a more detailed schematic and discussion of TWAIN's implementation in the Windows 98 STI, see "Technical Notes on Imaging" later in this chapter.

Acquiring Images from within TWAIN-Compliant Applications

TWAIN-compliant applications present two commands on the **File** menu for acquiring images from TWAIN-compliant input devices: **Select Source**, and **Acquire** or **Scan**.

The **Select Source** command allows a user to select a specific input device from which to acquire the image. The **Select Source** dialog box lets the user select from the available input devices.

The **Acquire** or **Scan** command begins the process of transferring image data from the selected or default input device to the application. When a user selects this command, a TWAIN-compliant input device will display that device's user interface, allowing the user to configure device-specific options.

Support for Scanners and Still Image Devices

The Windows 98 STI incorporates ICM 2.0 and TWAIN APIs to provide broad support for a variety of still image devices, including physical devices such as scanners and still image digital cameras, and logical devices, such as an image database.

You can now use Plug and Play to install physical devices easily. You can also install, configure, and test specific devices using the new Scanners and Cameras option or the Add New Hardware option in Control Panel. You can install still image devices from serial, parallel, SCSI, and universal serial bus (USB) ports.

Note The Scanners and Cameras option in Control Panel does not appear until you have installed a Plug and Play–compliant still image device or installed a still image device using the Add New Hardware option in Control Panel.

The new still imaging architecture provides simple, seamless transfer of image data between still image devices and applications. You can select input devices, configure device options, and acquire images directly from within any TWAIN-compliant authoring application, or from within any TWAIN-compliant editing application, such as Adobe PhotoShop. For more information about the still imaging architecture, navigate to **http://www.microsoft.com/hwdev/desinit/** and follow the link for "WDM Still Image Architecture."

For a detailed schematic and discussion of the still imaging architecture, see "Technical Notes on Imaging" later in this chapter.

Win32 Driver Model

The new Win32 Driver Model (WDM) defines a device-driver architecture that provides a common set of I/O services understood by both Windows 98 and future versions of Windows NT. With WDM, developers writing drivers for scanners and still image digital cameras can write a single bus driver or device driver for both operating systems.

For information about support for still imaging devices and drivers in WDM, see Chapter 30, "Hardware Management."

Installing Devices

Windows 98 uses a new INF format for installing still image devices. You can install a scanner, still image digital camera, or other physical still image device in the following ways:

- Using Plug and Play.
- Using the Add New Hardware option in Control Panel or the new Scanners and Cameras option in Control Panel.

Installing Plug and Play Devices

For Plug and Play–compliant still image devices, all you need to do is plug the device into the appropriate port and start Windows 98. The device reports its device ID to Windows 98, which searches INF files to find the ID that matches the values reported by the device.

- If the device ID matches, Windows 98 automatically installs the correct drivers and support for the device.
- If the device ID does not match, but a compatible driver is found, Windows 98 displays a New Hardware Found dialog box showing that information. You can then:
  - Provide a disk containing the device manufacturer's INF file.
  - Instruct Windows 98 to install the compatible driver it has found.
  - Instruct Windows 98 not to install a driver at all.

Installing non–Plug and Play Devices Using the Installation Wizard

You can install non–Plug and Play still image devices using the Add New Hardware option in Control Panel, or using the new Scanners and Cameras option in Control Panel.

If you have previously installed a still image device, click the Scanners and Cameras option in Control Panel to install the new device, and then respond to the wizard.

If you have not previously installed a still image device, there is no Scanners and Cameras option in Control Panel. Instead, click the Add New Hardware option, and then respond to the Add New Hardware Wizard to add the still image device. When the wizard prompts you, supply the location (on a floppy disk, compact disc, or network server) of the INF file provided by the device's manufacturer.

Configuring Devices

You can use the Scanners and Cameras option in Control Panel to configure device-specific options (such as the default size or resolution for scanned images) for an installed still image device. Select the device you want to configure, and then specify options on the **Properties** tab for that device.

Testing Devices

You can use the Scanners and Cameras option in Control Panel to test a still image device's installation and operation (for example, to calibrate a scanner or scan a test page).

Associating Applications with Device Events

The Windows 98 still image architecture allows you to associate events from a still image device with applications. For example, you can associate data transfer from a scanner with Kodak Imaging. When you begin scanning an image, the still image architecture starts Kodak Imaging and transfers the image data to Kodak Imaging automatically.

To associate applications with device events, use the **Events** tab of the new Scanners and Cameras option in Control Panel.

Technical Notes on Imaging

This section discusses technical issues about still imaging support in Windows 98.

Image Color Matching 2.0

Image Color Matching (ICM) 2.0 enhances the functionality and performance of ICM 1.0, introduced in Windows 95, while maintaining compatibility. ICM 2.0 supports all of ICM 1.0's capabilities and extends them to include:

- Support for sRGB as the default color space for images without embedded ICC profiles or specifically tagged color information.
- Support for more color spaces, such as CMYK and CIELAB, a theoretical color space defined by the Commission Internationale de L'Eclairage.

- Support for up to eight color channels for enhanced printing processes, such as HiFi Color.

- A faster, higher-quality default Color Management Module (CMM) and support for multiple CMMs.

- Cross-platform compatibility through ICC profiles and the ability to define custom profiles.

With ICM 2.0, applications can support either of two levels of API—one for RGB and one for multiple color spaces. This allows users to manage different device profiles and select alternate CMMs. Figure 11.6 illustrates the architecture of the ICM 2.0 API.

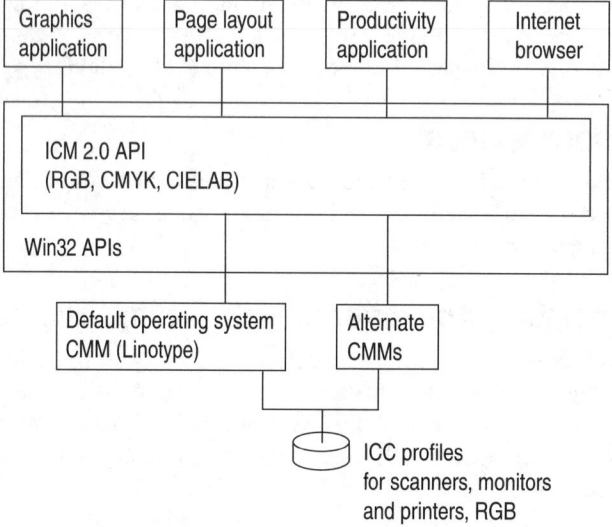

Figure 11.6   ICM 2.0 architectural overview

For detailed information and specifications on ICM 2.0, visit the Microsoft SDK Web site at **http://www.microsoft.com/msdn/sdk/**.

TWAIN

Hardware vendors can write only one TWAIN-compliant driver for a device, from that device which is then used by all TWAIN-compliant applications when acquiring images. Application developers no longer need to write and support device-specific drivers. Figure 11.7 presents a detailed schematic of the relationship between TWAIN-compliant input devices and applications in the Windows 98 still imaging architecture (STI).

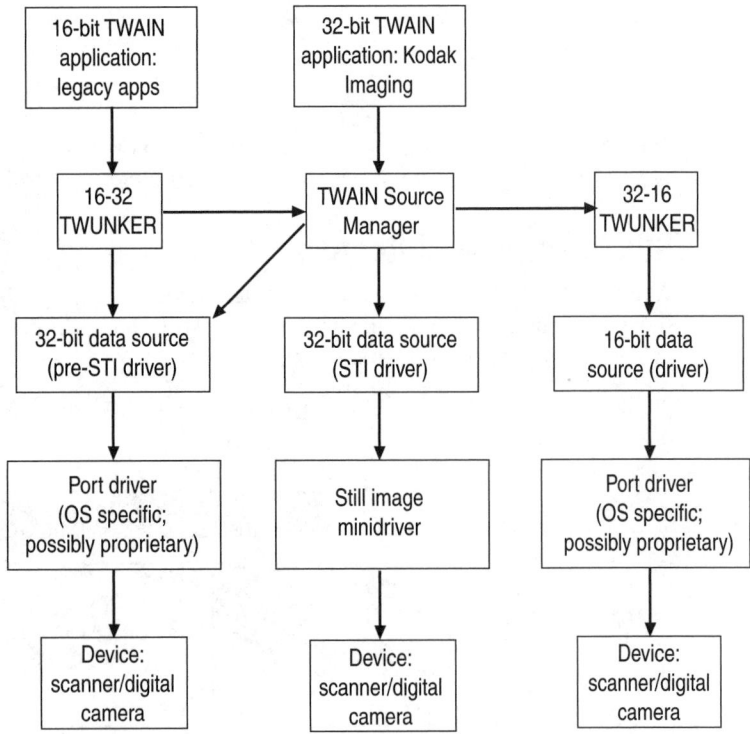

Figure 11.7   TWAIN implementation in the Windows 98 still imaging architecture

Figure 11.7 uses the following four general groupings of components to illustrate how TWAIN-compliant applications and input devices communicate. Following are descriptions of these components:

- The top component contains 16-bit and 32-bit TWAIN-compliant applications, such as Microsoft Picture It! These applications communicate with input devices through the TWAIN Source Manager and TWUNKERs. A *TWUNKER* is a virtual device that allows communications between 32-bit and 16-bit applications.

- The next component level, the TWAIN Source Manager and TWUNKERs, use TWAIN APIs to provide communication between applications and TWAIN-compliant data sources, such as input devices and drivers. The TWAIN Source Manager is implemented as a Windows DLL that can manage simultaneous sessions between multiple applications and multiple input devices. The 16-32 and 32-16 TWUNKERs translate commands and data between 16-bit and 32-bit applications.

- The TWAIN data sources are essentially 16-bit and 32-bit drivers for TWAIN-compliant input devices provided by hardware vendors. These drivers enable Plug and Play installation of input devices and configuration of device-specific options.

- Finally, the still image minidriver represents STI APIs and low-level device minidrivers that convert device-specific commands into hardware commands and actions.

For more detailed information and specifications on TWAIN, visit the TWAIN Working Group Web site at **http://www.twain.org/**.

Still Imaging Architecture

Windows 98 supports physical still image devices, such as flatbed scanners, sheet-fed scanners, handheld scanners, and still image digital cameras, as well as such logical devices as image databases.

Figure 11.8 provides a detailed schematic of the still imaging architecture in Windows 98.

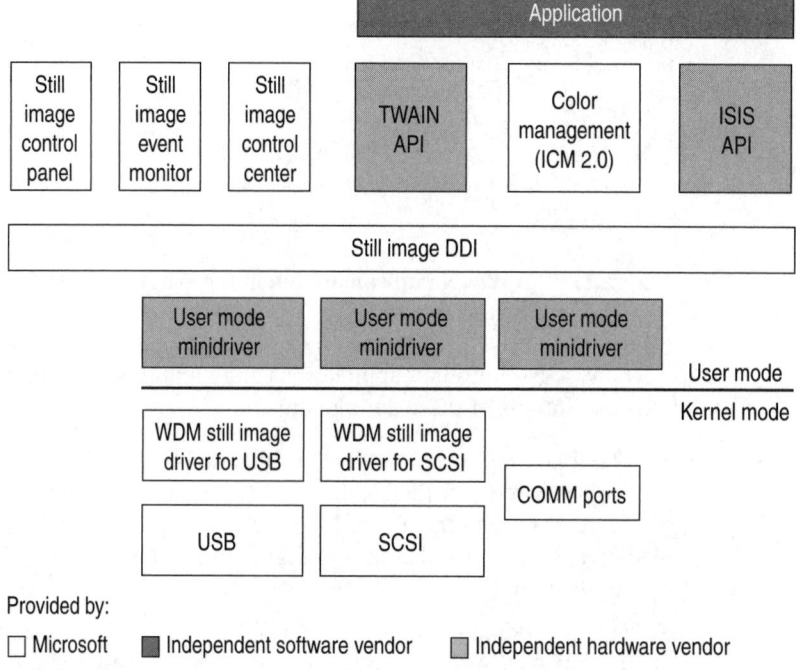

Figure 11.8   The Windows 98 still image architecture (STI)

The following discussion describes each of these components.

TWAIN or other API. This component represents the TWAIN or other API that acquires and interprets data from still image devices.

ICM 2.0 API. The ICM 2.0 API maintains device color profiles and provides for color space conversion. To define color output from a scanned image, a scanner must either create sRGB output or embed the ICC profile for the image into the image file. A scanner can create sRGB output in two ways:

- The scanner data source has a proprietary system that corrects from the scanner color space to sRGB. This method is not flexible and requires additional code from the scanner manufacturer that may not be as good as, and may not be compatible with, the method that the operating system uses to generate colors.

- The scanner data source calls into ICM, passes ICM the appropriate scanner profile, and points it to the sRGB profile. ICM then generates sRGB output that the device can pass onto the application.

Still image control panel. This component represents the Scanners and Cameras option in Control Panel. The Scanners and Cameras option lets you install, remove, and test still image devices. You can also associate specific still image device events with the applications to be notified of these events. The Scanners and Cameras option does not appear in Control Panel until you have installed a Plug and Play–compliant still image device or installed a still image device using the Add New Hardware option in Control Panel.

Still image event monitor. This component works behind the scenes to detect events coming from still image devices and dispatch those events to the still image control center.

Still image control center. This component determines how events initiated by still image devices are distributed to applications. The Scanners and Cameras option in Control Panel lets you configure specific device event or application associations.

Still image device driver interface (DDI). This component provides communications with a specific still image device, including enumeration, device capabilities, data and command I/O, and notification of device events, including polling for device activity. The still image DDI uses ICM 2.0 as a repository for a given device's color profile.

The still image DDI provides support for SCSI, parallel, serial, IR, and USB devices. Support for IEEE 1394 and multifunction peripherals (MFP) devices is also incorporated using the Win32 Driver Model (WDM).

User-mode minidrivers. These components are supplied by still image device manufacturers to implement device-specific DDI functionality (such as test, status, and data I/O). They inform the DDI of the device's capabilities and communicate with the specific kernel device driver.

WDM still image drivers. These components use the new Win32 Driver Model to provide a mechanism for packaging a command or data for delivery on a USB or SCSI bus.

Font Support in Windows 98

Fonts are used to print text, display text on screen, and send text to other output devices. Windows 98 provides a set of Win32-based functions that developers can use to install, select, and query different fonts.

Understanding Fonts

Windows 98 provides four basic kinds of fonts, which are categorized according to how the fonts are rendered for screen or print output:

- TrueType fonts are stored as mathematical models that define the outline of each character. They are much easier to work with than vector fonts because they appear the same on the screen as they do on the printed page. TrueType fonts can be scaled and rotated.

  You can distinguish TrueType fonts by the "TT" designation. Fonts without this designation are bitmap fonts.

- Raster fonts are stored in files as bitmaps and are rendered as an array of dots for displaying on the screen and printing on paper. Raster fonts cannot be cleanly scaled or rotated.

- Vector fonts are rendered from a mathematical model, in which each character is defined as a set of lines drawn between points. Vector fonts can be scaled to any size or aspect ratio. Windows 98 provides one vector font (Modern.fon) to ensure backward compatibility with plotter devices. It is installed in the \Windows\Fonts folder as a hidden file.

- OpenType fonts can be used with PostScript outlines only if you have installed Adobe Type Manager (ATM) on your computer. For information about obtaining and installing ATM, contact Adobe Systems.

Table 11.2 shows the types of fonts that can be printed on different kinds of printers.

Table 11.2   Printer and font compatibility

Printer type	Device fonts	Raster fonts	Vector fonts	TrueType fonts
Dot matrix	X	X	–	X
HP PCL	X	–	X	X
PostScript	X	–	X	X
Plotter	X	–	X	–

Font File Names and File Types

Raster and vector font files have .fon file name extensions. TrueType font files have .ttf file name extensions.

In Windows 98, information in the registry points to a single TTF file for TrueType fonts. In addition, Windows 98 includes a hidden file named Ttfcache that contains FOT type data for TrueType fonts to ensure backward compatibility with Windows 3.1. There are two files for each TrueType font in Windows 3.1: the FOT file contains a relatively short header with pointer information, and the TTF file contains the actual font data.

How Windows 98 Loads Fonts

In Windows 98, the locations for all fonts are stored only in the registry. Fonts are moved automatically when an application created for an earlier version of Windows installs a new font in the [fonts] section of Win.ini.

When Windows 98 starts, it loads the raster fonts and TrueType fonts listed in the registry. Following are descriptions of these components:

- The raster fonts are resolution-dependent and are listed in the registry key named **Hkey_Current_Config\Display\Fonts**. This supports multiple docking scenarios for portable computers in which there can be a different resolution on the LCD screen from the one on the docking station. The master list of all possible resolutions for raster fonts is stored in the registry under the following key:

  Hkey_Local_Machine\Software\Microsoft\Windows\CurrentVersion\Font size

- The TrueType fonts are loaded from the location specified in the following key:

  Hkey_Local_Machine\Software\Microsoft\Windows\CurrentVersion\Fonts

Printer drivers, which are loaded later in the startup process, look in Win.ini to load any available soft fonts. These fonts appear within an application's list of available fonts.

Note You can install approximately 1,000 TrueType fonts in Windows 98. Almost all of the installed fonts can be used simultaneously, and the same number can be printed in the same document. The 1,000-font maximum occurs because of the size of registry keys and available storage space for font names in the Graphics Device Interface (GDI).

How Windows 98 Matches Fonts

Windows 98 uses three methods of font matching: table mapping, numeric classification, and manual.

Basic Rules for Font Matching

When an application requests characters to print or display, Windows 98 must find the appropriate font to use from among the fonts installed on your computer. Finding the font can be complex. For example, a document might contain fonts that are not available on the current printer, or there may be more than one font with the same name installed on the computer.

Windows 98 uses the following basic rules for matching a font:

- If the font is a TrueType font, TrueType renders the character, and the result is sent to the display or to the printer.
- If the font is not a TrueType font, Windows 98 uses the font mapping table to determine the most appropriate device font to use.

Font Mapping Table

When Windows 98 uses the font mapping table to match screen fonts to printer fonts, the characteristics used to find the closest match are, in descending order of importance: the character set, the pitch (variable versus fixed), family, typeface name, height, width, weight, slant, underline, and strikethrough. If the necessary size and bitmap are available, font mapping proceeds in the following sequence:

1. Use the font found in the printer's ROM.
2. Use the font found in the printer's cartridge slot.
3. Use the downloadable soft font.
4. Use the TrueType font.

Note The Windows 98 search algorithm for finding fonts is the same as the one in Windows 95 and Windows 3.1.

Manual Matching

You can manually choose from among fonts by comparing their similarities in the Fonts folder.

▶ **To manually match fonts**

1. In Control Panel, double-click Fonts.

2. Click the **View** menu, and then click **List Fonts By Similarity**.

   In general, if you choose a TrueType font, Windows 98 sorts the list of fonts in descending order, with the least similar font listed last.

What Happens if a TrueType Font Becomes Corrupted?

If a TrueType font becomes corrupted, Windows 98 marks that font as unavailable during the remainder of that Windows session and prevents it from being rendered any longer. You can choose to uninstall the font at that point.

Installing Fonts

In Windows 98, fonts are installed on your computer in several ways:

- Windows 98 automatically installs its screen fonts and TrueType fonts during Setup.

- Some applications install soft fonts on your computer as part of the application Setup process.

- You can install additional TrueType or other soft fonts from disks or network locations.

- You can install printer-resident fonts and cartridge fonts using the printer's **Properties** sheets in the Printers folder.

You can view the fonts installed on your computer by opening the Fonts option in Control Panel. The Fonts folder lets you view fonts, compare fonts by similarity, and install new fonts from disks or network locations.

You can remove fonts by dragging their font icons from the Fonts folder to the Recycle Bin.

For more information about adding fonts, in the Windows 98 Help index, search for **adding fonts**.

Installing Soft Fonts from Disks or Network Locations

You can use the following procedure to install soft fonts from disks or network locations.

Note If you are installing soft fonts from a disk that includes an installation utility supplied by the vendor, you may not need to use the following procedure. The installation utility may automatically install the fonts in Windows 98. Consult the documentation supplied by the vendor.

▶ **To install soft fonts from disks or a network location**

1. In Control Panel, double-click Fonts.

2. Click the **File** menu, and then click **Install New Font**.

3. In the **Add Fonts** dialog box, use the **Folders** and **Drives** boxes to specify the drive and folder containing the fonts you want to install.

4. In the **List of fonts**, select the fonts you want to install, and then click **OK**.

Installing Printer-Resident and Cartridge Fonts

You can also install printer-resident or cartridge fonts by using the installation utility (such as HP JetAdmin) that came with the cartridge or printer, if any, or by using a printer's **Properties** sheets in the Printers folder.

▶ **To open the Printers folder**

- On the **Start** menu, point to **Settings**, and then click **Printers**.

  –Or–

  In Control Panel or My Computer, click the **Printers** option.

▶ **To install printer-resident or cartridge fonts**

- Use the installation utility that came with the font cartridge or printer.

  –Or–

1. In the Printers folder, right-click the printer's icon, and then in the shortcut menu, click **Properties**.

2. Click the **Fonts** tab. The options on the **Fonts** tab vary depending on the make and model of the printer, and whether any additional printer support software—such as HP JetAdmin—is installed on your computer.

3. Select from the list of fonts or font cartridges installed on the printer, and then click **OK**.

   –Or–

   Click the **Install Printer Fonts** or similar button, and then select the fonts you want to install.

Troubleshooting Printing and Fonts

This section describes the most common problems you might encounter with printing and fonts, and explains the best ways to resolve these problems.

Troubleshooting Printing

Windows 98 provides print troubleshooting topics in Help, which you should use first to resolve printing problems. In Windows 98 Help, select the **Index** tab, and then type **print troubleshooting**. If you cannot resolve the problem by using the print troubleshooting topics in Help, check the procedures in this section.

For information on specific printer models and printing problems, read the Printers.txt file in the \Windows directory. This document describes the latest printer models and troubleshooting issues for Windows 98.

Correcting Problems with Printer Installation

This section describes conditions that may interfere with installing a printer and explains how to fix them.

No printers are listed in the Print dialog box.

If you cannot select a specific model because no list appears, verify that the printer INF file exists. The Msprint*x*.inf file in the Windows INF directory stores the information displayed in the Manufacturer and Model lists.

A file-copy error occurs during printer installation.

If an error occurs with a file copying operation while running the Add Printer Wizard, the wizard displays the specific error information, including the source and destination paths and file names it was trying to copy when the error occurred. To continue, verify the location of the specified files, and then retry the installation.

Correcting Specific Printing Problems

This section describes problems or errors that might occur when printing and explains how to fix them.

You cannot print to a local or network printer.

If you encounter this problem, do the following:

- Clear the print buffer. Turn the printer's power off, wait about five seconds, turn the printer on, and then try printing again.

- Try printing a test page.

- Verify that there is paper in the printer, the printer is not jammed, and there are no problems with the printer cartridge or toner.
- Try printing to a file.
- If you can print to a file, try copying the file to the printer port (for local printers).

▶ **To copy a file to a printer port**

- At the MS-DOS prompt, type

  copy /b *filename* lpt1:

  The switch **/b** directs the system to print a binary file.

If copying the file to the printer port prints the document correctly, the problem is in the communication between Windows 98 and the printer. Check the following (and consult your printer's documentation as needed for further information):

- Check the printer, making sure it is plugged in, turned on, and online.
- Check the printer's self-test program.
- Check the printer connection and printer cable.
- Check the printer configuration.

You cannot print because of a network-specific printing problem.

If you encounter this problem, do the following:

- Make sure other network resources are available.
- Try connecting over the network to the print server.
- Try removing and adding network protocols.

If you still cannot print, the printer driver might not be working correctly.

You cannot print because of a printer driver.

If you encounter this problem, do the following:

- Try printing using another printer driver. For example, use the Generic/Text Only Printer driver. If this works, check the version of your printer driver, and either reinstall or upgrade the driver.
- Try printing from the MS-DOS command prompt to determine whether the description for the printer driver in the registry is invalid.

▶ **To check the printer driver**

1. In the Printers folder, right-click the printer's icon, click **Properties**, and then click the **Details** tab.

2. Verify that the driver name is correct.

3. Click the **Paper** tab, and then click the **About** button. Verify that the driver version is the same as the one listed in the manual from the printer manufacturer.

▶ **To fix the registry description for the printer driver**

- Remove the current printer driver and reinstall it.

If you still cannot print, an application might be conflicting with the printer driver.

You cannot print because of an application conflict.

If you encounter this problem, do the following:

1. Try printing from a different application.

2. If successful, check the failing application's configuration, and reinstall the application if needed.

If you still cannot print, determine whether you have a spooling problem.

You cannot print because of spooler problems.

To determine whether you have a spooling problem, print directly to the port.

▶ **To disable all spooling and print directly to the port**

1. In the Printers folder, right-click the printer's icon, click **Properties**, and then click the **Details** tab.

2. Click **Spool Settings**.

3. Click **Print directly to the printer**.

You cannot print to a printer shared using a non-Microsoft print server.

Redirect LPT1 to the shared printer, and then run the Add Printer Wizard to set up the printer on LPT1. For example, if a network printer is connected to LPT1, type the following at the MS-DOS prompt:

```
net use lpt1: \\servername\sharename
```

This command depends on the network you are using. Consult your network documentation to find out how to redirect an LPT port, and then use the Add Printer Wizard in the Printers folder to set up the printer on the LPT port.

You cannot access remote NetWare servers when making a dial-up connection.

This problem occurs when the computer making the remote connection is also running File and Print Sharing for NetWare Networks. In this case, the file and printer sharing service automatically becomes the default server, but it cannot receive the information needed to find the remote servers. To avoid this problem, disable File and Printer Sharing for NetWare Networks before you make the dial-up connection.

You cannot print because of a bidirectional printer problem.

▶ **To disable bidirectional printing support**

1. In the Printers folder, right-click the printer's icon, click **Properties**, and then click the **Details** tab.
2. Click **Spool Settings**.
3. Click **Disable bi-directional support for this printer.**

If you can now print successfully, make sure you have an IEEE 1284–compliant printer cable.

Graphic images do not print correctly, or output is garbled.

If you encounter this problem, do the following:

- Disable enhanced metafile (EMF) spooling (see "Enhanced Metafile Spooling" earlier in this chapter).

- Print with a PostScript driver, if supported by the printer. If this prints, the problem is a Unidrv.dll error.

- If PostScript fails, there is either a problem with the GDI or with the application. To verify that it is an application problem, try printing another file, or try printing from another application.

- Try printing shorter jobs or fewer jobs at a time. If you are printing a long document or several documents, the spooler may be printing one page over another.

- If the graphic is in encapsulated PostScript (EPS) format, try copying the PostScript file to the printer.

- For a PostScript printer, try changing from vector-graphics to raster-graphics mode. Raster-graphics mode uses less memory.

- For a PostScript printer, try adjusting the virtual memory settings.

Pages are only partially printed.

If you encounter this problem, do the following:

- If the printed page is missing part of a graphic image, this may mean that the printer has insufficient memory. To check for insufficient printer memory, try reducing print resolution.

- Try printing the same graphic image from a different document and application.

- Check the printable region by running a print test from the printer.

- If the printed page is missing a section of text, check the font that is used, and verify that the font is valid and correctly installed (check the Fonts option).

- Try printing from a different document with the same font.

- Try printing from the same document with a different font.

- Try enabling **Print TrueType As Graphics** in the **Fonts** tab of the printer's **Properties** sheet.

- Try simplifying the page by reducing the number of objects, such as lines, or reduce the number of fonts.

Printing is slow.

You can try the following:

- Use the Disk Defragmenter utility to check for excessive hard disk fragmentation, and defragment the hard disk drive.

- Check for available disk space for temporary files.

- Check for available system resources.

- Check the printer driver and reinstall it, if necessary.

- Disable the option to send TrueType fonts as bitmaps, as described in the following procedure.

▶ **To disable printing TrueType fonts as bitmaps**

1. In the Printers folder, right-click the printer's icon, and then click **Properties**.
2. Click the **Fonts** tab, click **Print TrueType as Graphics**, and then click **OK**.

A PostScript printer does not have enough virtual memory.

▶ **To change virtual memory settings for a PostScript printer**

1. In the Printers folder, right-click the printer's icon, and then click **Properties**.
2. Click the **Device Options** tab, and then increase the value in the **Available printer memory (in KB)** box.

You cannot print more than 256 copies of a document.

Some printers cannot print more than 256 copies of a document. Consult the documentation for your printer to determine the maximum number of copies it can print. This is a known limitation for the following printer models:

- Canon Bubble-Jet BJ-230
- CoStar LabelWriter Pro
- HP LaserJet 4
- HP LaserJet 4MV PostScript
- HP LaserJet Series II

The computer stalls while printing.

▶ **To troubleshoot a computer that stalls while printing to a local printer**

1. Check the printer driver version, and reinstall the printer driver if needed.

2. Check the video driver, and reinstall the video driver if needed.

3. Check for adequate free disk space in the Temp folder.

4. Delete residual spool files, and then retry printing. (See the procedure "To clear residual spool files" later in this section.)

You send a document to the printer, but nothing is printed.

If you encounter this problem, do the following:

- Check that the system has enough free hard disk space.
- If necessary, disable enhanced metafile spooling, as described in "Enhanced Metafile Spooling" earlier in this chapter.
- Check that the spooler has cleared the unprinted spool file.

▶ **To clear residual spool files**

1. Delete spool jobs by deleting SPL files in the Windows System\Spool\Printers directory.

2. Check the Temp folder and delete all TMP files. All EMFs have file names similar to EMF*xxxxx*.tmp.

3. Restart the computer, and then try printing again. Windows 98 cleans up corrupted SPL files and their corresponding EMFs when you restart the computer.

Troubleshooting Fonts

This section describes problems with fonts that may occur and explains how to fix them.

A font does not print correctly.

▶ **To ensure that a font is installed correctly**

1. Double-click the Fonts option in Control Panel, and make sure the font is installed.
2. Double-click the font, and then click **Print**.

You can also try the following:

- Print using a different font.

- Print a different document using the same font.

- Print with a different application using the same font.

- Print to a different printer using the same font.

- Verify the printer driver version, size, and date.

- Try using a printer-resident font.

- Print to a file, and then copy the file to a port to see if the driver or the spooler is causing the problem. For example:

  copy *filename.prn* /b lpt1:

- If the printer supports PostScript and page composition language (PCL), try printing in each format.

- If the font is a TrueType font, open the printer's **Properties** sheet, and then on the **Fonts** tab, click **Print TrueType As Graphics**.

- Print with a different minidriver, such as the Generic/Text Only.

When printed, a font appears distorted or unreadable.

If you encounter this problem, do the following:

- In the application, change to Print Preview mode to see if the font appears correct on-screen.

- Change the font size to see if the problem recurs with a larger or smaller font.

- Use a different font to see if the original font is corrupted.

- Check printer resolution. Most non-TrueType fonts are optimized for 300 dpi or greater.

- Cut and paste the formatted text into another application and print it. If the font errors still occur, the problem may be related to the specific font.

- Load a PostScript driver, and select **Download As TrueType**. If the job prints correctly, the problem lies in the printer driver or Unidrv.dll. Otherwise, the problem is probably in the GDI.

- Check printer memory. If there are many fonts on the page, you may need more memory.

- For a laser printer, in the **Fonts** tab of the printer's **Properties**, click **Download TrueType fonts as bitmap soft fonts** in the **TrueType fonts** box.

When printed, fonts overlap.

- Try different resolutions, using the same printer. If a higher or lower print resolution works, the printer driver is probably at fault. Try using another printer driver.

Note If the problem persists with more than one printer driver, the problem is likely to be at the GDI level.

- For a laser printer, in the **Fonts** tab of the printer's **Properties** sheet, click **Download TrueType Fonts as Bitmap Soft Fonts**.

- Try printing the same information with a different font.

A font does not print properly when underlined or strikethrough text is selected.

- Try a different application with the same font.

- Print in a different orientation (that is, if portrait, change to landscape).

- For a laser printer, in the **Fonts** tab of the printer's **Properties** sheet, click **Download TrueType Fonts as Bitmap Soft Fonts**.

You cannot convert PostScript Type1 fonts to TrueType fonts in the Fonts folder.

Windows 98 does not support this capability. PostScript Type1 fonts will work with Windows 98, but you need to install Adobe Type Manager to manage them on the screen and install them for a printer.

Fonts are clipped when printed.

- Recheck the printable region by running a print test from the printer. (There is usually a test button on the printer; press this to run a test.) Adjust the paper orientation if you can.

- For a laser printer, in the **Fonts** tab of the printer's **Properties** sheet, click **Download TrueType Fonts as Bitmap Soft Fonts**.

- Check the printer memory settings for the driver and printer. If you are printing large images, the printer memory may be insufficient; try printing small images.

Some parts of a TrueType font are rotated, but other parts are not.

- If this occurs because the printer can only print 180-degree and 90-degree rotation (not odd-degree rotations), redefine the degrees of rotation for the image.

- For a laser printer, in the **Fonts** tab of the printer's **Properties** sheet, click **Download TrueType Fonts as Bitmap Soft Fonts**.

- If the problem is font-related, try using another character set, or download TrueType fonts to the printer, and then try again.

TrueType fonts do not display in an MS-DOS window.

Changing the displayed font to a TrueType font in an MS-DOS window sometimes does not change the font on the screen. TrueType fonts cannot be displayed in an MS-DOS window if the MS-DOS-based application is running in graphics mode. To work around this problem, run the MS-DOS-based application in text mode, and use bitmap fonts in the MS-DOS window.

▶ **To change the font used in an MS-DOS window**

1. In the MS-DOS window, click the MS-DOS icon in the upper-left corner of the window (or press ALT + SPACEBAR).

2. Click **Properties**, and then click the **Font** tab.

3. Under **Available Types**, click **Both Font Types**.

4. In the **Font Size** list, click the font size you want to display, and then click **OK**.

C H A P T E R   1 2

Multimedia

12

This chapter describes the multimedia architecture and features in Microsoft Windows 98. Windows 98 provides an immediate multimedia upgrade for users of multimedia applications and equipment in your organization. Its Plug and Play architecture makes it simple to install and operate compatible multimedia devices.

The 32-bit Windows 98 architecture ensures that Windows 98 multimedia titles can include digital video and sound of excellent quality. At the same time, Windows 98 is completely compatible with most 16-bit multimedia titles.

In This Chapter

See Also

- For information about devices, see Chapter 24, "Device Management."

- For information about Broadcast Architecture, see Chapter 13, "WebTV for Windows 98."

- For information about Internet-related multimedia applications such as NetShow, see Chapter 20, "Internet Access and Tools."

- For information about the Win32 Driver Model (WDM), see Chapter 30, "Hardware Management."

Overview of Multimedia

Windows 98 contains several components to enhance your multimedia experience, whether you are creating, displaying, or simply playing titles. The multimedia features of Windows 98 include Microsoft DirectX®, the Media Control Interface (MCI), AutoPlay, and improved support for multimedia files and devices.

DirectX

Microsoft DirectX is a set of application programming interfaces (APIs) that allow applications to gain access directly to a system's multimedia hardware. The DirectX APIs included in Windows 98 can be broken down into the following components:

- DirectDraw®, a 2-D graphics interface, supports accelerated animation techniques by providing direct access to bitmaps in off-screen display memory as well as extremely fast access to the blitting and buffer-flipping capabilities of a computer's video adapter.

- DirectSound® provides an interface between applications and an audio adapter's sound mixing, playback, and capture capabilities. .

- Direct3D®, a 3-D graphics interface, supports the 3D-rendering functionality built into modern display adapters.

- DirectPlay® allows for easy connectivity of games over a modem link or network.

- DirectInput® provides functionality to process input from joysticks, gamepads, keyboards, mice, Human Interface Device (HID) devices, and force feedback devices. Although DirectInput is similar to Windows 98 input components, it provides advanced joystick input capabilities for games and scalability for future Windows hardware input APIs and drivers.

- DirectAnimation™ makes it possible to have titles that combine different types of media, such as images, 3-D objects, sounds, movies, and text, where any or all the media types can be animated and respond to user input. DirectAnimation enables multimedia content on Web pages, on your desktop, and in standalone titles.

- DirectShow™, formerly known as ActiveMovie™, provides support for a Digital Video Disk (DVD) Navigator/Splitter, proxy filters for video and audio streams, a video mixer, a video renderer, and an audio renderer.

Media Control Interface

The *Media Control Interface* (MCI) provides applications created for Windows 98 with device-independent capabilities for controlling such media devices as audio hardware, videodisc players, and animation players. This interface works with MCI device drivers to interpret and run such MCI commands as **pause**, **play**, and **stop**.

MCI provides a set of core commands for a broad range of media devices. For example, MCI uses the same command to begin playback of a waveform-audio file, a videodisc track, and an animation sequence. It also provides extended commands for using particular device types with unique capabilities, such as a frame-based time format used in animation. For more information about MCI drivers and commands, see the *Microsoft Windows 98 Device Development Kit*.

A *device type* identifies a class of MCI devices that respond to a common set of commands. Table 12.1 lists the currently defined MCI device types.

Table 12.1   MCI device types

Device type	Description
animation	Animation device
cdaudio	Compact disc (CD) audio player
dat	Digital audio tape player
digitalvideo	Digital video in a window (not graphics device interface [GDI]–based)
other	Undefined MCI device
overlay	Overlay device (analog video in a window)
scanner	Image scanner
sequencer	MIDI sequencer
vcr	Videocassette recorder or player
videodisc	Videodisc player
waveaudio	Audio device that plays digitized waveform-audio files

Multimedia Files

A multimedia file is usually maintained in one of the formats described in Table 12.2.

Table 12.2   Multimedia file formats

Format	Corresponding file name extension
Video for Windows	.avi
Waveform-audio	.wav
Moving Picture (MPEG)	.mpg
Quick Time for Windows	.mov
Musical Instrument Digital Interface (MIDI)	.mid

Multimedia files are stored on a compact disc, a local hard disk drive, a network file server, or another storage medium. The amount of data that the storage medium can continuously supply to the file system for streaming formats constrains the playback quality.

A multimedia data stream (such as an AVI file) generally contains multiple components, such as digital-video data, audio data, text, and perhaps other data (such as hot spot information, additional audio tracks, and so on). As multimedia information is read from the CD-ROM drive, the multimedia subsystem determines what the data stream contains and then separates and routes the data accordingly.

To provide the best possible performance from double-speed and faster CD-ROM drives, Windows 98 includes the 32-bit CD-ROM file system (CDFS) for reading files from CD-ROM drives quickly and efficiently. For more information about CDFS, see Chapter 26, "Performance Tuning," and Chapter 28, "Windows 98 Architecture."

CDFS replaces most Windows version 3.1 MSCDEX drivers.

Support for Multimedia Devices

Built-in support for common multimedia authoring devices makes it easy to set up a computer for *step capture*, a process in which a user captures digital-video data one frame at a time; the data is usually compressed later. This is a slow process, but it results in the highest possible quality of digital video.

To play the contents of a videotape on a computer, you must connect the video and audio outputs from the VCR to the video-capture or overlay and to the audio inputs of the computer. You might also need to install an MCI digital-video device driver.

WDM Audio

WDM audio class architecture performs all audio processing in kernel mode. Any number of filters can be connected into the filter graph to manipulate audio/video streams. WDM also provides a more complete architecture than was possible earlier. Code common to all audio hardware on a given bus is now part of the operating system, making for faster development with more consistent results.

WDM audio supports the following features for games under Windows 98:

- Software emulation of legacy hardware to support MS-DOS-based games. WDM drivers, which run in kernel mode, provide virtual Sound Blaster Pro, MPU 401, and legacy joystick interfaces.

- DirectSound support for software-simulated 3-D sound (interaural time delay and volume).

- A wave-table General MIDI synthesizer entirely in kernel-mode software. This provides 32 voices of music synthesis with 22.05-kHz output. DirectShow, DirectMusic™, MMSYS, and virtual MPU 401 (via Sound Blaster emulation) can use the synthesizer functions. The architecture supports optimal configuration based on CPU performance and installed hardware.

- A high-quality kernel-mode software sample rate conversion (SRC) capability, which converts data streams (including composite mixes of all 11.025-kHz or 22.05-kHz sources) to the final output mix format, typically 16-bit 44.1 kHz (general SRC support includes other rates).

- A kernel-mode system-wide software mixer, which supports DirectSound, DirectShow, and MMSYS clients, as well as kernel-mode WDM filters, including CD-ROM and MIDI drivers. The mixer implements highly optimized pulse code modulation (PCM) mixing at 8-bit or 16-bit 11.025, 22.05, 44.1, and 48 kHz.

- Flexible control of the output destination. The WDM drivers can send the master 16-bit 44.1-kHz or 48-kHz or other format output to an Industry Standard Architecture (ISA), Peripheral Component Interconnect (PCI), Universal Serial Bus (USB), or IEEE 1394 audio device.

- Native 32-bit DirectSound support for simultaneous audio input and output, not dependent on 16-bit MMSYS components.

WDM audio supports the following features for CD and DVD media playback under Windows 98:

- A kernel-mode, system-wide software mixer, which supports DirectSound, DirectShow, and MMSYS clients, as well as kernel-mode WDM filters, including CD-ROM and MIDI drivers. The architecture provides the ability for algorithms from any vendor to decode the DVD audio, and it supports mixing at any sampling rate from 100 Hz to 100 kHz.

- Flexible control of the output destination. The WDM drivers can send the master 16-bit 44.1-kHz or 48-kHz or other format output to an ISA, PCI, USB, or IEEE 1394 audio device. Additionally, support is provided for redirection of the PCI-device final-mix output to USB speakers.

- A kernel-mode CD-ROM driver that emulates MSCDEX commands and implements reading, parsing, and streaming of CD digital audio to the kernel-mode WDM system-wide mixer at 16-bit 44.1 kHz.

- A Universal Disk Format (UDF) DVD file reader, splitter, and navigator that provides access for DirectShow clients to separate video and audio streams.

WDM Streaming Class Driver

Windows 98 contains support for technologies that require data to be moved in real time. Digital audio, video, and scanner/camera support may contain data streams that can overwhelm the PCI bus. The Streaming Class Driver (file name Stream.sys) was written to address this issue.

How WDM Streaming Works

WDM Streaming is directly based on the DirectShow model of user mode filters. In the context of WDM Streaming, a filter represents a kernel-mode driver. The Streaming Class Driver takes the API calls that normally communicate back and forth from the user level (ring 3) to the kernel level (ring 0) and pushes them down so they occur mostly at the kernel level. This allows data streams to be passed through the operating system and to move at a faster pace, because CPU cycles are not used to pass the information back and forth between the user mode and kernel levels.

Efficient Streaming

Typically, time-sensitive applications are divided into several tasks.

Figure 12.1 shows the typical path that a data stream follows. The data stream (for instance, an MPEG-2 data stream with audio) is passed to the first filter to decompress the video stream. Then the entire stream is handed back to the device driver in kernel mode. When the audio portion of the data stream needs to be decoded, the entire data stream is passed back up to the user level. These transitions are CPU-intensive and are not the most efficient way to pass the data stream, because each transition carries the extra load to switch between the two levels, and the data may have to go through various validation stages.

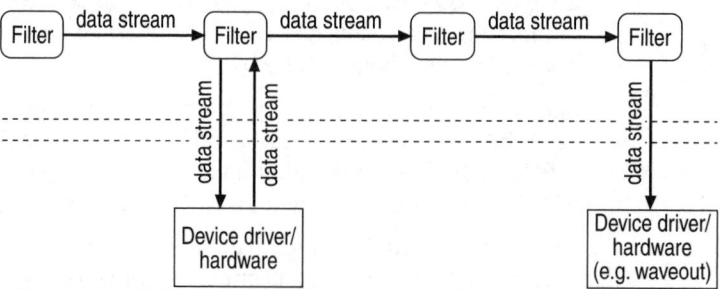

Figure 12.1   Typical data stream path in a non-WDM case

WDM Streaming enables more efficient data streaming, as shown in Figure 12.2. In this example, almost all data streaming takes place in kernel mode. The filter modules executing in user mode apply controls only to the kernel-mode device drivers/hardware. For example, in the case of an audio data stream, a user-mode filter can apply a loudness control to the kernel-mode driver/hardware renderer.

Note Kernel streaming (KS) filters are not necessarily bound to any piece of hardware.

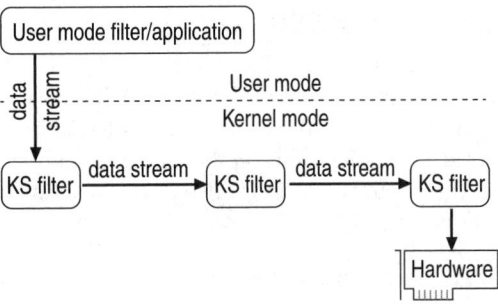

Figure 12.2   WDM data stream path

Additionally, a stream may be produced and consumed entirely in kernel mode, with only mechanisms exposed to the user-mode client, as shown in Figure 12.3. In this case, a source filter reading a file, for example, or picking up data off a 1394 bus passes it through some hardware-based codec and on through the remaining filters. If the filters in between reside on the same physical hardware, they may negotiate a faster transfer mechanism, or interface, which avoids memory copies and may avoid use of the host CPU in their communication.

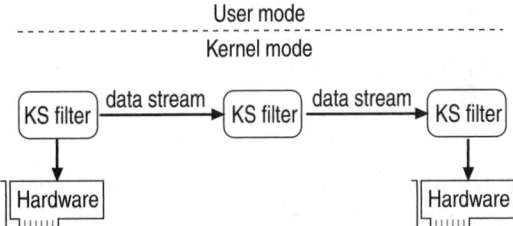

Figure 12.3   Data stream produced and consumed in kernel mode

DVD

DVD places full-length motion pictures on digital disc-sized media. DVD hardware and software are specifically tailored to read multiple digitally stored data streams concurrently. DVD is not computer-only media; many DVD players (which are similar to laser disc players) on the market are designed to feed the images directly to a television. DVD has two major compression technologies, MPEG-2 and Dolby Digital (sometimes referred to as AC-3), which are used to store video and audio on a disc. This allows more than two hours of better-than-laser-disc video and better-than-CD audio to be stored on a single disc, opening up new possibilities for content providers. Such possibilities include the ability to have different screen formats (for instance, letterbox, pan and scan, and so on), different soundtracks, different languages, and different ratings (such as both R and PG versions of a movie) all on the same disc.

Hardware Requirements for DVD

DVD requires a special drive as well as a decoder (a hardware decoder card, a software decoder, or a combination of the two). DVD drives use a laser with a shorter wavelength than that used on standard CD-ROM drives, which allows it to read data stored in smaller areas on the media. Standard CD-ROM drives cannot read DVD discs. However, DVD drives can read standard CD-ROM data and audio CDs.

Full-motion video is stored on DVD in the MPEG-2 format. Because high rates of transfer are necessary to read and display full-screen, real-time data, most of the decoding is done at the hardware level, so your DVD system must have a decoder.

Capacity

The current capacity of a DVD disc starts at 4.7 billion bytes. Vendors have developed technology to make both sides of the media readable and to layer data on each side (for example, a gold layer of data can be placed above a silver layer). Lower laser power is used to read the top layer, and increased laser power allows the bottom layer to be read. Combining these two options increases the total possible capacity of a single DVD disc to 17 billion bytes.

Uses

A DVD drive has many uses. Although it was specifically designed to handle the challenges that come with displaying full-motion video, its massive storage capacity allows it to perform in other ways, including the following:

- Support for DVD movie playback is especially important for Entertainment computers, but is also important for any multimedia hardware platform used to provide support for playback of movies. This support includes the full range of interactivity and quality playback found on a standard DVD video player. Because computers can achieve greater image quality than can television sets, a DVD disc on a computer running Windows 98 achieves even better quality than what is available on standard DVD video player devices.

- DVD discs and devices provide cost-effective storage for large data files. In the future, DVD will allow for writable devices, opening a larger range of options.

DVD Software Components

DVD technology includes several software components: MPEG-2, AC-3 (audio streaming), Subpicture, two class drivers (a ROM class driver and WDM), UDF file system, DirectShow, DirectDraw, and a copyright-protection encryption key.

MPEG-2

MPEG-2 is a type of video compression that saves space by saving only the data that changes on the screen. So rather than storing a 640 x 480 x 12 (12-bit color depth) for each frame, only those pixels that change are encoded.

Dolby Digital (AC-3)

AC-3 is a type of audio stream developed by Dolby Labs. It allows up to five separate audio channels (left and right front, left and right rear, and center) and a subwoofer channel.

Subpicture

DVD discs contain a third data stream called Subpicture. The Subpicture stream delivers the subtitles and any other movie add-on data, such as director's comments, that can be displayed while playing the movie.

DVD-ROM Class Driver

DVD-ROM drives use a specific command set referred to as the *Mt. Fuji specification*. The Windows 98 implementation of this command set is provided using the class driver/minidriver architecture conforming to WDM. A class driver is used to provide support for the full Mt. Fuji specification, while the manufacturer of the DVD drive provides a device-specific minidriver that handles device-specific functions. This allows both Windows 98 and Windows NT version 5.0 to read DVD disc data sectors.

WDM Streaming Class Driver

Issues with playing a full-length movie include the fact that data is moved in a different way. Data is usually thought of as being read from the media, loaded into memory, and then used. With multimedia applications, the process is slightly different. Because a full-length movie requires that a large amount of data be moved while playing the movie—the data must be read sequentially, displayed, and cleared by the time the next frame is ready to be displayed. The Streaming Class driver was introduced to address this real-time need. For more information about this driver, see "WDM Streaming Class Driver" earlier in this chapter as well as Chapter 30, "Hardware Management."

UDF file system

Data on a DVD disc is stored using a file system called Universal Disc Format (UDF). Support for this file system is implemented using installable file system architecture of Windows 98.

DirectShow

DirectShow (formerly known as ActiveMovie) provides support for a DVD Navigator/Splitter, proxy filters for video and audio streams, a video mixer, a video renderer, and an audio renderer. DVD movies have the equivalent of channels for the various data streams necessary for a full-length movie. Data streams consist of not only the MPEG portion but also digital audio, which may have Dolby surround sound and close captioning information. For a single video image, DVD can provide up to 8 languages/sound tracks and 32 subtitle tracks, and supports up to 9 angles and 8 ratings. DirectShow 2.0 provides support for keeping track of these various data streams and passing them to the proper codec.

DirectDraw HAL with VPE

Decoded video can become quite large. An MPEG-2 stream starts out at a rate of around 5–10 megabits per second (Mbps). After the stream is decoded, it can easily exceed 100 Mbps. The processing of this amount of information in a continuous stream could overwhelm the PCI bus. So most of the decoding of the information has been moved back to the hardware level by using dedicated MPEG decoder cards. Support for these decoder cards is built in to DirectX 5.0, with DirectDraw's support for Video Port Extensions (VPEs). Video Port Extensions allow the MPEG stream to be written directly to the frame buffer memory of the Video Card from the MPEG decoder card. Data transfer occurs through a special cable that connects the video card and the decoder card at the hardware level. DirectDraw 5.0 allows the data stream to be moved through the hardware layer while keeping track of such things as synchronization.

Copyright Protection

Copyright protection for DVD is provided by encrypting key sectors on a disc and then decrypting those sectors before decoding them. Microsoft provides support for both software and hardware decrypters using a software module that enables authentication between the decoders and the DVD-ROM drives in a computer.

As part of the Copyright Protection scheme used for DVD, the DVD Consortium has set up six worldwide regions. Discs are playable on DVD devices in some or all of the regions according to regional codes set by the creators of the content. Microsoft provides software that responds to the regionalization codes as required by the DVD Consortium and as part of the decryption licenses.

DVD in Windows 98

DVD hardware and software requirements are described in the following sections.

Hardware

A DVD-ready system must meet the specifications listed in the *PC 97 Hardware Design Guide*. These requirements are described in Table 12.3.

Table 12.3   DVD hardware requirements

Hardware	Required	Recommended
Processor	P120 (or equivalent) with 256-KB cache	P166 (or equivalent) with 256-KB cache; MMX enabled
RAM	16 MB	32 MB
Graphics display	800 x 600 x 16 bpp with Video Port Extensions (VPEs)	1024 x 786 x 16 bpp; 2-D accelerator
Decoder	Supported Decoder Card	Supported Decoder Card; NTSC / PAL TV Output

The following decoder cards and DVD drives are directly supported in Windows 98:

- Toshiba, Toshiba Infinia
- Quadrant, Dell XPS series
- Luxsonor, Creative PC-DVD (not Dxr2 and prior)

Software

Windows 98 ships with a DVD player named Dvdplay.exe. Dvdplay.exe is a stand-alone executable and has no program-specific DLLs associated with it. Like most applets shipped with Windows, DVDPlay has only basic functionality and may be replaced by a third-party application. If you have a supported decoder, DVD Player can be installed and uninstalled from the Control Panel using the Add/Remove Programs option.

Note   When the DVD Player is launched, it searches all local drives in alphabetical order, starting with C, looking for a folder called Video_TS. When this folder is located, the data file within it is loaded, and video streaming begins. If this folder exists on a drive that comes before the DVD drive, the player will try to play the data in the first folder it finds. This is also an issue with systems that have multiple DVD drives.

The basic DVD program is shown in Figure 12.4. It contains, from left to right, buttons for choosing a channel; VCR style controls for controlling playback; and menu navigation buttons for using the on-screen menu choices.

Figure 12.4   Basic DVD player

Recording, Editing, and Playing Audio

Windows 98 multimedia services provide extensible, device-independent audio support. Windows 98 features services for sound control for computers that have sound cards and for waveform-audio, MIDI, and mixer devices.

With audio support in Windows 98, users can do the following:

- Use Media Player or ActiveMovie Control to play WAV or MIDI files.
- Use applications that take advantage of DirectSound audio acceleration.
- Use the Sound option in Control Panel to assign sound clips to play each time a specific event occurs.
- Use CD Player to play audio CDs.
- Use Sound Recorder to record sound.
- Use built-in Windows 98 OLE support to copy or link audio clips in other documents. For more information, see Chapter 25, "Application Support."

For more information about recording, editing, and playing multimedia files, see Help.

Windows 98 Support for MIDI

Musical Instrument Digital Interface (MIDI) is a serial interface standard that allows for the connection of music synthesizers, musical instruments, and computers. The MIDI standard is based partly on hardware and partly on a description of the way in which music and sounds are encoded and communicated between MIDI devices.

MIDI is used as a development tool for musicians. Virtually all advanced music equipment supports MIDI, and MIDI offers a convenient way to control the equipment precisely. MIDI is the electronic equivalent of sheet music. For example, if you buy a CD that contains a particular performance of a piece of music, the data on the CD requires no interpretation at all—it is straightforward playback. If you buy the sheet music and have someone play it, it requires very little data, but, depending on the quality of the instruments, the hardware, and the software, you can get a good or a bad interpretation of that piece of music.

Windows 98 supports the General MIDI Specification to request particular instruments and sounds. This specification is an industry standard that defines how MIDI should be used, and it is supported by Microsoft and most MIDI sound card manufacturers.

Windows 98 supports MIDI streams. This technology is used in advanced sound cards to play very complex MIDI sequences with less CPU use. This technology allows Windows 98 to receive requests for multiple MIDI instructions at once and process the instructions in the operating system. As a result, playing MIDI files now requires even less computing power than before, and it allows developers to process MIDI instructions, graphics, and other data even more successfully.

MIDI devices supported by Windows 98 include the following:

- FM Synthesis
- Hardware Wavetable Synthesis
- Software Wavetable Synthesis
- MPU401

For more information about playing a MIDI sound file and installing a sound card, see Help.

Recording Sound

If you have a microphone connected to your computer, you can record sound by using Sound Recorder.

When using Sound Recorder, you can use a real-time audio compression filter to reduce the amount of disk space required to store audio. For example, to turn on voice compression when recording so the file is compressed in real-time, use the GSM 6.10 format in the **Convert Now** dialog box in **Properties** from the **File** menu.

▶ **To enable real-time compression while recording**

1. On the **Start** menu, point to **Programs**, point to **Accessories**, point to **Entertainment,** and then click **Sound Recorder**.
2. Click the **File** menu, and then click **Properties**.
3. From the drop down box, choose **Recording formats**.
4. Click **Convert Now**, choose a compression format, and then click **OK**.
5. Click **OK** to start recording.

For more information about recording sound with a microphone, see Help.

Controlling Audio Input Levels

Windows 98 includes a Volume Control tool that provides audio line routing services to manage the different audio lines installed on a computer. An audio line consists of one or more channels of waveform-audio data coming from one origin or system resource. For example, a stereo audio line has two data channels, yet it is considered a single audio line. A mixer control can take on many different characteristics (such as controlling volume), depending on the characteristics of the associated audio line.

The number of lines users can mix by using Volume Control depends on the number of audio source lines the computer has and whether they are using Volume Control for input or output.

For more information about mixing sounds, see Help.

Recording and Playing Digital Video

Windows 98 video services provide the resources for capturing video clips, compressing the content, and controlling playback.

Displaying digital video involves moving and processing huge streams of data continuously and efficiently. In earlier versions of Windows, the process of displaying digital video relied on a series of 16-bit systems—from reading data from the disk, to decompressing the video data, to displaying it on the screen. With the Windows 98 32-bit architecture, users can display bigger, smoother, and more colorful digital video, without adding any hardware.

Windows 98 multimedia is fully compatible with 16-bit multimedia titles. Testing has shown that the 32-bit improvements in file access speed and stream handling result in performance gains for 16-bit multimedia applications and especially for the new generation of 32-bit applications developed for Windows 98.

▶ **To determine the format in which an existing video clip was authored**

- Right-click the icon for the digital-video file, click **Properties**, and then click the **Details** tab.

For more information about playing video clips, see Help.

Buying a Multimedia Computer

Make sure to select a balanced computer, in which all components work together to meet the demands of supporting multimedia applications. In multimedia systems, balance is more important than speed, because multimedia playback places heavy demands on the CD-ROM (for reading data), on the hard disk (for writing data), on the CPU (for decompressing data), and on the video and audio subsystems (for playback). A fast CPU alone does not guarantee a great playback system.

The *PC 97 Hardware Design Guide* introduced the *Entertainment PC* as a distinct category of Windows-based computer, differentiated from the Basic PC by its ease of use and the breadth and quality of its multimedia capabilities. For example, the graphics, video, and audio subsystems for Entertainment PCs are designed to optimize the capabilities of software that uses Microsoft DirectX interfaces.

An Entertainment PC 98 system is optimized for the following uses:

- Games, including the best titles, with the most complex, realistic graphics and audio.

- Education, using the most engaging titles, with full-screen video, interactive animation, and so on.

- Active Internet, providing enhanced Web communications capabilities, with personalized and animated Web sites, chat rooms, and so on.

- Personal communications through multimedia e-mail, Internet audio phone, video phone, and so on.

- Interactive, high-resolution television and movie viewing through higher video quality, real-time links to content producers, and so on.

- Connection with traditional consumer-electronics devices, providing home theater surround audio such as Dolby Digital (AC-3) for games and DVD movies, and fast and easy capture, editing, and playback of personal video.

The following sections provide guidelines for what to look for in a multimedia system, along with specifics for audio components, MIDI components, and video components.

What to Look for in Basic Computing Power

This section presents a summary of general system recommendations for a multimedia computer, including system board, memory, and BIOS. The minimum PC 98 performance recommendations consist of the following:

- 200-MHz Pentium processor with Intel MMX technology, or equivalent. The minimum microprocessor capability is specified to support the demands of rich media, Internet access, and conferencing.

- Minimum 256-KB Level 2 (L2) cache or equivalent.

- 32-MB minimum system memory. Recommended: 64 MB. Memory should be 66-MHz Dynamic Random Access Memory (DRAM) or better.

- Graphics adapter using PCI, AGP, or other high-speed bus.

- Adapter support for screen resolutions as defined by VESA up to the PC 98 required maximum, including 640 x 480 x [8, 15, 16, 24] bpp, 800 x 600 x [8, 15, 16, 24] bpp, and 1024 x 768 x [8, 15, 16] bpp.

- Two USB ports to support connection of auxiliary input devices, such as game pads, joysticks, and track balls.

- Two IEEE 1394 ports to support camcorders and other digital consumer electronics devices.

- Keyboards, pointing devices, and game pads and their connections compliant with the USB Device Class Definition for Human Interface Devices, Version 1.0 or higher, and with the USB HID Usages Table, whether implemented as wired or wireless devices.

- Data/fax/voice modem that supports V.pcm.

What to Look for in Audio Hardware

Audio for a multimedia computer should meet PC 98 audio requirements, which include requirements for audio hardware capabilities, performance metrics, and external connections. The following are some key features to look for when you want to purchase a multimedia computer with high-quality audio :

- A sound card with a 16-bit digital-to-analog converter (DAC) for playback and a 16-bit analog-to-digital converter (ADC) for recording (necessary for applications developers).

- Full-duplex support to record and play sounds at the same time. The device should be capable of capturing audio at one sample rate while playing audio at another sample rate.

- Full-duplex audio capability for audio hardware supporting H.323/H.324 video and audio conferencing.

- Audio hardware supporting CD-ROM and DVD media playback, made possible by built-in or external audio codec support for playback of 16-bit stereo PCM data at both a 44.1-kHz and 48-kHz sample rate.

- Audio hardware featuring the acceleration supporting 3-D games, made possible by built-in or external audio codec support for playback of 16-bit stereo PCM data at a 44.1-kHz sample rate.

- CD-ROM drive providing 12x or higher performance. The CD-ROM drive must support 1200 KB per second average throughput or higher performance when running in the fully on power state.

- Audio system providing support for basic data formats. The audio system must provide full-duplex support of the following audio formats:

  - Mono/stereo

  - 8-bit unsigned

  - 16-bit signed

- Audio system support for both recording and playing back of sample rates that include 8, 11.025, 16, 22.05, 44.1, and 48 kHz waveforms. Compact disc–quality sound uses 44 kHz. The 11 kHz and 22 kHz waveforms are fractions of 44 and are often used for compressed waveforms that are meant to save CPU processing. The 8 kHz waveform is used for compatibility with telephone audio, and 16 kHz waveform is used for speech recognition.

- Audio system with sufficient externally accessible inputs and outputs. At a minimum, the audio system must have the following features:

  - A monaural microphone, stereo line input, or both

  - Stereo line-level output

- Audio system support of full-duplex operation at independent sampling rates. Voice recognition and audio/video conferencing require the audio system to play back and record simultaneously. Incoming and outgoing audio should be capable of operating at independent sampling rates. This recommendation considers the entire system, including the possibility of USB speakers or microphones.

- Audio system providing hardware or software support for the Downloadable Samples (DLS) specification. Support for DLS as defined by the MIDI Manufacturers Association is recommended. For more information, see *DLS Specification*, version 1.0 or higher, at **http://www.midi.org/**.

For computers that support software or hardware decoding and playback of DVD-Video or MPEG-2 video, the audio decoder must be capable of supporting the following formats:

- One or both of the following formats, depending upon the local requirements for DVD audio:

  - AC-3 (Dolby Digital) less than or equal to 5.1 channels, at 48 kHz less than or equal to 384 Kbps.

  - MPEG-2 multichannel less than or equal to 5.1 channels, at 48 kHz less than or equal to 912 Kbps.

- MPEG-1 Layer 2 stereo, at 44.1 and 48 kHz less than or equal to 384 Kbps.

- Linear PCM (LPCM) less than or equal to 8 channels, 16-bit, 20-bit, and 24-bit at 48 or 96 kHz less than or equal to 6.144 Mb/s.

Note Conversion to 48-kHz 16-bit stereo is acceptable when the content exceeds the available resolution, sampling rates, or number of output channels.

What to Look for in MIDI Support

Microsoft recommends that sound cards for both consumer and developer systems include the following:

- General MIDI support. General MIDI refers to a system of assigning numbers to each kind of instrument, so that, for example, instrument 12 on one computer is the same as instrument 12 on all others.

- Support for polyphony, the ability to play multiple sounds at the same time. Systems should include at least 32-voice polyphony. Support for more concurrent sounds means a fuller sounding playback.

- Wave table sound rather than FM synthesis.

- Standard MIDI port. This is normally implemented as an MPU-401 port. If you play a MIDI stream to the MPU-401 port, you will not hear anything unless you have a MIDI playback device attached to the port. You can use this port to plug in MIDI devices such as piano-style keyboards; it also supports joysticks.

Note An external MIDI port is needed only if you have external MIDI equipment to connect to the computer.

- System audio hardware acceleration features, such as Downloadable Samples (DLS) wave-table MIDI synthesis and multistream Head Related Transfer Function (HRTF) 3-D.

- Hardware for higher quality or concurrency DLS wave-table MIDI synthesis, with associated mixing and SRC support. A wave table card should send the audio to the same speakers as their wave output.

What to Look for in Video and Broadcast Support

Video and broadcast television are becoming integral elements of computer usage, especially for an Entertainment PC. For Entertainment PC 98, important design issues include the following:

- Increased quality of video capture and playback. This includes increased image resolution and increased frame rates.

- Low-latency video delivery, displaying video from both internal and external video devices.

- Implementation of a graphics adapter video port for use by one or more video sources.

The Entertainment PC 98 hardware recommendations for video capture, television output, and DVD playback support include the following:

- DVD-Video support with MPEG-2 hardware.

- WDM support implemented for all video input and capture capabilities.

- Support for National Television System Committee (NTSC), Phase Alternation by Line (PAL), or both types of television output, except for systems bundled with a large-screen super VGA (SVGA) monitor.

- Super VGA resolution. At a minimum, the consumer system should have a Super VGA display, which provides at least 800 x 600-pixel resolution with approximately 64,000 colors (16 bpp) for users working with complicated graphics.

- Hardware-assisted DirectDraw acceleration, Direct3D acceleration, and video playback.

Troubleshooting Multimedia

This section describes how to identify and resolve multimedia software problems.

For information about troubleshooting related hardware problems, see Chapter 24, "Device Management."

For information about general troubleshooting issues, see Chapter 27, "General Troubleshooting."

Correcting Problems with Playing WAV Files

When a multimedia application is unable to play waveform-audio (WAV) files, it is usually caused by one or more of the following problems.

The sound card is not installed properly.

Most sound cards come with MS-DOS-based programs for playing sounds or testing card configurations. Run these programs in MS-DOS mode; if the sound card does not work with these programs, it will not work with Windows 98 sound support.

Make sure the sound card settings do not conflict with other hardware. Use the Add New Hardware icon in Control Panel to detect your hardware, thereby determining if you have any hardware for which the appropriate driver is not yet installed. Verify port and IRQ settings.

Note If the sound card can play MIDI files, the card is probably properly installed.

The volume is muted or too low.

Check to see that the volume in Volume Control is not muted or too low.

▶ **To check the volume**

• Click the Volume Control icon on the system tray, and make sure the **Mute all** check box for **Wave** is not enabled, or raise the volume slider for **Wave** if it is too low.

Note If the Volume Control icon is not on the system tray, click **Start** and point to **Programs**, **Accessories**, and **Entertainment**, and then click **Volume Control**.

A waveform-audio driver is not installed.

If you are running Sound Recorder and there is no waveform-audio driver installed, you will receive an error message. In this case, make sure that the waveform-audio driver is listed in the **Multimedia devices** list; you can see this list by clicking the **Devices** tab in the Multimedia option in Control Panel. Check with the manufacturer of the sound card to ensure you have the proper drivers. If you cannot find the correct driver for the sound card in the list, try using the Windows 95 driver for that card or connecting to the manufacturer's Web site and downloading a current driver.

You should also make sure the correct codec is installed. You can check the codec by clicking Multimedia in the Control Panel and then clicking the **Devices** tab. The codecs are listed under **Audio Compression Codecs**.

A waveform-audio MCI driver is not enabled.

If you are running Media Player and cannot play WAV files, perform the following procedure to correct the problem.

▶ **To enable the waveform-audio MCI driver**

1. In Control Panel, double-click Multimedia, and then click the **Devices** tab.
2. In the **Multimedia devices** list, click the plus (+) sign next to **Media Control Devices**.

   If **Wave Audio Device (Media Control)** does not appear in the list, the driver is not installed.
3. Click **Wave Audio Device (Media Control)**, and then click **Properties**.
4. In the **Properties** dialog box, click **Use this Media Control device**.

Correcting Problems with Playing MIDI Files

A multimedia application's inability to play MIDI files is commonly caused by one or more of the following problems.

The sound card is not installed properly.

Most sound cards come with MS-DOS-based programs for playing sounds or testing card configurations. Run these test programs; if the sound card does not work with these programs, it will not work with Windows 98 sound support.

Make sure that the sound card settings do not conflict with other hardware. Use the Add New Hardware option in Control Panel to detect your hardware, thereby determining whether you have any hardware for which the appropriate driver is not yet installed. Verify port and IRQ settings.

> **Note** If the sound card can play WAV files, the card is probably properly installed.

The volume is muted or too low.

Check to see that the volume in Volume Control is not muted or too low.

▶ **To check the volume**

- Click the Volume Control icon on the system tray, and make sure the **Mute all** check box for **MIDI** is not enabled, or raise the volume slider for **MIDI** if it is too low.

  > **Note** If the Volume Control icon is not on the system tray, click **Start** and point to **Programs**, **Accessories**, and **Entertainment**, and then click **Volume Control**.

A MIDI driver is not installed.

If you are using Media Player and cannot play a MIDI file, it might be because there is no MIDI driver installed. Try installing the driver that came with the hardware. Or, if you do not find the correct driver for the sound card in the list, try using the Windows 95 driver for that card.

A MIDI MCI driver is not installed or enabled.

In Media Player, make sure that the option named **MIDI Sequencer** appears in the **Device** menu. If not, the MIDI MCI driver is not installed or not enabled.

▶ **To verify that the MIDI MCI driver is enabled**

1. In Control Panel, double-click Multimedia, and then click the **Devices** tab.

2. In the **Multimedia devices** list, click the plus (+) sign next to **Media Control Devices**.

    If **MIDI Sequencer Device (Media Control)** does not appear in the list, the driver is not installed. See the following procedure for instructions.

3. Click **MIDI Sequencer Device (Media Control)**, and then click **Properties**.

4. In the **Properties** dialog box, click **Use this Media Control device**.

▶ **To install the MIDI MCI driver**

1. In Control Panel, double-click Add New Hardware, click **No, I want to select the hardware from a list** when prompted to have Windows 98 search for your hardware, and then click **Next**.

2. In the **Hardware Types** list, click **Sound,** click **Video And Game Controllers**, and then click **Next**.

3. Click **Microsoft MCI** in the Manufacturers list, and then click **MIDI Sequencer Device (Media Control)** in the Models list.

4. Click **Next**.

5. To complete the installation, click **Finish**.

The incorrect MIDI output device is selected.

If the selected midi device is incorrect, you hear no MIDI output. Choose only External MIDI or MIDI OUT for an add-on MIDI daughter card or if an external MIDI device (for example, a synthesizer) is connected to the MIDI port of a sound card.

For example, if you do not have an MPU-401 compatible synthesizer plugged into the MIDI port, make sure that MPU-401 is *not* selected as your default MIDI device.

▶ **To select the correct MIDI output device**

1. In Control Panel, double-click Multimedia.

2. Select the **MIDI** tab.

3. Choose the proper MIDI playback device under MIDI output so that it appears in the box under **Single Instrument**.

4. Click **OK**.

Correcting Problems with Playing a DVD Disc

Because DVD uses several pieces, the first step in troubleshooting a DVD issue is to narrow down which piece is not functioning correctly.

- Make sure that the DVD drive is displayed as functioning correctly in Device Manager.

- Make sure that Windows 98 can read the data on the CD by using Windows Explorer to see the contents of the DVD disc. There can be at least two folders: Video_TS and Audio_TS.

- Make sure that ActiveMovie is working correctly by playing an AVI file.

Correcting Problems with Playing or Hearing an Audio CD

When a you are unable to hear an audio CD being played, it is commonly caused by one or more of the following problems.

The CD-ROM drive is not properly installed.

Place a data CD in the CD-ROM drive, and make sure you can view the files in Windows Explorer or list the files at the command prompt. If you can, the CD-ROM drive is properly installed. If not, verify your disk drivers (ESDI, SCSI, Proprietary, MSCDEX), and make the appropriate configuration changes so that you can view the files on a data CD.

The volume is muted or too low.

Check to see that the volume in Volume Control is not muted or too low.

▶ **To check the volume**

- Click the Volume Control icon on the system tray, and make sure the **Mute all** check box for **CD Audio** is not enabled, or raise the volume slider for **CD Audio** if it is too low.

Note   If the Volume Control icon is not on the system tray, click **Start** and point to **Programs**, **Accessories**, and **Entertainment**, and then click **Volume Control**.

Digital CD audio for the CD-ROM device is not enabled.

You can have Windows use digital playback of a CD audio for digital devices, such as USB speakers. This feature works with only certain CD-ROM devices.

▶ **To verify the digital CD audio is enabled**

1. In Control Panel, double-click Multimedia, and then click the **CD Music** tab.

2. Select the **Enable digital CD audio for this CD-ROM device** check box.

The CD audio MCI driver is not installed.

In Media Player, make sure that the option CD Audio appears in the **Device** menu. If not, the CD audio MCI driver is not installed or not enabled.

▶ **To verify the CD audio MCI driver is enabled**

1. In Control Panel, double-click Multimedia, and then click the **Devices** tab.

2. In the **Multimedia devices** list, click the plus (+) sign next to **Media Control Devices**.

   If **CD Audio Device (Media Control)** does not appear in the list, the driver is not installed. See the following procedure for instructions.

3. Click **CD Audio Device (Media Control)**, and then click **Properties**.

4. In the **Properties** dialog box, click **Use this Media Control device**.

▶ **To install the CD audio MCI driver**

1. In Control Panel, double-click Add New Hardware, click **No, I want to select the hardware from a list** when prompted to have Windows 98 search for your hardware, and then click **Next**.

2. In the **Hardware Types** list, click **Sound,** click **Video And Game Controllers**, and then click **Next**.

3. Click **Microsoft MCI** in the Manufacturers list, and then click **CD Audio Device (Media Control)** in the Models list.

4. Click **Next**.

5. To complete the installation, click **Finish**.

The CD-ROM is not connected to the sound card.

If the CD-ROM is playing and there is no sound coming from the sound card speakers, try plugging the speakers or headphones into the audio jack on the face of the CD-ROM drive. If you get sound, check the internal or external audio connection between the CD-ROM drive and the sound card.

Correcting Problems with Hearing from Headphones

Verify that the sound card is correctly installed by reviewing the card's properties.

▶ **To view your sound card's properties**

1. In Control Panel, double-click Multimedia, and then click the **CD Music** tab.

2. Make sure that the volume level is set to produce sound from the headphones. If not, use the slider to adjust the **CD Music Volume**.

Note If you have **Digital Playback** enabled on the **CD Music** tab, the headphone output for the CD-ROM drive is disabled.

Additional Resources

For more information about	See this resource
Multimedia in Windows 98	*Microsoft Windows 98 Device Development Kit*
Video support	**http://www.microsoft.com/hwdev/pc98.htm**
Implementing drivers that support simultaneous use of devices	*Microsoft DirectX Driver Development Kit*
MIDI Manufacturers Association	**http://www.midi.org/**
Computer design guidelines	**http://www.microsoft.com/hwdev/desguid/**

CHAPTER 13

WebTV for Windows 98

13

This chapter provides a brief overview of Microsoft WebTV for Windows 98 and how new broadcast technologies provide innovative methods for disseminating information.

In This Chapter

See Also

- For more information about Microsoft WebTV for Windows visit the World Wide Web at **http://www.microsoft.com/DTV/.**

Overview of Microsoft WebTV for Windows

Microsoft WebTV for Windows 98, included in Windows 98, integrates the interactivity of the Web with the medium of television, providing interative television on a computer. With Windows 98 and a TV tuner adapter card supported by Windows 98 installed on your computer, you can:

- Find your favorite television programs with an electronic program guide that is always up-to-date.

- Watch television programs on your monitor, even while you are using other software applications.

- View interactive television programs that enhance television shows with additional, more interactive information about the show.

- Receive information such as Web pages, multimedia files, and software upgrades over the broadcast airwaves, so you do not have to tie up a phone line.

Many kinds of applications can be run on Microsoft WebTV for Windows 98, from traditional Windows-based applications to standard broadcast TV programs. In between is a new application space: interactive television, is the melding of interactive content with an audio/video source.

For example, an interactive baseball game or cricket match might provide a score card, player stats, and a continuous ticker of scores from around the league, in addition to the television signal.

Currently, WebTV for Windows 98 supports both cable and over-the-air broadcast transmissions for National Television System Committee (NTSC) programming. Satellite and other broadcast transmission standards will be supported in the future.

In designing interactive content, internal Microsoft producers have been using a set of standards based on open, standard Internet technologies.

Interactive Television

The concept of interactive television is at the heart of WebTV. Interactive television combines television with interactive content and enhancements to provide better, richer entertainment and information, blending traditional TV-watching with the interactivity of a personal computer. Programming can include such items as: additional background text, richer pictures and graphics, one-click access to Web sites, electronic mail and chats, and online commerce with the use of a phone line back channel.

The process for creating interactive television is fairly simple. First, enhancement producers collect interactive elements on the set of a TV show. Then a Web developer assembles the elements using industry-standard languages and tools. Finally, the elements are transmitted within the live broadcast to the viewer's Windows 98 supported TV tuner. The signal is sent over narrow bandwidths in the vertical blanking interval (VBI) of a television signal.

Interactive Programming

There are three basic levels of interactive programming:

- TV Crossover Links
- Low Bandwidth (Analog) Interactivity
- High Bandwidth (Digital) Interactivity

Each of these options offers varying degrees of interactivity. Each of these types of interactivity is viewable by both Windows 98 and the WebTV Plus set top box. In other words, a broadcaster can send one signal and have it received, decoded, and rendered by both clients.

TV Crossover Links

TV Crossover Links are very easy, yet a very powerful way to marry television programs to their associated Web sites. TV Crossover Links enable producers to integrate a Uniform Resource Locator (URL), or what is considered the common Web page address, directly into an actual TV program through closed captioning. A "trigger" in the form of a graphic "i" appears as a small "watermark" overlaying the program. Viewers can click on the "i" with their mouse or remote control to visit the associated Web site. By sending a trigger over the closed-caption signal, shows can add static or dynamic Web links to their programming.

Since the closed captioning space is available throughout the duration of the program, multiple TV Crossover Links can be sent during a broadcast. Most programs currently include closed captioning information, so the tools needed to add TV Crossover Links to a program already exist.

Low Bandwidth (Analog) Interactivity

The second level of interactive programming is the ability to integrate Web-based information and video programming using current analog transports. By using the bandwidth available in the vertical blanking interval (VBI) of a television broadcast, show producers can synchronize useful and timely information with an existing television program. An integrated page is created combining the television's video signal with content that enhances the viewer's TV experience. This second level of programming allows for a more user-driven experience than TV Crossover Links by delivering interactivity to each viewer.

Using well defined and understood Internet Protocols (IPs), broadcasters can send additional information alongside their signal. Although this is available today, there is limited bandwidth in the VBI for sending data (essentially what amounts to the bandwidth of an Integrated Services Digital Network [ISDN] line), so only limited interactivity and information access is currently attainable. However, when combined with a back channel, the option to add e-mail and chat rooms expands the possibilities of this current technology.

High Bandwidth (Digital) Interactivity

The third level of interactive programming consists of delivering integrated video and multimedia programs through fully digital transports such as digital terrestrial high-definition television or digital satellite. When this level of programming is realized show producers will have greater bandwidth for delivering program enhancements, finer control over the synchronization of information and video, and more flexibility in the layout and integration of pages.

Technologies Involved

The following is a list of the technologies that Microsoft WebTV for Windows 98 uses:

- NDIS 5.0 Miniport Drivers
- Microsoft Win32
- Component Object Model (COM)
- Microsoft ActiveX / Java Components
- Winsock 2
- Transport Control Protocol/Internet Protocol (TCP/IP)
- Internet Explorer 4
- Microsoft Active Desktop
- DHTML
- Microsoft active scripting (Microsoft Visual Basic® Scripting Edition [aka VBScript], Microsoft JScript™)
- Microsoft DirectShow
- Microsoft DirectX 5.0/DirectDraw
- Microsoft Visual Basic
- Database/Jet/DAO/Loaders

Installing Microsoft WebTV for Windows 98

Microsoft WebTV for Windows 98 components are optionally installed during the Setup of Windows components, or by using the following procedure.

▶ **To install PrintServer Software for Windows 98**

1. In Control Panel, double-click Add/Remove Programs.
2. On the **Windows Setup** tab, click **WebTV for Windows**.

Microsoft WebTV for Windows 98 requires 31 MB of available hard-disk space, and there will be an optional component called "WaveTop" under WebTV for Windows 98. WaveTop is a free service to consumers, operated by WavePhore, Inc., which transmits high-value Web page content over the Public Broadcasting System's (PBS's) VBI signal. Examples of this content includes The Wall Street Journal, Time, Fortune, USA Today, and so. Since the PBS signal reaches 99 percent of all U.S. households over the air or via cable, this means that almost anyone in the United States will have access to this content 24 hours a day, 7 days a week starting at the launch of Windows 98. Installation requires Windows 98 to reboot at least twice, depending on hardware configuration, for complete hardware installation.

The program is run from the QuickLaunch toolbar or by using the following procedure.

▶ **To run WebTV**
  - Click **Start**, point to **Programs**, **Accessories**, and **Entertainment**, and then click **WebTV**.

Microsoft WebTV for Windows 98 Hardware Requirements

The minimum hardware to use Microsoft WebTV for Windows 98 is as follows:

- Intel Pentium 166 MHz processor or compatible
- 16 MB of memory (RAM)
- Super VGA monitor supporting 800 x 600 or higher resolution
- Microsoft Mouse or compatible pointing device with two buttons
- Television tuner card with Windows 98–compatible drivers

The recommended hardware to use Microsoft WebTV for Windows 98 is as follows:

- Intel Pentium 200 MHz processor
- 32 MB or more memory (RAM)
- 28,800 bps or higher internal fax modem (AT command set compatible)
- Microsoft Mouse or compatible pointing device with two buttons
- Super VGA monitor supporting 800 x 600 or higher resolution
- ATI All-inWonder Card or ATI All-in-Wonder Pro Card or any television tuner card with Windows 98–compatible drivers
- Cable connection to the card
- Sound card

To display video in WebTV for Windows 98, the requirement is an ATI All-in-Wonder Card or ATI All-in-Wonder Pro Card. However, third-party drivers will be available soon after the release of Windows 98.

Troubleshooting the Program Guide

There are steps you can take if you cannot connect to the Electronic Program Guide (EPG).

▶ **To connect to the Electronic Program Guide**

1. In the Internet Explorer 4 browsing software, click the **View** menu and select **Internet Options**. Click the **Security** tab. In the **Zone** list, click **Trusted sites zone**.

2. Click **Add Sites**. Type **http://*.microsoft.com** in the **Add this Web site to the zone** text box.

3. Click **Add** to add it to the Web site.

Note Make sure there is no check mark in **Require server verification (https: for all sites in this zone)**.

---

4. Click **OK**.

5. Set the security level for this zone as **Low**.

6. Try to connect again.

Program Guide Web Page

If the previously mentioned troubleshooting does not work, try the following steps.

Connect to **http://webtv.microsoft.com** for more information.

Troubleshooting Microsoft WebTV for Windows 98

The following list should help you answer some of the more common questions from customers about Microsoft WebTV for Windows 98.

I cannot get your TV software to work with my video card.

There are many TV tuner cards available in the market including STB TV PCI, IX-Micro Turbo TV, or the ATI All-in-Wonder VGA Card. At this time it is recommended that the ATI All-in-Wonder and ATI All-in-Wonder Pro Cards are used for WebTV.

The drivers in Microsoft WebTV for Windows 98 are written specifically for the chip sets in the two ATI cards. Customers using other cards should be able to use the software that ships with their TV tuner card. They will not, however, be able to use Microsoft WebTV for Windows 98.

I get a "WebTV for Windows could not find the necessary hardware" error.

Often times this error means that the drivers between your sound card and the ATI card are not "binding" together.

Make sure your devices are listed in Device Manager. If they are not, run Add New Hardware from the Control Panel.

Nothing happens.

"I have WebTV for Windows 98 installed with an ATI All-In-Wonder Pro video card. The ATI Movie Player will find the channels but WebTV for Windows 98 does nothing. I click on Start Scan and it just sits there. I clicked on Start Scan for every channel and after I got to channel 99 it gave me a broadcast error."

Or, "I downloaded the Program Guide from my cable TV provider and it says 'Loader running may take approximately 10 minutes.' I let that stand for about one hour and it did nothing."

Make sure the end-user did not install the release version of Windows 98 over a beta version. Make sure all the ATI drivers are present in the Sound Video and Game Controllers section of Device Manager. It should list the following:

- ATI TuneP, WDM TVTuner
- ATIXBar, ATI WDM Video Audio Crossbar
- Bt829, WDM Video Capture
- Closed Caption Decoder
- NABTS/FEC VBI Codec

If these devices are not listed, run Add New Hardware in Control Panel.

P A R T 3

Networking and Intranets

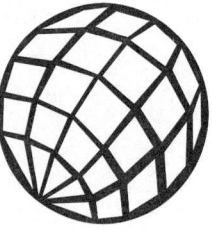

CHAPTER 14

Introduction to Networking Configuration

14

This chapter provides an overview of Microsoft Windows 98 networking and network configuration. It includes a discussion of compatibility and operational improvements introduced with Windows 98, and streamlined steps for network configuration.

In This Chapter

See Also

- For more information about configuring network adapter drivers and protocols, see Chapter 15, "Network Adapters and Protocols."

- For more information about using Windows 98 on Microsoft networks, see Chapter 16, "Windows 98 on Microsoft Networks."

- For more information about using Windows 98 on third-party networks, see Chapter 17, "Windows 98 on Third-Party Networks."

- For more information about network architecture, see Chapter 29, "Windows 98 Network Architecture."

Overview of Windows 98 Network Configuration

The Windows 98 operating system includes built-in networking support, including built-in support for popular networks and an open, extensible networking architecture.

If you are performing a clean install of Windows 98 (that is, if you format the hard disk and then install Windows 98), what Setup installs depends on whether you have a network adapter card and whether you choose to accept the default Dial-Up Networking component.

- If you have a network adapter card, Setup installs Dial-Up Networking (unless you choose not to), the network card, Microsoft Transport Control Protocol/Internet Protocol (TCP/IP), and Client for Microsoft Networks.

- If you do not have a network adapter card and you let Setup install Dial-Up Networking, Setup installs Dial-Up Networking and Microsoft TCP/IP, and Microsoft Family Logon.

- If you add virtual private networking (VPN) to either of the configurations listed in the previous bullets, then Setup also installs a second dial-up adapter and the network driver interface specification wide area network (NDISWAN) protocol for the virtual private networking adapter. The second dial-up adapter appears in the Network option in Control Panel as **Dial-Up Adapter #2 (VPN Support)**.

- If you do not have a network adapter card and you do not let Setup install Dial-Up Networking, no network components are installed.

When you are upgrading from Windows 95, in most cases Setup retains the components from your original network configuration. However, Setup does not always retain the Novell NETX and VLM real-mode clients. For more information, see Chapter 17, "Windows 98 on Third-Party Networks."

Note In the *Microsoft Windows 98 Resource Kit*, NETX is used to refer to the Novell NetWare workstation shell for NetWare version 3.*x*; VLM (Virtual Loadable Module) is used to refer to the workstation shell for version 4.*x*.

When you are upgrading, Setup also adds Dial-Up Networking, and if no network protocol was present in Windows 95, Setup adds Microsoft TCP/IP. If you have a network adapter card, and no previous network client was installed, Setup also adds Client for Microsoft Networks.

You can add any Windows 95 or Windows 98–compatible network client after you run Setup. You can also upgrade to Windows 98 from Windows 95 or Windows for Workgroups if you have any of the following networks already installed and running.

- Artisoft LANtastic version 7.0 or later
- Banyan Enterprise Client version 7.32 or later (32-bit client)

- Banyan VINES version 7.1 or later (16-bit client)

- Digital Equipment Corporation (DEC) PATHWORKS 32

- Microsoft networking—Microsoft LAN Manager, Windows for Workgroups 3.*x*, Windows 95, and Windows NT

- Novell NETX, VLM, and Novell Client for Windows 95/98

- IBM Networks Client for Windows 95

- Solstice NFS Client version 3.1 or later

For information about upgrading real-mode clients, see Chapter 17, "Windows 98 on Third-Party Networks."

The built-in networking components include support for a wide range of network transports (such as TCP/IP and IPX/SPX), industry-wide communications protocols (such as remote procedure calls [RPC], NetBIOS, and named pipes), and existing network device standards (such as network driver interface specification [NDIS] and Open Datalink Interface [ODI]). Because of the extensible architecture, other network vendors can add network connectivity enhancements and application support, and you can mix and match components at every layer. For more information, see Chapter 29, "Windows 98 Network Architecture." See also Chapter 15, "Network Adapters and Protocols."

Note For information about how to install other network components during Setup, see Chapter 3, "Custom Installations."

The following list summarizes the benefits of networking features that are new in Windows 98.

Secure access to remote servers with virtual private networking (VPN). *Virtual private networking* is a new technology by which you can securely connect to a remote server by tunneling through an intermediary network. In essence, you can use a network such as the Internet or your intranet as a substitute for your network wire. For example, you can make a virtual private networking connection to a Windows NT RAS tunnel server on your LAN, or you could make a dial-up connection to the Internet, then use virtual private networking to connect to a tunnel server on the Internet. The tunnel server can then grant you access to any public or private network that is connected to it. For more information, see Chapter 19, "Remote Networking and Mobile Computing."

Windows Sockets 2 application programming interfaces (APIs). The Windows Sockets 2 APIs support Quality of Service (QoS), by which an application can request or require certain network characteristics for a specific network connection. For example, a video application might request that a certain amount of bandwidth be available for a video transmission, and that all the packets it sends travel at a constant rate.

Enhancements to TCP/IP. Windows 98 provides several enhancements to TCP/IP. It provides an automatic private Internet Protocol (IP) addressing feature that enables TCP/IP clients on small LANs to automatically assign themselves IP addresses when no dynamic host configuration protocol (DHCP) server is available. It also provides performance enhancements for certain types of high-speed, high-bandwidth networks. Additionally, it supports IP multicasting, enabling a Windows 98 client to join IP multicast groups. For more information, see Chapter 15, "Network Adapters and Protocols."

Enhancements to network driver interface specification (NDIS), including support for connection-oriented media. Network driver interface specification 5 drivers add to the functionality provided by NDIS 3.1 drivers. For example, by using NDIS 5 drivers, Windows 98 can support a wide range of network media, including Ethernet, fiber distributed data interface (FDDI), token-ring, asynchronous transfer mode (ATM), and wide area network (WAN) technology. Additional features include NDIS power management, support for QoS, and support for a single INF file format across Windows operating systems. For more information, see Chapter 15, "Network Adapters and Protocols.

Simpler logon with Microsoft Family Logon. With Windows 95, you logged on to the computer using Windows Logon. Windows 98 provides a new option called Microsoft Family Logon. If user profiles are enabled and Microsoft Family Logon has been configured, the Microsoft Family Logon prompt will list all users that have been configured for that computer, enabling users to simply select their names from a list rather than having to type it in. For more information, see Chapter 18, "Logon, Browsing, and Resource Sharing."

Distributed File System (DFS) support. Windows 98 supports the Windows NT Distributed File System. This allows a user to access the content of several servers from one Windows NT share point. For more information, see Chapter 16, "Windows 98 on Microsoft Networks."

Client support for Novell Directory Services (NDS). With the optional service Microsoft Service for NetWare Directory Services, Client for NetWare Networks provides the ability to log on to NDS and integrates the NDS logon with the Windows 98 logon. The logon prompt for NDS contains the name of the user object and password and enables the user to set the NDS tree and workstation default name context. For more information, see Chapter 17, "Windows 98 on Third-Party Networks."

Distributed application management with Distributed Component Object Model (DCOM). The Distributed Component Object Model extends the Component Object Model (COM) to allow components of a distributed application to communicate over the network securely and transparently. With DCOM, application developers can create location-independent distributed applications using a language of their choice. Network administrators can then deploy those components on Windows 98 computers, Windows NT Server computers, and Windows NT Workstation computers anywhere in the network. For more information, see Chapter 29, "Windows 98 Network Architecture."

Planning for Microsoft Networking

Microsoft recommends using the 32-bit, protected-mode networking components wherever possible. With protected-mode networking components, all configuration settings are stored in the registry, so you do not have to maintain configuration files such as Autoexec.bat, Protocol.ini, or Net.cfg. The protected-mode networking components also allow you to take advantage of such related benefits as:

- Performance and reliability.

- Peer resource sharing capabilities.

- Use of system policies for administrative control, remote administration of the registry, and use of network agents such as the Simply Network Management Protocol (SNMP) agent included on the Windows 98 Resource Kit compact disc.

If you must run a real-mode client, networking settings are required in Autoexec.bat, and a Netstart.bat file might be required to start the network during system startup. Configuration settings are maintained in Protocol.ini or a similar file, depending on the particular network.

If you are upgrading from a real-mode network client, in most cases Windows 98 Setup retains your original network configuration. When Setup detects existing network components, it installs the appropriate supporting software automatically and moves the configuration settings to the registry, wherever possible.

Configuring Networks

Setup installs the default network configuration described at the beginning of this chapter. You can also install and configure networking support after installing Windows 98 by using the Network option in Control Panel. In the Network option, you can set properties for the following:

- Configuration of network clients, adapters, protocols, and services.
- Identification of the computer on the network.
- Access control, to specify the security used when other users access this computer over the network.

In the procedures presented in the following sections, it is assumed that Windows 98 and the appropriate networking hardware have already been installed on your computer. You might also need to install or configure various supporting components, such as security, mobile networking components, agents for remote administration software, and support for user profiles and system policies.

Installing Networking Components

This section summarizes how to install networking support by using the Network option in Control Panel after Windows 98 is installed. Specific issues for installing various network components are discussed in other chapters of the *Microsoft Windows 98 Resource Kit*. The following procedures describe the general steps that are required for installing networking components.

The following procedure describes how to install a driver for a legacy network adapter card.

Important You should not add Plug and Play–compatible network adapters manually. Instead, you should let Windows 98 detect the network adapter. If the **Select Device** box prompts you to select a network adapter, click the **Have Disk** button and type in the location of your network adapter drivers.

▶ **To install a driver for a legacy network adapter after Windows 98 is installed**

- In Control Panel, double-click Add New Hardware, and then run the Add New Hardware Wizard. Be sure to answer **Yes** when asked whether Windows 98 should search for your new hardware.

Tip You can configure network properties either from the Network option in Control Panel, or by right-clicking the Network Neighborhood icon on the desktop, and then clicking **Properties** on the context menu.

▶ **To install networking components after Windows 98 is installed**

1. In Control Panel, double-click Network, and then click the **Configuration** tab.
2. Click **Add**.
3. In the **Select Network Component Type** dialog box, double-click the type of component to install, as described in Table 14.1.

   Table 14.1   Network component types

Component	Description
Client	Installs client software for the types of networks the computer is connected to. You can use either a 32-bit network client (which needs no real-mode components) or older real-mode networking clients. There is no limit to the number of 32-bit network clients you can install, but you can have only one real-mode network client installed at a time. Some clients are supported only as primary network clients. For information, see Chapter 17, "Windows 98 on Third-Party Networks."
Adapter	Installs drivers for the network adapters in the computer. However, the recommended method for installing a new legacy adapter is to use the Add New Hardware option in Control Panel. For Plug and Play network adapters, you should let Windows 98 detect the network adapter. Then, if the **Select Device** dialog box prompts you to select a network adapter, you should click the **Have Disk** button and type in the location of your network adapter drivers. You can configure the type of driver to use (such as enhanced-mode NDIS, real-mode NDIS, or ODI), specify the resources for the adapters you are using (such as I/O, interrupt request [IRQ], and transceiver type), and define other options for the adapter. For information, see Chapter 15, "Network Adapters and Protocols."
Protocol	Installs network protocols and sets related options. For information, see Chapter 15, "Network Adapters and Protocols."
Service	Installs peer file and printer sharing services and other types of network services, such as Service for NetWare Directory Services, Microsoft Remote Registry, and Network Monitor. For information, see Chapter 23, "System and Remote Administration Tools."

4. In the **Select** dialog box, select the name of the component manufacturer and the name of the specific component.
5. Click **OK**.

Note Most network components require that you shut down and restart the computer after installing them.

You can also install and configure networking components by using custom setup scripts or system policies. For information, see Chapter 3, "Custom Installations," and Chapter 8, "System Policies."

Setting Computer Names and Workgroups

Windows 98 requires that you define a workgroup and computer name for each networked computer, independent of the type of networking software you use. You can also change the computer name or workgroup after Setup is complete.

▶ **To specify the computer name, workgroup, and description for a computer**

1. In Control Panel, double-click Network, and then click the **Identification** tab.

2. Type the values for the computer identification settings as described in Table 14.2.

Table 14.2   Computer identification settings

Setting	Description
Computer name	The computer name must be unique on the network. It can be up to 15 characters long, with no blank spaces. The computer name can contain only alphanumeric characters, as well as the following special characters: ! @ # $ % ^ & ( ) - _ ' { } . ~
Workgroup	The workgroup name does not need to be unique, but it uses the same naming conventions as the computer name. For information about using Wrkgrp.ini for specifying the workgroup that can be selected, see Chapter 3, "Custom Installations."
Computer Description	This information is displayed as a comment next to the computer name when users are browsing the network while viewing it in **Details** mode.

Caution Because computer and workgroup names can contain the special character %, and Msbatch.inf uses the special character % to indicate variables, Windows 98 does not behave as you expect if you use variables in Msbatch.inf for computer and workgroup names. For more information about this problem, see Knowledge Base Article Q170846, "Computer or Workgroup Name Not Set Properly Using Msbatch.inf."

Installing and Configuring WinPopup

You can use *WinPopup* to send a message to one person or to a whole workgroup. WinPopup can also display a message from someone else on your network or from a printer on a Windows NT server when your print job is done. With WinPopup, you can send and receive messages and alerts from LAN Manager, Windows for Workgroups, Windows NT, and Windows 98 servers and clients.

On a NetWare network, you can also use WinPopup to send messages in the following cases:

- If you are running a NetWare-compatible client, you can receive pop-up messages from the server you are attached to. You can also receive messages from other users running Novell-supplied network clients if the message is sent to you on the server using NetWare utilities.

- You can use WinPopup to send a message to a user on a computer running Client for NetWare Networks or a Novell-supplied client if that user is attached to your preferred server. However, you can send messages to bindery users only, not NDS users.

Note If you are running both Client for NetWare Networks and Client for Microsoft Networks, and if the message reaches the specified computer or user through Windows 98 networking, the message is not also sent through the NetWare server.

WinPopup is installed automatically with either Microsoft Client for NetWare Networks or Client for Microsoft Networks. You can configure it to start automatically every time the user starts the computer, or you can start it manually.

▶ **To configure WinPopup to start automatically on a client computer**

1. Place Winpopup.exe in the Startup folder on each computer that you want to receive messages.

2. In the **WinPopup** dialog box on each computer, click the **Messages** menu, and then click **Options** to specify choices for how WinPopup will present messages.

▶ **To start WinPopup manually**

- In the **Start** menu, click **Run**, and then type **winpopup**.

Starting Your Network During System Startup

If your computer uses 32-bit, protected-mode networking components exclusively, you do not need statements in Autoexec.bat or other startup batch files to start the network when you start the computer. The installation of the correct protected-mode network client, protocol, and network adapter driver, as shown in the Network option in Control Panel, is all you need to ensure that networking is available whenever you start Windows 98.

If your computer uses any real-mode components for the client, protocol, or network adapter driver, you must include commands to start the network in Autoexec.bat or a batch file that is called from Autoexec.bat. This is because real-mode components must be inserted properly in the startup sequence to be available to other parts of the system.

For real-mode components on NetWare networks, the Net.cfg or similar file is used to start and configure networking during system startup. The user or network administrator must maintain this file. For Microsoft networks, the **net start** statement in Autoexec.bat is used to start any real-mode networking components.

The Protocol.ini file stores settings for real-mode networking components. The only sections that might be read are [Protman$], [*netcard*], and [Ndishlp$]. For information about the content of Protocol.ini, see Chapter 16, "Windows 98 on Microsoft Networks."

Using Scripts to Automate Tasks

Windows 98 includes the Windows Scripting Host, a language-independent scripting host for 32-bit platforms. With Windows Scripting Host, scripts written with the Visual Basic Scripting Edition or JScript scripting engine, or any other language that provides a Microsoft ActiveX scripting engine can be executed directly on the Windows desktop or command console.

Windows Scripting Host supports several functions that make it easier to configure networking features on your user's computers, such as mapping drives and printers, launching applications, modifying registry keys, and managing your users' environment.

For more information about Windows Scripting Host, see Chapter 23, "System and Remote Administration Tools." See also **http://www.microsoft.com /management/**.

Troubleshooting Basic Networking Configuration

This section provides basic troubleshooting information for installing network components and solving connectivity problems. The section describes general factors to check and then describes in more detail how to check specific elements of your networking configuration.

For additional information about troubleshooting for particular networks, see Chapter 16, "Windows 98 on Microsoft Networks," and Chapter 17, "Windows 98 on Third-Party Networks." For information about general troubleshooting procedures and the supporting tools provided with Windows 98, see Chapter 27, "General Troubleshooting." See also online Help.

When troubleshooting network installation and connectivity problems, start by verifying the network operations status prior to and during the error condition. To evaluate the network problem, consider the following questions:

- Did the network work before? If so, what has changed? If any hardware or software has been added or removed, reset the original network hardware or software, and try again.

- Have any protocols been added or removed? In the Network option in Control Panel, check protocol settings, protocol bindings, and the compatibility of the protocol with the network.

- If you installed a new network component, did it install correctly? Are there duplicate network components or conflicting devices? Check the Microsoft System Information utility to find problem devices and device conflicts. If you find problems, you can change your settings from within Device Manager. For more information about Microsoft System Information, see Chapter 27, "General Troubleshooting."

- Are the network adapter settings correct? Check network adapter settings in Device Manager. Consult the documentation for the correct settings. Reset the adapter settings to the correct values if necessary. Restart the computer and try again.

- Has any network adapter been moved or added? Are other nearby network connections working? Check the adapter connection, and check any other working adapter.

- Has any network cable been moved or added? Check cables, connections, and terminators.

- Are the network connections alive? Look at the status lights on the back of the network adapter or on the media attachment unit. If the status lights show activity, the connection is live. If the status lights show no activity, disconnect and reconnect the network cable and check for activity. If the lights on the adapter are off, try a different network outlet.

- If the network was provided by another vendor, was it installed previously and working? If not, reinstall the other vendor's network. Verify that the network operates correctly. Reinstall Windows 98.

Tip You can quickly view, print, and save information about all your network components by using the Microsoft System Information utility. For more information about Microsoft System Information, see Chapter 27, "General Troubleshooting."

The following sections describe in more detail how to check specific elements of your network configuration.

Note On a clean installation, Windows 98 does not configure Client for Microsoft Networks to log on to a Windows NT domain. If you want Client for Microsoft Networks to log on to a Windows NT domain, follow the instructions in the procedure "To check the logon setting," later in this chapter.

Check domain or server validation.

Verify that the network domain or server is validating the user account. If the logon is not validated, connections to required servers cannot be made, logon scripts will not run, and so on. If the network domain or server does not validate the account, perform each of the following procedures.

▶ **To check the logon setting**

1. In Control Panel, double-click Network, and then click the **Configuration** tab.

2. Double-click the network client (for example, Client for Microsoft Networks or Microsoft Client for NetWare Networks).

3. Click the **Properties** button and then do the following:

   - For Client for Microsoft Networks, verify that logon validation is enabled and that the correct domain name is shown.

   - For Microsoft Client for NetWare Networks, verify that the correct server is specified as the preferred server.

4. If you are running Service for NetWare Directory Services, double-click **Service for NetWare Directory Services** and verify that the correct tree and context are specified.

▶   **To check the user and workgroup names**

- In Control Panel, double-click Network, and then click the **Identification** tab. Check the computer name and workgroup name.

Also check basic logon requirements. For example, verify that the user password and the domain or preferred server account are correct, and test basic network functionality, such as viewing or connecting to other servers.

You can also make Windows 98 display a dialog box that lists the server that validates a Windows 98 client logging on to a Microsoft Windows NT or LAN Manager domain. To do so, use Registry Editor to add a DWORD value named **DomainLogonMessage** to the following registry key:

HKEY_LOCAL_MACHINE\Network\Logon

Set the data value for **DomainLogonMessage** to 1.

For more information about this procedure, see Knowledge Base Article Q150898, "How to Display Domain Logon Confirmation in Windows 95."

Check connections to network resources.

Double-click Network Neighborhood on your desktop and determine whether domains, workgroups, and workstations appear. If they appear, try connecting to a server or workstation. If they do not appear, verify that at least one server exists on the local network and that client services and protocols are installed. If no resources appear in Network Neighborhood but all connectivity appears to be working, attempt to access a network resource by mapping to it using the **Map Network Drive** dialog box or by choosing **Start/Run** from the taskbar and typing in the universal naming convention (UNC) syntax of the resource (*computername**sharename*). If you can connect, browsing is an issue. Also, check cable termination.

Tip   You can access the **Map Network Drive** dialog box either by right-clicking the Network Neighborhood icon and then selecting **Map Network Drive**, or by selecting **Map Network Drive** from the **Tools** menu in Windows Explorer. You can also make the **Map Drive** button appear on the Windows Explorer toolbar by clicking the **View** menu and then clicking **Folder Options**.

If you cannot connect to the server or workstation you want, review the error messages. At the command prompt, use the **net use** command (as described in Chapter 18, "Logon, Browsing, and Resource Sharing") to verify that you can connect to at least one server and workstation. If you cannot connect to any server or workstation, check workgroup assignment, domain assignment, domain logon, and basic network operations.

If you still cannot connect, determine whether you can connect to a server from another computer. If this does not work, it probably indicates a problem with the server you are trying to connect to, or with the cabling or routing to that server.

If you are connecting to resources on a Windows 95 or Windows 98 server running file and printer sharing, verify that the file and printer sharing service appears in the list of installed network components on the server to ensure that peer resource sharing is enabled. Also verify that the correct settings for the browsing method are configured in the properties for the file and printer sharing service on that server. Finally, verify that something is being shared on the server. For information, see Chapter 18, "Logon, Browsing, and Resource Sharing."

Check network adapter and protocol configuration.

The following procedure summarizes how to check settings for network adapters. For more information about configuring network adapters, or for detailed troubleshooting steps for protocols, see Chapter 15, "Network Adapters and Protocols."

Note On networks with a bus topology, if the network adapter is not properly terminated both on the client and on the server, the Windows 98 networking component might not initialize during system startup. Make sure the network segment is terminated properly.

▶ **To check network adapter settings**

1. In Control Panel, double-click Network, and then double-click the entry for the network adapter in the list of installed components.

2. Click the **Advanced** tab, and verify that each entry in the **Property** area has an appropriate value specified in the **Value** area. For information, see your hardware documentation.

3. Click the **Driver Type** tab, and then verify that the appropriate driver type is selected. (If you are using a protected-mode network client, the default is an enhanced mode NDIS driver.)

4. Click the **Bindings** tab, and verify that each protocol is checked. If a protocol is not checked, it is not providing network functionality using that adapter.

5. In Control Panel, double-click System, and then select the **Device Manager** tab.

6. Expand the **Network adapters** tree, click the adapter you wish to check, and then click **Properties.**

7. Click the **Resources** tab, if it exists, and verify that the configuration type, I/O address range, and interrupt request (IRQ) are correct. Device Manager will also report any device conflicts and enable you to resolve those device conflicts by changing your settings. For information about the settings required for your specific adapter, see your hardware documentation. For information about using Device Manager, see Chapter 24, "Device Management."

Check real-mode network components.

To check basic network communications, at the command prompt you can use the **net diag** command with a second computer connected to the same local network segment. As a diagnostic tool, **net diag** can assist you in troubleshooting network connectivity problems by establishing a diagnostic server and then verifying that the local computer can connect to this server.

Note In order for **net diag** to work, you must be running either the Internet Packet Exchange (IPX) or NetBIOS extended user interface (NetBEUI) protocol.

▶ **To establish a diagnostic server on a second local computer**

1. At the command prompt, type:

   net diag

2. When a message appears showing you the protocols in use, press the first letter of the protocol indicated in the message to specify the protocol to test.

3. When a message appears prompting you to specify whether a diagnostic server exists, press **N**.

▶ **To verify that the diagnostic server is detected**

1. On the computer you are trying to troubleshoot, at the command prompt, type:

   net diag

2. When a message appears showing the protocols in use, specify the same protocol to test as that of the diagnostic server established in the previous procedure.

   A message should appear stating that the diagnostic server has been detected. If a message appears stating that no diagnostic servers have been detected, there may be a problem with the network adapter, configuration, or cables.

▶ **To remove and reinstall the protected-mode drivers in Windows 98**

1. In Control Panel, double-click Network, and make note of each installed component.

2. For each component, click the component, and then click **Remove**.

3. Install the components by following the procedure "To install networking components after Windows 98 is installed" in "Installing Networking Components" earlier in this chapter.

Caution Removing your network components causes you to lose network connectivity. You will not be able to reinstall your network components over the network. Make sure you have your original installation media available before removing your network components.

Additional Resources

For more information about	See this resource
Basic information about networks and network adapters	*Networking Essentials, Second Edition*
Advanced networking information, information about networking with Windows NT Server, and information about deploying large networks	*Microsoft Windows NT Server Networking Guide* in the *Microsoft Windows NT Server Resource Kit* (for Microsoft Windows NT Server version 4.0)

CHAPTER 15

Network Adapters and Protocols

15

This chapter describes technical issues related to network adapters and protocols for Microsoft Windows 98 and explains how to install and configure network adapters and protocols. It also presents some technical notes and tips for networking.

In This Chapter

See Also

- For an overview of network configuration, see Chapter 14, "Introduction to Networking Configuration."

- For more information about using Windows 98 on Microsoft networks, see Chapter 16, "Windows 98 on Microsoft Networks."

- For more information about using Windows 98 on third-party networks, see Chapter 17, "Windows 98 on Third-Party Networks."

- For more information about logon, browsing, and resource sharing, see Chapter 18, "Logon, Browsing, and Resource Sharing."

- For more information about Dial-Up Networking, see Chapter 19, "Remote Networking and Mobile Computing."

- For more information about network architecture, see Chapter 29, "Windows 98 Network Architecture."

Overview of Network Adapter Drivers and Protocols

A network adapter (sometimes called a network interface card, or NIC) is a hardware card installed in a computer so it can communicate on a network. The network adapter provides one or more ports for the network cable to connect to, and it transmits and receives data onto the network cable.

Every networked computer must also have a network adapter driver, which controls the network adapter. Each network adapter driver is configured to run with a certain type of network adapter.

A networked computer must also have one or more protocol drivers (sometimes called a transport protocol or just a protocol). The protocol driver works between the upper-level network software and the network adapter to package data to be sent on the network.

In most cases, for two computers to communicate on a network, they must use identical protocols. Sometimes, a computer is configured to use multiple protocols. In this case, two computers need only one protocol in common to communicate. For example, a computer running File and Printer Sharing for Microsoft Networks that uses both NetBEUI and TCP/IP can communicate with computers using only NetBEUI or only TCP/IP. Common protocols are not necessary if the computers are using an intermediary device or application such as the gateway. For a brief explanation of gateways, see "Using Gateways for Connectivity" in Chapter 17, "Windows 98 on Third-Party Networks."

In Windows 98, you configure all network adapter drivers and protocols supporting protected-mode clients by using the Network option in Control Panel rather than by manually editing configuration files. Configuration values are stored in the registry.

Windows 98 Setup automatically configures a computer to use protocols and drivers to match network components that are running when Setup is started.

If you are setting up Windows 98 for a new networking option, you must choose which types of network adapter drivers and protocols to use. Because Windows 98 has an open architecture, you have a lot of flexibility in this decision. Windows 98 supports both network driver interface specification (NDIS) and transport driver interface (TDI) standards, allowing Windows 98 to communicate with many other networking products and making it possible to choose from a variety of network adapters and protocols.

This section describes basic issues for choosing network adapter drivers and protocols to support your networking needs.

Choosing Adapters and Drivers for Best Performance

Network adapters have become exceptionally reliable and inexpensive. The low cost of Ethernet adapters, including new Plug and Play hardware, means that usually the cost-effective way to improve network performance is to replace an older network adapter with a new model. The cost of the new hardware is offset almost immediately by savings in support time and improved performance. Also, you should buy an adapter that matches one of your computer's buses. For example, peripheral component interconnect (PCI) network adapters are available for use in PCI computers.

Choosing Protected-mode Protocols and Adapter Drivers

Microsoft recommends that you choose separate 32-bit, protected-mode protocols and drivers rather than real-mode protocols and drivers. However, Windows 98 includes mapping technology for users who must continue to use real-mode NDIS 2 or Open Datalink Interface (ODI) drivers.

Overview of Protocols

Windows 98 network protocols are implemented as 32-bit, protected-mode virtual device drivers (VxDs) that offer high performance. Windows 98 can support multiple protocols simultaneously, and protocol stacks can be shared among the installed network clients. For example, the Internet Packet Exchange/Sequenced Packet Exchange (IPX/SPX)–compatible protocol can support both Client for NetWare Networks and Client for Microsoft Networks. The following protocols are included with Windows 98:

- TCP/IP
- IPX/SPX-compatible
- NetBEUI
- 32-bit DLC

All four protocols are Plug and Play–compliant, so they can be loaded and unloaded automatically. For example, if a PC Card network adapter is removed from the computer so that the network is no longer available, the protocols are unloaded automatically after any dependent applications have been notified.

Windows 98 can support multiple network protocols and can share a protocol among the network providers that are installed. You might choose more than one protocol to ensure communication compatibility with all systems in the enterprise. However, choosing multiple protocols can cause more network traffic, more memory used on the local computers, and more network delays.

The following sections briefly describe the benefits of using each protocol and issues to consider when using each protocol.

Microsoft TCP/IP Protocol

This is a complete implementation of the standard, routable Transmission Control Protocol/Internet Protocol (TCP/IP) protocol. Windows 98 includes only protected-mode support for this protocol. Microsoft TCP/IP provides the following benefits:

- Support for Internet connectivity and the Point-to-Point Protocol (PPP).
- Connectivity across interconnected networks with different operating systems and hardware platforms, including communication with many non-Microsoft systems, such as Internet hosts, Apple Macintosh systems, IBM mainframes, UNIX systems, and Open VMS systems.
- Support for automatic TCP/IP configuration using Dynamic Host Configuration Protocol (DHCP) servers such as Windows NT servers.
- Support for automatic IP-address-to-NetBIOS computer name resolution using Windows NT Windows Internet Naming Service (WINS) servers.
- Support for Windows Sockets 1.1 and 2.0, which are used by many client/server applications and many public-domain Internet tools.
- Support for the NetBIOS interface, commonly known as NetBIOS over TCP/IP.
- Support for many commonly used utilities, which are installed with the protocol.

Consider the following issues when using this protocol:

- TCP/IP in general has been known to require careful planning and management of the Internet Protocol (IP) address space. However, this problem is vastly reduced when you use DHCP servers to manage assignment of IP addresses for computers running Microsoft TCP/IP.
- If you want to take advantage of DHCP for private IP addressing or use WINS for name resolution on computers running Windows 98, the appropriate DHCP servers must be in place on the network.
- The Microsoft TCP/IP stack does not bind to NetWare client; therefore, you cannot use TCP/IP as a substitute for NetWare/IP when connecting to a NetWare server.

Microsoft IPX/SPX-compatible Protocol

This protocol is compatible with the Novell NetWare Internetwork Packet Exchange/Sequential Packet Exchange (IPX/SPX) implementation. Windows 98 includes both 32-bit, protected-mode and real-mode support for this protocol. This protected-mode protocol provides the following benefits:

- Works with Microsoft Client for NetWare Networks and Novell Client for Windows 95/98.
- Supports packet-burst mode to offer improved network performance.
- Supports the Windows Sockets, NetBIOS, and ECB programming interfaces.
- Support for automatic detection of frame type, network address, and other configuration settings.
- Routable connectivity across all network bridges and routers configured for IPX/SPX routing.

Consider the following issues when using this protocol:

- This protocol is required for Microsoft Client for NetWare Networks and installed automatically with the client. When Windows 98 Setup determines that it cannot install Client for NetWare Networks on a computer running a Novell-supplied network client, Setup still tries to install this protected-mode protocol. For information about how Setup determines whether to install this protocol automatically, see Chapter 17, "Windows 98 on Third-Party Networks."
- This protocol cannot be used to configure Windows 98 to support NetWare over ArcNet. Instead, you must use real-mode IPX drivers with NetBIOS support on ArcNet network adapters.
- With this protocol, it is not necessary to load the Novell-supplied Vipx.386 driver, because the Microsoft protocol provides virtualized services to all virtual machines (VMs) and applications.

Microsoft NetBEUI Protocol

This protocol is compatible with existing networks that use the NetBIOS extended user interface (NetBEUI), including Windows for Workgroups peer networks, Windows NT Server, LAN Manager, and other networks, and includes support for the NetBIOS programming interface. Windows 98 provides both protected-mode and real-mode support for this protocol.

NetBEUI was first introduced by IBM in 1985, when it was assumed that LANs would be segmented into workgroups of 20 to 200 computers and that gateways would be used to connect one LAN segment to other LAN segments or to a mainframe. NetBEUI is optimized for high performance when used in departmental LANs or LAN segments. Microsoft NetBEUI under Windows 98 is completely self-tuning.

One common method for setting up a network is to use NetBEUI plus a protocol such as TCP/IP on each computer that needs to access computers across a router. If you set NetBEUI as the default protocol, Windows 98 uses NetBEUI for communication within the LAN segment and uses TCP/IP for communication across routers to other parts of the WAN.

Consider the following issues when choosing this protocol:

- NetBEUI is a nonroutable protocol that cannot cross routers, although it can cross bridges and source routing bridges.
- NetBEUI is optimized for high performance only for use in departmental LANs or LAN segments.

Microsoft DLC Protocol

The 32-bit DLC protocol provides connection and communication with mainframe computers using DLC. With the 32-bit Data Link Control (DLC) protocol, you can establish multiple connections to different IBM host and AS/400 computers over the same network token-ring, FDDI, or Ethernet adapter. Host terminal emulation programs use the 32-bit DLC to communicate directly with host computers. The 32-bit DLC protocol also allows multiple 32-bit applications to use the same network adapter at the same time to connect to different host computers. You can also use the 32-bit DLC protocol to provide connectivity to local area printers connected directly to the network.

The 16-bit DLC protocol is also available; however, in most cases, it is recommended that you use the 32-bit DLC protocol.

Microsoft TCP/IP Protocol

Microsoft Transmission Control Protocol/Internet Protocol (TCP/IP) provides communication across interconnected networks that use diverse hardware architectures and various operating systems. TCP/IP can be used to communicate with computers running Windows 98, with devices using other Microsoft networking products, or with non-Microsoft systems such as UNIX.

Microsoft TCP/IP in Windows 98 extends the functionality that Microsoft TCP/IP offered in Windows 95. In Windows 95, Microsoft TCP/IP provided the following elements:

- Core TCP/IP protocols, including the Transmission Control Protocol (TCP), Internet Protocol (IP), User Datagram Protocol (UDP), Address Resolution Protocol (ARP), Internet Control Message Protocol (ICMP), and Domain Name System Protocol (DNS). This suite of Internet protocols provides a set of standards for how computers communicate and how networks are interconnected.

- Support for application programming interfaces (APIs), including Windows Sockets and NetBIOS.

- TCP/IP diagnostic tools to detect and resolve TCP/IP networking problems, including **arp**, **ftp**, **nbtstat**, **netstat**, **ping**, **route**, **telnet**, **tracert**, and **ipconfig**, plus Windows-based Telnet and IP Configuration (**winipcfg**) utilities.

- Client for DHCP, for automatic configuration of computers running TCP/IP on networks that have DHCP servers.

- Client for WINS, for dynamic resolution of IP addresses to computer names on networks that have WINS servers.

- Point-to-Point Protocol (PPP) for asynchronous communication, as described in Chapter 19, "Remote Networking and Mobile Computing."

With Windows 98, the following enhancements are added:

- Automatic private IP addressing by the client, as described in the section "Configuring IP Addresses Using Automatic Private IP Addressing" later in this chapter.

- Multihoming, as described in the section "Configuring Multihoming" later in this chapter.

- Windows Sockets 2 support, as described in "Enhancements to TCP/IP in Windows 98" later in this chapter.

- Support for IP Multicast (Request for Comments [RFC] 1112), including support for Internet Draft for IGMP version 2.

- Support for Internet Control Message Protocol (ICMP) Router Discovery (RFC 1256).

- Performance enhancements for certain types of high-speed, high-bandwidth networks. These include support for TCP Large Windows (RFC 1323), support for Selective Acknowledgments (RFC 2018), and support for TCP Fast Retransmit and Fast Recovery.

- DHCP enhancements, including address assignment conflict detection and longer timeout intervals.

For information about the Resource Reservation Protocol (RSVP) and Generic Quality of Service (GQoS) architecture, see Chapter 29, "Windows 98 Network Architecture." For more information about GQoS, see also the specification on **ftp://ftp.microsoft.com/bussys/winsock/winsock2/**. For more information about RSVP, see also the Internet Engineering Task Force (IETF) RSVP specification at **http://www.ietf.org**.

For other RFCs and Internet drafts listed above, see **http://www.ietf.org**.

Planning for TCP/IP

This section gives a broad overview of IP addressing. Then it presents a few common types of networks and explains issues you might want to consider when implementing each type of network.

For information about the architecture of TCP/IP and its Windows Sockets 2 socket API, see Chapter 29, "Windows 98 Network Architecture."

For more conceptual information about TCP/IP, information about routing, and information about using TCP/IP in a large installation with Windows NT Server, see the following publications:

- *Microsoft Windows NT Server Networking Guide for Microsoft Windows NT Server version 4.0.*

- *Network Supplement for Microsoft Windows NT Server version 4.0.*

- *Networking with Microsoft TCP/IP* by Drew Heywood (New Riders Publishing, 1996).

See also the TCP/IP white paper "Microsoft TCP/IP and Windows 95 Networking" at **http://www.microsoft.com/win32dev/netwrk/**.

For TCP/IP shareware tools such as *finger*, *chat*, *whois*, and *nslookup*, visit the following Web sites:

- **http://www.download.com**
- **http://www.shareware.com**
- **http://www.tucows.com**
- **http://www.windows95.com**

Understanding IP Addressing

Each workstation needs an IP address to communicate on a TCP/IP network such as the corporate network or the global public Internet. The section "Configuring IP Addresses" later in this chapter describes IP addresses in more detail, but for now it is just important to understand that there are two kinds of IP addresses, globally unique IP addresses and private IP addresses.

- Globally unique IP addresses, which you can use on the global Internet.

  On the Internet, the Internet Assigned Numbers Authority (IANA) assigns groups of IP addresses to organizations. The organizations can then assign IP addresses within those groups to individual computers. This prevents multiple computers from having the same IP address.

  For a computer to be visible on the Internet, it must be reachable through a globally unique IP address.

- Private IP addresses, which you cannot use on the global Internet.

  The IANA has reserved a certain number of IP addresses that will never be used on the global Internet. You can use these addresses for computers that will never be used to access the Internet.

  In some cases, you can also use these addresses for computers that need partial connectivity to the Internet but do not need to be directly reachable from the Internet. For example, if you need only Web browsing and e-mail connectivity on a computer, that computer does not necessarily have to be directly reachable from the Internet.

  However, in order to enable computers to use private IP addresses, you must deploy a firewall with proxy or Network Address Translator (NAT) capabilities. A proxy or NAT sits between a private network (a network of computers using private IP addresses) and the Internet. The firewall has a globally unique IP address that can be used on the Internet. When a computer on the private network sends a packet to the Internet, the NAT substitutes the source IP address on that packet for the NAT's own IP address. Thus, the packets appear to originate from the NAT.

  This configuration provides flexibility and a certain level of security: hosts on the Internet cannot directly send IP packets to the computer on the private network because they do not know and cannot use its IP address. The firewall can provide a level of administrative control for which machines and which applications can reach computers on the Internet, and vice versa.

  For more information about private IP addresses, see Request for Comments (RFC) 1918. For more information about NATs, see RFC 1631.

Depending on your needs, you can use either private IP addresses or globally unique IP addresses for each workstation. You could also use both a private IP address and a globally unique IP address if you have a multihomed computer (a computer that has two different adapters, each connected to a different network). For example, a workstation could be connected both to the corporate network (using an adapter that is configured with a private IP address) and to the Internet (using a dial-up adapter that is configured with a globally unique IP address). For information about multihoming and this type of special configuration, see the section "Configuring Multihoming" later in this chapter.

Regardless of the type of IP address you choose, you have two options for configuring the IP addresses:

- Dynamic IP addressing.

  With dynamic IP addressing, the IP address can be configured automatically. This method is much simpler, decreases your management time, and enables you to reuse IP addresses. It is recommended for all sizes of networks.

  In Windows 95, two types of dynamic IP addressing were available. For corporate networks, if there was a Dynamic Host Configuration Protocol (DHCP) server on the network, the computer could automatically obtain the IP address from the DHCP server. And for dial-up Internet connections, some Internet Service Providers (ISPs) automatically assigned your computer a dynamic IP address.

  Windows 98 provides a third option, automatic private IP addressing. This option is recommended for simple networks that have one LAN (subnet) and no DHCP servers. With automatic private IP addressing, if no DHCP server is available, the computer automatically assigns itself a private IP address. (If a DHCP server later becomes available, the computer obtains an IP address from the DHCP server instead.) Computers using private IP addresses can communicate only with other computers using private IP addresses, on the same subnet. They are not directly reachable from the Internet.

- Static IP addressing.

  With static IP addressing, you must manually configure the IP address. This method is time-consuming, especially on medium to large networks. It is not recommended except as a last resort.

For more information about automatic private IP addressing, see "Configuring IP Addresses Using Automatic Private IP Addressing" later in this chapter.

For more information about DHCP, see "Automatically Configuring IP Addresses with DHCP" later in this chapter.

Planning for a Dial-Up Networking Connection to the Internet

If you plan to use Dial-Up Networking to connect to the Internet, you must configure the Dial-Up Networking connection. Your ISP might automatically assign you an IP address. If not, you must configure information such as the following:

- An IP address
- A default gateway (default router)

For more information about creating a Dial-Up Networking connection, see Chapter 19, "Remote Networking and Mobile Computing."

For more information about configuring an IP address for a Dial-Up Networking connection, see Chapter 20, "Internet Access and Tools."

Planning for Small Networks

Figure 15.1 shows an example of a small (single-subnet) network that is connected to the Internet by a gateway. In this example, all the computers use globally unique IP addresses and are all visible on the Internet.

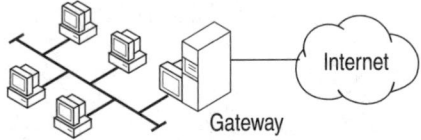

Figure 15.1   Small network with gateway

For this type of network, you must obtain a network ID that is valid on the Internet. You must also configure a gateway to reach the Internet, and each computer needs the address of the gateway in order to reach the Internet. A Windows 98 computer cannot be configured to act as a gateway.

For addressing, you should add a DHCP server and let it automatically assign IP addresses. You could also use static IP addressing, but to do so you must manually configure each computer not only now but whenever you make a change to your network that requires new IP addresses.

Now, suppose that the network includes a NAT. You must still obtain a network ID that is valid on the Internet, configure a gateway to reach the Internet, and configure each computer with the address of the gateway. Also, you can still use either DHCP or static addressing. However, because the NAT shields the IP addresses on your network from the Internet, you can also use private IP addressing. On a simple LAN you can use either DHCP to assign private IP addresses, or you can use the automatic private IP addressing feature to let the computer assign itself a unique private address on the LAN.

Planning for Large Networks

Figure 15.2 shows an example of a large network that is divided into several subnetworks and is connected to the Internet by a gateway.

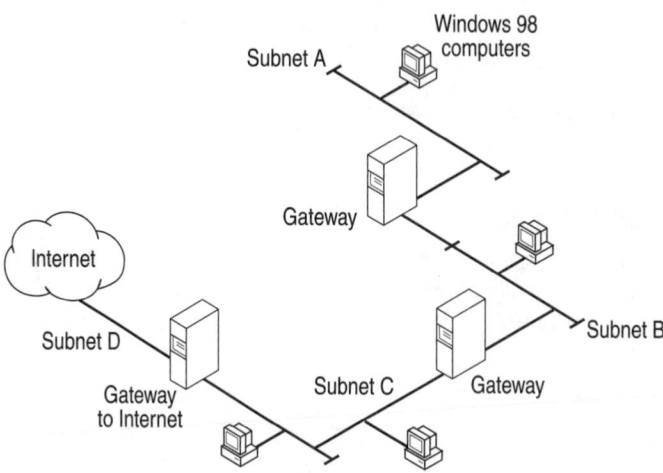

Figure 15.2   Large network with gateway

As with the previous example, you must obtain a network ID that is valid on the Internet. You must also set up one or more gateways. If you have multiple gateways, at least one must be configured as the *default gateway* (the gateway that is used to connect to the rest of the network). For more information about default gateways, see the section "Configuring Multihoming" later in this chapter.

For this type of network, you should use DHCP addressing. If your network does include a NAT, you can assign private IP addresses to each computer, but you should not do so using the Windows 98 automatic private IP addressing feature because the automatic private IP addressing feature guarantees uniqueness only on a LAN-per-LAN basis. Computers that use the automatic private IP addressing feature can communicate only with computers in their immediate subnet. Thus, you should use DHCP when there are routers on the network, even if each computer uses private IP addresses. You could, however, use the automatic private IP addressing feature as a backup method if your DHCP server fails.

If your computer does not include a proxy server or a NAT firewall and you want your machines to communicate on the Internet, you must use DHCP for IP address assignment and not the automatic private IP addressing feature.

Installing Microsoft TCP/IP

Setup installs Microsoft TCP/IP by default if you are installing Windows 98 (instead of upgrading to Windows 98) and you have a network adapter or modem in your computer. If you are upgrading to Windows 98, however, Setup generally keeps your network configuration and you will need to install Microsoft TCP/IP if you want to use it.

If your original Windows installation included a third-party TCP/IP protocol stack, Setup keeps the existing TCP/IP protocol stack instead of installing Microsoft TCP/IP. However, you might want to use Microsoft TCP/IP instead. For example, many third-party TCP/IP stacks do not yet support Windows Sockets 2. If you want to use Microsoft TCP/IP instead of your third-party stack, you must uninstall the third-party stack by using the uninstall utility provided by your network vendor, then install Microsoft TCP/IP.

▶   **To install Microsoft TCP/IP after Windows 98 Setup**

1. In Control Panel, double-click Network.

2. On the **Configuration** tab, click **Add**.

3. Select **Protocol**.

4. Click **Add**.

5. In **Manufacturers**, select Microsoft.

6. In **Network Protocols**, select TCP/IP.

7. Click **OK**.

Configuring TCP/IP

This section discusses the following topics:

- Configuring IP addresses.

- Configuring a multihomed computer.

- Using the route table to view your IP configuration and to add routes to hosts on the network.

Configuring IP Addresses

Every computer on a TCP/IP network is identified by a unique 32-bit *IP address*, which also specifies routing information in an internetwork. An IP address looks like this:

`172.16.94.97`

This is referred to as dotted decimal notation, with each eight bits of an IP address (called an octet) separated from the next eight bits by a period. An IP address is a single value that contains two pieces of information:

- The *network ID*, which is the portion of the IP address that identifies a group of computers and other devices that are all located on the same logical network.

- The *host ID*, which identifies a particular computer within a particular network ID. A *host*, or node, is any device that is attached to the network and uses TCP/IP.

Each host on the network uses the network ID and host ID to determine which packets it should receive or ignore, and to determine the scope of its transmissions (only hosts with the same network ID accept each other's IP-level broadcasts).

The Internet community uses *address classes* to differentiate networks of various sizes. The network class can be determined from the first octet of its IP address. Table 15.1 summarizes the relationship between the first octet of an IP address and its network ID and host ID, using *w.x.y.z.* to designate the four octets of the IP address. As Table 15.1 shows, the value of the first octet determines which portion of the IP address will be the network ID and which portion will be the host ID.

For example, the first octet of the sample IP address 172.16.34.1 is 172. The **w values** portion of Table 15.1 shows that if the first octet has a value of 128-191, it is a Class B address. Thus, the sample IP address is a Class B address. Its first octet (172) is the network ID, and the remaining octets (16.34.1) are its host ID.

Note The sample IP addresses used in this chapter are private IP addresses, not IP addresses that are valid on the global Internet.

The table also identifies the total number of network IDs and host IDs for each address class that participates in the Internet addressing scheme.

Table 15.1 IP address classes

Class	w values[1,2]	Network ID	Host ID	Available networks	Available hosts per net
A	1–126	*w*	*x.y.z*	126	16,777,214
B	128–191	*w.x*	*y.z*	16,384	65,534
C	192–223	*w.x.y*	*z*	2,097,151	254

[1] Inclusive range for the first octet in the IP address.

[2] The address 127 is reserved for loopback testing and interprocess communication on the local computer; it is not a valid network address. Addresses 224 and above are reserved for special protocols (IGMP multicasting and others), and cannot be used as host addresses.

Because the sender's IP address is included in every outgoing IP packet, the receiving computer can derive the originating network ID and host ID from the IP address field. This is done by using *subnet masks*, which are 32-bit values that allow the recipient of IP packets to distinguish the network ID and host ID portions of the IP address.

The value of a subnet mask can also be represented in dotted decimal notation. Subnet masks are determined by assigning ones to bits that belong to the network ID and zeroes to bits that belong to the host ID. When the bits are in place, the 32-bit value is converted to dotted decimal notation, as shown in Table 15.2.

Table 15.2   Default subnet masks for standard IP address classes

Address class	Bits for subnet mask	Subnet mask
Class A	11111111 00000000 00000000 00000000	255.0.0.0
Class B	11111111 11111111 00000000 00000000	255.255.0.0
Class C	11111111 11111111 11111111 00000000	255.255.255.0

The result allows TCP/IP to determine the host ID and network ID of the local computer. For example, if the IP address is 172.16.34.1 and the subnet mask is 255.255.0.0, then the network ID is 172.16 and the host ID is 34.1.

Subnet masks are also used to further segment an assigned network ID among several local networks. For example, a network using the Class B network address 10.100 is one of over 16,000 Class B addresses capable of serving more than 65,000 nodes each. But if this corporate network includes 12 international LANs with 75 to 100 nodes each, it is better to use subnetting to make effective use of 10.100 than to apply for 11 more network IDs. In this case, the third octet of the IP address can be used as a subnet ID, using the subnet mask 255.255.255.0, which splits this Class B address into 254 subnets: 10.100.1 through 10.100.254, each of which can have 254 nodes. Any of these network addresses could be assigned to the 12 international LANs in this example. Within each LAN, each computer is assigned a unique host ID, and they all have the subnet mask 255.255.255.0.

Note   All systems connected to the same local area network must have the same subnet mask.

Host IDs 0 and 255 should not be assigned to a computer; they are used as broadcast addresses that are typically recognized by all computers.

Windows 98 provides three methods of IP addressing:

- DHCP addressing, in which DHCP servers such as computers running Windows NT Server 3.5 or later automatically assign IP addresses to Windows 98 clients.

- Automatic private IP addressing, in which the computer automatically assigns itself an IP address.

- Static IP addressing, in which network administrators manually configure IP addresses for all the computers on the network.

The following sections describe each of the three configurations.

Automatically Configuring IP Addresses with DHCP

In an effort to make implementing the TCP/IP protocol more manageable, Microsoft worked with other industry leaders to create an Internet standard called Dynamic Host Configuration Protocol (DHCP) for the automatic allocation of IP addresses. DHCP is not a Microsoft standard, but a public Request for Comments (RFC 1541) that Microsoft has implemented.

DHCP allows you to establish a range of valid IP addresses to be used per subnetwork. An individual IP address from the range is assigned dynamically to any DHCP client requesting an address. DHCP also allows you to establish a lease time that defines how long an IP address is to remain valid. Other configuration parameters can also be assigned using DHCP, such as subnet mask, DNS and WINS server identification, and so on.

A computer running Windows 98 cannot be a DHCP server. A DHCP server runs as a service on Windows NT Server 3.5 or later. If DHCP is available company-wide, users can move from subnet to subnet and always have a valid IP address. The IP Configuration utility (**winipcfg**) allows users or administrators to examine the current IP address assigned to the computer, the IP address lease time, and other useful data about the TCP/IP configuration.

When TCP/IP is installed, Windows 98 automatically enables the option to obtain an IP address from a DHCP server. You can disable this option if you want to manually enter IP addresses; however, in general you should not need to disable DHCP.

▶ **To disable DHCP**

- You disable DHCP by configuring static IP addresses, following the instructions outlined in the section "Manually Configuring IP Addresses" later in this chapter.

If Microsoft TCP/IP is configured to obtain an IP address from a DHCP server when a DHCP server is not available on the network, an error message announces that the DHCP client could not obtain an IP address and your Windows 98 computer automatically assigns itself a private IP address (using automatic private IP addressing). When the DHCP server becomes available again, it will assign your computer an IP address.

Configuring IP Addresses Using Automatic Private IP Addressing

With Windows 98, Microsoft TCP/IP provides a new mechanism for automatic IP address assignment for simple LAN-based network configurations, called automatic private IP addressing. With automatic private IP addressing, DHCP clients can automatically assign themselves an IP address if a DHCP server is not present. This might happen, for example, on very small networks without a DHCP server, or on any size network if a DHCP server is temporarily down. The DHCP client can use B-node NetBIOS naming to assign the adapter a unique IP address from a special address space. These IP addresses must lie in the following range:

169.254.*x.x*

These addresses are used only for private, internal addressing and are not valid for hosts that are visible on the global Internet.

After the adapter has been assigned an IP address, the computer can use the TCP/IP protocol to communicate with any other computer that is connected to the same LAN hub and that also uses automatic private IP addressing. However, the computer cannot communicate with computers on other subnets, or with computers that do not use automatic private IP addressing.

A Windows 98 computer that is configured for automatic private IP addressing can assign itself a private IP address if either of the following circumstances applies:

- A computer that is not configured as a laptop can assign itself a private IP address at boot time if the computer does not have a valid DHCP lease, and no DHCP server is found on the network.

- If the computer is configured as a laptop, the computer can assign itself a private IP address if no DHCP server is found on the network, regardless of whether it has a DHCP lease. This is useful, for example, for a computer that is sometimes located on a network with a DHCP server, and sometimes located on a network without a DHCP server.

In either case, if a DHCP server is later found, the computer stops using the private IP address and instead uses the IP address assigned by the DHCP service.

Automatic private IP addressing is automatically enabled. You might want to disable it in the following cases:

- Your network uses routers.

- Your network is connected to the Internet without a NAT or proxy server.

Unless you have turned DHCP messages off, DHCP messages inform you when you change between DHCP addressing and automatic private IP addressing. If you do accidentally turn DHCP messages off, you can turn them back on by changing the value of the registry entry **PopupFlag** from 00 to 01 in the following registry location:

HKEY_LOCAL_MACHINE\System
\CurrentControlSet\Services\VxD\DHCP

You must reboot for the change to take effect.

You can also determine whether your computer is using automatic private IP addressing by using **winipcfg**, as the following procedure explains.

▶ **To determine whether automatic private IP addressing is currently enabled**

- Click **Start**, click **Run**, type **winipcfg**, and then click **More info**. The resulting screen identifies your IP address and other information. Look at the box immediately beneath your adapter address. If the name of the box is "IP Autoconfiguration Address" and the IP address lies in the 169.254.*x.x* range, automatic private IP addressing is enabled. If, on the other hand, the name of the box is "IP Address," automatic private IP addressing is not currently enabled.

You can disable automatic private IP addressing in one of two ways:

- You can manually configure TCP/IP by following the procedure outlined in the section "Manually Configuring IP Addresses" later in this chapter. However, this method also disables DHCP.

- You can disable automatic private IP addressing (but not DHCP) by editing the registry.

You disable automatic private IP addressing but not DHCP by adding the **IPAutoconfigurationEnabled** registry entry with a value of DWORD 0x0 in the following registry location:

HKEY_LOCAL_MACHINE\System
\CurrentControlSet\Services\VxD\DHCP

Use the Registry Editor to add this entry, then shut down and restart the computer.

Caution Using Registry Editor incorrectly can cause serious problems that may require you to reinstall Windows 98. Microsoft cannot guarantee that problems resulting from the incorrect use of Registry Editor can be solved. Use Registry Editor at your own risk.

You can change this registry entry for your entire network by creating an Msbatch.inf file. For more information about Msbatch.inf, see Chapter 3, "Custom Installations."

Manually Configuring IP Addresses

If you cannot use DHCP or automatic private IP addressing for automatic configuration, the network administrator must configure TCP/IP manually. Or, if custom setup scripts are used to install Windows 98, the correct values can be defined in the setup script. The required values include the following:

- The IP address and subnet mask for each network adapter installed on the computer.

- The IP address for the default gateways (hardware routers or servers running routing software with the ability to interpret IP addresses, usually used to find remote destinations).

- Whether the computer will use Domain Name System (DNS) and, if so, the IP addresses of the DNS servers on the internetwork.

- WINS server addresses, if WINS servers are available on the network.

The following procedure describes the basic configuration options for TCP/IP. If you want to configure the computer to use DNS or WINS for name resolution, see the procedures in "Using DNS for Name Resolution" later in this chapter and "Using WINS for Name Resolution" later in this chapter.

▶ **To configure the TCP/IP protocol manually**

1. In Control Panel, double-click Network.

2. Double-click the instance of the TCP/IP protocol that is bound to your network adapter.

Note If your computer has multiple network adapters, the list includes an instance of TCP/IP for each network adapter. You must configure each adapter with its own IP address, subnet mask, and gateway. There is one exception: you should configure TCP/IP settings for your dial-up adapter from your Dial-Up connection icon.

All other settings apply system-wide.

---

3. In the **TCP/IP Properties** dialog box, click the **IP Address** tab.

4. Select the **Specify an IP address** check box.

5. Type an IP address and subnet mask in the respective boxes.

   The network administrator must provide these values for individual users, based on the network ID and the host ID plan for your site.

   - The value in the **IP Address** box identifies the IP address for the local computer or, if more than one network adapter is installed, for the network adapter selected in the **Configuration** dialog box.

   - The value in the **Subnet Mask** box identifies the network membership and its host ID for the selected network adapter. The subnet mask defaults to an appropriate value, as shown in the following list.

Address class	Range of first octet in the IP address	Subnet mask
Class A	1–126	255.0.0.0
Class B	128–191	255.255.0.0
Class C	192–223	255.255.255.0

6. To view or specify which network clients are bound to the TCP/IP protocol, click the **Bindings** tab.

   - To keep a network client from using the TCP/IP protocol, make sure the check mark beside the client name is cleared.

   - If the network client for which you want to use TCP/IP does not appear in this list, that client might not be installed properly. Return to the **Configuration** tab in the **Network** dialog box and reinstall that network client.

   Note The only network client provided with Windows 98 that can use Microsoft TCP/IP is Client for Microsoft Networks. Client for NetWare Networks does not use Microsoft TCP/IP.

   NetWare/IP from Novell allows the NetWare Core Protocol (NCP) request to be sent over an IP header. You can use NetWare/IP only with a Novell-provided client.

7. Click the **Gateway** tab. Type at least one IP address for the default gateway (IP router) on the network, and then click **Add**.

8. To specify an IP address for an additional gateway, type the IP address in the **New gateway** box, and then click the **Add** button.

   The first gateway in the list is the default gateway, which is used to reach destinations on remote networks. Gateway addresses can be prioritized by dragging the IP address in the list of installed gateways. Windows 98 attempts to connect to other gateways only if the primary gateway is unavailable.

9. Click **OK**.

10. Restart the computer for changes to take effect.

If you are using Dial-Up Networking to connect to the Internet, you can manually configure DNS and IP addresses for each connection that you define. For more information about defining IP addresses for each connection and about IP addresses on TCP/IP networks, see Chapter 20, "Internet Access and Tools." For more information about TCP/IP registry entries, see Chapter 31, "Windows 98 Registry."

Configuring Multihoming

When a computer is configured with more than one IP address, it is referred to as a *multihomed system*. With Windows 98, network administrators create multihomed configurations for purposes such as the following:

- To connect a computer simultaneously to the local network and (through Dial-Up Networking or PPTP) to the Internet.
- To connect to different subnets when the computer is on a single physical network that contains multiple logical IP networks.
- To allow a computer to communicate simultaneously on two otherwise isolated networks.

For example, in the most common configuration, a computer might have a LAN connection and a dial-up (PPP) or Point-to-Point Tunneling Protocol (PPTP) connection to the Internet or another IP network.

For more information about this configuration, see Chapter 19, "Remote Networking and Mobile Computing."

As another example, a computer on the local area network at a branch office that also requires a network connection to certain computers on the corporate enterprise network might require a multihomed configuration. Such a configuration might be used, for example, by financial or human-resources personnel who must access servers on a private subnet.

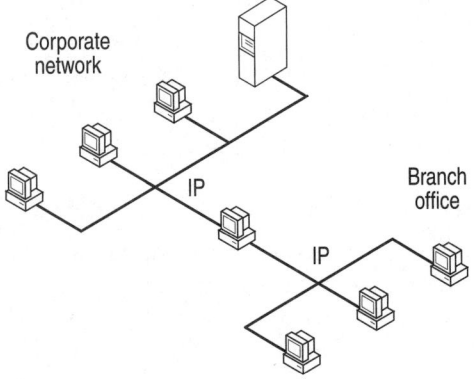

Figure 15.3   Multihomed Windows 98 computer connected to two separate networks

This section provides information about configuring multihomed computers running Windows 98.

Note Multihoming on a Windows 98 computer is suitable only as a limited solution for connecting a single computer to other networks. For corporate computing environments that require routing among subnetworks, you should use dedicated routers such as a Cisco routers, UNIX hosts, or a computer running Windows NT Server 3.5 or later.

Configuring TCP/IP on Multihomed Computers

You can configure multihoming by using multiple network adapters on a single computer, multiple media, or multiple IP addresses for a single network adapter.

For a multihomed computer that uses multiple network adapters for physical connections to the LAN, or a dial-up adapter for remote access, there is an instance of Microsoft TCP/IP for each adapter in the Network option in Control Panel.

Instances of Microsoft TCP/IP —

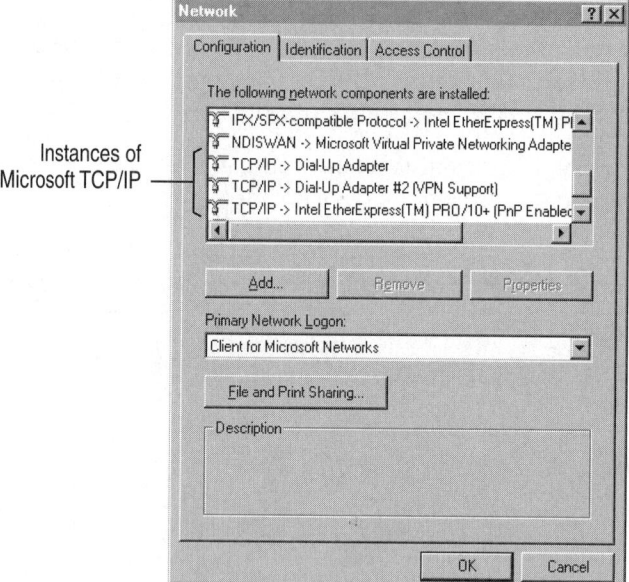

Configuring multiple network adapters per physical network.

Windows 98 places no restrictions on such configurations, so you can add as many network adapters as the computer hardware can accommodate, and assign each a separate address. However, you can only have six instances of TCP/IP and four instances of IPX/SPX installed on the system.

▶ **To configure a multihomed system using multiple network adapters**

- Add TCP/IP configuration information for each network adapter in the Network option in Control Panel, either by using DHCP or by entering information for static IP addresses.

Caution You should not use this method to configure a multihomed system for a Dial-Up or virtual private networking connection. When Dial-Up Networking or virtual private networking are installed, adapters are automatically added and appear automatically in the Network option in Control Panel.

Configuring multiple networks and media types.

You can have only six instances of TCP/IP and four instances of IPX/SPX. This means that only six adapters can bind to TCP/IP and only four to IPX/SPX. Otherwise, there are no restrictions for this type of configuration other than hardware and media support. Microsoft TCP/IP supports the following:

- Ethernet (and 802.3 SNAP).

- Token-ring (802.5).

- Fiber distributed data interface (FDDI), using NDIS 2 real-mode network adapter drivers (only a few protected-mode adapter drivers are available for FDDI supporting TCP/IP).

- WAN, using switched virtual-circuit wide-area media such as ISDN, X.25, and dial-up or dedicated asynchronous lines.

Configuring multiple IP addresses per network adapter.

This option is not supported through the Network option in Control Panel. Additional addresses can be added directly in the registry. However, this is not a recommended method for configuring TCP/IP. NetBIOS name registration using NetBIOS over TCP/IP supports only one IP address per network adapter. Moreover, if DHCP is enabled for configuring TCP/IP, only one DHCP-assigned address can be provided per adapter.

Issues When Implementing Multihoming

If TCP/IP is configured for multiple network adapters, or for both LAN and Dial-Up connections, you must consider the following issues:

A unique IP address and subnet mask are defined for each adapter.

For each network adapter or dial-up adapter, an instance of TCP/IP is bound to the adapter. You can choose to have IP addresses dynamically assigned by DHCP or automatic private IP addressing or defined manually as static addresses.

Domain Name System (DNS) configuration settings are global.

The settings on the **DNS Configuration** tab in TCP/IP properties are used for all adapters on the computer. For example, if you change the DNS settings in the TCP/IP properties for the dial-up adapter to enable DNS, then DNS is also enabled for every LAN adapter on the computer.

However, the settings on the **WINS Configuration** tab are used only for the adapter you are configuring. If you enable the option named **Use DHCP For WINS Resolution** for a LAN adapter, this option is enabled only for that adapter, not for the dial-up adapter or for other LAN adapters on the computer.

Therefore, for a multihomed computer, you must carefully define options for DNS that are applicable for all adapters using TCP/IP. Usually, this means that you want the following:

- If you want to use DNS or the Hosts file for name resolution with any TCP/IP connection, then make sure DNS is enabled.

Note In the case when WINS is used for name resolution on the network (including using WINS servers for host-name resolution) and when DNS is used only for dial-up connections, it is easy for a user to mistakenly disable DNS in the TCP/IP properties for the LAN adapter, without realizing that this also disables DNS for the remote connection. The result would be an inability to find remote hosts when using the remote connection.

The default gateway can be different for each adapter.

For multiple physical connections to the WAN, you can assign a different default gateway for each network connection; however, a Windows 98 computer uses only one default gateway at a time. The default gateway for the dial-up adapter is assigned by the access provider. You can also assign different gateways for a Dial-Up Networking connection by using the Make New Connection Wizard.

Only one default gateway is used at a time.

Although you can have a different default gateway for each adapter, Windows 98 uses only one default gateway at a time. This means that only certain hosts are reachable:

- Hosts on the local subnet
- Hosts that are reachable by the default gateway

As a result, in some cases you may lose network connectivity. For example, suppose your computer is first connected to the corporate TCP/IP network and you make a PPP dial-up connection to the Internet. Your computer stops using the default gateway that connects your computer to the corporate network and instead uses the default gateway that connects your computer to the Internet. Therefore, you can reach hosts on your local subnet, but you cannot reach other hosts on your network.

For a detailed example of a computer changing default gateways, see Chapter 19, "Remote Networking and Mobile Computing."

If you want to restore connectivity to the corporate network, you can use one of the following three methods:

- You can manually add routes to destinations on your local network. For information about adding routes, see "Using the Route Table" later in this chapter.

- In the properties for your dial-up connection, you can deselect the option named **Use default gateway on remote network**, then manually add routes to dial-up destination. For information about how to do this, see Chapter 19, "Remote Networking and Mobile Computing."

- If any of the routers on your corporate network uses the Routing Information Protocol (RIP), you can configure your computer to listen in on those broadcasts. For information about this configuration, see "Support for RIP Listening" later in this chapter.

Using the Route Table

The route table controls where IP packets are sent. It is maintained automatically in most cases, but in some cases you may want to manually add a route. This section describes the route table and explains how to add routes.

To see the route table for your computer, at the command prompt type **route print**.

Note You can reach the command prompt from the **Start** menu, either by clicking **Run** or by clicking **Programs**, and then clicking **MS-DOS Prompt**.

The following table is a sample route table from a single-homed computer.

Table 15.3   Route table sample

Network address	Netmask	Gateway address	Interface	Metric
0.0.0.0	0.0.0.0	172.16.34.1	172.16.34.232	1
127.0.0.0	255.0.0.0	127.0.0.1	127.0.0.1	1
172.16.34.0	255.255.255.0	172.16.34.232	172.16.34.232	1
172.16.34.232	255.255.255.255	127.0.0.1	127.0.0.1	1
172.16.255.255	255.255.255.255	172.16.34.232	172.16.34.232	1
10.0.0.0	10.0.0.0	172.16.34.232	172.16.34.232	1
255.255.255.255	255.255.255.255	172.16.34.232	172.16.34.232	1

Table 15.3 shows a computer with the IP address 172.26.34.232. The table contains the following seven entries:

1. The first line is the default route. This is the route to which the computer sends IP packets if the other route entries do not specify where to send them.
2. The second line is the loopback address. This is the address a host uses to send packets to itself. The loopback address is always 127.0.0.0, and the netmask is always 255.0.0.0.
3. The third line is a network route.
4. The fourth line is a host route for the local host (the route for this host computer).
5. The fifth line is the subnet broadcast address.
6. The sixth line is the IP multicast address. This is the address the computer sends packets to in order to reach an IP multicast group.
7. The seventh line is for limited broadcast address. This is the address a host uses to reach all other addresses on the subnet.

Network Address

The network address in the route table is the destination address. The network address column can have four different types of entries, listed here in the order in which they are searched for a match.

1. Host address (a route to a single, specific destination IP address).

2. Subnet address (a route to a subnet).

3. Network address (a route to an entire network).

4. Default gateway (a route used when there is no other match).

If no match is found, the packets are discarded.

Netmask

The *netmask* defines which portion of the network address must match in order for that route to be used. When the mask is written in binary, a 1 is significant (must match) and a 0 need not match.

For example, the mask of all 255s (all 1s) means that the destination address of the packet to be routed must exactly match the network address in order for this route to be used. For another example, the network address 172.20.232.0 has a netmask of 255.255.255.0. This netmask means that the first three octets must match exactly, but the last octet need not match.

Gateway Address

The gateway address is where the packet must be sent. This can be the local network card or the address of a gateway (router) on the local subnet.

Interface

The interface is the address of the network card over which the packet should be sent. 127.0.0.1 is the software loopback address.

Metric

The metric is the number of hops to the destination. Anything on the local subnet is one hop, and each router crossed after that is an additional hop. The metric is used to determine the best route.

Configuring Routes for a Multihomed Computer

If your computer is multihomed and has connections to two separate IP networks, such as the corporate network and the Internet, the default gateway for only one network is used. For the computer to be able to communicate with the other network, routes must be added to the route table. This can be accomplished in one of two ways:

1. If a router on the network sends RIP broadcasts and your computer is configured to listen to RIP broadcasts, routes will be added automatically. (For more information about configuring your computer to listen to RIP broadcasts, see the section "Support for RIP Listening" later in this chapter.)

2. You can manually add static routes to the route table.

   To add static routes, use the following format:

   ```
   Route add [subnet] mask [netmask] [gateway] metric [metric]
   ```

   The following is an example route:

   ```
   Route add 172.20.255.0 mask 255.255.255.0 172.20.234.232 metric 2
   ```

   The route in this example means that to get to the subnet 172.20.255.0 with a mask of 255.255.255.0, use gateway 172.20.234.232, and that the gateway is 2 hops away.

Configuring TCP/IP Name Resolution

Computers use IP addresses to identify each other, but users usually find it easier to work with computer names. A name resolution mechanism must be available on a TCP/IP network to resolve names to IP addresses.

Windows 98 provides several different types of name resolution, including DNS, WINS, broadcast name resolution, and name resolution using Hosts or LMHosts files. Generally, a Windows 98 computer uses a combination of these name resolution types, summarized in this section.

Domain Name System name resolution. Domain Name System (DNS) is a global, distributed database based on a hierarchical naming system. DNS name resolution is used on the Internet to map friendly names to IP addresses, and vice versa. Notice that DNS replaces the functionality of the Hosts file. For more information, see "Using DNS for Name Resolution" later in this chapter.

Windows Internet Naming Service. Windows Internet Naming Service (WINS) name resolution provides static and dynamic mapping of names to IP addresses. (This contrasts with DNS name resolution, which provides only static mapping.) Computers running Microsoft TCP/IP can use WINS if one or more Windows NT Server computers configured as WINS servers are available. WINS can be used in conjunction with broadcast name resolution for an internetwork, where other name resolution methods are inadequate. Notice that WINS is a dynamic replacement for the LMHosts file. For more information, see "Using WINS for Name Resolution" later in this chapter.

Broadcast name resolution. Computers running Microsoft TCP/IP can use local broadcast name resolution, which is a NetBIOS-over-TCP/IP mode of operation defined in RFC 1001/1002 as b-node. It is restricted to only one subnet. This method relies on a computer making IP-level broadcasts to register its name by announcing it on the network. Each computer in the broadcast area is responsible for challenging attempts to register a duplicate name and for responding to name queries for its registered name.

Hosts or LMHosts files. Hosts and LMHosts files, also called *host tables*, are files that Windows 98 can use for local name resolution if other methods are not available. An LMHosts file specifies the NetBIOS computer name and IP address mappings. When WINS in not available, it is used as a WINS equivalent to resolve NetBIOS names to IP addresses. Likewise, a Hosts file specifies the DNS name and IP address. It is used as a local DNS equivalent to resolve host names to IP addresses. You must manually enter the name-to-IP address mappings in Hosts and LMHosts files.
For more information about creating and editing Hosts and LMHosts files, see Appendix F, "Hosts and LMHosts Files for Windows 98."

Windows 98 provides support for multiple DNS servers and up to twelve WINS servers. Support for either service can be configured automatically from a DHCP server or after Windows 98 Setup by using the Network option in Control Panel.

Note To ensure that both the name and the address are unique, the computer using Microsoft TCP/IP registers its name and IP address on the network during system startup.

Using DNS for Name Resolution

This section provides an overview of DNS, then describes how to configure your Windows 98 client to use DNS.

Understanding DNS

Although TCP/IP uses IP addresses to identify and reach computers, users typically prefer to use host names. For example, users prefer the friendly name **ftp.terrafirminc.tld** instead of its IP address 172.16.23.55. Domain Name System, defined in Requests for Comments (RFCs) 1034 and 1035, is the naming service used on the Internet to provide standard naming conventions for IP computers.

Although DNS may seem similar to WINS, there are two major differences. First, DNS requires static configuration of IP addresses for name-to-address mapping. WINS, on the other hand can provide name-to-address mapping dynamically and requires far less administration.

Second, whereas WINS uses a flat name space (all names are located in the same domain), DNS uses a tree structure called the domain name space, where each node or domain is named and can contain subdomains. DNS is a global, distributed database based on a hierarchical naming system. The naming system was developed to provide a method for uniquely identifying hosts on the Internet.

In Windows 98, the DNS name consists of two parts—the domain name and the host name—known together as the fully qualified domain name (FQDN). For example, using the fictional domain name of Terrafirminc, an FQDN for a workstation in the nursery division could be **jeff.nursery.terrafirminc.tld**. Note that the DNS name can actually be multipart with a period (.) separating each part. Also note that the host portion of the name, **jeff**, is analogous to a NetBIOS computer name.

Note In Windows 98, a computer's globally known system name is its host name (for example, **jeff**), appended with a DNS domain name (for example, **nursery.terrafirminc.tld**). The host name defaults to the computer name (NetBIOS name) defined during Windows 98 Setup. The default name can be changed in the **DNS Configuration** tab when you are configuring TCP/IP properties.

The top-level domains were assigned organizationally and by country. These domain names follow the International Standard 3166. Two-letter and three-letter abbreviations are used for countries, and various abbreviations are reserved for use by organizations, as shown in Table 15.4.

Table 15.4   DNS domain names

DNS domain name	Type of organization
com	Commercial (for example, microsoft.com)
edu	Educational (for example, mit.edu for Massachusetts Institute of Technology)
gov	Government (for example, nsf.gov for the National Science Foundation)
org	Noncommercial organizations (for example, fidonet.org for FidoNet)
net	Networking organizations (for example, nsf.net for NSFNet)

DNS uses a client/server model, where the DNS servers contain information about a portion of the DNS database and make this information available to clients, called *resolvers*, that query the name server across the network. DNS *name servers* are programs that store information about parts of the domain name space called *zones*. The administrator for a domain sets up name servers that contain the database files with all the resource records describing all hosts in their zones. DNS resolvers are clients that use name servers to gain information about the domain name space.

All the resolver software necessary for using DNS on the Internet is installed with Microsoft TCP/IP. Microsoft TCP/IP includes the DNS resolver functionality used by NetBIOS over TCP/IP and Windows Sockets connectivity applications such as File Transfer Protocol (FTP) and Telnet to query the name server and interpret the responses.

The key task for DNS is to present friendly names for users and then resolve those names to IP addresses, as required by the internetwork. If a local name server does not contain the data requested in a query, it then queries the other name servers until it finds the specific name and address it needs. This process is made faster because name servers continuously cache the information learned about the domain name space as the result of queries.

Configuring DNS

You need to determine whether users should configure their computers to use DNS. Usually you will use DNS if you are using TCP/IP to communicate over the Internet or if your private internetwork uses DNS to distribute host information. You can use DNS either instead of or in conjunction with WINS, which is described in the next section.

You also need to determine whether or not you want to use DHCP for automatic configuration. (For information about circumstances in which you might want to use DHCP, see "Planning for TCP/IP" earlier in this chapter.) If you use DHCP for automatic configuration, a DHCP server can automatically configure the list of DNS servers the client should use. If you do not use DHCP, however, you will need to configure these parameters yourself.

Using DNS with WINS Lookup

If you are already using WINS servers for local name resolution but you want to make those servers visible to the global Internet, you can do so without configuring configure DNS on each computer. Windows NT Server 4.0 and later includes a feature called DNS with WINS Lookup. If you configure a Windows NT Server 4.0 and later to use DNS with WINS Lookup, that Windows NT Server can query the WINS servers for the "friendly names" of your computers, then use the information to construct a name that can be used on the global Internet.

For example, suppose the network **terrafirminc.tld** contains a Windows 98 computer named Annuals. On the internal network, the Windows NT Server is using DHCP to automatically assign IP addresses and WINS to resolve those IP addresses to the computer's "friendly names." You want Internet users to be able to connect to Annuals using the fully qualified domain name **annuals.terrafirminc.tld**. If you have Windows NT Server 4.0 or later, you can configure Microsoft DNS server on that computer to query WINS for the IP address for Annuals. WINS returns the IP address, and DNS then successfully resolves the IP address to the FQDN **annuals.terrafirminc.tld**.

For more information about this configuration, see the *Microsoft Windows NT Resource Kit* (for Microsoft Windows NT Server version 4.0).

This section describes how to configure a Windows 98 computer to use DNS for name resolution. You only need to follow the procedures outlined in this section if you are not using DHCP to configure name resolution. If you are using DHCP to configure name resolution, you need only configure DHCP by following the steps in "Automatically Configuring IP Addresses with DHCP" earlier in this chapter.

Figure 15.4 shows sample DNS configuration settings.

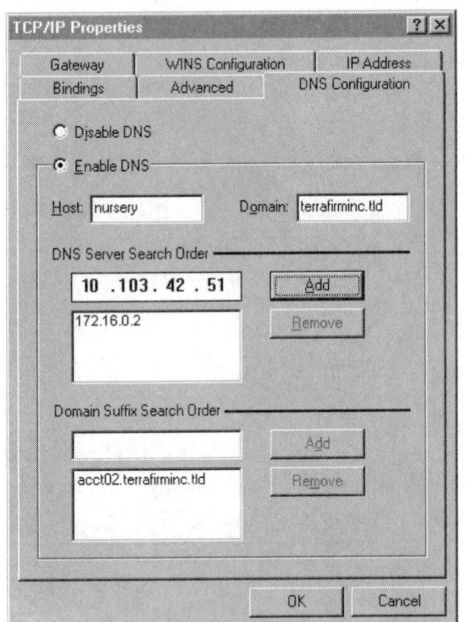

Figure 15.4   Sample DNS configuration settings

▶ **To configure a computer to use DNS for name resolution**

1. In Control Panel, double-click Network.

2. Double-click the TCP/IP protocol that is bound to your network adapter.

3. In the **TCP/IP Properties** dialog box, click the **DNS Configuration** tab.

4. If a DNS server is available, click **Enable DNS**. Then specify a host name and complete the other configuration information as described in the following procedure.

Tip You must enable DNS on each computer that needs to use Hosts for name resolution.

The host name is used to identify the local computer for authentication by some utilities. Other TCP/IP-based utilities can use this value to learn the name of the local computer. Host names are stored on DNS servers in a table that maps names to IP addresses for use by DNS.

▶ **To set the host name for DNS**

- Type a name in the **Host** box.

  The name can be any combination of the letters A through Z, the numerals 0 through 9, and the hyphen (-), plus the period (.) character used as a separator. By default, this value is the Microsoft networking computer name, but the network administrator can assign another host name without affecting the computer name.

Note Some characters that can be used in computer names, especially the underscore, cannot be used in host names. This is a limitation imposed in the character set defined by the Internet Engineering Task Force (IETF) standard for DNS. For more information, see RFC 1123.

▶ **To set the DNS domain name**

- Optionally, type a name in the **Domain** box.

  This is usually an organization name followed by a period and an extension that indicates the type of organization, such as **microsoft.com**. The name can be any combination of the letters A through Z, the numerals 0 through 9, and the hyphen (-), plus the period (.) character used as a separator.

This DNS domain name is appended to the host name (or short name) to create the fully qualified domain name (FQDN) for your computer. If you have not specified a domain in the Domain Suffix Search Order and you are querying for a short name, then this DNS domain name is appended to your query.

Note A DNS domain is not the same as a Windows NT or LAN Manager domain. A DNS domain is a hierarchical structure for organizing TCP/IP hosts and provides a naming scheme used on the Internet. A Windows NT or LAN Manager domain is a grouping of computers for security and administrative purposes.

You can add up to three IP addresses for DNS servers. For a given DNS query, Windows 98 attempts to get DNS information from the first IP address in the list. If no response is received, Windows 98 goes to the second server in the list, and so on. To change the order of the IP addresses, you must remove them and retype them in the order that you want the servers to be searched.

▶ **To set the DNS server search order**

1. In Control Panel, double-click Network.

2. Double-click the TCP/IP protocol that is bound to your network adapter.

3. In the **TCP/IP Properties** dialog box, click the **DNS Configuration** tab.

4. In the **DNS Server Search Order** box, type the IP address of a DNS server that will provide name resolution. Then click the **Add** button to add the IP address to the list.

   The network administrator should provide the correct values for this parameter, based on the IP address assigned to the DNS server used at your site.

5. To remove an IP address from the list, select it, and then click the **Remove** button.

Note If you have two servers listed in this dialog box, Windows 98 checks the second server only if no response is received from the first server. If Windows 98 attempts to check a host name with the first server and receives a message that the host name is not recognized, the system does not try the second DNS server.

The Domain Suffix Search Order specifies the DNS domain suffixes to be appended to short names during name resolution. For example, with the DNS configuration settings shown in Figure 15.4, the domain name acct02.terrafirminc.tld would be appended to the short name to create an FQDN. However, if the Domain Suffix Search Order list is blank, the domain name terrafirminc.tld would be appended instead.

You can add up to five domain suffixes. Place domain suffixes in the list in the order you want them to be searched.

▶ **To set the domain suffix search order**

1. In Control Panel, double-click Network.

2. Double-click the TCP/IP protocol that is bound to your network adapter.

3. In the **TCP/IP Properties** dialog box, click the **DNS Configuration** tab.

4. In the **Domain Suffix Search Order** box, type the domain suffixes to add to your domain suffix search list, and then click the **Add** button.

5. To remove a domain name from the list, select it, and then click the **Remove** button.

Using WINS for Name Resolution

Windows Internet Naming Service (WINS) is a service that runs on Windows NT Server to optimize NetBIOS name resolution. It provides a distributed database for registering and querying dynamic computer name-to-IP address mappings in a routed network environment. You can use WINS either alone or in conjunction with DNS.

WINS reduces the use of local broadcasts for name resolution and allows users to locate computers on remote networks automatically. Furthermore, when dynamic addressing through DHCP results in new IP addresses for computers that move between subnetworks, the changes are updated automatically in the WINS database. Neither the user nor the network administrator needs to make manual accommodations for name resolution in such a case.

WINS consists of two components: the WINS server, which handles name queries and registrations, and the client software (NetBIOS over TCP/IP), which queries for computer name resolution. A WINS server is a Windows NT Server 3.5 or later computer with WINS server software installed. When Microsoft TCP/IP is installed under Windows 98, WINS client software is installed automatically.

On a Windows-based network, users can browse transparently across routers. To allow browsing without WINS, you must ensure that the users' primary domain has Windows NT Server computers on both sides of the router to act as master browsers. These computers need to contain correctly configured LMHosts files with entries for the domain controllers across the subnet.

With WINS, such strategies are not necessary, because the WINS servers and proxies provide the support necessary for browsing Windows NT domains across routers. For a technical discussion of how WINS works and how it can be set up on the network, see *Windows NT Server 4.0 TCP/IP* in the Windows NT Server 4.0 documentation set.

If there are WINS servers installed on your network, you can use WINS in combination with broadcast name queries to resolve NetBIOS computer names to IP addresses. If you do not use this option, Windows 98 can use name query broadcasts (b-node mode of NetBIOS over TCP/IP) plus the local LMHosts file to resolve computer names to IP addresses. Broadcast resolution is limited to the local network, as described earlier in this section.

If DHCP is used for automatic configuration, these parameters can be provided by the DHCP server. Otherwise, you must configure information about WINS servers manually. WINS configuration is global for all network adapters on a computer.

Configuring WINS

The following procedure describes how to configure WINS and how to enable DHCP.

▶ **To configure a computer to use WINS for name resolution**

1. In Control Panel, double-click Network.

2. Double-click the TCP/IP protocol that is bound to your network adapter.

3. In the **TCP/IP Properties** dialog box, click the **WINS Configuration** tab.

4. If a DHCP server is available that is configured to provide information on available WINS servers, select the **Use DHCP For WINS Resolution** check box.

   – Or –

   If a WINS server is available but not a DHCP server, select **Enable WINS Resolution** and type the IP addresses of the Primary and Secondary WINS servers. These values should be provided by the network administrator, based on the IP addresses assigned to these Windows NT Server computers.

5. If WINS is enabled, in the **Scope ID** box, type the computer's scope identifier, if required on an internetwork that uses NetBIOS over TCP/IP.

   Usually this value is left blank. Scope IDs are used only for communication based on NetBIOS over TCP/IP. In such a case, all computers on a TCP/IP internetwork must have the same scope ID. A scope ID can be assigned to a group of computers if those computers communicate only with each other and not with computers outside the group. Such computers can find each other if their scope IDs are identical.

Enabling WINS Persistent Connection Attempts

Windows 98 includes an enhancement to the WINS client (called NetBIOS over TCP/IP, or NetBT), a session-layer network service that performs name-to-IP address mapping for name resolution. (For more information, see the following section, "WINS Technical Notes.") In Windows 95, NetBT queried only one WINS server, and returned a failure for a setup session attempt if the first IP address it tried to use failed to establish a session. This caused a problem because replication delays between two or more WINS servers on the network can cause WINS servers to return stale IP addresses when queried.

You can configure Windows 98 to work around this problem by configuring NetBT to continue querying multiple WINS servers if it failed to establish the initial session. Thus, it first queries the primary WINS server for an IP address and tries to establish a connection using that IP address. If this fails, it tries to get another IP address from the next WINS server, or by using broadcast name resolution. It will continue to query WINS servers until either all of the WINS servers specified have been queried or a connection is established.

To enable WINS persistent connection attempts, set the registry entry **TryAllNameServers** (String data type) to a value of 1. **TryAllNameServers** is found in the following registry key:

HKEY_LOCAL_MACHINE\System
\CurrentControlSet\Services\Vxd\MSTCP

WINS Technical Notes

The WINS protocol is based on and is compatible with the protocol defined for WINS server in Requests for Comments (RFCs) 1001 and 1002, so it is interpretable with any other implementations of these RFCs.

Microsoft TCP/IP uses NetBIOS over TCP/IP as specified in RFCs 1001 and 1002, which define a software interface that supports name resolution for NetBIOS client and server programs in the WAN environment.

RFCs 1001 and 1002 define the following four node types:

- B-node, which uses broadcasts to resolve names.
- P-node, which uses point-to-point communications with a NetBIOS server to resolve names.
- M-node, which uses broadcasts first (b-node), then name queries (p-node) if broadcasts are not successful.
- H-node, which uses name queries first (p-node), and then uses broadcasts (b-node) if the name server is unavailable or if the name is not registered in the WINS database.

If WINS is enabled on a Windows 98 computer, the system uses h-node by default. Without WINS, the system uses b-node by default. Non-WINS clients can access WINS through proxies, which are WINS-enabled computers that listen to name query broadcasts and then respond for names that are not on the local subnet or are h-nodes.

▶ **To see which node type is configured on a Windows 98 computer**

1. Click **Start**, click **Run**, and then, type **winipcfg**.
2. Click the **More info** button.
3. In **Host Information**, look at the **Node type** box.

Viewing Your WINS and DNS Configuration

Regardless of how you configure your computer to use name resolution, you can view your settings using the **winipcfg** utility. For instructions on using **winipcfg**, see "Using Diagnostic Utilities to Troubleshoot," later in this chapter.

Technical Notes on TCP/IP

This section discusses technical information about TCP/IP. First it describes the enhancements to TCP/IP in Windows 98. Next, it lists the supported standards. Finally, it lists and briefly describes TCP/IP command-line utilities.

For information about using these utilities to troubleshoot TCP/IP problems, see "Troubleshooting TCP/IP" later in this chapter.

Enhancements to TCP/IP in Windows 98

Microsoft TCP/IP in Windows 98 includes many enhancements over the version of Microsoft TCP/IP that was included in Windows 95. It includes performance enhancements, support for Windows Sockets 2 and multimedia applications, and greatly improved support for IP multicast. Additionally, it includes RIP listening, a feature that can improve network connectivity for multihomed computers in large corporate networks. This section describes some of the enhancements to Microsoft TCP/IP in Windows 98.

Support for Windows Sockets 2

In Windows 98, Windows Sockets 2 is the preferred application programming interface (API) for TCP/IP socket programming.

Microsoft TCP/IP contains the following enhancements to support Windows Sockets 2:

- Support for Resource Reservation Protocol (RSVP), and Quality of Service (QoS). For more information, see the next section.
- Support for IP multicast, as described in Request for Comment (RFC) 988. This includes support for the Internet Draft for IGMP version 2 and for RFC 1256, ICMP Router Discovery. For more information, see "Support for IP Multicast" later in this section.
- Support for raw sockets, enabling application developers to write applications that directly access Windows Sockets 2. Raw sockets can be used if an application does not want to use either UDP or TCP but instead wants to encapsulate its data in an IP packet to send it.

For more information about Windows Sockets 2, see Chapter 29, "Windows 98 Network Architecture." For information about troubleshooting setup problems associated with Windows Sockets 2, see Chapter 5, "Setup Technical Discussion." For information about incompatibilities between Windows Sockets 2 and third-party networking clients, see Chapter 17, "Windows 98 on Third-Party Networks."

Support for Quality of Service and Resource Reservation Protocol

Microsoft TCP/IP supports the Generic Quality of Service (GQoS) and Resource Reservation Protocol (RSVP) APIs.

The GQoS APIs let applications request certain characteristics for a network connection. The GQoS APIs can request attributes such as the following:

- Peak bandwidth (average or peak bit rate available).

- Latency (the maximum acceptable delay between transmission of a bit and its receipt by the receiver).

- Delay variation (the difference between a packet's minimum and maximum delay).

RSVP is a signaling protocol that is used to establish connections with the requested GQoS characteristics. It handles QoS requests, reserving network bandwidth when possible and when requested, then ensuring that the network can provide that bandwidth.

GQoS is available only if you have the most recent version of Microsoft TCP/IP (which includes Windows Sockets 2).

For more information about the RSVP and QoS architecture, see Chapter 29, "Windows 98 Network Architecture." For more information about GQoS, see also the specification on **ftp://ftp.microsoft.com/bussys/winsock/winsock2/**. For more information about RSVP, see also the Internet Engineering Task Force (IETF) RSVP specification at **http://www.ietf.org**.

For more information about installing Microsoft TCP/IP, see the section "Installing Microsoft TCP/IP" earlier in this chapter.

Support for IP Multicast

With Windows 98, Microsoft TCP/IP supports RFC 1112 IP Multicast, or the transmission of IP packets to a group of zero or more hosts in a multicast group. Windows 98 computers can create, join, and leave multicast groups, and they can send IP packets to groups they belong to.

Microsoft TCP/IP also supports the Internet Draft for IGMP version 2. IGMP version 2 specifies a way for hosts to quickly report termination of multicast group membership. This is useful for low-bandwidth connections. For example, suppose a user is listening to a radio broadcast over a slow dial-up link and wants to change the channel to listen to a different radio station. With IGMP 2, the computer can send a message to the upstream multicast router to stop forwarding the group's packets.

Support for ICMP Router Discovery

Microsoft TCP/IP supports Internet Control Message Protocol (ICMP) Router Discovery, described in RFC 1256. ICMP Router Discovery enables hosts attached to broadcast networks to learn IP addresses of neighboring routers.

Performance Enhancements

With Windows 98, Microsoft TCP/IP includes several features that improve network performance. These features include the following:

- Support for TCP Large Windows and time stamps
- Support for Selective Acknowledgments
- Support for Fast Retransmission and Recovery

Support for TCP Large Windows

Windows 98 TCP/IP supports TCP Large Windows (TCPLW) and time stamps as documented in RFC 1323. Time stamps enable computers to measure round trip times and to reject old duplicate packet segments. TCPLW and time stamps are useful for networks that have high bandwidth and high delay, such as high-speed transcontinental connections or satellite links.

Support for TCPLW and time stamps are enabled by default. By default, TCPLW will be used if an application requests a Windows Sockets 2 socket to use a buffer size greater than 64 KB or if a **DefaultRcvWindow** size of more than 64 KB is used in the registry. To change the default value, you must add the registry entry **Tcp1323Opts** to the following location:

HKEY_LOCAL_MACHINE\System
\CurrentControlSet\Services\VXD\MSTCP\Parameters

The registry entry **Tcp1323Opts** is a string value type. The values for the key are:

0 - No window scaling and time stamp options

1 - Window scaling options but no time stamp options

2 - Time stamp but no window scaling options

3 - Window scaling and time stamp options

Support for Selective Acknowledgments

Windows 98 TCP supports Selective Acknowledgments (SACK) as documented in RFC 2018. Selective Acknowledgments allows TCP to recover from IP packet loss without resending packets that were already received by the receiver. Selective Acknowledgments is most useful in combination with TCPLW and time stamps. SACK support is enabled by default. To disable SACK support, you must add the registry entry **SackOpts** to the following location:

**HKEY_LOCAL_MACHINE\System
\CurrentControlSet\Services\VXD\MSTCP\Parameters**

The registry entry **SackOpts** is a string value type. The values for the entry are:

0 - No SACK options

1 - SACK option enabled

The default value is 1 - SACK option enabled.

Support for Fast Retransmission and Fast Recovery

Windows 98 TCP/IP supports Fast Retransmission and Fast Recovery on TCP connections that are incurring IP packet loss. These mechanisms allow a TCP sender to quickly infer a single packet loss and resend the packet after receiving duplicate acknowledgments for a previously sent and acknowledged TCP/IP packet. This mechanism is useful when the network is intermittently congested and intervening routers or switches are dropping packets.

By default, the sender must receive three duplicate acknowledgments before resending the last unacknowledged TCP/IP packets. You can change this default value by adding a registry entry to the following location:

**HKEY_LOCAL_MACHINE\System
\CurrentControlSet\Services\VXD\MSTCP\Parameters**

The registry entry **MaxDupAcks** is data type DWORD and accepts integer values from 2 to N. The value data of MaxDupAcks indicates the number of duplicate acknowledgments the sender receives before resending the last unacknowledged TCP/IP packet.

Support for RIP Listening

In some large networks, a computer might be configured as a multihomed system and connected to two different networks. Figure 15.3 (earlier in this chapter) shows this configuration.

To communicate with both networks at the same time, the computer must be able to communicate with both routers. However, as the section "Configuring Multihoming" described, Windows 98 computers can use only one default gateway at a time.

There is a solution to this problem. If one or both of the routers uses the Routing Information Protocol (RIP) to send routing information, the computer can be configured to "listen in" to the RIP messages. Your computer can learn other routes on the network, by listening to RIP messages, and then add their IP addresses to the route table. Thus, you do not need to manually add routes to the route table. This process is called *RIP listening* or *silent RIP*. Figure 15.5 shows an example of a multihomed host that uses RIP listening.

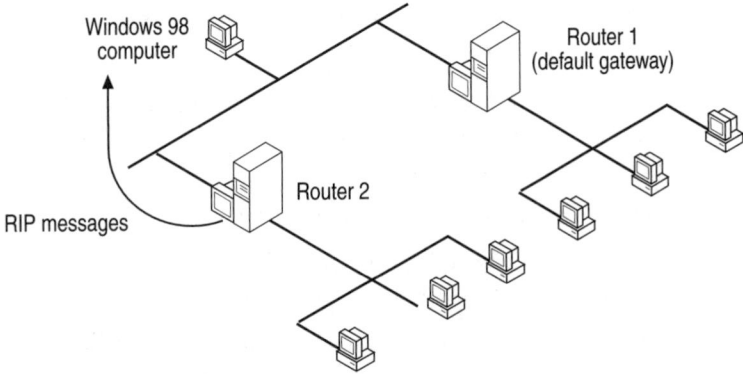

Figure 15.5   Multihomed host using RIP listening

Router 2 sends RIP messages, and the Windows 98 computer listens in on those messages. Router 1 does not send RIP messages, so the Windows 98 computer is configured to use Router 1 as the default gateway. Thus, the Windows 98 computer can communicate with hosts on both networks.

The following procedure describes how to enable RIP listening.

▶ **To enable RIP listening**
1. In Control Panel, double-click **Network**, and then click **Add**.
2. In **Select Network Component Type**, select **Service**, and then click **Add**.
3. Click **Have Disk**, and then type the location of the RIP listening files. They are located on the Windows 98 CD, in the \Tools\RIP directory. Select the file Irip.inf, and then click **OK**.

You must restart your computer for the changes to take effect.

Supported Standards

TCP/IP standards are defined in Requests for Comments (RFCs) published by the Internet Engineering Task Force (IETF) and other working groups. Table 15.5 lists the RFC standards supported by Microsoft TCP/IP. To find these standards, visit **http://www.ietf.org/**.

Table 15.5   Request for Comments standards supported

RFC number	RFC standard
768	User Datagram Protocol (UDP)
783	Trivial File Transfer Protocol (TFTP)
791	Internet Protocol (IP)
792	Internet Control Message Protocol (ICMP)

Table 15.5   Request for Comments standards supported (*continued*)

RFC number	RFC standard
793	Transmission Control Protocol (TCP)
816	Fault Isolation and Recovery
826	Address Resolution Protocol (ARP)
854	Telnet Protocol (TELNET)
862	Echo Protocol (ECHO)
863	Discard Protocol (DISCARD)
864	Character Generator Protocol (CHARGEN)
865	Quote of the Day Protocol (QUOTE)
867	Daytime Protocol (DAYTIME)
894	IP Over Ethernet
919,922	IP Broadcast Datagrams (broadcasting with subnets)
950	Internet Standard Subnetting Procedure
959	File Transfer Protocol (FTP)
1001,1002	NetBIOS Service Protocols
1034,1035	Domain Name System (DNS)
1042	IP over Token-Ring
1055	Transmission of IP over Serial Lines (IP-SLIP)
1122,1123	Host Requirements (communications and applications)
1134	Point-to-Point Protocol (PPP)
1144	Compressing TCP/IP Headers for Low-Speed Serial Links
1157	Simple Network Management Protocol (SNMP)
1179	Line Printer Daemon Protocol
1188	IP over Fiber Distributed Data Interface (FDDI)
1191	Path Maximum Transmission Unit (MTU) Discovery
1201	IP over ArcNet
1231	IEEE 802.5 Token-Ring MIB (MIB-II)
1323	TCP Extensions for High Performance
1332	PPP Internet Protocol Control Protocol (IPCP)
1334	PPP Authentication Protocols
1518	An Architecture for IP Address Allocation with Classless Inter-Domain Routing (CIDR)
1519	Classless Inter-Domain Routing (CIDR): An Address Assignment and Aggregation Strategy
1533	Dynamic Host Configuration Protocol (DHCP) Options and Bootstrap Protocol (BOOTP) Vendor Extensions

Table 15.5   Request for Comments standards supported (*continued*)

RFC number	RFC standard
1534	Interoperation between DHCP and BOOTP
1541	Dynamic Host Configuration Protocol (DHCP)
1542	Clarifications and Extensions for the Bootstrap Protocol (BOOTP)
1547	Requirements for Point-to-Point Protocol (PPP)
1548	The Point-to-Point Protocol (PPP)
1549	PPP in High-level Data Link Control (HDLC) Framing
1552	PPP Internetwork Packet Exchange Control Protocol (IPXCP)
1553	IPX Header Compression
1570	Link Control Protocol (LCP) Extensions
2018	TCP Selective Acknowledgment Options
2131	Dynamic Host Configuration Protocol (DHCP)
Draft RFCs	NetBIOS Frame Control Protocol (NBFCP); PPP over ISDN; PPP over X.25; Compression Control Protocol

TCP/IP Utilities

The TCP/IP utilities offer network connections to non-Microsoft hosts such as UNIX system computers. You must have the TCP/IP network protocol installed to use the TCP/IP utilities. The tools listed in Table 15.6 are installed automatically when you install Microsoft TCP/IP.

Table 15.6   Tools installed with TCP/IP

Command	Purpose
arp	Displays and modifies the IP-to-Ethernet address translation tables.
ipconfig	Command-line utility that displays IP address and other configuration information
ftp	Transfers files to and from a node running **ftp** service.
nbtstat	Displays protocol statistics and current TCP/IP connections using NetBIOS over TCP/IP.
netstat	Displays protocol statistics and current TCP/IP connections.
ping	Verifies connections to a remote host or hosts.
route	Manually controls network routing tables.
telnet	Starts terminal emulation with a remote system running a Telnet service. Windows 98 provides a graphical version of this utility as well as the older, MS-DOS-based version.
tracert	Determines the route taken to a destination.
Winipcfg	Graphical utility that displays IP address and other configuration information

---

Important The FTP and Telnet utilities rely on password authentication by the remote computer. Passwords are not encrypted before being sent over the network. This allows another user equipped with a network analyzer on the same network to steal a user's remote account password. For this reason, it is strongly recommended that users of these utilities choose different passwords for their workgroups, computer, or domain from the passwords used when connecting to computers that are not on Microsoft networks.

The following describes most of the TCP/IP commands included with Windows 98. For information about the syntax of those commands, use the help provided in the MS-DOS virtual machine.

For information about **winipcfg**, see "Using Diagnostic Utilities to Troubleshoot," later in this chapter.

▶ **To get help on TCP/IP utilities**

- At the command prompt, type the command name followed by a space and **-?**. For example, type **arp -?** to get help on the **arp** command. For some commands, you do not need to type the dash and question mark.

Arp

This diagnostic command displays and modifies the IP-to-Ethernet or IP-to-token-ring address translation tables used by the Address Resolution Protocol (ARP).

Ftp

This connectivity command transfers files to and from a computer running a File Transfer Protocol (FTP) service. The **ftp** command can be used interactively or by processing ASCII text files.

▶ **To use the ftp command**

- At the command prompt, type **ftp** plus any desired switches and press ENTER.

  For example, you might type **ftp -s:myfile.scr**

▶ **To get help with the ftp command**

- From within FTP, type **help** *command*, where *command* is the name of the command you need help with. For a list of commands, simply type **help**.

Table 15.7 shows the FTP commands available when Microsoft TCP/IP is installed on a computer.

Table 15.7   FTP commands in Microsoft TCP/IP

Command	Purpose
!	Runs the specified command on the local computer.
?	Displays descriptions for **ftp** commands. Identical to **help**.
append	Appends a local file to a file on the remote computer, using the current file type setting.
ascii	Sets the file transfer type to ASCII, the default.
bell	Toggles a bell to ring after each file transfer command is completed. By default, the bell is off.
binary	Sets the file transfer type to binary.
bye	Ends the FTP session with the remote computer and exits **ftp**.
cd	Changes the working directory on the remote computer.
close	Ends the FTP session with the remote server and returns to the command interpreter.
debug	Toggles debugging. When debugging is on, each command sent to the remote computer is printed, preceded by the string --->. By default, debugging is off.
delete	Deletes files on remote computers.
dir	Displays a list of a remote directory's files and subdirectories.
disconnect	Disconnects from the remote computer, retaining the **ftp** prompt.
get	Copies a remote file to the local computer, using the current file transfer type. Identical to **recv**.
glob	Toggles file name globbing. Globbing permits use of wildcard characters in local file or path names. By default, globbing is on.
hash	Toggles hash-mark (#) printing for each 2048 bytes data block transferred. By default, hash-mark printing is off.
help	Displays descriptions for FTP commands.
lcd	Changes the working directory on the local computer. By default, the current directory on the local computer is used.
literal	Sends arguments, verbatim, to the remote FTP server. A single FTP reply code is expected in return. Identical to **quote**.
ls	Displays an abbreviated list of a remote directory's files and subdirectories.
mdelete	Deletes multiple files on remote computers.
mdir	Displays a list of a remote directory's files and subdirectories. Allows you to specify multiple files.
mget	Copies multiple remote files to the local computer using the current file transfer type.

Table 15.7   FTP commands in Microsoft TCP/IP (*continued*)

Command	Purpose
mkdir	Creates a remote directory.
mls	Displays an abbreviated list of a remote directory's files and subdirectories.
mput	Copies multiple local files to the remote computer, using the current file transfer type.
open	Connects to the specified FTP server.
prompt	Toggles prompting. During multiple file transfers, **ftp** provides prompts to allow you to selectively retrieve or store files; **mget** and **mput** transfer all files if prompting is turned off. By default, prompting is on.
put	Copies a local file to the remote computer, using the current file transfer type. Identical to **send**.
pwd	Prints the current directory on the remote computer.
quit	Ends the FTP session with the remote computer and exits **ftp**.
quote	Sends arguments, verbatim, to the remote FTP server. A single FTP reply code is expected in return. Identical to **literal**.
recv	Copies a remote file to the local computer, using the current file transfer type. Identical to **get**.
remotehelp	Displays help for remote commands.
rename	Renames remote files.
rmdir	Deletes a remote directory.
send	Copies a local file to the remote computer, using the current file transfer type. Identical to **put**.
status	Displays the current status of FTP connections and toggles.
trace	Toggles packet tracing; displays the route of each packet when running an FTP command.
type	Sets or displays the file transfer type.
user	Specifies a user to the remote computer.
verbose	Toggles verbose mode. If on, all FTP responses are displayed; when a file transfer completes, statistics regarding the efficiency of the transfer are also displayed. By default, verbose is on.

Nbtstat

This diagnostic command displays protocol statistics and current TCP/IP connections using NetBIOS over TCP/IP.

Notes on Nbtstat

The column headings generated by the **nbtstat** utility have the following meanings.

Input
  Number of bytes received.

Output
  Number of bytes sent.

In/Out
  Whether the connection is from the computer (outbound) or from another system to the local computer (inbound).

Life
  The remaining time that a name table cache entry will live before it is purged.

Local Name
  The local NetBIOS name associated with the connection.

Remote Host
  The name or IP address associated with the remote host.

Type
  This refers to the type of name. A name can either be a unique name or a group name.

<03>
  Each NetBIOS name is 16 characters long. The last byte often has special significance, because the same name can be present several times on a computer. This notation is the last byte converted to hexadecimal. For example, <20> is a space in ASCII.

State
  The state of NetBIOS connections as shown in Table 15.8

Table 15.8   NetBIOS connection states

State	Meaning
Accepting	An inbound session is currently being accepted and will be connected shortly.
Associated	A connection endpoint has been created and associated with an IP address.
Connected	The session has been established.
Connecting	The session is in the connecting phase where the name-to-IP address mapping of the destination is being resolved.
Disconnected	The local computer has issued a disconnect, and it is waiting for confirmation from the remote computer.
Disconnecting	A session is in the process of disconnecting.
Idle	This endpoint has been opened but cannot receive connections.

Table 15.8   NetBIOS connection states (*continued*)

State	Meaning
Inbound	An inbound session is in the connecting phase.
Listening	This endpoint is available for an inbound connection.
Outbound	A session is in the connecting phase where the TCP connection is currently being created.
Reconnecting	A session is trying to reconnect if it failed to connect on the first attempt.

Netstat

This diagnostic command displays protocol statistics and current TCP/IP network connections.

Notes on Netstat

The **netstat** utility provides statistics on network components. Table 15.9 outlines these statistics.

Table 15.9   Netstat statistics

Statistic	Purpose
Foreign Address	The IP address and port number of the remote computer to which the socket is connected. The name corresponding to the IP address is shown instead of the number if the Hosts file contains an entry for the IP address. In cases where the port is not yet established, the port number is shown as an asterisk (*).
Local Address	The IP address of the local computer, and the port number the connection is using. The name corresponding to the IP address is shown instead of the number if the Hosts file contains an entry for the IP address. In cases where the port is not yet established, the port number is shown as an asterisk (*).
Proto	The name of the protocol used by the connection.
(state)	Indicates the state of TCP connections only. The possible states are the following:

close_wait	fin_wait_1	syn_received
closed	fin_wait_2	syn_send
established	listen	timed_waitlast_ack

Ping

This diagnostic command verifies connections to one or more remote hosts.

Notes on Ping

The **ping** command verifies connections to a remote host or hosts, by sending Internet Control Message Protocol (ICMP) echo packets to the host and listening for echo reply packets. The **ping** command waits for up to 1 second for each packet sent and prints the number of packets transmitted and received. Each received packet is validated against the transmitted message. By default, 4 echo packets containing 64 bytes of data (a periodic uppercase sequence of alphabetic characters) are transmitted.

You can use the **ping** utility to test both the host name and the IP address of the host. If the IP address is verified but the host name is not, you may have a name resolution problem. In this case, be sure that the host name you are querying is in either the local Hosts file or in the DNS database.

Route

This diagnostic command manipulates network routing tables.

Telnet

This connectivity command starts terminal emulation with a remote system running a Telnet service. Telnet provides Digital Equipment Corporation (DEC) VT 100, DEC VT 52, or TTY emulation, using connection-based services of TCP.

To provide terminal emulation from a Windows 95 computer, the foreign host must be configured with the TCP/IP program, the Telnet server program or daemon, and a user account for the computer running Windows 95.

The Telnet application is found in the Accessories program group if you install the TCP/IP connectivity utilities. Telnet is a Windows Sockets–based application that simplifies TCP/IP terminal emulation with Windows 98. HyperTerminal can also be used as a Telnet client.

Note   Microsoft does not provide the Telnet server daemon (**telnetd**).

Tracert

This diagnostic utility determines the route taken to a destination by sending Internet Control Message Protocol (ICMP) echo packets with varying Time-To-Live (TTL) values to the destination. Each router along the path is required to decrement the TTL on a packet by at least 1 before forwarding it, so the TTL is effectively a hop count. When the TTL on a packet reaches 0, the router is supposed to send back an ICMP Time Exceeded message to the source system. The **tracert** command determines the route by sending the first echo packet with a TTL of 1 and incrementing the TTL by 1 on each subsequent transmission until the target responds or the maximum TTL is reached. The route is determined by examining the ICMP Time Exceeded messages sent back by intermediate routers. Notice that some routers silently drop packets with expired TTLs and are invisible to **tracert**.

Notes on Tracert

When you type **tracert** *destination*, where *destination* is the host you wish to reach, four columns are displayed. The first column is the hop number, which is the TTL value set in the packet. Each of the next three columns contains the round-trip times in milliseconds for an attempt to reach the destination with that TTL value. An asterisk (*) means that the attempt timed out. The fourth column is the host name (if it was resolved) and IP address of the responding system.

IPX/SPX-compatible Protocol

The Microsoft Internetwork Packet Exchange/Sequenced Packet Exchange (IPX/SPX)–compatible protocol (nwlink.vxd) supports the 32-bit Windows Sockets 1.1 programming interface, so that any Win32-based Windows Sockets 1.1 application can run on IPX/SPX with Windows 98. (There are no 16-bit Windows Sockets applications using IPX/SPX.)

The IPX/SPX-compatible protocol can be used by Client for NetWare Networks to communicate with NetWare servers or computers running File and Printer Sharing for NetWare Networks.

This protocol can also be used by Client for Microsoft Networks to communicate with computers running Windows for Workgroups 3.11 or Windows NT that are also running IPX/SPX.

The IPX/SPX-compatible protocol uses the nwnblink.vxd module to support computers that use NetBIOS over IPX and to support the NetBIOS programming interface. This protocol can also use NetWare servers configured as routers (and other IPX routers) to transfer packets across LANs.

Configuring the IPX/SPX-compatible Protocol

The Microsoft IPX/SPX–compatible protocol is installed automatically when Client for NetWare Networks is installed. You can also install this protocol to support other network clients, including Client for Microsoft Networks.

▶ **To install the IPX/SPX-compatible protocol**

1. In Control Panel, double-click Network, and then click **Add**.

2. In the **Select Network Component Type** dialog box, click **Protocol** and then click the **Add** button.

3. In **Manufacturers**, click **Microsoft**, and then in **Network Protocols**, click **IPX/SPX-compatible Protocol**, and then click **OK**.

4. Click **OK**. Setup copies the files you need.

When you install the IPX/SPX-compatible protocol, Windows 98 automatically detects and sets appropriate values for the frame type, network address, and other settings. However, in some cases you might need to configure settings for this protocol manually.

▶ **To configure the IPX/SPX-compatible protocol**

1. In Control Panel, double-click Network.

2. Double-click the instance of **IPX/SPX-compatible Protocol** that is bound to your network adapter.

Note If the computer has multiple network adapters, the list will contain an instance of the IPX/SPX-compatible protocol for each network adapter. You must configure each adapter with its own settings. You can only have four instances of IPX/SPX on your system, so if you have more than four adapters are installed, you should bind IPX/SPX only to the adapters that will use this protocol.

---

3. Click the **Advanced** tab.

4. Most values have correct defaults in typical installations. If you need to change a value for a particular purpose, select the item in the **Property** list and specify a setting in the **Value** list based on the information in the Table 15.10.

Table 15.10   IPX/SPX configuration values

Property	Value
Force even-length IPX packets	Enabled only for Ethernet 802.3 on monolithic implementations that cannot handle odd-length packets.
Frame type[1]	Specifies the frame type based on detection. This value is used for network adapters that support multiple frame types. The possible values are: • Auto-detect (recommended) • Ethernet 802.2 (default for NetWare 3.12 and later) • Ethernet 802.3 • Ethernet II • Token-ring • Token-ring Subnetwork Access Protocol (SNAP)
Maximum connections	Specifies the maximum number of connections that IPX will allow. Configured dynamically.
Maximum sockets	Specifies the maximum number of IPX sockets that IPX assigns. Configured dynamically.
Network address	Specifies the IPX network address as a four-byte value. Configured dynamically.
Source routing[2]	Specifies the cache size to use with source routing. This parameter is used only on token-ring networks, where it is used to turn on source routing. **Important** Cache size is specified by entry count, not byte count. The recommended value of 16 entries is the most efficient and best setting for most installations.

[1] Each time the computer starts, Windows 98 detects the frame type by sending a general RIP request in each frame format. Based on the responses received from routers, Windows 98 determines the most prevalent frame type used and sets that as the default frame type.

[2] Source routing is a method of routing data across bridges. For NetWare networks, this means forwarding NetWare frames across an IBM token-ring bridge. With NDIS protocols, source routing is done by the protocol. With ODI-based protocols, source routing is configured with the network adapter driver or using the NetWare route.com utility.

You should not need to change bindings in most circumstances. However, you can disable the bindings for a protocol if you do not want other computers using that protocol to see this computer. At least one protocol, however, must be bound to the network client for the computer to communicate with the network.

▶ **To change bindings for the IPX/SPX-compatible protocol**

1. In Control Panel, double-click Network.

2. Double-click the instance of **IPX/SPX-compatible Protocol** that is bound to your network adapter.

Note If the computer has multiple network adapters, the list will contain an instance of the IPX/SPX-compatible protocol for each network adapter. You must configure each adapter with its own settings. You can only have four instances of IPX/SPX on your system, so if you have more than four adapters are installed, you should bind IPX/SPX only to the adapters that will use this protocol.

3. Click the **Bindings** tab.

4. Click any network component to change its bindings.

    If the option is checked, it is bound to the protocol. If it is not checked, that network component is not using the IPX/SPX-compatible protocol. For more information, see "Configuring Network Adapters" earlier in this chapter.

Note Microsoft Client for NetWare Networks is always bound only to the IPX/SPX-compatible protocol. This network client cannot use another protocol.

Using NetBIOS over IPX

NetBIOS is an interface used by network applications to communicate with other NetBIOS-compliant applications. The NetBIOS interface is responsible for the following:

- Establishing logical names on the network.

- Establishing connections (called sessions) between two computers by use of their logical names on the network.

- Transmitting data between networked computers.

Windows 98 provides a 32-bit, protected-mode driver to support NetBIOS services over IPX (Vnetbios.386). This implementation is compatible with the Novell NetBIOS support driver. Performance enhancements include acknowledgment of previous frames in response frames (called PiggyBackAck), plus a "sliding window" acknowledgment mechanism.

These NetBIOS enhancements are used only when the computer is communicating with other computers using IPX over NetBIOS, such as other computers running Windows 98, Windows NT, or NetWare when running Lotus Notes or other NetBIOS applications. NetBIOS over IPX is not necessary for computers running Windows 98 to be able to communicate with each other. The redirector and server networking components in Windows 98 communicate with the IPX protocol directly without NetBIOS.

Novell provides a terminate-and-stay resident (TSR) NetBIOS driver named Netbios.exe, which is a Level 1 NetBIOS provider that consumes about 40K of conventional memory. This driver acknowledges each frame received, thus increasing the amount of traffic generated when NetBIOS is used. With the Microsoft implementation of NetBIOS over IPX, you can remove the real-mode Netbios.exe TSR.

Note A Windows 98 computer that uses IPX without NetBIOS can connect to a Windows NT 3.5 or later server that uses IPX without NetBIOS. However, the Windows NT 3.5 or later computer service can only connect to a Windows 98 computer running File and Printer Sharing for Microsoft Networks when the Windows 98 computer is using NetBIOS over IPX.

▶ **To use the IPX/SPX-compatible protocol with NetBIOS on a computer**

1. In Control Panel, double-click Network.

2. Double-click the instance of **IPX/SPX-compatible Protocol** that is bound to your network adapter.

Note If the computer has multiple network adapters, the list will contain an instance of the IPX/SPX-compatible protocol for each network adapter. You must configure each adapter with its own settings. You can only have four instances of IPX/SPX on your system, so if you have more than four adapters are installed, you should bind IPX/SPX only to the adapters that will use this protocol.

3. Click the **Bindings** tab.

4. Click the **NetBIOS** tab, and then click **I want to enable NetBIOS Over IPX/SPX**.

Technical Notes on IPX/SPX on NetWare Networks

- There is no need to enable source routing on token-ring networks if the communication is on the same ring, even if one computer has it enabled.

- SPX-II is a protocol definition for windowing and transmitting large packets over SPX. The IPX/SPX-compatible protocol included with Windows 98 (Nwlink.vxd) does not support SPX-II. Some third-party dynamic-link libraries (DLLs) provide SPX-II support when you are using Nwlink.vxd. However, if you are using a third-party DLL that provides SPX-II support and a program communicates directly with Nwlink.vxd, SPX-II support will not be available for that program.

- When you install Windows 98 with the IPX/SPX-compatible protocol, parameters in Net.cfg and Shell.cfg will be moved to the registry if they are not already there. (If you are upgrading over an installation of Windows 95 that included the IPX/SPX-compatible protocol, those parameters will already have been moved to the registry.)

- To determine the network address in IPX packets, Windows 98 checks the wire for RIP packets and chooses the most likely address. The network address is dynamic and changes when a new network address becomes more prevalent.

- All transport layer interface (TLI) libraries can run on the IPX/SPX-compatible protocol in Windows 98. TLI is similar to TDI in Microsoft networking as a layer between the protocol and network adapter driver; this implementation is similar to STREAMS and provides a STREAMS environment for NetWare, but Windows 98 uses Windows Sockets instead.

Microsoft NetBEUI Protocol

Windows 98 provides the NetBIOS extended user interface (NetBEUI) protocol for compatibility with existing networks that use NetBEUI. Because NetBEUI is nonroutable and was designed for smaller LANs, you should use the TCP/IP or IPX/SPX-compatible protocol for enterprise-wide networks that require a routable protocol.

NetBEUI in Windows 98 provides two types of traffic:

1. Unreliable connectionless traffic, in which the sender sends packets to the receiver without setting up a connection and with no guarantee that the packets will arrive. NetBEUI connectionless traffic are used for name resolution, datagrams, and miscellaneous traffic.

2. Reliable connection-oriented traffic, in which the sender and receiver establish a reliable connection before sending data. NetBEUI connection oriented traffic is used for commands such as **net use**, **net view**, and **net start**.

NetBEUI in Windows 98 supports a NetBIOS programming interface that conforms to the IBM NetBEUI specifications and includes several performance enhancements. The NetBEUI module, Netbeui.vxd, is accessible through the NetBIOS interface.

If Windows 98 Setup detects NetBEUI during installation, it installs support for Microsoft NetBEUI automatically. If you are upgrading from a computer that did not have NetBEUI, Windows 98 does not automatically install it; however, you can add it at any time.

▶ **To install NetBEUI**

1. In Control Panel, double-click Network.

2. On the **Configuration** tab, click **Add**.

3. In the **Select Network Component Type** dialog box, click **Protocol**, and then click the **Add** button.

4. In **Manufacturers**, click **Microsoft**, and then in **Network Protocols**, click **NetBEUI**, and then click **OK**.

5. Click **OK**. Setup copies files from your original installation media and prompts you to restart your computer.

The **Advanced** properties for NetBEUI affect only real-mode NetBEUI. These values are set dynamically for protected-mode NetBEUI.

▶ **To configure real-mode NetBEUI manually**

1. In Control Panel, double-click Network.

2. On the **Configuration** tab, double-click the instance of **NetBEUI** that is bound to your network adapter.

Note If your computer has multiple network adapters, an instance of NetBEUI appears for each network adapter. You must configure each adapter with its own settings.

The **Bindings** tab shows which clients and services are currently using the NetBEUI protocol. For information about configuring bindings, see "Configuring Network Adapters" later in this chapter.

3. Click the **Advanced** tab to modify settings for **Maximum Sessions** and **NCBs** for the real-mode NetBEUI. The following list outlines the options in NetBEUI advanced configuration.

Option	Description
Maximum Sessions	Used to identify the maximum number of connections to remote computers that can be supported from the redirector. This is equivalent to the **sessions=** parameter formerly specified in Protocol.ini.
NCBs (network control blocks)	Used to identify the maximum number of NetBIOS commands that can be used. This is equivalent to the **ncbs=** parameter formerly specified in Protocol.ini.

4. Click **OK**. Then shut down and restart the computer.

Microsoft DLC Protocol

Windows 98 includes both a protected-mode DLC driver (Dlc.vxd), which supports 32-bit and 16-bit DLC applications, and a real-mode DLC driver (Msdlc.exe), which supports only 16-bit applications. Microsoft DLC is used primarily to access IBM mainframe computers and Hewlett-Packard network-ready printers. Microsoft recommends that you use the protected-mode driver in most cases. However, some 16-bit DLC applications will work only with the real-mode DLC driver. For more information about applications that require the 16-bit DLC, see "Using 32-bit DLC for Connectivity" later in this chapter.

The following sections how to use 32-bit, protected-mode DLC protocol and the 16-bit, real-mode DLC protocol.

Using 32-bit DLC for Connectivity

The 32-bit DLC protocol provides connection and communication with mainframe computers using DLC. With the 32-bit Data Link Control (DLC) protocol, you can establish multiple connections to different IBM host and AS/400 computers over the same network token-ring, FDDI, or Ethernet adapter. Host terminal emulation programs use the 32-bit DLC to communicate directly with host computers. The 32-bit DLC protocol also allows multiple 32-bit applications to use the same network adapter at the same time to connect to different host computers.

You can also use the 32-bit DLC protocol to provide connectivity to local area printers connected directly to the network. For example, you can use the DLC protocol to print to a printer that uses an adapter to connect directly to the network rather than to a port on a print server. The DLC protocol must be installed and running on the print server for the printer. The protocol does not need to be installed on the computers that send print jobs to the print server. To take advantage of the DLC protocol device driver, you must create a network printer in the printers folder by using a third-party utility such as Hewlett Packard's Jet Administration Utility.

The 32-bit DLC protocol software supports the following 32-bit and 16-bit DLC programs:

- Windows-based 32-bit programs that use Command Control Block 2 (CCB2).
- 16-bit programs that use Command Control Block 1 (CCB1).

Microsoft recommends that in most cases you use the 32-bit DLC protocol rather than the 16-bit DLC protocol or IBM's LAN Support drivers, because it supports both 32-bit applications and most 16-bit applications, provides better performance, and can access protected memory.

However, the 32-bit DLC protocol does not support certain 16-bit DLC applications. Some 16-bit DLC applications load TSRs to check the existence of DLC before Windows 98 loads. If you need to run any of those applications, you may want to use the 16-bit DLC protocol. For more information about the 16-bit programs the 32-bit DLC protocol does not support, see "Running 16-bit Applications" later in this chapter. The 32-bit DLC protocol also does not support 32-bit programs created to run under OS/2.

Client for Microsoft Networks does not use the 32-bit DLC protocol to communicate with the Microsoft network. Also, the 32-bit DLC protocol does not have a NetBIOS interface. 32-bit terminal emulation programs usually call the protected-mode DLC protocol by loading a TSR that acts as an interface to the DLC protocol. A 16-bit terminal emulation program can call the 32-bit DLC protocol by using the Int 0x5C (NetBIOS) interrupt vector. The 32-bit DLC protocol can coexist with other protocols, and it conforms to the network driver interface specification (NDIS) 3.1 and later.

Windows 98 supports the Ethernet multivendor standard DIX 2.

The following sections describe how to install the Microsoft 32-bit DLC protocol and how to configure it with Novell NetWare ODI drivers and IBM LAN Support.

For information about the architecture of Microsoft DLC, see Chapter 29, "Windows 98 Network Architecture."

Installing the 32-bit DLC Protocol

Before you install the 32-bit DLC protocol, you must perform the following tasks:

- Make sure you have access to your original Windows 98 setup files.

- If you are installing the 32-bit DLC protocol over the IBM LAN Support program (DXM mode drivers), first remove the existing IBM DLC from the Network option in Control Panel.

- If you are installing the 32-bit DLC protocol over an existing Madge Smart.exe (token-ring), you must first remove the existing ODI driver from the Network option in Control Panel. Then you must add the NDIS 3.1 or later Madge driver and the Microsoft 32-bit DLC protocol stack.

▶ **To install the 32-bit DLC protocol**

1. In Control Panel, double-click Network.

2. On the **Configuration** tab, click **Add**.

3. Click **Protocol**, and then click **Add**.

4. In the **Manufacturers** box, click **Microsoft.**

5. In the **Network Protocols** box, click **Microsoft 32-bit DLC**.

6. Click **OK**.

7. Setup prompts you to shut down and reboot your computer.

Windows 98 Setup removes any previous configuration settings for 16-bit Microsoft DLC, and adds an entry in the Autoexec.bat file for Dlchlp.exe, the file that supports 16-bit DLC programs. If no 16-bit DLC programs are used, you can save real-mode and 32-bit DLC protected-mode memory by disabling 16-bit support. For more information about disabling 16-bit support, see "Disabling 16-bit Support" later in this chapter.

Windows 98 setup also associates a unique CCB adapter number to the adapter that is bound to the DLC protocol.

For information about changing the CCB adapter number, see "Configuring the 32-bit DLC Protocol" later in this chapter.

For information about using multiple CCB adapter numbers, see "Adding a Second Network Adapter" later in this chapter. After you have installed the 32-bit DLC protocol, you can verify that the protocol is bound to the adapter by using the following procedure.

▶ **To verify bindings**

1. In Control Panel, double-click Network, and then click the name of your adapter.

2. Click **Properties.**

3. Click the **Bindings** tab.

4. Make sure **Microsoft 32-bit DLC** is selected.

Note You cannot check the bindings by clicking the 32-bit DLC protocol, because only clients and services can be bound to protocols.

Configuring the 32-bit DLC Protocol

After you have installed the 32-bit DLC protocol, you can configure adapter settings and settings for the 32-bit DLC protocol.

For information about configuring adapter settings, see Chapter 15, "Network Adapters and Protocols."

This section covers the following topics:

- Configuring settings for the 32-bit DLC protocol.
- Configuring Service Access Points (SAPs) and link stations.
- Configuring timer values.
- Adding a second network adapter.
- Disabling 16-bit support.

Configuring Settings

This section describes the 32-bit DLC settings you can manually configure.

Note In most cases, you do not need to change the default values. However, if you are loading multiple terminal emulation sessions, you might want to increase values for SAPs and link stations.

▶ **To configure 32-bit DLC settings**

1. In Control Panel, double-click Network.
2. Click the **Microsoft 32-bit DLC** protocol.
3. Click **Properties**.
4. Click the **Advanced** tab.

Table 15.11 shows the default settings you can change. Applications can also change these settings.

Table 15.11   DLC configuration settings

32-bit DLC parameter	Description	Range	Default
CCB Adapter Num (equivalent to LANA-number in NCB)	Specifies a unique number used by 32-bit DLC to identify each instance of a driver that is associated with a network card. [1]	1-15	0
Ethernet DIX	Sets the frame format. For 802.3 Ethernet format, set the value to 0. For Ethernet DIX 2.0 (Ethertype 0x80D5) format, set the value to 1 (enable). (Ethernet DIX frames have an extra type field.)	0- 1 (Boolean)	0

Table 15.11   DLC configuration settings (*continued*)

32-bit DLC parameter	Description	Range	Default
Max Grp Member	Specifies the maximum number of SAPs that can belong to each Group SAP.	1- 127	0
Max Grp SAPs	Specifies the maximum number of Group SAPs that can be opened simultaneously.	1- 126	0
Max Links	Indicates the number of link stations that can be opened simultaneously. [2]	1- 255	20
Max SAPs	Indicates a service access point. [3]	1- 255	3
Maximum Adapters	Indicates the maximum number of network adapter cards you can have in your computer.	1- 16	4
Maximum Frame Size	Indicates the maximum size of a frame that can be sent across the network. The maximum value of this setting depends on the network type. [4]	96- 17960 bytes	4464
Maximum Users	Indicates the maximum number of logical adapters that can be open at the same time. Typically, each 32-bit program opens a logical adapter of its own.	1-40	5
NDIS Pkt Descriptors	Specifies the number of packets that the adapter driver can store in its packet buffer before sending them to the network.	24-128	24
Support CCB1	If this setting is set to 1, 16-bit programs that use CCB1 are supported. If it is set to 0, only 32-bit DLC programs are supported. [5]	0-1 (Boolean)	1
Swap Addr Bits	When DLC is bound to an Ethernet or token-ring driver, set this parameter to 1 (enable) to turn on address bit-swapping.	0- 1 (Boolean)	1
Timer T1 (1)	Sets the retransmission-timer "short tick" value. This timer determines the delay (in units of 40 milliseconds) before retransmitting a link-level frame if no acknowledgment is received. [6]	1- 255	5
Timer T1 (2)	Sets the retransmission-timer "long tick" value. This timer determines the delay (in units of 40 milliseconds) before retransmitting a link-level frame if no acknowledgment is received.	1- 255	25
Timer T2 (1)	Sets the delayed-acknowledgment timer "short tick" value. This timer determines the delay (in units of 40 milliseconds) before acknowledging a received frame when the receive window has not been reached.	1- 255	1
Timer T2 (2)	Sets the delayed-acknowledgment timer "long tick" value. This timer determines the delay (in units of 40 milliseconds) before acknowledging a received frame when the receive window has not been reached.	1- 255	10

Table 15.11   DLC configuration settings (*continued*)

32-bit DLC parameter	Description	Range	Default
Timer Ti (1)	Sets the inactivity-timer "short tick" value (in units of 40 milliseconds). This timer determines how often DLC checks an inactive link to see whether it is still operational.	1- 255	25
Timer Ti (2)	Sets the inactivity-timer "long tick" value (in units of 40 milliseconds). This timer determines how often DLC checks an inactive link to see whether it is still operational.	1- 255	125
Trace Mask	Indicates the default mask setting used by the Trcdlc.exe command-line utility. [7]	–	–

[1] For more information about setting the CCB number for an alternate or secondary network card, see "Adding a Second Network Adapter" later in this chapter.

[2] For more information about link stations, see "Determining Links and SAPs Settings" later in this chapter.

[3] For a description of SAPs, see the *IBM Local Area Network Technical Reference*. For more information about SAPs, see "Determining Links and SAPs Settings" later in this chapter.

[4] For example, token ring networks can support frame sizes of up to 4 kilobits per second (Kbps), whereas Ethernet networks can support frame sizes of less than 2 Kbps. For more information about the maximum frame size, see your network documentation.

[5] For more information about CCB1, see "Disabling 16-bit Support" later in this chapter.

[6] For more information about timer settings, see "Configuring Timer Settings" later in this chapter.

[7] For more information about Trdlc.exe, see "Installing the 32-bit DLC Protocol" earlier in this chapter.

Choosing 16-bit DLC Protocol Settings

Table 15.12 shows 16-bit DLC protocol settings that are still available with the 32-bit DLC protocol. Note that the names have changed.

Table 15.12   Available 16-bit DLC protocol settings

16-bit DLC	32-bit DLC
Swap	Swap Addr Bits
UseDIX	Ethernet DIX
SAPs	Max SAPs
Stations	Max Links

Determining Links and SAPs Settings

Each program requires a certain number of Service Access Points (SAPs) and link stations. Because each SAP or link station takes up memory, you should provide just enough for your program to run.

If you do not know the number of SAPs and link stations your program requires, and you want to minimize the memory your terminal emulation programs use, start with large values and gradually reduce them until the program no longer works.

The Microsoft 32-bit DLC protocol uses defaults of 5 SAPs and 20 link stations. This should be sufficient for most programs. If needed, you can increase the number of SAPs and link stations. For more information about configuring 32-bit DLC settings, see "Configuring Settings" earlier in this chapter.

For information about which SAP and link station settings to use with your DLC programs, see the documentation for those programs.

Configuring Timer Settings

The Microsoft DLC protocol uses three timers:

- t1 (retransmission)
- t2 (acknowledgment)
- ti (inactivity)

Each timer has a "short tick" rate and a "long tick" rate that individual commands use to determine timer values. A command such as Dlc.Open.Sap specifies a timer value with a number range of 1 through 10 units of milliseconds.

For example:

- When the number is in the range of 1 through 5 units of milliseconds, the actual timer value is:

  ```
  (number selected) * (short-tick value) * 40 milliseconds
  ```

- When the number is in the range of 6 through 10 units of milliseconds, the actual timer value is:

  ```
  (number selected  - 5) * (long-tick value) * 40 milliseconds
  ```

Some network programs adjust these timer entries automatically. The Dlc.Open.Adapter command overrides the default value.

Adding a Second Network Adapter

If you add a second DLC32-compatible network adapter to your computer, a new copy of the 32-bit DLC protocol is created and automatically bound to your secondary network adapter. When you restart your computer, the CCB adapter number setting for that copy of the 32-bit DLC protocol automatically changes to a unique number.

Note If you remove your primary network adapter, the CCB adapter number for the second adapter does not change.

Disabling 16-bit Support

If your users will use only 32-bit network programs, you can disable support for 16-bit programs. This speeds up network access and saves real-mode and protected-mode memory.

▶ **To disable 16-bit support**

1. In Control Panel, double-click Network, and then click the Microsoft 32-bit DLC protocol for which you wish to disable 16-bit support.

2. Click **Properties**.

3. Click the **Advanced** tab.

4. Click the **Support CCB1** setting, and set it to 0. The reference in your Autoexec.bat file to Dlchlp.exe is removed.

Caution Do not manually remove Dlchlp.exe from your Autoexec.bat file.

Switching from IBM LAN Support

The 32-bit DLC protocol cannot be upgraded over IBM LAN Support. If you are adding the 32-bit DLC protocol to a computer that used IBM LAN Support, you must first remove the IBM DLC protocol from the Network option in Control Panel, then add the Microsoft 32-bit DLC protocol. Otherwise, you may not be able to connect to your host, and the Windows 98 computer could stop responding.

Note Before upgrading over IBM LAN Support, record the parameters for the DXM driver line(s) so that you can configure the equivalent Microsoft 32-bit DLC protocol settings. If you are using an NDIS configuration with IBM LAN Support, you should also record the parameters for your Protocol.ini file.

Windows 98 Setup does not migrate the IBM LAN Support program settings will to the Microsoft 32-bit DLC protocol. You will need to make sure that the settings for the Microsoft 32-bit DLC properties correlate to the prior settings for IBM LAN Support. Table 15.13 shows how to convert the Xmit_swap setting in Dxme0mod.sys to the Swap Addr Bits and Ethernet DIX settings for the 32-bit DLC protocol.

Table 15.13   IBM LAN Support program settings

Xmit_swap setting in Dxme0mod.sys	Swap Addr Bits setting	Ethernet DIX setting
0	1	0
1	1	1
2	0	0
3	0	1

Note You can configure the alternate adapter by using the **CCB Adapter Num** setting. For more information about the **CCB Adapter Num** setting, see "Adding a Second Network Adapter" earlier in this chapter.

Running 16-bit Applications

If you are running 32-bit Microsoft DLC with 16-bit applications that use DLC, you will need to update your Autoexec.bat file. Make sure that Net.exe is loaded before Dlchlp.exe.

Applications that require a terminate-and-stay-resident (TSR) program to connect to a host computer before starting Windows 98 will not work with the Microsoft 32-bit DLC protocol stack. The following applications require TSRs:

- IBM PC SUPPORT (versions V2R1 - V2R3)
- RELAY GOLD version 5.0 and 6.0a
- EICON ACCESS 5250 version 3.21

Contact your vendor for updated information about these applications.

Technical Notes for the 32-bit DLC Protocol

Table 15.14 describes the files included with the 32-bit DLC protocol.

Table 15.14   32-bit DLC files

File name	Description
Netdlc32.inf	The Windows 98 device information file, which provides settings used by Windows 98 setup to install DLC.
Dlc.vxd	The Windows 98 device driver for DLC.
Dlcapi.dll	The DLL file that supports 32-bit DLC programs.
Dlcndi.dll	A DLL file used by Windows 98 setup for custom installations.

Table 15.14   32-bit DLC files (*continued*)

File name	Description
Trcdlc.exe	A command-line trace utility for viewing DLC commands that are running 32-bit calls. This utility helps developers troubleshoot 32-bit DLC programs.
Dlchlp.exe	A TSR that allows 32-bit DLC to also support 16-bit DLC programs. This file is loaded in the Autoexec.bat file, but is not required if you do not need support for 16-bit DLC programs.

Note If you do not need support for 16-bit DLC programs, do not remove Dlchlp.exe from your Autoexec.bat file manually. Instead, disable support for 16-bit DLC programs by using the Support CCB1 setting.

Using 16-bit DLC for Connectivity

The 16-bit DLC protocol provides connection and communication with mainframe computers using DLC. To provide connection and communication, the DLC protocol must be installed on the client computer that is running Windows 98. The Microsoft DLC protocol works with either token-ring or Ethernet network adapter drivers.

Microsoft DLC is also used to provide connectivity to local area printers connected directly to the network. For example, DLC can be used for printing to a printer such as an HP LaserJet 4Si that uses an HP JetDirect network adapter to connect directly to the network (rather than to a port on a print server). The DLC protocol must be installed and running on the print server for the printer. Computers sending print jobs to a print server for a DLC network printer do not need the DLC protocol—only the print server requires DLC. To take advantage of the DLC protocol device driver, you must create a network printer in the Printers folder.

In addition to the 16-bit DLC protocol, Windows 98 includes a 32-bit DLC protocol. In most cases, Microsoft recommends that you use the 32-bit DLC protocol. It provides better performance and can access protected memory. However, certain applications require Microsoft's 16-bit DLC because they require a TSR program to connect to a host computer before starting Windows 98. For more information about these applications, see "Running 16-bit applications" earlier in this chapter.

The following sections describe how to install the Microsoft DLC protocol and how to configure it with Novell NetWare ODI drivers and IBM LAN Support.

Installing and Configuring Real-Mode Microsoft DLC

This section describes how to install the real-mode NDIS 2 Microsoft DLC protocol to bind with an NDIS 2 network adapter driver. This is an NDIS 2 protocol that, when installed, is bound to an NDIS 2 network adapter driver. The Windows 98 protected-mode protocols use the Ndis2sup.vxd module to coexist with and run over the real-mode NDIS 2 network adapter drivers.

When you install Windows 98, Windows 98 Setup detects whether the computer already has the Microsoft DLC protocol installed; if so, Setup migrates the protocol and its settings to Windows 98. Otherwise, you can add Microsoft DLC as a protocol after Windows 98 is installed.

Note   You must install the version of Microsoft DLC provided with Windows 98. You cannot use the Microsoft DLC INF file from Windows for Workgroups 3.*x* to install this protocol; Windows 98 uses a new INF file format.

You can also install Microsoft DLC using setup scripts, as described in Appendix D, "Msbatch.inf Parameters for Setup Scripts."

▶ **To install the Microsoft DLC protocol on a computer running Windows 98**

1. In Control Panel, double-click Network.

2. On the **Configuration** tab, click **Add.**

3. In the **Select Network Component Type** dialog box, double-click **Protocol**.

4. In the **Select Network Protocol** dialog box, click **Microsoft** in the Manufacturers list, and then click **Microsoft DLC** in the Network Protocols list. Then click **OK**.

5. Shut down and restart the computer for the changes to take effect.

6. Make sure that there is only one **net start** entry in Autoexec.bat, because Setup automatically adds an entry to support DLC, even if such an entry already exists.

The properties in Table 15.15 are set by default for real-mode Microsoft DLC. You can use the Network option in Control Panel to change these default values, or to set values for other parameters that you might use, in the Advanced properties for Microsoft DLC protocol.

Table 15.15 DLC properties

Value	Description
Saps	Indicates the number of SAPs that can be opened simultaneously. The range for SAPs is 1 to 255 inclusive. The default is 3.
	For a description of SAPs, see the *IBM Local Area Network Technical Reference*.
Stations	Indicates the number of link stations that can be opened simultaneously. The range for stations is 1 to 255 inclusive. The default is 20.
	Each application requires a certain number of SAPs and stations. Because each SAP or station takes up memory, you should provide only enough for your application to run.
Swap	Turns on address bit-swapping when it is enabled and Microsoft DLC is bound to an Ethernet driver. The default is 1 (enabled).
Usedix	Sets the frame format. By default, this value is 0 (disabled), which is the correct value for 802.3 Ethernet format. Set this value to 1 for Ethernet DIX 2.0 (Ethertype 0x80D5) format. Ethernet DIX frames have an extra type-field.

The default values for SWAP and UseDIX are appropriate for most token-ring LAN environments. If the computer has an Ethernet adapter, then you should set the correct values for these parameters in the Advanced properties for Microsoft DLC. If you previously used the IBM Dxme0mod.sys driver, use Table 15.16 to map the Xmit_swap parameter to set values for the two Microsoft DLC parameters.

Table 15.16 Mapping Xmit_swap parameters

Dxme0mod.sys xmit_swap	Microsoft DLC parameters
0	swap=1 usedix=0
1	swap=1 usedix=1
2	swap=0 usedix=0
3	swap=0 usedix=1

Table 15.17 shows some typical settings in Autoexec.bat and Protocol.ini for Microsoft DLC with an Intel EtherExpress PRO LAN NDIS 2 network adapter driver on an Ethernet network. Notice that the [msdlc$] section is added automatically by Windows 98 when the protocol is installed.

Table 15.17   Sample configuration file settings for Microsoft DLC with NDIS 2 adapters

File name	Required settings
| autoexec.bat | ```
net init
msdlc.exe
net start
``` |
| protocol.ini | ```
[netbeui$]
DriverName=NETBEUI$
Lanabase=0
sessions=10
ncbs=12
Bindings=EPRO$

[nwlink$]
DriverName=nwlink$
Frame_Type=4
cachesize=0
Bindings=EPRO$

[epro$]
DriverName=EPRO$
INTERRUPT=10
ioaddress=0x300

[protman$]
priority=ndishlp$
DriverName=protman$

[ndishlp$]
DriverName=ndishlp$
Bindings=EPRO$

[data]
version=v4.00.000
netcards=EPRO$,*PNP8132

[msdlc$]
DriverName=msdlc$
stations=20
saps=3
swap=0
usedix=1

Bindings=EPRO$
``` |

Configuring Real-mode Microsoft DLC with ODI Drivers

For computers that are running Microsoft DLC with ODI drivers using the Novell-supplied Odinsup.exe file, Windows 98 Setup installs over this configuration and leaves entries for ODINSUP and MSDLC in Autoexec.bat. Microsoft does not provide direct support for Microsoft DLC used with Odinsup.exe.

If you must run a real-mode network redirector or TSR (Netx.exe, Vlm.exe, and so on), you need to configure Microsoft DLC by binding the Microsoft DLC protocol to an ODI network adapter driver. Otherwise, install Microsoft DLC over NDIS 2 with the protected-mode Microsoft Client for NetWare Networks. For information about these configurations, see "Architecture for DLC" in Chapter 29, "Windows 98 Network Architecture."

Table 15.18 shows settings used to configure Microsoft DLC with ODI drivers.

Note This manual editing of Protocol.ini will remove "Microsoft DLC" from the Network Configuration dialog. The usage of Odinsup.exe prevents Windows 98 from correctly identifying the "Microsoft DLC" as being used by the Ethernet adapter and therefore will not be displayed even though the protocol will still function.

Table 15.18   Configuration file settings for real-mode Microsoft DLC with ODI drivers

File name	Required settings	
autoexec.bat	`lsl`	`;Novell-supplied component`
	`mlid_driver.com`	`;Novell-supplied component`
	`odihlp.exe`	`;Windows 98 component`
	`odinsup.exe`	`;Novell-supplied component`
	`msdlc.exe`	`;Windows 98 component`
	`net start netbind`	`;Windows 98 component`
net.cfg	`Protocol ODINSUP`	
	`    Bind EPROODI`	
	`    BUFFERED`	
	`Link Driver EPROODI`	
	`    Port 300`	
	`    Frame Ethernet_802.2`	
	`    Frame Ethernet_802.3`	
	`    Frame Ethernet_II`	
	`    Frame Ethernet_Snap`	

Table 15.18   Configuration file settings for real-mode Microsoft DLC with ODI drivers (*continued*)

File name	Required settings

protocol.ini	`[protman$]`
	`priority=ndishlp$`
	`DriverName=protman$`
	
	`[ndishlp$]`
	`DriverName=ndishlp$`
	`Bindings=`
	
	`[data]`
	`version=v4.00.000`
	`netcards=`
	
	`[nwlink$]`
	`Frame_Type=4`
	`cachesize=0`
	`DriverName=nwlink$`
	
	`[msdlc$]`
	`DriverName=msdlc$`
	`xstations0=0`
	`xstations1=0`
	`stations=20`
	`saps=3`
	`xsaps0=1`
	`xsaps1=1`
	`swap=0`
	`usedix=1`
	`Bindings=EPROODI`
	
	`[EPROODI]`
	`Drivername=EPROODI`
	`INTERRUPT=10`
	`ioaddress=0x300`

Upgrading Existing IBM LAN Support Installations

If you are using DLC support supplied by IBM to connect to host computers, Windows 98 Setup can detect IBM DLC; it leaves the installation intact and configures Windows 98 to run over that configuration. Although support for IBM DLC can be installed using the Network option in Control Panel, the required components must be provided by your network vendor.

This section describes two typical IBM LAN Support configurations, using Dxmc0mod.sys and Dxme0mod.sys.

Dxmc0mod.sys, the monolithic IBM DLC driver. For this configuration, Windows 98 Setup does one of two things:

- If the computer is running NetWare, Setup keeps the Dxmc0mod.sys driver and related settings, and installs the Generic ODI driver plus Microsoft Client for NetWare Networks, or keeps the real-mode client.

- If the computer is running Dxmc0mod.sys and no other networking components, Setups keeps the Dxmc0mod.sys driver and does not install any Windows 98 networking components.

Table 15.19 shows a sample configuration for IBM Dxmc0mod.sys with Microsoft Client for NetWare Networks.

Table 15.19   Example of configuration settings for Dxmc0mod.sys with ODI drivers

File name	Required settings	
autoexec.bat	`lsl`	`; Novell-supplied component`
	`lansup`	`; Novell-supplied component`
	`odihlp.exe`	`; Microsoft component`
config.sys	`device=path\dxmaood.sys`	`;IBM-supplied component`
	`device=path\dxmcomod.sys`	`;IBM-supplied component`

Dxme0mod.sys, the NDIS driver for IBM DLC.

For this configuration, Windows 98 Setup does one of three things:

- If the computer is running Dxme0mod.sys and no other networking components, Setup keeps the Dxme0mod.sys driver and does not install any Windows 98 networking components.

- If the computer is running Dxme0mod.sys and Novell NetWare, Setup installs an NDIS network adapter driver plus Microsoft Client for NetWare Networks, and leaves the Dxme0mod.sys driver intact.

- If the computer is running Dxme0mod.sys with the IBM MS-DOS LAN Requestor, Setup installs an NDIS 2 adapter driver, keeps the Dxme0mod.sys driver, installs Client for Microsoft Networks, and removes the IBM MS-DOS LAN Requestor redirector components.

Table 15.20 shows a sample configuration for IBM Dxme0mod.sys with Client for Microsoft Networks using an NDIS 2 adapter driver. The same basic kinds of settings are used for a computer running Microsoft Client for NetWare Networks with an NDIS 2 adapter driver.

Table 15.20   Example of settings for Dxmce0mod.sys with Client for Microsoft Networks

File name	Required settings
autoexec.bat	`net start netbind`

config.sys	`device=c:\windows\protman.dos /i:c:\windows`
	`device=c:\windows\epro.dos          ;ndis2 driver`
	`device=c:\lsp\dxma0mod.sys          ;IBM-supplied`
	`device=c:\lsp\dxme0mod.sys ,,3     ;IBM-supplied`
	`device=c:\windows\ndishlp.sys       ;Windows 98`

protocol.ini	`[protman$]`
	`priority=ndishlp$`
	`DriverName=protman$`
	
	`[ndishlp$]`
	`DriverName=ndishlp$`
	`Bindings=EPRO$`
	
	`[data]`
	`version=v4.00.000`
	`netcards=EPRO$,*pnp8132`
	
	`[netbeui$]`
	`DriverName=NETBEUI$`
	`Lanabase=0`
	`sessions=10`
	`ncbs=12`
	`Bindings=EPRO$`
	
	`[nwlink$]`
	`DriverName=nwlink$`
	`Frame_Type=4`
	`cachesize=0`
	`Bindings=EPRO$`
	
	`[EPRO$]`
	`DriverName=EPRO$`
	`INTERRUPT=10`
	`ioaddress=0x300`

Table 15.20   Example of settings for Dxmce0mod.sys with Client for Microsoft Networks (*continued*)

File name	Required settings

protocol.ini
(*continued*)
	`[DXMAIDXCFG]`
	`dxme0_nif=dxme0.nif`
	`dxmj0mod_nif=dxmj0mod.nif`
	`smcdosjp_nif=smcdosjp.nif`
	`smcdosjp2_nif=smcdosjp.nif`
	`smcdosat_nif=smcdosat.nif`
	`smcdosat2_nif=smcdosat.nif`
	`smcdosmc_nif=smcdosmc.nif`
	`smcdosmc2_nif=smcdosmc.nif`
	
	`[ETHERAND]`
	
	`DriverName=DXME0$`
	`Bindings=EPRO$`

Overview of Network Adapters

Windows 98 Setup automatically detects most network adapters, installs the appropriate driver for the adapter, and provides appropriate default settings to configure the adapter. If you add a new network adapter, its driver is bound automatically to all network driver interface specification (NDIS)–compatible protocols currently running on the computer. If any protocols are added later, they will also be bound automatically to the network adapter driver. TCP/IP can be bound to a maximum of six network adapters.

This section provides technical details for configuring network adapters, setting LAN adapter numbers, and other technical notes.

For specific information about PC Card adapters, see Chapter 24, "Device Management."

Note For information about specific network adapters, see the Windows 98 Adapter Card Configuration Help File on the Microsoft Windows 98 Resource Kit compact disc.

Understanding the Benefits of NDIS Adapter Drivers

The network driver interface specification (NDIS) describes the interface that network adapter drivers use to communicate with underlying hardware, with overlying protocol drivers, and with the operating system. All network adapter drivers and protocols provided with Windows 98 conform to NDIS. Windows 98 provides NDIS 5.0, an extension of NDIS 4.0 that supports NDIS versions 2.*x* 3.1, 4.0, and 5.0 protocol and adapter drivers. Windows 98 also provides a replacement for version 3.0 drivers, which are incompatible with Windows 98.

You should use NDIS 3.1 or later drivers whenever possible with Windows 98. If you are using a Novell-supplied network client, you should use ODI-based client software rather than monolithic IPX drivers.

NDIS 5 drivers add to the functionality provided by NDIS 3.1 drivers. For example, by using NDIS 5 drivers, Windows 98 can support a wide range of network media, including Ethernet, fiber distributed data interface (FDDI), token-ring, asynchronous transfer mode (ATM), and WAN technology. The NDIS 5 specification accommodates Plug and Play features, so that in many cases network adapters can be added and removed dynamically while the computer is running. NDIS 5 drivers also provide performance improvements, and compatibility with Windows NT Server 5.0.

This section summarizes the related benefits.

For information about NDIS architecture, see Chapter 29, "Windows 98 Network Architecture." See also the introduction to NDIS at **http://www.microsoft.com /hwdev/devdes/ndis5.htm.**

Plug and Play support for network protocols and adapters. Windows 98 can automatically determine the adapters to which each protocol should bind. Additionally, if you are using a PC Card or CardBus adapter, and a Plug and Play event occurs, such as the removal of an adapter from a portable computer, the NDIS protocols and network adapters can detect the event and remove themselves from memory automatically.

NDIS miniport driver model. In releases of NDIS before 3.1, adapter drivers implemented not only the media access functionality that was specific to the network adapter, but also the media access functionality that is common to all NDIS drivers.

For NDIS 3.1 and later adapter miniport drivers, the Windows 98 NDIS wrapper implements the half of the media access functionality that is common to all NDIS drivers. Thus, the miniport driver provided by the adapter manufacturer must implement only the half of the media access layer that is specific to the network adapter. These include specific details such as establishing communications with the adapter, turning on and off electrical isolation for Plug and Play, providing media detection, and enabling any value-added features the adapter might contain.

The Windows 98 miniport drivers are binary-compatible with Windows NT 3.5 and later miniport drivers, which means they can be used on either operating system without being recompiled. (You can recognize a miniport driver by its .sys file name extension; other drivers have .vxd extensions.)

Real-mode NDIS 2 support. An NDIS 2.*x* protocol under Windows 98 must use an NDIS 2.*x* network adapter driver. Both the protocol and network adapter drivers must load and bind in real mode before Windows 98 runs. Values in Protocol.ini are used to load the real-mode NDIS drivers, as described in Chapter 16, "Windows 98 on Microsoft Networks." However, you still use the Network option in Control Panel to configure NDIS 2 adapters.

When you run a real-mode network, Windows 98 uses NDIS 2 versions of NetBEUI and IPX/SPX protocols. These protocols are not intended for everyday use, since Windows 98 supplies faster protected-mode versions of these protocols.

Windows 98 also supports existing ODI drivers with Novell NetWare–compatible network clients. For information, see Chapter 17, "Windows 98 on Third-Party Networks."

Support for Windows Management Infrastructure. Windows Management Interface (WMI) collects a wealth of information about the entire system as well as device configuration. This information is stored in the registry and made available through extensions to the Registry API.

NDIS 5 supports the Windows Management Infrastructure (WMI) for Web-Based Enterprise Management (WBEM) of NDIS miniports and their associated adapters, providing the architecture for user-mode management of NDIS drivers and network adapters. This will enable network administrators and support technicians to remotely monitor and control systems using NDIS 5 compliant drivers.

For more information about WMI, see **http://www.microsoft.com/hwdev /devdes/ndis5.htm**.

Support for broadcast media. NDIS 5 includes extensions to support Broadcast Architecture. It supports high-speed unidirectional broadcast media such as services provided by DirectTV, PrimeStar, and Intercast. The extensions include definitions for receiver tuning, multiple media stream negotiation, fast data streaming, and support for UDP/IP multicast packets using a Microsoft LAN Emulation driver.

For more information about Broadcast Architecture, see Chapter 13, "WebTV for Windows 98."

Support for connection-oriented media. In addition to supporting connectionless media such as Ethernet, token-ring, FDDI, Wireless WAN, and infrared, with NDIS 5 Windows 98 now supports raw access to connection-oriented media such as ATM, integrated services digital network (ISDN), X.25, and Frame Relay. This support is provided only if you are using miniport drivers.

For more information about NDIS support for connection-oriented networks, see Chapter 29, "Windows 98 Network Architecture."

Plug and Play Networking

Plug and Play is an independent set of computer architecture specifications that hardware manufacturers use to produce computer devices that can be configured with no user intervention. With Windows 98, you can install Plug and Play–compliant devices such as network adapters simply by plugging in the device and turning on the computer. If Windows 98 has support for the device it automatically adds its configuration information to the registry, ensures that the correct files are installed, and ensures that the configuration options are set properly.

The networking components in Windows 98 are designed for dynamic Plug and Play operation with most ISA, EISA, PCI, IBM Micro Channel, CardBus, and PC Card network adapters. To take advantage of these features, the computer must be running all protected-mode networking components, including client, protocols, and network adapter drivers.

NDIS 3.1 and later supports adding and removing Plug and Play network adapters dynamically while the computer is running. For example, if you undock a portable computer (called *hot undocking*), the Windows 98 protocols can remove themselves from memory automatically.

Additional Plug and Play networking benefits are available when you use 32-bit socket services with PC Card cards. You can click the PC Card icon on the taskbar to remove the card without shutting down Windows 98 or turning off the computer. Clicking the PC Card icon causes the operating system to perform an orderly shutdown of the affected network components. Windows 98 notifies applications that the network is no longer available and automatically unloads any related drivers or protocols.

To help mobile users who might need to change adapters in their hardware, Windows 98 uses 32-bit Card and Socket Services to support hot removal and insertion of PC Cards, including network adapters. Support for hot docking means that users do not have to restart their computers each time they make a change to their hardware configuration by docking or undocking their computers. For information about using and configuring PC Cards, including how to enable 32-bit Card and Socket Services, see Chapter 30, "Hardware Management."

Network Plug and Play support in Windows 98 includes application-level support. An application created for Windows 98 might be designed with the ability to determine whether the network is available. Therefore, if a network adapter is removed, for example, the application automatically puts itself into "offline" mode to allow the user to continue to work, or it shuts down.

Configuring Network Adapters

This section describes how to configure network adapters for Windows 98 computers. First, the section "Installing and Configuring Network Adapters" provides a brief overview of how to install both Plug and Play and legacy network adapters. Next, the section "Configuring Network Adapter Settings in Windows 98" explains how to configure network adapter driver properties from within Windows 98. Finally, the section "Binding Network Adapter Drivers to Protocols" describes how to bind network adapter drivers to protocols.

Installing and Configuring Network Adapters

How you install your network adapter depends on what type of network adapter you have.

If you have a Plug and Play network adapter, Windows 98 automatically detects the adapter and performs most of the required configuration.

If you have a non-Plug and Play network adapter (also called a *legacy network adapter*), the Add New Hardware wizard starts and should automatically configure the network adapter. However, you might need to perform software or hardware configuration. For example, with some legacy network adapters you must set jumpers or switches on the hardware itself. With others, you must run a vendor-supplied software configuration program from within an MS-DOS window.

Note that this configuration is separate from the configuration you must do from within Windows 98. As the section "Configuring Network Adapter Settings in Windows 98" explains, you must configure settings from the Network option in Control Panel to match the settings you have configured using jumpers, switches, or a software configuration program.

Configuring Network Adapter Settings

This section discusses how to configure properties for network adapter drivers.

The properties you must configure from within Windows 98 depend on whether you are installing Plug and Play or non-Plug and Play devices.

If you install a Plug and Play network adapter, Windows 98 should automatically configure it. You should not need to change most of the settings, including any of the settings described in "Configuring Network Adapter Resource Settings" later in this chapter. However, if your network configuration is not working properly, you might want to review this section.

If you install a non-Plug and Play network adapter, the Add New Hardware Wizard should automatically configure it. When asked whether you want Windows to search for your new hardware (that is, to perform hardware detection), make sure to click **Yes**. This helps Windows 98 choose the correct driver and resource assignments. If hardware detection fails, you might need to configure Windows 98 settings to match the settings for the network adapter itself. For example, if you used a software configuration utility to set an Interrupt Request (IRQ), you must configure Windows 98 to use the same IRQ for the network adapter.

If you experience problems with the settings for a network adapter, you should begin troubleshooting by removing the network adapter driver from the Network option in Control Panel. Then reboot, and if the card is not detected, use the Add New Hardware option to reinstall support for the network adapter, using hardware detection to ensure that Windows 98 determines the correct adapter driver and standard settings for that network adapter. If you experience problems after installing a Plug and Play device or after automatically detecting a non-Plug and Play device from the Add New Hardware option, you might need to manually configure properties for network adapter drivers.

Specifying the Driver Type for a Network Adapter

Generally, you will not need to specify the driver type for a network adapter. In fact, some network adapters do not let you specify the driver type. However, if you need to use a real-mode driver you must specify the driver type.

▶ **To specify the driver type for a selected network adapter**

1. In Control Panel, double-click Network.

2. On the **Configuration** tab, select the name of the network adapter driver from the list of installed components.

3. Click the **Properties** button.

4. In the properties for the network adapter, click the **Driver Type** tab.

5. Click one of three options (if available for the specific adapter), as described in the following list.

Network adapter driver type	Description
Enhanced mode (32-bit and 16-bit) NDIS driver	Installs an NDIS 3.1 or later–compliant driver. This is the preferred driver type for use with 32-bit, protected-mode network clients.
Real-mode (16-bit) NDIS driver	Installs an NDIS 2.x–compliant driver.
Real-mode (16-bit) ODI driver	Installs a real-mode driver created to support ODI for Windows 3.1 on NetWare networks.

Configuring Network Adapter Resource Settings

Windows 98 can determine hardware settings for Plug and Play network adapters. Thus, for Plug and Play network adapters you should let Windows 98 go through its Plug and Play installation process. You should not change any settings described in this section unless you are absolutely sure they are incorrect. In fact, you cannot change network adapter resource settings for most Plug and Play network adapters.

For non-Plug and Play network adapters, you should use the Add New Hardware option in Control Panel, using detection to determine the correct driver and resource settings. You should accept the proposed settings unless you are absolutely sure they are incorrect.

Most ISA devices cannot share IRQ settings, memory buffer addresses, or ROM addresses. Where possible, Windows 98 identifies and resolves conflicts. However, if one of the supported devices does not seem to work, the problem may be the particular hardware configuration. To make sure there are no conflicts among network adapters or other peripherals, or between the system board and adapters, check the settings in Device Manager.

For information about checking the settings in Device Manager, see Chapter 24, "Device Management."

If Device Manager shows that any of these settings conflict, you can use the Network option in Control Panel to make sure that the settings match the settings for your network adapter.

▶ **To configure resources in a network adapter's properties**

1. In Control Panel, double-click Network.

2. In the list of installed components, click the network adapter and then click the **Properties** button. Make sure to click the network adapter, not the protocol binding for that adapter.

3. In the properties for the network adapter, if a **Resources** tab appears, click it.

   Note If a **Resources** tab does not appear, you cannot configure the network adapter's resources from the Network option in Control Panel.

4. Select a configuration from the **Configuration type** box. Confirm values for the listed settings by comparing the proposed settings with the values recommended in the documentation for the adapter.

5. To select from the available values for a setting, click the arrow beside the setting's current value.

- A hash (#) character appears by current settings.

- An asterisk (*) appears beside settings that conflict with another device in the system. You should avoid this setting or reconfigure the other devices to use different settings.

The settings available depend on the type of network adapter. For example, for Intel adapters, you cannot set the IRQ using the adapter's properties. Table 15.21 describes a few typical settings. Each setting must match the adapter's settings, as specified in the documentation for the adapter.

Table 15.21   Example hardware resource settings for a network adapter

Setting type	Description
I/O Address Range	Specifies the reserved I/O address range (as a hexadecimal value).
Interrupt Request (IRQ)	Specifies the hardware line over which the device can send interrupts (requests for service) to the computer's CPU.
Memory Address	Specifies the base memory address (as a hexadecimal value) used by this network adapter.

If the settings in the **Resources** tab do not match the adapter's settings, you must either change the settings in the **Resources** tab or, in some cases, change the adapter's settings. To determine how to change the adapter's settings, refer to the documentation for your network adapter.

Note For some legacy adapters, it is possible that the adapter uses resources not listed with the Resource properties. For these adapters, the NDIS driver determines the resource settings directly from the adapter itself. Even though these resources do not appear in the list, they can still conflict with other devices. For example, the resource list for the IBM token-ring adapter shows only the I/O settings, but this adapter also uses IRQ and Memory resources.

Configuring Advanced Properties for Network Adapters

You can configure Advanced properties for both Plug and Play and non-Plug and Play devices. The options available in the **Advanced** tab of the **Properties** dialog box vary, depending on the type of network adapter. For information about specific settings that appear for a selected network adapter, see the documentation provided by the manufacturer for the adapter and driver. The manufacturer can also provide guidelines for when to change the default values for advanced configuration options.

▶ **To specify advanced settings for the network adapter**

1. In Control Panel, double-click Network.

2. In the list of installed components, click the network adapter and then click the **Properties** button.

3. In the properties for the selected network adapter, click the **Advanced** tab.

   The following figure shows the advanced options for an Intel EtherExpress network adapter.

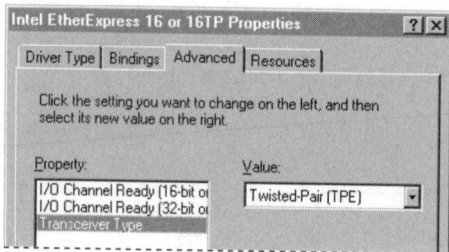

4. To change these values, select an item in the **Property** list, and then select a setting in the **Value** box.

5. Click the **OK** button.

6. Restart the computer.

Table 15.22 shows some typical settings for general types of network adapters. Network adapters that use the new, fast Ethernet technology might have many more settings. Examples of such adapters include SMC EtherPower 10/100 (9332) PCI Ethernet Adapter, DEC Etherworks 435, and Intel EtherExpress PRO/100. For an explanation of specific settings for a network adapter, see the documentation provided by the adapter manufacturer. You should not change the default settings unless you know they are incorrect.

Table 15.22   Typical network adapter settings

Example setting	Description
For Ethernet adapters:	
Transceiver type (cable connector)	The transceiver is the device that connects a computer to the network, defined as one of the following values:

- Thick Net, for an AUI or Digital/Intel/Xerox (DIX) connection.
- Thin Net, for a BNC or coaxial (COAX) connection.
- Twisted pair, for a TPE RJ-45 connection.

Table 15.22   Typical network adapter settings (*continued*)

Example setting	Description
For token-ring adapters:	
I/O port base address	This value specifies the base memory address used by the adapter. To set the I/O address of an IBM 4/16 token-ring adapter, select either Primary (A20) or Secondary (A24) for this value. In this case, the driver ignores the I/O settings in the **Resource** tab of the **Network Adapter Properties** dialog box.
Network Address	By default, Windows 98 network detection uses the address burned into the adapter. To use another network address, type the network address in hexadecimal form, in the format *XX-XX-XX-XX-XX-XX*; for example, 01-02-03-4E-2D-1F.
Ring speed	The ring speed is 4 or 16 megabits per second, and is set by changing a jumper on the adapter or by running the adapter's configuration utility. For example, for an Intel TokenExpress 16/4 adapter, this is set on the adapter itself. The value in Windows 98 should match the physical or software setting.

Binding Network Adapter Drivers to Protocols

For a protocol to communicate with each network adapter on your computer, the network adapter driver must be bound to the protocol. (This applies to both Plug and Play and non-Plug and Play network adapters.) The bindings define the relationships between networking software components. Windows 98 automatically binds the appropriate protocols to the network adapter.

You might want to change the bindings if you have multiple network adapters and you do not want to use a specific protocol with a particular network adapter. Or, if the computer is on a local area network and is also connected to the enterprise internetwork, you might not want the computer's shared resources to be seen on the internetwork. In that case, you can disable the binding between the related protocol and the adapter that connects the computer to the internetwork.

▶ **To configure bindings between a network adapter and installed protocols**

1. In Control Panel, double-click Network.

2. In the list of installed components, click the network adapter and then click the **Properties** button.

3. In the properties for the selected network adapter, click the **Bindings** tab.

   In the list, the protocols that are bound to the selected adapter are checked. If a particular protocol does not appear in the list, check that it is installed correctly by returning to the **Configuration** tab of the **Network** dialog box and reinstalling it.

4. If you do not want this network adapter to be bound to a particular protocol, clear the check box beside the protocol.

Setting LAN Adapter Numbers

NetBIOS defines the interface between the network client and the protocol layers using a set of function calls that allow an application to use the protocol services. Because many network applications use NetBIOS to send commands to the protocol driver, the NetBIOS interface is supported by all protocols provided with Windows 98.

Each combination of a NetBIOS network protocol and a network adapter forms a logical network over which computers can communicate with each other. For example, a computer can have a token-ring adapter and an Ethernet adapter, and might use NetBEUI on the token-ring network and both NetBEUI and TCP/IP on the Ethernet network. In this case, the computer is connected to three logical networks, each of which is assigned a NetBIOS LAN adapter (LANA) number that Windows 98 uses for communication.

When Windows 98 uses multiple protocols, it transmits data first using one protocol, then again using the next protocol, and so on. When multiple protocols are installed on a computer, the first protocol to be used is called the primary protocol.

On a computer running Windows 98, each binding of a protocol to a network adapter has a LAN adapter number assigned to it. (For example, one protocol bound to two network adapters requires two LAN adapter numbers; two protocols each bound to two adapters requires four LAN adapter numbers.)

In Windows 98, LANA numbers are assigned dynamically in sequence of binding order for the protocols, beginning with 7 and then 0, 1, and so on. This accommodates dynamic Plug and Play events such as the removal of a network adapter while the computer is running. If you are running Windows 98 in such a dynamic environment, Windows 98 cannot guarantee that a given protocol will receive the same LANA number each time the system is started. If the computer's network hardware never changes, the LANA numbers might not change at each startup. However, the default protocol is always LANA 0.

You need to change a LAN adapter number only if you have a NetBIOS application that needs to know the LANA number. For example, Lotus Notes requires that you enter the LANA number that Lotus Notes will use. To configure Windows 98 to use Lotus Notes, set the default protocol to be the NetBIOS-based protocol on which you want to run Lotus Notes. (Setting the default protocol makes it LANA 0.) This protocol can be NetBEUI, IPX/SPX-compatible with NetBIOS support, or TCP/IP.

▶ **To select a default protocol for LANA settings**

1. In Control Panel, double-click Network.

2. Double-click the protocol you want to be the default.

3. In the protocol's **Properties** dialog box, click the **Advanced** tab.

4. Click the option named **Set this protocol to be the default protocol** so that the check box is checked. Then click **OK**, and shut down and restart the computer for the changes to take effect.

Configuring Asynchronous Transfer Mode and LAN Emulation

Transport protocols such as TCP/IP and IPX are connectionless. That is, they do not need to establish a connection before transmitting data; computers using those protocols simply send packets out to the network. However, asynchronous transfer mode (ATM) is connection-oriented and must establish a connection before transmitting any data. LAN Emulation provides the bridge between the connectionless protocols and ATM, enabling them to function transparently over ATM networks.

This section describes how to configure LAN Emulation on Windows 98 computers.

For more information about the ATM and LAN Emulation architecture, see the section "Architecture for NDIS" in Chapter 29, "Windows 98 Network Architecture."

The following procedure describes how to configure a computer as a LAN Emulation client, so it can communicate with other devices on the ATM network.

Note Windows 98 Setup automatically installs TCP/IP only if it detects a network adapter. However, it does not automatically install TCP/IP on computers that have only an ATM card. Thus, if you want to use TCP/IP over the ATM network, you must also install TCP/IP by following the procedures outlined in "Installing Microsoft TCP/IP" earlier in this chapter. If you want to use another network protocol instead, you must install it by following the procedures outlined in the section for that protocol, earlier in this chapter.

▶ **To configure a Windows 98 computer as a LAN Emulation client**

1. In Control Panel, double-click Network.

2. On the **Configuration** tab, click the **Add** button.

3. In the **Select Network Component Type** dialog box, click **Protocol**, then click the **Add** button.

4. In the **Manufacturers** box, click **Microsoft**.

5. In the **Network Protocols** box, click **ATM Call Manager**, and then click **OK**.

6. Repeat steps 2 through 4 one time.

7. In the **Network Protocols** box, click **ATM Emulated LAN**, and then click **OK**.

8. Repeat steps 2 through 4 one time.

9. In the **Network Protocols** box, click **ATM LAN Emulation Client** and then click **OK**.

The previous procedure configures the computer to be part of the *default emulated LAN*. An *emulated LAN* is a virtual network that acts like a traditional LAN. ATM networks can consist of one or more emulated LANs: for example, a network administrator might want to create different emulated LANs for users in the Marketing and Accounting departments. However, all ATM networks have one default emulated LAN, which is the emulated LAN that all computers belong to unless they have been specifically configured as part of a different emulated LAN. Thus, after you have configured your computer as a LAN Emulation client, it automatically belongs to the default emulated LAN and can communicate with other devices on the ATM network.

In some circumstances, the ATM network administrator might configure additional emulated LANs. If so, and if you are given the name of an emulated LAN to which you should belong, you can configure your computer to be part of that emulated LAN.

Note When you are using ATM LAN Emulation, any network protocol that you will use on the emulated LAN must be installed on your computer. If you have not yet installed the network protocol you will use, you should do so now. For more information about installing network protocols, see the section for that protocol, earlier in this chapter.

▶ **To configure your computer as part of an Emulated LAN other than the default LAN**

1. In Control Panel, double-click Network.

2. In the list of installed components, select the network adapter binding for **ATM LAN Emulation Client**.

3. In the **Value** box, enter the name of the emulated LAN.

Technical Notes on Network Adapters

NDIS 3.0 network adapter drivers that worked with Windows for Workgroups 3.11 do not work under Windows 98. You must use an NDIS 2.x real-mode driver, an ODI driver, or an updated NDIS 3.1 or later protected-mode driver for the network adapter. The driver must have a Windows 98 INF file. Many real-mode drivers, updated protected-mode drivers, and supporting INF files are included with Windows 98.

Troubleshooting Network Adapters and Protocols

This section contains information about troubleshooting problems related to network protocols. For general information about troubleshooting the network installation, including how to use **net diag**, see Chapter 14, "Introduction to Networking Configuration." For information about troubleshooting procedures and tools provided with Windows 98, see Chapter 27, "General Troubleshooting."

Correcting Problems with Network Adapters

This section describes specific problems you might encounter using network adapters with Windows 98.

For information about specific network adapters, see the Windows 98 Adapter Card Configuration Help File on the Windows 98 Resource Kit compact disc.

For general troubleshooting steps, see the "Troubleshooting Basic Networking Configuration" section in Chapter 14, "Introduction to Networking Configuration."

Plug and Play card does not function with 16-bit network drivers.

If you are running Plug and Play with a 16-bit, real-mode driver, your Plug and Play network adapter might not function properly. If this happens, disable Plug and Play support for that network adapter.

▶ **To disable Plug and Play support for a network adapter**

1. Run the software setup utility that comes with your Plug and Play card.
2. Set the card to non-Plug and Play Mode.
3. In Control Panel, double-click System, and then click the **Device Manager** tab.
4. Expand the **Network adapters** tree, and then select your network card.
5. Click **Remove**.
6. In Control Panel, double-click Add New Hardware.
7. Manually reinstall the network adapter.

Note For some network adapters, you will also need to install a non-Plug and Play driver.

If you later need to re-enable Plug and Play support, follow these steps:

▶ **To re-enable Plug and Play support for a network adapter**

1. In Control Panel, double-click System, and then click the **Device Manager** tab.

2. Remove the network adapter.

3. Run the software setup utility that comes with your Plug and Play card.

4. Set the card to Plug and Play Mode.

5. Reboot the computer. Windows 98 automatically detects the network adapter.

Correcting Problems with TCP/IP

This section describes TCP/IP utilities that you can use to diagnose TCP/IP connectivity problems. Next, it discusses general troubleshooting methods to solve TCP/IP connectivity problems. Finally, it lists common problems you might experience.

Using Diagnostic Utilities to Troubleshoot

Use the TCP/IP diagnostic utilities included with Microsoft TCP/IP to diagnose connectivity problems. The following list describes which MS-DOS utility helps to identify various problems. For a more detailed description of these utilities, see "TCP/IP Utilities" earlier in this chapter.

Table 15.23   Using TCP/IP diagnostic utilities

Use this utility	To accomplish this action
ipconfig /all	Check host name, host IP address, and TCP/IP configuration.
	Note: The graphical utility **winipcfg**, described in this section, also provides this information.
ping	Verify physical connection and remote TCP/IP computer.
arp	Detect invalid entries in the ARP table on the local computer.
nbtstat	Check the state of NetBIOS over TCP/IP connections, update LMHosts cache, and determine registered name and scope ID.
net view	Determine if destinations on TCP/IP networks are reachable using WINS.
netstat	Display statistics and state of current TCP/IP connections.
tracert	Check the route to a remote computer. Also test connectivity to PPTP servers, which generally do not respond to ping requests.

For more information about these utilities, see "TCP/IP Utilities" earlier in this chapter.

You can also use the graphical IP Configuration utility **winipcfg** to display, update, or release TCP/IP configuration values, including DHCP values.

Winipcfg can also show you whether or not your computer is using automatic private IP addressing for its IP address. For more information about automatic private IP addressing, see "Configuring IP Addresses Using Automatic Private IP Addressing" earlier in this chapter.

▶ **To use winipcfg**

1. Click Start, click Run, and then type:

   winipcfg

2. The resulting screen identifies your IP address and the IP address of your default gateway.

3. Click **More info**.

4. The resulting screen tells you your IP address, subnet mask, and default gateway for each of your network interfaces. It also shows your DNS and WINS settings.

▶ **To test TCP/IP using ping**

- Check the loopback address by typing **ping 127.0.0.1** and pressing ENTER at the command prompt. The computer should respond immediately. To determine whether you configured IP properly, use **ping** with the IP address of your computer, your default gateway, and a remote host. (If you are using DHCP, use **winipcfg** to find the IP address.)

If you cannot use **ping** successfully at any point, verify the following:

- The computer was restarted after TCP/IP was installed and configured.
- The local computer's IP address is valid and appears correctly in the **TCP/IP Properties** dialog box.
- The IP address of the default gateway and remote host are correct.
- IP routing is enabled on the router, and the link between routers is operational.
- The local computer's registry includes an entry for **lmhosts=c:**_directory_ that correctly indicates the location of LMHosts.

If you can **ping** other computers running Windows 98 on a different subnetwork but cannot connect using Windows Explorer, **net use** *server**share*, or **net view** *server**share*, verify the following:

- The host is functioning.

- The correct host computer name was used.

- Using **tracert**, make sure that a router path exists between your computer and the target computer.

- LMHosts contains correct entries, so the computer name can be resolved.

- The computer is configured to use WINS, the WINS server addresses are correct, and WINS servers are functioning.

You can use **winipcfg** to verify your TCP/IP configuration settings. For information about using **winipcfg**, see "Using Diagnostic Utilities to Troubleshoot," earlier in this chapter.

Troubleshooting TCP/IP Gateway Problems

If a host computer on one subnet has problems communicating to computers on another subnet when using TCP/IP, the following information can help you determine whether the problem is with the gateway. For these troubleshooting steps, it does not matter whether the gateway that provides routing capabilities is a hardware router or a Windows NT or UNIX server configured to act as a router.

First, to troubleshoot gateway problems, you need a network map, plus the IP addresses and subnet masks for the host computer with problems, the near side of the hardware or software router that acts as the gateway, the remote side of the gateway, and the destination computer (node). For example, Figure 15.6 shows two subnets connected by a router.

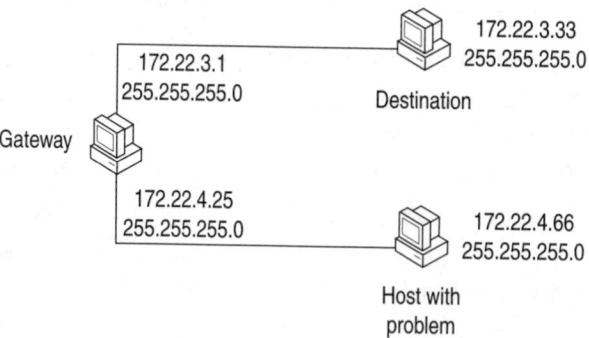

Figure 15.6   Two subnets connected by a router

The following example of troubleshooting steps uses the IP addresses from this illustration.

▶ **To troubleshoot possible gateway (router) problems**

1. Use **ping** to access the host computer that is having problems communicating outside the subnet. For example:

   ```
   ping 172.22.4.66
   ```

   If this works, this host is probably healthy at the IP level.

   If this does not work, use the usual methods to check the IP configuration and network connections on this host.

2. If the problem is not solved, use **ping** to access the near side of the router (that is, the default gateway). For example:

   ```
   ping 172.22.3.1
   ```

   If this works, this side of the router is healthy.

   If this does not work, use the usual methods to check the actual IP configuration and network connection for the near side of the router. Adjust the gateway settings on the problem host computer, if required.

   Notice, however, that if you can use **ping** to get a response from this address, it does not necessarily mean that this is actually a router.

3. If the problem is not solved, use **ping** to access the far side of the router. For example:

   ```
   ping 172.22.4.25
   ```

   If this works, the router is working.

   If this does not work, have another user use the same **ping** command from the destination node (172.22.4.66 in the example).

   If this works, the router is not working correctly.

4. If the problem is not solved, use **ping** to access the remote host. For example:

   ```
   ping 172.22.4.66
   ```

   If this works and all problems in the previous steps have been resolved, TCP/IP should be working fine.

   If this does not work, check the IP configuration and network connections on the destination computer. Typically, at this point the problem is that the remote computer has not route configured back to the original host computer. That is, the remote computer's routers or routing table does not contain the information necessary to send packets back to the original host computer.

When troubleshooting router connections, note the following:

- Do not use the host name when you are testing the router; instead, use the IP address. This will avoid any problems related to the Hosts or LMHosts files, DNS server, WINS server, or any other methods of name resolution.

- In most cases, the subnet mask should be the same for all hosts on the same side of the router.

- There could be two routers at separate sites performing the same job as described above; if this is the case, treat this situation the same as above, keeping in mind that each router could have a near and far side, depending on the configuration.

- If multiple routers exist between the source and destination, use **tracert** to see an ordered list of routers used. **Tracert** can also help you determine how many hops there are between the source and destination, and how much time it takes a packet to travel from the source to the destination.

Tip for using SNMP for routing   The TCP/IP utilities use the public interface provided by inetmib1.dll in both Windows NT and Windows 98. This API can be used with Simple Network Management Protocol (SNMP) for actions such as setting and getting routing information programmatically on Windows 98 computers. For information about the management information base (MIB) object types provided for Microsoft networking, see the *Microsoft Windows NT Server Resource Kit* (for Microsoft Windows NT Server version 4.0).

Notice, however, that you cannot use a Windows 98 computer to run the SNMPUTIL tool provided with the Windows NT Resource Kit utilities.

Troubleshooting Other TCP/IP Problems

This section describes how to troubleshoot other problems with TCP/IP.

Windows 98 does not retain primary WINS server IP address.

If the setting for your primary WINS server IP address is not retained when you reboot, check that a secondary WINS server IP address is also configured. If not, add a secondary WINS server IP address.

Windows 98 does not send DHCP request packet.

If the DHCP key in the registry contains eight MAC address entries, Windows 98 cannot create a new entry for the current session and will not send a DHCP request packet. If this happens, use the Registry Editor to remove all keys except for the Dhcpinfo00 key from the following registry entry:

**HKEY_LOCAL_MACHINE\System
\CurrentControlSet\Services\VxD\DHCP**

Then restart the computer.

Windows 98 detects an IP address conflict.

If your Windows 98 computer uses static IP addressing (described in the section "Manually Configuring IP Addresses" earlier in this chapter) and you receive a message that Windows 98 has detected an IP address conflict, another computer on the network is using the same IP address and you must change the IP address.

▶ **To change your IP address**

1. In Control Panel, double-click Network.

2. Click your TCP/IP protocol.

3. Click the **Properties** button.

4. Click the **IP Address** tab.

5. Configure the protocol to use a different IP address that is not already in use on the network.

Cannot log on to Windows NT domain.

If you cannot log on to a Windows NT domain, check that your computer uses NetBIOS name services. Windows 98 needs NetBIOS name services to log on to a Windows NT domain.

IP address connects but host names do not.

Verify that the Hosts file and DNS settings have been configured for the computer by checking settings on the **DNS Configuration** tab.

- If you are using a Hosts file, verify that the DNS host name of the remote computer is identical—especially in terms of spelling and capitalization—to the name in the file and the application using it.

- If you are using DNS, verify that the IP addresses of the DNS servers are correct and in proper order. Use **ping** with the remote computer, and type both the host name and IP address to determine if the host name is resolved properly.

Use the **netstat -a** command to show the status of all activity on TCP and UDP ports on the local computer. A good TCP connection is usually established with 0 bytes in the send and receive queues. If data is blocked in either queue or if the state is irregular, there might be a problem with the connection. If not, you are probably experiencing network or application delays.

Connect times are long after adding to LMHosts.

You might experience long connect times with a large LMHosts file if there is an entry at the end of the file. If so, mark the entry in LMHosts as a preloaded entry by following the mapping with the #PRE tag, or place the mapping higher in the LMHosts file. Then use the **nbtstat -R** command to update the local name cache immediately. The LMHosts file is parsed sequentially to locate entries without the #PRE keyword. You should place frequently used entries near the top of the file, and place the #PRE entries near the bottom.

You see a message stating computer is unable to connect to a server.

This message appears if name resolution fails for a particular computer name. If the computer is on the local subnetwork, confirm that the target server name is spelled correctly and that the target server is running TCP/IP. If the computer is not on the local subnetwork, be sure that its name and IP address mapping are available in the LMHosts file or the WINS database. If all TCP/IP elements appear to be installed properly, use **ping** with the remote computer to be sure that its TCP/IP software is working.

Use the **nbtstat -n** command to determine what name (or names) the server registered on the network. The **nbtstat** command can also display the cached entries for remote computers from either #PRE entries in LMHosts or recently resolved names. If the remote computers are using the same name for the server, and the other computers are on a remote subnetwork, be sure that they have the computer's mapping in their LMHosts files.

Correcting Problems with NetBEUI and IPX/SPX

This section describes problems that might occur with the NetBEUI and IPX protocols.

You cannot connect using NetBEUI

- Use **net diag** to test for NetBIOS connectivity over the LANA that NetBEUI is using. If it fails, check the transceiver type, cabling, and adapter.
- Check the NetBEUI protocol bindings.
- Verify that routing is not involved.

A NetBIOS application fails to start

This might be because the application is hard-coded to use the protocol on LANA 0 (such as Lotus Notes). You can force a particular protocol to always occupy LANA 0 by selecting it as the default protocol, as described in "Setting LAN Adapter Numbers" earlier in this chapter.

You cannot connect using the IPX/SPX-compatible protocol

Verify that both computers trying to connect are using the same frame type and that other settings are correct for this protocol.

- Verify the following in the **Advanced** tab of the **IPX/SPX-compatible Protocol Properties** dialog box, as described in "Configuring the IPX/SPX-compatible Protocol" earlier in this chapter:

  - The correct frame type is set. The recommended setting is Auto, but this frame type only checks SAP broadcast traffic on the network and might be selecting an incorrect frame type in a mixed frame-type environment.

  - Source Routing is enabled and a cache size is set if needed.

  - The option named Force Even Length Packets is set properly. NetWare servers with older NetWare Ethernet drivers or older IPX routers may require even-sized packets. If required, change this setting to make sure the computer transmits only even-length IPX frames.

- On the IPX routers, check the setting for Type 20 Packets (NetBIOS packets). When using NetBIOS over IPX, the IPX packet type is set to 14h (decimal 20). Manufacturers of routers might consider all NetBIOS traffic as being nonroutable LAN traffic even when carried over the routable IPX protocol, and so, by default, will not pass Type 20 NetBIOS IPX packets. To use NetBIOS over IPX connectivity, Type 20 packet passing must be enabled on the router.

- Use **net diag** to test for IPX connectivity over the related LANA number used by NetBIOS over IPX.

- Use System Monitor to view statistics for the IPX/SPX-compatible protocol. Then retry network operation and check the activity. If there is none, remove and reinstall the protocol, and then retry and retest the operation.

Correcting Connection Problems with Microsoft 32-bit DLC

This section describes common problems you might encounter while using the 32-bit DLC protocol.

Windows 98 reports a Dlchlp error message.

This error message appears if you have removed or renamed your Autoexec.bat file, or removed the reference to Dlchlp.exe from your Autoexec.bat file. To correct this error, add the Dlchlp.exe entry to your Autoexec.bat file.

Setting 32-bit DLC as the default protocol does not change the LANA number for NetBIOS protocols.

The 32-bit DLC protocol does not use a LANA number, so there is no reason to set DLC as the default protocol.

The 32-bit DLC protocol does not bind to the Dial-Up adapter.

Currently, the Microsoft 32-bit DLC protocol cannot bind to the Dial-Up adapter. When the Dial-Up adapter is installed and you then install the 32-bit DLC protocol, the 32-bit DLC protocol appears to be bound to the Dial-Up adapter. However, after you restart your computer, Windows 98 removes the binding. This is by design.

You cannot use Extra SAPs and Extra Stations settings.

Manual configuration of Extra SAPs and Extra Stations is no longer necessary with the Microsoft 32-bit DLC protocol.

After removing an adapter driver, programs cannot connect to the host.

When your computer is configured with multiple network adapters, removing an adapter driver may prevent the DLC program from connecting properly to the host. The connection fails when the removed network adapter driver is the adapter for which the DLC program is configured. To prevent this problem, if the DLC program is configured for the primary adapter, make sure the CCB Adapter Num is set to 0. If the DLC program is configured for the alternate (or secondary) adapter, make sure the CCB Adapter Num is set to 1. The 32-bit DLC protocol allows CCB2 adapter numbers 0 through F.

You cannot connect to the host over Ethernet after adding the 32-bit DLC protocol.

The most common issues you will face when using the DLC protocol on Ethernet are problems with bit swapping and Ethernet DIX. Check to see whether the host uses frame type 802.3 or Ethernet DIX 2.0, and whether address swapping is required on your network. For more information about configuring the 32-bit DLC protocol, see "Configuring the 32-bit DLC Protocol" earlier in this chapter.

After you have installed the 32-bit DLC protocol on a token-ring network adapter, Windows 98 stops responding.

Sometimes a token-ring network adapter has an RcvBufsize setting that is too small for the size of the frame being sent across the wire. If this happens, restart Windows 98 in Safe Mode, and increase the RcvBufSize setting for the network adapter driver. For more information about the appropriate settings for your network adapter, see the documentation for your network adapter. For information on getting to Safe Mode, see Chapter 7, "General Troubleshooting."

Correcting Connection Problems with Microsoft 16-bit DLC

If you encounter problems using the real-mode Microsoft DLC protocol, check the following items:

- When adding the Microsoft DLC protocol, make sure that there is only one **net start** entry in Autoexec.bat. Setup adds an entry for Microsoft DLC, even if an entry already exists. Also, make sure that Autoexec.bat is configured properly, as described in "Installing and Configuring Real-Mode Microsoft DLC" earlier in this chapter.

- Do not make direct entries or changes in Protocol.ini for Microsoft DLC. Instead, make all changes in the **Advanced** properties for Microsoft DLC by using the Network option in Control Panel. If you make changes directly in Protocol.ini, the next time you change any values by using the Network option in Control Panel, all settings in Protocol.ini for Microsoft DLC will be overwritten.

- Some terminal emulation applications use TSRs to communicate with the Microsoft DLC protocol. If your emulation application uses a TSR that runs from Autoexec.bat, make sure that the entry for the TSR still exists (usually, the TSR entry occurs after the **msdlc** and **net start** lines). Windows 98 Setup removes or comments out many TSRs.

- The option named **Set This Protocol To Be The Default Protocol** in the **Advanced** properties for Microsoft DLC does not provide any functionality. This option should not be checked, because Microsoft DLC does not use LANA settings.

- Real-mode Microsoft DLC is an NDIS 2 protocol, so the network adapter must have an NDIS 2-compatible network adapter driver for use with Windows 98. Windows 98 includes many compatible drivers, but some Windows 98 drivers for certain PCI and PC Cards do not have a corresponding NDIS 2 driver to allow loading real-mode Microsoft DLC.

Additional Resources

For more information about	See this resource
Conceptual information about TCP/IP	*Networking with Microsoft TCP/IP* by Drew Heywood (New Riders Publishing, 1996).
Network adapters and protocols	*Microsoft Windows NT Server Networking Guide for Microsoft Windows NT Server version 4.0.*
	See also the *Network Supplement for Microsoft Windows NT Server version 4.0.*
GQoS specification	**ftp://microsoft.com/bussys/winsock/winsock2/**
Requests for Comments (RFCs) and Internet drafts	**http://www.ietf.org/**
TCP/IP White Paper	**http://www.microsoft.com/win32dev/netwrk/**
TCP/IP and Dial-Up Networking shareware and technical information	**http://www.download.com/**
	http://www.shareware.com/
	http://www.tucows.com/
	http://www.windows95.com/

CHAPTER 16

Windows 98 on Microsoft Networks

16

Computers running Microsoft Windows 98 can communicate and share resources with other computers running Windows 98, Windows 95, Windows for Workgroups, Windows NT Server, Windows NT Workstation, LAN Manager, and Workgroup Add-on for MS-DOS on Microsoft networks. This chapter presents procedures and technical information about using Windows 98 on Microsoft networks.

Important Each computer running Windows 98 must have a client access license if it will access Window NT Server version 3.5 or later servers on a network. For more information, see "Client Access Licenses for Windows NT Server" later in this chapter.

In This Chapter

See Also

- For technical and architectural information about Client for Microsoft Networks and Microsoft's support for clients from other network vendors, see Chapter 29, "Windows 98 Network Architecture."

- For information about protocols and adapter drivers, see Chapter 15, "Network Adapters and Protocols."

- For information about using Client for Microsoft Networks with third-party networks, see Chapter 17, "Windows 98 on Third-Party Networks."

- For information about logon, browsing, and resource sharing, see Chapter 18, "Logon, Browsing, and Resource Sharing."

- For information about security options with Client for Microsoft Networks, see Chapter 9, "Security."

Overview of Windows 98 and Microsoft Networking

Client for Microsoft Networks is the 32-bit, protected-mode network client for Windows 98 that provides the redirector and other software components for Microsoft networking. Client for Microsoft Networks also supports limited interoperability with other Microsoft-compatible server message block–based (SMB) servers such as Samba, IBM LAN Server, IBM OS/2 Warp Server, and DIGITAL PATHWORKS.

You can install Client for Microsoft Networks to serve as the sole network support for Windows 98 or to coexist with Client for NetWare Networks or clients from other network vendors, as described in Chapter 17, "Windows 98 on Third-Party Networks." For technical information about these optional configurations, see Chapter 29, "Windows 98 Network Architecture."

Support for computers running Client for Microsoft Networks includes all the robust networking features built into Windows 98:

- Automatic setup, user profiles, and system policies for configuring computers.
- Dial-Up Networking, share-level and pass-through user-level security, and remote administration capabilities.
- Unified logon and automatic reconnection to network resources.

The following paragraphs summarize the additional key benefits of using Client for Microsoft Networks.

A high-performance system using no conventional memory. Client for Microsoft Networks uses only 32-bit, protected-mode supporting networking components and, as a file system driver, uses Windows 98 caching (VCACHE). Client for Microsoft Networks uses 32-bit versions of NetBIOS Extended User Interface (NetBEUI), Microsoft Transmission Control Protocol/Internet Protocol (TCP/IP), and the Microsoft Internetwork Packet Exchange/Sequenced Packet Exchange (IPX/SPX)–compatible protocol and network driver interface specification (NDIS) version 3.1–compliant network adapter drivers. This protected-mode client is designed to be used in a multitasking environment, providing robust performance and using no MS-DOS conventional memory space. For information about supporting protocols and network adapter drivers, see Chapter 15, "Network Adapters and Protocols."

Protected-mode peer resource sharing services. You can configure computers running Client for Microsoft Networks to provide peer server capabilities using File and Printer Sharing for Microsoft Networks. For information, see Chapter 18, "Logon, Browsing, and Resource Sharing."

Security and other support on Windows NT networks.   You can use Windows NT servers to validate user logon and to provide pass-through security for shared resources on computers running Windows 98. For information, see Chapter 9, "Security." Also, computers running Windows 98 can recognize and use long file names on Windows NT servers, because the two operating systems use the same algorithm for long file names and aliases.

Accessing Samba Servers

By default, a Samba server is installed with the ability to answer only unencrypted passwords. By default, Windows 98 sends only encrypted passwords. To enable unencrypted passwords, add the registry entry **EnablePlainTextPassword** (as a DWORD), and set the value to 1 in the following registry location:

HKEY_LOCAL_MACHINE\System
\CurrentControlSet\Services\VxD\Vnetsup

Planning for Windows 98 and Microsoft Networking

This section summarizes some issues you should consider when using Windows 98 with Client for Microsoft Networks, whether your site uses server-based or peer-to-peer networking.

If you are currently using a peer-to-peer network but you want to take advantage of remote administrative features or user-level security, consider a small server-based network using Windows NT. For example, the Microsoft BackOffice® Small Business Server provides server software for companies with 25 or fewer personal computers. For more information about Small Business Server, see **http://www.microsoft.com/backofficesmallbiz/**.

Planning for Server-based Microsoft Networks

On server-based networks, central servers running Windows NT Server or Microsoft LAN Manager version 2.*x* act as file and print servers and provide support for managing network logon and security. For information about the benefits of server-based networks using Windows NT Server, see "Running Windows 98 with Windows NT" later in this chapter.

The following list describes issues to consider when planning for a server-based network:

- You must configure Client for Microsoft Networks as the Primary Network Logon client if you want to take advantage of user profiles for configuring or managing custom desktops on a Microsoft network, or if you want users to use system policies stored on a Windows NT server.

- To share resources with computers running other Microsoft networking products, the computers must be running a common protocol.

- Client for Microsoft Networks can use a LAN Manager domain controller for logon validation. However, File and Printer Sharing for Microsoft Networks cannot use a LAN Manager domain controller for pass-through validation. To take advantage of the user-level security support on Microsoft networks, the user must have an account on a Windows NT domain.

Planning for Distributed File System

With Windows 98, Client for Microsoft Networks includes the capability to connect to a distributed file system (Dfs) tree.

The Microsoft distributed file system for Windows NT Server enables Windows NT Server administrators to build a single, integrated directory tree that spans many
servers and shares in the corporate network. This directory tree presents data logically, no matter where that data is physically located. This provides the following advantages:

- Users can more easily browse, search, and gain access to data.

- The network administrator can change the network by moving data or adding additional resources, such as file storage, without affecting the way users see and get at data.

- The network administrator can organize resources on the Dfs tree according to their purpose instead of by the server and share where they are physically located.

For example, suppose the network contains the following servers and shared network directories:

- \\Retail\Accounting

  This share includes a directory called Forms, which includes the files Tulip_Form and Begonia_Form.

- \\Supply\TerraCotta

  This share includes a directory called Inventory, which is currently empty.

- \\Supply\\Flower_Seeds

  This share includes two directories: Tulip_Seeds and Begonia_Seeds. Each directory includes a file named Seeds.txt.

With Dfs, Windows NT network administrators can construct the following Dfs tree:

\\TerraFirm\Corp

\Retail\Forms	(points to \\Retail\Accounting\Forms)
\Supply	(points to \\Supply\Flower_Seeds)
\Inventory	(points to \\Supply\TerraCotta\Inventory)

Note   This Dfs tree contains several different *junction points* (places where the Dfs path points to a destination share and subdirectories). For example, \\TerraFirm\Corp\Supply is a junction point.

Figure 16.1 shows what a Windows 98 user will see. Items in bold are part of the Dfs tree.

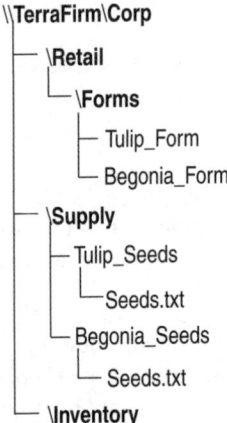

Figure 16.1   Dfs directory structure

With Windows 98, users can now gain access to Dfs volumes. Windows 98 users can browse directory trees created using Dfs in exactly the same way they browse ordinary servers and shares. For example, the user can gain access to the file Seeds.txt in the directory Tulip_Seeds in the following location:

```
\\TerraFirm\Corp\Supply\Tulip_Seeds\Seeds.txt
```

Users can also map one drive to the root of the Dfs tree and then transparently gain access to any resources in that part of the tree. For example, a user could map a drive to the root of the Dfs tree by using the following command:

```
net use Z: \\TerraFirm\Corp
```

The user can then gain access to the same file in the following location:

```
Z:\Supply\Tulip_Seeds\Seeds.txt
```

Thus, users can connect to many different servers without needing to map drives to each server.

Administrators can also create multiple Dfs directory trees and then merge them using interlinks. With *interlinks*, the leaf of one Dfs tree is the same as the root of another Dfs tree.

Windows 98 Dfs support is limited to server message block (SMB)–based resources, such as Windows NT servers. Any non-SMB resources will be invisible to Windows 98. For example, NetWare servers, which use NetWare Core Protocol (NCP), will be invisible. There is one exception: If the Windows NT server also uses Gateway for NetWare Networks, the Windows NT server network administrator can configure the gateway so that Windows 98 can also access NetWare servers by using NCP.

For more information about Dfs, see **http://www.microsoft.com/.**

Planning for Peer-to-Peer Networks

In the peer-to-peer networking model, at least one computer must act as both a client and a server. If desired, every computer can act as both a client and a server. As a client in a peer network, the computer can access the network resources shared on another computer.

A peer network can be easy to set up for a small number of users, but it becomes slower, less secure, and harder to maintain with a large number of users. Thus, a peer network is more appropriate for small offices with about five to ten users.

Any computer running Windows 98 can act as both a client and a server on peer networks. If you have the technical expertise, you can establish the wiring for a small peer network of Windows 98 computers; otherwise, use the services of a system integrator. The following sections summarize issues either you or the system integrator need to consider for peer networking with Windows 98. For technical information about configuring and using File and Printer Sharing for Microsoft Networks, see Chapter 18, "Logon, Browsing, and Resource Sharing."

Choosing Thinnet or Twisted Pair for Cabling

Thinnet (also called *thin Ethernet* or *thin coax*) is the simplest method of cabling ten or fewer connections on a network. It is appropriate only for Ethernet networks, not token-ring networks. Thinnet cabling uses coaxial cable with a BNC connector at each end. The cable attaches to each computer with a BNC T-connector. The major disadvantage in using thinnet cabling is that a fault in the cabling at any computer affects all computers on the network. Thinnet cabling is appropriate only for Ethernet topologies.

Unshielded twisted-pair (also called *UTP* or simply *twisted-pair*) cabling is based on standard telephone wiring technology, using connectors similar to those inserted in telephone jacks. Twisted-pair cabling is appropriate if your network has (or will have) more than ten computers, and if computers are located in low-interference environments such as an office—it is not appropriate for manufacturing or warehousing environments. You can use twisted-pair cabling for Ethernet or token-ring networks.

When cabling the network, make sure not to use twisted-pair wiring that was previously used for telephone systems or that is more than five years old, because it might not be reliable enough for network activity. For networks of more than two computers, you need additional components such as hubs and concentrators. These components can also help to isolate cabling failures. For more information about cabling, see *Networking Essentials, Second Edition* from Microsoft Press.

Choosing the Peer Network Components

This section summarizes issues for the following tasks:

Choosing protocols and other networking components. Microsoft NetBEUI is a fast protocol, requiring no additional configuration settings; it is a good choice for peer-to-peer networks. Microsoft TCP/IP and the IPX/SPX-compatible protocol are other alternatives for small peer-to-peer networks. You also need an NDIS 3.1 or later network adapter driver. For information about these components, see Chapter 15, "Network Adapters and Protocols."

Setting up security and automated backup. Share-level security is the only security option available on peer-to-peer networks. With share-level security, you create passwords to restrict access to shared resources on a peer server, so that only users with the password can gain access to the resources. For information about managing passwords in Windows 98, see Chapter 9, "Security." If you need to control access to individual files or to particular computers based on user identity, you must create a server-based network using Windows NT Server.

You can use any backup software that is compatible with Windows 98 to back up files on peer servers and other computers. To make sure data on the network is backed up automatically, use a server-based network.

Setting up peer servers. Each computer that is running File and Printer Sharing for Microsoft Networks can act as a server, so that other computers can connect to it to use files or printers created on that peer server. Because a peer server can slow down if many users are requesting services from it, you might want to dedicate one computer to servicing print requests. In this configuration, users can return to work immediately after printing, while the dedicated computer can perform the printing tasks.

For optimal performance on a computer used extensively as a file or print server, use the System option in Control Panel to optimize the performance of the file system for network server activities. For information, see Chapter 26, "Performance Tuning."

Managing a peer network. Most of the remote administration features in Windows 98 rely on user-level security, which requires a server running Windows NT or NetWare to provide pass-through authentication of users for access to resources on remote computers. Therefore, on peer-to-peer networks, you cannot use Microsoft Remote Registry Services or any administrative features that require remote access to the registry. However, you can use Net Watcher to manage the file system on remote computers, as described in Chapter 23, "System and Remote Administration Tools."

Installing Client for Microsoft Networks

In Windows 98, Client for Microsoft Networks provides the redirector (Vredir.vxd) to support all Microsoft networking products that use the SMB protocol. This includes support for connecting computers running Windows 98, LAN Manager, Windows NT, Windows for Workgroups, and Workgroup Add-on for MS-DOS networking software for personal computers running MS-DOS.

Because Windows 98 network redirectors are implemented as file system drivers, Client for Microsoft Networks provides mechanisms for locating, opening, reading, writing, and deleting files; submitting print requests; and making available such application services as named pipes and mailslots.

If a previous Microsoft network client is running when Windows 98 Setup is started, Client for Microsoft Networks automatically replaces the previous client. Depending on your configuration, Windows 98 Setup might add Client for Microsoft Networks. (For more information, see Chapter 14, "Introduction to Networking Configuration.") You can also add Client for Microsoft Networks after you add network hardware to the computer.

▶ **To install Client for Microsoft Networks**

1. In Control Panel, double-click Network, and then click **Add**.

2. In the **Select Network Component Type** dialog box, double-click **Client**.

3. In the **Select Network Client** dialog box, click **Microsoft** in the **Manufacturers** list, and then click **Client for Microsoft Networks** in the **Network Clients** list. Click **OK**.

Configuring Client for Microsoft Networks

To configure Client for Microsoft Networks, you need to consider the following:

- Will Client for Microsoft Networks be the Primary Network Logon client?

- Will users log on to a Windows NT domain, a single Windows NT computer, or a LAN Manager domain?

- Will persistent connections to network drives be restored when the user logs on to Windows 98 or only if the resource is used?

This section describes these options and how to configure the network client.

Note On a clean installation, Windows 98 does not configure Client for Microsoft Networks to log on to a Windows NT domain. If you want Client for Microsoft Networks to log on to a Windows NT domain, follow the procedure in "Configuring Logon and Reconnection Options," later in this chapter.

Configuring the Primary Client for Network Logon

If you set Client for Microsoft Networks as the Primary Network Logon, the computer downloads system policies and user profiles from the Windows-based network, and the first logon prompt that appears is for the Windows NT network. Also, if more than one network client is installed, the last logon script is run from Windows NT (or LAN Manager, depending on your network).

▶ **To make Client for Microsoft Networks the Primary Network Logon client**

1. In Control Panel, double-click Network.

2. In the **Primary Network Logon** box, click **Client for Microsoft Networks**. Click **OK**.

Configuring Logon and Reconnection Options

In the Network option in Control Panel, you can specify logon validation and resource connection options. If you enable logon validation, Windows 98 automatically attempts to validate the user by checking the specified domain. You must enable this option if you want to gain access to user profiles and system policies on a Windows NT domain. If logon validation is required on your network but is not enabled on your computer, you might not have access to most network resources. If logon validation is enabled and you do not provide the correct password, you might not have access to network resources.

Note For logon validation to work, the user's user name and password must be specified in a user account on the specified Windows NT domain, LAN Manager domain, or Windows NT computer.

You can also set logon validation by using system policies. With system policies, you can prevent the user from booting Windows 98 until the user is validated by either a Windows NT server or a NetWare server. For more information, see Chapter 8, "System Policies."

Note Windows 98 does not support using a LAN Manager domain controller as a pass-through security provider, but LAN Manager can provide logon validation.

▶ **To enable logon validation for Client for Microsoft Networks**

1. In Control Panel, double-click Network, and then double-click **Client for Microsoft Networks** in the list of network components.

2. Select the **Log on to Windows NT domain** check box if you want to log on to a Microsoft Windows NT or LAN Manager domain automatically when starting Windows 98.

   If you do not want to log on to a domain when starting Windows 98, make sure this check box is cleared.

3. If you select logon validation, you can also specify the domain to be used for validation by typing a name in the **Windows NT Domain** box.

   You can specify a Windows NT or LAN Manager domain name or the name of a Windows NT computer (version 3.1 or later) where you have a user account.

You can also specify whether Windows 98 should restore and verify each persistent connection at system startup.

▶ **To configure how persistent connections are restored**

1. In Control Panel, double-click Network, and then double-click **Client for Microsoft Networks** in the list of network components.

2. To map the drive letters when you log on without actually establishing a session for each persistent network connection, in the **Network logon options** area, click **Quick logon**.

   –Or–

   To have Windows 98 verify each persistent network connection at startup by establishing a session for each persistent connection, click **Logon and restore network connections.**

With *Quick logon*, Windows 98 initializes data structures for mapping local drives and local printer ports to network resources, but Windows 98 does not attach to the network resource until the user tries to get access to the resources.

When you use Quick logon (the default), Windows 98 starts faster than if the actual connections are made during startup. However, the first time you try to access a network drive, it will take a little longer for the contents of that drive to appear.

Note Quick logon requires password caching to function properly. If system policies are used to disable password caching, users cannot use Quick logon successfully with peer servers configured with share-level security.

Running Windows 98 in a Mixed Microsoft Environment

This section presents some technical information to consider if your network includes computers running Windows NT or earlier versions of Microsoft networking products in addition to computers running Windows 98.

Running Windows 98 with Windows NT

Microsoft Windows NT Server networks use a domain structure and provide both client/server and peer networking with user-level security. You can run Windows 98 on a Windows NT network.

For a description of the support for running logon scripts from Windows NT Server, see Chapter 18, "Logon, Browsing, and Resource Sharing." For information about installing Windows 98 as a dual-boot operating system with Windows NT, see Chapter 5, "Setup Technical Discussion."

Running Windows 98 in a Mixed Environment with Windows NT

In Windows 98, computers are grouped logically in workgroups, where each computer in the workgroup maintains its own security system for validating local user logon and access to resources. Computers in workgroups do not share security with other computers, and they do not rely on other computers to provide security. On Windows NT–based networks, computers can be grouped into domains, which allow multiple servers and workstations to be grouped for unified administration. With Windows NT domains, centralized user accounts are used to validate user logon and access to resources. Thus, if you have five users on five computers, you can configure your network so you need to create and maintain only five user accounts.

Windows 98 and Windows NT use the same workgroup model for browsing network resources, so computers running File and Printer Sharing for Microsoft Networks can appear in the same workgroup as computers running Windows NT. A computer running Windows NT will always be the *master browse server* (the computer that maintains the list of servers in a workgroup), but Windows 98–based computers might act as backup browse servers.

Users running Client for Microsoft Networks can gain access to the shared resources on a computer running Windows NT if both computers are using a common protocol. For a user running Windows 98 to get to Windows NT resources, the user must have been granted access to those resources and must have a valid user name and password. For a user running Windows NT to get to Windows 98 resources protected with share-level security, the user does not need to have been granted explicit access to the resource and needs only to know the password for the resource. For a user running Windows NT to get to Windows 98 resources protected with user-level security, the user must have been granted explicit access to those resources and must have a valid user name and password.

Benefits of Using Windows 98 with Windows NT Server

The Microsoft Windows NT Server operating system is the high-end member of the family of Microsoft Windows operating systems, providing a powerful, reliable, and scalable operating system to support the demands of client/server computing for workstations running Windows 98 or other operating systems.

Windows NT Server provides the ideal platform for the server backbone in a mixed-network environment. It is especially versatile and powerful for enterprise networks made up of LANs that use a variety of network types and require dial-in support for network access. Also, on a peer-to-peer network on which the computers are running Client for Microsoft Networks, you can add Windows NT to the network without changing the networking software on the existing computers.

Windows NT Server is designed to support complex business applications and administrative requirements. The following list summarizes important features.

Networking and workgroup support.   Windows NT Server provides built-in file and printer sharing capabilities for workgroup computing, and an open network system interface that includes built-in support for IPX/SPX, TCP/IP, NetBEUI, and other protocols. Windows NT Server also provides administrative tools for controlling network services, auditing system events, changing hardware configuration and system performance, managing and backing up disks, and so on. Additionally, Windows NT provides robust support for server-based and client/server applications.

Interoperability.   Windows NT Server is compatible with such networks as Windows 98, Novell NetWare, Banyan, UNIX, LAN Manager 2.*x*, and Microsoft Windows for Workgroups. Windows NT Server can add value to your current network environment without disruption. Even though networks and interoperability are complicated, a Windows NT network is easy to use and reliable, with automatic configuration provided wherever possible and remote administration available for most administration tasks.

A single network logon.   With Windows 98 with Windows NT Server, users can gain access to network resources, including client/server applications, using one user account and one password per user.

Centralized management of user accounts.   Using Windows 98 with Windows NT Server, network administrators can work from a single computer across divisions, departments, and workgroups.

Advanced data-protection features.   Using Windows NT Server, network administrators can take advantage of such features as disk mirroring, disk striping with parity (RAID 5), and uninterruptible power supply support.

Remote Access Service (RAS).   Users can gain access to network resources even when they are off-site, as when traveling or working at home. They can dial in over asynchronous telephone lines or Integrated Services Digital Network (ISDN) lines to reach the network from computers running Windows 98, MS-DOS, Windows for Workgroups, or Windows NT operating systems. Using RAS point-to-point tunneling protocol (PPTP), they can also dial an Internet Service Provider (ISP) and make a secure connection to their network over the Internet. Windows NT RAS also supports X.25 networks.

Access to Apple Macintosh resources.   When Services for Apple Macintosh is installed on a Windows NT server, Macintoshes and computers running Windows 98 can work together to share files, printers, and client/server applications. Macintosh users can gain access to resources on a computer running Windows NT Server.

Client Access Licenses for Windows NT Server

Microsoft licenses Windows NT Server and Windows NT Workstation separately, allowing you to purchase only the components you need to build a network solution for your organization.

To get access to Windows NT Server from Windows 98–based workstations, you need three types of licenses:

- Your Windows 98 license, required to run Windows 98.
- One Server License for Microsoft Windows NT Server for each Windows NT Server on the network.
- One Client Access License for Windows NT Server for each computer running Windows 98 or other operating systems that will access the Windows NT file, print, and remote access services.

Microsoft offers two licensing options for Windows NT Server:

- In *Per Seat* licensing, the Client Access License applies to a specific workstation ("seat"). Using this alternative, an unlimited number of computers or workstations running Windows 98 or other operating systems can access Windows NT Server, provided each is licensed with a Client Access License. After a workstation has been licensed, it has permission to access all Windows NT Server products installed throughout your organization.

  A Client Access License is required whether you use client software supplied by Microsoft or software from another vendor. In particular, for each computer running Windows 98, Windows for Workgroups, Windows NT Workstation, or any client software that Windows NT Server supports, a separate Client Access License is required.

- In *Per Server* licensing, each Client Access License is assigned to a particular server and allows one connection to that server for basic network services. Under this option, you designate during setup the number of licenses that apply to this server.

You can convert a Per Server License to a Per Seat License at no cost and without notifying Microsoft. You cannot, however, switch from a Per Seat option to a Per Server option. Also, you are not required to license all your servers using the same option.

Note It is a violation of the terms of the Server License to use Windows NT Server without an appropriate number of Client Access Licenses. For more information, see your Server License.

Client Access Licenses are available in single-client and 20-client configurations and in volume quantities through the Microsoft Select licensing program. For more information, contact your Microsoft reseller. If you have questions, in the United States, contact the Microsoft Sales Information Center at (800) 426-9400. In Canada, contact the Microsoft Canada Sales Information Centre at (800) 563-9048. For other locations, contact your local Microsoft subsidiary.

Running Windows 98 with LAN Manager

A workgroup in Windows 98 is analogous to a LAN Manager domain, in that it is a logical grouping of workstations. However, a workgroup in Windows 98 does not share any of the advanced security features offered as part of a LAN Manager domain. Windows 98 does not support using a LAN Manager domain controller as a security provider, so only share-level security can be used for computers running Windows 98 on LAN Manager networks. (User-level security requires a Windows NT domain.)

To ensure that computers running Windows 98 can browse for LAN Manager servers, make sure that at least one computer running Client for Microsoft Networks sets its workgroup name to the LAN Manager domain name. After a computer running Windows 98 becomes a member of the LAN Manager domain, it can distribute the names of LAN Manager servers in that domain to other computers running Windows 98 on the network. The configuration must be duplicated for each LAN Manager domain.

▶ **To ensure that LAN Manager workstations can see and access resources on computers running File and Printer Sharing for Microsoft Networks**

1. Make sure that all the computers are using a common protocol.

2. Make sure that users running LAN Manager clients have been granted access to the resources on the computers running Windows 98.

3. Set the value of the **LM Announce** property to **Yes** on each computer running Windows 98 with file and printer sharing services, as described in "Using File and Printer Sharing for Microsoft Networks" in Chapter 18, "Logon, Browsing, and Resource Sharing."

The **LM Announce** setting ensures that the computer running Windows 98 peer resource sharing services announces its presence to LAN Manager workstations and servers. By default, the **LM Announce** property is set to **No** to reduce broadcast traffic on the network.

Note IBM OS/2 LAN Server supports a domain model and is equivalent to LAN Manager for interoperating with Windows 98. Just as with Windows for Workgroups, the Client for Microsoft Networks in Windows 98 does not support LAN Server aliases.

Running Windows 98 with Windows for Workgroups

Windows 98 uses the same workgroup model as Windows for Workgroups. Therefore, computers running File and Printer Sharing for Microsoft Networks can be seen by computers running Windows for Workgroups. A computer running Windows NT or Windows 98 will always be the master browse server. For a computer running Windows 98 and Windows for Workgroups to communicate, both computers must be running a common protocol.

Shared resources on Windows for Workgroups computers are password-protected. Therefore, a user running Client for Microsoft Networks can gain access to shared resources on a computer running Windows for Workgroups only if that user knows the password.

To get to Windows 98 resources protected with user-level security, a user running Windows for Workgroups must have been granted access to those resources and must have a valid user name and password. To get to Windows 98 resources protected with share-level security, this same user does not need to have been granted explicit access to the resource and needs only to know the password for the resource.

Running Windows 98 with Workgroup Add-on for MS-DOS

Computers running File and Printer Sharing for Microsoft Networks can appear in the same workgroup as a computer running the peer server supported in Workgroup Add-on for MS-DOS. For a list of peer servers to be available in the workgroup, there must be at least one computer in the workgroup configured as the master browse server that is running Windows 98, Windows 95, Windows for Workgroups, or Windows NT. A computer running Workgroup Add-on for MS-DOS cannot be a master browse server.

Users running Client for Microsoft Networks can gain access to the shared resources on a computer running Workgroup Add-on for MS-DOS if both computers are using a common protocol and if the user knows the password for the resource.

To get to Windows 98 resources protected with user-level security, a user running Workgroup Add-on for MS-DOS must have been granted access to those resources and must have a valid user name and password. To get to Windows 98 resources protected with share-level security, this same user does not need to have been granted explicit access to the resource and needs only to know the password for the resource. In both cases, both computers must be running a common protocol.

Working with Protocol.ini: Real-Mode Network Initialization File

For real-mode networking, Windows 98 uses a file called Protocol.ini in the Windows directory to determine the parameters for the protocol and network adapter drivers. Setup creates and modifies Protocol.ini from information in INF files if any real-mode networking components, such as NDIS version 2 adapter drivers, are installed.

Caution   Never edit Protocol.ini manually. Actual settings are stored in the registry, and changes in Protocol.ini will be overwritten automatically. Instead, always use the Network option in Control Panel and the setup software for your network hardware to configure network settings.

The information presented in this section is for troubleshooting purposes only.

Protocol.ini also contains network adapter configuration information, such as the I/O address, direct memory access (DMA), and interrupt requests (IRQs). The Protocol.ini file contains sections for [protman$] and separate sections for each network adapter and network protocol.

Configuring Adapters with Real-Mode Networking

When multiple hardware adapters are used on a computer, some entries in Protocol.ini, such as interrupt settings and shared memory addresses, might need adjustments to avoid hardware conflicts. Because Windows 98 Setup cannot anticipate every possible conflict, watch for error messages when you start the computer in real-mode networking.

For example, if both a network adapter and a video controller adapter try to use the same memory address, you must adjust one of the adapters to a different address by using either the setup software for the adapter or the switches on the adapter (or both, which is the typical case). Also, the Protocol.ini entries must agree with the jumper setting on each adapter.

[Protman] section. This section provides the settings for the system component that manages protocols. The following list explains the format for this section.

[Protman] entry	Description
drivername=	Defines the driver name for the component that manages protocols.
priority=	Determines the order in which incoming frames are processed.

The following shows an example of entries in this section for a computer configured with multiple NDIS protocols:

```
[protman$]
priority=ndishlp$
DriverName=protman$
```

[Netcard] section. This section lists the set of parameters for an NDIS network adapter. A [netcard] section is present for each network adapter configured in the computer, and the specific entries present in this section vary depending on the network adapter installed. The following is an example of entries in this section for an Intel EtherExpress 16 or 16TP adapter:

```
[EXP16$]
DriverName=EXP16$
transceiver=Twisted-Pair (TPE)
iochrdy=Late
irq=5
ioaddress=0x300
```

[Protocol] section. This section defines the settings used by a network protocol. A [protocol] section is present for each network transport protocol installed on the computer, and the specific entries present in this section vary depending on the protocol installed. The following list explains the format for entries common to each configured protocol.

[Protocol] entry	Description
bindings=	Indicates the network adapter drivers to which each transport protocol binds. The netcard name for the network adapter driver must appear in the bindings= entry for at least one of the protocol drivers. The entry can specify one or more [netcard] sections (separated by commas).
Lanabase=	For NetBIOS protocols only, defines the first LANA number the protocol is to accept.

The following is an example of entries in this section for an IPX/SPX-compatible protocol and Microsoft NetBEUI:

```
[nwlink$]
DriverName=nwlink$
Frame_Type=4
cachesize=0
Bindings=EXP16$

[NETBEUI$]
DriverName=NETBEUI$
Lanabase=0
sessions=10
ncbs=12
Bindings=EXP16$
```

Troubleshooting Windows 98 on Microsoft Networks

For information about troubleshooting Windows 98 on Microsoft networks, see the chapter describing the aspect of your network setup that you need to troubleshoot. For information about troubleshooting basic network configuration issues, see Chapter 14, "Introduction to Networking Configuration." For information about troubleshooting network adapter drivers and network protocols, see Chapter 15, "Network Adapters and Protocols." For information about troubleshooting problems with Windows NT Server, see the *Microsoft Windows NT Server Networking Guide* in the *Microsoft Windows NT Server Resource Kit* (for Windows NT version 4.0).

Additional Resources

For more information about	See this resource
Basic information about networks and network adapters	*Networking Essentials, Second Edition*
Advanced networking information, information about networking with Windows NT Server, and information about deploying large networks	*Microsoft Windows NT Server Networking Guide* in the *Microsoft Windows NT Server Resource Kit* (for Windows NT version 4.0)

CHAPTER 17

Windows 98 on Third-Party Networks

17

This chapter describes how to install and configure Microsoft Windows 98 on Novell® NetWare® and other third-party networks. It discusses the issues you should consider before configuring Windows 98 for third-party networks, including issues to consider when installing real-mode clients. For NetWare networks, it also explains how to choose between Microsoft-supplied and NetWare-supplied networks.

In This Chapter

See Also

- For information about how to install third-party networks using custom setup scripts, see Chapter 3, "Custom Installations."
- For an overview of Windows 98 networking, see Chapter 14, "Introduction to Networking Configuration."
- For a discussion of logon, browsing, and resource sharing, see Chapter 18, "Logon, Browsing, and Resource Sharing."
- For a discussion of network architecture, see Chapter 29, "Windows 98 Network Architecture."
- For information about networking printing and support for printing when using a 16-bit network client, see Chapter 11, "Printing, Imaging, and Fonts."

Overview of Windows 98 on Third-Party Networks

Networking support is built into Windows 98. The Windows 98 network architecture includes a network provider interface, which defines a set of APIs that Windows 98 uses to access the network for actions, such as connecting to, logging on to, and browsing servers. Microsoft has made this set of APIs widely available to network vendors so that they can develop new protected-mode network providers (drivers for network clients) that are compatible with Windows 98.

Windows 98 includes two protected-mode network clients (Client for Microsoft Networks and Client for NetWare Networks). Windows 98 also includes built-in support for several 16-bit, real-mode network clients; however, in most cases, you also need to use supporting software from the appropriate network vendors. Additionally, the Windows 98 network provider interface enables you to use third-party network clients. Furthermore, because the Windows 98 network architecture supports multiple network providers, you can use multiple network clients on one computer. You can use one 16-bit, real-mode client, and as many 32-bit, protected-mode network clients as you need. Contact your network vendor to obtain a 32-bit, protected-mode network client for your network.

This chapter discusses the following networking software:

- Artisoft LANtastic version 7.0 (client and server components)
- Banyan Enterprise Client version 7.32 and later
- Banyan VINES client version 7.1 and later
- DIGITAL PATHWORKS 32 client
- IBM Networks Client for Windows 95

- Client for NetWare Networks
- NETX, the real-mode Novell NetWare workstation shell client for servers running NetWare version 3.*x* and later
- VLM (Virtual Loadable Module), the real-mode workstation shell client for servers running NetWare version 4.*x*.
- Novell Client for Windows 95/98 (also known as Client 32)
- Solstice NFS Client version 3.1 and later

Note   See the Network.txt file for a list of clients and servers that Windows 98 does not support.

For information about how to install third-party networks using custom setup scripts, see Chapter 3, "Custom Installations."

Overview of Windows 98 on NetWare Networks

With Windows 98, you can use the built-in features and commands to perform most common network operation and administration tasks on NetWare networks. The following networking features are available in Windows 98 to support computers running on NetWare networks:

- Automatic setup and customization of Windows 98 on NetWare workstations, as described in Chapter 3, "Custom Installations," and Chapter 4, "Automated Installations."
- System policies to enforce desktop and system settings for individual or multiple computers, as described in Chapter 8, "System Policies."
- Integration of network resources in Network Neighborhood, and common controls, such as the **Open** or **Save As** dialog boxes, as described in Chapter 18, "Logon, Browsing, and Resource Sharing."
- Password caching for network connections and user-level security with pass-through validation to NetWare servers, as described in Chapter 9, "Security."
- Printing to NetWare print queues using Point and Print. For information, see Chapter 11, "Printing, Imaging, and Fonts." You can use several different NetWare clients, and different features are available depending on the client you choose.

Additionally, the Windows 98 Resource Kit includes an agent for simple network management protocol (SNMP), as described in Chapter 23, "System and Remote Administration Tools."

Planning for Windows 98 on NetWare Networks

When planning for Windows 98 on NetWare networks, you will need to consider the following issues:

- The network client you will use.
- The protocols you will use.

Choosing the Network Client

Windows 98 runs on workstations that can connect to Novell NetWare versions 3.x, and 4.x servers. You can use several different networking clients:

- The 32-bit, protected-mode Microsoft Client for NetWare Networks.

  If you use Microsoft Client for NetWare Networks, you can also use the optional Microsoft Service for NetWare Directory Services. This service provides tight integration with Novell Directory Services (NDS).
- Novell Client for Windows 95/98 (also known as Client 32), a 32-bit, protected-mode client.
- NETX, the real-mode networking client for servers running NetWare version 3.x and later
- VLM, the real-mode networking client for servers running NetWare version 4.x.

Note Microsoft does not support connecting to servers running versions of NetWare earlier than NetWare 3.11. Microsoft also does not support using Novell Client for DOS/Windows 3.x. When using Novell Client for Windows 95/98, Microsoft recommends using version 2.2 or later with updated versions of Vmlid.nlm and Odiload.vxd, which you obtain from Novell.

You should use a protected-mode client rather than a real-mode client. Protected-mode clients offer the following benefits:

- Provide easy installation and configuration using built-in Windows 98 tools.
- Use no real-mode memory.
- Provide faster data I/O across the network than do real-mode clients.
- Offer greater stability than do real-mode clients.
- Enable you to run additional protected-mode clients.

The following sections describe the issues you will need to consider before choosing each client.

Note For computers that use Microsoft Client for NetWare Networks, all the files required for networking are included with Windows 98. However, you will need some Novell-supplied files in order to run NetWare utilities. Additionally, Windows 98 does not include any Novell-supplied components required for Novell clients. For information about obtaining updates for Novell-supplied files, see "Obtaining Current Novell-Supplied Files" later in this chapter.

For information about configuring Novell-supplied components and running NetWare utilities, consult your Novell documentation. For information about licensing requirements, see your Novell NetWare license agreement.

Issues with Microsoft-supplied NetWare Clients

You might choose not to use Client for NetWare Networks in the following cases:

- If you want to use Novell-supplied utilities, such as Novell Application Launcher, Novell IP Gateway, Remote Access Dialer, and NetWare Distributed Print Services, you should use Novell Client for Windows 95/98.

- If you want to take advantage of NetWare NCP packet signature for enhanced protection of servers and client computers using NCP, you must use Novell Client for Windows 95/98 or VLM, because Client for NetWare Networks does not support this feature.

- If your site needs to use NetWare Internet Protocol (IP), you should use Novell Client for Windows 95/98, the NETX client, or the VLM client. Client for NetWare Networks does not support NetWare IP, and you cannot use Microsoft TCP/IP to communicate with NetWare servers using NetWare IP.

- If you use 3270 emulators that rely on MS-DOS-helper terminate-and-stay-resident (TSR) programs or need 3270 emulation for applications in MS-DOS sessions, you should use NETX or VLM.

- If you are using custom VLM components, such as PNW, you should use VLM.

- If you have problems with programs that make proprietary or undocumented API calls, you should use a Novell-supplied client.

Issues with Novell-supplied NetWare Clients

If you are using a Novell-supplied NetWare client, you should use Novell Client for Windows 95/98. It is a 32-bit, protected-mode client that provides access to Novell Directory Services (NDS) and newer Novell-supplied utilities.

You might choose not to use Novell Client for Windows 95/98 and instead use Client for NetWare Networks in the following cases:

- If you have problems with Setup using MsBatch.
- If you want to take advantage of Windows 98 peer resource sharing without running another network client.

Choosing Protocols on NetWare Networks

This section discusses issues you should consider when using the following protocols:

- Microsoft's 32-bit, protected-mode IPX/SPX-compatible protocol.
- Novell's 32-bit, protected-mode IPX/SPX-compatible protocol.
- Novell's real-mode IPX protocol.
- Microsoft's TCP/IP.
- Novell's NetWare/IP.

Microsoft provides a 32-bit, protected mode IPX/SPX-compatible protocol that is compliant with network driver interface specification (NDIS) 3.1 and later and with the IPX specification. This protocol can use IPX routers, such as Novell NetWare servers configured as routers to transfer packets across LANs to access resources on other computers running any IPX/SPX protocol. With the Microsoft IPX/SPX-compatible protocol, you do not need to load the Novell-supplied Vipx.386 driver.

Consider the following issues when using Microsoft's 32-bit, IPX/SPX-compatible protocol:

- You can use this protocol with Client for NetWare Networks and Novell Client for Windows 95/98, but you cannot use it with Novell's real-mode clients, NETX and VLM.
- The Microsoft IPX/SPX-compatible protocol is installed automatically if you install Client for NetWare Networks. However, if you configure Windows 98 to maintain the existing NetWare client and protocol software instead, you can later try to install the Microsoft IPX/SPX-compatible protocol by following the instructions in Chapter 15, "Network Adapters and Protocols."
- You can install both protected-mode and real-mode IPX drivers on the same adapter with ODI drivers.

Novell provides a 32-bit, IPX/SPX-compatible protocol that works with Novell Client for Windows 95/98. Novell Client for Windows 95/98 does not work with the Novell IPXODI protocol, the 16-bit module for the NETX and VLM clients.

Client for NetWare Networks does not support NetWare IP. Also, Microsoft TCP/IP cannot provide TCP/IP support on NetWare networks. NetWare IP uses other protocol implementations for IP functionality, so the two protocol suites cannot communicate with each other.

Although you cannot use Microsoft TCP/IP as the supporting protocol for Client for NetWare Networks or for Novell-supplied, real-mode networking clients, you can use Microsoft TCP/IP to support Novell Client for Windows 95/98 and other networking clients on the same computer. Use this configuration when TCP/IP-based communications are used on the network.

Setting Up Windows 98 for NetWare Networks: An Overview

If you are administering a NetWare network, the move to Windows 98 will involve incremental planning, testing, and gradual implementation of Windows 98 on many computers on the network. Typically, the administrator will take time to complete the following tasks:

1. Install Windows 98 on a single workstation, and experiment with various configuration alternatives.

   This task includes experimenting with the typical applications used at your site and working over the network to assess the performance, reliability, and robustness available under Windows 98.

   For information about choosing protocols and a network client, see the section "Planning for Windows 98 on NetWare Networks."

2. Prepare an implementation strategy, as summarized in Chapter 1, "Deployment Strategy."

3. Test the selected configuration of network clients, protocols, and drivers on a small network.

4. Create default user profiles, system policies, and setup scripts, and perform other customization tasks for automatic installation and configuration, based on the inventory and implementation strategy.

5. Test automatic installation on a small network.

6. Prepare and implement the strategy for rollout on the larger network.

Windows 98 Setup detects whether a Novell NetWare workstation shell client is running on the computer. During the detection phase, Windows 98 Setup also tries to determine whether the computer is using real-mode TSRs that cannot be replaced (such as Dosnp.com, TCP/IP client software, or 3720 emulators).

After detection is complete, Windows 98 Setup determines whether to remove the existing components and install Client for NetWare Networks. If Setup finds the NETX client, it removes NETX and automatically configures Client for NetWare Networks. See "Installing or Upgrading a Real-Mode client" for issues you should consider before upgrading NETX or VLM.

However, Windows 98 Setup does not automatically install Client for NetWare Networks if detection finds the following:

- The computer is using Novell Client for Windows 95/98 or VLM with NetWare 4.*x* NDS, and you call Login.exe either in Autoexec.bat or a batch file referenced by it (such as Startnet.bat). In this case, Setup leaves all existing networking components in place.

- Certain TSRs are present that require ODI. In this case, Setup installs Client for NetWare Networks but configures it to run over ODI.

- Certain TSRs are present that are not compatible with the protected-mode client, but can use the new implementation of the IPX/SPX-compatible protocol. In this case, the real-mode network client and adapter drivers are left in place, but Setup installs the new protocol.

- Certain TSRs are present that are not compatible with Client for NetWare Networks or other protected-mode components. In this case, Setup leaves all existing real-mode networking components in place.

To install Client for NetWare Networks and other protected-mode networking components, Setup might perform the following actions:

- Comment out NetWare-related TSRs in Autoexec.bat that are not required with Client for NetWare Networks or other Windows 98 components.

- Move certain TSRs from Autoexec.bat to Winstart.bat so that this software can be loaded at the appropriate time during system startup.

- Install new 32-bit, protected-mode versions of networking components such as protocols and network adapter drivers.

- Comment out entries from System.ini that are not required when using protected-mode networking components.

- Configure settings in the registry related to support for NetWare networks

The actions for software detection and installation of new networking components are defined in a file named Netdet.ini in the \Windows directory. Installation actions are defined in Netdet.ini for the software listed in Table 17.1. For a complete and current list, see Netdet.ini in your \Windows directory.

Table 17.1   Windows 98 Setup software detection and installation

Software detected	Windows 98 Setup default action
Btrieve (Brequest.exe)	Installs Client for NetWare Networks, with all protected-mode components.
Dosnp.exe	Keeps the real-mode IPX protocol in place.
LAN Workplace	Installs Client for NetWare Networks, but keeps the real-mode ODI network adapter and IPX protocol in place.
Novell NetBIOS TSR	Installs the Microsoft IPX/SPX-compatible protocol and enables NetBIOS support.
NACS/NASI (Nasi.exe)	Retains all existing Novell-supplied networking components.

For information about the format of entries in Netdet.ini and how to customize this file, see Chapter 3, "Custom Installations."

Windows 98 Setup automatically configures settings for network adapters and protocols. The specific issues for configuring drivers and protocols depend on whether the computer is using Client for NetWare Networks or a Novell-supplied workstation shell.

Note Windows 98 Setup does not automatically install the Microsoft Service for NetWare Directory Services, which provides integration with NDS. To install Microsoft Service for NetWare Directory Services, follow the procedure "To add Microsoft Service for NetWare Directory Services after installing Windows 98" in "Setting Up Microsoft Service for NetWare Directory Services" later in this chapter.

Configuring NetWare Servers to Support Windows 98

This section presents information about installing Windows 98 source files on NetWare servers, automating Setup for NetWare workstations, support for long file names on NetWare servers, and where to place user profiles and system policy files on NetWare servers.

Installing Windows 98 Source Files on NetWare Servers

The Windows 98 master files can be placed on a NetWare server to be used as source files for installing Windows 98 locally on NetWare workstations.

▶ **To set up Windows 98 source files on a NetWare server**

- On the network administrator's computer, log on to the NetWare file server where you want to place the Windows 98 source files. Make sure you log on with security privileges that allow you to create directories and copy files to the file server. Then copy the Windows 98 source files to the NetWare file server.

Automating Setup for NetWare Workstations

You can create automatic installation procedures for installing Windows 98 on multiple workstations. The steps include the following:

- Creating setup scripts for installing Windows 98 on computers connected to NetWare networks, specifying the network client and supporting components, plus defining other software components to be installed.
- Defining user and computer settings to be used in setup scripts for specific NetWare workstation configurations.
- Creating logon scripts to set up Windows 98 automatically on NetWare workstations when users log on.

For a complete description of the procedures for preparing and managing automatic installation of Windows 98 on multiple computers, see Chapter 4, "Automated Installations."

Supporting Long File Names on NetWare Servers

Computers running a 32-bit, protected mode client with Windows 98 can use long file names on NetWare 3.*x* and 4.*x* volumes configured to use the OS/2 name space, which emulates a high-performance file system (HPFS) volume. File names on such NetWare volumes have a maximum length of 254 characters and use an 8.3 truncation on the first instance of the file name. For example:

```
longfilenameold.tst --> LONGFILE.TST
longfilenamenew.tst --> LONGFIL0.TST
```

The following procedures describe how to enable long file names on NetWare servers.

▶ **To enable long file names on NetWare servers running versions 4.10 or earlier**

1. At the NetWare server console prompt, type the following lines:

```
load os2
add name space os2 to volume sys
```

2. Then add the following line to Startup.ncf:

```
load os2
```

3. Shut down the file server. Then copy Os2.nam from the NetWare distribution disks or compact disc to the same disk and directory that contains Server.exe on the NetWare file server.

4. Restart the NetWare file server.

▶ **To enable long file names on NetWare servers running versions later than 4.1x**

- At the NetWare server console prompt, type the following lines:

```
load long
add name space long to sys
```

▶ **To verify that long file names have been added**

- At the NetWare server console prompt, type **volume**.

If you have problems with these procedures, contact Novell for more information.

When you use long file names for files on a NetWare volume while running Windows 98, the following exceptions occur:

- You cannot use a combination of short names and long names for a path used in an MS-DOS prompt window.

- You cannot use **cd** in an MS-DOS prompt window to switch directories using first a long file name, then a truncated name, or vice versa.

- You cannot use **dir** in an MS-DOS prompt window to check a directory on a NetWare server if you used a truncated name to switch to that directory.

To avoid these problems, use Windows Explorer. Otherwise, avoid long directory names if you do a lot of work at the command prompt.

NetWare 3.11 servers experience problems with applications that open a large number of files. Error messages report these problems as sharing or lock violations, or report a "file not found" error when you know the file exists, or report other errors in opening files. Novell supplies a patch for this problem, which you can obtain from **http://support.novell.com/**.

However, if you have not applied the patch, this problem affects how NetWare 3.11 servers handle long file names, even if the OS/2 name space is enabled. To avoid such problems, Windows 98 Setup enables long file name support only with NetWare servers version 3.12 or later.

To support long file names on all NetWare servers, you should apply all proper NetWare patches at your site. You must also set the value of SupportLFN to 2, expressed in binary as "**10**," in the following registry subkey:

Hkey_Local_Machine\System
   \CurrentControlSet\Services\VxD\Nwredir

Important Enter the value for this registry subkey in binary notation. Thus, enter the binary value "**10**" for a decimal value of 2.

The possible values for this registry key are the following:

- 0, which indicates that long file names are not supported on NetWare servers.
- 1 (the default), which indicates that long file names are supported on NetWare servers version 3.12 and later.
- 2, which indicates that long file names are supported if the NetWare server supports long file names. This can include NetWare 3.11 servers where the patch has been applied.

These values can also be set globally using system policies. The related policy name is Support Long File Names under the policies for Client for NetWare Networks.

Supporting Pass-Through Security for Peer Resource Sharing

If computers running Windows 98 will be providing File and Printer Sharing Services for NetWare Networks, then the NetWare server providing access validation can be configured with a special WINDOWS_PASSTHRU account. This special account is used to support pass-through validation for user-level security. It is not necessary for users who already have an account on that server.

For more information about configuring and managing pass-through and user-level security for Windows 98 on NetWare networks, see Chapter 9, "Security."

Placing Profile and Policy Files on NetWare Servers

User profiles, which consist of the user-specific information in the registry, can be used to ensure a consistent desktop for individual users who log on to multiple computers, or for multiple users logging on to the same computer. User profiles can be used on a NetWare network with computers configured to use Microsoft Client for NetWare Networks. When a user account is created on a NetWare server, a subdirectory of the MAIL directory is created automatically for that user. Because a MAIL directory is always available for each user, Windows 98 uses these individual directories to store user profiles. If you want to use user profiles to enforce a mandatory desktop, place the related User.man file in the users' MAIL directories.

If you are using system policies to enforce specific desktop or system settings, the appropriate Config.pol file must be stored in the SYS:PUBLIC directory on each NetWare server that users use as a preferred server. Windows 98 automatically downloads policies from this file.

Note Novell Client for Windows 95/98 always looks for Config.pol in the SYS:SYSTEM directory of the preferred server, not the logon server. If you have not set the preferred server, Config.pol does not automatically download.

For more information about using user profiles or creating system policies, including information about using profiles and policies with Service for NetWare Directory Services, see Chapter 7, "User Profiles," and Chapter 8, "System Policies."

Installing and Configuring Microsoft Client for NetWare Networks

The redirector provided by Client for NetWare Networks (Nwredir.vxd) is a file system driver that supports the NCP file sharing protocol for NetWare 3.x and NetWare 4.x. Client for NetWare Networks also supports Microsoft File and Printer Sharing for NetWare Networks (Nwserver.vxd, the NCP peer server provided with Windows 98).

In addition to installing Client for NetWare Networks, you can install the optional Microsoft Service for NetWare Directory Services. Microsoft Service for NetWare Directory Services adds several features, such as support for NDS and for logon scripts. If you install Microsoft Service for NetWare Directory Services, Client for NetWare Networks will be automatically installed.

This section describes how to install and configure Client for NetWare Networks and Microsoft Service for NetWare Directory Services, and provides some technical notes on supporting files.

For information about how to configure logon for Client for NetWare Networks and Microsoft Service for NetWare Directory Services, see Chapter 18, "Logon, Browsing, and Resource Sharing."

Setting Up Microsoft Client for NetWare Networks

When using Client for NetWare Networks, you generally do not need to load any Novell-supplied drivers or components. This client runs with the Microsoft IPX/SPX-compatible protocol and NDIS-compliant, protected-mode drivers, which Windows 98 Setup installs automatically when you select this client.

However, you may need to load Novell-supplied files if you are running NetWare-aware utilities and they do not function correctly with Microsoft Client for NetWare Networks, or if you have installed Microsoft Service for NetWare Directory Services and you need to run NDS-based utilities. For a list of these files, see "NetWare API Support in Client for NetWare Networks" later in this chapter.

When Windows 98 is installed with Client for NetWare Networks, Windows 98 Setup automatically moves any relevant Net.cfg settings to the Windows 98 registry. You can configure the related settings using the Network option in Control Panel. You can also configure the network adapter driver and the IPX/SPX-compatible protocol, as described in Chapter 15, "Network Adapters and Protocols."

If you did not install Client for NetWare Networks before Windows 98 Setup, you can switch to this client any time after Windows 98 is installed. If you need to connect to the NDS tree, follow the procedures outlined in "Setting Up Microsoft Service for NetWare Directory Services" later in this chapter. However, if you do not need to connect to the NDS tree, follow the procedure "To add Client for NetWare Networks after Windows 98 has been installed" in this section.

You can also install Client for NetWare Networks and configure related options when installing Windows 98 using custom setup scripts, as described in Chapter 3, "Custom Installations."

Tip To display the Network option without opening Control Panel, right-click the Network Neighborhood icon on the desktop. Then click **Properties** on the context menu.

Note Windows 98 Setup copies files from your original Windows 98 installation media, so make sure your original Windows 98 installation media are ready before you perform this procedure.

▶   **To add Client for NetWare Networks after installing Windows 98**

1. In Control Panel, double-click Network and examine the list of installed components. If the computer currently has NETX or VLM installed, select that NetWare Workstation Shell client in the list of installed components, and then click **Remove**. Also, select and remove the IPXODI protocol if it appears in the list.

2. Click **Add**, and then double-click **Client** in the **Select Network Component Type** dialog box.

3. In the **Select Network Client** dialog box, click **Microsoft** in the **Manufacturers** list, and then click **Client for NetWare Networks** in the **Network Clients** list. Then click **OK**.

You must shut down and restart the computer for the changes to take effect.

Caution Do not click **Cancel** during the installation. If you decide that you do not want to install Client for NetWare Networks, you must complete the installation process and then remove Client for NetWare Networks.

Setup automatically installs and configures all related components. Windows 98 Setup also adds the value **lastdrive=32** to the parameters for the network client in the registry. This value makes room for entries in a table to store drive information. For Microsoft networking, the last drive would be set to Z (or 26), but NetWare allows six additional entries in its drive table.

Setting Up Microsoft Service for NetWare Directory Services

If you install Microsoft Service for NetWare Directory Services, Client for NetWare Networks will also be automatically installed. You do not need to install Microsoft Client for NetWare Networks if you install Microsoft Service for NetWare Directory Services.

Adding Microsoft Service for NetWare Directory Services after Installing Windows 98

You can add Microsoft Service for NetWare Directory Services whether or not you have already installed Client for NetWare Networks.

> **Note** Windows 98 Setup copies files from your original Windows 98 installation media, so make sure your original Windows 98 installation media are ready before you perform this procedure.

▶ **To add Microsoft Service for NetWare Directory Services after installing Windows 98**

1. In Control Panel, double-click Network and examine the list of installed components. If the computer currently has NETX or VLM installed, select that NetWare Workstation Shell client in the list of installed components, and then click **Remove**. Also, select and remove the **IPXODI protocol** if it appears in the list.

2. Click **Add**, and then double-click **Service** in the **Select Network Component** dialog box.

3. In the **Select Network Service** dialog box, click **Microsoft** in the **Manufacturers** list, and then click **Service for NetWare Directory Services** in the **Network Services** list. Then click **OK**.

You must shut down and restart the computer for the changes to take effect.

After your computer restarts, you will be prompted to log on to the NDS tree. Make sure the dialog box identifies the correct context and tree.

> **Caution** Do not click **Cancel** during the installation. If you decide that you do not want to install Microsoft Service for NetWare Directory Services, you must complete the installation process, and then remove Microsoft Service for NetWare Directory Services.

Automated Installation of Microsoft Service for NetWare Directory Services

You can include Microsoft Service for NetWare Directory Services in automated installations that work with Msbatch.inf. For more information about automated installations, see Chapter 4, "Automated Installations."

▶ **To include the Service for NetWare Directory Services in an automated installation**

1. Copy the following two lines to the [Network] section in Msbatch.inf.

   ```
   Clients=NWREDIR
   Services=NWREDIR4
   ```

> **Note** You can also include entries for other networking clients and services on the above lines. Each entry should be separated by a comma. For example:
>
> ```
> Clients=VREDIR,NWREDIR
> ```

2. If you want to set the preferred tree and default context in Msbatch.inf, add the following lines:

   ```
   [NWRedir4]
   PreferredTree = <Tree>
   NameContext = <MyNameContext>
   ```

3. Save and exit Msbatch.inf.

4. At the command prompt, type:

   ```
   setup <drive letter>:<path>\msbatch.inf
   ```

   – Or –

   Place Msbatch.inf in the same directory as Setup.exe and then run Setup.

If you are doing an automated installation of Microsoft Service for NetWare Directory Services on computers that are running the NETX or VLM client, you should be aware of the following issues:

- Setup does not automatically comment out the line in Startnet.bat or Autoexec.bat that loads NETX or VLM. This will not cause any problems, but you may want to delete the line or comment it out.

- If Windows is not already installed on the computers, an error message may appear during Windows 98 Setup saying that you should run the Novell Workstation Shell install program after Windows 98 Setup. Disregard this message.

Configuring Microsoft Client for NetWare Networks

This section presents information for configuring and using Microsoft Client for NetWare Networks, including the following topics:

- Configuring protected-mode NDIS network adapter drivers for Client for NetWare Networks.

- Configuring Client for NetWare Networks with ODI network adapter drivers.

- Running NetWare utilities with Client for NetWare Networks and Microsoft Service for NetWare Directory Services.

For information about configuring logon options for Client for NetWare Networks, see Chapter 18, "Logon, Browsing, and Resource Sharing."

Configuring Protected-Mode NDIS Network Adapter Drivers for Client for NetWare Networks

When you install Client for NetWare Networks, a 32-bit, protected-mode, NDIS 3.1 and later compliant network adapter driver is installed automatically, unless the computer is running software cited in Table 17.1.

Although it is possible to run Client for NetWare Networks over ODI drivers, Microsoft recommends that you install a 32-bit, protected-mode network adapter driver to take advantage of the performance improvements offered by these drivers, as described in Chapter 15, "Network Adapters and Protocols." If you do configure Client for NetWare Networks to use ODI drivers instead, you can switch to the protected-mode drivers at any time.

Depending on when you install Client for NetWare Networks, you might have to install the 32-bit, protected-mode network adapter driver before you can install the network client. Setup prompts you to do this if it is necessary.

▶ **To switch to a 32-bit, protected-mode network adapter driver**

1. In Control Panel, double-click Network, and then double-click the network adapter in the list of installed network components.

2. In the **Driver Type** tab, click the option named **Enhanced mode (32 bit And 16 bit) NDIS driver**, and then click **OK**.

3. Shut down and restart the computer.

For more information about using NDIS, see Chapter 15, "Network Adapters and Protocols."

Configuring Client for NetWare Networks with ODI Network Adapter Drivers

This section describes how to configure Client for NetWare Networks with ODI network adapter drivers. For more information about ODI, see "Configuring Network Adapter Drivers for Real-Mode Novell Clients" later in this chapter.

Figure 17.1 shows the architecture for Client for NetWare Networks with ODI network adapter drivers. Novell-supplied components appear in bold.

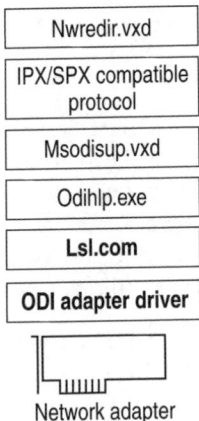

Figure 17.1   **Architecture for protected-mode client with ODI drivers**

Using an ODI driver instead of an NDIS 3.1 or later driver with Client for NetWare Networks has the following drawbacks:

- There is some use of conventional memory, and overall performance on the network is not as good as with NDIS 3.1 or later drivers.
- There are no Plug and Play capabilities for the networking components.

If you want to use the current ODI driver instead of a Windows 98 NDIS network adapter driver, you can select that driver using the Network option in Control Panel. For more information about using ODI drivers, see "Configuring Windows 98 with ODI Drivers" later in this chapter. For information about the related files, see "Obtaining Current Novell-Supplied Files" later in this chapter.

▶ **To use ODI drivers with Client for NetWare Networks**

1. In Control Panel, double-click Network.
2. In the list of installed components, double-click your network adapter.
3. In the **Properties** dialog box for your network adapter, click the **Driver Type** tab.
4. Click **Real mode (16 bit) ODI driver**, and then click **OK**. Then shut down and restart the computer.

Running NetWare Utilities with Client for NetWare Networks and Microsoft Service for NetWare Directory Services

With Client for NetWare Networks, you can use the 32-bit, protected-mode graphical tools built into Windows 98 as well as the 16-bit command-line utilities provided with NetWare for managing and sharing resources. You can run all NetWare 3.x utilities that reside on the NetWare server, such as SYSCON. You can also run most bindery-based NetWare 4.x utilities. However, you cannot use the VLM NWUSER utility, and you cannot use utilities that require NDS.

If you are running Microsoft Client for NetWare Networks along with Microsoft Service for NetWare Directory Services, you can use all the tools listed above, as well as graphical tools and utilities that require NDS, including NWAdmin, CX, and NETADMIN.

Tip SYSCON, a tool for NetWare 3.x servers, and NETADMIN, a tool for NetWare 4.x servers, are located in the SYS:PUBLIC directory. To access them using NetWare 3.x, map a drive to them either in a logon script or while you are running Windows 98. If you are using NetWare 4.x, you can also access NETADMIN from Network Neighborhood. Both SYSCON and NETADMIN are MS-DOS utilities, so whichever way you access them, you must run them from a command prompt (either a virtual machine or the **Run** prompt).

▶ **To run NetWare utilities from an MS-DOS prompt**

1. Map a drive to the volume containing the NetWare utilities by using statements in a logon script or by using the **Map Network Drive** dialog box.

   When you use **Map Network Drive**, you can make this a persistent connection by clicking the **Reconnect at logon** box.

2. From **Start**, point to **Programs**, and then click **MS-DOS Prompt** to start an MS-DOS session.

3. Switch to the mapped network drive, and then run the utilities in the usual way.

If you are running Microsoft Service for NetWare Directory Services and you are logged on to an NDS tree, you can also run NetWare utilities by clicking on their icons in Network Neighborhood.

▶ **To run NetWare utilities from Network Neighborhood**

1. In the NDS tree, double-click the volume that contains the utility.

2. Double-click the utility.

Note To run NetWare 4.*x* NDS utilities, you must install Microsoft Service for NetWare Directory Services. You also need access to, and the appropriate license to use, the NetWare dynamic link libraries (DLLs) listed in "NetWare API Support in Client for NetWare Networks" later in this chapter.

Installing and Configuring Novell NetWare Clients

Windows 98 can run with the following Novell-supplied clients:

- Novell Client for Windows 95/98, a 32-bit, protected-mode client that supports NDS.
- NetWare VLM, a 16-bit, real-mode client that supports NetWare 3.*x* and 4.*x* servers.
- NetWare NETX, a 16-bit, real-mode client that supports NetWare 3.*x* servers, as well as NetWare 4.*x* servers in bindery mode.

It is strongly recommended that you use Novell Client for Windows 95/98 instead of a real-mode client. Novell Client for Windows 95/98 provides more efficient memory use than the real-mode clients. It also provides such capabilities as support for NDS, support for optional components, such as IP Gateway, and integrated Windows logon.

Note If you are running Windows 98 Setup from a Windows for Workgroups computer that has Novell Client for DOS/Windows 3.x, Setup will fail. You should delete Novell Client for DOS/Windows 3.x Client before running Windows 98 Setup.

The following section describes how to set up and configure Windows 98 with Novell-supplied clients. For more information, contact Novell.

Note Before installing Windows 98, make sure that you have the necessary Novell-supplied files for Windows support, which can be obtained from Novell.

If you are upgrading to Windows 98 from another version of Windows, and you had Novell-supplied NetWare client software on your previous version of Windows, make sure that the Novell-supplied NetWare client software is working properly before you start Windows 98 Setup. To verify that the Novell-supplied software is working, make sure you can successfully connect to and use resources on a NetWare server.

This section describes how to install Novell Client for Windows 95/98 after Windows 98 Setup. First, it describes how to prepare the installation, then it describes how to perform the installation, and finally, it describes how to remove Novell Client for Windows 95/98.

Removing Incompatible Software

Before you install Novell Client for Windows 95/98, make sure that none of the following software is installed on your Windows 98 computer:

- Microsoft Client for NetWare Networks.
- Microsoft File and Printer Sharing for NetWare Networks.
- Microsoft Service for NetWare Directory Services.
- NETX or VLM.
- Novell IPXODI protocol (the 16-bit protocol for NETX and VLM clients). This is the 16-bit module for the NETX and VLM clients. The Novell Client for Windows 95/98 uses the IPX 32-bit protocol.

These network components conflict with Novell Client for Windows 95/98. If any of these components are installed, the Client installation program detects the conflict and removes the conflicting network components.

Preparing NetWare servers for the Installation

You must also prepare your servers for the installation. For NetWare 3.x and 4.x servers (except NetWare 4.11 servers), make sure the patches shipped with Novell Client for Windows 95/98 are installed.

Also, to support long file names, load Long.nam on each NetWare 4.11 server and on each volume. (See the Novell Client online help for more information.) For versions of NetWare earlier than NetWare 4.11, use the OS/2 name space instead of Long.nam.

Each name space uses up to 252 kilobytes (KB) of disk space. Each name space added to a volume requires additional server memory. If you add name space support to a volume, but do not have enough memory, the server cannot mount that volume. Once you add a name space to a volume, you cannot remove that name space unless you delete the volume and re-create it or use VREPAIR.

For information about how to calculate the memory required for name space support and for how to remove a name space, contact Novell.

Installing Novell Client for Windows 95/98

If you have installed Microsoft Client for NetWare Networks or an old version of a Novell protected-mode NetWare client, Setup for Novell Client for Windows 95/98 replaces it with the Novell Client.

You can run Setup in one of four ways:

- From the Network option in Control Panel.
- From a Novell-provided Novell Client for Windows 95/98 CD-ROM.
- By downloading the Novell Client for Windows 95/98 files from Novell's Web site at **http://www.novell.com/**.
- By placing the Novell Client for Windows 95/98 files on a Windows NT or NetWare server and then running Setup from the mapped drive.

This section discusses the first two methods.

Regardless of which method you choose, you should have your original Windows 98 installation media ready before running Setup.

Take the following steps to install Novell Client for Windows 95/98 from the Network option in Control Panel.

▶ **To install Novell Client for Windows 95/98 from the Network option in Control Panel**

1. Start Windows 98.
2. In Control Panel, double-click Network.
3. Remove any installed NetWare clients and components, and then click **Add**.
4. Click **Client**, and then click **Add**.
5. In the **Select Network Client** dialog box, click **Have Disk**.
6. Enter the directory where your Novell Client installation files are located, and then click **OK**.
7. In the **Network** dialog box, select the Novell Client and then click **Properties**.
8. Type the preferred server, tree, and context, click **OK**, and then click **OK** again.
9. When Windows 98 asks you whether to restart the computer, click **Yes**.

Take the following steps to install the Novell Client for Windows 95/98 from the Novell-provided Novell Client for Windows 95/98 CD-ROM.

▶ **To install Novell Client for Windows 95/98 from the CD-ROM**

1. Start Windows 98.
2. Insert the CD-ROM for Novell Client for Windows 95/98. The setup file, Setup.exe, loads automatically.
3. Click a language for the installation.

4. Click a set of components to install.

5. Click **Install the Novell Client for Windows 95/98**.

6. Accept the Novell License Agreement by clicking **Yes**.

7. Click **Typical** and then **Install**. Setup installs default settings.

8. If prompted to select a network adapter, choose one that matches your hardware. The **Select Device** dialog box displays a list. After you choose one, you may be asked to set the Interrupt Request (IRQ) and I/O Address Range. Note that asterisks help you avoid settings that conflict.

9. If prompted to set a Preferred Server, Preferred Tree, and Name Context, click **Yes**, enter information, and then click **OK**.

    For NetWare 3.x, set a Preferred Server. For NetWare 4.x, set a Preferred Server, Preferred Tree, Name Context, and First Network Drive.

10. Click one of the following:

    - Reboot. (The new client and settings do not take effect until you do this.)

    - Return to Windows.

      This option takes you to the Network option in Control Panel and allows you to install optional components or configure your workstation.

Removing Novell Client for Windows 95/98

You can remove Novell Client for Windows 95/98 in one of two ways:

- From the Network option in Control Panel. If you choose this option, client configuration information remains in the registry.

- By running Novell's Uninstall utility. If you choose this option, all client configuration information is removed from the registry.

▶ **To use the Control Panel**

1. In Control Panel, double-click Network, and then click the Novell Client for Windows 95/98.

2. Click **Remove**.

3. Remove any other Client networking components in the same way.

   Examples of other networking components are Novell ODINSUP and the IPX 32-bit Protocol for Novell Client for Windows 95/98.

4. Click **OK**.

5. Click **Yes** and restart the workstation.

▶ **To use Novell's Uninstall utility**

1. Locate and open the Unc32.exe file on the CD-ROM.

   The file is on the Novell Client for Windows 95/98 CD-ROM in the Products\Win98 \IBM_ENU\Admin folder.

2. Optionally, if you want to remove any ODI drivers installed on the workstation, check the **Remove Novell 32-bit ODI Adapter** check box.

   This check box appears only if a 32-bit ODI adapter has been installed on the workstation.

3. Click **Continue**.

   The uninstall process begins.

Caution Do not try to cancel the uninstall process by turning off your computer. If you do so, your registry might become corrupt. If you do turn off your computer during the uninstall process, run the Uninstall utility again to finish uninstalling the client and to clean up the registry.

---

4. Click **Reboot** when the uninstall process is complete.

Configuring Network Adapter Drivers for Novell Client for Windows 95/98

Novell Client for Windows 95/98 works with Microsoft-provided, 32-bit NDIS network drivers and with Novell's 32-bit ODI drivers. If you want to use Novell Client for Windows 95/98 with Novell's 32-bit ODI drivers, you must install them by running Novell's Setup.exe instead of by using the Network option in Control Panel.

Novell Client for Windows 95/98 might also work with NDIS 2 or 16-bit ODI drivers; however, this configuration is not recommended.

Installing or Upgrading a Real-Mode Novell Client

Windows 98 works with the real-mode NETX and VLM clients; however, it is strongly recommended that you upgrade to the protected-mode Client for NetWare Networks or Novell Client for Windows 95/98.

By default, Windows 98 Setup automatically replaces NETX with Microsoft Client for NetWare Networks. To install Windows 98 with NETX, you must use a custom setup script.

However, Microsoft supports upgrading from NETX to Client for NetWare Networks only if you are logged on to a NetWare server at the time of the upgrade. For more information, see the troubleshooting step "Upgrade from NETX to Client for NetWare Networks fails," later in this chapter.

If you are running VLM and you do not call Login.exe either in Autoexec.bat or a batch file referenced by it (such as Startnet.bat) when you install Windows 98, Windows 98 Setup might replace VLM with Client for NetWare Networks.

However, Windows 98 Setup does not replace VLM with Microsoft Client for NetWare Networks if you are logged on to NDS when you start Windows 98 Setup. If you are running VLM and you are logged on to NDS using the Login.exe command either in Autoexec.bat or a batch file referenced by it (such as Startnet.bat), Windows 98 uses the existing networking configuration specified in Net.cfg for protocols, adapter drivers, and other values.

If you currently use Ipx.com, Microsoft recommends that you upgrade to the latest versions of NetWare client software that use ODI drivers before you install Windows 98. Windows 98 does not support Ipx.com.

Caution NETX and VLM require that you log on to the appropriate NetWare server before starting Windows 98. Thus, if you are using these clients, you should not log on to a NetWare server from within Windows 98.

Instead, log on to the server from Autoexec.bat or from a batch file that is called from Autoexec.bat. You should also continue to load the necessary MS-DOS-based TSR programs using Autoexec.bat or Startnet.bat.

For information about where a logon command should be placed in system startup files, see Chapter 18, "Logon, Browsing, and Resource Sharing."

This section describes how to install Windows 98 with ODI drivers, how to verify that you are using the correct drivers, how to retain VLM and NETX when you are upgrading to Windows 98, and how to install them after Windows 98 Setup. For architectural information about ODI drivers and for information about Net.cfg settings, see "Configuring Network Adapter Drivers for Real-Mode Novell NetWare Clients" later in this chapter.

Installing Windows 98 with ODI Drivers

Before you install Windows 98 on a computer, the real-mode IPXODI network should be configured and working properly using your Novell-supplied installation program. Test to confirm that there are no errors when loading the Novell-supplied files Lsl.com, Ipxodi.com, the ODI driver, and Netx.exe or Vlm.exe, or when accessing resources on NetWare servers.

If Windows 98 Setup cannot identify the ODI driver being used, you might have to configure the network adapter driver manually.

▶ **To configure the network adapter driver manually**

1. In Control Panel, double-click Network, and then click **Add**.

2. In the **Select Network Component Type** dialog box, click **Adapter**, and then click **Add**.

3. In the **Select Network Adapters** dialog box, click **Have Disk**. You must provide an INF file for the correct IPXODI support driver to match the type of network adapter used, using a file supplied by Novell or the adapter manufacturer.

Verifying Drivers for Real-Mode Clients After Windows 98 Setup

Before installing a real-mode client, make sure the correct adapter driver is installed. Real-mode clients require 16-bit ODI drivers, and some cards do not work with those drivers. If you cannot install the correct adapter driver, you will not be able to install the real-mode client.

▶ **To determine whether the correct adapter driver is installed after Windows 98 Setup**

1. In Control Panel, double-click Network, and then double-click the network adapter (or your existing ODI driver) in the list of installed components.

2. In the **Properties** dialog box for the network adapter, click the **Driver Type** tab.

3. Make sure the **Real mode (16 bit) ODI driver** option is selected.

Upgrading Windows 98 with VLM

This section describes how to upgrade Windows 98 and retain the VLM client if VLM support was previously installed under Windows 3.*x* or Windows 95 and you are upgrading from the \Windows directory, or if VLM was previously installed under DOS.

If you run Windows 98 Setup without the proper preparation, Setup replaces VLM with Client for NetWare Networks. You can prevent VLM from being replaced in one of two ways:

- By including VLM in Msbatch.inf. For more information about Msbatch, see Chapter 3, "Custom Installations," and Appendix D, "Msbatch.inf Parameters for Setup Scripts."

- By following the steps in the following procedure.

▶ **To retain VLM during Windows 98 upgrade**

1. Make sure that you have the files Netware.hlp, Nwpopup.exe, Vipx.386, Vetware.386, Ipxodi.com, Lsl.com, Netware.drv, and the driver for your network adapter.

Note If you are upgrading from a version of Windows, those files should be located in you /Windows/System and network client directories.

Otherwise, use the NetWare **Nwunpack** command to expand the following files from your VLM installation media: Netware.hl_, Nwpopup.ex_, Vipx.38_, Vnetware.38_, Ipxodi.co_, Lsl.co_, Netware.dr_, and the driver for your network adapter.

---

2. Add the Login.exe command in Autoexec.bat or a batch file referenced by Autoexec.bat, such as Startnet.bat.

3. Reboot.

4. When prompted to log on to the NetWare server, log on and make sure your Novell-supplied software is functioning correctly.

5. Run Windows 98 Setup.

6. If Windows 98 asks for the Novell-supplied files that you expanded using **Nwunpack**, enter the path for those files.

7. If prompted, run the Novell Workstation Shell Install program. Consult your NetWare documentation for information about the Novell-supplied installation program.

Note Setup might place the entry **device=*vnetbios** in System.ini, which causes a blue screen error to appear when you restart the computer. You can safely ignore this screen.

---

8. After Setup finishes, in Control Panel, double-click **Network**.

You must reboot your computer for the changes to take effect.

In the Network option in Control Panel, you will see that Setup has added Novell NetWare (Workstation Shell 4.0 And Above [VLM]) as a network client. You might also need to modify configuration files, such as Net.cfg and Autoexec.bat. Consult your NetWare documentation for more information.

Installing VLM for the First Time After Windows 98 Setup

This section describes how to install the VLM client after Windows 98 Setup if it has not been previously installed. For information about how to upgrade VLM from Windows 95, see the sections "Upgrading Windows 98 With VLM in Typical Installations" and "Upgrading Windows 98 With VLM in Special Cases," earlier in this chapter.

> **Note** Before attempting to install VLM, you should follow the procedure in "Verifying Drivers for Real-Mode Clients After Windows 98 Setup," earlier in this chapter.

▶ **To install VLM after Windows 98 Setup**

1. On your VLM installation disk, locate the files Netware.hl_, Nwpopup.ex_, Vipx.38_, Vnetware.38_, Ipxodi.co_, Lsl.co_, Netware.dr_, and the driver for your network adapter. Use the NetWare **Nwunpack** command to expand them.

2. Remove all NetWare clients from the Network option in Control Panel.

3. In Control Panel, double-click Network, and then click **Add**.

4. In the **Select Network Component Type** dialog box, double-click **Client**.

5. In the **Select Network Client** dialog box, click **Novell** in the **Manufacturers** list, and click **Novell NetWare (Workstation Shell 4.0 and above [VLM])** in the Network Clients list. Then click **OK**, and then click **OK** again. The computer copies files, then prompts you to reboot to the command prompt.

6. Reboot the computer.

7. After rebooting, run the Novell-supplied installation program. Consult your NetWare documentation for information about the Novell-supplied installation program.

8. After the installation program has finished copying files, exit to MS-DOS and then type **win** at the **c:** prompt.

> **Note** You will see an error message stating that you have a bad or missing VnetBIOS. Continue past this error message.

9. In Control Panel, double-click Network. Windows 98 should notify you that the VLM installation program has been run.

You must reboot your computer for the changes to take effect. You might also need to modify configuration files, such as Net.cfg and Autoexec.bat. Consult your NetWare documentation for more information.

Upgrading Windows 98 with NETX

By default, if Windows 98 Setup detects the NETX client, it replaces NETX with Microsoft Client for NetWare Networks. If you want to retain NETX when you upgrade to Windows 98, follow these steps.

▶ **To select Novell-supplied NETX client support during Windows 98 Setup**

1. Have your NETX files available before you run Setup.

2. In Msbatch.inf, add the value **netware3** to the parameter **Clients**.

3. Run Setup with the Msbatch.inf parameter.

   – Or –

   Place Msbatch.inf in the same directory as Setup.exe and then run Setup.

   For information about creating and using Msbatch.inf files, see Chapter 3, "Custom Installations." For information about Msbatch.inf parameters, see Appendix D, "Msbatch.inf Parameters for Setup Scripts."

Alternatively, you can install the Novell-supplied NETX client software after you have run Windows 98.

Note Before attempting to install NETX, you should follow the procedure in "Verifying Drivers for Real-Mode Clients After Windows 98 Setup," earlier in this chapter.

▶ **To reinstall NETX after Windows 98 Setup**

1. Back up your NETX files.
2. Run Windows 98 Setup.
3. After Windows 98 Setup is complete, in Control Panel, double-click Network.
4. Remove all other NetWare clients from the Network option in Control Panel.

   Important Make sure you remove Client for NetWare Networks before installing NETX.

   ---

5. Click **Add**, and then double-click **Client**.
6. In the **Select Network Client** dialog box, click **Novell** in the **Manufacturers** list, and click **Novell NetWare (Workstation Shell 3.X [NETX])** in the **Network Clients** list. Then click **OK**.

   Windows 98 automatically installs IPXODI support.

7. Click **OK** in **Network** properties, and provide a disk or a location for any files that Windows 98 requests to complete the installation. Then shut down and restart the computer.

Usually, you will have to reinstall Novell-supplied files at this stage, because Windows 98 Setup previously replaced these files with versions required by Client for NetWare Networks. You must also make sure that Net.cfg is present and contains correct settings, and that the required settings are present in Config.sys and Autoexec.bat. See your Novell documentation for information about these required settings.

Configuring Network Adapter Drivers for Real-Mode Novell Clients

Before attempting to install a real-mode client, you should make sure your network adapter card and drivers work with your real-mode client. In some cases, you must obtain a driver that works with ODI. After you install a real-mode client, you might need to make changes to Net.cfg, the Novell NetWare configuration file that specifies settings for the adapter, protocol, and client.

This section presents some technical information related to the network adapter drivers used when configuring Windows 98 to run with Novell-supplied network clients. The topics include configuring Windows 98 with ODI drivers and setting options in Net.cfg.

For information about how to ensure your network adapter card and drivers work with your real-mode client, see "Verifying Drivers for Real-Mode Clients After Windows 98 Setup" earlier in this chapter. For information about installing ODI drivers, see "Installing Windows 98 with ODI drivers" earlier in this chapter. For information about the format and contents of Net.cfg, consult your Novell documentation.

Note Windows 98 does not support the monolithic IPX configuration. You should use ODI drivers with real-mode clients. Also, Windows 98 does not support ArcNet network adapters. For information about ArcNet network adapters, see the *Microsoft Windows 95 Resource Kit*.

Configuring Windows 98 with ODI Drivers

The Open Datalink Interface (ODI) specification was defined by Novell and Apple Computer to provide a protocol and a consistent API for communicating with a network adapter driver and to support the use of multiple protocols by a network adapter driver.

Figure 17.2 shows the architecture for ODI drivers.

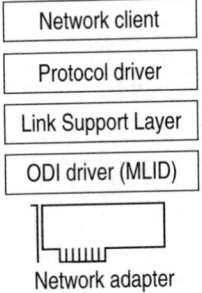

Figure 17.2   Architecture for ODI drivers

ODI consists of the following components:

An ODI-compliant version of the IPX/SPX protocol. This component provides the network protocol for communicating between NetWare clients and servers. With NETX or VLM clients, this must be the Novell-supplied Ipxodi.com. With Novell Client for Windows 95/98, it must be the 32-bit IPX protocol that ships with it.

For Client for NetWare Networks, you can also use the Microsoft IPX/SPX-compatible protocol.

The Link Support Layer (LSL). This component, provided in the Novell-supplied Lsl.com file, sets the foundation for the network adapter and multiple protocol drivers to communicate.

The ODI driver. Also called the Multiple Link Interface Driver (MLID), the ODI-compliant network adapter driver is created by the adapter manufacturer. This component usually identifies the name of the supported adapter in the file name, such as Ne2000.com for the Novell NE-2000 adapter, 3c5x9.com for the 3Com EtherLink III adapter, and Exp16odi.com for the Intel EtherExpress 16 adapter. Windows 98 supports using these drivers, but they are not included with Windows 98.

For information about required files, see "Obtaining Current Novell-Supplied Files" later in this chapter.

Setting Network Adapter Options in Net.cfg

Because a computer using ODI drivers can have multiple ODI drivers and multiple protocols loaded and bound, the networking software uses Net.cfg to identify the network adapters, protocol configuration, and binding information. Net.cfg is responsible for configuring the network environment for a Novell-supplied client, and is used to configure custom parameters for VLM, NETX, IPX, NetBIOS, or the general NetWare environment. To configure any options, edit Net.cfg as described in your Novell documentation.

NetWare uses Net.cfg as the configuration file name for ODI. You should not use Shell.cfg. If neither file exists, default settings are used.

If you are using ODI drivers, the Novell-supplied Lsl.com file uses information from Net.cfg to configure the ODI driver before the NETX workstation shell does. For the LSL driver to load and initialize information from Net.cfg, the proper Net.cfg file should reside in the same directory as Lsl.com and the Novell-supplied Netx.exe network client, or Lsl.com should take the path to the proper Net.cfg file as a parameter. To verify that there is not more than one Net.cfg file present on a computer, type **dir /s net.cfg** at the command prompt (or from **Start**, click **Find** and search for Net.cfg).

Network adapter configuration information is contained in a "Link Driver" section in Net.cfg, where you can specify the network adapter's interrupt, I/O address, memory address, frame types, and protocols. The following example shows Net.cfg entries for an SMC Ethercard Plus Elite 16 adapter:

```
show dots=on
file handles=60
preferred server=nw_311
link driver smc8000
    int 5
    port 240
    mem d000
    frame ethernet_802.3
```

Table 17.2 describes selected information commonly found in Net.cfg under the "Link Driver" section. For information not found in Net.cfg, default settings for the network adapter are assumed. For more information, consult your Novell documentation.

Table 17.2   Network adapter driver settings in Net.cfg

Net.cfg setting	Description
DMA	DMA channel number. Can assign up to two DMA channels by designating them DMA #1 x and DMA #2 y.
FRAME	Alternate media access control layer frame encapsulations for the network adapter. Frame types are: ETHERNET_802.3 ETHERNET_SNAP ETHERNET_802.2 TOKEN_RING ETHERNET_II TOKEN_RING_SNAP You must add the ETHERNET_II frame type for Microsoft TCP/IP to work over ODI drivers.
INT	Interrupt Request (IRQ) number. Can assign up to two IRQs by designating them IRQ #1 x and IRQ #2 y.
MEM	Memory address in upper memory area (UMA). Can assign up to two UMA addresses by designating them MEM #1 x and MEM #2 y.
NODE ADDRESS	12-digit media access control address assigned to the network adapter.
PORT	I/O port address. Can assign up to two I/O port addresses by designating them PORT #1 x and PORT #2 y.
PROTOCOL	Protocols to be used with ODI drivers. You do not need to specify this in Net.cfg if NETX is running only the IPX protocol. If other protocols are running, you must specify the protocol, protocol ID, and frame type.
SLOT	Network adapter slot number (MCA, EISA).

Technical Notes for Windows 98 on NetWare Networks

This section contains information about obtaining current Novell-supplied files and technical notes on the IPX/SPX-compatible protocol.

Obtaining Current Novell-Supplied Files

If your computer is not configured with the necessary NetWare software, or if you do not have the support files that Windows 98 Setup requires to configure your computer, several sources are available for these files.

Important Use the latest available version of Novell-supplied driver files. If the latest version of VLM does not work, use version 120.

▶ **To obtain current NetWare software files**

- Check with your NetWare network administrator or your local Novell representative to see if the latest client files are available locally.

  – Or –

  Over the Internet, obtain files from **http://support.novell.com/**.

Required Support Files for Novell-supplied Clients

In addition to the base Novell-supplied NetWare client software required to communicate with a NetWare server, some additional NetWare support files are necessary for the Novell-supplied components to work properly in the Windows 98 environment. When Windows 98 is configured to support a Novell NetWare client, Setup checks to see if the required supporting files for Windows are in the \Windows directory. If the files are not in the \Windows directory, Setup asks for a disk or network drive location for these files.

The required Novell-supplied supporting files for NetWare connectivity under Windows are shown in Table 17.3.

Table 17.3 Novell-supplied files for Windows support

File	Description
Netware.drv, Netware.hlp	Windows-compatible network driver and associated help file to provide access to network redirector functionality from 16-bit applications. Notice that this must be the version 2.*x* WinNet16 driver for the NETX client. Also, the Novell-supplied version of Netware.drv for NETX is approximately 124 KB in size; for VLM, the size is approximately 144 KB or 162 KB, depending on the version.

Table 17.3   Novell-supplied files for Windows support (*continued*)

File	Description
Nwpopup.exe	NetWare messaging utility. Used to receive messages and alerts from a NetWare server.
Vnetware.386	Virtual device driver providing virtualization services for the NetWare redirector in the Windows environment and across virtual machines (VMs).
Vipx.386	Virtual device driver providing virtualization services for the NetWare IPX protocol for the Windows environment and across VMs.
Nw16.dll[1]	A thunk layer for passing 32-bit calls to 16-bit NETX APIs.

1 Required for VLM, but not for NETX.

Required Support Files for ODI Drivers

A computer using Novell-supplied ODI and the IPX/SPX protocol requires certain files, depending on whether you choose to keep the Novell-supplied client when installing Windows 98 on a NetWare network. Table 17.4 lists the required files.

Table 17.4   Required support files for ODI drivers with Novell-supplied client

Type of driver	Support files	
Windows 98 drivers	Vnetbios.386	
Novell-supplied NETX drivers	Ipxodi.com Lsl.com Netware.drv Netware.hlp Netx.exe	Nwpopup.exe Vipx.386 Vnetware.386 A network adapter driver, such as Ne2000.com.
Novell-supplied VLM drivers	Netx.vlm version 4.0 or later. VLM client supporting files, version 1.02 or later.	
Windows 98 driver	Msodisup.vxd[1] Ndis.vxd Nwlink.vxd Nwnblink.vxd Nwnet32.dll	Nwnp32.dll Nwredir.vxd Odihlp.exe Vnetbios.386
Novell-supplied drivers	Lsl.com A network adapter driver, such as Ne2000.com.	

1 Msodisup.vxd is the ODI support layer that maps NDIS 3.1 and later protocols to an ODI driver, and Odihlp.exe is the real-mode stub that allows LSL to complete its binding process in real mode.

Search Mode with Windows 98 on NetWare Networks

Many applications, when started, also open a number of other files (such as overlay files and data files) that are used as application resources. To find these files, older NetWare-aware applications, such as the FILER version 3.*x* NetWare utility look for files in NetWare search drives in two ways:

- Using the PATH environment to search for executable files.
- Using a NetWare search path to find supporting files, such as required data files.

Under Windows 98, the search mode defines how files are found, depending on the network client you use, as described in Table 17.5.

Table 17.5   Search mode for NetWare networks

Client	Search mode
Client for NetWare Networks	Search from a drive mapped to the server where the utility is stored.
Novell-supplied Novell Client for Windows 95/98	Configured in the client's properties.
Novell-supplied NETX	Search from any local drive or any network drive.
Novell-supplied VLM	Search from any network drive. Cannot search from a local drive.

Technical Notes on Client for NetWare Networks

This section presents some technical issues you should be aware of when using Client for NetWare Networks, including a summary of configuration settings and required support files, and configuration notes, as well as notes about NetWare API support and running NetWare utilities with Client for NetWare Networks.

Summary of Settings for Client for NetWare Networks

Client for NetWare Networks does not require you to change any settings in Autoexec.bat, Startnet.bat, or Config.sys. However, it does modify some configuration files automatically. For information about configuration files that are modified automatically, see "Required Support Files for Client for NetWare Networks," later in this chapter.

Login.exe is not loaded from any configuration file. Windows 98 Setup removes this entry automatically. If you install Client for NetWare Networks over a real-mode client, Setup does not always remove references to the real-mode client from Autoexec.bat or another batch file. If either NETX or VLM is initialized from Autoexec.bat or another batch file, Client for NetWare Networks will not be loaded, and your computer might lock up. Therefore, you should remove real-mode clients before installing Client for NetWare Networks.

No real-mode drivers are needed if a network adapter driver appears in the list of installed components in the Network option in Control Panel.

Table 17.6 summarizes the minimum settings that you should see in the Network option in Control Panel after you install Client for NetWare Networks.

Table 17.6   Required network settings for Client for NetWare Networks

Network component	Configuration options
Client for NetWare Networks	If the computer will be downloading system policies or user profiles from NetWare servers, Client for NetWare Networks should be selected in the Primary Network Logon box.
	In the **General** properties for Client for NetWare Networks, Preferred Server should show the name of the NetWare server to be used for initial logon. If login scripts are used, the option that enables login scripts should be checked.
Network adapter	In the properties for the adapter, the driver type should be **Enhanced mode (32 bit and 16 bit) NDIS**.[1]
IPX/SPX-compatible protocol	In its **Advanced** properties, the **Frame Type** should be **Auto**, or **802.2** if you have problems connecting to a NetWare server. If any network applications at your site require support for NetBIOS over IPX, that option should be checked in the NetBIOS properties.

[1] You can also specify 16-bit ODI drivers. You do not need to load such drivers from Config.sys or another configuration file.

Required Support Files for Client for NetWare Networks

Table 17.7 summarizes the support files required for Client for NetWare Networks. All of these files are found in the \Windows\System directory and are provided with Windows 98; no Novell-supplied components are required. For more information about these components, see Chapter 29, "Windows 98 Network Architecture."

Table 17.7   Required files for Client for NetWare Networks[1]

File	Description
Netware.drv	Emulates a WinNet driver required by some NetWare-aware applications that check for this file, such as Lotus Notes. Notice that this file is supplied with Windows 98, and is not the same as the similarly-named Novell-supplied file and, therefore, does not support applications that make direct function calls to Novell's Netware.drv. (The Windows 98 version is approximately 2 KB in size.)
Nwlink.vxd	Provides the IPX/SPX-compatible protocol.
Nwlsproc.exe, Nwlscon.exe	Optionally, provides the 32-bit login script processor and console used by Client for NetWare Networks.

Table 17.7   Required files for Client for NetWare Networks[1] (*continued*)

File	Description
Nwnet32.dll	Provides common NetWare networking functions for the 32-bit network provider and print provider.
Nwnp32.dll	Provides access to NetWare network resources using Windows Explorer, Network Neighborhood, and so on. This 32-bit network provider for NetWare networks is the service provider interface to the Multiple Provider Router.
Nwpp32.dll	Provides the print provider interface to the print router in Spoolss.dll. This 32-bit print provider supports the ability to print to NetWare printing resources.
Nwredir.vxd	Provides a 32-bit file system driver (redirector) to support applications that use the NCP file sharing protocol.

[1] These files are all supplied on the Windows 98 product disks. Netware.drv in this configuration replaces an identically named Novell-supplied file.

Tables 17.8 and 17.9 summarize entries that are changed automatically in configuration files when Client for NetWare Networks is installed with Windows 98.

Table 17.8   Configuration file deletions for Client for NetWare Networks

File	Deletions		
Autoexec.bat	bnetx	ipx	odihlp
	brequest	lsl	odinsup
	emsnetx	msipx	startnet
	emsnet5	netbios	vlm
	emsnet4	net3	xmsnet3
	emsnet3	net4	xmsnet4
	int2f	net5	xmsnet5
	ipxodi	netx	xmsnetxp
System.ini	[386enh]	[Boot]	[boot.description]
	network=	network.drv=	network.drv=
	uniquedospsp=		
	pspincrements=		
	timercriticalsection=		
	reflectdosint2a=		
Net.cfg	msipx		

Table 17.9   Configuration file additions for Client for NetWare Networks

File	Additions	
Protocol.ini	[nwlink$]	
	DriverName=nwlink$	
	Frame_Type=4	
	cachesize=0	
	bindings=*device driver(s)*	; for adapters that support NDIS 2

The following list shows files that are renamed in the Windows and System directories when Client for NetWare Networks is installed. Files are renamed to *file name.??~*. (For example, the file Nwuser.exe is renamed to Nwuser.ex~.)

- Nwuser.exe
- Netware.drv
- Netware.hlp
- Nwgdi.dll
- Nwpopup.exe
- Vnetware.386
- Vipx.386

Client for NetWare Networks Configuration Notes

This section presents some configuration notes for Client for NetWare Networks.

- When Windows 98 attempts to connect to a NetWare server, it first silently tries to use the user's logon name and password to make the connection. If you use system policies, you can set a policy that turns off this behavior for Client for NetWare Networks. For information, see Chapter 8, "System Policies."

- If you are running both the Client for NetWare Networks and the Client for Microsoft Networks, Windows NT logon scripts always run before NetWare login scripts.

- Client for NetWare Networks is always bound only to the IPX/SPX-compatible protocol. This is the only protocol this network client can use. If you require an additional protocol for your network, such as TCP/IP, you must install an additional network client, such as Client for Microsoft Networks.

  Notice, however, that you can install Microsoft TCP/IP to connect to the Internet without installing an additional network client.

- With Client for NetWare Networks, you cannot map drives for individual virtual machine (VM) sessions; drive mappings are always global. This is the equivalent of the behavior specified in versions of Windows earlier than Windows 95 by the System.ini setting **NWShareHandles=True** (when using NETX or VLM). Notice, however, that with Client for NetWare Networks, each VM can have a different current directory on network drives, unlike versions of Windows earlier than Windows 95.

- If you are using File and Printer Sharing for NetWare Networks, Config.sys should not have a **LastDrive=** statement.

- The NWPopUp messaging utility is not supported with Client for NetWare Networks. You can use WinPopup to broadcast pop-up messages, as described in Chapter 14, "Introduction to Networking Configuration."

Additional Settings for Client for NetWare Networks

This section describes some additional settings that can be added to the registry for Client for NetWare Networks or for File and Printer Sharing for NetWare Networks. For information about how to add registry values, see Chapter 31, "Windows 98 Registry."

Setting maximum IPX packet size for the LIP protocol. You can set a global value for the maximum IPX packet size for the LIP protocol. To do this, add a registry entry named **MaxLIP** and specify a binary or DWORD value that is the greatest value allowed on any one network segment. The value should be a binary value entered in hexadecimal in reverse order. This global setting is also used on the local network. For example, if a client on a token-ring segment (which allows 4 KB packet sizes) communicates over an Ethernet segment (which allows 1.5 KB packets) to a server on another token-ring segment, the size specified for **MaxLIP** should be limited to the lowest packet size allowed.

Add **MaxLIP** as an entry under the following registry key:

Hkey_Local_Machine\System
   \CurrentControlSet\Services\VxD\Nwredir

To continue the earlier example, you would specify a value for 1.5 KB (**0x000005DC** in hexadecimal). The actual optimal value depends on the frame-header size, which is the IPX portion of the packet. You might want to experiment to get the right size, but in general, specifying a size that is too small is better than too large, because you want to make sure that the echo packet goes through on the first try.

Turning off support for packet-burst protocol. If you want to turn off support for the packet-burst protocol (which is enabled by default for File and Printer Sharing for NetWare Networks), set **SupportBurst=0** in the following registry key:

**Hkey_Local_Machine\System
\CurrentControlSet\Services\VxD\Nwredir**

Setting the shell version for OVL files. The versions of NetWare available for the United States that run on *x*86-based computers use Novell-supplied Ibm*.ovl (overlay) files to present the NetWare shell. This is the default assumed by Windows 98. However, other locales use other versions of OVL files to account for different architecture. For example, Table 17.10 shows the overlay files that NetWare 3.*x* J (for Japan) uses for various computer types.

Table 17.10   Overlay Files

Overlay file	Computer architecture
Pc98$run.ovl	NEC PC9800
Dosv$run.ovl	IBM PC-compatible
J31$run.ovl	Toshiba J3100
Fmr$run.ovl	Fujitsu FMR
Ps55$run.ovl	IBM Japan

For real-mode clients, alternate OVL files are specified in Net.cfg as the SHORT MACHINE TYPE. For Microsoft Client for NetWare Networks, you can specify alternate OVL files as the **ShellVersion** value in the following registry key:

**Hkey_Local_Machine\System
\CurrentControlSet\Services\VxD\Nwredir**

The default value is **MDOS\0V7.00\0IBM_PC\0IBM\0**, where **\0** indicates a binary zero (null value). This value represents the four concatenated strings returned by the INT 21 function 0xEA. You must replace the last string (0IBM) with the one used to generate the *$Run.ovl name. The value in the registry must have a binary type; however, you can enter the required combination of raw ASCII and binary data in the **Enter Binary Data** dialog box.

NetWare API Support in Client for NetWare Networks

Client for NetWare Networks includes built-in support for MS-DOS-based APIs defined by Novell for NetWare 3.*x*, as summarized in Table 17.11.

Table 17.11   APIs for MS-DOS

API for MS-DOS	Description
INT21H	Used by applications for NetWare information, bindery services, and so on.
INT64 and INT7A	Used by applications to submit IPX/SPX requests.

Client for NetWare Networks supports MS-DOS-based API calls documented in the Novell *NetWare Client SDK*. If problems occur with applications that make proprietary or undocumented API calls, then you should use a real-mode Novell-supplied client. Also, please report this problem to both Microsoft and the application vendor.

The Windows 3.*x* APIs for NetWare consist of a series of DLLs provided by Novell with the version 3.*x* WinNet16 driver for the VLM client. The 16-bit Novell-supplied DLLs for Windows can run with Client for NetWare Networks. This ensures that Windows-based applications and utilities that are NetWare-aware will run with Microsoft Client for NetWare Networks.

If any of your applications requires one or more of these DLLs when running on a real-mode Novell-supplied client (NETX or VLM), you must also run the same DLLs when using that application under Client for NetWare Networks. For example, you need the DLLs listed in Table 17.12 to run Novell's NWAdmin utility. You also need access to these files if you want to change passwords for a bindery server by using the Passwords option in Control Panel.

Table 17.12   NetWare dynamic-link libraries (DLLs)

API for Windows	Description
Nwcalls.dll	APIs for NCP communication between the file server and the client computer.
Nwgdi.dll	NetWare Graphical Device Interface.
Nwipxspx.dll	APIs for IPX/SPX communication.
Nwlocale.dll	APIs for localization of applications.
Nwnetapi.dll	Network API support for NDS.
Nwpsrv.dll	Print server services APIs.

Microsoft Service for NetWare Directory Services searches for these files in locations in the user's search path statement. If you put these files in a directory on a server, make sure the directory is in each of your users' search path statements. Microsoft recommends that you place these files in the SYS:PUBLIC directory of your users' preferred servers.

These Novell-supplied DLLs are not provided with Windows 98. They are provided by Novell with NetWare versions 3.12 and 4.*x*, and are updated on **http://support.novell.com/**. To install these files, you must follow the directions provided in your Novell documentation. For information about obtaining the most recent files, see "Obtaining Current Novell-Supplied Files" earlier in this chapter.

Technical Notes on Novell Client for Windows 95/98

This section provides technical information about Novell Client for Windows 95/98. It describes the files Novell's Setup program copies to your computer and the changes the Setup program makes to system files. It also briefly discusses changes the Setup program makes to your registry.

File Locations

Setup.exe copies or creates the listed Client files into the folders shown in Table 17.13.

Table 17.13   Files copied during Novell Client installation

Folder	Files copied	
\Novell\Client32	Client32.nlm	Nwpopup.exe
	Cmsm.nlm	Nwsipx32.nlm
	Cne2000.lan	Pc32mlid.lan
	Cne3200.lan	phasers.wav
	Ethertsm.nlm	Readme.txt
	Fdditsm.nlm	Setupnw.cnt
	Ipx.nlm	Setupnw.hlp
	Loginw95.exe	Spx_skts.nlm
	Lslc32.nlm	Sroute.nlm
	Nios.log	Tokentsm.nlm
	Nmr.nlm (if NMR is installed)	Vmlid.nlm
	NWIP95.NLM (if NetWare/IP is installed)	
\Novell\Client32\Install	Admin.cfg	Nwlinks.exe
	Net2reg.log (created during install)	Nwsetup.ini
\Windows\NLS*language*[1]	Login.dat	
	Login.msg	
\Novell\Nwclient[2]	Driver.com	Net.cfg
	Lsl.com	Route.com (if a token-ring driver)
	N16odi.com	
	Nesl.com	
\Windows\Help[3]	Loginw95.hlp	
	Nwcfg95.hlp	
	Nwover95.hlp	
	Nwtips95.hlp	
	Nwtsg95.hlp	
	Nwuse95.hlp	

Table 17.13   Files copied during Novell Client installation (*continued*)

Folder	Files copied	
\Windows\Inf	Ne1000.inf	Ntr2000.inf Nwclient.inf
	Ne15_21.inf	Nwip.inf
	Ne2.inf	Nwlayout.inf Nwserv.inf
	Ne2_32.inf	Nwtrans.inf
	Ne2000.inf	Odinsup.inf
	Ne3200.inf	
	Netdef.inf	
\Windows\NLS*language*4	Novelnpr.dll	
\Windows\System	Calwin16.dll	Nwdrvlgo.bmp
	Calwin32.dll	Nwgdi.dll
	Clnwin16.dll	Nwipxspx.dll
	Clnwin32.dll	Nwlink2.vxd
	Clnwinth.dll	Nwlocale.dll
	Clxwin16.dll	Nwnet.dll
	Clxwin32.dll	Nwpasswd.dll
	Lgnw9532.dll	Nwpsrv.dll
	Locwin16.dll	Nwrrnsp.dll
	Locwin32.dll	Nwsetup.dll
	Ncpwin16.dll	Nwshellx.dll
	Ncpwin32.dll	Nwsipx32.dll
	Netware.drv	Odiload.vxd
	Netwin16.dll	Odinsup.sys
	Netwin32.dll	Odipage.dll
	Nios.vxd	Prtwin16.dll
	Nioslib.dll	Prtwin32.dll
	Novellnp.dll	Tli_spx.dll
	Novpp32.dll	Tli_win.dll
	Nwcalls.dll	

[1] The name of this folder varies depending on the language being used. For example, for English, the folder name is ENGLISH.

[2] Setup adds the following files to the NWCLIENT folder on workstations that use 16-bit ODI LAN drivers.

[3] Each of these help files might also have files with the following file types associated with them:
.cnt ,.fts*.gid.

[4] The name of this folder varies depending on the language being used. For example, for English, the folder name is ENGLISH.

Changes to System Files

Table 17.14 shows the changes Novell Client installation makes to Windows 98 system files.

Table 17.14   Changes to Windows 98 system files

System file	Changes
Autoexec.bat	Removes lines that reference the following: IP NETX SERVER STARTNET VLM Removes the NWCLIENT folder from the SET PATH statement.
Config.sys	Removes LASTDRIVE=*drive letter*
System.ini	Adds the following lines to the [386Enh] section: NWHOMEDIR=[drive]\NOVELL\CLIENT32 FileSysChange=Off NWEnableLogging is a feature that logs status messages from the Novell Client. You can set the path and file name for the log from the Log File parameter in the Network Control Panel **Advanced Settings** page.
Netdef.inf	Sets the NetClient= line to NOVELL32.

Changes to the Windows Registry

Novell Client makes several changes to the registry. You can reverse these changes by removing the Novell Client software. The INF files document all changes Setup makes to the registry.

Technical Notes on Novell's NETX

This section provides technical information about using the Novell-supplied NetWare 3.*x* client software (NETX) with Windows 98.

When running NETX with Windows 98, you keep all the same functionality that you had when running NETX with MS-DOS, Windows 3.*x*, and Windows 95.

Using NETX with Client for Microsoft Networks

If you are using NETX as the network client, you might also choose to install the 32-bit, protected-mode Client for Microsoft Networks if you want to connect to other Microsoft network computers, such as computers running Windows for Workgroups 3.*x*, LAN Manager, or Windows NT.

When you run the NetWare NETX client with Windows 98 in this configuration, you should continue to load the necessary Novell-supplied client components and MS-DOS-based TSR programs (LSL, ODI driver, IPXODI, and NETX) in Autoexec.bat or Startnet.bat, just as you did with MS-DOS, Windows 3.1, or Windows 95. Windows 98 Setup automatically adds the configuration settings if they are not present. For information about required configuration settings, see your Novell documentation.

You will need a Microsoft Windows NT Client Access license if the computer will be connecting to servers running Windows NT Server. For information, see Chapter 16, "Windows 98 on Microsoft Networks."

Figure 17.3 shows the architecture for this configuration. Novell-supplied components appear in bold.

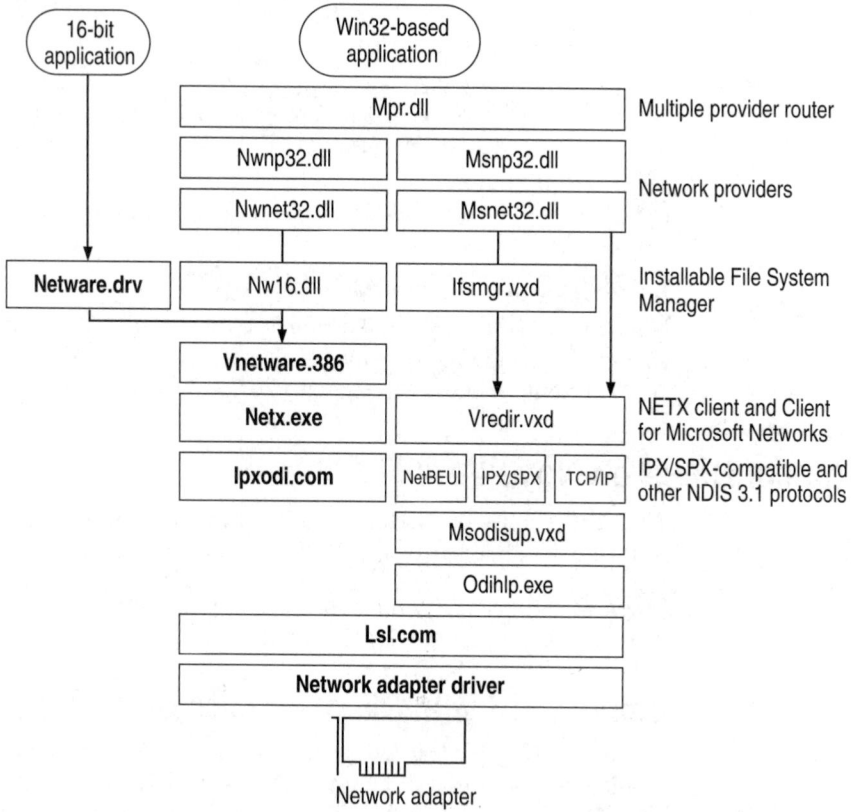

Figure 17.3   Architecture for Novell-supplied NETX with Client for Microsoft Networks

In this configuration, the Novell-supplied version of Netware.drv is installed and loaded only for applications that call it directly. Because this driver is not used by Windows 98, all access to NetWare resources occurs by using the Windows 98 user interface, not the Netware.drv dialog boxes provided by Novell. The Nw16.dll component translates 32-bit network calls to 16-bit network calls that can be passed to Vnetware.386.

Using NETX as the Sole Client

You might want to use NETX as the sole client if you do not need to connect to other computers running Windows for Workgroups 3.*x*, LAN Manager, or Windows NT.

If you use NETX as the sole client, you can still connect to computers running Microsoft File and Printer Sharing Services for NetWare.

To use only NETX client support, use the Network option in Control Panel to remove Client for NetWare Networks and Client for Microsoft Networks, if either of these clients is installed. Then add the Novell NetWare (Workstation Shell 3.*x* [NETX]) client, as described in "Installing or Upgrading a Real-Mode NetWare Client" earlier in this chapter.

Figure 17.4 shows the architecture for this configuration. Novell-supplied components appear in bold.

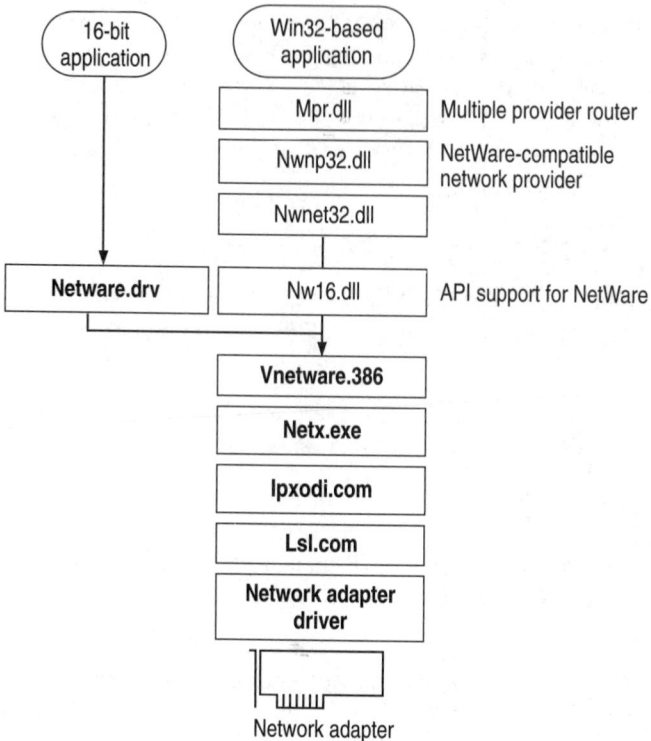

Figure 17.4   Architecture for Novell-supplied NETX as the sole client

Table 17.15 lists the required settings for Config.sys and Autoexec.bat files if you use NETX as the sole network client.

Table 17.15   Configuration file settings for NETX as the sole network client

Filename	Required settings
Config.sys	lastdrive=*drive letter*
Autoexec.bat[1]	lsl.com *odi_driver* ipxodi.com netx.exe q: ; that is, lastdrive+1 login c:

[1] Or this could be the name of a batch file called from Autoexec.bat.

Table 17.16 summarizes the minimum settings that you should see in the Network option in Control Panel if you use NETX as the sole network client.

Table 17.16   Network settings for NETX as the sole network client

Component	Options
NetWare (Workstation Shell 3.x [NETX])	Novell NetWare (Workstation Shell 3.x [NETX]) appears in the list of installed components. All other settings are configured in Net.cfg.
Network adapter	In the properties for the adapter, the **Real mode (16 bit) ODI Driver** option should be selected.
Novell IPXODI	Settings are configured in Net.cfg.

Setting the LastDrive Parameter for NETX

Windows 98 uses the value of the **LastDrive=** entry in the registry (or in Config.sys) to allocate enough storage space in the internal memory structures to recognize drive letters for devices. For example, a setting of **LastDrive=Z** tells Windows 98 to recognize drive letters from A to Z. Windows 98 uses all drive letters up to the letter assigned as the last drive.

In contrast, NETX clients can use only the drive letters following the last drive. For example, if you specify **LastDrive=P**, you will be able to map NetWare volumes only to drives Q-Z. This can cause problems if you have a setting of **LastDrive=Z**, because you will then have no drives available for mapping to NetWare servers.

NETX clients always use the drive letters following the drive specified in the **LastDrive=** entry, even if they are local drives. Also, when you install NETX, Windows 98 adds **LastDrive=E** to the registry. This can cause problems: for example, if you have a local drive **F**: and a network drive is mapped to **F**:, you will no longer be able to access the local drive. If this happens, you will need to modify the **LastDrive=** entry in Config.sys.

Setting Show Dots and File Access Limits

A NetWare file server does not include the directory entries dot (.) and double dot (..) as MS-DOS and Windows 98 do. However, the NetWare Workstation Shell client version 3.01 or later can emulate these entries when applications attempt to list the files in a directory.

▶ **To turn on the Show Dots feature**

- If you have problems listing files or deleting directories, add the following line to the beginning of Net.cfg:

```
show dots=on
```

By default, NetWare client software allows you access to only 40 files at a time. When you are running many applications under Windows 98, it is possible to exceed this limit, so you will want to increase the settings for file limits.

▶ **To increase the file access limit**

1. Add the following line to the beginning of Net.cfg:

```
file handles=60
```

2. Add the following line to Config.sys for the local computer:

```
files=60
```

Technical Notes on Novell's VLM

VLM, the network client provided with Novell NetWare version 4.*x*, provides the same support and behavior under Windows 98 as it does under MS-DOS or Windows 3.1.

If the computer is using VLM, you should still load the Novell-supplied client components and TSR programs and log on from either Autoexec.bat or Startnet.bat. Logon scripts also work in the same way they do with MS-DOS, Windows 95, and Windows 3.*x*. After Windows 98 starts, you can use the Windows 98 user interface to make drive and printer connections, or you can run NetWare utilities by running NWUSER or other commands at the command prompt. Notice, however, that you cannot use NDS names in Windows 98 dialog boxes.

This section presents specific notes related to using the Novell-supplied NetWare 4.*x* client software with Windows 98.

Using VLM with Client for Microsoft Networks

If you are using VLM as the network client, you might also choose to install the 32-bit, protected-mode Client for Microsoft Networks if you want to connect to other Microsoft networking computers, such as computers running Windows for Workgroups 3.*x*, LAN Manager, or Windows NT. Figure 17.5 shows the architecture for this configuration. Novell-supplied components appear in bold.

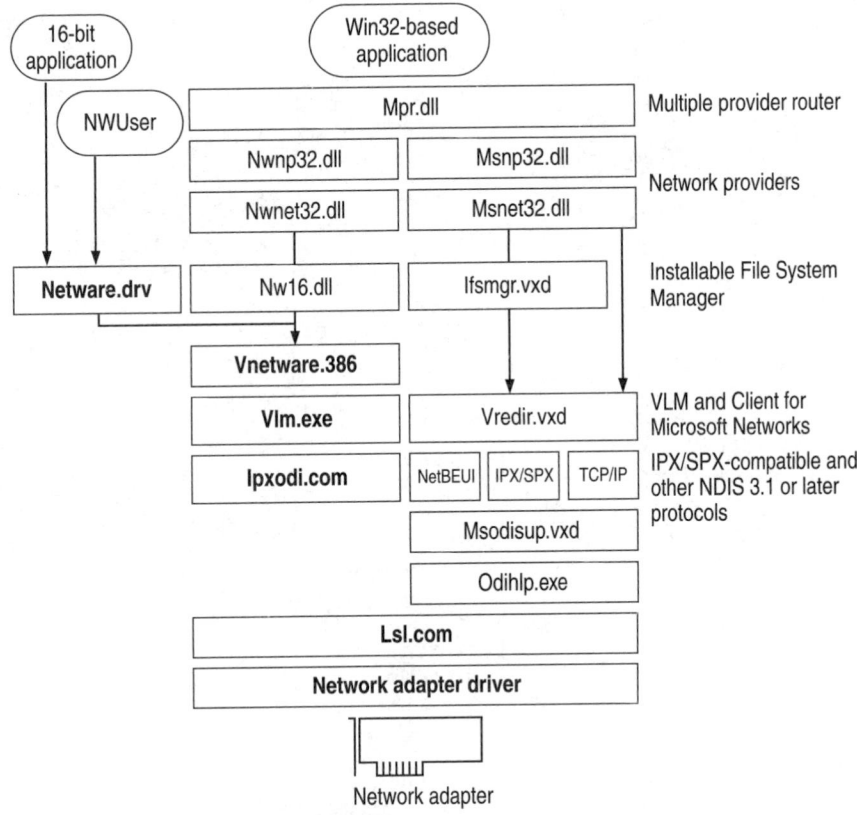

Figure 17.5   Architecture for Novell-supplied VLM with Client for NetWare Networks

In this configuration, the Novell-supplied version of Netware.drv is not used by Windows 98. It is installed and loaded only for applications that call it directly. All access to NetWare resources is through the Windows 98 user interface, not the Netware.drv dialog boxes. The NWUSER utility calls Netware.drv directly to bring up the central NetWare Version 3.0 WinNet16 dialog box.

Notice that this configuration requires a Microsoft Windows NT Client Access License if this computer will be connecting to servers running Windows NT Server. For more information, see Chapter 16, "Windows 98 on Microsoft Networks."

Using VLM as the Sole Client

You can use VLM as the sole client if you do not need to connect to other computers that are running Windows for Workgroups 3.x, LAN Manager, or Windows NT. (If you use VLM as the sole client, you can still connect to a Windows 98 computer running Microsoft File and Printer Sharing for NetWare.)

Figure 17.6 shows the architecture for this configuration. Novell-supplied components appear in bold.

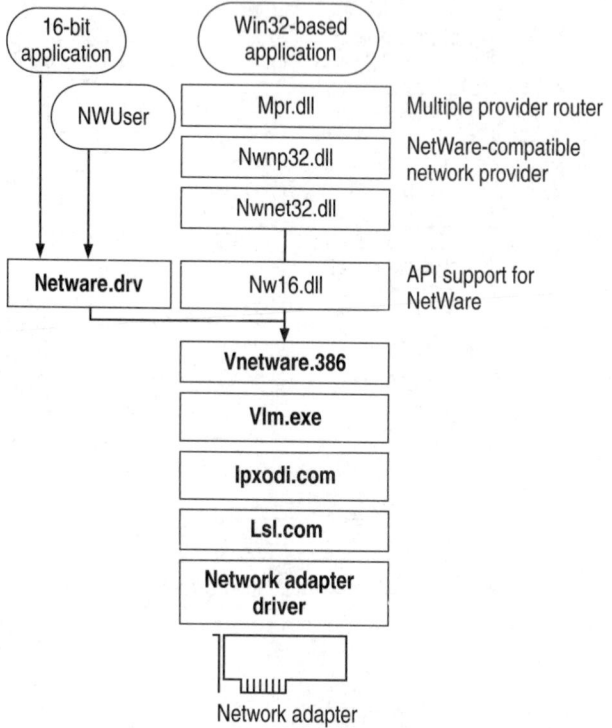

Figure 17.6   Architecture for Novell-supplied VLM as the sole client

Table 17.17 lists the required settings for Config.sys and Autoexec.bat files if you use VLM as the sole network client.

Table 17.17   Configuration file settings for VLM as the sole network client

File name	Required settings
Config.sys	lastdrive=*drive_letter*
Autoexec.bat	startnet.bat
Startnet.bat	lsl.com odi driver ipxodi.com vlm.exe f: ; that is, first network drive in net.cfg login c:

Table 17.18 summarizes the minimum settings that you should see in the Network option in Control Panel if you install Windows 98 with VLM as the sole network client.

Table 17.18   Network settings for VLM as the sole network client

Component	Options
NetWare (Workstation Shell 4.*x* [VLM])	Novell NetWare (Workstation Shell 4.*x* [VLM]) appears in the list of installed components. All other settings are configured in Net.cfg.
Network adapter	In the properties for the adapter, the **Real mode (16 bit) ODI Driver** option should be checked.
Novell IPXODI	Settings are configured in Net.cfg.

Setting the LastDrive Parameter for VLM

Windows 98 uses the value of the **LastDrive=** entry in the registry to allocate enough storage space in the internal memory structures to recognize drive letters for devices. For example, a setting of **LastDrive=Z** tells Windows 98 to recognize drive letters from A to Z.

The Novell-supplied NetWare 4.*x* redirector handles the **LastDrive=** entry the same way that Windows 98 does. That is, both the NetWare 4.*x* redirector and Windows 98 allow drive letters to be used to connect to redirected network drives up through the drive letter specified by the **LastDrive=** entry. For example, a setting of **LastDrive=Z** tells the NetWare 4.*x* redirector to recognize drive letters up through Z.

The NetWare 4.*x* redirector uses the **First Network Drive=** entry in the Net.cfg file to identify the first network drive that can be mapped. For more information about this setting, consult your Novell documentation.

Overview of Windows 98 on Other Third-Party Networks

In addition to its support for Novell's network clients, Windows 98 includes built-in support for 32-bit, protected-mode clients and for several types of 16-bit, real-mode network clients.

Tip for Using Protected-Mode Network Clients from Other Vendors

The network provider interface defines a set of APIs used by Windows 98 to access the network for actions, such as logging on to the server, browsing and connecting to servers, and so on. Microsoft has made this set of APIs widely available to network vendors so that they can develop new protected-mode network providers that are compatible with Windows 98.

For example, Windows 98 can support Microsoft networks, Novell NetWare, and Banyan VINES 32-bit connectivity at the same time through Network Neighborhood.

Multiple network support in Windows 98 consists of the following components:

- Win32 WinNet API.

- Multiple provider router and service provider interface.

- Network providers, including the WinNet16 interface, as described in "Using Real-Mode WinNet16 Drivers" later in this chapter.

This section describes how to install and configure Windows 98 on third-party networks other than Novell NetWare. It discusses the following network software:

- Artisoft LANtastic version 7.0 (client and server).

- Banyan Enterprise Client version 7.32 and later.

- Banyan VINES version 7.1 and later (a 16-bit, real-mode client).

- Digital PATHWORKS 32 client.

- IBM Networks Client for Windows 95.

- Solstice NFS Client version 3.1 and later.

It also includes information about host (that is, mainframe) connectivity for Windows 98.

For information about the system components that provide multiple network support, see Chapter 29, "Windows 98 Network Architecture." For information about networking printing and support for printing when using a 16-bit network client, see Chapter 11, "Printing, Imaging, and Fonts."

Issues with Windows 98 on Other Third-Party Networks

Both protected-mode, 32-bit, and real-mode, 16-bit network clients are available for most network clients. You should use 32-bit, protected mode network clients whenever possible. Protected-mode, 32-bit clients offer the following benefits:

- Easy installation and configuration using built-in Windows 98 tools.
- Performance enhancements, such as Plug and Play networking support, long file names, client-side caching, and automatic reconnections.
- Greater stability than with real-mode clients.
- Ability to run additional 32-bit, protected-mode clients simultaneously.
- Integration with the Windows 98 environment, including the Windows 98 unified logon, Network Neighborhood, and Windows 98 network management tools.

You should install 32-bit clients after you have finished Windows 98 Setup. If you have a 16-bit client on your computer before Windows 98 Setup, contact your network vendor for information about how to upgrade to the 32-bit clients.

Contact your network vendor for their latest installation INF file.

Note Be sure to read the Windows 98 Readme.txt, Setup.txt, and Network.txt notes on networking. Also check the Microsoft WinNews forums on online services for specific information about your network and about particular adapters.

Overview of Installing Support for Other Networks

This section gives an overview of installing both 32-bit clients and 16-bit clients, and it describes how to install Microsoft Client for Microsoft Networks after another network client has been installed.

Installing 32-bit Clients

You should install 32-bit clients after you have run Windows 98 Setup. For installation details related to your specific network, see the section for that network.

Installing 16-bit Clients

This section describes how to install Windows 98 16-bit clients from another vendor. For installation details related to your specific network, see the section for that network or contact your network vendor.

You can add real-mode, third-party support to Windows 98 in one of two ways:

- Add network support before upgrading to Windows 98. In most cases, Setup retains networking components. (One exception is Novell NETX. For more information about upgrading Novell NETX, see "Installing or Upgrading a Real-Mode Novell Client" earlier in this chapter.) You should be sure that the network client is installed correctly under MS-DOS, Windows 3.1, Windows for Workgroups, or Windows 95.

- Add network support after upgrading to Windows 98.

On most computers running multiple clients, Windows 98 Setup stores all real-mode networking components, including Protocol.ini, in the \Windows directory. (For computers running Novell's VLM, Windows 98 Setup stores these components in the Nwclient directory.) On computers running a real-mode client as the primary network, the networking components are left in place. The settings in Protocol.ini affect only real-mode NDIS drivers. Changing these values has no effect on protected-mode NDIS drivers. If you need to change settings in Protocol.ini, use the Network option in Control Panel whenever possible. For information about Protocol.ini entries, see Chapter 16, "Windows 98 on Microsoft Networks."

Note Microsoft does not support upgrading over any real-mode clients other than NETX, VLM, and Banyan VINES 7.1 or later. Consult the Network.txt file for more information about support boundaries for real-mode clients.

Installing Client for Microsoft Networks with Other Networks

If you want to install the 32-bit, protected-mode Client for Microsoft Networks in addition to a network client from another vendor, and if the client is not already installed, follow these steps. For more information about configuring and using Client for Microsoft Networks, see Chapter 16, "Windows 98 on Microsoft Networks."

▶ **To install Client for Microsoft Networks after another client has been installed**

1. After Windows 98 Setup, in Control Panel double-click Network.

2. In the **Network** dialog box, click **Add**. In the **Select Network Component Type** dialog box, double-click **Client**.

3. In the **Select Network Client** dialog box, click **Microsoft** in the **Manufacturers** list, and click **Client for Microsoft Networks** in the **Network Clients** list. Click **OK**.

4. Usually hardware detection detects the correct network adapter and selects the corresponding driver. If you must add a network adapter, follow the steps in Chapter 14, "Introduction to Networking Configuration."

5. In the **Network** dialog box, double-click the network adapter in the list of components. Verify the settings in the properties for the network adapter. Then click **OK**. For information, see Chapter 15, "Network Adapters and Protocols." See also the documentation for your network adapter to verify its software settings.

   Setup automatically installs a protected-mode version of any protocol that the installed network clients are using. If you need to install another protocol, follow the steps in Chapter 14, "Introduction to Networking Configuration."

6. Shut down and restart the computer.

Using Real-Mode WinNet16 Drivers

In addition to multiple 32-bit Windows 98 network providers, Windows 98 can also support a single 16-bit WinNet driver. This is the basic configuration that must be used for a network product that does not offer a 32-bit network provider.

If the 16-bit network provider from another network vendor does not provide a browsing scheme, Network Neighborhood will be empty. This indicates that it is not a browsable network. You must use the **Map Network Drive** dialog box for network access. Also, notice that a drive connected through the Windows 98 user interface is accessible in all command prompt boxes. (However, it is accessible only from Windows 98 command prompt boxes, not when you reboot in MS-DOS mode.) A connection made at a command prompt, however, will be available in that command prompt box only and will not be available throughout the Windows 98 user interface.

Table 17.19 summarizes the components for the 16-bit, real-mode network drivers.

Table 17.19   Components for real-mode network drivers

Component	Description
Winnet16.dll	Provides a 32-bit to 16-bit thunk and translation between the 32-bit Windows 98 network provider interface and the 16-bit WinNet API.
Winnet16.drv	A 16-bit Windows 3.x network driver that provides a basic **Map Network Drive** dialog box.
Network.vxd (or .386)	A Windows 3.x virtual device driver that allows virtualized access to the real-mode network software for all virtual machines (including Winnet16.drv).
Real-mode network software	This can include proprietary network adapter drivers, protocol drivers, client (redirector), and network utilities loaded through Config.sys and Autoexec.bat (or another batch file).

Artisoft LANtastic 7.0

This section describes how to install Windows 98 with the protected-mode client and server for Artisoft LANtastic 7.0. Microsoft recommends that you do not use any earlier versions of Artisoft LANtastic.

If you want to run Windows 98 with Artisoft LANtastic for Windows 95, contact Artisoft at **http://www.artisoft.com/**.

Note Real-mode versions of Artisoft LANtastic do not work with Windows 95. Also, If you are running Windows 98 Setup from a Windows for Workgroups computer that has a real-mode version Artisoft LANtastic, Setup will fail. You should remove the real-mode version of Artisoft LANtastic before running Windows 98 Setup.

Artisoft LANtastic 7.0 includes the following components:

- A client component.
- A server component.
- The Artisoft NetBIOS protocol.
- File and printer sharing.
- Modem sharing, which enables several users to share one modem.
- The Internet Gateway Server, which enables several users to share the same Internet connection.

You should install Artisoft LANtastic 7.0 after Windows 98 Setup is complete. You can also install LANtastic on Windows 95, and then upgrade to Windows 98.

Artisoft has patches and other program updates, which you should apply after installing Artisoft LANtastic. Contact Artisoft for more information.

Artisoft LANtastic can be run in conjunction with Client for Microsoft Networks and Client for NetWare Networks. However, in some cases you might not be able to get Artisoft LANtastic to work with non-Artisoft networking components. If so, disable multicast addressing on all computers running LANtastic. See the section "Correcting Problems with Other Third-Party Networks" later in this chapter, or contact Artisoft for more information.

LANtastic servers appear in Network Neighborhood and Windows Explorer. You can map to a network drive as you normally do. You can also use the LANtastic Custom Control Panel. However, network drive mappings made through the LANtastic Custom Control Panel will not show the universal naming convention (UNC) extension label when viewed through Explorer, My Computer, or the LANtastic Custom Control Panel utilities.

▶ **To install Artisoft LANtastic after Windows 98 Setup**

1. If you have a previous real-mode version of Artisoft LANtastic, contact Artisoft for information about how to uninstall it.

2. Double-click the Setup.exe file provided by Artisoft.

3. Follow the instructions on the screen.

Note LANtastic Setup asks you for Msrrdir.vxd approximately 6 to 8 times. To move past this more quickly, click **Skip File** or **Cancel** at each prompt. The file is an Artisoft Modem Sharing component and has already been copied to its proper location, in your \Windows\System directory.

---

4. Restart the computer.

5. In the **Start** menu, click **Programs** and then click **LANtastic 7.0**. Follow the instructions on the screen. This sets up the LANtastic Custom Control Panel.

▶ **To configure Artisoft LANtastic**

- You configure most Artisoft LANtastic options from the LANtastic Custom Control Panel icon. You can also configure the LANtastic NetBIOS protocol from the Network option in Control Panel.

You can uninstall Artisoft LANtastic in one of two ways.

▶ **To uninstall Artisoft LANtastic completely**

1. In Control Panel, double-click Network.

2. Remove all LANtastic components.

3. Click **OK**.

4. In Control Panel, double-click Add/Remove Programs.

This method is not recommended if you plan to reinstall Artisoft LANtastic later, because it also removes any security and share information you have set up.

▶ **To uninstall Artisoft LANtastic but preserve settings**

- Remove LANtastic by running LANtastic's setup utility. The setup utility detects the LANtastic components from the Network option in Control Panel and then asks you if you want to remove LANtastic from your system.

This method preserves your security and share information in case you want to reinstall later.

Banyan Enterprise Clients and Banyan VINES

Windows 98 can be installed and run with the following Banyan clients:

- Banyan Enterprise Clients for Windows 95, protected-mode, 32-bit clients.
- Banyan VINES 7.1 and later, real-mode, 16-bit clients.

You should run a protected-mode client rather than a real-mode, 16-bit client.

This section discusses how to run Windows 98 with Banyan Enterprise Client 7.32 or later and Banyan VINES 7.1 and later. For information about running Windows 98 with Banyan Enterprise Clients for Windows 95, contact Banyan.

If you are using a 16-bit client, Banyan VINES servers do not show up in Network Neighborhood or Windows Explorer. You must use the **Map Network Drive** dialog box in Windows 98 to connect to servers.

However, if you are using a Banyan Enterprise 32-bit client, you can view Banyan file and print services from within Network Neighborhood.

Banyan Enterprise Client 7.32 or later supports system policies, and Banyan Enterprise Client 8.02 or later supports user profiles. Refer to your Banyan documentation for more information.

Banyan Enterprise Clients

This section describes how to install, uninstall, and configure Banyan Enterprise Clients on Windows 98. For information about how to upgrade to Banyan Enterprise Client from real-mode versions of Banyan clients, contact your Banyan vendor.

Installing Banyan Enterprise Client on Windows 98

This section describes how to install and uninstall Banyan Enterprise Client.

▶ **To install Banyan Enterprise Client after Windows 98 Setup**

1. In Control Panel, double-click Network.
2. On the **Configuration** tab, click **Add**.
3. In the **Select Network Component Type** dialog box, select **Client**.
4. Click **Add**.
5. In the **Select Network Client** dialog box, click **Have Disk**.
6. Enter the directory where your installation files are located, and then click **OK**.
7. Follow the instructions on the screen.

▶ **To uninstall Banyan Enterprise Client after Windows 98 Setup**

1. In Control Panel, double-click Network.

2. On the **Configuration** tab, select **Banyan Client for Windows**.

3. Click **Remove**.

4. Select **Banyan Vines Protocol for 95**.

5. Click **OK**.

6. When prompted, reboot the computer.

Configuring Banyan Enterprise Client

Banyan Common Logon is enabled by default. If you want to disable it, you must do so from the Network option in Control Panel.

The following example shows a sample Autoexec.bat entry when Banyan Enterprise Client protected-mode network support is installed with Client for Microsoft Networks either as a primary network or as a secondary network:

```
c:\win95\system\bansvc
```

Table 17.20 shows Banyan system files and their functions.

Table 17.20   Banyan system files and functions

Primary Banyan system files	Function
Bancom.vxd	Banyan IP communications stack
Vinesifs.vxd	Network redirector
Bansvc.com	MS-DOS interface enabler
Vsnet32.dll	Net provider
Vnsprn32.dll	Print provider
Vnsapi32.dll	Banyan Toolkit API

Banyan VINES 16-bit Client

You should use the 32-bit clients Banyan Enterprise Client version 7.32 or later instead of the Banyan VINES 16-bit client. For information about the benefits of using 32-bit, protected-mode clients see "Issues with Windows 98 on Other Third-Party Networks" earlier in this chapter. Also, Banyan no longer supports the 16-bit client.

If you are already using the Banyan VINES 16-bit client and you want to upgrade to the 32-bit client, you cannot do so using Msbatch.inf. Instead, you should wait until after Windows 98 Setup to upgrade to the 32-bit client.

If you do choose to use the Banyan VINES 16-bit client, you should upgrade to version 7.1 or higher. Microsoft no longer supports versions lower than 7.1. You should upgrade before you run Windows 98 Setup.

▶ **To upgrade to version 7.1**

1. Obtain a patch from Banyan and apply it to at least one Banyan server on your network.
2. Run **Newrev** to upgrade all the Banyan clients on which you will be installing Windows 98.
3. Run Windows 98 Setup.

Banyan can be installed as an additional 16-bit network client, and you can install 32-bit, protected-mode clients, such as Client for Microsoft Networks or Client for NetWare Networks.

Installing the Banyan VINES 16-bit Client

If you want to set up Windows 98 with Banyan VINES real-mode network client support on an Ethernet network, make sure that the Banyan VINES client is already installed and working under MS-DOS, Windows 3.1, Windows for Workgroups, or Windows 95 before you run Windows 98 Setup.

Note If you are running Banyan VINES with monolithic drivers, you must use the PCCONFIG utility provided by Banyan to change Banyan drivers to NDIS drivers. Make sure that the section name matches the driver name.

Configuring the Banyan VINES 16-bit Client

Tables 17.21 and 17.22 show the entries required in configuration files when Banyan VINES real-mode network support is installed with Windows 98, depending on whether Banyan VINES is installed as the primary network only (connecting to a Banyan server) or is installed with Client for Microsoft Networks. These entries are for NDIS drivers.

Table 17.21   Banyan VINES as primary network, using NDIS

Configuration file	Entries
Autoexec.bat	cd *banfiles* ban ndisban ; ndtokban for token ring redirall netbind arswait z:login c: cd\\

Table 17.21   Banyan VINES as primary network, using NDIS (*continued*)

Configuration file	Entries
Config.sys	device=c:*banfiles*\\protman.dos /i:c:*banfiles* device=c:*banfiles**ndis2driver* eg: exp16.dos
Protocol.ini	[PROTOCOL MANAGER] drivername=protman$ [VINES_XIF] drivername=ndisban$; ndtokban$ for token ring bindings=MS$EE16 [MS$EE16] drivername=EXP16$ interrupt=5 ioaddress=0x300 iochrdy=late

Table 17.22   Banyan VINES with Client for Microsoft Networks

Configuration file	Entries
Autoexec.bat	c:\windows\net initialize cd *banfiles* ban ndisban ; ndtokban for token ring redirall c:\windows\net start arswait z:login c: cd\
Config.sys	rem device=c:*banfiles*\\protman.dos /i:c:*banfiles* rem device=c:*banfiles**ndis2driver* eg: elnkii.dos
Protocol.ini	[NDISBAN$] ; NDTOKBAN$ for token ring drivername=NDISBAN$; NDTOKBAN$ for token ring bindings=ELNKII$ [NWLINK$] drivername=NWLINK$ frame_type=4 cachesize=0 bindings=ELNKII$ [NETBEUI$] drivername=NETBEUI$ lanabase=0 sessions=10 ncbs=12 bindings=ELNKII$

Table 17.22   Banyan VINES with Client for Microsoft Networks (*continued*)

Configuration file	Entries
| Protocol.ini (*continued*) | ```
[ELNKII$]
drivername=ELNKII$
transceiver=external
interrupt=2
ioaddress=0x280
maxtransmits=12
datatransfer=pio_word
xmitbufs=2

[PROTMAN$]
priority=ndishlp$
drivername=protman$

[NDISHLP$]
drivername=ndishlp$
bindings=ELNKII$
``` |

DIGITAL PATHWORKS 32

This section describes how to install and run Windows 98 with the protected-mode client DIGITAL PATHWORKS 32. Digital Equipment Corporation (DEC) does not support any earlier versions of PATHWORKS, and it might not be possible to make earlier versions work with Windows 98.

DIGITAL PATHWORKS 32 is a set of communication software products that enables users and applications to connect to nodes on the network that are running the DECnet protocol. It includes the following components:

- DECnet protocol and related utilities and APIs, including Windows Sockets 2 support.
- LAT service.
- VT Terminal emulation.
- File transfer.
- X server software.
- Print services.
- Remote access services including support for asynchronous links using digital data communications message protocol (DDCMP), support for Point-To-Point Protocol (PPP), and support for Microsoft Dial-Up Networking.
```

▶ **To install DIGITAL PATHWORKS 32 after Windows 98 Setup**

1. Insert the PATHWORKS 32 compact disc into your CD-ROM drive.

2. If you have not disabled the Autoplay function, the CD-ROM Autoplay displays a banner window with several options. Click **Install**.

   – Or –

   If you have disabled the Autoplay function, double-click the executable file Autoplay.exe provided by DEC on the PATHWORKS 32 CD-ROM.

3. Follow the instructions on the screen.

4. After installing DIGITAL PATHWORKS 32, shut down and restart your workstation.

For information about uninstalling DIGITAL PATHWORKS 32, consult the Release Notes included in version 7.0a or later, or contact Digital Equipment Corporation.

IBM Networks Client for Windows 95

Users must be running Client for Microsoft Networks in order to take advantage of all the features that IBM Networks Client for Windows 95 offers. If users are running Client for Microsoft Networks alone, they can access non-secure shares on IBM OS/2 LAN Servers and IBM OS/2 Warp Servers. Using the IBM Networks Client for Windows 95 with Client for Microsoft Networks, they can also log on to IBM OS/2 LAN Servers and IBM OS/2 Warp Servers, access secure shares, and execute scripts.

Users can connect to servers using the **Map Network Drive** dialog box or the command prompt. Users can also browse OS/2 Warp Servers as long as those servers have been configured as browse masters. They can be configured as browse masters using the IBM Neighborhood Browser Enabler for OS/2 Warp Server, which is available from IBM.

Important Client for Microsoft Networks must be installed before you install IBM Networks Client for Windows 95.

▶ **To set up Windows 98 with IBM Networks Client for Windows 95 after Windows 98 Setup**

1. Make sure that the Client for Microsoft Networks and other standard networking components are already installed.

2. Make sure that a NetBEUI or TCP/IP network protocol is installed.

3. In Control Panel, double-click Network, and then click **Add**.

4. In the **Select Network Component Type** dialog box, select **Client**, and then click **Add**.

5. In the **Select Network Client** dialog box, click **Have Disk**.

6. Enter the directory path where your IBM Networks Client for Windows 95 installation files are located, and then click **OK** three times. You must restart the computer for the changes to take effect.

Solstice NFS Client

Windows 98 can be installed and run with Solstice NFS Client version 3.1 and later. Solstice NFS Client uses the Microsoft TCP/IP network protocol for its network connection and can be supported as either the primary network client or as an additional 32-bit client.

The installation process consists of the following three procedures:

- Installing and configuring Microsoft TCP/IP.

  For information about how to install and configure Microsoft TCP/IP, see Chapter 15, "Network Adapters and Protocols."

- Installing Solstice NFS.

- Optionally, verifying the installation.

Note If you want to access NetWare servers, install Microsoft Client for NetWare Networks before installing the Solstice NFS Client.

▶ **To install Solstice NFS**

1. Insert the Solstice Network Client compact disc into your CD-ROM drive.

2. If you have not disabled the Autoplay function, the CD-ROM Autoplay displays a banner window with several options. Click **Install**.

   – Or –

   If you have disabled the Autoplay function, at the command prompt type

   `<drive_letter>:\pcpro3\setup`

   where *<drive_letter>* is the letter of your CD-ROM drive.

3. Click **Next** and follow the instructions on the screen. The installation program copies files from the compact disc to your computer and enters information into your system files.

> **Note** During installation, Solstice Setup asks you which name service to use and lists Windows Default as the default. Do not change this configuration unless you are using an NIS server. If you are using an NIS server, contact your network administrator for configuration information.

4. After installing Solstice NFS, shut down and restart your computer. When the computer reboots, you can log on.

You can change your configuration later, from the Network option in Control Panel.

▶ **To configure Solstice NFS from the Network option in Control Panel**

1. In Control Panel, double-click Network.

2. Click each Solstice component and then click the **Properties** button, to view its properties.

3. Make any necessary changes. For more information, contact Sun Microsystems.

After you have installed and configured it, make sure your configuration works properly.

▶ **To verify your configuration**

1. Use the **Ping** utility to make sure you can connect to another computer on the network. If not, you have a problem with your TCP/IP configuration.

2. Use the **Winipcfg** utility to verify TCP/IP configuration information.

3. In Network Neighborhood, double-click the Entire Network icon, click the NFS Servers icon, and then select a remote computer to make sure you can browse it. If no remote computers appear, try adding a computer by following the procedure "To add NFS hosts to Network Neighborhood," later in this section.

For information about using the Ping and Winipcfg utilities, see the section "Troubleshooting TCP/IP" in Chapter 15, "Network Adapters and Protocols."

After you have installed and configured Solstice NFS, you will see the following new workgroups in Network Neighborhood:

- NFS Automount Maps

  This workgroup includes all the NFS Automount Maps on the network that have been predefined by the network administrator.

- NFS Servers

  This workgroup includes all the NFS hosts on your subnet and all other hosts on your network that you have added to Network Neighborhood.

▶ **To add NFS hosts to Network Neighborhood**

1. In Network Neighborhood, double-click the Entire Network icon, and then click the NFS Servers icon.

2. In the **File** menu, select **Add/Remove NFS Servers**.

▶ **To uninstall Solstice NFS**

1. In Control Panel, double-click Add/Remove Programs.

2. Click **Solstice** and then click **Add/Remove**.

3. When you are asked whether you want to completely remove the selected application, click **Yes**.

4. When you are asked whether you want to delete shared files, click **No** unless you know that no other program is using the files.

5. Click **OK**.

Host Connectivity and Windows 98

Host connectivity in this section refers to connecting to legacy IBM System 370/390-compatible mainframe computers, the mid-range IBM AS/400 computers, DEC VAX/VMS, UNIX, and HP 3000 computers. Host terminal emulation applications running in Windows 98 require network protocols to connect to their respective hosts.

The common network protocols used to support host connectivity include the following:

- IPX/SPX. The IPX/SPX-compatible transport provided with Windows 98 is compatible with Novell NetWare IPX/SPX, and can be installed to support host connectivity using terminal emulation programs and gateways supporting an IPX/SPX interface.

- NetBEUI. The NetBEUI protocol provided with Windows 98 supports a NetBIOS programming interface and conforms to the IBM NetBEUI specifications. It also includes performance enhancements related to NetBIOS 3.0. Microsoft NetBEUI can be installed on computers running Windows 98 to provide NetBIOS support for host connectivity using terminal emulation programs and gateways supporting a NetBIOS interface.

- TCP/IP. The TCP/IP protocol provided with Windows 98 is a complete implementation of the most common and accepted protocol available. It allows connectivity between interconnected networks with different operating systems and hardware architectures, such as UNIX, IBM mainframes, and Microsoft networks. Usually, host connectivity with the TCP/IP protocol is provided using Telnet services, such as TN3270 connecting to legacy mainframes, TN5250 connecting to an IBM AS/400, and using gateways supporting a TCP/IP interface. Microsoft TCP/IP supports the Windows Sockets 2.0 interface.

- Data Link Control (DLC). Windows 98 includes both a protected-mode DLC driver (Dlc.vxd), which supports 32-bit and 16-bit DLC applications, and a real-mode DLC driver (Msdlc.exe), which supports only 16-bit applications. It is used primarily to access IBM mainframe computers and Hewlett-Packard network-ready printers. Microsoft recommends that you use the protected-mode driver in most cases. However, some 16-bit DLC applications will work only with the real-mode DLC driver. For more information about applications that require the 16-bit DLC, see "Using 32-bit DLC for Connectivity" in Chapter 15, "Network Adapters and Protocols."

This section provides tips for using TCP/IP, terminal emulation applications, and gateways for connectivity.

For information about using Microsoft TCP/IP, Microsoft NetBEUI, the IPX/SPX-compatible protocol, and Microsoft DLC, see Chapter 15, "Network Adapters and Protocols."

Using TCP/IP for Host Connectivity

Many utilities and terminal emulation programs from other vendors allow direct communication with a mainframe or host computer using a TCP/IP protocol stack. The protected-mode version of Microsoft TCP/IP included with Windows 98 relies on the Windows Sockets version 1.1 or 2.0 interface. Any terminal emulation program or utility that you use to connect to a mainframe or host computer over Microsoft TCP/IP must support Windows Sockets 1.1 or 2.0. If the application does not support Windows Sockets 1.1 or 2.0, contact the application vendor to obtain a version that does; otherwise, do not use Microsoft TCP/IP.

If you want to connect to a host computer using Telnet or TCP/IP and you are running an application that emulates an IBM 3270 or 5250, or a DEC VT *xx* computer terminal, you can use Microsoft TCP/IP.

Some third-party TCP/IP stacks cannot be installed after Windows 98 Setup due to conflicts with Windows Sockets 2.0, which is installed with Microsoft TCP/IP. If you want to use a third-party TCP/IP stack with Windows 98, you should install it before running Windows 98 Setup. In almost all cases, this ensures that your third-party stack is successfully upgraded. If you do not do install the stack before running Setup, you can try restoring Windows Sockets 1.1, then installing the third-party TCP/IP stack. However, this method does not always work, and Microsoft does not support it. Also, if you restore Windows Sockets 1.1, you will not be able to use features, such as Quality of Service. For more information, see Chapter 15, "Network Adapters and Protocols."

▶ **To restore Windows Sockets 1.1**

1. In Control Panel, double-click Add/Remove Programs.

2. On the **Install/Uninstall** tab, click **Restore Winsock 1.1 Configuration**, and then click **Add/Remove**.

3. When asked whether you want to restore your original configuration, click **Yes**.

Note Microsoft does not support using 16-bit TCP/IP stacks.

If your emulation software requires a TSR to communicate with another vendor's TCP/IP protocol stack, you must remove the TSR and reconfigure the emulation software for Windows Sockets in order to communicate using Microsoft TCP/IP in Windows 98. To determine the proper configuration with Windows Sockets, see the documentation for the emulation software.

For more information about TCP/IP, see Chapter 15, "Network Adapters and Protocols."

Using Terminal Emulation Applications

Terminal emulation applications offer several different connectivity options for connecting to an IBM System 370/390-compatible mainframe host, IBM AS/400, or DEC VAX computer. This section describes configuration and other issues related to using terminal emulation programs.

Connecting to a NetWare for SAA gateway. For most 32-bit terminal emulation applications, configuring Windows 98 with the Microsoft IPX/SPX-compatible protocol enables connectivity to a NetWare for SAA gateway or to any gateway supporting IPX/SPX connectivity. If you are using a token-ring network with source routing, use the Network option in Control Panel to make sure that Microsoft IPX/SPX-compatible protocol appears in the list of network components. In **Advanced** properties for the protocol, set the Source Routing property to a 16-entry cache size.

Connecting to a Windows NT SNA 2.0 or later server. Windows 3.*x* client software supports connectivity to a Windows NT SNA 2.0 or 2.1 server. The Windows NT 32-bit client for SNA should not be used; it was designed to work only with client computers running Windows NT Workstation.

Connecting to an IBM AS/400 with IBM PC Support software. You can use Windows 98 to connect to an AS/400 using the IBM PC Support software. To do so, configure the PC Support application for Basic Mode; do not use Extended Mode. If the PC Support application was configured to connect using DLC, make sure that Microsoft DLC or IBM Lan Support is already installed on the computer.

You can also use Windows 98 to connect to an AS/400 using the NetWare for SAA gateway and the IBM PC Support application. Configure the PC Support application for Basic Mode; do not use Extended Mode. The IBM-supplied Dos16m.386 file is not compatible with Windows 98.

If Windows 98 is configured to use the IPX/SPX-compatible protocol, then you must create a Winstart.bat batch file in the \Windows directory and add entries in this file to run Pcswin.com and Strnrtr.exe (the Novell-compatible router). If you encounter problems using the protected-mode IPX/SPX-compatible transport with the Novell-compatible PC Support router, then configure Windows 98 to use the Novell-supplied NETX or VLM client with IPXODI, as described in "Configuring Network Adapter Drivers for Real-Mode Novell Clients" earlier in this chapter.

For information about using TCP/IP with IBM 3270 terminal emulation, see "Using TCP/IP for Host Connectivity" earlier in this chapter.

Using Gateways for Connectivity

When your network uses a gateway to communicate with a host computer, the client computer running Windows 98 communicates with the gateway computer just as it does with any other computer on the network. The gateway computer translates requests from the client into a form that can be understood by the host, then communicates with the host, and returns the information to the client. In this configuration, the client computer can connect to the gateway using any protocol that the gateway supports. The gateway uses some form of the DLC protocol to communicate with the host.

Table 17.23 shows commonly used gateways and the supported operating systems.

Table 17.23   Commonly used gateways and supported operating systems

Gateway	Operating system
Microsoft SNA Server 2.0 or later	Microsoft Windows NT 3.*x* and later
NetWare for SAA	Novell NetWare server 3.*x* and 4.*x*
Attachmate Gateway 4.0 or later	MS-DOS Microsoft Windows NT 3.*x* and later
Attachmate IRMALAN SNA Gateway	MS-DOS

Many of the gateways in the preceding table have MS-DOS versions, which run only under MS-DOS, not under Windows. Windows 98 does not support running the MS-DOS-based gateways in a VM. For information about support for a particular gateway under Windows 98, contact your gateway vendor.

Troubleshooting Windows 98 on Third-Party Networks

This section presents troubleshooting tips for some common problems that might occur when using Windows 98 on third-party networks.

As a general troubleshooting step, you should upgrade to 32-bit clients whenever possible. You should also apply all the latest patches for your network software.

For information about general troubleshooting issues, see Chapter 27, "General Troubleshooting."

Important   For the most current information about problems that might occur, consult the Relnotes.doc and Network.txt files included with Windows 98.

For more troubleshooting tips related to system logon and browsing on NetWare networks, and for information about File and Printer Services for NetWare Networks, see Chapter 18, "Logon, Browsing, and Resource Sharing."

Correcting Problems with Client for NetWare Networks

This section discusses some common problems that might occur while installing, configuring, or using Microsoft Client for NetWare Networks.

As a general troubleshooting step, make sure that the Netware.drv has a size of about 2 KB. If it is much larger, remove Client for NetWare Networks in the Network option in Control Panel, and then reinstall it.

Microsoft Service for NetWare Directory Services Installation over Novell Client for Windows 95/98 fails.

If you install Novell Client for Windows 95/98, the Novell setup program removes and renames the setup files Netdef.inf and Nwnds.dll, making it impossible to install Microsoft Service for NetWare Directory Services later. Follow the procedure outlined below to install Microsoft Service for NetWare Directory Services over Novell Client for Windows 95/98.

▶ **To install Service for NetWare Directory Services after installing Novell Client for Windows 95/98**

1. In Control Panel, examine the list of installed components.

2. If present, remove the Novell Client for Windows 95/98 and all instances of the IPX 32-bit Protocol for the Novell Client for Windows 95/98, and then click **OK**. Windows 98 deletes Novell Client for Windows 95/98.

3. When prompted to reboot, do so.

4. Insert your original Windows 98 installation media.

5. Extract the files Netdef.inf and Nwnds.dll by using System File Checker. For information about System File Checker, see "Using System File Checker," in Chapter 27, "General Troubleshooting."

6. Reboot your computer.

7. Install Service for NetWare Directory Services by following the procedure in the section "Setting Up Microsoft Service for NetWare Directory Services" earlier in this chapter.

For more information, see Knowledge Base article Q150925: "How to Uninstall Novell's 32-bit Client."

Upgrade from NETX to Client for NetWare Networks fails.

If you upgrade from NETX to Client for NetWare Networks without first logging on to a NetWare server, the Client for NetWare Networks installation might fail. Microsoft does not support upgrading over NETX before first logging on using Autoexec.bat (or a batch file called by Autoexec.bat). If your installation does fail, you can try one of the following fixes:

- Change the frame type in the IPX/SPX-compatible protocol from **Auto** to the frame type in use on your network.
- Verify that the correct preferred server is listed.

No network is available after Windows 98 starts.

Use the Network option in Control Panel to view a list of installed clients, protocols, and services. Verify that Client for NetWare Networks is installed and that the IPX/SPX-compatible protocol is in the list of installed components.

The login script does not run.

Make sure the correct preferred server is set and that **Enable logon script processing** is checked in the properties for Client for NetWare Networks.

Passwords do not work in NetWare 4.1 environment.

In a NetWare 4.1 environment, Microsoft Client for NetWare does not support passwords that use certain lowercase extended characters. Users must change their passwords to use all uppercase characters.

Cannot disable default password in Policy Editor.

Microsoft Service for NetWare Directory Services uses the Windows 98 logon password as the master password for both the bindery and the NDS tree logon attempts. You cannot disable this feature in Policy Editor. Instead, you must modify the **DisableDefaultPassword** registry entry with a value of **1** in the following registry location:

**HKEY_LOCAL_MACHINE\System
    \CurrentControlSet\Services\NWNP32\NetworkProvider**

You are asked for a Windows 98 password and a NetWare password at each logon.

Client for NetWare Networks might ask you for a Windows 98 password after you log on to the network. This can happen if the user name and password for your NetWare preferred server differs from your Windows 98 password, because in some cases the password is not stored in the cache. You can solve this problem in either of two ways:

- You can make the passwords the same for both the NetWare preferred server and Windows 98.
- You can save the password in the cache by using "attach as" from the server's context menu.

NetWare servers cannot be found.

You might not be able to see NetWare servers if you are using an incorrect frame type for the servers. To ensure that you are using the correct frame type for the server, verify the frame type set in the **Advanced** properties for the IPX/SPX-compatible protocol in the Network option in Control Panel. You can switch the setting from **Auto** to the specific frame type used on the server.

Client for NetWare Networks supports NetWare 4.*x* bindery emulation. Be sure that the bindery context you set for your NetWare server directory includes the Windows 98 users who should have access to the servers. To view and set your bindery context on NetWare 4.*x* servers, load the SERVMAN NetWare Loadable Module (NLM) and then view and set the SET BINDERY CONTEXT parameter. Or, you can type **set** at the command prompt to view the miscellaneous SET parameters. For more information, see your NetWare 4.*x* server documentation. Client for NetWare Networks also supports NDS, if you are running Service for NetWare Directory Services. Be sure that you have specified the correct context for your NetWare 4.*x* servers. Also, be sure that you have set your preferred server to be a 4.*x* server in the NDS tree you are logging onto.

Access to NetWare servers is denied.

By default, Client for NetWare Networks uses the credentials provided for preferred server authentication to access other NetWare servers. To see files on NetWare servers for which you have access, synchronize your credentials on all the NetWare servers, using the Novell SETPASS command at the command prompt.

You cannot map drive to SYS volume in login script with Microsoft Service for NetWare Directory Services.

With Microsoft Service for NetWare Directory Services, if you are using a login script to map a drive to a SYS volume, the drive might not map correctly. You must edit your login script. Replace the following text

```
map n server\sys:
```

with

```
#MAP N server\sys
```

Cannot open Nwadmn3x.exe using Microsoft Service for NetWare Directory Services.

If you are using Microsoft Service for NetWare Directory Services and you try to open Nwadmn3x.exe, you will see the error message "This program has performed an illegal operation and will be shut down." To work around this problem, you should instead use Nwadmin.exe, the version of NetWare Administrator that gives you access to the NDS tree.

▶ **To install Nwadmin.exe**

1. Install version 4.10.2 or later of Nwadmin.exe on the NetWare server. For information about how to install Nwadmin.exe, contact Novell.

2. Make sure that you have the required DLL files on the public folder from which you are running Nwadmin.exe. These DLL files are supplied by Novell.

3. Make sure that the Netware.drv file you are using is the one included with Microsoft Service for NetWare Directory Services.

4. Make sure that you have the latest DLL files from Nwdll2.exe in your Windows\System folder. Nwdll2.exe is supplied by Novell.

For more information, see Knowledge Base article Q124712.

You cannot access NDS drives after making dial-up connection.

With Microsoft Service for NetWare Directory Services, you might not be able to access NDS drives from Windows Explorer after making a dial-up connection. To solve this problem, you can either connect to the drives using Network Neighborhood or modify your Dial-Up Networking connection.

▶ **To modify your Dial-Up Networking connection**

1. From the **Start** menu, point to **Programs**, point to **Accessories**, and then click **Dial-Up Networking**.

2. In the Dial-Up Networking folder, right-click the connection.

3. Click the **Server Type** tab.

4. Clear the **Log on to Network** box.

Note Clearing the **Log on to Network** box on a Dial-Up Networking connection will prevent you from logging on to Windows NT and NetWare servers for that connection.

You experience problems opening files on NetWare 3.11 servers.

Programs that open a large number of files in rapid succession might not work properly on NetWare 3.11 servers. Also, you might have problems when opening a file in a folder for which you do not have file scan rights. To solve this, obtain the file Os2opnfx.nlm from Novell.

Passwords do not function in NetWare 4.1 environment.

If users have problems logging on to NetWare 4.1 servers, check that their passwords use only uppercase characters. Microsoft Client for NetWare does not support passwords that use certain lowercase extended characters.

Cannot print to NDS printers.

If you install Microsoft Service for NetWare Directory Services and your NDS printers appear to be offline, remove and reinstall Service for NetWare Directory Services.

Experience problems with Packet Burst.

You may experience dropped connections, decreased performance, or file copy fails if you are connecting to NetWare 3.12 and 4.01 servers and packet burst is turned on. Novell provides a fix for this problem. To solve it, download the file Pburst.exe from the Novell Web site **http://www.novell.com/**.

Correcting Problems with Novell NetWare Clients

This section provides general troubleshooting steps for running a Novell-supplied client with Windows 98, then describes some common problems that might occur.

As a general troubleshooting step for Novell Client for Windows 95/98, try using NDIS drivers instead of ODI drivers, and make sure you are using the latest version of your ODI or NDIS driver.

As a general troubleshooting step for VLM, verify that your computer is not using the Netware.drv file version 3.10.96.201. One version of Netware.drv that is known to work is Netware.drv 3.03.94.280.

As a general troubleshooting step for NETX, verify that your computer is using the Netware.drv file 2.02 or later.

If necessary, restore this file from the Novell-supplied installation source. The following list provides other general troubleshooting steps.

- Check the version numbers of all Novell-supplied NetWare workstation shell components, including IPX, NETX, VLM, LSL, IPXODI, and the ODI driver files. Make sure the latest versions are being used.

  To get the version number for the Novell-supplied software you are using, run *driver_name* **i** or *driver_name* **?** at the command prompt. For example, type **netx i** to get the version number for the Novell-supplied Net*.com or Net*.exe file.

  If you are not using the latest software, upgrade as described in "Obtaining Current Novell-Supplied Files" earlier in this chapter.

- Check for multiple instances of the NetWare files, specifically the ODI driver and Net.cfg. If there are multiple instances, remove all but the most recent version.

- Verify that IPXODI is binding to the network adapter by running the NetWare NVER utility, using the same settings as Net.cfg and the same [**link driver** *ODI_driver*] name. If IPXODI is not bound to the network adapter, change the entries in Net.cfg to correct this problem.

The following section describes common problems that might occur.

You see Hardware Troubleshooting Agent with ODI drivers.

With versions of Novell Client for Windows 95/98 2.2 and earlier, if you upgrade Windows 98 over a Novell-provided 32-bit ODI driver, you might see the Hardware Troubleshooting Agent every other boot. Novell has solved this problem with an ODI update pack available from **http://www.novell.com/**. For more information, contact Novell.

Network adapter drivers will not load with Novell Client for Windows 95/98.

TSRs that need to be loaded after a network connection is established or after IPX loads should be loaded from the Winstart.bat file. Otherwise, they will not load. If they fail to load, load the TSRs from the Winstart.bat file. If the file does not already exist, you can create it in the subfolder where Windows 98 is installed.

Novell Client for Windows 95/98 installation fails.

If the Novell Client for Windows 95/98 installation fails, make sure that all installation files have been placed in folders that conform to the standard MS-DOS 11-character (8.3) naming convention.

NetWare 4.11 server is missing DLL files needed for Nwadmn3x.exe.

You might have trouble opening Nwadmn3x.exe when you are using the Novell Client for Windows 95/98. You can solve this problem by in two different ways:

- Run Install.nlm on the server and selecting the option that lets you install the legacy NWADMIN utility. This installs Nwadmin.exe on the server, which works as documented by Novell. Contact Novell for technical support for this procedure.

- Use Nwunpack to expand the DLL files to a location in your MS-DOS path, such as a NetWare search drive or the \Windows\System directory. Do no overwrite existing DLL files. This procedure is not supported by Microsoft.

Setup requires Novell Workstation Shell Installation Program.

If, during installation, Setup fails to load Novell drivers and displays a message that it requires the Novell Workstation Shell Install Program for installing the VLM network client with Windows 98, follow the instructions presented in "Technical Notes on Novell's VLM" earlier in this chapter.

You cannot attach to the NetWare file server after installing Windows 98.

Verify the frame type being used by the NetWare server. If the NetWare server is using a different frame type from the one configured for the computer running Windows 98, the user cannot see the server. The Novell-supplied IPXODI protocol binds only to the first logical board, which is the first frame type in the **link driver** *ODI_driver* section in Net.cfg.

To correct this problem, manually edit Net.cfg so that the correct frame type is first in the **link driver** *ODI_driver* section.

You cannot see other computers running Windows 98 or NetWare servers.

- Determine which frame type is used at your site, and then verify that the correct frame type you want to use on the network is listed in Net.cfg. The frame type that IPXODI will use must be first or must be set explicitly.

- Verify that the correct Net.cfg is being processed by Lsl.com. To do this, check the local drive for other Net.cfg files. There should be only one, and it should be in the same directory as the NetWare driver files. If you are loading these files from Autoexec.bat or another batch file, modify the batch file to change to this directory, run the necessary ODI drivers, and change back to the directory you want. This ensures that the current directory is the same as the location of the Lsl.com file when it is being loaded.

- Verify that Net.cfg contains the correct settings for the network adapter. If necessary, restore this file from a correct backup version, or edit it to include correct settings.

- Verify that you are running the latest version of the Novell-supplied ODI drivers and support files. Check with your network adapter manufacturer to determine whether a newer ODI driver is available.

- Verify that both client computers are running the same protocols. If the client computers are on different sides of a router, make sure that an IPX/SPX-compatible protocol is being used on both computers.

You cannot access the logon drive after installing Windows 98.

A common misconception is that users must log on to their NetWare server using the drive letter F. However, this is not true. For a client computer using the NETX workstation shell, the NetWare logon drive is the next drive letter available after the **LastDrive=** statement in Config.sys.

You can alter the **LastDrive=** statement to change the logon drive, but you must leave enough drives before the **LastDrive=** that Windows 98 can use for its own connections.

You see an error message after you install VLM support under Windows 98.

If a message says that the system cannot find a device file needed to run Windows, make sure that the VLM client has been installed using the Network option in Control Panel. To do so, double-click the Network option after running Setup. This step ensures that the correct VLM information is placed in System.ini.

The Windows directory contains Nwsysvol\Login\login.???.

This stub file is installed with File and Printer Sharing for NetWare Networks to prevent the computer from incorrectly responding as the preferred server for other NetWare clients.

You cannot connect to the network using TCP/IP when ODI drivers are installed.

If you are using a Novell NetWare ODI driver and you can use the Ping tool to ping your own computer, but you cannot access the network using TCP/IP, check to make sure that the Ethernet_II frame type is listed properly in Net.cfg. If not, add it.

▶ **To add the Ethernet_II frame type to Net.cfg**

1. Use any text editor (such as WordPad) to open the Net.cfg file.

   Note Make sure you edit the correct Net.cfg file. It is usually read from the same directory as Lsl.com.

2. Add **Ethernet_II** so that it is the last frame type listed in the LINK DRIVER *<MLID>* section.

3. Save and close the Net.cfg file.

4. Restart your computer.

Correcting Problems with Artisoft LANtastic

This section lists problems you might experience while using Artisoft LANtastic. As a general troubleshooting step, if you are using the 16-bit version, you should upgrade to the 32-bit version. This will solve most problems.

For the most current troubleshooting steps, see Relnotes.doc and Network.txt.

Installing Windows 98 disables LANtastic Internet Gateway Client.

If installing Windows 98 disables the LANtastic Internet Gateway Client, remove and reinstall LANtastic using LANtastic's setup utility.

Caution Do not uninstall LANtastic using Add/Remove Programs in Control Panel if you think you might reinstall LANtastic later. If you uninstall LANtastic using Add/Remove Programs, you will lose your user and resource settings.

You see a LANtastic Modemshare error during Windows 98 upgrade.

If you have LANtastic 7.0 installed on your Windows 95 computer and you upgrade to Windows 98, you might see a Modemshare error message stating that the modem is not responding. Press a key, and Setup continues normally. When Setup is finished, LANtastic Modemshare will work properly.

You cannot access files on LANtastic servers.

If LANtastic 7.0 uses your computer name for its file and printer sharing capabilities, you might have problems accessing files on the system if you also have File and Print Sharing for Microsoft Networks installed. To solve this problem, you can either change the name that LANtastic 7.0 uses for its server in the LANtastic Custom Control Panel, or change your computer name in the Network option in Control Panel.

You cannot see servers with LANtastic 7.0.

You may have problems seeing other computers on the network. If so, disable Multicast using the following procedure:

▶ **To disable Multicast**

1. In Control Panel, double-click Network.

2. Double-click the **Artisoft LANtastic NetBIOS** protocol and then click the **Advanced** tab.

3. In the **Property** field select **Multicast,** and in the **Value** field select **Off,** and then click **OK**.

You must restart your computer for the changes to take effect.

Drives mapped to LANtastic shares appear without names.

When you map a drive to a LANtastic share, the drive name does not appear anywhere in the LANtastic or Windows graphical user interface. However, you can still use the mapped drive as you usually would.

You cannot disconnect mapped drives from within LANtastic utility.

If you map a drive to a LANtastic share, you will not be able to disconnect that mapped drive using LANtastic's Custom Control Panel utilities. You can still disconnect mapped drives using the Windows 98 user interface, by right-clicking the mapped drive in My Computer and selecting **Disconnect**.

You cannot print to a LANtastic network printer.

If you are using LANtastic 7.0 and you cannot print to a LANtastic network printer, you might need to change the properties for the network printer.

▶ **To change the printer's properties**

1. In the Printers folder, right-click the printer's icon, and then select **Properties** from the context menu.

2. In the printer's properties, click the **Details** tab.

3. Examine the printer's name in the **Print to the following port:** box.

4. If the name uses a syntax similar to the following:

```
Port: \\Server\Share
```

change that syntax to the following:

```
\\Server\Share
```

Correcting Problems with Other Third-Party Networks

This section lists problems you might experience while using a third-party network client. As a general troubleshooting step, if you are using a 16-bit client, you should upgrade to a 32-bit client. This will solve most problems.

For the most current troubleshooting steps, see Relnotes.doc and Network.txt.

You see a "Reinstall Windows" error message while installing 16-bit Banyan VINES client, or Windows constantly restarts.

If you are installing Windows 98 and the setup program is interrupted, you might see the error message "Cannot connect to Z:\Wnewrev.exe, you must reinstall Windows." During the installation program for the Banyan VINES 16-bit client, you might also encounter an error in which Windows 98 constantly restarts. If this happens you will need to edit your System.ini file.

▶ **To edit your System.ini file**

1. Reboot your computer.

2. During startup, press the left CTRL key until the Microsoft Windows 98 Startup Menu message appears.

3. Select **Safe mode command prompt only**.

4. Open System.ini and change the entry **Shell=Z:\Wnewrev.exe** to read **Shell=Explorer.exe**.

5. Reboot the computer.

You see an error message asking you to run Newrev.

If you are installing the 16-bit Banyan VINES client and you do not install the latest version, you will see an error message stating that you are not running the latest VINES version and that you need to run Newrev. If this happens, type the following line from the Banyan subdirectory:

```
Newrev /I
```

This command copies the latest Banyan files to your local drive.

You cannot install Banyan VINES 16-bit Client with Msbatch.inf.

Windows 98 does not support the following lines in Msbatch.inf setup files:

```
Clients=vines552
Protocols=ndisban, ndistok
```

If you wish to install support for Banyan VINES networking, you must do so after Windows 98 setup is complete.

You cannot map a drive using Banyan VINES 16-bit client.

If you lose graphical user interface functionality for the Banyan VINES 16-bit client (for example, if you can no longer map a drive from within Windows 98 or view a previously mapped Banyan VINES drive), your path might be lost or corrupt. You must have Z:\ set to the end of their path. You can either do so from Autoexec.bat or ask a VINES administrator to place the path in the VINES login script.

You lose Windows functionality after overwriting Ver.dll during Banyan VINES 16-bit installation program.

The installation program for the Banyan VINES 16-bit client prompts you to overwrite the file Ver.dll. If you do so, you will lose Windows functionality such as printing or using the Control Panel. To restore Windows functionality, manually extract Ver.dll from your original installation media and add it to your \Windows and \Windows\System directories. For information about how to manually extract files, see Knowledge Base Article Q129605, "How to Extract Original Compressed Windows Files."

Third party TCP/IP stack does not work with Windows Sockets 2.

Many third-party TCP/IP stacks, such as FTP Software's OnNet32 TCP/IP stack, do not support Windows Sockets 2. If you want to use one of these stacks with Windows 98, you should install the TCP/IP stack before installing Windows 98. In some cases, you can also remove Windows Sockets 2 after upgrading to Windows 98, then install the third-party stack. However, this second method does not always work.

Note that if you install the third-party TCP/IP stack before installing Windows 98, Windows Sockets 2 will not be installed. For information about removing Windows Sockets 2, see Chapter 5, "Setup Technical Discussion."

Samba server does not accept your password.

For security reasons, Windows 98 no longer allows you to send plain text passwords. It sends only encrypted passwords. However, Samba servers require plain text passwords, so you will not be able to connect to Samba servers unless you change a registry entry to enable plain text passwords.

Caution Enabling plain text passwords will decrease your computer's security.

To enable plain-text passwords, add the registry entry EnablePlainTextPassword (as a Dword) and set the value to **1** in the following registry location:

**HKEY_LOCAL_MACHINE\System
  \CurrentControlSet\Services\VxD\Vnetsup**

Additional Resources

For more information about	See this resource
Any third-party networking product	Your network vendor's documentation
Artisoft products	**http://www.artisoft.com/**
Banyan products	**http://www.banyan.com/**
Digital Equipment Corporation (DEC) products	**http://www.digital.com/**
IBM products	**http://www.ibm.com/**
Novell products	**http://www.novell.com/**
Microsoft products	**http://www.microsoft.com/**
Sun products	**http://www.sun.com/**

CHAPTER 18

Logon, Browsing, and Resource Sharing

18

This chapter describes how to configure and use the logon, network browsing, and peer resource sharing capabilities of Microsoft Windows 98. It is intended for advanced users and network administrators who need to know how to configure and use logon, browsing, and resource sharing.

In This Chapter

See Also

- For more information about installing and using Client for Microsoft Networks, see Chapter 16, "Windows 98 on Microsoft Networks."

- For more information about other networking clients, see Chapter 17, "Windows 98 on Third-Party Networks."

- For more information about system policies, see Chapter 8, "System Policies."

- For more information about security, see Chapter 9, "Security."

Overview of Logon, Browsing, and Peer Resource Sharing

This section summarizes key Windows 98 features that you can use to make network logon, resource browsing, and peer resource sharing easier and more secure for computers running Windows 98 on your network.

Unified System Logon Overview

Windows 98 offers a consistent user interface for logging on to and validating access to network resources. The first time the user logs on to Windows 98, logon dialog boxes appear for each network client on that computer and for Windows 98. For a Windows 95 upgrade, your Primary Network Logon setting and all Windows 95 password caching settings remain the same; therefore, you might not see a logon box for each client and for Windows 98 depending on how you have configured your computer.

Windows 98 includes the following features that enable you to see only one logon prompt (or no logon prompts) when you log on:

- Unified system logon
- Password caching

For more information about these features, see "Understanding System Logon," later in this chapter.

For Novell NetWare networks, Windows 98 provides graphical logon to Novell NetWare version 3.x, or version 4.x if the network is configured for bindery emulation or if your computer is running Microsoft Service for NetWare Directory Services. Windows 98 also provides a NetWare-compatible Login Script Processor. This means that if you are using Microsoft Client for NetWare Networks, Windows 98 can process NetWare login scripts.

For Microsoft networks, Windows 98 supports network logon using domain user accounts and logon script processing (as supported by Windows NT and LAN Manager version 2.x).

The Windows 98 logon processor can parse most statements in the NetWare login scripts. However, any statements loading terminate-and-stay-resident (TSR) programs must be removed from the scripts and loaded from Autoexec.bat. Because the Windows 98 logon processor operates in protected mode, it is not possible to load TSRs for global use from the login script. These TSRs should be loaded from Autoexec.bat before protected-mode operation begins, or you can use other methods described in "Using Logon Scripts" later in this chapter.

In some cases, logon scripts load backup agents as TSRs. In such cases, you can use protected-mode equivalents compatible with Windows 98, making it unnecessary to load these TSRs.

Network Browsing Overview

Network Neighborhood is the central point for browsing in Windows 98. It offers the following benefits:

- Users can browse the network as easily as browsing the local hard disk.

- Users can create shortcuts to network resources on the desktop and hard disk.

- Users can easily connect to network resources by using the **Map Network Drive** dialog box.

- Users can easily connect to network resources using universal naming convention (UNC) connections, which are described later in this section.

- Users can open files and complete other actions by using new common dialog boxes in applications. This standard provides a consistent way to open or save files on both network and local drives.

- The network administrator can customize Network Neighborhood by using system policies, as described in Chapter 8, "System Policies." A custom Network Neighborhood can include shortcuts to commonly used resources, including Dial-Up Networking resources.

In any situation in which you can type a path for connecting to a server—such as in the **Map Network Drive** dialog box or at the command prompt—you can specify the server name with two backslashes (\\) if your network uses UNC path names. For example, to connect to the server CORP, volume DOCS, directory WORD, and subdirectory Q1, type the UNC name **\\corp\docs\word\q1**.

Network browsing issues include the following:

- You can plan ahead to configure workgroups for effective browsing by using Wrkgrp.ini to control the workgroups that people can choose. For more information about configuring Wrkgrp.ini, see Chapter 3, "Custom Installations."

- If your enterprise network is based on Microsoft networking, is connected by a slow-link wide area network (WAN), and includes satellite offices running only Windows 98, users in the satellites cannot browse the central corporate network. Consequently, they can connect to computers outside their workgroups only by typing the computer name in a **Map Network Drive** dialog box. To provide full browsing capabilities, the satellite office must have a Windows NT Server.

Note   There is one exception: if one computer in the satellite office has a workgroup name that corresponds to the corporate network's domain name, users will be able to browse the central corporate network. For more information, see Knowledge Base article Q149941, "Windows Clients Not Able to Browse Remote Workgroups."

- You can use system policies, such as Hide Drives In My Computer or Hide Network Neighborhood, to limit or prevent browsing by users. For more information, see Chapter 8, "System Policies."

Peer Resource Sharing Overview

The two peer resource sharing services in Windows 98—Microsoft File and Printer Sharing for NetWare Networks and File and Printer Sharing for Microsoft Networks—are 32-bit, protected-mode networking components that allow users to share directories, printers, and CD-ROM drives on computers running Windows 98. File and printer sharing services work with existing servers to add complementary peer resource sharing services. These components are required for any computer whose name will appear in a browse list.

For example, using File and Printer Sharing for NetWare Networks produces the following benefits:

- Users can share files, printers, and CD-ROM drives without running two network clients. This saves memory, improves performance, and reduces the number of protocols running on your network.

- Security is user-based, not share-based. You can administer user accounts, passwords, and group lists from the NetWare server, because File and Printer Sharing for NetWare Networks uses the NetWare server's authentication database.

Note In the Windows 98 Resource Kit, NETX is used to refer to the Novell NetWare workstation shell for NetWare version 3.*x*; VLM (Virtual Loadable Module) is used to refer to the workstation shell for version 4.*x*.

- Users running VLM or NETX clients can access shared resources on computers running Windows 98. The computer running Windows 98 looks as if it were just another NetWare server if it uses Service Advertising Protocol (SAP) Advertising, as described in "Using File and Printer Sharing for NetWare Networks" later in this chapter. The computer providing file and printer sharing services can handle up to 250 concurrent connections.

- You can add secure storage space and printing to the network inexpensively, while using familiar NetWare tools to manage these resources. You can reduce the load and improve the performance of NetWare servers by moving selected shared resources to one or more computers running file and printer sharing services. This allows you to manage load balancing for users without adding a new NetWare server.

- You get a scalable, high-performance 32-bit peer server that uses multiple 32-bit threads, the Windows 98 Virtual File Allocation Table (VFAT) 32-bit file system, 32-bit network driver interface specification (NDIS) drivers, a 32-bit Internet Packet Exchange/Sequenced Packet Exchange (IPX/SPX)–compatible protocol, and the Packet Burst protocol.

Similar benefits are available when you use File and Printer Sharing for Microsoft Networks. You can also use either share-level security or, on a Windows NT network, user-level security to protect access to peer resources.

Resource sharing issues include the following:

- You can install only one file and printer sharing service at a time.

- If you want to configure a computer to share its files or printers, the choice of which file and printer sharing service you install depends on whether users who will be browsing for shared resources are running Microsoft or NetWare network clients.

- If you want to use File and Printer Sharing for NetWare Networks, a NetWare server must be available on the network. This peer resource sharing service uses only user-level security, not share-level security, so a NetWare server must be available to validate user accounts. Also, the NetWare server must include a Windows_Passthru account (with no password) in its user accounts database.

- If you plan to use File and Printer Sharing for Microsoft Networks with user-level security, a Windows NT Server or domain must be available to validate user accounts.

- If you are configuring a user's workstation to act as a peer server, you might also want to specify that this computer cannot run MS-DOS-based applications that take exclusive control of the operating system, shutting down file and printer sharing services. To do this, you can set the system policy named **Disable Single-Mode MS-DOS Applications**.

Logging on to Windows 98

This section discusses how to configure logon for Windows 98 computers.

Understanding System Logon

There are two levels of system logon on Windows 98 computers:

- Log on to Windows 98 by using a user name and password.

  With Windows 95, you logged on to the computer using the Windows Logon. Windows 98 provides a new option called Microsoft Family Logon. If user profiles are enabled and Microsoft Family Logon has been configured, Microsoft Family Logon lists all users for that computer. For more information about the Microsoft Family Logon, see "Configuring Microsoft Family Logon" later in this chapter. For more information about user profiles, see Chapter 7, "User Profiles.

- Log on to a Windows NT domain, NetWare network, or another network for which you are using a 32-bit, protected-mode networking client.

Windows 98 provides a single unified logon prompt that allows the user to log on to all networks and Windows 98 at the same time. The first time a user starts Windows 98, there are separate logon prompts for each network, as well as one for Windows 98. If these passwords are made identical, the system logon prompt for Windows 98 is not displayed again.

Note The Passwords option in Control Panel provides a way to synchronize logon passwords for different networks so they can be made the same if one is changed. For more information, see Chapter 9, "Security."

Windows 98 also includes a related feature, called password caching. With password caching, when a user logs on to other networks with different passwords and chooses to save them, the passwords are stored in a password cache. Thereafter, the user sees only the Windows 98 logon prompt, or no prompt, even if the Windows 98 password is different from the password for the primary network client. You can enable password caching for a network client simply by selecting the check box for the **Save this password in your password list** option on the logon prompt for your network client (if the check box appears). You can also enable password caching later, by using the following procedure:

▶ **To set up password caching of network passwords**

1. In Control Panel, double-click Network.

2. In **Primary Network Logon**, select **Windows Logon**, and then click **OK**.

3. In Control Panel, double-click **Passwords**, click **Change Windows Password**, and then click **OK**.

4. Make your Windows password blank, and then click **OK** two times.

5. Restart your computer.

6. When asked for a password to log on to Windows 98, enter a password, and then press **OK**.

7. For each network prompt, enter your network password and make sure the check box for **Save this password in your password list** is selected.

Note This check box does not appear for Client for NetWare Networks unless you are using Service for NetWare Directory Services. Therefore, to use password caching with Client for NetWare Networks, you must install Service for NetWare Directory Services.

The next time you log on to Windows 98 using that password, Windows 98 uses the passwords stored in this cache to log the user on to other networks, you do not need to type any additional passwords.

You can also configure Windows 98 to perform an automatic or "silent" logon, by opening the user's password file with a blank password. To do so, follow the procedure above, but instead of entering a password in Step 5, simply click **OK**. On subsequent boots, you will not need to log on either to Windows 98 or to the network.

You might choose this configuration, for example, for peer servers that are physically secure from user access and that must be able to automatically recover from power outages or other failures without user intervention.

If you are concerned about users compromising network security by using automatic logon, you can disable this feature by using system policies. For more information, see Chapter 9, "Security."

The following procedures describe how to log on to Windows 98 and to Microsoft and NetWare networks.

▶ **To log on to Windows 98 when no network logon has been configured**

- When the **Welcome to Windows** dialog box appears, type the user name and password.

The following screen appears.

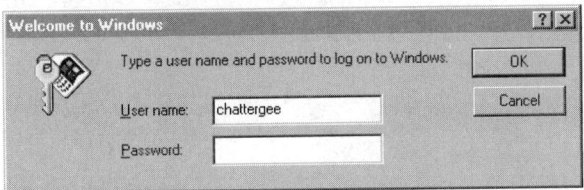

Windows 98 uses this logon information to identify the user and to find any user profile information. User profiles define user preferences, such as the fonts and colors used on the desktop, and access information. For more information on user profiles, see Chapter 7, "User Profiles."

▶ **To log on to Windows 98 on a Microsoft network for the first time**

1. When the **Enter Network Password** dialog box appears after starting Windows 98 for the first time, type the user name and password.

Note This dialog box appears without the **Domain** box unless your computer is configured to log on to a Windows NT domain. For information, see Chapter 16, "Windows 98 on Microsoft Networks."

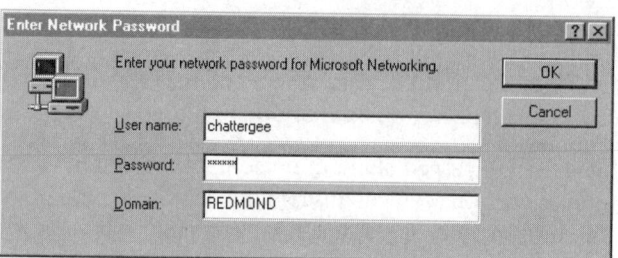

For network logon on a Microsoft network, type the name of the Windows NT domain, LAN Manager domain, or Windows NT computer that contains the related user account.

After the user name and password pair are validated by the network server, the user is allowed to use resources on the network. If the user is not validated, the user cannot gain access to network resources.

2. If you do not already have a Windows password for this computer or if your Windows password and network password are different the first time Windows 98 starts, the **Set Windows Password** dialog box appears, prompting you to type the user name and password defined for Windows 98.

▶ **To log on to Windows 98 on a NetWare network for the first time using Client for NetWare Networks**

1. The following dialog box appears if you are running Service for NetWare Directory Services (Microsoft's service for accessing Novell Directory Services):

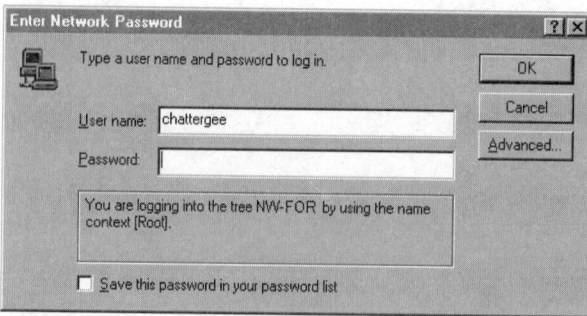

To log on, type your user name and password.

– Or –

If you are not running Service for NetWare Directory Services, the following dialog box appears instead:

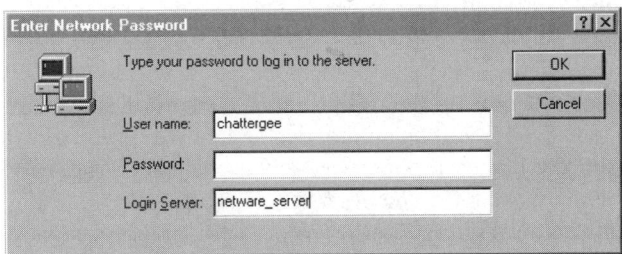

To log on to a NetWare network using Client for NetWare Networks, type your user name, password, and the name of the NetWare server, which is the preferred server where the related user account is stored.

2. If you are running Service for NetWare Directory Services, click the **Advanced** button and verify that the correct context and tree are selected.

   After the user name and password pair are validated by the NetWare server, the user can use resources on the network. If the user is not validated, the user will be prompted to type a password when connecting to a NetWare server during this work session.

3. If you do not already have a Windows password for this computer or if your Windows password and network password are different the first time Windows 98 starts, the **Set Windows Password** dialog box appears, prompting you to type the user name and password defined for Windows 98.

▶ **To log on to Microsoft or NetWare networks after the first time**

- The next time this computer is started, Windows 98 displays the name of the last user who logged on and the name of the domain or preferred server used for validation. If the same user is logging on again, only the password for the network server or domain needs to be entered. If a different user is logging on, that user's unique user name and password must be entered. If the passwords are the same for the network and Windows 98, the second dialog box for logging on to Windows 98 does not appear again.

Configuring Microsoft Family Logon

Microsoft Family Logon is a new feature that works in combination with user profiles to prevent any user from gaining access to your computer unless you have configured a user profile for that user. Before you can use or configure Microsoft Family Logon, you must enable user profiles. (For more information about enabling user profiles, see "User Profiles and Windows 98 Logon" later in this chapter.) Windows 98 includes a new way to enable user profiles: the Users option in Control Panel. If you enable user profiles with this option, Microsoft Family Logon will be automatically enabled. If you already have user profiles enabled on your computer, however, you can configure Microsoft Family Logon by using the Network option in Control Panel. This section describes both methods of configuring Microsoft Family Logon.

▶ **To enable user profiles with the Users option in Control Panel**

1. In Control Panel, double-click Users.

2. A wizard appears and asks you to enter a user name and password. After you do so, it automatically enables user profiles and installs the Microsoft Family Logon Client.

▶ **To configure Microsoft Family Logon if you have already enabled user profiles**

1. In Control Panel, double-click Network, and then click **Add**.

2. In the **Select Network Component Type** dialog box, select **Client**, and then click **Add**.

3. In the **Manufacturers** box, select **Microsoft**.

4. In the **Network Clients** box, select **Microsoft Family Logon**, and then click **OK**.

You must restart the computer for the changes to take effect. If you have selected a network logon as your primary logon, you will see only the **Enter Network Password** dialog box when you restart.

If you have selected the Microsoft Family Logon as your primary logon, and if user profiles have been enabled, the **Enter Password** dialog box appears:

If your Windows password and your network logon password have not been synchronized, you will also see the **Enter Network Password** dialog box.

Just as with Windows logon, if your user name and password for Microsoft Family Logon are the same as your user name and password for your network, you will not need to perform both a system logon and a network logon.

Configuring Network Logon

If you install either Client for Microsoft Networks or Client for NetWare Networks, you can configure a computer running Windows 98 to participate on a Windows NT or NetWare network.

Before you can access domain resources on a computer running Windows 98, however, you must have a Windows NT domain controller or NetWare server on the network that contains user account information for the Windows 98 user. (A Windows NT or NetWare server is not necessary for a peer-to-peer network.) For more information about setting up permissions on a Windows NT or NetWare server, see the administrator's documentation for the server. For related information, see Chapter 16, "Windows 98 on Microsoft Networks" and Chapter 17, "Windows 98 on Third-Party Networks."

The validation of a user's network password at system startup might not be required for accessing network resources later during that work session. However, the logon script can run only in one of two circumstances:

- During system startup.
- If your computer is configured to use Dial-Up Networking only, and there is no active network adapter installed that forces network components to load on system startup, a logon script can run after you connect to a network using Dial-Up Networking.

Because those are the only two cases in which logon scripts can be run if you are using a Microsoft-provided network client, they are the only times at which user profiles and system policies can be downloaded on the local computer. (However, profiles and policies are disabled by default over Dial-Up Networking connections and require special configuration to be enabled.) Therefore, proper network logon is extremely important.

The following sections provide information about configuring network logon for computers on Windows NT and NetWare networks when using a 32-bit, protected-mode network client. You can also use system policies to control network logon options, as summarized at the end of this section. For more information about enforcing logon password requirements, see Chapter 9, "Security."

Tip Logon validation controls only user access to network resources, not access to running Windows 98. To require validation by a network logon server before allowing access to Windows 98, you must use system policies. For information, see "Setting Network Logon Options with System Policies" later in this chapter.

Notice, however, that Windows 98 security cannot prevent a user from starting the computer by using Safe Mode or a floppy disk. If you require complete user validation before starting the computer in any way, use Windows NT as the sole operating system.

Configuring Logon for Client for Microsoft Networks

When the computer is configured to use Client for Microsoft Networks as the Primary Network Logon, you can specify Microsoft Windows NT logon options in the Network option in Control Panel. This section discusses these options.

If your network includes a Windows NT domain, you can configure your computer to automatically validate you on the specified domain during the logon process. If this option is not configured, you cannot access most network resources. If this option is configured and you do not provide a correct password, you will not have access to most network resources.

You can also specify whether you want to automatically establish a connection for each persistent connection to a network resource or verify whether to reestablish connections at system startup. You can also specify basic network logon options in custom setup scripts used to install Windows 98.

For complete procedures for configuring network logon and persistent connections for Client for Microsoft Networks, see Chapter 16, "Windows 98 on Microsoft Networks." For more information about defining network logon options in custom setup scripts, see Chapter 3, "Custom Installations." For more information about controlling network logon by using system policies, see Chapter 8, "System Policies."

Configuring Logon for NetWare Networks

Each Windows 98 user must have an account on the NetWare server before being able to use its files, applications, or print queues. The NetWare server account contains user credentials (a user name and password).

With Client for NetWare Networks, there is no real-mode logon before Windows 98 starts, just the single, unified logon prompt for Windows 98 that allows users to log on to the system and to all networks at the same time. The first time a user starts Windows 98, there are two separate logon prompts: one for Windows 98 and one for the NetWare preferred server. If the two passwords are the same, the second logon prompt for Windows 98 is not displayed again. If you are using password caching, only the Windows 98 dialog box is displayed.

Like Client for NetWare Networks, Novell Client for Windows 95/98 uses a protected-mode logon instead of a real-mode logon. However, unlike Client for NetWare Networks, Novell Client for Windows 95/98 does not cache passwords in a PWL file. Thus, you will see separate logon prompts unless you set Novell Client for Windows 95/98 as the Primary Network Logon.

If the computer uses a Novell-supplied real-mode network client, network logon occurs in real mode and uses all the NetWare configuration settings that were in place before Windows 98 was installed. There are no required changes. However, the logon prompt for Windows 98 always appears when these clients are used because the unified logon process is not available.

Passwords on Windows 98 and NetWare Servers

If you are using a protected-mode network client, maintaining the same user name and password for both Windows 98 and the NetWare network makes it easier for network administrators to coordinate user accounts. For more information about passwords, including brief information on changing passwords on a NetWare server, see Chapter 9, "Security."

To configure Client for NetWare Networks for network logon, you need to specify whether Client for NetWare Networks is the Primary Network Logon. If Client for NetWare Networks is the primary network logon, the following happens:

- System policies and user profiles are downloaded from NetWare servers, if you use these features.

- Users are prompted first to log on to a NetWare server for validation when Windows 98 starts (before being prompted to log on to any other networks).

- The last login script runs from a NetWare server.

Tip When you start Windows 98 with Client for NetWare Networks configured as the Primary Network Logon, Windows 98 automatically prompts you to provide logon information, such as your password on the NetWare server.

Therefore, you should never run the Novell-supplied Login.exe utility from a batch file or at the command prompt when you are using Client for NetWare Networks.

When you designate Client for NetWare Networks as the Primary Network Logon, you can also specify a preferred NetWare server. Windows 98 uses the preferred server to validate user logon credentials and to find user profiles and system policy files. You can change the preferred NetWare server at any time.

With Client for NetWare Networks, you can log on only to specific servers, not to the NDS tree. However, with Service for NetWare Directory Services, you can log on to either the NDS tree or to specific bindery-based servers. The following sections explain how to use Client for NetWare Networks and Service for NetWare Directory Services to log on to NetWare servers and to the NDS tree.

Configuring Client for NetWare Networks to Log on to a NetWare Network

The following procedure describes how to configure Client for NetWare Networks to log on to a NetWare network. If you use a NETX or VLM client, you can configure the setting for the preferred server using Net.cfg or using the **/ps** option (/ps=*server*) in Startnet.bat, Autoexec.bat, or wherever you start NETX or VLM. For more information, consult your Novell-supplied documentation.

Note In the Windows 98 Resource Kit, NETX is used to refer to the Novell NetWare workstation shell for NetWare version 3.*x*; VLM (Virtual Loadable Module) is used to refer to the workstation shell for version 4.*x*.

▶ **To use a NetWare server for network logon**

1. In Control Panel, double-click Network.

2. Select **Client for NetWare Networks** in the **Primary Network Logon** dialog box.

3. Double-click **Client for NetWare Networks** in the list of installed components.

4. In the **General** tab set values for the configuration options, as described in Table 18.1.

Table 18.1   Client for NetWare configuration options

Property	Meaning
Preferred Server	Designates the name of the NetWare server that appears automatically in the **Network Logon** dialog box. Windows 98 obtains the NetWare login script from this server, unless you specify a different NetWare server in the **Enter Network Password** dialog box. This is also the server used to store user profiles and system policies, if these are used on your network. The **Preferred Server** setting applies to the computer, not for individual users. If you are running Service for NetWare Directory Services, this setting will be used only if the preferred server is a 4.*x* server in the same NDS tree that you are logging on to. If you want to log on to a bindery-based server when running Service for NetWare Directory Services, follow the procedures outlined in "Configuring Microsoft Service for NetWare Directory Services to Log on to a NetWare Bindery Server" to log on to a NetWare bindery server.
First network drive	Specifies the first drive letter that you want assigned to the first NetWare network connection.
Enable login script processing	Specifies that this computer will process NetWare login scripts when a user logs on to the network.

If the preferred server has been specified, Client for NetWare Networks attempts to connect to the preferred server rather than the first server that responds to the Get Nearest Server broadcast. Client for NetWare Networks also attempts a number of server connections in case the client computer cannot establish a connection with the preferred server.

Configuring Microsoft Service for NetWare Directory Services to Log on to the NDS Tree

This section describes how to configure Service for NetWare Directory Services to log on to the NDS tree. For more information about Service for NetWare Directory Services and how to install it, see Chapter 17, "Windows 98 on Third-Party Networks."

To log on to an NDS tree, you must select a default context and a preferred NDS tree. The default context determines what the user will be able to see and use in Network Neighborhood. You can also configure a preferred server by following the procedure in "Configuring Client for NetWare Networks to Log on to a NetWare Network," earlier in this chapter. For more information about configuring the default context and directory tree, see Help.

The logon context is the context where your user object is located. In many cases, a user's default context and logon context will be the same, so he or she can log on without using a full or partial distinguished name.

Depending on how your directory tree is set up, a user who travels to other locations in your organization (such as other people's offices or other sites) may need to log on from a different context from the one that contains his or her user object. You may want to encourage such users to type their full distinguished name when they log on. They may also need to change the context they are logging on to. For information on changing the logon context, see Chapter 17, "Windows 98 on Third-Party Networks."

Note When a user logs on using a different logon context than the computer's default context, the current context does not switch to the user's logon context, but the container script from the user's logon context is run. For example, suppose Ann has a user object in the APPS container object. She logs on to a machine whose default context is set to MARKETING, using the full distinguished name .CN=ANN.O=APPS. Even though her logon context is APPS, the current context stays in MARKETING, but the APPS container login script is run.

Logging on to a NetWare Bindery Server using Microsoft Service for NetWare Directory Services

If you want to log on to a bindery server instead of to an NDS directory tree, you can do so at system startup.

▶ **To log on to a bindery server**

1. Restart your computer

2. In the **Enter Network Password** dialog box, enter your name and password and then click the **Advanced** tab.

3. Click **Log in to a bindery server**.

4. Select a bindery server, and then click **OK**, and then click **OK** again.

Configuring Novell Client for Windows 95/98 to Authenticate to NDS Trees and Servers

You are first prompted to authenticate to an NDS tree when you log on to Windows 98. However, you can also authenticate to other NDS trees or NetWare servers during the same session, so you can be authenticated to more than one NDS tree at once.

▶ **To authenticate to NDS Trees and NetWare servers**

1. Right-click the server or tree you want to attach to.

2. In the context-sensitive menu, click **Authenticate**.

3. If prompted, specify your user name and password for the tree or server you are authenticating to.

▶ **To view the trees and servers you are authenticated to**

- Right-click Network Neighborhood, and then click **NetWare Connections**.

▶ **To view a specific connection**

1. From Network Neighborhood, right-click a server or tree.
2. In the context-sensitive menu, click **WhoAmI.**

Setting Network Logon Options with System Policies

The network administrator can define system policies to enforce requirements for network logon. For example, you may want to make sure that users cannot access the local computer without network validation, or you may want to disable password caching.

Note System policies are not installed on Windows 98 by default. For more information, see Chapter 8, "System Policies."

For network logon in general, use the following policies:

- Logon Banner, to specify a caption and other text, such as a legal notice, to be displayed before the logon dialog box appears.

- Require Validation By Network For Windows Access, to specify that each logon must be validated by a server before access to Windows is allowed.

For Client for Microsoft Networks, use the following policies:

- Log On To Windows NT, to specify that this computer can participate in a Windows NT domain.

- Display Domain Logon Validation, to display a message when the domain controller has validated user logon.

- Disable Caching of Domain Password, to specify that no caching is used for the network password. However, do not enable the Quick Logon features when password caching has been disabled using system policies. The Quick Logon feature requires password caching to function properly.

For Microsoft Client for NetWare Networks, use the following policy:

- Disable Automatic NetWare Logon, to specify that when Windows 98 attempts to connect to a NetWare server, it does not automatically try to use the user's network logon name and password and the Windows logon password to make the connection.

For Microsoft Service for NetWare Directory Services, use the following policies:

- Preferred Tree, to specify the preferred NDS tree.
- Default Name Context, to specify the default context.

For more information about these policies and others that enforce password requirements, see Chapter 8, "System Policies."

If a computer has the Microsoft Remote Registry agent installed, you can use System Policy Editor to remotely set network logon options on individual computers without using system policies. This is useful in cases in which you have not previously enforced logon requirements using system policies but you want to make sure that network logon is configured properly on a specific computer.

Using Logon Scripts

This section summarizes some information about using logon scripts on Windows NT and NetWare networks. For details about using logon scripts for a push installation of Windows 98, see Chapter 4, "Automated Installations."

Using Logon Scripts with Microsoft Networking

This section summarizes how to use logon scripts for Windows 98 on Windows NT networks.

Logon scripts are batch files or executable files that run automatically when a user logs on to a computer running either Windows NT, Windows 98, or MS-DOS. Logon scripts are often used to configure users' working environments by making network connections and starting applications.

There are several reasons that you might want to use logon scripts:

- You want to manage part of the user environment (such as network connections) without managing or dictating the entire environment.
- You want to create common network connections for multiple users.

To assign a user a logon script, designate the path name of the logon script file in the user's account on the server. Then, whenever that user logs on, the logon script is downloaded and run. You can assign a different logon script to each user or create logon scripts for multiple users.

To create a batch-file logon script, create an MS-DOS batch file. (For more information about creating batch files, see your MS-DOS documentation.)

A logon script is always downloaded from the server that validates a user's logon request. For users with accounts on Windows NT server domains that have one or more backup domain controllers and a primary domain controller, any one of the domain controllers can authorize a user's logon attempt. To ensure that logon scripts always work for users, you should be sure that logon scripts for all user accounts in a domain exist on every primary and backup domain controller in the domain. You can do this by using the Windows NT Replicator service.

Home directories on Windows NT networks are used to store user profiles and can also serve as private storage spaces for users. To ensure access to user profiles, you should assign each user a home directory on a server. You can also assign users home directories on their own workstations (although this means that users will not have access to their user profiles from other computers).

Using the Windows Scripting Host to Run Logon Scripts

The Windows Scripting Host is a tool that allows you to run scripts natively on Windows 95, Windows 98, or Windows NT version 4.0 or later. If you are a network administrator and you want to run a logon script on Windows NT Server 4.0 or later, you can write that script using the Microsoft Visual Basic Scripting Edition or the Microsoft JScript scripting engine, then run it using the Windows Scripting Host. The Windows Scripting Host supports several features commonly used in logon scripts, such as mapping drives and printers and managing your users' environments, so it can help you automate routine logon tasks.

For more information about the Windows Scripting Host, see Chapter 23, "System and Remote Administration Tools." See also **http://www.microsoft.com/management/scrpthost.htm**.

Using Login Scripts on NetWare Networks

NetWare clients that support NDS use the NDS login script when connecting to NDS. When connecting in bindery mode, they use the bindery login script. Bindery clients always use the bindery script.

Login scripts are stored differently on NetWare 3.x servers using bindery services than on NetWare 4.x servers using NDS. On a bindery server, the system login script is stored in the Net$log.dat file in the \Public directory, and individual user login scripts are stored in the Login file in Mail subdirectories that correspond to the users' internal IDs. On an NDS server, the Container, Profile, and User login scripts are stored in the NDS database as properties of those objects.

The network administrator can use SYSCON for NetWare 3.*x* bindery-based servers or NETADMIN or NWADMIN for 4.*x* servers to edit login scripts for any NetWare-compatible client running under Windows 98.

The issues related to running login scripts depend on whether the computer is configured with Client for NetWare Networks or uses a Novell-supplied network client.

Running Login Scripts with Client for NetWare Networks

If the computer is running Client for NetWare Networks, the special Windows 98 Login Script Processor runs the login script after the user completes entries in the network logon dialog box during system startup. If you are also running Service for NetWare Directory Services, your computer can make NDS-based connections and can use the NDS login script if you log on as an NDS user. If you are not running Service for NetWare Directory Services, Client for NetWare Networks makes only bindery connections.

When a computer running Client for NetWare Networks but not Service for NetWare Directory Services connects to a NetWare 4.*x* server, the server must be running bindery emulation, so that the login scripts can be accessed in the same way as on a bindery server. If bindery-type login script files are not available, you can create login scripts by enabling bindery emulation on the server, then using NETADMIN to create accounts.

The Windows 98 Login Script Processor runs NetWare system and user login scripts, using commands in these scripts, such as MAP and CAPTURE, to make global changes to the system environment. For example, a script might include SET statements or PATH statements to specify search drives.

The login script appears in a window if the user's login script contains the WRITE, DISPLAY, FDISPLAY, PAUSE, or WAIT commands.

You can use any NetWare or MS-DOS command (in conjunction with NetWare login script commands) in a login script, except those that load TSRs. The Windows 98 Login Script Processor operates in protected-mode, so loading real-mode TSRs from a login script is not possible because login scripts are run after all real-mode actions are completed at system startup. Any TSR that is run from a login script is loaded in a single virtual machine, which is subsequently shut down when login script processing is completed. In these cases, the Login Script Processor displays an error message.

For loading components, such as backup agents, you can use protected-mode equivalents in Windows 98 instead of running TSRs. If you need to run a TSR to support an application, use one of the options described in the Table 18.2.

Table 18.2   Loading TSRs with Client for NetWare Networks

What the TSR must support	Where to load the TSR
With NDIS 3.1 drivers:	
All applications created for MS-DOS or Windows, without IPX/SPX support	Autoexec.bat
All Windows-based applications that require IPX/SPX support[1]	Winstart.bat in the \Windows directory
All MS-DOS-based applications that require IPX/SPX support[2]	At the command prompt before running the application
With ODI drivers:	
All applications created for MS-DOS or Windows with IPX/SPX support	After the entry that loads IPXODI in Autoexec.bat or Winstart.bat

[1] The IPX/SPX-compatible protocol (NWLINK) is loaded after real mode is complete but before login scripts are processed, so this protocol is available for TSRs loaded from Winstart.bat.

[2] The TSR must be loaded in each separate virtual machine for each application that requires that TSR before the application is loaded. This can be done in a batch file used to run the application.

The network administrator might want to warn users that, in the following circumstances, the Login Script Processor can display special windows and messages, and that this is not an error condition:

- When the login script runs, a message announces that the operating system is processing login scripts. The user can click a button to see details. However, if any statement in the script writes to the screen or if there is a PAUSE statement, the Login Script Processor window appears and displays all subsequent statements as they run.

- If a *#DOS_command* statement is included in the script, a special virtual machine is used to process the command. An MS-DOS Prompt window appears while the command is running and then closes automatically when the command is complete.

The following list presents some tips for testing and running login scripts with Client for NetWare Networks:

- Insert PAUSE statements frequently in the scripts you are testing so that you can study each screen of information as it appears in the Login Script Processor window.

- While testing scripts, check carefully for script errors that appear in the Login Script Processor window.

- Insert PAUSE statements following any text that you want the user to read during system logon.

> **Note** The Windows 98 Login Script Processor can handle any documented NetWare login script commands. Any undocumented variations on NetWare commands might not be processed as legal statements.

You can make persistent connections (using the same drive letter each time) to NetWare volumes and directories by using the Windows 98 user interface. Using persistent connections eliminates the need for some NetWare MAP commands in login scripts. However, if persistent connections are made to a server, you should avoid using the ATTACH command in login scripts.

Running Login Scripts with Novell-Supplied Clients

If a computer is running the Novell-supplied Novell Client for Windows 95/98, login scripts are processed when you log on to a NetWare network. (Logging on is different from authenticating to either a NetWare server or an NDS tree, which you can also do after logging on to the network.)

If you are running Novell Client for Windows 95/98, if you run an external command in your login script, such as "**send /a=n**" the MS-DOS box does not automatically close when the program terminates.

If a computer is running the Novell-supplied NETX or VLM networking client, login scripts are processed as they were before Windows 98 was installed.

With NETX or VLM, login scripts are run in real mode during system startup. Therefore, all statements and TSRs will run as expected and be available globally for all applications created for Windows or MS-DOS.

> **Important** Users running a Novell-supplied real-mode client should always log on to the NetWare server before running Windows 98. Otherwise, many operational problems will occur. For example, if a user instead logs on at the command prompt while already running Windows 98, then all the drive mappings created by the login scripts will be local only to that virtual machine.

User Profiles and Windows 98 Logon

The notes in this section provide a brief overview of the logon process in Windows 98. User profiles can be enabled in three ways:

- From the Users option in Control Panel.
- From the Passwords option in Control Panel.
- From the System Policy Editor.

If user profiles are enabled, then a network or Windows logon dialog box will always appear at system startup (even if the user's password is blank) because the user must be identified so the operating system can load the correct profile.

If user profiles are not enabled, what happens in the logon process depends on the setting specified in the **Primary Network Logon** box in the Network option in Control Panel. If the **Primary Network Logon** setting is for a network provider, such as Client for NetWare Networks or Client for Microsoft Networks, then an **Enter Network Password** dialog box will always appear at system startup if the network is active. These network providers cannot allow automatic logon without the user entering a password because the provider does not know which network account the user wants to use.

If the user selects **Windows Logon** as the value in the **Primary Network Logon** box in the Network option in Control Panel, then the **Windows Logon** dialog box will appear first, followed by logon dialog boxes for any other network providers. In this case, if the user has entered a Windows password but has cached the network passwords, the user needs to enter only the Windows password. If the user has configured the computer to perform an automatic logon by using password caching, the user will not need to enter a password to gain access to Windows 98 or the network. (For more information about password caching, see "Understanding System Logon," earlier in this chapter.)

If the user selects **Microsoft Family Logon** from the value in the **Primary Network Logon** box in the Network option in Control Panel, and user profiles are enabled, then the **Microsoft Family Logon** dialog box appears.

Note   The administrator can use system policies to restrict users' access to the Passwords option in Control Panel or to require a minimum password length to prevent automatic logon using blank passwords.

Browsing

This section describes how to configure browsing.

For more information about browsing, see the white paper "Browsing and Windows 95 Networking" at **http://www.microsoft.com/win32dev /netwrk/browser.htm**, and also the *Microsoft Windows NT Server Resource Kit* (for Windows NT Server version 4.0).

Understanding Browsing

Browsing in Windows 98 is the same for all network providers, whether the network is based on Windows NT Server, Novell NetWare, another network, or Windows 98 itself.

Users can browse network resources to connect to them. For example, users on NetWare networks can see NetWare servers and printers, plus computers running File and Printer Sharing for NetWare Networks. Users on Microsoft networks can find network resources by scrolling through a list of available workgroups, a list of available computers in a given workgroup, and a list of available resources on a given computer.

For technical details about network computing with Windows 98 on Microsoft and NetWare networks, see "Browsing on Microsoft Networks" and "Browsing on NetWare Networks" later in this chapter.

Using Network Neighborhood

When you use Network Neighborhood, you can access shared resources on a server without having to map a network drive. Browsing and connecting to the resource consists of a single step: clicking an icon.

For more information about what happens internally when Network Neighborhood is used to browse multiple networks, see the description of the multiple provider router in Chapter 29, "Windows 98 Network Architecture."

Using Workgroups in Windows 98

On Microsoft networks, computers are logically grouped in workgroups for convenient browsing of network resources. If share-level security is used, each computer in the workgroup maintains its own security system for validating local user log on and access to local resources.

NetWare networks do not use the workgroup concept, so computers running Windows 98 with only VLM or NETX clients cannot be members of workgroups. However, computers running File and Printer Sharing for NetWare Networks with Workgroup Advertising enabled can appear in workgroups.

To set the workgroup for a computer, click the **Identification** tab in the Network option in Control Panel and type a name.

For more information about using Network Neighborhood, see online Help.

▶ **To browse a server quickly without mapping a drive**

1. From the **Start** menu, click **Run**, and then type the server name. For example:

   \\nwsrv1

2. To browse any shared directory in the window that appears, double-click its icon.

3. To browse this server's workgroup, press BACKSPACE. This is the equivalent of clicking the **Up One Level** button on the toolbar.

▶ **To create a shortcut on the desktop to a network resource**

1. In Network Neighborhood, find the network resource for which you want to create a shortcut.

2. Click the right mouse button and drag the icon for that resource onto the desktop.

3. In the context-sensitive menu, click **Create Shortcut**.

4. Double-click the shortcut icon to view the contents of the network directory in a new window. This shortcut is available every time you start Windows 98.

As the network administrator, you can use system policies to create a custom Network Neighborhood for individuals or multiple users. As part of the custom Network Neighborhood, you can create shortcuts using UNC names for any network connections, including Dial-Up Networking connections. However, do not place directories in the custom Network Neighborhood. Neither the **Up One Level** icon nor the BACKSPACE key will return the user to the Network Neighborhood from a directory. In System Policy Editor, enable the policy named Custom Network Neighborhood:

- Use Registry mode to enable this option on a local or a remote computer.

- Use Policy mode to create or modify a policy file for one or more users.

You can also set system policies to control users' access to built-in Windows 98 browsing features. For more information, see "Restricting Access to Shell Settings" in Chapter 8, "System Policies."

Connecting to Drive and Printer Resources

You can connect to network drives from the **Map Network Drive** dialog box, which you can display in one of two ways.

▶ **To connect to network drives**

- Right-click Network Neighborhood, and then select **Map Network Drive** from the context-sensitive menu.

  – Or –

  In Windows Explorer, select the **Tools** menu and then click **Map Network Drive**.

In this dialog box, you can type the name of a network server and shared directory using the UNC name. For example, the UNC name for the server CORP and the shared directory DOCS is \\CORP\DOCS. On NetWare networks, you can also type any remote computer name understood by the network (for example, TRIKE/SYS:public). However, you cannot type a remote computer name understood by a NetWare network from other places in the operating system, such as the **Run** dialog box or a common control.

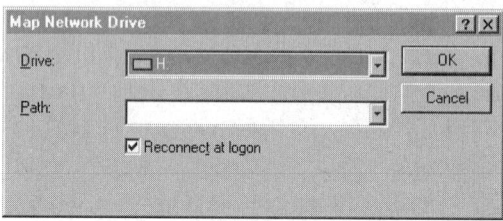

You can make a persistent connection to any drive (that is, you can store its name and automatically reconnect to it at startup) by clicking the **Reconnect at logon** check box in the **Map Network Drive** dialog box. Persistent connections are restored to the same drive letters each time Windows 98 is started.

When installing a new printer, you can specify a shared printer resource by using the UNC name or the Point and Print method. For example, for the shared printer named HP_III on the server CORP, the UNC name is \\CORP\HP_III. For more information about Point and Print, see Chapter 11, "Printing, Imaging, and Fonts."

You can also map drives and printers by using the Windows Scripting Host to execute scripts to map drives and printers. For more information about Windows Scripting Host, see Chapter 23, "System and Remote Administration Tools." See also **http://www.microsoft.com/management/scrpthost.htm**.

Browsing with the Net Commands

Browsing network resources at the command prompt is handled by the real-mode networking components. You can use the **net view** command to perform most of the same browsing actions as Network Neighborhood or Windows Explorer, except that it cannot provide a list of workgroups.

▶ **To get help for the net view command**

- At the command prompt, type **net view /?**.

You can use the **net use** command to connect and disconnect from shared resources, such as shares and printers. Additionally, you can see all the servers that you are connected to.

▶ **To get help for the net use command**

- At the command prompt, type **net use /?** | **more**.

    For specific notes about using the **net** commands on NetWare networks, see "Using Commands to Connect to NetWare Servers" later in this chapter.

Browsing on Microsoft Networks

The Windows 98 browsing scheme for Microsoft networks is based on the scheme currently used for Windows NT and Windows for Workgroups. The Windows 98 browse service attempts to minimize the network traffic related to browsing activity, while also providing an implementation that scales well to support both small and large networks.

This section describes how the browse service designates browse servers and maintains the browse list. It also provides information about connecting to network resources on Microsoft networks.

For more information about how browsing works on Windows 98 networks, see the *Microsoft Windows NT Resource Kit for Windows NT Server Version 4.0.*

Designating a Browse Master for Microsoft Networks

The Windows 98 browse service maintains a list of all the available servers in a given workgroup. This list is called the *browse list*. One server, called a *master browse server*, maintains the browse list for the workgroup and responds to queries from client computers. To minimize network traffic to the master browse server, one or more *backup browse servers* can also be designated to resolve some query requests. The master browse server periodically sends copies of the browse list to the backup browse servers.

When Windows 98 starts on a computer, the computer first checks to see if a master browse server is already present for the given workgroup. If a master browse server does not exist, an *election* creates a master browse server for the workgroup. To determine which computer in a workgroup will become the master browse server, if a computer boots up and either does not find a master browse server or has the Browse Master option enabled, then an election occurs in which the highest ranked server version becomes the browse master. For example, Windows NT is a higher version than Windows 98, so a Windows NT computer will be chosen before a Windows 98 computer.

If a master browse server already exists, Windows 98 checks the number of computers in the workgroup, and the number of browse servers present. If the number of computers in the workgroup exceeds the defined ratio of browse servers to computers in a workgroup (usually one browse server for every 15 computers), an additional computer in the workgroup might become a backup browse server.

The **Browse Master** parameter provides a mechanism for controlling which computers can become browse servers in a workgroup. If this parameter is set to **Automatic**, the master browse server can designate that computer as a backup browse server when needed, or that computer can be elected as master browse server.

Tip It is a good idea to set the **Browse Master** parameter to **Disabled** on computers that are frequently powered off or removed from the network, such as laptop. This helps you ensure that a browse server is always available.

For information about configuring the **Browse Master** parameter, see "Using File and Printer Sharing for Microsoft Networks" later in this chapter.

Using the Net View Command to Check the Browse Server

The **net view** command is a valuable troubleshooting tool if you suspect the browse list maintained by a browse server is incomplete or inaccurate. You can use **net view /workgroup**: *workgroupname* at the command prompt to get the list of known computers directly from the master browse server. The request is not handled by a backup browse server.

If the list of computers returned by a master browse server is inaccurate, you can reset the master browse server by shutting it down. Another computer will then be promoted to master browse server for the workgroup.

Building the Browse List for Microsoft Networks

In Windows 98, the browse service maintains an up-to-date list of domains, workgroups, and computers, and provides this list to applications when requested. The user sees the list in the following types of circumstances:

- If a user requests a list of computers in a workgroup, the browse service on the local computer randomly chooses one of the browse servers it is aware of and sends the request.

- If a user selects a workgroup to which the computer does not belong, Windows 98 requests a list of computers defined in the selected workgroup from a browse server in the selected workgroup.

The selected browse server also sends a list of the other workgroups it knows about that are defined on the network, along with a list of computers in the workgroup to which the user belongs. The browse list is displayed anywhere that Windows 98 presents lists of browsable resources. The browse list can also be displayed by using the **net view** command. The list can contain the names of domains, workgroups, and computers running the file and printer sharing service, including the following:

- Computers running Windows 98, Windows 95, Windows for Workgroups, and Windows NT Workstation.

- Windows NT domains and servers.

- Workgroups defined in Windows 98, Windows 95, Windows for Workgroups, Windows NT Server, and Windows NT Workstation.

- Workgroup Add-on for MS-DOS peer servers.

- LAN Manager 2.*x* domains and servers.

Adding New Computers to the Browse List

When a computer running Windows 98 is started on the network, it announces itself to the master browse server for its workgroup, and the master browse server adds that computer to the list of available computers in the workgroup. The master browse server then notifies backup browse servers that a change to the browse list is available. The backup browse servers then request the new information to update their local browse lists. It might take as long as 15 minutes before a backup browse server receives an updated browse list, and new computers on the network do not show up in a user's request for a browse list until then.

Removing Computers from the Browse List

When a user shuts down a computer properly, the operating system informs the master browse server that it is shutting down. The master browse server then notifies backup browse servers that a change to the browse list is available. The backup browse servers then request the changes to the browse list.

If a user turns off the computer without shutting down, the computer does not get a chance to send the message to the master browse server. In this case, the computer name might continue to appear in the browse list until the name entry times out, which can take up to 45 minutes.

Technical Notes on Browsing on Microsoft Networks

This section includes a table of NetBIOS special names and presents some brief notes related to browsing on Microsoft networks.

NetBIOS Special Names

When a computer connects to the network, it receives a NetBIOS special name that indicates what role it will play in browsing for the network. For example, a computer might have a special name to indicate that it is a master browse server. Table 18.3 shows those names. You can use the utility **nbtstat** to find your computer's special names, and you can use Network Monitor to find special names for other computers on the network.

For more information about **nbtstat**, see "Technical Notes on TCP/IP" in Chapter 15, "Network Adapters and Protocols." For more information about Network Monitor, see Chapter 23, "System and Remote Administration Tools."

Table 18.3   NetBIOS special names

Special name	Description
computer\0x00	Used by Microsoft networking workstations to receive second class mailslot requests. All workstations must add this name in order to receive mailslot requests. This is the computer name registered for workstation services by a WINS client.
computer\0x03	Used as the computer name that is registered for the messenger service on a computer that is a WINS client.
computer\0x20	Used as the name that is registered for the peer server service on a Windows 98 computer (or the server service on a Windows NT computer) that is a WINS client.
computer\0xBe	Used as the unique name that is registered when the Network Monitor agent is started on the computer.
computer\0x1f	Used as the unique name that is registered for Network dynamic data exchange (DDE) when the NetDDE service is started on the computer.

Registered group names:

.._MSBROWSE_.	Used by master browser servers to periodically announce their domain on a local subnet. This announcement contains the domain name and the name of the master browser server for the domain. In addition, master browser servers receive these domain announcements to this name and maintain them in their internal browse list along with the announcer's computer name.
domain\0x00	Used by workstations and servers to process server announcements to support Microsoft LAN Manager. Servers running Windows 98, Windows NT, Windows NT Server, and Windows for Workgroups do not broadcast this name unless the LMAnnounce option is enabled in the server's properties.

Table 18.3   NetBIOS special names (*continued*)

Registered group names:

Special name	Description
domain\0x1b	Used to identify the domain master browser name, which is a unique name that only the primary domain controller (PDC) can add. The PDC processes GetBrowserServerList requests on this name. WINS assumes that the computer that registers a domain name with the \0x1b character is the PDC.
domain\0x1c	Used for the Internet group name, which the domain controllers register. The Internet group name is a dynamic list of up to 25 computers that have registered the name. This is the name used to find a Windows NT computer for pass-through authentication.
domain\0x1d	Used to identify a master browser (not a domain master browser). The master browser adds this name as a unique NetBIOS name when it starts. Workstations announce their presence to this name so that master browsers can build their browse list. For peer servers, this name has the form *workgroup*\0x1d.
domain\0x1e	Used for all workgroup or domain-wide announcements by browser servers in a Windows network workgroup or Windows NT Server domain. (Notice, however, that workstations use the domain\0x1d form, not \0x1e.) This name is added by all browser servers and potential servers in the workgroup or domain. All browser election packets are sent to this name.
computer\0xBf	Used as the group name that is registered when the Network Monitor agent is started on the computer. If this name is not 15 characters in length, it is padded with plus (+) symbols.
username\0x03	Used to register the name of the currently logged on user in the WINS database, so that users can receive **net send** commands sent to their user names.

Other Notes

- The Windows 98 browser supports browsing across Transport Control Protocol/Internet Protocol (TCP/IP) subnetworks. You can take advantage of this feature if one of the following applies:

  - The network uses a WINS server.

    – Or –

    You use #DOM entries in LMHOSTS files for name resolution.

    – Or –

    You give one Windows 98 client computer a workgroup name that corresponds to the domain name on the remote subnet you wish to reach.

- Microsoft LAN Manager–compatible networks, such as IBM LAN Server and Microsoft LAN Manager for UNIX support browsing of servers, and shared directories using the Windows 98 user interface or **net view**.

- Digital PATHWORKS is an example of a Microsoft LAN Manager–compatible network that does not support browsing. AT&T StarLAN is an example of a Microsoft Network–compatible network that is not based on Microsoft LAN Manager and that does not support remote browsing of servers and shared directories. These servers do not appear in Network Neighborhood; with Windows 98, however, users can still access the servers and shared directories through a network connection dialog box.

- When a known slow network connection is used (for example, the remote access driver), Windows 98 is automatically configured not to designate that computer to be a browse server for the network connection. The **SlowLanas** parameter in the registry identifies the network LANA numbers for which the local computer will not serve as a master browse server. However, the user can still request a list of available workgroups and computers on the network across the slow network connection.

Browsing on NetWare Networks

The Windows 98 user interface includes support for browsing and connecting to network resources on Novell NetWare and other networks. Except for workgroups, this support is the same whether you use Client for NetWare Networks or a Novell-supplied client. After you connect to a NetWare volume or a computer running File and Printer Sharing for NetWare Networks, you can drag and drop directories and files to move and copy them between your computer and the NetWare server.

For more information about printer connections, see Chapter 11, "Printing, Imaging, and Fonts."

Using Network Neighborhood on NetWare Networks

Network Neighborhood is the primary way you can browse the network. What you see using Network Neighborhood depends on which network client you are using.

If you are using Microsoft Client for NetWare Networks without Service for NetWare Directory Services, or if you are using a real-mode Novell NetWare Client, you can see all the NetWare bindery-based servers your computer is connected to. You will also see all computers running File and Printer Sharing for NetWare Networks that use Workgroup Advertising.

If you have installed Service for NetWare Directory Services, you will also see all the NDS objects in the current context. For more information, see "Browsing the NDS Tree Using Service for NetWare Directory Services" later in this chapter.

If you have installed Novell Client for Windows 95/98, you will see bindery-based servers and computers running File and Printer Sharing for NetWare Networks, but you will also see a separate folder for the NDS tree and workstation context. You can click this icon to browse the network as usual.

Clicking the Entire Network icon displays a list of all NetWare servers on the network. This list also contains a list of workgroups that include computers running File and Printer Sharing for NetWare Networks. You can view the contents of any server without having to map a network drive.

If you are running Service for NetWare Directory Services and you are logged on to the NDS tree, clicking the Entire Network icon will also display the NDS tree. If you are running Novell Client for Windows 95/98, you will see NetWare servers and NDS trees in separate folders.

If your computer has both Client for Microsoft Networks and Client for NetWare Networks installed, then you will also see a list of computers running Windows for Workgroups, Windows 98, and Windows NT. The list of NetWare servers is along with the list of workgroups or domains in the Entire Network window.

In both the Network Neighborhood and Entire Network views, you can open a server to access its contents without having to map a network drive. If you are running Service for NetWare Directory Services or Novell Client for Windows 95/98 and you are authenticated to the NDS tree, you will not need to enter a password if you are connecting to a NetWare 4.*x* server. However, if you are not running Service for NetWare Directory Services, you are not authenticated to the NDS tree, or you are connecting to a NetWare 3.*x* server, you may be asked to enter a password. If you are running Client for NetWare Networks, you can choose to save your password in the password cache so that you will not have to type it again.

If the computer is running Client for NetWare Networks, drive mappings are limited to the available drive letters. However, Windows 98 supports unlimited UNC connections. (If the computer is running NETX or VLM, it is limited to only eight server connections.)

Connecting to Resources Using Client for NetWare Networks

This section describes how to connect to resources using Client for NetWare Networks. The procedures in this section assume that you are logged on using Client for NetWare Networks.

▶ **To connect to a bindery-based NetWare server in Network Neighborhood**

1. In Network Neighborhood, right-click a bindery-based NetWare server.

2. In the context-sensitive menu, click **Attach As**. Then type a user name and password, and click **OK**.

3. If you want to map a directory on this server, double-click the server icon. Right-click the volume you want to map, and click **Map Network Drive** in the context-sensitive menu. Select a drive, and click **OK**.

Tip You can also create a shortcut to frequently used resources. For information, see "Using Network Neighborhood" earlier in this chapter. When you double-click a shortcut, you have to supply only a password to connect to it.

You can also use the **Map Network Drive** dialog box to specify the name of a NetWare server and volume (or directory) that you want to map to a drive letter.

▶ **To connect to a directory as the root of the drive**

1. In Network Neighborhood, right-click a directory on a NetWare server.

2. In the context-sensitive menu, click **Map Network Drive**.

3. If you are connecting to a bindery-based server and if you see the option **Connect as Root of the drive**, select that option.

4. Click **OK**.

With this option enabled, if you switch to this mapped directory in a command prompt window, you will see the prompt as *drive*:\> not *drive*:*directory*>. You cannot go further up the directory tree from the command prompt.

The context-sensitive menu for a NetWare server shows everything you can do with the related server, volume, or directory. To view the context-sensitive menu, in Network Neighborhood, right-click a NetWare server.

Table 18.4 describes the commands available on the context-sensitive menu.

Table 18.4   Shortcut commands for NetWare servers

Command	Description
Open	Connects to that server.
Explore	Shows the resources available on that server without making a connection.
Who Am I	Specifies whether the user is logged on or attached to the server; if a user is logged on and the computer is attached, specifies that user's name.
Detach	Logs the user off a bindery-based server.

Table 18.4   Shortcut commands for NetWare servers (*continued*)

Command	Description
Attach As	Presents a dialog box for typing a password to log on to a bindery-based server. This dialog box allows the user to connect to the server by using a different user name from the one used to log on to the network.
Map Network Drive	Presents a dialog box for mapping a network drive to a drive letter.
Create Shortcut	Creates a shortcut on the desktop for the selected server.
Properties	Shows the properties for the server. Listing the properties of a NetWare server creates an attachment without logging on, thereby using up one of the allowable connections.

If a computer running File and Printer Sharing for NetWare Networks has been configured to allow remote administration, and if you have the authority to administer that server, you can use the administration options in the computer's properties. To do this, in Network Neighborhood, right-click the computer's icon. In the context-sensitive menu, click **Properties**, and then click the **Tools** tab. Use the buttons to run Net Watcher or System Monitor, or to administer the file system.

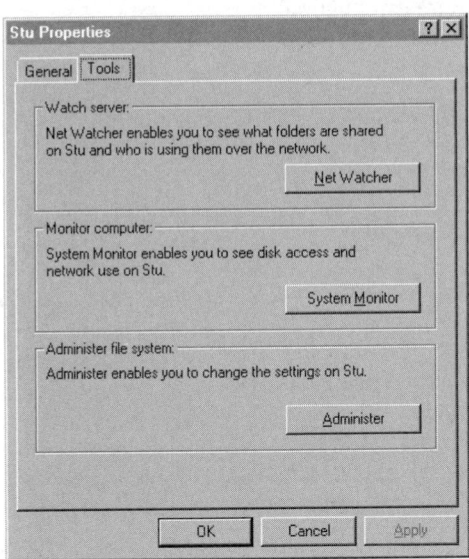

For more information about preparing computers for remote administration under Windows 98, and about using Net Watcher and other tools, see Chapter 23, "System and Remote Administration Tools."

Browsing the NDS Tree Using Service for NetWare Directory Services

If your computer is running Service for NetWare Directory Services and you are logged on to the NDS tree, you will be able to see NDS objects. The following NDS objects are visible in Network Neighborhood:

- Organizations
- Organizational unit
- Servers
- Volume objects
- Directory maps
- Printers
- Print queues
- Aliases for NDS objects

If you are logged on to the NDS tree, you are automatically logged on to all servers in that tree. Therefore, you do not need to use the ATTACH command to connect to those servers.

Service for NetWare Directory Services also enables you to change your preferred logon server and your current context.

▶ **To change contexts**

1. In Network Neighborhood, click the Organization or Organizational Unit you want to change your current context to.
2. Click **File**.
3. Click **Set Current Context**.

▶ **To specify a preferred server**

1. In Control Panel, double-click Network.
2. Click **Client for NetWare Networks**.
3. Click **Properties**.
4. In **Preferred Server**, type the name of the server.

Note You can change your preferred server only if it is a 4.*x* server in the same NDS tree you are logging on to.

Browsing the NDS Tree Using Novell Client for Windows 95/98

If your computer is running Novell Client for Windows 95/98, you can see the same NDS objects that are listed in "Browsing the NDS Tree Using Service for NetWare Directory Services" earlier in this chapter. From within Network Neighborhood you will see bindery-based servers and computers running File and Printer Sharing for NetWare Networks, as well as a separate folder for the NDS tree and workstation context.

If you are logged on to the NDS tree, you are automatically logged on to all servers in that tree. Therefore, you do not need to use the ATTACH command to connect to those servers.

With Novell Client for Windows 95/98, you can be authenticated to multiple NDS trees. However, not all applications can use multiple trees. To support those applications, Novell Client for Windows 95/98 enables you to specify a "current tree," that is, the tree that applications will use if they cannot use multiple trees.

Novell Client for Windows 95/98 also enables you to change your current server and your current context.

▶ **To view the current tree and current server**

1. From the Windows 98 desktop, right-click Network Neighborhood.

2. Click **NetWare Connections**.

▶ **To change the current tree**

1. From Network Neighborhood, right-click the tree you want to change to.

2. In the context-sensitive menu, click **Set Current Tree**.

▶ **To change the current server**

1. From the Windows 98 desktop, right-click Network Neighborhood.

2. In the context-sensitive menu, click **NetWare Connections**.

3. Click the server you want to change to.

4. Click **Set Current**.

▶ **To change the current context**

1. From Network Neighborhood, right-click the tree you want to change to.

2. In the context-sensitive menu, click **Change Context**.

3. Enter the context under Enter New Default Context.

4. Click **Change**.

5. To see the new context, refresh Network Neighborhood by pressing F5.

Managing Connections with Client for NetWare Networks

With Client for NetWare Networks, you can manage connections to the NetWare network by using Network Neighborhood and common network-connection dialog boxes, such as **Open** and **Save**. (These are the same techniques used for Microsoft networks.)

With Client for NetWare Networks, you can define persistent connections (which use the same drive letter each time the computer starts) to NetWare volumes and directories. Using persistent connections eliminates the need for NetWare MAP commands in login scripts; however, you can still use MAP, ATTACH, and other commands at the command prompt or in login scripts, as described in the following section.

Using Commands to Connect to NetWare Servers

If you are running Client for NetWare Networks, all NetWare commands run in the same way as they do for a Novell-supplied networking client.

Note the following about certain Novell-supplied commands:

- If you are running Service for NetWare Directory Services and you are logged on to the NDS tree, you do not need to use the ATTACH command to connect to servers in the NDS tree.

- For the ATTACH command, configure the networking client to use SAP browsing. You can configure SAP browsing from the **Properties** window for **File and printer sharing for NetWare Networks**.

- It is recommended that you do not use the LOGIN utility to create an attachment to a computer running File and Printer Sharing for NetWare Networks. Use the ATTACH command instead.

- For the MAP command, drive mappings in Windows 98 are global to all sessions.

You can also use the Microsoft networking **net** commands at the command prompt or in login scripts to manage connections on NetWare networks.

For Client for NetWare Networks or Novell real-mode clients, you can use the Windows 98 **net view** command to perform the same function as the NETX SLIST or VLM NLIST SERVER commands.

The **net view** command creates an attachment without logging on. Viewing a NetWare server or a computer running File and Printer Sharing for NetWare Networks does not show print queues. However, viewing a computer running File and Printer Sharing for Microsoft Networks shows both shared directories and shared printers.

▶ **To get help for the net view command**

- At the command prompt, type **net view /?**.

You can use the **net use** command to do the following:

- Perform the same functions as the NetWare ATTACH and MAP commands. The **net use** command maps only to the root of a volume.
- Supply similar functionality to the CAPTURE utility for printing when programs require printing to a specific port, and the ENDCAP utility for deleting a print connection.

▶ **To get help for the net use command**

- At the command prompt, type **net use /? | more**.

The following brief procedures show built-in Windows 98 commands that can be used at the command prompt or in scripts to manage resource connections.

The **net** command in Windows 98 does not support the following:

- The functionality of the NetWare MAP ROOT command or search drive mappings.
- Any of the command-line options of the CAPTURE command, except the equivalents for specifying port, server name, and queue name. To use specific CAPTURE options, use the Novell CAPTURE command.
- The functionality of the Novell NetWare print job designations (the J=*jobname* parameter for the CAPTURE command).

Note You can still use the NetWare commands SLIST and NLIST instead of **net view**, MAP instead of **net use**, or CAPTURE instead of **net use** to connect to a printer. With Service for NetWare Directory Services, you can map drive letters to NDS objects, such as directory map objects and volume objects.

Using Windows NT to Connect to NetWare Servers

If your site includes both a Novell NetWare network and a Windows NT Server network, computers using Microsoft networking will need to communicate and share resources with the NetWare network. This section summarizes several options using Windows NT.

For more information about these features, contact your Microsoft sales representative.

NWLink. With *NWLink*, Microsoft's IPX/SPX-compatible protocol, you can give NetWare-compatible clients access to Windows NT Server–based applications, such as Microsoft SQL Server™ and Internet Information Server. You can also give Windows 98 clients access to databases running as NetWare Loadable Modules on NetWare servers.

Windows NT Gateway Service for NetWare. For Microsoft networking clients that cannot use multiple protocols, you can configure a computer running Windows NT Server 3.5 or later as a file or print gateway using Windows NT Gateway Service for NetWare to connect to and share NetWare resources. Windows NT Gateway Service for NetWare acts as a translator between the server message block (SMB) protocol used by Microsoft networks and the NetWare Core Protocol (NCP), used on NetWare networks. With Windows NT Server 4.0, Gateway Service for NetWare also supports Novell Directory Services (NDS) and login scripts.

Because access over the gateway is slower than direct access from the client for computers running Windows 98 that require frequent access to NetWare resources, Client for NetWare Networks is a better solution.

Notice that a Microsoft Windows NT Client Access License is required if the computer will be connecting to servers running Windows NT Server. For information, contact your Microsoft reseller. For more information about setting up a Windows NT Server computer with Gateway Service for NetWare, see the *Microsoft Windows NT Server Networking Guide* in the *Microsoft Windows NT Server Resource Kit* (for Windows NT Server version 4.0).

Microsoft File and Print Services for NetWare. This utility for Windows NT Server provides users running a NetWare-compatible client with access to basic NetWare file and print services and to powerful server applications on the same Windows NT Server–based computer, without changing users' network client software.

Microsoft Directory Service Manager for NetWare. This utility for Windows NT Server allows you to maintain a single directory for mixed Windows NT Server, NetWare 2.*x* and 3.*x* servers, and bindery-based NetWare 4.*x* servers .

Peer Resource Sharing

This section describes how to configure and use peer resource sharing.

Understanding Peer Resource Sharing

When a computer is running file and printer sharing services, other users running a compatible network client can connect to shared printers, volumes, CD-ROM drives, and directories on that computer by using the standard techniques for connecting the network resources, as described in "Browsing on Microsoft Networks" and "Browsing on NetWare Networks" earlier in this chapter.

Using computers running Windows 98 as peer servers allows you to add secure storage space and printing to the network at a low cost. The peer service is based on a 32-bit, protected-mode architecture, which means all the Windows 98 benefits for robust, high performance are available. In addition, administrators can take advantage of tools, such as system policies (included in the Windows 98 Resource Kit) and Net Watcher (included in Windows 98) to centrally administer peer servers. In addition, user-level security is available as an additional enhancement beyond the peer server capabilities built into Windows for Workgroups.

Tip Using Net Watcher, a network administrator can remotely monitor and manage files on any computer running file and printer sharing services if remote administration has been enabled for that computer. Net Watcher allows an administrator to disconnect users, change access rights, and administer the file system on remote computers. For more information, see Chapter 23, "System and Remote Administration Tools."

Installing Peer Resource Sharing

If you use custom setup scripts, you can specify that file and printer sharing services be installed with Windows 98. Otherwise, you can add the service later by using the Network option in Control Panel.

Tip For a computer that will share resources with other users on the network, choose which file and printer sharing service to install based on what other users require:

- If most users who need to share these resources are running NETX, VLM, or Client for NetWare Networks, then install File and Printer Sharing for NetWare Networks.

- If most users who need to share these resources are running Client for Microsoft Networks, Windows NT, Windows for Workgroups, or Workgroup Add-on for MS-DOS, then install File and Printer Sharing for Microsoft Networks.

▶ **To install file and printer sharing after setup**

1. In Control Panel, double-click Network, and then click **Add**.

2. In the **Select Network Component Type** dialog box, double-click **Service,** and then click **Add**.

3. If you are installing File and Printer Sharing for Microsoft Networks, select **File and printer sharing for Microsoft Networks**, and then click **OK**.

   – Or –

   If you are installing File and Printer Sharing for NetWare Networks, select **File and printer sharing for NetWare Networks**, and then click **OK**.

For information about enabling file and printer sharing in custom setup scripts, see Chapter 3, "Custom Installations." For information about controlling peer resource sharing capabilities using system policies, see Chapter 8, "System Policies."

Implementing Security for Peer Resource Sharing

Figure 18.1 shows how Windows 98 supports share-level and user-level security for File and Printer Sharing for Microsoft Networks. Windows 98 supports share-level security similar to the security provided with Windows for Workgroups. This level of security associates a password with a shared disk directory or printer. Share-level security for peer resource sharing can be implemented in a Windows 98–only peer-to-peer network or on a network supported by Windows NT or other Microsoft Windows network-compatible servers.

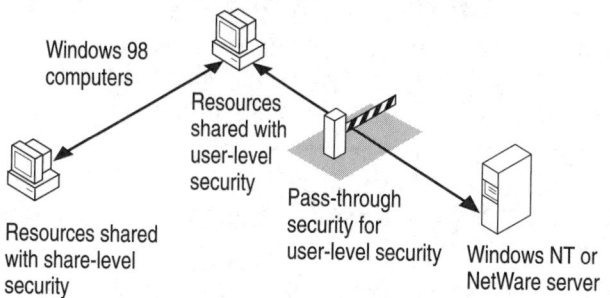

Figure 18.1   Security for peer resource sharing under Windows 98

For file and printer sharing services on both Windows NT and NetWare networks, Windows 98 supports user-level security by linking a peer server directly to another server for user account validation. For network administrators, the user account list is centrally controlled at the Windows NT domain controller or NetWare server; on a Windows NT network, the user account list on a single server can also be used for validation. The resources on the Windows 98 peer server can be accessed only by users with accounts in the central database. Users can also be assigned specified access rights in Windows 98 for particular resources. For more information about using and managing security, see Chapter 9, "Security."

The 32-bit, protected mode-network client and the file and printer sharing service are separate network processes, but they share connection information and pass requests to each other when validating a user-level security request.

For user-level security on a computer running either version of file and printer sharing service, you specify the server that contains the database of user accounts that are allowed to connect to this peer resource sharing server. You can do the following to customize access to a shared resource:

- You can use the Windows 98 user interface to specify which users can access the shared resources and which rights they have. For details, see "Controlling Access to Peer Server Resources on NetWare Networks" later in this chapter.

- For File and Printer Sharing on NetWare Networks, you can set up user rights remotely on the computer running Windows 98 by using NetWare utilities.

- For File and Printer Sharing on Microsoft Networks, you can set up user rights remotely with User Manager for Windows NT.

- You can use Net Watcher to monitor, add, and remove shared resources, as described in Chapter 23, "System and Remote Administration Tools."

When a user requests access to a shared resource under user-level security, Windows 98 checks for the user's logon name against the list of user accounts maintained on the server. If this is a valid user logon name, Windows 98 then checks whether this user has access privileges for this resource. If the user has access privileges, then the requested operation is allowed.

For an example of how pass-through validation works with peer resource sharing, see Chapter 9, "Security."

Using File and Printer Sharing for Microsoft Networks

File and Printer Sharing for Microsoft Networks is the 32-bit, protected-mode Windows 98 SMB server (Vserver.vxd) that supports all networking products that use the SMB file-sharing protocol, including Windows for Workgroups, Windows NT, LAN Manager, Samba, IBM LAN Server, IBM OS/2 Warp Server, and DIGITAL PATHWORKS 32. Windows 98 enhances the features of Windows for Workgroups peer services by providing administrative control over whether peer sharing services are enabled, by adding user-based security capabilities, and by supporting long file names.

The following summarizes some requirements for File and Printer Sharing for Microsoft Networks:

- The computer must use Client for Microsoft Networks.

- File and Printer Sharing for Microsoft Networks cannot run at the same time as NCP-based File and Printer Sharing for NetWare Networks.

- If user-level security is used, a Windows NT domain controller must be used for authentication.

The default settings for File and Printer Sharing are correct for most installations. You should need to change these settings only in the following circumstances:

- You need to set **Browse Master** properties, as described in "Browsing on Microsoft Networks" earlier in this chapter.

- You want LAN Manager 2.*x* clients on your network to use resources on a computer running File and Printer Sharing for Microsoft Networks.

Use the Network option in Control Panel to configure the Browse Master and LM Announce parameters for the file and printer sharing service. For information about configuring security in the **Access Control** tab of the **Network** dialog box, see Chapter 9, "Security."

▶ **To specify Browse Master settings**

1. In Control Panel, double-click Network, and then examine the list of installed components to see if **File and printer sharing for Microsoft Networks** is installed. If not, click the **File and Print Sharing** button and follow the instructions on the screen.

2. On the **Configuration** tab, double-click **File and printer sharing for Microsoft Networks** in the list of installed components.

3. In the **File and printer sharing for Microsoft Networks** dialog box, select **Browse Master** in the **Property** list.

4. Select an option in the **Value** list, as described in Table 18.5.

Table 18.5   Browse Master settings for Microsoft networks

Option	Description
Automatic	Specifies that this computer will maintain the browse list if Windows 98 determines that it is necessary. This is the default.
Disabled	Specifies that this computer is never used to maintain the browse list. Use this setting if the computer has little free memory, if it is connected by a slow link (such as a dial-up connection), if it is frequently disconnected from the network, or if other conditions create special performance problems.
Enabled	Specifies that this computer is to be used to maintain the browse list for computers in this workgroup.

At least one computer in the workgroup must have the value of **Automatic** or **Enabled** for this parameter to ensure the browse list is available to network computers. This parameter is equivalent to the **MaintainServerList=** entry in the [network] section of System.ini in Windows for Workgroups 3.11.

The LM **Announce** property controls whether a computer running File and Printer Sharing for Microsoft Networks can be seen by LAN Manager 2.*x* clients.

▶ **To specify LM Announce settings**

1. In Control Panel, double-click Network, and then double-click **File and printer sharing for Microsoft Networks** in the list of installed components.

2. In the **File and printer sharing for Microsoft Networks** dialog box, select **LM Announce** in the **Property** list.

3. Select an option in the **Value** list, as described in Table 18.6.

Table 18.6   LM Announce settings for Microsoft networks

Option	Description
No	Specifies that you do not want this computer to broadcast its presence to other computers by using LAN Manager broadcast announcements. Setting this value to No minimizes the level of network traffic. The Browse Master ensures that this computer appears in its browse list.
Yes	Specifies that you want this computer to announce its presence to other Microsoft networking computers in the workgroup multiple times, because there is a LAN Manager 2.*x* domain on the network. This value should be set to Yes if other computers in your workgroup need to see this computer when browsing the network.

This parameter is the equivalent of the **LMAnnounce=** entry in the [Network] section of System.ini in Windows for Workgroups 3.11. This value should be **No** unless there is a LAN Manager 2.*x* domain on your network.

A LAN Manager 2.*x* domain is known by browse servers in a workgroup only if at least one computer running Windows 98 (or Windows NT in the domain) is a member of that LAN Manager 2.*x* domain.

▶ **To make a computer running Windows 98 a member of a LAN Manager 2.*x* domain**

- Set the workgroup name for the computer to be the same as the LAN Manager 2.*x* domain name.

You can share a folder (or other resource) by selecting it in Windows Explorer or in My Computer and then configuring the related options. The following procedure describes how to share a directory on a computer where user-level security has been specified in the Network option in Control Panel. The steps f or sharing resources with share-level security are similar to those for user-level security except that you do not select specific users. Rather, you specify the type of access and define a password for the shared resource.

▶ **To share a directory (folder) with user-level security**

1. In Windows Explorer, right-click the icon for the directory you want to share. In the context-sensitive menu that appears, click **Sharing**.

2. On the **Sharing** tab, click the **Shared As** button, and then type a share name for the directory.

Tip If you add a dollar sign ($) to the end of the share name, the resource will not appear in Network Neighborhood or elsewhere when people browse network resources.

---

3. Click the **Add** button, and use the **Add Users** dialog box to specify which users can access the directory.

For more information about sharing folders on a Microsoft network, see Help.

Using File and Printer Sharing for NetWare Networks

If you want to use File and Printer Sharing for NetWare Networks:

- The computer must use Client for NetWare Networks, rather than Novell-supplied client software.

- Only user-level security (not share-level security) is available.

- The service cannot run on the same computer as SMB-based File and Printer Sharing for Microsoft Networks.

- For pass-through validation when user-level security is enabled, there must be a Windows_Passthru account (with no password) on the NetWare server that is used as the security provider.

A computer configured with File and Printer Sharing for NetWare Networks uses the NCP file-sharing protocol to share resources with MS-DOS-based Novell NetWare computers, computers running Windows NT, and computers that have Client for NetWare Networks installed.

File and Printer Sharing for NetWare Networks supports long file names and is Plug and Play–aware. This implementation differs from peer resource sharing in Windows for Workgroups in two fundamental ways:

- File and Printer Sharing for NetWare Networks uses the NCP protocol instead of the SMB protocol. This means that any NetWare-compatible client (Client for NetWare Networks, Novell Client for Windows 95/98, NETX, or VLM) can connect to a computer running File and Printer Sharing for NetWare Networks.

- File and Printer Sharing for NetWare Networks uses user-level security. Access to a shared resource is based on the user's identity instead of on a password associated with that resource. The user database for verifying user identity is the bindery on a specified NetWare server.

This feature means that hundreds of NetWare users can, for example, access a shared CD-ROM using a single NetWare server connection. Also, trustee or other access rights can be defined per directory for a shared CD-ROM.

When File and Printer Sharing for NetWare Networks is running on a computer, how that peer server appears to users browsing the network depends on how the peer server advertises itself:

- For another computer running Microsoft Client for NetWare Networks, the resources on the peer server appear exactly as any shared resources on the network. If the peer server is using Workgroup Advertising, it appears in a workgroup. A peer server using SAP (the NetWare broadcasting protocol) will not appear in a workgroup, but it will appear in the Entire Network list.

- For a computer running NETX or VLM, any shared directory on a peer server that uses SAP Advertising appear the same as volumes on any server. Any shared printers appear as print queues. Most NetWare administrative commands work as expected, including RIGHTS, FILER, SYSCON, MAP, SLIST, VOLINFO, PCONSOLE, and CAPTURE. If the peer server is not using SAP Advertising, then users running NETX or VLM cannot see or connect to the peer server when browsing the network.

- You cannot access resources on a peer server if you are running Novell Client for Windows 95/98.

Sharing Resources on a NetWare Network

To allow NETX and VLM clients on the network to access resources on the peer server, you must enable SAP Browsing in the properties for File and Print Sharing for NetWare Networks. The computer then appears as a server in SLIST or NLIST, and users can map drives to connect to this computer. To see a list of volumes, users can use the VOLINFO command.

Note Administrative control over File and Printer Sharing for NetWare Networks is coupled with the printer sharing control—the option controlling the user's ability to share a local printer. If these sharing options are not selected in the Network option in Control Panel, then the file and printer sharing service is not loaded. However, if the administrator disables printer sharing or file sharing by setting the related option in a system policy file, the file and printer sharing service still runs on the computer, but the related sharing options are not available.

Configuring Browsing for Resource Sharing on NetWare Networks

After you install File and Printer Sharing for NetWare Networks, you must choose the method that computers browsing on the network will use to find this computer. You can browse by using either of two options:

- Workgroup Advertising, which uses the same broadcast method as used by workgroups on Microsoft networks.

- SAP Advertising, which is used by Novell NetWare 2.15 and later servers to advertise their presence on the network. You must enable this option if you want the shared resources to be available to computers running NETX or VLM.

Note SAP Browsing has a theoretical limit of 7000 systems for browsing, and a practical limit of about 1500 systems. For a large peer network, use Workgroup Advertising.

For a general discussion of browsing when using NetWare-compatible clients, see "Browsing on NetWare Networks" earlier in this chapter.

▶   **To specify the browsing preference**

1. In Control Panel, double-click Network, and then double-click **File and printer sharing for NetWare Networks** in the list of installed components.

2. In the **File and printer sharing for NetWare Networks** dialog box, select **Workgroup Advertising** in the **Property** list, and then choose a value from the options listed in Table 18.7.

   – Or –

   If you want NETX and VLM clients to be able to connect to this peer server Select **SAP Advertising** and set the **Value** box to **Enabled**.

Table 18.7   Workgroup Advertising settings for NetWare networks

Option	Description
Disabled	This computer will not be added to the browse list, and it cannot be seen by other members of the workgroup using any method for browsing network resources.
Enabled: May Be Master	This computer is added to the browse list and can be promoted to master browse server if the preferred master is not available.
Enabled: Preferred Master	This computer is the master browse server for the workgroup.
Enabled: Will Not Be Master	This computer is added to the browse list by the master browse server, but it cannot be promoted to master browse server.

For more information about master browse server options, see "Building the Browse List for Microsoft Networks" earlier in this chapter.

Note If Workgroup Advertising is used, each workgroup must have a master browse server at all times to track names and addresses for computers in the workgroup.

If you select **SAP Advertising**, you can set the options shown in Table 18.8.

Table 18.8   SAP Advertising settings for NetWare networks

Option	Description
Disabled	This computer will not advertise its presence, and NETX or VLM clients cannot see it by using SLIST or other browsing options, and cannot connect to it. Users running Client for NetWare Networks can see it if Workgroup Advertising is enabled on the peer server.
Enabled	This computer will advertise its presence. It will appear in the Entire Network list. Users running VLM, NETX, and Client for NetWare Networks can see it by using any browsing methods, and they can connect to it as they do for any server.

By default, computers running File and Printer Sharing for NetWare Networks are placed in and browsed by workgroups. To specify the workgroup and computer name for the computer, in Control Panel, double-click Network, and then click the **Identification** tab.

Although computers that use SAP Advertising appear in the list of NetWare servers, you cannot use them in all the same ways that you use NetWare servers.

- When using NETX, you cannot log on to a computer running Windows 98 at the command line, although you can attach to one and map drives to its directories.

- When using VLM, you cannot log on to a computer running Windows 98 at the command line, but you can run a **login /ns** command and use the Login button in the NWUSER utility.

- If you run SYSCON on a NetWare server, you can change the server to one of the computers running Windows 98. However, the computer running Windows 98 does not have a bindery, so when you display all the users (or groups) in SYSCON, you will see the user list (or group list) from the NetWare server that was selected as the user-level security provider.

- If you run VOLINFO on a NetWare server, you can select one of the computers running Windows 98 and display its volume information (if you are attached to it). This shows all the available shared disk resources for the computer running Windows 98.

In Windows 98, you can do the same things to resources on computers running File and Printer Sharing for NetWare Networks as you can to any other network resource.

Note Each computer configured with File and Printer Sharing for NetWare Networks logs on to the NetWare server that provides security, to get access to the bindery, using the Windows_Passthru account. This logon process takes place in the background, without user intervention.

If a connection to the server already exists, Windows 98 uses that connection and makes a new connection only when required.

Controlling Access to Peer Server Resources on NetWare Networks

You can add to the list of users who can access the resources on the peer server. To do this, add the users to the NetWare pass-through server that provides security. You can then give these users access to the peer server by adding them to the **Sharing** properties associated with the shared resource.

Passwords for users' resources on the peer server are the same as those for the NetWare pass-through server. Passwords must be changed at that server, as described in "Unified System Logon Overview" earlier in this chapter.

▶ **To make sure all users have the required server access**

- Make sure that one NetWare server on the network has the accounts for all users or all servers, and then set that server as the security provider for every computer configured with File and Printer Sharing for NetWare Networks.

▶ **To share a directory and specify users on a NetWare network**

1. In Windows Explorer, right-click the directory you want to share. In the context-sensitive menu, click **Sharing**.

2. In the **Sharing** tab of the **Properties** dialog box, type a share name for the directory.

3. Click the **Add** button. In the **Add Users** dialog box, select the user name in the list on the left, and then click the related button to specify the kind of access that user is allowed.

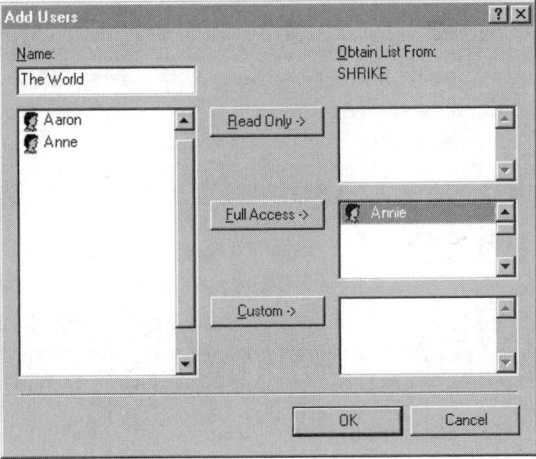

Notice in the illustration that the list of users shown in the **Add Users** dialog box is from the SHRIKE server's bindery. This means two things:

- All user management is done in the name space of the existing NetWare server. The NetWare server is administered by using all the same tools that are currently in place; Windows 98 has not added another name space to administer.

- Only valid user accounts and groups on SHRIKE can be specified for shared resources on the peer server.

For more information about using the **Add Users** dialog box, see Help. For more information about specifying directory access rights, see Chapter 9, "Security."

When the computer running Windows 98 receives a request from a user attempting to access a shared device, Windows 98 uses the NetWare server to validate the user name or group membership. If the name or group membership is validated, Windows 98 then checks to see if this validated name or group has been granted access rights to the shared resource, and then it grants or denies the connection request.

Share Names Versus NetWare Volume Names

When you share resources on a local hard disk drive using File and Printer Sharing for NetWare Networks, the share name associated with the shared directory structure becomes a volume name in the Novell designation *server/volume:* or the UNC designation *server\volume*.

You can use the UNC designation with **net** commands to connect to and disconnect from *server\sharename* shares.

Windows 98 does not make the distinction between shares and volumes because all shares and volumes appear as directories (also called folders). This distinction becomes important when you use NETX or VLM and NetWare utilities. NetWare does not use or understand the concept of share names. NetWare uses volumes for drive resources and print queue names for print resources.

Therefore, for a shared drive or printer resource to be available to all the different types of clients, when a computer configured with File and Printer Sharing for NetWare Networks shares a drive resource, the share name becomes equivalent to a NetWare volume. When this same computer shares a printer resource, the share name becomes equivalent to the NetWare print queue.

```
DIRECTORY SHARE NAME ---->   VOLUME
PRINTER SHARE NAME ------>   PRINT QUEUE
```

Using Bindery Emulation for Pass-through Security

File and Printer Sharing for NetWare Networks grants access to printers and directories on a per-user basis, which requires the name of the server to retrieve the names of users on a network. For NetWare versions 2.15 and 3.x servers, all the information for users, groups, passwords, and rights is stored in a database on the server called the bindery. NetWare version 4.x servers can appear to have a bindery using bindery emulation, which is enabled by default. Windows 98 can use the bindery of one NetWare server.

Usually, companies have multiple NetWare servers for different departments, and individual users log on to a different server by department. Problems can occur when the list of accounts differs between NetWare servers. For example, assume that Pat and Yoshi log on to the SALES server, and Hanna is on the R&D server. Pat can select only one server for pass-through validation, so she must select the SALES server, because that is where this account is located for log on. She can grant access to Yoshi, but not to Hanna.

Troubleshooting Logon, Browsing, and Resource Sharing

This section provides some general troubleshooting steps and explains how to solve common problems that might occur with logon, browsing, and resource sharing.

Troubleshooting Logon

This section describes common problems that might occur with system and network logon.

Setup does not run the logon script.

If the network logon server or domain controller is not validating the user account, the logon script will not run. Check the following:

- The network connection
- The user name
- The user password
- The basic network functionality
- The domain or server logon validation

If the network logon server or domain controller is validating the user account, do the following:

- Check the network connection.
- Verify that the login script is present in the home directory (on a Windows NT network) or in the user's mail directory (on a NetWare network).
- Check for enough memory on the client computer.
- Check for and remove unnecessary drivers and TSRs, and then try to log on again.

Logon script net use command does not work.

If your Windows NT domain is organized into a multiple master domain and a user's logon script **net use** command does not work, verify that you do not have two user accounts with the same user name and different passwords.

Logon fails with Novell Client for Windows 95/98.

After installing Novell Client for Windows 95/98, if you do not see a NetWare logon screen and NetWare servers do not appear in Network Neighborhood, check the following:

- Make sure the frame type conforms to your particular network.
- In the Novell Client **Properties** pages, make sure the Preferred Server and Preferred Tree settings are correct.
- Make sure the GUI logon utility Loginw95.exe is located on the local drive on the client workstation, not on a network server.

Troubleshooting Browsing

This section describes common problems that might occur with network browsing. As a general troubleshooting step, before performing the steps listed in this section, verify that you have a browsing problem rather than a problem with network connectivity.

▶ **To verify that you have a browsing problem**

1. On the **Start** menu, point to **Find**, and then click **Computer**.
2. In the **Named** box, type the computer name for the network server you want to browse.
3. Click **Find Now**.

If you can find the computer, you have a browsing problem. If not, you have a problem with your network connection.

As another general troubleshooting step, verify that the master browse server is functioning correctly. At the command prompt, type

net view /workgroup:*workgroup_name*

If your workgroup name contains spaces, enclose the workgroup name in quotation marks.

This command retrieves a browse list from the master browse server. If you can retrieve a browse list, a backup browse server might not be functioning correctly or might not have an updated browse list. (It can take up to 15 minutes to retrieve an updated browse list.)

You can also test browse master functionality with the **net use** command. At the command prompt, type

net use \\server\share

If you can connect but not browse, you might have a problem with your master browse server.

For more information about troubleshooting browsing, see the *Microsoft Windows NT Server Resource Kit* (for Windows NT Server version 4.0).

You cannot browse to find SMB-based servers in the workgroup while using Client for Microsoft Networks.

There might be no SMB-based servers in the workgroup (computers running Windows NT, LAN Manager, or File and Printer Sharing for Microsoft Networks). Windows 98 does not support browsing in a workgroup that does not contain an SMB-based server if the computer is running Client for Microsoft Networks. The following presents a solution.

▶ **To make sure there is an SMB-based server in the workgroup**

- On a computer running File and Printer Sharing for Microsoft Networks, make sure the service is configured as the master browser server.

    – Or –

    Make sure that a Windows NT server computer is a member of the workgroup (or domain).

Samba server does not accept your password.

For security reasons, Windows 98 no longer allows you to send plain text passwords. It sends only encrypted passwords. However, Samba servers require plain text passwords, so you will not be able to connect to Samba servers unless you change a registry entry to enable plain text passwords.

Caution   Enabling plain text passwords will decrease your computer's security.

To enable plain-text passwords, add the registry entry EnablePlainTextPassword (as a DWORD) and set the value to 1 in the following registry location:

HKEY_LOCAL_MACHINE\System
\CurrentControlSet\Services\VxD\Vnetsup

Access to an NCP-based server changes if SAP Advertising is defined.

Where you access an NCP-based peer resource server in Network Neighborhood can change, depending on whether the server is configured for Workgroup Advertising or SAP Advertising.

- If the computer running File and Printer Sharing for NetWare Networks is configured for Workgroup Advertising, that peer server appears as a computer in its workgroup.

- If the file and printer sharing server is configured for SAP Advertising, it appears with the other Novell NetWare servers at the beginning of the list of workgroups in the Entire Network window of Network Neighborhood.

To set SAP Advertising or Workgroup Advertising, follow the procedures in "Configuring Browsing for Resource Sharing on NetWare Networks" earlier in this chapter.

A user cannot connect to any network resource.

- Verify that the user is connected to the network.

- Check the network cable termination.

- Verify that the correct network client is loaded.

- Verify that a common NetBIOS protocol is installed. NetBIOS-compliant protocols include NetBEUI, TCP/IP, and IPX/SPX.

- Check the workgroup assignment.

- Check the domain or preferred server assignment for the protected-mode network client.

- Check the rights for the user as defined on the domain or preferred server.

- Use **net view \\computer name** to view shared resources.

Others cannot connect to my shared resources.

- In Control Panel, double-click Network, and verify that the file and printer sharing service appears in the list of installed components.

- Make sure other users are running a common protocol.

Network Neighborhood does not show servers.

- Verify that at least one active server is on the local network.

- Verify that the proper network clients are installed and, if necessary, reinstall them.

- Verify that the user is logged on to the particular network.

- Check the network protocol settings.

- Check that the IPX Frame Type is set to **Auto** or to the same type as the server.

- Check the network cable termination.

- Verify that you are connected to the correct workgroup. If you do not know what the correct workgroup is, contact your network administrator.

You cannot connect to a specific server.

- Check error message details, if available.

- Verify that you can connect to any server.

- Verify that you can connect to a specific server from other computers. If you cannot connect to the specific server from other systems, it probably indicates a problem with that server or the cabling or routing to it. Also verify termination of the local network cable.

The network redirector or server is not responding.

If the computer running Windows 98 is not responding properly as a client or server, use System Monitor to view statistics about the activity of the installed network servers and redirectors. If there is no activity, remove the client or server on the Network option in Control Panel, and then reinstall and try again.

You cannot see computers running Windows 98 on the other side of a router on a NetWare network.

This might be related to the IPX network number. An IPX client (such as a computer running Client for NetWare Networks) determines its network number by sending Routing Information Protocol (RIP) requests to the nearest IPX router. If the router is configured incorrectly, all IPX clients on that network can be adversely affected. Network numbers are assigned in the server's Autoexec.ncf file when the network adapter drivers are loaded and IPX is bound to the logical adapter.

Troubleshooting Resource Sharing

This section describes common problems that might occur with resource sharing.

Access is denied for Windows for Workgroups users trying to connect to shared resources on a computer running File and Printer Sharing for Microsoft Networks.

If the user with the Windows for Workgroups client computer is logging on to a different domain than the computer running file and printer sharing services (the peer server), then Windows 98 cannot confirm logon validation for access to shared resources. To solve this problem, do one of the following:

- Upgrade the Windows for Workgroups clients to Windows 98 (recommended).
- Switch to share-level security on the peer server.
- Change the logon domain for the Windows for Workgroups clients.

This problem will not occur in these cases: if the client computers are running Windows 98 or Windows NT; if the peer server uses share-level security; or if the same domains are used for the client computer's logon domain and the domain specified for pass-through validation in the peer server's **Access Control** properties.

A user is incorrectly denied access to resources on a peer server on a Windows NT network.

If a user is denied access to resources on a computer running File and Printer Sharing for Microsoft Networks with user-level security, you should first determine which security provider is specified for the peer server. Then, see if the client can be validated by that security provider directly without going through the peer server.

If this is successful, verify that the user is on the access control list for the shared resource on the peer server. Remove that user from the list of users and then add the name back. If this is unsuccessful, reconfigure the peer server to use another security provider that you know can validate the user.

File and Printer Sharing for Microsoft Networks does not work.

If the **Sharing** command does not appear on the context-sensitive menu when you use the right mouse button to click a drive, folder, or printer, check the following items:

- Verify that File and Printer Sharing for Microsoft Networks is installed.
- Verify that File and Printer Sharing for NetWare Networks is not installed.

You need to manage SAP Advertising on computers running File and Printer Sharing for NetWare Networks.

The SAP Advertising option is disabled by default for File and Printer Sharing on NetWare Networks. If you need to enforce the configuration of the file and printer sharing service, you can set the Disable SAP Advertising policy under the Default Computer policies.

In general, you will want to enable SAP Advertising only on computers with resources, such as CD-ROM drives that you want to share with NETX and VLM clients. SAP Advertising is not required for sharing resources only among computers running Windows 98. Notice the following:

- SAP Advertising is not required if you want to use Net Watcher to administer the file system on a computer running File and Printer Sharing for NetWare Networks.

- Neither SAP Advertising nor File and Printer Sharing for NetWare Networks is required for remote registry administration. The only requirement is user-level security with a pass-through server specified.

Windows 98 peer servers with SAP Advertising enabled will respond to **GetNearestServer** broadcasts. If this causes a NETX or VLM client to attempt to log on to a peer server, Windows 98 makes sure these NETX and VLM clients connect to a real NetWare server by using a stub file named Login.exe in the \Windows\Nwsysvol\login directory. This directory is created automatically when File and Printer Sharing for NetWare Networks is installed, and it is automatically shared with read-only privileges whenever SAP Advertising is enabled on the peer server.

Additional Resources

For more information about	See this resource
Windows NT	*Microsoft Windows NT Server System Guide*
	Microsoft Windows NT Server Resource Kit (for Windows NT Server version 4.0)
NetWare	**http://www.novell.com/**
Browsing white paper "Browsing and Windows 95 Networking"	**http://www.microsoft.com/win32dev/netwrk/**

CHAPTER 19

Remote Networking and Mobile Computing

19

This chapter describes how to use Dial-Up Networking and virtual private networking (VPN) to access a network from a remote location. It also describes how other Windows 98 mobile computing tools, such as Briefcase and Direct Cable Connection, can be used to connect to desktop computers or the network. This chapter benefits network administrators who need to install remote access service on clients and servers, implement virtual private networking, or add mobile computing features to clients on the network. It also explains to advanced users how to use Dial-Up Networking, virtual private networking, and mobile computing features.

In This Chapter

See Also

- For information about network protocols, see Chapter 15, "Network Adapters and Protocols."

- For information about setting up modems and Integrated Services Digital Network (ISDN) devices, see Chapter 21, "Modems and Communications Tools."

- For information about connecting to the Internet, see Chapter 20, "Internet Access and Tools."

Overview of Remote Networking and Mobile Computing

Dial-Up Networking, virtual private networking (VPN), and mobile computing allow users not directly connected to the network to work as if they were. *Dial-Up Networking* allows them to make a dial-up connection to remote networks such as the Internet over a telephone or ISDN line. *Virtual private networking* allows users to connect securely to resources on a remote network by "tunneling" over an intermediary network (an existing Internet or local area network [LAN] connection) to a server on the remote network. The intermediary network is used as a substitute for a network wire, enabling you to connect to a server on a remote network even if you are not directly connected to the remote network. Finally, *mobile computing* tools allow intermittently-connected users to access network resources more easily.

Windows 98 Dial-Up Networking allows you to use a computer running Windows 98 as a dial-up client. From a remote site, you can use Dial-Up Networking to connect to a remote access server such as Windows NT version 3.1 or later Remote Access Service (RAS), a Windows 98 dial-up server, a Windows 95 dial-up server, any Point-to-Point Protocol (PPP) server, Novell NetWare Connect version 1.0 or 1.1, or Shiva NetModem or LanRover, using the IP, IPX, and NetBEUI protocols. If the client and server are running the same network protocols, the dial-up client can connect to the network to access its resources. For information about using Windows 98 Dial-Up Networking to dial in to other remote access servers, or using other remote access software to dial in to Windows 98, contact your network vendor or software supplier.

Note A Microsoft Windows NT Client Access License is required if the computer will be connecting to servers running Windows NT Server. For information, see Chapter 16, "Windows 98 on Microsoft Networks," or contact your Microsoft reseller.

Dial-Up Networking also allows you to designate a computer running Windows 98 as a single-connection dial-up server. A remote user can dial in to the dial-up server and access resources on the dial-up server.

For clients running the IPX or the NetBEUI protocol, the dial-up server can be used to provide access to the network. However, if you need a dial-up server that provides access to the network using Transmission Control Protocol/Internet Protocol (TCP/IP), you should use a Windows NT Server. For more information about the capabilities of the Windows 98 dial-up server, see "Configuring and Using the Windows 98 Dial-Up Server" later in this chapter.

Windows 98 provides the following tools to help users stay as functional as possible with the limited resources of a mobile site:

- Briefcase allows users to update documents on a portable computer with source documents on a desktop computer or network.
- Direct Cable Connection allows users to connect a portable computer to a desktop computer to synchronize files and share other resources.
- Microsoft Outlook Express provides remote access to electronic mail.
- Deferred printing allows users to generate print jobs when no physical printer is available.

Overview of Dial-Up and Virtual Private Networking

Windows 98 includes the following enhancements to Dial-Up Networking:

- Client support for a single virtual private networking connection.
- Support for ISDN modems and adapters.
- Multilink capabilities.
- Connection-time scripting to automate nonstandard logons.
- Improved performance and stability.

This section provides an overview explanation of how you can use these enhancements and other Dial-Up Networking features for remote access. For information about ISDN, see Chapter 21, "Modems and Communications Tools."

With Dial-Up Networking and virtual private networking, you can connect from a remote site to a computer that has been configured as a remote access server, or connect to a network through the remote access server. For example, as Figure 19.1 shows, if you connect to a Windows NT Remote Access Server, you can access its shared resources (if the Microsoft File and Printer Sharing service has been enabled), or you can use it as a gateway to a network that is running the TCP/IP, IPX/SPX, and NetBEUI network protocols.

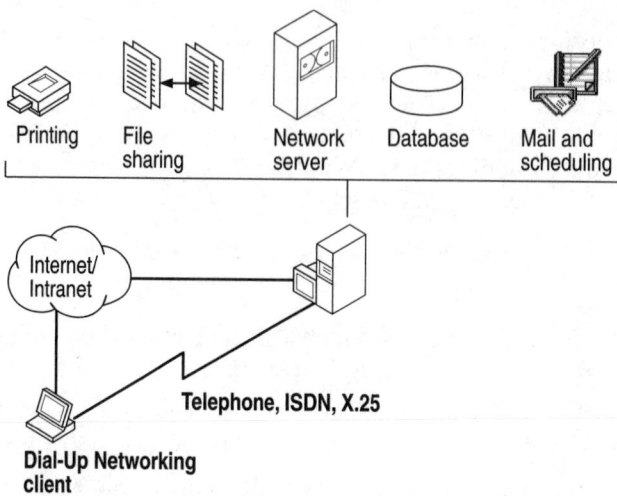

Figure 19.1   Connecting to a remote access server

Figure 19.1 illustrates two types of connections: a dial-up connection and a virtual private network connection through the Internet. You would use either the dial-up connection or the virtual private network connection to access those resources.

Note You can also access shared resources by connecting to a Windows 98 dial-up server. For a description of the capabilities and limitations of the Windows 98 dial-up server, see "Configuring and Using the Windows 98 Dial-Up Server" later in this chapter.

As Figure 19.2 shows, a Windows 98 dial-up client can connect to a wide variety of networks, because Windows 98 supports a variety of connection and network protocols.

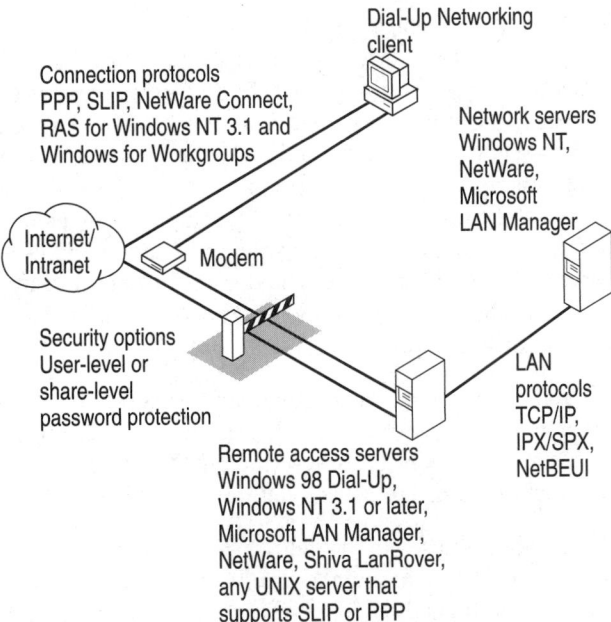

Figure 19.2   Connecting to remote networks

With virtual private networking, you can connect to remote servers not only over telephone lines, but also over Internet connections and the corporate intranet. This provides the following benefits:

Inexpensive remote access With virtual private networking, remote users can connect to your company's network from the Internet instead of over a telephone line, so you do not need to maintain modem pools or pay long-distance charges. Your network must have a Windows NT Remote Access Server (RAS) virtual private networking server and a dedicated connection to the Internet, such as a 56Mbits, fractional T-1, T-1 connection. Users simply dial in to their local Internet Service Providers (ISPs) and then connect to the RAS VPN server over the Internet.

Secure access to private data In Windows, 98, virtual private networking is implemented using Point-to-Point Tunneling Protocol (PPTP). Because PPTP is a secure protocol, only authenticated users can gain access to your dial-up server. Also, you can encrypt data transfer to prevent Internet intruders from listening in.

Private addressing schemes   Using certain types of routers and gateway servers, it is possible to connect your network to the Internet so that all your computers and their IP addresses are visible on the Internet. However, this configuration presents two drawbacks. First, your computers are vulnerable to attack by intruders on the Internet. Second, you must obtain IP addresses that conform to the Internet addressing scheme. Using virtual private networking, on the other hand, you can configure all the computers on your private intranet by using a private addressing scheme that does not need to conform to the Internet addressing scheme. The VPN server then shields the internal addresses from the rest of the Internet. The IP addresses of the computers on your private intranet remain hidden, providing additional security for those computers.

Different remote access servers provide different security systems to protect access to a network. The Windows 98 dial-up server uses pass-through (user-level) or share-level security as described in "Configuring Security Options for a Windows 98 Dial-Up Server" later in this chapter.

Dial-Up Networking uses the Windows 98 communications architecture to communicate through a modem to a network. It initializes the modem, determines device status, and dials the telephone number by using the telephony application program interface (TAPI) and the Unimodem driver. For more information about the communications architecture and the Dial-Up Networking architecture, see Chapter 29, "Windows 98 Network Architecture."

A Windows 98 Dial-Up Networking configuration includes the components described in the following sections

Dial-Up Client

With Dial-Up Networking, you can configure a remote computer running Windows 98 as a dial-up client to dial in to a remote access server. A dial-up client, running the appropriate connection protocol, can connect to many types of remote access servers, including the following:

- Windows NT 3.51 or later Server computer.
- Windows NT 3.51 or later Workstation computer.
- Windows 98 dial-up server.
- Windows 95 dial-up server.
- Windows for Workgroups version 3.11.
- NetWare Connect 1.0 or 1.1.
- Any network access server that supports PPP (including NetWare Connect 2.0).
- Any UNIX server that runs Serial Line Internet Protocol (SLIP) or PPP.

Connection Protocols

Connection protocols control the transmission of data over the wide-area network (WAN). A Windows 98 dial-up client can use the following connection protocols to connect to a remote access server:

- PPP.
- Novell NetWare Connect 1.0 and 1.1.
- Windows NT 3.1 or Windows for Workgroups RAS (Asynchronous NetBEUI).
- SLIP.

The type of connection protocol you choose depends on the server you are connecting to. Some connection protocols support a subset of the common network protocols. For example, PPP allows you to connect to a network server or a computer running Windows 98 with TCP/IP, IPX/SPX-compatible, or NetBEUI network protocols.

This section describes the connection protocols.

Point-to-Point Protocol   Point-to-Point Protocol (PPP) provides a standard method for transporting multi-protocol datagrams over point-to-point links. It has become the standard for remote access because of its flexibility, password encryption security, and compatibility with future client and server hardware and software. A dial-up client running PPP can connect to a network running IPX, TCP/IP, or NetBEUI protocols. Windows 98 dial-up clients can use PPP to connect to any remote access server running PPP, including Windows NT Server version 3.51 or later. PPP is the default protocol for the Microsoft Dial-Up adapter.

Novell NetWare Connect   NetWare Connect 1.0 and 1.1 is a proprietary connection protocol. It allows a computer running Windows 98 to connect directly to a NetWare Connect 1.0 or 1.1 server and, if running a NetWare-compatible network client, connect to NetWare servers.

Windows 98 can connect to NetWare Connect 2.0 using PPP. For information about PPP, see "Technical Notes for PPP-Compatible Servers" later in this chapter.

Note   Windows 98 can act only as a client for connecting to a NetWare Connect 1.0 or 1.1 server. NetWare Connect 1.0 or 1.1 clients themselves cannot directly connect to a Windows 98 dial-up server through a dial-up connection.

RAS for Windows NT 3.1 or Windows for Workgroups 3.11 (Asynchronous NetBEUI)

Asynchronous NetBEUI is used to connect computers running Windows 98 to remote access servers running Windows NT Server 3.1 LAN Manager, or Windows for Workgroups 3.11. It is also supported by Windows NT Server 3.5 and later. The remote access server must also be running NetBEUI.

Serial Line Internet Protocol SLIP is an older remote access standard that is typically used by UNIX remote access servers. Use SLIP only if your site has a UNIX system configured as a SLIP server for Internet connections. The remote access server must be running TCP/IP.

Windows 98 does not provide SLIP server capabilities; SLIP is used for client dial-out only.

Local Area Network Protocols

Windows 98 makes it easy to configure dial-up clients to access a network. When you install Dial-Up Networking, any protocols already installed on the computer are automatically enabled for Dial-Up Networking. Windows 98 includes support for TCP/IP, IPX/SPX, and NetBEUI network protocols.

Note In Properties for your Dial-Up Networking connection, all network protocols show up as automatically enabled. However, remember that you cannot use them unless they have actually been installed on your computer. For information about how to install network protocols, see Chapter 15, "Network Adapters and Protocols."

The following list presents the combinations of protocols you can use to run either Windows Sockets or NetBIOS applications on a network.

Connection protocol	Network protocols (APIs)
NetWare Connect 1.0 or 1.1	IPX/SPX (Windows Sockets/NetBIOS)
PPP	TCP/IP (Windows Sockets/NetBIOS) IPX/SPX (Windows Sockets/NetBIOS) NetBEUI (NetBIOS)
RAS for Windows NT 3.1 or Windows for Workgroups 3.11	NetBEUI (NetBIOS)
SLIP	TCP/IP (Windows Sockets/NetBIOS)

Figure 19.3 shows the protocols Dial-Up Networking clients can use to connect to host servers and to remote networks.

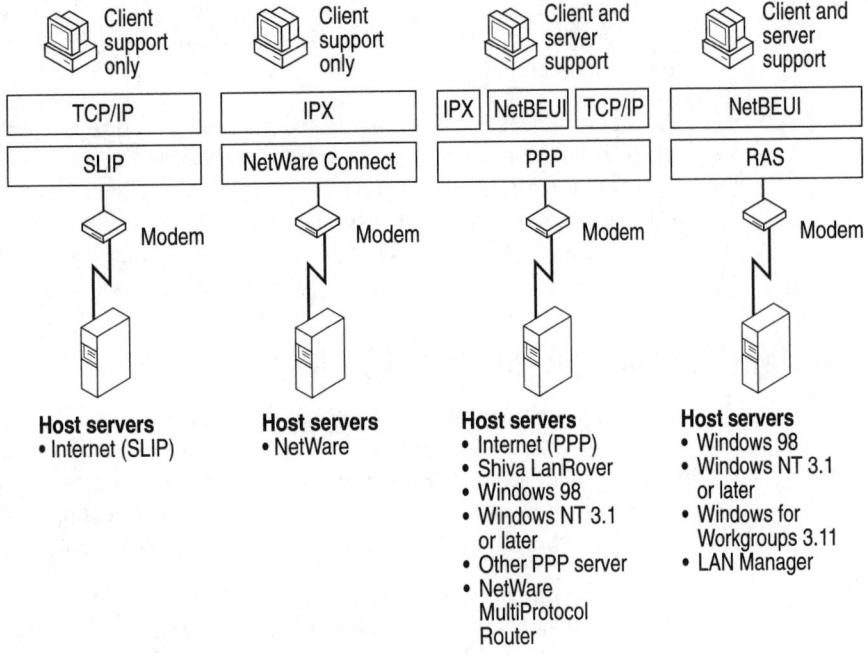

Figure 19.3   Connection protocols

Dial-Up Server

You can designate a computer running Windows 98 a single-connection dial-up server. If both the server and the client are running IP, IPX, or NetBEUI, the dial-up server can provide access to its shared resources. If both the server and the client are running IPX or NetBEUI, the dial-up server can act as a gateway to a network running the same protocol. For more information about the capabilities of the Windows 98 dial-up server, see "Configuring and Using the Windows 98 Dial-Up Server" later in this chapter.

Using Software and Hardware Compression to Transfer Data

To improve the throughput and transfer times when you use Dial-Up Networking, Windows 98 supports dynamic compression of information when you are connected to another computer that also supports compression—for example, a computer running Windows 98 or Windows NT.

You do not need to perform any special configuration to enable hardware and software compression. Software compression on the client is enabled by default and is available for PPP connections. You should leave it enabled. Hardware compression is also enabled by default and is performed by the modem. You should leave it enabled. For more information about hardware compression, see Chapter 21, "Modems and Communications Tools."

Using Data Encryption for Dial-Up Clients

You do not need to perform any special configuration to enable data encryption on dial-up clients. This option can be required by either the server or the client. For instructions on how to configure a Dial-Up connection so that the dial-up client will refuse to connect to a server that does not support data encryption. For instructions, see "Configuring a Dial-Up Connection," later in this chapter.

Data encryption requires that the client and server share a common key, which is generated at connection time using Microsoft Challenge Handshake Authentication (MS-CHAP).

Security Options for Dial-Up Clients and Servers

Dial-Up Networking servers can be configured with either user-level or share-level security. Additionally, a Dial-Up Networking client can be configured to use encrypted passwords if the server it is connecting to supports that feature. For more information, see "Configuring Security Options for a Windows 98 Dial-Up Server" later in this chapter.

Planning for Dial-Up and Virtual Private Networking

To use Dial-Up Networking to connect to the Internet or a remote network, you need the following hardware:

- One or more compatible modems or ISDN devices, as described in Chapter 21, "Modems and Communications Tools."

- Enough available hard disk space to install Dial-Up Networking. Currently, about 2 to 3 MB of free disk space are required to install the client and server portions of Dial-Up Networking.

In most cases, you will need the same hardware to use virtual private networking to connect to a remote network through the Internet. If you will be connecting to a remote network through a VPN server on your corporate network and you will never make a dial-up connection, you will not need a modem or ISDN device, but you will need a network adapter that is physically connected to the LAN.

To use a Dial-Up Networking client to connect to the network, you need to decide the following:

- The kind of remote access server remote users will connect to. For example, a Windows 98 dial-up server allows only 1 remote connection at a time, whereas a Windows NT Server 3.5 or later remote access server allows 256 connections. Depending on the size and needs of your network, you might configure a Windows 98 dial-up client to connect to a Windows NT Server 3.5 or later remote access server or another remote access server. For a list of the types of remote access servers that a Windows 98 dial-up client can be configured to connect to, see "Dial-Up Client" earlier in this chapter.

- The type of connection protocol your dial-up client will use to connect to the remote access server. Windows 98 provides support for PPP, RAS for Windows for Workgroups 3.11 and Windows NT 3.1, NetWare Connect 1.0 and 1.1, and SLIP. The dial-up client and the remote access server must both be running the same connection protocol. For a complete list of protocol types, see "Connection Protocols" earlier in this chapter.

- The kind of network protocol to install on the dial-up client to connect the client to the network. Windows 98 dial-up clients support IPX/SPX, TCP/IP, and Microsoft NetBEUI protocols. For more information about network protocols and Dial-Up Networking, see "Local Area Network Protocols" earlier in this chapter.

If you want to add a Windows 98 dial-up server to your network, you need to decide the following:

- Which computers on the network will function as Windows 98 dial-up servers.

- Whether you want to connect the client to the network and what kind of network protocol you need to install on the dial-up server. Windows 98 dial-up servers support only the IPX/SPX and Microsoft NetBEUI protocols; to use TCP/IP to connect the client to the network, you must use a Windows NT Server instead of a Windows 98 dial-up server.

- The level of security you need for dial-up servers. You can enable either user-level or share-level security on a Windows 98 dial-up server. For more information, see "Configuring Security Options for a Windows 98 Dial-Up Server" later in this chapter.

Installing Dial-Up Networking

By default, Windows 98 Setup automatically installs Dial-Up Networking, other communications tools, and most of the components you need to connect to a network. Table 19.1 shows the communications tools that appear in the **Add/Remove Programs** option in Control Panel. For information about which of these tools are installed by default under the Typical, Portable, Compact, or Custom installations, see Chapter 2, "Setting Up Windows 98."

Table 19.1   Communications tools available in Windows 98

Tool	Purpose
Dial-Up Networking	Allows a Windows 98 computer to access a network or the Internet from a remote location.
Dial-Up Server	Gives a Windows 98 computer the ability to provide remote access to a single dial-up client.
Direct Cable Connection	Allows you to establish a direct serial or parallel cable connection between two computers.
HyperTerminal	Provides file transfer and terminal emulation capabilities.
Infrared	Allows a Windows 98 computer to communicate with other computers or the network using infrared.
Microsoft Chat 2.0	Allows you to chat with people on a chat server.
Microsoft NetMeeting	Allows you to call people on the Internet or a corporate intranet and talk, share applications, draw on a shared whiteboard, or share files and messages.
Phone Dialer	Allows a Windows 98 computer to make voice calls.
Virtual private networking	Allows a Windows 98 computer to connect securely to a remote server over telephone lines, the Internet, or a corporate intranet.

If you want to add an additional component, you must install it after running Windows 98 Setup.

▶ **To add an additional component**

1. In Control Panel, double-click **Add/Remove Programs,** and then click the **Windows Setup** tab.

2. Double-click **Communications** in the list of components.

3. Select the component.

4. Click **OK**, and then click **Apply.**

Windows 98 Setup also installs most of the components you need to connect to a network. For example, Windows 98 installs the Microsoft Dial-Up adapter, connection protocols, and the Microsoft TCP/IP network protocol if TCP/IP has not already been installed on the computer.

Note If you are upgrading from Windows 3.1 or Windows for Workgroups, Setup does not upgrade your phonebook entries (your connection information). You must reenter all connection information. However, if you are upgrading from Windows 95, Setup does upgrade your connection information.

However, Windows 98 Setup does not automatically install network protocols such as IPX/SPX and NetBEUI. If you need to use those protocols but they are not already installed on your computer, you must install them.

To verify that the correct protocols are installed, in Control Panel, double-click Network, and then check the list of installed components.

For information about adding protocols, see Chapter 15, "Network Adapters and Protocols."

Configuring and Using Dial-Up Networking Clients

Configuring computers as Dial-Up Networking clients consists of four tasks:

- Running the Install New Modem Wizard to install a modem.
- Configuring Telephony Dialing Properties.
- Running the Make New Connection Wizard in Dial-Up Networking to set up a connection to a remote access server for the dial-up client.
- Optionally, configuring the connection by selecting the remote access server type it will connect to, and by choosing whether to log on to the network after connecting to the remote access server. Selecting the server type automatically enables the correct connection protocol, such as PPP or SLIP.

This section explains how to perform these four tasks.

Installing a Modem

If you have not already installed a modem, the Install New Modem wizard appears when you start Dial-Up Networking. It guides you through the process of installing a modem. For more information about modems, see Chapter 21, "Modems and Communications Tools."

Configuring Telephony Dialing Properties

After the Install New Modem wizard installs your modem, a **Location Information** dialog box appears. This dialog box asks for such information as what country you are in and what area code you are in. Windows 98 uses this information to establish a dialing rule (called a *dialing location*). Whenever you dial a call, Windows 98 uses this dialing rule to automatically adjust your dialing string. For example, if you enter "425" as your area code in the **Location Information** dialog box, then later try to dial the number "425-555-1212," Windows 98 adjusts the dialing string to "555-1212."

If you have a portable computer and frequently dial from different places, you might also want to use the Dialing Properties utility to create different dialing locations for each place. You can also define calling card rules that you can use with one or more of your dialing locations.

Note The information you entered in the **Location Information** dialog box also appears in the Dialing Properties utility, as your default dialing location.

The remainder of this section describes how to establish and use different calling locations using the Dialing Properties Utility. For more information about the Dialing Properties utility, including how to define calling card rules, see "Using Dialing Properties" in Chapter 21, "Modems and Communications Tools."

The Dialing Properties utility allows you to define different locations from which you dial. For each location, enter your country code, area code, and other information about the place you are dialing from. You can then dial a number using Dial-Up Networking, and Windows 98 automatically adjusts your dialing string based on the location from which you are calling.

For example, suppose you commonly dial from two different places:

- **Your home** in the 206 area code region. You do not need to dial an outside line, but you dial ***70** for each call to disable call waiting.

- **Your office** in the 801 area code region. To reach an outside line, you must dial **9**.

You can create two different locations (home and office) and enter area code and other information for each location. Then, whenever you make a dialing location, Dialing Properties automatically adjusts the telephone number based on the place you are calling from.

For example, suppose you have defined a Dial-Up Networking Connection to your ISP at 206-555-5555.

If you are dialing from home, Dialing Properties adjusts the telephone number to *70,555-5555. But if you are dialing from your office, Dialing Properties changes the telephone number to 9,1-206-555-5555.

You can access Dialing Properties from several different places, including the Modems icon in Control Panel, the Telephony icon in Control Panel, and the connection you are dialing.

▶ **To define a new dialing location**

- In Dialing Properties, enter the name of your new dialing location, the area code you are dialing from, and other information about your location. Optionally, enter information about your calling card. This information will then be available to any Dial-Up Networking connection that you create.

▶ **To use the dialing location**

1. When you configure the General properties for a Dial-Up Networking connect (described in "Configuring General Properties" later in this chapter), make sure that the check box "**Use area code and Dialing Properties**" is selected.

2. When you dial the connection (described in "Making a Dial-Up Networking Connection" later in this chapter), make sure that you have selected the correct dialing location.

Defining a Dial-Up Networking Connection

When you first start Dial-Up Networking, the Make New Connection Wizard appears. You can define two different types of remote connections:

- A dial-up connection allows you to use modems or ISDN devices to connect to the Internet or your intranet.

- A VPN connection uses two connections. With the first connection, you use a network adapter, modem, or ISDN device to connect to a remote access server on the Internet or your intranet. With the second connection, you can "tunnel through" the first connection to a VPN tunnel server, in order to gain access to any server that the VPN tunnel server allows you to access.

Before creating a new dial-up connection, you should install a modem, ISDN device, or network adapter. If you have not yet installed a modem and did not install a modem when Dial-Up Networking started, you can install one by using the Install New Modem Wizard in the Modems option in Control Panel. For information about modems and ISDN devices, see Chapter 21, "Modems and Communications Tools."

Additionally, if you are configuring a VPN connection, you must first install virtual private networking. To do so, follow the procedure "To add an additional component" described in "Installing Dial-Up Networking" earlier in this chapter.

▶ **To create a Dial-Up Networking connection using the Make New Connection Wizard**

1. From My Computer, double-click the Dial-Up Networking folder.

2. In the **Dial-Up Networking** window, double-click the Make New Connection icon.

3. In the **Type a name for the computer you are dialing** dialog box, enter a name for your connection.

4. If you are creating a dial-up networking connection, in the **Select a device** box select a modem or ISDN device.

   –Or–

   If you are creating a VPN connection, in the **Select a device:** box select **Microsoft VPN Adapter**.

5. If you are creating a dial-up networking connection, the Make New Connection Wizard prompts you for information about your connection, such as a name for the computer you are dialing, modem type, area code, telephone number, and country code.

   –Or–

   If you are creating a VPN connection, the Make New Connection Wizard prompts you for the host name or address of the VPN server.

6. The new icon for your connection appears in the **Dial-Up Networking** window. You need to provide this information only once for each connection you define.

   Once a connection has been established, remote network access becomes transparent to the user.

Configuring a Dial-Up Connection

The Dial-Up Networking defaults for the dial-up connection are designed for Internet connections and for most other types of connections. You can change these defaults, but you should do so only if you want to change the default behavior.

There is one exception. By default, Dial-Up Networking uses the PPP protocol to connect to servers. This default will work for most Internet connections and many other types of connections. But if you are connecting to a server that does not use PPP, you must change the server type by following the procedure in "Configuring Options for the Server to Which You Are Connecting" later in this chapter.

You can configure the following options:

- General properties
- Server properties
- Scripting
- Multilink

You can predefine Dial-Up Networking connections for users by including them as part of system policies. If you enable user profiles, different users sharing the same computer can use separate dialing configurations. For more information, see Chapter 7, "User Profiles," and Chapter 8, "System Policies."

Configuring General Properties

This section describes how to configure basic options for a dial-up connection.

▶ **To configure general properties for the connection**

1. In Dial-Up Networking, right-click a connection icon, and then select **Properties** from the **File** menu.

2. Review the information on the **General** tab to ensure that the telephone number is correct and that the correct modem or ISDN device is selected. Ensure that **Use area code and Dialing Properties** is selected if you have defined one or more dialing locations as described in "Configuring Telephony Dialing Properties" earlier in this chapter. Make any necessary changes.

3. Click **Configure**, and then click the **Options** tab.

4. Optionally, click **Bring up terminal window before dialing** or **Bring up terminal window after dialing**. For modem connections, these options allow you to use a terminal window for an interactive logon session with the server.

Configuring Options for the Server to Which You Are Connecting

Dial-Up Networking allows you to configure options for the server to which you are connecting. You do not need to change any values in this section if you are connecting to an ISP and your ISP's remote access server supports PPP.

▶ **To configure options for the server to which you are connecting**

1. In Dial-Up Networking, right-click a connection icon, and then click **Properties**.

2. Click the **Server Types** tab.

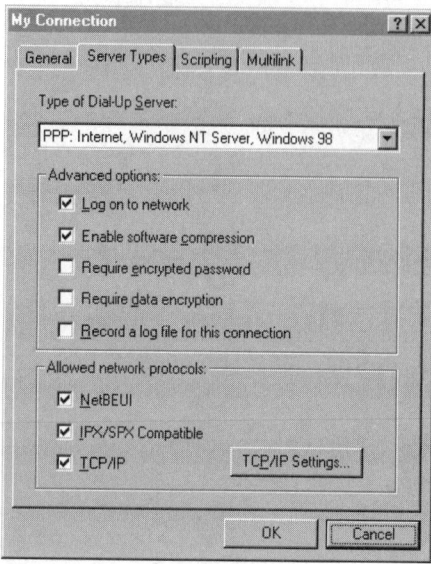

3. In the **Type of Dial-Up Server** box, ensure that the correct remote access server type is selected. If it is not selected, you will not be able to connect to the server. The possible connections are as follows:

This server type	Connects to
PPP: Internet, Windows NT Server, Windows 98	The default; selecting it allows Windows 98 to automatically detect and connect to other remote access servers that are running TCP/IP, NetBEUI, or IPX/SPX over PPP. Select this option for connections to your ISP.
NRN: NetWare Connect version 1.0 and 1.1	Novell NetWare Connect 1.0 or 1.1 running IPX/SPX over NetWare Connect 1.0 or 1.1.
SLIP: UNIX Connection	Any SLIP server over TCP/IP.
Windows for Workgroups and Windows NT 3.1	Windows 98 dial-up server; Windows NT 3.1 or 3.5; Windows for Workgroups version 3.11 running NetBEUI over RAS.
CSLIP: UNIX Connection with IP Header Compression	Any SLIP server over TCP/IP that supports IP header compression.

4. Optionally, if you are making a connection to an ISP, deselect **Log on to network** to speed connection time. This option is selected by default, but it is unnecessary for Internet connections.

5. Optionally, select **Require encrypted password**. If this option is selected, the client will use only Challenge Handshake Authentication Protocol (CHAP) and MS-CHAP encryption when generating a password. If this option is not selected, the client can also perform Password Authentication Protocol (PAP) if the server requests it. However, PAP encryption is less secure. For more information about encryption, see "PPP Dial-Up Sequence" later in this chapter.

6. Optionally, select **Require data encryption**. If this option is selected, the client will refuse to connect with any server that does not use data encryption. However, most ISPs do not support data encryption. For more information, see "Using Data Encryption for Dial-Up Clients," earlier in this chapter.

7. Optionally, select **Record a log file for this connection**. If this option is selected, Dial-Up Networking will create a PPP log file that shows information about your connection. For information about PPP log files, see "PPP Log File" later in this chapter.

8. In the **Allowed network protocols** box, ensure that the network protocols used on the target network are selected. For example, if you are configuring a connection to the Internet, ensure that TCP/IP is selected.

Note   By default, all network protocols (TCP/IP, IPX/SPX, and NetBEUI) are selected in the **Allowed network protocols** box. However, for you to use those protocols, they must also be installed on the client workstation you are configuring. For information about how to install protocols, see Chapter 15, "Network Adapters and Protocols."

---

9. Optionally, if you are configuring a connection to your ISP and your ISP requires you to enter information such as a static IP address for your computer or a DNS server to which you must connect, click **TCP/IP Settings**. However, in most cases you do not need to do so. For more information, see Chapter 20, "Internet Access and Tools."

Configuring Scripting for Modem Connections

Windows 98 supports scripting on modem connections (not on ISDN or VPN connections.) In most cases, you do not need to create a script. Many ISPs do not require a manual logon, and ISPs that do require a manual logon almost always provide a script file you can use. Contact your ISP for more information.

However, if you need and do not have a logon script, you can create one. Windows 98 provides four sample scripts you can use as starting points. The sample scripts are located in your **\Program Files\Accessories** directory. Windows 98 also includes a document that explains how to write and modify logon scripts. The file is called Script.doc and located in your Windows directory.

After you have created a script, save it in your **\Program Files\Accessories** directory, using the file extension SCP.

> **Important**   Microsoft does not support logon scripts you create. Also, Microsoft does not support modifications to the four sample scripts.

After you have created the script, you must configure scripting for each connection that will use the script. Make sure your connection is working properly before you configure scripting.

▶ **To configure scripting for the Windows 98 dial-up client**

1. In Dial-Up Networking, right-click a connection icon, and then click **Properties**.

2. Click the **Scripting** tab, and then click **Browse** .

3. Locate the script, and then click **Open**.

4. Optionally, select the **Step through script** box.

   Selecting the **Step through script** box enables you to step through the script to verify that each line is working correctly, or to troubleshoot the script if the connection fails.

5. Click **OK**.

Configuring Multilink

The PPP Multilink protocol allows you to use two or more devices (such as modems or ISDN devices) for a single dial-up link. With Multilink, you combine the bandwidth capabilities of both devices, thus inexpensively increasing the bandwidth on your dial-up connections. This section describes how to use Multilink. For additional information about Multilink, and for information about ISDN, see Chapter 21, "Modems and Communications Tools."

The Windows 98 PPP Multilink implementation complies with the Internet Engineering Task Force (IETF) PPP Multilink standard defined by Request for Comments (RFC) 1717.

Before using Multilink, consider the following issues:

- Multilink is available only for Windows 98 dial-up clients, not for the Windows 98 dial-up server.

- The server or ISP you connect to must also support PPP Multilink. Otherwise, Multilink will not function correctly.

- You can use Multilink only when your computer is configured with multiple devices that can be combined to form the logical PPP pipe over the communication link.

- For best performance, the devices you use should be the same speed.

- When you combine both B channels under ISDN, you cannot use your second channel for other applications, such as fax or voice calls.

▶ **To configure Multilink for the Windows 98 dial-up client**

1. In Dial-Up Networking, right-click your connection icon, and then click **Properties**.

2. Click the **Multilink** tab.

3. Select **Use additional devices**.

4. Click **Add.**

5. Specify the additional device you wish to use.

6. If you need to edit an entry, click **Edit**.

▶ **To use Multilink**

- After you have configured Multilink, click the connection icon and click **Connect**. Dial-Up Networking connects using the primary device, then the secondary device.

▶ **To view information about your link**

1. Click the Dial-Up Networking icon displayed on your taskbar.

2. In the dialog box, click **Details**.

Configuring a Connection to the Internet

To configure a Windows 98 Dial-Up Connection to dial the Internet, follow the procedures outlined in "Configuring and Using Dial-Up Networking Clients" earlier in this chapter. Keep in mind the following issues:

- Before you begin, check to make sure TCP/IP is correctly installed on your computer.

- If you want to use a terminal window for an interactive logon session with the server, in the modem's Properties, click **Bring up terminal window before dialing** or **bring up terminal window after dialing**.

- If you are using SLIP instead of PPP to connect to the Internet, in the **Server Types** dialog box, select **SLIP: UNIX Connection**.

- If you want to speed your connection time, in the **Server Types** dialog box, deselect **Log on to network**. This option is not necessary for Internet connections.

- If your ISP requires you to enter information such as an IP address for your computer or the IP address of a DNS server, enter this information in the **Server types** dialog box. In most cases, you will not need to enter information here. For more information, see Chapter 20, "Internet Access and Tools."

Making a Dial-Up Networking Connection

After you have defined a remote connection by using the Make New Connection Wizard, you can make a connection.

Note If you selected **Use area code and Dialing Properties** in the General Properties for your connection, Dial-Up Networking automatically adjusts the dialing string (telephone number) according to your dialing location (the place you're dialing from). For more information about your dialing location, see "Configuring Telephony Dialing Properties" earlier in this chapter.

▶ **To make a Dial-Up Networking Connection**

1. Double-click its connection icon in the Dial-Up Networking folder.

2. Optionally, enter a user name and password.

3. If you selected **Use area code and Dialing Properties** in the General Properties for your connection, in the **Dialing from** area, ensure that you have selected the correct dialing location (the place you are dialing from). If necessary, select another dialing location or click **Dial properties** to define a new dialing location.

After a connection has been made, a connection icon appears in the system tray. You can double-click this icon to see information about the connection, such as the server type it is using, the protocols it is using, and whether it is using authentication and compression.

Note If you are using PPP to connect to the remote server and you are dialing in to an IPX network, you will lose IPX connectivity to your local network. Thus, after you make a dial-up networking connection, NetWare servers on the local network will no longer be visible.

You might also lose IP connectivity to your local network if you are dialing in to an IP network. For specific details and for ways to restore IP connectivity, see "Technical Notes on Dial-Up and Virtual Private Networking" later in this chapter.

Dial-Up Networking starts automatically in certain circumstances, through an autodial feature included in Dial-Up Networking and an autodial feature included in the Internet Explorer 4 browsing software. The following sections describe the two features.

Using the Dial-Up Networking Autodial Feature

Dial-Up Networking provides an autodial feature. If autodial is enabled, Windows 98 starts Dial-Up Networking when you try to perform one of the following tasks:

- You try to access a network resource when your computer is not connected to any network.

- You try to access a network resource that you have accessed before using Dial-Up Networking.

- Your application specifies a UNC name (which uses the form *servername*\ *sharename*) that cannot be accessed by using the network.

Note The Dial-Up Networking autodial feature is separate from the Internet Explorer browsing software autodial feature, described below.

When you choose a remote connection, Windows 98 retrieves the server information from the addresses stored in the registry. If the information is not available, you are asked to select a server from the connection icons in Dial-Up Networking, or to type a new server name.

If Dial-Up Networking cannot find the network resource, it displays a network error message. If the connection is successful, Windows 98 remembers the connection for future use.

You can disable the prompt that asks if you want to use Dial-Up Networking when you are attempting to connect to a network resource.

▶ **To disable the Dial-Up Networking prompt**

1. In Dial-Up Networking, click the **Connections** menu, and then click **Settings**.

2. Click **Don't prompt to use Dial-Up Networking**.

Using the Internet Explorer Browsing Software Autodial Feature

The Internet Explorer browsing software includes an autodial feature that can automatically start Dial-Up Networking while you are browsing. When you start the Internet Explorer browsing software or try to access a URL that is not locally available, and you have not already established a Dial-Up Networking connection, a dialog box appears and asks you if you want to use Dial-Up Networking.

Note The Internet Explorer autodial feature is separate from the Dial-up Networking autodial feature, described above.

The Internet Explorer browsing software starts Dial-Up Networking only if you have a modem and you have configured the Internet Explorer browsing software to automatically start Dial-Up Networking.

The following procedure shows how to do so.

▶ **To configure the Internet Explorer browsing software to automatically start Dial-Up Networking**

1. In Control Panel, double-click Internet, and then click the **Connection** tab.

2. In the **Connection** box, select **Connect to the Internet using a modem**.

3. Optionally, click the **Settings** box to specify a particular Dial-Up Networking connection and to enter information about that connection.

The following procedure shows how to configure the Internet Explorer browsing software to not start Dial-Up Networking.

▶ **To configure the Internet Explorer browsing software to not start Dial-Up Networking**

1. In Control Panel, double-click Internet, and then click the **Connection** tab.

2. In the **Connection** box, select **Connect to the Internet using a local area network**.

Configuring and Using the Windows 98 Dial-Up Server

With Dial-Up Networking, you can configure a computer running Windows 98 to be a remote access server for dial-up clients running Windows 98, Windows 95, Windows for Workgroups, or Windows 3.1, or any other client running PPP. The Windows 98 dial-up server can act as a server to the client, sharing its file and printer resources with one dial-up client at a time. Both the dial-up server and the dial-up client must be running the same protocol (IP, IPX, or NetBEUI). The Windows 98 dial-up server can also act as a gateway to an IPX/SPX or NetBEUI network, as long as both the client and the server are using the same protocol that is used on the network.

The Windows 98 dial-up server supports software compression. It also works with ISDN; however it can use only one B channel.

A Windows 98 dial-up server differs from the Windows NT 3.5 and later dial up servers in the following ways:

- Windows NT Server 4.0 and later can act as a VPN server; Windows 98 cannot.

- Windows NT Server 3.5 and later can act as an IP router; Windows 98 cannot. IP router capabilities permit access to a TCP/IP network, such as the global Internet. Windows 98 provides all the protocols you need to connect to the Internet but cannot act as an IP router.

- Windows NT Server 3.5 and later support 256 remote connections, whereas Windows 98 provides one remote connection.

A Windows 98 dial-up server with the appropriate network protocols installed can act as a NetBIOS gateway, as shown in Figure 19.4.

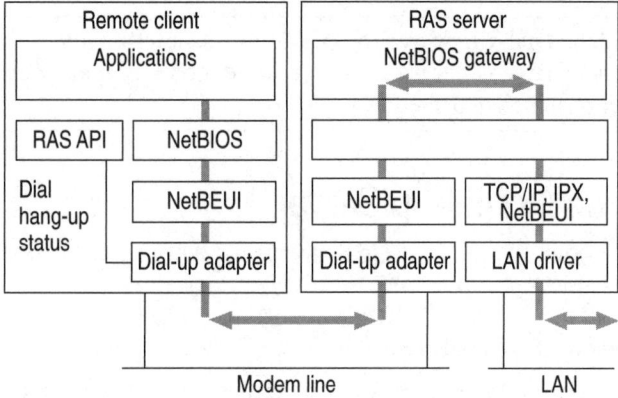

Figure 19.4   Dial-up server as NetBIOS gateway

Configuring a computer running Windows 98 to be a dial-up server consists of the following steps:

- Installing the Dial-Up Server, as described in "Installing a Windows 98 Dial-Up Server," later in this chapter.

- Optionally, enabling file and printer sharing services for either Microsoft or NetWare networks on the dial-up server. Perform this step only if you want the dial-up server to share files with the dial-up clients. For more information, see Chapter 18, "Logon, Browsing, and Resource Sharing."

- Enabling user-level or share-level security on the dial-up server. For information, see "Configuring Security Options for a Windows 98 Dial-Up Server" later in this chapter.

- Configuring the server type for the dial-up server, as described in the section "Configuring the Server Type for the Dial-Up Server" later in this chapter.

After you perform the steps previously listed, your Dial-Up Server will be ready to answer incoming calls.

▶ **To disconnect any users who are currently connected to this computer through Dial-Up Networking**

- In the **Dial-Up Server** dialog box, click **Disconnect User**.

Note The Dial-Up Server for Windows 98 can use only one modem at a time. You can enable caller access on multiple modems at any one time, but only one modem can be connected.

Installing a Windows 98 Dial-Up Server

In Windows 98, the Dial-Up Server is not automatically installed. To install it, follow this procedure.

▶ **To install the Dial-Up Server**

1. In Control Panel, double-click **Add/Remove Programs**, and then click the **Windows Setup** tab.

2. In **Add/Remove Programs Properties**, double-click **Communications**.

3. Select the **Dial-Up Server** check box, and then click **OK**, and then click **OK** again.

Configuring Security Options for a Windows 98 Dial-Up Server

Dial-Up Networking gives you the option of requiring a password to connect to the remote access server, depending on whether the Windows 98 dial-up server is protected with share-level or user-level security.

- Share-level security assigns a password to the Windows 98 dial-up server. When users dial in, they must provide the password before they can gain access to the server. After the connection is established, users can browse the resources on the dial-up server, subject to whatever level of security has been applied to them. Users can also log on to the network after connecting to the dial-up server if logging on to the network is enabled on the dial-up client. Because users can distribute passwords, this method is less secure than user-level security.

- User-level security restricts access to a network resource until a security provider, such as a Windows NT domain controller or a NetWare server, authenticates the request. You can require that a user's logon password to a remote access server be the same as the network and Windows 98 logon passwords.

  With user-level security, when the user accesses shared resources on the dial-up server, Windows 98 controls a user's rights to the shared resources, such as whether the user has read-only access or full access to files. Access rights are specified in the sharing properties for each resource protected by user-level security. For more information, see Chapter 9, "Security," and Chapter 18, "Logon, Browsing, and Resource Sharing."

The following procedure assumes that you have completed the installation procedure described in the previous section, "Installing a Windows 98 Dial-Up Server."

▶ **To configure the dial-up server for user-level security**

1. Make sure that your computer has file and printer sharing services installed and that user-level security is enabled. For more information, see Chapter 18, "Logon, Browsing, and Resource Sharing."

2. In Dial-Up Networking, click the **Connections** menu, and then click **Dial-Up Server**.

3. In the **Dial-Up Server** properties, click **Allow caller access**, and then click **Add**.

4. In the **Add Users** dialog box, specify the users who will have permission to access the dial-up server, and then click **OK**.

5. In the **Dial-Up Server** properties, click **Server Type**, and make sure **Require encrypted password** is checked if your Dial-Up client supports encrypted passwords.

   Clicking the **Require encrypted password** option requires the client to send an encrypted as opposed to a text password. Some clients support only text passwords; however, encrypted passwords are preferred. Clearing this option does not disable password protection.

▶ **To configure the dial-up server for share-level security**

1. Make sure that your computer has File and Printer Sharing services installed and that share-level security is enabled. For more information, see Chapter 18, "Logon, Browsing, and Resource Sharing."

Note Share-level security is not available on NetWare networks.

---

2. In Dial-Up Networking, click the **Connections** menu, and then click **Dial-Up Server**.

3. In the **Dial-Up Server** dialog box, click **Allow caller access**, and then click **Change Password** to provide password protection for the Dial-Up Server.

4. Optionally, to require password encryption, click **Server Type**. In the **Server Type** dialog box, make sure **Require encrypted password** is checked, and then click **OK**.

Configuring the Server Type for the Dial-Up Server

This section explains how to configure the server type for the dial-up server. It assumes that you have already followed the procedures in the sections "Installing a Windows 98 Dial-Up Server" and "Configuring Security Options for a Windows 98 Dial-Up Server," earlier in this chapter.

▶ **To configure a computer as a dial-up server**

1. From the **Connections** menu in the Dial-Up Networking folder, click **Dial-Up Server**.

2. Click **Server Type**, and then select the server type.

   Make sure that the server type is the same for both the dial-up server and the dial-up client. If the dial-up client uses PPP, you can also select the Default server type. If you select the Default server type, the dial-up server will automatically start in PPP mode for incoming calls and switch to Windows for Workgroups and Windows NT 3.1 if the PPP negotiation fails.

3. Click **OK**, and the dial-up server is ready to answer incoming calls.

Notice that changes to the server type do not apply to a currently open connection. Changes will apply to any future connections made to this computer.

Disabling Dial-Up Server Support

You can disable dial-up server support in several different ways. You can disable it from within Dial-Up Networking, as the following procedure explains.

▶ **To disable the dial-up server on a single computer**

1. From the **Connections** menu in the Dial-Up Networking window, click **Dial-Up Server**.

2. In the **Dial-Up Server** dialog box, click **No caller access**.

You can also completely remove Dial-Up Server capabilities from a user's computer by using the Add/Remove Programs option in Control Panel.

Finally, you can disable dial-up support on each computer or on a system-wide basis by using System Policy Editor to change a single computer's registry or to define policies that can be shared by multiple computers.

To disable dial-up support by using System Policy Editor, click **Disable Dial-in**. The **Dial-Up Server** menu option still appears on the **Connections** menu after dial-up support has been disabled, but no dialog box for setting up the dial-up server will appear. For more information, see Chapter 8, "System Policies."

Configuring and Connecting to Remote Servers

With Dial-Up Networking, you can connect to many different kinds of servers. This section discusses how to connect to and configure a Windows NT Remote Access Server and a Novell NetWare Connect 1.0 or 1.1 server. It also provides technical information about PPP-compatible servers.

Connecting to a Windows NT Remote Access Server

Connecting to a Windows NT remote access server is the same as connecting to a Windows 98 Dial-Up Networking server. All you need is the telephone number of the Windows NT server when creating a connection. Dial-Up Networking negotiates the proper protocols and server connection type. You do not need to specify a default server type.

Planning the Connection to a Windows NT Remote Access Server

Windows NT Server 3.5 and later remote access servers support PPP and RAS clients. PPP is the recommended protocol. Windows NT Server 3.5 and later support IPX/SPX, NetBEUI, and TCP/IP network protocols and can function simultaneously as a NetBIOS gateway, IPX router, and IP router. Windows NT Server 4.0 and later can act as a VPN server, so you can set up a VPN connection to Windows NT 4.0 RAS servers using the PPTP protocol.

Note Windows NT 3.1 supports only the RAS protocol, which is a proprietary protocol that supports only NetBEUI. It is a fast connection type but does not allow for multiple protocols over the connection. RAS in Windows NT 3.1 cannot support the IPX/SPX or TCP/IP protocols.

Microsoft recommends that you upgrade from Windows NT RAS to Windows NT Server 3.5 or later, which provides many additional benefits, including PPP support.

A Windows NT 3.5 or later remote access server provides several features that a Dial-Up Networking server does not. For an explanation of these differences, see "Configuring and Using the Windows 98 Dial-Up Server" earlier in this chapter.

For more information about Windows NT remote access servers, see the *Microsoft Windows NT Server Networking Guide* in the *Microsoft Windows NT Server Resource Kit* (for Microsoft Windows NT Server version 4.0). See also the *Networking Supplement* for Windows NT Server version 4.0.

Configuring a Windows NT Server for Windows 98 Dial-Up Clients

To configure a computer running Windows NT Server 3.5 or later so that Windows 98 dial-up clients can remotely access it, you need to install and configure RAS.

You must be logged on as a member of the Administrators group to install and configure RAS. It can be installed during Custom Setup of Windows NT or afterward. During Express Setup, if there is not a network adapter in a computer, you are given the option to install RAS.

RAS installation varies slightly depending on which network protocols are installed. If you use TCP/IP or IPX/SPX protocol with RAS, you should install the protocol before you install RAS, although selecting a protocol that is not installed causes that protocol to be installed at the conclusion of RAS Setup. For information about installing either protocol, see the *Networking Supplement* for Microsoft Windows NT Server 4.0.

For information about installing RAS, see the *Microsoft Windows NT Server Resource Kit* (for Microsoft Windows NT version 4.0).

Note Microsoft does not recommend granting guest accounts dial-in permission. If you do, be sure to assign a password to the guest account.

Connecting to a Novell NetWare Connect 1.0 or 1.1 Server

Windows 98 Dial-Up Networking supports connecting to Novell NetWare resources in three ways:

- Connecting directly to a Novell NetWare Connect 1.0 or 1.1 server.
- Connecting directly to a Novell NetWare Connect 2.0 server. NetWare Connect 2.0 uses the PPP protocol, so you can connect to a NetWare Connect 2.0 server as you would to any other PPP server.
- Using a computer running Windows 98 or Windows NT 3.5 or later as a gateway into a network where NetWare servers are connected.

NetWare Connect 1.0 or 1.1 allows a Windows 98 client to dial in to a NetWare server running NetWare Connect 1.0 or 1.1

Note Windows 98 can act only as a client for connecting to a NetWare Connect 1.0 or 1.1 server. NetWare Connect 1.0 or 1.1 clients themselves cannot dial up a Windows 98 dial-up server.

The NetWare Connect 1.0 or 1.1 connection type allows a Windows 98 client to connect directly to a NetWare Connect 1.0 or 1.1 server and to connect to NetWare servers on the connected network.

To use Dial-Up Networking to connect to a NetWare Connect 1.0 server, you must specify NetWare Connect 1.0 as the server type in the properties for a Dial-Up Networking connection. You also need to use the Network option in Control Panel to make sure the following are enabled on a Windows 98 dial-up client or server:

- Microsoft Client for NetWare Networks.
- The IPX/SPX-compatible protocol bound to the Microsoft Dial-Up adapter driver.

If you use Dial-Up Networking to access NetWare Connect 1.0 or 1.1 servers, you can access data remotely, but you cannot control a computer remotely as you can with the NetWare Connect 1.0 or 1.1 client software supplied by Novell.

Technical Notes for PPP-Compatible Servers

This section provides technical information about connecting to PPP-compatible servers. It covers the following topics:

- PPP architecture
- PPP dial-up sequence
- PPP log file

PPP Architecture

The Point-to-Point Protocol (PPP) provides a standard method for transporting multi-protocol datagrams over point-to-point links. PPP does so by establishing and configuring different link and network-layer protocols to carry traffic from point to point. Control and data flow modules make up the PPP control protocols as illustrated in Figure 19.5.

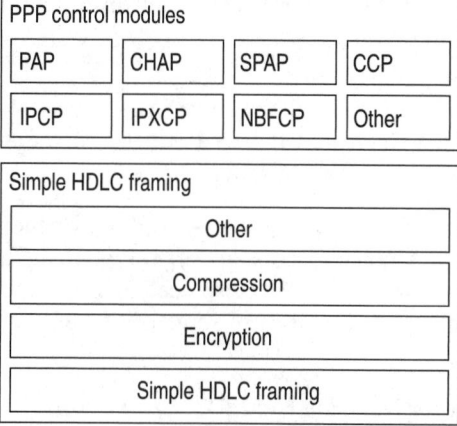

PPP control modules			
PAP	CHAP	SPAP	CCP
IPCP	IPXCP	NBFCP	Other

Simple HDLC framing
Other
Compression
Encryption
Simple HDLC framing

Figure 19.5   Microsoft PPP control modules

Figure 19.5 shows Password Authentication Protocol (PAP), Challenge Handshake Authentication (CHAP), and Shiva Password Authentication Protocol (SPAP), which perform password authentication of PPP clients. Compression Control Protocol (CCP) is used to negotiate encryption with PPP clients. IPCP, IPXCP, NBFCP, and Other are the Internet Protocol (IP), NetWare IPX, NetBIOS Extended User Interface (NetBEUI), and Other protocol modules, respectively, which control PPP client sessions. *HDLC* is the High-level Data Link Control protocol.

PPP Dial-Up Sequence

When a user dials in to a PPP-compatible server, four things happen:

1. The Data Link Control Layer (HDLC) defines how data is encapsulated before transmission on the WAN. By providing a standard framing format, PPP ensures that various vendors' remote access solutions can communicate and distinguish data packets from each other. PPP uses HDLC framing for serial, ISDN, and X.25 data transfer.

   The PPP Data Link Control layer is a slightly modified version of the HDLC layer. The HDLC format, extensively used by IBM and others for synchronous data transfer, was modified by adding a 16-bit protocol field that allows PPP to multiplex traffic for several Network Control Protocol (NCP) layers. This encapsulation frame has a 16-bit checksum, but the size of the protocol field and address can be compressed.

2. Link Control Protocol (LCP) establishes, configures, and tests the integrity of the data-link connection. LCP also negotiates which authentication protocol (listed in step 3) will be used. When LCP negotiates authentication of protocols, it determines what level of security validation the remote access server can perform and what the server requires. LCP also determines whether Multilink will be used.

3. The authentication protocol negotiated by LCP is used. Any of the following authentication protocols can be used.

   - PAP uses a two-way handshake for the peer to establish its identity. This handshake occurs only when the link is initially established. With PAP, passwords are sent over the circuit in text format, which offers no protection from playback.

   - SPAP offers encryption of PAP passwords and Novell NetWare bindery access for user account information. When Windows 98 is set up for user-level security using a NetWare server account list, this is the security type used for remote access clients.

   - CHAP periodically verifies the identity of the peer, using a three-way handshake. The authenticator sends a challenge message to the peer. The peer returns the user name and an MD5 hash of the challenge, session ID, and client's password. The authenticator then checks this response and, if the values match, the authentication is acknowledged; otherwise, the connection is ended. CHAP provides protection against playback attack, because the challenge value changes with every message. Because the password is never sent unencrypted over the link, it is virtually impossible to learn it.

- MS-CHAP is an encrypted authentication mechanism similar to but more secure than CHAP. As with CHAP, the authenticator sends a challenge to the peer. The peer must return the user name and an MD4 hash of the challenge string, the session ID, and the MD4-hashed password. This design, which manipulates a hash of the MD4 hash of the password, provides an additional level of security because it allows the authenticator to store hashed passwords instead of clear-text passwords. MS-CHAP also provides additional error codes, including a password expired code, and additional encrypted client-server messages that permit users to change their passwords. In Microsoft's implementation of MS-CHAP, both the peer and the authenticator independently generate an initial key for subsequent data encryption. During phase 2 of PPP link configuration, the authenticator collects the authentication data and then validates the data against its own user database or against a central authentication database server.

4. After authentication, the client and server begin negotiating NCPs. NCPs establish and configure different network protocol parameters. The type of NCP that PPP selects depends on which protocol (NetBEUI, TCP/IP, or IPX) is being used to establish the Dial-Up Networking connection. Windows 98 supports the following:

- NetBIOS Frames Control Protocol (NBFCP) is used to configure, enable, and disable the NetBEUI protocol modules on both ends of the link. For information about NBFCP, see Request for Comments (RFC) 2097, "The PPP NetBIOS Frames Control Protocol."

- Internet Protocol Control Protocol (IPCP) is used to configure, enable, and disable IP protocol modules at both ends of the link. IPCP is defined in RFC 1332, "The PPP Internet Protocol Control Protocol (IPCP)"

- Internet Packet Exchange Control Protocol (IPXCP) is used to configure, enable, and disable IPX protocol modules on both ends of the link. IPXCP is widely implemented by PPP vendors. IPXCP is defined in RFC 1552, "The PPP Internetwork Packet Exchange Protocol (IPXCP)."

PPP Log File

You can record how the PPP layers process a call by enabling the PPP log file. This file contains some of the basic layers and points of any Dial-Up Networking session, and is especially useful for monitoring PPP sessions. It is recorded and stored in the Windows directory.

Windows 98 improves over the PPP logging feature in Windows 95 in a few ways. It allows you to enable PPP logging per connection, rather than per adapter. Thus, you can enable PPP logging for only the connections you need, and you do not need to know which adapter is used for which connection. Also, you do not need to reboot for PPP logging to take effect. Moreover, PPP logging is more sophisticated in Windows 98 than in Windows 95. As the sample at the end of this section shows, with Windows 98, the PPP log shows the actual packets that are being passed.

▶   **To enable PPP logging for a connection**

1. In Dial-Up Networking, single-click a connection icon, and in the **File** menu, select **Properties**.

2. Click the **Server Types** tab.

3. Select the option named **Record a log file for this connection**.

The following example is sample content of a ppplog.txt file. This is only a partial log of a connection; it stops before authentication. For information about the format of PPP packets, see RFC 1662, "PPP in HDLC-like Framing."

```
03-19-1998 13:17:16.04 - Microsoft Dial Up Adapter log opened.
03-19-1998 13:17:16.04 - Server type is  PPP (Point to Point Protocol).
03-19-1998 13:17:16.04 - FSA : Adding Control Protocol 80fd (CCP) to
control protocol chain.
03-19-1998 13:17:16.04 - FSA : Protocol not bound - skipping control
protocol 803f (NBFCP).
03-19-1998 13:17:16.04 - FSA : Adding Control Protocol 8021 (IPCP) to
control protocol chain.
03-19-1998 13:17:16.04 - FSA : Protocol not bound - skipping control
protocol 802b (IPXCP).
03-19-1998 13:17:16.04 - FSA : Adding Control Protocol c029 (CallbackCP)
to control protocol chain.
03-19-1998 13:17:16.04 - FSA : Adding Control Protocol c027 (no
description) to control protocol chain.
03-19-1998 13:17:16.04 - FSA : Encrypted Password required.
03-19-1998 13:17:16.04 - FSA : Adding Control Protocol c223 (CHAP) to
control protocol chain.
03-19-1998 13:17:16.04 - FSA : Adding Control Protocol c021 (LCP) to
control protocol chain.
03-19-1998 13:17:16.04 - LCP : Callback negotiation enabled.
03-19-1998 13:17:16.04 - LCP : Layer started.
```

```
03-19-1998 13:17:16.05 - PPP : Transmitting Control Packet of length: 25
03-19-1998 13:17:16.05 - Data 0000: c0 21 01 01 00 17 02 06 | .!...·..
03-19-1998 13:17:16.05 - Data 0008: 00 0a 00 00 05 06 00 02 | ........
03-19-1998 13:17:16.05 - Data 0010: 50 17 07 02 08 02 0d 03 | P·......
03-19-1998 13:17:16.05 - Data 0018: 06 00 00 00 00 00 00 00 | ........
03-19-1998 13:17:19.05 - PPP : Transmitting Control Packet of length: 25
03-19-1998 13:17:19.05 - Data 0000: c0 21 01 02 00 17 02 06 | .!...·..
03-19-1998 13:17:19.05 - Data 0008: 00 0a 00 00 05 06 00 02 | ........
03-19-1998 13:17:19.05 - Data 0010: 50 17 07 02 08 02 0d 03 | P·......
03-19-1998 13:17:19.05 - Data 0018: 06 00 00 00 00 00 00 00 | ........
03-19-1998 13:17:22.05 - PPP : Transmitting Control Packet of length: 25
03-19-1998 13:17:22.05 - Data 0000: c0 21 01 03 00 17 02 06 | .!...·..
03-19-1998 13:17:22.05 - Data 0008: 00 0a 00 00 05 06 00 02 | ........
03-19-1998 13:17:22.05 - Data 0010: 50 17 07 02 08 02 0d 03 | P·......
03-19-1998 13:17:22.05 - Data 0018: 06 00 00 00 00 00 00 00 | ........
03-19-1998 13:17:22.11 - PPP : Received Control Packet of length: 8
03-19-1998 13:17:22.11 - Data 0000: c0 21 04 03 00 06 08 02 | .!......
03-19-1998 13:17:22.11 - LCP : Received configure reject for address
field compression option.
03-19-1998 13:17:22.11 - PPP : Transmitting Control Packet of length: 23
03-19-1998 13:17:22.11 - Data 0000: c0 21 01 04 00 15 02 06 | .!...·..
03-19-1998 13:17:22.11 - Data 0008: 00 0a 00 00 05 06 00 02 | ........
03-19-1998 13:17:22.11 - Data 0010: 50 17 07 02 0d 03 06 00 | P·......
03-19-1998 13:17:22.16 - PPP : Received Control Packet of length: 23
03-19-1998 13:17:22.16 - Data 0000: c0 21 02 04 00 15 02 06 | .!...·..
03-19-1998 13:17:22.16 - Data 0008: 00 0a 00 00 05 06 00 02 | ........
03-19-1998 13:17:22.16 - Data 0010: 50 17 07 02 0d 03 06 00 | P·......
03-19-1998 13:17:23.27 - PPP : Received Control Packet of length: 32
03-19-1998 13:17:23.27 - Data 0000: c0 21 01 00 00 1e 03 05 | .!...-..
03-19-1998 13:17:23.27 - Data 0008: c2 23 80 05 06 00 00 6e | .#.....n
03-19-1998 13:17:23.27 - Data 0010: 21 07 02 11 04 06 4e 13 | !.....N.
03-19-1998 13:17:23.27 - Data 0018: 09 03 00 80 5f e2 d8 a8 | ...._...
03-19-1998 13:17:23.27 - LCP : Received and accepted authentication
protocol c223 (CHAP).
03-19-1998 13:17:23.27 - LCP : Received and accepted magic number 6e21.
03-19-1998 13:17:23.27 - LCP : Received and accepted protocol field
compression option.
03-19-1998 13:17:23.27 - PPP : Transmitting Control Packet of length: 19
03-19-1998 13:17:23.27 - Data 0000: c0 21 04 00 00 11 11 04 | .!......
03-19-1998 13:17:23.27 - Data 0008: 06 4e 13 09 03 00 80 5f | .N....._
03-19-1998 13:17:23.27 - Data 0010: e2 d8 a8 00 00 00 00 00 | ........
03-19-1998 13:17:23.30 - PPP : Received Control Packet of length: 19
03-19-1998 13:17:23.30 - Data 0000: c0 21 01 01 00 11 03 05 | .!......
03-19-1998 13:17:23.30 - Data 0008: c2 23 80 05 06 00 00 6e | .#.....n
03-19-1998 13:17:23.30 - Data 0010: 21 07 02 00 00 00 00 00 | !.......
03-19-1998 13:17:23.30 - LCP : Received and accepted authentication
protocol c223 (CHAP).
03-19-1998 13:17:23.30 - LCP : Received and accepted magic number 6e21.
03-19-1998 13:17:23.30 - LCP : Received and accepted protocol field
compression option.
```

```
03-19-1998 13:17:23.30 - PPP : Transmitting Control Packet of length: 19
03-19-1998 13:17:23.30 - Data 0000: c0 21 02 01 00 11 03 05 | .!......
03-19-1998 13:17:23.30 - Data 0008: c2 23 80 05 06 00 00 6e | .#.....n
03-19-1998 13:17:23.30 - Data 0010: 21 07 02 00 00 00 00 00 | !.......
03-19-1998 13:17:23.30 - LCP : Layer up.
```

Implementing Virtual Private Networking

Networking provides a way to connect a client computer to a server by means of a transmission medium such as a network wire or a dial-up connection. It contains three key elements: the client, the transmission media, and the server.

Similarly, virtual private networking (VPN) provides a way to connect a client computer to a server by means of a tunnel through an intermediary network. That is, it uses a network as a transmission medium. The virtual private network consists of the two computers (one at each end of the connection) and a route, or *tunnel*, over the public or private network.

For example, suppose you want to access the resources on your corporate LAN, but you have only an Internet connection. With virtual private networking, you can "tunnel through" the Internet to access resources on your corporate LAN.

In another example, suppose you are connected to your corporate LAN (LAN A), but you want to access the resources on a server on another LAN (LAN B). LAN A and LAN B are connected by means of a private TCP/IP network. With virtual private networking, you can tunnel through the private network to access the resources on the server on LAN A just as if you were directly connected to it.

In Windows 98, virtual private networking is implemented using the *Point-to-Point Tunneling Protocol* (PPTP). PPTP allows you to tunnel through TCP/IP-based data networks to securely access resources on remote servers. PPTP supports multiple network protocols (IP, IPX, and NetBEUI) and can be used for virtual private networking over public and private networks. You can use PPTP to provide secure, on-demand, virtual networks by using dial-up lines, LANs, WANs, or the Internet and other public, TCP/IP-based networks.

The networking technology of PPTP is an extension of the remote access PPP protocol defined in the IETF document "The Point-to-Point Protocol" (RFC 1661). PPTP is a network protocol that encapsulates PPP packets into IP datagrams for transmission over the Internet or other public TCP/IP-based networks. PPTP can also be used in private LAN-to-LAN networking.

For more information about virtual private networking, visit Microsoft's Web site at **http://www.microsoft.com/communications/**. You can also download the IETF Internet draft "Point-to-Point Tunneling Protocol—PPTP" from **http://www.ietf.org/**.

Planning for Virtual Private Networking

There are two common virtual private networking scenarios:

- You can connect your workstation to a remote network by making a Dial-Up Networking connection to a network access server at an ISP facility, and then tunneling through the Internet to a VPN server that is attached to both the Internet and the remote network. Once you are connected to the VPN server, you can transparently gain access to any public or private network that is connected to it.

- If you have a permanent IP connection to a VPN tunnel server (such as a LAN connection), you can use that VPN server to tunnel to any public or private network that is connected to it.

Some less common virtual private networking scenarios require a server provided by a third party. For instance, some VPN tunnel servers, called front end processors (FEPs), can be used for modem pooling. If your PC is on a network with a FEP that has modems available for dialing out, users can simply connect to that tunnel server, dial out, and establish a connection to a PPP access server on another network.

The following section describes the first scenario, in which you use the Internet as the network through which the client tunnels. However, keep in mind that you could use any TCP/IP network in place of the Internet. If so, you must have a permanent TCP/IP connection to a VPN server, and you do not need a dial-up connection to a network access server.

Typical Virtual Private Networking Deployment

A typical deployment of virtual private networking starts with a remote or mobile Windows 98 client that uses a local ISP to access the Internet. The client then tunnels through the Internet to a private enterprise LAN.

A Windows 98 client must make two connections to establish a VPN tunnel: one physical connection and one logical connection. Figure 19.6 shows these connections. The client first uses Dial-Up Networking and the remote access protocol, PPP, to connect to a network access server at an ISP's facility. Once connected, the client can send and receive packets over the Internet. The network access server uses the TCP/IP protocol for all traffic to the Internet.

Note Network access servers are also referred to as dial-in servers, or point-of-presence (POP) servers.

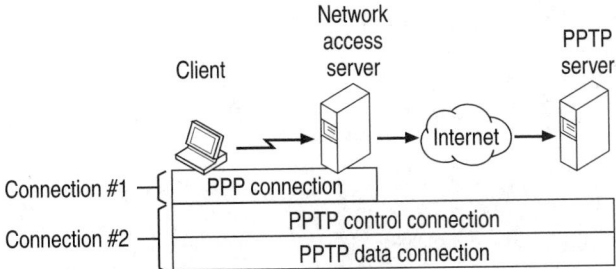

Figure 19.6   Creating a VPN tunnel

The client then uses Dial-Up Networking to make a second logical connection over the existing PPP connection. Data sent using this second connection is in the form of IP datagrams that contain PPP packets, referred to as encapsulated PPP packets.

The second connection creates the VPN connection to a VPN server on the private enterprise LAN (a computer running Windows NT Server 4.0 and configured as a VPN server). This connection is referred to as a *tunnel*.

Tunneling is the process of sending packets to a computer on a private network by routing them over some other network, such as the Internet. The other network's routers cannot access computers on the private network. However, tunneling enables the routing network to transmit the packet to an intermediary computer, a VPN server that is connected to the both the routing network and the private network. Both the VPN client and the VPN server use tunneling to route packets securely to a computer on the private network by using routers that know only the address of the private network intermediary server.

When the VPN server receives the packet from the routing network, it sends it across the private network to the destination computer. The VPN server does this by processing the PPTP packet to obtain the private network computer name or address information in the encapsulated PPP packet. Note that the encapsulated PPP packet can contain multi-protocol data such as IP, IPX, or NetBEUI protocols. Because the VPN server is configured to communicate across the private network by using private network protocols, it is able to read multi-protocol packets.

Figure 19.7 illustrates the multi-protocol support built into virtual private networking. A packet sent from the VPN client to the VPN server passes through the VPN tunnel to a destination computer on the private network.

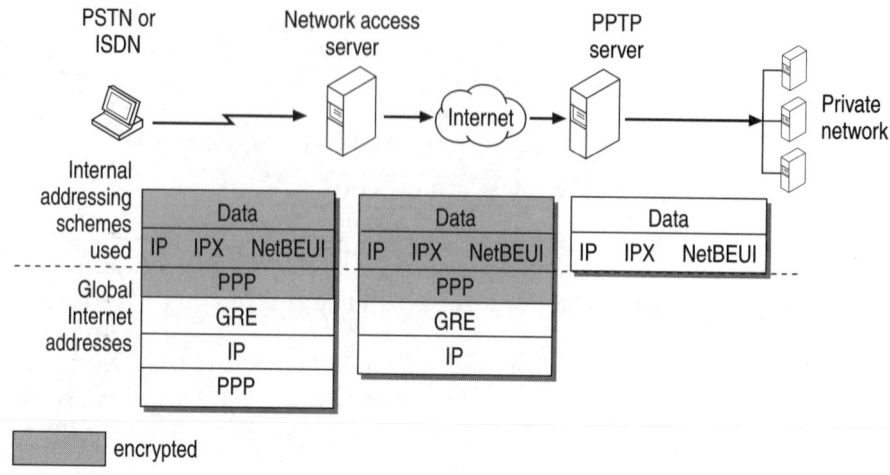

Figure 19.7   Connecting a Dial-Up Networking VPN client to the private network

PPTP encapsulates the encrypted and compressed PPP packets into IP datagrams for transmission over the Internet. The IP datagrams are created using a modified version of the Internet Generic Routing Encapsulation (GRE) protocol. (defined in RFCs 1701 and 1702).These IP datagrams are routed over the Internet until they reach the VPN server that is connected to both the Internet and the private network. The VPN server disassembles the IP datagram into a PPP packet and then decrypts the PPP packet. It then sends the de-encapsulated IP, IPX, or NetBEUI packet on the private network.

Using Network Protocols with Virtual Private Networking

Virtual private networking allows you to create a tunnel over a public TCP/IP network but retain existing network protocols, network node addresses, and naming schemes on the private enterprise network. Thus, no changes to existing network configurations or network-based applications are required when using virtual private networking to tunnel across the Internet or other TCP/IP-based public networks. For example, IPX or NetBEUI clients can continue to run applications on the private network that require these protocols.

Name resolution methods used on the private network—such as Windows Internet Naming Service (WINS) for NetBIOS computers, Domain Name System (DNS) for TCP/IP host names, and Service Advertisement Protocol (SAP) for IPX networking—do not need to be changed.

Note The address and name resolution schemes on the private enterprise network must be correctly configured. If they are not, VPN clients are unable to communicate with computers on the private network.

Virtual Private Networking Issues

Consider the following issues when using virtual private networking:

- A VPN server can be placed behind a firewall on the private enterprise network to ensure that traffic in and out of the private network over the VPN server is secured by the firewall computer. (For more information, visit **http://www.microsoft.com/communications/** and download "Understanding PPTP.")

- Using the Internet to establish a connection between a VPN client and a VPN server means that the VPN server must have a globally unique IP address that is valid for the global Internet. However, the encapsulated IPX, NetBEUI, or TCP/IP packets sent between the VPN client and the VPN server can be addressed to computers on the private enterprise network using private network addressing or naming schemes. The VPN server disassembles the PPTP packet from the VPN client and forwards the packet to the correct computer on the private network. For more information about private network addressing, see Chapter 15, "Network Adapters and Protocols."

Configuring Virtual Private Networking

Depending on how you will be using virtual private networking, you will need to configure different types of connections.

If you have a permanent TCP/IP connection (such as a LAN connection) to a VPN tunnel server, and you want to connect to a remote network that is connected to your VPN server, you need only configure the connection to that VPN tunnel server.

If you want to connect your workstation to a remote server by tunneling through the Internet, you must configure two connections: a connection to the Internet through your ISP and a tunnel connection to the VPN server on the target network.

To configure the connection to your ISP or your VPN tunnel server, follow the procedures outlined in "Defining a Dial-Up Networking Connection" and "Configuring and Using Dial-Up Networking Clients" earlier in this chapter.

Using Virtual Private Networking

This section describes how to use the two common VPN configurations.

> **Note** If you are using PPP or PPTP to connect to another IPX network, you will lose IPX connectivity to your local network. Thus, after you make a dial-up or virtual private networking connection, you will no longer be able to see NetWare servers on the local network.

Using Virtual Private Networking over the LAN to Connect to a Tunnel Server

VPN clients with a permanent IP connection to a VPN tunnel server can use VPN tunneling over that IP connection. For example, suppose that you are in a networked office environment and your network has a VPN tunnel server. You can then use that VPN server to tunnel to any private network that is connected to that VPN server, such as the personnel department's private network. Thus, you can create a virtual private network by using your direct LAN connection. Data sent from your VPN client to another computer on the LAN is encrypted and secure because you are using a VPN server to connect to the remote computer.

In the following scenario, the VPN client uses Dial-Up Networking over a LAN connection instead of a telephone line. Only one connection to the VPN server is required.

▶ **To connect to a VPN server over a LAN connection**

1. Double-click My Computer, and then double-click Dial-up Networking.
2. Click the icon that you have created for your VPN server.
3. Enter the user name and password required for the target network.
4. Click **Connect**.
5. You now have a connection to your VPN server.

Note The connection speed displayed is only an estimate. If you see a connection speed that seems too high or too low it will not impact performance and should not be cause for concern.

After you successfully connect to a VPN server, all traffic from your computer is first routed to your VPN server, which then forwards your data across the LAN to the remote computer. Your computer behaves as if it were physically connected to the remote network. While the tunnel is open, you continue to see computers and servers on your immediate LAN subnet. However, you might not be able to see hosts and servers on other subnets on your LAN. Contact your network administrator for more information.

Dialing an ISP to Connect to a Virtual Private Networking Server

With virtual private networking, you can connect your workstation to a remote network by tunneling through the Internet to a VPN server on that network. To do so, you must make two connections. First, you must connect to the Internet through an ISP. Next, you must create a tunnel to the target network. This section explains how to make these connections.

▶ **To connect to the Internet**

1. In My Computer, double-click Dial-Up Networking.

2. Double-click the connection icon that was created for your ISP.

3. In the **Connect To** dialog box that appears, enter the user name and password required by your ISP, and then click **Connect**.

▶ **To connect to the target network using a tunnel to the VPN server**

1. After connecting to your ISP, click the icon that was created for your VPN server.

2. Enter the user name and password required for the target network.

3. In the **Connect To** window, click **Connect**.

You now have two connections, as seen in the two following similar boxes.

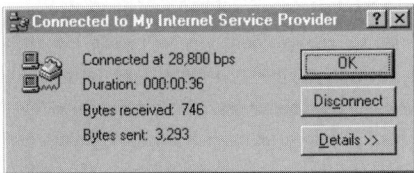

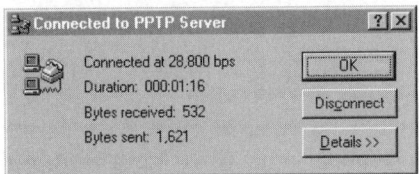

After you connect successfully to the VPN server on the remote network, the ISP routes all traffic sent from your workstation over the Internet to the VPN server. The VPN server then routes the traffic to the correct computer on the remote network. Consequently, you see only computers and servers on the remote network. You no longer see the Internet unless the remote network itself provides access to the Internet.

Virtual Private Networking Security

This section describes VPN security and discusses how to use virtual private networking with firewalls.

Authentication

When you dial an ISP network access server (NAS), the NAS requires require initial dial-in authentication. This authentication is required only to log on to the NAS; it is not related to Windows NT-based authentication. Check with your ISP for their authentication requirements.

When you dial a VPN tunnel server to connect to a private network, the VPN server requires a standard Windows NT-based logon. Therefore, remote access logon using a computer running Windows 98 is as secure as logging on from a Windows-based computer connected to the local LAN.

Authentication of remote VPN clients is performed using the same PPP authentication methods used for any Dial-up Networking client dialing directly to a RAS server. Microsoft's implementation of Dial-up Networking supports the CHAP, MS-CHAP, and PAP authentication schemes.

Access Control

After authentication, all access to a private LAN continues to use the Windows NT-based security model. Access to resources on NTFS drives or to other network resources requires the proper permissions.

For more information about using security on NTFS drives or other network resources, see your product documentation or the *Microsoft Windows NT Server Resource Kit* (for Microsoft Windows NT version 4.0).

Data Encryption

For data encryption, virtual private networking uses the RAS "shared-secret" encryption process. Both the client and the server share a secret, the user's password. Both the client and the server uses the secret to generate an initial 40-bit encryption key, then uses the key to encrypt and decrypt all data that it passes over the Internet. When you are connecting to a Windows NT 4 RAS Server with Service Pack 4 or later, the key changes on every packet. For earlier versions of Windows NT 4, the key changes every 256 packets.

Note The process by which the client and server generate the initial key occurs only when MS-CHAP is used.

Users in the United States and Canada can obtain a 128-bit session key through a cryptography pack for use inside the US. Contact your Microsoft reseller for more information. When 128-bit encryption is used, the initial key is based on the password and a unique MS-CHAP challenge.

PPTP Packet Filtering

To protect the VPN server from malicious attacks, you can enable PPTP filtering on the VPN server. With PPTP filtering, the VPN server on the private network accepts and routes *only* authorized, encrypted PPTP packets from authenticated users.

PPTP filtering is enabled on the VPN server. For step-by-step instruction on enabling PPTP filtering, see the white paper "Installing, Configuring, and Using PPTP with Microsoft Clients and Servers" at **http://www.microsoft.com/ communications/**.

Virtual Private Networking with Firewalls and Routers

PPTP traffic uses TCP port 1723, and IP protocol uses ID 47, as assigned by the Internet Assigned Numbers Authority (IANA). Virtual private networking can be used with most firewalls and routers by enabling traffic destined for TCP port 1723 and protocol 47 to be routed through the firewall or router.

Firewalls ensure corporate network security by strictly regulating data that comes *into* the private network from the Internet. An organization can deploy a VPN server running Windows NT Server 4.0 behind its firewall. The VPN server accepts PPTP packets passed to the private network from the firewall and extracts the PPP packet from the IP datagram, decrypts the packet, and forwards the packet to the computer on the private network.

Technical Notes on Dial-Up and Virtual Private Networking

In Windows 98, computers can be *multihomed*, or configured with multiple IP addresses. This enables them to connect to multiple networks that are physically separate, such as a corporate network and the Internet, with certain limitations. This section describes those limitations as they apply to Dial-Up Networking. For general information about multihoming, see Chapter 15, "Network Adapters and Protocols."

If you are connected to a LAN and you make a PPP dial-up connection or a VPN connection, you might lose connectivity to some of the servers on your LAN. Likewise, if you connect to the Internet, then make a VPN connection to another network, you might lose connectivity to the Internet itself.

This is because of the default routing changes that Dial-up Networking makes when setting up a connection. Clients on TCP/IP networks can send packets directly to hosts on their immediate network segment. However, to reach other network segments and other networks, they send their packets to a default gateway instead. That gateway then determines where to send the packets. Thus, clients can send packets to servers anywhere in a very large, complex network without having to know how to reach each server. Figure 19.8 shows how TCP/IP clients use default gateways.

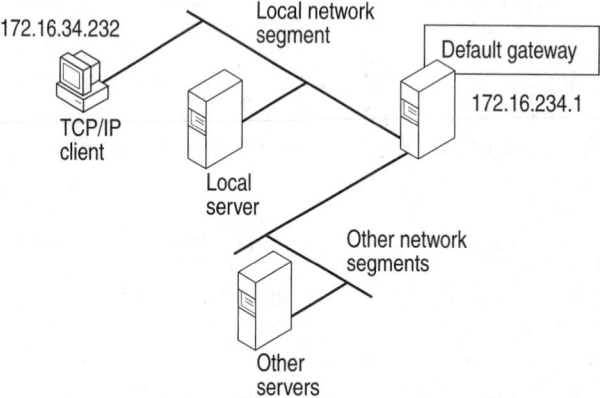

Figure 19.8   Default gateway for a TCP/IP client

You can find out what your default gateway is by looking at the route table for your computer. The *route table* shows all the routes your computer uses to reach other computers on the network.

For more information about the route table and to see the complete route table for the network shown in Figure 19.8, see Chapter 15, "Network Adapters and Protocols."

▶ **To view the route table**

• At the command prompt, type **route print**.

Table 19.2 shows a partial route table for the network shown in Figure 19.8.

Table 19.2   Partial route table for TCP/IP client

Network address	Netmask	Gateway address	Interface	Metric
0.0.0.0	0.0.0.0	172.16.34.1	172.16.34.232	1
…	…	…	…	…

Notice that the first line of the route table shows the address for the default gateway, and that it has a metric of 1. The *metric* indicates which gateway will be used and what the gateways that will be used if the first is removed from the route table. TCP/IP clients always use the default gateway with the smallest metric.

TCP/IP clients can be configured with several different default gateways. If one default gateway fails, the clients automatically switch to another. However, because TCP/IP clients always use the default gateway with the smallest metric, they cannot use more than one default gateway at a time.

Figure 19.9 shows what happens when you make a PPP dial-up connection to the Internet. Dial-Up Networking assigns a new default gateway, that of the PPP server. Because the client can use only one default gateway, it sends all network traffic through that gateway. You can no longer gain access to some of the servers on your LAN.

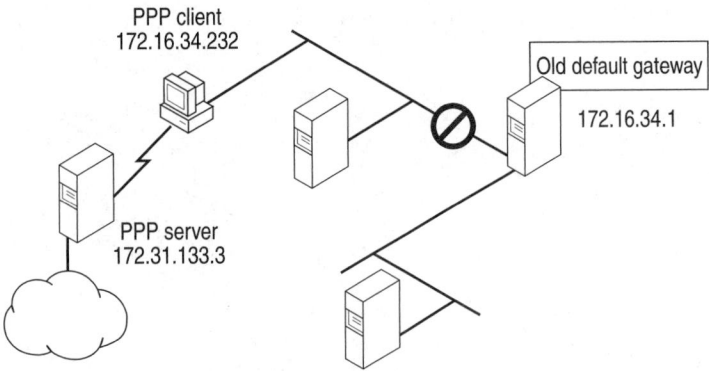

Figure 19.9   New default gateway for PPP client

The partial route table displayed in Table 19.3 shows what happens to the default gateway.

Table 19.3   New partial route table for PPP client

Network address	Netmask	Gateway address	Interface	Metric
0.0.0.0	0.0.0.0	172.16.34.232	172.16.34.232	1
0.0.0.0	0.0.0.0	172.16.34.1	172.16.34.232	2
...	...	...	...	...

The first line now shows the new default gateway for the PPP server, and the second line shows the old default gateway on your LAN. Because the old default gateway has a metric of 2, the TCP/IP stack does not use it.

If you need to reach servers on your network while connected to the Internet, you can manually add host routes to those servers. Use the **route** command to add a route manually to the gateway, IP subnet, or IP network you want to reach. For more information about adding routes, see Chapter 15, "Network Adapters and Protocols." See also the *Windows NT Server Networking Guide for Windows NT version 4.0.*

Finally, Figure 19.10 shows what happens when you make a VPN tunnel connection over the PPP connection. (For more information about PPP, see "Implementing Virtual Private Networking" earlier in this chapter.) Dial-Up Networking assigns a third default gateway to the VPN server, invalidating the first two default gateways. You lose access not only to servers on your LAN but to hosts on the Internet.

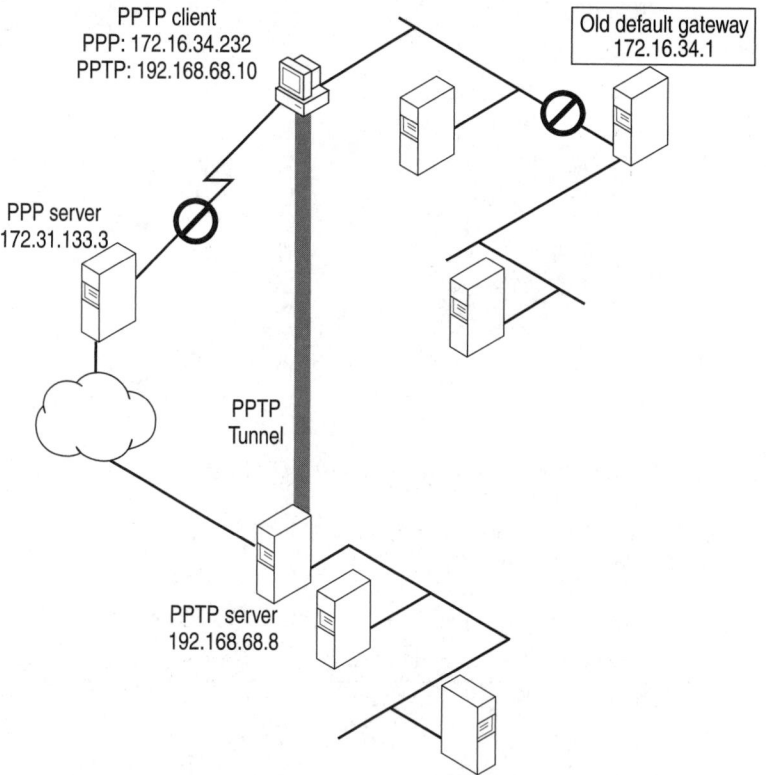

Figure 19.10   New default gateway for PPTP client

The partial route table displayed in Table 19.4 shows the default gateways.

Table 19.4   New partial route table for VPN client

Network address	Netmask	Gateway address	Interface	Metric
0.0.0.0	0.0.0.0	192.168.68.10	192.168.68.10	1
0.0.0.0	0.0.0.0	172.16.34.232	172.16.34.232	2
0.0.0.0	0.0.0.0	172.20.232.1	172.20.234.232	2
...	...	...	...	...

If you want to regain lost connectivity to servers on your local network or to the Internet, you have the following options:

- You can manually add host routes to servers on your network, as described in Chapter 15, "Network Adapters and Protocols."
- For VPN connections, you can disable the default gateway to the VPN tunnel server. You must then add routes to the virtual private network.

The following procedure describes how to disable the default gateway to the VPN tunnel server. After you disable the default gateway, you might need to configure routes to servers on the remote network. However, you do not need to configure a route to the VPN tunnel server, because Dial-Up Networking automatically assigns a host route to that server.

▶ **To disable the default gateway to the VPN tunnel server**

1. In the Dial-Up Networking folder, right-click the VPN server connection icon, and then click **Properties**.
2. Click the **Server Types** tab.
3. Click **TCP/IP Settings**.
4. Clear the **Use default gateway on remote networks** check box.

Dial-up Networking automatically creates a host route to the VPN tunnel server, so you can still reach it.

Using Windows 98 Mobile Computing Features

You can be productive away from the office by using the following Windows 98 mobile computing tools:

Windows 98 Briefcase   Briefcase allows you to update documents on a portable computer with source documents on a desktop computer or network, thus minimizing the task of keeping track of the relationships between files on a portable computer and on a desktop computer. With Briefcase, you can simultaneously update related files.

Direct Cable Connection Direct Cable Connection (DCC) allows you to establish a connection between two computers quickly and easily by using a parallel cable, a null-modem serial cable, or an infrared connection. After the connection is established, Direct Cable Connection facilitates the transfer of files from the host computer to the guest computer. The host can act as a gateway to an IPX/SPX or NetBEUI network for the guest.

Infrared Windows 98 supports infrared devices, so you can wirelessly connect a laptop or a computer to infrared cameras, other computers, or printers. Infrared works with file sharing tools such as Direct Cable Connection, so you can quickly and easily take a laptop with you wherever you go and then update files on a standalone computer or the network.

Deferred printing Windows 98 supports deferred printing, which allows you to generate print jobs when you are not connected physically to a printer. The print jobs are stored until a printer becomes available. Windows 98 detects the printer connection and automatically spools the print jobs in the background. For information, see Chapter 11, "Printing, Imaging, and Fonts."

Internet Mail and News With Outlook Express, you can dial into your internet service provider and download your e-mail from an IMAP4 or POP3 server. You can also download news from your newsgroups located on an NNTP server. For information, see Chapter 22, "Electronic Mail with Outlook Express."

Other mobile computing tools, such as the following, help you manage a portable computer's limited battery power and disk space:

- With Advanced Power Management, you can use the battery indicator on the taskbar and a **Suspend** command on the **Start** menu to save power without turning off your computer. For more information, see Chapter 30, "Hardware Management."

- With DriveSpace, you can free space on their portable computer's hard disk drive and floppy disks by compressing them. For more information, see Chapter 10, "Disks and File Systems."

- With Outlook Express, you can view the headers of mail messages before deciding whether to download, preventing unnecessary messages from taking up disk space.

- With Quick View, you can view the contents of a file in Windows Explorer by right-clicking a file icon. For information, see Chapter 25, "Application Support."

Using Direct Cable Connection

With Direct Cable Connection, you can establish a direct serial connection, parallel cable connection, or infrared connection between two computers in order to share the resources of the computer designated as the host. If the host is connected to a network, the guest computer can also access the network.

For example, if you have a portable computer, you can use a cable to connect it to your work computer and network. To establish a local connection between two computers, you must connect a compatible serial or null-modem parallel cable to both computers, or both computers must be equipped with infrared devices. For information about using Direct Cable Connection with infrared devices, see the section "Using Infrared" later in this chapter.

Before you can transfer files from the host to the guest computer, the files must be in a shared directory, and File and Printer Sharing services for either Microsoft or NetWare networks must be enabled in the Network option in Control Panel. You can also apply share-level security to the shared files. For information, see Chapter 18, "Logon, Browsing, and Resource Sharing," and Chapter 9, "Security."

Before you install and configure Direct Cable Connection, you need to decide:

- What remote access and network protocols do you need to install on the guest and host computers? They must both be running at least one common network protocol in order to connect. A broadcast protocol such as NetBEUI is simplest.

- Do you want the host computer to act as a gateway to a TCP/IP network? If so, you must install NetBEUI.

- What kind of cable or infrared device do you need?

- Do you want to assign a password to the host computer? If you assign a password on the host, all users connecting from the guest computer will be prompted for it. After connecting, the guest can access resources on the host computer according to the type of security applied to it, that is, user-level or share-level security.

Note You cannot use Direct Cable Connection and Dial-Up Networking at the same time. Both applications use the same network interface (Pppmac.vxd). Before using Direct Cable Connection, make sure to shut down any active Dial-Up Networking connections.

Installing and Configuring Direct Cable Connection

To install Direct Cable Connection during Windows 98 Setup, you must run Setup from the DOS prompt and choose Custom or Portable as the setup type. You can also install Direct Cable Connection after installing Windows 98.

▶ **To install Direct Cable Connection after Windows 98 Setup**

1. In Control Panel, click Add/Remove Programs, and then click the **Windows Setup** tab.

2. In the **Components** list, click **Communications**, and then click **Details**.

3. In the **Components** dialog box, click **Direct Cable Connection**, and then click **OK**.

Windows 98 provides a Direct Cable Connection Wizard for establishing the connection between two computers. The wizard runs when you open Direct Cable Connection the first time. It allows you to designate one computer as the guest and the other as a host. Before you run the wizard, you must install Direct Cable Connection on each computer and connect them with a null-modem serial or parallel cable, or with an infrared device.

For more information about setting up and using Direct Cable Connection, see Help, or the Networks troubleshooter section on "I am unable to connect my Windows 95 computer to my Windows 98 computer."

Cables Compatible with Direct Cable Connection

Windows 98 supports a serial null-modem standard (RS-232) cable and the following parallel cables:

- Standard or Basic 4-bit cable, including LapLink and InterLink cables available before 1992.

- Extended Capabilities Port (ECP) cable. This type of cable works on a computer with ECP-enabled parallel ports, which must be enabled in BIOS. This kind of parallel cable allows data to be transferred more quickly than a standard cable.

- Universal Cable Module (UCM) cable. This cable supports connecting different types of parallel ports. Using this cable between two ECP-enabled ports allows the fastest possible data transfer between two computers.

Parallel cables transmit data simultaneously over multiple lines, whereas serial cables transmit data sequentially over one pair of wires. Thus, parallel cables are faster than serial cables.

You can also use Direct Cable Connection over an infrared link. For more information, see "Using Infrared" later in this chapter.

Using Briefcase to Synchronize Files

If you can use a portable computer and a desktop computer, or you are connected to a network, you must constantly work to keep the files synchronized. Windows 98 Briefcase minimizes this task by keeping track of the relationships between files on two or more computers.

With Briefcase, you can do the following:

- Create a Briefcase folder.
- Add files to Briefcase.
- Check the status of files in Briefcase and their related files.
- Update related files, either individually or all at once.
- Split related files to maintain them separately.

Windows 98 provides a set of OLE interfaces that allow applications to bind reconciliation handlers to it, track the contents of Briefcase, and define the outcome of any reconciliation on a class-by-class basis. For example, when both the file in Briefcase and its synchronized copy outside have changed, Windows 98 calls the appropriate reconciliation handler to merge the two files. This could be handy when several users are simultaneously updating one large document.

Caution   Do not place one Briefcase inside another Briefcase. You cannot drag a file into a Briefcase that is in another Briefcase.

Creating and Configuring a Briefcase

To install Briefcase during Windows 98 Setup, you must run Setup from the DOS prompt and choose Custom or Portable as the setup type. You can also install Briefcase after installing Windows 98.

▶ **To install Briefcase after Windows 98 installation**

1. In Control Panel, double-click Add/Remove Programs.
2. Click the **Windows Setup** tab, in the **Components** list click **Accessories**, and then click **Details**.
3. In the **Accessories** dialog box, click **Briefcase**, and then click **OK**.

If you install Briefcase, it appears as an icon on your Windows 98 desktop. To run Briefcase, double-click its icon.

▶ **To uninstall Briefcase**

- Drag the Briefcase icon to the Recycle bin.

Tip You can use Briefcase to synchronize files between a portable computer running Windows 98 and a desktop computer running Windows NT Server 3.5 or later.

Updating Files with Briefcase

When you update files by using Briefcase, Windows 98 automatically replaces unmodified files with modified files. If both files have changed, Windows 98 calls the appropriate application (if available) to merge the disparate files. The host and guest can be connected in the following ways:

- You can copy files from your desktop to Briefcase and then load Briefcase onto your portable computer. If you are using a Plug and Play BIOS docking station, Briefcase automatically updates files when you later dock your portable computer.

- You can update files using Briefcase and a floppy disk. For information, see Windows 98 Help.

- You can synchronize files between a portable computer and a network if the portable computer has a network connection.

- You can use Direct Cable Connection to connect two computers running Windows 98, and then use Briefcase to synchronize their files. For more information about Direct Cable Connection, see "Using Direct Cable Connection" earlier in this chapter.

For more information about Briefcase, and for instructions for using Briefcase to update two connected computers, see Help.

Tip To find the copy of a file that is outside Briefcase, click **Find Original** in the **Update Status** dialog box.

Using Infrared

Windows 98 includes Microsoft Infrared version 3.0, which allows you to use infrared devices to connect to computers, printers, or other devices such as infrared cameras. Microsoft Infrared 3.0 supports the Infrared Data Association (IrDA) standards IrDA 1.0, for Serial Infrared Devices (SIR); and IrDA 1.1, for Fast Infrared Devices (FIR). Because of its low cost and simple implementation, infrared is the first widely used wireless transmission technology. It can be used for the following purposes:

- Exchanging files wirelessly between two computers.
- Printing wirelessly on infrared-capable printers.

- Connecting to the network wirelessly instead of using cabling, through a computer connected by Direct Cable Connect.

The Windows 98 implementation of Infrared provides the following benefits:

- Device drivers for SIR devices capable of sending and receiving at speeds up to 115.2 kbps.

- Support for FIR devices capable of sending and receiving data at 4 Mbps.

Windows 98 also includes Microsoft Infrared Transfer, an application that enables a suitably enabled computer to quickly send files using their infrared device.

Installing an Infrared Device

This section describes how to install infrared devices.

Note If you change the infrared adapter model that is connected to the computer, you should reinstall it.

The procedure for installing an infrared device varies depending on whether it is a Plug and Play device. All Fast Infrared devices are Plug and Play–compatible.

▶ **To install a Plug and Play device**

1. If it is an external device, attach it. The Infrared 3.0 software loads automatically.

2. Double-click the Infrared icon in Control Panel to activate the infrared device. If there is no Infrared icon in Control Panel, press F5 to make the icon appear.

▶ **To install a non-Plug and Play infrared device**

1. If it is an external device, attach it.

2. In Control Panel, double-click the Add New Hardware wizard. Follow the instructions on the screen, making the following choices:

   - If asked whether the device you want is in the list, click **No**.

   - When asked whether you want Windows to search for your new hardware, click **No**.

   - When the **Hardware Types** box appears, click **Infrared devices**.

   - When asked to select a device, accept the default selection **Generic Infrared Serial Port or dongle**. (The other devices listed are Plug and Play devices.)

   - When asked for such information as the communications port that the infrared device is physically connected to, if you are not sure, accept the defaults.

Using the Infrared Monitor

You can use the Infrared Monitor to keep track of your computer's infrared activity. You can activate Infrared Monitor once your infrared device is installed by double-clicking the Infrared icon in Control Panel or by clicking the animated Infrared icon in the system tray on the Taskbar. The Infrared Monitor contains the tabs and options shown in Table 19.5.

Table 19.5   Infrared Monitor tabs

Tab name	Tab option	Description
Status		Tells you whether infrared is working properly and displays information about the infrared connections.
Options	Enable infrared communication	Enables and disables infrared services on the physical serial port.
	Search for and provide status for devices in range	Starts and stops the infrared device's ability to detect other devices that are in range.
	Enable software install for Plug and Play devices in range	Enables and disables Microsoft Infrared Support software from automatically configuring a device across the infrared communication link when the computer comes into range of a new Plug and Play device.
	Limit connection speed	Configures the maximum speed for the infrared. Limiting this speed may improve communication.
	Restore defaults	Restores settings to defaults.
Preferences	Display the infrared icon in the taskbar	Determines whether the infrared icon displays in the system tray.
	Open Infrared Monitor for interrupted communication	Specifies whether to open the Infrared Monitor when infrared communication is interrupted.
	Play sounds for devices in range and interrupted communication	Specifies whether sounds will be played for various infrared events.
Identification	Computer name	Contains the name assigned to the computer. This is the same name used to identify your computer on the network. If no name appears here, enter one.
	Computer description	Contains a description of the computer. This is the same description used to identify your computer on the network. If no description appears here, enter one.

▶ **To verify your connection using Infrared Monitor**

1. On one of the computers, in the system tray on the Taskbar, double-click the animated infrared icon. Infrared Monitor appears.

2. Click the **Status** tab. It shows all devices visible to the computer.

3. Repeat steps 1 and 2 for the other computer.

Transferring Files Using Infrared Transfer

Windows 98 includes Infrared Transfer, a new application for transferring files through an infrared connection.

When an infrared device has been installed, an icon called Infrared Recipient is added to My Computer, and a shortcut to it is added to the **\Windows\Send To** folder. This shortcut adds an item to the **Send To** menu option that appears when you right-click a file or folder.

The first time Infrared Transfer is used to send a file or folder, a folder called My Received Files is created, and all sent files or folders will be copied to this folder. If a file or folder is sent that already exists in the My Received Files folder, a copy of the file or folder is made.

You can transfer files using one of several different methods. Before attempting to transfer files, make sure the infrared communications driver is properly installed and the infrared devices are enabled by carrying out the procedures in "Installing an Infrared Device" and "Using the Infrared Monitor" earlier in this chapter.

▶ **To transfer files or folders using Infrared Recipient**

1. In My Computer, double-click Infrared Recipient.

2. Select an available infrared device.

3. Click **Send Files**.

4. Select the files to send.

5. Click **Open**.

▶ **To transfer files or folders using Send To**

1. Select the files you want to send.

2. Right-click the selected files, and then point to **Send To**.

3. Click **Infrared Recipient**.

▶ **To transfer files or folders using Drag and Drop**

1. In My Computer, open Infrared Recipient.

2. If there is more than one infrared device in range, select an available infrared device.

3. In Windows Explorer, select files you want to send.

4. If there is only a single infrared device in range, drag and drop files onto the Infrared Recipient icon in my computer.

-Or-

5. If there is more than one infrared device in range, drag and then drop files onto the computer selected in **Available** devices within range.

Transferring Files using Direct Cable Connection and Infrared

You can use Direct Cable Connection over an infrared link to connect a host and guest computer. This section describes how to transfer files over an infrared link, using Direct Cable Connection. Before transferring files, you must install Direct Cable Connection on both computers by following the procedure outlined in "Using Direct Cable Connection" earlier in this chapter. Both computers must also use a common network protocol; a broadcast protocol such as NetBEUI is easiest to configure.

Additionally, the files must be in a shared directory, and File and Printer Sharing services for either Microsoft or NetWare networks must be enabled in the Network option in Control Panel. You can also apply share-level security to the shared files. For information about File and Printer Sharing, see Chapter 18, "Logon, Browsing, and Resource Sharing." For more information about share-level security, see Chapter 9, "Security."

▶ **To transfer files using Direct Cable Connection**

1. Make sure the infrared communications driver is properly installed and the infrared devices are enabled by carrying out the procedures in "Installing an Infrared Device" and "Using the Infrared Monitor" earlier in this chapter.

2. On one of the computers, open the Infrared Monitor and click the **Options** tab. It lists the virtual COM port the infrared device uses. Note this information.

3. On the host computer, click **Start**, point to **Accessories**, and then click **Direct Cable Connection**.

4. Follow the steps in the Direct Cable Connection Wizard to set up the host computer.

   When the wizard prompts you for it, select the Host option. When the wizard prompts you to choose a port, use the same virtual port you found in Step 2.

   The wizard also offers password protection. It is not necessary to establish password protection on the host computer for this test of the infrared link. When you have finished the wizard, click **Finish**. Direct Cable Connection starts running on the infrared link and displays the following message: "Status: Waiting to connect via Serial cable on Com*x*," where Com*x* is the name of the virtual port the infrared link is using.

5. Repeat steps 3 and 4 for the guest computer, except select the Guest option instead of the Host option. When you have finished the wizard, click **Finish**.

The connection is automatically made over the infrared link, and all the shared folders on the host computer are displayed on the guest computer's screen.

When you run Direct Cable Connection to establish the connection between the host and guest computers, the guest computer might display the message "Direct Cable Connection was unable to display shared folders of the host computer" and prompt you to enter the computer name of the host computer. If this happens, check the **Status** tab of the Infrared Monitor interface screen.

If you are working on the guest computer, and you want to copy a shared folder from the host computer to the guest computer, select the folder's icon in the window that displays all the shared folders that are on the host computer, and drag the icon to the desktop.

To work on a shared folder on the host computer without copying it to the guest computer, double-click the folder in the display on the guest computer. Note that if the host computer is connected to a network, the guest computer can reach shared resources on the network through the connection to the host.

Printing with Infrared Transfer

Before attempting to print, make sure the infrared communications driver is properly installed and the infrared devices are enabled by carrying out the procedures in "Installing an Infrared Device" and "Using the Infrared Monitor" earlier in this chapter.

▶ **To print to an Infrared-Capable Printer**

1. Make sure the infrared communications driver is installed on the computer.

2. Bring an infrared-enabled printer within range.

3. Your computer might automatically detect and install the printer. If not, make sure the printer driver for the infrared-capable printer is installed on the computer.

4. Try the Print option in a program.

You can make printers without built-in infrared ports infrared-capable by connecting an infrared adapter made for printers into the printer's parallel port. An example of an infrared adapter for printers is the Extended Systems JetEye Infrared Printer Port ESI-9580. If a parallel cable is also used to connect the computer to the infrared printer adapter, you can use either the infrared link or the parallel cable to print. The infrared link is used when you select the virtual parallel port; the cable is used when you select the physical parallel port.

To validate the infrared link to the printer, make sure the correct printer driver is installed for the infrared-capable printer. (Most printers with built-in infrared ports are Plug and Play devices, which are installed automatically.) Then use a program to print over the infrared link.

If the program prints on an infrared-capable printer, the infrared driver installation is validated. If there is trouble printing, see "Troubleshooting Infrared" later in this chapter for more information.

Troubleshooting Remote Networking and Mobile Computing

This section describes problems you may encounter in using Dial-Up Networking, virtual private networking, and Mobile Computing.

Troubleshooting Dial-Up Networking

This section describes problems that you may encounter in using Dial-Up Networking and how to resolve them. Windows 98 provides a troubleshooting aid for Dial-Up Networking in Help. Try using the troubleshooting aid before taking the troubleshooting steps included in this section.

You can monitor any Dial-Up Networking session for possible problems by enabling the Record a Log File option. This produces a Ppplog.txt file in the Windows directory, which you can reference to find out the cause of a problem. For more information, see Knowledge Base Article Q156435, "How to Interpret the Ppplog.txt File."

Dial-Up Networking does not install properly.

If you cancel Setup while Dial-Up Networking is copying files and then restart the computer, you will see an error message stating that the following files are missing:

- Vnetsup.vxd
- Nwlink.vxd
- Nwredir.vxd
- Nscl.vxd
- Vredir.vxd
- Ndis.vxd
- Ndis2sup.vxd
- Vnetbios.vxd

If these files are missing, Dial-Up Networking will not function correctly. You must remove and reinstall Dial-Up Networking.

▶ **To remove Dial-Up Networking**

1. In Control Panel, click Add/Remove Programs.

2. Remove all Dial-Up Networking components.

3. Restart your computer.

To reinstall Dial-Up Networking, follow the procedures outlined in "Installing Dial-Up Networking" earlier in this chapter.

Caution   Never remove Dial-Up Networking components using Network in Control Panel.

Dial-Up Networking cannot find modem.

If you see an error message stating that Dial-Up Networking cannot find the specified modem, check the following:

- Check that the modem is properly installed and configured.

- In Modems in Control Panel, check the **General tab** to make sure it lists your modem.

- Check the connection to make sure the modem you have specified is the modem connected to your computer.

The remote server does not respond.

If you receive an error message that the computer you are connecting to has not responded, check the following items:

- Check your connection to make sure it is configured to use the network protocols used on the remote server.

- If you are using TCP/IP, check your connection to make sure that the network protocols are configured correctly.

- In Control Panel, check the Network option to make sure it lists all the network protocols used on the remote server.

- Check your connection to make sure it is configured to access the correct server type.

- Check that the server is configured correctly.

- If a terminal logon is required, check that you have configured the **Options** tab in your connection to bring up a terminal window before dialing.

You cannot access the Dial-Up Networking server because a user name is not valid.

In the properties for the Windows 95 or Windows 98 dial-up server, verify that the user name is in the list of users that are allowed access.

▶ **To set Dial-Up Networking Server to allow caller access options**

1. In Dial-Up Networking, click the **Connections** menu, and then click **Dial-Up Server**.

2. In the **Dial-Up Server** properties, click **Allow Caller Access**, if this is not already selected, and then view the User name list to ensure the user's name appears.

   The User name list appears only if you have chosen user-level security for the dial-up server. The type of security is selected in the Network option in Control Panel.

If the dial-up client is also running File and Printer Services for NetWare Networks, the File and Printer Sharing service automatically becomes the default server, but it cannot receive the information needed to find the remote servers.

You cannot access remote NetWare servers when making a dial-up connection.

Disable File and Printer Sharing Service for NetWare Networks when you make the dial-up connection.

Software compression does not work.

Check the settings for the dial-up server type and software compression.

▶ **To verify dial-up server and compression options in Dial-Up Networking**

1. In the **Connections** menu, click **Dial-Up Server**.

2. Click **Server Type** and verify that the correct type of dial-up server is selected.

3. Check that **Enable software compression** is selected. Compression will occur only if the dial-up client and server have enabled it.

The modem is dialing but not connecting.

- Check the modem configuration; change the configuration if necessary.

- Verify all parameters, such as access codes, area code, country code, and dialing properties.

- Try choosing the driver for **Generic Modem Drivers**.

- If you are using an external modem, check the cable and verify that it is connected correctly.

- Check the COM port configuration in Device Manager.

For more information, see the troubleshooting section in Chapter 21, "Modems and Communications Tools."

Dial-Up Networking Server is not answering incoming calls.

- If you are using an external modem, check the cable and verify that it is connected correctly.

- If you are using an internal modem with a nonstandard IRQ selection, use Device Manager to check the IRQ setting for the COM port and change it if necessary.

- Disable **Allow Caller Access** and shut down the computer. Turn off the computer to reset the COM port. If the modem is external, turn off the modem. Turn the computer back on and reconfigure the Dial-Up Networking server, and then try again.

- If these steps fail, disable **Allow Caller Access** and see if any modem software can manually answer the incoming call.

- Try choosing the **Generic Modem Drivers** on the dial-up server.

The password for the Dial-Up Networking server is stored in the Rna.pwl file. However, simply deleting this file or removing and reinstalling Dial-Up Networking may not remove the password. If you set the Dial-Up Networking server to monitor for calls and then delete the Rna.pwl file, the password is not removed, because it is stored in memory. If you shut down Windows 98 at this point, the Rna.pwl file is re-created with the password in memory.

▶ **To replace a forgotten password in a Dial-Up Networking server**

1. Disable **Allow Caller Access**, and then shut down and restart Windows 98.

2. Delete the Rna.pwl file, and then restart Dial-Up Networking.

Note   When you first connect to the Dial-Up Networking server, an error message states that the password file is missing or corrupt for every modem device you have installed. If you have any null modem devices installed (for example, when you run Direct Cable Connection it installs a modem device for every COM and LPT port you have), this error message also appears.

You lose connectivity to servers on your network or to the Internet.

If you are connected to a LAN and you make a PPP or VPN connection, you might lose connectivity to some of the servers on your LAN. Likewise, if you connect to the Internet, then make a VPN connection to another network, you might lose connectivity to the Internet itself. For information about the cause of this problem and its solution, see "Technical Notes on Dial-Up and Virtual Private Networking," earlier in this chapter.

Multilink does not provide additional bandwidth.

- Check that the server you are connecting to supports Multilink.

- Check that you have two modems or a dual-channel ISDN card. If you do not have two modems or a dual-channel ISDN card, you cannot use Multilink.

- Check that your modems are exactly the same speed. Performance degrades if the modems connect at different speeds.

- Check that your modems or ISDN card are configured correctly. For more information about the correct configuration, see Chapter 21, "Modems and Communications Tools."

TAPI codes do not work properly.

If you entered TAPI codes, an area code, or a country code in one connection, but Dial-Up Networking does not use those codes when you use the connection, make sure that all your connections use the TAPI codes.

▶ **To verify that all your connections use the TAPI codes**

1. Right-click each connection icon, and then select **Properties** from the context menu.

2. In the **General** tab for each connection, check that **Use area code and Dialing Properties** is selected.

Troubleshooting Your Virtual Private Networking Connection

This section describes common virtual private networking problems and explains how to correct them.

Two Dial-Up networking adapters appear in Network in Control Panel.

This is by design. Do not attempt to remove Dial-Up Networking components using Network in Control Panel. If you need to remove virtual private networking, do so using Add/Remove Programs in Control Panel.

You cannot connect to a VPN server.

If you cannot connect to a VPN server, you can begin to diagnose the problem by looking at the status messages that appear when you attempt to make a connection. If the connection is successful, you will see the following messages:

- a message stating that your computer is dialing a server.

- a message that says the server is verifying your name and password.

- a message that says the client is logging on to the network.

If the connection fails before you see the "Verifying name and password" message, you might have a problem with DNS name resolution, or the VPN server might not be responding. If the connection fails before you see the "Verifying name and password" message and gives you the error message that the other computer is not responding, a computer along the way might be filtering out Generic Routing Encapsulation (GRE) packets, which are required for VPN to work.

However, if you do see the message "verifying name and password," your PPP connection succeeded and PPTP is working, and you probably have a problem with your user name and password.

You can also check the following items.

Verify that you are properly connected to the Internet.   Make sure that your Internet connection is working properly.

▶   **To check that your connection to the Internet is working properly:**

1. Ping a host that you can normally reach using **ping**.

   If **ping** succeeds, your Internet connection is working properly.

2. If **ping** does not reach that host, type its IP address.

   If **ping** succeeds, you are properly connected to the Internet, but you are not properly connected to your DNS server. You should be able to connect to your VPN server by typing its IP address instead of its host name.

   – Or –

   If **ping** fails, you might not be connected to the Internet. Contact your ISP.

Ping the VPN server.   Ping the host name or IP address of the VPN server.

If you receive a response, you are properly connected to the VPN server, and you might have entered an incorrect user name or password.

If you do not receive a response, the administrator of the VPN server might have turned on PPTP filtering. This prevents you from pinging the VPN server. Contact the administrator of that server.

Check for a firewall.   Firewalls sometimes filter out PPTP packets. Contact your ISP and the administrator of your corporate server and ask if they are using a firewall. If they are, request that they pass TCP port 1723 and IP protocol 47 (the GRE protocol).

Because PPTP is a secure protocol, adding TCP port 1723 and IP protocol 47 will not affect the security of the firewall.

Make sure your ISP is not filtering out PPTP. Contact your ISP and ask if it filters out GRE packets. If so, request that it pass GRE protocol 47.

Check for a proxy server. It is not possible to create a VPN tunnel that passes through a proxy server such as a computer running Microsoft Proxy Server. Therefore, if your internal network's proxy server handles all Internet traffic, including PPTP traffic, you will not be able to create a VPN tunnel to access resources on the internal network.

You cannot log on to the target network.

If you can connect to the VPN tunnel server, but you cannot perform a domain logon to the target network, verify that you have configured the connection to your VPN server to allow you to perform a domain logon to the target network.

▶ **To verify your VPN configuration**

1. In the Dial-Up Networking folder, right-click the icon for your VPN server connection.

2. Click **Properties**.

3. Click the **Server Types** tab.

4. In the **Advanced options** dialog box, make sure the **Log on to the network** check box is selected.

Your VPN connection is slow.

If your VPN connection is slow, follow the procedures outlined below.

- Check your ISP connection.

   You might be able to improve your performance by changing settings in your ISP connection. Specifically, you can improve performance by deselecting the option **Log on to network** and by deselecting all network protocols you are not using. To do so, follow the steps outlined in the procedure in the "Configuring Options for the Server to Which You Are Connecting" section earlier in this chapter. For information about other issues you should consider when setting up a connection to the Internet, see "Configuring a Connection to the Internet" earlier in this chapter.

- Check the connection to other Internet sites.

   To check the speed of your Internet connection, ping Internet sites you can normally ping. If **ping** shows a response time of more than five seconds, you have a slow Internet connection. Contact your ISP.

- Check the connection to your VPN server.

   If you do not have problems with your Internet connection, but the connection to your VPN server is still slow, the VPN server might be overloaded. Contact the administrator of the VPN server.

You cannot connect after disconnecting from a LAN.

If you have a mobile computer that has a directly attached network adapter card that you use to access resources on your corporate network, you might have trouble connecting to some of your network's hosts after disconnecting a mobile computer such as a laptop from your corporate network and then making a VPN connection to your corporate network. This happens because your computer is still forwarding all its network traffic to the network adapter instead of over the VPN connection. To force your computer to forward its network traffic over the VPN connection, disable your network adapter using the following procedure.

▶ **To disable your network adapter**

1. In Control Panel, double-click System.

2. Click the **Device Manager** tab.

3. Double-click **Network adapters**.

4. Select your network adapter.

5. Click **Properties**.

6. In the **Device usage** box, select the **Disable in this hardware profile** check box.

If this procedure does not work, but you are using DHCP to automatically assign IP addresses, you can try using **winipcfg** to release your IP address. For more information, see Chapter 15, "Network Adapters and Protocols."

▶ **To release your IP address**

1. Click **Start**, click **Run**, type **winipcfg**, and then press the ENTER key.

2. In the **IP Configuration** dialog box, click **Release All**.

Troubleshooting Direct Cable Connection

This section presents problems that might occur when you are using Direct Cable Connection.

As general troubleshooting steps, verify the following:

- Verify that your cable is properly connected.

- Make sure that you are using a compatible cable, listed in "Using Direct Cable Connection" earlier in this chapter. Make sure that you are not using such devices as gender-benders or devices that convert 25-pin cables to 9-pin cables.

- Check Device Manager to make sure that you do not have an IRQ port conflict.

- Verify that both computers have the same network protocol installed. A broadcast protocol such as NetBEUI is simplest.

You cannot find the host computer.

If you cannot find the host computer using Direct Cable Connection, follow the procedures in "Using Direct Cable Connection" earlier in this chapter to make sure Direct Cable Connection has been installed correctly on the host computer and is working.

If Direct Cable Connection is working properly but you still cannot find the host computer, make sure you have Client for Microsoft Networks is installed. For more information, see Chapter 16, "Windows 98 on Microsoft Networks."

You can connect to the host computer but you cannot use it as a gateway to the network.

The host computer and guest computer can communicate using the TCP/IP protocol, which is generally installed by default. However, if you want the host computer to act as a gateway to a TCP/IP network, you should make sure that NetBEUI is installed as well. For more information, see Chapter 15, "Network Adapters and Protocols."

You cannot use Direct Cable Connection with Dial-Up Networking.

Both Dial-Up Networking and Direct Cable Connection use the same network interface (Pppmac.vxd). You cannot have more than one instance of Pppmac.vxd running at one time, so you cannot use both Direct Cable Connection and Dial-Up Networking at the same time. You must close either Direct Cable Connection or Dial-Up Networking.

Troubleshooting Infrared

Following are several factors to check as you begin to troubleshoot your infrared connection:

- Check distance between infrared adapters.

  Try moving the devices closer together or farther apart. The devices must be no more than three feet apart, and some devices work best if kept at least six inches apart. Make sure that there are no obstructions between the devices.

- Check alignment between infrared adapters.

  Infrared devices produce an "arc" of infrared light. This arc is usually between 15 and 30 degrees. Try realigning the devices so that they fall within this arc.

- Check for interference with infrared transmission.

  Direct sunlight contains infrared light and can cause degradation of the infrared signal between devices. If this occurs, try blocking the sunlight or moving the devices closer together.

- Experiment with connection speed.

  Use the **Limit Connection Speed To** option in the Infrared Monitor **Options** tab to limit the connection speed to 19.2 kbps. If this is successful, you can experiment with establishing a connection at a higher speed. This is especially important if an infrared adapter is attached to a COM port that is using an 8250 UART instead of a 16550 UART or if the adapter is connected to a relatively slow computer.

- Ensure that application is set to use virtual infrared port.

  Ensure that the application you are using is configured for the virtual port, not the physical port that the infrared device is attached to. Keep in mind that, as with all communications and printer ports, only one application can use the virtual port at one time.

- Verify infrared adapter settings.

  Open the Infrared Monitor and verify that all settings are correct.

- Verify the physical COM port.

  If you select the wrong physical COM port during installation of the infrared communications driver, the infrared device will be unable to discover another infrared device within range. If this happens, put an actively searching infrared device close to the computer's infrared device and reinstall infrared on a different COM port until the infrared device on the computer discovers the nearby infrared device.

- Verify that the infrared adapter has power.

  You might need to change the batteries in an infrared adapter or plug the AC power into an infrared adapter.

Troubleshooting General Infrared Problems

This section discusses general problems that might occur when using infrared. For information about specific infrared hardware, see the next section.

Communication over a virtual COM port link is unreliable with printer's infrared adapter in range.

Communication over a virtual COM port link between two computers might not be reliable if a printer's infrared adapter is also within range. You should move the adapter out of range.

Zmodem fails over infrared.

You might experience problems transferring files over an infrared link. If the Zmodem protocol fails with a link speed of 115.2 kbps, use the Infrared Monitor Limit Connection Speed To tab to limit the link speed to 19.2 kbps and then retry the Zmodem file transfer.

Troubleshooting Specific Infrared Hardware

This section discusses common problems you might experience with specific infrared hardware. For information about general problems you might encounter, see the previous section.

The Texas Instruments TravelMate 5000 might communicate over an infrared link only at very low speeds (9600 bps). The Sharp PC 3050 might communicate over an infrared link only at speeds between 9600 bps and 19.2 kbps.

For the Hewlett Packard Omnibook 4000C or the Hewlett Packard Omnibook 600CT, which have built-in infrared ports, you must install a special echo-canceling serial driver in addition to the components that make up the infrared communications driver. The echo-canceling driver, and instructions on how to install it, are available from Hewlett-Packard.

Serial port does not provide sufficient power for Adaptec AIRport 2000.

The Adaptec AIRport 2000 infrared adapter can be powered in three ways: by the serial port, by installed AA batteries, or by an external power supply. In some cases the serial port might not provide sufficient power for the operation of the adapter. This can cause reduced operating range and/or a failure to find another infrared device that is nearby and aligned correctly. If you suspect this problem, connect an AC adapter or add four AA batteries to the battery compartment in the infrared adapter. This will assure sufficient power. In some instances, you might also need to separate the adapter by at least six inches from the other infrared device.

Cannot print from ActiSys 220L infrared adapter.

If an ActiSys 220L infrared adapter is attached to a computer and used to print to a printer that is using an Extended Systems ESI-9580 printer infrared adapter, or a Hewlett Packard DeskJet 340, you must use the **Options** tab in the Infrared Monitor properties to limit the connection speed to 19.2 kbps in order to print successfully. If the infrared devices are allowed to negotiate the connection speed automatically without setting this limit, they will negotiate a higher connection speed, and a program will be unable to print.

Additional Resources

For more information about	See this resource
Internet drafts and RFCs	**http://www.ietf.org/.**
Virtual private networking	**http://www.microsoft.com/communications/.**
Windows NT remote access servers	*Windows NT Server Networking Guide for Windows NT Server version 4.0* and the *Networking Supplement* for the Windows NT Server 4.0.

P A R T   4

Internet and Communication Tools

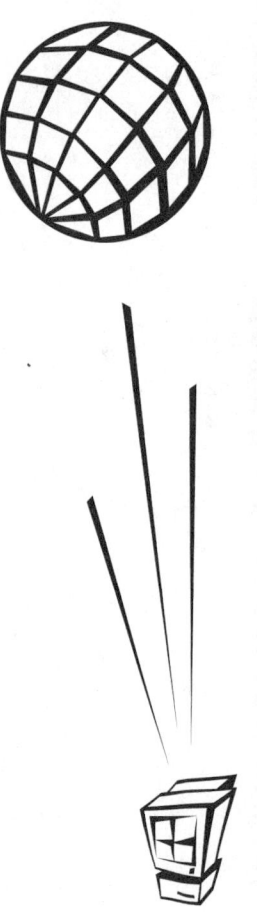

C H A P T E R   2 0

Internet Access and Tools

20

This chapter describes some of the Internet tools available with Microsoft Windows 98, including the Internet Explorer 4 browsing software and a complete set of communication and collaboration tools. It also includes a comprehensive discussion of the various options provided in Windows 98 to connect computers to the Internet.

Internet Explorer is an integrated suite of Internet software that includes a customizable browser built on open Internet standards. It delivers an Internet solution to network administrators, who can customize and control their users' Web-browsing capabilities and ensure the security of their corporate intranets. Users and Web authors value the possibilities allowed with Internet Explorer support for Dynamic HTML, ActiveX, and Java.

In This Chapter

See Also

- For information about Outlook Express, the Internet Explorer e-mail client, see Chapter 22, "Electronic Mail with Outlook Express."

- For information about configuring Web site and channel subscriptions, see Chapter 6, "Configuring the Active Desktop and Active Channels."

- For information about configuring Internet Explorer, see the *Microsoft Internet Explorer Resource Kit* (ISBN 1-57231-842-2), or download it from **http://www.microsoft.com/ie/corp/**.

Overview of Internet Explorer

Internet Explorer is the Windows 98 suite of Internet communication tools that includes an easy-to-use Web browser. Internet Explorer integrates the PC and the Internet by providing a single Explorer view and Web-savvy Start menu and taskbar. It also delivers information directly to the desktop with support for Webcasting and Active Channels. For information about Webcasting and Active Channels, see Chapter 6, "Configuring the Active Desktop and Active Channels."

The Internet Explorer browsing software gives users a more integrated and personalized browsing experience, providing an easy way to browse the Internet, their intranets, and their local computers. Users can interact with Web sites and find information faster than ever.

For corporate information systems (IS) and information technology (IT) managers, the ability of the Internet Explorer browsing software to combine the browser and the operating system reduces overall cost of ownership, as it allows users to be more productive. It extends existing functionality, thereby leveraging the investment made in training and reducing training costs. New and improved administration tools, including security features, ease migration to the intranet and administrator maintenance and control of internal Webs.

Installing and Configuring Internet Explorer

Internet Explorer is a suite of Internet software that includes several communication and collaboration tools in addition to the Internet client. It is completely integrated with the Windows 98 operating system and cannot be uninstalled. Various optional components, however, can be uninstalled at any time.

Adding/Removing Components

Certain Internet Explorer components are optionally installed when you install Windows 98. If you do not choose a particular component and wish to install it later, you can do so using the Add/Remove Programs function of Control Panel and selecting the desired components from Windows Setup. You can also install Internet Explorer components from the Add-Ons page of the Internet Explorer Web site. For more information and to download components, see **http://www.microsoft.com/ie/ie40/download/addon.htm**.

Configuring Internet Explorer with the IEAK Profile Manager

The *Internet Explorer Administration Kit (IEAK) Profile Manager* is an administrative tool that can be installed on your computer from the Microsoft Windows 98 Resource Kit compact disc. The Profile Manager simplifies the creation and maintenance of custom Internet Explorer configurations. Network administrators can use the Profile Manager to create, save, and load Internet Explorer profiles that customize settings for Internet Explorer. These profiles are stored in INS files that encapsulate Internet Explorer parameters and are structured very much like Windows INI files.

Understanding IEAK Profiles

There are three types of IEAK profiles, all of which work together to give you the flexibility you need:

Per-user profile. The INS file that contains settings for an individual user. The file name usually consists of the user logon name plus the .ins file extension.

Group profile. The INS file that contains settings for a group (such as a division or department). The file name usually consists of the group name plus the .ins file extension.

Default profile. The INS file that contains settings that Internet Explorer uses if it does not find a per-user or group INS file. The file name is Default.ins.

The Profile Manager can also read Windows policy template (ADM) files. This ability means that administrators can create their own custom templates to define additional settings and restrictions for Internet Explorer and import them to the Profile Manager using **Import** on the **Policy** menu. When you use custom policy templates, the Profile Manager generates an INF file using the file prefix from the ADM file. For example, if you import a file called Custom.adm, a Custom.inf file is created.

Important When you import custom policy (ADM) files to the Profile Manager, it is wise to select **Check Duplicate Keys** on the **Policy** menu to check for duplicate registry keys in the templates, and delete any duplicates from your templates.

For more information about policy template files, see Chapter 8, "System Policies."

Using the IEAK Profile Manager

The IEAK Profile Manager can be installed from the Netadmin\Profmgr directory on the Microsoft Windows 98 Resource Kit compact disc.

▶ **To start the IEAK Profile Manager**

1. Click **Start**, point to **Programs**, point to **Windows 98 Resource Kit**, and then click **Tools Management Console**.

2. In the left pane, click the Tool Categories folder, and then click the Deployment Tools folder.

3. In the right pane, click **Profmgr.exe**.

The Profile Manager is organized into a left-hand pane showing a hierarchical tree of objects and a right-hand pane showing the options. When you select an object in the tree in the left-hand pane, the options and settings for that object appear in the right-hand pane. You can change options or specify settings as necessary to manage automatic browser configurations.

The Profile Manager provides two categories of settings that you can specify: Wizard Settings and System Policies & Restrictions.

Furthermore, you can specify desktop, shell, and security settings across your organization. You can customize numerous settings, ranging from default Start and Search pages to users' permission to transfer files when using NetMeeting.

You can control or lock down features and functions. For example, you can use the **System** options under the **Shell** category to prevent Windows 98 users from restarting their systems in MS-DOS mode. You can also use the **Security** option under **Internet Properties** to prevent users from changing any of the security settings on the **Security** property page in Internet Explorer. When features are locked down, they either do not appear or appear in gray type on the user's desktop.

Before changing system policies and restrictions, you should understand the impact of the security settings on your users, especially if you have roaming users who share computers with other users. Consider, for example, the implications of removing icons from the desktop, or not allowing users to change their security settings. Make sure that your users understand what features they have access to and what features need to be configured by your IT organization.

For more information about the IEAK Profile Manager, see Help in the Profile Manager or the *Microsoft Internet Explorer Resource Kit*. The *Microsoft Internet Explorer Resource Kit* (for Internet Explorer 4) is available from Microsoft Press, or you can download a copy from the Internet Explorer Web site at **http://www.microsoft.com/ie/corp/**.

Configuring Proxy Servers

To ensure the security of corporate networks while allowing users access to the World Wide Web, many organizations use a proxy server. A *proxy server* can run on a company's firewall computer, which acts as a security barrier between the local network and outside networks, such as the Internet. The proxy server can also speed up access to certain Web sites, because it caches frequently requested uniform resource locators (URLs).

The Internet Explorer browsing software supports the use of proxy servers. You can configure it to use a different proxy for each Internet Protocol (IP). You can do this configuration either manually or automatically using the **Connection** tab of the **Internet Options** property page.

Manual Proxy Server Configuration

You may want to configure your proxy settings manually.

▶ **To configure proxy settings manually**

1. On the **View** menu, click **Internet Options**.
2. Click the **Connection** tab.
3. Under **Proxy server**, select **Access the Internet using a proxy server**, and type the Address and Port.
4. Click the **Advanced** button to specify different proxy addresses and ports for each Internet protocol server type, or to instruct Internet Explorer to **Use the same proxy server for all protocols**.
5. Under **Exceptions**, you can also enter Internet Protocol (IP) address prefixes or machine names (such as 207.68*.* or *.microsoft.com) for which a proxy server is not to be used.

Important When you enter exceptions, be sure to enter both the relevant names and the relevant IP numbers; if you enter only IP numbers, users who browse a site by name will still be sent by way of the proxy server and vice versa.

Automatic Proxy Server Configuration

The Internet Explorer browsing software allows administrators to configure proxy settings, such as server addresses and bypass lists, automatically. Administrators can use the IEAK Profile Manager to configure proxy settings or to create a settings file (JS, JVS, or PAC) using JScript.

Internet Explorer can be configured to retrieve proxy settings automatically for each Internet Protocol (Hypertext Transport Protocol [HTTP], File Transfer Protocol [FTP], Secure [HTTPS], Gopher, SOCKS), from an INS file created with the Profile Manager or from an HTML file that contains JScript or JavaScript, which executes whenever a network request is made. Multiple proxies can be configured for each protocol type, and Internet Explorer can automatically cycle through the different proxy servers to avoid overloading any particular server.

Benefits of Automatic Proxy Configuration

Automatic Proxy Configuration provides the following benefits:

Centralized management and compatibility. Automatic Proxy Configuration makes it easy to administer a distributed network of PCs running Windows 98 by allowing administrators to set proxy configurations in a central location for all users. Any changes are propagated to all users as they run their browsers, without disrupting the work process.

Most compatible management solution. With Internet Explorer, support for both IEAK Profile Manager settings and JScript configurations ensures maximum compatibility with existing installations.

Automatic Proxy Configuration Files

You can use a text editor to create automatic proxy configuration (JS or PAC) files that dynamically assign browser proxy settings based on the location of hosts. *Automatic proxy configuration files* are JScript files. When an automatic proxy configuration file is specified, the Internet Explorer browsing software uses the proxy auto-configuration script to determine if it should connect directly to a host or use a proxy server. You can use automatic proxy configuration files to configure users automatically to use different proxy servers for different domains.

The following example shows a proxy auto-configuration function that checks to see whether the host name is a local host, and if it is, whether the connection is direct. If the host name is not a local host, the connection is made through the proxy server. In the following example the server name is "proxy1."

```
function FindProxyForURL(url, host)
    {
        if (isPlainHostName(host))
            return "DIRECT";
        else
            return "PROXY proxy1:80";
    }
```

The isPlainHostName() function checks to see if there are any dots in the host name. If there are, it returns **false**; otherwise, the function returns **true**.

Automatically Configuring Internet Explorer After Deployment

Although it is advantageous to use the IEAK Profile Manager to customize Internet Explorer so that automatic configuration is enabled before you deploy Windows 98, it is not difficult to turn it on after the fact. This procedure can be done in Automatic Browser Configuration under Wizard Settings in the Profile Manager. You can specify the URL of the INS file to be used for automatic configuration, as well as a time interval (in minutes) for auto-configure to occur.

Important If you set up auto-configuration with the IEAK Profile Manager, you should then prevent your users from changing the auto-configuration settings. This step can be done under **System Policies & Restrictions** in the **Connection** tab of Internet Properties.

Users can manually point Internet Explorer to the URL of the auto-configuration file. This task needs to be done once, and then you can lock down the settings (as described earlier) so that your users cannot change them.

▶   **To set up automatic configuration manually**

1. On the **View** menu, click **Internet Options**.

2. Click the **Connection** tab.

3. Under **Automatic configuration**, click **Configure**.

4. Type the URL for the auto-configuration file name.

5. Click the **Refresh** button to update settings immediately.

Note Some auto-configuration settings require the system to be restarted before changes to the system registry take effect.

Configuring Cache Settings

As you view Web pages, the Internet Explorer browsing software stores them in the Temporary Internet Files folder on your hard disk to make browsing more efficient. Internet files are also stored in this "cache" when you subscribe to Web sites or use offline browsing.

▶ **To configure cache settings**

1. On the **View** menu, click **Internet Options**.
2. Click the **General** tab.
3. Under **Temporary Internet files**, click **Settings**.
4. In the **Settings** dialog box, you can select an option specifying how often Internet Explorer checks for newer versions of stored pages, specify how much disk space is used for the cache, and change the folder where temporary files are stored.

Note If you change the folder where temporary Internet files are stored, viewing the %Windows%\Temporary Internet Files folder will still reflect files in the cache. This is because that folder is referencing a Shell Handler, not the actual files.

▶ **To view temporary Internet files or downloaded objects**

1. On the **View** menu, click **Internet Options**.
2. Click the **General** tab.
3. Under **Temporary Internet files**, click **Settings**.
4. Click **View Files** to view temporary files.

    –Or–

    Click **View Objects** to view downloaded program files.

Security

Internet Explorer supports many existing and emerging security standards, such as digital certificates, making it the most secure browser available. With it, you can conduct private communications, protect your identity on the Internet, protect your computer from potentially damaging code, prevent others from tracking your activities, and restrict the viewing of certain sites on your computer. You can even verify the identity of Web servers and positively identify yourself to those servers when desired. This restriction means that online consumer transactions and banking can be conducted with privacy and security.

Security Features

The following security features make it easier for you to protect your computer and your privacy while using the Internet Explorer browsing software:

Security zones. This feature allows you to divide the Web into zones and have Internet Explorer provide different levels of security, depending on which zone you have assigned to a Web site.

Authenticode technology. Microsoft Authenticode™ certificates identify the publisher of a piece of software and verify that it has not been tampered with to help you decide whether to download it.

Privacy Protection. Internet Explorer supports all standard Internet security protocols to ensure your privacy when you communicate over the Web.

Certificate management. Digital certificates are electronic credentials that establish an individual's or organization's identity on the Internet. With certificate management, you can control which Java applets, ActiveX controls, and other software can be run on your intranet, based on who published the software.

Trust-based security for Java. The new Internet Explorer security model for Java makes it easy to control how Java applets can interact with your computer system. This cross-platform security model provides fine-grained administration of the permissions granted to Java applets and libraries.

These security features are described in more detail in the following sections.

Configuring Security Zones

The Internet Explorer *security zones* divide the Internet or intranet into zones with different levels of security. This capability permits setting global browser defaults for allowing all content on "trusted" sites or disallowing content, such as Java applets or ActiveX controls, depending on the Web site of origin.

The Internet Explorer browsing software comes with four predefined zones: local intranet, trusted sites, Internet, and restricted sites. Using the **Internet Properties** dialog box, you can set the security options you want for each zone and then add or remove sites from any zone (except Internet), depending on your level of trust in the site. In corporate environments administrators can set up zones for users and even add or remove, in advance, the authentication certificates of software publishers that they do or do not trust so that users do not have to make security decisions while they are using the Internet.

For each security zone you can choose a high, medium, low, or custom security setting. Although Microsoft recommends the high setting for sites in a zone of uncertain trustworthiness, you can safely use the medium setting in a trusted zone. The custom choice gives advanced users and administrators more control over all security options, including the following:

- Access to files, ActiveX controls, and scripts.
- The level of capabilities given to Java applets.
- Site identity designation with Secure Socket Layer (SSL) authentication.
- Password protection with Windows NT LAN Manager (NTLM) authentication. (Depending on which zone a server is in, Internet Explorer can send password information automatically, prompt the user for user and password information, or simply deny any logon request.)

Table 20.1 shows the default settings for each security zone.

Table 20.1   Security zone default settings

Zone	Default setting
Trusted sites zone	Low (do not warn before running potentially damaging content).
Local intranet zone	Medium (warn before running potentially damaging content).
Internet zone	Medium (warn before running potentially damaging content).
Restricted sites zone	High (exclude content that could damage your computer).

▶ **To configure security zones**

1. On the **View** menu, click **Internet Options**.

   –Or–

   In Control Panel, click the Internet icon.

2. Click the **Security** tab.

3. Select the zone you wish to configure from the **Zone** menu.

4. Click the desired security level for that zone.

5. If you click **Custom**, you can then click **Settings** to modify specific security settings.

Adding Sites to Security Zones

You can add sites to the Local intranet, Restricted sites, and Trusted sites security zones. The local intranet zone is comprised of all the sites behind your company's proxy server or firewall. All Web sites that are not included in one of the other zones are automatically assigned to the Internet zone.

Note   Web sites can be addressed by either Domain Name System (DNS) name or IP address. For sites that use both, it is important to configure both references to the same zone.

▶ **To add sites to the Trusted or Restricted zone**

1. On the **View** menu, click **Internet Options**.

   –Or–

   In Control Panel, click the Internet icon.

2. Click the **Security** tab, and then select **Trusted sites zone** or **Restricted sites zone** from the Zone list.

3. Click **Add Sites**.

4. Enter the addresses of the sites you want to add to this zone, and then click **Add** after each site you enter.

▶ **To add sites to the Local intranet zone**

1. On the **View** menu, click **Internet Options**.

   –Or–

   In Control Panel, click the Internet icon.

2. Click the **Security** tab, and then select **Local intranet zone** from the Zone list.

3. Click **Add Sites**, and then select the types of sites you want included in this zone.

4. Click **Advanced**.

5. Enter the addresses of the sites you want to add to this zone, and then click **Add** after each site you enter.

Note   The Internet Explorer browsing software allows you to use a wildcard character (*) when entering the address of a Web site you wish to add to a security zone.

For more detailed information about Internet Explorer security zones and security settings, see the *Microsoft Internet Explorer Resource Kit*. The *Internet Explorer Resource Kit* is available from Microsoft Press, or you can download a copy from the Internet Explorer Web site at **http://www.microsoft.com/ie/corp/**.

Configuring Security in the IEAK Profile Manager

Administrators can use the IEAK Profile Manager to configure Internet Explorer security zones and keep users from changing security zone settings on their computers. Click **Security Zones and Content Ratings Customization** under **Wizard Settings** to customize security zones settings. Lock down these settings by expanding **Internet Properties** under **System Policies & Restrictions** and then clicking the **Security** tab.

Important If you have users who roam from one computer to another, consider the implications of selecting the first option, **Use machine settings for security zones ONLY**. This prevents users from having their own security settings when they are logged on to a different computer, and they inherit whatever settings are associated with that computer.

Microsoft Authenticode Technology

Microsoft Authenticode technology allows you to verify both the publisher and the integrity of specific code found on the Internet. You can make informed decisions about whether to download the specific code, as well as whether to block execution of specific types of downloadable code, such as Java applets.

Authenticode works with VeriSign, a leading certificate authority. VeriSign is responsible for issuing digital certificates (which the company refers to as "digital IDs") and continuously verifying that the certificates are still valid.

If a piece of software has been digitally signed, Internet Explorer can verify that the software originated from the named software publisher and that it has not been tampered with. Internet Explorer displays a verification certificate if the software passes the test.

The new Authenticode time-stamping feature establishes that a piece of software was properly signed during the valid lifetime of a publisher's certificate. (Certificates have a limited lifetime to prevent giving counterfeiters enough time to eventually crack the code associated with the certificate.)

Developers can find tools for signing their code through the ActiveX software development kit (SDK).

Privacy Protection

This section describes the various aspects of privacy protection built into the Internet Explorer browsing software.

Secure channel services. Support for Secure Socket Layer (SSL) version 2.0/3.0 and Personal Communications Technology (PCT) version 1.0 ensures that personal or business communications using the Internet or intranet are private. The SSL and PCT protocols create a secure channel so that no one can eavesdrop on communications. With secure communications guaranteed, you can buy consumer goods, reserve airplane tickets, or conduct personal banking on the Internet.

Transport Layer Security. Transport Layer Security (TLS) is a new secure channel protocol under development by the Internet Engineering Task Force (IETF). TLS builds on existing protocols to create an improved Internet secure channel protocol.

Personal Information Exchange. The Personal Information Exchange (PFX) is a set of public key-based security technologies that is part of the Microsoft Internet security framework. PFX supports such Internet standards as X.509 and Public Key Cryptography Standards (PKCS) #7 certificate formats. Microsoft has submitted PFX for consideration as a new PKCS standard.

Cookie privacy. Some Web sites use cookie technology to store information on a client computer. These cookies are usually used to provide Web site personalization features. With Internet Explorer, you can choose whether to store a cookie by making the desired selection on the **Advanced** tab of the **Internet Options** dialog box.

SOCKS firewall support. Many corporations provide their employees with access to the Internet through firewalls that protect the corporation from unwanted access. SOCKS is a standard protocol for traversing firewalls in a secure and controlled manner. Internet Explorer is compatible with firewalls that use the SOCKS protocol. Hummingbird Communications, a leading provider of firewalls, provides this support.

Windows NT Server challenge/response. Corporations can take advantage of the Microsoft Windows NT Server LAN Manager (NTLM) challenge/response authentication that is already in use on their Windows NT Server networks. This provides users with increased password protection and security while remaining interoperable with their existing Internet information servers.

CryptoAPI.   CryptoAPI version 2.0 provides the underlying security services for secure channels and code signing. Through CryptoAPI, developers can easily integrate strong cryptography into their applications. Cryptographic Service Provider (CSP) modules interface with CryptoAPI and perform functions, including key generation and exchange, data encryption and decryption, hashing, digital signatures, and signature verification. CryptoAPI is included as a core component of the latest versions of Windows. Internet Explorer automatically provides this support for earlier versions of Windows.

PICS standards for Internet content.   Parents want assurances that children can be blocked from visiting sites that display inappropriate information. Corporations have similar concerns, wanting to block the use of sites that offer no business value to their employees. Microsoft has been working closely with the Platform for Internet Content Selection (PICS) committee to help define standards for rating Internet content. Internet Explorer supports the PICS standard, which means that you can control access to rated Web sites or use third-party rating bureaus to control access based on content. For more information about third-party rating bureaus, see the PICS specification at **http://www.w3.org/pics/**.

Microsoft Wallet.   Microsoft Wallet supports securely storing important and private information, such as credit cards, electronic driver's licenses, ATM cards, and electronic cash. No application or person can view this information without your permission. In addition, you decide where to store the information (on a computer, smart card, or floppy disk). You have to enter password or account information only once and do not have to remember many different passwords. You have complete control over who can see or use this information. Wallet allows information to be securely transferred to any computer and used with any application through the use of PFX technology. Wallet supports additional payment methods (such as Internet cash) as well as other credentials and confidential information.

Note   Microsoft Wallet is an optional component of Internet Explorer and must be selected under Internet Tools when installing Windows 98.

▶ **To add or modify personal information or payment methods**

1. On the **View** menu, click **Internet Options**.

    –Or–

    In Control Panel, click the Internet icon.

2. Click the **Content** tab.

3. Under **Personal Information**, click **Addresses** or **Payments** to add or change personal information and payment methods to be used by Internet Explorer.

Certificate Management

With Certificate Management, administrators can control which Java applets, ActiveX controls, and other software can run on their intranets based on who published the software. This control makes administering network security relatively easy. Certificates are assigned only to software publishers who meet industry guidelines for security and integrity.

Managing Certificates with the Internet Explorer Administration Kit

Through the IEAK, administrators can pre-install certificates on users' computers and block them from downloading any other certificates. The benefit of such pre-installation is two-fold. First, it gives administrators greater control. Second, it reduces the number of warnings and choices that are presented to users when they download software from the Internet.

After initially installing Windows 98, administrators can remotely manage all allowed publisher and site certificates by adding new certificates or removing certificates from the list.

For more information, or to license and download a copy of the IEAK, visit the IEAK Web site at **http://ieak.microsoft.com/**.

Obtaining and Using Personal Certificates

Personal certificates verify your identity on the Web. You can obtain a certificate from a certifying authority, an organization responsible for issuing certificates and continuously verifying that the certificates are still valid. The certificate provider preferred by Microsoft is VeriSign.

For more information on obtaining a personal certificate, see Chapter 22, "Electronic Mail with Outlook Express."

Viewing Security Certificates

You can view both personal and site certificates at any time in the Internet Explorer browsing window.

▶ **To view security certificates**

1. On the **View** menu, click **Internet Options**.

   –Or–

   In Control Panel, click the Internet icon.

2. Click the **Content** tab.

3. Under **Certificates**, click **Personal**, **Authorities**, or **Publishers** to view the current certificates.

Note You can also import or export personal certificates. (The file extension is .cer or .p7c.)

Trust-Based Security for Java

Trust-based security is a cross-platform security model that adds intermediate levels of trust to the Java security model. It enhances administration of the Java Virtual Machine (VM) by providing flexible control over permissions granted to Java classes, such as access to scratch (storage) space, local files, and network connections. This allows an application to be given some additional permissions without being offered unlimited access to all other permissions in the system.

For more information about Java and the Java VM, see "Java" later in this chapter, or visit the Microsoft Java Web site at **http://www.microsoft.com/java/**.

Trust-based security zones. Administrators can manage Java classes with the same trust level as a group by assigning them to the same zone. For more information about Internet Explorer Security Zones, see "Configuring Security Zones" earlier in this chapter. Administrators can configure three different sets of permissions for each zone, for both signed and unsigned code:

- Permissions granted without user intervention are available without user intervention to Java applets from the zone. They can be specified for signed and unsigned applets.

- Permissions granted with user intervention are determined by a user's responses to queries about whether to grant permissions to specific applets from the zone.

- Permissions that are fully denied are considered too dangerous to allow under any circumstances and, therefore, are denied automatically.

Permissions model. This model supports a rich set of permissions that administrators can control with parameters and individually grant or deny for a particular zone. To reduce the number of options that administrators have to specify in common cases, the administrative user interface for trust-based security supports several preset permission sets that can be applied.

Permission signing. Permission signing extends signed Cabinet (CAB) file functionality by allowing a signed CAB file to specify securely not only the identity of the signer, but also the set of permissions being requested for the signed classes. Because the permissions are understood by the Java VM, a Java component can read the signature and provide an accurate warning about the risks of each permission.

Permission scoping. Permission scoping prevents permissions granted to a trusted component from being misused, either intentionally or inadvertently, by a less trusted component. Permission scoping allows a class to precisely limit the range of code for which a granted privilege is enabled for use.

Package Manager. Package Manager allows the installation of local class libraries that are not fully trusted, using permission signing. This is important for components, such as JavaBeans, that need to reside on the local computer and have some expanded privileges but should not have unlimited power.

Trust User Interface. The user interface defined by trust-based security for Java shields users from complicated security decisions and reduces the number of security-related dialogs they must answer. When deciding whether to trust an application, users need only make a simple "Yes/No" choice, because an administrator has already made the fine-grained decisions of what is left to the discretion of users for a particular zone.

Using Profile Assistant

The Internet Explorer Profile Assistant provides a simple way for you to store personal information that can be shared with specified Web sites. This information is completely private and secure, in that others cannot view or access it without your permission. Profile Assistant saves you from having to type in registration or demographic information each time it is requested. The Profile Assistant secure client profile is populated by default with registration information collected by Internet Explorer. If there is no data, or you wish to edit the information previously collected, you can access your profile at any time.

▶ **To access personal information in Profile Assistant**

1. On the **View** menu, click **Internet Options**.

   –Or–

   In Control Panel, click the Internet icon.

2. Click the **Content** tab.

3. In the **Personal Information** area, click **Edit Profile**.

4. Click the desired tabs to enter personal, demographic, and security information.

Note Profile Assistant can be disabled using the **Advanced** tab of the **Internet Options** dialog box. If you disable Profile Assistant, all requests from Web sites for personal information must be handled manually.

When a Web site requests user information, such as an e-mail address, Profile Assistant opens a dialog box that provides you with the URL of the site, the specific information requested, the purpose of the request, and whether the site has a secure connection. You can then decide what information, if any, you wish to share. There is also an option you can choose to always allow this site to see the specific items you have selected.

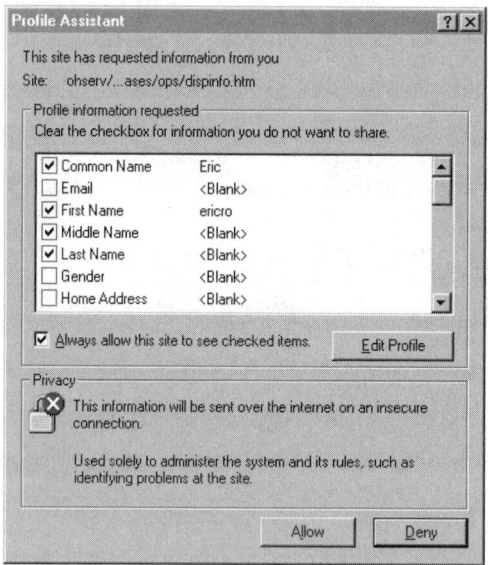

If you have given permission for certain sites to always have access to some or all of your personal profile information, you can revoke that access at any time.

▶ **To revoke permissions previously granted to sites**

1. On the **View** menu, click **Internet Options**.

   –Or–

   In Control Panel, click the Internet icon.

2. Click the **Content** tab.

3. In the **Personal Information** area, click **Reset Sharing**, and then click **Yes**.

Using the Internet Explorer Browsing Software

The Internet Explorer browsing software is powerful and easy to use. The following section highlights some important features and describes how you can customize and personalize Internet Explorer.

Making Browsing Easy and Personalized

Internet Explorer includes improvements in browsing and personalization capabilities.

Explorer Bars

Explorer bars are ways to browse through a list of links, such as your History or Favorites, while displaying the pages those links open in the right side of the window. For example, if you click **Search** on the toolbar, the Explorer bar opens and you can use it to search for the Web site you want. You can use several different Explorer bars:

- The **Search** bar displays a list of services that offer different kinds of searching capabilities. You can use the IEAK Profile Manager to specify a custom Search bar that points to the URL of your workgroup's favorite search engine.

- The **Favorites** bar displays the list of Favorite Web site URLs, files, folders, and applications added using **Add to Favorites**.

- The **History** bar displays a list of folders containing links for URLs visited in previous days and weeks.

- The **Channels** bar displays a list of subscribed Active Channels.

Explorer Bars slightly reduce the available content area and remain visible until you again click the button that opened the particular Explorer bar.

AutoComplete

AutoComplete makes it easy to type in an Internet address and reduces the risk of typographical errors. The Address bar automatically completes addresses for you based on sites you have already visited, adds prefixes and suffixes to Internet addresses, and corrects syntax errors. You can easily override the suggestions by typing over them. AutoComplete is similar to the AutoFill feature in Microsoft Excel.

AutoComplete includes the following features and shortcuts:

- You can skip to break and separation characters in URLs (that is, // / . , ? +) by pressing and holding CTRL and then pressing the right or left arrow key.
- You can search your History file by typing the beginning of an Internet address and then pressing the up or down arrow key to find the desired URL.
- By pressing CTRL and ENTER, you can browse directly to "http://www.<what you typed>.com." You can customize this shortcut through a registry key, as described in Chapter 31, "Windows 98 Registry."

Improved Favorites

The Favorites function has been improved in the following ways:

Drag and drop ordering. This feature allows you to drag and drop your favorite sites and links to the Favorites menu and arrange them in any way you choose.

Thumbnail view. This option allows you to preview multiple Web sites simultaneously without visiting the sites.

▶ **To enable Thumbnail view**

1. On the **Favorites** menu, click **Organize Favorites**.
2. Right-click the window background, and then click **Properties**.
3. Click the **Enable thumbnail view** check box.
4. Right-click the window background, and then click **Refresh**
5. Right-click the window background, point to **View**, and then click **Thumbnails**.

Browse in a New Process

This optional feature enables you to open multiple browsing windows simultaneously. For example, if you have an Internet Explorer browsing window open, and you open an HTML document in My Computer, another browsing window opens for the HTML document. If you click a link on a Web site that calls for a new Internet Explorer window, a new window opens for that link. This feature helps minimize disruption to other programs on your computer if the content or programs you are running in a browsing window are unstable.

Note Enabling this option can degrade system performance due to the additional system resources required by each Internet Explorer browsing window. If your computer is low on resources or only meets the base system requirements for Windows 98, you may want to consider not enabling browsing in a new process.

▶ **To enable browsing in a new process**

1. On the **View** menu, click **Internet Options**.

2. On the **Advanced** tab, select **Browse in a new process**.

RealPlayer 4.0

With the inclusion of RealPlayer version 4.0 in Windows 98, you can easily access RealAudio and RealVideo content from the Web. The RealPlayer 4.0 is automatically launched from the Internet Explorer browsing software when you choose to play RealAudio and RealVideo clips. You can continue to use your browsing window while RealPlayer is playing the clip, and you can minimize the RealPlayer 4.0 window while you use other applications. The RealPlayer 4.0 continues playing the selected clip until it is finished, or until you stop or pause it.

For information about how to use the RealPlayer, refer to online Help in RealPlayer 4.0. To obtain technical support from RealNetworks, go to their Web site at **http://service.real.com/**.

On a corporate intranet, the RealPlayer may need to be configured to work with your company's firewall. For information about using RealPlayer 4.0 with a firewall refer to the information at **http://www.real.com/firewall/**.

Creating Web Page Subscriptions

You can choose to subscribe to a Web page as you add it to your Favorites. Web pages that you subscribe to are automatically checked for updates since the last time you accessed them, and, if there have been any updates, the new content can be downloaded automatically or you can choose to be notified of changes by e-mail.

▶ **To create a Web page subscription**

1. Open a Web page you wish to subscribe to.
2. On the **Favorites** menu, click **Add to Favorites**.
3. Click **Yes, but only tell me when this page is updated**.
4. Click the **Customize** button, and select **Yes, send an e-mail message to the following address** to configure Internet Explorer to send you an e-mail message when the Web page is updated.

Configuring Web Page Subscriptions for Offline Reading

Using a large network, such as a corporate intranet or the Internet, has traditionally required having a direct connection from your computer to the network. This prevents access to network content for computers without a network connection, such as portable computers. Furthermore, even for a computer with a network connection, browsing can be slow, because the browser must traverse the network from the local machine to the Web server and back to the local machine again to download and refresh the content on the screen.

The offline capabilities of the Internet Explorer browsing software allow you to access subscription Web pages without being connected to the Internet. Internet Explorer downloads the pages in the background based on a schedule you set up, automatically disconnects from the Internet, and then notifies you of changes to these pages. You can also download the pages manually, if desired.

▶ **To configure new Web page subscriptions for offline reading**

1. Open a Web page you wish to subscribe to.
2. On the **Favorites** menu, click **Add to Favorites**.
3. Click **Yes, notify me of updates and download the page for offline viewing**.
4. Click **Customize** to start the Subscription Wizard.
5. Select the desired download option for this subscription, and then click **Next**.
6. Select the desired e-mail option for this subscription, and then click **Next**.

7. Select the desired scheduling option for this subscription, and then click **Next**.

8. Specify any password data if applicable, and then click **Finish**.

Note If you do not designate a schedule for downloading updates to Web pages, Internet Explorer defaults to a daily update between 12:00 A.M. and 12:30 A.M.

You can also modify download and scheduling options for existing subscriptions.

▶ **To modify an existing subscription**

1. On the **Favorites** menu, click **Manage Subscriptions**.

2. Select the desired subscription.

3. On the **File** menu, click **Properties.**

    –Or–

    Right-click the subscription, and then click **Properties**.

4. Click the **Receiving** tab and select the desired subscription and notification options.

5. If you select **Notify me when updates occur, and download for offline viewing**, you can click **Advanced** to configure options for specific content and items to be downloaded, and for the maximum number of bytes to be downloaded at one time. You can also configure the subscription to follow links outside of the subscribed Web site.

6. Click the **Schedule** tab to designate whether downloading of content should occur automatically or manually, and when to perform manual downloading.

▶ **To update subscriptions manually**

• On the **Favorites** menu, click **Update All Subscriptions**.

Controlling Subscriptions with the IEAK Profile Manager

Administrators can use the IEAK Profile Manager to control whether and how their users subscribe to Web sites. The time of day that downloads can occur, as well as the maximum size of the content downloaded, can be specified as well. These and other options are accessible in **Channels & Subscriptions** under **System Policies & Restrictions**.

For more information about configuring subscriptions, see Chapter 6, "Configuring the Active Desktop and Active Channels."

Customizing Your Start Page with the Personal Home Page Wizard

Whenever you start the Internet Explorer browsing software, the first page you see is the Internet Start page. This page always includes articles and features to help you benefit more from the Internet. You can customize this page through the Internet Start Personalization feature so that it keeps you up to date with information about topics of interest to you.

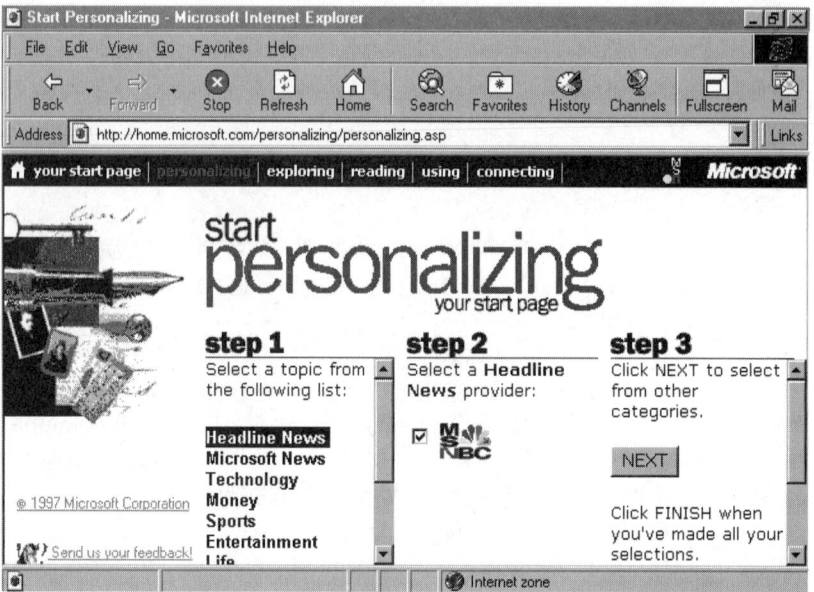

You can also add headlines from news providers, including Wired, MSNBC, and Forbes. In addition, you can search the Web from your Internet Start page.

Through its Exploring section, Internet Start also includes regularly updated links to the latest sites from around the world that qualify as the Best of the Web in such categories as sports, travel and entertainment, and computers and technology.

▶ **To use the Personal Home Page Wizard**

1. Start Internet Explorer. By default, your start page is set to Internet Start: **http://home.microsoft.com/**.

2. Click **Personalizing** on the toolbar at the top of the Internet Start page.

3. Follow the instructions on the screen to select the type of content you want to see each time you start Internet Explorer.

Changing Your Default Home Page

You can also change your default home page to another Web site or to a blank page. Administrators can do this globally through a setting in the IEAK Profile Manager and can disable users from changing the setting.

▶ **To change your default home page**

1. On the **View** menu, click **Internet Options**.

2. Click the **General** tab.

3. Type the URL of the page you want to designate as your home page.

   –Or–

   Click **Use Current** to make the current page your default home page.

   –Or–

   Click **Use Blank** to have Internet Explorer start with a blank page.

Using Internet Explorer with Netscape Browsers

The Internet Explorer browsing software may coexist with any Netscape browser. Keep in mind that the Netscape user settings are imported by Internet Explorer only at the time you upgrade your system to Windows 98. After that, separate user settings may be applied to each of the browsers.

Migration of Existing Netscape Configurations

Windows 98 Setup imports proxy settings, bookmarks, and cookies from Netscape Navigator or Communicator to the Internet Explorer browsing software.

The following Netscape Navigator settings are always imported:

- The Proxy settings.
- Netscape bookmarks adopted as Internet Explorer Favorites. With Navigator, only custom bookmarks are adopted. With Communicator, all default bookmarks are adopted.

The following Navigator settings are adopted only if they are not default settings:

- Security settings: personal certificate list and site certificate list.
- Option to match up the Toolbar view in Internet Explorer to that in Netscape Navigator.

The following Navigator settings are imported by Outlook Express:

- SMTP server information.
- POP3 server settings (POP3 server name and POP3 user name).
- Identity information (name, e-mail address, reply address, organization, and signature information). This information is stored in a different tab from **View/Options/Server**.
- Personal address book.
- Internet telephone application Web-based telephone book.
- Send and post settings (8-bit characters in headers, and MIME compliance) if different from the Navigator Default.
- Settings for checking new messages every x minutes if different from the Navigator Default.

The following Navigator settings are imported by the Web Publishing Wizard:

- Author's name
- Document template location
- Publisher user name
- Publisher password

Using Public Domain Tools

There are a variety of navigation applications available in the public domain on the Internet, including Gopher, Archie, and Wide Area Information Server (WAIS). These applications allow you to find information on the Internet easily. The following sections provide information about several of these applications. You should contact your Internet service provider (ISP) to find these public domain and shareware applications. To download them, you can use the File Transfer Protocol (FTP).

Note Many TCP/IP applications from non-Microsoft vendors offer Internet browsing, viewing, and connection capabilities. Many of these applications are 16-bit and do not currently work with the 32-bit version of TCP/IP provided with Windows 98.

Caution Windows 98 provides a 32-bit Windows Sockets interface (Winsock.dll). Any attempt to override the Windows 98 interface could cause TCP/IP applications to fail or could cause the computer to stop responding.

Using Gopher

Gopher offers menu-based access to Internet information. Gopher hides the intricacies of FTP servers and bypasses complicated TCP/IP addresses and connections. You choose information from a list of menus, and Gopher makes the connections necessary to retrieve the files. Gopher is most helpful when you need to find specific pieces of information on the Internet.

Using Archie

Archie is a server that supports a database of anonymous FTP sites and their contents. Archie stores the contents, descriptions, and file names of many FTP sites. Archie applications are available from many major Internet sites.

Using Wide Area Information Server

With *Wide Area Information Server* (WAIS), you can browse the hundreds of databases and library catalogs on the Internet in an organized way. WAIS searches the contents of documents based on words as opposed to titles. After a search, WAIS displays a list of documents. This list, however, can be extremely large, so WAIS sorts the documents based on how many times a key word is found in each one. If the list is too large, you can narrow the search by specifying categories.

Tips for Adding a Gateway Server

A dedicated connection to the Internet provides many advantages over a modem connection with a telephone line to your ISP. Having a gateway server can improve performance and reduce costs. You will need to set up hardware and obtain a domain name so others can send information to your gateway.

If you set up a dedicated computer to act as a router or gateway server to the Internet, it should use a high-speed connection, such as T1 or 56 KB lines, instead of a slower telephone line. The T1 line connects to the computer using a special network adapter.

Networks that connect to the Internet must obtain an official network ID from the InterNIC to guarantee unique IP network IDs. Contact the InterNIC by sending electronic mail to info@internic.net. In the United States call (800) 444–4345; from Canada and overseas call (619) 455–4600.

Send Internet registration requests to hostmaster@internic.net. You can also use FTP to connect to **rs.internic.net/templates** where you will find a template for registering a domain name. The template also contains details on the registration process and procedures. After receiving a network ID, the local network administrator must assign unique host IDs for computers within the local network.

Microsoft TCP/IP Utilities

Windows 98 provides several TCP/IP utilities for copying files, initiating host sessions with other servers, checking the status of your IP configuration, and verifying your connection.

Using File Transfer Protocol

File Transfer Protocol (FTP) allows the transfer of text and binary files between a host computer and a computer. FTP requires you to log on to the remote host for user authentication. Sometimes, you may log on as "anonymous" and use your e-mail address as your password. Some FTP servers limit the number of anonymous users they can handle at any one time, so you might have to attempt to connect more than once to get a connection.

You can use FTP to gain access to the Microsoft FTP server for troubleshooting help and other information. This support service uses anonymous FTP to provide documentation, utilities, updated drivers, and other information for many Microsoft systems products.

▶ **To get support from Microsoft using FTP**

1. Make sure you are connected to your Internet provider.

2. From the **Start** menu, click **Run**, type **ftp**, and then click **OK**.

3. At the command prompt, type **open ftp.microsoft.com**

4. When you are prompted to specify a user name, type **anonymous**

5. Type your Internet account name (your e-mail name) as your password, using the format userid@hostname.domain.

   As you type your Internet account name, characters might not appear on the screen. This is a security measure to protect your password.

   You are now connected to the root directory of the Microsoft FTP site.

Note   You can also use FTP from the Internet Explorer browsing software. To navigate to ftp.microsoft.com, use the following URL format: **ftp://ftp.microsoft.com/**.

Working with Directories and Folders at an FTP Site

You can view a list of directories and files at an FTP site, change directories, and download files. Most FTP servers contain text files that describe the layout of their entire directory structure to help you find what you need. For example, the text file Dirmap.txt may describe that server's directory structure.

▶ **To list the directories and folders at an FTP site**

- At the ftp> prompt, type **ls**

▶ **To view more details about the current directory**

- At the ftp> prompt, type **ls -l**

This command provides a detailed listing similar to the following:

```
dr-xr-xr-x    1    owner    group    0       Aug 23   16:23    advsys
dr-xr-xr-x    1    owner    group    0       Aug 24   5:37     deskapps
dr-xr-xr-x    1    owner    group    0       Aug 24   10:52    developer
-r-xr-xr-x    1    owner    group    4161    Sep 19   7:43     dirmap.txt
-r-xr-xr-x    1    owner    group    712     Aug 25   15:07    disclaimer.txt
-r-xr-xr-x    1    owner    group    860     Sep 1    8:40     index.txt
```

In this list:

- The left column indicates whether the item is a file (r) or a directory (dr).
- The fifth column indicates the size of each file in bytes.
- The last column describes the name of the file, directory, or link. A link can be to a file or directory somewhere else on the FTP site (similar to a shortcut to a folder or file in Windows 98).

▶ **To change directories**

- At the ftp> prompt, type **cd** *directory_name*

  For example, to get more information about desktop applications, you might type **cd deskapps**

▶ **To go back to the previous directory**

- At the ftp> prompt, type **cd**

  If you have navigated through many directories and want to go back to the beginning, instead of typing **cd ..** again and again, you can type **cd /** to return to the root directory of the host.

Tip Notice that the forward slash "/" is used (as opposed to the backslash "\" that MS-DOS and Windows users are accustomed to). On most UNIX computers, the way to change directories is the forward slash. Thus UNIX FTP servers typically understand only directory names using the forward slash, while Windows NT FTP servers, such as ftp.microsoft.com, understand directories using both the forward slash and the backslash.

Downloading Files with FTP

To download files from the Internet using FTP, you must indicate whether the file is an ASCII or a binary (for example, Microsoft Word) file. By default, when you begin using FTP, you are working in ASCII mode. To transfer text files, it is not necessary to change modes; however, you cannot transfer a binary file while you are in ASCII mode.

Tip Most text-based FTP clients are case-sensitive, so make sure you use the correct case when you attempt to transfer resources from these FTP sites.

▶ **To switch from ASCII to binary transfer mode**

- At the ftp> prompt, type **binary**

  The following message appears to confirm the change to binary transfer mode:

  ```
  200 Type set to I
  ```

▶ **To switch from binary transfer mode to ASCII**

- At the ftp> prompt, type **ascii**

  The following message appears to confirm the change to ASCII:

  ```
  200 Type set to A
  ```

▶ **To transfer a file to your computer**

- At the ftp> prompt, type **get** *filename*

  For example, to get the directory map on the Microsoft FTP server, type **get dirmap.txt**

  To place the file on a computer with a name other than the one it had on the server, type **get** *filename newname*

If you receive an error message, remember that you are using software that is case-sensitive, so make sure you typed **dirmap.txt** exactly.

When you see the ftp> prompt again, look in Windows Explorer for the Dirmap.txt file and open it by using a text processor, such as Microsoft WordPad.

▶ **To disconnect from your host**

- At the ftp> prompt, type **disconnect**

▶ **To quit the FTP client**

- At the ftp> prompt, type **quit**

Using Telnet

Some of the information on the Internet is still available only if you use telnet. Windows 98 provides a version of telnet that you can run from the **Start** menu.

▶ **To run telnet**

1. From the **Start** menu, select **Run**, type **telnet**, and then click **OK**.
2. In Telnet, click the **Connect** menu, and then click **Remote Session**.
3. In the **Connect** dialog box, type the host name of the telnet site to which you want to connect.
4. In the **Term Type** box, select a terminal mode. The default is VT-100.
5. In the **Port** box, select a port. The default is telnet.
6. To start the telnet session, click the **Connect** button.
7. To capture data to a file, type **terminal/start logging**

For more information about using telnet, see Help.

Supported Standards and Technologies of Internet Explorer

Users can now view and listen to real-time netcasts, watch videos, run ActiveX controls and Java applets, and play interactive multiplayer games while they are connected to the World Wide Web. This capability is made possible by the extensive support of Internet Explorer for Internet standards and its innovative underlying technologies, such as Dynamic HTML, ActiveX, and Java. Using this set of technologies, Web authors can produce more enticing content and develop consumer and business applications that create a more rewarding Web experience.

Dynamic HTML

Because of the limitations of earlier browser technology, Web authors often have to choose between page interactivity and speed. After a page is loaded, changing the display or content of the page typically requires the entire page to be reloaded. Or, depending on how extensive the changes are, additional pages may have to be retrieved from the server. The Internet Explorer browsing software solves this dilemma with Microsoft's *Dynamic HTML*, a collection of features that extends the capabilities of traditional HTML, giving Web authors more flexibility, design options, and creative control over the appearance and behavior of Web pages as well as an easier and faster way to author interactive Web pages.

Dynamic HTML is consistent with the direction of the Document Object Model, being defined by the World Wide Web Consortium (W3C) Document Object Model Working Group. Dynamic HTML allows Web authors to add a new dimension of interactivity without slowing performance in the process.

Dynamic HTML offers a new way for Web authors to control the HTML tags they already know. Every element on a Web page—whether it be an image, link, Java applet, heading, or the like—is now an object to which Web authors can add functionality. Much of Dynamic HTML's functionality and flexibility comes from adding "intelligence" to the user's computer. When the user places the mouse over the object or clicks on it, the element can deliver additional information or options—without having to go back to a Web server to do so. In this way, you can use Dynamic HTML to pack greater value into your Web sites.

The following paragraphs describe some of the key aspects of Dynamic HTML.

Document Object Model for Dynamic HTML

The central Document Object Model for Dynamic HTML gives authors access to every HTML tag on a page. You do not need to be an expert programmer to create a dynamic experience for the user—add a little JavaScript or VBScript to the standard tags already in use throughout the Web. You can also extend the capabilities of Dynamic HTML through Java applets or ActiveX controls.

What you see is only the start of what you get from a Web page when you create it using the Dynamic HTML Document Object Model. Consider an organizational chart, for example. The new Document Object Model allows you to build the chart so that when a user moves the mouse over a person's name, a pop-up box tells the user more about that person and his or her group. For additional information, the user can simply click a link in the box. This way of presenting the information saves space on the page—and the user's valuable time—by hiding information and options until the user wants them.

Another example of how you can use the Object Model is building a table of contents that users can expand or contract to see key information on a page quickly. Such a table of contents is easy to generate in Dynamic HTML—even for sites that already exist—because the Object Model gives authors control over all the HTML tags on a page. In this case, you add a few lines of scripting to take the existing heading tags and arrange them into a linked table of contents on the user's command.

Here are some of the things you can do with the Dynamic HTML Object Model by adding a little JavaScript or VBScript to standard HTML:

- Build in text that changes and images that move and hide, changing dynamically according to what the user does with the mouse.
- In a picture, have text display when the user moves the mouse over any button.
- Hide and show text as well as move objects around the page.
- Add several layers of information—and color—to ordinary text. Set up a title to display main headings dynamically with a mouse click. Set up the headings to change font color as the user points to them. Allow another click to display subheadings that link the user to pages within the Internet Explorer site.

Dynamic HTML 2-D Positioning

Web authors can position elements to make sites look as they want them to. The Internet Explorer browsing software supports cascading style sheets (CSS) positioning, or the ability to position HTML elements in x- and y- coordinates, and the z-plane. With this capability, authors can overlap objects make them transparent. Combined with other Dynamic HTML features, these new positioning capabilities allow authors to move elements around and animate their pages.

With the Dynamic HTML 2-D positioning feature, you have complete control over the positioning of images and elements and can determine what happens where on every page you create. In addition to being able to specify the exact placement of text and images on a page, you can create multiple layers using standards-based cascading style sheets so that images overlap and appear transparent, creating new visual effects that animate pages. You can also build interactivity into your sites by combining 2-D positioning with scripting.

Data Binding in Dynamic HTML

The data awareness functionality of the Internet Explorer browsing software allows Web authors to use native HTML so that users can manipulate and input data efficiently, with minimal load on the server. After users receive data from a Web site that is enabled with Dynamic HTML, they can sort, filter, and modify the data repeatedly—without using the server again. By reducing the number of hits to the server, *data binding* speeds up operations for both the user and the Web site.

Until now, sending and receiving data over the Web have been difficult and inefficient. Whenever you wanted to look at the data a different way, you had to go back to the Web server and then wait for the page to reload. With Internet Explorer, Web authors can take advantage of the Dynamic HTML data awareness, or data binding, capabilities to create powerful and useful Web-based business applications.

After you receive information from a site that takes advantage of Dynamic HTML and data binding, you can sort and filter the data repeatedly without initiating another round trip to the server. For example, you may be shopping for a car and request a list of all cars costing between $15,000 and $20,000. After receiving the list, you decide to narrow the search to sports cars within that price range. Your computer does all the subsequent processing, refreshing the page to reflect the result of the sort operation. The result is faster performance and less traffic on the Web server. Data binding creates pages that display such information as lists of prices, product descriptions, airline flights, and company benefits.

Data binding requires little or no additional programming. Instead, it allows authors to insert data into a Web page as a Java applet or an object that can be manipulated. The HTML Data Binding extensions can bind HTML elements that have been proposed to the W3C for incorporation into the HTML standard. Authors can choose from data source objects included in the Internet Explorer browsing software or in third-party data source objects, or they can build new ones. After the object is dropped into an HTML page, Internet Explorer recognizes it as a data provider.

For more examples of data source objects, see the Data Source Object Gallery on the Site Builder Network Web site at:

http://www.microsoft.com/gallery/files/datasrc/.

Data binding delivers all the Best-of-the-Web content when you first download the site. Then, as you select various categories of information, data binding filters the information on your computer—without revisiting the server. In this way, the content you want to read displays instantly, no matter how many pages you view or the number of times you filter the information.

Data binding gives you quick access to information and enables you to enter information, make selections, and manipulate data any way you want. Best of all, Data Binding allows you to view pages instantly—even while building complex tables.

Dynamic HTML Scriptlets

Dynamic HTML *scriptlets* let Web authors create reusable objects with Dynamic HTML. These reusable objects, known as Web components, are simply Web pages in which script has been written according to certain conventions. The functionality of a scriptlet can be written in any scripting language, including Microsoft JScript and Visual Basic Scripting Edition (VBScript).

The following benefits of using scriptlets make the Internet Explorer browsing software an ideal platform for anyone building applications for the Web:

- Because they are isolated from their surrounding program, errors elsewhere in a program will not affect the scriptlet. This makes debugging programs simpler and less time consuming.

- Scriptlets can be reused in many programs without having to be modified. This can eliminate many problems that can arise from copying and modifying source code.

- Due to the support of the underlying component architecture, scriptlets written in different languages can be combined. This allows applications to be built more quickly since code does not have to be translated to another language.

To download samples of Dynamic HTML scriptlets, see the Dynamic HTML Scriptlets Gallery on the Site Builder Network Web site at:

http://www.microsoft.com/gallery/files/scriptlets/.

ActiveX

With *ActiveX*, you can create dramatic multimedia effects, interactive objects, and sophisticated applications. Internet Explorer ActiveX controls allow you to uninstall controls quickly.

ActiveX technology creates innovative Web-based software components. Developers can write ActiveX controls in any language, including Visual C++, Microsoft Visual Basic, and Java with low-bandwidth effects on the Web pages. Also, ActiveX controls have full access to the Object Model in Internet Explorer, which allows developers to manipulate pages dynamically.

Following are some examples of ActiveX controls:

Windowless controls. Allow developers to create transparent and nonrectangular controls—a crucial feature for overlapping controls with the 2-D layout feature of Internet Explorer.

Apartment model controls. Increase performance by taking advantage of the fact that Internet Explorer is a multithreaded container.

Quick activation. Greatly simplifies the process of initializing controls.

Support for downloading data asynchronously. Boosts performance for controls that need to download images or other complex data.

ActiveX Scripting

Web authors can use ActiveX Scripting to make pages more interactive—capable of asking questions, responding to queries, checking user data, calculating expressions, and connecting to other controls. You can view Web pages that use any popular scripting language—including VBScript and JScript.

ActiveX Scripting lets ActiveX controls "talk" to each other and to other Web programs. It allows ActiveX and Java controls to access the Object Model in Internet Explorer, which in turn allows developers to author pages that users can manipulate.

In addition to the scripting support in the Internet Explorer browsing software, Microsoft provides the following powerful scripting options.

The Windows Scripting Host (WSH) is a simple, powerful, and flexible scripting solution for the 32-bit Windows platform. WSH allows scripts—including those written in VBScript and JavaScript—to be run directly on the Windows desktop without being embedded in an HTML document. This low-memory scripting host is ideal for non-interactive scripting needs, such as logon and administrative scripting. WSH can be run from either the Windows-based host (Wscript.exe) or the command-shell–based host (Cscript.exe).

For more information about the Windows Scripting Host see **http://www.microsoft.com/management/**.

Microsoft Internet Information Server now supports Active Server Pages, which allows scripts to run on Web servers. In other words, it enables server-side scripting over the Internet or an intranet.

Java

With Internet Explorer support for Java, developers and users can enjoy the benefits of compelling, high-performance multimedia applications. The following paragraphs describe some of the features that make it easy for developers to create rich, full-featured Java applications for the Web.

High performance. Internet Explorer maintains its performance leadership as the fastest way to run Java applications, delivering performance improvements in the Virtual Machine, Just-in-Time (JIT) compiler, and class libraries.

Full integration with ActiveX. Developers can now access ActiveX controls as Java Beans (components), and Java Beans as ActiveX controls. This integration is seamless, automatic, and bidirectional. In addition, developers now have a seamless operation for debugging between Microsoft Visual Basic Scripting Edition (VBScript), JScript, and Java.

Full Object Model capability. The Internet Explorer Document Object Model is exposed through Java libraries, allowing Java developers to manipulate pages dynamically and tightly integrate Java applications with Web pages.

Application Foundation Classes. Support for Java includes Microsoft's recent introduction of Application Foundation Classes (AFC), a comprehensive set of cross-platform class libraries that help software developers quickly create commercial-quality applications for Java. AFC delivers a rich suite of graphics as well as user interface and multimedia capabilities.

Java Development Kit 1.1 compatibility. Internet Explorer is fully compatible with all the cross-platform features of Java Development Kit (JDK) version 1.1, the current version of Java.

New multimedia class libraries. All the functionality of DirectX 5 media and the DirectX 5 foundation is provided as cross-platform Java class libraries, enabling developers to manipulate and animate a full set of media types.

Capabilities-based security model. Internet Explorer expands the code-signing Authenticode feature to specify at a granular level which system capabilities—for example, the file system—a Java application can access through the use of digital signatures. For more information about Internet Explorer security, see "Security" earlier in this chapter.

Virtual Machine for Java

Windows 98 includes Microsoft's Virtual Machine for Java, which enables the Internet Explorer browsing software to interpret Java code. The Virtual Machine makes Java code platform-independent, meaning that the same code can run on many different machines. When Internet Explorer encounters a Web page that contains a Java applet, it uses the Virtual Machine to compile the Java bytecode into hardware-specific code and run the applet. Figure 20.1 illustrates the various components of the Virtual Machine for Java.

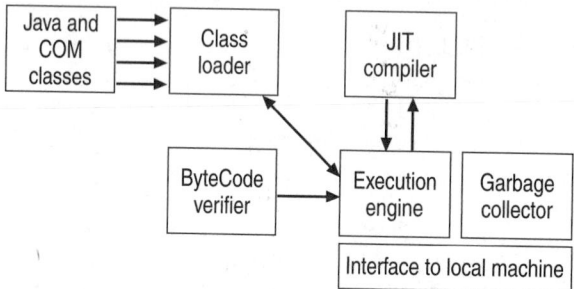

Figure 20.1   Virtual Machine for Java

The Virtual Machine for Java includes the following components:

- Class loader. Responsible for loading classes. A class is Java source code compiled into bytecode.

- ByteCode verifier. Prevents hostile classes from being loaded, and verifies the overall integrity of the class files.

- Execution engine. Compiles Java bytecode in-line. It can also use the Just-in-Time (JIT) compiler to compile code on the fly for faster running.

- Garbage collector. Keeps track of memory usage, freeing the developer from having to make explicit calls to allocate and deallocate memory.

- Just-in-Time (JIT) compiler. Compiles bytecode into machine specific code at runtime. This provides for enhanced performance, because the code is not interpreted instruction by instruction.

Note The JIT compiler can be turned off in Internet Explorer by clicking **Internet Options** in the **View** menu and then deselecting the **Java JIT compiler enabled** option on the **Advanced** tab.

Conferencing with NetMeeting

NetMeeting version 2.1 is a powerful conferencing tool that allows you to take full advantage of the global reach of the Internet or corporate intranets to communicate and collaborate effectively in real time.

The video, audio, and data conferencing functions of NetMeeting 2.1 are all based on industry standards, so you can communicate with people who use compatible products from companies other than Microsoft.

NetMeeting 2.1 is compatible with earlier versions of NetMeeting; with the Microsoft Internet Locator Server (ILS), which lets you find and connect with other people on the Internet; and with applications and solutions built using the *Microsoft NetMeeting 2.1 Software Development Kit* (SDK). The NetMeeting 2.1 SDK can be downloaded from the NetMeeting SDK Web site at **http://www.microsoft.com/netmeeting/sdk/**.

For more information about NetMeeting 2.1, see the NetMeeting Web site at **http://www.microsoft.com/netmeeting/** or the *NetMeeting Resource Kit*, which is on the Microsoft Windows 98 Resource Kit compact disc, or can be downloaded from the NetMeeting Resource Kit Web site at **http://www.microsoft.com/netmeeting/reskit/**.

Conferencing Options

With NetMeeting 2.1, you can take advantage of the following conferencing options:

Audio conferencing. NetMeeting 2.1 serves as an Internet telephone with high-quality audio, letting you talk with others in real time over the Internet or an intranet. All you need are a sound card, a microphone, and speakers. While you are conversing, you can bring data or video conferencing capabilities into NetMeeting 2.1.

Video conferencing. When you add a video capture card and camera to your computer, you can hold a face-to-face conversation over the Internet or an intranet with high-quality video. (You do not need a video camera on your computer to receive video, and there are some cameras that do not require a video capture card.) You can even take a snapshot of a person or an object with your video camera and place it on the Whiteboard for discussion or markup.

Multipoint conferencing. The comprehensive suite of data conferencing tools in NetMeeting 2.1 lets you collaborate and exchange information with two or more people in real time. You can share information from one or more applications on your computer, exchange graphics or draw diagrams on an electronic Whiteboard, send messages or take notes with the text-based chat program, and send files to other meeting members using the binary file transfer capability.

Installing and Configuring NetMeeting

This section describes hardware requirements and steps for installing and configuring NetMeeting 2.1.

Hardware Requirements for NetMeeting

The following hardware is required for data and audio conferencing:

- 486/66 MHz computer.
- 5 MB of free hard disk space.
- 8 MB of RAM.
- 14,400-baud or faster modem, Integrated Services Digital Network (ISDN), or local area network (LAN).
- Sound card with microphone and speakers.
- TCP/IP connection, which is supported by the data conferencing features of NetMeeting. For real-time audio conferencing you must use a TCP/IP network, such as the Internet or your corporate LAN.

The following hardware is required for data, audio, and video conferencing:

- Pentium 90 MHz or higher processor.
- 5 MB of free hard disk space.
- 16 MB of RAM.
- 28,800-baud or faster modem, ISDN, or LAN connection.
- Sound card with microphone and speakers.
- Video capture card or camera that provides a Video for Windows capture driver (required only to *send* video images).

NetMeeting 2.1 works with any video card or camera that provides a Video for Windows capture driver. Some video cameras can plug into the parallel port; other cameras require a video capture card installed in your computer. Camcorders can often be plugged into these adapters.

In general, parallel port cameras are less expensive but can be more CPU-intensive, yielding decreased video performance. Cameras connected to separate video capture cards typically offer better performance. Also, a black and white camera typically offers better performance than an equivalent color camera, because fewer bits need to be sent across the connection.

Installing NetMeeting

The NetMeeting 2.1 component of Internet Explorer is selected and installed by default in the full installation of Windows 98. If you do not wish to install it, you can easily deselect it during installation. You can install it later using the Add/Remove Programs option in Control Panel.

▶ **To install NetMeeting if it was not installed with Windows 98**

1. In Control Panel, click Add/Remove Programs.
2. Click the **Windows Setup** tab.
3. Click **Communications,** and then click **Details**.
4. Select the **Microsoft NetMeeting** check box, click **OK**, and you will be guided through the installation process.

Configuring NetMeeting Client

When you run NetMeeting 2.1 the first time, a one-time Configuration Wizard runs to help you set up your personal information, the directory server you want to connect to, and your audio and video device preferences. It then runs an Audio Tuning Wizard that prompts you to select options to tune your audio settings.

After running the Configuration Wizard, you can always change your NetMeeting configuration from within the program by clicking the **Tools** menu and then clicking **Options**.

Note Sound quality can vary depending on your sound card and microphone. To run only the Audio Tuning wizard at any time after you initially run NetMeeting, on the **Tools** menu, click **Audio Tuning Wizard**.

Configuring NetMeeting Settings with the IEAK Profile Manager

The IEAK Profile Manager allows system administrators to control their users' implementation of NetMeeting 2.1. They can restrict NetMeeting activities, such as file transfer and application sharing, disable or lock down certain options, and specify a default directory server.

For an overview of the IEAK Profile Manager, see "Configuring Internet Explorer with the IEAK Profile Manager" earlier in this chapter.

▶ **To set NetMeeting policies and restrictions**

1. In the left-hand pane of the IEAK Profile Manager, expand **Microsoft NetMeeting** under **System Policies & Restrictions**.

2. Click **NetMeeting Settings** to display options for NetMeeting restrictions in the right-hand pane.

3. Select the desired restrictions, and enter the appropriate information.

4. Save the settings in the INS file that will be used to configure your users' installation.

Setting NetMeeting policies with the System Policy Editor

Administrators can also implement NetMeeting system policies with the System Policy Editor. Using system policies, administrators can predefine settings and restrictions, and provide standard NetMeeting configurations for their user community.

NetMeeting system policies are set using the Conf.adm template.

For more information about setting system policies, see Chapter 8, "System Policies," or see the *NetMeeting Resource Kit*, which is on the Microsoft Windows 98 Resource Kit compact disc or is available at **http://www.microsoft.com/netmeeting/reskit/**.

Using NetMeeting

The main window of NetMeeting 2.1 contains four navigation icons in the left-hand pane which provide single-click access to the major functions of NetMeeting:

Directory. The Directory icon opens a window containing a list of users connected to the selected server, including e-mail address, name, and location, the category of the directory (such as Personal or Business) and the server name.

SpeedDial. If you make a connection to another user through an ILS, the person's contact information is stored as a SpeedDial entry. You can add anyone to your SpeedDial list by selecting an entry in your Directory and clicking the SpeedDial icon on your toolbar.

Current Call. When you connect to someone, this window is automatically selected. This window is where you conduct data, voice, and video conferencing.

History. Select the History icon to see a log of each incoming call. The log includes the name of the caller, your response to the call (accepted or ignored), and the time the call was received.

Note The navigation icons are part of the default view in NetMeeting 2.1. They can be optionally hidden by deselecting them on the **View** menu, in which case you can gain access to the particular function by selecting it on the **View** menu.

The Internet Locator Server

The *Microsoft Internet Locator Server* (ILS) provides a Lightweight Directory Access Protocol (LDAP) service that allows NetMeeting 2.1 users to locate each other on the Internet or corporate intranets. These servers create a directory of NetMeeting users. From this directory, you can select participants to connect to for real-time conferencing and collaboration.

The ILS provides a memory-resident database for storing dynamic directory information. This database allows you to find dynamic information, such as an IP address, for people currently logged on to an Internet service or site. The ILS database maintains the entries, which clients refresh periodically. This process ensures that clients can always access the most current information about each user's Internet location.

The ILS provides a graphical setup program to help you easily install server components. Administrators can set options for user logon, security, and server access.

Note If you are an Internet Webmaster or an intranet administrator, you can set up your own Intranet Locator Server on the Internet or your corporate intranet. For more information, refer to the *Microsoft Internet Locator Server Operations Guide*, or to its companion, the *Microsoft Internet Locator Service Operations Reference*. Both documents are packaged with the product, or you can download the ILS and the accompanying documents from **http://www.microsoft.com /netmeeting/ils/**.

Entering Your Personal Information

If you want to change any of the personal information that you have entered in the Configuration Wizard, you can do so at any time using **Options** on the **Tools** menu, and then clicking the appropriate tab to access the information you want to change.

If your network administrator used the IEAK Profile Manager to restrict the use of the **Options** dialog box, one or more of the **Options** tabs may not be visible.

Video Conferencing

With the video conferencing feature of NetMeeting 2.1, you can send and receive real-time visual images with another conference participant using any Video for Windows-compatible equipment. You can conduct "face-to-face" meetings and use the camera to view any item instantly by placing it in front of the lens. Note that you do not need video hardware to receive images.

NetMeeting 2.1 video has many features, including remotely adjustable video quality, detachable video window, ability to control the size of the video window dynamically, Clipboard accessibility, and the ability to switch video to another meeting member.

If another meeting participant has a camera, receiving video is automatically enabled when you begin a conference. You can disable these options and choose to send or receive video manually at the start of a conference by setting these options on the **Video** tab of the **Options** dialog box.

Audio Conferencing

The audio conferencing feature of NetMeeting 2.1 allows you to conduct real-time, point-to-point conversations over the Internet or corporate intranet. NetMeeting 2.1 audio conferencing has many features, including half-duplex and full-duplex audio support, automatic microphone sensitivity level setting, microphone muting, and the ability to switch audio to another meeting participant.

You automatically enable audio when you begin a conference.

Note For video and audio conferencing, support is limited to TCP/IP connections, and only two people at a time can send and receive audio or video during a meeting.

▶ **To switch your audio connection to someone else**

- Right-click the person's name in the Current Call window, and then click **Switch Audio and Video**.

  –Or–

  On the toolbar, click **Switch**, and then click the name of the person to whom you want to switch.

▶ **To stop sending audio to someone**

1. Click the Speaker icon next to the name of the person.
2. Click **Stop Using Audio and Video**.

Multipoint Data Conferencing

Using Multipoint data conferencing, two or more people can share information in real time over the Internet or corporate intranet. Meeting participants can share applications, exchange information between shared applications through a shared clipboard, transfer files, collaborate on a shared Whiteboard, and communicate with a text-based chat feature.

Sharing Applications

Participants in the conference can share a program running on one computer. They can review the same data or information and watch the actions of others as they work on the program (for example, editing content or scrolling through information). Participants can share Windows-based applications transparently, without any special knowledge of the application capabilities. The person sharing the application can choose to collaborate with other conference participants, and the participants can take turns editing or controlling the application. Only the person sharing the program needs to have the given application installed on his or her computer.

Caution When you share an application and collaborate, meeting participants can use the **File Open** and **File Save** dialog boxes in your application to open or delete files on your computer or network. To stop someone from using your shared program while you do not have control of the cursor, press ESC. To stop them when you do have control, click **Collaborate** or press ESC.

Sharing the Clipboard

The shared Clipboard allows you to exchange its contents with other participants in a conference using familiar cut, copy, and paste operations. For example, you can copy information from a local document and paste the contents into a shared application as part of group collaboration. This capability provides seamless exchange of information between shared and local applications.

Transferring Files

With the file transfer capability, you can send one or more files in the background to one or all of the conference participants. You can send files to a particular person by right-clicking on that person's name in the Current Call window or by dragging and dropping the file into the Microsoft NetMeeting 2.1 window and having it sent automatically to all meeting participants, each of whom can then accept or decline receipt. Again, this file transfer occurs in the background as everyone continues sharing an application, using the Whiteboard, or chatting. This file transfer capability is fully compliant with the T.127 standard.

Using the Whiteboard

The Whiteboard program is a multipage, multiuser drawing application that allows conference participants to sketch diagrams, create organization charts, or display other graphic information. Whiteboard is object-oriented, allowing you to move and manipulate its contents by clicking and dragging with the mouse. In addition, you can use the Remote Pointer to point out specific contents or sections of shared pages. This capability extends the application-sharing feature of NetMeeting 2.1 by supporting ad hoc collaboration on a common drawing surface.

Using Chat

Using Chat, you can type text messages to share common ideas or topics with other conference participants or record meeting notes and action items as part of a collaborative process. Conference participants can also use Chat to communicate in the absence of audio support. A new "whisper" feature lets you have a separate, private conversation with another person during a group chat session. From the Chat window, click on the person's name in the **Send to** list, and type your text message that only you and the selected person see.

Using NetMeeting with a Firewall

You can configure firewall components in a variety of ways, depending on the specific security policies and overall operations of your organization. While most firewalls are capable of allowing primary (initial) and secondary (subsequent) TCP and User Datagram Protocol (UDP) connections, they might be configured to support only specific connections based on security considerations. For example, some firewalls allow only primary TCP connections, which are considered the most secure and reliable.

To enable NetMeeting 2.1 multipoint data conferencing (application sharing, Whiteboard, chat, file transfer, and directory lookups), your firewall needs to pass through only primary TCP connections on assigned ports. For NetMeeting 2.1 to make calls with audio and video conferencing, your firewall must be able to pass through secondary TCP and UDP connections on dynamically assigned ports. Some firewalls can pass through primary TCP connections on assigned ports but cannot pass through secondary TCP or UDP connections on dynamically assigned ports. In such cases, you are not able to use the audio or video features of NetMeeting 2.1.

Establishing a NetMeeting Connection with a Firewall

When you use NetMeeting 2.1 to call other users over the Internet, several IP ports are required to establish the outbound connection. If you use a firewall to connect to the Internet, you must configure it so that the IP ports shown in Table 20.2 are not blocked.

Table 20.2   Required IP ports in NetMeeting connections with firewalls

This port	Is used for
389	Internet Locator Server (TCP)
522	User Location Service (TCP)
1503	T.120 (TCP)
1720	H.323 call setup (TCP)
1731	Audio call control (TCP)
Dynamic	H.323 call control (TCP)
Dynamic	H.323 streaming (RTP over UDP)

To establish outbound NetMeeting 2.1 connections through a firewall, the firewall must be configured to do the following:

- Pass through primary TCP connections on ports 389, 522, 1503, 1720, and 1731.
- Pass through secondary TCP and UDP connections on dynamically assigned ports (1024-65535).

The H.323 call setup protocol (over port 1720) dynamically negotiates a TCP port for use by the H.323 call control protocol. Also, both the audio call control protocol (over port 1731) and the H.323 call setup protocol dynamically negotiate UDP ports for use by the H.323 streaming protocol, called the real-time protocol (RTP). In NetMeeting 2.1, two UDP ports are determined on each side of the firewall for audio and video streaming, for a total of four ports for inbound and outbound audio and video. These dynamically negotiated ports are selected arbitrarily from all ports that can be assigned dynamically.

NetMeeting directory services require either port 389 or port 522, depending on the type of server you are using. ILSs, which support LDAP for NetMeeting 2.1, require port 389. The User Location Service (ULS), developed for NetMeeting 1.0, requires port 522.

Microsoft Proxy Server Example

The following steps describe how to set up the Microsoft Proxy Server to enable the necessary ports for NetMeeting outbound calls. Use this example as a guideline for configuring your proxy server for NetMeeting. For additional information about configuring the Microsoft Proxy Server, refer to the *Microsoft Proxy Server Installation and Administration Guide.*

▶ **To configure the Microsoft Proxy Server for NetMeeting**

1. Start the Microsoft Internet Service Manager, and then click **Winsock Proxy Service**.

2. Click the **Protocols** tab, and then click **Add**.

3. Add each port required for NetMeeting 2.1 (listed earlier in this section) by typing or selecting values for the following fields:

   - Protocol Name
   - Type
   - Direction

   For example, if you want to add port 389, you would enter the following settings:

   - Protocol Name   NetMeeting 2.1
   - Port   389
   - Type   TCP (default)
   - Direction   Outbound

   For TCP-only ports, click **OK** after adding information for each port. For ports that require UDP connections, continue with step 4.

4. For ports that require secondary UDP connections, click **Add** in the **Port Ranges for Subsequent Connections** dialog box.

5. Enter the following values:

   - Port or Range   0-65535
   - Type   UDP (default)
   - Direction   Inbound or Outbound

6. Click **OK** to add the UDP connection information. Repeat this process to add both Inbound and Outbound dynamic port ranges. Then, click **OK** to add the protocol definition.

Firewall Limitations

Some firewalls cannot support an arbitrary number of virtual internal IP addresses or cannot do so dynamically. With these firewalls, you can establish outbound NetMeeting 2.1 connections from computers inside the firewall to computers outside the firewall, and you can use the audio and video features of NetMeeting 2.1. Other people, however, cannot establish inbound connections from outside the firewall to computers inside the firewall. Typically, this restriction is due to limitations in the network implementation of the firewall.

Note Some firewalls are capable of accepting only certain protocols and cannot handle TCP connections. For example, if your firewall is a Web proxy server with no generic connection handling mechanism, you are not able to use NetMeeting 2.1 through the firewall.

Optimizing Bandwidth

Microsoft designed NetMeeting 2.1 as a "bandwidth-smart" application with built-in mechanisms for caching, compressing, and optimizing information dynamically. NetMeeting 2.1 includes system policies to limit throughput for audio and video and to restrict audio and video features. These system policies provide additional assurance that corporations can control the impact on bandwidth utilization. NetMeeting 2.1 bandwidth testing confirms these assumptions.

NetMeeting 2.1 achieves optimal bandwidth use by focusing on the most efficient and effective methods for minimizing network traffic while maximizing performance. This effort encompasses intelligent bandwidth management and control, and optimization of data through compression, caching, and other tools.

Bandwidth Characteristics of NetMeeting Data Conferencing

The following characteristics typify NetMeeting 2.1 data conferencing scenarios:

- NetMeeting 2.1 creates bandwidth traffic only when an action is occurring, as when a person is updating information. If no action is occurring (for example, a person is viewing information on the screen), network bandwidth is not impacted.

- There will be intermittent spikes in the bandwidth during intense activity, with a return to zero bandwidth use when no activity is occurring. (Screen updates due to mouse or cursor activity may prevent the bandwidth from returning to zero.) This type of activity is similar to standard file traffic on the network.

- For increased efficiency, NetMeeting 2.1 transmits data in a series of smaller packets rather than in one large packet. This method spreads out the bandwidth traffic to reduce large spikes, in contrast to the output you would see during a typical file copy.

- NetMeeting 2.1 data compression varies depending on the size of the data packet and the speed of the network, so that more compression will occur over slower network connections.

- NetMeeting 2.1 optimizes the available bandwidth (through caching, compression, and other tools), but response time varies depending on the amount of bandwidth available for NetMeeting operations. If less bandwidth is available, responsiveness decreases.

Bandwidth Characteristics of NetMeeting Audio and Video Conferencing

The following characteristics typify NetMeeting 2.1 audio and video conferencing scenarios:

- Audio-only conferencing (normal conversations) produces more predictable, less sporadic bandwidth results than do data or video conferencing.

- By default, NetMeeting 2.1 uses low-bandwidth codecs for audio (G.723.1) and video (H.263). For example, the G.723.1 audio codec requires only 6.4 kbps, plus ~40% for the IP packet header and overhead. Higher bandwidth codecs are used only if they are selected manually by the user or are required by another application for interoperability.

- Video performance can dynamically scale higher or lower, depending on the available network bandwidth, but audio remains constant.

- NetMeeting uses bandwidth during video and audio activity and returns to zero when no activity is present.

- During video conferencing, NetMeeting 2.1 transmits a complete video frame every 15 seconds to refresh an image and then sends successive deltas throughout the transmission.

Supported Standards

The conferencing functionality in NetMeeting 2.1 is based on international communication and conferencing standards, including the International Telecommunication Union (ITU) H.323 standard for audio and video conferencing and the ITU T.120 standard for multipoint data conferencing. The H.323 standard specifies the use of T.120 for data conferencing functionality, allowing audio, data, and video to be used together. H.323 gateway services are being developed that will allow NetMeeting 2.1 users to access the Internet and call any telephone in the world through the public switched telephone network (PSTN).

The T.120 standard protocols assist developers in creating applications that allow real-time multipoint data connections and conferencing. These T.120-based applications permit users to transmit and receive data and to collaborate using compatible data conferencing features, such as sharing applications using a Whiteboard and transferring files. The H.323 standard is a hardware standard for audio and video. Because it defines how audio and video information is formatted and packaged for transmission over a network, it allows users on different platforms to use products from different vendors to speak with each other and communicate face to face.

Support for these standards ensures that you can call, connect, and communicate with other users who are using compatible conferencing products. You can also take advantage of conferencing services that support these standards. (For more information about this functionality, see "Multipoint Data Conferencing" earlier in this chapter.)

Troubleshooting NetMeeting

This section contains a brief description of a troubleshooting strategy for NetMeeting, as well as procedures on how to access NetMeeting's online Help. For more information about troubleshooting NetMeeting, see the *NetMeeting Resource Kit,* which is on the Microsoft Windows 98 Resource Kit compact disc, or can be downloaded from the NetMeeting Resource Kit Web site at **http://www.microsoft.com/netmeeting/reskit/**.

Checking for Common Problems

Check to see if the problem is a commonly reported one in the online Help for NetMeeting 2.1, or in the Netmeet.txt readme file which is in the \Program Files\NetMeeting directory. Online Help includes troubleshooting aids for solving problems related to NetMeeting features and components.

▶ **To get troubleshooting help from NetMeeting online Help**

1. In NetMeeting, click **Help**, and then click **Help Topics**.
2. On the **Contents** tab, double-click **Troubleshooting**.
3. Click **If you have trouble using NetMeeting**, and then click **Display**.
4. Click the button to the left of the appropriate scenario description.

Isolating and Testing Error Conditions

You can resolve a problem more quickly by systematically isolating and testing error conditions. Use the following methods for isolating your error conditions:

- Eliminating variables helps to determine a problem's cause. For example, consider closing all other programs except NetMeeting to eliminate the other programs as the potential cause of your problem.

- You can isolate the cause by changing a specific value and then testing to see if the problem is corrected or altered. For example, if you experience audio problems, switching between full-duplex and half-duplex options might resolve the issue.

- If a component fails after you upgrade to new hardware or software, replace the new version with the original item and then retest. For example, if you install a new sound card driver and lose audio capability, you can replace the new driver with the original version and retest to see if the problem still occurs.

Test each modification individually to see if the change resolves your problem. Make note of all modifications and their effect on symptoms. If you contact product support personnel, this information helps them troubleshoot your problem. Also, the information provides an excellent reference for future troubleshooting.

Consulting Online Troubleshooting and Support Options

When possible, check the appropriate online forum. Other users might have discovered, reported, and found workarounds for your problem. Suggestions from others could save you time in tracking down the source of the problem and might give you ideas that can help with troubleshooting.

▶ **To get online support**

1. In NetMeeting 2.1, click **Help**.

2. Click **Online Support**. The NetMeeting Technical Support page on the World Wide Web is displayed. From this page, you can choose from several topics, including Knowledge Base articles, Frequently Asked Questions, Troubleshooting wizards, newsgroups, and other support options.

Multimedia Streaming with NetShow

Microsoft NetShow version 2.0 is a platform for streaming multimedia over networks ranging from low-bandwidth dial-up Internet connections to high-bandwidth switched local area networks. Using NetShow, companies can offer new streaming content for such applications as training, corporate communications, entertainment, and advertising to users all over the world. NetShow is a powerful broadcast system that is easy to acquire and operate and that empowers companies to offer rich, high-quality interactive content over networks.

Microsoft NetShow 2.0 provides a complete platform for integrating audio and video into online applications, bringing the power of networked multimedia to the Internet and corporate intranets. With its leading-edge live and stored media-streaming technology, Microsoft NetShow 2.0 allows users to receive audio and video broadcasts from their personal computers. It uses a client/server architecture and sophisticated compression and buffering techniques to deliver live and on-demand audio, video, and illustrated audio (synchronized sound and still images) to users of the NetShow Player. The NetShow Player continuously decompresses and plays the content in real time. Users can listen and watch live audio and video programs or navigate on-demand audio and video content.

Note   NetShow complements NetMeeting, and the two make up Internet Explorer's main delivery systems for multimedia communication. Whereas NetShow delivers content from one source to many on the Internet or an intranet, NetMeeting allows person-to-person and group interactive sessions.

Advanced Streaming Format

Advanced Streaming Format (ASF) represents the file format in which NetShow content is created. It is a low-overhead storage and transmission file format that encapsulates multimedia data types (images, audio, and video) as well as embedded text (URLs, for example) and allows for the synchronization of these objects within a stream. When you create NetShow content, you create ASF streams or files.

ASF provides industry-wide multimedia interoperability, with ASF being adopted by all major streaming solution providers and multimedia authoring tool vendors.

Each ASF file is composed of one or more media streams. The file header specifies the properties of the entire file, along with stream-specific properties. Multimedia data, stored after the file header, references a particular media stream number to indicate its type and purpose. The delivery and presentation of all media stream data is synchronized to a common timeline.

NetShow Player

There are two ways of using NetShow Player to play content:

- As a standalone player. When you use NetShow Player as a standalone application, you can decide how you want to have access to the NetShow content. If you play the NetShow content file locally, you are not streaming the file. NetShow Player reads the content file from the hard drive and then plays it. If you play a content file from a remote location, it streams to your computer. You can start the standalone player from a link in a Web page.

- Embedded in a Web page, Visual Basic script application, or another ActiveX container application. An easy way of providing NetShow Player to people who do not already have it on their computers is to embed the player in a Web page. When a user gains access to the page, the player is optionally downloaded. The script commands used to embed the player can identify the NetShow content to play as well as show how to play it. The properties can be set to check the version of the player on the computer. If the player is outdated, the computer downloads the newest version.

Installing and Configuring the NetShow Player

Playing ASF files requires prior installation of the Microsoft NetShow Player, a third-party player that supports ASF files, or an application that supports the NetShow ActiveX control. After the player is installed, a user either clicks on a link to the NetShow content and it plays in an external help application, or it plays embedded in an HTML page or application that uses the NetShow ActiveX control. Whether content plays in the external player or is embedded is determined at the time the content is authored. The NetShow ActiveX control ships with the NetShow Player installation.

Where to Find the NetShow Player

The NetShow Player is available in the full installation of Windows 98. If you select the full installation when installing Windows 98, it gives a choice of components to install. Choose the category Multimedia, and you will be allowed to select Microsoft NetShow Player 2.0.

It is also available on the Microsoft NetShow Web site at **http://www.microsoft.com/netshow/**. Additional NetShow products, such as the NetShow Tools, Software Development Kits, and NetShow Server are also available there, as well as versions of the player for Windows NT 3.51, Windows NT 4.0, Windows 3.1, Macintosh, and UNIX computers.

The NetShow Player installed with Windows 98 is the same as the one on the NetShow Web site. However, it does not contain the Netscape plug-in that allows you to play NetShow content embedded in an HTML page and played back by a computer running Netscape Navigator.

Installing the NetShow Player

If you choose the standard installation of Windows 98, the NetShow Player will not be installed automatically. It is easy to install later, however.

▶ **To install NetShow Player after installing Windows 98**

1. In Control Panel, click Add/Remove Programs.
2. Click the **Windows Setup** tab.

3. Click **Multimedia**, and then click **Details**.

4. Select the **Microsoft NetShow Player 2.0** check box, click **OK**, and you will be guided through the installation process.

Configuring the NetShow Player

You can use the **Advanced** tab of the **File/Properties** menu or the **View/Play Settings** menu to control the buffering and protocols settings for NetShow. The **Advanced** tab gives you control in two areas: Buffering and Protocols.

The Buffering option can be used to decrease or increase the amount of time it takes before content begins to play. Normally the default time is sufficient and users under normal circumstances would not need to change it. However, if network conditions make playback quality unacceptable, you can increase the buffer time to try to improve performance. Most content is normally set to buffer between five and ten seconds.

You can also make some selections in the Protocol area, as shown in Table 20.3.

Table 20.3   NetShow Player protocol settings

Setting	Description
Multicast	Multicast enables the client to receive multicast streams. It allows the administrator to send one copy of the content to many users on the network, as long as that network is multicast-enabled. Networks that are not multicast-enabled and ASF files not being streamed from a NetShow server are sent through unicast. Unicast means that one stream is sent for every request.
UDP	UDP enables the client to receive streams through UDP. It is well-suited to audio because it sends packets regardless of connection quality. Therefore, users hear fewer delays or pauses. The problem with UDP is that if a company's firewall does not accept UDP streams, the stream stops at the firewall, and the user gets an error message. If the company's network administrator has set up their firewall to support UDP streams on a particular port, the user can specify that port. If UDP does not work, the stream automatically rolls over to TCP transmission.
TCP	TCP transmission sends the stream through more firewalls. TCP forms a reliable stream—if packets are lost, the stream stops and lost packets are recovered. This means that users experience more delays and pauses over a network that is congested.
HTTP	HTTP transmission sends the stream through almost all firewalls and proxy servers through port 80, using either the existing browser proxy settings or a customized setting.

Using the NetShow Player

Playing NetShow content is straightforward. Normally, a user clicks on a link to the content, and it starts playing. This allows the user to listen to or watch the content and continue to browse the Web or run other applications.

Markers

Markers are like bookmarks in the file. They can allow you to quickly skip from one part of the content to another. This feature becomes very important to developers who wish to create interactive applications using NetShow, because they can use VBScript or JavaScript to present questions to the user and respond to the selection given by skipping directly to a particular part in the ASF file. For example, a developer writing an interactive training application could present material and, at a specific point in the file, insert a URL flip command in the stream that flips the user's browser to an HTML page with quiz questions on it. Based on the answer to the quiz question, the developer can automatically make the user repeat a section if the answer is incorrect or continue to the next section if the answer is correct.

To see whether the person who created an ASF file used markers, look for the tick marks under the slider bar on the player. If you hover your mouse over the tick marks, you can see their description:

Notice the "Road Work Ahead" label that appears when the mouse hovers over the corresponding marker.

If you would like to see a marker list, right-click the ASF while it is playing, and select **Marker List**.

You can skip to a specific marker by clicking on the marker number and clicking **Go To Marker**. This feature is especially convenient for content embedded in an HTML page with no controls showing.

Advanced Player Features

After users learn that playing content over the Internet means compromises in the size of images, frame rate, or clarity of the images, they often become curious about the bandwidth the file uses for adequate playback. They also learn how to find out more about the ASF file in case they are having problems getting it to run. Here is how to find out the details of the ASF file, even if it is embedded in an HTML page. First, right-click on the content while it is playing. Then select **Properties**.

You are presented with a separate window with multiple tabs to choose from. The **General** tab details the ASF title, author, copyright, rating and description. The **Details** tab gives you the following information:

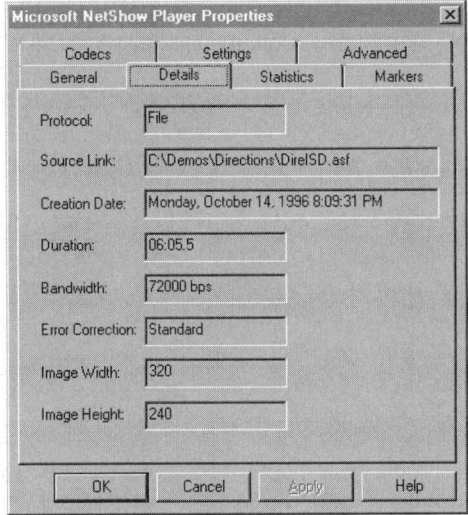

Protocol. Shows what protocol is being used between the player and the NetShow server or HTTP server or file server running the content. Choices are **File** for play from a local drive or file server, **MMS** or **HTTP** for play from a NetShow server, or **HTTP** for play from an HTTP server such as Microsoft's Internet Information Server or some other HTTP server (such as a UNIX server).

Source link. Shows the server or share location for the file or stream. **Bandwidth** shows how much bandwidth the file will take up when playing back. In the example above, it takes 72,000 bps or a LAN connection or dual-channel ISDN connection. **Error Correction** shows whether the file was created with error correction features enabled.

If playback of a file is inconsistent or the picture or sound is poor, checking the **Statistics** tab can be helpful.

On networks, such as the Internet, where varying traffic conditions mean varying performance, you can see that the reception quality and numbers of packets lost vary when the Internet gets busy. When the connection is poor, you see the red part of a pie chart that gets bigger and smaller with connection variances.

Hosting NetShow Content

After NetShow content has been created, it can be hosted in several ways.

From a Local Drive. You can play ASF files from a local drive. When linking to the content, use file://c:\directory\filename.asx as the path.

From a File Server. You can play ASF files from a file server or network drive. When linking to the content, use file://\\servername\share\filename.asx as the path.

From a NetShow Server. You can play ASF files from a NetShow server. The NetShow server software is available from **http://www.microsoft.com/netshow/**. It allows you to stream using UDP, TCP, or HTTP, which means a great degree of flexibility in configuration to support the widest array of networks. It also provides the ability to do live streaming, multicast, unicast, scheduling of programs, and administration. When you play content from a NetShow server, use mms://servername/path/filename.asx as the path.

From an HTTP Server. You can play ASF files from a standard HTTP server (such as Microsoft Internet Information Server or a UNIX-based HTTP server). First, you need to register the ASF and ASX MIME types on your HTTP server. Instructions on registering MIME types are at **http://www.microsoft.com /netshow/**. Then just store the ASF on the HTTP server and link to it (see "Linking to NetShow Content" later in this chapter for information).

Linking to NetShow Content

After NetShow content is created and hosted, the content developer can link to it in a variety of ways.

Links from HTML Pages

Most users start by using a standard anchor tag to link directly to an ASF file (like **<a href="http://servername/path/filename.asf">**). However, browsers by nature understand how to send files from a server to a user's computer. For example, when you link to a Word document (.doc) or an Excel spreadsheet (.xls), the browser sends the entire file to the client. When you link directly to an ASF file, the same thing happens—the entire ASF file is downloaded to the user's cache directory, and the file plays back from there. This defeats the purpose of streaming, however. So to cause the browser to stream, we have to introduce a redirector file called an ASX.

When a user links to an ASX file, the user's browser downloads the entire ASX file to the user's cache directory. (Do not worry. The files are only about 1 KB in size.) Then the user's computer receives the signal in the file associations table that when it reaches an ASX file, it should start the NetShow Player. The NetShow Player opens, looks in the ASX for instructions on where to get the ASF file, and starts the stream playing.

If you have an ASF file that you want users to be able to connect to on demand, or in a unicast fashion, create an ASX file by going into your favorite text editor, such as Notepad, and type the following:

ASF *path*

where *path* is one of the following, depending on where you are streaming the content from:

- mms://servername/path/asfname.asf (for content on a NetShow server)
- http://servername/path/asfname.asf (for content on an HTTP server)
- file://\\servername\path\asfname.asf (for content on a network server)
- file://c:\path\asfname.asf (for content on a fixed drive, such as your hard drive)

For example, you might use the following text in an ASX file:

ASF mms://netshow.microsoft.com/welcome.asf

After you enter this data into Notepad, save the file as *Filename*.asx and host it on the HTTP server that contains your HTML pages. Make sure the ASX is working by double-clicking its name in Windows Explorer. It should bring up the NetShow Player and start the content streaming. To make the link to the ASF file, therefore, link to the ASX file instead, and use the following syntax:

<a href=http://servername/path/filename.asx >Description</a>

To edit an existing ASX file, open up a text editor, such as Notepad, and open the file.

Note There are two types of ASX files: handcrafted, for use with stored content, and machine-generated for use in multicasting content from the NetShow server. The machine-generated files are encrypted and allow you to publish an announcement that supports multicast. They are generated in the NetShow Program Manager and are created by right-clicking an existing NetShow program and choosing Announce. This process creates an ASX file that you can link to in the standalone player, use with an embedded object on an HTML document, use with an anchor tag in an HTML document, or distribute as appropriate.

Embedding Content in HTML Pages

Internet Explorer

To embed ASF files in an HTML page for the Internet Explorer browsing software, use the following code:

```
<OBJECT ID="NSPlay" WIDTH=160 HEIGHT=128 CLASSID="CLSID:2179C5D3-EBFF-
11CF-B6FD-00AA00B4E220">
<PARAM NAME="FileName" VALUE="http://server/path/myvideo.asx">
</OBJECT>
```

You need to change the VALUE for the ASX to reflect the location of the ASX on your HTTP server, and you need to change the WIDTH and HEIGHT to reflect the actual size of the ASF.

Netscape

The NetShow Player installed from **http://www.microsoft.com/netshow/** includes a Netscape plug-in for Windows 95 and Windows NT clients. (The NetShow Player installed with Windows 98 does not include the Netscape plug-in.) To use it, just add some code to the <object> tag used earlier:

```
<OBJECT ID="NSPlay" WIDTH=160 HEIGHT=128
CLASSID="CLSID:2179C5D3-EBFF-11CF-B6FD-00AA00B4E220">

<Embed type="video/x-ms-asf-plugin"
src="http://server/path/myvideo.asx"
filename="http://server/path/myvideo.asx"
pluginspage="http://www.microsoft.com/netshow/download/player.htm"
ControlType=1
width=290
height=250>
</embed>
</OBJECT>
```

The <embed> part of this code invokes the NetShow plug-in for Netscape.

For additional information about how to embed NetShow content in an HTML page while using the codebase property to auto-install the NetShow Player, see **http://www.microsoft.com/netshow/**.

Starting NetShow Content from E-Mail Messages

First, you need an ASX file. Insert the file into an e-mail message as an attachment. When the user receives it, he or she can double-click it, and the NetShow content starts streaming from the specified server.

There are some big advantages to inserting ASX files into e-mail messages as a way to encourage people to view live or stored content. First, this method saves bandwidth. Instead of sending an e-mail message to large numbers of people with big multimedia files that could clog network bandwidth, when you send ASX files, you send only a tiny (approximately 1 KB) file that does not take up network bandwidth until the user starts playing the file. Also, sending ASX files means that the NetShow content plays in its external player, freeing the user to continue reading e-mail or work on other applications. Last, it allows the content developer to sidestep the entire browser issue by not requiring that the user have a browser installed.

Placing NetShow Content on the Active Desktop

One of the features of Internet Explorer is its ability to embed content onto the Active Desktop. This can be especially useful to allow you to put live NetShow streaming audio or video content directly onto the desktop so you can listen to your favorite radio station on a site, such as AudioNet (**http://www.audionet.com/**) or your favorite live video-based business news on a site, such as MSNBC Business Video (**http://businessvideo.msnbc.com/**).

▶ **To place NetShow content on the Active Desktop**

1. Right-click on the desktop and select **Properties**.

2. Click the **Web** tab and make sure **View my Active Desktop as a web page** is selected.

3. Click **New**, and then click **No** to indicate that you do not want to connect to the gallery.

4. Enter the URL for the Web page you would like to have displayed on your desktop.

It is easy to resize the window so you can see only the part of the page that contains the NetShow content.

Configuring for Play over a Variety of Networks

One of the new features of NetShow 2.0 is the ability to do protocol rollover.
Protocol rollover allows you to try sending the ASF over a default protocol
(such as MMS using UDP from the NetShow server). If it fails, it tries sending
over an alternative server or protocol that you specify in the ASX file. This is
especially convenient when you are concerned whether your content will
penetrate customers' firewalls. You can set it up to try UDP first, and if that
fails because the users' companies do not accept UDP traffic through their
corporate firewalls, you can tell it to try the same content over HTTP or from a
different server. This procedure uses the advanced capabilities of ASX files.

You can also insert the program title, description, author, and copyright
information from the ASX. This information appears in the properties of the
ASF when the user plays the file.

To use these features, go into Notepad and create and type the following lines
that apply to what you are trying to do:

```
[Reference]
Ref1=mms://servername/path/asfname.asf (this is the first reference to
try)
Ref2=http://servername/path/asfname.asf (this is the second reference to
try)
BaseURL = http://servername/path/dir/ (this is the Base URL for relative
references in the ASF stream to use as a base path)
[Description]
Program Title=Title of the ASF here
Program Description=Description of your ASF here
Program Author=Your name here
Program Copyright=Copyright or other information here
```

Base URL is used when you want to create NetShow content that uses URL flips
but does not rely on the ASF being on one particular server. For example, if you
created an ASF that included URL flips to a specific directory on an HTTP server,
to duplicate the content on another server using protocol rollover, previously you
would have had to rebuild the ASF with new hard-coded URL flips for every
server. With NetShow 2.0, you specify a Base URL in the ASX file, which allows
you to move or duplicate the NetShow content to other servers.

Save this text file as *Asxname*.asx and post it to your HTTP server or network
server, as before. Also, note that you do not need REF1 and REF2 if the virtual
path is the same for both protocols. For example, if you had HTTP streaming
enabled on the NetShow server or had a WWW virtual root that was the same,
the first REF1 would be sufficient because of the protocol rollover feature of
NetShow version 2.0 clients.

Technical Notes on the NetShow Player

NetShow provides a wide range of audio and video compression models to accommodate various forms of content and different bandwidths and bit rates. Following is a partial listing of codecs supported by NetShow:

- H.263 video
- G.723.1 audio
- MPEG layer-3 audio
- MPEG-4 video

NetShow has the following minimum system requirements:

- 486/66 MHz computer.
- 8 MB of RAM.
- 16-color display card.
- 16-bit sound card.
- 14 KBps modem.
- Windows 95 (audio, audio and images, some video).

NetShow has the following recommended system requirements:

- Pentium 120 MHz or higher processor.
- 16 MB or more RAM.
- 256-color or more display card.
- 28.8 KBps or higher modem or Ethernet card.
- Windows 95, Windows 98, or Windows NT 4.0 (audio, audio and images, video).

Troubleshooting the NetShow Player

If you encounter problems when playing back NetShow content, they are usually in one of the following areas:

Codecs

Codecs (compressors/decompressors) are required on the content creation side as well as the client side to play the content back. If the content creator uses a codec that is not installed on the client computer, then the content does not play back. While playing the content, the user can right-click on the ASF, select **Properties**, and then click the **Codecs** tab. If any of the codecs listed say **NO** in the Installed column, the user is missing a codec necessary for playing the audio or video. The quickest way to get the largest set of NetShow codecs is to re-install the NetShow Player from **http://www.microsoft.com/netshow/**.

Firewalls

Many corporations administer firewalls to prevent unauthorized access to corporate networks. Most firewalls are based on packet filtering. Packet filtering takes place when the computer examines the source and destination IP addresses of a packet and forwards only those packets for which access has been granted. When playing NetShow content, if it is being sent using a protocol that is not allowed through the corporation's firewall, it will not play. Therefore, if NetShow content does not play at all, make sure the company's firewall supports the protocol used (for example, UDP, TCP, or HTTP). For a list of firewalls that support NetShow, go to **http://www.microsoft.com/netshow/firewall.htm**.

Common Errors

When NetShow Player opens, the animation stops.

If all you see is a black screen, you should see if you have the correct codec installed to render the video.

▶ **To check if you have the right codec installed**

1. Right-click in the player window and select **Properties**.

2. In the **NetShow Player Properties** dialog box, select the **Codecs** tab. The codecs used to compress the ASF information are displayed.

3. Verify that the video codec used to compress the ASF information is installed on your computer. If the codec is not installed, contact the person who created the ASF stream for information about how to get the proper codec. Most content creators either use standard NetShow codecs or provide a way for you to download the codec before watching the ASF information.

Audio is distorted or video is choppy.

Distorted audio and video are usually caused by one of two things: there is a large amount of network traffic, or the audio and video were created that way.

▶ **To determine if network traffic is the problem**

1. Right-click in the Player window and select **Statistics**.

2. In the **NetShow Player Properties** dialog box, determine how many (or what percentage of) packets have been lost. If you are losing more than five percent of the packets, network traffic is your problem.

3. If NetShow Player is losing only a few packets, check to see if **Buffering** appears in the Current Time/Total Time indicator. If NetShow Player must constantly buffer information, there is network traffic, and NetShow Player must wait to receive ASF information.

If you are not losing any packets and there is no significant network traffic, the content was likely created that way. Take into consideration the type of ASF content you are watching. Video requires considerably more network bandwidth than image flipping, and the higher the audio quality, the more bandwidth is required.

Audio sounds scratchy, hisses or pops, or is silent.

This problem can often be caused by problems with incompatible or improperly implemented sound devices.

▶ **To determine if the problem is due to poorly implemented or incorrect sound devices**

1. Open Sound Recorder.
2. Open the Microsoft Sound directory (in the Media directory under your Windows directory).
3. Play one of the sounds. If it sounds OK, then proceed to the next step. If the sound does not play correctly, you may need to check the directions for installing your sound device and re-install it.
4. On the **File** menu, click **Save As**, and then click **Change**.
5. Select the same **Format** and **Attributes** as the clip you are having the problem with, and then click **OK**.
6. Save this file with a different name or in a different directory, so as not to overwrite the Microsoft Sound file.
7. Open the file saved in the previous step and play it. If it does not play correctly, check the drivers you are using to ensure that they are the most recent and proper drivers for your sound card.

Note Another possible cause of audio problems can be the sampling rate of the content. Sampling rates of 12 and 24 kilohertz (kHz) are not supported in many hardware sound devices and drivers. Content authors should choose a sampling rate other than 12 or 24 kHz when creating content.

You have problems when using dial-up networking to gain access to a network.

These problems are usually caused by incorrect settings for the proxy server the firewall is using.

▶ **To verify that your proxy settings are correct**

- On the **Advanced** tab of the **NetShow Player Properties** dialog box, for the HTTP protocol, select **No proxy**.

You get a Failed Network Connection message.

One possible reason for this message is that your NetShow Player settings may conflict with your Internet Explorer settings. This occurs if you adjust the NetShow Player protocol settings in the **Advanced Settings** tab and do not restart NetShow Player. Clicking **Apply** does not cause these changes to take effect.

Getting Help on the World Wide Web

For more information, see the NetShow Web site at **http://www.microsoft.com /netshow/**. Material here includes NetShow Software Development Kits, online documentation, tools, and the Content Creation Authoring Guide. The Content Creation Authoring Guide is a detailed resource for people who want to understand how to create NetShow content for the highest quality and performance. The NetShow Web site also includes demonstrations, NetShow-based tutorials on NetShow, lists of companies providing services and products based on NetShow, support information, and white papers.

Web Authoring with FrontPage Express

FrontPage Express is a Web page editor with a graphical user interface that gives you full access to Hypertext Markup Language (HTML 3.2). When you work with FrontPage Express, you are in a WYSIWYG ("what you see is what you get") view mode, which gives you a clear picture of how your pages are going to appear.

FrontPage Express takes you step by step through the process of creating Web pages, and it is also a tool for editing existing HTML documents. When you have FrontPage Express installed, start it by clicking the **Edit** button on the Internet Explorer browsing window toolbar to start editing the page you are viewing. Then you can use the Microsoft Web Publishing Wizard to post the modified page back to the server.

FrontPage Express offers many of the features of Microsoft FrontPage 97 Editor, in a smaller package. If you need the added features of FrontPage Editor and FrontPage Explorer, it is easy to upgrade to FrontPage 97 or FrontPage 98 without having to learn a new software package.

Key Features of FrontPage Express

FrontPage Express includes all the features of the FrontPage 97 editor except for the following: editing frames, image maps, and proofing tools; support of Advanced Server Pages; Preview In Browser; most of the FrontPage WebBot® components, and the site management features. Some of the key features included in FrontPage Express are the Include, Search, and Timestamp WebBot components; capabilities for editing tables, forms, plug-ins, Java applets, JavaScript; and some of the FrontPage page templates and wizards.

Note FrontPage WebBot components are referred to simply as FrontPage components in FrontPage 97 and FrontPage 98.

Some of the FrontPage Express features are explained in the following paragraphs:

Personal Home Page Wizard. This wizard takes you step by step through the process of creating a personal home page. For more details about this wizard, see "Customizing Your Start Page with the Personal Home Page Wizard" earlier in the chapter.

Table creation and editing. Generating tables is easy with the Insert Table feature. Once you insert a table into a Web page, you can edit the entire table or individual cells.

Forms. You can add forms to your Web page that can be filled out and submitted to your Web site. Your forms can include text boxes, check boxes, drop-down menus, images, and more.

Page templates and wizards. If you are connected to a server running the FrontPage Server Extensions, you can also use forms-related wizards and templates that let you create the following items without having to write any code:

- A form, by selecting the types of information you need to collect.
- A page to acknowledge that you have received a user's input.
- A survey to collect information from readers and store it on your Web server.

You do not have to be connected to a server running the FrontPage Server Extensions to use these features. However, in that case you do not have the advantage of having the HTML code written for you.

FrontPage Express supports major Internet technologies, such as Java applets, JavaScript, plug-ins, and ActiveX to make your pages more engaging.

WebBot Components

FrontPage Express *WebBot components* are dynamic objects you can insert on your Web pages. They provide complex functionality that would otherwise require you to write scripts. WebBot components require the FrontPage Server Extensions to be installed on the Web server in order to function properly.

FrontPage Express offers three WebBot components:

- The Include component lets you insert the body of another HTML page into the current page. This is useful for serial elements, such as headers and footers that appear on multiple pages. Instead of having to edit every instance of a serial element, you simply edit the included file once.

- The Search component builds an index of the current Web site's content so that it can be searched.

- The Time Stamp component automatically inserts the date and time of the last update to a page.

Most WebBot components are added to a page using the **WebBot Component** command on the **Insert** menu in the FrontPage Express editor. When you insert a WebBot component, dialog boxes help you configure it. A graphical representation of the WebBot component is then visible in the editor at that position in the page. The HTML that a WebBot component generates depends on conditions in your FrontPage Web at the time the WebBot component is activated. For example, a WebBot Search component is associated with a search form that FrontPage Express creates. When a user enters a word to search for and submits the form, the WebBot Search component searches the FrontPage Web and generates an HTML list of hyperlinks to all the pages in the FrontPage Web that contain the word. The WebBot component supplies this HTML list to the Web browser, which automatically displays it to the user.

When you view a page that includes a WebBot component, the interactive or programming properties of it are available. The WebBot components themselves are stored in a page using a specially formatted HTML comment, although the FrontPage Express author does not typically see this representation.

Installing and Configuring FrontPage Express

The FrontPage Express component of Internet Explorer is selected by default in the full installation of Windows 98. If you do not wish to install it, you can easily deselect it. You can install it at a later time using the Add/Remove Programs option in Control Panel.

▶ **To install FrontPage Express if it was not installed with Windows 98**

1. In Control Panel, click Add/Remove Programs.

2. Click the **Windows Setup** tab.

3. Click **Internet Tools**, and then click **Details**.

4. Select the **Microsoft FrontPage Express** check box, click **OK**, and you will be guided through the installation process.

You can also install FrontPage Express from the Internet Explorer Add-Ons Page on the Web at **http://www.microsoft.com/ie/ie40/download/addon.htm**.

Benefits of Web Authoring

Writing your own Web pages offers two main benefits:

Fast Web page development. With FrontPage Express, you do not need to learn HTML, because the application has a graphical user interface. FrontPage Express even lets novices insert Java applets, ActiveX controls, or scripts without knowing any programming. For those who still like to edit HTML directly, FrontPage Express offers a new color-coded HTML editing mode.

Tight suite integration. As mentioned earlier, when you have FrontPage Express installed, the **Edit** button on the Internet Explorer browsing window toolbar allows you to edit the currently viewed page.

How Web Authoring Works

While you are browsing any Web page, you can click the **Edit** button on the Internet Explorer browsing window toolbar to open FrontPage Express with all of the tables, controls, and pictures displayed inside the editor. FrontPage Express makes it easy to download pages from the Web locally because it lets you save an entire Web page (pictures included) in a single step.

Most WebBot components are added to a page using the **WebBot Component** command on the **Insert** menu in the FrontPage Express editor. When you insert a WebBot component, a graphical representation of the WebBot component is then visible in the editor at that position in the page. A few of the WebBot components are specifically associated with forms and can be reached through the **Form Properties** dialog box rather than the **Insert WebBot Component** command.

When you view a page that includes a WebBot component, the interactive or programming properties of it are available. The WebBot components themselves are stored in a page using a specially formatted HTML comment, although the FrontPage Express author does not typically see this representation.

Publishing Web Pages with Personal Web Server

Microsoft Personal Web Server (PWS) version 4.0 is the answer to your personal information sharing and Web development needs. PWS is a desktop Web server that performs Web site setup, creates a personalized home page automatically, and allows drag-and-drop publishing of documents.

On the corporate intranet, Personal Web Server can be used to share documents in their native format quickly; or you can convert documents to HTML and then use PWS to share them across different operating systems.

Because Personal Web Server supports Advanced Server Pages, it can be used as a development and testing platform for Web sites. You can create your site in the office or at home and test it by using Personal Web Server before hosting it on the corporate server or an Internet service provider.

Installing Personal Web Server

Personal Web Server is included on your Windows 98 compact disc. You can install it using the Add/Remove Programs option in Control Panel.

▶ **To install Personal Web Server**

1. In Control Panel, double-click Add/Remove Programs.
2. Click **Install**, and insert the Windows 98 compact disc.
3. Browse to \add-ons\pws.
4. Double-click the PWS application icon and follow the instructions on your screen.
5. When you are finished, restart your computer for the changes to take effect.

After installation, PWS appears as an item on your Program menu and includes four components: FrontPage Server Administrator, Personal Web Manager, Personal Web Server Set up, and Personal Web Server Documentation.

Using Personal Web Server

You can use Personal Web Server to create and maintain a Web site in addition to using features, such as the guest book and message drop box.

PWS online Help shows you how to do the following:

- Create a Web page without learning HTML.
- Create a Web page with a text editor.
- Make documents available on your site.
- Add links on the home page to documents on your hard disk or the Internet.
- View and edit your guest book.

- View and delete your drop box messages.
- Add new publishing directories.
- Track activity on or performance of your site.

Posting a Web Site with the Web Publishing Wizard

The Internet Explorer Web Publishing Wizard allows you to post your own Web site to a server. The Web Publishing Wizard allows you to publish Web pages on the Internet or an intranet by automating the process of copying files from your computer to a Web server or an Internet Service Provider (ISP).

The Web Publishing Wizard can automatically post to a variety of Web servers and offers support for standard protocols, such as FTP, universal naming convention (UNC), HTTP Post; third-party services, such as America Online, America Online Primehost, and SPRYNET Primehost; and system-independent protocols, such as CRS and FrontPage Extended Web.

The Web Publishing Wizard can post to local ISPs, IIS, intranet servers on your local area network, and FrontPage. It supports the following languages: English, French, German, Italian, Japanese, and Spanish.

ISPs that have their own protocol schemes for uploading files to their Web servers can write a custom WebPost provider dynamic-link library (DLL) and distribute it from the Microsoft Web site at **http://www.microsoft.com/windows /software/webpost/**.

If you want details about this procedure, send e-mail to WebPost@lists.msn.com expressing your interest in writing a provider DLL. Code for a sample WebPost provider is included in the *ActiveX SDK*.

The Web Publishing Wizard connects to the ISP, determines the protocol needed to copy the files, and then uploads the files to the appropriate directory on the ISP computer. Before publishing a Web site with the Web Publishing Wizard, you will need to have the following information:

- The local path to the Web content you want to publish (such as C:\webfiles).
- The protocol used by the ISP to upload files. You can choose from FTP, HTTP Post, or CRS (FTP is the most commonly used protocol).
- The URL that files are to be uploaded to (for example, ftp.my_isp.com if the ISP requires users to post files via FTP).
- The URL for your root on the Web server. This is often the URL for the ISP, plus the username (http://www.my_isp.com/username).
- The username and password for the account.

The Web Publishing Wizard will guide you through the steps of connecting to your ISP or intranet site and will automatically upload Web files from a directory you specify. Because it saves all of the information that you enter, you will not be asked to enter it during subsequent publishing efforts, making subsequent publishing efforts quick and convenient.

▶ **To begin publishing on the Internet with the Web Publishing Wizard**

1. Create a Web page using FrontPage Express or your favorite authoring tool.

2. Sign up for an account with an ISP.

3. Use the Web Publishing Wizard to copy the Web pages to the Internet.

Other Tools for Authors and Developers

Internet Explorer provides new technology that you can use to increase interactivity for your customers without slowing down server performance. Internet Explorer includes the following technologies to help you create Web pages and applications:

ActiveX scripting. Lets ActiveX controls talk to one another and to other Web programs.

ActiveX technology. Helps you create Web-based software components using your existing knowledge and code base.

Dynamic HTML. Gives you design options and control, as well as the ability to add a new dimension of interactivity without slowing performance in the process.

Java with AFC. Provides a powerful set of building blocks for developing Java applets and other Internet applications. Application Foundation Classes (AFCs) deliver a rich suite of graphics as well as user interface and multimedia capabilities to authors who use Java in their Web pages.

Upgrading to FrontPage

When you install FrontPage 97 or FrontPage 98 on a computer that has FrontPage Express installed, the **Edit** command on the Internet Explorer browsing window toolbar and the Internet Shortcuts from the Windows 98 desktop use FrontPage 97/98 as the default editor. In other words, the most recently installed HTML editor takes precedence over any previously installed HTML editors.

Using the Registry to Change the Default Editor

You can also edit the Windows 98 registry to set a different default HTML editor in Windows 98.

The registry key that needs to be changed is:

HKEY_CLASSES_ROOT\htmlfile\shell\edit\command

The value for FrontPage Express is: "C:\Program Files\FPXpress\bin \fpexpress.exe %1."

This value can be changed to: "C:\Windows\Notepad.exe %1" for Notepad or "C:\Program Files\Microsoft FrontPage\bin\fpeditor.exe %1" for FrontPage 97 or FrontPage 98.

Warning Changing the registry by using a registry editor can have unforeseen effects that can prevent you from starting your system. In some cases, you might need to reinstall Windows 98. Wherever possible, use programs, such as Control Panel or System Policy Editor, to configure Windows 98.

Connecting to the Internet

Whether you connect to the Internet through your corporate LAN or you use a modem to dial in to an ISP, you can configure your connection easily in Windows 98. The Internet Connection Wizard is the primary Internet connection tool provided with Windows 98. It takes you through all of the steps required to set up your connection, and uses "smart" code to detect existing configurations. Depending on your requirements, you can also perform these steps manually.

The following choices are provided in Windows 98 to connect to the Internet:

- You can use the Internet Connection Wizard to help you sign up with an ISP if you need to and configure your connection to the Internet.

- You can join the Microsoft Network (MSN) online service from the Windows 98 desktop to send and receive mail on the Internet and to gain access to Internet newsgroups. For more information about how to install and connect to MSN, see Help.

- You can use the Online Services folder on the Windows 98 desktop to set up accounts with a variety of ISPs.

- You can use TCP/IP and Dial-Up Networking—both of which are provided in Windows 98—to connect to ISPs. You connect to an ISP by using Dial-Up Networking to dial in to their Point-to-Point Protocol (PPP) or Serial Line IP (SLIP) servers, which are connected directly to the Internet.

- You can use TCP/IP and a network adapter so that you can connect to a company's network server that is connected directly to the Internet.

Windows 98 supports all the protocols you need to connect to an ISP, including a 32-bit implementation of TCP/IP, as PPP or SLIP. In addition, Windows 98 provides File Transfer Protocol (FTP) and telnet clients, which can be used to browse the Internet and download files from Internet servers. Also, you can use the Internet Explorer browsing software to browse the World Wide Web. Figure 20.2 illustrates how your Windows 98 computer can be connected to the Internet.

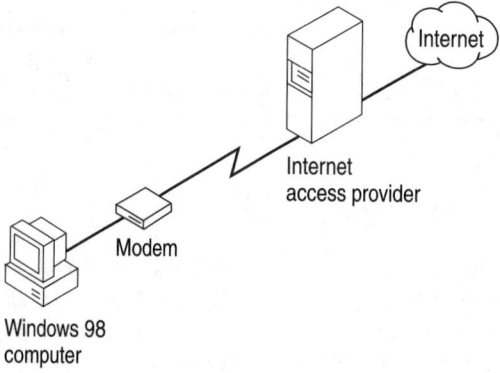

Figure 20.2   A Windows 98 computer connected to the Internet

For more information about using telnet and FTP, see "Using Public Domain Tools" earlier in this chapter.

Preparing to Connect to the Internet

To connect a computer running Windows 98 to an ISP, do the following:

- Obtain an Internet account with an ISP. This is provided automatically if your company has a direct connection to the Internet.

- Make sure TCP/IP and Dial-Up Networking are installed, and make sure TCP/IP is bound to the Microsoft Dial-Up adapter or a network adapter.

- Install a modem (if you dial in to the Internet) or a network adapter (if you have a direct network connection to the Internet).

- Define a Dial-Up Networking connection to an Internet Service Provider, and define IP address information for each connection, or for your network adapter, if required.

Before you connect to the Internet, you need to decide what kinds of information you want to provide or exchange. The most common tools for finding and exchanging information and the most common sources of information are described briefly in the following sections.

Sending and Receiving E-mail

You can exchange e-mail with individuals on the Internet or join an Internet mailing list. To do this, you run an electronic mail application, known as a Simple Mail Transport Protocol (SMTP) client, and connect to an SMTP or Post Office Protocol (POP) server. Most ISPs provide this support. For information about Outlook Express, the Windows 98 e-mail client, see Chapter 22, "Electronic Mail with Outlook Express."

Usenet Newsgroups

Newsgroup servers, supporting Net News Transport Protocol (NNTP), share information and commentary on defined topics. Each newsgroup is an electronic bulletin board where members post and reply to messages. Most ISPs offer NNTP access. To connect to a newsgroup, you need the following:

- Access to an NNTP server.

- A newsgroup account provided by an ISP.

- An NNTP reader (an application that allows you to view newsgroup information), which is available as a feature of most Word Wide Web browsers, including the Internet Explorer browsing software.

Internet Tools

A variety of tools are available to help you find the information you need on the Internet. For information about these tools, see "Using Public Domain Tools" earlier in this chapter.

Note Network administrators can configure Internet connections for their users using the Internet Explorer Administration Kit. This will prevent the Internet Connection Wizard from being launched automatically on users' computers. For information about using the Internet Explorer Administration Kit, see "Configuring Internet Explorer with the IEAK Profile Manager" earlier in this chapter.

Connecting to the Internet with the Internet Connection Wizard

The Internet Connection Wizard is included in Windows 98. This wizard is a fully automated process with two main functions. It can sign you up with an ISP if you do not already have an account with one, and it can help you configure your Internet software if you do not need to sign up with an ISP. The four possible paths that the wizard can take once it is started are determined in part by the wizard, and in part by the tasks you wish to accomplish.

Understanding the Internet Connection Wizard

There are five possible ways you can run the Internet Connection Wizard in Windows 98:

- From the Windows 98 Welcome screen.

- From the Connect to the Internet icon on the desktop. This is only for new computers, or computers that have been upgraded to Windows 98 and had no previous Internet connection.

- From the **Start** menu. This is only for new computers, or computers that have been upgraded to Windows 98 and had no previous Internet connection.

- From the Internet Explorer browsing software or Outlook Express. This is only if you have not already configured an Internet connection the first time you run one of them.

- From the **Connections** tab of Internet Options in the Internet Explorer **View** menu.

When the Internet Connection Wizard starts, it analyzes your computer to determine if there is an existing Internet connection. If it finds one, the path it follows is determined by where the wizard was run from. If the wizard does not find an Internet connection, then it gives you the option of signing up with an ISP or using the Manual Internet Configuration Wizard (Inetwiz.exe) to manually configure Internet settings for an existing ISP account.

The code that the Internet Connection Wizard runs during Windows 98 Setup searches your computer for evidence of an existing Internet connection. Once this determination is made, there is either a Connect to the Internet icon on the desktop (in lieu of the Internet Explorer and Outlook Express icons) and an Internet Connection Wizard shortcut in the Start menu, or the regular Internet Explorer and Outlook Express icons appear on the desktop and an Internet Connection Wizard shortcut appears in the Internet Explorer program group.

Starting the Internet Connection Wizard

As mentioned earlier in this section, there are a number of different ways you can start the Internet Connection Wizard. The entry points from the Windows Welcome, the desktop icon, and the Start menu are only available if no existing Internet connections were detected during Windows Setup. Similarly, the only way that Internet Explorer or Outlook Express will run the Internet Connection Wizard when they are started is if you have not already configured an Internet connection. You can however, always run the Internet Connection Wizard from the Internet Explorer program group, and from the **Connection** tab of Internet Options in the Internet Explorer **View** menu.

Signing Up with an ISP

If you choose the path in the Internet Connection Wizard that allows you to sign up for an Internet account with an ISP, you will be connected to the Internet Referral Server. If the Internet Connection Wizard detects that there is no modem configured, it will run the Install New Modem Wizard to help you configure your modem. Once you have configured your modem, the Internet Connection Wizard gathers location information from the dialing properties to pass to the Referral Server.

Once you are connected to the Referral Server, you can choose from a list of ISPs available in your area, and set up an account with any one of them. Certain ISPs will provide a free trial period of Internet service. With this option, you will not have to supply any credit card or other billing information when you sign up. When the trial period expires, the ISP will contact you to offer a continuation of service and request your billing information then.

Configuring Settings with the Manual Configuration Wizard

If you choose the option to set up an Internet connection for an existing Internet service in the initial screen of the Internet Connection Wizard, the Manual Internet Configuration Wizard does the following:

- Checks that your modem is set up properly. If it is not, the wizard runs the Install New Modem Wizard so that you can configure your modem.
- Checks that your dialing settings are set up properly. If they are not set up properly, the wizard displays the **Dialing Properties** dialog box.
- Sets up the TCP/IP protocol.
- Sets up Dial-Up Networking, and then creates a Dial-Up Networking connection to assist you in creating an Internet account.

If you are connecting to the Internet over a corporate network, you may need to supply the Internet Connection Wizard with proxy server information and, in some cases, TCP/IP information. You can check with your network administrator, and obtain the appropriate information.

If you are connecting to the Internet by dialing in to an ISP with a modem, you will need to supply the Internet Connection Wizard with the following information:

- Telephone number, account ID, and password
- Mail account information: server types and names, and password
- TCP/IP information if required

Once you have completed all of the tasks required to configure a connection to the Internet, and exited the Internet Connection Wizard, you can return to it at any time by pointing to **Programs** on the Start menu, pointing to **Internet Explorer**, and then clicking **Connection Wizard**.

Installing and Configuring a Modem

Windows 98 supports a variety of modems for dial-in access. You do not need to configure a modem differently to connect to the Internet than you would for any other Dial-Up Networking connection.

For information about installing and manually configuring modems and communications ports, see Chapter 21, "Modems and Communications Tools."

Obtaining an Internet Account

Most users connect to the Internet by dialing in to an ISP's server that is directly connected to the Internet.

Tip Using an ISP for remote access is a fairly inexpensive way to reach the Internet, but its effectiveness is limited by the speed of the connection and the modem. For a good modem and a normal phone line, this speed tends to be roughly between 14.4 and 28.8 kilobytes per second (KBps).

For better performance at greater expense, you can use one or more Integrated Service Digital Network (ISDN) lines to achieve 64 KBps or 128 KBps. Many ISPs now offer ISDN packages.

In deciding which ISP to use, you should consider the following:

- Does the ISP offer full Internet access?
- Does the ISP support PPP?
- Does the ISP offer technical support?
- What kind of connection speeds does the ISP support?

- Does the ISP have an adequate number of phone lines and a large enough pipe to the Internet in order to provide good response time?
- Does the ISP offer a local dial-up number?
- What range of services, such as mail, does the ISP offer, and at what charge?

After you have chosen an ISP, obtain the following information from the ISP when you establish a PPP or a SLIP account. You need this information in order to configure Windows 98 to gain access to the Internet:

- Access phone number, preferably local.
- Logon name.
- Logon password.
- Your host and domain name. If electronic mail is part of your connection services, your host name can include a POP3 host name and an SMTP host name.
- The NNTP server name, if Internet newsgroups are part of your connection service.
- The Domain Name System (DNS) server and IP address (only if they will not be assigned automatically by the ISP).

All SLIP accounts require you to manually configure an IP address on your computer when you connect. Service providers who support PPP usually assign an IP address automatically each time you dial in to the service provider. However, some PPP service providers might require manual configuration of an IP address. In most cases you also need to configure the IP address of the service provider's DNS server.

For more information about these settings, refer to the following sections.

Installing TCP/IP

Connecting the millions of computer networks on the Internet would not be possible without a standard set of protocols. TCP/IP is the protocol used on the Internet. It combines many different protocols, making it possible to communicate across interconnected networks that have diverse hardware and operating systems.

To connect to the Internet, you must install TCP/IP. Windows 98 automatically allows (binds) TCP/IP to work with a network adapter or with the Microsoft Dial-Up adapter. You can install TCP/IP when you install Windows 98, or you can install it after Setup by using the Network option in Control Panel.

▶ **To install TCP/IP**

1. In the Network option in Control Panel, click **Add** on the **Configuration** tab.

2. In the **Select Network Component Type** dialog box, double-click **Protocol**.

3. In the **Select Network Protocol** dialog box, select **Microsoft** from the **Manufacturers** list.

4. In the **Network Protocols** list, click **TCP/IP**.

5. Click **OK**.

▶ **To verify that TCP/IP is bound to the Microsoft Dial-Up adapter or a network adapter**

1. In the Network option in Control Panel, scroll through the list of network components on the **Configuration** tab, and select the **TCP/IP** icon. It may include an arrow that indicates which adapter it is bound to.

2. If no adapter is indicated, click **Properties**. The **TCP/IP Properties** dialog box appears.

3. Click the **Bindings** tab. This tab lists the adapter(s) to which TCP/IP can be bound and indicates binding with a selected check box next to the bound component.

When you install Dial-Up Networking or another network adapter, Windows 98 automatically binds TCP/IP to the adapters if TCP/IP was previously installed. If your computer has multiple network adapters, an entry for TCP/IP is displayed for each one. You must configure each adapter with its own TCP/IP settings.

Setting the Domain Name System Server and IP Addresses

The Internet uses the DNS to translate computer and domain names into IP addresses. A DNS server maintains a database that maps domain names to IP addresses as specified by network administrators. The DNS organizes the names of hosts in a hierarchical fashion, similar to a file system.

Most ISPs dynamically assign IP addresses for DNS servers, especially for PPP or SLIP connections. If yours does not, you must configure a computer to recognize DNS information. If an ISP does not dynamically assign either a DNS IP address or your IP address, you should set these in the **TCP/IP Settings** dialog box in Dial-Up Networking for each connection you create.

If your LAN's Internet access server dynamically assigns your IP address and the DNS IP address, you do not need to set this information yourself. For example, if you are using a server with Dynamic Host Configuration Protocol (DHCP) capabilities, such as a DHCP server on a Windows NT Server network, it assigns IP address information dynamically If you have a static, direct LAN connection to the Internet or other TCP/IP network, then you should set the DNS IP address and your IP address in **TCP/IP Properties** in the Network option in Control Panel.

For more information about configuring IP addresses, see Chapter 15, "Network Adapters and Protocols."

Note   The following procedures assume that your computer has Microsoft TCP/IP installed as a network protocol. If your site uses another vendor's version of TCP/IP, you must configure the protocol as recommended by the protocol vendor.

It is important that each host on a network be assigned a unique IP address that is valid for its particular network. Before assigning any IP addresses, read the related material in Chapter 15, "Network Adapters and Protocols."

▶ **To set the DNS IP address for a direct LAN connection without DHCP**

1. In the Network option in Control Panel, double-click **TCP/IP** for the network adapter in the network component list on the **Configuration** tab.

2. In the **TCP/IP Properties** dialog box, click the **DNS Configuration** tab.

3. Click **Enable DNS**, and then, in the **Host** and **Domain** boxes, type your host name and domain name, respectively. These names identify you on the Internet.

4. In the **DNS Server Search Order** dialog box, type the address of your LAN's DNS server.

   If your network has more than one DNS server, type the address of each DNS server, and then click **Add**. DNS settings are currently global across all instances of TCP/IP. This allows you to rely on a secondary DNS server if the primary DNS server is down. The first server listed is the first one searched.

▶ **To define the IP address for a direct LAN connection to the Internet**

1. In the Network option in Control Panel, double-click **TCP/IP** for the network adapter on the **Configuration** tab.

2. In the **TCP/IP Properties** dialog box, click the **IP Address** tab, and then select **Specify an IP address**.

3. Type your IP address in the **IP Address** dialog box. After you type the address, the subnet mask is provided automatically.

4. Click **OK**.

The following procedures are for setting IP addresses on a computer that uses Dial-Up Networking to connect to the Internet.

▶ **To set the DNS IP address for each connection in Dial-Up Networking**

1. In Dial-Up Networking, right-click the connection you have defined for the Internet, and then click **Properties**.

2. In the connection's properties, click **Server Types**, and then click **TCP/IP Settings**.

3. In the TCP/IP Settings dialog box, select the **Specify an IP address** option, and type your IP address.

4. Select the **Specify name server addresses** option, and then type the IP address of the DNS server in the **Primary DNS** dialog box.

▶ **To define an IP address if the service provider does not dynamically assign one**

- In the **TCP/IP IP Address** dialog box, click **Specify an IP address**, and then type your IP address.

For more information about assigning DNS and IP addresses, see Chapter 15, "Network Adapters and Protocols."

Making a Dial-Up Networking Connection

After you configure TCP/IP, you need to configure a Dial-Up Networking connection to an ISP. The way you configure the connection settings depends on the type of Internet server you are using.

The Dial-Up Networking defaults for the dial-up connection are designed for Internet connections and for most other types of connections. You can change these defaults, but you should do so only if you want to change the default behavior.

There is one exception. By default, Dial-Up Networking uses the PPP protocol to connect to servers. This default will work for most Internet connections. But if you are connecting to a server that does not use PPP, you must change the server type as illustrated in the following section.

Note You can predefine Dial-Up Networking connections for users by including them as part of system policies. If you enable user profiles, different users sharing the same computer can use separate dialing configurations. For more information, see Chapter 7, "User Profiles," and Chapter 8, "System Policies."

Configuring Options for the Server to Which You Are Connecting

Dial-Up Networking allows you to configure options for the server to which you are connecting. You do not need to change any values in this section if you are connecting to an ISP and your ISP's remote access server supports PPP.

Before you begin, make sure that TCP/IP is correctly installed on your computer.

▶ **To configure options for the server to which you are connecting**

1. In Dial-Up Networking, right-click a connection icon, and then click **Properties**.

2. Click the **Server Types** tab.

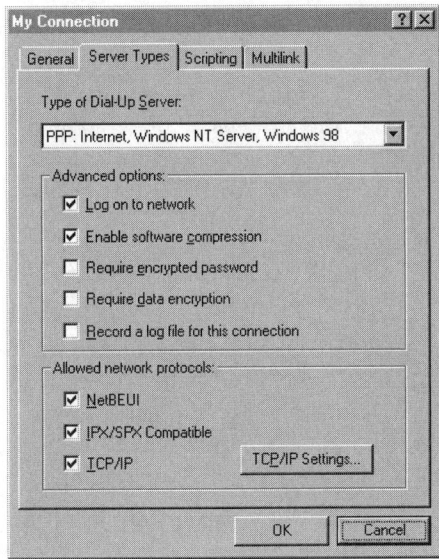

3. In the **Type of Dial-Up Server** box, ensure that the correct remote access server type is selected. If it is not selected, you will not be able to connect to the server. The possible connections are as follows:

This server type	Connects to
PPP: Internet, Windows NT Server, Windows 98	The default; selecting it allows Windows 98 to automatically detect and connect to other remote access servers that are running TCP/IP, NetBEUI, or IPX/SPX over PPP. Select this option for connections to your ISP.
NRN: NetWare Connect version 1.0 and 1.1	Novell NetWare Connect 1.0 or 1.1 running IPX/SPX over NetWare Connect 1.0 or 1.1.
SLIP: UNIX Connection	Any SLIP server over TCP/IP.
Windows for Workgroups and Windows NT 3.1	Windows 98 Dial-Up Server; Windows NT 3.1 or 3.5; Windows for Workgroups version 3.11 running NetBEUI over RAS.
CSLIP: UNIX Connection with IP Header Compression	Any SLIP server over TCP/IP that supports IP header compression.

4. Optionally, if you are making a connection to an ISP, deselect **Log on to network** to speed connection time. This option is selected by default, but it is unnecessary for Internet connections.

5. Optionally, select **Require encrypted password**. If this option is selected, the client will use only Challenge Handshake Authentication Protocol (CHAP) and MS-CHAP encryption when generating a password. If this option is not selected, the client can also perform Password Authentication Protocol (PAP) if the server requests it. However, PAP encryption is less secure.

6. Optionally, select **Require data encryption**. If this option is selected, the client will refuse to connect with any server that does not use data encryption. For more information, see Chapter 19, "Remote Networking and Mobile Computing."

7. Optionally, select **Record a log file for this connection**. If this option is selected, Dial-Up Networking will create a PPP log file that shows information about your connection. For information about PPP log files, see Chapter 19, "Remote Networking and Mobile Computing."

8. In the **Allowed network protocols** box, make sure that TCP/IP is selected.

Note By default, all network protocols (TCP/IP, IPX/SPX, and NetBEUI) are selected in the **Allowed network protocols** box. However, for you to use those protocols, they must also be installed on the client workstation you are configuring. For information about how to install protocols, see Chapter 15, "Network Adapters and Protocols."

9. Optionally, if you are configuring a connection to your ISP and your ISP requires you to enter information such as a static IP address for your computer or a DNS server to which you must connect, click **TCP/IP Settings**. However, in most cases you do not need to do so. For more information, see "Setting the Domain Name System Server and IP Addresses" earlier in this chapter.

For more information about defining a Dial-Up Networking connection, see Chapter 19, "Remote Networking and Mobile Computing."

Connecting to a SLIP Server

Windows 98 Dial-Up Networking clients support SLIP and can connect to any remote access server using the SLIP standard.

There are two types of SLIP accounts: uncompressed SLIP and compressed SLIP (CSLIP). You set what type of SLIP account you have for each connection you create in Dial-Up Networking.

▶ **To select the type of SLIP account for a connection in Dial-Up Networking**

1. Right-click a connection icon, and then click **Properties**.

2. In the connection's properties, click **Server Type**.

3. In the **Server Type** dialog box, select the Slip option **UNIX Connection** or **CSLIP Connection With IP Header Compression** in the **Type of Dial-Up Server** dialog box.

Tip If you have difficulty running TCP/IP applications after connection, you might need to change the server type from CSLIP to SLIP or from SLIP to CSLIP.

SLIP servers cannot negotiate your TCP/IP address. Therefore, you must set Dial-Up Networking to display a terminal window after you dial the Internet server. After you type your user name and password, IP address information is displayed in the terminal window as described in the following procedure.

▶ **To connect to a SLIP server**

1. In Dial-Up Networking, right-click the connection icon you created for the Internet, and then click **Properties** to specify that a terminal window be displayed. Click **OK**.

2. In General Properties, click **Server Types**.

3. In the **Server Types** dialog box, select **SLIP UNIX Connection** or **CSLIP UNIX Connection With IP Header Compression**, and then click **OK**.

   Make sure the **Log on to network** check box is not selected, because SLIP servers allow you to log on only in a terminal window. Notice that the only protocol allowed is TCP/IP.

4. In Dial-Up Networking, double-click the icon for the connection.

5. In the **Connect To** dialog box, click **Connect**.

6. After the modem establishes a connection, the **Post Dial Terminal Screen** dialog box appears for you to log on to the SLIP server and receive your IP address.

   You must follow the ISP's guidelines for logging on to its server. Most ISPs require only that you type a user name and a password. However, ISPs require additional information.

   In most cases, after you type your user name and password, the ISP displays two IP addresses, a host IP address and your IP address. (If the ISP does not display the IP addresses, you should ask about them.) The second address displayed is usually your IP address, which you may wish to record for future reference. Then click F7.

7. In the **SLIP Connection IP Address** dialog box, type your IP address, and then click **OK**.

8. If your Internet Service Provider assigns you the same IP address each time you connect, then, after you finish an Internet session, type your IP address in the **TCP/IP settings** dialog box for that connection in Dial-Up Networking. The next time you connect to the Internet SLIP server using this connection, you will not have to type your IP address.

Note You can use the **ping** command at the command prompt to differentiate the local from the host IP address. At the command prompt, type **ping** and the local IP address (for example, **123.45.6.7**), and then try ping with another server on the Internet. If the local address works, and the server address does not, contact the ISP.

After you connect to an ISP, Windows 98 displays a dialog box named **Connected To Internet** (or whatever name you gave the Dial-Up Networking connection to the Internet). You can minimize this dialog box and begin your Internet session by running Internet Explorer, FTP, telnet, or other Internet browsing applications.

Troubleshooting Internet Connections

Using Winipcfg to Verify Internet Connections

The IP Configuration utility (Winipcfg) is a troubleshooting utility that displays all current TCP/IP network configuration values for any computer running Microsoft TCP/IP. Network configuration values include the current IP address allocated to the computer and other useful data about the TCP/IP allocation. This utility is of particular use on networks using DHCP, allowing users to determine which TCP/IP configuration values have been configured by DHCP.

The IP Configuration utility does not dynamically update information. If you make any changes, such as disconnecting, you must exit the IP Configuration utility and restart it.

To run Winipcfg, select **Run** from the Start menu, type **winipcfg,** and click **OK**.

For more information about IP addresses on TCP/IP networks, see Chapter 15, "Network Adapters and Protocols."

This following paragraphs describe how to identify and resolve common Internet connection problems.

Your modem does not dial.

Use the troubleshooting aid for modems in online Help. See also the modem troubleshooting section in Chapter 21, "Modems and Communications Tools."

You cannot connect to your Internet service provider.

- In Dial-Up Networking, check the **Server Types** dialog box to make sure your server type is correct.

  - If you have a PPP account, make sure the server type is not SLIP or CSLIP.

  - If you have a SLIP account, make sure you have the correct type selected, either CSLIP or SLIP. Also, make sure you typed the correct IP address in the **SLIP Connection IP Address** dialog box.

- Select the Network option in Control Panel to make sure TCP/IP is bound to the Dial-Up or network adapter.

You connect to the Internet service provider but cannot obtain information from other Internet sites.

Try using the **ping** command to connect to other Internet sites.

▶ **To test a connection using the ping command**

1. At the command prompt, type **ping** followed by the name of the host you are trying to reach.

   If **ping** succeeds, your connection to the Internet is working properly.

2. If **ping** does not succeed, type **ping** followed by the IP address of the host.

   If this works, you are properly connected to the Internet, but not properly connected to your DNS server.

   –Or–

   If this does not work, you may not be connected to the Internet. In either case, contact your ISP.

You cannot view or download hypertext documents.

To view or download hypertext documents, such as World Wide Web home pages, you must use an Internet browser, such as the Internet Explorer browsing software. The telnet and FTP utilities provided with Windows 98 support only basic navigation on the Internet.

For more information about troubleshooting Dial-Up Networking connections, see Chapter 19, "Remote Networking and Mobile Computing."

Additional Resources

For more information about	See this resource
Proxy Server	*Microsoft Proxy Server Installation and Administration Guide*
Windows Scripting Host	**http://www.microsoft.com/management/**
Java	**http://www.microsoft.com/java/**
Third-party rating bureaus	**http://www.w3.org/pics**
Internet Explorer	**http://www.microsoft.com/ie/corp/**
	http://ieak.microsoft.com/
	http://www.microsoft.com/ie/ie40/download/ addon.htm
NetMeeting	**http://www.microsoft.com/netmeeting/**
Internet Locator Server Service	**http://www.microsoft.com/netmeeting/ils/**
NetShow	**http://www.microsoft.com/netshow/**
RealPlayer	**http://service.real.com/**
Data source objects	**http://www.microsoft.com/gallery/files/datasrc/**
Dynamic HTML scriplets	**http://www.microsoft.com/gallery/files/scriptlets/**

C H A P T E R   2 1

Modems and Communications Tools

21

This chapter illustrates how to install and use modems with Microsoft Windows 98, and describes other communications tools included in Windows 98, such as HyperTerminal, Phone Dialer, and Integrated Services Digital Network (ISDN). It also contains technical information relating to modems and communications tools. The chapter is written for system and network administrators.

In This Chapter

See Also

- For more information about remote networking and mobile computing, see Chapter 19, "Remote Networking and Mobile Computing."

- For more information about access to the Internet and Internet tools, see Chapter 20, "Internet Access and Tools."

- For more information about e-mail and Outlook Express, see Chapter 22, "Electronic Mail with Outlook Express."

Overview of Modems and Communications Tools

The Windows 98 communications subsystem allows users to make simultaneous connections to a variety of communications services, including electronic mail and online services. With Windows 98, connecting to a communications service is as easy as connecting to your network.

Users need select and configure a modem only once for it to work with all applications created for Windows 98. You can install a modem in the Modems option in Control Panel, or in an application created for Windows 98—the first time the application is run.

Two other communications tools facilitate modem calling: *HyperTerminal* connects two computers over a modem or a serial connection and transfers files between them, and *Phone Dialer* dials voice telephone calls.

Windows 98 provides the basic protocols and utilities users need to connect a computer to a server that has access to the Internet, and the software they need to browse and download information from the Internet.

The Windows 98 communications subsystem allows applications to transmit data quickly and reliably, and to cooperatively share communications devices. The new kernel and new communications architecture in Windows 98 provide the following benefits.

High-speed reliability. The data-transmission speed in Windows 98 is limited only by the hardware characteristics of the computer, such as the processor speed and the type of communications port. Windows 98 supports communications with devices of high transmission speeds, such as ISDN, which can communicate at speeds of 64 or 128 kilobits per second (Kbps).

High data throughput. The 32-bit communications subsystem and preemptive multitasking architecture provide high data throughput and an instant response.

Support for Plug and Play and legacy communications devices. Plug and Play support and device installation wizards, simplify installation and configuration of Plug and Play and legacy modems and communications devices.

Device sharing among communications applications. The Telephony Application Programming Interface (TAPI) arbitrates among applications that want to share the same communications ports and devices.

Summary of Modems and Communications Tools

This section contains a brief summary of the communications tools included in Windows 98. The tools are described in more detail later in this chapter.

Modems

Modem is short for modulator/demodulator. It is a communications tool that enables a computer to transmit information over a standard telephone line. Because a computer is digital (works with discrete electrical signals representing binary 1 and binary 0) and a telephone line is analog (carries a signal that can have any of a large number of variations), modems are required to convert digital to analog and vice versa.

HyperTerminal

You can use HyperTerminal with a modem to connect two computers so you can send and receive files or connect to computer bulletin boards and other information programs. For example, you can use HyperTerminal to connect to an online service and to download files from a bulletin board on the online service. You can also use HyperTerminal to connect a computer directly to another computer.

Phone Dialer

The Phone Dialer application lets you dial telephone numbers using the calling card and location information defined in Dialing Properties. It also stores frequently dialed numbers, dials stored telephone numbers, and logs telephone calls.

Dial-Up Networking and Mobile Computing

Dial-Up Networking provides remote users with complete network capabilities, including downloading and browsing electronic mail, accessing shared files, and running a client/server application. Dial-Up Networking lets you make a dial-up connection to remote networks, such as the Internet over a telephone or ISDN line.

Mobile computing features include Briefcase, which keeps documents up-to-date on two computers; Direct Cable Connection, which allows two computers to share resources when connected by a serial cable; and deferred printing capability, which lets you generate print jobs from a remote site and print them when you return to the office.

For more information about Dial-Up Networking, see Chapter 19, "Remote Networking and Mobile Computing."

Outlook Express

Microsoft Outlook Express is a universal information client that can read and send electronic mail from any message application that supports MAPI services.

For more information about Outlook Express, see Chapter 22, "Electronic Mail with Outlook Express."

Windows Telephony API

The Win32 communications APIs in Windows 98 provide an interface for using modems and communications devices. Applications call the Win32 communications APIs to configure modems and perform data I/O through them.

Windows TAPI provides a standard way for communications applications to control telephony functions for data, fax, and voice calls. The TAPI manages all signaling between a computer and a telephone network, including basic functions, such as dialing, answering, and hanging up a call. It also supports supplementary functions, such as hold, transfer, conference, and call park found in PBX, ISDN, and other telephone systems.

Universal Modem Driver

The universal modem driver (Unimodem) is a layer that provides services for data and fax modems and voice so that users and application developers will not have to learn or maintain difficult modem AT commands to dial, answer, and configure modems. Instead, Unimodem does these tasks automatically by using INF files supplied by modem hardware vendors.

Unimodem is both a VCOMM device driver and a TAPI Service Provider. Other Service Providers (for example, those supporting other devices, such as an ISDN adapter, a telephone on a PBX system, or an AT command modem) can also be used with TAPI.

Integrated Services Digital Network

Microsoft provides Integrated Services Digital Network (ISDN) for remote computing in Windows 98. ISDN, with speeds of up to 128 Kbps, offers higher bandwidth than modems over analog telephone lines. ISDN can be used over an existing telephone network and can provide connections to the Internet that support World Wide Web browsing, multimedia, and video presentation applications.

Requirements for Communications Tools

To use your modem with the built-in communications features of Windows 98, including HyperTerminal and Dial-Up Networking, you must configure your modem using the Modems option in Control Panel. Settings made in the **Modems Properties** dialog box do not affect modem operation in programs designed for MS-DOS or Windows version 3.1.

Communications Tools Management

Windows 98 includes the following tools for expanding communications capabilities:

- HyperTerminal lets you connect two computers through a modem and TAPI for transferring files.

- Phone Dialer lets you use a computer to dial telephone numbers for voice telephone calls. It includes a telephone dial pad, user-programmable speed dials, and a call log.

- Microsoft NetMeeting is a set of application and network components that enable real-time audio and data communication over the Internet. For more information about NetMeeting, see Chapter 20, "Internet Access and Tools."

- Microsoft Outlook Express is an Internet standards-based e-mail and news reader. For more information about Outlook Express, see Chapter 22, "Electronic Mail with Outlook Express."

With Windows 98, you can do the following:

- Configure HyperTerminal to predefine computers to which your computer can connect.

- Configure Phone Dialer for voice telephone calls.

- Define the location you are calling from for all applications and tools.

- Dial a telephone call or display a terminal window before or after dialing.

- Connect to a remote computer.

Using a Modem

A modem is a communications tool that enables a computer to transmit information over a standard telephone line. With Windows 98, you can install a modem in one of four ways:

- Using the Modems option in Control Panel.

- Running a communications application that causes Windows 98 to prompt you to install a modem.

- Adding a modem through the Add New Hardware option in Control Panel.

- Plugging in your Plug and Play modem and letting Windows 98 connect to it.

In these cases, the Install New Modem Wizard appears and asks if you want Windows 98 to automatically detect the modem, or if you want to manually select a modem from the list of known manufacturers and modem models. If you choose the detection option, the wizard detects and then queries the modem to configure it. If it cannot detect the modem, it prompts you to select one.

Once the modem has been selected, you can adjust its properties (if necessary), such as the volume for the modem speaker, the time to wait for the remote computer to answer the call, and the maximum speed.

Depending on the type of modem you have, installing and configuring it might vary slightly as follows:

- If you install an internal legacy (non–Plug and Play) modem adapter, its built-in COM port must be configured by using the Add New Hardware Wizard, before it is installed by using the Modems option in Control Panel. In most cases, the Install New Modem Wizard does this automatically for you.

- If you are using Windows 98 PC Card drivers, Windows 98 will detect and configure PC Card modem cards automatically when they are first inserted. Otherwise, you might need to run the Add New Hardware Wizard in Control Panel to configure the card's built-in COM port. Then install the modem card by using the Modems option in Control Panel. For more information, see Chapter 24, "Device Management."

Note Before you install a modem, check the Modems section in the Windows 98 Readme.txt for possible information.

▶ **To install a modem by using the Modems option in Control Panel**

1. In Control Panel, double-click Modems.

2. If no modem is currently installed on your computer, the Install New Modem Wizard starts automatically to lead you through the steps for installing a modem. Follow the online instructions.

    – Or –

    If you are installing a second modem, click **Add** to start the Install New Modem Wizard.

In most cases, it is best to let the Install New Modem Wizard detect the modem for you. If it cannot detect the exact manufacturer and model, the wizard picks a standard configuration that is usually compatible. Your modem will still function at its maximum speed and according to factory default settings. A few advanced features, such as enabling and disabling compression, error control, and flow control, might be disabled.

Note This procedure is for both internal and external modems. PC Card modems automatically install when inserted; they require protected-mode PC Card drivers.

For information about installing a modem if your modem is not detected or listed, or about finding a better match than any of the Standard Modem Types, see "Correcting Problems with Modem Installation" later in this chapter.

Windows 98 automatically assigns COM names to communications ports, internal modem adapters, and PC Card modem cards according to their base I/O port addresses, as described in Chapter 24, "Device Management."

Defining Your Location

A *location* contains information that Dialing Properties uses to analyze telephone numbers in international format and to determine the correct sequence of numbers to be dialed. It need not correspond to a particular geographic location, but it usually does. The first time you set up a modem, the Install New Modem Wizard prompts you for information about the location you will usually be calling from (the default location), including your area code and country code. This information is stored in Dialing Properties, a communications utility that is accessible from all communications applications created for Windows 98, and in the Modems option in Control Panel.

▶ **To set dialing location information**

- Run the Install New Modem Wizard, and then type the area code and country code information in **My Locations**.

   – Or –

   In Control Panel, double-click Telephony, and type the country code and the area code in **My Locations**.

After you install the modem, more specific location information, such as calling card numbers or the number you must dial to access an outside line, can be entered into the **My Locations** tab in the **Dialing Properties** dialog box. For more information, see "Using Dialing Properties" later in this chapter.

Setting Modem Properties

In the Modems option in Control Panel, you can change default modem settings.

▶ **To view General properties for a modem**

1. In Control Panel, double-click Modems, click a modem, and then click the **Properties** button.

2. View the default settings for the modem that will be used by all applications created for Windows 98. Table 21.1 explains these settings.

Table 21.1   Default modem settings

Option	Description
Port	A port is either a COM or an LPT port to which an external modem is attached, or a COM port name that identifies an internal or PC Card modem. Windows 98 automatically assigns a port name (COM1, COM2, COM3, or COM4) to any device it detects. Usually, the name is adjusted only if you move an external modem from one COM port to another. For PC Card modem cards, the port cannot be changed. The port can also be a virtual infrared COM port.
Speaker volume	This option sets the volume for the telephone speaker, which broadcasts the dial tone, modem connection, and voices (if applicable) on the other end. To change the volume, move the slider bar to the right or left.
Maximum speed	This is the speed at which Windows 98 communicates with the modem. It is limited by the CPU speed of the computer and the speed supported by the communications port. Windows 98 selects a conservative default speed so that slower computers do not lose data during transfers.

Set the speed lower if the faster rate causes data errors. Set it higher for faster performance if you are using a computer with an 80486 or a Pentium processor. For example, 57,600 might work better than the Windows 98 default setting of 38,400 for v.32bis (14,400 bps) modems on fast computers. If applications report data errors, set a lower speed (for example, change it from 38,400 to 19,200 for v.32bis modems). |

Tip If you have a slower computer and an external modem, you can install a 16550A universal asynchronous receiver transmitter (UART)–based COM port adapter to increase speeds. Some internal modems have an integrated 16550A UART adapter.

▶ **To change or view the Connection properties**

- In **General Properties** for your modem, click the **Connection** tab to display its connection options, which are explained in Table 21.2.

Table 21.2   Modem connection options

Option	Description
Connection preferences	Connection settings usually correspond to what the computer on the other end is using. Therefore, do not change connection settings by using the Modems option in Control Panel. Rather, use a specific tool or application, such as HyperTerminal, to change these settings connection by connection.

Preferences include Data bits, Parity, and Stop bits. For information about these values, see Help. |

Table 21.2   Modem connection options (*continued*)

Option	Description
Call preferences	Specifies dialing and connections options for connections you make using this modem and port. The following preferences are available: **Wait for dial tone before dialing.** Clear this option if you are making calls from a country other than where your modem was purchased and your modem fails to properly detect the dial tone. **Cancel the call if not connected within.** Change the number of seconds listed in this field if it takes a long time to make a connection; for example, this might occur when you are making an international call and there are long delays before the call is connected. **Disconnect a call if idle for more than.** Change the number of minutes listed in this option if there is no activity on the line; for example, increase the number if you want to stay connected to a computer bulletin board even though there is no activity.

▶ **To view or change Advanced Connection properties**

• Click **Advanced** in the **Connection** properties to display the **Advanced Connection Settings** dialog box. In this box you can set error control, flow control, and modulation, and audit the modem operations, as explained in Table 21.3.

Table 21.3   Modem advanced connection options

Option	Description
Use error control	Check this option to boost file transfer speeds by eliminating errors caused by noise on a telephone line. This feature is available on most newer modems. When it is enabled, modems sometimes have trouble connecting. If this occurs, clear the check box and try again.
Required to connect	Check this option when you want your modem to connect with another modem, only if error control is enabled on a call. This is useful in areas with very noisy telephone lines, where connecting at a slower speed can improve data throughput.
Compress data	Check this option to boost transmission speeds by compressing data between the modems. This feature is available on most modems. When it is enabled, modems sometimes have trouble connecting. If this occurs, clear the check box and try again. Using modem compression can sometimes reduce performance if the data being sent is already compressed by the application.
Use cellular protocol	Check this option when you want your modem to use special protocols designed to reduce errors over cellular connections. You might want to clear this when making a call on a normal non-cellular telephone line.

Table 21.3   Modem advanced connection options (*continued*)

Option	Description
Use flow control	Check this option for all external modems to avoid loss of data. If your modem cable has RTS and CTS wires connected, you can use hardware flow control; otherwise, use software flow control.
Modulation type	Switches modulation type to be compatible with the modem signals for the computer to which you are trying to connect. Both computers must use the same type of modulation to exchange information successfully.
Extra settings	Use this field to type modem commands that Windows 98 will include in the initialization sequence that it sends to the modem before dialing. Do not include the "AT" prefix in this box. The option is intended only for debugging purposes and should be used only by experienced modem users.
Append to log	Windows 98 records commands and responses to and from the modem in a text file in the Windows folder. If the box is not checked, Windows 98 erases the old log and records a new log at the beginning of each call. If the box is checked, Windows 98 appends new call logs to this file. The file name is Modemname.txt, where *modemname* is the name of the modem in the **General** tab of the Control Panel Modem option.
View Log	The modem log is a powerful tool for diagnosing problems, particularly with connection problems. However, the interpretation of the contents of the file requires modem documentation, technical support, and/or experience with modems. The problems diagnosed may be in the local modem, its configuration, the telephone system, the remote modem (for example, the Internet Service Provider's), or in some combination.

You can also click **Port Settings** in the **Connection** properties to set **Receive Buffer** and **Transmit Buffer**.

Dialing Manually

Windows 98 lets you dial your modem manually if you are having difficulty making an international call or other connection. To do so, you need a separate telephone headset and keypad. You can request manual dialing, using slightly different procedures from within any Windows 98–based communications applications, such as HyperTerminal or Dial-Up Networking. The following procedure describes how to dial your modem manually by using Dial-Up Networking.

▶ **To control modem dialing manually**

1. In My Computer, double-click Dial-Up Networking.

2. Right-click the connection icon you want to change, and then click **Properties**.

3. Click **Configure**, and then click the **Options** tab.

4. Select the **Operator assisted or manual dial** check box, and then click **OK**.

5. Connect to the shared resource that uses this connection, or click the icon for this connection in Dial-Up Networking.

6. Click **Connect**.

7. When instructed, pick up the telephone and dial the number.

8. When you hear the other computer answer, click **Connect** and hang up the telephone.

Displaying the Terminal Window

Before or after dialing, you can display a terminal window to type AT modem commands if a connection requires them. A terminal window can be used to log on for security purposes, for establishing connections with servers that require a specific logon procedure, and for other reasons. The following procedure describes this process for Dial-Up Networking.

▶ **To display a terminal window before or after dialing**

1. In Dial-Up Networking, right-click a connection icon, and then click **Properties**.

2. Click **Configure**, and then click the **Options** tab.

3. Select the **Bring up terminal window before dialing** check box or **Bring up terminal window after dialing** check box, and then click **OK**.

Using Hardware Compression

Hardware compression at higher connection speeds is available on most newer modems. For example, V.42bis is an industry standard that allows modems to compress all data sent through them. Compressing the data decreases communication time.

▶ **To choose hardware compression**

1. In Control Panel, double-click Modems, click **Properties**, and then click the **Connection** tab.

2. Click **Advanced**, select **Use error control**, and then click **Compress Data**.

Using HyperTerminal

HyperTerminal lets you connect two computers with a modem so you can send and receive files, or connect to computer bulletin boards and other information programs. For example, you can use HyperTerminal to connect to an online service and to download files from a bulletin board on that service. You can also use HyperTerminal to connect a computer directly to another computer, such as a debugging terminal.

You can install HyperTerminal with Custom setup during Windows 98 installation. Select HyperTerminal when selecting components to install. See Chapter 3, "Custom Installations" for more information about custom installations.

▶ **To install HyperTerminal after Windows 98 Setup**

1. In Control Panel, double-click Add/Remove Programs, and then click the **Windows Setup** tab.

2. In the **Components** list, click **Communications**, and then click **Details**.

3. In the **Communications** dialog box, click **HyperTerminal**, and then click **OK**.

▶ **To start HyperTerminal**

1. Click **Start**, point to **Programs, Accessories,** and then **Communications**.

2. Click **HyperTerminal**, and then click **Hypertrm.exe**.

For more information, see the online Help in HyperTerminal.

File Transfer Protocols

HyperTerminal supports the File Transfer Protocols (FTPs) described in Table 21.4.

Table 21.4   HyperTerminal File Transfer Protocols

Protocol	Description
Xmodem	The most common error-correcting data communications protocol. Most communications packages support (and some will *only* support) Xmodem. This protocol is also supported by most online services. Xmodem is slower than other protocols.
1K Xmodem	A variant of traditional Xmodem, which sends data in 1 KB (1024-byte) blocks instead of 128-byte blocks. On some bulletin boards, this protocol is called Ymodem.
Ymodem	A faster version of Xmodem, transferring data in 1 KB blocks.
Ymodem-G	A variant of Ymodem designed for use with modems that support hardware error control. If you cannot transfer files by using Ymodem-G, your modem might not support error control; use Ymodem instead.
Zmodem	The fastest data transfer protocol and the primary choice of most bulletin-board users. Zmodem dynamically changes its block size based on line conditions, and it is extremely reliable. You can also choose Zmodem with crash recovery.
Kermit	An extremely flexible protocol, found most often on Digital Equipment Corporation (DEC) VAX computers, IBM mainframes, and other minicomputers. However, Kermit is quite slow and should not be used if faster options are available on the other computer.

Note You can choose a File Transfer Protocol to use when you send or receive a file by using the **Send** or **Receive File** options in the **Transfer** menu, as described in Help.

Terminal Emulation Types

HyperTerminal supports the following terminal emulation types:

- American National Standards Institute (ANSI)
- Minitel (for France)
- Auto Detect
- TTY/TDD
- Viewdata (for the United Kingdom)
- DEC VT 100
- VT 52

▶ **To choose a terminal emulation type**

1. Right-click a connection icon, and then click **Properties**.
2. In the connection's properties, click the **Settings** tab, and then select the emulation type.

Note Some modems might not be able to connect to French Minitel in HyperTerminal using the Windows 98 default settings. To correct this, you need to add an extra command in the **Extra settings** field in the **Advanced Connection Settings** dialog box in the modem's properties. Check the modem manual for the command that enables the modem to connect in V.23 modulation to Minitel, and then add this to the **Extra settings** field.

Using Phone Dialer

The Phone Dialer application in Windows 98 allows you to use your computer and a modem to dial telephone calls using the calling card and location information defined in Dialing Properties. It also stores frequently dialed numbers, dials stored phone numbers, and logs telephone calls.

You can install Phone Dialer by choosing Custom Setup during Windows 98 installation or by using the following procedure. See Chapter 3, "Custom Installations" for more information about custom installations.

You can also install it after installing Windows 98 by choosing the Add/Remove Programs option in Control Panel.

▶ **To install Phone Dialer after Window 98 installation**

1. In Control Panel, double-click Add/Remove Programs, and then click the **Windows Setup** tab.

2. In the **Components** list, click **Communications**, and then click **Details**.

3. In the **Communications** dialog box, click **Phone Dialer**, and then click **OK**.

▶ **To start Phone Dialer and make a call**

1. Click **Start**, point to **Programs**, **Accessories**, **Communications**, and then click **Phone Dialer**.

2. In the **Phone Dialer** dialog box type a telephone number using either your keyboard or the Phone Dialer numeric keypad.

3. Click **Dial**.

When you dial a number with Phone Dialer, the number is automatically stored in a list of your most recently used telephone numbers. All local, domestic long distance, and international telephone numbers are stored when you type all the digits needed to dial in the **Number to dial** box. You can also store phone numbers as speed-dial numbers.

Important The **Number to dial** box can hold up to 40 digits. Therefore, you can type a local, domestic long distance, or international long distance telephone number in this text box. The same is true when you create speed-dial numbers.

If you type the area code and local telephone number, Phone Dialer automatically precedes the dialed number with a "1" if you have typed this information in the **Area Code Rules** properties of the **Dialing Properties** dialog box. Dialing Properties is a separate communications tool described in "Using Dialing Properties" later in this chapter.

If you type nonnumeric characters (such as a hyphen or a parenthesis) in a telephone number, Phone Dialer ignores them except when you type a plus sign (+) at the beginning of your number, which is international format. If you type a number in international format, you must put parentheses around the area code, for example, **+1 (425) 882-8080**. For more information, see the online Help in Phone Dialer.

Using Windows 98 Telephony

Computer telephony lets desktop computers interact with telephone hardware. The Microsoft Windows Telephony Application Programming Interface (TAPI) is an interface that provides a method for applications to support telephone communication easily. Windows 95 shipped with TAPI version 1.4, which provided support for the direct connection to a telephone network, automatic phone dialing, and interfaces for conference calling, voice mail, and caller ID.

Windows 98 supports TAPI version 2.1. In addition to being compatible with previously released versions of TAPI (including TAPI 2.0 in Windows NT version 4.0), TAPI 2.1 gives developers additional extensions for the creation of client/server telephony applications. TAPI helps make Windows 98 a powerful and flexible platform for developing and using computer-telephony integration (CTI) applications. It provides services that allow applications to share a line so that more than one application can wait for an incoming call while another dials out.

Windows 98 includes two TAPI Service Providers, Unimodem V and network driver interface specification wide area network (NDISWAN):

Unimodem V   Unimodem V is the TAPI Service Provider available for Windows 95. Support for the following has been added in Windows 98:

- Sierra modems
- Sparacom modem pooling
- Denmark support
- Intel H.324 support
- Controller-less modems

NDISWAN   NDISWAN interfaces with ISDN cards and the Point-to-Point Tunneling Protocol (PPTP). It acts as a translation layer between TAPI and ISDN. For more information about NDISWAN, see Chapter 29, "Windows 98 Network Architecture."

Using Telephony Dialing Properties

Windows 98 includes a Telephony option in Control Panel from which users can adjust dialing properties and view installed telephony drivers.

The **My Locations** tab contains the information that was previously found in the Modems option in Windows 95, and the tab is still available from that option. It contains information regarding dialing location. The **Telephony Drivers** tab lets you identify, install, configure, and remove TAPI Service Providers.

Windows 98 includes the Dialing Properties utility, which enables you to do the following:

- Establish different locations (dialing rules) depending on where you are dialing from.
- Define calling card rules that you can use with one or more of your locations.

The Dialing Properties utility enables you to define different locations from which you dial. For each location, you enter your country code, area code, and other information about the place you are dialing from. You can then dial a number using Dial-Up Networking, and Windows 98 automatically adjusts your dialing string (telephone number) based on the location you are calling from. For example, suppose you commonly dial from three different places:

- Home
- Office
- Hotel

You can create three different locations, and enter area code and other information for each location. Then, whenever you make a dialing location, Dialing Properties automatically adjusts the telephone number based on the place you are calling from.

In Windows 98, you can access Dialing Properties from the following sources:

- From the **Tools** menu in Phone Dialer.
- From the Telephony icon in Control Panel.
- By clicking **Dialing Properties** when you make a new connection in HyperTerminal.

See "Using Dialing Properties" later in this chapter for details about setting up dialing properties.

▶ **To define a new dialing location**

1. In Control Panel, double-click Telephony.
2. In the **My Locations** tab, enter the name of your new dialing location, the area code you are dialing from, and other information about your location. Optionally, enter information about your calling card. This information will then be available to any Dial-Up Networking connection that you create.

▶ **To use the dialing location**

1. When you define a Dial-Up Networking Connection, make sure that **Use area code and dialing properties** is selected.

2. When you dial the connection (described in "Making a Dial-Up Networking Connection" later in this chapter), make sure that you have selected the correct dialing location.

For more information about Dial-Up Networking, see Chapter 19, "Remote Networking and Mobile Computing."

Making a Dial-Up Networking Connection

After you have defined a remote connection by using the Make New Connection Wizard, you can make a connection.

Note If you selected **Use area code and Dialing Properties** in the **General** properties for your connection, Dial-Up Networking automatically adjusts the dialing string (telephone number) according to your dialing location.

▶ **To make a Dial-Up Networking Connection**

1. In My Computer, double-click Dial-Up Networking.

2. Double-click **My Connection**.

3. Optionally, enter a user name and password.

4. Optionally, if you selected **Use area code and Dialing Properties** in the **General** properties for your connection, in the **Dialing from:** box, ensure that you have selected the correct dialing location. If necessary, select another dialing location or select **Dial Properties** to define a new dialing location.

Installing a Dial-Up Networking Connection

You need an installed and correctly configured modem. If the Dial-Up Networking option is not installed, add it by opening Control Panel and then double-clicking Add/Remove Programs. Click the **Windows Setup** tab, and then follow the instructions on your screen.

Open the Dial-Up Networking folder in My Computer, and start the Connection Wizard.

Dial-Up Networking uses the Windows 98 communications architecture to communicate through a modem to a network. It initializes the modem, determines device status, and dials the telephone number by using TAPI and the Unimodem driver. For more information about the communications architecture and the Dial-Up Networking architecture, see Chapter 29, "Windows 98 Network Architecture."

A Windows 98 Dial-Up Networking configuration can include the following components:

- The dial-up client.
- Connection protocols.
- Local area network (LAN) protocols.
- The dial-up server.
- Security options for the dial-up client and server.
- Hardware and software compression.

The Point-to-Point Protocol (PPP) protocol is a connection protocol installed by default because it has become the standard for remote access because of its flexibility, password encryption security, and compatibility with future client and server hardware and software. If a dial-up client is running PPP, it can connect to a network running the IPX, TCP/IP, or NetBEUI protocol. Windows 98 dial-up clients can use PPP to connect to any remote access server running PPP, including Windows NT Server version 3.5 or later. PPP is the default protocol for the Microsoft Dial-Up Adapter.

Using Dialing Properties

Dialing Properties is a utility integrated with Telephony, Phone Dialer, HyperTerminal, the Internet Connection Wizard, Dial-Up Networking, and other communications applications created for Windows 98. The options you set with Dialing Properties are stored in the registry.

With Dialing Properties, you can do the following:

- Define locations, specifying area code, country code, and in-house dialing rules.
- Define calling card rules.
- Define area code rules with 10-digit dialing.

In Windows 98, you can access Dialing Properties from the following sources:

- From Telephony in Control Panel.
- From the **Tools** menu in Phone Dialer.
- By clicking **Dialing Properties** from one of several applications, such as HyperTerminal, MSN, or the Internet Connection Wizard.

For purposes of discussion, procedures in this section describe accessing Dialing Properties from the Telephony Control Panel applet. The procedures are the same, however, no matter how you access Dialing Properties.

Defining Locations

You can name locations anything you choose to help you remember and select them later. Dialing Properties allows you to add new locations, edit existing locations, and remove locations. For more information, see "Defining Your Location" earlier in this chapter.

▶ **To define a location in Dialing Properties**

1. In Control Panel, click Telephony.

2. In the **My Locations** tab, type information about where you are calling from, including the following:

   - Name of your location (for example, home or office).

   - Name of your country.

   - Area code.

   - Access number required to make a local or long distance call.

   - Whether your telephone has call waiting and whether it should be disabled.

   - Whether your telephone uses pulse or tone dialing.

   - Whether you use a calling card to make calls.

3. If you live in an area that requires 10-digit dialing, click **Area Code Rules** and specify which area codes do not have to be dialed as long distance. Click **OK**.

4. If you want to change calling card information, click **Calling Card**. For more information about calling cards, see "Defining Calling Card Rules" later in this chapter.

Defining Calling Card Rules

The *calling card* contains information that Dialing Properties uses to create the sequence of numbers to be dialed on a particular call. The calling card can include a calling card number that can be dialed at a specified time during call placement. You can choose any name for the calling cards to help you remember them.

Dialing Properties include predefined settings for several popular calling cards, including AT&T, Sprint, MCI, British Telecom, France Telecom Mercury, Telecom New Zealand, and others. You can modify and use these directly. Dialing Properties allows you to add new calling cards, edit existing calling cards, and remove calling cards.

The information stored in a calling card includes the name, the card number, and the dialing rules for local, long distance, and international calls.

▶ **To specify that you are using a calling card in Dialing Properties**

1. Run Phone Dialer, click the **Tools** menu, and then click **Dialing Properties**.

2. In the **My Locations** tab, click **Calling Card**.

3. In the **Calling Card** dialog box, click your calling card type in the list (for example, **AT&T**), or click **New** and type the calling card name.

4. Type your calling card personal ID number, and then click **OK**.

If you are making a calling card telephone call from outside the United States and do not want Windows telephony applications to automatically add a "0" prefix to the number you are calling, precede the telephone number with a different numeric code.

▶ **To redefine numbers that automatically precede the phone number**

1. In the **Calling Card** dialog box, click **New**.

2. Type the name of the calling card. A dialog box tells you that you must enter dialing "rules" for this calling card. Click **OK**.

3. Type the personal ID number. Settings for the card also include the access numbers for long distance calls and international calls, and the calling card sequences.

Using Integrated Services Digital Network

Integrated Services Digital Network (ISDN) is the digital telephone service that works over existing copper telephone wiring. To use ISDN, you need either an ISDN modem or an ISDN adapter. You might also need an NT-1 (the equivalent of the phone jack into which you plug your device) and an ISDN line from your telephone company.

ISDN modems hook up to your computer through a serial port, just as regular modems do. This means that, because a serial port can go no faster than 115 Kbps (which is lower than the total effective bandwidth of the ISDN line), some throughput will be lost if you are using the maximum ISDN bandwidth. An ISDN adapter, which operates at bus speed, provides the higher rate that ISDN needs. With most ISDN modems and adapters, you also need an NT-1. Some ISDN equipment comes with the NT-1 built in.

In addition to the configuration the telephone company must do at their end of your ISDN line, you must do some configuration at your end. You need to know three pieces of information supplied by the telephone company to make your ISDN service work with your Windows 98:

- Switch type
- Telephone numbers
- Service Profile Identifiers (SPIDs)

Switch type   Most ISDN hardware adapters need to know what type of switch they are connected to. The switch type simply refers to the brand of equipment and software revision level that the telephone company uses to provide you with ISDN service. There are only a few types of switches in the world and usually just one in countries other than the United States.

Telephone number   The second type of information is your telephone number or numbers. In some cases, each B channel on an ISDN line has its own number, while in other cases both B channels share a single telephone number. (See "Technical Notes on Communications Tools" later in this chapter.) Your telephone company will tell you how many numbers your ISDN line will have. Separate numbers may be useful if you plan to take incoming calls on your ISDN line.

Service Profile Identifier   The last type of information is the Service Profile Identifier (SPID), which is used only in the United States and Canada. The SPID usually consists of the telephone number with some additional digits added at the beginning and end. The SPID helps the switch understand what kind of equipment is attached to the line. If multiple devices are attached, it helps route calls to the appropriate device on the line.

ISDN Versus POTS

ISDN is typically supplied by the same company that supplies analog service, also referred to as Plain Old Telephone Service (POTS). However, ISDN differs from analog telephone service in several ways, including:

- Data transfer rate
- Available channels per call
- Availability of service
- Cost of service
- Quality of connection

Data transfer rate   ISDN can provide data transfer rates of up to 128 Kbps. These speeds are slower than those of local area networks (LANs) supported by high-speed data communications technology, but faster than those of analog telephone lines. In addition to the difference in data transfer rates, ISDN calls can be set up much faster than analog phone calls. While an analog modem can take up to a minute to set up a connection, you usually can start transmitting data in about two seconds with ISDN. Because ISDN is fully digital, the lengthy handshaking process of analog modems is not required.

Channels   POTS provides a single channel, which can carry voice or digital communications, but not both at the same time. ISDN service is available in several configurations of multiple channels that provide simultaneous voice and digital communications. In addition to increasing data throughput, multiple channels eliminate the need for separate voice and data telephone lines.

Availability   POTS is generally available throughout the United States. Although increasing in availability, ISDN is not as widely available as POTS.

Cost   The cost of ISDN hardware and service is generally higher than for POTS modems and service.

Connection quality   ISDN transmits data digitally and, as a result, is less susceptible to static and noise than are analog transmissions. Analog modem connections must dedicate some bandwidth to error correction and retransmission. This overhead reduces the actual throughput. In contrast, an ISDN line can dedicate all its bandwidth to data transmission.

Configuring Windows 98 for ISDN

Windows 98 provides built-in support for ISDN. To connect to the Internet by using ISDN, you need to install and configure the Dial-Up Networking feature in Windows 98.

Before configuring ISDN on a computer running Windows 98, you need the following:

- Installed internal or external ISDN adapter.

- ISDN telephone line service at the location where you will use Dial-Up networking to connect to the Internet.

- ISDN telephone line service at the remote location to which you want to connect, usually either your Internet Service Provider (ISP) or a Remote Access Service (RAS) server.

In general, it is recommended that you also use PPP with ISDN for connections to the Internet. This protocol is the one typically used to access the Internet over dial-up connections. To use PPP, you must have a PPP account with your ISP. If you currently have a Serial Line Internet Protocol (SLIP) account, you should ask your ISP to change the account to PPP.

After you have installed your ISDN adapter and received notice from your telephone company that your ISDN service has been installed, you can configure Windows 98 for your ISDN service.

For more information about ISDN services, see "Technical Notes on Communications Tools" later in this chapter.

▶ **To install your ISDN device**

1. In Control Panel, double-click Network.

2. Click **Add**, and then click **Adapter**.

3. Select the appropriate manufacturer and model, and then click **OK**.

Note If your ISDN adapter is Plug and Play–compatible, Windows 98 will automatically install the required support.

---

4. The ISDN Configuration Wizard starts automatically. Follow the directions on the screen. The following information needed by the Wizard must be provided by your telephone carrier and ISDN provider.

Information	Supplied by
Switch protocol	Telephone company
Telephone numbers	ISDN provider
SPID numbers	ISDN provider

After you have configured ISDN on your computer, you can enable PPP Multilink protocol by using the procedure described in the following section.

Enabling Multilink

ISDN increases speed from a single 64 Kbps channel by providing dual-channel support for up to 128 Kbps performance on standard ISDN lines. This dual-channel support is commonly referred to as *multilinking*. The protocol for multilinking is called PPP Multilink Protocol.

Multilink is available when you have more than one dial-up device (such as two B channels of an ISDN connection). If you have only one dial-up device configured, you will not be able to use Multilink. Multilink depends upon the capabilities of the service or corporate network that you are dialing into in order to function properly. To use Multilink, the answering ISP, online service, or corporate LAN must provide Multilink support.

Dial-Up Networking Multilink combines multiple physical links into a logical "bundle." This aggregate link increases your bandwidth. The most common use is bundling ISDN channels, but you can also bundle two or more modems or a modem and an ISDN line.

Before using Multilink, consider the following issues:

- The server or ISP you connect to must also support PPP Multilink. Otherwise, Multilink will not function correctly.

- You can use the Multilink protocol feature only when your computer is configured with multiple devices that can be combined to form the logical PPP pipe over the communication link.

- For best performance, the devices you use should function at the same speed.

- When you combine both B channels under ISDN, you cannot use your second channel for other applications, such as fax or voice calls.

- If you are dialing a server that is configured to call you back for security purposes, that server will call only one telephone line. If you are using ISDN, you can solve this problem by configuring both ISDN lines with the same telephone number.

Example You can provide up to 128 Kbps wire speeds on a single ISDN-BRI line by combining the two B channels. Each B channel provides a 64 Kbps line, and the two combined achieve speeds of up to 128 Kbps. You can also combine an analog line with an ISDN line to increase bandwidth.

▶ **To configure Multilink**

1. Double-click My Computer.

2. Double-click Dial-Up Networking.

3. Double-click **Make New Connection** if this is a first-time connection. Define the connection to the dial-up service you want to use. Double-click the icon that represents your new connection in the Dial-up Networking folder. For more information about creating a new Dial-up Connection, see Chapter 19, "Remote Networking and Mobile Computing."

   – Or –

   Right-click the existing connection that you want to configure for Multilink.

4. Click **Properties**, and then click the **Multilink** tab.

5. Click **Use Additional Devices**.

6. Click **Add**, and then specify the devices to bundle to form the multilink connection.

   Use the **Add**, **Remove**, and **Edit** buttons to change the list of additional devices. You can enter a different telephone number for each device, and both numbers will be stored. If you subsequently change the telephone number for the connection icon, the numbers associated with additional devices on this page will not change.

Using Multilink

After configuring your additional devices, you are ready to dial your Multilink connection. When you dial the connection, Dial-Up Networking dials the primary number of the primary device specified for the connection. Once the first connection has been established, Dial-Up Networking dials the other devices specified in the **Additional Devices** list.

Once the connections are established, you can view status information about the link by double-clicking the communicating computers icon displayed in the taskbar, or you can disconnect.

Note Using Multilink with two modems requires that both modems be connected to separate telephone lines. Communication will be at the highest common connect speed. For example, if you have modems with baud rates of 14.4 and 28.8, the highest speed you can use is 14.4.

The status information includes the number of bytes sent and received, the network protocols negotiated for use on the connection, and additional devices. When you select an additional device, a **Suspend** or **Resume** button is displayed. If a **Suspend** button is displayed, the device is in use and bundled into the multilink connection. Clicking **Suspend** disconnects that line and removes it from the bundled connections.

If the **Resume** button is displayed, click it to dial that connection and add that line to the bundle. You can suspend and resume individual links without dropping the connection.

▶ **To use Multilink**

- After you have configured Multilink, click the connection icon and click **Connect**. Dial-Up Networking will connect using the primary device and then the secondary device.

▶ **To view information about your link**

1. Click the Dial-Up Networking icon displayed on the taskbar.
2. In the dialog box, click **Details**.

Technical Notes on Communications Tools

This section provides further information about Windows 98 communications tools.

Windows Telephony API

The Windows Telephony API (TAPI) is an important part of the Windows Open System Architecture (WOSA). TAPI lets developers of virtually any skill level create powerful, easy-to-use, and effective telephony applications. TAPI provides full client/server telephony, and is open, comprehensive, scalable, and integrated.

Open TAPI was defined with substantial, ongoing input from the telephony and computing industries from all over the world, so it is truly an open industry standard. TAPI-compatible applications can be run on a wide variety of personal computer and telephony hardware and can support a variety of network services.

Comprehensive TAPI supports many telephony features. A developer can program telephone capabilities into most general-purpose applications. TAPI supports Unicode, so it is easier to make applications work globally. In addition, it integrates call control and other WOSA elements. With Active Controls for telephony provided by a variety of vendors, corporate developers can put together powerful telephony applications.

Scalable With TAPI, you can have CTI applications that are affordable for one person or can scale to support thousands, because TAPI supports the widest array of call models. With TAPI you can run several telephony applications simultaneously on a client or server computer, unlike with other competitive APIs.

Integrated TAPI is tightly integrated with Windows 98.

Telephony Drivers from Other Vendors

There are several ways to add telephony drivers from other vendors, if necessary. Some telephony drivers work over the network and consist of software only. If this is the case, the software can be installed through the Add/Remove Programs option in Control Panel.

Hardware drivers can be installed through the Add New Hardware option in Control Panel, unless the hardware requires its own class installer. In this case, the hardware should come with a standard Setup program to install it.

Integrated Services Digital Network

Integrated Services Digital Network (ISDN) is the digital telephone service that works over existing copper telephone wiring. There are several types of ISDN service, but the most appropriate type for individual computer users—and the type that this section focuses on—is the ISDN Basic Rate Interface (BRI).

Basic Rate ISDN divides the telephone line into 3 digital channels: 2 B channels and one D channel, all of which can be used simultaneously. The B channels are used to transmit data, at rates of 64 Kbps or 56 Kbps (depending on your telephone company). The D channel does the administrative work, such as setting up and terminating the call and communicating with the telephone network. With two B channels, you can make two calls simultaneously.

Most of the world's existing telephone network is already digital. The only section that typically is not digital runs from the local exchange to your house or office. ISDN makes that final leg of the network digital.

Unlike analog telephone service, ISDN service is not yet available everywhere. Your telephone company must have installed the necessary equipment in the central office that serves you.

Provisioning is a telephone company term for the configuration of your line on the telephone company's end. A normal analog telephone line comes with a few options, such as Call Waiting or Caller ID, but it is not necessary to choose any of them. An ISDN line, on the other hand, has many, many options, and choices for all of them must be defined in order for the line to function.

In addition to the configuration the telephone company must do at their end of your ISDN line, there is also some configuration you must do at your end. You need to know three pieces of information supplied by the telephone company to make your ISDN service work with Windows 98:

- Switch type
- Telephone numbers (also known as directory numbers)
- Service Profile Identifiers (SPIDs)

Most ISDN hardware adapters need to know what type of switch they are connected to. The switch type simply refers to the brand of equipment and software revision level that the telephone company uses to provide you with ISDN service. There are only a few types of switches in the world and usually just one in countries other than the United States.

The second type of information is your phone number or numbers. In some cases, each B channel on an ISDN line has its own number, while in other cases both B channels share a single phone number. Your telephone company will tell you how many numbers your ISDN line will have. Separate numbers may be useful if you plan to take incoming calls on your ISDN line.

The last type of information is the Service Profile Identifier (SPID), which is only used in the United States and Canada. The SPID usually consists of the phone number with some additional digits added to the beginning and end. The SPID helps the switch understand what kind of equipment is attached to the line, and if there are multiple devices attached, helps route calls to the appropriate device on the line.

Internal and External ISDN Adapters

There are two types of ISDN hardware adapters: internal and external. *Internal ISDN adapters* are cards that you put inside your computer. *External adapters* connect though a port on the back of your computer.

These ports impose certain limitations. Most personal computer serial ports will not transmit information faster than 115 Kbps, which is less than ISDN's maximum data speed of 128 Kbps. These serial ports impose overhead on the transfer of information between the computer and the external adapter, further slowing data speeds. An external ISDN modem can impact the performance of your system, because an external adapter places heavy requirements on the CPU. To use an external ISDN adapter, it is recommended you have a 486/66 MHz or faster processor.

There are also potential interoperability issues with external adapters, because higher level protocols like PPP or authentication are implemented in the modem itself. These protocols are evolving quickly and can be difficult to update in the modem should you want to install new protocols or fix bugs.

U and S/T Interfaces

Once you have ISDN service, you need to know which ISDN interface your equipment expects. There are two ISDN interfaces. The *U-Interface* carries ISDN signals over a single pair of wires between your location and the central office. This interface is designed to carry ISDN signals over long distances. The *Subscriber/Termination (S/T) Interface* uses two pairs of wires to deliver the signal from the wall jack to your ISDN adapter or other ISDN equipment.

Some ISDN adapters sold in North America connect directly to a U-Interface. If the computer is the only equipment to be connected to an ISDN line, this type of adapter is the easiest to install.

Wiring and Jacks

ISDN service from the phone company officially ends at what is called the demarcation point ("demarc"), usually just inside the building. You are responsible for the "inside wiring" from the demarc to your ISDN equipment, including the wall jacks. Direct wiring between the ISDN wall jack and the demarc (also known as a "home run") is recommended. The telephone company or an electrical contractor will install and maintain the inside wiring for an additional charge.

If you are just connecting your personal computer to the ISDN line, the wiring requirements may be very simple. Many homes and offices are wired with extra sets of telephone wires, and one of those sets can be used for your ISDN line. There are a number of possible wiring pitfalls, however:

- Your "extra" wires may already be in use for analog line(s).

- Your "extra" wires may already be in use to power lighted phone buttons.

- Your "extra" wires may not be connected directly to the demarc.

- The wiring may be daisy-chain rather than home-run.

For more information on wiring issues, consult your telephone company or an electrical contractor.

The NT-1 (Network Termination 1) is a device that is required to connect ISDN terminal equipment to an ISDN line. The NT-1 connects to the two-wire line that your telephone company has assigned for your ISDN service. Your ISDN service will not work if the NT-1 plug is not connected to a working electrical outlet.

Two types of jacks are associated with ISDN:

- RJ11 — the standard analog phone jack. The RJ11 has 4 wires. The wire from the wall to the NT-1 usually has RJ11 jacks.

- RJ45—a jack is slightly wider than the RJ11, with 8 wires. The wire from the NT-1 to the ISDN adapter usually has RJ45 jacks.

Connecting Multiple Devices to an ISDN Line

It is possible to connect up to eight devices to a single ISDN line. These devices can include network routers and bridges, Group 4 ISDN fax machines, and ISDN telephones, as well as traditional analog telephone devices. ISDN is intelligent enough to arbitrate the use of the two B channels between these devices (up to two devices can be in use simultaneously) and route incoming calls to the appropriate device.

Instead of connecting the ISDN line to a single computer, it is possible to connect an ISDN line to a LAN so that all the computers on the LAN can share the ISDN line. This requires an ISDN network bridge or router.

It is also possible to connect several ISDN devices to a single ISDN line. For example, you might wish to have an ISDN adapter in your computer, an ISDN telephone for voice calls, and a Group 4 ISDN fax machine, all connected to the same ISDN line. Incoming data calls would go to the personal computer, voice calls to the telephone, and fax calls to the fax machine. To support this configuration, you need an NT-1 that supports multiple S/T Interface connections. Each device must be connected to the NT-1. Each device also needs its own SPID to ensure that the telephone company can route calls to the appropriate device.

In addition to ISDN devices, some NT-1s or ISDN adapters also support analog telephone devices, such as telephones, data modems, Group 3 fax machines, and answering machines. The NT-1 or the ISDN adapter converts the analog signal into ISDN and vice versa.

Connection Quality

Because ISDN is a digital service, it is sensitive to outside interference, and certain factors affect the quality of ISDN connections to the telephone network and the Internet. The computer connecting to the ISDN line must be within a given distance of the telephone company's central office equipment that serves the computer for the ISDN connection to work. The maximum distance allowed between the computer and the central telephone office is typically 18,000 feet. Additionally, ISDN connections can be adversely affected by telephone lines that are not wired using twisted-pair wiring.

The most appropriate type of service for small Internet Information Server sites is ISDN-Basic Rate Interface (ISDN-BRI). The most appropriate type of service for medium to large Internet Information Server sites is ISDN-Primary Rate Interface (ISDN-PRI).

ISDN - Basic Rate Interface   ISDN-BRI divides the telephone line into three digital channels: two bearer channels, commonly referred to as B channels, and one D channel. All three channels can be used simultaneously. The B channels can be used to send voice, circuit-switched data, or packet-switched data at rates of 56 Kbps to 64 Kbps. The maximum available transfer rate is determined by your local telephone company. The B channels function independently of one another. They can be used simultaneously for separate calls or combined to provide a total bandwidth of 128 Kbps. The D channel can transfer data at 16 Kbps and is used for signaling and control information sent between the computer and the telephone office. D channel signaling provides such functions as call setup, call monitoring, call termination, and enhanced telephony features.

When using ISDN-BRI, it is possible to perform several types of connections. For example, it is possible to have a voice conversation on one B channel, a circuit-switched data call on the second B channel, and a packet-switched data call on the D channel. The D channel can simultaneously complete all necessary signaling and call control functions.

ISDN-Primary Rate Interface   The U.S. standard for ISDN-PRI consists of 24 digital channels: 23 B channels and 1 D channel, commonly referred to as a 23 B+D connection. ISDN-PRI provides a total bandwidth of 1.544 megabits per second (Mbps) and is designed for transmission over a North American-standard T1 line connection.

The European standard for ISDN-PRI provides a total of 31 or 32 digital channels. Each of these channels is a 64 Kbps B channel, except for one that is the D channel for the entire group. In Europe, ISDN-PRI is designed for transmission over a European-standard E1 line connection. A PRI D channel can be used to control one or multiple T1 or E1 lines.

Ordering ISDN Service

ISDN is a powerful but complex service and is not yet available throughout the United States. For this reason, getting ISDN can sometimes be confusing or frustrating. Microsoft provides an online service that can guide you through the ordering process. This service and useful information is available for computers running Windows-based operating systems. This service can simplify and streamline the process of getting ISDN for your Windows-based computer by helping you:

- Identify which telephone companies offer ISDN. Most but not all telephone companies offer this service.

- Check whether the necessary ISDN equipment has been installed in your area.

- Learn about the ISDN service options and pricing in your area.

- Send an electronic order for ISDN to your telephone company.

- Automatically tell the telephone company how to configure your ISDN line.

To use this online service, connect to the Microsoft World Wide Web site at **http://www.microsoft.com/windows/getisdn/**.

Note   Even if the right equipment is installed in your area, ISDN may not be available. To determine whether your particular wiring supports ISDN, your telephone company must perform what is known as a line qualification.

Windows 98 Architecture Support for ISDN

Support for ISDN is a built-in feature of Windows 98. ISDN requires Transmission Control Protocol/Internet Protocol (TCP/IP) and Point-to-Point Protocol (PPP), which Windows 98 fully supports. PPP is an industry standard that enables Windows 98–based computers to support remote access networking in multi-vendor networks.

Troubleshooting Modems and Communications Tools

This section describes how to solve problems with installing modems, making connections, and using applications to access the modem. Windows 98 provides a troubleshooting aid for modems in online Help. Windows 98 captures call control information in a log file, for troubleshooting connections.

Try using online Help for troubleshooting before trying the steps included in this section. In addition, a general modem diagnostic tool is located in the Modems option in Control Panel. It provides information about each modem or COM port that has been configured on the computer.

This section also includes troubleshooting information for ISDN.

▶   **To use the Modems Diagnostics Tool**

1. In Control Panel, double-click Modems, and then click the **Diagnostics** tab.

2. In **Diagnostics** Properties, click **Driver** to find out which communications driver is installed. For these applications, the driver should be Comm.drv. If a different driver is listed and you are having problems with using Win16-based applications, the driver is probably the cause.

3. In **Diagnostics** Properties, click **More Info** to make sure Windows 98 can communicate with the modem. Clicking this button causes Windows 98 to send commands to and read responses from the modem, and then to display information about the modem and its COM port.

   The **Port Information** box displays the following information:

   - The interrupt request (IRQ) and I/O address of the modem's COM port. These should match the physical configuration of the port or modem adapter.

   - The UART type of COM port, for example, 8250 or 16550A. Notice that 16550A UART ports can sustain faster connection speeds with fewer errors.

   - The highest port speed supported by the modem. Never set the modem's speed higher than the speed listed here.

   The **Modem Information** box displays the modem's responses to various AT commands that Windows 98 previously sent to it. Some modems return a response that indicates their make and model. This can help you select the correct modem if the Install New Modem Wizard did not detect it correctly. Notice that many modems return **ERROR** for some AT commands. This means that the modem does not support that particular AT command.

Tip   You can access the Windows 98 Modems Troubleshooter by clicking **Help**.

Windows 98 helps you identify modem problems by recording modem commands and responses in a text file, as described in "Setting Modem Properties" earlier in this chapter. This log file always contains a log of the most recent call, and, if the **Append a Log File** option is checked, it records successive calls in the same log file. The file name consists of the name of the modem as displayed in the Modem applet of the Control Panel with a .txt extension. For example, if the modem is called Modem1, the name of the log file is Modem1.txt.

Correcting Problems with Modem Installation

This section describes situations that can interfere with installation of a modem and how to fix them.

Modem detection is incorrect.

If Windows 98 detects your modem as a Standard Modem Type or incorrectly detects its make and model, use the **Change** button in the Install New Modem Wizard to make a different selection. However, if you manually select an incorrect type, your modem may not work with Windows 98 communications features. If this happens, double-click Modems in Control Panel, remove the modem, and then add it as one of the Standard Modem Types.

Windows 98 will use your modem with its factory default settings if you have configured it as a Standard modem. The modem will make optimal high-speed connections with Windows 98 communications features. However, you will not be able to adjust some of the modem's settings, such as those for speaker volume and cellular protocols.

You can also specify a location to load the drivers from by inserting the disk that came with your modem, and from the Install New Modem Wizard, click the Have disk button. Select your modem from the list.

Your Racal modem does not respond.

If you have a Racal modem, do not use detection in the Install New Modem Wizard. Instead, click **Don't detect my modem**, and then pick one of the **Standard Modem Types**. If you have already run detection and your modem is not responding, turn the modem off and then back on again.

Your Minitel modem (France) does not connect.

Some modems may not be able to connect to French Minitel in HyperTerminal if you use the Windows 98 default settings.

Check your modem manual for a command that will enable your modem to connect in V.23 modulation to Minitel.

▶ **To reset your modem to connect to French Minitel**

1. In Control Panel, double-click Modems, click the name of your modem, and then click **Properties**.

2. Click the **Connection** tab, and then click **Advanced**.

3. In the **Extra Settings** box, type the correct command.

Modem detection may start AutoRun CDs.

On some computers, running modem detection may start the CD AutoRun application.

PC Card Power Management Modem not found or not ready.

When PC Card Power Management is enabled, some PC Card modems require an extra delay before they are ready. If you encounter this with your PC Card modem, the symptom is that it may not work when you try to use it, but it works if you try again right away.

▶ **To increase the delay, use the following procedure.**

Caution Before modifying any registry values, always back up your system. See "Backing Up and Recovering the Registry" in Chapter 31, "Windows 98 Registry." If you use Registry Editor to change values in the registry, you will not be warned if any entry is incorrect. Editing the registry directly by using Registry Editor can cause errors in loading hardware and software, and can prevent users from being able to log on to the computer.

---

1. Click **Start**, click **Run**, and then type **regedit**.

2. Go to the **\HKEY_LOCAL_MACHINE\System\CurrentControlSet \Services\Class\Modem** subkey.

3. Click the key for the modem that you are trying to use.

4. To add a key in the root of the modem, click the **Edit** menu, and then point to **New**.

5. Click **DWORD Value**, and create a DWord named **ConfigDelay**.

6. Set the value equal to "3000" for a three-second delay.

The Install New Modem Wizard detects the modem as a Standard Modem Type.

This does not indicate a problem. Rather, it means that Windows 98 was unable to detect the exact make and model of a modem. Most communications applications work correctly with the standard modem; that is, you can successfully make connections using the modem's factory default settings. However, advanced control of some features, such as speaker volume, error control (for example, V.42 protocol), and compression (for example, V.42bis protocol) will be disabled in the modem's properties.

If you do not want to use the standard modem, you can run the Install New Modem Wizard to select a specific type of modem similar to the modem you are using. If you specify another, similarly named model from the same manufacturer—for example, if you configure the modem as a Practical Peripherals PM9600HC when a Practical Peripherals PM9600FX modem is actually installed—Windows 98 usually treats the models as being identical, and the specified configuration will probably work well.

To determine whether other modem models are compatible with the one you are using, check the modem manual. Many modems are compatible with Hayes, Microcom, Rockwell, or U.S. Robotics models.

You can also use the disk that came with the modem to install the modem drivers by clicking the Have disk button in the Install Wizard.

The Install New Modem Wizard did not detect any new modems.

Take the following steps:

- Make sure the modem does not already appear in the list of installed modems. Windows 98 will not redetect already installed modems.

- Make sure no other programs are running that might be using the modem or its COM port.

- If the modem is external, check the connection between it and your computer, and reset it by turning it off and on again. If the modem's power was turned off, turn it on and run modem detection again.

- If the modem is internal, make sure that its built-in COM port has been configured properly in **Device Manager** in the System option in Control Panel. If it does not appear, run the Add New Hardware Wizard to allow Windows 98 to detect and configure it.

- Make sure the modem's COM port is active and has a correct IRQ by checking its **Resources** configurations in **Device Manager,** in the System option in Control Panel. Make sure the IRQ does not conflict with one in use by another device. For details, see Chapter 24, "Device Management."

- Make sure the modem is not listed under **Other Devices**.

If the Install New Modem Wizard still does not detect a modem, there is probably a problem with the port, the cable, or the modem itself. Try the modem with another computer, if possible.

You cannot install a PC Card modem.

If you are using a PC Card modem for your Dial-Up Networking connection to the Internet and have not yet installed the modem, you may have to enable Windows 98 PC Card socket support before running the Internet Setup Wizard.

▶ **To enable PC Card socket support**

1. Click **Start**, point to **Settings**, and then click **Control Panel**.

2. Double-click the PC Card icon to start the PC Card Wizard, and then follow the instructions on your screen.

If you cannot find the PC Card icon, you may need to install the PC Card drivers.

The Install New Modem Wizard does not detect PC Card modem drivers.

If the Windows 98 PC Card drivers are loaded, Windows 98 should automatically detect and configure a PC Card modem when it is installed. Use the Add New Hardware option in Control Panel to check the configuration of a PC Card socket driver.

If the Windows 98 PC Card drivers are *not* being used, the modem card must be configured as a COM port before the Install New Modem Wizard can detect and configure it as a modem.

▶ **To detect and configure a PC Card modem when Windows 98 PC Card drivers are not used**

1. Configure the modem according to the instructions that came with your original PC Card driver software.

2. Run the Add New Hardware Wizard to detect and configure the card as a COM port.

3. Run the Install New Modem Wizard to detect and configure the card as a modem.

Correcting Problems with Modem Connections

This section describes basic steps for troubleshooting modem connections and explains specific communications errors or problems and how to correct them.

The modem will not dial or will not answer.

If your modem is not set up correctly, communications features might not function properly. The following procedures list steps in verifying the correct operation of your modem and the Windows 98 communications subsystem.

Because some communications programs designed for Windows 3.1 install incompatible driver files, which can cause COM ports and modems to stop working, start by verifying that the correct Windows 98 files are being loaded.

▶ **To verify that the required communications files are present**

1. Verify file sizes and dates of Comm.drv and Serial.vxd in the System directory against the original versions from the Windows 98 floppy disks or compact disc.

2. Confirm that the following lines are present in System.ini:

```
[boot]
comm.drv=comm.drv
[386enh]
device=*vcd
```

3. To revert to the default communications drivers for Windows 98, delete communications port entries in **Device Manager**.

4. Run the Add New Hardware Wizard in Control Panel to detect and install the Windows 98 drivers.

Note   Windows 98 does not load the Serial.vxd driver in System.ini. Rather, Windows 98 loads it on demand by using the registry. Also, there is no corresponding file for the *vcd entry in System.ini. This is an internal file built into Vmm32.vxd.

▶ **To verify the modem configuration by using the Modems option in Control Panel**

1. In Control Panel, double-click Modems.

2. In **General** properties, verify that the manufacturer and model for your modem are correct. If not, you might have changed the modem and failed to reconfigure it. In this case, run the Install New Modem Wizard to detect the modem, and confirm it with the current registry configuration.

3. If your modem does not appear in the list of installed modems, click **Add**, and then select the appropriate modem.

4. If the manufacturer and model are not correct and are not available from the list, try the **Hayes-compatible** option or the **Standard Modem Types** driver option, set to the maximum speed supported by the modem. Click **OK**.

5. Try removing any other modem entries in the list to eliminate any conflicts.

▶ **To verify that the modem is enabled by using the System option in Control Panel**

1. In Control Panel, double-click System.

2. Click the **Device Manager** tab, click a modem from the list, and then click **Properties**.

▶ **To verify that the port is correct by using the Modems option in Control Panel**

1. In **General** Properties, click a modem, and then click **Properties**.

2. In **General** Properties for that modem, verify that the listed port is correct. If it is not, select the correct port. Click **OK**.

3. Select the **Diagnostic** tab, highlight the modem, and then click the **More Info** button. This will verify the system can communicate with the modem.

▶ **To determine if a serial port's I/O address and IRQ settings are properly defined by using the System option in Control Panel**

1. Click the **Device Manager** tab, click **Ports**, and then click a specific port (such as **COM2**).

2. Click **Properties**, and then click the **Resources** tab to display the current resource settings (IRQ and I/O) for that port. To find the correct settings, consult the modem manual.

3. In the **Resources** properties, check the **Conflicting Devices List** to see if the modem is using resources in conflict with other devices.

4. If the modem is in conflict with other devices, click **Change Setting**, and then click a **Basic Configuration** that does not cause resource conflicts.

Note Interrupt (IRQ) conflicts are common when using a modem on COM1 and a serial mouse on COM3. Usually, COM1 and COM3 ports use the same IRQ, meaning that they cannot be used simultaneously on most computers. The COM2 and COM4 ports may also use the same IRQ. If possible, change the COM3 or COM4 port to an IRQ setting that is not in conflict.

Also, some display adapters (especially S3, 8514A and ATI mach8) have an address conflict with COM4 ports. You can work around this by using another COM port or replacing your display adapter.

Click **System** in the **Control Panel**, and then click **Device Manager** to see how **Ports (COM and LPT)** are currently assigned.

▶ **To check the port settings by using the Modems option in Control Panel**

1. Click a modem in the list box, and then click **Properties**.

2. Click the **Connection** tab to check the current port settings, such as bits per second (speed), data bits, stop bits, and parity.

3. Click **Advanced** to check error control and flow control. If you are using Win16-based applications, turn off these advanced features.

4. Verify the UART type.

   Data transmission problems can occur if a speed greater than 9600 is selected on a computer not equipped with a 16550 UART, or when performing other tasks during a file download. If problems or errors occur during transmission, try lowering the speed. Attempting to use speeds greater than 9600 on computers equipped with 8250 or 16450 UARTs will probably result in dropped characters.

▶ **To check the modem speed by using the Modems option in Control Panel**

1. Click a modem in the list box, and click **Properties**.

2. In **General** Properties, check the speed to make sure it is not set too high for either the modem or computer. Lower speeds might work, especially when using an older, slower computer.

3. Click **Only Connect At This Speed** if it is not already selected.

Tip   To optimize communications performance, you can set the speed higher if your computer has an 80486 or a Pentium processor.

▶ **To disable hardware flow control if your modem cable does not support it**

1. In Control Panel, double-click Modems, click a modem in the list box, and then click **Properties**.

2. Click the **Connection** tab, and then click **Advanced**.

3. If a check appears in the **Use Flow Control** check box, click the box to clear it.

▶ **To remove VxDs from other vendors that might be interfering with modem operation**

- Use MSConfig to search for and comment out (type a semicolon as the first character of the line) any related entries in the System.ini file. When commenting out a line in System.ini, it is useful to add a comment line noting this. For more information about MSConfig, see Chapter 27, "General Troubleshooting."

The initialization (dialing) string is improper for the modem.

If the modem will not pick up the line and dial, the problem might be due to an improper initialization string. Typically, the manufacturer's recommended dial command string is loaded from the corresponding modem INF file; however, if your modem driver is not available and you select a compatible modem, the dial command string might not work correctly. Try using the **Standard Modem Types** option, and retest the modem dialing the selected number.

The modem repeatedly drops the connection.

Take the following actions:

- Check for a bad or loose serial cable to the modem. If all connections are tight, test for a faulty cable by replacing it with a working cable, and retest the modem communications.

- Check the connection between the RJ-11 telephone outlet and the modem. Verify that the connection is firmly plugged in and well connected.

- Try using a different telephone line. If you have ruled out other factors, consistent modem errors might be due to problems in the telephone line used for communication.

- Disable call waiting, if it is in use. The call waiting feature can interfere with remote connections and file transfers. If you use this feature regularly, disable it only temporarily, when the modem is in use.

- Check communications with the host computer. The communications problems might be due to the host computer not connecting or repeatedly dropping the line.

- Try using a lower speed in **Modem** Properties, in the Modems option in Control Panel.

The COM ports remain in Device Manager after the modem has been removed.

After you have installed an internal modem and assigned it to a COM port that does not physically exist on your computer, the port appears in **Device Manager**. After removing this adapter, you might also need to manually remove the port in **Device Manager**, as described in Chapter 24, "Device Management."

You are unable to dial international calls.

Windows 98 allows you to set specific modem properties that assist you when making international calls over your modem. You set these properties in Dial-Up Networking, Dialing Properties, and in Modems Properties.

▶ **To check location and calling card settings**

1. In Control Panel, double-click Telephony.

2. In the **My Locations** properties, verify that your calling location and calling card settings are correct.

▶ **To disable dial tone detection if your modem fails to detect a dial tone**

- In Control Panel, double-click Modems, click the **Connection** tab, and then clear the check box next to **Wait for dial tone before dialing**.

▶ **To increase the time between dialing if connections are taking a long time**

- In Control Panel, double-click Modems, click the **Connection** tab, and then increase the number of seconds in the **Cancel the Call If Not Connected Within** option.

To control modem dialing manually, see "Dialing Manually" earlier in this chapter. To display a terminal window to type AT commands before or after dialing, see "Displaying the Terminal Window" earlier in this chapter.

Correcting Problems with Modem Access Through Applications

This section describes troubleshooting problems with applications using a modem.

You cannot send or receive binary files by using HyperTerminal.

Take the following actions:

- Make sure that both computers are using the same file transfer protocol (Xmodem, 1K Xmodem, Ymodem, Ymodem-G, Zmodem, or Kermit).

- If you are using the Ymodem-G file transfer protocol, ensure that your modem supports hardware error control. If it does not, try using Ymodem instead.

- If you are trying to use an alternative protocol (such as Kermit) and you encounter transmission errors, try Xmodem instead. Most communications packages, bulletin boards, and online services support Xmodem.

- If a session is open, HyperTerminal does not recognize when a PC Card modem is inserted.

- When receiving a file, HyperTerminal does not know if the disk is full.

- To use the CTRL keys for **Cut**, **Copy**, and **Paste** in HyperTerminal, you need to use Windows keys instead of Terminal keys. To change this setting, in HyperTerminal, click the **Settings** tab.

- In File Transfer, HyperTerminal does not send files with attributes marked as **System** or **Hidden**.

You cannot dial with Phone Dialer.

Take the following actions:

- In the **Dialing Properties** dialog box, make sure your area code and country code are correct.

- Under the **Tools** menu, select **Connect Using** and verify that the modem you are dialing out with is selected.

- For each access number you want to use for calling out, specify at least the country code, area code, and telephone number.

- Verify basic modem and port configurations.

Win16-based applications cannot access the modem, but MS-DOS-based or Windows 98–based applications can.

Make sure the communications driver for Windows 3.1–based applications in the System.ini file is Comm.drv. Some applications replace this driver for various reasons.

MS-DOS-based applications cannot access the modem (especially a PC Card modem), but all Windows-based applications can.

Take the following actions:

- If possible, adjust the IRQ setting in the MS-DOS-based application according to the application's documentation.

- If the MS-DOS-based application's IRQ settings cannot be adjusted, adjust the IRQ settings for the modem COM port as described earlier in this section.

Errors occur during MS-DOS-based applications communications sessions, especially file transfers.

Increase the **COMxBuffer** setting in the [386Enh] section of System.ini. The default value is 128 bytes.

Correcting Problems with Integrated Services Digital Network

To connect through ISDN, you must specify a telephone number for each channel you request when requesting more than two. For example, if you request three channels, you must specify three telephone numbers (separated by colons, with no spaces). Insert the telephone numbers in the **Phone number** box in the **Basic** tab, as you would when adding, editing, or cloning any other entry—for example:

555-1234:555-1234:555-5678

If you request four channels, specify four telephone numbers—for example:

555-1234:555-1234:555-5678:555-5678

Note If there are more channels specified than telephone numbers given, the extra channels will attempt to use the last number. For this reason you can use one number for a two-channel call, because ISDN lines normally support two channels each. However, some ISDN telephone companies require a unique number for each channel. Check with your ISDN provider.

ISDN fails to connect.

When you dial through ISDN and fail to connect, the error message "**No answer**" appears. This message means one of several things may be wrong:

- The remote access server does not answer because it is turned off or the modem is not connected.
- The line is busy.
- There is a problem with your hardware. Make sure your ISDN cards have been installed and configured correctly.
- A poor line condition, such as too much static, interrupted your connection. Wait a few minutes and try dialing again.
- You did not enable line-type negotiation in the **ISDN Settings** dialog box, and a connection could not be made with the line type you chose in the dialog box.
- Your ISDN switching facility may be busy. Try again later.

Check for any of these potential problems. When you have solved the problem, redial the number.

Your ISDN adapter can support only a single channel.

Not all ISDN adapters can support more than one channel. Read the documentation included with your adapter to identify whether your ISDN adapter can support Multilink PPP.

Your ISDN line is not set up for dual-channel connections.

When you have your ISDN line installed, you may need to specify to your ISDN provider that you need support for two channels on your line. This is not always the default configuration from an ISDN provider.

Your ISDN adapter settings are not correct.

With most ISDN adapters that can support Multilink PPP, you must change the settings to enable dual-channel capabilities. Use the documentation included with your adapter to identify which settings to use for Multilink PPP. Then you can change the settings using the following steps.

1. In Control Panel, double-click Modems.
2. Click the ISDN adapter you are using, and then click **Properties**.
3. Click the **Connection** tab, and then click **Advanced**.
4. In the **Extra Settings** box, type the dual-channel settings for your ISDN adapter. You can find these settings in the documentation for your adapter.

The two ISDN channels are connected to different access boxes.

Internet access numbers sometimes have more than one access box to handle a large number of incoming calls at once. Sometimes, when you connect with two channels, the channels get separated into two different access boxes. This situation is called *straddling*. When straddling occurs, your second channel might not make a connection. And in some cases, your adapter might not make a connection at all. If this happens, you must wait and try your connection again later.

The telephone numbers for your adapter are not configured correctly.

ISDN lines usually come configured with two telephone numbers. When you use dual-channel ISDN, your adapter uses only one telephone number. The second number might be the reason your second line is not connecting. This problem is especially common with the 3Com Impact adapter running firmware version 2.02. If you think the second telephone number might be the problem, try reconfiguring your adapter to use only one of your ISDN numbers.

Drivers are not supported in Windows 98.

ISDN drivers from the ISDN version 1.0 Accelerator Pack are not supported in Windows 98. Contact your ISDN adapter's manufacturer if you require updated drivers. For a list of known vendor drivers that work with ISDN 1.1 included with Windows 98, see **http://www.microsoft.com**.

Additional Resources

For more information about	See this resource
ISDN	**http://www.microsoft.com/windows/getisdn/**

C H A P T E R   2 2

Electronic Mail with Outlook Express

22

This chapter describes the electronic messaging and mail features in Microsoft Windows 98, which are provided through the Outlook Express client. Outlook Express is a mail and newsgroup reader that provides a simple, consistent user interface that is closely integrated with the Web.

In This Chapter

See Also

- For more information about the Internet Explorer browsing software and connecting to the Internet, see Chapter 20, "Internet Access and Tools."

- For more information about Internet security, see Chapter 9, "Security."

Overview of Outlook Express

Outlook Express is a standards-based Internet messaging application integrated with the Microsoft Internet Explorer browsing software. Outlook Express contains services to read and send e-mail messages, browse and post within newsgroups, sort and store messages on the local drive or e-mail server (for Internet Message Access Protocol [IMAP] servers), and create and edit contacts in the Address Book.

Outlook Express Features

Built on Internet standards, including POP3, SMTP, IMAP4, LDAP, S/MIME, MHTML, and NNTP, Outlook Express offers a set of versatile features that are easy to use.

HTML support. This feature allows users to send and receive messages in Hypertext Markup Language (HTML) format. HTML messages can incorporate graphics, hyperlinks, and multimedia files. Also, with its support for the Multipurpose Internet Mail Extensions (MIME) HTML (MHTML) standard, Outlook Express allows users to embed images in their messages so recipients do not need to be connected to the Internet or intranet to view the embedded images.

Multiple accounts. Users of Outlook Express can easily maintain multiple e-mail and news accounts. When checking for new e-mail, users can specify to check all accounts or just a specific one. Likewise, when composing a message, there is a choice of which account to send the message from.

Stationery. This unique feature of Outlook Express allows you to personalize your e-mail and news messages. Outlook Express stationery makes it easy to create messages with personalized background images, graphics, and fonts. In addition, for special occasions like birthdays or anniversaries, Outlook Express includes a variety of stationery designs from Microsoft Greetings Workshop and Hallmark. You can also download additional stationery from the Microsoft Greetings Workshop Web page.

Safe and secure e-mail. Outlook Express uses the Internet Explorer browsing software security zones for HTML messages. The *security zones* feature of Internet Explorer allows you to control whether scripts and active content can be run in messages you receive.

For more information about the Internet Explorer browsing software security zones, see Chapter 20, "Internet Access and Tools." For more information about Outlook Express, see the Outlook Express Web site at **http://www.microsoft.com /ie/ie40/oe/**.

Outlook Express also supports Secure/Multipurpose Internet Mail Extensions (S/MIME), which allows you to digitally sign and encrypt your messages with digital certificates. Using digital signing and encryption, you can verify the source and integrity of any messages you receive, and protect messages from being read by anyone other than the intended recipients.

Outlook Express Architecture

Table 22.1 shows the main files used for Outlook Express.

Table 22.1   Outlook Express main files

File name	Definition
Inetcomm.dll	Parses MIME information and communicates with mail servers.
Msimnimp.dll	Internet Mail and News setting importer/exporter.
Msimnui.dll	Dialog boxes and other e-mail and news functions comprising most of the user interface.
Msoeacct.dll	Account manager DLL file.
Msoemapi.dll	Provides Simple MAPI support in Outlook Express.
Msoert.dll	Run-time utility functions.
Wab32.dll	Windows Address Book (WAB) core functionality.
Wabfind.dll	WAB search user interface.
Wabimp.dll	WAB import back end.
Wldap32.dll	Lightweight Directory Access Protocol (LDAP) support file for WAB and LDAP searches.
Msimn.exe	Outlook Express main program; loads Msimnui.dll.
Wab.exe	Windows Address Book; uses Wab32.dll.
Wabmig.exe	WAB import user interface.

Outlook Express Directories

When Outlook Express downloads e-mail messages and news articles, it stores them on the local hard disk. Unless you specify a different location when you first start Outlook Express, it will use the default. The path for the default location varies slightly depending on whether the User Profiles feature is turned on or not. For more information about user profiles, see Chapter 7, "User Profiles."

Without User Profiles:

Windows\Application Data\Microsoft\Outlook Express

With User Profiles (and on Windows NT):

<windir>\Profiles*username*\Application Data\Microsoft\Outlook Express

Within this directory are folders for mail, and possibly for news and IMAP mail as well. The News folder has a subdirectory for each news account that is in use.

The Mail directory has no subdirectories, only a collection of files used to manage mail accounts. The three types of files in the Mail directory are:

- **MBX files.** These files contain the text of all messages stored on the system.
- **IDX files.** These files function as indexes for MBX files. The IDX and MBX files are always paired.
- **NCH files.** These files are used to retain the folder hierarchy and to cache newsgroup and IMAP information.

Each IDX file has pointers to each message that is stored in its companion MBX file. The MBX files store the content of each message, including the addressing information. For HTML messages, the raw HTML source code is visible in the MBX file.

Inside the News directory, a folder is created for each news account. Two types of files are used to manage newsgroups:

- **NCH files.** These files store a cache of articles downloaded from the server.
- **DAT files.** These files store two types of newsgroup lists. The names of all current newsgroups are stored in Grplist.dat, while the names of all subscribed newsgroups are stored in Sublist.dat.

Outlook Express places data in two registry keys. User accounts and LDAP services are stored in:

HKCU\Software\Microsoft\Internet Account Manager\Accounts

Setting and configuration options are stored in:

HKCU\Software\Microsoft\Outlook Express

Installing and Configuring Outlook Express

Outlook Express is the default e-mail client for Windows 98 and is included with a standard installation. You can configure Outlook Express settings from within the product as described in the following sections.

Administrators can configure certain Outlook Express settings, such as default e-mail and news servers, and default views, using the Internet Explorer Administration Kit (IEAK) Profile Manager, which is supplied on the Microsoft Windows 98 Resource Kit compact disc. For more information about configuring Outlook Express with the IEAK Profile Manager, see "Configuring with the IEAK Profile Manager" later in this chapter.

Uninstalling Outlook Express

Outlook Express is installed with Windows 98. You can uninstall or reinstall it at any time by double-clicking Add/Remove Programs in Control Panel, clicking the **Windows Setup** tab, and then selecting or clearing the **Microsoft Outlook Express** check box.

Creating an E-mail Account

The first time you run Outlook Express, it starts the Internet Connection Wizard if you have not previously configured Windows for Internet use in the Internet Explorer browsing software. The wizard guides you through the process of setting up Outlook Express for e-mail (based on POP3 or IMAP4), news (NNTP), and directory service (LDAP) accounts for use with either an Internet Service Provider (ISP) or a local area network (LAN). For more information about the Internet Connection Wizard, see "Connecting to the Internet with the Internet Connection Wizard" in Chapter 20, "Internet Access and Tools."

Before creating an e-mail account, you need to know several pieces of information:

- The name and type (POP3 or IMAP4) of the incoming e-mail server.
- The name of the outgoing e-mail server. (It is not necessary to specify the type of server as it is always Simple Mail Transfer Protocol [SMTP].)
- Logon and security information, such as whether your ISP uses secure password authentication (SPA) for connecting to your accounts. SPA describes any authentication scheme where the actual password is not sent over the network.
- The type of Internet connection, including dial-up parameters if not using an existing connection.

You can access the Internet Connection Wizard at any time from within Outlook Express to modify existing account information or add new accounts.

▶ **To create an additional e-mail account**

1. On the **Tools** menu, click **Accounts**.
2. Click **Add**, and then click **Mail**. This launches the Internet Connection Wizard.
3. In the **Display name** box, type the name you want others to see when you send a message, and then click **Next**.
4. In the **E-mail address** box, type the e-mail address for your account, and then click **Next**.

5. Under **E-mail Server Names**, select the appropriate incoming e-mail server type, type the names of your incoming and outgoing e-mail servers, and then click **Next**.

6. Depending on your logon type, type your account name and password in the **[POP/IMAP] account name** and **Password** boxes.

   –Or–

   Click **Log on using Secure Password Authentication (SPA)**.

   Note Whether you need your account name and password to log on, or you use SPA, needs to be determined before you can create an e-mail account. Contact your ISP or, if you are connected to the Internet on your corporate network, your network administrator to get this information.

   ---

7. In the **Internet mail account name** box, type a friendly name to identify the e-mail account you are configuring, and then click **Next**.

8. Select the connection type you use to connect to the Internet, and then click **Next**.

9. If you select **Connect using my phone line**, you are prompted to either create a new Dial-Up Networking connection or use an existing one. If Dial-Up Networking has been configured for your ISP, select **Use an existing dial-up connection**, select the name for your Dial-Up Networking connection in the list, and then click **Next**. If you already have an account set up with one ISP and you are setting up another account with a different ISP, you must create a new Dial-Up Networking connection.

10. Click **Finish.**

Configuring Outlook Express

You can configure and customize many aspects of Outlook Express, such as default views and e-mail servers, using the Outlook Express interface. As an administrator, you can configure additional settings, control which ones can be changed by your users, and customize certain views and functions of Outlook Express using the IEAK Profile Manager.

Configuring News, E-mail, and Directory Service Accounts

A news account is an account on a news server that you can use to read and post messages on newsgroups. News servers are maintained by ISPs, companies, groups, and individuals, and can host thousands of newsgroups.

You must have an e-mail account to read and send e-mail messages. This account specifies the e-mail servers, connection types, and server logon information for Outlook Express.

A directory service is an account that Outlook Express uses to look up e-mail addresses when you send messages. By default, Outlook Express is configured to connect to directory services provided by Bigfoot, Yahoo!, InfoSpace, SwitchBoard, VeriSign, and WhoWhere.

Creating News Accounts

Creating a news account for Outlook Express is much like creating an e-mail account. To create a news account, you need the server name and, if required, logon information (an account name and password).

▶ **To create a news account**

1. On the **Tools** menu, click **Accounts**.

2. Click **Add**, and then click **News**.

3. Follow the instructions in the Internet Connection Wizard, supplying your name and e-mail address, the actual and "friendly" names of your news server, and the type of Internet connection you use.

4. Click **Finish** to exit the wizard and create the account.

5. Click **Close** to close the **Internet Accounts** dialog box. At this point you are asked if you want to download the list of newsgroups.

6. Click **Yes** if you wish to see a list of newsgroups available on the news server.

▶ **To subscribe to a newsgroup**

1. In the Folder List (tree view of folders), click the desired news server.

2. Click the Newsgroups icon on the toolbar. A newsgroup window appears, which lists your newsgroup servers and the groups available for subscription.

3. Click the desired newsgroup, and then click the **Subscribe** button. Outlook Express tags the newsgroup with a subscription icon.

   - Once you subscribe to a newsgroup, you can click **Go to** for a list of the subjects or headers in that newsgroup. As you click a subject, its content is downloaded and displayed.

   - To quit downloading, click **OK**. Outlook Express returns you to the list of newsgroups that appeared in step 1.

▶ **To unsubscribe from a newsgroup**

- Follow steps 1 and 2 in the previous procedure, click the **Subscribed** tab, select the desired newsgroup, and then click **Unsubscribe**.

▶ **To view messages in a newsgroup**

- Click on a newsgroup title, and then click **Go to**.

Tip It is helpful to use the **Display newsgroups which contain** box to narrow down the list of newsgroups to just those that interest you. The list narrows down as you type each word.

Adding Directory Services

In addition to the directory services that it provides, Outlook Express allows you to connect to any other LDAP server.

▶ **To add a directory service account**

1. On the **Tools** menu, click **Accounts**.

2. Click **Add,** and then click **Directory Service**.

3. Follow the instructions in the Internet Connection Wizard, supplying the actual and "friendly" names for your Internet directory server, and specifying whether you want Outlook Express to automatically check addresses using this directory server.

4. Click **Finish** to exit the wizard and create the account.

5. Click **Close** to close the **Accounts** dialog box.

▶ **To remove a directory service account**

- Follow step 1 in the previous procedure, click the desired directory service, and then click **Remove**.

Managing Your Newsgroups

Once you have connected to a news server and subscribed to one or more newsgroups, two files are created on your local machine for each news server:

- The Grplist.dat file contains a list of all available newsgroups. If the **Notify me if there are any new newsgroups** option in the **General** tab, under **Options** in the **Tools menu** is selected (this is the default), this list is compared against available newsgroups upon connection, and you are given the opportunity to view the newsgroups that have been added since your last connection.

- The Sublist.dat file contains a list of the newsgroups to which you have subscribed.

After newsgroups have been selected, Outlook Express downloads message header and/or body information to a corresponding NCH file. These files are located in a directory that matches the corresponding server name, and there is an NCH file for each newsgroup you subscribe to.

Note The first time you view a newsgroup, it may take several minutes to download the messages. The next time you go to that newsgroup, it downloads faster because Outlook Express downloads only new messages.

Creating Newsgroup Filters

You can filter messages based on the following criteria:

- The sender's e-mail address.
- The contents of the subject line.
- The size of the message.
- The length of time the message has been on the server.

You can filter all messages from all servers, only messages from a specific server, or messages from a specific newsgroup on a specific server.

▶   **To create a newsgroup filter**

1. In the Folder List, click a news server.
2. On the **Tools** menu, click **Newsgroup Filters**.
3. Click **Add**.
4. In the **Group(s)** box, click the news server or newsgroups you want to filter.
5. Enter the desired criteria for the filter.
6. Click **OK** when you are finished.

▶   **To change the order of a filter**

- Click the filter, and then click **Move Up** or **Move Down**.

Changing Existing E-mail or News Servers

▶   **To change an existing e-mail or news server**

1. On the **Tools** menu, click **Accounts**.
2. On either the **Mail** or **News** tab, click on a server, and then click **Properties**.
3. Change the server information as needed on the appropriate tabs.

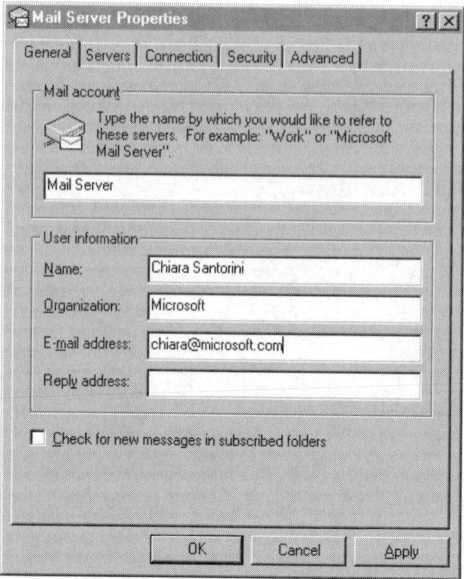

Managing Multiple E-mail Accounts

It is becoming common for users to have more than one e-mail account. With Outlook Express, you can retrieve messages from multiple accounts and send e-mail from any of these accounts when composing a message.

Note When you have more than one account and you only want to retrieve messages from one, click the **Tools** menu, point to **Send and Receive**, and then click the account name.

▶ **To add an e-mail or news account**

1. On the **Tools** menu, click **Accounts**.

2. Click **Add**, and then click **Mail** or **News**. Follow the instructions in the Internet Connection Wizard.

3. Click **Finish** to exit the wizard and create the account.

Configuring for Multiple Users

Outlook Express uses Windows profiles to handle multiple user scenarios. Users can log on to their respective profile and access their own *mail store* (file of incoming messages that have been retrieved). The **Log Off** *user name* option in the Outlook Express **File** menu or the Windows **Start** menu allows you to switch from one user to another. If profiles have not been set up on the user's computer, the **Profiles Setup** dialog box appears, guiding the user through the process of setting up a new profile.

When the new user logs on and runs Outlook Express, they will have access to all of their own e-mail and newsgroup folders, rules, filters, and preferences.

Important When you use the **Log Off** *user name* option in Outlook Express, it is important to realize that you are actually logging off of your Windows 98 session. If you have unsaved work in any other applications you are running, you should save it and then exit those applications correctly before logging off.

For more information about setting up Windows user profiles, see Chapter 7, "User Profiles."

Setting Processing Rules with Inbox Assistant

The Inbox Assistant allows you to configure how messages are processed when they enter the Inbox. You can create rules on a per-account basis to easily sort and filter messages. You can construct rules based on the following criteria:

- Sender
- Addressees on the To: line
- Addressees on the Cc: line
- Subject
- Message size

At the present time, the Inbox Assistant only works with POP accounts. It does not work with IMAP4 accounts because IMAP4 keeps the e-mail on the server and there is no mechanism for applying rules on an e-mail server.

Tip You can specify multiple filters or rules for incoming messages. If a message matches more than one of your criteria, it is sorted according to the first one it matches. You can also create rules after the fact and apply them to existing folders. For example, if your Inbox gets too large, you can create a rule and apply it to your Inbox even though you have already received the messages.

▶ **To create an Inbox rule**

1. On the **Tools** menu, click **Inbox Assistant**.
2. Click **Add**. A **Properties** dialog box for the rule appears.
3. In the **When a message arrives with the following criteria** area, type the criteria you want to apply to the incoming messages.
4. In the **Perform the following action** area, select a check box, and then click the folder, person, or file you want to send the matching incoming messages to.

5. Click **OK** to add the rule.

6. To specify the priorities by which rules are applied to incoming messages, click the **Move Up** or **Move Down** button in the **Inbox Assistant** dialog box.

Important The criteria for rules in Outlook Express are handled differently than for Windows Messaging or Outlook. In the **Subject** criteria, if more than one word is used as the conditional, the words are "and'ed" together, rather than "or'ed."

Storing Messages on E-mail Servers

If you use more than one computer to retrieve your e-mail, it can be useful to leave a copy of your messages on your mail server. When you log on to your account, Outlook Express downloads your messages according to the options you have set.

Note If your account uses an IMAP4 e-mail server, messages will always be stored on the server. If your account uses a POP3 e-mail server, messages will be downloaded and deleted from the server unless you instruct Outlook Express to leave a copy of them there.

▶ **To store messages on an e-mail server**

1. On the **Tools** menu, click **Accounts**.

2. On the **Mail** tab, click the account, and then click **Properties**.

3. Click the **Advanced** tab.

4. Under **Delivery**, select the **Leave a copy of messages on server** check box.

Tip When you configure Outlook Express to leave a copy of messages on the POP3 e-mail server, it is a good idea to select **Remove from server when deleted from 'Deleted Items'**; this prevents the number of messages on the server from growing without bound.

Security Options

Outlook Express takes advantage of the Internet Explorer browsing software security zones. Security zones provide fine-grained control over scripts and active content in HTML messages. Outlook Express also supports the industry security standard called Secure/Multipurpose Internet Mail Extensions (S/MIME),which enables users to encrypt and digitally sign messages.

Configuring Security Zones

The Security zones feature of the Internet Explorer browsing software allows for custom security configurations. The default security zone for Outlook Express messages is the Internet zone. This zone allows scripts and active content to be run in HTML messages. To change that, you can choose the Restricted sites zone, or you can customize the settings for the Internet zone to disallow script execution, ActiveX controls, Java applets, and other Web features.

▶ **To change security zones**

1. On the **Tools** menu, click **Options**.

2. Click the **Security** tab.

3. Select a zone from the **Zone** list.

▶ **To customize security settings**

1. On the **Tools** menu, click **Options**.

2. Click the **Security** tab.

3. Click **Settings**.

4. Select a **High**, **Medium**, or **Low** security level.

    – Or –

    Select **Custom**, and then click **Settings** to modify the desired custom settings.

Note Changing settings for a security zone in Outlook Express also changes them for the Internet Explorer browsing software.

For more information about the Internet Explorer browsing software security zones, see Chapter 20, "Internet Access and Tools," and Chapter 3, "Custom Installations."

Obtaining a Digital Certificate

In order to make full use of the security features included in Outlook Express, you must obtain a digital certificate. *Digital certificates*, which are also called digital IDs, provide a means for proving your identity on the Internet similar to the way a driver's license does for people on a daily basis.

Digital certificates allow you to sign your e-mail in a way that recipients can be sure the message you send is actually from you and has not been tampered with. Also, digital certificates allow others to send you encrypted messages.

You obtain a digital certificate from a certifying authority, an organization that issues and verifies digital certificates. Microsoft's preferred certificate provider is VeriSign, a leading provider of digital authentication products and services.

Before you can send signed e-mail, you must associate your digital certificate with the e-mail account you want to use. The following procedure lists the steps you would follow to obtain a Class I certificate from VeriSign. Other certificate providers may have different policies and procedures for issuing digital certificates.

▶ **To obtain a digital certificate**

1. On the **Tools** menu, click **Options**.

2. Click the **Security** tab.

3. Click **Get Digital ID**.

4. This will launch the Internet Explorer browsing software and open a site where you will be able to enroll for a digital certificate, through either VeriSign or another certificate provider.

5. Once the enrollment is completed and accepted, verification mail is generated and sent to the e-mail name specified on the enrollment form. This e-mail contains instructions for the installation of the digital certificate, a personal identification number (PIN), and a Web location for final certificate validation and installation.

6. The final step in the process is validation and installation of the digital certificate. After navigating to the page specified in the verification e-mail, entering the supplied PIN will display the details of the digital certificate.

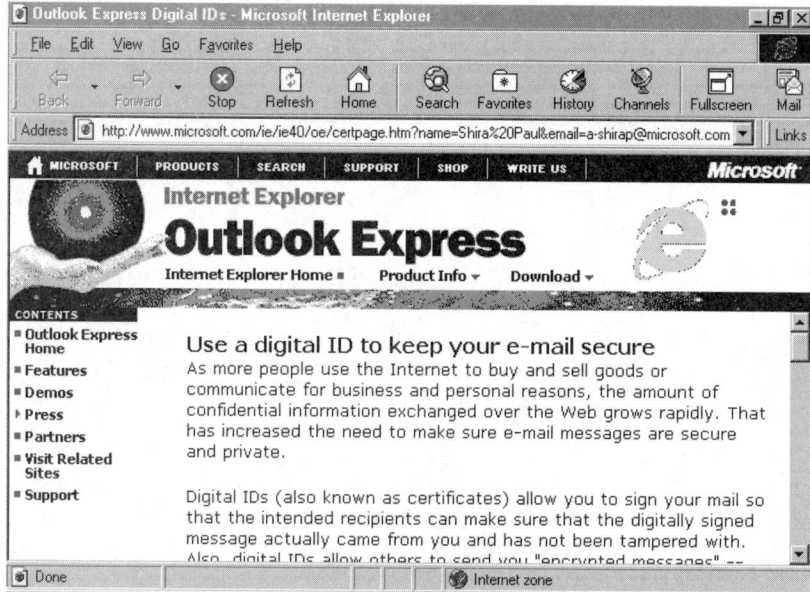

Important The previous process must be completed using the same browser on the same computer as was used during the enrollment process.

Installation is then simply a matter of clicking **Install** at the bottom of this screen. Final installation status will be displayed in a message box with either success text or an error code.

You must associate your digital certificate with an e-mail account before you can send digitally signed e-mail from that account.

▶ **To associate your digital certificate with an e-mail account**

1. On the **Tools** menu, click **Accounts**.

2. Select the account you want to use your digital certificate with, and click **Properties**.

3. Click the **Security** tab.

4. Select **Use a digital ID when sending secure messages from**.

5. Click **Digital ID**, and then select the default certificate for this account.

Sending and Receiving Encrypted Messages

Encrypting a message prevents other people from reading it while it is in transit over a network. To encrypt a message, you need to have a digital certificate, and you need to know the digital certificate of the person you are sending the message to. The digital certificate must be part of the person's entry in the Address Book.

▶ **To send an encrypted message**

- Before you send a message, click the **Tools** menu in the New Message window, and then click **Encrypt**.

  – Or –

  Click the Encrypt message icon on the New Message toolbar.

▶ **To add a digital certificate to your Address Book from a digitally signed message that you receive**

1. Open the digitally signed message.

2. On the **File** menu, click **Properties**.

3. Click the **Security** tab, and then click **Add digital ID to the address book**.

▶ **To add a digital certificate to your Address Book from another source**

1. In the Address Book, create a new entry for the contact, or double-click an existing contact.

2. In the **Properties** dialog box for the contact, click the **Digital IDs** tab, and then click **Import**.

3. Find the digital certificate file, and then click **Open**.

Note When a contact has a digital certificate, a red ribbon is added to their card in the Address Book.

Sending and Receiving Digitally Signed Messages

Once you have obtained a digital certificate and associated it with an e-mail account, you can send digitally signed messages. It is not necessary for your recipients to have digital certificates.

▶ **To send a digitally signed message**

- Before you send a message, click the **Tools** menu in the New Message window, and then click **Digitally Sign**.

  – Or –

  Click the Digitally sign message icon on the New Message toolbar.

For more information about security in Windows 98, see Chapter 9, "Security."

Configuring for Offline Use

You can make more efficient use of your time online by downloading messages or newsgroups and reading them at a later time. You can also download just the message headers to view offline, and mark those you want to read next time you are connected to your ISP. Finally, you can compose messages offline and send them at a later time. After you have composed a message, select **Send Later** from the **File** menu, and Outlook Express will store the message in your Outbox until you click **Send and Receive**. Then it will prompt you to return to the online mode and attempt to establish your Internet connection.

▶ **To configure Outlook Express to work offline**

1. On the **Tools** menu, click **Options**.

2. Click the **Dial Up** tab.

3. Under **When Outlook Express starts**, select **Do not dial a connection**.

4. Select the **Hang up when finished sending, receiving, or downloading** check box, and then click **OK**.

▶ **To set up newsgroups for offline reading**

1. In the Folder List, select a newsgroup.

2. On the **File** menu, click **Properties**.

3. Click the **Download** tab, select the **When downloading this newsgroup, retrieve** check box, and then select the option you want.

4. Repeat steps 1 through 3 for as many newsgroups as you want.

5. Whenever you want to download the messages, click the **Tools** menu, and then click **Download All**.

Configuring with the IEAK Profile Manager

The Internet Explorer Administration Kit (IEAK) Profile Manager, which is supplied on the Microsoft Windows 98 Resource Kit compact disc, is a tool that administrators can use to preconfigure some Outlook Express settings. The Profile Manager is also the only way to turn on the *Outlook Express InfoPane*. This is a window that is displayed at the bottom of the main Outlook Express screen, and can contain a customized welcome message, frequently asked questions (FAQ), and support numbers.

Outlook Express policy settings that can be preset are the ability to send HTML messages, the security zone for HTML messages, and the elements in the default view.

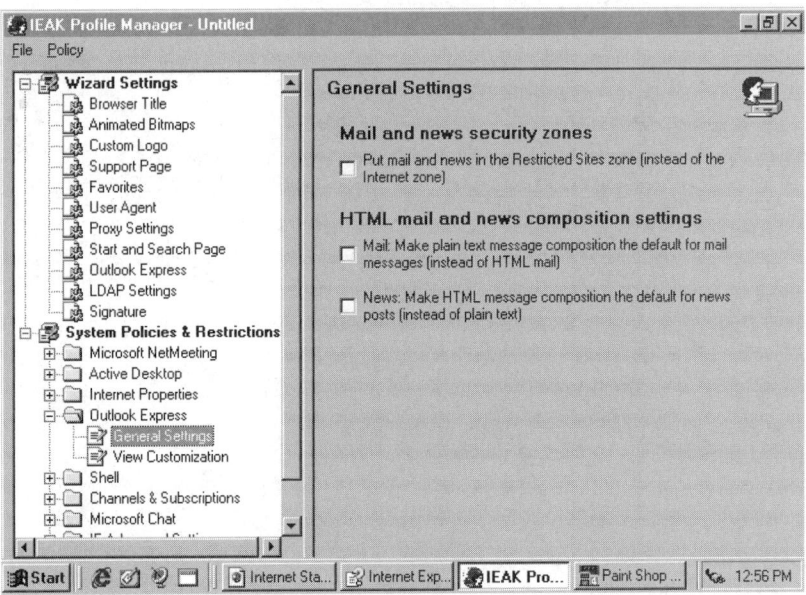

▶ **To install the IEAK Profile Manager**

1. Insert the Windows 98 Resource Kit compact disc into your CD-ROM drive. When the autorun screen appears, click **Browse this CD**.

2. Locate the Netadmin\Profmgr directory.

3. Copy the entire contents of this directory and its subdirectories to the desired location on your hard disk, making sure to maintain the directory structure.

▶ **To start the IEAK Profile Manager**

1. On the **Start** menu, click **Run**.

2. Type the path to the location where you installed Profile Manager, and then type **Profmgr.exe**.

For more information about the IEAK Profile Manager, see the *Microsoft Internet Explorer Resource Kit*, which is available from Microsoft Press or can be downloaded from the Internet Explorer browsing software Web site at **http://www.microsoft.com/ie/corp/**.

Using Outlook Express

By default, the Outlook Express Start page is the first page you see after starting Outlook Express. The Start page allows you to move quickly to the tasks you are most interested in performing.

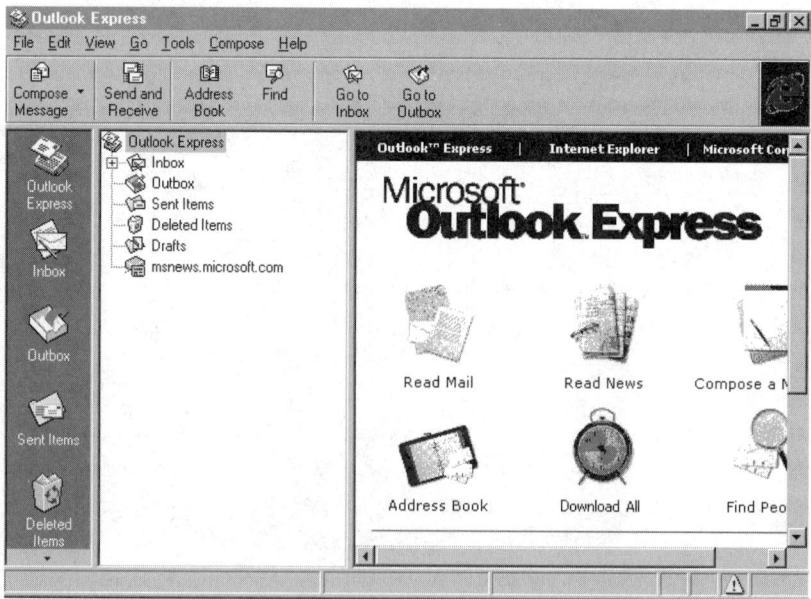

Directly from the Start page, you can do the following:

- Compose or read e-mail and newsgroup messages.
- Access or set up the Address Book.
- Download new e-mail.
- Locate people on the Internet through a corporate Lightweight Directory Access Protocol (LDAP) server or built-in LDAP directories, such as Bigfoot, Yahoo!, InfoSpace, SwitchBoard, VeriSign, and WhoWhere.
- Read helpful online tips.
- See statistics for unread messages and drafts.

Note   You can return to the Start page at any time by clicking the Outlook Express icon in the Folder List.

Using the 3-Pane View

The *3-pane view* of the Outlook Express Inbox allows you to see all of your folders and the contents of a selected folder, preview your messages, and drag-and-drop messages all within one window. The three panes are the Folder List, the contents of the selected folder, and the Preview Pane. The Folder List is a tree view of your folders which provides single-click access to different folders and modules, as well as drag-and-drop support. In the Preview Pane, you can view your messages quickly in a Preview mode without opening them.

This default view in Outlook Express can be customized using the **Layout** option of the **View** menu. You can select which components of the basic view you want to see, customize the contents and placement of your toolbar, and modify or remove the Preview Pane.

Administrators can preset or change their users' default views using the IEAK Profile Manager. They can do this in the **View Customization** object under **Outlook Express**, which is in the **System Policies and Restrictions** category.

Sending and Receiving Messages

To connect to an e-mail server and check for new messages, or to send current messages from your Outbox, click **Send and Receive** on the toolbar. **Send and Receive** uses the account connection data to establish a connection to your e-mail server, validate access to your e-mail account, and then download or upload any new messages. Alternatively, you can use the **Send and Receive** option on the **Tools** menu.

Note If you have enabled *background polling* (check for new messages every *n* minutes), Outlook Express will automatically send and receive messages upon startup.

Creating Messages

To create a new message, click **Compose Message** on the toolbar. Enter the recipient data, or click the Address Card icon on the **To:** line to access recipient data in the Address Book or to create new e-mail contacts.

Using Stationery

You can personalize and enhance your e-mail and news messages by composing them using stationery. Recipients using any e-mail client that supports HTML messages will be able to view your stationery correctly.

Stationery is a combination of background images, graphics, and font styles and colors that appear in a message. When you create stationery, you can designate a default stationery for both e-mail and news messages. This means that it will automatically be used when you compose messages. With the **Apply Stationery** option, you can also apply any stationery to a message even after you have composed it. This is also true for messages that are replies or messages that you are forwarding.

Note If you are applying stationery to a new message, you need to have your sending format set to **HTML**. On the **Tools** menu.click **Options**, and then click the **Send** tab to check your sending format. HTML is the default setting.

▶ **To compose a message using stationery**

1. On the **Compose** menu, point to **New Message using**.

2. Click the stationery design you want to use.

   – Or –

   Click **More Stationery** to view more stationery designs.

▶ **To apply stationery to an existing message**

- On the **Format** menu, point to **Apply Stationery**, and then click the stationery design you want to use.

   – Or –

   Click **More Stationery** to view more stationery designs.

> **Note** When you format a message with the **Apply Stationery** command, you will only get the background image of the stationery.

▶ **To configure default stationery**

1. On the **Tools** menu, click **Stationery**.
2. Click the **Mail** tab to configure the default e-mail stationery.

    – Or –

    Click the **News** tab to configure the default news stationery.
3. Under **When composing new messages use**, select **This stationery**.
4. Click **Select** to choose the default stationery type.

> **Note** The stationery you choose will only be used by default if you have **HTML** selected as your sending format. On the Tools menu click **Options**, and then click the Send tab to check your sending format. HTML is the default setting.

In addition to the stationery designs it provides, Outlook Express includes a mechanism for downloading additional designs from the Microsoft Greetings Workshop Web page.

▶ **To download additional stationery**

1. On the **Tools** menu, click **Stationery**.
2. Click the **Mail** tab to configure the default e-mail stationery.

    – Or –

    Click the **News** tab to configure the default news stationery.
3. Under **When composing new messages use**, select **This stationery**.
4. Click **Select**.
5. Click **Get More** to access the Microsoft Greetings Workshop Web page.
6. Select a stationery design to download. This stationery is now available in Outlook Express.

Creating Stationery

Outlook Express comes with several default stationery templates that can be modified, and you can also create your own custom templates using HTML.

Using a Signature or Business Card (vCard)

You can personalize and enhance your e-mail and news messages by composing them using signatures and electronic business cards (vCards).

If you have a signature or electronic business card, you can add it to your messages as an option. Signatures typically contain contact information and can be as simple as a few lines of text that are appended to the end of your messages. You can also choose to append a file with a text or HTML format as your signature. You can also include a personal business card with your messages as a means of providing your recipients with contact information. Your business card is your personal contact information from the Address Book in vCard format. This standards-based format allows your information to be interpreted by a variety of other software programs. For more information about creating business cards, see "Creating and Importing Business Cards" later in this chapter.

You can add a signature or electronic business card to individual messages, or automatically to all messages.

▶ **To add a signature to your messages automatically**

1. On the **Tools** menu, click **Stationery**.
2. Click **Signature**, and then select the **Add this signature to all outgoing messages** check box.
3. Type the desired signature in the box.

   – Or –

   Select **File** and then enter a file name to use as your signature.

▶ **To add a personal business card to your messages automatically**

1. On the **Tools** menu, click **Stationery**.
2. Click **Signature**.
3. Under **Personal Business Card (vCard)**, select the **Attach card to all outgoing messages** check box.
4. In the **Card** box, click the desired contact name.

   – Or –

   Click **New** and enter the desired contact information.

Checking for New E-mail

You can check for new e-mail as you want to see it, or you can have Outlook Express check for new e-mail automatically.

▶ **To check for new e-mail messages yourself**

- Click **Send and Receive** on the toolbar.

  – Or –

  On the **Tools** menu, click **Send and Receive**.

▶ **To have Outlook Express check for new e-mail messages automatically**

1. On the **Tools** menu, click **Options**.

2. On the **General** tab, select **Check for new messages every** *n* **minute(s)**.

3. Use the arrow buttons to adjust the number of minutes.

Importing Messages from Other E-mail Programs

Outlook Express provides an Import Wizard that allows you to easily import messages from a variety of popular Internet e-mail programs, as well as from Windows Messaging and Microsoft Outlook.

▶ **To import messages from another e-mail program**

1. In the Folder List, click the Inbox icon.

2. On the **File** menu, point to **Import**, and then click **Messages**.

3. Select the e-mail program you want to import messages from, and then click **Next**.

4. Follow the instructions on the screen.

Deleting Newsgroup Messages and Headers

You can save space on your computer by removing message bodies and headers, removing message bodies only, or compacting wasted space. These options only apply to messages downloaded from newsgroups that are locally stored. The messages on the server are not affected.

▶ **To delete messages or headers, or to compact files**

1. On the **Tools** menu, click **Options**.

2. Click the **Advanced** tab.

3. Select the appropriate check box to activate or deactivate it:

   Delete messages (*n*) days after being downloaded.

   n is the number of days. The default value is 5 days.

Don't keep read messages.

This deletes all read messages when you exit Outlook Express.

Compact files when there is (*n*) percent wasted space.

n is the percent of space that is wasted. The default value is 20 percent.

Note For any of the three options in this step, it is important to understand that only the message bodies and not the headers are deleted from local storage. If you want to delete the message headers as well, you must select **Clean Up Now** and choose either **Delete** or **Reset**.

The **Delete** option deletes message headers and bodies according to the parameters you have set. The **Reset** option deletes all message headers and bodies for the newsgroup, effectively allowing you to start from scratch.

---

4. Select **Clean Up Now**.
5. Select the server or newsgroup from which you want to delete the messages.
6. Click the appropriate button.
7. Click **Close**.

HTML Support

Outlook Express fully supports Hypertext Markup Language (HTML). Together with the Internet Explorer browsing software, which supports Multipurpose Internet Mail Extensions (MIME) HTML, it provides a new way to share Web content through e-mail. You can send full Web pages or links from the Internet or intranet to another user, even when you and the other user are offline.

Sending Web Pages or Links

You can send a Web page—or a link to that page—to another user while you are browsing it with Internet Explorer. If you know the address, you can also send it while you are composing a message in Outlook Express. If you have selected **Plain Text** as your default e-mail message format, you must first change it to **Rich Text (HTML)** from the **Format** menu in a New Message window.

Administrators can change the default e-mail message format to **Plain Text** using the IEAK Profile Manager.

Note In order to have the Internet Explorer browsing software use Outlook Express to send Web pages or links, it must be the default e-mail program for the Internet Explorer browsing software. You can verify that it is by clicking **Internet Options** on the **View** menu of the Internet Explorer browsing software and checking the mail program on the **Programs** tab, or by clicking the Internet icon in Control Panel and checking the mail program on the **Programs** tab.

▶ **To send a Web page to another user**

1. Open the page in the Internet Explorer browsing window.

2. Click **Mail** on the toolbar, and then click **Send Page**. Outlook Express drops the entire page into the e-mail message.

   – Or –

   On the **File** menu, point to **Send**, and then click **Page By Email**.

3. Fill in an e-mail address, or click the Address Book icon on the **To:** line. If you cannot find the address you need, click **Find** in the **Select Recipients** dialog box.

4. When you have located the correct person, click **OK**, and then click **Send**.

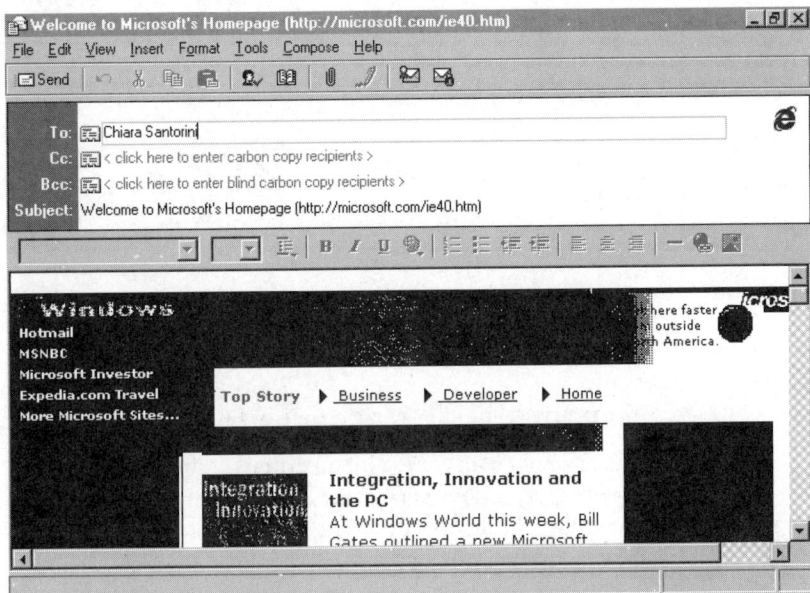

If you decide that you would rather send a link to a Web page than send an entire Web page, you can insert the link into a message directly from the Web page, or you can type the link into the message and Outlook Express will automatically turn it into a hyperlink. Alternatively, you can drag and drop a shortcut into the message.

▶ **To send a link to another user**

1. Open the page in the Internet Explorer browsing window.

2. Click **Mail** on the toolbar, and then click **Send a Link**. Outlook Express drops the link into the e-mail message.

   – Or –

   On the **File** menu, point to **Send**, and then click **Link By Email**.

3. Fill in an e-mail address, or click the Address Book icon on the **To:** line. If you cannot find the address you need, click **Find** in the **Select Recipients** dialog box.

4. When you have located the correct person, click **OK**, and then click **Send**.

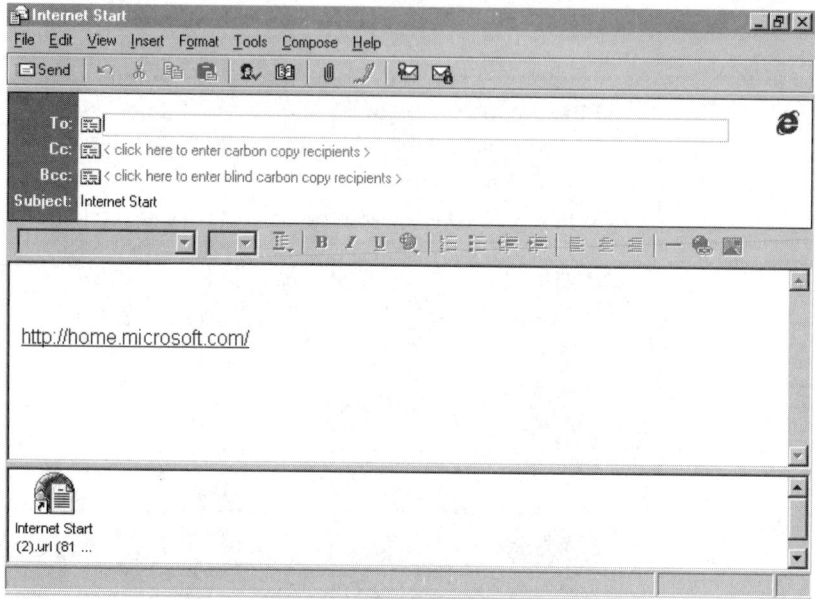

Sending HTML Messages to People Without HTML Clients

Because not everyone with an e-mail address has a MIME HTML messaging client, Outlook Express makes sure that the appropriate message comes across regardless of the technology on the recipient's side. Here are some examples of how an e-mail message can be displayed to a recipient:

- If the recipient supports MIME and HTML mail, the full Web page in native format is displayed inside the e-mail message.

- If the recipient supports MIME, the message displays the text-based information first and may include the HTML as an attachment, which the recipient can view in their default browser.

- If the recipient does not support MIME, the message displays the text-based information first and then, after a separator, the raw HTML follows.

If you want to make sure that you send e-mail in a format your recipients can view, you can use the Smart Reply feature of Outlook Express (which is on by default). This option automatically responds to a message in the same format it was sent.

▶ **To automatically reply to messages in a like format**

1. On the **Tools** menu, click **Options**.

2. On the **Send** tab, select the **Reply to messages using the format in which they were sent** check box.

You can easily keep track of your contacts' HTML capabilities in the Address Book. That way, when you compose a message, you can format it accordingly. For more information about using the Address Book, see "Using the Address Book" later in this chapter.

LDAP Support

Finding e-mail addresses is easy in Outlook Express because it fully supports the Internet standard Lightweight Directory Access Protocol (LDAP) directory services, which provide access to virtual Internet white pages. You can locate people on corporate LDAP servers, and you can also use the built-in support for LDAP directories like Bigfoot, Yahoo!, InfoSpace, SwitchBoard, VeriSign, or WhoWhere to locate an individual on the Internet.

Using the new LDAP-enabled Address Book, you can search popular Internet white page directories using an individual's first name, last name, or e-mail name. You type the name on the **To:** line in any message, and Outlook Express automatically searches the selected white page directories to fill in the e-mail name. Because this may slow down the performance of Outlook Express, it is not the default behavior.

▶ **To use an Internet directory service to check e-mail addresses**

1. On the **Tools** menu, click **Accounts**.

2. On the **Directory Service** tab, select the desired account and then click **Properties**.

3. On the **General** tab, select **Check names against this server when sending mail**.

Finding People on the Internet

The **Find People** option on the **Edit** menu in Outlook Express performs the same task as opening the **Start** menu, pointing to **Find**, and selecting **People**. It launches Wabfind.dll and allows you to search the local Address Book or any of the configured Internet Directory Services.

Creating a Search Hierarchy

Outlook Express supports partial name checking against various LDAP servers. The search engine looks for partial names against whatever hierarchy you create. For example, by typing in a partial name, you can tell Outlook Express to search your local Address Book first, then your corporate LDAP servers, and finally, the Internet. Once the information is found, Outlook Express can store the address for later use.

The LDAP search engine implements a form of fuzzy logic to help you find others on the Internet. For example, if you entered *Ann Devon*, Outlook Express would look for successful matches according to the following:

- Exact match for Ann Devon.
- First name exact match for Ann, last name match beginning with Devon.
- First name beginning with Ann, last name exact match for Devon.
- First name beginning with Ann, last name beginning with Devon.
- The whole e-mail address beginning with Ann Devon.

▶ **To set up a directory service to check for e-mail addresses**

1. On the **Tools** menu, click **Accounts**.
2. Click the **Directory Service** tab.
3. Select a directory service, and then click **Properties**.
4. On the **General** tab, make sure the check box **Check names against this server when sending mail** is selected.

Using the Address Book

Windows 98 provides an Address Book for storing contact information such as e-mail addresses and whether a contact can receive HTML messages. Once you create an entry in the Address Book for a contact, you do not need to remember their e-mail address when you send them e-mail. By simply clicking the Address Book icon on the Outlook Express toolbar or in the **To:**, **Cc:**, or **Bcc:** line of a message, you can access the Address Book and easily address a message to any of your contacts. The Address Book is also accessible from the Internet Explorer browsing software and from the **Start** menu.

In Outlook Express, even when you do not explicitly open the Address Book, you benefit from the convenience of its *AutoComplete* feature. When you begin typing a contact name on the **To:**, **Cc:**, or **Bcc:** line of a message, Outlook Express tries to complete it for you using the names in the Address Book.

Understanding the Address Book

The Address Book, provided by the Wab.exe program, locally stores contact information. When you invoke the Address Book, Wab.exe creates and searches the file named *Username*.wab, which is found in the Application Data directory. The full path varies depending on whether the User Profiles feature is enabled:

%windir%\Application Data\Microsoft\Address Book*username*.wab (without User Profiles)

%windir%\Profiles*user name*\Application Data\Microsoft\Address Book*username*.wab (with User Profiles)

Adding Names from E-mail Messages

When you receive e-mail, you can easily add the sender's name and e-mail address to your Address Book. This can be done by opening the message, right-clicking the person's name, and then clicking **Add to Address Book**. You can also set up Outlook Express to automatically add contact information to your Address Book whenever you reply to e-mail.

▶   **To automatically add the names of people you reply to**

1. On the **Tools** menu, click **Options**.
2. Click the **General** tab, and then select the **Automatically put people I reply to in my Address Book** check box.

Of course, you can always add contact information to your Address Book manually as well.

Importing an Address Book

You can import Address Book contacts from a variety of Internet e-mail programs, such as Netscape Communicator, as well as from Windows Messaging Personal Address Book and any text (CSV) file. For example, in Microsoft Outlook, you can export your Address Book to text (CSV) file format, and then import it into Outlook Express using the **Import** option.

▶   **To import an Address Book**

1. On the **File** menu, point to **Import,** and then click **Address Book**.
2. Click the Address Book or file that you want to import, and then click **Import**. If you select Microsoft Exchange or Microsoft Internet Mail, you are prompted for a user profile. For other formats, Outlook Express attempts to auto-detect the existing Address Book, or prompts you for a path to the file's location.

> **Note** If you do not see listed the program that you want to import address book information from, you can export it to a text (CSV) file using your current mail program, and then import it to Outlook Express using the **Text File** option.

Creating and Importing Business Cards

The easiest way to exchange contact information with people over the Internet is by attaching an electronic business card to e-mail messages. A business card is your personal contact information from the Address Book in vCard format. The vCard format can be used with a wide variety of digital devices and operating systems.

You must have your own contact information in the Address Book before you can create a business card.

▶ **To create a business card**

1. On the **Tools** menu, click **Address Book**.

   – Or –

   Click the Address Book icon on the toolbar.

2. Select your name from the list.

3. On the **File** menu, point to **Export**, and then click **Business Card (vCard)**.

4. Select a location to store the VCF file, and then click **Save**.

▶ **To import a business card**

1. On the **Tools** menu, click **Address Book**.

   – Or –

   Click the Address Book icon on the toolbar.

2. On the **File** menu, point to **Import**, and then click **Business Card (vCard)**.

3. Point to the location of the VCF file, and then click **Open**.

4. Modify or add to the contact information in the **Properties** dialog box.

Using Windows Messaging

If you have installed Windows 98 on a computer that had any Windows Messaging components on it, they will be left intact. These components, which include Microsoft Exchange, Internet Mail, and Microsoft Fax, will continue to function as they did with your old operating system, and your e-mail icon will remain on the desktop unless you remove it.

The first time you click the Outlook Express icon, Windows detects the presence of any other e-mail programs, and asks if you would like to make Outlook Express your default e-mail client.

Additional Functionality of Windows Messaging

The core of the Windows Messaging subsystem is the messaging application programming interface (MAPI), an industry standard that enables applications to interact with many different messaging systems using a single interface. MAPI is a set of API functions and object linking and embedding (OLE) interfaces that allows messaging clients, such as Microsoft Exchange, to interact with various message service providers, such as Microsoft Mail and Microsoft Fax.

The Exchange and Outlook e-mail clients also provide features like scheduling, groupware applications, and custom application development. If you need this additional functionality, you may want to keep one of these e-mail clients on your system, or if you do not currently have them, you can install them.

To download the Microsoft Exchange mail client, go to the Windows Update Web site at **http://www.microsoft.com/windows95/info/exupd.htm**.

Troubleshooting Outlook Express

For help identifying and solving some common problems, Outlook Express provides an excellent troubleshooting resource called the Outlook Express Troubleshooter. You can access it by opening the Troubleshooting topic in online Help.

Setting Logging Options

Outlook Express provides three different logging options to aid in troubleshooting. When an option is selected, a LOG file that contains all activity within the specified process is created. The following LOG files are created, depending on the options that are selected.

- Pop3.log
- Smtp.log
- Inetnews.log
- Imap.log

▶ **To configure logging options**

1. On the **Tools** menu, click **Options**.

2. Click the **Advanced** tab, and then select the desired logging options.

Note The LOG files are created in different directories depending on whether Internet Mail and News existed previously on your computer. If it did, the locations are:

C:\Program Files\Outlook Express\<*username*>\Mail for mail protocol logs, and \News for news logs

If Internet Mail and News were not previously installed, the file locations will vary slightly depending upon whether the user profiles feature is turned on or not:

C:\Windows\Application Data\Microsoft\Outlook Express\Mail for mail protocol logs, \News for news logs, and \IMAP for IMAP protocol logs (without user profiles)

C:\Windows\Profiles\<*username*>\Application Data\Microsoft\Outlook Express\Mail for mail protocol logs, \News for news logs, and \IMAP for IMAP protocol logs (with user profiles)

Verifying Internet Connection Wizard Files

The Icwconn1.exe file should be located in the C:\Program Files\Internet Explorer\Connection Wizard folder, and should be version 4.71.465.5.

The following files should be located in the Windows\System folder:

File	Version
Inetcfg.dll	4.71.465.6
Icfg95.dll	4.71.465.5
Inet16.dll	4.71.465.5

If any of these files are missing, reinstall Outlook Express. If any of these files are the wrong version, rename the file, and then reinstall Outlook Express.

Additional Resources

For more information about	See this resource
IEAK Profile Manager	*Microsoft Internet Explorer Resource Kit*

P A R T 5

System Management

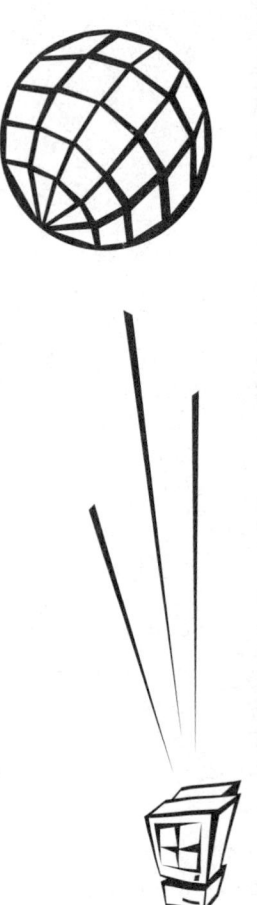

CHAPTER 23

System and Remote Administration Tools

This chapter describes the Microsoft Windows 98 management tools that allow you to configure and manage your own computer, manage remote computers, and monitor network statistics. This chapter also includes information about other system management products and technologies.

In This Chapter

See Also

- For more information about system policies, see Chapter 8, "System Policies."
- For more information about security issues, see Chapter 9, "Security."
- For more information about device management, see Chapter 24, "Device Management."
- For more information about System Monitor, see Chapter 26, "Performance Tuning."

Overview of System and Remote Administration Tools

Businesses need the ease-of-use, productivity, and cost benefits of personal computers, but they also want the control of mainframe computing. In today's distributed environments, the distinction between systems and network management disappears, and management issues are more difficult to resolve.

The system management tools and agents provided with Windows 98 support system management in three areas:

- Operating system software, including drivers, system services, and user interface components. These require system software distribution, system and user configuration management, security, and data backup.

- Hardware, including the computer's motherboard, add-in cards, hard disk and CD-ROM drives, monitors, tape drives, pointing devices, and keyboards.

- Application software that must be licensed and installed.

Windows 98 also provides registry-based support for remote management of configuration settings for hardware and software settings—either on individual computers or on multiple computers (through system policies) on the network.

The remote management tools provided with Windows 98 make it easier for you to identify and solve problems encountered by users without dispatching support personnel to make changes at the users' work sites. The tools include System Policy Editor, Registry Editor, System Monitor, and Net Watcher.

You can enable remote administration capabilities on a computer as part of the process for installing Windows 98 from custom scripts. For more information, see Appendix D, "Msbatch.inf Parameters for Setup Scripts."

You can manage file systems remotely by browsing specific computers in Network Neighborhood, as described in "Using Network Neighborhood" later in this chapter.

Windows 98 also provides an agent for Microsoft Network Monitor and a Simple Network Management Protocol (SNMP) agent for administration with SNMP system management products, as described in "Using Microsoft Network Monitor" and "Using an SNMP Agent" later in this chapter.

Figure 23.1 provides an overview of system and remote administration.

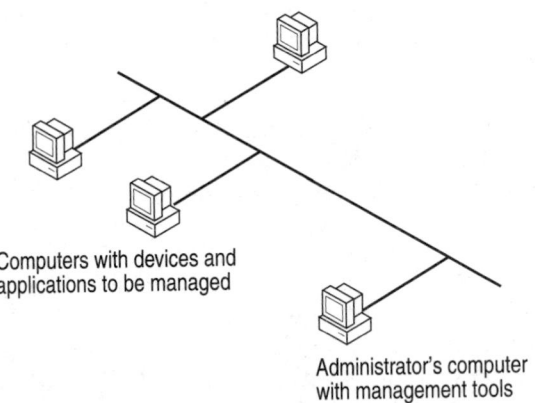

Computers with devices and
applications to be managed

Administrator's computer
with management tools

Figure 23.1   System and remote administration overview

The following sections summarize features in Windows 98 that support system
and remote management on corporate networks.

Security for system logon and resource access. Administrators can take
advantage of centralized user accounts on Windows NT or Novell NetWare
networks to restrict network logon and access to shared resources on computers
running Windows 98. Windows 98 provides password caching to make it easier
for users to manage connections to password-protected resources yet also allows
network administrators to restrict users' capabilities. Consequently, administrators
can enforce strict security policies. For information, see Chapter 9, "Security."

User profiles. When user profiles are enabled, individual users and desktop
configurations are available wherever they log on to the network. This solution
permits multiple users to share one computer and "roving" users to log on to other
networked computers while maintaining their personal settings. Administrators
can also enforce a mandatory user profile, which can be useful for managing a
common desktop for novice users. For information, see Chapter 7, "User
Profiles."

System policies. Administrators can use system policies to specify required
system settings and to restrict network access, security privileges, and system
settings from a convenient central source. Policies can be specified for groups,
for specific users, and for multiple computers, providing administrators significant
control over users' ability to configure computer and desktop settings. For
information, see Chapter 8, "System Policies."

Remote administration. Built-in capabilities for remote administration assist administrators in managing networking computers from a central location, reducing the burden of supporting system configuration and troubleshooting on the corporate network.

Backup capabilities. Windows 98 includes an improved version of the Microsoft Backup utility. The improved version supports a wider range of backup devices than the Windows 95 backup utility. For information about Microsoft Backup, see Chapter 27, "General Troubleshooting."

Windows 98 registry. In Windows 98, the operating system collects information about the hardware, system configuration settings, and applications and stores it in the registry. The Windows 98 registry is a structured database that consolidates configuration and status information for hardware and software components. As a result, this information is available to system management applications, ensuring flexible system management capabilities. For information, see Chapter 31, "Windows 98 Registry."

Configuration Tools in Windows 98

Microsoft Windows 98 includes several tools and built-in features that make it easy to configure hardware and software on a computer.

Automatic hardware detection. Hardware designed to work with Windows 98 is virtually self-configuring. When you run Windows 98 Setup, an automatic hardware detection routine determines the hardware components that are installed. Whether your system includes Plug and Play–compliant or legacy components, Windows 98 can automatically detect and configure them.

Configuration wizards. Windows 98 includes wizards for installing new hardware; adding modems, infrared devices, scanners, digital cameras, and printers; installing applications; and tuning up your system. These tools lead you through the steps for configuring the new component on a computer.

Point and Print. When you copy a printer icon from the server's window to your Printers window or desktop, Windows 98 automatically installs the correct printer driver and configures the network connection to a network printer.

Control Panel options for system configuration. Control Panel includes several tools for configuring various parts of your system. Table 23.1 describes some of these tools.

Note The tools in Control Panel vary depending on the setup of your computer.

Table 23.1   Control Panel tools

Icon	Description of tool
	Accessibility Options. Use this tool to adjust keyboard, sound, display, mouse, and general options to make Windows 98 easier to use for individuals with disabilities. For information, see Appendix H, "Accessibility."
	Add New Hardware. Use this wizard to configure newly installed hardware through detection or by selecting the corresponding driver from a list. For information, see Chapter 24, "Device Management."
	Add/Remove Programs. Use this wizard to install a program from a setup disk. You can also remove any application installed with this tool, add components from the Windows 98 compact disc, or create a new startup disk. For information, see Chapter 25, "Application Support."
	Date/Time. Use this tool to change date, time, and time zone settings for your computer. For information, see Help.
	Display. Use this tool to change background and screen saver choices. Modify settings for on-screen fonts, colors, color palette, active desktop, and so on. For information on configuring the display, see Chapter 24, "Device Management" and Chapter 30, "Hardware Management."
	Fonts. Use this tool to view installed fonts or install new fonts. For information, see Chapter 11, "Printing, Imaging, and Fonts."
	Game Controllers. Use this tool to add, remove, or change settings for game controllers. For information about game controllers, see Chapter 24, "Device Management," and Chapter 30, "Hardware Management."
	Infrared. Use this tool to configure and monitor infrared communication. (This is available to users who have infrared devices on their computers.) For information about Infrared devices, see Chapter 19, "Remote Networking and Mobile Computing."
 Internet	**Internet**. Use this tool to change your Internet settings. For information about the Internet, see Chapter 20, "Internet Access and Tools."
	Keyboard. Use this tool to change options for the style of keyboard you use and for the rate at which the characters you type are displayed. (The appearance of the icon might be different, depending on the type of keyboard used.) For information, see Help.
	Modems. Use this wizard to add a new modem. You can also use this tool to configure or diagnose installed modems. For information, see Chapter 21, "Modems and Communications Tools."
	Mouse. Use this tool to change mouse or pointer options. (The appearance of the icon might be different, depending on the type of mouse used.) For information, see Chapter 24, "Device Management."
	Multimedia. Use this tool to change options for audio playback and recording, MIDI output and schemes, and compact disc playback volume. Use the **Advanced** properties to install or configure multimedia hardware, drivers, and codecs. For information, see Chapter 12, "Multimedia."

Table 23.1   Control Panel tools (*continued*)

Icon	Description of tool
	Network. Use this tool to configure network hardware and software. For information about networks, see Chapter 14, "Introduction to Networking Configuration."
	Passwords. Use this tool to change passwords and set security options. For information about passwords, see Chapter 9, "Security."
	Power Management. Use this tool to change power management settings. For information about power management, see Chapter 24, "Device Management."
	Printers. Use this tool to configure existing printers or add a new printer. For information, see Chapter 11, "Printing, Imaging, and Fonts."
	Regional Settings. Use this tool to change how numbers, currencies, dates, and times are displayed on your computer. For information, see Help.
	Scanners and Cameras. Use this tool to install, remove, or change properties for a scanner or a digital camera. (This is available to users who have scanners or digital cameras on their computers.) For information, see Help.
	Sounds. Use this tool to create or modify sound schemes. (This is available to users who have sound cards on their computers.) For information, see Help.
	System. Use this tool to view general information about your computer. Use Device Manager to list or configure hardware properties. You can also list, copy, or rename hardware profiles and view performance status settings. For information, see Chapter 24, "Device Management."
	Telephony. Use this tool to configure telephony drivers and dialing properties. For information about telephony, see Chapter 21, "Modems and Communications Tools."
	Users. Use this tool to set up and manage multiple users on your computer. For information, see Chapter 7, "User Profiles."

Setting Up Remote Administration

This section provides details about how to set up remote administration after Windows 98 has been installed.

To take advantage of the remote administration capabilities of Windows 98, you should do the following:

- Enable remote administration and user-level security on every computer that you will administer remotely. If you want to administer a remote computer using System Policy Editor, Registry Editor, or System Monitor, the Microsoft Remote Registry service must be installed on both your computer and the remote computer. Although the remote computer requires user-level security, it does not also require file and printer sharing services.

Optionally, install the SNMP agent or the Microsoft Network Monitor agent if required for your administrative tools. For information, see "Monitoring Your Network" later in this chapter.

- Run a common network protocol, such as the Microsoft version of the Transmission Control Protocol/Internet Protocol (TCP/IP), Internetwork Packet Exchange/Sequenced Packet Exchange (IPX/SPX)–compatible protocol, or NetBIOS Extended User Interface (NetBEUI).

- Train help desk personnel on System Monitor if they will use it. They should understand what each measurement provided by System Monitor means and what course of action is required in response to these measurements. For information, see Chapter 26, "Performance Tuning."

- Train help desk personnel on what problems can be identified and repaired by using System Policy Editor or Registry Editor.

Table 23.2 describes what you need to set up on the remote computer to complete an administrative task.

Table 23.2   Remote computer setup requirements

Remote administration task	Requirement on the remote computer
Browse and manage shared resources on a remote computer by using Net Watcher.	Enable user-level security, remote administration, and file and printer sharing services; grant remote administration privileges to the network administrator.
Manage the file system of a remote computer by using Net Watcher.	Enable user-level security and remote administration; grant remote administration privilege to the network administrator.
Edit a remote computer's registry by using Registry Editor or System Policy Editor.	Enable user-level security and remote administration, and install Microsoft Remote Registry service.
Monitor performance of a remote computer by using System Monitor.	Enable user-level security and remote administration, and install Microsoft Remote Registry service.

Granting remote administration privilege gives a person full access to all shared resources on the system (including the ability to add and remove other remote administrators). Granting or removing access to remote administration capabilities for a user does not take effect until the next time the user connects to the computer running Windows 98.

When remote administration is enabled on a computer, two special shared directories are created:

- Admin$ gives administrators access to the file system on the remote computer.

- Ipc$ provides an interprocess communication (IPC) channel between the two computers.

Important If you enable user-level security by using the Network option in Control Panel or in a setup script, remote administration is enabled automatically for the Domain Administrator group on a Windows NT domain. On a Novell NetWare network, the Supervisor account (for version 3.*x*) or the Admin account (for version 4.0) is enabled automatically. For more information, see Chapter 9, "Security."

If you want to enable user-level security without automatically enabling remote administration, you can use system policies to enable the **User-level access control** option. In this case, you must enable remote administration manually by using the Passwords option in Control Panel on each individual computer.

▶ **To enable remote administration manually**

1. In Control Panel, double-click Passwords, and then click the **Remote Administration** tab.

2. Make sure the **Enable remote administration of this server** check box is selected.

3. If the computer is configured for share-level access control and you have configured file and printer sharing, the following dialog box appears. Specify the password for remote administration.

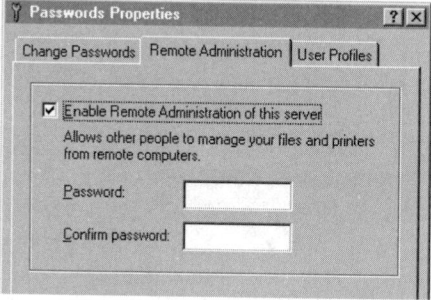

If the computer is configured for user-level access control, the following dialog box appears. Click **Add**, and add the appropriate administrators. Then click **OK**.

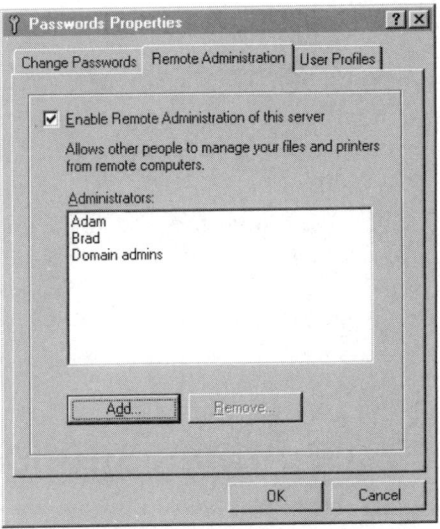

▶ **To install the Microsoft Remote Registry service**

1. In Control Panel, double-click Network, and then click **Add**.

2. In the **Select Network Component Type** dialog box, double-click **Service**.

3. In the **Select Network Service** dialog box, click **Have Disk**.

4. In the **Install From Disk** dialog box, type the path to the Tools\Reskit\
   Netadmin\Remotereg directory on the Windows 98 compact disc, and then
   click **OK**.

5. In the **Install From Disk** dialog box, click **OK**.

6. In the **Select Network Service** dialog box, click **Microsoft Remote Registry**,
   and then click **OK**.

7. If you are prompted to specify the location of additional files, specify the
   path to the Windows 98 source files on a shared network directory or on
   the Windows 98 compact disc.

For more information about installing the Microsoft Remote Registry service
and enabling remote administration by using setup scripts, see Appendix D,
"Msbatch.inf Parameters for Setup Scripts."

Technical Notes on the Microsoft Remote Registry Service

- You must also install the Remote Registry service on the administrator's computer to ensure that the Winreg.dll file is in the Windows System directory on that computer.

- Make sure that both the administrator's and the user's computers have at least one protocol in common. That can be Microsoft NetBEUI, Microsoft TCP/IP, or the IPX/SPX-compatible protocol (with or without the network basic input/output system [NetBIOS]).

Using System and Remote Administration Tools

The tools and agents that network administrators can use for system management are available from various installation sources. Tools come with Windows 98 that help you manage your system, and several other system and remote management tools are available from Microsoft. This section describes how to access the management tools in Windows 98 and where to find tools available from other sources.

Setup installs Registry Editor, the utility used to modify the registry, and Registry Checker, a utility that backs up and, if necessary, fixes the registry. The following tools are also installed during Windows 98 Setup: Disk Defragmenter, DriveSpace 3, and ScanDisk, as described in Chapter 10, "Disks and File Systems."

Microsoft Backup can be installed optionally from the Windows 98 installation compact disc. For more information about Microsoft Backup, see Chapter 27, "General Troubleshooting."

Some agents and tools are provided on the Windows 98 compact disc. Users can install these agents and tools directly from the compact disc, or the administrator can copy the software to the shared network directory that contains the Windows 98 source files. This software can be installed from custom setup scripts during Windows 98 installation or by using Control Panel after Windows 98 has been installed.

The following tools are available only in the Tools\Reskit\Netadmin directory on the Windows 98 compact disc. You can run these tools directly from the compact disc or install them locally by using the Add/Remove Programs option in Control Panel:

- Password List Editor (in the Pwledit subdirectory), as described in Chapter 9, "Security."

- System Policy Editor (in the Poledit subdirectory), as described in Chapter 8, "System Policies."

The following agents and services are available only in the Tools\Reskit \Netadmin directory on the Windows 98 compact disc. You can install them on a local computer by using the Network option in Control Panel.

For remote administration:

- Microsoft Remote Registry service (in the Remotreg subdirectory)
- Microsoft SNMP agent (in the Snmp subdirectory)
- Microsoft Network Monitor agent (in the Netmon subdirectory)

Note Both System Policy Editor and Registry Editor allow you to gain access to a remote computer's registry. However, System Policy Editor allows you to gain access to only a subset of keys, whereas Registry Editor allows you to gain access to the entire registry. This means that to use Registry Editor, users may require significantly more training. Also, remember that some changes made to the registry on a remote computer require the user to shut down and restart the computer, whereas other changes take effect immediately. As a rule, if you must restart the computer when changing a setting by using Control Panel or other tools, you must restart it when directly changing that setting in the registry.

This section discusses how to control remote registries; view a remote computer; and use Net Watcher, Network Neighborhood, and various agents. It also describes other system management tools and technologies. In addition to the tools discussed in this section, you can use other system management tools provided by Microsoft or by other vendors to remotely administer computers running Windows 98. Such tools include the following:

- Microsoft Systems Management Server
- Microsoft Windows NT Server
- Novell NetWare Management System (NMS)
- Hewlett-Packard Open View for Windows
- Intel LANDesk
- IBM LAN NetView
- Sun NetManager

Controlling Remote Registries with System Policy Editor

When you run System Policy Editor in registry mode, you have direct, real-time access to the registry for a local or remote computer. This section discusses how to gain access to the registry on a remote computer by using System Policy Editor. You can also use System Policy Editor to create, edit, and manage system policies to control system settings for multiple computers on the network. For information about installing and using System Policy Editor, see Chapter 8, "System Policies."

As with Registry Editor, most of the changes you make with System Policy Editor in registry mode modify the remote registry as soon as you save the changes. These registry changes apply to the user or to the computer. Some of them require the user to log off and then log back on to take effect.

▶ **To edit the registry on a remote computer by using System Policy Editor**

1. In System Policy Editor, click the **File** menu, and then click **Connect**.

2. In the **Connect** dialog box, type the name of the computer you want to administer remotely, using the name for that computer as it appears in the Network option in Control Panel. Windows 98 connects to the registry on the specified computer (assuming you have appropriate permissions).

   The title bar of System Policy Editor shows whether you are viewing a local or a remote registry.

3. Make changes by using the methods described in Chapter 8, "System Policies."

After you have made a connection to the remote computer, you can use System Policy Editor to modify user and computer properties just as you would on a local computer.

Controlling Remote Registries with Registry Editor

You can use Registry Editor to read and write values directly in the registry. You can read settings, create new keys and entries, or delete existing keys. Registry Editor should be used only by those who have appropriate access rights to identify and correct problems. You can also use Registry Editor to solve a problem on a remote computer running Windows 98. To solve a problem on a remote computer running Windows 98, you might need to gain access to the entire registry for the computer. In this case, you should use Registry Editor, because System Policy Editor allows access to only a subset of registry settings.

Note To use Registry Editor to edit the registry on a remote computer, the Microsoft Remote Registry service must be installed on the remote computer, as described in "Setting Up Remote Administration" earlier in this chapter.

▶ **To edit the registry on a remote computer by using Registry Editor**

1. In Registry Editor, click the **Registry** menu, and then click **Connect Network Registry**.

2. In the **Connect Network Registry** dialog box, type the name of the computer you want to administer remotely.

   Windows 98 adds the contents of the remote registry below the contents of the local registry.

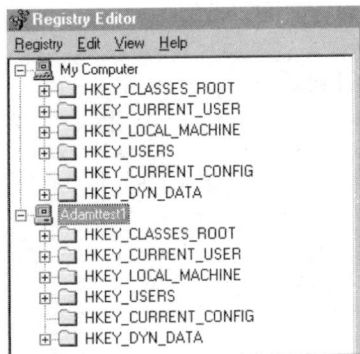

3. Make changes by using the methods described in Chapter 31, "Windows 98 Registry."

Viewing a Remote Computer with System Monitor

System Monitor is a tracking tool that monitors the real-time performance of various computer components, functions, and behaviors and displays the results in graphs or charts. You can use System Monitor to troubleshoot performance problems by monitoring virtual device drivers across the network. System Monitor can provide you with performance information from many system components, including the file system and network clients. This information is useful in locating bottlenecks and solving other performance problems.

With the appropriate administrative privileges, you can use System Monitor over the network to track the performance of remote computers. To monitor more than one computer simultaneously, you can start multiple instances of System Monitor and connect to the appropriate computers.

For more information about installing and using System Monitor, see Chapter 26, "Performance Tuning."

Note To use System Monitor to connect to a remote computer, the Microsoft Remote Registry service must be installed on the remote computer.

▶ **To view performance data on a remote computer by using System Monitor**

1. In System Monitor, click the **File** menu, and then click **Connect**.

2. In the **Connect** dialog box, type the name of the computer, and then click **OK**.

Using Net Watcher

If you use file and printer sharing services, you can use Net Watcher to create, add, and delete shared resources on remote computers, and to monitor and manage connections to shared resources. This is especially useful when you need to know who is connected to a computer and which files are open.

Note If you are not using file and printer sharing services, you can skip this section.

Net Watcher includes a set of icons that make it easy to do the following:

- Add a shared resource or stop sharing a resource.
- Show all shared resources, connected users, and open files.
- Close files users have opened.
- Disconnect a user.

▶ **To install Net Watcher**

1. In Control Panel, double-click Add/Remove Programs, and then click the **Windows Setup** tab.
2. Click **System Tools**, and then click **Details**.
3. Select the **Net Watcher** check box, and then click **OK**.

▶ **To connect to a remote computer by using Net Watcher**

1. On the **Start** menu, click **Run**, type **netwatch** in the **Open** box, and then click **OK.**
2. On the **Administer** menu, select **Select Server**, and then type the name of the computer you want to connect to.
3. Type the password for remote administration on the computer you are connecting to.

   The password depends on the type of security used on the remote computer, as follows:

   - For share-level security, the password is the Remote Administration password specified in the Passwords option in Control Panel.
   - For user-level security, the password is the one for an Administrator account specified in the Passwords option in Control Panel.

When using Net Watcher to view a remote computer, consider the following constraints:

- The remote computer must be running file and printer sharing services.
- If your computer uses share-level security, you can use Net Watcher to connect only to other computers that use share-level security. However, if the computer uses user-level security, you can use Net Watcher to connect to any other remote computers running file and printer sharing services. The pass-through server or domain does not have to be the same for the two computers.
- For computers running File and Printer Sharing for NetWare Networks, you can use Net Watcher to connect only to other computers running File and Printer Sharing for NetWare Networks. The pass-through server does not have to be the same for the two computers.
- On a NetWare network, you cannot use Net Watcher to close documents on remote computers. You can, however, use Net Watcher to disconnect users.

Tip You can prevent a user from sharing files, although the user must have file and printer sharing services running to allow remote administration. To do this, set the system policies named Disable File Sharing Controls and Disable Print Sharing Controls. Disabling these options by using system policies does not remove the file and printer sharing services, whereas using the Network option in Control Panel does disable the service.

▶ **To share a resource on a remote computer by using Net Watcher**

1. To connect to a remote computer, follow the procedure "To connect to a remote computer by using Net Watcher" earlier in this section.
2. On the **View** menu, click **By Shared Folders**.
3. On the **Administer** menu, click **Add Shared Folder**.
4. In the **Enter Path** dialog box, type the drive and complete path of the resource that you want to share, and then click **OK**.

Using Network Neighborhood

Another way to use System Policy Editor, Registry Editor, System Monitor, or Net Watcher remotely is to right-click the remote computer from within Network Neighborhood.

▶ **To manage remote computers in the local workgroup by using Network Neighborhood**

1. In Network Neighborhood, right-click the icon of the computer you want to administer, and then click **Properties**.

2. In the computer's **Properties** dialog box, click the **Tools** tab.

3. Click the button for the remote management task you want to perform, as described in the following list.

Option	Description
Net Watcher	Runs the Net Watcher tool and automatically connects to the specified computer.
System Monitor	Runs the System Monitor tool and automatically connects to the specified computer.
Administer	Opens a folder on the desktop for the specified remote computer and allows you to gain access to the remote computer's hard disk drive.

Scheduling Tasks

The Scheduled Task Wizard lets you run useful utilities and routine tasks at regular intervals. You can set the tasks to run at times that are most convenient for you.

Once you have a task scheduled, an icon appears in the Windows taskbar.

Note If you are upgrading a Windows 95 computer on which System Agent is installed, the System Agent tasks are inherited by the Scheduled Task.

The Scheduled Task Wizard is automatically installed when you install Windows 98. The executable file, Mstask.exe, is located in your \Windows \System folder.

▶ **To schedule tasks**

1. Double-click My Computer, and then double-click Scheduled Tasks.

2. Double-click **Add Scheduled Task** to start the Scheduled Task Wizard.

3. Click **Next**, and then enter the information as prompted by the wizard.

Configuring the Scheduled Tasks

Each task in Scheduled Tasks can be reconfigured once it has been set up in the Scheduled Task Wizard.

▶   **To change the configuration for a scheduled task**

1. Double-click My Computer, and then double-click Scheduled Tasks.

2. Double-click the task you want to reconfigure.

   The following information describes the three tabs that you can use to reconfigure each task:

   - **Task** provides the source location of the program.

   - **Schedule** provides options to configure the frequency, date, and time that the program should be run.

   - **Settings** provides options to configure when to delete or stop the program, and how to run the program if the computer is idle, is in use, or has Power Management options enabled.

Technical Notes on Scheduled Tasks

Consider the following issues when you are using Scheduled Tasks:

- During Suspend mode, the computer can perform tasks in Scheduled Tasks only if it has Advanced Power Management (APM) version 1.2 or Advanced Configuration and Power Interface (ACPI). Check for this in Device Manager, Systems, Devices in Control Panel.

- Tasks are stored as a JOB file in the \Windows\Tasks folder. This file can be copied and pasted to different machines.

- A task must be sage-aware in Task Scheduler; otherwise, the task will open and wait for **OK** to be clicked. A task is *sage-aware* if it displays a **Settings** button in its user interface. All Microsoft disk utilities are sage-aware.

Using Windows Scripting Host

The Windows Scripting Host (WSH) is a language-independent scripting host that enables scripts to be executed directly on the Windows desktop or command console, without the need to embed the scripts in an HTML document. You can run scripts directly from the desktop simply by clicking on a script file, or from the command console. WSH provides a low-memory scripting host that is ideal for noninteractive scripting needs, such as logon scripting or administrative scripting.

For more information about the WSH, see the following Web site:

- **http://www.microsoft.com/management/**

Using Microsoft Management Console

Microsoft Management Console (MMC) is a general-purpose management display framework for hosting administration tools built by Microsoft and third parties. It is provided in the Windows 98 implementation for compatibility with Windows NT. MMC is task-focused. It is implemented with an object architecture, which gives MMC the foundation for its modularity and customizability and provides administrators with the flexibility to build and distribute task-oriented tools from modular components called *snap-ins*.

MMC can be used from within an existing enterprise console or can launch enterprise consoles. Unlike enterprise consoles, MMC imposes no protocol dependencies or object repositories; these remain the responsibility of each snap-in. Working within the MMC, the administrator can use a series of snap-ins to create task-oriented administrative displays customized to provide the appropriate management functions. Snap-ins can work independently or act to extend functionality of other snap-ins. Allowing administrators to create their own views and removing technology discipline boundaries, makes it possible to create a display of network, system, and user information—providing a single point of management that is integrated, comprehensive, and easy to use.

For more information about the Microsoft Management Console, see the following Web sites:

- **http://www.microsoft.com/management/**
- **http://www.microsoft.com/msdn/sdk/mmc/gallery/**

Using Other Management Tools

Microsoft has launched an initiative called the *Zero Administration Initiative for Windows*. Zero Administration Initiative for Windows (ZAIW) encapsulates many technologies, some of them already available and some under development. It equates to establishing a management infrastructure in Microsoft Windows, exposing the infrastructure, and building the tools to use it.

Zero Administration Initiative for Windows includes infrastructure components, such as Windows Management Instrumentation (WMI), Web-based Enterprise Management (WBEM), and management tools, such as Systems Management Server and Microsoft Management Console (MMC). This section describes technologies that combine to provide the Zero Administration Initiative for Windows. It also describes the Internet Explorer Administration Kit Profile Manager, which ships as a Resource Kit tool.

Internet Explorer Administration Kit Profile Manager

After you create a custom Windows 98 Active Desktop and Active Channel configurations on your computer, you can use the Internet Explorer Administration Kit (IEAK) Profile Manager to import the custom configurations and deploy them to users or workgroups.

You can also use IEAK Profile Manager to:

- Specify system policies and restrictions, such as whether users can close toolbars or modify their **Start** menus, and additional options, such as proxy settings.

- Customize additional components of the Internet Explorer browsing software, such as Outlook Express and Microsoft NetMeeting.

- Package these and additional applications that you want to distribute to users or workgroups into files that can be downloaded, distributed on floppy disk or compact disc, or installed by Active Setup.

- Deploy updates to Active Desktop and Active Channel configurations when a user starts the Internet Explorer browsing software, or at scheduled intervals, using automatic browser configuration.

- Set up and maintain software distribution channels, which you can use to distribute new applications or software updates.

For more information about setting up the Active Desktop, see Chapter 6, "Configuring the Active Desktop and Active Channels."

The *Internet Explorer Administration Kit* provides extensive details, procedures, and technical discussions about planning, creating, and deploying custom configurations, creating software distribution channels, and using the Profile Manager.

The IEAK ships as a tool on the Windows 98 Resource Kit compact disc.

For more information about the IEAK, see the Windows 98 Resource Kit compact disc. See also the following Web sites:

- **http://www.microsoft.com/ie/corp/**
- **http://ieak.microsoft.com/**

Systems Management Server

Systems Management Server is a systems management application for medium and large organizations that require a highly scalable and extensible management infrastructure for the management of distributed Windows-based systems. Providing automated software and hardware inventory, software distribution, and remote diagnostics, Systems Management Server integrates with leading enterprise management platforms while also providing an integration point for a range of third-party management applications.

For more information about Microsoft Systems Management Server, see the following Web site:

- **http://www.microsoft.com/smsmgmt/**

Web-based Enterprise Management

Web-based Enterprise Management (WBEM) is a collection of technologies designed to facilitate management of the enterprise. These technologies were developed by a group of companies and are intended to work independently of their vendors, protocols, and management standards. Typically, enterprise management has been tied to different protocols for different disciplines; for example, SNMP for network management. WBEM assumes that management problems are task-oriented and require tools that work together to provide a single management methodology. The WBEM technologies are strongly influenced by advancing Internet technology, which has opened up a new perspective on system management.

For more information about WBEM, see the following Web sites:

- **http://www.microsoft.com/management/**
- **http://wbem.freerange.com/wbempdk/**

Windows Management Instrumentation

Windows Management Instrumentation (WMI) provides the basis for instrumentation in future Windows environments. Close coupling of WMI with services developed to conform to the Web-based Enterprise Management initiative will allow Microsoft to simplify instrumentation and provide consistent, open access to management data. WMI is a set of extensions to the Win32 Driver Model (WDM) and provides an operating system interface through which instrumented components can provide information and notification.

For more information about WMI, see the following Web site:

- **http://www.microsoft.com/management/**

Monitoring Your Network

This section describes the following tools for monitoring your network:

- The Network Monitor protocol and agent, which you can use with System Monitor to obtain network statistics.
- An SNMP agent that allows you to monitor, from an SNMP console, remote connections to computers running Windows 98.

Using Microsoft Network Monitor

The Windows 98 compact disc includes a protocol driver and an agent for Microsoft Network Monitor. The protocol driver provides performance counters that can be viewed by using System Monitor if you want to assess certain network traffic statistics for network driver interface specification (NDIS) version 5.0 protected-mode network adapters. The Network Monitor Agent, which runs as a Windows 98 service, works with the protocol driver for use with the Microsoft Network Monitor application. You can use this application to detect and troubleshoot problems on LANs, WANs, and Microsoft Remote Access Service (RAS) connections.

Note The Network Monitor application is provided with Microsoft Systems Management Server, a client-server system that allows administrators to perform key management functions for distributed computers from a central location.

Installing the Network Monitor Agent and Driver

When you install the Network Monitor Agent, the protocol driver is also installed automatically. You must have both the agent and the driver installed if you want to use the agent with Network Monitor to conduct remote captures of network traffic to and from a computer running Windows 98.

However, if you want only to view the performance counters in System Monitor and you want to prevent anyone from gaining access to the local computer by way of the Network Monitor Agent, you can choose to install only the protocol driver.

Note The Network Monitor application uses NetBIOS to control the remote-capture computer. If you are using the IPX/SPX-compatible protocol to connect the agent and manager computers, you must enable NetBIOS support for IPX/SPX.

▶ **To install the Microsoft Network Monitor Agent on a single computer**

1. In Control Panel, double-click Network, and then click **Add**.

2. In the **Select Network Component Type** dialog box, double-click **Service**.

3. In the **Select Network Service** dialog box, click **Have Disk**.

4. In the **Install From Disk** dialog box, type the path to the Tools\Reskit \Netadmin\Netmon directory on the Windows 98 compact disc, and then click **OK**.

5. In the **Select Network Service** dialog box, select **Microsoft Network Monitor Agent** from the Models list, and then click **OK**.

▶ **To install only the Microsoft Network Monitor protocol driver**

1. In Control Panel, double-click Network, and then click **Add**.

2. In the **Select Network Component Type** dialog box, double-click **Protocol**.

3. In the **Select Network Protocol** dialog box, click **Have Disk**.

4. In the **Install From Disk** dialog box, type the path to the Tools\Reskit \Netadmin\Netmon directory on the Windows 98 compact disc, and then click **OK**.

5. In the **Select Network Protocol** dialog box, select **Microsoft Network Monitor Driver** from the Models list, and then click **OK**.

Running Network Monitor Agent

You can run Network Monitor Agent as a service, or you can start and stop the agent as an executable application.

▶ **To start Microsoft Network Monitor Agent**

• On the **Start** menu, click **Run**, type **nmagent** in the **Open** box, and then click **OK**.

Network Monitor Agent is removed from the system each time you log off and must be restarted for each user who logs on if the agent is not scheduled to run as a service.

▶ **To run Network Monitor Agent as a service**

1. In Registry Editor, select the following registry key:

   HKEY_LOCAL_MACHINE\Software\Microsoft\Windows \CurrentVersion\RunServices

2. On the **Edit** menu, select **New**, and then click **String Value**.

3. Type a label for the value name, such as **nmagent**, and then press ENTER.

4. On the **Edit** menu, click **Modify**.

5. In the **Value Data** box, type **nmagent.exe**.

6. Click **OK**.

If Network Monitor Agent has been started as a service, it continues to run after a user logs off. You can, however, type a command to stop running the agent, whether the agent was started as a service or run from the command prompt.

▶ **To stop Microsoft Network Monitor Agent**

- On the **Start** menu, click **Run**, type **nmagent -close** in the **Open** box, and then click **OK**.

Configuring the Network Monitor Driver

You can configure options for Network Monitor by defining properties for the Network Monitor protocol driver.

▶ **To configure the Microsoft Network Monitor protocol driver**

1. Make sure that Network Monitor Agent is not running and that System Monitor is not monitoring the performance statistics provided by the Network Monitor protocol driver.

2. In Control Panel, double-click Network, and then double-click **Microsoft Network Monitor Driver**.

3. In the **Microsoft Network Monitor Driver Properties** dialog box, click the **Password** tab. You can define the password that users must specify to capture data, view capture files, or access the computer remotely. The following options are available:

   - If you want to change any previously defined password, type a password in the **Old Capture Password** area.

   - If you want to define a password to restrict users to viewing only previously saved capture files by using the Microsoft Network Monitor application, type a password in the **Display Password** area.

   - If you want to define a password to authorize users to connect to the computer and capture files by using the Microsoft Network Monitor application, type a password in the **Capture Password** area. You can define only one password for all network adapters on a computer with multiple adapters.

   - If you want to allow free access to the computer by anyone running the Microsoft Network Monitor application, make sure the **No Password** check box is selected.

4. If the computer has more than one network adapter, click the **Describe** tab, and then select the network adapter you want to monitor.

   You can also define a description for each network adapter in this dialog box, so that the administrator running the Network Monitor application can determine which adapter to select.

5. Click the **Advanced** tab. In the **Value** box, type the user name to be shown when an administrator running the Network Monitor application selects the **Identify Network Monitor Users** command.

This additional information, which is similar to a comment, is not updated or changed if another user logs on to this computer.

Using an SNMP Agent

For networks that use Simple Network Management Protocol (SNMP) for system management, Windows 98 includes an SNMP Agent that conforms to the SNMP version 1 specification. This agent allows you to monitor, from an SNMP console, remote connections to computers running Windows 98. After this agent has been installed, you do not need to make any other modifications to client computers to use SNMP.

Installing Microsoft SNMP Agent

The SNMP Agent is implemented as a Win32-based service and works using Windows Sockets over both TCP/IP and IPX/SPX. The extension agents are implemented as Win32 dynamic-link libraries (DLLs). (For more information about writing SNMP management information bases [MIBs] under Windows 98, see the *Microsoft Windows Platform Software Development Kit*.) The configuration information for the RFC 1156 extension agent is placed in the registry under the following key:

HKEY_LOCAL_MACHINE\System\CurrentControlSet\Services \SNMP\Parameters

▶ **To install Microsoft SNMP Agent**

1. In Control Panel, double-click Network, and then click **Add**.

2. In the **Select Network Component Type** dialog box, double-click **Service**.

3. In the **Select Network Service** dialog box, click **Have Disk**.

4. In the **Install From Disk** dialog box, type the path to the Tools\Reskit \Netadmin\SNMP\ directory on the Windows 98 compact disc, and then click **OK**.

5. In the **Select Network Service** dialog box, select **Microsoft SNMP Agent** from the Models list, and then click **OK**.

If you are prompted to specify the location of additional files, specify the path to the Windows 98 source files on a shared network directory or on the Windows 98 compact disc.

Configuring Microsoft SNMP Agent

Use System Policy Editor to set the following policies for the computer:

Policy	Description
Communities	Specifies one or more groups of hosts to which this computer belongs for purposes of administration using the SNMP service. These are the communities allowed to query the SNMP Agent.
Permitted Managers	Specifies Internet Protocol (IP) or Internetwork Packet Exchange (IPX) addresses allowed to obtain information from an SNMP Agent. If this policy is not selected, any SNMP console can query the agent.
Traps for Public Community	Specifies trap destinations, or IP or IPX addresses of hosts in the public community to which you want the SNMP service to send traps.
Internet MIB (RFC 1156)	Allows you to specify the contact name and location if you are using Internet MIB.

If you want to configure the Windows 98 SNMP Agent to send traps to a community other than the public community, you must either edit the registry directly or add a new system policy.

▶ **To add SNMP communities by editing the registry**

1. In Registry Editor, select the following key:

   **HKEY_LOCAL_MACHINE\System\CurrentControlSet\Services
   \SNMP\Parameters\TrapConfiguration**

2. On the **Edit** menu, select **New**, and then click **Key**.

3. Type the name that you want to specify for a new community.

4. Create a new string value for each console to which SNMP should send traps:

   - The first value name should be **1**, the second value name should be **2**, and so on.

   - The value data must be the IP or IPX address of the SNMP console to which traps will be sent.

   - You can use Registry Editor to create new string values or to modify the string value by using commands on the **Edit** menu.

The following screen shows an example of what the registry should look like after adding a new community named **Prv1**.

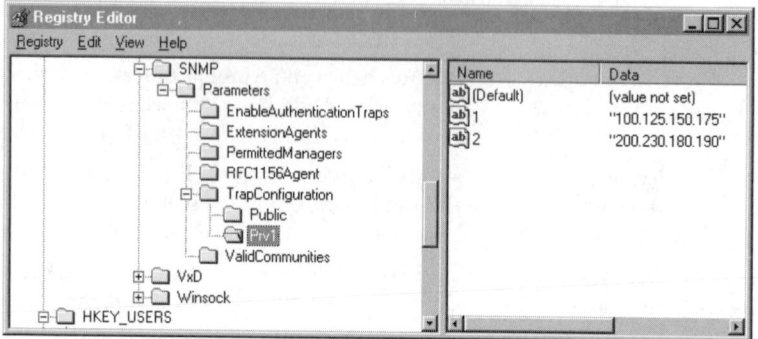

▶ **To add SNMP communities by using system policies**

1. Start a text editor, and open the Windows.adm file in the INF subdirectory of the Windows directory.

2. Add an entry in the section named CATEGORY !!SNMP, specifying the following new values:

   - *Name Of New Policy*, which defines the text that you want to appear in System Policy Editor for this policy. You do not need to include "!!" if you use quotation marks around the name. The "!!" string is used only for Windows 98 localization, and the strings are defined at the bottom of Windows.adm.

   - *Name Of New Community*, which defines the name of the community for which you are adding support.

The following shows the complete syntax for this entry:

```
POLICY "Name Of New Policy"
    KEYNAME
    System\CurrentControlSet\Services\SNMP\Parameters
            \TrapConfiguration\Name Of New Community
    PART !!Traps_PublicListbox LISTBOX
        VALUEPREFIX ""
    END PART
END POLICY
```

Note The registry key and value names are case-sensitive. Also, the registry key name (System\...*Name Of New Community*) must be one continuous line in the Windows.adm file.

For example, the following adds a policy for a community named Prv1:

```
POLICY "Traps for Prv1 Community"
    KEYNAME
System\CurrentControlSet\Services\SNMP\Parameters\TrapConfiguration\Prv1
    PART !!Traps_PublicListbox LISTBOX
    VALUEPREFIX ""
    END PART
END POLICY
```

After editing and saving Windows.adm, you can see this new policy by running System Policy Editor and selecting the Computer policy under Network named SNMP. You can use this policy exactly as you would use the policy named Traps for Public Community.

Removing Remote Agents and Services

You can remove any agent that runs as a network service and that appears in the Network option in Control Panel. To do this, select the agent, and then click **Remove**.

You can use System Policy Editor to turn off services by setting system policies or by using registry mode to modify a computer's registry. To do this, in the computer properties, click **System**. Then delete the services you no longer want under the Run and Run Services policies.

You can remove some agents, such as the SNMP Agent, only by modifying the registry. For a single computer, you can do this by using either Registry Editor or System Policy Editor. The following registry keys list the services running on the computer:

HKEY_LOCAL_MACHINE\Software\Microsoft\Windows
 \CurrentVersion\RunServices
HKEY_LOCAL_MACHINE\Software\Microsoft\Windows
 \CurrentVersion\Run

Additional Resources

For more information about	See this resource
Profile Manager	*Microsoft Internet Explorer Administration Kit*
Microsoft Management Console	**http://www.microsoft.com/management/** **http://www.microsoft.com/msdn/sdk/mmc/gallery/**
Windows Management Instrumentation and Windows Scripting Host	**http://www.microsoft.com/management/**
Systems Management Server	**http://www.microsoft.com/smsmgmt/**
Internet Explorer Administration Kit	**http://www.microsoft.com/ie/corp/** **http://www.microsoft.com/ie/ieak/**

C H A P T E R   2 4

Device Management

24

This chapter describes how Microsoft Windows 98 manages system devices. It also provides instructions for installing and configuring both Plug and Play–compliant and legacy devices, including PC Cards (also known as Personal Computer Memory Card International Association [PCMCIA] cards), display adapters, mouse devices, and communications ports.

See Also

- For information about the components that work together in Windows 98 to configure the system, see Chapter 28, "Windows 98 Architecture."

- For information about the Windows 98 registry, see Chapter 31, "Windows 98 Registry."

- For information about Universal Serial Bus (USB) and the IEEE 1394 bus, see Chapter 30, "Hardware Management."

Overview of Device Management

Windows 98 allows you to configure and manage your system devices by using Device Manager, which you gain access to by clicking the System icon in Control Panel. Using Device Manager is recommended and is described in the sections that follow.

Note If Windows 98 does not include a driver for your device, check the \Drivers directory on the Windows 98 compact disc.

Understanding Device and Bus Classes

To install and manage device drivers and allocate resources, Windows 98 groups devices and buses into classes. The registry contains a subkey for every class of device supported, and the hardware tree (described in "The Hardware Tree" later in this chapter) is organized by bus type. Windows 98 uses class installers to install drivers for all hardware classes. Device Manager, for example, sends messages to the various class installers to tell them to add, remove, or configure specific hardware.

The following are some examples of class names defined in the Windows 98 registry.

Adapter	Keyboard	MTD	Ports
CD-ROM	Media	Net	Printer
Display	Modem	NetService	SCSI Adapter
FDC	Monitor	Nodriver	System
HDC	Mouse	PC Card	USB devices
HID			

The Hardware Tree

The Windows 98 hardware tree is a record of the current system configuration, based on the configuration information for all devices in the hardware branch of the registry. The hardware tree is created in random access memory (RAM) each time the system is started or whenever a dynamic change occurs to the system configuration.

Each branch in the tree defines a *device node* with the following requirements for system configuration:

- Unique identification code, or device ID.
- List of required resources, including resource type, such as interrupt request (IRQ) and memory range.
- List of allocated resources.
- Indication that the device node is a bus, if applicable (each bus device has additional device nodes under it in the tree).

For more information about the components that work together in Windows 98 to configure the system, see Chapter 28, "Windows 98 Architecture."

Displaying Hardware Tree Information in Device Manager

Most information in the Windows 98 hardware tree can be accessed by using Device Manager, shown in Figure 24.1. Device Manager contains a representation of the active hardware device tree, listing the system device nodes. Under each node are listed the actual devices configured for your system; double-clicking a device node exposes its device list. You can reconfigure the device driver and resource settings for a specific device from the **Device Properties** dialog box, reached by clicking the device name and then **Properties**.

For more information about using Device Manager to configure devices, see "Configuring Device Settings" later in this chapter.

Note You can also see the information in the hardware tree in the Windows 98 registry. For more information about the Windows 98 registry, see Chapter 31, "Windows 98 Registry."

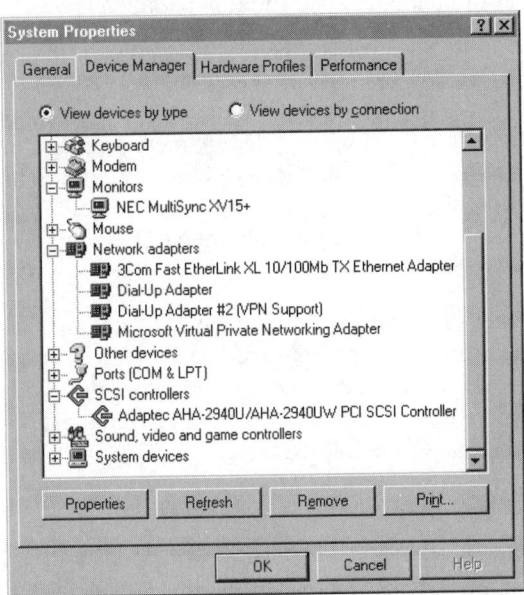

Figure 24.1   Device Manager dialog box

Plug and Play Support

Plug and Play is an independent set of computer architecture specifications that hardware manufacturers use to produce computer devices that can be configured with no user intervention. When you install a device, you do not need to know its Plug and Play requirements, because they will be set automatically.

You can install hot-pluggable Plug and Play–compliant devices simply by plugging in the device. For other devices, such as Plug and Play Industry Standard Architecture (ISA) cards, you must plug in or install a device while the computer is off and then turn the computer back on to initialize the device.

For example, a user can do the following:

- Insert and remove such Plug and Play–compliant devices as PC Cards without having to configure them.
- Connect to or disconnect from a docking station or network without restarting the computer or changing configuration parameters.
- Add a new monitor by plugging it in and turning it on.

Windows 98 detects the presence of a Plug and Play–compliant device. This is known as *enumerating* the device. After enumeration, the device driver can be configured and then loaded dynamically, requiring little or no user input. Certain buses (for example, peripheral component interconnect [PCI] and Universal Serial Bus [USB]) are also automatically enumerated; these buses take full advantage of Plug and Play capability.

You can add some Plug and Play functionality by adding Plug and Play–compliant devices on legacy computers. Therefore, it is best to add Plug and Play–compliant devices on legacy computers rather than adding non–Plug and Play devices. To be able to use *all* Plug and Play features, however, your system must also include one of the following:

- An Advanced Configuration and Power Interface (ACPI) BIOS.
- A Plug and Play BIOS (for Plug and Play devices on the system board).
- The Plug and Play–compliant hardware devices (including buses).

The Plug and Play implementation in the Windows 98 operating system provides the following benefits:

- Dynamically loads, initializes, and unloads drivers in protected mode.
- Supports a wide range of device types (as described in "Plug and Play Device Types" later in this chapter).

- Provides enumeration of devices, which is critical for Plug and Play on legacy computers.
- Notifies other drivers and applications when a new device is available for use. Windows 98 also includes an automatic installation procedure to ensure that appropriate drivers are installed and loaded.
- Provides robust, seamless operation through the integration of all subsystems and the startup process.
- Provides an architecture with a consistent driver and bus interface for all devices.

For more information about ACPI, see Chapter 30, "Hardware Management."

For more information about the supporting architecture, see Chapter 28, "Windows 98 Architecture."

Plug and Play Device Types

A variety of devices are compliant with Plug and Play. The following sections describe the types of devices and provide details for Plug and Play.

Note Windows 98 assigns resources first to ISA, EISA, and Micro Channel Architecture (MCA) devices, next to PCI devices, and finally to Accelerated Graphics Port (AGP) devices.

USB Devices

Universal Serial Bus is a bus standard that brings Plug and Play capability to external hardware devices, such as keyboards, mouse devices, speakers, and cameras. USB devices are *hot pluggable*. This means that they can be connected at any time, even when the computer is running. USB devices are automatically configured as soon as they are physically attached—without the need to reboot or run the setup sequence. Windows 98 supports USB and includes a driver for a digital camera. Contact your hardware manufacturers for other drivers.

IEEE 1394 Devices

The IEEE 1394 bus is designed for high-bandwidth PC devices such as digital camcorders, cameras, and videodisc players. Windows 98 supports hot plugging of IEEE 1394 devices. To use an IEEE 1394 device, you must obtain the appropriate Win 32 Driver Model (WDM) driver. Windows 98 includes a driver for a digital camera; for other drivers, contact your hardware manufacturer.

For more information about USB and the IEEE 1394 bus, see Chapter 30, "Hardware Management."

SCSI Devices

Small computer system interface (SCSI) is a multiple-device chained interface used for many devices such as hard disks and CD-ROM drives. Plug and Play SCSI devices support dynamic changes to the adapter and automatic configuration of device ID and termination, as long as the driver supports it.

Configuration of a SCSI device can be separated into two distinct processes:

- Configuring the SCSI bus itself, for example, by terminating both ends of the SCSI bus and setting device IDs.
- Configuring the SCSI host adapter, for example, by assigning an interrupt request (IRQ) channel, direct memory access (DMA) channel, and so on.

Configuring a SCSI bus that is not Plug and Play–compliant is difficult for most users. The long list of issues related to configuring a SCSI bus includes the following:

- SCSI device ID assignment
- Termination
- SCSI parity
- Command sets
- Disk geometry and software

For example, the SCSI-2 specification does not define an automated ID assignment mechanism, so the user is responsible for making sure that no two SCSI devices on the same SCSI bus share the same SCSI ID. Also, you might replace a SCSI host adapter with one from another company and find it does not work because of differences in disk geometries or the way devices are mapped to hardware interrupt 13 (INT13) parameters.

For more information about hardware interrupts as well as support for SCSI devices and drivers, see Chapter 10, "Disks and File Systems."

PC Card Devices and CardBus

Windows 98 supports the new features of products designed for the *PC Card* standard, also known as the Personal Computer Memory Card International Association (PCMCIA) standard. These products include multifunction cards, 3.3-V cards, and 32-bit PC Cards (CardBus). These advances add the modularity and bus-independence of Plug and Play without affecting device drivers.

Windows 98 also supports *CardBus*, a 32-bit implementation of PC Card also known as PC Card 32. CardBus brings 32-bit performance and the benefits of the PCI bus to the PC Card format. CardBus allows laptop PCs to run high-bandwidth applications such as Video Capture. For more information about how Windows 98 supports Video Capture, see Chapter 30, "Hardware Management."

Windows 95 and Windows 98 have the same driver development structure. This means many of the drivers that worked under Windows 95 should work under Windows 98.

VL Devices

The Video Electronic Standards Association (VESA) Local (VL) bus standard allows high-speed connections to peripherals (compared to ISA devices). VL bus devices are not totally Plug and Play–compliant but work similarly to ISA devices.

PCI Devices

The *peripheral component interconnect (PCI)* local bus has become the industry-standard bus and is used in most Pentium computers as well as in the Apple Power Macintosh. It is considered the successor to the VL bus. The PCI bus architecture meets most Plug and Play requirements, because the PCI bus and devices use agreed-upon mechanisms for identifying themselves and declaring their resource settings and/or requirements. Windows extracts PCI and ISA Plug and Play–compliant device resource information from the system BIOS, and the BIOS provides the PCI IRQ Steering Table for PCI devices. With the information from the PCI IRQ Steering Table, Windows 98 can reassign PCI device resource requirements dynamically, if necessary. For example, when a PCI-based laptop is hot-docked into a docking station, Windows 98 might have to reassign a PCI device's IRQ on the fly to accommodate the new hardware.

Note Windows 98 can manipulate only the ISA IRQ that is mapped to a particular PCI INT#. It cannot alter the link value for the PCI device listed in the PCI IRQ Routing Table. (The *link value* is the combination of the device's INT# assignment and the specific PCI slot the device is installed in.)

ISA Devices

Industry Standard Architecture (ISA) bus design is the architecture specified for the IBM PC/AT. Plug and Play ISA devices can be used on existing computers, because the specification does not require any change to ISA buses. To configure Plug and Play ISA devices, the system performs the following actions:

- Isolates each card and retrieves a unique device ID and a unique serial number.

- Reads the resource requirements and capabilities stored on each card.

- Allocates resources to each card, reserving these resources so that they cannot be assigned to other Plug and Play cards in the computer.

- Activates the Plug and Play ISA cards.

For legacy devices, standard ISA cards can coexist with Plug and Play ISA cards in the same computer. Windows 98 determines the type of hardware and its configuration during Setup, by either polling the hardware or asking the user to supply values. This configuration information is stored as static values in the registry and cannot be changed dynamically, but it is used to determine resource assignments for Plug and Play–compliant devices.

EISA Devices

Extended Industry Standard Architecture (EISA) is a bus design for *x*86-based computers, specified by an industry consortium. EISA devices use cards that are upwardly compatible from ISA. EISA devices use standard software mechanisms for identification and configuration. Windows 98 includes a bus enumerator that makes configuration information from these devices accessible to the operating system. This means that Windows 98 does not reconfigure EISA cards but instead uses the information that hardware detection derives from the EISA nonvolatile RAM storage to determine which resources are used.

Other Device Types

Other device types can take advantage of Plug and Play if they provide mechanisms for identification and configuration. These include integrated device electronics (IDE) controllers, Extended Capability Ports (ECPs), and communications ports.

Parallel ports (ports designated as LPT) can also take advantage of Plug and Play. The most common parallel port type is the Centronics interface. Plug and Play parallel ports meet Compatibility and Nibble mode protocols defined in IEEE P1284. Compatibility mode provides a byte-wide channel from the computer to the peripheral. Nibble mode provides a channel from the peripheral to the host through which data is sent as 4-bit nibbles using the port's status lines. These modes provide two-way communication between the host and the peripheral. Nibble mode is also used to read the device ID from the peripheral for device enumeration.

For totally Plug and Play–compliant computers, the BIOS also meets Plug and Play specifications. For computers that comply with the Plug and Play BIOS specification, the file Bios.vxd provides the BIOS Plug and Play enumerator. For computers that conform to the ACPI specification, the file Acpi.sys provides the motherboard Plug and Play enumerator.

Technical Notes on Plug and Play

With Plug and Play, the operating system and the BIOS can communicate with each other to share information about system resources. This communication channel is not new, but with newer system BIOSs combined with either Windows 98 or OSR2, this process is more effective than with previous Plug and Play implementations.

Many newer motherboards, with newer Plug and Play BIOSs, can store individual device settings in an area of non-volatile CMOS memory. This area, called the Extended System Configuration Database (ESCD), is a data structure that stores resource requirement data about Plug and Play, non-Plug and Play, EISA, ISA, and PCI devices. It also contains information about the standard devices in the system, such as serial and parallel ports. If a Plug and Play BIOS supports the ESCD, on shutdown Windows 98 actually writes to the CMOS, telling the Plug and Play BIOS which PCI and Plug and Play ISA devices have forced configurations (that is, if the user fixed their resource settings) and which legacy devices Windows 98 has already assigned. Windows 98 writes this information to the CMOS so that the Plug and Play BIOS will not attempt to reassign those resources to another Plug and Play device on the next boot. An added benefit is that if system hardware has not changed, Plug and Play–compliant devices will initialize with the same resources, from boot to boot.

In previous implementations, the operating system wrote to the CMOS using Plug and Play BIOS functions 9 and A. This method, called the bitmap method, allowed only the most primitive form of data exchange to occur. Instead of providing complete device descriptions and their resource requirements, the operating system described only IRQs and I/O addresses that were off-limits to the Plug and Play BIOS. If a Plug and Play BIOS does not support the ESCD but does support the bitmap method, Windows 98 uses the bitmap method to communicate with the Plug and Play BIOS.

Installing Devices

In Windows 98, how you install a device depends on whether the device and the computer are Plug and Play–compliant. To take full advantage of Plug and Play technology, a computer needs the following:

- Plug and Play operating system (Windows 98).
- Plug and Play BIOS or ACPI BIOS.
- Plug and Play–compliant hardware devices with drivers.

The Plug and Play components perform the following tasks:

- Identify the installed devices.
- Determine the device resource requirements.
- Create a nonconflicting system configuration.
- Program the devices.
- Load the device drivers.
- Notify the system of a configuration change.

Windows 98 automatically installs and configures most Plug and Play–compliant devices. For devices that are not automatically configured, the Add New Hardware Wizard, shown in Figure 24.2, installs and configures legacy and Plug and Play devices that require installation information, such as the driver location. Microsoft recommends that, whenever possible, you choose new Plug and Play–compliant devices, even for a legacy computer that does not have a Plug and Play BIOS.

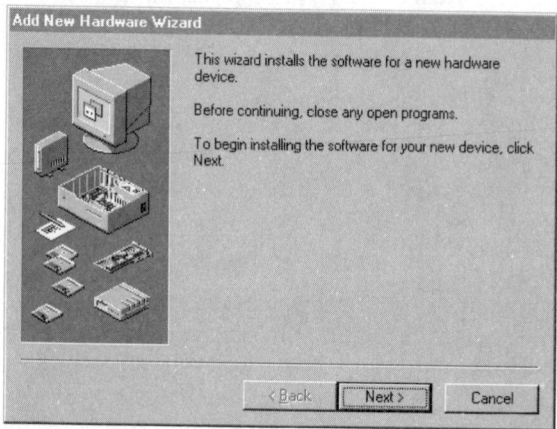

Figure 24.2   Add New Hardware Wizard

Classes of Devices

Windows 98 uses a large number of subsystems to control various classes of devices that identify logical device types, such as the display, keyboard, and network. For many devices, you must use Device Manager in the System option in Control Panel for configuration if you need to make manual changes.

Table 24.1 lists the default classes and devices and shows where you can find the installation tools for changing the device drivers. Your computer might have additional classes, depending on what you have installed.

Table 24.1   Configuration information for default classes and devices

Class and devices	Where to configure devices
Disk class: Disk drives and adapters	Device Manager, under the **Disk drives** option.
Display class: Display adapters	Device Manager, under the **Display adapters** option. -Or- Display option in Control Panel. See "Configuring the Display" later in this chapter.
Modem class: Data and fax modems	Device Manager, under the **Modem** option. -Or- Modems option in Control Panel. See Chapter 21, "Modems and Communications Tools."
Mouse class: Mouse devices	Device Manager, under the **Mouse** option. -Or- Mouse option in Control Panel. See Help. See also "Configuring the Mouse" later in this chapter.
Multimedia class: Multimedia devices	Device Manager, under the **Sound, video and game controllers** option. -Or- Multimedia option in Control Panel. See the related media devices in Device Manager for game ports; see also Chapter 12, "Multimedia."
Network class: Network adapters	Device Manager, under the **Network adapters** option. -Or- Properties for the network adapter under the Network option in Control Panel. See Chapter 15, "Network Adapters and Protocols."
PC Card class: PC Card sockets	Device Manager, under the **PC Card socket** option. See "Using PC Cards" later in this chapter.
Ports class: Ports	Device Manager, under the **Ports (COM and LPT)** option. See "Configuring Communications Resources" later in this chapter.
Printer class: Printers	Printers Folder (no class installer). See Chapter 11, "Printing, Imaging, and Fonts."
System class: System devices	Installation handled by the system. Configure using the **System devices** option in Device Manager.
Unknown class: Detected devices with no driver for Windows 98	Device Manager -Or- Add New Hardware option in Control Panel. See "How Windows 98 Installs a Device" later in this chapter.

How Windows 98 Installs a Device

Windows 98 Setup performs an inventory of all devices on the computer and records the information about those devices in the registry. Setup gets configuration information for system devices from the INF file associated with each device and, with Plug and Play devices, from the device itself. To maintain compatibility, Setup also checks entries in Win.ini, System.ini, and Config.sys.

When a new device is installed, Windows 98 uses the device ID to search Windows 98 INF files for an entry for that device. Windows 98 uses this information or a default driver to create an entry for the device under the **Hkey_Local_Machine** branch in the registry, and it copies the drivers needed. Then the registry entries are copied from the INF file to the driver's registry entry, including the **DevLoader=** and **DriverDesc=** values for the Driver entry, and the **Driver=** and **ConfigFlags=** values for the Enum entry.

Tip If you use custom setup scripts to install Windows 98, you can include the setting **devicepath=1** in the [Setup] section to specify that Windows 98 should check a source installation path to find INF files, rather than looking only in the Windows INF directory when installing devices. When you use this parameter in setup scripts, you can later add INF files to a single network source location to ensure that up-to-date drivers are used any time a new device is installed on computers running Windows 98. For information, see Appendix D, "Msbatch.inf Parameters for Setup Scripts."

When you need to install a new device, rely first on Windows 98 to detect and configure it. How you do so depends on what type of device you have, as the following list explains:

- For hot-pluggable Plug and Play–compliant devices, simply insert the device into the computer.

- For PCI and ISA Plug and Play cards, turn the computer off before installing. When you power the machine back on, Windows 98 enumerates the device and starts the Plug and Play installation procedures automatically.

- For legacy devices, run the Add New Hardware Wizard and let Windows 98 detect the device.

▶ **To install a new Plug and Play–compliant device**

1. Check the documentation for your new device. If you are told to do so, turn off the power before inserting the device. (For hot-pluggable devices, such as USB or PC Cards, you do not need to turn off the power.)

2. Insert the device, and turn the power back on if you turned it off.

   The computer detects your device and, if you are installing a PC Card, beeps when the device is configured and loaded. If the computer does not detect your device, it is a legacy device, and you should follow the steps in the procedure "To install a legacy device" later in this section. If the computer does not appear to detect your device, check for your device in the **Unknown Device** section in Device Manager. You might need to install a driver from within Device Manager.

You can begin working with the device immediately. Windows 98 notifies other drivers and applications that the device is available.

If your computer uses PC Cards or other Plug and Play cards and if a driver is not available for the new device, the Add New Hardware Wizard gives you the following four options:

- Floppy drive
- CD-ROM
- Windows Update Web site (Internet search)
- Other (you must specify a search path)

For more information about the Windows Update Web site, see Chapter 27, "General Troubleshooting."

▶ **To install a legacy device**

1. In Control Panel, double-click the Add New Hardware icon. The Add New Hardware Wizard is displayed. Click **Next** twice.

2. Windows 98 checks for Plug and Play devices on your system. If one is found, you are asked if it is the hardware you want to install. If you answer **Yes**, the device is installed, and the installation is finished. If you answer **No**, the wizard continues.

3. You are asked if you want to install any devices that have problems running (a disabled device, one that has a resource conflict, and so on). If you answer **Yes**, Windows 98 proceeds to fix the chosen device. If you answer **No**, the wizard continues.

4. The wizard now asks if you want to let Windows 98 search for the device. If you answer **Yes**, the wizard attempts to find and install the device. If the wizard then fails to find the device, or if you answer **No**, you are prompted to select a device from the list.

5. In the list of hardware devices, click a device class, and then click **Next**.

6. In the next **Add New Hardware** dialog box, specify the manufacturer and model of the device, and then click **Have Disk**.

7. In the **Install From Disk** dialog box, type the path to the driver files, and then click **OK**.

Using PC Cards

Under Windows 98, Plug and Play support for the PC Card socket is enabled automatically. If you must use old drivers, Windows 98 should work well with your previous PC Card drivers, although some Plug and Play capabilities such as automatic installation and friendly device names will not be available.

To take advantage of Plug and Play, a PC Card must contain information that Windows 98 can use to create a unique device ID for the card. This is called the *card information structure (CIS)*. Device drivers can be implemented under three possible schemes:

- A standard Plug and Play device driver for PC Card (the preferred driver) can handle dynamic configuration and removal, and receive configuration information from the operating system without knowledge of the card in the PC Card bus. The recommended choices are NDIS version 5.*x* drivers for network adapters and miniport drivers for SCSI cards.

- Generic Windows 98 device drivers are supported automatically for such devices as modems and disk drives. If the card contains complete configuration information, the operating system initializes the device and passes configuration information to the driver.

- Manufacturer-supplied drivers are required for device classes that Windows 98 does not natively support.

Windows 98 supports many PC Cards, including modems, network adapters, SCSI cards, and others. If Windows 98 includes supporting drivers for the PC Card and for the socket, installation and configuration should be automatic. This section provides some guidelines for enabling Windows 98 protected-mode PC Card support when automatic detection and configuration are not available for your card.

For more information, see the topic "PC Cards" in Help. See also the PC Card Troubleshooter.

Important If you are using a network card, your PC Card socket driver and network driver both must be Plug and Play–compliant drivers (that is, developed for Windows 98 and compliant with NDIS version 3.1 or later) or both must be real-mode drivers. If these drivers are of mixed types, the computer might hang, or you might not be able to connect to the network.

If you are performing a clean install, Windows 98 Setup automatically detects the presence of a PC Card socket and automatically enables it. If you are not performing a clean install, you can use the Add New Hardware Wizard to make Windows 98 automatically detect the socket.

▶ **To verify that Windows 98 has properly detected your PC Card socket**

1. In Control Panel, double-click System, and then click the **Device Manager** tab. The **Device Manager** dialog box appears.

2. Look for a **PC Card Socket** listing.

   If Windows 98 has not detected a PC Card socket, your socket controller might not be supported by Windows 98.

▶ **To find out if a PC Card socket is supported**

1. In Control Panel, double-click Add New Hardware.

2. On the first screen in the Add New Hardware Wizard, click **Next**.

3. When the Add New Hardware Wizard asks you if the device you want is in the list, click **No**, and then click **Next**.

4. When the Add New Hardware Wizard asks you whether you want Windows to search for your new hardware, click **No**, and then click **Next**.

5. In the **Hardware Types** list, select **PCMCIA Socket**, and then click **Next**.

6. Select the manufacturer for your device, and examine the **Models** list.

If your socket does not appear in the list, you might want to find out if this type of socket is supported. Most likely, if it did not install automatically, the socket type is not supported.

If your PC Card does not appear in Device Manager after you insert it, you might need to enable protected-mode support for that PC Card by using the following procedure.

▶ **To enable protected-mode support for PC Card by running the PC Card Wizard**

- In Control Panel, double-click PC Card.

  –Or–

  In Device Manager, double-click the PC Card controller.

  –Or–

  In the Windows 98 Help index, look up "PC Cards" and then "enabling support."

▶ **To find out if Windows 98 has enabled PC Card support**

1. In Device Manager, double-click your PC Card controller, and then click **Properties**.

2. Click the **General** tab.

   In the **Device Usage** box, if the box labeled **Disable in this Hardware Profile** is not checked, PC Card support is enabled.

Real-Mode Drivers and the los.ini Safe Driver List

Microsoft strongly recommends that you use 32-bit, protected-mode drivers wherever possible. With protected-mode drivers, much of the configuration information is stored in the registry rather than in Config.sys or other files.

General Guidelines

The following lists the general guidelines for device entries in Config.sys and whether such entries are required or can be removed under Windows 98:

- When you use only protected-mode drivers, the only configuration information the operating system needs to know for system startup is the location of the Windows 98 system files and the directory for the swap file. You do not need to load drivers in Config.sys or Autoexec.bat.

- Any boot device in your computer that needs real-mode support does not require an entry in Config.sys. In the unusual case that the CD-ROM is part of system startup, entries for this device must be included in Config.sys.

- If your computer requires any real-mode drivers, an entry for loading the driver must be included in Config.sys and Autoexec.bat, as was true under earlier versions of MS-DOS.

Windows 98 automatically unloads any real-mode drivers for which it has protected-mode drivers to provide the same functionality. For example, the real-mode Dblspace.bin driver is unloaded, and the protected-mode Dblspace driver, Drvspacx.vxd, takes over. However, the protected-mode device driver should take over only when it guarantees functionality similar to that of the real-mode driver, not merely because it can drive the hardware.

Tip To determine whether a particular driver is running in real mode versus protected mode, click the **Performance** tab in the System option in Control Panel.

Safe Drivers

Real-mode drivers that can safely be used are identified in the list of safe drivers, which identifies drivers and terminate-and-stay-resident (TSR) programs that Windows 98 can replace with corresponding protected-mode drivers. The list of safe drivers (Ios.ini in the Windows directory) can include the following information:

- Name of the driver or TSR, using the same name as used in Config.sys or Autoexec.bat.
- Driver requirements.
- Whether the driver hooks INT13.
- Whether the driver monitors INT13 (regardless of whether I/O is controlled by a protected-mode driver).
- Whether the driver accesses hardware directly.

Windows 98 does not store the version number of the driver or the TSR in the list, so the vendor must change the name of the driver if a future version is enhanced so that the driver is safe or unsafe.

By default, the following drivers are considered safe:

- MS-DOS version 5.0–compatible real-mode block device drivers.
- INT13 driver (provides INT13 functionality and directly accesses hardware).
- INT13 monitors (hooks INT13 for monitoring I/O but does not access hardware directly or modify the I/O buffer).
- INT13 hooker (hooks INT13 for altering I/O but does not access hardware directly).
- ASPI Manager (implements the Advanced SCSI Programming Interface for the MS-DOS specification).
- CAM Manager (implements the MS-DOS Common Access Method specification).

For more information on interrupts, see Chapter 10, "Disks and File Systems."

Unsafe Drivers

A real-mode driver is considered *unsafe* if it implements functionality that is not supported. For example, a real-mode IDE or enhanced small device interface (ESDI) driver that uses dynamic encryption is an unsafe driver because Windows 98 does not support encryption. Windows 98 protected-mode drivers do not implement the following functions, so if a real-mode driver uses any of them, it is considered unsafe and should not be added to the list of safe drivers:

- Data compression (other than DriveSpace-compatible compression).
- Data encryption.
- Disk mirroring.
- Bad sector mapping.
- Fault tolerance (maintaining error correction code [ECC] correction on a separate disk).
- Input/output controls (IOCTL) defined or extended by the vendor.

If Windows 98 provides an appropriate protected-mode driver, you should use only the real-mode driver in the following cases:

- The real-mode driver is used for a boot device.
- An MS-DOS mode application uses the driver's device, in which case the protected-mode driver must be unloaded to load the real-mode driver.

Ios.ini Formats

The following is the syntax of the list of safe drivers in Ios.ini:

filename, qualifier_string ; *comments*

qualifier_string is optional.

Qualifier string	Meaning
do_not_care	Indicates that it is acceptable to load the protected-mode driver and not use the mapper for this real-mode driver, because it doesn't matter whether it sees any I/O requests. This is the default.
must_chain	Implies that the device driver or TSR is safe, but it has an INT13 hook that needs to see INT13 requests. In this case, the protected-mode drivers are loaded, but the system routes the logical requests through the real-mode mapper and then switches back to protected-mode at the end of the INT13 chain.
must_not_chain	Implies that the driver is safe as long as it does not see any INT13 requests. In this case, the protected-mode drivers are loaded, and the real-mode mapper is not used.

Qualifier string	Meaning
non_disk	Indicates a driver that controls a device that is not a disk, such as Interlnk.exe. Integrated office system (IOS) issues INT25 calls to all logical volumes in the system and determines whether the request is mapped to INT13, ASPI, or CAM. If the request is not mapped, this is a monolithic driver, as is the case for Interlnk.exe. Adding **non_disk** prevents IOS from considering Interlnk.exe in its safe-driver processing.
monolithic	Similar to **non_disk**. Any driver that is monolithic and safe must have this qualifier set to indicate to IOS that the protected-mode port drivers can be loaded and the driver's entry point can be handled to prevent contention.

Ios.ini also contains an Unsafe CD section. Adding a driver to this section indicates that this compact disc file system (CDFS) will not be loaded on the CD drives that this driver controls.

The following is an example of some Ios.ini entries:

```
386max.sys      ; Qualitas
4dos.com        ; 4DOS shell program
ad-dos.com      ; Afterdark
ad_wrap.com     ; Afterdark
adi2.com        ; Afterdark
aspi3x90.sys    ; DTC SCSI no PM driver
ramdrive.sys, non_disk; MS-DOS
interlink.exe, non_disk; MS-DOS
laddrv.sys, non_disk; MS-DOS
```

Tip for Troubleshooting Protected-Mode Drivers

If you believe that a protected-mode driver should be controlling a device, but the device appears with a real-mode driver in the System option in Control Panel, you can check entries in Ios.log. The Ios.log file in the Windows directory is created when a protected-mode driver is not available or the operating system detects that an unknown device driver is controlling a device.

In most cases, the first line in Ios.log states why the protected-mode driver was not loaded. If the first line mentions Mbrint13.sys, the problem most likely is a virus (unless you are using a driver that replaces the master boot record).

Configuring Device Settings

For Plug and Play–compliant devices, there are no true default settings. Instead, Windows 98 identifies devices and their resource requests and then arbitrates requests among them. If no device requests the same resources as another device, their settings should not change. If another device requests the same resources, the settings might change to accommodate the request. Consequently, you should never change resource settings for a Plug and Play–compliant device unless absolutely necessary. Doing so will fix its settings, making it impossible for Windows 98 to grant another device's request to use that resource. Changed resource settings can be brought back to the original values by checking the **Use automatic settings** box under the **Resources** tab of the **Device Properties** dialog box in Device Manager. See the procedure "To change a device's resource settings using Device Manager" later in this section.

All legacy devices have fixed resource settings, which are discovered either during Windows Setup or through the Add New Hardware Wizard in Control Panel.

Certain circumstances might require users to change resource settings after Windows 98 has configured a device. For example, Windows 98 might not be able to configure one device without creating conflicts with another device. In such a case, a message usually appears to explain what is happening and what you can do about the problem—turn off a device to make room for the new device, disable the new device, or reconfigure a legacy device to make room for the new device.

The best source for resolving any conflicts that might occur is the Hardware Conflict troubleshooting aid in Windows 98 Help. For more information, see "Troubleshooting Device Management" later in this chapter.

When you must manually change a device's configuration, you can use the **Device Manager** tab in the System option in Control Panel. Never attempt to edit registry entries directly. Editing registry entries directly is not supported and can cause serious problems.

If you need or want to resolve device conflicts manually, you can use Device Manager and try the following strategies:

- Identify a free resource, and assign the device to use that resource.
- Disable a conflicting Plug and Play–compliant device to free its resources.
- Disable a legacy device to free its resources, by removing the legacy device card and not loading the device drivers.

- Rearrange resources used by another device or devices to free resources needed by the device with a conflict.

- After powering down and unplugging your computer, change jumpers on your hardware to match the new settings.

Caution Changing default settings using either Device Manager or Registry Editor can cause conflicts that make one or more devices unavailable on the system.

To get assistance in resolving device conflicts, go to the Hardware Conflict troubleshooting aid in Windows 98 Help. For more information, see "Troubleshooting Device Management" later in this chapter.

▶ **To use Device Manager**

1. In Control Panel, double-click System, and then click the **Device Manager** tab.

   –Or–

   Right-click My Computer, click **Properties** from the shortcut menu, and then click the **Device Manager** tab. The **Device Manager** dialog box is displayed.

2. Double-click the device type in the list to display the specific devices of that type on your computer.

3. Double-click the device you want to configure. Or select the device, and then click **Properties** to view or change its settings.

In Device Manager, you can print reports about system settings, including reports on the following:

- System summary

- Selected class or device

- All devices and system summary

▶ **To print a report about system settings**

1. In Device Manager, click **Print**.

2. In the **Print** dialog box, click the type of report you want.

Important You should quit all MS-DOS-based applications before printing the report named "All devices and system summary," because the device detection code might cause problems for some MS-DOS-based applications. If you do not do this, some applications might report the system is out of memory.

The following procedure explains how to change a device's resource settings using Device Manager. Change resource settings only if absolutely necessary. Also, before changing resource settings, make sure that your problem is a resource conflict instead of a missing driver.

▶ **To change a device's resource settings using Device Manager**

1. In Device Manager, double-click the device class, or click the plus sign (+) next to a device class. The tree expands to show the available devices.

2. Click a device, and then click **Properties**. The **Device Properties** dialog box is displayed.

3. Click the **Resources** tab. Notice that the **Conflicting device list** shows any conflicting values for resources used by other devices.

4. In the **Resource type** list, select the setting you want to change. Make sure the **Use automatic settings** box is unchecked.

5. Click **Change Setting**. The dialog box for editing the particular setting is displayed.

   If there is a conflict with another device, a message is displayed in the **Conflict Information** field.

   Note When you click **Change Setting**, you might see an error message saying, "This resource setting cannot be modified." If this is the case, you must choose a different basic configuration until you find one that allows you to change resource settings.
   ---

6. Choose a setting that does not conflict with any other devices, and then click **OK**.

7. Shut down and restart Windows 98. Then verify that the settings are correct for the device.

Note Most legacy devices have jumpers or switches that set the IRQ, DMA, and I/O addresses. If you change these settings in Device Manager, you must also change the settings on the device to match them.

Changing Device Drivers

If your device is not working properly and you suspect that you have either an outdated device driver or the wrong device driver for your device, you can change your device driver from within Device Manager.

You might also want to change your device driver from within Device Manager if you need to switch between WDM and VxD drivers. You might want to do this, for example, if your WDM driver doesn't work with a specific application, or if you are using VxD drivers and you want the enhanced performance and functionality available with WDM drivers.

▶ **To change the device driver using Device Manager**

1. In Device Manager, double-click the device class of the driver you want to change, or click the plus sign (+) next to the device class. The tree expands to show the available devices.

2. Click the device whose driver you want to change, and then click **Properties**. The **Device Properties** dialog box is displayed.

3. Click the **Driver** tab.

4. Click **Update Driver** in the **Device Properties** dialog box. The Upgrade Device Driver Wizard is displayed.

5. Click **Next**.

6. The wizard asks whether you want to search for a better driver. If you want Windows 98 to detect your driver automatically, click **Search for a better driver than the one your device is using now**.

   – Or –

   If you want to choose a driver yourself, click **Display a list of all the drivers in a specific location, so you can select the driver you want**.

7. Click **Next** and follow the instructions to upgrade the driver.

Using Hardware Profiles for Alternate Configurations

Windows 98 uses hardware profiles to determine which drivers to load when system hardware changes. Hardware profiles are an especially important feature for portable computers that can be docked. Windows 98 uses one hardware profile to load drivers when the portable is docked and another when it is undocked—for example, at a customer site that has a different monitor from the one at the office.

Configurations are created when Windows 98 queries the BIOS for a dock serial ID and then assigns a name for the docked and undocked configurations. Windows 98 then stores the hardware and software associated with these configurations. Applications access and store information for each of the different hardware configurations used by the mobile user. The registry support enables applications to adapt gracefully to different hardware configurations.

Note It is not necessary to use a different hardware profile for a fully Plug and Play–compliant portable computer, because the computer automatically knows when it is docked or undocked.

The only time Windows 98 prompts you for the name of a hardware profile is when two profiles are so similar that Windows 98 cannot differentiate between them. If this happens, Windows 98 displays a **Hardware Profile** menu from which you can choose the correct one.

▶ **To create a hardware profile**

1. In Control Panel, double-click System, and then click the **Hardware Profiles** tab.

2. Click the name of the hardware profile on which you want to base the new hardware profile, and then click **Copy**.

3. Type a name for the hardware profile you are creating.

4. Change which hardware is enabled or disabled in this profile by using the **Device Manager**, as described in the following procedure.

▶ **To enable or disable hardware in a hardware profile**

1. In Device Manager, click the plus sign (+) next to the hardware type, and then double-click the hardware.

2. In the **Device Usage** box, click to clear or add the check mark in the **Disable in this hardware profile** check box.

3. If you see a message prompting you to restart your computer, click **Yes**.

▶ **To delete or rename a hardware profile**

1. In Control Panel, double-click System, and then click the **Hardware Profiles** tab.

2. Click the name of the hardware profile you want to change.

3. If you want to remove this profile, click **Delete**.

    – Or –

    If you want to change the name of the profile, click **Rename**, and then type a new name.

Configuring the Display

Windows 98 consolidates display properties in the Display option in Control Panel, so you can easily customize display adapter settings. You can use the Display option in Control Panel to do the following:

- Change the display type or driver.

- Change screen resolution and color depth (without restarting the computer when using display drivers that support this functionality).

- Change color schemes and text styles in all screen elements, including fonts used in dialog boxes, menus, and title bars.

- View changes in colors, text, and other elements of display appearance before the changes are applied.

- Configure display settings for each hardware profile, for example, docked and undocked configurations.

- Configure monitors as multiple displays. For information, see "Configuring Multiple Displays" later in this chapter.

Tip To set display options quickly, right-click the desktop, and then click **Properties**. Click the **Help** button to get help for setting display properties.

Display Driver Overview

Windows 98 provides enhanced functionality and easy configuration for display adapters, in addition to resolving many problems inherent in Windows 3.1 display drivers. By using a minidriver architecture for display drivers, Windows 98 provides better support for a wide range of hardware and provides more stable and reliable drivers.

If you are upgrading from Windows 95, Setup uses the existing display driver. Otherwise, if Windows 98 supports the display adapter, Setup automatically detects it and installs the correct display driver, or an updated driver, if one is available in Windows 98. If the display adapter is not supported, the user is asked to provide the search locations for the appropriate driver. If no appropriate driver is found, Windows 98 installs the standard Video Graphics Array (VGA) driver. In some cases, if an existing driver has been shown to cause problems with Windows 98, Windows 98 replaces an existing display driver with the Microsoft-provided driver.

Windows 98 contains a universal display driver called the device-independent bitmap (DIB) engine. The DIB engine provides 32-bit graphics code for fast, robust drawing on high-resolution and frame buffer-type display adapters. Windows 98 display minidrivers use the DIB engine for all in-memory graphics operations and on-screen operations that do not pass to the adapter for hardware acceleration. This architecture makes it easy for hardware developers to write drivers for a new controller type and to add hardware acceleration features incrementally.

To ensure broad support for display adapter devices in Windows 98, Microsoft developed many display drivers in cooperation with the major display controller hardware manufacturers. The Microsoft development team also worked closely with hardware manufacturers to write additional display drivers and assisted in optimizing existing drivers to enhance display speed for improved graphics performance.

Windows 98 also includes mechanisms to ensure that incompatible display drivers cannot prevent a user from accessing the system. If a display driver fails to load or initialize when Windows 98 is started, Windows 98 automatically uses the generic VGA display driver. This ensures that you can start Windows 98 to fix a display-related problem.

For displays, colors are described in bits per pixel (bpp). Table 24.2 lists the bpp-to-color conversions.

Table 24.2   Bpp-to-color conversions

Bits per pixel	Color conversion
1 bpp	Monochrome
4 bpp	16 colors
8 bpp	256 colors
15 bpp	32,768 (32K) colors
16 bpp	65,536 (64K) colors
24 bpp	16.7 million colors
32 bpp	16.7 million colors [1]

[1] This is another description of true color that includes an 8-bit alpha component in addition to the 24-bits used for 16.7 million colors. Alpha is a degree of transparency or translucency.

Resolutions are described in the horizontal number of pixels multiplied by (x) the vertical number of pixels—for example, 640 x 480.

Tip You can identify the Windows 98 version of a display driver by clicking the display adapter from within Device Manager. If you can boot only to the command prompt, you can also identify the driver by examining the following line in the [boot.description] section of the System.ini file:

```
display.drv=pnpdrvr.drv.
```

For example:

```
[boot.description]
system.drv=Standard PC
keyboard.typ=Standard 101/102-Key or Microsoft Natural Keyboard
mouse.drv=Standard mouse
aspect=100,96,96
display.drv=S3 ViRGE-DX/GX PCI (375/385)
```

The actual display driver is loaded from the registry. This supports docking computers that have different adapters for the portable computer as opposed to the docking station.

Configuring Plug and Play Monitors

Windows 98 can automatically detect a Plug and Play monitor as soon as you plug it in. If you are using a legacy monitor, this option is disabled by default. If you want to enable it, follow the procedure below.

▶ **To enable Windows 98 to detect Plug and Play monitors automatically**

1. In Control Panel, double-click the Display icon.

   – Or –

   Right-click the desktop, and then click **Properties** from the shortcut menu.

2. In the **Display Properties** dialog box, click the **Settings** tab, and then click **Advanced**.

3. Click the **Monitor** tab, select the **Automatically detect Plug & Play monitors** check box, and then click **Apply**. Windows 98 detects and installs the monitor.

If you are having problems with a Plug and Play monitor, you might need to disable this option by following the procedure below.

▶ **To prevent Windows 98 from automatically detecting Plug and Play monitors**

1. In Control Panel, double-click the Display icon.

   – Or –

   Right-click the desktop, and then click **Properties** from the shortcut menu.

2. In the **Display Properties** dialog box, click the **Settings** tab, and then click **Advanced**.

3. Click the **Monitor** tab, clear the **Automatically detect Plug & Play monitors** check box, and then click **Apply**.

4. Reboot your computer.

   When the computer reboots, Windows 98 runs the Add New Hardware Wizard and configures your monitor as an Unknown Device, with a default refresh rate of 60 Hz.

After your computer has been configured as an Unknown Device, you can change the device driver by following the procedure in "Changing the Display Type and Driver" later in this chapter.

Changing the Display Type and Driver

You can change or upgrade a display driver by using the Display option in Control Panel or by using Device Manager. For more information about adding or changing a device driver, see Help.

Warning Some monitors can be physically damaged by incorrect display settings. Carefully check the manual for your monitor before choosing a new setting.

▶ **To change or upgrade the display driver by using the Display option in Control Panel**

1. In Control Panel, double-click the Display icon.

   – Or –

   Right-click the desktop, and then click **Properties** from the shortcut menu.

2. In the **Display Properties** dialog box, click the **Settings** tab. If you have configured multiple displays, the highest framed number indicates the number of monitors configured for the system.

3. Click **Advanced**. The properties dialog box for your display driver appears.

4. If you've chosen a specific monitor, a **Refresh Rate** menu appears in the lower portion of the dialog box.

5. Click the **Adapter** tab, and then click **Change**.

6. If you are using a Plug and Play monitor and you have chosen to have Windows 98 automatically detect Plug and Play monitors by selecting the **Automatically detect Plug & Play monitors** check box, the Upgrade Device Driver Wizard is displayed. Click **Next** and follow the instructions to upgrade the driver.

   – Or –

   If you are not using a Plug and Play monitor or have not selected the **Automatically detect Plug & Play monitors** check box, the **Select Device** dialog box is displayed. Follow the instructions to change your driver.

Changing Hardware Acceleration Settings

Windows 98 uses hardware acceleration to improve display performance. In some cases, this might cause problems. (These problems are rare with newer hardware.) If so, you can turn off part or all of your hardware acceleration.

Note If you are using multiple monitors, changing hardware acceleration settings affects all monitors.

The following procedure describes how to turn off hardware acceleration.

▶ **To turn off hardware acceleration**

1. In Control Panel, double-click the Display icon.

   – Or –

   Right-click the desktop, and then click **Properties** from the shortcut menu.

2. In the **Display Properties** dialog box, click the **Settings** tab, and then click **Advanced**.

3. Click the **Performance** tab. In the **Graphics** box, choose a setting based on the level of hardware acceleration you need. For information about which setting corresponds to what level of hardware acceleration, see the section "Setting Graphics Compatibility Options" in Chapter 26, "Performance Tuning."

Configuring Display Resolution and Colors

You can configure the display resolution and color choices for your display or customize the font size used by using the Display option in Control Panel.

New features in Windows 98 allow you to change resolution and color depth without rebooting, if the installed display adapter is using a video driver provided by Windows 98. However, if you select to change or customize the font size, you must reboot your computer regardless of what video driver you are using. You must also reboot the computer if you are not using a Plug and Play–compliant display adapter and driver that support on-the-fly changes (such as an older Windows 3.1 driver).

▶   **To configure your display resolution**

1. In Control Panel, double-click the Display icon.

    –Or–

    Right-click the desktop, and then click **Properties** from the shortcut menu.

2. In the **Display Properties** dialog box, click the **Settings** tab.

3. To change your display settings, use the options described in Table 24.3.

Table 24.3   Display setting options

Option	Description
Colors	Select from this list the number of colors you want for your display adapter. The larger the number, the greater the number of colors.
Screen Area	Drag the slider to change the visible screen area used by the display. The larger the desktop area, the smaller everything looks on your screen.
Extend my Windows desktop onto this monitor	Active when multiple display support is enabled and monitors are configured as multiple displays. A checked box activates the display adapter for a particular monitor. For information, see "Configuring Multiple Displays" later in this chapter.

Table 24.3   Display setting options (*continued*)

Option	Description
Advanced	Click to display a dialog box with tabs for selecting display font size, adapter type, monitor type, and restart options. Notice that the monitor type setting has no impact on system performance. This setting identifies the characteristics of the monitor to define the maximum resolution and power management capabilities that it supports. For information, see "Changing the Display Type and Driver" earlier in this chapter.

Note Sometimes selecting a supported, higher color-depth (for example, from 16bpp to 24bpp) requires you to reduce the desktop area (for example, from 1024 x 768 to 800 x 600 pixels). Conversely, selecting a supported, lower color-depth gives you the option to select a higher resolution. In nearly all cases, these traits are a function of the amount of video RAM installed on the display adapter.

▶ **To customize display of fonts in dialog boxes**

1. In Control Panel, double-click the Display icon, and then click the **Settings** tab.

2. Click **Advanced**. The properties dialog box for your display adapter is displayed.

3. With the **General** tab selected, pull down the **Font Size** menu and select **Other**. The **Custom Font Size** dialog box is displayed.

4. Drag the controls until the sample shows the size you want, and then click **OK**.

Note You must shut down and restart Windows 98 for the font size changes to take effect.

Configuring Display Appearance

You can use the Display option in Control Panel to set the screen saver and the background pattern used on the desktop.

You can also use settings in Screen Saver properties to take advantage of Energy Star Monitor support in Windows 98 if your hardware supports this feature. This is similar to the standby mode commonly used in portable computers to save power. Windows 98 can support screen saver power management if both of the following conditions are true for your computer:

- In the properties dialog box for your display adapter with the **Monitor** tab active, the option **Monitor Is Energy Star Compliant** is checked.

  This option is checked automatically if, during Setup, hardware detection determined that the monitor supports the VESA Display Power Management Signaling (DPMS) specification. You can also check this option manually.

- The device driver for this display uses either the Advanced Power Management (APM) version 1.1 or later BIOS interface with support for device "01FF" (which is not supported by every APM 1.1 or later BIOS), or the VESA BIOS Extensions for Power Management. For information about whether your display adapter supports these BIOS interfaces, see the documentation for your device driver.

The display monitor is typically one of the most "power-hungry" components of a computer. Manufacturers of newer display monitors have incorporated energy-saving features into their monitors based on the DPMS specification. Through signals from the display adapter, a software control can place the monitor in standby mode or even turn it off completely, thus reducing the power the monitor uses when inactive.

▶ **To use Energy Star power consumption features**

- In Control Panel, click the Power Management icon, select a power scheme, and specify the time intervals to place the system on standby, to turn off the monitor, and to turn off hard disks.

Configuring Multiple Displays

Multiple Display allows you to configure multiple monitors so that the Windows 98 desktop can be spread out over their display areas. For each display, you can adjust its position, resolution, and color depth.

Windows 98 has been tested successfully with up to nine monitors; however, because of such limitations as the limited number of PCI slots available on current motherboard designs, real-world implementations generally work on three or fewer additional monitors.

For you to be able to use a monitor as a secondary monitor, it must meet certain criteria. It must be a PCI or AGP device, and it must be able to run in GUI mode or without using VGA resources. It also must have a Windows 98 driver that enables it to be a secondary display. For a list of these drivers, see "Technical Notes on Multiple Display" later in this chapter.

For more information about Multiple Display, see Chapter 30, "Hardware Management."

▶ **To add a second display to your computer**

1. Verify that your primary display adapter works properly.

2. Add your second adapter. The system BIOS then decides which adapter will be the primary one. Windows 98 then autodetects the new adapter.

Note To test which card will be primary, watch to see which card performs a Power On Self Test (POST). The one that performs a POST will be primary, and the one that seems inactive will be secondary. If you want the order to be changed, reverse the order of the cards in the PCI slots.

---

3. When you are prompted to reboot, do so. When Windows 98 reboots, it will display a message that the card initialized properly.

4. If the primary display comes up in a 640 x 480 resolution with 16 colors, try changing to 256 colors or higher, and reboot.

5. In Control Panel, double-click the Display icon.

   – Or –

   Right-click the desktop, and then click **Properties** from the shortcut menu.

6. In the **Display Properties** dialog box, click the **Settings** tab. Windows 98 lists each adapter in the system.

7. Select the adapter you want to use.

8. The **Extend my Windows desktop to this monitor** check box appears. Click it, and then click **Apply**.

▶ **To configure multiple displays**

Note This procedure applies only if your system contains multiple displays. A system with a single display will have a different **Display Properties** dialog box.

---

1. In Control Panel, double-click the Display icon.

   – Or –

   Right-click the desktop, and then click **Properties** from the shortcut menu.

2. In the **Display Properties** dialog box, click the **Settings** tab. The number in the framed area indicates a particular monitor configured for the system. Frame 1 is for the primary display; frames 2 through 9 are for the secondary displays.

3. Double-click frame 1 to activate it. In the **Monitor** menu, select the display adapter for the primary display. Click the **Extend my Windows Desktop to this monitor** box to place a check mark in it. In the **Colors** menu, select the color depth. In the **Screen area** menu, select the resolution.

4. Double-click frame 2 to activate it. In the **Monitor** menu, select the display adapter for the first secondary display. Click the **Extend my Windows Desktop to this monitor** box to place a check mark in it. In the **Colors** menu, select the color depth. In the **Screen area** menu, select the resolution.

5. If there are additional secondary displays, repeat step 4 for each one.

6. Make sure that the on-screen arrangement of the monitors matches the physical configuration of your monitors.

7. Click **Apply**.

8. Optionally, right-click a display.

   From the context-sensitive menu that appears, you can enable or disable the display, show the number of the display on the desktop, or select which monitor to use.

9. Click **OK**.

Technical Notes on Multiple Display

Table 24.4 lists Microsoft-supplied drivers that can be used for secondary displays and that are included with Windows 98:

Table 24.4   Microsoft-supplied drivers that can be used for secondary displays

Monitor	Driver
ATI Mach 64 GX (GX, GXD, VT) ATI Graphics Pro Turbo PCI	Atim64.drv
ATI Rage I, II, & II+ ATI All-In-Wonder ATI 3D Xpression+ PC2TV ATI 3D Xpression ATI 3D Xpression+	Atim64.drv
ATI Rage Pro (AGP & PCI)	Atir3.drv
S3 765 (Trio64V+)	S3mm.drv, revisions 40, 42, 43, 44, 52, 53, and 54 [1]
S3 Trio64V2(DX/GX) Diamond Stealth 64 Video 2001 STB PowerGraph 64V+ STB MVP 64 Miro TwinHead 22SD Hercules Terminator 64/Video Number Nine 9FX Motion 331	S3mm.drv
California Graphics V2/DX Videologic GraphicsStar 410	
Cirrus 543 Cirrus Alpine	Cirrusmm.drv

Table 24.4   Microsoft-supplied drivers that can be used for secondary displays
(*continued*)

Monitor	Driver
Cirrus 5446 STB Nitro 64V	Cirrusmm.drv
S3 ViRGE (ViRGE (325), ViRGE VX (988), ViRGE DX (385), ViRGE GX (385)) Diamond Stealth 3D 2000 Diamond Stealth 3D 3000	S3v.drv
Number Nine 9FX Reality 332 STB Nitro 3D STB Powrgraph 3D STB Velocity 3D STB MVP/64 3D Miro Crystal VR4000	
ET600 Hercules Dynamite 128/Video STB Lightspeed 128	Et6000.drv
S3 Aurora Compaq Armada	S3mm.drv

[1] If the card is at one of these revisions, then Windows 98 will recognize the card as a Trio 64V+, provided the Microsoft driver is used. If the card is not at one of these revisions then it is recognized as a Trio 32/64. Please note carefully which Microsoft driver Windows 98 selects with this card.

Table 24.5 lists third-party drivers that can be used for secondary displays. These drivers are provided by third-party manufacturers and are not supported by Microsoft.

Table 24.5   Third-party drivers that work with Multiple Display

Monitor	Driver
Permedia 2	Glint.drv
TI TVP4020, 8 MB (Reference board)	
InterGraphics Systems (IGS) CyberPro 2000A, 2MB	Iga2k.drv

Configuring the Mouse

Mouse drivers based on the Windows 98 mini-driver architecture are protected-mode drivers that provide better support for MS-DOS-based applications in the Windows 98 environment. Windows 98 makes mouse configuration and customization easier by providing a single Control Panel option for mouse settings.

Windows 98 Setup detects Microsoft, Logitech, and Microsoft-compatible mouse device drivers, and then replaces these with new drivers.

Mouse and Pointing Device Driver Overview

Windows 98 provides the following improvements in mouse and pointing device support:

- Supports Plug and Play for easy installation of pointing devices. For example, the VMOUSE driver interface supports Plug and Play.

- Supports USB mouse devices.

- Provides smooth, reliable input when using the new protected-mode drivers.

- Supports multiple simultaneous devices, for example, when using PS/2 and serial devices at the same time.

- Eliminates the need to use separate MS-DOS-based mouse drivers.

  Windows 3.1 required that an MS-DOS-based mouse driver be loaded before starting Windows to use a mouse in an MS-DOS-based application running in a window or running in a full screen.

The protected-mode Windows 98 Virtual Device Driver (VxD) mouse driver provides mouse support for Windows-based applications, MS-DOS-based applications running in a window, and MS-DOS-based applications running in a full screen. This results in zero use of conventional memory for mouse support in the Windows 98 environment. (However, most legacy real-mode drivers will run in Windows 98.)

In addition to better mouse services, Windows 98 allows the use of serial ports COM1 through COM4 for connecting a mouse or another pointing device.

▶ **To see the improvements in mouse driver support**

1. Be sure the real-mode mouse driver from such entries as Mouse.com or Mouse.sys has been removed from Config.sys or Autoexec.bat.

2. Restart the computer, and start an MS-DOS-based application that supports the use of a mouse.

   For example, use an application such as Edit, and try the MS-DOS-based application both in a window and in a full screen. Notice that the mouse is available in both modes.

Changing Mouse Drivers

The Mouse option in Control Panel provides customization options, including setting the behavior of the mouse buttons and the mouse pointer. You can use Device Manager to change drivers for a pointing device. For information, see Help.

For pointing device drivers that do not appear in the **Select Device** dialog box (that is, those that are not provided with Windows 98), the Windows Driver Library (WDL) provides support for additional drivers from other vendors. For information about obtaining drivers, check the Windows Update Web site by clicking **Windows Update** on the **Start** menu.

Configuring Mouse Behavior

You can use the Mouse option in Control Panel to configure buttons, customize mouse cursor appearance, set mouse speed, and make other changes. Different functions might be available, depending on the pointing device used with your computer.

▶ **To specify mouse behavior**

1. In Control Panel, click the Mouse icon. The **Mouse Properties** dialog box is displayed.

2. Click the tab for the behavior you want to set.

3. After changing the settings to the ones you want, click **Apply**.

   For information about the configuration options, see Help.

Configuring Communications Resources

A communications resource is a physical or logical device that provides a single, asynchronous data stream. Communications ports, printer ports, and modems are examples of communications resources. In Windows 98, *VCOMM* is the 32-bit protected-mode VxD that manages all access to communications devices. Port drivers use VCOMM to register themselves and to manage access to communications devices.

Two types of ports appear in Device Manager:

- Communications ports, also known as COM ports, serial ports, or RS-232 ports, are used to connect RS-232-compatible serial devices, such as modems and pointing devices, to the computer.

- Printer ports, also known as LPT ports or parallel ports, are used to connect parallel devices, such as printers, to the computer. For more information about configuring printer ports, see Chapter 11, "Printing, Imaging, and Fonts."

Several types of communications ports might be listed in Device Manager:

- Serial ports, also known as RS-232 COM ports, are ports to which external serial devices can be attached. These usually require a 9-pin or 25-pin plug. Serial ports designed for Windows 98 use the 16550A buffered UART, which has a 16-byte FIFO that gives the CPU more time to serve other processes and that can serve multiple characters in a single interrupt routine.

- An internal modem adapter may be installed in Device Manager. In addition, internal modems should also be installed and configured in the Modems option in Control Panel. For information, see Chapter 21, "Modems and Communications Tools."

When you install a communications device, Windows 98 automatically assigns COM names to communication ports, internal modem adapters, and PC Card modem cards according to their base I/O port addresses as shown in the following list:

- COM1 at 3F8 (input/output range)
- COM2 at 2F8
- COM3 at 3E8
- COM4 at 2E8

If a device has a nonstandard base address, or if all four standard ports have been assigned to devices, Windows 98 automatically assigns the modem to COM5 port or higher. Some 16-bit Windows 3.1–based applications might not be able to access ports higher than COM4. Consequently, in the System option in Control Panel, you must adjust the base address in Device Manager or delete other devices to free up a lower COM port.

In addition, if some of the devices installed on a computer are not Plug and Play–compliant, you might have to change resource settings for their communications ports. You can change communications port settings by using Device Manager, as described in "Installing Devices" earlier in this chapter.

Tip For future reference, you might want to record the settings that appear on the Resources sheet for each communications port.

Troubleshooting Device Management

This section describes specific problems in device configuration and how to correct them. For information about general procedures and Windows 98 tools that can be used in troubleshooting, see Chapter 27, "General Troubleshooting." Chapter 27 also includes information about what to do if you are having trouble booting to Safe Mode.

As a general troubleshooting step, always make sure that you are using updated drivers. You can get updated drivers from the Windows Update Web site, as described in Chapter 27, "General Troubleshooting." Also, check the \Drivers directory on the Windows 98 compact disc. Also, make sure that your drivers have been digitally signed by Microsoft by using the Digital Signature Tool, also described in Chapter 27. If they have not been digitally signed, try the Windows Update Web site. If you do not find drivers there, contact your hardware manufacturer and ask for drivers that bear the "Designed for Microsoft Windows 98/Windows NT" logo.

Your first and best resource for diagnosing problems due to changing device settings is the Hardware Conflict troubleshooting aid in Help.

▶ **To use the Hardware Conflict troubleshooting aid**

1. In any Help window, click the **Contents** button.

2. Click **Troubleshooting**, click the listing called **Windows 98 Troubleshooters**, and then click the topic called **Hardware Conflict**. Follow the instructions on the screen.

Correcting Problems with Enabling PC Cards

If you have the correct drivers and protected-mode PC Card support is activated, but the device is still not available, your computer is probably using the wrong memory window for the device. Windows 98 selects a default set of commonly supported settings. Your socket might not support certain interrupt settings, so you might be able to get a PC Card socket to work by changing the IRQ. Similarly, your socket might not work on certain memory windows, and changing the memory window might solve your problem.

▶ **To change the memory window for a PC Card device**

1. In Device Manager, click your PC Card socket, and then click **Properties**.

2. In the PC Card controller properties, click the **Global Settings** tab.

3. Make sure that the **Automatic Selection** check box is not checked.

4. Change the Start address according to information from your hardware manual.

   Typically, selecting a Start value higher than 100000 will work.

5. Restart Windows 98.

▶ **To change the interrupt for a PC Card device**

1. In Device Manager, click your PC Card socket, and then click **Properties**.

2. Change the IRQ from its default to a value that does not conflict with other IRQ settings used on your computer.

3. Restart Windows 98.

If Windows 98 still does not detect your PC Cards, you should disable the Windows 98 protected-mode PC Card support. If you do so, you will be able to use your PC Card only with real-mode drivers.

▶ **To disable protected-mode PC Card support**

1. In Device Manager, click your PC Card socket controller, and then click **Properties**.

2. In the Device Usage box, select the Disable in this hardware profile box.

   The new configuration should appear in Device Manager. If not, restart Windows 98.

Correcting Problems with the Display

If your computer has problems with the display, determine whether the problems persist when you use lower screen resolutions and different color depths with the display driver. If the display driver fails and changing resolutions does not resolve the problem, check or replace the current display driver. Also, make sure the installed display driver is the correct one for the installed display adapter.

Windows 98 includes safeguards that in most cases prevent unsupported settings from being implemented. However, problems can result when Windows 98 has incorrect information that a monitor or display adapter can support certain functionality. This usually happens only if Windows 98 misidentifies the display adapter or Plug and Play–compliant monitor, or the user misidentifies a legacy monitor, and Windows 98 attempts to exceed the display adapter's resolution or color depth capabilities or the monitor's supported refresh rates.

If Windows 98 correctly identifies your display adapter, and you attempt to set the adapter to a setting it does not support, in most cases you will see an error message stating that the display adapter does not support the chosen resolution or color depth. Less commonly, Windows 98 might try to set the chosen resolution or color depth, and your system might lock up.

Windows 98 can identify Plug and Play–compliant monitors and automatically adjust refresh rates available in the user interface to correspond to the settings provided in the monitor's INF file listing the monitor's capabilities. This results in reliable monitor operation and usually prevents users from setting incorrect or incompatible refresh rates.

With older legacy monitors, however, it is possible to set refresh rates incorrectly. Because Windows 98 does not communicate with legacy monitors, it is possible for a user to select an INF file of a monitor with a greater range of refresh rate capabilities than that of the actual monitor installed. If you select a higher refresh rate than the monitor can support, you will see corrupted display with an image that looks like a misadjusted horizontal with oscillating multiple images. If this happens, Windows 98 should return the monitor to its original refresh rate after a few moments.

Note If the video signal is set to an unsupported refresh rate, newer monitors may mute the video signal and generally return an error message such as "Invalid sync" or "Unsupported mode."

To determine whether any performance problems might be related to the display adapter, you can progressively disable enhanced display functionality using the System option in Control Panel. On the **Performance** tab, click **Graphics**, and then use the slider to select new settings. For information, see Chapter 26, "Performance Tuning."

If Windows 98 does not recognize the display adapter, try using the basic VGA driver (by definition, a generic 640 x 480, 16-color driver). However, keep in mind that multiple display support is not available when you are using a basic VGA driver. If you have a vendor-supplied driver disk for the display adapter, you can install the OEM drivers. If the drivers were not written for Windows 95 or Windows 98, some advanced display features might be disabled.

If an error occurs during display adapter initialization, the computer stops responding. To restart the computer, press CTRL+ALT+DEL. This problem might occur if you are using a video accelerator card and you change the display from the default setting (640 x 480, 16 colors) to 1024 x 768, 256 colors in the properties dialog box for your display adapter. Although Windows 98 might accept the changes, the error still results. The Super VGA (SVGA) driver (1024 x 768) included with Windows 98 is designed only for nonaccelerated SVGA display adapters. To correct this problem, change the display driver back to the default VGA setting.

▶ **To see if the display error is corrected by changing the screen color setting**

1. In the Display option in Control Panel, click the **Settings** tab.

2. Check the setting in the **Colors** menu. If the selection is other than **16 Colors**, select **16 Colors**.

3. Click **Apply**.

4. Retest the condition that was causing the display error. If the error does not recur, you might want to temporarily operate at a lower resolution until you can upgrade the display driver to a version that functions without error.

▶ **To check the display drivers**

1. In Device Manager, click the plus sign (+) next to **Display Adapters**.

2. Double-click the specific display adapter shown (for example, Cirrus Logic).

3. In the **Adapter properties** dialog box, click the **Driver** tab, and then click **Driver File Details**.

4. Click each file shown in the **Driver files** box. If available, the **Provider**, **File version**, and **Copyright** information appears below the file tree (some vendors' display drivers might not contain version information).

5. Check displayed file versions for compatibility. Windows 98 display driver files have version numbers starting at 4.00 or higher.

6. If you have an incompatible driver, you can reinstall the original driver from the Windows 98 disks or get new drivers from the Microsoft Download Service (MSDL) as described in Appendix I, "Windows 98 Resource Directory." If Microsoft drivers do not support the display adapter, contact the display adapter vendor for updated drivers, or check the Microsoft Windows Update Web site.

▶ **To check where the driver is loading from**

• To ensure that a Windows 98 version of the display driver is installed, check the [boot] section of System.ini for the following entry:

```
display.drv=pnpdrvr.drv
```

If this entry is specified, the display entries in System.ini are ignored, and the display drivers are loaded from the registry. If the entry specifies any driver other than Pnpdrvr.drv, the display drivers are loaded from System.ini.

▶ **To find out if an incorrect display driver is installed**

1. Restart the computer, and then press the left CTRL key until the Microsoft Windows 98 Startup Menu message appears.

2. Choose **Safe Mode**, which uses the standard VGA (640 x 480 x 16-color) driver.

   If this resolves the display problem, the display driver is probably involved. Try replacing the driver with a newer version, or reinstall the driver from the original disks.

▶ **To see if the display error is corrected by changing screen resolution**

1. In Control Panel, double-click Display, and then click the **Settings** tab.

2. Check the setting in the **Screen area** menu. Select a setting with a lower resolution.

3. Click **Apply**.

4. Retest the condition that was causing the display error.

▶ **To load VGA on your next boot**

• In the [boot] section of System.ini, change the value of DisplayFallBack from 0 to 1.

▶ **To change your display driver back to VGA**

1. Restart the computer, hold down the left CTRL key until the Microsoft Windows 98 Startup Menu message appears, and then choose **Safe Mode**.

2. After you have successfully booted to Safe Mode, in Control Panel, double-click Display, and then click the **Settings** tab.

3. Click **Advanced**, and then click **Change**. The Upgrade Device Driver Wizard is displayed. Click **Next**, and then follow the instructions on the screen.

If you want to use a high-resolution display driver with Windows 98, consult your display adapter manufacturer for the proper driver to use.

To correct jerky motion during multimedia playback.

• Use the Add New Hardware option in Control Panel to verify that the appropriate display driver is installed for the display adapter you are using.

• Check to see if Mscdex.exe is installed. If so, remove it and use Windows 98 CDFS drivers.

• If the problem occurs with MS-DOS-based applications, check and maximize available extended memory specification (XMS) memory in the virtual memory (VM).

Correcting Problems with Multiple Displays

This section describes problems that might occur with multiple displays. As a general troubleshooting step, make sure that your video card is on the list of supported video cards listed in Tables 24.4 and 24.5 and that you are using an updated driver.

An additional display does not appear in Display Properties.

If an additional display does not appear in the **Display Properties** dialog box, or if you cannot use additional monitors, check the following:

- Check the driver you are using for your displays. If you are using VGA or a Windows 3.1 driver, Multiple Display will not work. Keep in mind that the standard VGA driver is used whenever the desktop resolution is 640 x 480 and the color depth is 16 colors, so you should also make sure you have selected a higher resolution and color depth.

- Make sure you are not using a Windows 3.1 driver for your primary monitor.

- Make sure that all the display adapters you use are PCI-based. One of them can be a PCI-based adapter embedded in the motherboard. The bulleted list later in this section provides information about potential problems with this configuration.

- Check to see if you are using any third-party display control panels; if so, try removing them.

You might also have a hardware problem. Following are several problems you might experience with motherboard or on-board PCI video:

- The PCI motherboard video is hidden from the enumerator and might be identified incorrectly.

- Some systems vendors hide the motherboard video from PCI when another video card is detected in the system. If Plug and Play cannot find the device, Setup cannot start it. To determine whether you have this problem, check Device Manager. If only your add-in card is shown as present and working, this is likely your problem.

- Windows 98 cannot read the ROM from a motherboard video device. It might be possible to overcome this problem if you set up Windows 98 without any other display adapters in the computer.

The computer will not boot with multiple displays, or you see a Code 12 in Device Manager.

If your computer won't boot or you see a Code 12, you might have a system BIOS bug. Try moving all the video cards to the slots closest to the motherboard.

In Device Manager, you are told that video card memory is in use.

If you check your video card in Device Manager and see a message stating that the region of memory the video card uses is already in use, try removing Emm386.exe, or set the following under the [386enh] section of System.ini:

```
Emmexclude C000-CFFF
```

Device Manager says your card will not work with Multiple Display.

If your card is on the list of supported cards listed in Tables 24.4 and 24.5, but Device Manager tells you that your card will not work with Multiple Displays, make sure that you are using the correct driver. For a list of supported drivers, see "Technical Notes on Multiple Display," earlier in this chapter.

You cannot use an absolute pointing device on your secondary display.

Absolute pointing devices work only on the primary display.

Correcting Problems with SCSI Devices

This section includes problems that might occur with SCSI devices.

A SCSI device fails to work.

The SCSI and CD-ROM support built into Windows 98 requires that CD-ROM drives provide SCSI parity to function properly. For many drives, this is a configurable option or is active by default. Examples of drives that do not provide or support SCSI parity are the NEC CDR-36 and CDR-37 drives.

If you have trouble with a SCSI drive, make sure the SCSI bus is set up properly (refer to your hardware documentation for specific details).

In some cases, adding or removing a SCSI adapter might prevent your computer from starting correctly. Check the following:

- The ends of the SCSI bus must have terminating resistor packs (also called terminators) installed.

  If you have only internal or only external SCSI devices, the ends of the bus are probably the SCSI adapter and the last device on the cable. If you have both internal and external SCSI devices, the adapter is probably in the middle of the bus and should not have terminators installed. If you disconnect a device that has terminators installed (such as an external CD-ROM drive), be sure to install terminators on whatever device then becomes the last one on the bus. One of the devices on the SCSI bus (usually the adapter) should be configured to provide termination power to the bus.

Windows 98 supports as many internal and external SCSI devices as the SCSI controller supports. In addition to the requirement that the last external and the last internal SCSI device be terminated, some hardware has additional requirements for where it must be placed in the SCSI chain.

- Removable media must be mounted on the drive before running Setup.

  If you have a SCSI removable media device, such as a cartridge drive, make sure the media are mounted on the drive before running Setup. If no media is mounted on the drive, errors might occur during Setup that prevent installation of Windows 98.

A SCSI device works with MS-DOS but not Windows 98.

For many SCSI hardware devices, you can specify command-line parameters when the driver is loaded. By default, the Windows 98 miniport driver runs without parameters (in the same way it does for real-mode drivers). If you want to use a command-line parameter, if the device has a Windows 98 MPD file, you can add the parameter to the **Settings** tab in the **Properties** for the SCSI controller.

For information about the switches that can be used for a particular SCSI device, see the documentation from the device manufacturer. There are no additional parameters added by Microsoft.

For example, if your SCSI adapter has full functionality under MS-DOS but not under Windows 98, you can add any device parameters previously specified in Config.sys to the **Adapter Settings** box. As another example, for Adaptec 7700 SCSI devices, you might specify **removable=off** to disable support for removable media if you want to load another ASPI removable disk.

Setup does not automatically detect the SCSI CD-ROM drive.

If Setup does not automatically detect a SCSI CD-ROM drive, try the following:

- Try loading real-mode drivers for the SCSI controller, the CD-ROM driver, and Mscdex.exe, and see if the CD-ROM drive works in MS-DOS.
- If the drive does work in MS-DOS, in Device Manager, examine the SCSI controller's properties to make sure it was detected correctly.
- Check your physical connections.
- Check the SCSI IDs for all devices to make sure they are unique.

Setup does not recognize the correct SCSI CD-ROM drive.

Windows 98 Setup can recognize multiple CD-ROM drives connected to the same SCSI host adapter. Therefore, if it does not recognize one of the CD-ROM drives, there is a hardware problem. For example, it could be caused by a legacy adapter with more than one device with the same SCSI ID.

You see an error message about your CD-ROM drive during Setup.

If you see an error message during Setup, and your SCSI or IDE CD-ROM drive does not appear in Device Manager, make sure your driver appears in the Ios.ini safe list. If a real-mode driver is loaded for the CD-ROM drive, and the driver does not appear in the Ios.ini safe list, Windows 98 Setup does not install protected-mode drivers for it, and it does not appear in Device Manager. If that happens, you must comment out the real-mode driver. For example:

```
rem device=c:\sbrpo\drv\sbpcd.sys/d:mscd001 /p:220
```

Then reboot your computer. Windows 98 should automatically detect and configure the CD-ROM drive.

A SCSI or IDE tape drive or scanner does not show up in Device Manager.

Windows 98 does not assign drive letters to tape drives and scanners, because they have no drive to assign a letter to; that is, they have no official hardware class designation. Therefore, they might appear as Unknown Devices in Device Manager. (If you run Microsoft Backup, however, they will be moved to a new device class and will not appear as Unknown Devices.) After you start Windows 98, it asks if you have a driver for these devices. If you have Windows 98 drivers, click **Yes**, and then type the path to where the drivers are located. To use existing real-mode drivers, click **No**. Windows 98 will continue to recognize and support these devices although they are listed as Unknown Devices.

A SCSI drive does not show up in My Computer.

This probably indicates that there is something wrong with the SCSI drivers in Config.sys and Autoexec.bat, or that the protected-mode SCSI drivers fail to load. Look for an Ios.log file and check its entries, as described in "Real-Mode Drivers and the Ios.ini Safe Driver List" earlier in this chapter.

Correcting Problems with Other Devices

This section describes problems that might occur with devices other than the display or SCSI devices.

You see Code 11 error when installing a PCI device.

If Windows 98 hangs or reboots when you are installing a PCI device and then gives you a Code 11 error, you might have a problem with IRQ steering in your BIOS (a mechanism that enables Windows 98 to dynamically allocate ISA interrupts). To find out whether this is the cause, try turning off IRQ steering.

▶ **To turn off IRQ steering**

1. In Device Manager, click your PCI bus, and then click **Properties**.

2. Click the **IRQ Steering** tab, and then clear the **Use IRQ Steering** check box.

When you reboot, Windows 98 will no longer dynamically allocate interrupts but will instead rely on your BIOS to do so.

The system stalls when accessing the CD-ROM.

After you press CTRL+ALT+DEL to shut down and restart the computer, Windows 98 might be unable to find the CD-ROM or might stall when trying to access the drive; sometimes, pressing CTRL+ALT+DEL will not reset the computer. This might occur if Windows 98 is relying on real-mode drivers for the Sound Blaster or Media Vision Pro Audio proprietary CD-ROM drive. If this is the case, you cannot access anything on the CD-ROM because its drivers cannot load. If this happens, turn off and then restart the computer. Use the Add New Hardware option in Control Panel to install the protected-mode drivers provided with Windows 98 for the specific CD-ROM device.

CD-ROM performance problems occur when AutoPlay is enabled.

This problem sometimes occurs with both protected-mode drivers and real-mode Microsoft Compact Disc Extensions (MSCDEX) drivers. To fix it, turn off AutoPlay, which is enabled by default, and then turn it back on again.

WAV files cannot be played.

If Windows 98 cannot recognize the sound card, you might not be able to play WAV files.

▶ **To verify sound card settings**

1. In Device Manager, double-click **Sound, video and game controllers**.

2. Double-click the specific sound card, and then in the card's properties, click the **Driver** tab so you can verify the drivers.

3. Click the **Resources** tab, and verify IRQ settings.

4. Check the **Conflicting device list**, and verify that no conflicts for the sound card settings appear in the list.

Ports for sound cards with multiple CD-ROM adapters are not detected.

If a sound card has multiple CD-ROM adapters, they often include a program that activates the port to be used. This program must run before Windows 98 runs. If it does not, Windows 98 will not detect the port.

An input device fails.

If an input device, such as the keyboard or the mouse, fails, do the following:

- Check the physical connection.
- In Device Manager, check the driver used for the device.
- Check for conflicts with the I/O and IRQ resources used.
- Check for conflicting drivers or applications.

The mouse moves erratically, or keyboard input fails.

For specific problems concerning mouse or keyboard operation, do the following:

- In Device Manager, check the mouse and keyboard drivers, replacing them if necessary.

- In Control Panel, click Mouse, and then check the **Motion** configuration for pointer speed.

- Check the port used for the mouse.

- Check the physical connection of the mouse and keyboard.

- Make sure there are no entries for real-mode mouse drivers in Config.sys, Autoexec.bat, Win.ini, and System.ini.

- Reboot the computer and hold down the left CTRL key until the Microsoft Windows 98 Startup Menu message appears, and then choose the **Logged** option. Check the Bootlog.txt file and verify that the mouse driver is loading.

Mouse reports GROWSTUB errors.

If you were using the Microsoft Mouse Manager with Windows 3.1, Windows 98 Setup automatically updates the Pointer.exe and Pointer.dll files in the Mouse directory. If these files are not updated correctly, the mouse might stall and report GROWSTUB as a running task in the **Close Program** dialog box. To fix this problem, remove all references to the mouse in the Autoexec.bat and Config.sys files, and make sure the correct POINTER files were copied to the Mouse directory and not just the Windows directory.

Additional Resources

For more information about	See this resource
Changing a PC Card device memory window SCSI device switches Display adapter support for BIOS interfaces	Device documentation
Card bus Adding or changing a device drive Configurations options	Windows 98 Help
INF files	Appendix C, "Windows 98 INF Files" Windows 98 DDK

Application Support

25

This chapter describes how to optimize support for applications in Microsoft Windows 98 using the new Distributed Component Object Model (Distributed COM). It also describes support and issues for using Win32-based, Win16-based, and MS-DOS-based applications.

In This Chapter

See Also

- For more information about setup, see Chapter 5, "Setup Technical Discussion."

- For more information about performance tuning, see Chapter 26, "Performance Tuning."

- For more information about the registry, see Chapter 31, "Windows 98 Registry."

- For more information about the Apps.inf file, see Appendix C, "Windows 98 INF Files."

Overview of Application Support in Windows 98

Windows 98 optimizes the performance of applications written for it, as well as existing applications created for MS-DOS and previous versions of Windows. Applications perform more smoothly than with MS-DOS, Windows for Workgroups, Windows 3.1, or Windows 95, because Windows 98 significantly increases system resources available to them and more efficiently manages how they use system memory.

Windows 98 also supports new and existing versions of COM technology, including ActiveX Controls and Automation for new Windows-based applications. It also supports other Web authoring technologies such as Dynamic Hypertext Markup Language (HTML) and JavaScript. For more information about ActiveX, Dynamic HTML, and JavaScript, see Chapter 20, "Internet Access and Tools." Finally, Windows 98 now supports the Distributed Component Object Model, which lets application components work with each other across a network or across the Internet.

Windows 98 offers the following general improvements in application support:

Distributed computing with the Distributed Component Object Model. New for Windows 98, Distributed COM extends the COM infrastructure to allow components of a distributed application to communicate over a network. Users can access and share information without needing to know the location of an application's components.

Increased system resources and other optimizations. Windows 98 increases system resources for all applications by using 32-bit heaps to store application data structures, making more resources available for the remaining data elements than with MS-DOS, Windows 3.1, or Windows for Workgroups. In addition, Windows 98 increases the number of timers, COM and LPT ports, Windows menu handles, and other resources available to applications.

Windows 98 also includes performance enhancements, such as a change to binaries and a change to Disk Defragmenter, that make applications run faster. For more information, see Chapter 26, "Performance Tuning." See also Chapter 10, "Disks and File Systems."

Improved memory management. The Virtual Machine Manager, an integral part of the Windows 98 architecture, manages the memory required by each application. A virtual machine (VM) is an environment in memory that functions like a separate computer for each application. All Win32-based and Win16-based applications run in the System VM, in which all system processes also run. Each MS-DOS-based application runs in its own VM. For more information, see Chapter 28, "Windows 98 Architecture."

Distributed Component Object Mode

The *Distributed Component Object Model (Distributed COM)* extends the Component Object Model (COM) to allow components of a distributed application to communicate over the network securely and transparently. Your existing COM applications can use Distributed COM without any modifications to the application code. Distributed COM provides the infrastructure for creating applications as a system of software objects (for example, sorting functions or database searches) designed to be reusable and replaceable.

In a corporate environment, Distributed COM lets application developers break down an application into a multitier design using smaller components that can communicate directly with each other across computers. Application developers can update a single component without having to recompile the entire application.

For example, as shown in Figure 25.1, your company might deploy a distributed order entry application that uses individual components for sales tax calculations, with each component designed for a different geographic sales region. Each of these sales channel components uses the same inventory component located on a network server. As the inventory changes, you can change the inventory component without having to rewrite and recompile the sales tax components for each of the sales regions.

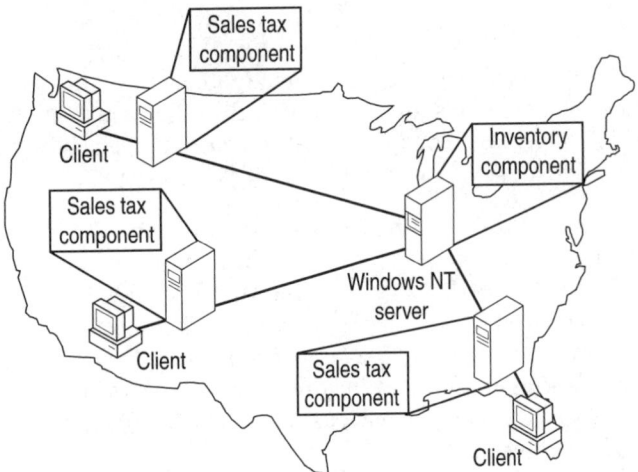

Figure 25.1   Overview of distributed applications using Distributed COM

Distributed COM is particularly powerful for component applications running across computers for the following reasons:

Distributed COM is transport-neutral. Components can communicate with each other over any network transport. In Windows 98, Distributed COM supports Transmission Control Protocol/Internet Protocol (TCP/IP).

Distributed COM is language-neutral. ActiveX controls, Java applets, and components written in many languages (such as Microsoft Visual Basic, Microsoft Visual C++®, or even COBOL or Pascal) can communicate with each other through COM.

Distributed COM is platform-independent. Distributed COM runs on Windows 98, Windows NT, UNIX, and legacy operating systems, providing a common application infrastructure across a company's entire information systems environment.

Distributed COM is based on open standards. Distributed COM uses the Open Group distributed computing environment (DCE) remote procedure call (RPC) mechanism for communication between clients and servers across the network.

For procedures on how to configure applications and establish permissions for using Distributed COM, see "Distributing Applications Across a Network" later in this chapter.

For schematic and detailed information about Distributed COM, see "Technical Notes," later in this chapter.

For more information about COM, go to **http://www.microsoft.com/com/**.

Win32-based Applications

Win32-based applications receive the full benefit of the performance enhancement features in Windows 98. Because each Win32-based application runs in a separate memory space, it can take complete advantage of the preemptive multitasking capabilities of Windows 98.

To get the best possible performance, use versions of applications designed for Windows 98 whenever possible. Applications written specifically for Windows 98 carry the "Designed for Microsoft Windows NT Windows 98" logo. To qualify for the logo, applications must meet the requirements outlined on the Microsoft Developer Network (MSDN) Web site at **http://www.microsoft.com/msdn/**. Windows 98 includes new requirements in areas such as power management, assumed hard disk size limitations, digital signing, and installation.

Win16-based Applications

Win16-based applications designed for Windows 3.1 run under Windows 98 without modification, but these applications run in a shared memory space and cannot take advantage of preemptive multitasking. However, they do benefit from improvements incorporated into the Windows 98 subsystem. For Win16-based applications that are known to need special parameters to run, Windows 98 includes an Apps.inf file that defines parameters for each application.

Because of default settings and other support in Windows 98, you do not need Config.sys, Autoexec.bat, and INI files to run Win16-based applications, although you can still use settings from existing files. When you upgrade by replacing Windows 3.1 with Windows 98, Windows automatically moves the current settings for your installed applications to the registry for use with Windows 98.

In general, Windows 98 does not allow you to specify a working directory in the properties sheet of a Win16-based application. (This is true for Win32-based applications as well.) This is because the program file has links assigned to it that rely on unchanging data. However, you can achieve the same effect by creating a shortcut for the application and specifying a working directory in the **Start In** box in the **Properties** dialog box for the shortcut.

MS-DOS-based Applications

MS-DOS-based applications can take advantage of the improved memory management and increased system resources that are made possible by the system architecture used in Windows 95 and Windows 98. Most applications can now run in a window. An MS-DOS-based application that does not run well under Windows can run in exclusive MS-DOS mode, which makes all system resources available to that application. For more information, see "Changing Memory Settings" later in this chapter.

For MS-DOS-based applications that need special parameters to run, Windows 98 includes an Apps.inf file that defines parameters for each application. When running under Windows 98, MS-DOS-based applications also benefit from the following:

- Improved robustness, including better virtualization for computer resources, such as support for timers and sound devices.

- Improved support for highly graphical MS-DOS-based applications. This allows you to run video-mode style applications in a window rather than in a full screen.

- Improved memory protection. Windows 98 includes a global memory-protection attribute in the **Properties** dialog box for executable files. This attribute allows the MS-DOS system area to be protected from errant MS-DOS-based applications.

- Improved printing performance and font support, including user-scalable windows with support for TrueType fonts in VMs.

- Local environment settings for VMs. You can also customize the VM environment by specifying a batch file in an executable file's properties.

Because of default settings and other support in Windows 98, you do not need Config.sys, Autoexec.bat, and INI files to run MS-DOS-based applications, although you can still use settings from existing files. Windows automatically moves the current settings for your installed applications to the registry when you install Windows 98.

Installing Applications

This section describes how to install and remove applications locally or on a network. It also describes how to configure distributed applications across a network using Distributed COM.

Considerations Before Installing Applications

Before you install and configure applications for use with Windows 98, consider the following questions:

- How will applications perform in your networking environment? After you set up Windows 98 on the network, you will need to install and test how applications perform. For example, for MS-DOS-based applications, test whether they can run in a window or if you need to run them in MS-DOS mode. After you test them, disperse information to users about how to run different applications.

- Which applications do you want to share over the network? With Windows 98, most applications can be shared across the network by installing them on a network server and then creating shortcuts to them on the client computers. Users can open them from the network location by double-clicking the shortcuts. For more information, see "Sharing and Installing Applications Across a Network" later in this chapter.

  To share some large applications, you must run a separate setup on the server and on the workstation. Check the documentation for the application before attempting to share it across the network.

- Can you use Distributed COM to configure distributed applications for use across a network? For more information, see "Distributing Applications Across a Network" later in this chapter.

- Do you want to use software distribution channels to automatically install or update applications? Internet Explorer 4.0 can subscribe to software distribution channels, a special type of Active Channel that updates subscribers' computers at regular intervals. For more information, see Chapter 6, "Configuring the Active Desktop and Active Channels."

- Do you want to simplify users' access to applications by customizing the **Programs** menu or the toolbar? For more information, see Chapter 6, "Configuring the Active Desktop and Active Channels."

- Do the default settings for each of your MS-DOS-based applications work well? You can use an executable file's **Properties** dialog box to modify settings as needed, as described in "Configuring MS-DOS-based Applications" later in this chapter.

- Which terminate-and-stay-resident (TSR) programs do you need to run to support applications? If you are running Client for NetWare Networks, you cannot process TSRs in a logon script. For information about how to load a TSR, see the section titled "Running Logon Scripts with Client for NetWare Networks" in Chapter 18, "Logon, Browsing, and Resource Sharing."

- Do you need to restrict users from running MS-DOS-based applications? For computers that run file and printer sharing services, where access to the shared resources is critical to other users, you may want to restrict the ability to switch to MS-DOS mode to ensure that shared resources are always available. Or do you want to allow only certain Windows-based applications to run on a computer? For more information about using system policies to restrict access to MS-DOS mode or restrict the applications that can run on a computer, see Chapter 7, "User Profiles," and Chapter 8, "System Policies."

Installing Applications Locally

How you install and configure an application depends on whether it was created for Windows 95, Windows 3.1, or MS-DOS. This section discusses how to install and configure applications written for each operating system and how to find out whether your application is compatible with Windows 98. For more information about installing and configuring distributed applications across a network using Distributed COM, see "Distributing Applications Across a Network" later in this chapter.

Using Add/Remove Programs with Win32-based Applications

Windows 98 simplifies installing Win32-based applications by providing an Add/Remove Programs option in Control Panel. When you install an application using this option, Windows 98 does the following:

- Searches specified drives for files named Install or Setup. If an application setup file uses a name other than Install or Setup, you can start setup by double-clicking the application setup file's icon in My Computer.

- Adds to the registry such information about the application as which parameters to use to run the application and which files to delete when removing the application from the computer.

Keeping Windows 3.1 Settings

If you upgrade by placing Windows 98 in the Windows 3.*x* directory, you do not need to reinstall applications. Setup automatically moves information about currently installed applications to the registry. Setup also converts existing Program Manager groups and adds them to the **Programs** menu on the **Start** menu.

If you install Windows 98 in a separate directory, you must reinstall all Windows-based applications to ensure that they work properly under Windows 98. Copying GRP and INI files from your previous \Windows directory is not sufficient to run applications under Windows 98.

Creating Application Groups and Icons

When a Windows-based setup application creates an application group and icons, Windows 98 creates folders and icons for the **Programs** menu on the **Start** menu. If a setup application fails to create a shortcut correctly, you can do it manually. For information about adding shortcuts to the **Start** menu, see the section titled "Configuring the Start and Programs Menus" in Chapter 6, "Configuring the Active Desktop and Active Channels."

Installing MS-DOS-based Applications

You generally install an MS-DOS-based application by running its Setup.exe file. When you install the application, Windows 98 copies information about the application from Apps.inf to the application's program information file (PIF). If the application was installed under an earlier version of Windows, Setup automatically moves its settings to the new Apps.inf. If there is no information about the application in Apps.inf, Windows 98 uses default settings instead, or you can manually set the properties, as described in "Configuring MS-DOS-based Applications" later in this chapter.

Note Windows 98 has no separate PIF Editor. To configure an application, right-click its executable file, and then click Properties.

Running Specific Applications

For more information about whether a specific application runs under Windows 98, check the Windows 98 Readme.txt file. If you do not find an application listed in Readme.txt, check with the application's manufacturer or your software vendor. Windows 98 provides a utility that makes an incompatible application compatible with Windows 98. This utility is a file named Mkcompat.exe in the \Windows\System directory. For more information, see "How Windows 98 Accommodates Application Problems" later in this chapter.

For more information about installing applications after you have installed Windows 98, see online Help.

Sharing and Installing Applications Across a Network

This section describes how to share and install applications over a network. It first explains how to make applications available over a network. It then explains an optional procedure for giving users a master list of available applications.

Sharing Applications

You can share most applications on a network by installing them on a network server and then creating shortcuts to them on the client computers. Users can run an application by double-clicking the shortcut or by double-clicking the application's icon in Network Neighborhood.

You can also install applications over a network by using software distribution channels, a type of Active Channel that updates subscriber's computers at regular intervals. For more information about software distribution channels, see Chapter 6, "Configuring the Active Desktop and Active Channels."

▶ **To share an application on a network**

1. Install an application on a network server or workstation, as described in the documentation from the vendor.

2. Make sure that users can access the network server or workstation. For information about sharing directories on Windows 98 computers, see Chapter 18, "Logon, Browsing, and Resource Sharing." For information about sharing directories on Windows NT–based computers, see the *Microsoft Windows NT Server Networking Guide* in the *Microsoft Windows NT Server Resource Kit* (for Microsoft Windows NT Server version 4.0) (ISBN 1-57231-343-9).

3. On a client computer, go to Network Neighborhood, right-click and hold down the icon for the application, drag it to the desktop, and then click **Create Shortcut**.

For more information about creating shortcuts, see online Help. For information about creating and distributing custom shortcuts using system policies, see Chapter 8, "System Policies." For more information about configuring Active Desktop toolbars, see Chapter 6, "Configuring the Active Desktop and Active Channels."

Creating an Apps.ini File

If users will be installing applications from source files stored on a network, you can create an Apps.ini file that contains a master list of applications and their network locations. When a user's registry contains a reference to Apps.ini, a new tab named **Network Install** appears under Add/Remove Programs, in Control Panel. The **Network Install** tab lists all the applications that appear in the Apps.ini file and that can be installed from the server.

▶ **To create an Apps.ini file on a network server**

1. Use a text editor to create a file that contains a list of applications using the following format:

   ```
   [AppInstallList]
   application name = [*] UNC path
   ```

   For *application name*, substitute the name that you want users to see on the **Network Install** tab. For *UNC path*, substitute the network location of the Setup application. If a Setup application cannot work with universal naming convention (UNC) names, include an asterisk before it. For example:

   ```
   Microsoft Word 97=*\\applications\forusers\word97\setup.exe
   ```

2. Save Apps.ini on a server to which users have read-only access.

▶ **To display the applications listed in Apps.ini on a client computer's Network Install tab**

1. In the registry on the client computer, click the following key:

   Hkey_Local_Machine/Software/Microsoft/Windows/Current Version

2. Right-click a blank area in the right pane, and then click **New**.

3. Click **String Value**, type **appinstallpath**, and then press ENTER.

4. Right-click the item you just created.

5. In the **Edit** menu, click **Modify**.

6. In the **Value Data** area, type the UNC path to Apps.ini, including the file name. For example:

   ```
   \\myserver\myshare\apps.ini
   ```

7. Click **Close**.

For information about adding registry settings in setup scripts, see Appendix D, "Msbatch.inf Parameters for Setup Scripts." For information about adding registry settings using system policies, see Chapter 8, "System Policies."

Distributing Applications Across a Network

This section describes how to use the Distributed COM Configuration tool to configure clients, servers, and applications. The Distributed COM Configuration tool lets you configure 32-bit COM and Distributed COM distributed applications to run across computers by specifying properties for the distributed application, such as the locations of application components and security for those components.

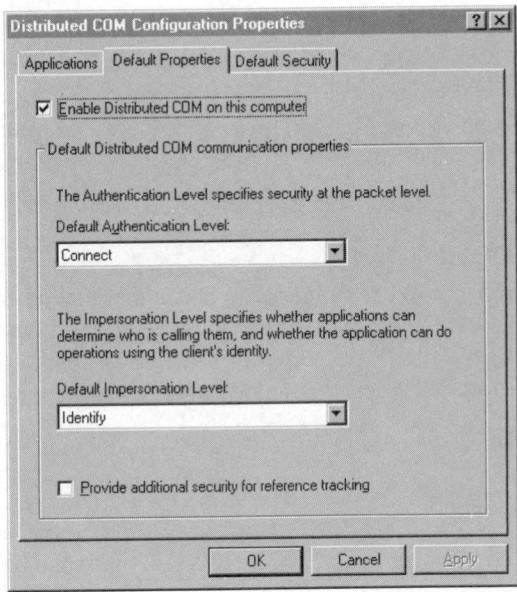

Note Application configuration can also be specified in the application itself. If so, the settings override any settings you choose in the DCOM Configuration tool.

For additional procedures on using the Distributed COM Configuration tool to configure applications, see the Distributed COM Configuration tool's online Help system.

For more information about setting security levels and permissions for Distributed COM applications, see Chapter 9, "Security."

Configuring Distributed COM Clients and Servers

A Distributed COM computer running Windows 98 can be either a client, a server, or both. A *client* makes calls to a component, and a *server* gets calls. Thus, if computer A is running an application that calls a component on computer B, computer A is acting as a client and computer B is acting as a server. If the component on computer B also calls a component on computer C, computer B is acting both as a client and as a server.

Using the Distributed COM Configuration tool, you can configure your computer as a client, a server, or both. By default, your computer is configured as a client but not as a server. Before you can use dcomcnfg your computer must be configured for user-level security. For more information, see Chapter 18, "Logon, Browsing, and Resource Sharing."

▶ **To configure your computer as a DCOM client and server**

1. On the **Start** menu, click **Run**, and then in the **Open** box, type **dcomcnfg**.

2. Click the **Default Properties** tab, and then select the **Enable Distributed COM on this computer** check box if it is not already selected. By default, this box is selected.

3. If you also want to configure your computer as a Distributed COM server (you want to receive calls from other computers), click the **Default Security** tab, and then select the **Enable Remote Connection** check box.

Setting Authentication Levels

You can configure the client computer to use authentication when a connection is made to the server. You can also configure the server to use authentication when a connection is made to a server. If either the client or the server requests authentication, both will need to use authentication.

It is highly recommended that you configure your computer to use authentication if it will be used as a server. Otherwise, client computers can call the server without being authenticated.

If your computer is not part of a Windows NT domain and has no access to Windows NT domain security, authentication will fail. If either the client or the server request authentication, the connection will fail. Thus, if you are certain that your computer is a client and not a server, and your computer is not part of a Windows NT domain, you might want to set that computer not to use authentication. However, even if you do so, the connection will fail if the server requests authentication.

If your computer is a server and is part of a Windows NT domain, but it is configured to use share-level security, a secure connection will fail. In that case, you might want to set your computer to use user-level security. For more information about user-level security, see Chapter 9, "Security" and Chapter 18, "Logon, Browsing, and Resource Sharing."

Before you can use dcomcnfg your computer must be configured for user-level security. For more information, see Chapter 18, "Logon, Browsing, and Resource Sharing."

▶ **To set authentication on communications between applications**

1. On the **Start** menu, click **Run**, and then in the **Open** box, type **dcomcnfg**.

2. Click the **Default Properties** tab, and then in the **Default Authentication Level** box, select the security level you want:

    ▪ To disable security checking on communications between applications, select (**None**).

    ▪ To enable security checking for the initial connection, select **Connect**.

Setting Impersonation Levels

With *impersonation*, one process can take on the security attributes of another process. For example, a server process can impersonate a client process to complete a task involving objects to which the server does not normally have access. The server application can impersonate the client application only on the computer running the server application.

You can set impersonation levels for a Distributed COM application on a Windows 98 Distributed COM client, enabling Windows NT Distributed COM servers to impersonate the client.

In most cases, the default settings are correct. However, if you want to change the impersonation level, see online Help.

Setting the Location for Distributed COM Applications

The first step in configuring an application for Distributed COM is to specify the location of the server application that will be accessed by the computer running the client application. You do this on the computer running the client application. Before you can use dcomcnfg your computer must be configured for user-level security. For more information, see Chapter 18, "Logon, Browsing, and Resource Sharing."

▶ **To set the location of a Distributed COM application**

1. On the **Start** menu, click **Run**, and then in the **Open** box, type **dcomcnfg**.

2. Click the **Applications** tab, click the application that you want to configure, and then click **Properties**.

3. Click the **Location** tab, and then specify where you want to run the server application.

Configuring User Accounts to Access Distributed Applications with Distributed COM

You can create an access control list that specifies the user accounts that will have permission to have access to or start applications, on either the server or the application, or both. Before a component can run, Distributed COM validates the user name using whatever authentication mechanism is configured and checks the user name against the access control list. The permissions you can set depend on the server's operating system:

- If the server is running Windows NT, you can set both access and start permissions.

- If the server is running Windows 98, you can set only access permissions. The server must have user-level security installed and must be using Windows NT domain security.

Note If you set custom permissions for a Distributed COM application, the custom permissions will override any default permissions that have been set for all applications.

For information about how to use the Distributed COM Configuration tool to configure users and permissions, see online Help.

Starting Distributed COM–enabled Applications

The extent to which a Distributed COM client computer running Windows 98 can start or access a Distributed COM–enabled application on a server depends on the server's operating system:

- If the server is running Windows NT, the client can start or access the server application.

- If the server is running Windows 98, the client cannot start the server application. The server application must be started manually on the server, and then the client can access it.

Removing Applications

If you installed applications through Add/Remove Programs in Control Panel, you can safely remove them in the same way. Because the application's components are tracked through the registry, Windows 98 deletes all of the application's files unless those files are being used by another application. Shared files are retained on the hard disk. You see a prompt if you try to remove a shared file.

Removing a Win16-based or MS-DOS-based application is not always straightforward. You can delete the directory that contains the application, but additional files belonging to the application (especially in a Win16-based application) are often located in the \Windows or \Windows\System directory. There is no way to determine which applications placed certain files in these directories, so some of the application's files may be left behind on your hard disk.

If you try to delete all the files of an application installed in the \Windows or \Windows\System directory, you might delete a system file used by other applications. If this happens, the other applications will not run properly and must be reinstalled.

To avoid problems when removing Win16-based or MS-DOS-based applications, check their documentation for instructions about removing them, and keep backup copies of dynamic-link libraries (DLLs) and other essential system files, in case you need to restore them.

Configuring Applications

This section describes how to optimize access to applications by configuring elements of the Active Desktop. It also discusses how to associate specific file types with applications and how to optimize the performance of MS-DOS-based applications.

Associating File Types with Applications

To open an application when you double-click a related file, the file's type must be defined in the registry. If the file type is defined in the registry, it appears in a list of file types that you can associate with applications.

For any standard Windows-based application, file types are automatically associated with the application when you install the application on your computer. You can use the following procedure to associate a file type with a different application. For example, if you wanted to make Internet Explorer open all GIF files, you could use this procedure to associate Internet Explorer with GIF files.

▶ **To associate a file type with an application**

1. In **My Computer** or **Windows Explorer**, click **View**, and then click **Folder Options**.

2. Click the **File Types** tab.

3. Click the type of file that you want to associate, and then click **Edit**.

4. In the **Actions** list, click **Open**, and then click **Edit**.

5. In the **Application used to perform action** area, type or browse the path to the application you want to associate the file type.

Some applications, such as Microsoft Word, associate multiple extensions with a file type. For example, a Microsoft Word document is associated by default with either a .doc or an .rtf extension. This can cause problems if a user wants to change which application opens a particular file. To re-associate a file type with an application under these conditions, follow the preceding procedure to delete all extensions registered to that application on the **File Types** tab, and then re-associate each file type with an application. In addition, you must redefine Open, Print, and Dynamic Data Exchange (DDE) actions for each file type.

Customizing the New Shortcut Menu

The **New** shortcut menu shows a list of options, such as **Folder**, **Shortcut**, **Text Document**, and **Microsoft Word Document**. It appears when you click **File** and then point to **New** in Windows Explorer, or when you right-click the Active Desktop and then point to **New** on the shortcut menu. Clicking an object on the **New** shortcut menu creates that new object in Windows Explorer or on the desktop. You can add an object to this list by adding a key called ShellNew to the corresponding file extension in the registry for the related file name extension:

Hkey_Classes_Root\.ext

After creating the ShellNew key, add a new string value called **FileName** with a data value that equals the path of a template file in the ShellNew subdirectory. For example:

```
filename="c:\windows\shellnew\excel.xls"
```

Customizing the Active Desktop for Applications

The Windows 98 Active Desktop lets you simplify a user's access to applications by customizing the Active Desktop **Start** and **Programs** menus. You can also create new toolbars containing only the applications and documents that you use most often.

You can also customize many other Active Desktop elements, such as channel bars, folders, and Active Desktop items. For more information about customizing the Active Desktop, see Chapter 6, "Configuring the Active Desktop and Active Channels."

Note Windows 98 adds your most recently used documents to **Documents** on the **Start** menu. However, documents opened in an application that is not Win32-based do not appear. Win16-based documents are added to the list only if you double-click the document's icon in Windows Explorer or My Computer.

Configuring MS-DOS-based Applications

Windows 98 configures conventional memory as do earlier versions of Windows, allowing MS-DOS-based applications to run smoothly in Windows 98. For more information about how Windows 98 makes system memory available to MS-DOS-based applications, see Chapter 26, "Performance Tuning."

Understanding the Apps.inf File

The Apps.inf file in Windows 98 (in the \Windows\Inf directory) contains a section named [PIF95] that acts as a master list of settings for MS-DOS-based applications. Each line in this section corresponds to a subsequent entry in Apps.inf that contains information about running that specific application. Table 25.1 explains these entries.

Each entry in the [PIF95] section uses the following syntax:

app file=%title%, icon file, icon num, set working, section, other file, set pif

Table 25.1   Syntax of [PIF95] entries in Apps.inf

Entry	Meaning
app file	The file name, with extension, of the application's executable file.
title	The name that appears in the application's title bar. The string identifier must appear in the [Strings] section of the INF file, set to the quoted name of the application.
icon file	The file from which to extract the application's icon.
icon num	The number from the icon extraction table. The default is **0**.
set working	Allows Windows 98 to set the working directory automatically to the one that contains the executable (**0**, the default) or prevents it from doing so (**1**).
section	The name of the corresponding section in Apps.inf that contains details about this application.
other file	The key file within a directory for this application, used when two *app file* entries are identically named.
set pif	The value allowing (**0**, the default) or preventing (**1**) creation of a PIF file for this application.

Following the [PIF95] section are sections for each application listed in [PIF95]. Each application section includes entries that define any parameters, required memory or other options, and options that can be enabled or disabled for that application. For example:

```
[WORD.EXE]
LowMem=384
Enable=cwe
Disable=win,bgd,asp
```

The **Enable=** and **Disable=** entries use the abbreviations shown in Table 25.2. To separate multiple entries, use commas.

Table 25.2   Abbreviations used in Enable= and Disable= [PIF95] entries in Apps.inf

Entry	Meaning	Entry	Meaning
aen	ALT+ENTER	eml	EMS memory locked
aes	ALT+ESC	ems	EMS memory
afp	Allow fast paste	emt	Emulate ROM
aps	ALT+PRINT SCREEN	exc	Exclusive mode
asp	ALT+SPACE	gmp	Global memory protection
ata	ALT+TAB	hma	Use HMA
awc	Automatic window conversion	lml	Low memory locked
bgd	Background	mse	Mouse
cdr	CD-ROM	net	Network
ces	CTRL+ESC	psc	PRINT SCREEN
cwe	Close on exit	rvm	Retain video memory
dit	Detect idle time	rwp	Run Windows applications
dos	Real mode	win	Run in a window
dsk	Disk lock	xml	XMS memory locked

Changing PIF Files

In addition to the information contained in the Apps.inf file, you can set unique properties for individual MS-DOS-based applications. You may want to do this to customize the way an application runs or to reset default properties used by Windows 98 that do not work correctly.

An application's settings are recorded in its program information file (PIF). Windows 98 has no separate PIF Editor. To configure an application, right-click the application's executable file, and then click **Properties**. Any settings you change in the **Properties** dialog box are recorded in the PIF file.

Windows 98 first searches for a PIF file in the directory that contains the executable file you are starting. If Windows 98 cannot find a PIF file there, it searches the \Windows\PIF directory. If there is no PIF file in the \Windows\PIF directory, Windows 98 searches the path specified in Autoexec.bat. If no PIF file is found, Windows 98 searches the Apps.inf file for a match.

If Windows 98 does not find an entry for an application in Apps.inf, it uses default settings for the application. If you replace Windows 3.1 with Windows 98, a _default.pif file remains in the directory. In this case, Windows 98 uses information in the _default.pif file to create a PIF file for the application.

If you do not have a _default.pif file and want to create one, you can do so by copying Dosprmpt.pif to _default.pif.

Regardless of how the settings for an application are initially established, you can change them by right-clicking the application's executable file and then clicking **Properties**.

Changing Memory Settings

Windows 98 provides a flexible environment for running MS-DOS-based applications, even those that must have exclusive access to system resources. Almost all MS-DOS-based applications should run under Windows 98. For MS-DOS-based applications that need sole access to computer resources, Windows 98 offers MS-DOS mode.

When an MS-DOS-based application starts in MS-DOS mode, Windows 98 removes itself from memory (except for a small stub) and provides the application with full access to all the computer's resources. Before running an application in this mode, Windows 98 ends all running tasks, loads a real-mode copy of MS-DOS, and uses customized versions of Config.sys and Autoexec.bat to run the application. After you quit the MS-DOS-based application, Windows 98 restarts and returns to the Windows 98 user interface.

MS-DOS mode is intended for applications that will not otherwise run in Windows 98. It does not necessarily improve the performance of MS-DOS-based applications that will run in Windows 98.

▶ **To configure an MS-DOS-based application to run in MS-DOS mode**

1. Right-click the icon for the application, and then click **Properties**.

2. Click the **Program** tab, and then click **Advanced**.

3. In the **Advanced Program Settings** dialog box, select the **MS-DOS mode** check box.

If an MS-DOS-based application, such as a game, performs badly because of insufficient memory or a lack of appropriate drivers, you can try the following:

- Run the application in MS-DOS mode.
- Adjust the amount of memory available.
- Create a custom startup configuration by modifying the contents of Config.sys and Autoexec.bat.

▶ **To adjust the amount of memory available to an MS-DOS-based application**

1. Right-click the icon for the application, and then click **Properties**.
2. Click the **Memory** tab, and then increase or decrease the amount of memory available to the application.

The following procedure describes how to create a custom PIF file for an MS-DOS-based application. Windows 98 includes two sample PIF files in the \Windows directory.

▶ **To create a custom startup configuration for an MS-DOS-based application**

1. Right-click the icon for the application, and then click **Properties**.
2. Click the **Program** tab, and then click **Advanced**.
3. In the **Advanced Program Settings** dialog box, select the **MS-DOS mode** check box, and then click **Specify a new MS-DOS configuration**.
4. Specify any custom startup instructions in the **Config.sys for MS-DOS mode** and **Autoexec.bat for MS-DOS mode** boxes.
5. If you want to enable or disable additional options, such as expanded memory specification (EMS) or Direct Disk Access, click **Configuration**, and then select the options you want to enable for your custom configuration.

Note Windows 98 automatically provides expanded memory for MS-DOS-based applications that require it to run. Windows cannot provide this memory, however, if you include a statement in Config.sys that loads Emm386.exe with the **noems** parameter. When you include Emm386.exe in Config.sys, use the **ram** parameter or use the x=*mmmm-nnnn* statement to allocate enough space in the upper memory area for Windows 98 to create an EMS page frame.

Setting Properties

In Windows 98, the properties sheets replace PIF Editor, which was used in versions of Windows earlier than Windows 95 to optimize settings for MS-DOS-based applications.

▶ **To view or modify the properties settings for an MS-DOS-based application**

1. Right-click the icon for the application, and then click **Properties**.

2. Click the tab you want to use, and change the options as appropriate.

For specific information about the options on each tab of the **Properties** dialog box, click the **Quick Help** button in the upper right of the tab, and then click the option you want to learn more about.

Setting Paths

You can set the path for a specific MS-DOS-based application that runs in MS-DOS mode using the following procedure.

▶ **To specify a path for an MS-DOS-based application that runs in MS-DOS mode**

1. Right-click the icon for the application, and then click **Properties**.

2. Click the **Program** tab, and then click **Advanced**.

3. In the **Advanced Program Settings** dialog box, select the **MS-DOS mode** check box, and then click **Specify a new MS-DOS configuration**.

4. In the **Autoexec.bat for MS-DOS mode** box, specify the correct path.

Note For MS-DOS-based applications that do not run in MS-DOS mode, you can set only a working directory.

You can set a global path for all MS-DOS-based applications by adding a path statement to Autoexec.bat. You can also write a batch file that sets a path for an MS-DOS-based application. For example:

```
path=%path%;c:\utils;c:\norton
```

After you write the batch file, carry out the following procedure to ensure that Windows runs it before starting your MS-DOS-based application.

▶ **To run a batch file before starting an MS-DOS-based application**

1. In the application's **Properties** dialog box, click the **Programs** tab.

2. In the **Batch file** box, type the batch file's path and name.

3. If you want the VM window in which the batch file is running to close after the batch file has finished, select the **Close on exit** check box.

Running Games

In most cases, MS-DOS-based games run under Windows 98 with no special adjustments. Most popular games are listed in the Windows 98 Apps.inf file. You do not need to specify certain PIF settings because Windows 98 manages them automatically. These settings include foreground and background priorities, exclusive priority, video memory usage, and video port monitoring.

If you run a game that uses graphics modes, and Windows 98 fails to run it in a full screen, press ALT+ENTER. To run the game in a full screen every time you start it, right-click its executable file, and then click **Properties**. Click the **Screen** tab, and then in the **Usage** area, click **Full-screen**. You can also use the **Properties** dialog box to adjust other settings that improve performance.

Using Applications

This section describes how to start applications and how you can use object linking and embedding (OLE) to share data between applications. It also discusses what to do when an application fails.

Starting Applications

There are several ways to start applications in Windows 98:

- Click the **Start** button, point to **Programs**, point to the folder that contains the application, and then double-click the application's name.

- In My Computer or Windows Explorer, double-click the application's icon.

- In My Computer or Windows Explorer, click the application's icon, click the **File** menu, and then click Open. Or right-click the application's icon, and then click **Open**.

- If the application has a shortcut on the desktop, double-click the application's shortcut icon.

- If the application has an icon on the QuickLaunch toolbar or on a custom toolbar, double-click the application's icon.

- Click the **Start** button, click **Run**, and then type the path and file name for the application's executable file.

Tip Instead of starting a Windows-based application to see the contents of a document, you can use the Windows Explorer **Quick View** option. You must first install **Quick View** using Add/Remove Programs in Control Panel. To use **Quick View**, in Windows Explorer, right-click the document you want to look at, and then click **Quick View** on the shortcut menu. This opens a Quick View window of the document. If you want to open the document, click **File** in the Quick View window, and then click **Open File for Editing**. For more information, see online Help.

Using Object Linking and Embedding to Share Data Between Applications

Windows 98 includes built-in object linking and embedding (OLE) functionality that enables you to share data between OLE-compliant applications. Using applications that take advantage of OLE technology, you can create compound documents that contain multiple types of data and that allow you (or other users) to edit or display that data without running other applications.

OLE version 2.0 is a technology built into Windows 98 that improves on the OLE version 1.0 standard. It provides services for sharing OLE objects (units of data) and the related functions needed to manipulate that data.

As Figure 25.2 shows, OLE technology provides a way of communicating between *container applications* and *object applications*. Container applications maintain compound documents, and object applications act as servers to provide various data objects (such as text, bitmaps, spreadsheets, spreadsheet cells, or sound clips) to be included in the compound document. The container application does not need any information about the object application or its data type to communicate with it.

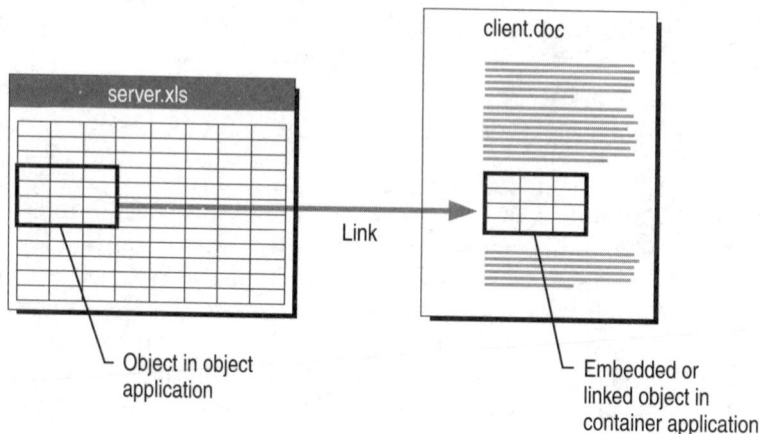

Figure 25.2   OLE objects in applications

Windows 98 keeps track of OLE objects by keeping an entry for each one in the registry. Each entry includes a unique identification tag for the object and an application identifier. The application identifier is also used as a class name when OLE objects are placed in OLE containers. For example, "Word.Document.8" is the application identifier for a Word 8.0 document.

Note With ClipBook Viewer, an OLE application that is located in the \Add-ons\Clipbook directory on the Windows 98 compact disc, you can share OLE objects for use in documents across a network. For more information, see Help in ClipBook Viewer.

OLE objects can be visually edited, meaning that users can activate objects and edit, play, or otherwise manipulate them in the location in which they are embedded.

To make visual editing possible, both the container application and the object application must be OLE-compliant and must support the OLE visual editing interface. This interface is a feature of Windows 98 OLE and is not supported by OLE 1.0. If either application meets only the OLE 1.0 specification, the object application will be launched in a separate window for editing. For example, Corel Draw version 4.0 implements some features of OLE that do not include the visual editing interface, so when a Corel Draw 4.0 object is opened for editing from a Word document, the Corel Draw 4.0 application will start in its own window.

Note OLE version 2.0 applications that do not support visual editing also open in separate windows.

If an embedded object has a file name extension that is not associated with any application, you may not be able to activate it successfully. You must first associate the file type with an application. For more information about associating file types with applications, see "Associating File Types with Applications" earlier in this chapter.

To move or copy an object, you can drag it from one container to another. When doing so, use the key combinations outlined in Table 25.3.

Table 25.3   Key combinations used for moving and copying objects

Mouse Action	Result
Drag and drop	Moves the object unless the source and target applications have the same data type, in which case the information is merely placed as native data.
SHIFT+drag and drop	Moves the object.
CTRL+drag and drop	Copies the object.
SHIFT+CTRL+drag and drop	Links the object from the source to the container.

Closing Failed Applications

If an application stops responding, or other parts of the computer, such as the keyboard, mouse, or display, no longer function correctly, you can end the malfunctioning process or application by pressing CTRL+ALT+DEL.

Some applications may have several processes running simultaneously. For example, a mail application may be running an executable application and a spooler. If a single process fails and you close that process, the rest of the application may continue to run.

Although it is possible to restart your computer by pressing CTRL+ALT+DEL twice, it is not recommended. For more information about restarting or shutting down a computer, see online Help.

Technical Notes

This section summarizes technical information about running applications under Windows 98. For more information about the supporting system components, see Chapter 28, "Windows 98 Architecture."

System Changes Affecting Application Support

The following sections describe how system changes affect 16-bit and 32-bit applications and MS-DOS-based applications.

Windows 98 changes the system configuration files, as described in Chapter 5, "Setup Technical Discussion." The following changes affect application support:

- If no **files=** line is specified in Config.sys, Windows 98 uses a setting of 60.

- Many application settings have moved from INI files to the registry. If you install an application after Windows 98 has been installed, and the setup application writes directly to Win.ini and System.ini instead of using documented functions, Windows 98 does not recognize those changes. To resolve this problem, obtain a version of the application designed for Windows 98 or Windows 95.

- Windows 98 enables file sharing by default. Therefore, it is no longer necessary to add Share.exe to Autoexec.bat or Vshare to System.ini. However, some applications check for the existence of Share.exe. To work around this problem, create a dummy file called Share.exe in your \Windows\Command directory. Depending on the application, you might also need to add a line to Autoexec.bat referring to the dummy Share.exe file. To do so, follow the procedure below:

▶ **To create a dummy Share.exe file**

1. At the command prompt, go to the \Windows\Command directory and type **Copy con share.exe**.

2. Press ENTER at least twice.

3. Press CTRL+Z, and then press ENTER again. A dummy file called Share.exe is created.

Distributed Component Object Model

The Distributed Component Object Model (Distributed COM) is based on the COM standard. With COM, an object can have multiple interfaces (the set of methods and properties the object supports). When an application accesses a COM object, it always uses an interface pointer. As a result, the calling application does
not need to know the location of the object or how it is implemented. Also, developers can modify the implementation of COM interfaces — or add support for additional interfaces to your components — without rebuilding the client applications that use them.

COM also provides location transparency. All method calls on objects are similar to in-process function calls. The operating system handles all the details of making the call across processes.

As Figure 25.3 shows, Distributed COM extends COM to make the call across computers and to add security mechanisms. An application does not need to know the details of local or remote procedure calls (RPCs).

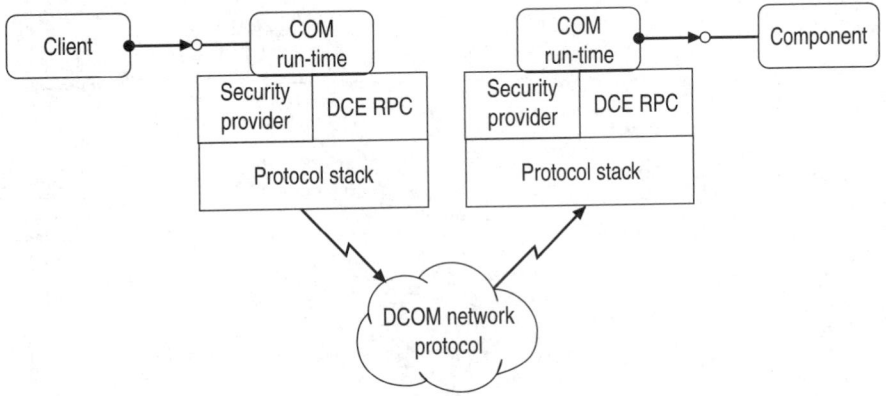

Figure 25.3   Distributed COM schematic overview

Win32-based Applications

Applications that use Win32 application programming interfaces (APIs) can take full advantage of all Windows 98 performance enhancement features. Win32-based applications can utilize multitasking, Win32 APIs, long file name support, separate message queues, and memory protection. Each Win32-based application runs in its own fully protected, private address space, preventing it from causing the operating system or other applications to fail and preventing interference from errors generated by other applications. In addition, you can manage files from the **Open** dialog box in Win32-based applications.

To support preemptive multitasking, the Windows 98 kernel schedules the time allotted for running applications. This results in smoother concurrent processing and prevents any one application from using all system resources without permitting other tasks to run. (An exception is when you run an MS-DOS-based application in MS-DOS mode, which gives the application exclusive use of system resources.) Win32-based applications can implement threads to improve the level of detail at which they can take advantage of multitasking. As Figure 25.4 shows, each Win32-based application has its own message queue and, consequently, is not affected by how other tasks access message queues.

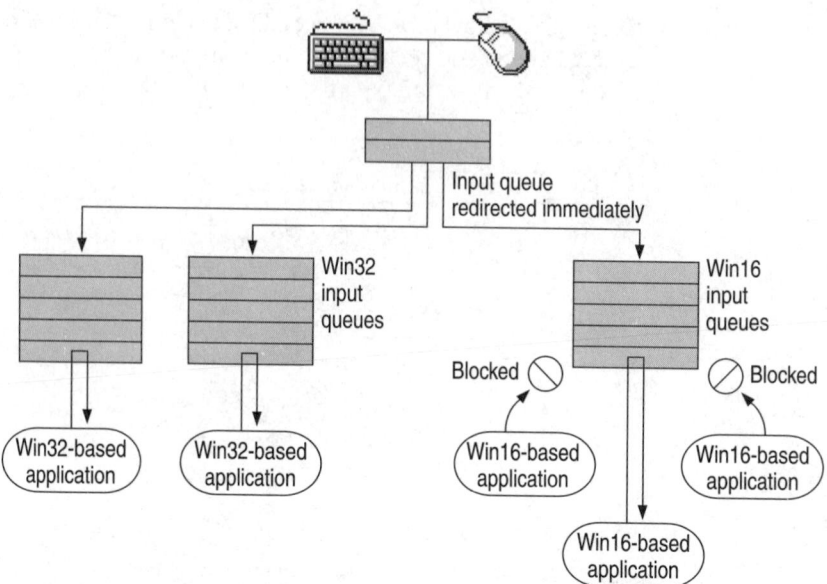

Figure 25.4   Message queues in Windows 98

Resources allocated for each Win32-based application tracked on a per-thread basis are automatically freed when the application ends. If an application stops responding, you can press CTRL+ALT+DEL to display the **Close Program** dialog box, and then close the unresponsive application without affecting other running tasks.

To make the most of Windows 98, your applications should:

- Be Win32-based.
- Be OLE-compliant to allow for data sharing with other applications.
- Use RPCs for networked NetBIOS applications.
- Use Windows Sockets for networked non-NetBIOS applications.

A Win32-based application that runs under Windows NT will run well under Windows 98 if it does not use any Windows NT–specific APIs (such as those for security) or if it has been designed to run under both Windows 98 and Windows NT.

Win16-based Applications

Win16-based applications designed for Windows 3.1 run under Windows 98 without modification. Windows 98 ensures that Win16-based applications running on a computer with 16 MB or memory or more perform as well as—or better than—they did under Windows 3.1. In addition, the performance of Win16-based applications is improved, because they can use operating system services provided by the 32-bit system components of Windows 98, including 32-bit device driver components and 32-bit subsystems.

Windows 98 provides the same system resources to both Win32-based and Win16-based applications, but Win16-based applications cannot take advantage of preemptive multitasking. Win16-based applications share memory as well as common input and message queues, and their processes are scheduled cooperatively.

Win16-based applications benefit from preemptive multitasking of other system components, including the 32-bit print and communications subsystems and improvements made in system robustness and protection for the Windows 98 system kernel.

Because all Win16-based applications run in the same VM, an errant application can cause other Win16-based applications to fail, but it should not adversely affect Win32-based applications. However, the improvements made to overall system-wide robustness significantly increase the system's ability to recover from an errant application. Improved cleanup of the system lessens the likelihood of application errors. Windows 98 tracks resources allocated by Win16-based applications and uses the information to clean up the system after an application exits or ends abnormally, thus freeing up unused resources that the rest of the system can use. If an application does fail, you can press CTRL+ALT+DEL to display the **Close Program** dialog box, and then close the unresponsive application without affecting other running tasks.

Note Win16-based applications cannot use long file names. The Windows 98 file system should preserve long file names while you use a Win16-based application to edit files. However, you will lose long file names if you copy files from within existing Win16-based applications, such as user interface replacements.

MS-DOS-based Applications

Windows 98 support for MS-DOS-based applications includes better printing support and improved capabilities for running hardware-intensive applications, such as games.

Each MS-DOS-based application runs in its own VM, allowing multiple 8086-compatible sessions to run on the CPU. This, in turn, allows existing MS-DOS-based applications to run preemptively with the rest of the system. The use of virtual device drivers (VxDs) provides common regulated access to hardware resources. Each application running in a VM appears to run on its own individual computer; this allows applications that were not designed for multitasking to run concurrently with other applications.

VMs are protected from each other and from other running applications. This prevents errant MS-DOS-based applications from overwriting memory that is occupied or used by system components or other applications. If an MS-DOS-based application attempts to access memory outside its address space, the system notifies the user and ends the MS-DOS-based application.

One of the major difficulties MS-DOS-based applications had in the VMs in versions of Windows earlier than Windows 95 was insufficient conventional memory space. By the time MS-DOS-based device drivers, TSR applications, and networking components were loaded with Windows, there often was not enough conventional memory left to allow the MS-DOS-based application to load or run. Windows 98 provides 32-bit, protected-mode driver components that replace many 16-bit, real-mode device driver and TSR counterparts, improving overall system performance and using no conventional memory. The savings in memory with protected-mode components can be significant. For example, a computer using only Windows 98 protected-mode components would save more than 225 KB of conventional memory over the amount used by real-mode networking software, drivers for a mouse and SCSI CD-ROM drive, and SMARTDrive.

How Windows 98 Accommodates Application Problems

Some Windows-based and MS-DOS-based applications may not run well under Windows 98 because they were written to take advantage of characteristics of older operating systems. For example, certain applications use a portion of the title bar to include items other than the title, such as a **Quick Help** button. Because Windows 98 title bars are not formatted in the same way as Windows 3.x title bars, some information may be overwritten when you run these old applications.

In addition, some applications use interrupts that are not automatically supported by Windows 98. Others do not handle long file names well, or they incorrectly check for the operating system's version number.

Windows 98 provides the Make Compatible utility to make compatible an application that is initially incompatible with Windows 98. You can use this utility to troubleshoot if you have trouble printing from an application, or if an application stalls or has other performance problems. This utility provides the means to increase stack memory to an application, emulate earlier versions of Windows, and solve other common problems that cause an application not to run with Windows 98. For more information, see online Help.

▶ **To run the Make Compatible utility**

- Click the **Start** button, click **Run**, and then type **mkcompat.exe**.

Note Many programming tools not specifically designed to run under Windows 98 may run satisfactorily, but the corresponding debugging tools usually do not. Make sure that both the programming and the debugging tools you use are designed for Windows 98.

Some Win16-based and MS-DOS-based disk utilities must be run with special care. In addition, some disk utilities do not perform correctly with long file names. For more information about using Win16-based and MS-DOS-based disk utilities with Windows 98, see Chapter 10, "Disks and File Systems."

Running Terminate-and-Stay-Resident Programs

Some older terminate-and-stay-resident programs (TSRs) rely on MS-DOS interrupts to monitor everything that happens on the system. However, because of its protected-mode file system, Windows 98 does not use MS-DOS interrupts. If Windows 98 detects that a TSR is trying to monitor these interrupts, it will accommodate the application and send all system information through MS-DOS interrupts. In this way, the TSR can monitor system events successfully. However, doing this will significantly slow the performance of the operating system.

Ios.ini, as described in Chapter 24, "Device Management," includes a list of "safe" drivers and applications. If Windows 98 finds the application listed in Ios.ini, it will not send system events through MS-DOS interrupts, thus avoiding slowed performance.

Fixing Version-Checking Errors

If you are using an MS-DOS-based application that was designed for an MS-DOS version other than 7.1 (which is the version that Windows 98 reports), you may receive a message that says you are not using the correct version of MS-DOS. If this is the case, you can add the application to the version table. The *version table* contains a list of executable files, followed by the version number of MS-DOS with which the applications were designed to run. Windows 98 cannot report the correct MS-DOS version to applications unless the version table is loaded into memory.

To display the version table, type **setver** in a command prompt window. For information about the syntax, parameters, and switches you can use to add an application to the version table, add the question mark (?) switch to the command (that is, type **setver /?** at the command prompt).

To load the version table, include a **device** command in Config.sys. For example:

```
device=c:\windows\setver.exe
```

If you modify the version table or Config.sys, restart the computer so the changes can take effect.

Some applications incorrectly check the version number of Windows 98. Incorrect version-checking techniques sometimes invert the two bytes that record the version number; thus, version 3.10 would be reported as 10.3. Windows 98 tries to accommodate this possible version-checking error by reporting 3.98 as the version. In this way, if an application looks for a version greater than 3.10 or its inverse, 10.3, the new Windows 98 version proves to be greater.

If the application looks for an exact match for the version number, such as Windows version 3.10, it may not run under Windows 98. To resolve this problem, add the following line to the [Compatibility] section of Win.ini:

```
compiled_module_name=0x00200000
```

To determine the compiled module name, right-click an executable file in Windows Explorer, and then click **QuickView**. The Module Name line provides this information. After you have obtained the module name, the section you add to Win.ini should look similar to the following entry for cc:Mail:

```
[Compatibility]
CCMAIL=0x00200000
```

Windows 98 Setup adds entries to Win.ini for many applications that are known to have this problem.

Note Do not add a permanent entry to Win.ini for an installation application. Install your application first, and then edit the compiled module name in Win.ini.

If a setup application incorrectly detects the version of Windows 98, you may not be able to install the application. In this case, add an entry to the [Compatibility] section of Win.ini for the setup application (for example, SETUP=0x00200000). Install the application, and then immediately remove the section that you added to Win.ini.

Running Applications That Replace System Dynamic-Link Libraries

Some setup applications do not check the version of the system files they are installing and overwrite the newer Windows 98 versions of those dynamic-link libraries (DLLs). Windows 98 restores its original DLLs after every setup application runs and for the first three startups thereafter. If an application stops running or behaves erratically after you install it, you may need to obtain an updated version of the application that does not overwrite Windows 98 system files.

Versions of Windows earlier than Windows 95 allowed applications to redistribute parts of the system with no ill effects. For example, an application might overwrite a system file with no adverse consequences. In Windows 98, multiple system files have been consolidated to expedite the startup process. If an application tries to overwrite a system file that is no longer used, Windows allows the application to copy the file, but does not use it.

If your application must run with a replacement file, you can add that file to the \Windows\System\Vmm32 directory (which is initially empty after you set up Windows 98).

After you install an application, Windows 98 checks for files that are commonly overwritten by setup applications. If any are found, a dialog box appears, enabling you to restore the files from the hidden \Windows\Sysbckup directory.

Windows 98 includes a new utility, System File Checker, that checks for replaced system files. For information, see Chapter 27, "General Troubleshooting."

Troubleshooting Applications

This section describes some problems that might occur with applications on Windows 98. For information about specific applications, see the Relnotes.txt file included on the Windows 98 compact disc.

Hot keys fail to start applications.

In Windows 98, you cannot use hot keys to run applications located on the desktop. You can use hot keys to run only those applications located in the Applications folder. To start an application located on the desktop, double-click its icon.

You cannot create a shortcut.

If you try to add an application to the **Start** menu by dragging the application's icon to the **Start** button, you may receive a message that says that you cannot create a shortcut. The message prompts you to place the shortcut on the desktop. This message appears if the \Start Menu directory is corrupted or deleted.

▶ **To repair a corrupted or missing \Start Menu directory**

1. Click the **Start** button, and then click **Shut Down**.

2. Click **Restart**.

    This creates a new Start Menu folder.

.Lnk extensions are never displayed.

Windows 98 never displays the .lnk extension in My Computer or Windows Explorer.

A disk utility cannot write to a disk.

Windows 98 does not support MS-DOS-based or Windows 3.1–based utilities that perform direct disk writes. Direct disk writes using the MS-DOS read sector (INT 26h) or absolute read sector (INT 13h) interfaces will fail unless the application has locked the volume for exclusive use. For information, see Chapter 10, "Disks and File Systems."

You cannot print from an application.

If you cannot print from an application, you can bypass spooling by sending printer output to a file and then dragging that file to a printer. For more information about printing to a file, see Chapter 11, "Printing, Imaging, and Fonts."

The taskbar is hidden.

Whenever you maximize an application, Windows 98 resizes the window so it does not cover the taskbar. However, if an application maximizes itself by using screen metrics to resize its window to take up the entire screen, the taskbar may be obscured. Because such an application commonly has problems with the taskbar, Windows 98 hides the taskbar when this occurs, giving the application the entire screen. To display the taskbar, manually resize the application's window or minimize the application. To display the **Start** menu, press CTRL+ESC.

An application on a compressed drive lacks sufficient memory to run.

Applications that require maximum available conventional memory should not be run on compressed drives. You might need to run such applications in MS-DOS mode.

Running an MS-DOS-based application causes Windows 98 to stall during startup.

To restore Windows 98, shut down and restart the computer, and then hold down the CTRL key until the Microsoft Windows 98 Startup Menu appears. In the Microsoft Windows 98 Startup Menu, select the option named Previous Version of MS-DOS. (This option does not appear unless you edit Msdos.sys, as described in Chapter 5, "Setup Technical Discussion.") Disable the following lines in Autoexec.bat by typing **rem** before them:

```
rem cd c:\windows\command
rem call c:\windows\command\<game.exe>
rem c:\windows\win.com/wx
```

Remove the following line in Config.sys by typing **rem**:

```
rem dos=single
```

Text on menus and other screen elements is truncated.

Applications that depend on the system font to be a certain size may truncate the text on menus and other screen elements if the text is larger than the default setting. This may occur if users customize their screen fonts. To resolve this problem, right-click the desktop, and then click **Properties**. Click the **Appearance** tab; then, in the **Scheme** list, click **Windows Standard**.

Strange colors and patterns appear on the desktop.

Some Windows 3.1 applications hook into the desktop so they can be aware of all the events that take place there. When all applications were minimized in Windows 3.1, the desktop was the background area. In Windows 98, however, the background area is always covered by the new Windows 98 shell. Applications that subclass the old desktop no longer monitor any activity. If such applications attempt to draw on the old background, images appear on the new desktop, but they conflict with images that the Windows 98 interface draws there. Users cannot interact with the images such applications draw.

This problem typically occurs with screen background and wallpaper applications and with replacement user interfaces, typically located in the StartUp folder. These types of applications may also be started by **run**= or **load**= lines in Win.ini.

To resolve this problem, remove the application from the StartUp folder or remove its entry in Win.ini. Or obtain a version of the application designed for Windows 98.

A setup program cannot create shortcuts.

Because of cooperative multitasking in Windows 3.1, Program Manager was always guaranteed to respond within a few seconds of a Dynamic Data Exchange (DDE) message. For that reason, many setup applications set the DDE timeout to a very short interval. In some cases, Windows 98 may be unable to process the DDE request within the same time because of preemptive multitasking. Setup applications may be unable to create an application group or shortcuts for this reason. If this occurs, you can manually add folders and shortcuts to the **Programs** menu.

You need to rebuild the Programs menu.

If Windows components are inadvertently deleted from the **Programs** menu, you can rebuild the menu. When you do, Windows 98 searches for installed components and adds shortcuts for them to the **Programs** menu. To rebuild the **Programs** menu, first rename Setup.old to Setup.ini. Then click the **Start** button, click **Run**, and type **grpconv -s** in the **Open** box.

For more information about manually rebuilding the **Programs** menu, see online Help. For more information about **grpconv**, see Chapter 5, "Setup Technical Discussion."

You need to save a Notepad or WordPad file using an unassociated file name extension.

If you are saving a file in Notepad or WordPad and you specify a file name extension that has not been associated with an application, Notepad or WordPad appends the default file name extension to the end of the file name. Notepad uses the extension .txt, and WordPad uses the extension .doc. For example, if you try to save the file "Cat.foo" in Notepad, Notepad saves it as "Cat.foo.txt."

To save a file using a file name extension that is not in the registry, enclose the file name in quotation marks.

An application requires Share.exe.

Windows 98 no longer supports real-mode MS-DOS Share.exe. However, some applications check for the existence of a file named Share.exe. To work around this problem, create a dummy file named Share.exe in the \Windows\Command directory.

For more information, see "System Changes Affecting Application Support," earlier in this chapter.

You are using Distributed COM and see run-time error 429.

Occasionally, when you attempt to access a Distributed COM server from a remote client application, you may see the following error:

```
Run-time error '429':
ActiveX component can't create object
```

If this happens, run **dcomcnfg** to check the following:

- In the application's properties, make sure that the **Run application on this computer** setting is checked.
- In the application's properties, make sure that the correct server is specified.
- In the **Default Security** tab, make sure that **Enable Remote Connection** is selected.

Also, make sure that the server application is started before the Windows 98 client tries to access it.

For more information about this troubleshooting step, see Knowledge Base Article Q177394, "HOWTO: Troubleshoot Run-Time Error '429' in DCOM Applications."

Additional Resources

For more information about	See this resource
COM and Distributed COM	**http://www.microsoft.com/com/**
Designed for Windows NT Windows 98 logo usage qualification	**http://www.microsoft.com/msdn/**
Sharing directories on Windows NT–based computers	*Microsoft Windows NT Server Networking Guide* in the *Microsoft Windows NT Server Resource Kit* (for Microsoft Windows NT Server version 4.0)

CHAPTER 26

Performance Tuning

26

Microsoft Windows 98 provides the easiest methods and best defaults ever offered for configuring system memory and ensuring good performance on an *x*86-based computer. This chapter summarizes system features related to performance and describes tools for monitoring and managing system performance.

In This Chapter

See Also

- For more information about DriveSpace and Disk Defragmenter, see Chapter 10, "Disks and File Systems."

- For more information about Registry Checker, see Chapter 31, "Windows 98 Registry."

- For more information about Task Scheduler and Maintenance Wizard, see Chapter 27, "General Troubleshooting."

Performance Tuning Overview

The Windows 98 architecture includes performance improvements over earlier versions of Windows. The changes, which strongly impact most areas of system performance, are as follows:

- 32-bit device drivers for all system components, ensuring better performance and better resource management.
- An application launch accelerator that uses Disk Defragmenter to optimize disks for quicker start of applications.
- Optimization for new Advanced Configuration and Power Interface (ACPI) computers with fast-boot basic input/output system (BIOS) support.
- Quicker system shutdown than with Windows 95.
- More efficient memory management with MapCache and lazy swap file writing.
- OnNow, which causes the computer to go into a low-power mode when not in use and to quickly start up when needed.

   For more information about OnNow, see Chapter 30, "Hardware Management."

Many Windows 98 features provide dynamic configuration, reducing or eliminating the need for users to adjust system settings. The following self-tuning features in Windows 98 are designed to improve performance and reduce support costs.

Dynamic swap file and dynamic caching using VCACHE. VCACHE is a 32-bit protected-mode cache driver. Windows 98 uses dynamic sizes for the virtual memory swap file, the cache for file and network access, and the CD-ROM cache. Both the swap file and cache sizes can grow or shrink, depending on the computer's memory configuration and the demand for memory from applications. This relieves users or administrators from having to change the cache parameters as new memory or new applications are added. Windows 98 can take advantage of new memory automatically and expand or reduce the file and cache sizes automatically based on demands when applications are loaded or unloaded. Because in Windows 98 some code is executed out of cache, cache sizes are larger in Windows 98 than they were in Windows 95 (the MapCache feature). Also, the networking, disk, CD-ROM, and paging caches are integrated and scale as more memory is added to the computer. For more information, see "Optimizing the Swap File" and "Optimizing File System Performance" later in this chapter.

Note Windows 98 does not delete an existing swap file on the boot drive during system boot, because that file automatically shrinks if it is not being used. This keeps system boot time to a minimum.

A user might see a large Win386.swp file immediately after system boot. This could be due to the system being stressed during the previous session; it has nothing to do with the current session.

32-bit disk and file access for fast hard disk access. These mechanisms allow Windows 98 to access the hard disk or file system directly, bypassing the computer's BIOS. Using 32-bit file and disk access improves performance and allows Windows 98 to handle BIOS requests in protected mode rather than in real mode. For more information, see Chapter 10, "Disks and File Systems."

Background print rendering. For a computer that has sufficient memory to take advantage of it, background print rendering is available automatically to reduce the return-to-application time for printing. With this feature, Windows 98 first writes an enhanced metafile (EMF) format file, which is a device-independent rendering of the print job that is much faster to produce than a device-specific rendering. In the background, Windows 98 uses the EMF file to create the device-dependent rendering while the user continues to work in the application. For more information, see "Optimizing Printing" later in this chapter.

Automatic system adjustments during Windows 98 Setup. During installation, Windows 98 Setup makes decisions about certain operating system features based on the hardware configuration. For example, in a computer with low memory, Windows 98 turns off background print rendering, because this feature increases the operating system working set that is loaded into memory and cannot be paged out to the swap file.

Built-in tools for monitoring and adjusting system performance. The following tools in Windows 98 are available for managing performance-related settings:

- The Maintenance Wizard is used to schedule several performance-improving tasks, such as Disk Defragmenter, ScanDisk, Disk Cleanup, and Compression Agent (on DriveSpace3 drives). You can:
    - Speed up frequently used programs.
    - Check the hard disk for errors.
    - Delete unnecessary files from the hard disk.
    - Remove programs from the Startup group.

For more information about Maintenance Wizard, see Chapter 27, "General Troubleshooting," and Chapter 10, "Disks and File Systems."

For more information about Disk Defragmenter, ScanDisk, and Disk Cleanup, see Chapter 10, "Disks and File Systems."

- System option in Control Panel provides settings for tuning and troubleshooting. For information, see "Optimizing the Swap File," "Optimizing File System Performance," and "Setting Graphics Compatibility Options" later in this chapter.

- System Monitor can be used to track the performance of key system components, as described in "Tracking Performance with System Monitor" later in this chapter.

- DriveSpace includes a protected-mode driver that is installed by default, providing faster performance than the earlier real-mode compression driver and using only an additional 10 or 15 percent overhead. If you are using any real-mode disk-compression utilities other than DriveSpace or DoubleSpace, plan to switch to a protected-mode version. Contact the manufacturer to determine availability of protected-mode drivers that are compatible with Windows 98.

Note A FAT32 volume cannot be compressed using Microsoft DriveSpace3.

- Disk Defragmenter can improve file access time by defragmenting uncompressed file allocation table (FAT) drives and compressed DriveSpace or DoubleSpace drives. Fragmentation occurs over time, as programs read from and write to the hard disk. Eventually, files must be stored in noncontiguous sectors on a disk. Fragmentation does not affect the validity of the information, but it takes much longer for the computer to read and write fragmented files. In addition, there is an application launch accelerator that uses Disk Defragmenter to optimize disks for quicker start of applications.

- Registry Checker is a system maintenance program that finds and fixes registry problems. Each time you start the computer, Registry Checker automatically scans the registry for inconsistent structures, and if no problem is found, it backs up the registry once a day. If a problem is found in the registry, Registry Checker can restore the registry from a good backup copy (Registry Checker generally maintains a set of registry backups that have successfully started the computer). If, for some reason, a backup cannot be found, Registry Checker will attempt to fix the registry. Registry Checker also removes unused space in the registry, reducing the size of the registry file and thus improving performance.

- Scheduled Tasks Wizard lets you run useful utilities and routine tasks at regular intervals. You can set the tasks to run at times that are most convenient for you. Each task can be reconfigured once it has been set up. Task configuration parameters include:

  - Source location of the program.

  - Frequency, date, and time that the program should be run.

  - When to delete or stop the program.

  - How to run the program if the computer is idle, is in use, or has power management options enabled.

- WinAlign is a tool that allows greater use of the *MapCache* feature, which optimizes memory usage and general system performance.

Understanding System Performance

Windows 98 cleans up resources that have not been freed to help reduce system resource limitations. When Windows 98 determines that an application that owned certain resources no longer needs those resources in memory, it reallocates remaining data structures, freeing the resources for use elsewhere in the system.

Wherever possible, Windows 98 is self-tuning, adjusting cache sizes or other elements of the system environment to provide the best performance for the current configuration. Windows 98 can also detect when the loaded drivers or other performance-related components are not providing the optimal performance.

▶ **To see a report of performance problems**

- In Control Panel, double-click System, and then click the **Performance** tab. Windows 98 reports the current performance status, including whether 32-bit, protected-mode components are being used.

System Resource Capacity in Windows 98

Windows 98 provides a significant increase in the system resources available to Windows-based and MS-DOS-based applications over what was available under earlier versions of Windows. The net result for users is that they can count on more system resources being available for creating windows, using fonts, running five or more applications simultaneously, and so on.

In Windows 98, to help reduce the system resource limitation, many data structures formerly stored in the 16-bit graphics device interface (GDI) and User heaps are now stored in 32-bit heaps. This provides more room for the remaining data elements to be created.

Table 26.1 shows the system limits in Windows 98, as compared to the constraining limits under Windows 3.1. For more information about how to assess performance of key system resources, see "Identifying Performance Problems with System Monitor" later in this chapter. For more information about the supporting architecture, see Chapter 28, "Windows 98 Architecture."

Table 26.1   Windows 3.1 and Windows 98 system limits

Resource	Windows 3.1[1]	Windows 98[2]
Windows Menu handles	~299	32 KB
Timers	32	Unlimited
COM and LPT ports	4 per type	Unlimited
Items per list box	8 KB	32 KB
Data per list box	64 KB	Unlimited
Data per edit control	64 KB	Unlimited
Regions	All in 64 KB segment	Unlimited
Physical pens and brushes	All in 64 KB segment	Unlimited
Logical pens and brushes	All in 64 KB segment	All in 64 KB segment
Logical fonts	All in 64 KB segment	750 – 800
Installed fonts	250 – 300 (best case)	1000
Device contexts	200 (best case)	16 KB

[1] Limits for GDI objects in Windows 3.1 are not exact, because all regions, physical objects, logical objects, device contexts (DCs), and installed fonts had to fit in a single 64 KB segment. Because many of these have been moved to the 32-bit heap, Windows 98 provides much more room for remaining items, such as logical pens, brushes, and so on. The remaining items in the Windows 98 local heap are all less than 10–20 bytes each.

[2] System-wide resources, unless otherwise noted.

Technical Notes on MS-DOS Components in Windows 98

Many users have wondered whether Windows 98 contains MS-DOS code and, if so, whether that means that Windows 98 is somehow built on top of MS-DOS. Many of these questions relate to how Windows 98 achieves the highest possible degree of compatibility with existing devices and applications created for MS-DOS and Windows 3.x. Three key questions are answered here:

- How does Windows 98 support internal processes and certain application services?

- How does Windows 98 reclaim memory from real-mode drivers?

- Why does Io.sys load Win.com rather than directly loading Vmm32.vxd?

The following services were written for Windows 95 and Windows 98, and are not revisions to MS-DOS code:

- Process and thread memory management.

- Interprocess communications and synchronization.

- Preemptive Win32 subsystem.

- CD-ROM, hard disk, and network input/output (I/O) services.

- High-level graphics operations and window management.

- Printing services.

Some functions, however, are handled by MS-DOS code, although the code itself is running in virtual 8086 mode, not real mode. Functions implemented in this manner ensure backward compatibility with existing real-mode software, such as the Novell NetWare client. The following list shows such functions:

Create Program Segment Prefix (function 55h)	Get MS-DOS Version (function 30h)
	International (function 65h)
Create Temp File (function 5Ah)	Set/Get Drive (functions 0Eh and 19h)
Dup File Handle (function 45h)	Set/Get Program Segment Prefix (functions 50h and 51h)
Exit (function 4Ch)	
Get Date/Time (functions 2Ah and 2Ch)	NetWare Get Station Num (function DCh)

An important example of how Windows 98 reclaims memory from real-mode device drivers is MSCDEX, the CD-ROM driver. After Windows 98 Setup is completed and Windows 98 starts from the hard disk for the first time, special code runs to determine whether the protected-mode compact disc file system (CDFS) drivers have taken over the CD-ROM drive completely. If so, the real-mode MSCDEX driver in memory is matched to the related lines in Autoexec.bat, and the MSCDEX entries are then commented out. This provides a trail in Autoexec.bat to show what has happened. Similar methods are used for other device drivers that Windows 98 knows to be safe to remove, such as other vendors' real-mode disk cache utilities and redundant protected-mode virtual device drivers (VxDs).

As a final example, some users have wondered whether the fact that Io.sys loads Win.com (rather than loading Vmm32.vxd directly) is an indication that Windows 98 is built on Windows 3.x code, with the addition of new VxDs. Actually, Io.sys is used to load Win.com only to ensure backward compatibility. Certain real-mode drivers and terminate-and-stay-resident (TSR) programs insert themselves at various places in the Windows 3.1 startup process. If Windows 98 were to bypass the loading of Win.com and instead load VxDs directly, any driver that needs to insert itself when Win.com is loaded would never be called. Instead, Windows 98 starts in precisely the same way as Windows 3.1 and loads the same components in the same order, ensuring compatibility with earlier versions of applications and device drivers.

Optimizing the Swap File

Windows 98 uses a special file on your hard disk called a *virtual memory swap file* (or paging file). With virtual memory under Windows 98, some of the program code and other information are kept in random access memory (RAM), while other information is swapped temporarily to virtual memory. When that information is required again, Windows 98 pulls it back into RAM and, if necessary, swaps other information to virtual memory. This activity is invisible, although you might notice that your hard disk is working. The resulting benefit is that you can run more programs at one time than the computer's RAM would usually allow.

The Windows 98 swap file is dynamic, so it can shrink or grow based on the operations performed on the system and based on available disk space. A dynamic swap file is usually the most efficient use of resources. It can also occupy a fragmented region of the hard disk with no substantial performance penalty.

Tip The single best way you can ensure high swap file performance is to make sure that the disk containing the swap file has ample free space so that the swap file size can shrink and grow as needed.

The Windows 98 swap file (Win386.swp) is not a permanent file. However, Windows 98 can also use a permanent Windows 3.1 swap file. In this case, the file cannot shrink below the permanent size set for it in Windows 3.1, although the file can grow bigger if required.

Under Windows 98, the swap file can reside on a compressed drive if a protected-mode driver (that is, Drvspace.vxd) controls the compressed drive. DriveSpace marks the swap file as uncompressible and places the swap file as the last file in the sector heap (to reduce the risk of fragmentation), allowing room for the swap file to grow.

Although the system defaults usually provide the best performance, you can adjust the parameters used to define the swap file. For example, to optimize swap file performance on a computer with multiple hard disk drives, you might want to override the default location of the Windows 98 swap file. The swap file should be placed on the drive with the fastest performance, unless that disk is overused. If a user usually loads all software from the same drive in a computer that has multiple drives, performance might be boosted by placing the swap file on one of the drives that is not as busy.

Caution   Completely disabling virtual memory might cause the computer to stop operating properly. You might not be able to restart the computer, or system performance might be degraded. Do not disable virtual memory unless instructed to do so by a product support representative.

▶ **To adjust the virtual memory swap file**

1. In Control Panel, double-click System, click the **Performance** tab, and then click **Virtual Memory**.

2. To specify a different hard disk, click the **Let me specify my own virtual memory settings** option. Then specify the new disk in the **Hard disk** box. Or type values (in kilobytes) in the **Minimum** or **Maximum** box. Then click **OK**

If you set the maximum swap file size in the **Virtual Memory** dialog box to the amount of free space currently on a drive, Windows 98 assumes that it can increase the swap file beyond that size if more free disk space becomes available. If you want to impose a fixed limit on the swap file size, make sure that the limit you choose is less than the current maximum.

Optimizing File System Performance

In Windows 98, the disk cache is dynamic. You do not need to configure its size as part of system configuration. Because of this, certain settings used for Windows 3.x are not required in Windows 98 and should be removed from the configuration files. Table 26.2 shows these settings.

Table 26.2   Configuration settings not required

Configuration file	Configuration setting to remove
Autoexec.bat	SHARESMARTDRV settings. Any entries for other disk cache software.[1]
Config.sys	SMARTDRV settings (double-buffer driver). Any entries for other disk cache software.

[1] For a list of the disk caching software that is removed by Windows 98 Setup, see Chapter 5, "Setup Technical Discussion."

The overall performance, for example, of a computer with 16 MB of memory is better under Windows 98 than under Windows 3.1. However, the amount of paging might increase under Windows 98 for the following reasons:

- Windows 98 aggressively writes the contents of dirty memory pages (pages that contain changes) during system idle time, even if it does not need the memory then. This causes more idle-time disk activity but speeds up future memory allocations by doing some of the work while the system is idle.

- Much more of Windows 98 can be paged out to disk than Windows 3.1.

Changing the cache size is not a good method of limiting paging. Paging through the cache would quickly overwhelm it and make it useless for other file I/O. Although swap file I/O operations do not go through the cache, memory-mapped files and executable files do. The cache, however, is designed to make sure it cannot be overwhelmed by such I/O operations.

Changing the cache size (even if you could) probably would not have much effect on paging. The cache grows and shrinks as needed. If the system begins to page a lot, the cache shrinks automatically. However, people often think they are seeing a lot of paging, but they are really seeing other disk activity, such as Windows 98 building its icon cache or the cache lazy writing.

A common reason for excessive paging is that the working set of the applications you are running is greater than the amount of physical RAM available. If the amount of paging is extreme, to the point where system performance is poor, a real-mode driver for the hard disk may be the cause, and should be replaced with a protected mode driver. If Windows 98 needs to use real-mode for its disk I/O operations, a lot of code has to be locked down that would otherwise be pageable, and your working set increases significantly.

Note Paging through a real-mode driver increases paging, and on a computer with 16 MB of memory (the minimum configuration for Windows 98), it can cause unacceptable performance.

Preventing Data Loss with 32-bit Disk Access

The 32-bit disk access feature is always turned on in Windows 98 unless Windows 98 detects a real-mode disk driver that does not have a protected-mode replacement. This could be, for example, an older Stacker driver or a hard-disk security or encryption driver for a disk drive.

To prevent the performance loss that occurs when Windows 98 is forced to use a real-mode disk driver, upgrade to a protected-mode replacement for that driver. If you need to determine why a Windows 98 real-mode disk driver was installed, check the Ios.log file. For more information, see Chapter 24, "Device Management."

Optimizing File System Performance with Profiles

In Windows 98, file system and disk performance can be controlled based on how the computer is used in most situations. The option for configuring file system performance is controlled only by the user. None of these settings are affected by other configuration changes that might be made in Windows 98, such as installing file and printer sharing services, or choosing the Portable option as the setup type when installing Windows 98.

Note   Application launch acceleration depends on cluster size and, therefore, the particular file system. Smaller cluster sizes give better application launch performance—the 4 KB cluster size (FAT32) is best; larger sizes (for example, FAT16) give less of a performance boost.

▶ **To optimize file system performance**

1. In Control Panel, double-click System, click the **Performance** tab, and then click **File System**.

2. In the **Typical role of this computer** box, select the most common role for this computer, and then click **OK**. Table 26.3 describes each role in the list.

   Table 26.3   Computer role descriptions

Role	Description
Desktop computer	A normal computer acting primarily as a network client, or an individual computer with no networking. This configuration assumes that there is more than the minimum required RAM, and that the computer is running on power (rather than battery).
Mobile or docking system	Any computer with limited memory. This configuration assumes that RAM is limited and that the computer is running on battery, so the disk cache should be flushed frequently.
Network server	A computer used primarily as a peer server for file or printer sharing. This configuration assumes that the computer has adequate RAM and frequent disk activity, so the system is optimized for a high amount of disk access.

Each disk performance profile adjusts the values of the following file system settings in the registry:

- **PathCache** specifies the size of the cache that the virtual file allocation table (VFAT) can use to save the locations of the most recently accessed directory paths. This cache improves performance by reducing the number of times the file system must seek paths by searching the file allocation table. The number of paths is 32 for the Desktop computer profile, 16 for Mobile or docking system, and 64 for Network server.

- **NameCache** stores the locations of the most recently accessed file names. The combined use of PathCache and NameCache means that VFAT never searches the disk for the location of cached file names. Both PathCache and NameCache use memory out of the general system heap. The number of file names is about 677 (8 KB) for the Desktop computer profile, 337 (4 KB) for Mobile or docking system, and 2729 (16 KB) for Network server.

- **BufferIdleTimeout**, **BufferAgeTimeout**, and **VolumeIdleTimeout** control the time between when changes are placed in the buffer to when they are written to the hard disk.

The values to be assigned to each disk performance profile are stored in the following registry key:

HKEY_LOCAL_MACHINE\Software\Microsoft\Windows\CurrentVersion \FS Templates

The following subkey contains the actual settings for the profile currently used:

HKEY_LOCAL_MACHINE\System\CurrentControlSet\Control\FileSystem

An additional performance setting in the **FileSystem** subkey, **ContigFile AllocSize**, can be used to change the size of the contiguous space that VFAT searches for when allocating disk space. Under MS-DOS, the file system began allocating the first available space found on the disk, which ensured a great deal of disk fragmentation and related performance problems. By default under Windows 98, VFAT first tries to allocate space in the first contiguous 0.5 MB of free space and then returns to the MS-DOS method if it cannot find at least this much contiguous free space. This optimizes performance for both the swap file and multimedia applications.

In some cases, you might choose to set a smaller value in the registry, as when you are not running demanding applications on the computer. A smaller value for **ContigFileAllocSize**, however, can lead to more fragmentation on the disk and, consequently, more disk access for the swap file or applications that require larger amounts of disk space.

Optimizing CD-ROM File System Performance

The CD-ROM cache is separate from the cache used for disk file and network access because the performance characteristics of the CD-ROM are different. This cache can be paged to disk (the file and network cache cannot), reducing the working set for Windows 98 but still allowing for better CD-ROM performance. When Windows 98 is retrieving data from a compact disc, it is still faster to read a record from the cache even if it has been paged to disk, because the disk-access time is much faster than the compact disc–access time.

Tip A small CD-ROM cache makes a big difference in streaming performance, but a much larger cache does not pay off as significantly, unless the cache is large enough to contain entire multimedia streams.

▶ **To set the supplemental cache size for CDFS**

1. In Control Panel, double-click System, click the **Performance** tab, and then click **File System**.

2. Click the **CD-ROM** tab, and drag the slider to set the **Supplemental cache size**.

   Move the Supplemental Cache Size slider to the right to allocate more RAM for caching data from the CD-ROM drive or to the left to allocate less RAM for caching data.

Note Many multimedia programs perform better with a smaller cache, because they tend not to reuse data.

---

3. In the **Optimize access pattern for** box, select a setting based on your computer's CD-ROM drive speed. Table 26.4 shows the size of the cache created for each CD-ROM drive speed setting.

   Table 26.4   Optimizing cache size

CD-ROM drive speed	Cache size
No read-ahead	1088 KB
Single-speed drives	1088 KB
Double-speed drives	1138 KB
Triple-speed drives	1188 KB
Quad-speed or higher	1238 KB

4. Click **OK**, and then shut down and restart the computer.

Optimizing DVD File System Performance

Digital video discs (DVDs) primarily use the Universal Disk Format (UDF) for their file systems. UDF uses the main file system cache (VCACHE), and there are no performance settings for end users to change.

For more information about UDF, see Chapter 10, "Disks and File Systems."

For more information about DVD, see Chapter 10, "Disks and File Systems," and Chapter 30, "Hardware Management."

Optimizing Removable Disk Drive Performance

Windows 98 gives you the option to use write-behind caching to improve the performance of removable disk drives, such as the ZIP or JAZ drive.

▶ **To set write-behind caching for removable disk drives**

1. In Control Panel, double-click System, click the **Performance** tab, click **File System**, and then click the **Removable Disk** tab.

2. Select the **Enable write-behind caching on all removable disk drives** check box. Click **OK**.

3. If this causes a problem with disk operations, follow step 1, and then click to clear the **Enable write-behind caching on all removable disk drives** check box. Click **OK**.

Optimizing I/O Transfers by Using Direct Memory Access

The advantage of using direct memory access (DMA) with integrated device electronics (IDE) CD-ROM and disk drives is that it allows much lower CPU usage during I/O transfers for drives that are part of an original equipment manufacturer (OEM) computer. DMA is enabled by default in OEM computers, but because certain older IDE drives can corrupt data when using DMA, care must be taken when enabling DMA in upgraded computers.

▶ **To enable DMA**

1. In Control Panel, double-click System, and then click the **Device Manager** tab.

2. Select an IDE device under the **CD-ROM** branch or the **Disk drives** branch, and click **Properties**.

3. Click the **Settings** tab, and then check off the **DMA** check box.

4. Click **OK**, and then shut down and restart the computer.

Using File System Troubleshooting Options

The System option in Control Panel presents a set of options for changing file system performance. You can use these options when you experience rare hardware or software compatibility problems.

Important Enabling any of the file system troubleshooting options will seriously degrade system performance. Typically, you want to enable these options only if instructed to do so by a product support representative. Otherwise, these options should rarely, if ever, be used.

▶ **To display the file system troubleshooting options**

1. In Control Panel, double-click System, and then click the **Performance** tab.

2. Click **File System**, and then click the **Troubleshooting** tab.

Table 26.5 summarizes the settings in **Troubleshooting** properties. Each option sets a value in the following registry key.

HKEY_LOCAL_MACHINE\System\CurrentControlSet\Control\FileSystem

Table 26.5   File system troubleshooting options

File system option	Description
Disable new file sharing and locking semantics.	This option alters the internal rules for file sharing and locking on hard disks, governing whether certain processes can have access to open files in certain share modes that guarantee a file will not be modified. This option should be checked only in the rare case that an MS-DOS-based application has problems with sharing under Windows 98. This sets **SoftCompatMode=0** in the registry.
Disable long name preservation for old programs.	This option turns off the tunneling feature, which preserves long file names when files are opened and saved by applications that do not recognize long file names. This option should be checked in the rare case that an important legacy application is not compatible with long file names. This sets **PreserveLongNames=0** in the registry.
Disable protected-mode hard disk interrupt handling.	This option prevents Windows 98 from terminating interrupts from the hard disk controller and bypassing the read-only memory (ROM) routine that handles these interrupts. Some hard disk drives might require this option to be checked in order for interrupts to be processed correctly. If this option is checked, the ROM routine handles the interrupts, slowing system performance. This sets **VirtualHDIRQ=1** in the registry. This setting is off by default in Windows 98.
Disable synchronous buffer commits.	The file commit API is used to guarantee integrity of user data that is being written by an application to a disk. Normally, the file commit API is used by applications to ensure that critical data that the application is writing is written to the disk before returning from a call made to the file commit API. Choosing this option disables this feature. Data is still written to disk, but it is written to disk in the background at the discretion of the file system. Choosing this option can compromise data written to disk by an application should the system crash before the data is actually written. This option was added to allow adequate performance of a defective database application that used the file commit API incorrectly and excessively.

Table 26.5   File system troubleshooting options (*continued*)

File system option	Description
Disable all 32-bit protected-mode disk drivers.	This option ensures that no 32-bit disk drivers are loaded in the system, except the floppy driver. Typically, you would check this option if the computer does not start because of disk peripheral I/O problems. If this option is enabled, all I/O will go through real-mode drivers or the BIOS. Notice that in this case, all disk drives that are visible only in protected mode will no longer be visible. This sets **ForceRMIO=1** in the registry.
Disable write-behind caching for all drives.	This option ensures that all data is flushed continually to the hard disk, removing any performance benefits gained from disk caching. This option should be checked only in the rare case that you are performing risky operations and must ensure prevention of data loss. For example, a software developer who is debugging data at Ring 0 while creating a VxD would check this option. This sets **DriveWriteBehind=0** in the registry.

Setting Graphics Compatibility Options

In Windows 98, graphics hardware acceleration features can be turned off when system performance indicates incompatibility problems. Specifically, problems can occur when Windows 98 assumes a display adapter can support certain functionality that it cannot. In such cases, the side effects might be anything from small irregularities on the screen to system failure. You can disable hardware acceleration features of the display adapter so that the computer can still be used if there is a problem with the display adapter. If changing these settings fixes otherwise unexplained system crashes or performance problems, the source of the problem is probably the computer's display adapter.

▶ **To change graphics performance settings**

1. In Control Panel, double-click System, click the **Performance** tab, and then click **Graphics**.

2. Drag the slider to change the **Hardware acceleration** setting, as summarized in the following list. Then click **OK**.

   - The default setting is **Full**, which turns on all graphics hardware acceleration features available in the display driver.

   - The first notch from the right can be set to correct mouse pointer display problems. This setting disables hardware cursor support in the display driver by adding **SwCursor=1** to the [Display] section of System.ini.

- The second notch from the right can be set to correct certain display errors. This setting prevents some bit block transfers from being performed on the display card and disables memory-mapped I/O for some display drivers. This setting adds **SwCursor=1** and **Mmio=0** to the [Display] section of System.ini, and **SafeMode=1** to the [Windows] section of Win.ini.

- The last notch from the right (None) can be set to correct problems if your computer frequently stops responding to input, or has other severe problems. This setting adds **SafeMode=2** to the [Windows] section of Win.ini, which removes all driver acceleration support and causes Windows 98 to use only the device-independent bitmap (DIB) engine rather than bit block transfers for displaying images.

  For example, an error message at system startup stating that an application caused "an invalid page fault in module <unknown>" would indicate a problem between the display driver and the Windows 98 DIB engine. In such cases, this setting should correct the problem.

For more information about the built-in graphics performance features in Windows 98, see Chapter 24, "Device Management," and Chapter 28, "Windows 98 Architecture."

Optimizing Printing

The way printing to a printer attached to a file or print server occurs depends on your server's operating system. If you print to a server running Windows 98, the rendering from the EMF format to the printer-specific language happens on the server. This means that less work is performed on the client computer, giving the user better performance.

When you print to NetWare or Windows NT servers, the rendering from EMF to the printer-specific format happens on the client computer. Although this happens in the background, it still means more work is performed on the client computer. Printing to a printer attached locally causes both the EMF rendering and the device-specific rendering to happen on the computer. For more information, see Chapter 11, "Printing, Imaging, and Fonts."

You also need to decide on the trade-off between disk use and return-to-application time when configuring printing in Windows 98.

▶ **To define spool settings for print performance**

1. In Control Panel, double-click Printers, right-click a printer icon, and then click **Properties**.

2. Click the **Details** tab, and then click **Spool Settings**.

3. Select **Spool print jobs so program finishes printing faster**, and then click one of the following options:

   - Click **Start printing after last page is spooled** if you want the return-to-application time to be faster. This requires more disk space and increases the total print time. The second rendering does not start until the entire file is written to the EMF file, decreasing the amount of work performed on the computer as you print, but increasing the disk space, because the entire file has to be written before the second rendering starts.

   - Click **Start printing after first page is spooled** if you want the second rendering to take place simultaneously with the writing of the EMF file. This reduces the total print time and disk space required, but it increases the return-to-application time.

Optimizing Network Performance

Windows 98 automatically adjusts system parameters to accommodate users' demands and various network configurations. For example, it alters the size of the system paging file and cache buffer as memory requirements change, and automatically tunes network time-out values to fit varying local area network (LAN) topologies.

With few exceptions, manual tuning of operating system parameters is not required to improve network performance. However, you can take several other measures that can increase file-sharing performance, such as reconfiguring or changing hardware components. This section summarizes these measures.

- Use a 32-bit, protected-mode network client.

  For example, the Microsoft Client for NetWare Networks significantly out-performs the Virtual Loadable Module (VLM) or NetWare 3.*x* workstation shell (NETX) version of the NetWare client.

- Do not add unnecessary protocols.

  If you can see all network connections with only Transport Control Protocol/Internet Protocol (TCP/IP) loaded, do not manually add Internetwork Packet Exchange/Sequenced Packet Exchange (IPX/SPX). Doing so only creates system overhead, which slows down network connections and consumes additional system memory.

- Use the new network driver interface specification (NDIS) version 3.1 or later network adapter drivers provided with Windows 98.

- If your system does not have a modem (or if you have one and do not use it), and you do not use Point-to-Point Tunneling Protocol (PPTP), remove all Dial-Up Networking components.

- Install a new network adapter. The adapters currently available provide markedly better performance than earlier models. If possible, select an adapter that matches the computer bus. For more information, see Chapter 15, "Network Adapters and Protocols."

  Network adapters have become exceptionally reliable and inexpensive. The low costs of Ethernet adapters, including new Plug and Play hardware, means that usually the most cost-effective way to improve network performance is to replace an older network adapter with a new model. The cost for the new hardware is offset almost immediately by savings in support time and improved performance.

The following measures can help you obtain the best performance from computers that provide file and printer sharing services:

- Let Windows 98 determine the right size for the swap file.

- Make sure the computer has enough memory, depending on the size of your network and the number of users who will be accessing the peer server.

- In the System option in Control Panel, set the typical role of the computer to Network server, as described in "Optimizing File System Performance with Profiles" earlier in this chapter.

- Install a high-performance network adapter on the peer server. If the computer uses an 8-bit adapter, you can increase performance significantly by replacing it with a high-performance 16-bit or 32-bit adapter.

- Disable rarely used network adapters. This improves overall network performance by decreasing the number of broadcast packets on the network. Each broadcast packet must be processed by every active adapter on the network. High broadcast rates adversely affect LAN performance by increasing network connection time. You can disable a network adapter by disabling its binding to protocols in the Network option in Control Panel.

- Install faster hard drives or disk controllers (or both). Typically, when setting up peer servers, you will want to choose computers configured with the best-performing hardware.

- On a computer running File and Printer Sharing for NetWare Networks, set the read-only attribute on shared files wherever possible. The network client can take better advantage of file caching with read-only files, improving network performance and reducing the load on the server.

Optimizing Conventional Memory

The methods for conventional memory management under Windows 98 are the same as for MS-DOS 6.x:

- In Config.sys, load **himem** and **emm386** (using either the **ram** or the **noems** switch), and load any required real-mode drivers and applications using **devicehigh** or **loadhigh** statements.

- Remove as many real-mode drivers and TSRs from Config.sys and Autoexec.bat as possible, and instead use new protected-mode drivers and applications created for Windows 98.

- Use **buffershigh**, **fcbshigh**, **fileshigh**, **lastdrivehigh**, and **stackshigh** to ensure that reserved memory is taken out of the upper memory area.

- Do not load **smartdrv** in your configuration files, except in configuration files for an application that you run in MS-DOS mode. Windows 98 uses an improved method for disk caching, so loading **smartdrv** typically wastes memory that could be used by MS-DOS-based applications.

You can still run the MEMMAKER utility provided with MS-DOS 6.2x to load real-mode drivers in the upper memory blocks (UMBs). This utility is available in the Tools\Oldmsdos directory on the Windows 98 compact disc.

For more information about MS-DOS mode and other configuration issues related to MS-DOS-based applications, see Chapter 25, "Application Support." For specific information about MS-DOS memory settings, consult the *Microsoft MS-DOS 6.2x Technical Reference* or other books on MS-DOS memory management.

MS-DOS Mode and Performance

Do not assume that running an MS-DOS-based application in MS-DOS mode provides better performance. When an application runs in MS-DOS mode, Windows 98 and all of its protected-mode drivers are unloaded, so the application is running in real mode with exclusive use of the computer's resources.

Although this might help with a few applications that otherwise cannot run under Windows 98, it does not benefit performance overall, because the application does not get the benefit of protected-mode drivers, VCACHE, 32-bit disk access, and so on. Also, real-mode device drivers must be loaded, reducing the amount of conventional memory available to the application.

Tracking Performance with System Monitor

System Monitor is a Windows 98 tool you can use to help determine the cause of problems on a local or remote computer by measuring the performance of hardware, software services, and applications. When you make changes to the system configuration, System Monitor shows the effect of your changes on overall system performance. You can also use System Monitor to justify hardware upgrades.

A new feature in Windows 98 is System Monitor's ability to log. This is useful for measuring system performance over time. For example, logging memory consumption while using a specific application could be helpful.

Before making major configuration changes, use System Monitor to evaluate your current configuration; this can help you determine whether a particular system or network component is acting as a performance bottleneck.

System Monitor is not automatically installed with the Windows 98 Setup.

▶ **To install System Monitor**

1. In Control Panel, double-click Add/Remove Programs.
2. Click the **Windows Setup** tab.
3. Click **System Tools**, and then click **Details**.
4. Click **System Monitor**, and then click **OK**.

▶ **To run System Monitor**

- On the **Start** menu, point to **Programs**, point to **Accessories**, point to **System Tools**, and then click **System Monitor**.

▶ **To start logging**

1. In System Monitor, click **File**, and then click **Start Logging**.
2. Type a file name for the log file, and then click **Save**.
3. On the **File** menu, click **Stop Logging** to stop logging.

▶ **To edit an item in a chart**

1. In System Monitor, click **Edit**, and then click **Edit Item**.
2. Click **Add Item**, **Remove Item**, or **Edit Item**, and then make the changes you want.

Note To view a definition of an item in the **Item** list, click the item, and then click **Explain**.

3. Click **OK**.

> **Note** You can edit only a chart that you are currently viewing.

▶ **To change the look of a chart**

- In System Monitor, click **View**, and then click **Line Charts**, **Bar Charts**, or **Numeric Charts**.

> **Note** You can edit only a chart that you are currently viewing.

▶ **To use System Monitor to monitor remote computers**

1. Install the Microsoft Remote Registry service on your computer and on the computer you want to monitor, as described in Chapter 23, "System and Remote Administration Tools."
2. In System Monitor, click the **File** menu, and then click **Connect**.
3. Type the name of the computer you want to monitor, and then click **OK**.

> **Note** Monitoring a remote computer requires user-level security.

Configuring Performance Charts in System Monitor

System Monitor uses the dynamic data information in the registry to report on the state of processes. You can use System Monitor to do the following:

- Monitor real-time system performance and compare it with historical performance to help identify trends over time.
- Determine system capacity and identify bottlenecks.
- Monitor the effects of system configuration changes.

▶ **To use System Monitor to track performance problems**

1. In System Monitor, click the **Edit** menu, and then click **Add Item**.
2. In the **Category** list, click the resource that you want to monitor.
3. In the **Item** list, select one or more resources that you want to monitor.

   To select more than one item, press CTRL while clicking the items that you want to select. To select several items in a row, click the first item, and then press and hold down SHIFT while clicking the last item.

4. Click **Explain** for more information about a selected resource.
5. Click **OK**. A performance chart of the resource is added to System Monitor.
6. To change the view of the data from a line chart to a bar chart or a numeric listing, click the related button on the toolbar.

System Monitor offers menu commands for configuring the charts:

- To change the update interval, click the **Options** menu, and then click **Chart**.
- To configure the color and scaling for a selected item, click the **Edit** menu, and then click **Edit Item**.
- To control the display of the toolbar, status bar, and title bar, click the **View** menu, and then click **Toolbar**, **Status Bar**, or **Hide Title Bar**, respectively.

Identifying Performance Problems with System Monitor

If you want to use System Monitor effectively, you need to run it frequently to become familiar with what typical performance looks like for a standard configuration so that you can recognize performance problems when they appear in System Monitor.

To become well-acquainted with System Monitor, run it while you are doing your usual work under Windows 98. To do this, add the System Monitor icon to your desktop. Then run System Monitor and use commands on the **View** menu to remove the title bar or to force the window to be always on top.

Following are some general guidelines and key settings for using System Monitor in troubleshooting performance problems:

- If you suspect an application might not be freeing memory when it finishes using it (sometimes called memory leaks), monitor the value of **Kernel: Threads** over time. This will indicate whether the application is starting threads and not reclaiming them. Windows 98 automatically removes such threads when the application closes, but if you identify a leak while the application is running, you might decide that you should restart the application periodically.
- If the values for **Memory Manager: Discards** and **Memory Manager: Page-outs** indicate a great deal of activity, performance problems might be related to system memory stress. These values might indicate a need for more physical memory.
- If a computer seems slow, check the values reported by **Kernel: Processor Usage (%)**, by **Memory Manager: Page Faults**, and by **Memory Manager: Locked Memory**, as described in the following list:
  - If values for **Kernel: Processor Usage (%)** are high even when the user is not working, check to see which application might be keeping it busy. To do this, press CTRL+ALT+DEL to see the list of tasks in the **Close Program** dialog box.
  - If the values for **Memory Manager: Page Faults** are high, the applications being used might have memory needs beyond the computer's capabilities.

- If the **Memory Manager: Locked Memory** statistics are continually a large portion of the **Memory Manager: Allocated Memory** value, inadequate free memory might be affecting performance. Also, you might be running an application that locks memory unnecessarily. (Locked memory indicates the portion of memory used that cannot be paged out.)

Summary of System Monitor Categories

System Monitor tracks functionality for the following categories:

- Dial-Up Adapter
- Disk Cache
- File System
- Kernel
- Memory Manager
- Microsoft Network Client
- Microsoft Network Server file and printer sharing services

Note Because System Monitor uses registry information, drivers can be written to report additional information in System Monitor. For more information about creating such drivers, see the *Microsoft Windows 98 Device Development Kit*.

Tables 26.6 through 26.12 describe the settings for the System Monitor categories.

Table 26.6   Dial-Up Adapter settings in System Monitor

Setting	Description
Alignment Errors	Serial port alignment errors.
Buffer Overruns	Serial port buffer overrun errors.
Bytes Received/Second	Number of bytes received per second.
Bytes Transmitted/Second	Number of bytes transmitted per second.
Connection Speed	Connection speed in bits per second.
CRC Errors	Number of frames with CRC errors.
Frames Received/Second	Number of good frames received per second.
Frames Transmitted/Second	Number of frames transmitted per second.
Framing Errors	Serial port framing errors.
Incomplete Frames	Number of incomplete frames received.

Table 26.6   Dial-Up Adapter settings in System Monitor (*continued*)

Setting	Description
Overrun Errors	Serial port overrun errors.
Timeout Errors	Serial port timeout errors.
Total Bytes Received	Total number of bytes received.
Total Bytes Transmitted	Total number of bytes transmitted.

Table 26.7   Disk Cache settings in System Monitor

Setting	Description
Cache buffers	Number of active buffers in a cache, including any and all compressed buffers.
Cache hits	Number of times data found in the cache resulting in I/O requests.
Cache misses	Number of times data not found in the cache resulting in I/O requests.
Cache pages	Current number of disk cache pages.
Failed cache recycles	Number of times a recycling request (either least recently used [LRU] or random) has failed. This can happen in low memory situations or when all cache buffers are currently in use.
LRU cache recycles	Number of times the cache is sequentially searched for a buffer to recycle, beginning with the oldest data. This happens when new data needs to be added to the cache, or when memory manager needs to borrow memory from the cache.
Maximum cache pages	Maximum number of disk cache pages.
Minimum cache pages	Minimum number of disk cache pages.
Random cache recycles	Number of times the cache is randomly searched for a buffer to recycle. This can happen whenever the cache becomes filled with data not used lately.

Table 26.8   File System settings in System Monitor

Setting	Description
Bytes read/second	The number of bytes read from the file system each second.
Bytes written/second	The number of bytes written by the file system each second.
Dirty data	The number of bytes waiting to be written to the disk. Dirty data is stored in cache blocks, so the number reported might be larger than the actual number of bytes waiting.
Reads/second	The number of read operations delivered to the file system each second.
Writes/second	The number of write operations delivered to the file system each second.

Table 26.9   Kernel settings in System Monitor

Setting	Description
Processor Usage (%)[1]	The approximate percentage of time the processor is busy.
Threads	The current number of threads present in the system.
Virtual Machines	The current number of virtual machines present in the system.

[1] Monitoring processor usage will increase processor usage slightly, so do not monitor this setting unless you are investigating a problem.

Table 26.10   Memory Manager VMM32 settings

Setting	Description
Allocated memory[1, 2]	The total amount in bytes of Other memory and Swappable memory. If this value is changing when there is no activity on the computer, it indicates that the disk cache is resizing itself.
Discards	The number of pages discarded from memory each second. (The pages are not swapped to the disk, because the information is already on the disk.)
Disk cache size	The current size, in bytes, of the disk cache.
Instance faults	The number of instance faults each second.
Locked memory[1]	The amount of allocated memory that is locked.
Locked non-cache pages	Number of non-cache locked pages.
Maximum disk cache size	The largest size possible for a disk cache. This is a fixed value loaded at system startup.
Mid disk cache size	The mid disk cache size. This is a fixed value loaded at system startup.
Minimum disk cache size	The smallest size possible for a disk cache. This is a fixed value loaded at system startup.
Other memory[1]	The amount of allocated memory not stored in the swap file, for example, code from Win32 dynamic link libraries (DLLs) and executable files, memory mapped files, nonpageable memory, and disk cache pages.
Page faults	The number of page faults each second.
Page-ins	The number of pages swapped into memory each second, including pages loaded from a Win32-based executable file or memory-mapped files. Consequently, this value does not necessarily indicate low memory.
Page-outs	The number of pages swapped out of memory and written to disk each second.
Pages mapped from cache	Used to monitor MapCache/WinAlign changes. The swap file size in use at the same time as this setting should be monitored for differences after running the WinAlign tool.

Table 26.10   Memory Manager VMM32 settings (*continued*)

Setting	Description
Swap file defective	The number of bytes in the swap file that are found to be physically defective on the swap medium. Because swap file frames are allocated in 4096-byte blocks, a single damaged sector causes the whole block to be marked as defective.
Swap file in use	The number of bytes being used in the current swap file.
Swap file size	The size, in bytes, of the current swap file.
Swappable memory[1]	The number of bytes allocated from the swap file. Locked pages still count for the purpose of this metric. This includes code from 16-bit applications and DLLs, but not code from Win32 DLLs and executable files.
Unused physical memory	Amount of physical memory (RAM) not currently in use.

[1] This number includes the disk cache. To see the actual size, subtract the value of Disk cache size.

[2] For any Windows-based application that uses common dialog boxes, the spooler, OLE, and so on, handles are cached for later use, so not all resources will be freed when the application closes.

Table 26.11   Microsoft Network Client settings in System Monitor

Setting	Description
Bytes read/second	The number of bytes read from the redirector each second.
Bytes written/second	The number of bytes written to the redirector each second.
Number of nets	Number of networks currently running.
Open files	Number of open files on the network.
Resources	Number of resources.
Sessions	Number of sessions.
Transactions/second	The number of server message block (SMB) transactions managed by the redirector each second.

Table 26.12   Microsoft Network Server file and printer sharing for Microsoft or NetWare networks settings in System Monitor

Setting	Description
Buffers	The number of buffers used by the server.
Bytes Read/sec	The total number of bytes read from a disk.
Bytes Written/sec	The total number of bytes written to a disk.
Bytes/sec	The total number of bytes read from and written to a disk.
Memory	The total memory used by the server.
NBs	Server network buffers.
Server Threads	The current number of threads used by the server.

WinAlign and MapCache

WinAlign is a tool designed to optimize the performance of executable code (binaries) on the Windows 98 platform. WinAlign works by formatting the sections of binary files along 4 KB boundaries. Because pages on the Intel *x*86 chip family are 4 KB, this aligns the executable sections with the memory pages, increasing the efficiency of data caching.

Caution WinAlign works by restructuring an executable's files and can cause problems with certain applications. Such damage can usually be corrected by restoring the files to their previous condition (type **WinAlign -r** on the command line). In some cases, it may be necessary to reinstall the application.

MapCache is a performance feature that causes programs to consume less memory. Simply installing Windows 98 gives you some of the benefits of aligned binaries running directly from the cache, but to gain the most benefit from aligned binaries, you should run Winalign.exe. The alignment process takes less than one minute on an empty drive (with only Windows 98 installed), and should not take longer than five or six minutes on a full drive.

Memory can be divided into two parts: the disk cache (VCACHE) and memory that is allocated to run programs (VMM). The cache is useful because memory I/O is faster than disk I/O. For example, if you close Microsoft Word and then shortly afterwards restart Microsoft Word, much of the application is brought into VMM to run from the cache rather than having to be read off the disk. The result is a faster application start.

The downside of this process is that the cache takes up memory that could be used for other applications. You have two copies of some data in physical memory: one copy in the cache and another in VMM, which is being used to run the application. Having more memory available to VMM in many other cases than the application reload lets your system run faster, as it prevents over committing memory and writing/reading from the swap file (another case of slow disk I/O).

Memory mapped I/O out of cache is the best of both worlds. This process keeps a single copy of many pages of memory in one place rather than two places. This gives you more memory available for running applications, and, at the same time, less of the swap file is being used.

The WinAlign.exe file is located on the Windows 98 Resource Kit compact disc. For more information about WinAlign, see *Microsoft Windows 98 Resource Kit Tools Help* on the Windows 98 compact disc.

Troubleshooting Performance Tuning

This section describes specific issues in performance and how to correct them. For information about general procedures and Windows 98 tools that can be used for troubleshooting, see Chapter 27, "General Troubleshooting."

Optimize performance of the floppy disk drive.

Some computers, especially portable ones, start Windows with a disk mounted in the floppy drive. If you commonly add or remove floppy disks between Windows sessions and the computer often does not recognize the new disk, use the **Search for new floppy disk drives each time your computer starts** feature to direct the floppy driver to scan for new disks at every startup.

If this feature is not selected, Windows starts faster, because a floppy driver uses the previous settings for drive information.

▶   **To optimize performance of the floppy disk drives**

1. In Control Panel, double-click System, and then click the **Performance** tab.

2. Click **File System**, and then click the **Floppy Disk** tab.

3. Select the **Search for new floppy disk drives each time your computer starts** check box to scan for new drives every time Windows starts

    – Or –

    Clear the check box so Windows will not scan for new drives at startup.

The DMA check box in Device Manager will not remain checked.

When you enable DMA support on the **Settings** tab in the properties for an IDE hard disk, the DMA check box in Device Manager may not remain checked even though the IDE controller supports bus mastering and DMA. This happens because the hard disk may not support a multiple-word DMA protocol.

DMA (also referred to as bus mastering) reduces CPU overhead by providing a mechanism for data transfers that do not require monitoring by the CPU. The transfer rate for a particular data transfer event will not noticeably increase. However, overall CPU overhead should be reduced using DMA mode.

A disadvantage of implementing DMA data transfer operations is that the PC/AT and IDE hard disk controller evolved around PIO data transfer methods. As a result, the system Int 13h BIOS and native operating system device drivers evolved around PIO transfers instead of DMA transfers. Modifications to the BIOS, as well as external device drivers, have been necessary to achieve the incremental performance that DMA offers.

To determine whether your IDE hard disk supports multiple-word DMA protocol, test the primary IDE drive and the secondary IDE drive.

▶ **To test the primary IDE drive**

1. Restart the computer. Press the CTRL key to get the Windows 98 **Startup** menu, and then choose **Command Prompt Only**.

2. At the command prompt, type **debug**.

3. At the hyphen prompt, type the following lines, pressing ENTER after each line. Do not type the comment.

Note The first character of each line is the letter *o*, not the numeral zero.

Type	Comment
o 1f6 a0	a0 (a-zero) is for a master drive; use b0 for a slave.
o 1f2 22	22 is for DMA mode 2; use 21 for DMA mode 1.
o 1f1 03	03 (zero-3) is to program the hard disk timing.
o 1f7 ef	ef is the set feature command for the hard disk.
i 1f1	Reads in the error status; a value is returned.

If the number returned after entering **i 1f1** is 00, the hard disk accepts the DMA protocol timing that you entered with the **o 1f2** statement, and the hard disk supports DMA. A return value of 04 indicates that the hard disk does not support a DMA multiple-word protocol. If the value returned is not 00 or 04, you may not have typed the characters correctly, or you may need to quit Windows.

PIO mode 3 hard disks may support multiple-word DMA mode 1. PIO mode 4 hard disks should support multiple-word DMA mode 2. If you have a PIO mode 4 drive that does not support multiple-word DMA mode 2, it is possible that the hard disk has a firmware problem. Contact the hard disk manufacturer, and verify the firmware version.

4. To quit Debug, type **q** and press ENTER.

▶ **To test the secondary IDE drive**

1. Restart the computer. Press CTRL to get the Windows 98 **Startup** menu, and then choose **Command Prompt Only**.

2. At the command prompt, type **debug**.

3. At the hyphen prompt, type the following lines, pressing ENTER after each line. Do not type the comment.

Note The first character of each line is the letter *o*, not the numeral zero.

Type	Comment
o 176 a0	a0 (a-zero) is for a master drive; use b0 for a slave.
o 172 22	22 is for DMA mode 2; use 21 for DMA mode 1.
o 171 03	03 (zero-3) is to program the hard disk timing.
o 177 ef	ef is the set feature command for the hard disk.
i 171	Reads in the error status; a value is returned.

If the number returned after entering **i 171** is 00, the hard disk accepts the DMA protocol timing that you entered with the **o 172** statement, and the hard disk supports DMA. A return value of 04 indicates that the hard disk does not support a DMA multiple-word protocol.

If your drive does support a DMA multiple-word protocol and the DMA check box will not remain enabled, the IDE controller may not be compatible with the Microsoft IDE bus mastering driver.

4. To quit Debug, type **q** and press ENTER.

Additional Resources

For more information about	See this resource
MS-DOS memory settings	*Microsoft MS-DOS 6.2x Technical Reference* or other books on MS-DOS memory management
Creating drivers	*Microsoft Windows 98 Device Development Kit*
Resource kit tools	*Microsoft Windows 98 Resource Kit Tools Help* on the Windows 98 compact disc

CHAPTER 27

General Troubleshooting

27

This chapter provides a general approach to troubleshooting. It presents a troubleshooting strategy and identifies tools that are available in Microsoft Windows 98 for finding and correcting problems on your system.

Note This is a general guide to troubleshooting. Most chapters in this book have troubleshooting sections for individual components. When you have the problem narrowed down to a known component, use the troubleshooting section in the chapter that describes that component.

In This Chapter

General Troubleshooting Strategy

This section discusses an approach for solving system problems. Meticulous record-keeping is essential to successful troubleshooting. You should keep readily accessible all records of the network layout, cabling, previous problems and their solutions, and dates of installation of hardware and software.

Many problems can be avoided with routine virus checks. Be sure to check for viruses before installing or upgrading Windows 98 on a computer that is already in use.

Caution Anti-virus software may interfere with the installation of Windows 98. Disable all anti-virus software before running setup for any operating system. Once Windows 98 is successfully installed, re-enable the anti-virus protection.

To troubleshoot a problem, follow these general guidelines:

- Analyze symptoms and factors.
- Check to see if the problem is a common issue.
- Isolate the source of the problem.
- Consult technical support resources.

Analyzing Symptoms

Start troubleshooting by gathering information. Develop a clear understanding of the symptoms and collect pertinent system information to understand the environment in which they occur. Precisely what is not working correctly? Under what conditions does the problem occur? Which aspects of the operating system control those conditions? Is the problem specific to an application, or is it specific to a subsystem (networks, video, and so on)?

Try to narrow down exactly what you *expect* to have happen versus what *is* happening.

Consider the following:

- What is the issue at hand? What do you expect to happen when the problem is resolved?
- Has the system or configuration ever worked? If so, what changed?
- Is the error condition reproducible or random?
- Is the error specific to a particular system, configuration, or application?
- What specific hardware and firmware are involved?
- Is software that Windows 98 does not load by default loaded when the problem occurs?
- Does the error still occur with Safe Mode?

One strategy for isolating the source of the problem is to attempt to reproduce the symptom using another application that offers similar functionality. If the problem is reproducible, it might be subsystem- or hardware-related. If the problem is not reproducible, investigate the application itself.

Checking for Common Issues

Check to see if the problem is a common issue by reviewing Help and the TXT files included on the Windows 98 compact disc. For example, check Setup.txt and Readme.txt.

See the Troubleshooting topic in Help for the Windows 98 Troubleshooters. Use the Troubleshooters to diagnose and solve technical problems with the following system components and events:

- Networking
- Modem
- Startup and shutdown
- Print
- DriveSpace 3
- Memory
- MS-DOS programs
- Display
- DirectX
- Sound
- The Microsoft Network
- Hardware conflict
- Dial-Up Networking
- Direct Cable Connection
- PC Card

▶ **To get troubleshooting assistance from Windows 98 Help**

1. On the **Start** menu, click **Help**.
2. On the **Contents** tab, click **Troubleshooting**, and then click **Windows 98 Troubleshooters**.
3. Pick a topic from the list.

Identifying the Source of the Problem

Try to identify all the variables that could affect the problem. As you troubleshoot the problem, try to progressively eliminate these variables to isolate the root cause of the issue. Keep records of what you do and the effect of each action. If you must eventually escalate your issue to a support provider, your detailed notes will be invaluable to the technician.

Eliminating variables helps determine the cause of a problem. Do symptoms manifest themselves when you run the system in Safe Mode? If not, you can use the System Configuration Utility (Msconfig.exe) to identify problems with software loading during a normal startup. By selecting **Diagnostic startup–interactively load device drivers and software** and following the instructions you can safely eliminate all of the items at once to determine if the problem can be isolated using the tool. If the symptoms are no longer reproducible, you can add items back in its **Selective startup** until the symptoms reappear, thus identifying the problem's source. The System Configuration Utility is described later in this chapter.

Caution Do not modify Config.sys and Autoexec.bat until you have determined it is safe to do so. Your system might require legacy software to access the hard disk through a drive overlay or compression. If your system will run in Safe Mode, you can modify these files without losing access to the drive.

Windows 98 does not load protected-mode device drivers when it is run in Safe Mode. If you determine that the problem is not with software loading at startup using Msconfig.exe, you could attempt to isolate the problem with the protected-mode configuration by disabling suspect devices' drivers. To do so, in Control Panel double-click System and then click the **Device Manager** tab.

Caution The Plug and Play specification allows an operating system to disable devices at the hardware level. For example, if you disable a COM port in Device Manager, you may be required to enter the CMOS or system setup to re-enable it.

If the problem is the result of a recent change to the system, undo that change. Microsoft System Information (MSInfo) maintains a history of device drivers installed on the system. If you are unsure of a system's recent history, use MSInfo to better understand what has happened. If a device fails and its history indicates a recent upgrade to a new driver, replace it with the original driver and retest. If an update installed from the Windows Update Web site fails to meet your expectations, restore the original files by running the Update Wizard Uninstall from the **Tools** menu in MSInfo. If everything was fine yesterday, try restoring yesterday's configuration files by running MS-DOS-based Registry Checker with the /restore command prompt option (Scanreg /restore). Restoring a previous day's backup set will result in the loss of any changes made in the interim. Registry Checker is described in "Using Registry Checker" and "Restoring the Registry" later in this chapter.

Test each modification individually to see if it solved the problem. Make note of all modifications and their effect on the symptoms. This provides you with the information product support personnel will request if you eventually determine you need their assistance, and it provides an excellent reference for future troubleshooting.

Checking Technical Support Resources

Technical newsgroups offer peer support for common computer problems. When possible, post persistent problems on the appropriate online forum. Other users may have already discovered, reported, and found workarounds for your problem. Suggestions from others may save you time in tracking down the source of the problem by giving you direction for your troubleshooting. For more information about technical support resources such as Microsoft TechNet, see **http://www.microsoft.com/**.

Microsoft Help contains information about getting online Microsoft technical support.

▶ **To get online Microsoft technical support information from Windows 98 Help**

1. On the **Start** menu, click **Help**.

2. Click **Web Help**, and then click **Support Online** to connect to Support Online from Microsoft Technical Support.

Troubleshooting Tools

This section provides an overview of tools that are available in Windows 98. The tools can help you maintain your system in the following ways:

- Keep your system running smoothly.
- Isolate problem areas.
- Diagnose problems.
- Fix problems.
- Seek further assistance.

Table 27.1 lists system tools installed during Windows 98 Setup. The table includes a brief overview of the tool, and some details about the files that make up the tool. The tools are described in more detail later in the section.

Note This chapter assumes that your Windows 98 files are in the \Windows folder, which is the default folder in which Setup copies the system files.

Table 27.1   Troubleshooting tools

Tool	Overview	File details
Microsoft System Information (MSInfo)	Displays system information, such as hardware resources, devices installed, and the corresponding device drivers. Use MSInfo to diagnose and solve computer problems. MSInfo can be used to view reports generated by WinRep or DOSRep on a remote system.	Name: Msinfo32.exe Location: \program files\common files\microsoft shared\msinfo
Dr. Watson	A program error debugger that traps application faults (running in ring 3 of the processor), generating a snapshot of the system to aid in the diagnosis of the fault. This tool interprets program errors in Windows-based applications and attempts a diagnosis. When you are running Dr. Watson, it automatically creates a log file when an application fault occurs. The log files are stored in the \Windows\Drwatson directory with a .wlg extension. The log file indicates the program that faulted, the program the fault occurred in, and the memory address where the fault occurred. Dr. Watson cannot create a snapshot in the event of a system hang.	Name: Drwatson.exe Location: \windows
System File Checker	Verifies the integrity of system files. This tool scans the system for changed, deleted, or corrupt files. If necessary, System File Checker can extract the original Windows 98 file.	Name: Sfc.exe Location: \windows\system
Digital Signature Check	Feature that network administrators can enable to identify drivers that have been digitally signed by Microsoft. This feature can be turned on using Policy Editor (Poledit) or by setting a key in the registry.	Enabled in registry key: HKEY_LOCAL_MACHINE \Software\Microsoft\Driver Signing
Signature Verification Tool	Tool that determines whether a file has been granted a digital signature and whether that file has been modified after being granted a digital signature.	Name: Sigverif.exe Location: \windows
Automatic Skip Driver Agent	Detects devices that prevent Windows from starting.	Name: Asd.exe Location: \windows
Windows Update	Windows Update is the Web-extension of Windows 98 designed to help your computer continue to work better and run better. Windows Update contains a central catalog of new product enhancements, including service packs and new Windows features. In addition, Windows Update lets you update new system files and device drivers, specific to your computer.	Name: Iexplore.exe Location: http://www.microsoft.com /windowsupdate
System Configuration Utility	Automates routine Windows troubleshooting steps. System Configuration Utility allows you to modify the system configuration with check boxes. This tool allows you to troubleshoot problems through a process of elimination using check boxes.	Name: Msconfig.exe Location: \windows\system

Table 27.1   Troubleshooting tools (*continued*)

Tool	Overview	File details
Registry Checker	Windows 98 includes both Windows-based and MS-DOS-based programs for scanning, fixing, backing up, and restoring the registry and system configuration files. Registry Checker runs each time Windows starts.	Names: Scanreg.exe and Scanregw.exe Locations: \windows\command \scanreg.exe and \windows \scanregw.exe
Microsoft Backup	A built-in application that you run to back up the data in your entire system to prevent the loss of data in the event of hardware failure	Name: Msbackup.exe Location: \program files\accessories \backup\msbackup.exe
Microsoft System Recovery	Operating system recovery tool that operates completely in protect mode. Installs a minimal Windows 98 environment with full access to Win32 APIs, drivers, and other resources, and then steps you through the process of recovering files through Microsoft Backup.	Name: Pcrestor.bat Location: \tools\sysrec on Windows 98 compact disc
Scheduling Tasks	The Scheduled Task Wizard enables you to run important utilities such as ScanDisk, Disk Defragmenter, and Backup at regular intervals.	Name: Mstask.exe Location: \windows\system
Maintenance Wizard	The Windows Maintenance Wizard is used to schedule the operation of ScanDisk, Disk Cleanup, Disk Defragmenter, and other tools.	Name: Tuneup.exe Location: \windows
Version Conflict Manager	Windows 98 Setup automatically installs Windows 98 files over a newer file that may be on the hard drive.	Name: Vcmui.exe Location: \windows
Windows Report Tool	Web-based reporting tool that gathers system information and uploads it using HTTP to a support provider. The report includes a snapshot of the system in Microsoft System Information's format.	Name: Winrep.exe Location: \windows
MS-DOS Report Tool	Web-based reporting tool used to gather system files and upload them to an FTP server when Windows is inaccessible.	Name: Dosrep.exe Location: \windows

Using Microsoft System Information

Microsoft System Information (MSInfo) collects system information, such as devices installed or device drivers loaded, and provides a menu for displaying the associated system topics. Use MSInfo to diagnose computer problems. For example, if you are having display problems, use MSInfo to determine the display adapter installed on the computer and the status of its drivers.

Use MSInfo to track down an error and to learn the appropriate support tool to resolve the problem. For example, if a device is not functioning, MSInfo reports the following when viewing problem devices:

```
This device has a problem: Code=##
```

MSInfo also provides links in the **Tools** menu to other tools used for troubleshooting.

▶ **To launch Microsoft System Information**

- Click **Start**, point to **Programs**, **Accessories**, and **System Tools**, and then click **System Information**.

Note You can also launch Microsoft System Information by typing **msinfo32.exe** *filename* at the command prompt. The command prompt option *filename* enables you to specify a CAB file that was generated by the Windows Report Tool. For information about the Windows Report Tool, see "Windows Report Tool" later in this chapter.

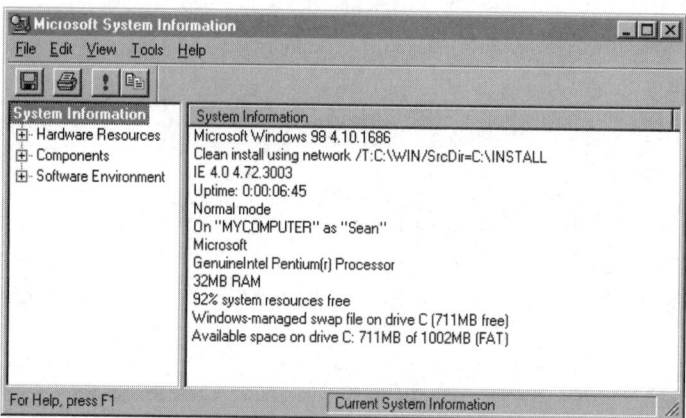

The information displayed in MSInfo is divided into three categories: Hardware Resources, Components, and Software Environment. The following sections describe the categories and sub-categories displayed in MSInfo, and explain how this information can be used when troubleshooting.

System Information

System Information provides a general profile of the system. This includes the version of Windows, the version of the Internet Explorer browsing software, CPU, memory, system resources, total and available disk space, and the file system for each partition. Use this information at the beginning of the troubleshooting process to develop a basic picture of the environment in which the problem occurs.

Hardware Resources

The Hardware Resources view displays hardware-specific settings, such as assigned or used interrupt requests (IRQs), I/O addresses, and memory addresses.

Conflicts/Sharing Lists identified resource conflicts between Industry Standard Architecture (ISA) devices, and identifies resources shared by peripheral component interconnect (PCI) devices. Use this information to help you identify some hardware conflicts.

DMA Reports the DMA channels in use, the devices using them, and those free for use.

Forced Hardware Lists hardware devices that have user-specified resources as opposed to system-specified resources. This information is useful when troubleshooting Plug and Play resource conflicts.

I/O Lists all I/O port ranges in use and the devices using each range.

IRQs Summarizes IRQ usage, identifying the devices using the IRQs and showing free IRQs.

Memory Lists memory address ranges in use by devices.

Components

Components displays information about your Windows 98 system configuration. The Components view includes the status of your device drivers, networking, and multimedia software. There is also a comprehensive driver history and a summary of problem devices.

Multimedia Lists sound card and game controller information.

Multimedia—Audio Lists audio CODECs loaded.

Multimedia — Video Lists video CODECs loaded.

Multimedia — CD-ROM Lists the drive letter and model of the CD-ROM drive. With a data CD-ROM in the drive, MSInfo also performs a data transfer test.

Display Lists video card and monitor information.

Infrared Lists Infrared device information.

Input Lists keyboard and mouse information.

Miscellaneous Lists information about any miscellaneous components.

Modems Lists modem information.

Network Lists network adapter, client, and protocol information.

Network—Winsock Lists Winsock version, description, and status information.

Ports Lists serial and parallel port information.

Storage Lists information on hard drives, floppy drives, removable storage, and controllers.

Printing Lists installed printers and printer drivers.

Problem Devices Lists devices with problems. Lists each device flagged in Device Manager, with the corresponding status information.

USB Lists controllers and drivers installed.

History Lists complete driver history or history for the past seven days. Useful for tracking changes to the system's configuration.

System Lists information on BIOS, motherboard, and other system devices.

Note The options to view Basic Information, Advanced Information, or History appear if the component has a device driver.

Software Environment

The Software Environment view displays a snapshot of the software loaded in computer memory.

Drivers — Kernel Drivers Lists kernel-mode (ring 0) device drivers loaded.

Drivers — MS-DOS Drivers Lists real-mode device drivers loaded.

Drivers — User-Mode Drivers Lists user-mode (ring 3) device drivers loaded.

16-bit Modules Loaded Lists loaded 16-bit system-level dynamic-link libraries (DLLs) and programs. Useful for debugging software problems, such as application faults.

32-bit Modules Loaded Lists loaded 32-bit system-level DLLs and programs. Useful for debugging software problems, such as application faults.

Running Tasks Lists currently running executable files. This provides a comprehensive view of the processes running on the system.

Startup Programs Lists programs started automatically either from the registry, the Startup group, or the Win.ini file.

System Hooks Lists programs that are resident in memory and hook system calls.

OLE Registration—INI File Lists OLE file associations controlled by various INI files.

OLE Registration — Registry Lists OLE file associations controlled by the registry.

Caution Hardware information is not available in Safe Mode. While MSInfo can run in Safe Mode, it will be limited to displaying system components and the software environment.

Launching System Tools

With Windows 98, Microsoft System Information should be the first place to go when troubleshooting. To reduce the time spent navigating through the **Start** menu, you can launch the following utilities from the **Tools** menu of Microsoft System Information:

- Windows Report Tool
- Update Wizard Uninstall
- System File Checker
- Signature Verification Tool
- Registry Checker
- Automatic Skip Driver Agent
- Dr. Watson
- System Configuration Utility
- ScanDisk
- Version Conflict Manager

These troubleshooting tools are covered later in this chapter.

Viewing, Saving, and Printing Information

▶ **To view files created by other programs**

1. Click **Start**, point to **Programs**, **Accessories**, and **System Tools**, and then click **System Information**.
2. From the **File** menu, click **Open**.
3. Click **Files of type**, click a file to open, and then click **Open**.

You can view the following file formats:

File	Description
*.cab	Report created by the Windows Report Tool (Winrep.exe) or MS-DOS Report Tool. This is the same CAB format used by Windows 95.
*.txt	File created by a text editor such as Notepad. You can paste specific information from MSInfo into Notepad, and send it to Technical Support so that they can view only that specific information.
*.dat	File created by Hwinfo.exe.
*.wlg	Dr. Watson log files. Dr. Watson is used to assist in determining the cause of failures in Windows-based applications.
*.nfo	File created by MSInfo. You can view NFO files created on another computer to see its system configuration.

▶ **To save system information**

- In MSInfo, go to the **File** menu, and click **Save**.

You can save system information in the following file formats:

File	Description
*.nfo	This is the MSInfo file format. These files are saved to the \Windows folder by default.
*.txt	Files created by a text editor such as Notepad. You can paste specific information from MSInfo into Notepad, and then send it to Technical Support.

▶ **To export system information**

- In MSInfo, go to the **File** menu, and then click **Export**.

  MSInfo exports information in text file (TXT) format. The files are saved to the \Windows folder by default.

▶ **To print system information**

- You can print a report of all system information by clicking **Print** on the **File** menu.

Note A typical MSInfo report can total more than 80 pages depending on the hardware and software installed.

▶ **To print specific information**

1. Highlight, and then copy the appropriate information.
2. Paste it into a text editor, such as Notepad, and then print the information from the text editor.

Using Dr. Watson

Dr. Watson (Drwatson.exe) collects detailed information about the state of your system at the time of and slightly before an application fault. Dr. Watson intercepts the software faults, identifying the software that faulted and offering a detailed description of the cause. When enabled, this tool automatically logs this information to the disk (\Windows\Drwatson*.wlg), and can display it on screen. Dr. Watson indicates the program that caused the application fault, the program the fault occurred in, and the memory address at which the fault occurred. This information can be used to assist product support personnel in determining the cause of the fault.

Starting Dr. Watson

You can configure Dr. Watson to load automatically when Windows starts by creating a shortcut to Drwatson.exe in the Startup folder. This is important when an issue is not easily reproducible. Once Dr. Watson traps the application fault and creates the log, you can contact support for further assistance.

Tip   Dr. Watson is best used with reproducible faults. Determining the cause of intermittent faults may prove difficult.

▶ **To start Dr. Watson**

- On the **Start** menu, click **Run**, and then type **Drwatson**. Click **OK**.

  – Or –

  Click **Start**, point to **Programs**, **Accessories**, and **System Tools**, and then click **System Information**. Select the **Tools** menu and click **Dr. Watson**.

Dr. Watson runs minimized, and the icon appears in the Taskbar. Dr. Watson monitors the system for application faults. If an application fault occurs, Dr. Watson generates a snapshot of the software environment. Click the **Details** button in the error message box to view the information gathered by Dr. Watson.

▶ **To generate a log file**

- Double-click the **Dr. Watson** icon in the Windows 98 system tray. Dr. Watson gathers information about the system, and then the **Dr. Watson** dialog box appears.

When Dr. Watson is loaded, you move out of the text box by clicking any tab. The Dr. Watson window closes if you press the ENTER key.

▶ **To view the Advanced tabs in Dr. Watson**

1. Double-click the **Dr. Watson** icon in the Windows 98 system tray. Dr. Watson gathers information about the system, and then the **Dr. Watson** dialog box appears.

2. Click **Options**, **View**, and then **Advanced View**.

   The following tabs, which provide detailed information about your system for a support technician, are added to the dialog box:

   - System
   - Tasks
   - Startup
   - Kernel Drivers
   - User Drivers
   - MS-DOS Drivers
   - 16-bit Modules

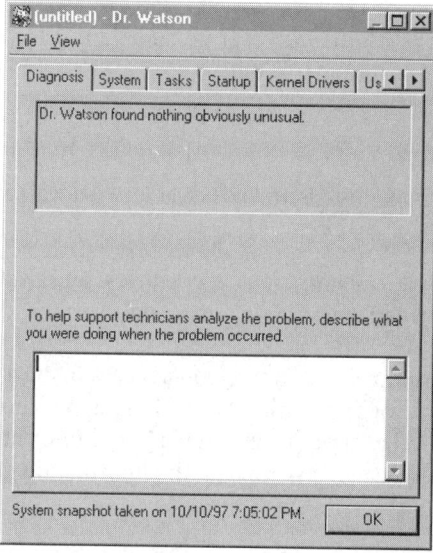

Using Dr. Watson with an Application Fault

If you get an application fault, use these general guidelines to isolate the problem.

1. Try to reproduce the fault to verify that it is not a random failure.

2. Click **Start**, point to **Programs**, **Accessories**, and **System Tools**, and then click **System Information**. Select the **Tools** menu and click **Dr. Watson**.

3. Reproduce the fault.

4. Click **Details** on the application fault message box.

5. Look in the **Diagnosis** box to determine the source of the fault.

If the problem is intermittent or not easy to reproduce, put Dr. Watson in your Startup folder so that it is always running. The **Dr. Watson** dialog box provides a text box to provide information about what you were doing when the problem occurred. You should provide which applications were running, and the steps that resulted in the application fault in this box.

Caution   After typing the information in the text box, choose **File Save** or **Save As** to save the file. If you click **OK**, the text entered in the text box is not saved.

Customizing Dr. Watson

You customize Dr. Watson by clicking **Options** from the **View** menu. Table 27.2 describes these options.

Table 27.2   Dr. Watson options in View menu

Option	Description
Log Files	Configures the number of log files to store on the computer and the folder that log files are saved in.
Disassembly	Configures the number of CPU instructions and stack frames that are reported in the log file. You need to configure these options only when requested to do so by technical support.
View	Configures Dr. Watson to display in **Standard View** or **Advanced View** the next time it runs.

Saving Log Files

When an application fault occurs, the Dr. Watson log file is automatically named Watson*xx*.wlg (where *xx* is an incremented number). By default, Dr. Watson log files are saved to the \Windows\Drwatson folder.

▶ **To save the information generated by Dr. Watson**

• Click **Save** on the **File** menu.

Caution   After typing the information in the text box, choose **File Save** or **Save As** to save the file. If you click **OK**, the text entered in the text box is not saved.

Viewing Log Files

You can view a Dr. Watson log file in the Dr. Watson program or from Microsoft System Information (MSInfo).

▶ **To view Dr. Watson log files from MSInfo**

1. Open Microsoft System Information (click **Start**, point to **Programs**, **Accessories**, and **System Tools**, and then click **System Information**).

2. Click **File**, and then click **Open**.

3. Go to the folder where you save your Dr. Watson log.

4. Select **Dr. Watson Log File (*.WLG)** from the **Files of type** list.

5. Select the file, and click **Open**.

Printing Log Files

Print Dr. Watson log files by selecting **Print** from the **File** menu. To print only specific information, use Microsoft System Information to view the log file, and then copy the specific information to a text editor, such as Notepad.

Note A typical Dr. Watson log can be over 15 pages, depending on the software running.

Using System File Checker

System File Checker verifies the integrity of your system files. After scanning for altered files, it offers to restore corrupted files. If a file is found to be corrupt, you will be prompted to restore the original file. By clicking **Settings**, System File Checker can also be configured to notify you of changed and deleted files. If you choose to restore the file, System File Checker attempts to extract the file from your original Windows 98 installation source.

System File Checker (Sfc.exe) helps you do two things:

- Scan system files for corrupt, missing, or changed files. Windows-based applications commonly install shared files that may not be compatible with another application in use. You can use System File Checker to track changes to your Windows configuration and identify the affected files.

- Restore original Windows 98 system files.

▶ **To start System File Checker**

1. Click **Start**, point to **Programs**, **Accessories**, and **System Tools**, and then click **System Information**.

2. Select the **Tools** menu and click **System File Checker**. The following dialog box appears:

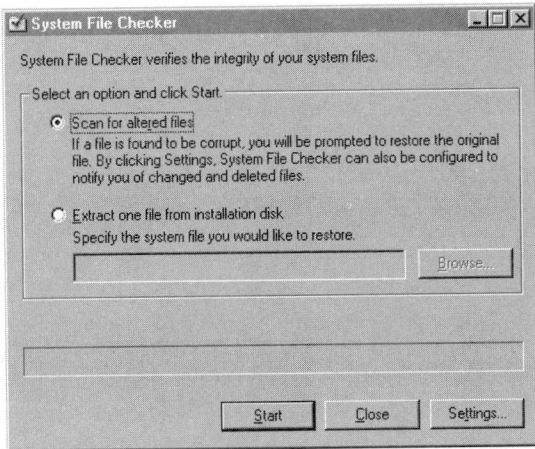

▶ **To scan for corrupt files**

- In System File Checker, click **Scan for altered files**, and then click **Start**.

  System File Checker scans the system using a default baseline contained in a file named Default.sfc. Default.sfc is copied from the Windows 98 installation source and contains the information shown in Table 27.3 about each system file:

Table 27.3   System File Checker Default.sfc contents

Information	Description
Cyclical Redundancy Check (CRC)	A checksum added to a file entry whenever a file is written to disk. This data is used to see if the file has changed.
	For example, the sum of all ones and zeros in a file equals a specific number. If a CRC is performed on the file and the sum does not equal the checksum associated with the file, then System File Checker assumes the file has changed. When a difference is detected between the information in the Default.sfc and the file on the disk, a message box appears. If all the verification data matches except for the CRC, the message indicates that there is possible file corruption and recommends you restore the file.
Date, time, size, and version information	If System File Checker determines a change in date, time, size, or version, it considers the file to be changed.

When System File Checker identifies a changed file, the user is given several choices to approach the situation. Table 27.4 describes these options.

Table 27.4   System File Checker options

Option	Used to
Update the verification information	Update the file data in Default.sfc. Choose this option when you have updated a system file without running System File Checker, and are certain that you want to update Default.sfc to use the updated information about the file the next time System File Checker is run.
Restore file	Specify the source location of the file to restore and where to save the new copy of the file. You are also prompted to back up the existing file to the \Windows\Helpdesk\SFC folder. Choose to back up the file in case there are problems using the new file.
Ignore	Skip the file. The next time System File Checker is run, this file will cause the **File Changed** dialog box to appear because it was not added to Default.sfc and it was not restored.

▶ **To verify the integrity of your system files**

1. In System File Checker, click **Scan for altered files**.

2. Click **Start**.

3. Note any files that display a dialog box requesting your action.

   When you uninstall a program, System File Checker reports that files necessary for that program (for example, files with .exe, .dll, and .ocx extensions) have been deleted. Select **Update verification information** to bring the baseline for System File Checker up to date.

If you know a specific system file is corrupt or missing, you can extract it from your original installation media using the following procedure.

▶ **To extract a specific system file**

1. In System File Checker, click **Extract one file from installation disk**.

2. Enter the name of the file, and then click **Start**.

3. In **Restore from**, type the location of your Windows 98 installation media.

4. In **Save file in**, type the location where you want to put the file, and then click **OK**.

Customizing System File Checker

You can customize the criteria that System File Checker uses to check files. Table 27.5 shows the items that you can customize in the **System File Checker Settings** dialog box:

Table 27.5   System File Checker custom settings

Option	Description
Settings	Used to configure how to back up files, log file options, and whether to check for changed or deleted files.
Search Criteria	Used to modify the files and folders to scan.
Advanced	Used to create a new verification data file, choose a different verification data file to use, or restore the original Default.sfc.

▶ **To customize System File Checker**

1. In System File Checker, click **Settings**.

2. Choose one of the three options for **Back up file before restoring**:

Option	Description
Always back up before restoring	Before restoring the original file, System File Checker will always create a copy of the current file.
Prompt for back up	Before restoring the original file, System File Checker will ask you if you want to save a copy of the current file.
Never back up before restoring	System File Checker will not create copies of the current files before restoring.

   The default backup location is C:\Windows\Helpdesk\sfc.

3. Choose one of the three options for **Log File**:

Option	Description
Append to existing log	Keeps one log file, and System File Checker adds to that file with every system check.
Overwrite existing log	Overwrites existing log file with every system check.
No log	Does not create a log file.

4. Click **View Log** to open the current System File Checker log text file in Notepad.

5. Check the **Check for changed files** box to enable System File Checker to prompt you when it finds files that have changed.

6. Check the **Check for deleted files** box to enable System File Checker to prompt you when it finds files that have been deleted.

▶ **To change the search criteria**

1. Click the **Search Criteria** tab.

   System File Checker shows the list of folders to be checked according to the verification data file.

2. Click **Add Folder** to add a folder to the verification data.

3. Click **Add Type** to add file extensions to the search criteria.

4. Enter a file extension. For example, type ***.TXT** to search for all TXT files.

5. Click **OK**.

More Information about System File Checker

Files that are renamed during Windows 98 Setup are not automatically extracted and renamed by System File Checker. For example, Winoa386.new in a CAB file cannot be extracted and renamed to Winoa386.mod.

There are files created during Windows 98 Setup that cannot be found by System File Checker Extract. System File Checker Extract looks for files in the cabinets to extract. If they do not exist in the CAB files, it cannot extract them. For example, files such as Control.ini, Exchange32.ini, and Msbatch.inf are not found.

If you save any changes for the search criteria in Default.sfc, those changes will overwrite the original file.

Points to remember about System File Checker:

- System File Checker lets you scan specific system files for errors and restore the original Windows 98 system files.

- Files that are renamed during Setup are not automatically extracted and renamed by System File Checker.

- Some files created during Setup cannot be found by System File Checker Extract.

- If you save any changes for the search criteria in Default.sfc, the changes will overwrite the original file.

Verifying Digital Signatures on Drivers

All drivers shipped with Windows 98 will be digitally signed by Microsoft. You can verify that the drivers you install on your Windows 98 system have met the Windows Hardware Quality Labs (WHQL) standards, and that they have not been modified since they were tested by WHQL. To ensure that the device drivers you are installing are compatible with Windows 98, look for vendors offering drivers signed by Microsoft.

Windows 98 includes the Signature Verification Tool and Signature Checking to identify files that have been signed. This section describes them.

Signature Verification Tool

The Signature Verification Tool (Sigverif.exe) determines whether or not a file is signed. With Sigverif.exe, you can do the following:

- View the certificates of signed files to ensure that the file has not been tampered with after being certified.
- Search for Signed files in a specific location.
- Search for Not signed files in a specific location.

▶ **To start the Microsoft Signature Verification Tool**

- On the **Start** menu, click **Run** and then type **Sigverif**. Click **OK**.

  – Or –

  Click **Start**, point to **Programs**, **Accessories**, and **System Tools**, and then click **System Information**. Select the **Tools** menu and click **Signature Verification Tool**.

Signature Checking on Drivers

Signature Checking can be enabled by system administrators to ensure that Windows 98 inspects files for digital signatures whenever drivers are installed.

Signature Checking has three levels:

- **Level 0** disables digital signature checking. The dialog box that identifies a digitally signed driver will not appear, and all drivers will be installed on the system if they are signed or not.
- **Level 1** determines if the driver has passed WHQL testing. A message appears whenever a user tries to install a driver that fails the signature check.
- **Level 2** blocks installation of a driver that fails the signature check. A dialog box appears with a message informing the user that the driver cannot be installed because it is not digitally signed.

You can start the Signature Checking feature using Policy Editor (Poledit).

▶ **To start Signature Checking using Policy Editor**

Note For information about setting up, starting, and using Policy Editor, see Chapter 8, "System Policies."

1. In Policy Editor, set the current Policy Template to Windows.adm, and then open the Default Computer policy.

2. Enable the check box in Default\Computer\Windows98 System\Install Device Drivers\Digital Signature Check.

   The system administrator can set the Security level using the list box.

Caution Making a mistake in editing the registry can cause your system to become unstable and/or unusable.

Wherever possible, use the administrative tools, such as Control Panel or System Policy Editor, to make configuration changes, rather than editing the registry. This is to ensure values are stored properly in the registry when changing the configuration.

If you use Registry Editor to change values, you will not be warned if any entry is incorrect. Editing the registry directly by using Registry Editor can cause errors in loading hardware and software, and can prevent users from being able to start the computer.

You can also start the Signature Checking feature by setting the following registry value:

HKEY_LOCAL_MACHINE\Software\Microsoft\Driver Signing

If the Policy Value is set to "00 00 00 00", the signature checking is set to level 0.

If the Policy Value is set to "01 00 00 00", the signature checking is set to level 1.

If the Policy Value is set to "02 00 00 00", the signature checking is set to level 2.

Using Automatic Skip Driver Agent

Automatic Skip Driver (ASD) Agent is used to detect and automatically disable device drivers or operations that fail during startup. Disabled items can be viewed and re-enabled by running the Automatic Skip Driver Agent (Asd.exe). If you run Asd.exe with no errors in the registry, you will receive a message stating that no critical operation failures occurred.

When Windows 98 starts, it attempts to load all device drivers required for the installed hardware. If a hardware device or its driver is defective, the device driver can fail to load and prevent Windows from starting. Automatic Skip Driver tracks the device load failure using the following steps:

1. Identifies the specific device(s) that failed to enumerate when Windows 98 started. Enumeration is the process of identifying which Plug and Play devices are in the computer and assigning the appropriate hardware resources to the devices.

2. After two failed attempts to load, ASD disables the device driver or stops the operation that caused system startup to fail. Windows will no longer attempt to enumerate the component.

If a device is disabled by ASD, it may be identified with a yellow exclamation point (!) in Device Manager. Device Manager identifies devices disabled by ASD with a Code 11.

Along with device drivers, certain problems during startup and during normal operating system operation can be detected by ASD. The following items are examples of operations that ASD monitors:

- Starting a device.
- Enumerating a device.
- Calling a PnP BIOS.
- Calling a PCI BIOS.
- Calling a VESA BIOS.
- Posting a video BIOS.
- Mapping an address space.
- Setting a graphics device power state.
- Posting a video BIOS after standby.
- Getting PCI IRQ routing table from a PCIBIOS 2.1 call.

▶ **To launch Automatic Skip Driver Agent**

- On the **Start** menu, click **Run** and then type **ASD**. Click **OK**.

  – Or –

  Click **Start**, point to **Programs**, **Accessories**, and **System Tools**, and then click **System Information**. Select the **Tools** menu and click **Automatic Skip Driver Agent**.

Every problem that ASD has ever detected on that computer is recorded in the Asd.log file.

More Information about Automatic Skip Driver Agent

Automatic Skip Driver Agent tracks device load failures by identifying specific device(s) that failed to enumerate when Windows 98 started.

If a device driver fails to load during startup, run Asd.exe. In the **Automatic Skip Driver** dialog box, click the operation that failed, and then click **Details**. The device's **Details** dialog box appears and provides a recommendation for solving the problem. This may include updating the driver.

Points to remember about Automatic Skip Driver Agent:

- The Automatic Skip Driver (ASD) Agent is used to detect device drivers that fail to load or certain operations that fail at startup.
- ASD tracks device load failures by identifying the specific device(s) that failed to enumerate when Windows 98 started.

Using Windows Update

Windows Update (Iexplore.exe) is an online extension of Windows 98. It helps your computer operate better by providing a central location to find customized files and product enhancements. Product enhancements include service packs, system files, device drivers, and new Windows 98 features.

When Windows 98 is installed, an Internet shortcut to the Windows Update page on **www.microsoft.com** is created on the **Start** menu. Windows Update uses Active Setup and ActiveX controls to provide product enhancements. The ActiveX controls are downloaded and installed on your system when you connect to the Windows Update Web page.

Note Windows Update requires browser software that supports ActiveX controls.

Once the controls are installed, they automatically compare device drivers installed on your computer with a database of updated drivers on the server. If any drivers are found to be newer than your current set, they are offered to you to install.

Note Device drivers, system patches, or hot fixes can be uninstalled using the Restore page from the Web site. If you are unable to connect to the Windows Update Web site, you can uninstall the latest updates by using Update Wizard Uninstall (Upwizun.exe) found on the **Tools** menu of Microsoft System Information. Existing files and drivers are automatically backed up before the new ones are installed.

▶ **To use Windows Update**

- Click **Start**, and then click **Windows Update**.

    – Or –

    Click **Start**, point to **Settings**, and then click **Windows Update**.

Follow the instructions on the screen to install the latest updates.

Windows Update scans your system, generates a list of items that can be updated, and then installs the files for the items you choose to update.

Restricting Access to Windows Update

You can use Policy Editor to restrict access to Windows Update. System administrators can control access to system updates to ensure the Windows 98 configuration remains consistent across all desktops. Use the following check boxes in System Policy Editor to restrict access:

- **Disable Windows Update** disables all access to Windows Update and removes its shortcut from the **Start** menu.

- **Override Local Web Page** redirects the user to a specified Web page the first time Windows Update is launched.

- **Override Windows Update Site URL** redirects the user to a specified URL when Windows Update is launched.

▶ **To restrict access to Windows Update using Policy Editor**

Note For information about setting up, starting, and using Policy Editor, see Chapter 8, "System Policies."

1. In Policy Editor, set the current Policy Template to Windows.adm, and then open the Default Computer policy.

2. Expand **Windows 98 System** by clicking the **+** box next to it, and then select **Windows Update**.

3. **Disable Windows Update**, **Override Local Web Page**, and **Override Windows Update Site URL** appear with check boxes next to them. The system administrator can restrict access to Windows Update using the check boxes.

Caution Making a mistake in editing the registry can cause your system to become unstable and/or unusable.

Wherever possible, use the administrative tools, such as Control Panel or System Policy Editor, to make configuration changes, rather than editing the registry. This is to ensure values are stored properly in the registry when changing the configuration.

If you use Registry Editor to change values, you will not be warned if any entry is incorrect. Editing the registry directly by using Registry Editor can cause errors in loading hardware and software, and can prevent users from being able to start the computer.

You can also restrict access to Windows Update by setting the following registry values:

HKEY_LOCAL_MACHINE\Software\Microsoft\Windows\CurrentVersion \Policies\Explorer\NoWindowsUpdate

If the value is set to "1", access to Windows Update is disabled.

If the value for NoWindowsUpdate is deleted, access is permitted.

HKEY_LOCAL_MACHINE\Software\Microsoft\Windows\CurrentVersion \RunOnce\WUCheckShortcut

If the value is set to "WUpdMgr.exe -shortcut", the shortcut to Windows Update is deleted on the subsequent system startup.

HKEY_LOCAL_MACHINE\Software\Policies\Microsoft\WindowsUpdate \Local URL

If a value is specified for a local URL, the first time Windows Update runs, it redirects the user to this location.

HKEY_LOCAL_MACHINE\Software\Policies\Microsoft\WindowsUpdate \Remote URL

If a value is specified for a remote URL, the link to Windows Update redirects the user to this location.

More Information about Windows Update

Points to remember about Windows Update:

- Windows Update is an online extension of Windows 98 that helps you maintain a current computer.

- You must have browser software that supports ActiveX controls to access Windows Update.

- Device drivers, system patches, or hot fixes can be uninstalled using the Restore page from the Web site. If you are unable to connect to the Windows Update Web site, use Update Wizard Uninstall (Upwizun.exe) found on the **Tools** menu of Microsoft System Information. The original files are automatically backed up to ensure a safe return to the prior state, if needed.

Using the System Configuration Utility

The System Configuration Utility (Msconfig.exe) provides a graphical interface for configuring the Windows 98 startup environment. The System Configuration Utility (MSConfig) lets you troubleshoot by creating a clean environment to test against. If a problem is not reproducible after performing a Diagnostic startup, a process of elimination can be used to identify the source of the issue.

The System Configuration Utility lets you edit lines of Windows 98 configuration files, like Config.sys or System.ini, and provides the ability to "remark" individual lines in the files, preventing the lines from executing or processing on subsequent boots of the computer.

The System Configuration Utility also lets you enable/disable items in your Startup group, and the RUN/RUN SERVICES keys of the registry. You can also use it to create a backup of system files.

▶ **To use the System Configuration Utility**

1. Click **Start**, point to **Programs**, **Accessories**, and **System Tools**, and then click **System Information**.

2. From the **Tools** menu, click **System Configuration Utility**.

   Table 27.6 describes the tabs in System Configuration Utility.

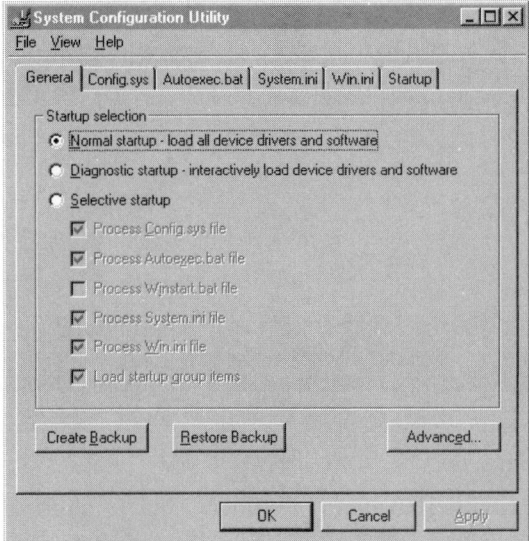

3. Select **Diagnostic startup** to create a clean software environment for troubleshooting, and then click **OK** to restart the computer.

4. The **Windows 98 Startup** menu appears. Select **Step-by-Step** from the menu options, and choose to process all but the Config.sys and Autoexec.bat files. If, while bypassing these files, the system hangs, restart the computer and step through them line by line, choosing to load all drive overlay and compression software the drive requires.

5. Determine if the symptoms are alleviated in the clean environment.

If the symptoms are alleviated, a process of elimination can be employed to identify the source of the problem using MSConfig. Continue with step 6 of this procedure to isolate the source of the issue using the Selective Startup Options.

– Or –

If the symptoms still manifest after a Diagnostic startup, investigate the following possibilities:

- Advanced troubleshooting options in the System Configuration Utility. For more information, see Table 27.7.

- Protected-mode device driver configuration. Launch Device Manager from the **View** menu in Microsoft System Configuration.

- A file is missing, corrupt, or has been replaced. For more information, see "Using System File Checker" earlier in this chapter.

- Registry corruption. For more information, see "Using Registry Checker" later in this chapter.

- Virus.

- Faulty hardware settings. Use the CMOS screen to check the hardware settings.

- Unsuccessful upgrade of previous Windows configuration.

6. Isolate the issue using the **Selective startup** options.

Using a process of elimination, enable options until the symptoms are reproducible. Once the problem reappears, isolate the issue by narrowing the suspect options down to one source.

7. Once you have identified the source of the problem, identify the problem using the appropriate tab(s).

- Identify issues with the real-mode configuration by disabling all but the Config.sys and Autoexec.bat files and restarting.

- Enable the System.ini and Win.ini files and restart as prompted to determine if the problem lies in the Windows configuration files.

- Test the software loading at startup by enabling the Winstart.bat and Startup options and restarting the system.

The **Config.sys** and **Autoexec.bat** tabs use the following conventions to identify settings and minimize the risks inherent in editing configuration files:

- Disabled check boxes indicate lines commented out by the tool.

- Settings used when the **Selective startup** option of the file is disabled are identified with a Microsoft Windows logo ⊞.

- Previously commented lines are listed without a check box.

- A yellow pencil identifies lines edited from within the tool.

The **System.ini** and **Win.ini** tabs also follow these conventions and identify sections with a yellow folder. Entire sections can by commented out by disabling the check box for the section.

The **Startup** tab lists items loading automatically at startup from the Windows 98 Startup group, Win.ini load= and run=, and the registry.

Table 27.6   System Configuration Utility dialog box tabs

Tab	Description
General	Enable or prevent the loading of all or specific device drivers and software. Prevent the loading of Config.sys, Autoexec.bat, System.ini, Win.ini, and Startup options. Back up or restore Config.sys, Autoexec.bat, System.ini, and Winstart.bat. The **Advanced** button contains the settings that are described in Table 27.7.
Config.sys	Enable or prevent the loading of specific lines in the Config.sys file. Checking a line item edits the Config.sys file and adds REM TSHOOT: to remark out the line.
Autoexec.bat	Enable or prevent the loading of specific lines in the Autoexec.bat file. Checking a line item edits the Autoexec.bat file and adds REM TSHOOT: to remark out the line.
System.ini	Enable or prevent the loading of specific lines in the System.ini file. Checking a line item edits the System.ini and adds ;REM TSHOOT: to remark out the line.
Win.ini	Enable or prevent the loading of specific lines in the Win.ini file. Checking a line item edits the Win.ini and adds ;REM TSHOOT: to remark out the line.
Startup	Enable or prevent specific items loaded by the operating system on startup. The information in the **Startup** tab comes from the registry, Win.ini items on the **Startup** menu under **Programs**.

Table 27.7   The Advanced button settings of System Configuration Utility

Setting	Description
Disable System ROM Breakpoint	Specifies whether Windows 98 should use ROM address space between F000:0000 and 1 MB for a breakpoint.
Disable Virtual HD IRQ	Allows Windows to terminate interrupts from the hard disk controller, bypassing the ROM routines that handle these interrupts. Some legacy hard drives might require that this setting be disabled in order for interrupts to be processed correctly. If this setting is disabled, the ROM routine handles the interrupts, which slows the system's performance.
EMM Exclude A000-FFFF	EMM Exclude specifies a range of memory that Windows will not use as an API buffer area. Using or attempting to use certain areas of the upper memory area can interfere with some ISA adapters that use the same memory area.

Table 27.7   The Advanced button settings of System Configuration Utility
(*continued*)

Setting	Description
Force Compatibility mode disk access	Forces Windows to use real-mode methods to access the hard drive. No 32-bit disk drivers are loaded in the system (except the floppy driver). Used as a troubleshooting tool to test for problems with protected-mode hard disk drivers. Note that this drastically affects performance.
VGA 640 x 480 x 16	Forces the display to use the industry-standard VGA mode. If the machine is not booting, and this setting allows the machine to boot successfully, then this could indicate a video-related problem.
Use SCSI Double-buffering	Grayed out if Windows detected that SCSI double-buffering is required. Enables SCSI double-buffering. Windows 98 detects whether this double-buffering is needed or not, so this should be enabled only if there is a disk access problem.
Enable Startup menu	Enables or disables a setting in the Msdos.sys file that controls whether the **Start** menu appears or not by default.
Disable ScanDisk after bad shutdown	Modifies a setting in the Msdos.sys file that controls whether ScanDisk runs automatically following an improper shutdown of Windows 98.
Limit memory to	Adds a setting to System.ini that artificially limits the amount of physical memory available to Windows 98. Note that a 16 MB or lower setting may prevent Windows from starting in normal mode.
Disable fast shutdown	Instructs Windows 98 to revert to the previous methods of shutting down Windows 98. Some software may not allow this feature, and could manifest problems if fast shutdown is enabled.
Disable UDF file system	Disables the Universal Disk Format (UDF) file system for all removable media. Use this to troubleshoot problems encountered with proprietary DVD movie players that are incompatible with UDF.
Enable Pentium F0 (Lock CmpXchg) workaround	If an illegal instruction sequence is issued, certain Pentium processors will hang. If this box is checked, Windows will enable the protection routine to avoid hanging under the illegal instruction sequence. Checking this box will write a SWORD registry key "FixP5Lock" with value 1 at **HKEY_LOCAL_MACHINE \System\CurrentControlSet\Services\VxD\VMM**. Note that this routine makes part of the interrupt description table to be not present, so it is recommended that this feature remain disabled while debugging programs.

In the **System Configuration Utility** dialog box, the **View** menu lets you open other controls in Windows 98, which include the following:

- Control Panel
- Device Manager

- Printers Folder
- Display Settings
- Multimedia Settings
- Fonts Folder

Disabling Entries

When you disable an entry in System.ini or Win.ini from the System Configuration Utility, the following entry is added to the front of the specified line:

;REM TSHOOT:

When you disable an entry in Config.sys or Autoexec.bat from the System Configuration Utility, the following entry is added above and before the specified line:

REM TSHOOT:

Creating Backup Files

Backups of Win.ini, System,ini, Autoexec.bat, and Config.sys can be created with the System Configuration Utility by clicking **Create Backup** from the **General** tab. These files have a .pss extension and can later be restored to their original name and configuration by clicking **Restore Backup**.

Important It is strongly recommended that you create a backup of these four system files before making any changes to an installation with System Configuration Utility.

▶ **To create backups of your files**

1. In the **System Configuration Utility** dialog box, click the **General** tab.
2. Click **Create Backup**.
3. Click **OK**.

More Information about System Configuration Utility

The **Startup** tab lists information about items loading from the registry's run and runservices keys, the Win.ini run= load=, and the Startup group. It does not list Static Virtual Device Drivers (VxDs) and Shell Extensions. Identify items loading automatically at startup as a Static VxD or Shell Extension by using information gathered by Dr. Watson and the software environment category in Microsoft System Information; refer to the product's documentation for instructions on disabling or uninstalling the software.

Points to remember about the System Configuration Utility:

- The System Configuration Utility can be used to control the Windows 98 startup environment.

- Use the System Configuration Utility to edit Config.sys, Autoexec.bat, System.ini, Win.ini files, and the Startup group.

- When changing any of the files listed in the previous bullet, the originals are renamed with the file extension .tsh and a new file is created.

- The **View** menu lets you open other troubleshooting controls in Windows 98, including Control Panel, Device Manager, Printers Folder, Display Settings, Multimedia Settings, and Fonts Folder.

- When you disable an entry in System.ini or Win.ini, ;REM TSHOOT: is added to the front of the particular line.

- When you disable an entry in Config.sys or Autoexec.bat, ;REM TSHOOT: is added above and before the particular line.

- When a line is editing in the System Configuration Utility, a pencil icon appears next to the edited line.

- When creating a backup, the files are renamed with the .pss extension in the same folder as the original.

Using Registry Checker

Registry Checker is a system maintenance program that finds and resolves some registry problems, and regularly backs up the registry. Windows 98 provides an MS-DOS-based version for scanning the registry, backing up, and restoring the registry and system configuration files, and a Windows-based version for scanning and backing up the registry.

Registry Checker backs up the registry each day following a successful Windows 98 system startup, maintaining one backup for each day. If a serious problem is found in the registry, Registry Checker will restore the most recent registry from a backup copy.

Note If you want to restore an earlier version of the registry, you must use the MS-DOS-based utility outside of Windows.

Registry Checker maintains compressed backups of the registry and configuration files that have successfully started the computer. Registry Checker will attempt to fix the registry only if a valid backup cannot be found.

ScanRegW is the Windows-based version. This program scans the registry for corruption and determines if it requires optimization, and then backs up the following system configuration files: registry (User.dat and System.dat), Win.ini, and System.ini. This scan occurs automatically when the system is started. You can run Scanregw.exe to force a scan and backup of these files. ScanRegW backs up the registry and configuration files using a compressed CAB file in the \Windows\Sysbckup directory.

ScanReg is the MS-DOS-based version. If ScanRegW detects a problem with the registry, it prompts you to restart the computer to fix the problem, and ScanReg will run automatically. It either restores a known good backup or, if no backups are available, attempts to repair the current registry by removing the corruption. If ScanRegW detects that optimization is required, ScanReg will optimize the registry on the subsequent startup.

For more information about the registry, see Chapter 31, "Windows 98 Registry." For information about restoring a registry, see "Restoring the Registry" later in this chapter.

ScanRegW versus ScanReg

Table 27.8 identifies the differences between ScanRegW and ScanReg.

Table 27.8   Differences between ScanRegW and ScanReg

Function	ScanRegW	ScanReg
Environment	Windows	MS-DOS
Real-mode or Protected- mode?	Protected-mode	Real-mode
Scan registry?	Yes	Yes
Fix registry?	No	Yes
Backup registry?	Yes	Yes
Runs in Safe Mode?	Yes	No
Compresses backup	Yes	No
Runs automatically?	Yes, every time computer is started.	Yes, if a registry problem is detected.
Restores the registry?	No	Yes

Command-line Options

Table 27.9 describes command line options for the ScanRegW and ScanReg utilities of Registry Checker.

Table 27.9   Command line options for Registry Checker

Command line option	Description	Available for
/backup	Backs up the registry with no prompts to the user.	ScanReg and ScanRegW
/restore	Displays a list of backup files available, sorted by date and time of the backup.	ScanReg
"/comment"	Specifies that a comment be associated with the backup. The comment is displayed with the /restore command. For example: "/comment=this is a backup comment."	ScanReg and ScanRegW
/fix	Repairs the registry files.	ScanReg
/autoscan	Scans the registry files every time it is run, but backs up the registry only once per day.	ScanRegW
/scanonly	Scans the registry files and returns an error, if appropriate; it does not back up the files.	ScanRegW

ScanReg.ini

Both ScanRegW and ScanReg use settings from the Scanreg.ini file. Table 27.10 lists the settings.

Table 27.10   Scanreg.ini settings

Keyname and default value	Function	Other values
Backup=1	Run ScanReg at startup and make a backup automatically.	0: ScanReg is not run at startup
Optimize=1	Run ScanReg to optimize the registry, reducing its size to improve performance.	0: Automatic optimization is skipped
MaxBackupCopies=5	Number of backups to store in the backup folder.	0 to 99
BackupDirectory=	Backup directory where CAB files are stored. Must be a full path, for example c:\tmp\backup.	Defaults to Windows\sysbckup

Table 27.10   Scanreg.ini settings (*continued*)

Keyname and default value	Function	Other values
Files=[dir code,] file1,file2,file3	Additional system files to backup into the CAB file. File names are separated by a comma (,). The dir code can be: 10: windir (ex. c:\windows) 11: system dir (ex. c:\windows\system) 30: boot dir (ex. c:\) 31: boot host dir (ex. c:\)	None

Note   If ScanReg cannot create a backup in the location specified by the Backup folder in the Scanreg.ini file, it defaults to placing the CAB file in the \Windows folder.

Using ScanRegW to Back up the Registry

Registry Checker automatically makes a backup of your registry once per day as the computer starts, but you can also manually make periodic backups of the registry using ScanRegW. There are several reasons to back up the registry, for example, before editing the registry using Registry Editor, or before installing an application.

ScanRegW stores the backup as a RB0##.cab file in \Windows\Sysbckup, which is a hidden folder. The symbols ## represent backups using digits from 01 to 99 (05 is the default for the number of backups). The files are compressed CAB files (like the files on the Windows 98 compact disc). If you run ScanRegW and your system already has the maximum RB0##.cab files as indicated in Scanreg.ini, the oldest one is deleted.

The RB0##.cab file contains the following files:

- System.dat
- System.ini
- User.dat
- Win.ini

▶ **To back up your registry**

1. On the **Start** menu, click **Run**.

2. Type **ScanRegW**, and then click **OK**.

   After scanning the system registry, ScanRegW displays a dialog box asking if you would like to back up the registry. Click **Yes**.

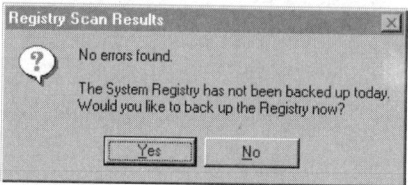

   – Or –

   Type **ScanRegW /autoscan** to automatically back up the registry without a dialog box. Use this command line switch to have ScanRegW scan and back up the registry as a scheduled task.

3. Click **OK** when backup is complete.

   ScanRegW informs you when the backup is complete. The backup is stored as the file RB0##.cab in the hidden \Windows\Sysbckup folder.

More Information about Registry Checker

Registry Checker runs automatically with each startup to determine if the system registry has errors, and to back up the registry. Some more points to remember about Registry Checker:

- ScanRegW scans and backs up registry (User.dat and System.dat), Win.ini, and System.ini files.

- Do not use backups of core configuration files from Windows 95 on a Windows 98 system. The computer will not start.

- Backups are stored by default as a file called RB0##.cab in a hidden \Windows\Sysbckup folder.

- ScanReg creates RB0##.cab files, where ## represents increments from 01 to 99 (5 is the default setting). The CAB files are compressed using the same compression as the Windows installation media. As such, they can be opened within Windows by double-clicking the file.

- To restore a backup, boot to a command prompt and type **Scanreg/Restore**. For more information, see "Restoring the Registry" later in this chapter.

Using Microsoft Backup

You should perform a full backup of your system regularly to have a current backup of your entire system available to restore in case of hard disk failures. Windows 98 includes a new backup utility called Microsoft Backup (Msbackup.exe), which supports a wider range of backup devices than the Windows 95 backup utility. Support has been added for parallel, IDE/ATAPI, and SCSI backup devices.

Several devices are supported, including the following:

- QIC-80 and 80 Wide, 3010 and 3010 Wide, and 3020 and 3020 Wide
- TR1, 2, 3, and 4 (Travan)
- DAT (DDS1 and 2)
- DC 6000
- 8mm
- DLT
- Removable media (floppy disks, Iomega Jaz or Syquest cartridges)

Note   QIC-40 backup devices are no longer supported by the Windows 98 backup utility.

Installing Microsoft Backup

Microsoft Backup is not a default selection for the Windows 98 installation process. If the utility is installed on Windows 95 before Windows 98 Setup is run, Microsoft Backup will be installed during Setup.

The tool can be added using Add/Remove Programs in Control Panel. It is located in the Disk Tools component. Microsoft Backup requires the same minimum configuration for Windows 98 as well as a hard drive with at least 5.2 MB free disk space. When the backup utility is installed, the program is added to the **System Tools** menu under **Start\Programs\Accessories**.

▶ **To install Microsoft Backup**

1. In Control Panel, double-click Add/Remove Programs.

2. Select the **Windows Setup** tab.

3. Double-click **System Tools**.

4. Check the box next to **Backup**.

5. Click **OK**.

6. Click **Apply**.

   Copying the files for the selected components runs automatically.

7. Click **OK** to complete the installation.

▶ **To configure a backup device**

- Most backup devices are automatically detected and configured either when you install the device and restart the computer or the first time you run Microsoft Backup. If you install a new device and it is not detected on Startup, go to Control Panel, and use Add New Hardware to detect the device.

▶ **To start Microsoft Backup**

1. Click **Start**, point to **Programs**, **Accessories**, and then **System Tools**.

2. Click **Backup**.

   If Windows 98 does not detect a backup device, it asks you if you want the Add New Hardware applet. Click **Yes**, and add the device, or click **No** to continue.

3. A dialog box displays three choices, **Create a new backup job**, **Open an existing backup job**, and **Restore backed up files**.

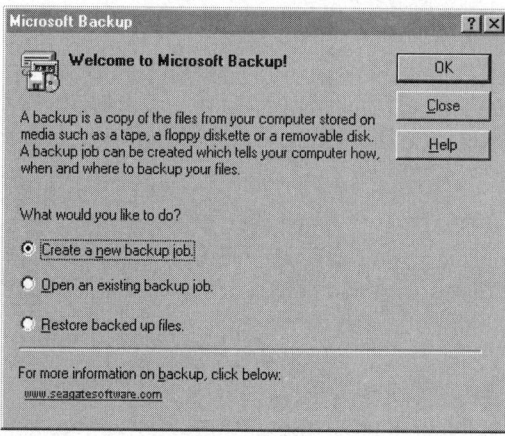

4. Click **Create a new backup job**, and then click **OK**.

    Backup Wizard leads you through the steps required to create a new backup job. The backup utility uses backup jobs to save and reuse file or option selections and to perform backups.

Note Backup Wizard is used only to create new backup jobs. It cannot be used to modify an existing job.

Backup Wizard Configuration

When naming a Backup, you cannot use these characters: \ / : ? * " < > |

To change a setting or review the backup job's summary while progressing through the wizard, use the **Back** and **Next** buttons.

If the medium being used to back up the files does not have a unique name, a prompt will be displayed for naming it.

Removable media devices are supported when specifying the option in Microsoft Backup to back up to a file rather than a removable drive.

Restore Wizard Configuration

You can select your files from the catalog stored on your hard disk or from the tape in your drive.

Files are restored in their original folder structure unless you choose to restore all files to an alternate location.

Using Restore Wizard

Restore Wizard presents a series of dialog boxes that lead you through the steps required to restore a backup job. Restore Wizard can be launched from the Microsoft Backup **Tools** menu or from the Microsoft Backup toolbar.

Note You can restore backups made with the Windows 95 backup. You cannot restore backups made with MS-DOS version 6.*x* or earlier.

▶ **To use Restore Wizard**

1. Click the **Restore Wizard** button on the Microsoft Backup toolbar, and follow the directions on the screen.

2. Restore is successful when the **Operation completed** dialog box appears. Click **OK**.

Using Reports

Both Backup and Restore create a report for the operation. If unsuccessful, the report can give an indication as to why.

A sample report is shown below.

```
Start Job Report
    Job Name: Restore
    Restore Job Started - 8/13/97 1:47:47PM
    Processed File Count: 1
    Total Bytes Before Compression: 180,736
    Operation Completed - Yes
    Restore Job Ended - 8/13/97 1:47:49PM
End Job Report
```

▶ **To set options for the report**

1. Start Microsoft Backup, and then click the **Close** button in the Welcome to Microsoft Backup window.

2. Click the **Options** button, and then click the **Report** tab.

▶ **To view or print a report**

1. Click the **Tools** menu, and then click **Reports**.

2. Click either **View** or **Print**.

Note A history of the backup and restore operations for the machine can be found in \Program Files\Accessories\Backup\Reports\Report.txt. You can open the file in Notepad.

Backing up without the Wizard

You can back up files without using Backup Wizard.

▶ **To back up without using Backup Wizard**

1. Start Microsoft Backup, and then click the **Close** button in the **Welcome to Microsoft Backup** dialog box.

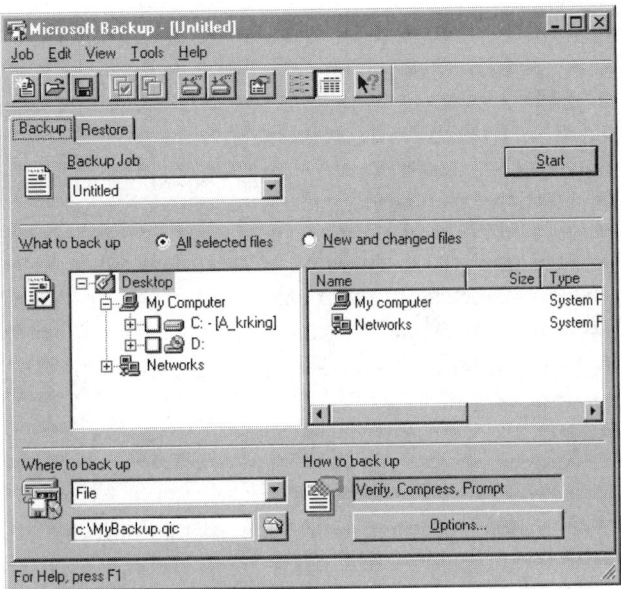

2. Type the name for the backup job in the **Backup Job** field.

3. In **What to back up**, if **All selected files** is selected, then all files chosen are backed up. If **New and changed files** is selected, only new and/or changed files from the previous backup are backed up.

4. Select which files to back up.

   To back up an entire drive, click the box next to the drive.

   – Or –

   To back up individual folders or files, click the + next to the drive and select the folders, or click the + next to a folder and select files.

Note Back up removable media as a File.

---

5. Select the media for the destination for the backup in **Where to back up**. Type the path to the backup destination, or click the folder icon to the right for the destination.

6. Click **Options** to select options for this backup.

   The **Backup Options** dialog box has the following tabs: **General**, **Password**, **Type**, **Exclude**, **Report**, and **Advanced**. Click **?** for a description of the features on these tabs. Click **OK** to return to the **Backup Options** dialog box.

7. Click **Start** to begin the backup.

Restoring without the Wizard

You can restore files without using Restore Wizard.

▶ **To restore without using Restore Wizard**

1. Start Microsoft Backup, click the **Close** button in the **Welcome to Microsoft Backup** dialog box, and then click the **Restore** tab.

2. Select the media where the backup job is located in **Restore from**.

3. Next to the **Restore from** box, type the name of a QIC file, or click the folder icon to the right and search for it.

4. Click **Refresh** to open the backup set(s) from the source location specified in **Restore from**.

5. Choose the **Original** or **Alternate** location for **Where to restore**.

6. Click **Options** for this restore.

   The **Restore Options** dialog box has the following tabs: **General**, **Report**, and **Advanced**. Click **OK** to return to the **Restore Options** dialog box. The restore general options are displayed in **How to Restore**.

7. Click **Start** to begin restoring files.

More Information about Microsoft Backup

Points to remember about Microsoft Backup:

- Supported devices for Microsoft Backup include (but are not limited to): QIC-80 and 80 Wide, 3010 and 3010 Wide, and 3020 and 3020 Wide, TR1, 2, 3, and 4 (Travan), DAT (DDS1 and 2), DC 6000, 8mm, DLT, and Removable media (for example, floppy disks, and Iomega Jaz or SyQuest cartridges).

- QIC-40 backup devices are no longer supported by the Windows 98 backup utility.

- You can restore backups made with the Windows 95 backup utility.

- You cannot restore backups made with MS-DOS version 6.*x* or earlier.

- Microsoft Backup is not a default selection for the Windows 98 installation process. If the utility is installed on Windows 95 before Windows 98 Setup is run, Microsoft Backup will be installed during Setup.

- Backup Wizard is used only to create new backup jobs. It cannot be used to modify an existing job.

Using Microsoft System Recovery

Microsoft System Recovery (Pcrestor.bat) is a quick and easy method to restore your system from a backup. The recovery tool operates completely from protect mode (within the Windows operating system environment).

Microsoft System Recovery takes advantage of the scripting extendibility of the Windows 98 Setup program to install Windows 98, while maintaining access to the Win32 APIs and other critical system resources (such as networks, removable media, and tape devices) needed to access your data.

Microsoft System Recovery uses Msbatch (Msbatch.inf), an automated setup process, to install a minimal Windows 98 environment. Microsoft System Recovery copies Msbatch to a directory called \Restore on the hard drive, and then starts the install process. There are no prompts during the setup process since Msbatch automates the entire setup program. Msbatch is described in detail in Appendix D, "Msbatch.inf Parameters for Setup Scripts."

Finally, Microsoft System Recovery uses a wizard to walk you through the process of recovering system files through Microsoft Backup.

Important You should perform a full backup of your system regularly to have a current backup of your system available to restore in case of hard disk failures. Microsoft System Recovery requires a backup to restore your system files.

It is recommended that you back up your system files at least once a week. For more information about backing up your files, see "Using Microsoft Backup" earlier in this chapter.

▶ **To start a system recovery using Microsoft System Recovery**

1. Start the computer using the Windows 98 Startup Disk.

2. At the command prompt, change the directory to \Tools\Sysrec.

3. Type **pcrestor**, and then follow the directions on the screen.

After Windows 98 is set up, Microsoft Recovery Wizard walks you through the process of restoring system and application files from Microsoft Backup. In addition to Microsoft Backup, the System Recovery Wizard installs Microsoft Notepad and Wordpad.

Tip Click the **Details** button in the wizard for help in recovering your files.

More Information about Microsoft System Recovery

Microsoft System Recovery operates completely in protect mode, and uses an automated batch program to install a minimal Windows 98 environment. It then uses a wizard to step you through a recovery process that lets you recover all or part of your system.

The following is a list of the benefits of Microsoft System Recovery:

- No need to create a separate set of disks. The Startup Disk has drivers for most CD-ROM drives, and contains tools to help solve startup problems.

- Microsoft System Recovery supports IDE and SCSI removable media devices. Most tape drives, removable drives, and network shares are supported for system restore.

- Operates completely in protect mode for faster input/output and system performance.

- Simple batch install script makes setup and recovery fast, automatic, and safe.

- You can restore the entire system or only certain parts of it.

Scheduling Tasks

Scheduled Task Wizard lets you run useful utilities and routine tasks at regular intervals. You can set the tasks to run at times that are most convenient for you.

Once you have a task scheduled, an icon appears in the Windows taskbar.

Note If you are upgrading a Windows 95 installation in which System Agent is installed, the System Agent tasks are inherited by the Scheduled Task.

▶ **To schedule tasks**

1. Double-click My Computer, and then double-click Scheduled Tasks.

2. Double-click **Add Scheduled Task** to start the Scheduled Task Wizard.

3. Click **Next**, and enter the information as prompted by the wizard.

For more information about Scheduled Task Wizard, see Chapter 23, "System and Remote Administration Tools."

Using Maintenance Wizard

Maintenance Wizard is used to schedule several performance-improving tasks, such as Disk Defragmenter, ScanDisk, Disk Cleanup, and Compression Agent (on DriveSpace 3 drives).

Note Microsoft Plus! for Windows 98 includes two additional features: you can clean up your **Start** menu, and you can clean up orphan links in Add/Remove Programs. To obtain Microsoft Plus! for Windows 98, contact your Microsoft reseller.

You can choose time of day or night, or customize the schedule to run the performance improving tasks.

The following list shows a typical schedule for these tasks:

- Defragmenter programs, every Wednesday at 1:00 A.M.
- ScanDisk, every Tuesday at 1:00 A.M.
- Disk Cleanup, every first day of the month at 12:30 A.M.
- Compression Agent, every Friday at 1:00 A.M.

For more information about Disk Defragmenter, ScanDisk, and Disk Cleanup, see Chapter 10, "Disks and File Systems."

▶ **To start Maintenance Wizard**

- Click **Start**, point to **Programs**, **Accessories**, **System Tools**, and then click **Maintenance Wizard**.

▶ **To view scheduled tasks**

- Double-click My Computer, and then double-click Scheduled Tasks. Your tasks appear in the Scheduled Tasks window, preceded by the word "Tune-up" or "Maintenance."

Note You can also launch Maintenance Wizard from the Welcome to Windows 98 screen, which appears after you set up the Windows 98 software.

You can start and run all the tasks in succession anytime with the Tune-Up/autorun switch.

▶ **To run the tasks in succession**

- On the **Start** menu, click **Run**, and then type **Tuneup /autorun**. Click **OK**.

  The tasks will run automatically in succession. This does not change the schedule for the tasks that you set in Maintenance Wizard.

Version Conflict Manager

Sometimes, when installing software, you may have a newer version of a file on your system than the one being installed. Windows 98 Setup automatically installs the Windows 98 file over the newer file and stores the newer version of the file in the \Windows\VCM folder. Those files can be viewed with Version Conflict Manager (VCM).

Note The determining factor in identifying an older file is the file version, not the file date.

You can use Version Conflict Manager (Vcmui.exe) to restore an application's version of a file. Reinstalling the entire application is no longer necessary.

▶ **To launch Version Conflict Manager**

- Click **Start**, point to **Programs**, **Accessories**, **System Tools**, and then click **System Information**. Select the **Tools** menu and click **Version Conflict Manager**.

Version Conflict Manager displays the file name, the backup date, and the backed- up version of every newer file that was replaced. It also lists the current version being used of that file.

When Version Conflict Manager restores an older file, the older file is moved in the \Windows\VCM folder with the extension changed to .000. You can then use Version Conflict Manager to determine the original configuration.

More Information about Version Conflict Manager

Points to remember:

- Windows 98 Setup automatically installs any older Windows 98 files over the newer files on your system.
- The determining factor in identifying an older file is the file version, not the file date.
- During Setup, newer version files are moved and stored in the \Windows\VCM folder.
- When VCM restores an older file, the older file is moved in the \Windows \VCM folder with the extension changed to .000. You can then use VCM to return to the original configuration (using the older file with the newer file stored in \Windows\VCM).

Using Windows Report Tool

The Windows Report Tool (Winrep.exe), is an Internet-based information gathering tool that is installed with Windows 98. This tool provides a means for uploading system information to a support provider for diagnosis.

With the Windows Report Tool, you can submit problem reports over the Internet to a technical support center, or across an intranet to a corporate help desk. The problem report includes system data and can include configuration files. To use Windows Report Tool, you connect to a Web page, and then, using ActiveX control and scripting, the Windows Report Tool is invoked on the local computer.

If you cannot connect to a Web page, you can launch the Windows Report Tool (Winrep) from the **Tools** menu in the Microsoft System Information utility and save the report as a CAB file. The report can then be transferred to support personnel another way, such as by using FTP or by copying the file to a computer that is connected to the Internet and using Winrep on that system to open and submit the report.

Support personnel using MSInfo to open the CAB file can view the report. For information about MSInfo, see "Using Microsoft System Information" earlier in this chapter. Winrep can write information to a SQL database to track the service requests.

This section describes how to generate a report using Windows Report Tool, and then submit it to a Web server. For information about how to design the Web server to accept Windows Report Tool reports and to update a database, see the paper "OEM and Corporate WinRep Integration" on the Microsoft Windows 98 Resource Kit compact disc.

Note For best results, establish a connection to the Internet before launching Windows Report Tool. If you need to create a new Internet connection, run the Internet Connection Wizard.

▶ **To use Windows Report Tool to submit a report**

1. Launch Windows Report Tool from your support Web page.

2. From the **Options** menu, click **User Information**. Fill out the demographic information. At the very least, include phone number(s) and e-mail address.

3. If you are experiencing problems submitting the report from behind a firewall, select **Use alternate data format proxy server**. This will reduce the size of the packets sent by Winrep, and use a different data format that is compatible with most proxy servers.

> **Note** Enabling the **Use alternate data format proxy server** feature will slow down the upload process.

4. Type a problem in the **Problem description** box that describes your experience. Include the exact text of any and all error messages encountered.

> **Tip** The first line of the problem description will become the report's title, so use this to summarize the contents of the report.

5. Type an explanation in the **Expected results** box detailing the behavior you expect when this problem has been addressed.

6. Type a detailed history of the events leading up to the issue in the **Steps to reproduce the problem** box. It is helpful if you number the steps.

7. From the **File** menu click **Save** to back up your work and maintain a record of your issue.

8. Click **Next** and follow the instructions given by the support provider to upload your report.

You can also use Windows Report Tool to generate a report, without first connecting to a Web page.

▶ **To use Windows Report Tool without first connecting to a Web page**

1. Click **Start**, point to **Programs, Accessories, System Tools**, and then click **System Information**.

2. Select the **Tools** menu and click **Windows Report Tool**.

3. Optionally, if your support provider asks you to do so, type a space and enter a product information number, including the dashes in the correct places.

4. Optionally, type a space and then type the name of a CAB file to open, then type another space. This lets you open a previously generated report.

5. Press the ENTER key to launch Winrep.

6. Fill out the report form as the procedure "To use Windows Report Tool to submit a report" instructs.

7. From the **File** menu, click **Save** to back up your work and maintain a record of your issue.

8. Optionally, save the report to a floppy disk, copy it to another system with Internet access, connect to your support provider's Web site, and follow the directions they provide to upload the report.

Using MS-DOS Report Tool

The MS-DOS Report Tool (Dosrep.exe) is an Internet-based reporting tool that can be run outside of Windows (in real-mode). This tool was created to upload system information to a Support Engineer when Windows is not accessible.

▶ To use MS-DOS Report Tool

- To launch MS-DOS Report Tool, boot to a command prompt outside of Windows and run Dosrep.exe from the Windows directory. Have your user name, password, and phone number to call your Internet Service Provider (ISP) available.

Note   The list of files uploaded by MS-DOS Report Tool is configurable. Edit the Dosrep.ini to add or remove files to be uploaded by the tool.

To receive reports generated by the MS-DOS Report Tool, you must use a File Transfer Protocol (FTP) server on the Internet. Provide users with either the Internet Protocol (IP) address or the friendly name (DNS or HOST) of the FTP server. Also, provide them with the name of the directory on your FTP server in which they will submit reports. The MS-DOS Report Tool then creates the specified directory on the FTP server share and uploads a cabinet (CAB) file to it. To view the uploaded report, use MSInfo to open the report in the directory you specified, and then access its contents.

More Information about MS-DOS Report Tool

Points to remember:

- MS-DOS Report Tool is a real-mode reporting tool. As such, you must have access to your modem outside of Windows. Controller-less modems, or Windows only modems, and PC Card modems may not work because they rely on Windows for functionality. To test your modem, type the following at the command prompt outside of Windows:

  ECHO ATDT > COMx [enter]

  Where x is the COM port your modem is using.

  If you do not hear a dial tone, your modem is not accessible at that COM port in real-mode. You can still use the MS-DOS Report Tool to gather system information by typing:

  DOSREP [enter]

  and then clicking the option named **Create and save report**.

  This will generate a CAB file comprised of the system files that could be uploaded using another machine connected to the Internet. The Windows Report Tool can be used to upload reports created using the MS-DOS Report Tool.

- MS-DOS Report Tool will only work with modems. ISDN adapters may not be recognized.

- For the MS-DOS Report Tool to be able to submit log files over the Internet, your ISP must support Point-to-Point Protocol (PPP) and clear-text password authentication protocol (PAP).

Troubleshooting Procedures

This section provides basic instructions for troubleshooting problems that may occur when running Windows 98.

Important Create and keep a Startup Disk, and verify that it works before you need it (create and test two Startup Disks for even better protection). Use Registry Checker (ScanRegW) often to backup system configuration files.

A particularly good time for backing up files and updating the Startup Disk is before you install new devices and applications, when you have a known good configuration.

Checking for Free Disk Space

Running out of space on the disk drive used for TEMP and swap files can cause a variety of operational and installation errors. If you need more disk space, see the troubleshooting aid for disk space problems in Help.

To check for free space, try the following:

- Click **Start**, point to **Programs**, **Accessories**, **System Tools**, and then click **System Information** to view the total and available disk space.

- Use the **chkdsk** *drive* command at the command prompt to display the available disk space in the Bytes Available on Disk line.

- Use the **dir** *drive* command at the command prompt to view the bytes free at the end of the DIR display.

You might want to check the swap file settings.

▶ **To check the swap file settings**

- Click **Start**, point to **Programs**, **Accessories**, **System Tools**, and then click **System Information** to view the location of the swap file and the available disk space on that drive.

  – Or –

  In Control Panel, double-click System, click the **Performance** tab, and then click **Virtual Memory**.

Important By default, Windows 98 manages the virtual memory settings automatically. Changing these settings manually can adversely affect system performance. The recommended setting in this dialog box is to let Windows manage virtual memory settings.

▶ **To check for lost allocation units from a command line**

1. Press and hold down the left CTRL key during system startup to access the **Windows Startup** menu, and when it appears, select **Command Prompt Only**.

   Note Selecting **Safe Mode Command Prompt Only** will not load the extended memory driver Himem.sys. The MS-DOS version of ScanDisk requires Himem.sys be loaded to check FAT32 drives.

2. Run ScanDisk from the \Windows\Command directory, and specify the drive to inspect. For example, you would type **SCANDISK C:** to inspect the C:\ drive.

   ScanDisk detects lost allocation units and prompts you to recover them as files. The files will have a .chk extension.

For information about running ScanDisk in Windows 98, see Chapter 10, "Disks and File Systems."

▶ **To check the TEMP variable**

1. At the command prompt, type **set** to display the TEMP variable.

2. Verify that the TEMP variable points to a valid drive and directory.

   Check for free disk space on the drive that contains the TEMP directory. If you are printing multiple copies of a large document, or printing large PostScript documents, increase the minimum available free disk space.

Checking for Disk Corruption

Key operating system data structures prevent system startup if they are damaged. These structures include the master boot record, the boot sector, the file allocation table, and the core operating system files.

Caution Back up key data files before performing any disk repair operations. Do not run any disk utilities that are not specifically designed for Windows 98. Earlier versions of disk repair utilities may not work properly. To prevent possible data loss, use a disk utility, such as ScanDisk, that is specifically designed for Windows 98. For details, see Chapter 10, "Disks and File Systems."

▶ **To check for disk corruption with Safe Mode Command Prompt Only**

1. Restart the computer, pressing and holding down the left CTRL key when the Starting Windows 98 message appears, and then select the **Safe Mode Command Prompt Only** option.

Note Selecting **Safe Mode Command Prompt Only** will not load the extended memory driver Himem.sys. The MS-DOS version of ScanDisk requires Himem.sys be loaded to check FAT32 drives.

---

2. Change to the \Windows\Command directory, and then type **scandisk**.

   This method also checks and repairs the file allocation table.

If corruption is detected, you may need to replace system files. For more information, see "Using System File Checker" earlier in this chapter.

Checking for Correct File Versions

With Windows 98, you can use System File Checker (SFC) to look for system files that have been changed by applications. You can configure System File Checker to notify you when a change is discovered. System File Checker will prompt you to restore the original file from the installation source of your Windows 98 files.

System File Checker scans specific system files for corruption, changes, and to determine if they have been deleted. When configured to do so, it prompts you to restore the original Windows 98 system files.

▶ **To scan system files**

1. Click **Start**, point to **Programs**, **Accessories**, and **System Tools**, and then click **System Information**.
2. Select the **Tools** menu.
3. Click **System File Checker**.
4. Click **Scan for altered files** and then click **Start**.

You can also view a file's properties to determine its version number and other information such as its date. You can use this information to determine whether a DLL or other system file is mismatched to your system.

▶ **To view information about a system file**

1. In Windows Explorer, right-click the file name, and then click **Properties** in the context menu.
2. For a supporting or executable file, click the **Version** tab. Use the **Other Version Information** list to see details about the file.

Replacing Corrupted Files

If you have isolated a corrupted file, use System File Checker to restore a working file.

▶ **To replace a corrupted file**

1. Click **Start**, point to **Programs**, **Accessories**, and **System Tools**, and then click **System Information**.
2. Select the **Tools** menu and then click **System File Checker**.
3. Select **Extract one file from installation disk** to restore the original system file, select the file to extract, and then click **Start**.
4. Ensure the path to **Restore from:** is correct and click **OK**.
5. In the **Backup File** dialog box, either accept the default or change the path.
6. If a dialog box appears explaining the folder does not exist, click **Yes**.

   System File Checker finishes extracting the file and notifies you when it completes the action.
7. Click **OK** to return to System File Checker.

Updating System Files and Drivers

Windows Update is the Web extension of Windows 98, and is designed to help your computer operate better. Windows Update contains a central catalog of new product enhancements, including service packs and new Windows features. In addition, Windows Update lets you update system files and device drivers specific to your computer.

To update a file, see "Using Windows Update" earlier in this chapter.

Checking Entries in Startup Files

The Config.sys and Autoexec.bat files contain system startup drivers, settings, and paths, and you may need to verify the accuracy of these entries.

Use the System Configuration Utility to check entries in files. See "Using the System Configuration Utility" earlier in this chapter.

Using Windows 98 Command-Line Switches

Starting Windows 98 with command-line switches is an effective method for isolating issues with your configuration. The switches should be used for troubleshooting only. Use the information to modify your existing configuration and eliminate the conflict. The following switches are available to start Windows 98 from the command prompt:

win [/d:[f] [m] [s] [v] [x]]

▶ **To use the command-line switches**

1. Start Safe Mode by starting the computer and pressing and holding down the left CTRL key as Windows 98 starts.

2. Choose **Command Prompt Only** at the **Windows 98 Startup** menu.

3. Start Windows 98 using the troubleshooting command-line switches by typing **win /d:** at the command prompt, and adding the appropriate switches

The **/d:** switch is used for troubleshooting when Windows 98 does not start correctly. The switches in Table 27.11 can be used with the **/d:** switch.

Table 27.11   Windows 98 command-line switches

Switch	Description
f	Turns off 32-bit disk access. This is equivalent to disabling the hard disk controller(s) in Device Manager. Try this if the computer appears to have disk problems, or if Windows 98 stalls. This is equivalent to **32BitAccess=FALSE** in System.ini.
m	Starts Windows 98 in Safe Mode.
s	Specifies that Windows 98 should not use ROM address space between F000:0000 and 1 MB for a break point. Try this if Windows 98 stalls during system startup. This is equivalent to **SystemROMBreakPoint=FALSE** in System.ini.
v	Specifies that the ROM routine will handle interrupts from the hard disk controller. This is equivalent to **VirtualHDIRQ=FALSE** in System.ini.
x	Excludes all of the adapter area from the range of memory that Windows 98 scans to find unused space. This is equivalent to **EMMExclude=A000-FFFF** in System.ini. If this switch resolves the issue, you may have a conflict in the upper memory area (UMA) that requires an Exclude statement.

Note Each of the System.ini file entries referenced in Table 27.11 belongs in the [386Enh] section of the System.ini file.

Troubleshooting Problems with System Startup

If a computer fails to start Windows 98, start the computer in Safe Mode to try to resolve the problem. Starting Windows 98 in Safe Mode can help you resolve issues that occur when you start Windows 98 normally. These issues include (but are not limited to):

- Setup hangs during the first reboot.
- Error messages.

- Hanging.
- Loss of functionality.

Starting Windows 98 in Safe Mode bypasses the current real-mode configuration and loads a minimal protected-mode configuration, disabling Windows 98 device drivers and using the standard VGA display adapter.

If the issue does not occur in Safe Mode, you may be experiencing a conflict with hardware settings, real-mode configuration issues, incompatibilities with legacy Windows programs or drivers, or registry damage.

From within Safe Mode, use the following tasks to find a problem in startup. Many of these steps require changes to system configuration files. The changes are not intended to be permanent; they are techniques for isolating the conflict that resulted in an issue with the normal configuration.

Note Before making changes, create a Windows 98 Startup Disk if you do not already have one. Use Add/Remove Programs in Control Panel to create a Startup Disk.

▶ **To troubleshoot system startup in Safe Mode**

1. Start Safe Mode by starting the computer and pressing and holding down the left CTRL key as Windows 98 starts. Determine if the symptom is alleviated.

2. Start Microsoft System Configuration Diagnostic Startup.

   If Microsoft System Configuration Diagnostic Startup starts, go to "Using the System Configuration Utility" earlier in this chapter.

   – Or –

   If Microsoft System Configuration Diagnostic Startup does not start, continue to step 3 of this procedure.

3. Enable these Windows Diagnostic switches in Microsoft System Configuration Advanced options:
   - Disable System ROM Breakpoint
   - Disable Virtual HD IRQ
   - EMM Exclude A000-FFFF
   - Force Compatibility mode disk access

4. Check protected-mode device configuration:
   - Check Microsoft System Information Problem Devices category to find problems.
   - Check Device Manager to disable device drivers to test and/or correct the configuration.

5. If you suspect a corrupt registry, use scanreg /restore to get a known good backup of the registry.

6. Check for device conflicts in Microsoft System Configuration's Conflicts/Sharing category below Hardware Resources.

7. Check for an outdated or damaged VxD by examining Bootlog.txt, and then do the following:

   - If it is in the Windows System\Iosubsys directory, rename it.

   - If it has a .386 filename extension, examine the [386Enh] section of System.ini and remark out its lines. When renaming VxDs, be sure to change the .vxd extension. Windows 98 loads all files in the Iosubsys subdirectory that have a .vxd extension.

   - If it is in Vmm32.vxd, check the \Windows System\Vmm32 directory for a Vmm32 file, and rename or move it.

Restoring the Registry

Windows 98 introduces the Registry Checker that scans the registry for corruption and backs up configuration files once a day. The utility maintains multiple backup sets that can be restored as required. For example, you might restore a previous day's backup if you have installed something on your computer with undesirable results but it did not corrupt the registry. In that event, you could run ScanReg /Restore to return the system to its previous state. ScanReg is the MS-DOS-based Registry Checker.

ScanReg provides a list of available backups and indicates whether the system configuration files stored in the CAB have been used to start Windows 98 successfully. Generally, you should choose the CAB file that was most recently used to start Windows 98. However, returning the system to an older configuration may be warranted when the origin of the undesirable behavior is unknown.

▶   **To restore a Registry Checker backup**

Note If the computer failed to start because the registry is corrupt, ScanReg will automatically fix the problem. If the computer failed to start because of a change to the registry's content, and the registry is not corrupt, then running ScanReg /Restore and choosing the most recent backup is an appropriate way to fix the problem.

---

1. Restart Windows 98. While the system is restarting, press and hold the left CTRL key until you see the **Windows 98 Startup** menu.

2. In the **Windows 98 Startup** menu, select **Command Prompt Only**.

3. From the MS-DOS command prompt, type **ScanReg /Restore**.

   A screen appears listing the available backup sets. Select the appropriate backup and determine if the symptom is alleviated on the subsequent start.

Checking Specific Driver Problems

Loading a specific driver in Config.sys, Autoexec.bat, or from the Windows 98 registry may cause a computer to stop responding. This could be due to a hardware or software (device driver or TSR) conflict.

Automatic Skip Driver (ASD) tracks device load failures by identifying the specific device(s) that failed to enumerate and stopped the system from starting. If Windows 98 stops responding when enumerating the same device on subsequent startups, ASD will automatically disable the device.

▶ **To check a device driver using Automatic Skip Driver**

1. If a device driver fails to load, launch **Automatic Skip Driver Agent** from the **Tools** menu in **System Information**.

2. In the **Hardware Troubleshooting Agent** dialog box, click the operation that failed, and then click **Details**.

   The **Enumerating a Device Details** dialog box appears and provides a recommendation for solving the problem. This includes updating the driver. It is possible that you will need to upgrade the driver disabled by Automatic Skip Driver.

To manually determine whether hardware or software is stalling the computer, try the following, stopping when the determination has been made.

▶ **To manually check a device driver**

1. Press and hold down the left CTRL key when starting Windows 98, and select **Safe Mode Command Prompt Only** from the **Startup** menu. If this option prevents the computer from stalling on startup, a device driver or terminate-and-stay-resident (TSR) program is a likely cause of the problem.

2. Restart the computer, pressing and holding down the left CTRL again, and then select the **Step-By-Step Confirmation** option to check for TSRs that are loading and may be causing the problem.

3. If you use disk compression and the computer still stalls after using **Safe Mode Command Prompt Only** to start the computer, restart the computer in **Safe Mode Without Compression** by pressing CTRL+F5 when the Starting Windows 98 message appears.

4. Check the CMOS settings in the computer's BIOS configuration menus, making sure the settings match your installed hardware.

5. Check the hardware installation and the manufacturer's documentation to verify that all devices are correctly installed.

6. Check resource settings in Device Manager for specific installed hardware to make sure no conflicts exist in the IRQ, I/O address, DMA channels, and memory addresses used. Compare your actual installation with your hardware documentation for inconsistencies in the settings used. For information, see Chapter 24, "Device Management."

▶ **To check whether a specific driver is stalling the computer**

1. Restart the computer.

2. Press and hold down the left CTRL key when the Starting Windows 98 message appears, and then select **Logged** (Bootlog.txt).

3. Search Bootlog.txt for errors.

Checking Whether a Required File Is Missing

Some computers contain devices that require a specific driver in Config.sys to correctly complete the startup process, such as drivers used for partitioning, compression, video, and hard disks.

▶ **To check for missing files**

1. Press and hold down the CTRL key when starting Windows 98, and select **Step-By-Step Confirmation** from the **Startup** menu.

2. Respond **Yes** to all prompts. For any error messages that appear, make note of the driver involved, its location, and the specific wording of the error message. Verify that the specified driver exists in the specified location.

Do not remove any hard disk drivers, disk partitioning drivers, or disk compression drivers when starting Windows 98 using the **Step-By-Step Confirmation** option or while editing startup files. The following is a partial list of drivers that should not be removed.

Hard disk drivers:

ah1544.sys	ilm386.sys	scsiha.sys	sstbio.sys
aspi4dos.sys	nonstd.sys	skydrvi.sys	sstdrive.sys
atdosxl.sys	scsidsk.exe	sqy55.sys	

Partitioning drivers:

dmdrvr.bin	evdr.sys	ldrive.sys	sstor.sys
enhdisk.sys	fixt_drv.sys	hardrive.sys	

Compression drivers:

dblspace.bin	drvspace.bin	sswap.com
devswap.com	sstor.exe	stacker.com

To find out about other system drivers, see the documentation for the hardware or software installed on the system.

Checking Device Configuration

Errors are sometimes caused by conflicts between devices trying to use the same system resources. There are two ways to view your device configuration:

- Microsoft System Information
- Device Manager

Microsoft System Information (MSInfo) collects system information, such as devices installed or device drivers loaded, and provides a menu for displaying the associated system topics.

▶ **To launch Microsoft System Information**

- Click **Start**, point to **Programs**, **Accessories**, and **System Tools**, and then click **System Information**.

Device Manager provides a central place where you can verify that devices are configured correctly.

▶ **To check for resource conflicts among devices**

1. Click **Start**, point to **Programs**, **Accessories**, and **System Tools**, and then click **System Information**.
2. Expand the **Components** category and select **Problem Devices**. Devices with hardware conflicts will be identified.
3. To determine the resource in conflict, expand the **Hardware Resources** category and select **Conflicts/Sharing**. Keep in mind that PCI devices can share resources—if neither of the devices are listed under **Problem Devices**, they are probably sharing the resource.
4. If necessary, change the devices' resource settings using **Device Manager**.

   To open **Device Manager**, click System in the Control Panel, and then click the **Device Manager** tab. For more information about Device Manager, see Chapter 24, "Device Management."

Note If you use multiple hardware profiles, you should first select the appropriate configuration using the list in the device's Resource properties.

Checking Upgrade Issues

The following sections describe how to check upgrade issues.

Microsoft MS-DOS Utilities

The MS-DOS utilities that are installed into the \Windows\Command directory have been enhanced to work with Windows 98. The disk repair utilities that shipped with older versions of MS-DOS and Windows 95 should not be used with Windows 98. Most of the other MS-DOS utilities that worked with Windows 3.1 should continue to work with Windows 98, but if they were bound to an older version of MS-DOS, you may need to use the SETVER command to enable them.

The following MS-DOS utility files will be deleted after you upgrade from an earlier version of Windows:

- Defrag.hlp
- Mwundel.exe
- Mwundel.hlp
- Networks.txt
- OS2.txt

The following MS-DOS utility files will be upgraded after you upgrade from an earlier version of Windows:

Ansi.sys	Doskey.com	Keyboard.sys	Scandisk.exe
Attrib.exe	Drvspace.exe	Label.exe	Scandisk.ini
Chkdsk.exe	Edit.com	Mem.exe	Setver.exe
Choice.com	Ega.cpi	Mode.com	Share.exe
Country.sys	Emm386.exe	More.com	Smartdrv.exe
Debug.exe	Fc.exe	Move.exe	Sort.exe
Defrag.exe	Fdisk.exe	Mscdex.exe	Subst.exe
Deltree.exe	Find.exe	Nlsfunc.exe	Sys.com
Diskcopy.com	Format.com	Ramdrive.sys	Xcopy.exe
Display.sys	Keyb.com	Readme.txt	

Disk Utilities

The disk utilities included with Windows 98 have been modified and fully support FAT32. DriveSpace 3 is included with Windows 98. It has been modified to detect FAT32 drives, but it will not compress them. In order to support FAT32, SHARE support has been disabled in the real-mode MS-DOS kernel (sharing support is still provided under protected-mode Windows 98).

Reinstalling Programs

If you upgrade your existing Windows 3.*x* or Windows 95 directory to Windows 98, then you do not need to reinstall your programs. If you install to a new directory, then you must reinstall all of your Windows-based programs. Copying files from your Windows 3.1 directory to Windows 98 is not supported.

MS-DOS-based Programs

Your existing MS-DOS-based programs should run from Windows 98. If you experience problems with an MS-DOS-based program, you can set it up to run in MS-DOS mode, the single application environment.

▶ **To run an MS-DOS-based program in an MS-DOS environment (MS-DOS mode)**

1. Create a shortcut to the MS-DOS-based program.
2. Right-click the shortcut icon, and then select **Properties**.
3. Click the **Program** tab, and then click **Advanced**.
4. Make sure that the **MS-DOS Mode** box is checked.

When you run a program in MS-DOS mode, it forces Windows 98 to shut down and loads the program in an MS-DOS environment. You will not have access to devices that require protected-mode (Windows) drivers.

If you find an MS-DOS-based program slowing down or stopping when it is in the background, use the following procedure.

▶ **To speed up MS-DOS-based programs**

1. Right-click the **MS-DOS Prompt** icon on the taskbar, and then click **Properties**.
2. Click the **Misc** tab.
3. Drag the **Idle Sensitivity** slider toward **Low**.
4. In the Background area, make sure that the **Suspend Always** box is not checked.

Note Applications that run in MS-DOS mode may require additional conventional memory, also referred to as the Transient Program Area (TPA). Optimize the TPA by loading MS-DOS support for devices in the upper memory area (UMA). Refer to the following examples provided with Windows 98:

- MS-DOS Mode for Games
- MS-DOS Mode for Games with EMS and XMS Support

Anti-Virus Software

Existing anti-virus software should be able to detect, but not always clean, viruses while running on Windows 98. This depends on where the virus was found and how the program chose to clean it. Also, virus shields may not be able to see all file activity, and therefore could miss some virus activity. It is recommended that you update your anti-virus software to a version that was designed to run with Windows 98.

Disk Repair and Optimization Utilities

Most legacy disk repair and optimization programs use direct disk reads and writes (INT25/INT26) for disk access. Because of this, Windows will block these disk repair and optimization programs from executing, in order to protect the data on your disk. This is necessary in a multitasking environment to prevent disk corruption caused by multiple utilities running simultaneously. It is strongly recommended that you upgrade to disk repair software that was designed for Windows 98. For more information, contact your software vendor.

Note If you bypass the disk-locking features of Windows 98 using the Lock <*drive letter*>: command at a real-mode prompt, and run one of these utilities on a FAT16 drive, you will destroy all long file names. This may not happen on a FAT32 drive as most of these utilities will see the physical FAT32 drives as "device-driven" and will not function.

Windows Shell Enhancements

Most Windows 3.1 and all Windows 95 shell replacements will run on Windows 98, but with many limitations because of the taskbar, 32-bit components, and the new Windows 98 shell. If you want to continue running one of these programs, you should upgrade to a version that was designed to run with Windows 98.

P A R T 6

Architecture

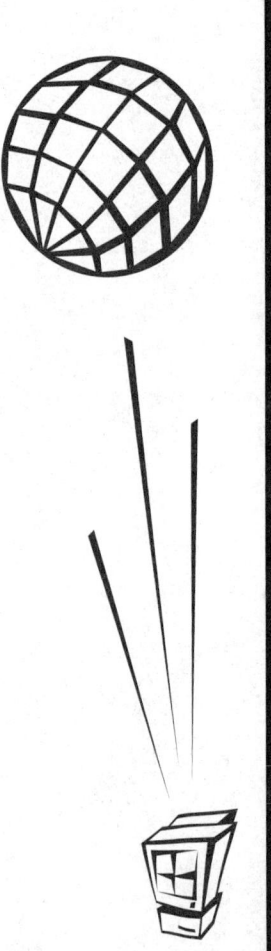

C H A P T E R   2 8

Windows 98 Architecture

28

This chapter provides a brief review of the Microsoft Windows 98 architecture to help you understand how the key operating system components function and interrelate.

In This Chapter

See Also

- For more information about the Win32 Driver Model (WDM) and hardware device classes, see Chapter 30, "Hardware Management."

Overview of Windows 98 Architecture Components

Microsoft Windows 98 is a 32-bit operating system that provides built-in Internet connectivity, Plug and Play hardware support, high performance, robustness, and backward compatibility with Windows 95. Windows 98 enhancements to Windows 95 include more sophisticated power management, multiple video display support, and integrated support for the latest hardware. Also included is support for the new Win32 Driver Model (WDM), allowing a WDM device to run under both Windows 98 and future versions of Windows NT using the same driver.

These features are supported by the components shown in Figure 28.1.

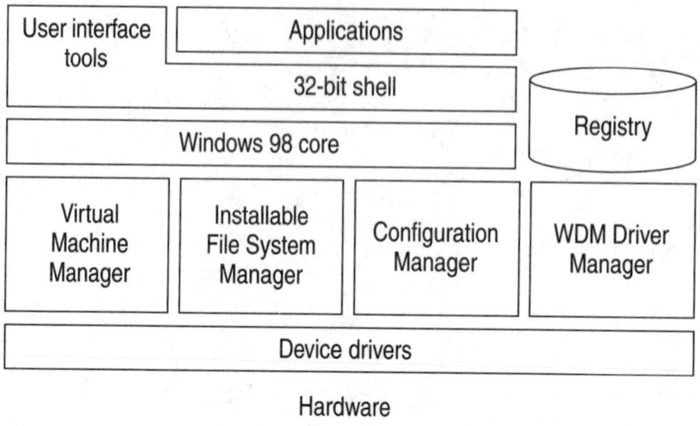

Figure 28.1   Windows 98 components

Like Windows 95, Windows 98 is derived from the Windows 3.1 platform and includes the following features:

- A complete 32-bit kernel, including memory management, and preemptive multitasking and multithreading support.

- A fully integrated 32-bit, protected-mode file system, which eliminates the need to rely on a separate copy of MS-DOS once the system boots up.

- 32-bit installable file system drivers supporting FAT, FAT32, ISO 9660 (CD-ROM), ISO 13346 (Universal Disk Format/Digital Video Disc [UDF/DVD]), network redirection, and high performance. These file system drivers also support the use of long file names and an open, modular architecture to handle future expansion.

- WDM support, which allows a WDM-supported device to run under both Windows 98 and future versions of Windows NT using the same driver.

- Improved system-wide robustness and "cleanup" after an application or driver fails. This delivers a more stable and reliable operating environment.

- A dynamic hardware and environment configuration, which reduces the need for users to adjust and restart their systems manually.

This chapter describes the key components that make up the Windows 98 architecture, beginning with its central information store, the registry, and proceeding from bottom to top.

Windows 98 Registry

The central information database for Windows 98 is called the *registry*. This hierarchical database both simplifies the operating system and makes it more adaptable. The registry simplifies the operating system by eliminating the need for Autoexec.bat, Config.sys, and INI files, however, Windows 98 still supports the use of these files when legacy applications require them. It makes the operating system more adaptable by storing user-specific and configuration-specific information so you can share one computer among multiple users and have more than one configuration (such as in-the-office and on-the-road configurations) for each computer.

A primary role of the registry in Windows 98 is to serve as a central repository for hardware-specific information for use by the hardware detection and Plug and Play system components. Windows 98 maintains information about hardware components and devices that have been identified through an enumeration or detection process, in the hierarchical structure of the registry, as described in "Configuration Manager" later in this chapter. When a new device is installed, the system checks for an existing configuration in the registry. If none is found, Windows 98 then searches all available media for the driver that best matches the device. Once the driver is found, it is added to the registry alongside the settings for the device.

Improvement over INI Files

Earlier versions of Windows used initialization (INI) files to store system-specific or application-specific information on the state or configuration of the system. For example, the Win.ini file stored information about the appearance of the Windows environment, the System.ini file stored system-specific information on the hardware and device driver configuration of the system, and various INI files (such as Msmail.ini and Winword6.ini) stored application-specific information.

The registry alleviates the issues of dealing with multiple INI files by providing a single location for the computer's configuration information. Table 28.1 illustrates other issues or limitations using multiple INI files, along with the solutions that are provided by using the registry.

Table 28.1   Registry solutions for problems with INI files

Problem	Solution
INI files are text-based, limited to 64 KB in total size.	The registry has no size restriction and can include both binary and text values.
Information stored in INI files is nonhierarchical and supports only two levels of information.	The registry is hierarchically arranged.

Table 28.1   Registry solutions for problems with INI files (*continued*)

Problem	Solution
Many INI files contain a myriad of switches and entries that are complicated to configure or are used only by operating system components.	The registry contains more standardized values.
INI files provide no mechanism for storing user-specific information, thus making it difficult for multiple users to share a single computer or for users who move around on the network to have access to their user-specific settings.	The **HKEY_USERS** key stores user-specific information.
Configuration information in INI files is local to each system, and no API mechanisms are available for remotely managing configuration, thus making it difficult to manage multiple computers.	The registry can be remotely administered, and system policies (stored as registry values) can be downloaded from a central server each time a new user logs on. For more information, see Chapter 7, "User Profiles," Chapter 8, "System Policies," and Chapter 23, "System and Remote Administration Tools."

When you upgrade from Windows 3.1 to Windows 98, system-specific information, such as the references to the loading of static virtualization drivers (VxDs), is moved (as appropriate) from the System.ini file to the registry.

For backward compatibility, Windows 98 supports the Autoexec.bat, Config.sys, and INI files, because many Win16-based applications still use them. For example, Windows 98 allows Win16-based applications to use INI files for their program settings, parameters, device drivers, and so on that the applications need to run. In addition, Windows 98 continues to scan the [386Enh] section of System.ini at startup to check for virtualization drivers to ensure that they are loaded.

Network Access to Registry Information

One advantage of the registry for Win32-based applications is that many of the Win32-based registry APIs can be used remotely through the remote procedure call (RPC) mechanism in Windows 98 to provide access to registry information across a network. This means that network administrators can use system management tools to access the contents of the registry for any computer on the network. (Of course, the remote computer must be configured to allow remote administration and must have user-level security.)

With Windows 98 remote administration, such industry management mechanisms as Simple Network Management Protocol (SNMP) can easily be integrated into Windows 98, lightening the network administrator's management and support burden. For more information, see Chapter 23, "System and Remote Administration Tools."

Windows Management Infrastructure

The Windows Management Infrastructure collects a wealth of information about the entire system as well as device configuration. This information is stored in the registry and made available through extensions to the registry API. This software is the foundation of Microsoft's support for Desktop Management Interface (DMI) and will provide device and system information to OLE Management Services (OLE MS) and Simple Network Management Protocol (SNMP) in the future.

For more information about the registry, see Chapter 31, "Windows 98 Registry."

Understanding Device Drivers

Windows 98 provides improved support for hardware devices, including disk devices, display adapters, pointing devices, modems, fax machines, and printers.

In Windows 3.1, device drivers were, for the most part, monolithic and complex to develop. In this case, monolithic means that the driver had to provide all services, user interfaces, API functions, and hardware-access services to operate under Windows 3.1. Starting with Windows 95, and continuing with Windows 98, we provide a universal driver/minidriver architecture that makes driver development easier for hardware vendors. By having the operating system provide basic device services for a given hardware class natively, the vendor is required to provide only device-specific code for their particular hardware. In addition, Windows 98 uses the WDM architecture, which provides a common set of I/O services understood by both Windows 98 and future versions of Windows NT. With WDM, developers can write a single device driver for both operating systems.

The Universal Driver

A universal driver includes most of the code necessary for devices of a particular class (such as printers or modems) to communicate with the appropriate operating system components (such as the printing or communications subsystems). A *minidriver* is the relatively small and simple driver that contains any additional instructions needed by a specific device. In many cases, however, the universal driver for a particular category of devices also includes the code needed to operate devices designed to the most common standard for that category. (For example, the Unimodem driver works with all modems supporting AT commands.) The universal driver architecture is shown in Figure 28.2.

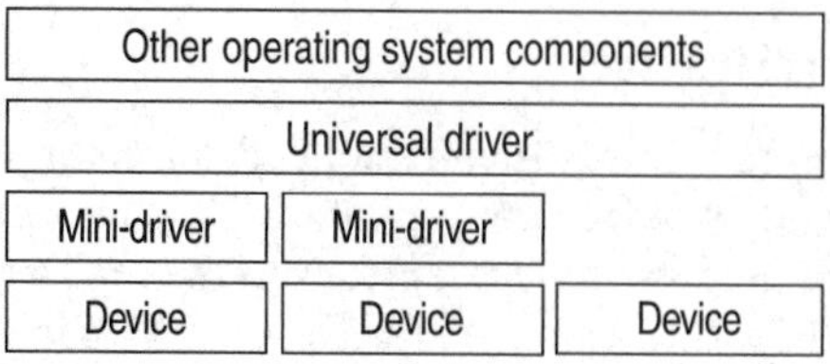

Other operating system components		
Universal driver		
Mini-driver	Mini-driver	
Device	Device	Device

Figure 28.2   Universal driver architecture

The Virtualization Driver

A virtualization driver (VxD) is a 32-bit, protected-mode driver that manages a system resource, such as a hardware device or installed software, so that more than one application can use the resource at the same time. *VxD* refers to a general virtualization driver; the *x* represents the type of device driver. For example, a virtualization driver for a display device is known as a VDD, a virtualization driver for a timer device is a VTD, a virtualization driver for a printer device is a VPD, and so forth.

Windows 98 dynamically loads VxDs—albeit only those that are needed at any given time are loaded into memory. In addition, the new VxDs do not require all of their memory to be page-locked, thereby further increasing the available memory in the system.

VxDs support all hardware devices for a typical computer, including disk controllers, serial and parallel ports, keyboard and display devices, and so on.

While the VxDs dynamically support device drivers, the virtual device keeps track of the status of the device for any application that uses the specific device. Within the Windows 98 environment the ability to switch between multiple applications is commonplace. Each application being used can interrupt the use of a device being used by another open application. Because this interruption can lead to problems with the use of an application trying to access the device, the virtual device checks and manages the state of the device for applications. Furthermore, the virtual device ensures that the device is in the correct mode of operation whenever an application continues. Although most virtual devices manage hardware, some, such as an MS-DOS device driver or a TSR program, manage only installed software. Such virtual devices contain code to emulate the software or ensure that the software uses data that applies only to the currently running application. Also, VxDs are often used to improve software performance.

Note   Windows 98 and Windows 95 virtualization driver files have a file name extension of .vxd; Windows 3.1 drivers used the .386 file name extension.

Win32 Driver Model Drivers

A Win32 Driver Model (WDM) driver can run under Windows 98 and future versions of Windows NT. WDM uses a *layered architecture* in which each layer isolates portions of the services required of a device driver. This design also allows hardware vendors to contain all hardware-specific functionality in a single file. Before WDM, device drivers had to include hooks for a particular operating system in addition to the elements necessary to interact with a specific piece of hardware. This nonlayered approach prevented device drivers from being supported across multiple operating systems.

The WDM layered architecture is shown in Figure 28.3.

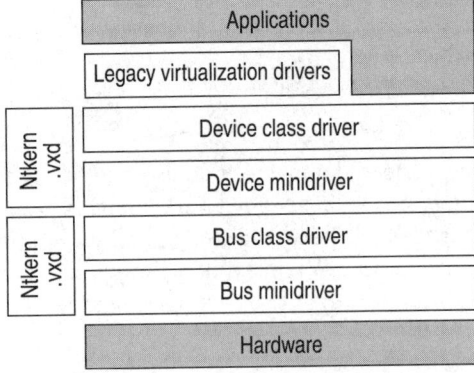

Figure 28.3   WDM layered architecture

The components of the WDM layered architecture are defined in the following sections.

Device Class Drivers

Device class drivers provide interfaces between different layers of the WDM architecture. The lower layer of a device class driver communicates with the class-specific interface exposed by a device minidriver. The upper edge of the device class driver is specific to the operating system. Device class drivers have the following attributes:

- They contain class functions (such as enumeration) not specific to hardware or buses.
- They are dynamically loaded and unloaded.
- They expose a single class-specific interface to multiple-client layers.

An example of a device class driver is Hidclass.sys. This is the generic layer for such input devices as keyboards, mouse devices, and joysticks.

For more information about device drivers, see Chapter 30, "Hardware Management."

Bus Class Drivers

Bus class drivers perform the same function as device class drivers but facilitate the communication between the hardware layer and bus minidrivers. Under Windows 98, WDM supports bus class drivers for the Universal Serial Bus (USB) and the IEEE 1394 bus. An example of a bus class driver is Usbd.sys, for the USB.

For more information about bus drivers, see Chapter 30, "Hardware Management."

Minidrivers

Minidrivers were implemented under Windows 95 in the classes of small computer system interface (SCSI) and network adapters. With Windows 98, the concept of minidrivers has been widened to include support for USB, the IEEE 1394 bus, digital audio, DVD players, still imaging, and video capture. Minidrivers either communicate directly with hardware or form the "glue" between two class drivers.

Hardware minidrivers have the following attributes:

- They are source-compatible and binary-compatible across platforms, allowing the minidriver to be used in Windows 98 as well as Windows NT.
- They are dynamically loaded and unloaded.
- They contain only hardware-specific functionality.
- They can expose multiple class interfaces. This functionality is very important in respect to multifunction (or composite) cards. Audio and video hardware are typical examples of multifunction devices.

Minidrivers that connect class drivers have the following attributes:

- They are source-compatible and binary-compatible across platforms, allowing the minidriver to be used in Windows 98 as well as future versions of Windows NT.
- They are dynamically loaded and unloaded.
- They indirectly control hardware through a specific bus class driver.

An example of a "bridging" minidriver is Hidusb.sys. This Human Interface Device (HID) class minidriver translates HID I/O into request packets that are understood by the USB class driver (Usbd.sys).

For more information about HID, see "Human Interface Device Drivers" later in this chapter and Chapter 30, "Hardware Management."

Legacy Virtualization Drivers

Though non-portable, virtualization drivers occasionally have a place in the WDM layer, Windows 98 virtualization drivers can allow legacy hardware interfaces to be used with WDM devices. For example, an MS-DOS-based game running on an MS-DOS virtual machine (VM) under Windows 98 might attempt to read a joystick's position by directly accessing the I/O ports associated with the legacy game port controller. The virtualization driver for HID joystick support would trap these requests and redirect them into the HID class driver. Another use for a VxD is to act as a "mapper" between the Windows 98 VxD architecture and the WDM architecture. For example, Joyhid.vxd forwards HID class driver information on to Vjoyd.vxd. For a detailed example of VxDs in the WDM stack, see "Human Interface Device Drivers" later in this chapter.

For more information about virtualization drivers, see "The Virtualization Driver" earlier in this chapter.

Ntkern.vxd

The Win32 Driver Model is implemented in Windows 98 by adding a new layer to the existing device driver architecture. *Kernel Services* handles device driver access for Windows NT, whereas Ntkern.vxd handles device driver access for Windows 98. Ntkern.vxd abstracts the Windows 98 architecture to look like the Windows NT architecture. This abstraction allows vendors to develop one driver for both operating systems.

For more information about WDM, see Chapter 30, "Hardware Management."

Human Interface Device Drivers

Windows 98 supports the Human Interface Device (HID) class, the standard for input devices, such as keyboards, mouse devices, joysticks, and game pads. Support is based on the HID specification developed by the USB Implementers' Forum. A HID-compliant device is self-describing, returning function, layout, and usage information. The HID architecture for Windows 98 (implemented with WDM drivers) is shown in Figure 28.4.

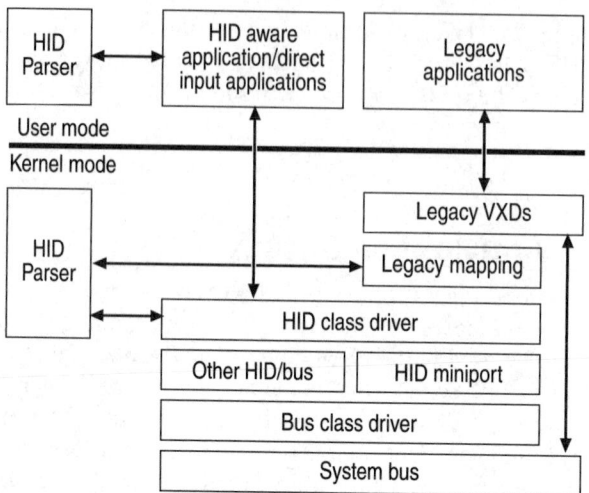

Figure 28.4   HID architecture

HID support is provided for USB keyboards, mouse devices, joysticks, and game pads. HID support for USB comes from the HID class minidriver (Hidusb.sys) provided by Microsoft. Game applications can communicate with USB devices by using the Microsoft DirectInput 5.0 COM interfaces.

The following HID modules are shown in Figure 28.4:

- Hidclass.sys is the HID class driver. It sends and receives HID reports to and from its minidrivers. Hidclass.sys also provides input queues so several processes can have handles open on the same device.

- Hidusb.sys is the USB HID class minidriver. It sends and receives HID reports over the USB bus.

- Hid.dll and Hidparse.sys are parsing services. Hid.dll is a User-mode parsing service. Hidparse.sys is a Kernel-mode parsing service. These modules aid User-mode applications and Kernel-mode drivers in parsing HID reports.

Figure 28.5 shows the Windows 98 HID keyboard implementation alongside the USB stack. In this example, the USB controller may be based on either the OpenHCI standard (Openhci.sys) or the Universal HCI standard (Uhci.sys). The system has two keyboards attached, one USB, another PS/2.

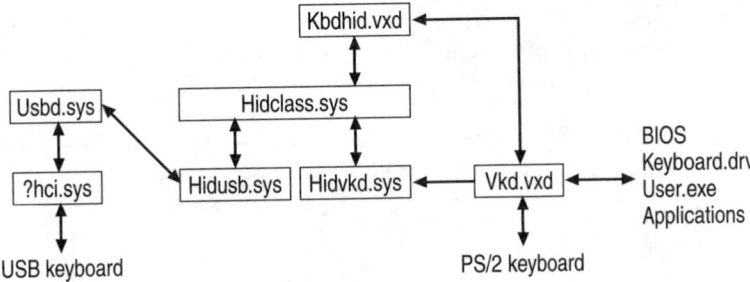

Figure 28.5   HID keyboard architecture example (with USB stack)

The WDM layered architecture and the role of "mapper" virtualization drivers (VxDs) is illustrated by considering how Windows 98 keeps the LED states of both keyboards consistent.

- When CAPS LOCK is pressed on the USB keyboard:

  A HID report containing the CAPS LOCK HID Usage is passed across the USB bus and progresses up the USB stack. It crosses over to the HID stack through Hidusb.sys and is presented to any driver or application that has the keyboard device open with the HID class driver, Hidclass.sys. In this case, Kbdhid.vxd is listening and translates the HID Usage into a legacy PS/2 SCAN CODE, and injects it into the legacy Vkd.vxd driver for routine processing by User.exe. User.exe eventually will cause Vkd.vxd to transmit a SET LED command to the PS/2 keyboard. Kbdhid.vxd hooks this service and also issues a HID report with the CAPS LOCK LED Usage set. This report propagates down through Hidclass.sys, Hidusb.sys, and the USB driver stack to the keyboard. In the meantime, Vkd.vxd sets the LED on the PS/2 keyboard in its usual way.

- When CAPS LOCK is pressed on the PS/2 keyboard:

  In the usual way, the PS/2 SCAN CODE propagates up from Vkd.vxd to User.exe. Eventually, User.exe sends a command to Vkd.vxd to set the LED. This command is noticed by Kbdhid.vxd, because it has the service hooked. It creates a HID report with the CAPS LOCK LED Usage set and writes it to Hidclass.sys, and the report propagates down through Hidusb.sys and the USB driver stack to the keyboard. In the meantime, Vkd.vxd sets the LED on the PS/2 keyboard in its usual way.

  Hidvkd.sys does much the same as Kbdhid.vxd, only Hidvkd.sys is looking for the power key scan codes available on newer PS/2 keyboards.

Just as Kbdhid.vxd is needed to connect HID keyboard support with the VxD keyboard subsystem (Vkd.vxd), similar mapping VxDs (as shown in Table 28.2) are needed to enable support for HID mouse devices, joysticks, and so on.

Table 28.2   Virtualization drivers that support HID class devices

Hidclass.sys device	Windows 98 mapping driver	Windows 98 core driver
Keyboard	Kbdhid.vxd	Vkd.vxd
Mouse device	Mouhid.vxd	Vmouse.vxd
Joystick	Joyhid.vxd	Vjoyd.vxd

For more information about HID, see Chapter 30, "Hardware Management."

Virtual Machine Manager

The Virtual Machine Manager manages resources needed for each application and system process running on the computer. Virtual Machine Manager creates and maintains the virtual machine environments in which applications and system processes run.

A *virtual machine* (VM) is an environment in memory that, from the application's perspective, looks as if it is a separate computer, complete with all the resources available on the physical computer that an application needs to run. The Virtual Machine Manager, shown in Figure 28.6, provides each application with the system resources it needs.

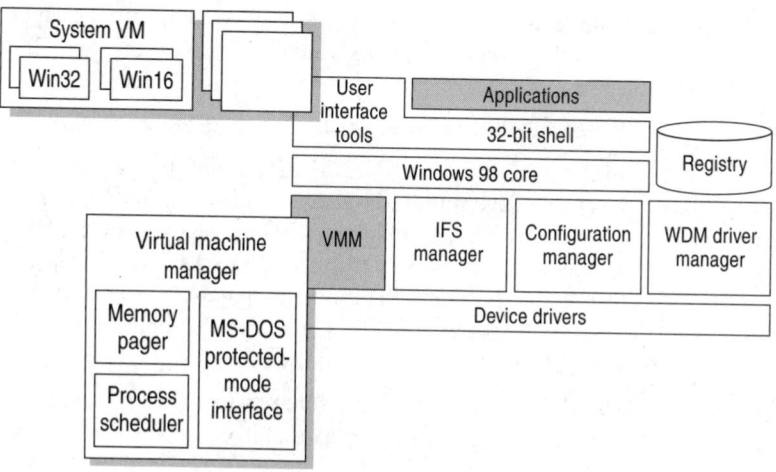

Figure 28.6   Virtual Machine Manager

Windows 98 has a single VM called the System VM, in which all system processes run. In addition, each Win32-based application runs in its own VM, whereas Win16-based applications share a single Win16 VM. Each MS-DOS-based application runs in its own VM.

Note   Windows NT has the ability to run each Win16-based application in its own VM.

The Virtual Machine Manager is responsible for three key areas of services:

- Process scheduling.
- Memory paging.
- MS-DOS Mode support (for MS-DOS-based applications that must have exclusive access to system resources).

The following sections describe these three areas of service.

Process Scheduling and Multitasking

The Process Scheduler is the component responsible for providing system resources to the applications and other processes you run, and for scheduling processes to allow multiple applications to run concurrently.

The Process Scheduler also schedules processes in a way that allows multiple applications and other processes to run concurrently. Windows 98 uses two methods for concurrent process scheduling—cooperative multitasking and preemptive multitasking.

With Windows 3.1, applications ran concurrently through a method known as *cooperative multitasking*. Using this method, the operating system required an application to check the message queue periodically and to relinquish control of the system to other running applications. Applications that did not check the message queue would effectively "hog" CPU time and prevent the user from switching to another application. For compatibility reasons, Windows 98 cooperatively multitasks Win16-based applications.

Windows 98 uses *preemptive multitasking* for Win32-based applications. This means that the operating system takes control away from or gives control to another running task, depending on the needs of the system.

Unlike Win16-based applications, Win32-based applications do not need to yield to other running tasks to multitask properly. Win32-based applications can take advantage of *multithreading*, a mechanism that Windows 98 provides to facilitate the ability to run applications concurrently. A Win32-based application running in the system is called a *process* in terms of the operating system. Each process consists of at least a single thread of execution that identifies the code path flow as it is run by the operating system. A *thread* is a unit of code that can get a time slice from the operating system to run concurrently with other units of code, and must be associated with a process. However, a Win32-based application can initiate multiple threads for a given process to enhance the application for the user by improving throughput, enhancing responsiveness, and aiding background processing. Because of the preemptive multitasking nature of Windows 98, threads of execution allow code to be smoothly processed in the background.

A good illustration of this is the Windows 98 shell itself. Although the shell is a Win32-based process, each folder window that opens is a separate thread of execution. As a result, when you initiate a copy operation between two, shell folder windows, the operation is performed on the thread of the target window. You can still use the other windows in the shell without interruption, or you can start a different copy in another window.

In another example, a word processing application (a process) can implement multiple threads to enhance operation and simplify interaction with the user. The application can have a separate thread that responds to keys typed on the keyboard by the user to place characters in a document, while another thread performs background operations, such as spelling checking or paginating, and a third thread spools a document to the printer in the background.

Note Some Win16-based applications may have provided similar functionality; however, because Windows 3.1 did not provide a mechanism for supporting multithreaded applications, it was up to application vendors to implement their own threading schemes. The use of threads in Windows 98 makes it easy for application vendors to add asynchronous processing of information to their applications.

Memory Paging

Windows 98, like Windows NT, uses a demand-paged virtual memory system. This system is based on a flat, linear address space, accessed using 32-bit addresses.

Each process is allocated a unique virtual address space of 2 gigabytes (GB). The upper 2 GB is shared, while the lower 2 GB is private to the application. This virtual address space is divided into equal blocks, or *pages*.

Demand paging is a method by which code and data are moved in pages from physical memory to a temporary paging file on disk. As the information is needed by a process, it is paged back into physical memory on demand.

The *Memory Pager* maps virtual addresses from the process address space to physical pages in computer memory. In doing so, the Memory Pager hides the physical organization of memory from the process threads. This ensures that the thread can access the memory of its process as needed, but not the memory of other processes. Therefore, as shown in Figure 28.7, the virtual memory of a thread process is much simpler than the real arrangement of pages in physical memory.

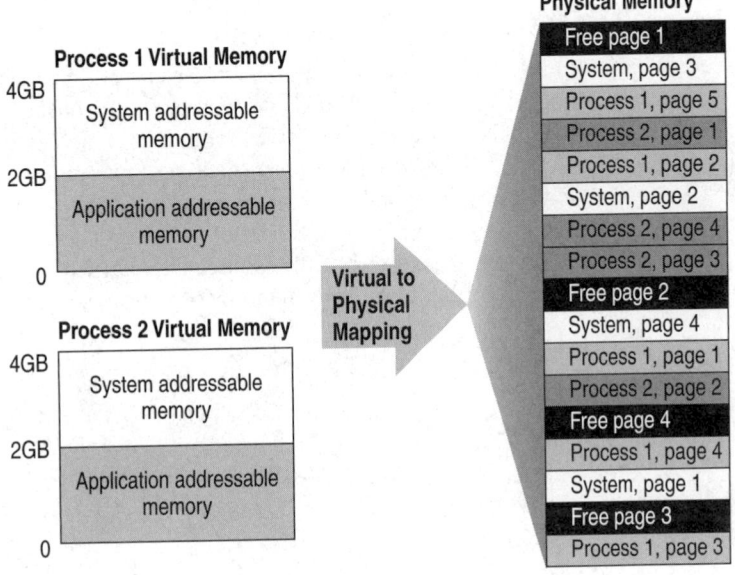

Figure 28.7   Memory mapping with Memory Pager

To support a 16-bit operating environment including Windows 3.1 and MS-DOS, the Intel processor architecture uses a mechanism called a *segment*. Segments reference memory by using a 16-bit segment address, and a 16-bit offset address within the segment. A segment is 64 KB in size, and performance of both applications and the operating system suffer for accessing information across segment boundaries. Windows 98 supports this memory model for backward compatibility to Win16-based applications that were written for it by providing emulation by the Win16 subsystem.

For the support of Win32-based applications and features, Windows 98 uses the 32-bit capabilities of the 80386 (and later) processor architecture to support a flat, linear memory model for 32-bit operating system functionality and Win32-based applications. A *linear addressing model* simplifies the development process for application vendors and removes the performance penalties imposed by the segmented memory architecture.

With this addressing model, Windows 98 allows full use of the 4 GB of addressable memory space for all 32-bit operating system components and applications. Each 32-bit application can access up to 2 GB of addressable memory space, enough to support the largest desktop application.

Support for MS-DOS Mode

Although most MS-DOS-based applications run well in Windows 98 and can run concurrently with other Win32-based and Win16-based applications, a small number of MS-DOS-based applications require exclusive access to system resources to run. The Virtual Memory Manager that creates for the application this exclusive operating environment, called *MS-DOS Mode*. When an MS-DOS-based application runs in MS-DOS Mode, no other applications or processes may compete for system resources—all resources are at the exclusive access of the MS-DOS-based application. For related information, see Chapter 25, "Application Support."

Installable File Systems

Windows 98 features a layered file system architecture that supports multiple file systems, including the virtual file allocation table (VFAT), CD-ROM file system (CDFS), and UDF.

The new file system architecture makes the computer easier to use and improves file and disk I/O performance. Features of the new file system architecture include long file name support and a dynamic system cache for file and network I/O.

Long file name support improves ease of use because users no longer need to reference files by the MS-DOS 8.3 file name. Instead, users can specify names of up to 255 characters to identify their documents. In addition, file names seem less cryptic and easier to read, because Windows 98 hides the file name extensions from users.

Windows 98 features 32-bit, protected-mode code for reading information from—and writing information to—the file system and the disk device. It also includes 32-bit dynamically sizable caching mechanisms, and a full, 32-bit code path is available from the file system to the disk device. Moreover, it includes an open file system architecture for future system support.

Figure 28.8 shows the file system architecture used by Windows 98.

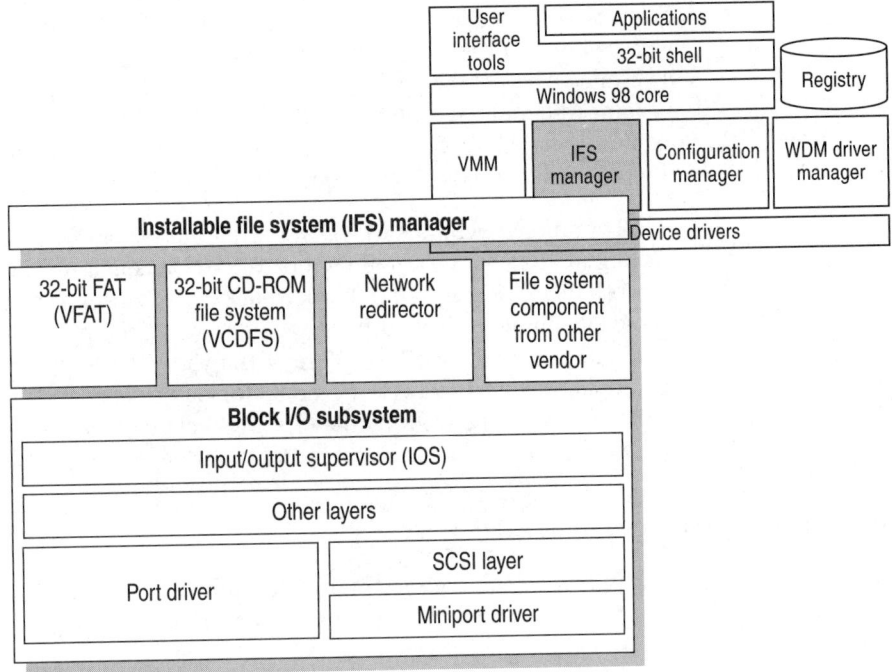

Figure 28.8   Windows 98 file system architecture

The Windows 98 file system architecture is made up of the following components:

- **Installable File System (IFS) Manager**. The IFS Manager is responsible for arbitrating access to different file system components.
- **File system drivers**. The file system driver layer includes access to FAT-based disk devices, CD-ROM file systems, and redirected network device support.
- **Block I/O subsystem**. The block I/O subsystem is responsible for interacting with the physical disk device.

The following sections describe these components.

Installable File System Manager

In Windows 98, the key to access of disk and redirected devices is the Installable File System (IFS) Manager. The IFS Manager arbitrates access to file system devices and other file system device components.

Under MS-DOS and Windows 3.1, INT21 provided access to the file system for reads and writes to a file-storage device. In order to support redirected disk services, such as a network drive, system components such as a network redirector would "hook," or intercept an INT21 function call, so that this redirector could determine whether the INT21 request was intended for it, or for the base file system. Although this "hooking" method allowed multiple device drivers to examine the INT21, some of these add-on components ran improperly, and at times, would not pass on the request for other drivers to examine it.

Another problem with the MS-DOS-based file system was the difficulty in loading multiple network redirectors to provide concurrent access to different network types. Windows for Workgroups provided support for running the Microsoft Windows Network redirector at the same time as an additional network redirector, such as Novell NetWare or Banyan VINES; however, support for running more than two network redirectors at the same time was not provided. In Windows 98, the network redirectors are implemented as file systems under IFS Manager, so an unlimited number of 32-bit redirectors can be used.

File System Drivers

With Windows 98, file system drivers are Ring 0 components of the operating system. Windows 98 includes support for all of the following file systems (others can be added by other vendors):

- VFAT driver.
- CDFS driver.
- 32-bit Universal Disk Format (UDF) file system driver
- 32-bit network redirector (for connectivity to Microsoft network servers, such as Windows NT Server, along with a 32-bit network redirector to connect to Novell NetWare servers).

For more information about network redirectors, see Chapter 29, "Windows 98 Network Architecture."

VFAT File System

The 32-bit VFAT driver provides a protected-mode code path for manipulating the file system stored on a disk. Because it is reentrant and multithreaded, it provides smoother multitasking performance.

The 32-bit VFAT driver interacts with the block I/O subsystem to provide disk access to more device types than were supported by Windows 3.1. Windows 98 also supports mapping to any installed real-mode disk drivers. The combination of 32-bit file access and 32-bit disk access drivers results in significantly improved disk and file I/O performance.

Benefits of the 32-bit file access driver over MS-DOS-based driver solutions include the following:

- Dramatically improved performance and real-mode disk caching software.
- No conventional memory used.
- Better multitasking when accessing information on disk.
- Dynamic cache support.
- More efficient utilization of memory for 32-bit applications (cache mapping).

Both MS-DOS and Windows 3.1 used 16-bit real-mode code to manipulate the file allocation table (FAT) and to read to and write from the disk. In Windows 3.1, most disk accesses still required the use of MS-DOS routines. This data manipulation required several processor mode-switches, from protected mode, reset to real mode to allow MS-DOS to access the disk, and a switch back to protect mode. The constant activity consumed many clock-cycles, and affected potential file access performance drastically. However, Windows 98 manipulates the disk file system from protected mode, which removes or reduces the need to switch to real mode to write information to the disk through MS-DOS, thus resulting in faster file I/O access.

The 32-bit VFAT works with a 32-bit, protected-mode cache driver (VCACHE). This driver replaces the 16-bit, real-mode SMARTDrive disk cache software provided with MS-DOS and Windows 3.1. The VCACHE driver features better caching algorithms than SMARTDrive, to cache information read from or written to a disk drive. The VCACHE driver also manages the cache pool for the Universal Disk Format File System (UDF) and the 32-bit network redirectors provided with Windows 98.

Another big improvement in VCACHE over SMARTDrive is that the memory pool used for the cache is dynamic and is based on the amount of available free system memory. Users no longer need to allocate a block of memory as a disk cache. The system automatically allocates or deallocates memory used for the cache, based on system use.

For example, as you perform a large number of activities on the network, Windows 98 increases the size of the cache. As network activity decreases and more applications are started, Windows 98 decreases the cache size.

Another improvement made to VCACHE in Windows 98 is the ability of VCACHE and the memory manager to execute applications that are present in the cache, directly out of the cache memory. This is referred to as *cache mapping* and improves the efficiency of memory utilization.

CD-ROM File System

The 32-bit, protected-mode CDFS implemented in Windows 98 provides improved CD-ROM access and performance over the real-mode MSCDEX driver in Windows 3.1. (CDFS conforms to the ISO 9660 standard.) The CDFS driver cache is also dynamic, requiring no configuration or static allocation on the part of the user. For more information about the CD-ROM cache, see Chapter 26, "Performance Tuning."

Benefits of the new 32-bit CDFS driver include the following:

- No conventional memory used.
- Improved performance over MS-DOS-based MSCDEX and real-mode cache.
- Better multitasking when accessing CD-ROM information.
- Dynamic cache support to provide a better balance between providing memory to run applications and providing memory to serve as a disk cache.

Note Because of the 32-bit CDFS, MSCDEX is no longer necessary under Windows 98, and is automatically removed from memory and from Autoexec.bat by Setup. It is possible that a legacy CD-ROM drive, using proprietary access methods might require the use of MSCDEX, along with its real-mode drivers. Such a configuration should still work under Windows 98.

Universal Disk Format File System

The 32-bit, protected-mode UDF file system in Windows 98 is implemented according to Revision 1.02 of Universal Disk Format Specification by Optical Storage Technology Association (OSTA). It provides read-only access to UDF-formatted media, such as DVD discs. The UDF file system uses VCACHE and is dynamic, requiring no configuration or static allocation on the part of the user.

Block I/O Subsystem

Figure 28.9 shows the block I/O subsystem in Windows 98. It improves on the 32-bit disk access "FastDisk" device architecture used in Windows 3.1 to enhance performance for the entire file system, and provides a broader array of device support.

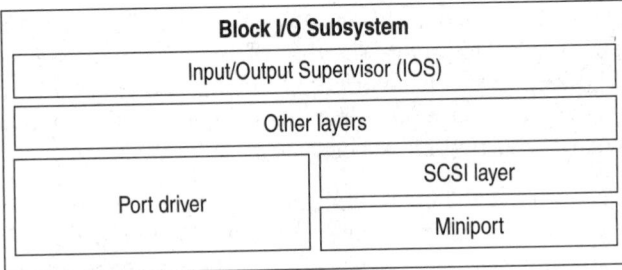

Figure 28.9   Block I/O subsystem

The block I/O subsystem includes the following components.

Input/Output Supervisor (IOS). This component provides services to file systems and drivers. The IOS is responsible for the queuing of file service requests and for routing the requests to the appropriate file system driver. The IOS also provides asynchronous notification of file system events to drivers. This component is described further in "Input/Output Supervisor and Driver Loading" later in this chapter.

Port driver. This is a monolithic, 32-bit, protected-mode driver that communicates with a specific disk device, such as a hard disk controller. This driver is Windows 98–specific and resembles the 32-bit disk access driver used in Windows 3.1 (for example, WDCTRL for Western Digital–compatible hard disk controllers). In Windows 98, the driver that communicates with IDE or ESDI hard disk controllers and floppy disk controllers is implemented as a port driver. A port driver provides the same functionality as the combination of the SCSI manager and the miniport driver.

SCSI layer. This component applies a 32-bit, protected-mode, universal driver model architecture for communicating with SCSI devices. The SCSI layer provides all the high-level functionality common to SCSI and similar devices, and then uses a miniport driver to handle device-specific I/O calls. The SCSI Manager, which is also part of this system, provides the compatibility support for using Windows NT miniport drivers.

Miniport driver. The Windows 98 miniport driver model makes it easier for a hardware disk device vendor to write a device driver. Because the SCSI stub provides the high-level functionality for communicating with SCSI devices, the hardware disk device vendor needs only to create a miniport driver tailored to the vendor's own disk device. The Windows 98 miniport driver is 32-bit, protected-mode code and is binary-compatible with Windows NT miniport drivers. However, older miniport drivers written for Windows NT do not include Plug and Play information. Therefore, they will not perform well on Windows 98.

In addition to these other layers, the block I/O subsystem provides a real-mode mapping layer. This layer provides compatibility with real-mode, MS-DOS-based device drivers for which a protected-mode counterpart does not exist. This layer allows the protected-mode file system to communicate with a real-mode driver as if it were a protected-mode component.

The layers above the block I/O and the real-mode mapper are protected-mode code, and the real-mode mapper translates file I/O requests from protected mode to real mode, so that the MS-DOS-based device driver can perform the appropriate operation to write or read information to or from the disk device. For example, the real-mode mapper is used when real-mode disk compression software is running and a protected-mode disk compression driver is not available.

Note Using MS-DOS-based device drivers may create a bottleneck, because all I/O must be serialized. Also, because all these VxDs must be page-locked, the working set used by the operating system increases.

Input/Output Supervisor and Driver Loading

The I/O Supervisor is a required system VxD that carries out all control and management tasks for the protected-mode file system and block device drivers in Windows 98. The I/O Supervisor loads and initializes protected-mode device drivers and provides services needed for I/O operations.

The I/O Supervisor receives requests from VFAT and CDFS file systems and loads the drivers for accessing local disk devices and drives, including SCSI and IDE. It supports WD1003-compatible drivers, takes control of real-mode drivers, and provides a mapper for real-mode drivers.

The real-mode mapper in the I/O Supervisor provides compatibility with real-mode MS-DOS device drivers for which protected-mode counterparts do not exist. For example, the real-mode mapper goes to work when real-mode disk compression software is running and a protected-mode disk compression driver is not available. This component ensures binary compatibility with existing MS-DOS-based disk device drivers in Windows 98.

The I/O Supervisor was first implemented in Windows 3.x as BLOCKDEV, and in Windows 98 it also provides BLOCKDEV services for older 32-bit disk access drivers. New responsibilities for the I/O Supervisor include:

- Registering drivers.

- Routing and queuing I/O requests, and sending asynchronous notifications to drivers as needed.

- Providing services that drivers can use to allocate memory and complete I/O requests.

Windows 98 loads and initializes the I/O Supervisor as specified in a **device=** entry in System.ini. The I/O Supervisor is initialized before clients and virtualization drivers, such as APIX and INT 13, so clients and virtualization drivers can call services in the I/O Supervisor to register and carry out tasks.

To load and initialize port drivers, miniport drivers, and value-added drivers, the I/O Supervisor requires the files for these drivers to be stored in the \System\IOSubsys directory with the file name extensions shown in Table 28.3.

Table 28.3   File name extensions for drivers in System\IOSubsys

File name extension	Description
pdr	Port drivers (such as SCSIPORT, ESDI_506, and NEC)
mpd	Miniport drivers
386 or vxd	Value-added drivers (such as the volume tracker and vendor-supplied drivers)

The \System\IOSubsys directory is reserved for device drivers specifically designed to be used with the I/O Supervisor. Other clients or virtualization drivers should be stored in other directories and explicitly loaded using **device=** entries in System.ini.

The I/O Supervisor initializes device drivers (as described in the following sections) from the bottom layer upwards, so port drivers are initialized before vendor-supplied drivers, vendor-supplied drivers before type-specific drivers, and so on. Value-added drivers are initialized in groups, layer-by-layer, with all drivers in one layer initialized before drivers in the next layer. The initialization order within a layer is not defined, so you cannot depend on the drivers in a group being initialized in a specific order, or even on the same order between startup operations.

For Plug and Play detection, the I/O Supervisor loads a specific port or miniport driver only if Configuration Manager requests that the driver be loaded after hardware detection locates an adapter.

Configuration Manager

To support Plug and Play functionality, Windows 98 architecture includes a component called Configuration Manager, which orchestrates the configuration process. This process might involve many bus and device architectures coexisting on a single system, with more than one device type using the same bus architecture, yet with each device having a separate set of configuration requirements. For example, a mouse and a keyboard can both use the same keyboard controller bus; a CD-ROM drive and a hard disk drive might both use the same SCSI bus.

As shown in Figure 28.10, Configuration Manager works with a number of subcomponents to identify each bus and each device on the system and to identify the configuration settings for each device. Configuration Manager ensures that each device on the computer can use an interrupt request (IRQ), I/O port addresses, and other resources without conflict with other devices.

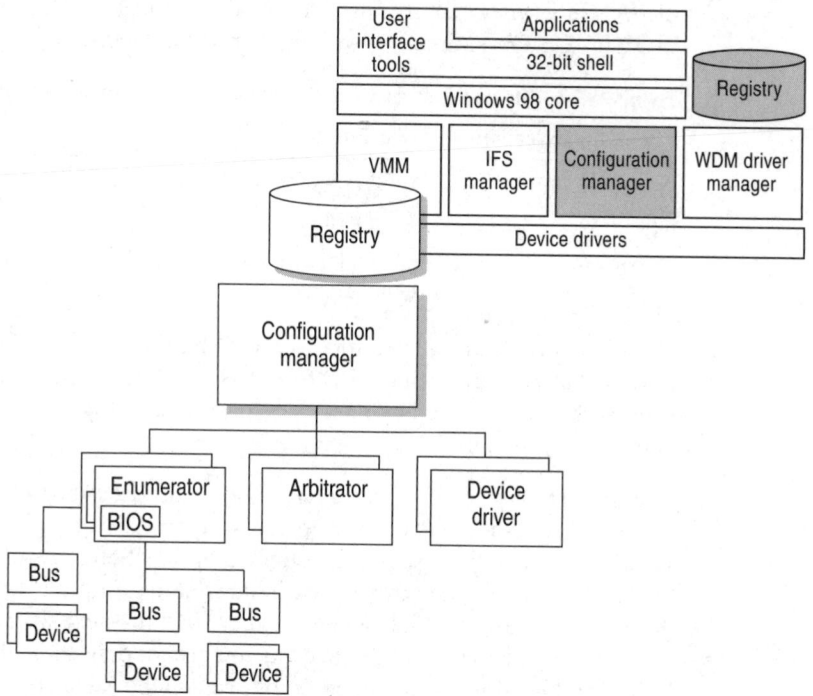

Figure 28.10   How Configuration Manager works in Windows 98

Configuration Manager also helps monitor the computer for changes in the number and type of devices present, and manages the reconfiguration of the devices, as needed, when changes take place. As these events occur, Configuration Manager communicates the information to applications.

To perform its role, Configuration Manager (implemented as part of the Virtual Memory Manager [VMM32]) calls on the bus enumerators to identify all the devices on their specific buses and their respective resource requirements.

Bus enumerators are new drivers that are responsible for creating the Windows 98 hardware tree. A *hardware tree* is the hierarchical representation of all the buses and devices on a computer. Each bus and each device is represented as a *node.* Figure 28.11 graphically represents a hardware tree.

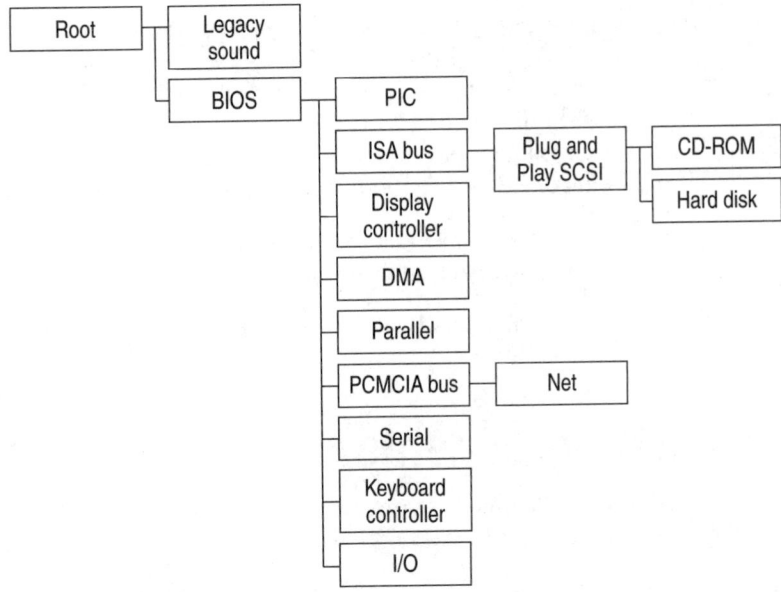

Figure 28.11   Example of a hardware tree

During the device enumeration process, the bus enumerator locates and gathers information from either the device drivers or the BIOS services for that particular device type. For example, the SCSI bus enumerator calls the SCSI drivers to gather information. (Some bus enumerators may instead check the hardware directly.)

A driver is loaded for each device. When loaded, the driver waits for Configuration Manager to assign specific resources (such as IRQs) to the device. Configuration Manager calls on *resource arbitrators* to allocate resources for each device.

Resource arbitrators resolve conflicts among devices that request identical resource assignments. Windows 98 provides arbitrators for the standard I/O, memory, hardware interrupt, and direct memory access (DMA) channel resources. (The arbitrators are separate components, rather than a part of Configuration Manager, to ensure extensibility to new types of resources, such as power allocation or automatic SCSI IDs.)

To complete the configuration process, Configuration Manager informs the device drivers about the device configuration. This process is repeated when the BIOS or one of the other bus enumerators informs Configuration Manager about an event that requires a change to the system configuration, such as the removal or insertion of a Plug and Play–compliant PC Card.

For more information about Plug and Play, see Chapter 24, "Device Management."

Win32 Driver Model Driver Manager

Win32 Driver Model (WDM) support is implemented in Windows 98 by adding a new layer to the existing VxD device driver architecture that mimics the Windows NT kernel. Ntkern.vxd exposes this interface for WDM drivers, allowing vendors to develop one driver for both Windows 98 and future versions of Windows NT.

For more information about the WDM driver architecture, see "Win32 Driver Model Drivers" earlier in this chapter.

For more information about WDM in general, see Chapter 30, "Hardware Management."

Core System Components

Windows 98 includes a core composed of three components—User, Kernel, and Graphics Device Interface (GDI)—as shown in Figure 28.12.

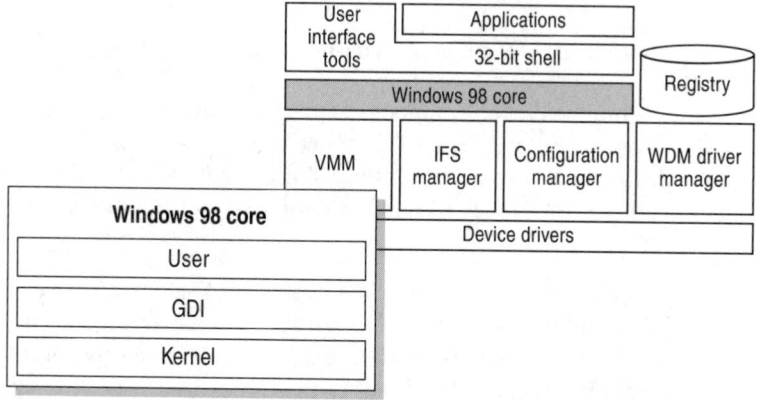

Figure 28.12   Windows 98 core system components

Each of these components includes a pair of dynamic-link libraries (DLLs) (one 32-bit and one 16-bit) that provide services for the applications you run. Windows 98 is designed to use 32-bit code wherever it significantly improves performance without sacrificing application compatibility. Windows 98 retains existing 16-bit code where it is required to maintain compatibility or where 32-bit code would increase memory requirements without significantly improving performance. All the Windows 98 I/O subsystems (such as networking and file systems) and device drivers are 32-bit, as are all the memory management and scheduling components, including the Kernel and Virtual Memory Manager.

As shown in Figure 28.13, the lowest-level services provided by the Windows 98 Kernel are implemented as 32-bit code to ensure a high-performance core. Most of the remaining 16-bit code consists of hand-tuned assembly language, delivering performance that rivals some 32-bit code used by other operating systems.

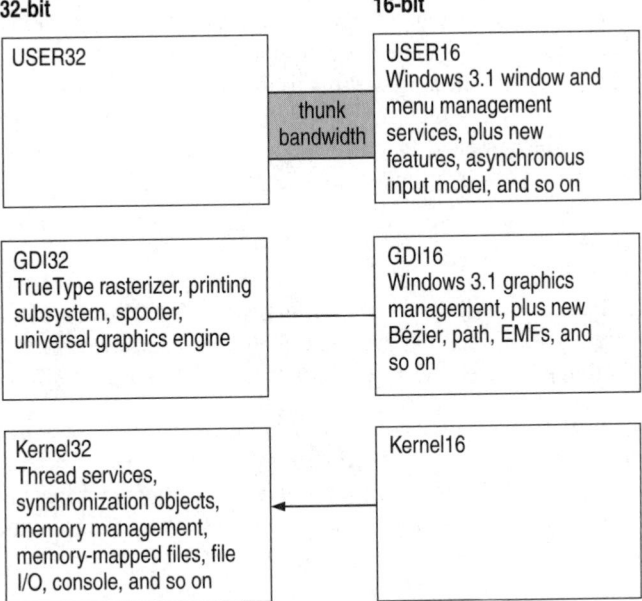

Figure 28.13   Windows 98 core services

Many functions provided by the GDI—which are mostly complex, CPU-intensive functions—have been rewritten as 32-bit code to improve performance. Much of the window management code in the User components (small, fast functions) remains 16-bit, thus retaining application compatibility.

Windows 98 also improves on the MS-DOS and Windows 3.1 environments by implementing many device drivers as 32-bit, protected-mode code. Virtualization drivers in Windows 98 assume the functionality provided by many real-mode, MS-DOS-based device drivers, eliminating the need to load them in MS-DOS. This results in a minimal conventional memory footprint, improved performance, and improved reliability and stability of the system over real-mode device drivers.

The following sections describe the services provided by these core components.

User

The User component manages input from the keyboard, mouse, and other input devices and output to the user interface (windows, icons, menus, and so on). It also manages interaction with the sound driver, timer, and communications ports.

Windows 98 uses an asynchronous input model for all input to the system and applications. As the various input devices generate interrupts, the interrupt handler converts these interrupts to messages and sends the messages to a raw input thread area, which in turn passes each message to the appropriate message queue. Although each Win32-based thread can have its own message queue, all Win16-based applications share a common one.

Kernel

The Kernel provides base operating system functionality, including file I/O services, virtual memory management, and task scheduling. When a user wants to start an application, the Kernel loads the EXE and DLL files for the application.

Exception handling is another service of the Kernel. *Exceptions* are events that occur as a program runs and that require software outside the normal flow of control to be run. For example, if an application generates an exception, the Kernel is able to communicate that exception to the application to perform the necessary functions to resolve the problem.

The Kernel also allocates virtual memory, resolves import references, and supports demand paging for the application. As the application runs, the Kernel schedules and runs threads of each process owned by an application.

The Kernel provides services to both 16-bit and 32-bit applications by using a translation process called *thunking* to map between 16-bit and 32-bit formats. Thunking converts a 16-bit value to its 32-bit equivalent.

Virtual Memory Management

Virtual memory refers to the fact that the operating system can actually allocate more memory than the computer physically contains. Each process is allocated a unique virtual address space, which is a set of addresses available for the process's threads to use. This virtual address space appears to be 4 gigabytes (GB) in size: 2 GB reserved for program storage and 2 GB for system storage.

Figure 28.14 illustrates where Windows 98 system components and applications reside in virtual memory.

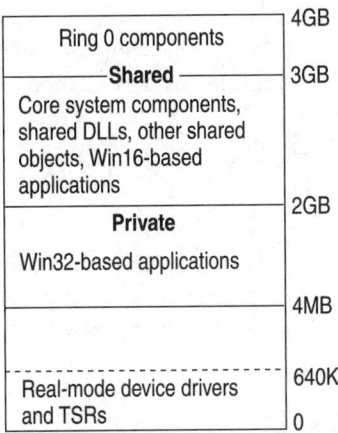

Figure 28.14   Windows 98 virtual memory structure

From top to bottom, here is where system and application components reside in virtual memory:

- All Ring 0 components reside in the address space above 3 GB.

- The Windows 98 core components and shared DLLs reside in the shared address space between 2 GB and 3 GB. This makes them available to all applications.

- Win32-based applications reside between 4 megabytes (MB) and 2 GB. Each Win32-based application has its own address space, which means that other programs cannot corrupt or otherwise hinder the application, or vice versa.

Windows 98 Swap File

The Windows 98 virtual memory swap file implementation addresses problems and limitations imposed in Windows 3.1.

Under Windows 3.1, users had to decide whether to use a temporary swap file or a permanent swap file, how much memory to allocate to the swap file, and whether to use 32-bit disk access to access the swap file. One of the benefits of a temporary swap file is that the swap file did not need to be contiguous; Windows allocated space on the hard disk when the user started Windows and freed up the space when the user exited Windows. A permanent swap file provided better performance; however, it required a contiguous block of space on a physical hard disk and was static, so it remained as a hidden file, taking up space, on the hard drive when the user exited Windows.

The swap file implementation in Windows 98 simplifies the configuration task for the user and combines the best of temporary and permanent swap files because of improved virtual memory algorithms and access methods. The swap file in Windows 98 is dynamic; it can shrink or grow, based on the operations that are performed on the system. The swap file can also occupy a fragmented region of the hard disk with no substantial performance penalty. The swap file can also reside on a compressed volume.

You can still adjust the parameters used for defining the swap file in Windows 98; however, the need to do this is reduced by using system defaults. For more information about swap file configuration options, see Chapter 26, "Performance Tuning."

Graphics Device Interface

The *Graphics Device Interface* (GDI) is the graphical system that manages what appears on the screen. It also provides graphics support for printers and other output devices. It draws graphic primitives, manipulates bitmaps, and interacts with device-independent graphics drivers, including those for display and printer output device drivers.

Graphics Subsystem

The graphics subsystem provides graphics support for input and output devices.

For reliability and better performance, Windows 98 uses a 32-bit graphics engine, also known as the device-independent bitmap (DIB) engine. This engine directly controls graphics output to the screen, providing more reliable system performance. It also provides a set of optimized generic drawing functions for monochrome (1-bit), 16-color (4-bit), 256-color (8-bit), 65,535-color (16-bit), and 16,777,215-color (24-bit) graphic devices and supports Bézier curves and paths.

Windows 95 introduced Image Color Matching (ICM) for better color-matching between display and color output devices. Microsoft has enhanced the capability of ICM to provide increased functionality and performance in Windows 98. ICM 2.0 supports more color spaces beyond RGB to CMYK, to device-independent color spaces such as CIELAB, a theoretical color space defined by the Commission Internationale de L'Eclairage (CIE), as well as support for additional colors for processes such as HiFi Color. See Chapter 11 "Printing, Imaging, and Fonts" for more information on ICM.

As with other parts of the operating system, the Windows 98 graphics subsystem includes a universal driver/minidriver model. As illustrated in Figure 28.15, display drivers for Windows 3.1 included hardware-specific instructions, in addition to general instructions for the operating system. Now, all instructions about drawing to the screen or output device are included in the universal display driver. Minidrivers for Windows 98 define only hardware-specific instructions. Minidrivers are available for most leading Super VGA adapters and graphics accelerators, including S3, ATI, Tseng, Paradise, Western Digital, and Cirrus Logic.

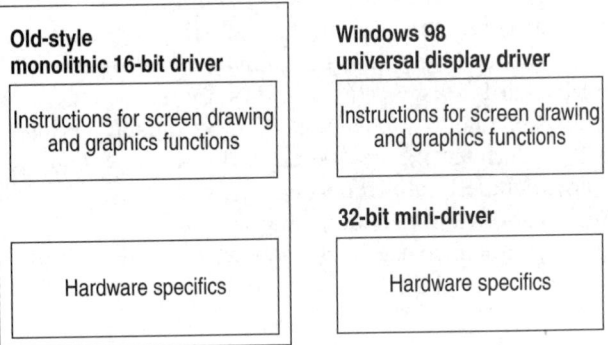

Figure 28.15   The 16-bit and 32-bit graphics subsystem driver models

---

Tip Problems can result when Windows 98 assumes that a display adapter can support certain functionality that, in fact, it cannot. If this occurs, the side effects might be anything from small display irregularities to system lockup.

To determine whether any performance problems might be related to the display adapter, you can progressively disable enhanced display functionality using the System option in Control Panel. For information, see Chapter 26, "Performance Tuning."

Printing Subsystem

The 32-bit Windows 98 printing subsystem provides performance through smoother background printing and faster return-to-application time. By using background thread processing, the Windows 98 spooler passes data to the printer, as the printer is ready to receive more information.

Windows 98 spools enhanced metafile (EMF) format files rather than raw printer data to ensure quick return-to-application time (up to twice as fast as with Windows 3.1). When spooled, the EMF information is interpreted in the background, and the output is sent to the printer.

The printing subsystem supports Point and Print. When users browse the network to choose the printers they want to use, Windows 98 automatically installs the appropriate printer driver from the Windows 98 or Windows NT server.

Another feature of the Windows 98 printing subsystem is deferred printing. If no printing device is available, the user can still "print" the job. Windows 98 generates the print job and then saves it for output to a print device when one is available. Then, when the user docks the portable computer after returning to the office, the print job that was "printed" begins generating pages at the print device.

The printing subsystem also provides system-level support of bidirectional communication protocols for printers adhering to the Extended Communication Port (ECP) printer communication standard, developed by Microsoft and Hewlett-Packard. This capability allows printers to send unsolicited messages to Windows 98 and to applications. For example, the printer might send an "out of paper" or "printer offline" message. Bidirectional communication enables much more detailed status reporting on a wider variety of information, such as information about a low toner condition, details about a paper jam, instructions related to maintenance needs, and so on. For more information on printing, see Chapter 11 "Printing, Imaging, and Fonts."

User Interface

Windows 98 features a new 32-bit user interface that unifies information access into one utility to universally view local, network, intranet, and Internet data. This new shell contains several desktop tools, including Network Neighborhood, the selectable Active Desktop interface, and the selectable Active Channel interface. As shown in Figure 28.16, these tools run at the same architectural level as other Win32-based, Win16-based, and MS-DOS-based applications.

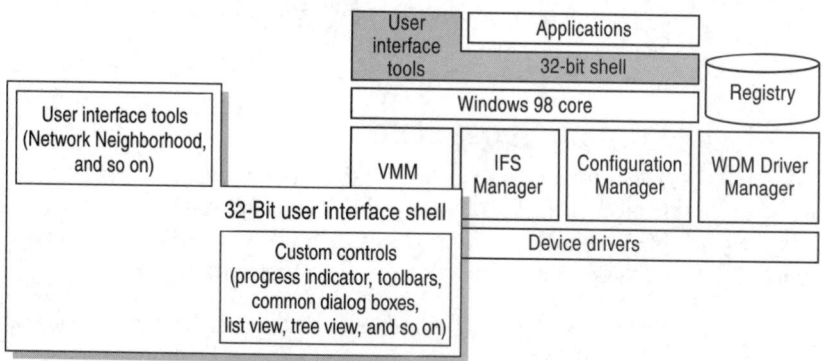

Figure 28.16   Windows 98 user interface shell

All applications and tools can take advantage of the common controls offered by the shell, such as common dialog boxes, tree views, and list views.

Application Support

Windows 98 supports Win32-based, Win16-based, and MS-DOS-based applications.

As illustrated in Figure 28.17, Win32-based and Win16-based applications run in the System VM. Win32-based applications each run in a separate address space, while Win16-based applications run together in a shared address space. Each MS-DOS-based application runs in its own VM.

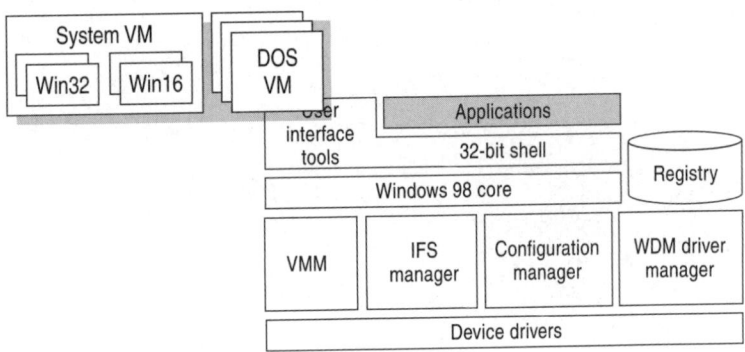

Figure 28.17   Windows 98 support for Win32-based and Win16-based applications

For more information about using Win32-based, Win16-based, and MS-DOS-based applications in Windows 98, see Chapter 25, "Application Support," and Chapter 29, "Windows 98 Network Architecture."

For more information about VMs, see "Virtual Machine Manager" earlier in this chapter.

CHAPTER 29

Windows 98 Network Architecture

This chapter presents information about the architecture for the networking components in Microsoft Windows 98.

In This Chapter

See Also

- For more information about configuring and using network adapters and protocols, see Chapter 15, "Network Adapters and Protocols."

- For more information about configuring and using Windows 98 on Microsoft networks, see Chapter 16, "Windows 98 on Microsoft Networks."

- For more information about configuring and using Windows 98 on third-party networks, see Chapter 17, "Windows 98 on Third-Party Networks."

- For more information about configuring and using Dial-Up Networking and Point-to-Point Tunneling Protocol (PPTP), see Chapter 19, "Remote Networking and Mobile Computing."

Overview of Windows 98 Network Architecture

Windows 98 provides multiple, simultaneous connections to a variety of networks (Windows NT, Novell NetWare, and others) and a variety of resources (files, programs, printers, host systems, and mail systems) over most popular media (Ethernet, Token Ring, X.25, ATM, and ISDN) from almost any location.

Windows 98 networking capabilities are implemented using a high-performance, reliable, and open architecture based on the Windows Open Services Architecture (WOSA) specification. This approach provides users with a consistent interface to different services on the front end, while giving system administrators the flexibility to mix and match multiple services on the back end.

Open Systems Interconnection Model

The modular networking architecture of Windows 98 is based on two industry standard models for a layered networking architecture, namely the International Standards Organization (ISO) model for computer networking, called the *Open Systems Interconnection (OSI) Reference Model*, and the Institute of Electrical and Electronics Engineers (IEEE) 802 model. Windows NT and Windows for Workgroups are also designed according to these standard models. The ISO OSI and IEEE 802 models define a modular approach to networking, with each layer responsible for some discrete aspect of the networking process. They are only models; they do not correspond exactly to any existing network. However, they can help you understand how networks function in general.

The OSI model describes the flow of data in a network, from the lowest layer (the physical connections) up to the layer containing the user's applications. Data going to and from the network is passed from layer to layer. Each layer is able to communicate with the layer immediately above it and the layer immediately below it. In this way, each layer is written as an efficient, streamlined software component. When a layer receives a packet of information, it checks the destination address, and if its own address is not there, it passes the packet to the next layer.

When two computers communicate on a network, the software at each layer on one computer assumes it is communicating with the same layer on the other computer. For example, the transport layer of one computer assumes that it is communicating directly with the transport layer on the other computer. However, the actual connection occurs only at the physical layer, as Figure 29.1 shows. The transport layer on the first computer has no regard for how the communication actually passes through the lower layers of the first computer, across the physical media, and then up through the lower layers of the second computer.

Figure 29.1 shows the OSI model.

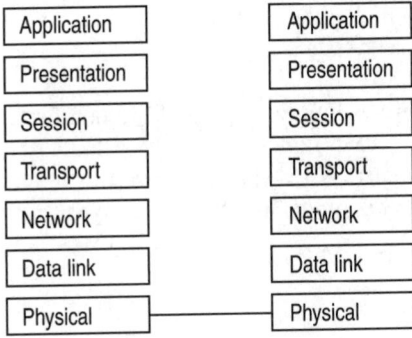

Figure 29.1   Layers in the OSI Model

The OSI model includes seven layers:

- The *application layer* represents the level at which applications access network services. This layer represents the services that directly support applications, such as software for file transfers, database access, and electronic mail.

- The *presentation layer* translates data from the application layer into an intermediary format. This layer also manages security issues by providing such services as data encryption, and compresses data so that fewer bits need to be transferred on the network.

- The *session layer* allows two applications on different computers to establish, use, and end a session. This layer establishes dialog control between the two computers in a session, regulating which side transmits, as well as when and how long it transmits.

- The *transport layer* handles error recognition and recovery. When necessary, it also repackages long messages into small packets for transmission and, at the receiving end, rebuilds packets into the original message. The receiving transport layer also sends receipt acknowledgments.

- The *network layer* addresses messages and translates logical addresses and names into physical addresses. It also determines the route from the source to the destination computer and manages traffic problems, such as switching, routing, and controlling the congestion of data packets.

- The *data link layer* packages raw bits from the physical layer into frames (logical, structured packets for data). This layer is responsible for transferring frames from one computer to another, without errors. After sending a frame, it waits for an acknowledgment from the receiving computer.

- The *physical layer* transmits bits from one computer to another and regulates the transmission of a stream of bits over a physical medium. This layer defines how the cable is attached to the network adapter and what transmission technique is used to send data over the cable.

The IEEE 802 model defines low-level protocol standards at the physical and data link layers of the OSI model, dividing the data link layer into two sublayers: logical link control (LLC) and media access control (MAC). Figure 29.2 compares the IEEE 802 model and the lower layers of the OSI model.

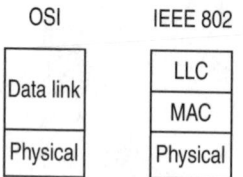

Figure 29.2   IEEE 802 model compared to the OSI model

The LLC sublayer performs the following tasks:

- Link establishment and termination
- Frame control
- Frame sequencing
- Frame acknowledgment

The MAC sublayer performs the following tasks:

- Media access management
- Frame delimiting
- Frame error checking
- Frame address recognition

Windows 98 Networking Model

Figure 29.3 shows the layered components that make up the Windows 98 networking model.

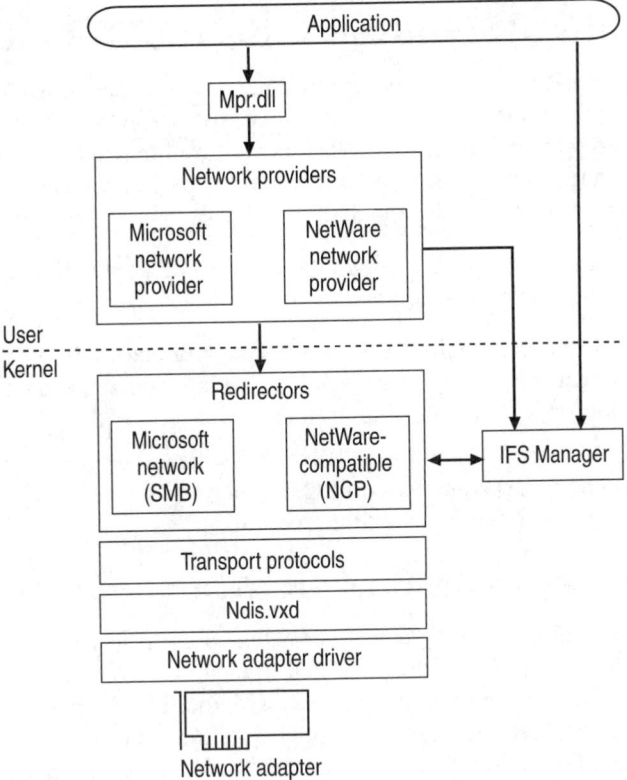

Figure 29.3   Windows 98 network architecture

These layers correspond roughly to the layers in the OSI model, as the following list describes:

- The network providers, Installable File System (IFS) Manager, and redirectors provide functionality described in the application, presentation, and session layers of the OSI model.

- The transport protocols provide functionality described in the transport and network layers of the OSI model.

- Network driver interface specification (NDIS) and the network adapter drivers provide functionality described in the data link layer of the OSI model.

The following sections describe these elements of the Windows 98 network architecture, beginning with redirectors. Network providers are described in "Multiple Network Support" later in this chapter.

Redirectors and Installable File System Manager

A network *redirector* provides mechanisms to locate, open, read, write, and delete files and submit print jobs. It also makes available such application services as named pipes and mailslots. When an application needs to send or receive data from a remote device, it sends a call to the redirector. The redirector provides the functionality of the application and presentation layers of the OSI model.

The redirectors are included in the Windows 98 network client software as the following file system drivers:

- In Client for Microsoft Networks, the redirector (Vredir.vxd) supports all networks based on Microsoft networking, which use the server message block (SMB) file sharing protocol.

- In Microsoft Client for NetWare Networks, the redirector (Nwredir.vxd) supports NetWare networking products, which use the NetWare Core Protocol (NCP) file sharing protocol.

Windows 98 also supports network redirectors created by other network vendors.

The *Installable File System (IFS) Manager* controls file I/O transfers for all the file systems. Each 32-bit, protected-mode redirector is implemented as a file system driver. The redirector works with the IFS Manager to map local names to network devices and to decide whether the application needs a local or remote device. For more information about IFS Manager, see Chapter 28, "Windows 98 Architecture."

In Client for Microsoft Networks, the redirector for Microsoft networks formats an application's request into SMB packets. In Microsoft Client for NetWare Networks, the NetWare redirector formats requests into NCP packets. In both cases, the data packet is then passed by the protocol to the adapter driver.

Windows 98 provides two server services for peer resource sharing:

- File and Printer Sharing for Microsoft Networks (the Windows 98 SMB-based server, Vserver.vxd), which supports resource sharing among all computers on the network that use the SMB file sharing protocol.

- File and Printer Sharing for NetWare Networks (the Windows 98 NCP-based server, Nwserver.vxd), which supports resource sharing among all computers on the network that use the NCP file sharing protocol.

Multiple Network Support

The Windows 98 modular network provider interface, as described in this section, supports concurrent communication with several different networks. For example, a computer can have simultaneous connections to computers running Windows 98 peer resource sharing services, to servers for Windows NT and NetWare networks.

In addition to the Windows 98 network client and peer sharing components, Windows 98 supports upgrading from several different third-party network clients. For a list of these clients, see Chapter 14, "Introduction to Networking Configuration."

Most of these network clients can be installed along with protected-mode Windows 98 networking components. Windows 98 does not include the supporting files for these networks; you must obtain them from the network vendor. For more information about these network clients, see Chapter 17, "Windows 98 on Third-Party Networks."

Multiple network support in Windows 98 consists of these components, as described in the following sections:

- Win32 WinNet application programming interface (API).
- Multiple provider router and service provider interface (SPI).
- Network providers (including the WinNet16 interface).

Figure 29.4 shows the architecture for multiple network support.

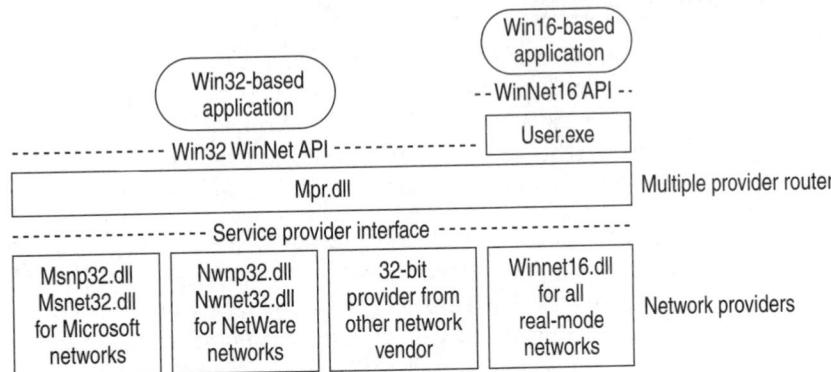

Figure 29.4   Multiple network support in Windows 98

Win32 WinNet Interface for Applications

The Win32 WinNet interface in Windows 98 provides an API that software developers can use to create single versions of applications that run unmodified on different networks. Applications that use Win32 APIs can take full advantage of all Windows 98 performance enhancement features. Win32-based applications can utilize multitasking, Win32 APIs, long file name support, separate message queues, and memory protection. Each Win32-based application runs in its own fully protected, private address space, preventing it from causing the operating system or other applications to fail and preventing interference from errors generated by other applications.

The Win32 WinNet interface is the successor to the WinNet16 interface introduced in Windows 3.0 and enhanced in Windows 3.1.

The expanded WinNet API set includes the following:

- Support for the Win32 WinNet APIs as defined in Windows NT. This set of functions and the other Win32 APIs together provide all the commonly used capabilities required by applications.

- Support for the Win32 WinNet APIs for browsing network resources (directories, printers, and other resources). This includes consistent handling of authentication requirements across multiple networks and support for the NetWare server security model.

- Backward compatibility with Windows for Workgroups 3.11 and support for networks that use a WinNet16 network driver.

Multiple Provider Router and Service Provider Interface

The multiple provider router in Windows 98 exports the Win32 WinNet APIs to applications. It provides seamless access to network services and resources, and it supports a way to access a single WinNet16 network driver. It routes incoming network requests to the appropriate network provider, using the same interface, whether one or more network providers are installed.

Features common to all networks are implemented once in the multiple provider router, reducing the code base for each network provider and ensuring common behavior among networks. For example, network providers do not implement persistent connections—this feature is implemented in the multiple provider router and is entirely transparent to a network provider.

Windows 98 uses an open, modular service provider interface (SPI) to allow multiple 32-bit network providers to be installed in Windows 98 simultaneously. The service provider interface is a single, well-defined set of functions used by Windows 98 to request network services to browse servers, connect to and disconnect from servers, and so on. The multiple provider router communicates with the network providers using the service provider interface.

The service provider interface provides the needed network services to honor a Windows 98 request for network-specific services. This model is similar to the Windows 98 design for various device driver interfaces: a well-defined set of interfaces used by the operating system, with services provided by a device driver (often written by another vendor) to honor requests. These requests are then passed to the network providers.

The service provider interface enables Microsoft or other network providers to integrate varied network services seamlessly into Windows 98. The service provider interface ensures that all supported networks are identically accessed and managed through Network Neighborhood and other user interface components.

Network Providers

Windows 98 uses an open, modular network provider interface to allow multiple network support simultaneously. Key benefits of the network provider interface architecture are the following:

- An open interface allowing any network vendor to supply tightly integrated support for Windows 98.
- Identical access to and management of network resources and components through the Windows 98 user interface, including Network Neighborhood and the Network option in Control Panel.

The network provider API calls are used by applications to request network services. Windows 98 passes a network provider call to the appropriate network provider, which then supplies the requested network service.

The *network provider* is a network-specific driver that implements the service provider interface call from the multiple provider router. The functions provided include authenticating users when they access a network server, managing passwords, adding or removing server connections, and browsing network resources.

Windows 98 includes the following network providers:

- Msnp32.dll for Microsoft networks.
- Nwnp32.dll for NetWare networks.
- Winnet16.dll for a single 16-bit network provider that uses WinNet16 APIs.

Windows 98 also supports any number of other 32-bit network providers, which must be supplied by other network vendors.

The Windows 98 system logon is an example of a network service provided by the network provider interface. Each network provider can provide a unique logon dialog box to suit the needs of its network server security model. After the logon is validated by the requested server, this information is passed back to Windows 98, which can then use this password to unlock any network resource linked to the logon validation. In this way, Windows 98 can accommodate the various ways that network servers provide their services, yet still offer a consistent user interface.

For example, the following summarizes the internal processes when a user double-clicks the Entire Network icon in Network Neighborhood:

1. The Windows 98 user interface generates a Win32-based network API call to enumerate servers and resources on the network.
2. The multiple provider router receives the API call and submits a service provider interface call to all the available network providers.
3. Each network provider browses its individual networks and returns the list to Windows 98, which displays all the networks and their hierarchies in the Entire Network window.

Because of the network provider support in Windows 98, users can specify server name strings in a drive connection dialog box using the syntax to which they are accustomed. A network provider knows how to correctly interpret the syntax of its own server name strings. The server name string is the syntax used by a particular network operating system to specify a shared disk resource. Microsoft network-compatible networks use the universal naming convention (UNC) format (*server_name**share_name*).

However, because the network provider knows how to interpret server name strings, users who are accustomed to using the NetWare server syntax (*server_name/volume_name:directory_name*) can type such server names wherever required in Windows 98 to access NetWare server resources. The Windows 98 user interface and the **net** command also support UNC names for connecting to NetWare resources.

Network Provider for Microsoft Networks

The network provider that supports Microsoft networks (Msnp32.dll) provides access to SMB-based Microsoft network resources using the Windows 98 user interface, such as Windows Explorer, Network Neighborhood, Control Panel, and other Windows-based applications.

As Figure 29.5 shows, Msnp32.dll provides the Microsoft network-specific dialog boxes (such as the Windows NT domain logon dialog box) and code to resolve a service provider interface call from the multiple provider router to a call to Client for Microsoft Networks.

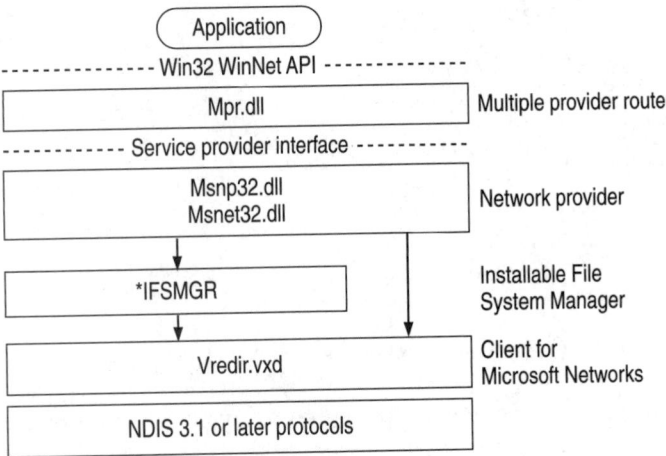

Figure 29.5   Network provider for Microsoft networks

Notice that there are three arrows, two going through IFS Manager and one going directly to Client for Microsoft Networks.

- When a network request is for a generic function, such as adding a connection, the call is submitted to the IFS interface.

- When a network request is specific to a redirector, such as logging on or browsing a server, the call is sent to Client for Microsoft Networks.

The network provider supports the following functions on Microsoft networks:

- Browsing Microsoft networks.

- Logging on to and off of a Windows NT or LAN Manager domain. The Microsoft network provider provides authentication services for validation by a domain controller and the ability to change the domain password using the Passwords option in the Windows 98 Control Panel.

- Adding and removing connections. The Microsoft network provider allows mapped drive and printer connections and UNC connections to SMB-based network resources.

Network Provider for NetWare Networks

Figure 29.6 shows the network provider that supports NetWare networks. The network provider (Nwnp32.dll and its support library, Nwnet32.dll) provides access to NCP-based NetWare network resources using Windows Explorer, Network Neighborhood, Control Panel, and other Windows-based applications.

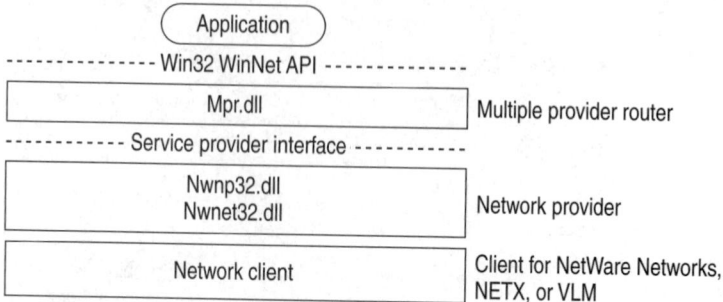

Figure 29.6   Network provider for NetWare networks

The network provider supports the following functions on NetWare networks:

- Browsing NetWare networks. Bindery-based NetWare networks (versions 2.15 and later, 3.*x*, and 4.*x* with bindery emulation) use a Server-Volume-Directory hierarchy.

- Logging on to and off of a NetWare network, providing dialog boxes for network logon, and performing attachments to bindery-based servers.

- Adding and removing connections, allowing remote drive and printer connections using the NetWare format (*server/volume:*) and the UNC connections to NCP-based network resources (mapped drive or printer port, and *server\share*).

WinNet16 Interface

The WinNet16 interface, shown in Figure 29.7, is the earlier set of network-independent APIs included in Windows 3.1 and Windows 95. WinNet16 provides such simple functionality as connecting to a drive letter or redirecting a printer port to a network printer. Windows 98 provides support for using a single WinNet16 driver.

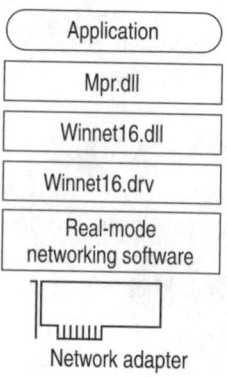

Figure 29.7   WinNet16 interface

If a network vendor provides a WinNet16 network driver developed for Windows 3.1 but has not written a 32-bit network provider and file system driver for Windows 95 or Windows 98, using the WinNet16 interface and Winnet16.dll is the only way to support that network in Windows 98. The WinNet16 driver that currently works with Windows 95 can be used without modification under Windows 98, using the Winnet16.dll.

If Windows 98 Setup detects a Windows 95 or Windows 3.1 installation that uses a WinNet16 network driver and there is no 32-bit network provider available, Windows 98 Setup keeps the 16-bit network driver in place and provides network functionality with the 16-bit network driver installed as the primary network.

Multiple Network Example

Figure 29.8 shows an example of multiple networks. In this example, the user has installed two Windows 98 network clients (Client for Microsoft Networks and Client for NetWare Networks) and has also installed support for a 32-bit Banyan VINES client.

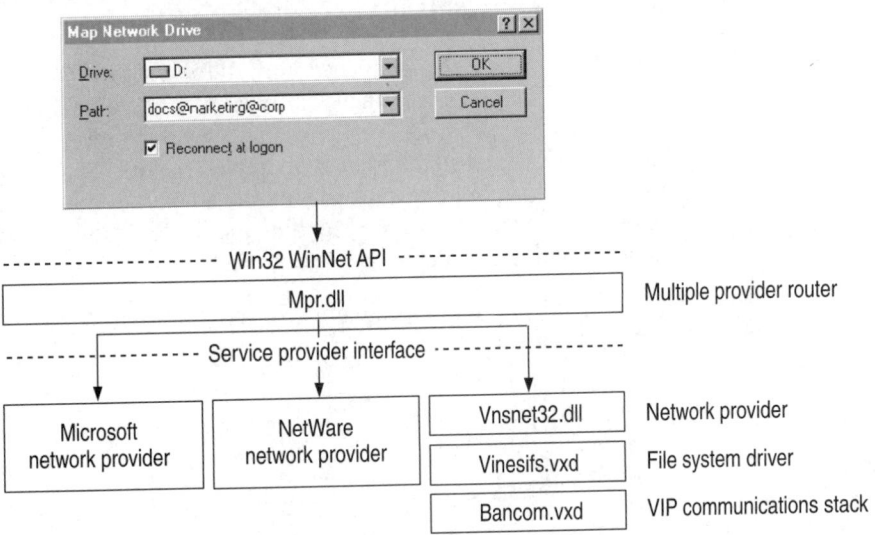

Figure 29.8   Network drive connection request with multiple networks installed

Banyan VINES uses the StreetTalk syntax (*item@group@organization*) to specify file service names. When the multiple provider router receives a request to connect to docs@marketing@corp from a network drive connection dialog box in Windows 98, the multiple provider router submits the request to all installed network providers. The Banyan VINES network provider, Vnsnet32.dll, queries StreetTalk to identify the path as a Banyan object. Then the network provider passes the connection request to the VINES file system driver.

Architecture for the Network Driver Interface Specification

The network driver interface specification (NDIS) describes the interface that network adapter card drivers use to communicate with underlying network interface cards, with overlying protocol drivers, and with the operating system.

Windows 95 included support for NDIS 2.*x* and 3.1 network adapter card and protocol drivers. Windows 98 still supports NDIS 2.*x* and 3.1 drivers, and adds support for extensions defined in NDIS 4.0 and NDIS 5.0.

This section provides technical background information about NDIS support in Windows 98.

NDIS Miniport Architecture

In releases of NDIS before 3.1, adapter drivers implemented not only the media access functionality that was specific to the network adapter card, but also the media access functionality common to all NDIS drivers.

For NDIS 3.1 and later adapter miniport drivers, the Windows 98 NDIS wrapper implements the functionality common to all NDIS drivers. Thus, the miniport driver provided by the adapter manufacturer must implement only the functionality specific to the network adapter. This includes specific details such as establishing communications with the adapter, turning on and off electrical isolation for Plug and Play, providing media detection, and enabling any value-added features the adapter might contain.

Figure 29.9 shows the architecture for NDIS 3.1 or later network adapter and protocol drivers.

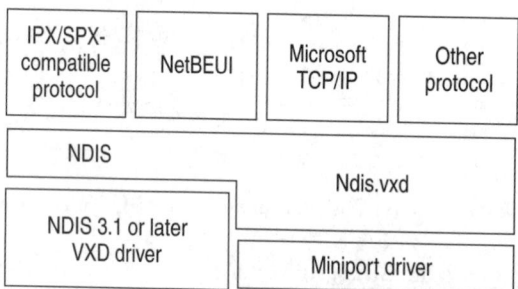

Figure 29.9   Windows 98 architecture for NDIS 3.1 or later protocols

Windows 98 provides miniport binary compatibility between Windows 98 and Windows NT 3.5 and later, so miniport drivers written for one operating system can also be used on the other.

NDIS Architecture for Connection-Oriented Networks and ATM

NDIS 5.0 adds support for connection-oriented networks. This section gives a brief overview of connection-oriented networks and describes the general NDIS architecture for them. Next, it describes the specific NDIS architecture for asynchronous transfer mode (ATM) networks.

NDIS Support for Connection-Oriented Networks

On connectionless networks such as Ethernet networks, computers do not wait to establish a connection before sending packets; they simply forward the packets. Both the sending and receiving computers then perform complex error-checking to ensure the packets arrived at their destination. In contrast, on *connection-oriented networks* such as Integrated Services Digital Network (ISDN) or ATM networks, two computers must establish a connection (sometimes called a virtual circuit [VC]) before either computer can transmit any data. NDIS 5.0 supports multiple virtual circuits on one network adapter. Computers use signaling protocols to establish virtual circuits.

On ATM networks, the signaling protocols may establish a particular *Quality of Service* (QoS), or level of service, during call setup. The QoS parameters defined by the ATM standards are used to negotiate such network attributes as the following:

- Peak bandwidth (average or peak bit rate available).
- Latency (the maximum acceptable delay between transmission of a bit and its receipt by the receiver).
- Delay variation (the difference between a packet's minimum and maximum delay).

Figure 29.10 shows how Windows 98 implements support for connection-oriented networks.

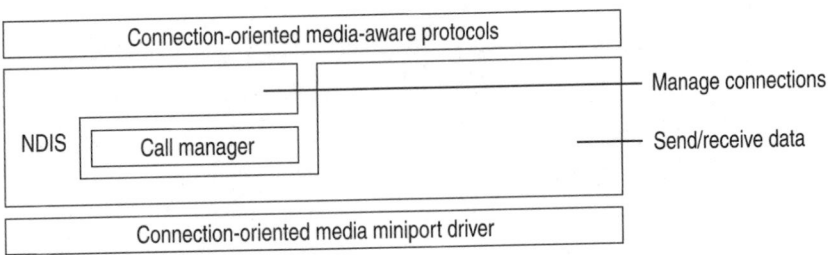

Figure 29.10   Windows 98 architecture for connection-oriented networks

NDIS 5.0 describes three entities in support of connection-oriented media:

Call manager. The call manager implements the media-specific signaling protocol for virtual circuit (connection) management on connection-oriented networks.

Connection-oriented miniport driver. Just as the connectionless local area network (LAN) miniport driver described in "NDIS Miniport Architecture" earlier in this section provides the hardware interface to connectionless media, the connection-oriented miniport driver provides the hardware interface to connection-oriented media.

Note With NDIS 5.0, network adapter driver manufacturers can also create a single driver that provides both call manager and miniport functionality.

Connection-oriented protocol. A connection-oriented protocol uses NDIS to establish and tear down virtual circuits and to send and receive data over those virtual circuits.

Windows 98 Support for ATM Networks

Figure 29.11 shows Windows 98 support for ATM networks.

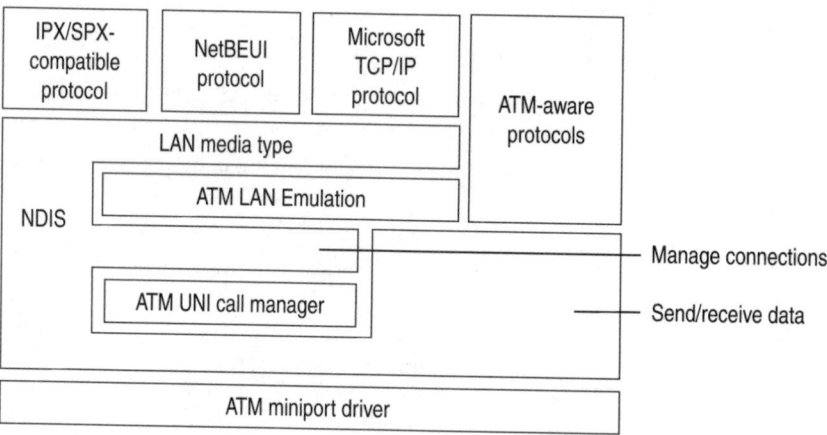

Figure 29.11   Windows 98 support for asynchronous transfer mode

Windows 98 contains the following components to support ATM:

Support for ATM miniport drivers. Windows 98 includes integrated support for many ATM miniport drivers. Microsoft distributes a driver development kit (DDK) and provides compatibility testing programs to ensure support for a variety of ATM adapters.

User-Network Interface (UNI) 3.1 call manager. This call manager complies with the ATM Forum's UNI specification for signaling on an ATM network.

ATM LAN Emulation 1.0. Windows 98 includes a LAN Emulation (LANE) 1.0 module, which works with the LAN Emulation Services on an ATM switch to translate Ethernet addresses into ATM addresses, thus allowing LAN applications and protocols to function transparently on an ATM network.

Native ATM access for kernel-mode drivers. NDIS 5.0 provides an API by which any kernel mode driver can establish and use connections on an ATM network, with full support for ATM's Quality of Service. This will also allow Microsoft to expose native ATM access to Win32-based applications through such network programming APIs as Windows Sockets version 2.0.

Architecture for Network Protocols

Microsoft Windows 98 includes support for Transport Control Protocol/Internet Protocol (TCP/IP), Internetwork Packet Exchange/Sequenced Packet Exchange (IPX/SPX)–compatible protocols, and NetBEUI. The following sections describe how support for each type of protocol is implemented in Windows 98.

Architecture for Microsoft TCP/IP

TCP/IP is a popular routable protocol for wide-area networks (WANs). The TCP/IP module, Vtcp.vxd, is accessible through the Windows Sockets interface or through the NetBIOS interface. For information about Windows Sockets and interprocess communication mechanisms, see "Architecture for Interprocess Communications" later in this chapter.

Figure 29.12 shows the TCP/IP architecture.

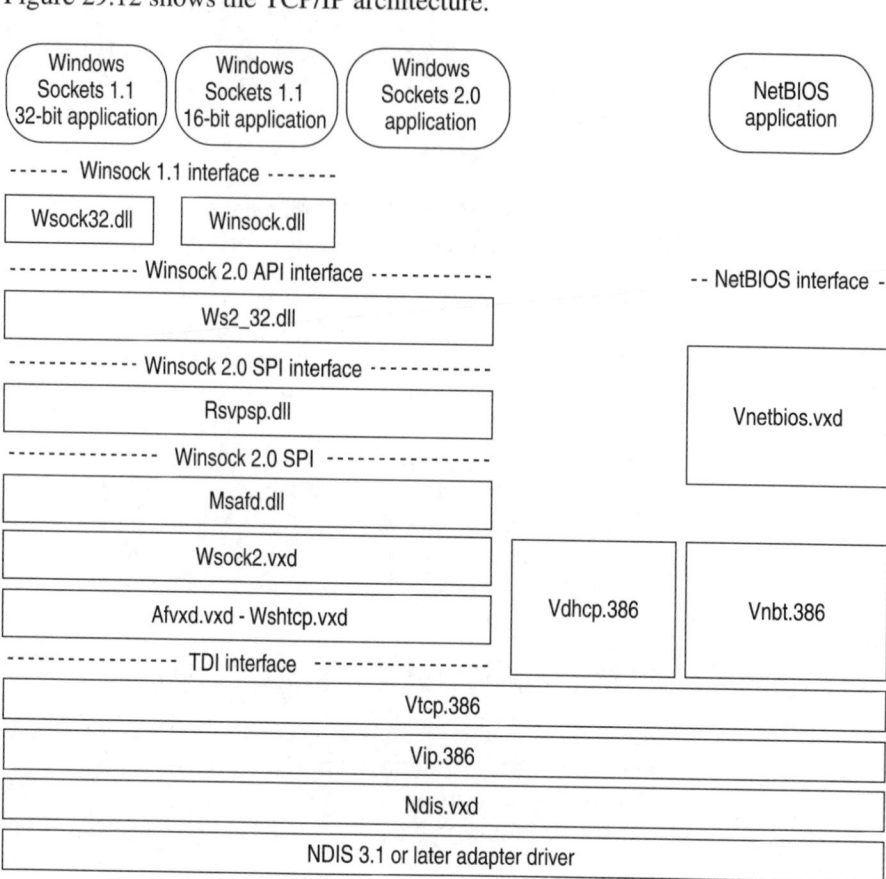

Figure 29.12   Windows 98 architecture for Microsoft TCP/IP

Architecture for the IPX/SPX-Compatible Protocol

The Microsoft IPX/SPX-compatible protocol uses the Nwnblink.vxd module to support NetBIOS over IPX and to support the NetBIOS programming interface. Figure 29.13 shows the architecture for the IPX/SPX-compatible protocol.

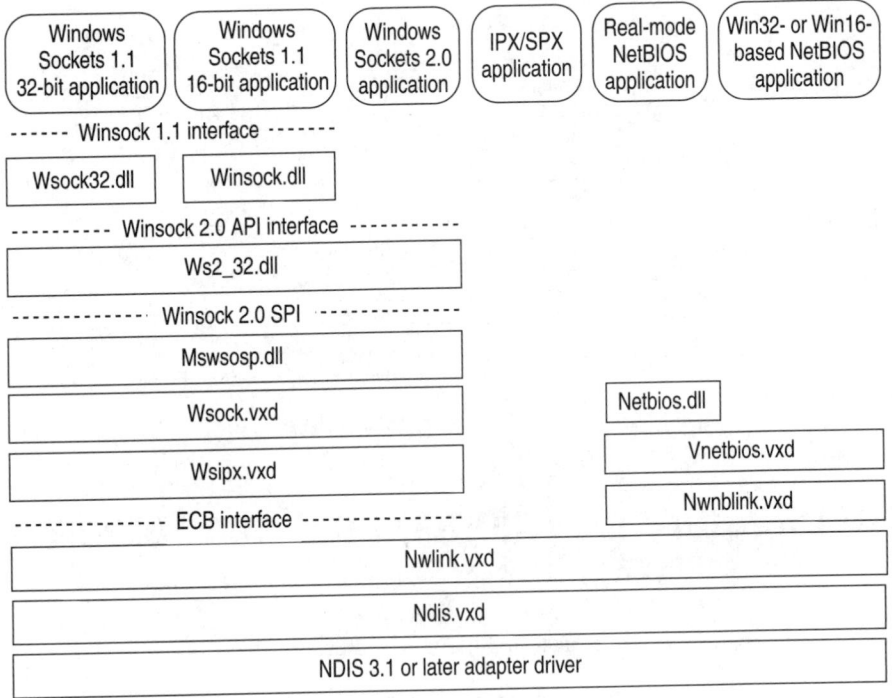

Figure 29.13   Windows 98 architecture for IPX/SPX-compatible protocol

The Microsoft IPX/SPX-compatible protocol is compliant with NDIS 3.1 and later and enables computers running Windows 98 to communicate over a routable IPX-compatible protocol. This protocol can use Novell NetWare servers configured as routers (as well as other IPX routers) to transfer its packets across LANs to access resources on other computers running Windows 98.

Architecture for the NetBEUI Protocol

As Figure 29.14 shows, the NetBEUI module, Netbeui.vxd, implements the NetBIOS framing protocol.

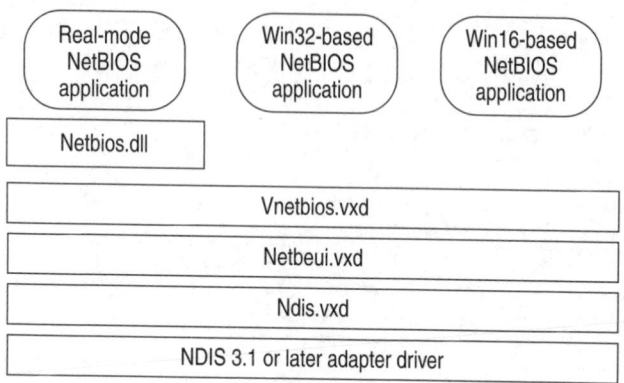

Figure 29.14   Windows 98 architecture for NetBEUI protocol

Architecture for Clients and Peer Servers

You can install either or both of the 32-bit, protected-mode networking clients, Client for Microsoft Networks and Client for NetWare Networks. The following sections describe the architecture for these two clients and the related peer servers.

Figure 29.15 shows the architecture for both network clients.

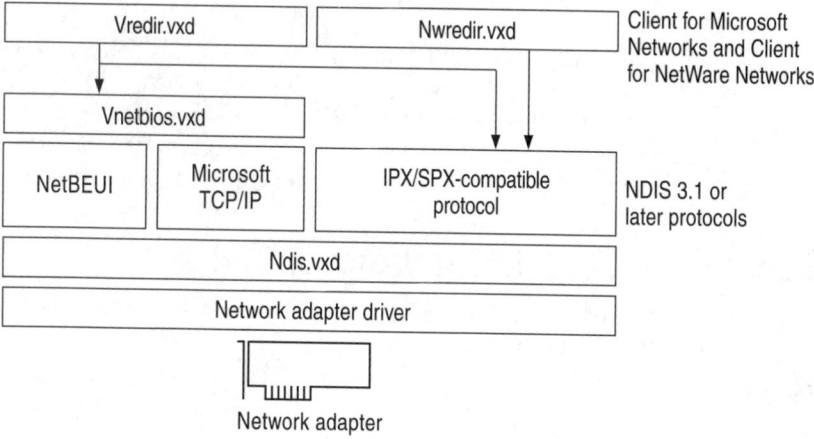

Figure 29.15   Architecture for Client for NetWare Networks used with Client for Microsoft Networks

Client for Microsoft Networks Architecture

Windows 98 provides a 32-bit, protected-mode file system driver to support all Microsoft networking products that use the SMB file sharing protocol. This includes LAN Manager, Windows NT, Windows for Workgroups 3.*x*, Workgroup Add-on for MS-DOS, Windows 95, and Windows 98. Also supported are network products from other vendors using the Microsoft network standard, such as IBM LAN Server, IBM OS/2 Warp Server, and Samba servers. Figure 29.16 shows the architecture for Microsoft networking.

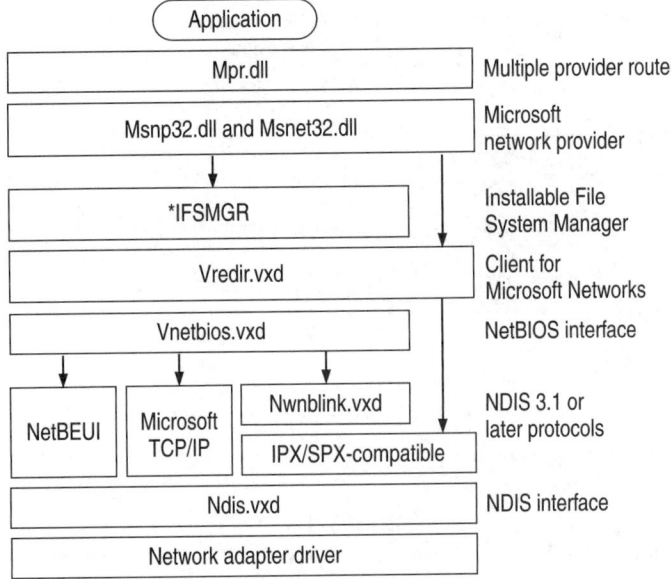

Figure 29.16   Windows 98 architecture for Microsoft networking

Client for Microsoft Networks supports connectivity over any NDIS protocol that supports a NetBIOS interface and is accessible through Vnetbios.vxd. The protected-mode protocols provided with Windows 98 that support a NetBIOS interface are the following:

- NetBEUI using Netbeui.vxd
- NetBIOS over TCP/IP using Vnbt.vxd and the TCP/IP components Vtcp.vxd and Vip.vxd
- NetBIOS over IPX/SPX using Nwnblink.vxd and Nwlink.vxd

Client for Microsoft Networks also supports connectivity over IPX/SPX using Nwlink.vxd without the NetBIOS interface.

Client for NetWare Networks Architecture

You can use Client for NetWare Networks in an environment where all that is needed is a 32-bit client to connect to existing NetWare servers (for example, if there is no need for SMB-based peer resource sharing services). Figure 29.17 shows the architecture for this configuration.

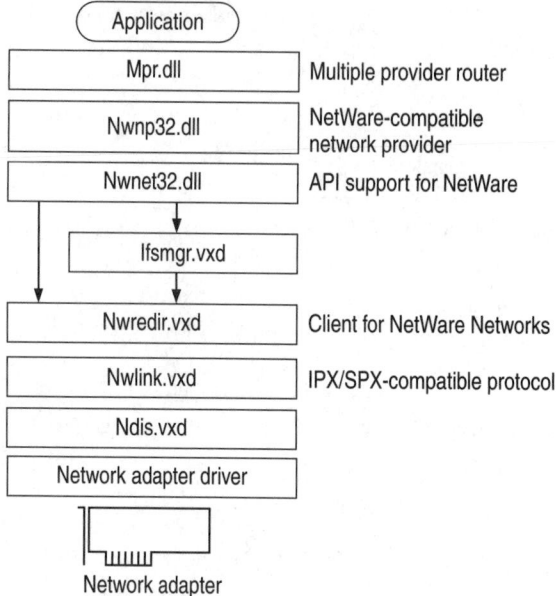

Figure 29.17   Architecture for Client for NetWare Networks as the sole client

For more details about the architecture for Windows 98 with Novell-supplied network clients, see Chapter 17, "Windows 98 on Third-Party Networks."

Architecture for Peer Resource Sharing

Windows 98 includes components to support file and printer sharing on Microsoft networks and NetWare networks.

When File and Printer Sharing for Microsoft Networks is installed, the Windows 98 SMB server (Vserver.vxd) is added to the computer's configuration. This component supports all Microsoft networking products that use the SMB file sharing protocol. Figure 29.18 shows the basic supporting files for File and Printer Sharing for Microsoft Networks in the Windows 98 networking architecture.

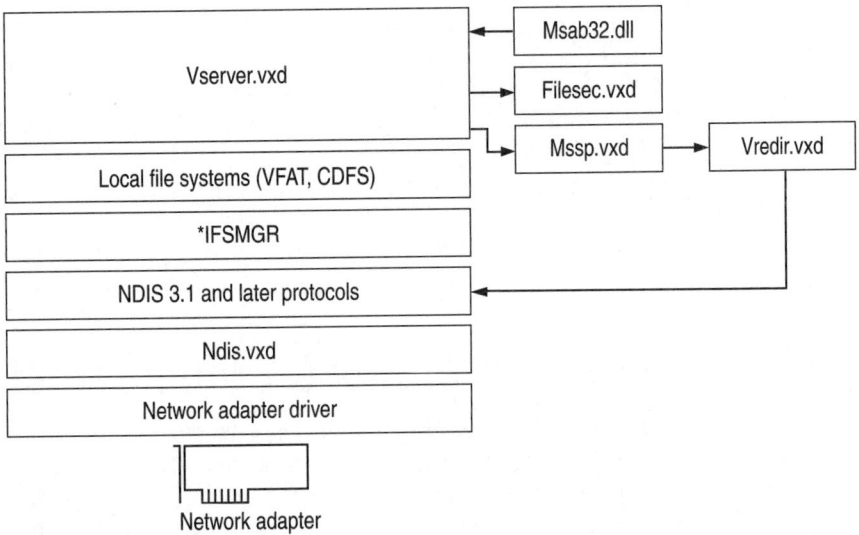

Figure 29.18   Architecture for File and Printer Sharing for Microsoft Networks

When File and Printer Sharing for NetWare Networks is installed, the Windows 98 NCP server (Nwserver.vxd) is added to the computer's configuration. Client for NetWare Networks is used to get NetWare server connection information and to enable user-level security based on a NetWare server's user accounts. Figure 29.19 shows the supporting files for File and Printer Sharing for NetWare Networks in the Windows 98 networking architecture.

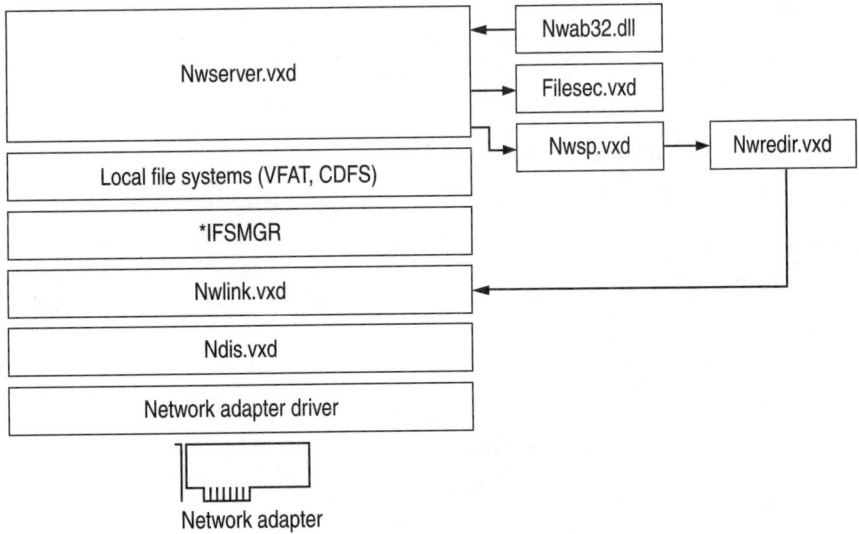

Figure 29.19   Architecture for File and Printer Sharing for NetWare Networks

For file and printer sharing services with user-level security, the security provider (Mssp.vxd or Nwsp.vxd) assists in validating user access when sharing a resource and in retrieving a user list when administrating the server. The network address book (Msab32.dll or Nwab32.dll) translates the account lists from the server and provides the **Add Users** dialog box for selecting which users get access rights. The file security component (Filesec.vxd) provides access control based on information in the registry. Notice that these same security components support features such as remote registry access even when file and printer sharing services are not present.

Architecture for Interprocess Communication

Windows 98 includes several mechanisms that support distributed computing. Typically, *distributed computing* means that a computing task (or process) is divided into two parts. The first part runs on the client computer and requires minimal resources. The other part of the process runs on the server and requires large amounts of data, number crunching, or specialized hardware.

Another type of distributed computing spreads the work among multiple computers. For example, one computer can work on a complex mathematical problem that would take a month to solve. But with distributed computing, 50 computers could work on the same problem simultaneously and solve it in less than a day.

In both cases, a connection between computers at a process-to-process level allows data to flow in both directions. Windows 98 includes the following interprocess communication (IPC) mechanisms to support distributed computing: Windows Sockets, remote procedure calls (RPCs), NetBIOS, named pipes, mailslots, and the Distributed Component Object Model (DCOM). The following sections provide details about these IPC implementations in Windows 98.

Windows Sockets 2.0

Windows Sockets is a Windows implementation of the widely used U.C. Berkeley Sockets API, the *de facto* standard for accessing datagram and session services over TCP/IP. Non-NetBIOS applications must be written to the Sockets interface to access Microsoft TCP/IP protocols. Applications written to the Sockets interface include File Transfer Protocol (FTP) and Simple Network Management Protocol (SNMP).

Windows Sockets in Windows 98 is a protocol-independent networking API tailored for use by programmers using the Windows family of products. Windows Sockets is a public specification that aims to do the following:

- Provide a familiar networking API to programmers using Windows or UNIX.

- Offer binary compatibility between heterogeneous Windows-based TCP/IP stack and utility vendors.

- Support both connection-oriented and connectionless protocols.

Windows 95 included the Windows Sockets version1.1 interface. Windows 98 includes a new version of Windows Sockets, Windows Sockets version 2.0. Windows Sockets 2.0 extends the Windows Sockets 1.1 interface to provide access to networks other than TCP/IP and to support real-time multimedia communications.

Note In Windows 95, both TCP/IP and IPX/SPX supported the Windows Sockets 1.1 interface. In Windows 98, only TCP/IP supports the Windows Sockets 2.0 interface. IPX/SPX still supports the Windows Sockets 1.1 interface.

Windows Sockets 2.0 provides the following enhancements over Windows Sockets 1.1:

Name registration and resolution. Windows Sockets 2.0 provides an interface that applications can use to access many different name spaces, such as DNS, NDS, X.500, and SAP.

Support for multimedia. Windows Sockets 2.0 provides several multimedia enhancements, including Quality of Service (QoS), which enables different applications to request different network characteristics.

Protocol-independent multipoint and multicast. Windows Sockets 2.0 enables applications to transparently take advantage of the multipoint and multicast capabilities of transport stacks that provide those capabilities.

Windows Sockets 2.0 Architecture

Windows Sockets 2.0 is a Windows Open Systems Architecture (WOSA)–compliant interface that enables a front-end application and a back-end service to communicate without having to speak each other's language.

As Figure 29.20 shows, the Windows Sockets 2.0 interface includes the following components:

- The Windows Sockets 2.0 API

- The Windows Sockets 2.0 DLL (Ws2_32.dll)

- The Windows Sockets 2.0 SPI (which defines transport providers and name space service providers)
- Layered service providers (optional)

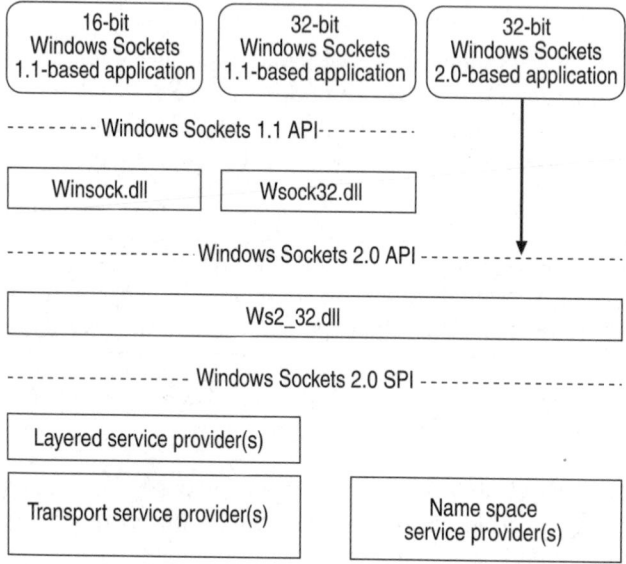

Figure 29.20   Windows Sockets 2.0 architecture

Windows Sockets 2.0 API

The Windows Sockets 2.0 API sits between the Windows Sockets 2.0 DLL and either a Windows Sockets 2.0–based application or a Windows Sockets 1.1 DLL. It provides backward compatibility with the Windows Sockets 1.1 API and adds such new APIs as Generic Quality of Service (GQoS) APIs. For more information about the GQoS APIs, see "Generic Quality of Service and Resource Reservation Protocol" later in this chapter.

Layered Service Provider Layer

The optional layered service provider layer can be inserted between the Windows Sockets 2.0 DLL and the underlying protocol stack. It can extend the underlying protocol stack by providing additional services such as authentication, encryption, or proxy server services. In Windows Sockets 1.1, application developers added such services by replacing and renaming the Windows Sockets DLL or by inserting themselves in an application's process address table in place of the Windows Sockets DLL. These methods will no longer work with Windows Sockets 2.0, and layered service providers should be used instead.

The Resource Reservation Protocol (RSVP), which handles QoS requests, can be implemented as a layered service provider layer but is implemented as a transport service provider in Windows 98.

Windows Sockets 2.0 SPI Transport Service Providers

Transport service providers enable applications to use a consistent interface for accessing multiple transport protocols. Above the transport service provider, the Windows Sockets 2.0 DLL takes requests from applications and sends those requests to the transport service provider. The Windows Sockets 2.0 DLL also provides traffic management. The transport service provider then supports one or more transport protocols.

In Windows 98, RSVP is implemented as a base transport provider. For more information about RSVP, see "Generic Quality of Service and Resource Reservation Protocol" later in this chapter.

Windows Sockets 2.0 SPI Name Space Service Providers

Name space service providers enable servers (services) and client applications to use a consistent interface for multiple name services. Services register with the Windows Sockets DLL, and client applications send the Windows Sockets DLL requests for the names of those services. The Windows Sockets DLL manages registration and loading of name space service providers and sends name space operations to the correct provider. Finally, the provider implements an interface with existing name services, such as Domain Name System (DNS).

Generic Quality of Service and Resource Reservation Protocol

Connectionless networks such as Ethernet networks make only a best effort to deliver packets to their destination. There is no guarantee that packets will arrive, or that they will arrive in the correct order. Instead, such protocols as TCP/IP were developed to ensure retransmission of lost packets and to ensure that out-of-order packets could be reassembled in the correct order. This is sufficient for most applications, such as e-mail. However, for newer applications, such as real-time audio and video, packets must arrive on time and in order or the transmission might be garbled.

Connection-oriented networks, on the other hand, can enable applications to request certain levels of service (Quality of Service, or QoS) such as bandwidth and reliability for specific connections. Additionally, they enable computers to set up several different connections with several different Qualities of Service. For example, on a connection-oriented network you could have two simultaneous connections: a high-delay connection to send e-mail and a high-bandwidth, low-delay connection for a videoconferencing application.

Windows 98 makes this possible through its Generic Quality of Service (GQoS) APIs and its support for the Resource Reservation Protocol (RSVP). Through the GQoS APIs, applications can request different network characteristics for a connection. RSVP then handles those requests by attempting to make bandwidth "reservations" for that connection.

This section briefly discusses GQoS and RSVP. For more information about GQoS, see the specification on **http://www.microsoft.com/**. See also **ftp://microsoft.com/bussys/winsock/winsock2/**. For more information about RSVP, see the Internet Engineering Task Force (IETF) RSVP specification at **http://www.ietf.org/**.

Generic Quality of Service

The Generic Quality of Service (GQoS) APIs in Windows Sockets 2.0 provide access to most common attributes of various QoS implementations without requiring specific knowledge of the underlying QoS providers. Applications can make calls to GQoS APIs and request such attributes as the following:

- Peak bandwidth (average or peak bit rate available).
- Latency (the maximum acceptable delay between transmission of a bit and its receipt by the receiver).
- Delay variation (the difference between a packet's minimum and maximum delay).

Figure 29.21 shows the architecture of QoS.

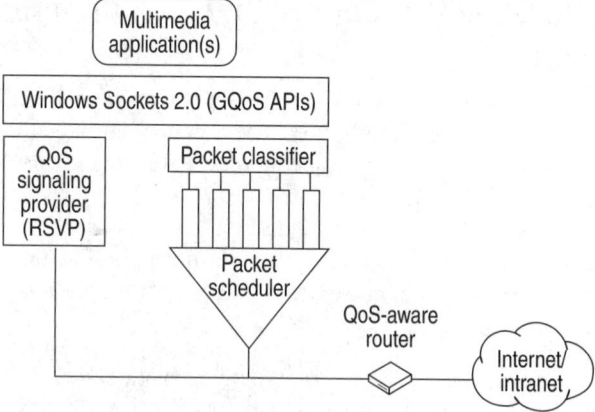

Figure 29.21   Quality of Service architecture

As Figure 29.21 shows, multimedia applications request the QoS attributes. The Resource Reservation Protocol (RSVP) signaling provider (discussed in "Resource Reservation Protocol" later in this chapter) then negotiates with the network for the requested attributes. The packet classifier and scheduler determine when to send the packets and with what priority. Finally, the QoS-aware router forwards the packets as requested.

Resource Reservation Protocol

The Resource Reservation Protocol (RSVP) is installed during the Windows 98 installation of Windows Sockets 2.0. It handles QoS requests, reserving network bandwidth when possible and when requested, and then ensuring that the network can provide that bandwidth. Figure 29.22 shows how RSVP works.

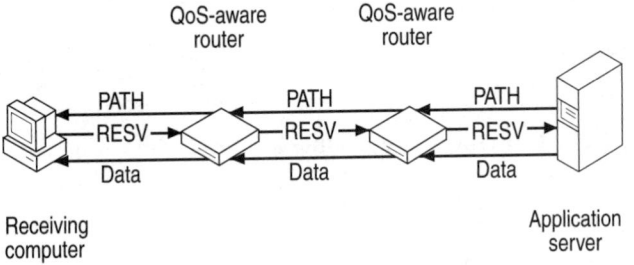

Figure 29.22   Resource Reservation Protocol

First, the receiving computer sends a non-RSVP request to the application server. Then the application server tells RSVP to send a PATH statement to the receiving computer. The PATH statement tells the receiving computer the path the data should follow and whether the requested characteristics are available. Next, the receiving computer sends a RESV statement, which reserves network bandwidth at each hop (at each RSVP-aware router or switch) along the way. The application server then transmits data with the required QoS characteristics.

As Figure 29.23 shows, RSVP can also be used to reserve bandwidth for multicast broadcasts. As in the previous case, the receiving computer uses RSVP to request bandwidth, and the application server sends out a PATH statement. In this case, the application server sends out only one PATH statement to multiple receiving computers, thus conserving network bandwidth. Computers on the network that did not send RSVP requests will not receive the broadcast.

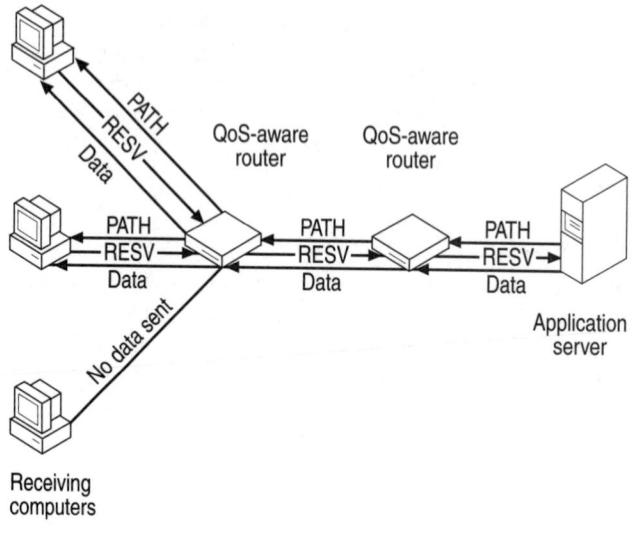

Figure 29.23   Resource Reservation Protocol with multicast

Supporting Files

Table 29.1 shows Windows Sockets supporting files.

Table 29.1   Windows Sockets supporting files

File	Description	Comments
WinSock.dll	16-bit Windows Sockets	Provides backward compatibility with existing 16-bit TCP/IP Windows Sockets applications (Windows Sockets 1.1 interface)
Ws2thk.dll	16- and 32-bit Windows Sockets Thunk	Thunking layer to convert 16-bit Windows Sockets API to 32-bit Windows Sockets API
Wsock32.dll	32-bit Windows Sockets 1.1	Provides backward compatibility with existing 32-bit TCP/IP Windows Sockets applications (Windows Sockets 1.1 interface)
Ws2_32.dll	32-bit Windows Sockets 2.0	Windows Sockets 2.0 application programming interface
Ws2help.dll	Operating system–dependent support for Windows Sockets 2.0	Abstracts operating system–dependent functionality in Windows Sockets 2.0 API library
Msafd.dll	TDI transport service provider	Microsoft Windows Sockets 2.0 transport service provider for transport, exposing TDI interface (currently TCP/IP)

Table 29.1   Windows Sockets supporting files (*continued*)

File	Description	Comments
Mswsosp.dll	Windows Sockets 1.1 transport service provider	Microsoft Windows Sockets 2.0 transport service provider for Windows Sockets 1.1–compatible transports (currently IPX/SPX). Supports only Windows Sockets 1.1 functionality.
Mswsock.dll	Windows Sockets 1.1 extensions	Microsoft extensions that are not part of general (supported by all providers) Windows Sockets 2.0 specifications but were present in Windows Sockets 1.1
Rnr20.dll	TCP/IP name space service provider	Microsoft Windows Sockets 2.0 TCP/IP name service provider.
Wsock2.vxd	Windows Sockets 2.0 transport service provider	Kernel mode support for Windows Sockets 2.0–compatible transport service providers (currently only TCP/IP)
Wsock.vxd	Windows Sockets 1.1 transport service provider	Kernel mode support for Windows Sockets 1.1–compatible transport service providers (currently only IPX/SPX)
Afvxd.vxd	TDI transport service provider	Kernel mode support for Windows Sockets 2.0 transport service provider exposing TDI interface (currently only TCP/IP)
Wshtcp.vxd	TCP/IP TDI transport support	Supports TCP/IP-specific functionality for Microsoft TDI transport service provider for Windows Sockets 2.0
Wsipx.vxd	Windows Sockets over IPX/SPX	Supports IPX/SPX Windows Sockets 1.1–compatible transport

If you are interested in developing a Windows Sockets 2.0–based application, specifications for Windows Sockets 2.0 are available on the Internet from **ftp://ftp.microsoft.com/** and on the MSDN compact disc. For more information, visit **http://www.microsoft.com/msdn/**.

Remote Procedure Calls

The Microsoft remote procedure call (RPC) facility is compatible with the Open Software Foundation (OSF) distributed computing environment (DCE) specification for remote procedure calls and is completely interoperable with other DCE-based RPC systems, such as those for Hewlett-Packard and IBM AIX systems. (The RPC facility is compatible but not *compliant* with the OSF specification—that is, it does not start with and build on the OSF source code).

RPC uses other IPC mechanisms, such as named pipes, NetBIOS, or Windows Sockets, to establish communications between the client and the server. With the RPC facility, essential program logic and related procedure code can exist on different computers, which is important for distributed applications.

As Figure 29.24 shows, Windows 98 provides RPC client support over the NetBIOS, named pipes, and Windows Sockets interfaces.

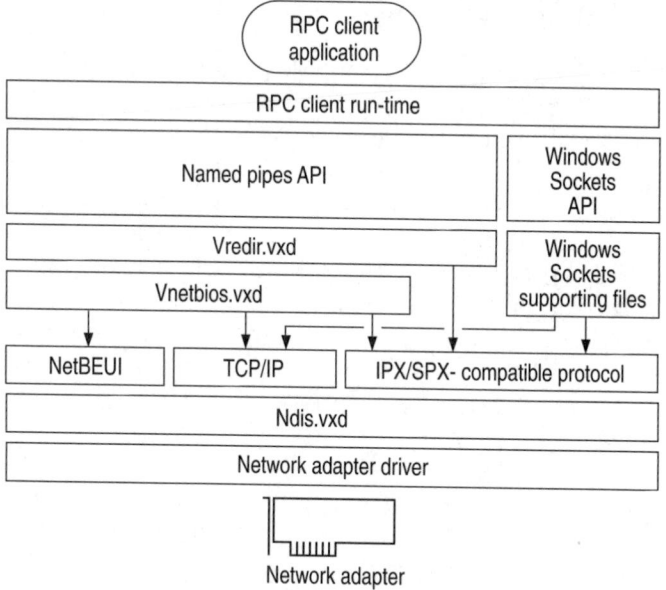

Figure 29.24   Remote procedure call client support in Windows 98

Figure 29.25 shows how Windows 98 provides RPC server support over NetBIOS and Windows Sockets. There is no server support for RPC over named pipes. With an RPC application using named pipes, the client can be run on Windows 98, but the server must be run on Windows NT.

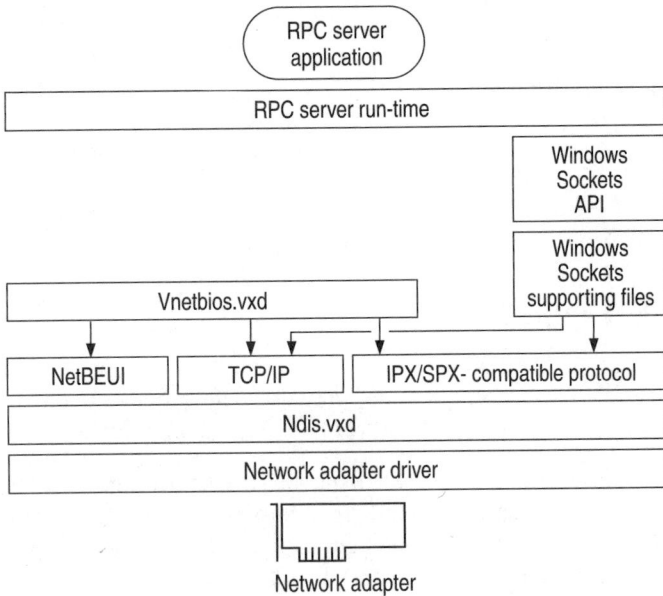

Figure 29.25   Remote procedure call server support in Windows 98

NetBIOS

NetBIOS can be used in Windows 98 for communication between protocols and upper-level software, such as the redirector and server service. NetBIOS provides backward compatibility for existing NetBIOS applications. It provides a protocol-independent way of creating sessions and datagrams, and supporting name resolution over multiple protocols. NetBIOS is supported by the Microsoft TCP/IP, NetBEUI, and IPX/SPX-compatible protocols in Windows 98. The additional NetBIOS driver and DLL allow Windows 98 to be compatible with NetBIOS applications and to run software that specifically requires NetBIOS. The NetBIOS software is used only for these situations.

NetBIOS defines the interface between the redirector and the protocol layers. The NetBIOS interface is a set of function calls that allow an application (such as the redirector in the Windows 98 protected-mode network client) to use the services of a transport-layer service provider, such as the NetBEUI protocol driver.

Many network applications use NetBIOS to send commands to the protocol driver. As long as a protocol driver recognizes NetBIOS commands issued by an application, that protocol driver can be used with any NetBIOS application. The NetBIOS interface in Windows 98 (Netbios.dll and Vnetbios.vxd) is supported by all three protocols provided with Windows 98.

The architecture for NetBIOS over the various protocols is described with the respective protocols earlier in this chapter.

Client-Side Named Pipes

Named pipes provide backward compatibility with existing LAN Manager installations and applications. Windows 98 supports client-side named pipes for Microsoft networks. Server-side named pipes are not supported.

Client for Microsoft Networks makes the named pipes API available for applications that use named pipes for IPC. However, Client for Microsoft Networks does not provide named pipes support for other networks, such as Novell NetWare and Banyan VINES. A user who needs Novell NetWare or Banyan VINES named pipes support must use the real-mode terminate-and-stay-residents (TSRs) and network components provided by Novell or Banyan.

Named pipes provide an easy-to-access conduit for a one-to-one, reliable, connection-oriented data transfer between two processes. These two processes are normally differentiated as a client process and a server process. The term *server* as applied to the server process in a named pipe application does not refer to the "server service" that is a component of the network operating system, although the server service may be involved in making the named pipe available to other computers.

- The named pipe server process creates the pipe and manages access to it. The resources that make up the pipe are owned by the server process and physically exist on the computer where the server process is running.

- The named pipe client process uses the services of the underlying network protocols to access the remote pipe resources.

Although named pipes are usually used bidirectionally, a named pipe can be configured to allow communication in only one direction, such as from server to client.

A common use for named pipes is in client/server applications based on the Structured Query Language (SQL). The SQL client application can be run on a computer running Client for Microsoft Networks. The Microsoft SQL Server application, however, must be set up on a LAN Manager, Windows NT, or other named pipes server.

Mailslots

Mailslots provide backward compatibility with existing LAN Manager installations and applications. Mailslot APIs in Windows 98 and Windows NT are a subset of the APIs in Microsoft OS/2 LAN Manager. Client for Microsoft Networks makes the mailslots API available for applications that use mailslots for interprocess communication (IPC).

Mailslots can be used for one-to-one or one-to-many communication. A mailslot can be created on any network computer. When a message is sent to a mailslot, the sending application specifies in the mailslot message structure whether the message is to be sent using first-class or second-class delivery.

First-class delivery is a session-oriented, guaranteed data transfer for one-to-one or one-to-many communication. Messages designated as first-class delivery can be sent only to a mailslot created on a server. (Windows 98 does not use first-class messaging.)

Second-class delivery is a datagram-based, unguaranteed data transfer for one-to-one or one-to-many communication. Messages designated as second-class delivery can be sent to a mailslot created on any computer, or even on multiple computers, if the message size is 400 bytes or less.

Windows 98 and Windows NT implement only second-class mailslots, which are most useful for identifying other computers or services on a network and for wide-scale identification of a service. Windows 98 uses second-class mailslots for WinPopup messages and browsing.

Distributed Component Object Model

The *Distributed Component Object Model (DCOM)* extends the Component Object Model (COM) to allow components of a distributed application to communicate over the network securely and transparently.

With DCOM, application developers can create location-independent distributed applications using a language of their choice, such as Java, Microsoft Visual Basic, or Microsoft Visual C++. Network administrators can then deploy those components on Windows 98 computers, Windows NT Server computers, and Windows NT Workstation computers anywhere in the network.

DCOM provides several benefits and optimizations, including the following:

- Renders the complexity of underlying network invisible to application components.

- Provides administrative options to enable remote use of existing COM applications.

- Provides a high level of control over such security mechanisms as permissions and authentication.

- Provides two-way, symmetric communication.

DCOM is based on the COM model. COM provides a binary model for components and a protocol for communicating with components. Clients and components can communicate with one another in one of three ways:

Method 1. If clients and components are in the same apartment, they can communicate directly. (For information about apartments, see Knowledge Base Article Q150777, "INFO: Descriptions and Workings of OLE Threading Models.")

Method 2. If clients and components are in a different process but on the same computer, COM injects itself between the client and the component and uses a local interprocess communication (LPC).

Figure 29.26 shows how COM is used within a single computer. Component A, a client component, calls component B, a server component.

Note Components that call other components are called *client components*, whereas components that are called by other components are called *server components*. Client and server components can reside on the same computer and be part of the same application.

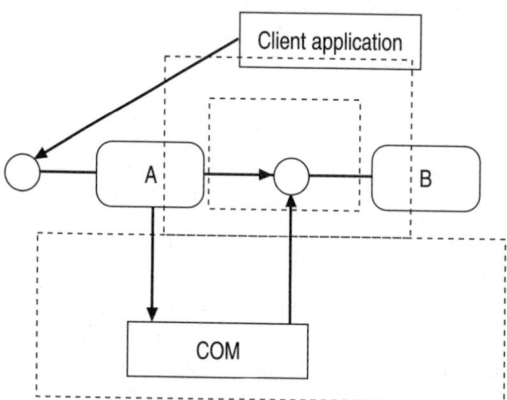

Figure 29.26   Component Object Model used in a single computer

Method 3. If the client and the component are on different computers, they still communicate with each other in the same way. However, in this case, DCOM injects itself between the client and component and uses RPC. Figure 29.27 shows this configuration.

Component A, located on one computer, uses DCOM to call component B, located on another computer.

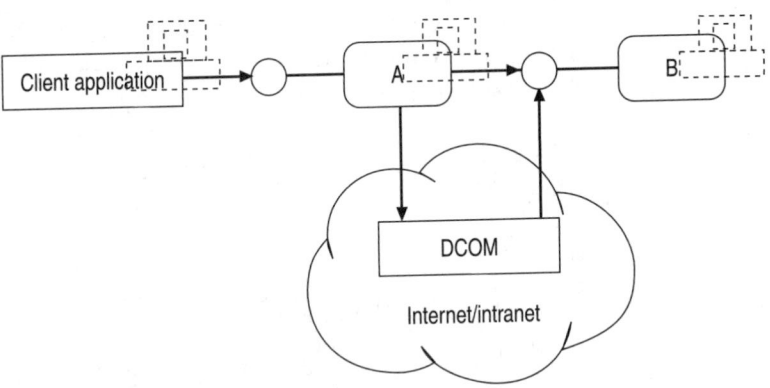

Figure 29.27   Distributed Component Object Model used on a network

DCOM shields the client and the component from the network protocol, so the client and the component are unaffected. Thus, COM components can be reused without modification. In addition, any number of components can also be distributed across any number of computers. Also, DCOM hides the location of the component and enables components to be moved without changes to the source code and without recompilation.

To download the COM standard, visit **ftp://ftp.microsoft.com/developr/drg /OLE-info/COMSpecification/**.

For more information about COM, and to download the informational DCOM Request for Comments (RFC), go to **http://www.microsoft.com/com/**.

Architecture for Communications and Remote Networking

This section describes the following topics:

- Serial Communications architecture
- Dial-Up Networking architecture
- Point-to-Point Tunneling Protocol (PPTP) architecture

Serial Communications Architecture

Windows 98 separates communications operations into three primary areas:
Win32 communications APIs and the Telephony API (TAPI), the universal
modem driver, and communications port drivers. Figure 29.28 shows the
communications architecture.

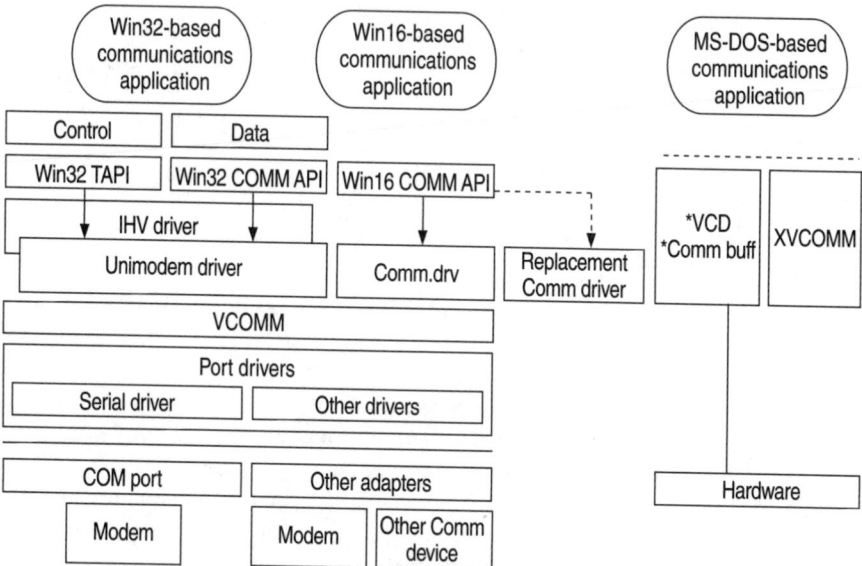

Figure 29.28   Serial Communications architecture

VCOMM is a communications device driver that provides protected-mode
services allowing Windows-based applications and drivers to use ports and
modems. To conserve system resources, communications drivers are loaded
into memory only when in use by applications. Also, VCOMM uses Plug and
Play services in Windows 98 to assist with configuration and installation of
communications devices.

Figure 29.28 also illustrates the flow path for a Win16-based application to show
how compatibility is maintained when hardware or software vendors replace the
Windows 3.1 Comm.drv driver. The vendor-specific communications driver,
however, communicates directly with the I/O port, rather than through VCOMM.

The following paragraphs describe the primary areas that make up the
architecture.

Win32 communications APIs and TAPI. The Win32 communications APIs in Windows 98 provide an interface for using modems and communications devices in a device-independent fashion. Applications call the Win32 communications APIs to configure modems and perform data I/O through them. Through the Windows Telephony API (TAPI), applications can control modems or other telephony devices.

Universal modem driver. The *universal modem driver* (Unimodem) is a layer that provides services for data and fax modems and for voice so that users and application developers will not have to learn or maintain difficult modem AT commands to dial, answer, and configure modems. Rather, Unimodem does these tasks automatically by using miniport drivers written by modem hardware vendors.

Unimodem is both a VCOMM device driver and a TAPI service provider. Other service providers (for example, those supporting other devices, such as an ISDN adapter, a telephone on a PBX system, or an AT-command modem) can also be used with TAPI.

Port drivers. Port drivers are specifically responsible for communicating with I/O ports, which are accessed through the VCOMM device driver. Port drivers provide a layered approach to device communications. For example, Windows 98 provides a port driver to communicate with serial communications and parallel ports, and other vendors can provide port drivers to communicate with their own hardware adapters, such as multiport communications adapters. With the port driver model in Windows 95 and Windows 98, it is not necessary for vendors to replace the communications subsystem as they did in Windows 3.1.

Windows Telephony API. TAPI-aware communications applications no longer need to provide their own modem support list because interaction with a modem is now centralized by Windows 98. All communications services provided with Windows 98 use these services.

TAPI provides a standard way for communications applications to control telephony functions for data, fax, and voice calls. TAPI manages all signaling between a computer and a telephone network, including basic functions such as dialing, answering, and hanging up a call. It also includes supplementary functions, such as hold, transfer, conference, and call park found in PBX, ISDN, and other telephone systems. TAPI also provides access to features specific to certain service providers, with built-in extensibility to accommodate future telephony features and networks as they become available.

TAPI services arbitrate requests from communications applications to share communications ports and devices cooperatively. Win32-based applications can use TAPI functionality to make outgoing calls while others are waiting for incoming calls. Of course, only one call can be performed at a time, but users no longer have to close applications that are using the same communications port.

TAPI consists of two interfaces: an API that developers use to write applications and the service provider interface (SPI) that applications use to establish the connection to the specific telephone network. This model resembles the computer industry model for printers, in that printer manufacturers provide printer drivers for Windows-based applications. Figure 29.29 shows the relationship between the front-end TAPI and the back-end SPI.

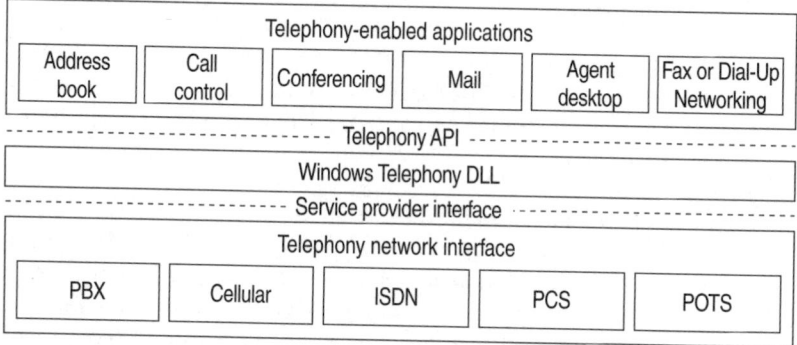

Figure 29.29   Telephony API and service provider interface

Dial-Up Networking Architecture

Windows 98 includes several new components in its Dial-Up Networking architecture. This section gives an overview of the new architecture and then breaks it down into the following areas:

- Dial-Up Networking call control
- Dial-Up Networking data transfer
- Point-to-Point Tunneling Protocol (PPTP) call control
- PPTP data transfer

For more conceptual information about Dial-Up Networking and PPTP, see Chapter 19, "Remote Networking and Mobile Computing."

Dial-Up Networking Overview

This section describes many of the components included in the Dial-Up Networking architecture, which is shown in Figure 29.30.

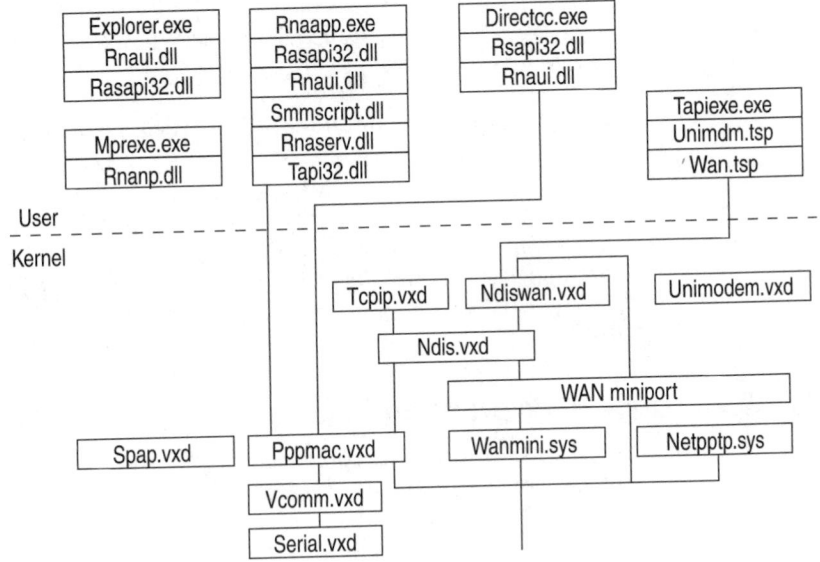

Figure 29.30   Dial-Up Networking architecture

Following are descriptions of the major user-mode components in this architecture.

Rnaui.dll. An Explorer extension that implements the Dial-Up Networking folder and invokes Rnaapp.exe to dial.

Rasapi32.dll. The main Windows 98 RAS API DLL. It supports the Phonebook APIs.

Smmscript.dll. Implements the session manager modules (SMMs), which enable new dial-up protocol implementations to be rolled under the RAS API and the user interface.

Rnanp.dll. A Windows 98 network provider DLL.

Directcc.exe. The Direct Cable Connect alternative user interface for connecting computers directly, using a serial or parallel cable. The first time it is run, it creates modem entries that are hidden from the Modems option in Control Panel but appear in the System option.

Following are descriptions of the major kernel-mode components in this architecture.

Pppmac.vxd. Implements the core RAS protocols: PPP, SLIP, Asynchronous NetBEUI, and NetWare Connect.

Ndiswan.vxd. Supports network driver interface specification wide area network (NDISWAN) miniport drivers. It is installed as a protocol and appears in the Network option in Control Panel as a protocol. Each adapter that is installed is bound to the NDISWAN protocol, and NDISWAN miniports bind only to the NDISWAN protocol.

Dial-Up Networking Call Control and Data Transfer

Figure 29.31 shows how the components of Dial-Up Networking work together when Dial-Up Networking is setting up a call over a modem or ISDN device.

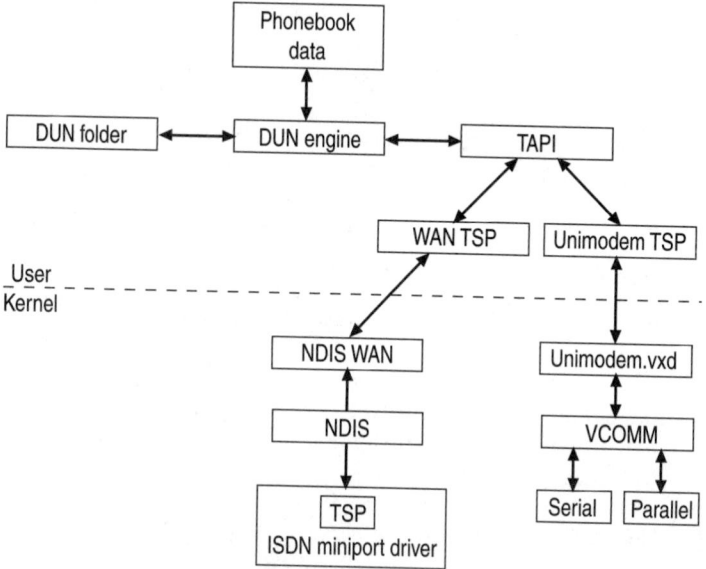

Figure 29.31   Call control for modems and Integrated Services Digital Network devices

To set up a connection over a modem, a user first starts a Dial-Up Networking connection. The Dial-Up Networking engine looks for information about the telephone call in the Phonebook and then queries TAPI for the available TAPI devices. Next, it places a call on the device specified in the Phonebook entry. TAPI translates the device to the correct TAPI service provider (TSP) (in this case, the Unimodem TSP). The Unimodem TSP translates the Dial-Up Networking command to specific modem commands, and then sends the modem commands to Unimodem.vxd. Unimodem.vxd sends them to VCOMM, which sends them out a serial or parallel port to a modem.

The process is similar for an ISDN card. However, TAPI uses the WAN TSP rather than the Unimodem TSP. The WAN TSP passes the commands through NDISWAN and to the ISDN driver's TSP, and the ISDN driver's TSP translates the commands.

Figure 29.32 shows an example of what happens after a call has been set up and data is being transferred. This example shows data transfer over a modem.

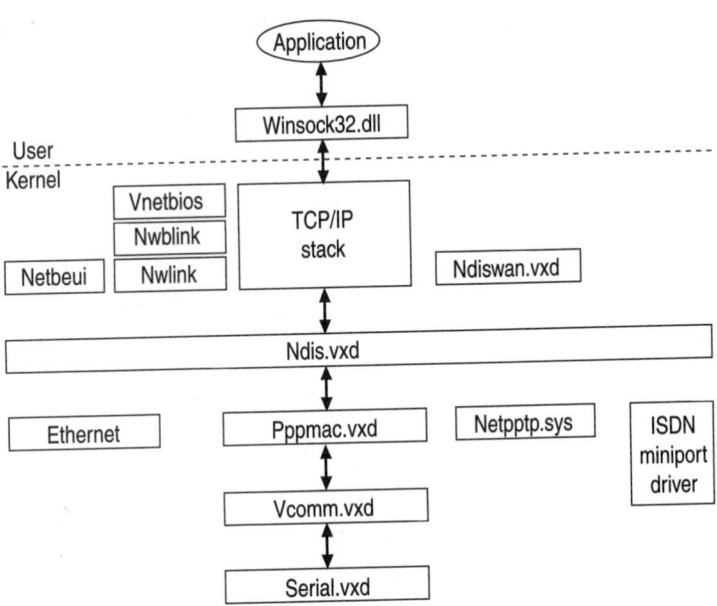

Figure 29.32   Data transfer for modems

In this example, data is sent through the Windows Sockets DLL. The TCP/IP stack then encapsulates the data in TCP and Internet Protocol (IP) and then sends it to Pppmac.vxd (the component that implements the RAS protocols). Finally, Pppmac.vxd encapsulates the packet in a PPP frame and sends it to VCOMM.

Point-to-Point Tunneling Protocol Call Control and Data Transfer

Virtual private networking (VPN) is a secure method for creating an on-demand connection between two computers in different locations. The virtual private network consists of the two computers (one computer at each end of the connection) and a route, or *tunnel*, over the public or private network. Virtual private networking is implemented in Windows 98 using the Point-to-Point Tunneling Protocol (PPTP).

This section describes the Windows 98 architecture that supports virtual private networking.

For more detailed information about virtual private networking, see Chapter 19, "Remote Networking and Mobile Computing."

Figure 29.33 shows call control for a PPTP connection over a modem. Contrast this diagram with Figure 29.31, which showed call control for an ordinary Dial-Up Networking connection. In Figure 29.31, the call request passes through the Unimodem TSP. In Figure 29.33, it passes through the WAN TSP instead.

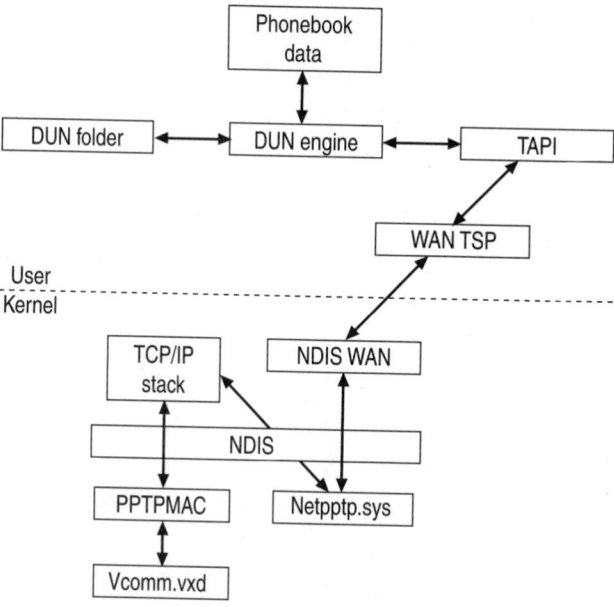

Figure 29.33   Call control for a Point-to-Point Tunneling Protocol tunnel over a modem

Figure 29.34 shows PPTP data transfer.

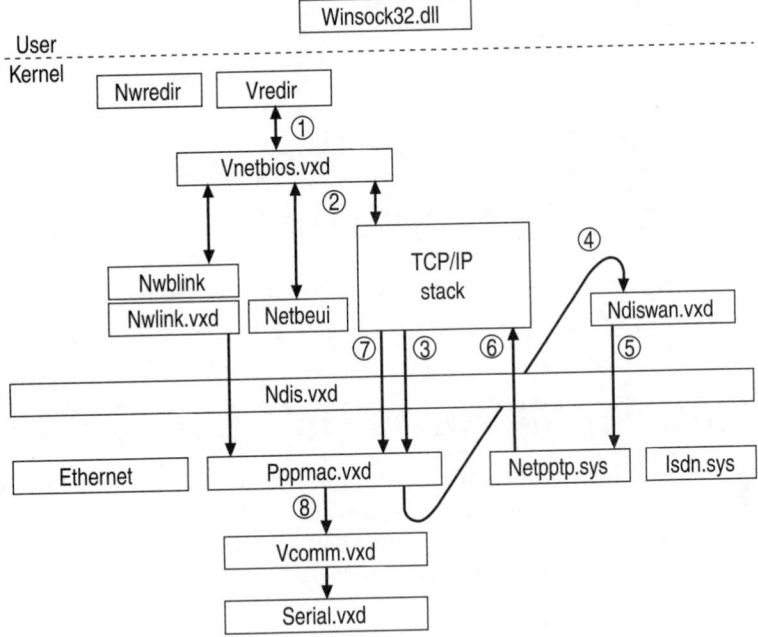

Figure 29.34   Data transfer for a Point-to-Point Tunneling Protocol tunnel over a modem

In this example, data is transferred using Client for Microsoft Networks and sent out over a modem. It could also be transferred using Client for NetWare Networks and sent out over an Ethernet connection or an ISDN device.

The data is sent by Vredir and encapsulated in IP. As with a normal data transfer, it is sent to Pppmac.vxd. In a normal data transfer, however, the data would have been sent through the Pppmac.vxd VCOMM interface to VCOMM. Here, it is rerouted instead through the Pppmac.vxd NDISWAN interface.

From there, it travels to Netpptp.sys, the component that handles the PPTP connection. Netpptp.sys transfers the PPP data to the TCP/IP stack, where it is encapsulated in GRE (defined in RFCs 1701 and 1702.).

It is next sent back through NDIS to Pppmac.vxd, which encapsulates it in PPP and sends it through VCOMM to the serial port and, finally, to the modem.

Figure 29.35 shows the encapsulated packet that is finally sent to the modem.

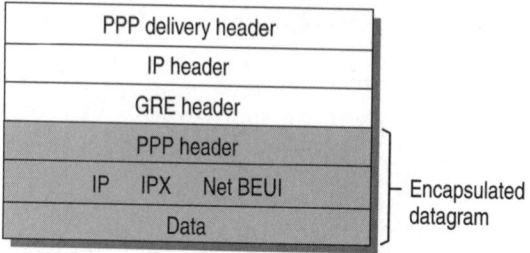

Figure 29.35   Internet Protocol datagram containing encrypted Point-to-Point Protocol packet

Architecture for Microsoft Data Link Control

Windows 98 includes both a protected-mode Data Link Control (DLC) driver (Dlc.vxd), which supports 32-bit and 16-bit DLC applications, and a real-mode DLC driver (Msdlc.exe), which supports only 16-bit applications. It is used primarily to access IBM mainframe computers and Hewlett-Packard network-ready printers.

This section shows the architecture for Microsoft 32-bit and 16-bit DLC.

Microsoft 32-bit Data Link Control

Figure 29.36 shows the architecture for Microsoft 32-bit DLC.

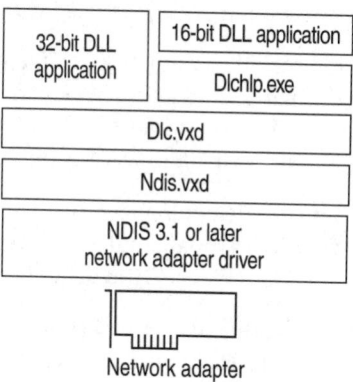

Figure 29.36   Architecture for Microsoft 32-bit Data Link Control

Microsoft 16-bit Data Link Control

Figure 29.37 shows the architecture for Microsoft 16-bit DLC with NDIS drivers, used with a protected-mode protocol.

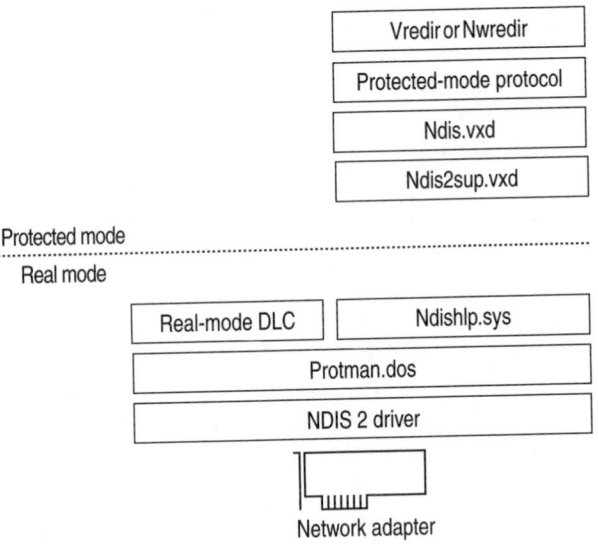

Figure 29.37   Architecture for Microsoft 16-bit Data Link Control

Figure 29.38 shows the architecture for Microsoft 16-bit DLC with Open Datalink Interface (ODI) network adapter drivers.

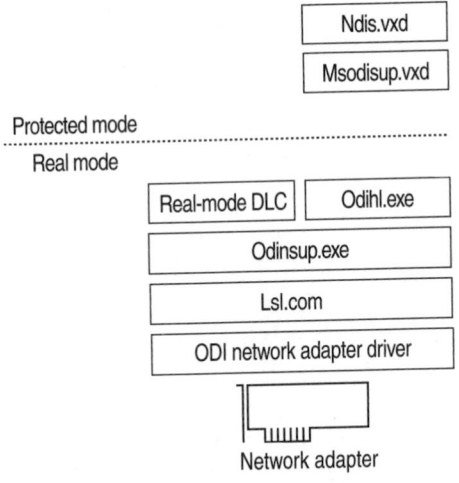

Figure 29.38   Architecture for real-mode Data Link Control with Open Datalink Interface network adapter drivers

Figure 29.39 shows the architecture for real-mode DLC with NDIS 2 network adapters and IBM LanSupport.

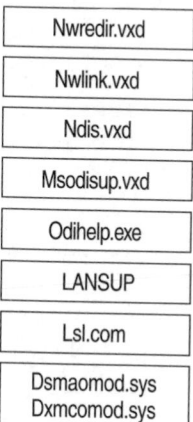

| Nwredir.vxd |
| Nwlink.vxd |
| Ndis.vxd |
| Msodisup.vxd |
| Odihelp.exe |
| LANSUP |
| Lsl.com |
| Dsmaomod.sys
Dxmcomod.sys |

Figure 29.39   Architecture for real-mode Data Link Control with NDIS 2 network adapter and IBM LanSupport

Additional Resources

For more information about	See this resource
Generic Quality of Service (GQoS)	**http://www.microsoft.com/**
	ftp://microsoft.com/bussys/winsock/winsock2/
Internet Engineering Task Force (IETF) Resource Reservation Protocol (RSVP) specification	**http://www.ietf.org/**
COM standard	**ftp://ftp.microsoft.com/developr/drg/OLE-info/COMSpecification/**
DCOM Request for Comments (RFC)	**http://www.microsoft.com/com/**

CHAPTER 30

Hardware Management

30

This chapter describes four major components of hardware management in Microsoft Windows 98: Win32 Driver Model (WDM)—the new driver model compatible with Windows 98 and future versions of Windows NT, system bus support, hardware device support, and power management. This chapter is intended primarily for writers of device drivers, computer technicians, system administrators, network administrators, and anyone else interested in how these components operate and are supported by Windows 98.

Note Although the material in this chapter is common to both Windows 98 and future versions of Windows NT, within this resource kit, WDM architecture, aspects of system bus support and hardware-device support, and certain power management capabilities are described only in relation to Windows 98.

In This Chapter

See Also

- For more information about the WDM architecture and its relationship with Windows 98, see Chapter 28, "Windows 98 Architecture."

- For more information about how to use the Windows 98 Device Manager, see Chapter 24, "Device Management."

Overview of Win32 Driver Model

Win32 Driver Model (WDM) defines a device-driver architecture that provides a common set of I/O services understood by both Windows 98 and future versions of Windows NT. With WDM, developers can write a single bus driver or device driver for both operating systems.

WDM is based on the concept of layers of driver classes. Each layer isolates portions of the services required of a device driver and allows hardware vendors to contain all hardware-specific functionality into a single file. Before WDM, device drivers had to include hooks for a particular operating system, in addition to the elements necessary to interact with a specific piece of hardware.

Understanding WDM

This section describes WDM. The WDM layered architecture, shown in Figure 30.1, is based on the concept of class drivers.

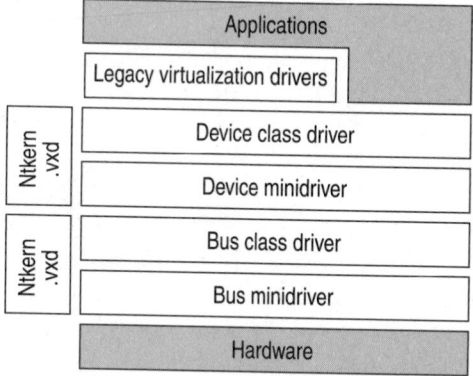

Figure 30.1   WDM layered architecture

There can be any number of driver layers, depending on the configuration of the computer. In this figure, there are six driver layers:

- Legacy Virtualization drivers
- Device Class drivers
- Device minidrivers
- Bus Class drivers
- Bus minidrivers
- Ntkern.vxd (platform abstraction layer)

The WDM layer contains the following types of drivers:

- Device Class drivers
- Device minidrivers
- Bus Class drivers
- Bus minidrivers

A bus minidriver and a bus class driver for a device are not fundamentally different from other device class drivers and device minidrivers.

The layers of the WDM architecture are detailed in Chapter 28, "Windows 98 Architecture."

Under Windows 98, WDM provides a set of kernel services, device drivers, and bus drivers that enables new bus and device classes to have a single driver for each class, while allowing Windows 98 to fully support existing virtual device drivers (VxDs).

For more information about the workings of the WDM kernel, see the WDM Device Driver Kit (DDK).

Microsoft supports the following technologies using WDM drivers: OnNow power management, Plug and Play, USB, the IEEE 1394 bus, and hardware device classes, including digital audio, Human Interface Device (HID), imaging (still image and video capture), and DVD. Besides providing a set of drivers for buses and mainstream hardware devices supported by WDM, Windows 98 allows you to create custom drivers for unsupported hardware devices as well.

For each bus class and hardware device class provided by WDM, Windows 98 provides a class driver. The interface for this driver is documented in the Windows 98 DDK. Because Microsoft provides all platform-specific integration support for WDM, you are required to write only minidrivers for hardware devices whose classes are supported by Microsoft. In addition, Windows 98 provides enhanced power management for these devices.

For more information about minidrivers, see Chapter 28, "Windows 98 Architecture."

Using the WDM Stream Class

Many devices rely on the WDM Stream class driver. It uses a standard interface for interconnecting device drivers to optimize the flow of data within the Windows 98 kernel. The WDM Stream class driver is used by some audio devices and video-capture devices, as well as hardware decoders (such as MPEG-2) used for playing DVD movies. In addition, the class driver helps to deal with common operating system tasks, such as direct memory access (DMA), scatter/gather memory use, and Plug and Play. The WDM Stream class driver functions on both internal and external buses.

The WDM Stream class lets you work with a single driver model for MPEG, video capture, USB audio and video, IEEE 1394 audio and video, and other streaming hardware. Therefore, if you are creating drivers for multifunction hardware devices, you can build on the Stream class and use a single driver model for all data types. Also, no driver needs to be written for USB audio drivers. This is a great improvement over previous architectures, which required the developer to create drivers using a different driver model for each type of hardware device (for example, audio, MIDI, and video capture).

The WDM Stream class driver is designed to cover an entire category of hardware devices, with each device supported by a minidriver supplied by the manufacturer. This significantly reduces the amount of code required to support a device—provided the device follows standard design specifications and principles.

For more information about the WDM Stream class, see the following:

- "Win32 Driver Model Connection and Streaming Architecture Functional Specification" in the Windows 98 DDK
- Help files in the Windows 98 DDK

Identifying Bus Classes Supported by WDM

The following WDM drivers are provided by Windows 98.

USB

Windows 98 provides a USB class driver and a PCI enumerator, and supports USB hubs, the Universal Host Controller Interface (UHCI) standard, the Open Host Controller Interface (OpenHCI) standard, and HID-compliant USB devices. The WDM Stream class provides additional infrastructure for most USB-compliant devices (most HID devices and imaging devices).

IEEE 1394

Windows 98 provides an IEEE 1394 bus class driver and a minidriver for Texas Instruments Lynx, Adaptec host controllers, and 1394 OpenHCI-compliant host controllers.

Identifying Hardware Device Classes Supported by WDM

The following hardware device classes are supported by Windows 98.

HID

Windows 98 provides built-in HID support for the following:

- System devices (such as keyboard and mouse).
- Gaming devices (such as joysticks and gamepads) using DirectInput.
- HID-compliant devices connected using USB (such as keyboards, mouse devices, gaming devices, personality modules, remote controls, and telephony devices).

Note Microsoft Windows 98 supports any HID-compliant device; however, the device may require additional device or vendor-specific drivers or applications to be installed before it is functional.

DVD

DVD support is based on the WDM Stream class driver. When an original equipment manufacturer (OEM) creates a decoder card, a WDM decoder-card minidriver has to be written. Non-WDM components include a class driver for the DVD-ROM drive, a collection of DirectMovie filters, and the Universal Disk Format (UDF) file system to ensure support for UDF-formatted DVD disks.

For more information about UDF, see Chapter 10, "Disks and File Systems."

Digital Audio

Windows 98 provides minidrivers for WDM audio and USB audio, and also provides a cross-application Kernel-mode mixer and a sample-rate converter as clients of the Stream class driver.

Still Image

Windows 98 provides WDM drivers for USB and SCSI still image devices, and supports still image devices (scanners, for example) plugged into serial and parallel ports.

Video Capture

WDM support for video capture is based on the Stream class driver. Windows 98 provides minidrivers for USB and IEEE 1394 cameras, as well as PCI and Videoport capture devices. Support includes DirectMovie filters for WDM video-capture interfaces, and for backward compatibility, a Video for Windows (VFW)-to-Stream class mapper.

Supporting Power Management

Windows 98 directs power management through the OnNow system. In the OnNow system, the operating system directs power management and integrates the activities of other components. The goal of OnNow is to turn the system on quickly through the use of power management techniques. The strategy for achieving that goal is to use power management techniques and have the operating system run the power management process.

WDM under Windows 98 supports OnNow power management for all USB devices. For more information about OnNow support under WDM, see "Supporting OnNow Through WDM" later in this chapter.

Understanding Driver Solutions Provided by Windows 98

To help you determine when to create custom drivers, this section describes the features and capabilities of the drive solutions provided in Windows 98, and how these solutions apply to various kinds of devices.

WDM Stream Class

The Microsoft WDM Stream class, through participation in WDM Connection and Streaming Architecture (CSA), abstracts a way to transport high-bandwidth, time-stamped, latency-sensitive data streams between kernel-mode components or between kernel-mode drivers and user-mode components. Support is provided for power management and Plug and Play.

Through CSA, the Stream class works well with Microsoft DirectShow (formerly known as ActiveMovie), in that it shares media types, has similar streaming states (Stop, Pause, Run), and shares the same concept of pins and connections. Although mainstream implementations of streaming include video capture, TV viewing, and DVD movie playback, the Stream class can also support other device types. An example is high-volume capture of instrumentation data, where time-stamping and data manipulation are important features. The ease with which DirectShow can use this data is an important consideration in deciding to use the Stream class to support a specific device.

For more information about writing WDM class drivers, see the WDM DDK.

HID Class

The HID class driver supports control devices, such as keyboards, mouse devices, and gaming devices. Any device with controls can benefit from the HID class driver. For example, remote controls and front panels are likely candidates for HID class-driver support. Support is also provided for power management and Plug and Play. Although a USB HID minidriver is provided with Windows 98, the HID class driver is not bus-specific. You can develop HID class minidrivers that support legacy input devices using HID emulation or that support HID devices using legacy ports or the IEEE 1394 bus.

For more information about the HID class, see the Windows 98 DDK Help file, "Human Interface Devices."

Port Class

The Microsoft Port class supports PCI and ISA/DMA audio devices. Existing Port drivers include Wave I/O using cyclic DMA, Wave I/O using scatter/gather, Topology (MixerLine support), and MIDI. You can use the Port class to support a specific audio device by writing one or more miniport drivers.

Like the Stream class, the Port class participates in CSA and has the same streaming capabilities and the same synergy with DirectShow. The Port class differs from the Stream class as follows:

- The Port class uses a three-tiered approach, combining the class driver, port drivers, and vendor-supplied miniports.
- Port drivers address a narrow class of audio functions, allowing the miniport interface to be positioned very close to the hardware.
- Multiple combinations of Port/miniport drivers can be associated with a single device. This explicitly addresses the need to support multifunction cards.

WDM miniport audio drivers are simpler to write than VxD drivers. For more information about the Port class, see the Windows 98 DDK document, "WDM Streaming Miniport Driver Model Specification."

Still Image Architecture

The Microsoft *Still Image (STI) architecture* is not a class, but an infrastructure that supports the use of still image devices, such as scanners and still image cameras with Windows 98. STI currently provides support for SCSI, serial, and USB devices. The architecture is extendible, so Infrared Data Association (IrDA) or IEEE 1394 devices, for example, can be easily incorporated. WDM abstracts the interfaces to which the vendor must write; the vendor need only write a miniport driver that exposes the specific functionality of the device.

For more information about STI, see the Windows 98 DDK Help file, "Architecture and Interfaces for Scanners and Digital Still Cameras Design Notes and Reference."

USB and the IEEE 1394 Bus

Each USB and IEEE 1394 bus class driver provided under Windows 98 is independent of its host bus and supports respective bus adapters or bridges on any other type of bus. Plug and Play support is provided. Both interfaces use I/O request packets (IRPs) to communicate with their respective bus drivers.

For more information about the USB driver and the IEEE 1394 bus driver, see the following Help files in the Windows 98 DDK:

- "Universal Serial Bus"
- "IEEE 1394 Bus Driver Design Notes and Reference"

Overview of System Buses

Windows 98 supports four system bus standards for connecting hardware devices to the computer. The two new standards are Universal Serial Bus (USB) and IEEE 1394, both supported by WDM. The other two are PCI and PC Card, both currently supported by Windows 95 but unsupported by WDM. The following sections describe the four system bus standards supported by Windows 98.

Using USB

USB is an external bus standard for the computer that brings the Plug and Play capability of hardware devices (such as keyboards, mouse devices, and hard drives) outside the computer, eliminating the need to install cards into dedicated computer slots and reconfigure the system. With USB, hardware devices can be automatically configured as soon as they are physically attached—without the need to reboot or run the setup sequence. USB is supported by WDM under Windows 98.

USB Topology

As seen in Figure 30.2, USB uses a tiered topology, allowing you to attach up to 127 devices to the bus simultaneously. USB currently supports up to five tiers. Each device can be located up to five meters from its hub.

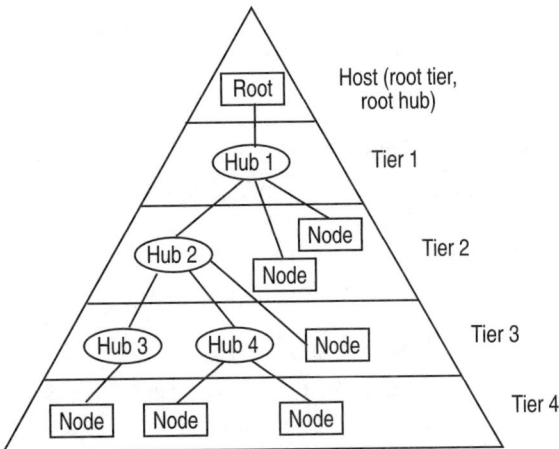

Figure 30.2   Example of the USB topology

The three types of USB components are:

- The *host*, which is also known as the *root*, the *root tier*, or the *root hub*. It is built into the motherboard or installed as an adapter card in the computer. The host controls all traffic on the bus and can also function as a hub.

- The *hub*, which provides a point, or *port,* to attach a device to the bus. Hubs are also responsible for detecting devices being attached or detached from the bus and for providing power management for devices attached to the hub. Hubs are either *bus-powered* (drawing power directly from the bus) or *self-powered* (drawing power from an external source). A self-powered device can be plugged into a bus-powered hub. A bus-powered hub cannot be connected to another bus-powered hub or support more than four downstream ports. A bus-powered device that draws more than 100 mA cannot be connected to a bus-powered hub.

- The *device*, which is attached to the bus through a port. USB devices can also function as hubs. For example, a USB monitor can have ports for attaching a USB keyboard and a mouse. In this case, the monitor is also a hub.

Note   When you plug a device into a particular port for the first time, Windows 98 must go through the detection and enumeration process with that device.

Choosing Devices Supported by USB

You can connect the following USB devices to your computer: monitor controls, audio I/O devices, telephones, modems, speakers, keyboards, mouse devices, joysticks, scanners, printers, low-bandwidth video devices, digital still cameras, data gloves, and digitizers. For computer-telephony integration, USB provides an interface for Integrated Services Digital Network (ISDN) and digital PBXs.

For USB, the computer host controller is implemented through the OpenHCI or UHCI standards. To work with USB, the host controller must comply with one of these standards.

The USB Connector and Cable

The USB specification defines a standard connector, socket, and cable, which all USB devices can use. This single standard eliminates the confusion caused by the current mixture of connector and cable types required for hardware devices. The USB hub uses a type A connector, and the device uses a type B connector.

Data Transfer Rates Supported by USB

USB supports four data transfer modes: interrupt, control, bulk, and isochronous. Each mode applies to the endpoints of the same name and has separate characteristics. Isochronous and interrupt endpoints reserve bandwidth and are guaranteed access to transfer data at the established rate. Bulk and control endpoints are scheduled for best fit or for whatever bandwidth is available, but 10% of the total bus bandwidth is reserved for bulk and control transfers. Guaranteed data delivery is required to support the demands of multimedia applications and devices.

The USB host determines the data transfer rate and the priority assigned to a data stream. USB supports the following maximum data transfer rates, depending on the amount of bus bandwidth a device requires:

- 1.5 megabits per second (Mbps) for devices that do not require a large amount of bandwidth, such as mouse devices and keyboards.

- 12 Mbps isochronous transfer rate for higher bandwidth devices, such as telephones, modems, speakers, scanners, video devices, and printers.

USB Support for Plug and Play

Windows 98 supports Plug and Play through USB in several ways.

Hot Plug-in Capability.   You can plug a USB device into the system anytime. The USB hub driver enumerates the device and notifies the system that the device is present.

Persistent Addressing.   USB devices use descriptors to identify the device and its capabilities and protocols used. The serial number generates the Plug and Play ID, and the port address indicates the port and hub the device is connected to. If the device does not provide a serial number, USB uses the device's port address.

Power Management Support.   USB supports three power modes: On, Suspend, and Off. USB devices can be placed in Suspend mode and still retain the ability to wake up the system.

USB Driver Interface

Windows 98 supports USB by allowing USB device drivers to communicate with the USB driver stack. Between the USB device drivers (for example, Human Interface [HID] drivers for keyboard, mouse, and joystick) and the USB driver stack is the USB Driver Interface (USBDI). In Windows 98, this communication takes place within the WDM layered architecture.

The USB driver architecture is shown in Figure 30.3.

Note   Although Windows 98 natively supports many USB devices, some devices might require additional drivers or application software (for example, a device developed after the release of Windows 98 might not be inherently recognized). Such a device would ship with a diskette or other medium containing the required driver or application software.

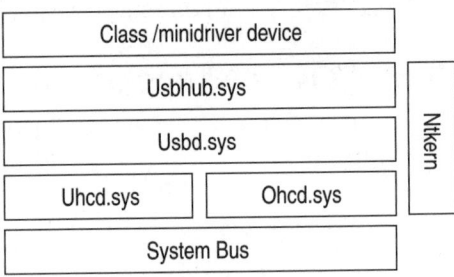

Figure 30.3   USB Driver Architecture

Figure 30.3 shows the following modules:

- Usbhub.sys is the USB hub driver. It is loaded when Usbd.sys enumerates the root hub built into each USB host controller as the driver for each host controller is loaded.

- Usbd.sys is the USB class driver.

- Uhcd.sys (Universal Host Controller Driver) and Ohcd.sys (Open Host Controller Driver) are USB host controller drivers.

In addition, Hidclass.sys, a WDM input class driver, sends and receives HID reports to and from its minidrivers. Hidusb.sys, an HID device driver, sends and receives HID reports over the USB. The PCI Enumerator loads the USB stack driver components when a USB bus is detected on a platform and always loads at least the other core components.

Windows 98 is able to recognize a USB device once the client device driver communicates with the USB driver stack. This requires that a WDM I/O request packet (IRP) be issued to pass information across the USBDI between the client device driver and the USB driver stack.

For more information about how device drivers communicate with the USB through the use of IRPs, see the Windows 98 DDK.

Using the IEEE 1394 Bus

Windows 98 supports the IEEE 1394 bus, also known as FireWire. It is designed for high-bandwidth computer devices, such as digital camcorders, cameras, and videodisc players. IEEE 1394 devices are supported by WDM in accordance with the OpenHCI standard.

You can connect up to 63 devices to one IEEE 1394 bus and interconnect up to 1023 buses to form a very large network with over 64,000 devices. Each device can have up to 256 terabytes of memory addressable over the bus. A built-in mechanism ensures equal access to the bus for all devices.

For more information about device support under IEEE 1394, see "Choosing Devices Supported by IEEE 1394" later in this chapter.

Looking at the IEEE 1394 Bus Topology

Figure 30.4 shows an example of an IEEE 1394 bus configuration.

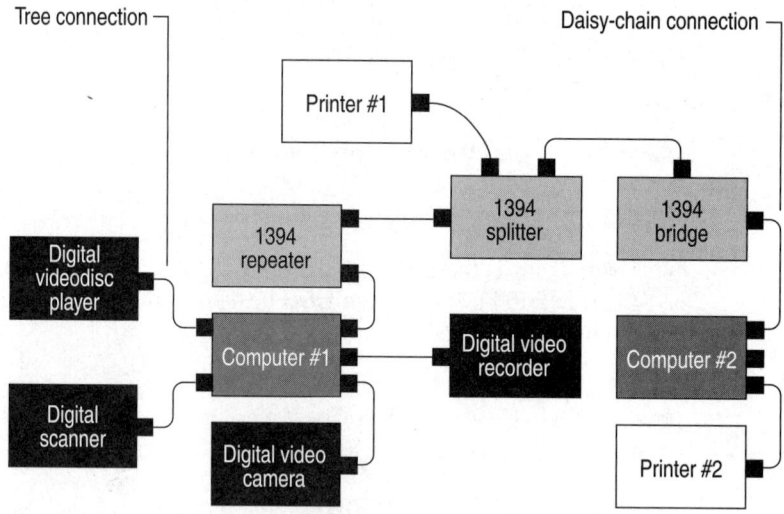

Figure 30.4   An IEEE 1394 bus configuration

The four types of IEEE 1394 bus components are:

- A *device*, which attaches to the bus. An IEEE 1394 device usually has 3 ports, although the maximum is 27. You can daisy-chain up to 16 devices—more than 16 devices can be connected in a tree topology. Windows 98 assigns physical addresses on power-up (this resets the bus) and whenever you add or remove a device from the system.

- A *splitter*, which allows considerable flexibility in designing and implementing IEEE 1394 bus topology by providing extra IEEE 1394 ports.

- A *bridge*, which isolates data traffic within a specific area of the bus.

- A *repeater*, which extends the distance between devices by retransmitting data signals across the bus.

Choosing Devices Supported by IEEE 1394

Windows 98 supports IEEE 1394 by allowing IEEE 1394 device drivers to communicate with the IEEE 1394 bus class driver. In accordance with the OpenHCI standard, Windows 98 currently includes the IEEE 1394 bus class driver with hardware-specific minidriver extensions for add-on and motherboard host controllers.

The IEEE 1394 Bus Connector and Cable

The IEEE 1394 specification defines a standard connector and socket based on the Nintendo GameBoy connector. An IEEE 1394 bus cable contains two power conductors and two twisted pairs for transmitting data.

Data Transfer Rates Supported by IEEE 1394

The IEEE 1394 specification currently supports the following bus transfer rates:

- S100 (98.304 Mbps)
- S200 (196.608 Mbps)
- S400 (393.216 Mbps)

Higher transfer rates are under development.

You can freely interconnect devices with different data rates; communication automatically takes place at the highest rate supported by the lowest-rate device.

IEEE 1394 supports two data transfer protocols: *isochronous* and *asynchronous*. An isochronous connection transfers data at a guaranteed, fixed rate of delivery. Guaranteed data delivery is required to support the demands of multimedia applications and devices. Asynchronous data can be transferred whenever there is no isochronous traffic on the bus.

IEEE 1394 Support for Plug and Play

Windows 98 supports hot plugging of nodes; you can plug an IEEE 1394 device into the system anytime.

IEEE 1394 Standards

IEEE 1394 device standards are currently under development. To simplify IEEE 1394 device development, Microsoft is participating with industry partners and the 1394 Trade Association to define the standards necessary to enable seamless integration of IEEE 1394 consumer devices with computers. Table 30.1 lists the standards.

Table 30.1   Proposed IEEE 1394 standards

Standard	Benefit
OpenHCI Standard interface for computer host controller hardware	Enables broad computer market adoption of IEEE 1394 by providing standard hardware and software much like IDE.
SBP-2 General-purpose command transport protocol for IEEE 1394	Simplifies device development by providing a common transport protocol that can be used to support a range of device classes.
Device power management Interfaces for centralized power management (proposed)	Provides standard power-control interfaces for centralized power management and OnNow devices, based on application demand.
Plug and Play design reference Requirements for interoperability (proposed)	Provides guidelines for configuration-ROM structure, bus-management capabilities, and electro-mechanical design for overall ease of use.

Each proposed standard has been submitted to the 1394 Trade Association for industry review and feedback. After this has been completed, many of the standards will be forwarded to an appropriate standards body, such as the Institute of Electrical and Electronics Engineers (IEEE) or the American National Standards Institute (ANSI). Wide adoption of these standards will ensure the interoperability of IEEE 1394 devices and computers.

Comparing the IEEE 1394 Bus and USB

The IEEE 1394 bus and USB are used for different classes of devices. The IEEE 1394 bus, with its fast data rates, is designed for high-bandwidth consumer electronics connections to the computer, such as those required by digital camcorders and digital videodisc players, storage, printers, and scanners. The slower data rate of USB is suited for more traditional computer connections, such as those required by keyboards, mouse devices, joysticks, and handheld scanners. USB is also suitable for advanced computer games, high-fidelity audio, and highly compressed video, such as MPEG-1.

The Simply Interactive PC (SIPC) is the Microsoft initiative to create computers that never have to be serviced by the user and are as simple to use as any household appliance. The SIPC concept requires that the ports for the IEEE 1394 bus and USB be easily accessible, that is, available on the front of the computer where you can easily walk up and plug in a hardware device. More permanent installations of IEEE 1394 or USB devices will be handled from the back of the computer.

Because the SIPC concept is compatible with the IEEE 1394 bus, USB, WDM, and OnNow power management, Windows 98 and future versions of Windows NT will be the operating systems of choice for computers designed under the SIPC concept.

Supporting Legacy Buses

The following sections describe how the buses supported previously by Windows now function under Windows 98.

The PCI Bus

The *PCI bus* is a high-performance bus well suited for transferring data between hardware devices, adapters, and other bus backplanes. Today, almost all computers ship with a PCI backplane or host bus. The PCI bus is usually connected to the host CPU and main memory through a bridge device that controls the data transfers between the CPU, cache, and main memory. This bridge also provides the major interface, and controls the data transfer between main memory and all the other devices on the PCI bus.

Because of its high bandwidth, the PCI bus is capable of high-performance data transfers.

Note This calculation is an approximation of the maximum transfer rate. Not every PCI bus cycle is used to transfer data, and the calculation does not include latency or guarantees of isochronous transfers.

▶ **To calculate the maximum transfer rate on the PCI bus**

1. Multiply the bus clock rate by the bus width in bits.

2. Divide by the number of clock cycles it takes for each data transfer (1 cycle for the PCI bus).

The following example illustrates this calculation:

Clock rate	33 MHz
Bus width	32 bits
Maximum transfer rate	1.06 Gbps

This is higher than the maximum IEEE 1394 bus rates (98.304, 196.608, and 393.216 Mbps) and considerably higher than the maximum USB rate (12 Mbps).

PC Card and CardBus

Windows 98 supports the new features of products designed for the Personal Computer Memory Card International Association (PCMCIA) standard, also known as *PC Card*. These products include multifunction cards, 3.3-V cards, and 32-bit PC Cards. These advancements add the modularity and bus-independence of Plug and Play without affecting device drivers. Driver development under Windows 98 is identical to that used in Windows 95, and many Plug and Play drivers that operated under Windows 95 can be used unmodified under Windows 98 to support the same controller implemented on the multifunction or 32-bit PC cards.

Windows 98 supports *CardBus*, a combination of PC Card 16 and PCI, also known as PC Card 32. CardBus brings 32-bit performance and the benefits of the PCI bus to the PC Card format. CardBus allows portable computers to run high-bandwidth applications, such as Video Capture.

As of this writing, CardBus implementations under Windows 98 are being developed.

The SCSI Bus

The *Small Computer Standard Interface (SCSI)* is used with such devices as hard disks and CD-ROM drives. Each device on the bus is connected in a daisy-chained topology. Plug and Play SCSI devices support dynamic changes to the adapter and automatic configuration of device ID and termination.

For more information about support for SCSI devices and drivers, see Chapter 10, "Disks and File Systems."

For more information about Plug and Play using SCSI devices, see Chapter 24, "Device Management."

The ISA Bus

The *Industry Standard Architecture (ISA) bus* is specified for the IBM PC/AT. Plug and Play ISA devices can be used on existing computers, because the specification does not require any change to ISA buses. For legacy devices, standard ISA cards can coexist with Plug and Play ISA cards on the same computer. Windows 98 determines the type of hardware and its configuration during Setup.

For more information about ISA devices, see Chapter 24, "Device Management."

The EISA Bus

The *Enhanced Industry Standard Architecture (EISA) bus* is specified for *x*86-based computers by an industry consortium. EISA devices use cards that are upwardly compatible from ISA. As with ISA, standard EISA cards can coexist with Plug and Play EISA cards on the same computer.

For more information about EISA devices, see Chapter 24, "Device Management."

Overview of Hardware Devices

Windows 98 supports standards for the following types of hardware devices: HID, DVD, Digital Audio, Still Image, Multiple Display Support, Video Capture, and Accelerated Graphics Port (AGP). Much of this support is either new or significantly improved over what was offered under Windows 95. For Windows 98, driver support is mostly WDM-based, which means the same set of drivers will also be used in future versions of Windows NT. The following sections describe the hardware device standards supported by Windows 98.

Using HID

Windows 98 supports devices compliant with the *Human Interface Device (HID)* firmware specification, the new standard for input devices, such as keyboards, mouse and pointing devices, joysticks, gamepads, and other types of game controllers. Support is based on the specification developed by the USB Implementers' Forum and is targeted towards devices connecting through USB. The HID-compliant device is self-describing, indicating its type and providing usage information when plugged into the host system.

For more information about the USB Implementers Forum, see **http://www.usb.org/**. The HID specification is also available at this Web site.

Under Windows 98, HID keyboards, mouse devices, joysticks, and gamepads that plug into USB are connected to the existing legacy input device infrastructure. This is done through a set of VxD-to-WDM mappers that map the HID data into the corresponding legacy format. This allows the operating system and existing applications to receive data transparently from these kinds of USB/HID devices.

In general, communication with HID devices is Win32 File I/O-based, and devices can be accessed in both kernel mode and user mode. Devices that connect through USB are Plug and Play and power-managed in accordance with the OnNow specification for input devices.

Supporting HID Devices

Windows 98 provides, through the built-in USB and HID drivers stacks and the HID parser, complete support for any HID-compliant device. Third-party drivers and applications can enumerate, open, and exchange data with any HID device and have this data parsed by the built-in HID parser. In addition, Windows 98 includes complete support for the following types of standard HID input devices:

- Keyboards and keypads
- Mouse and pointing devices
- Joysticks and gamepads

These types of HID devices can be plugged into the system and be used immediately. They do not require installation of additional software drivers.

The generality of the HID specification opens up the opportunity for new kinds of input devices. For example, HID usage pages and usages are defined for the following types of devices:

- Simulation devices (for example, automobiles, planes, tanks, spaceships, and submarines)
- Virtual reality devices (for example, belts, body suits, gloves, head trackers, head-mounted displays, and oculometers)
- Sports-equipment devices (for example, golf clubs, baseball bats, rowing machines, and treadmills)
- Consumer appliance devices (for example, audio and video appliances, and remote controls)
- Advanced game controllers (for example, 3-D game controllers and pinball devices)

For more information about HID usage, see the supplemental HID Usages Table specification at **http://www.usb.org/**.

Understanding the HID Architecture

The HID class driver (Hidclass.sys), the USB-specific HID class minidriver (Hidusb.sys), and the HID kernel-mode parser (Hidparse.sys) comprise the heart of the Windows 98 HID architecture. The HID architecture in Windows 98 is shown in Figure 30.5.

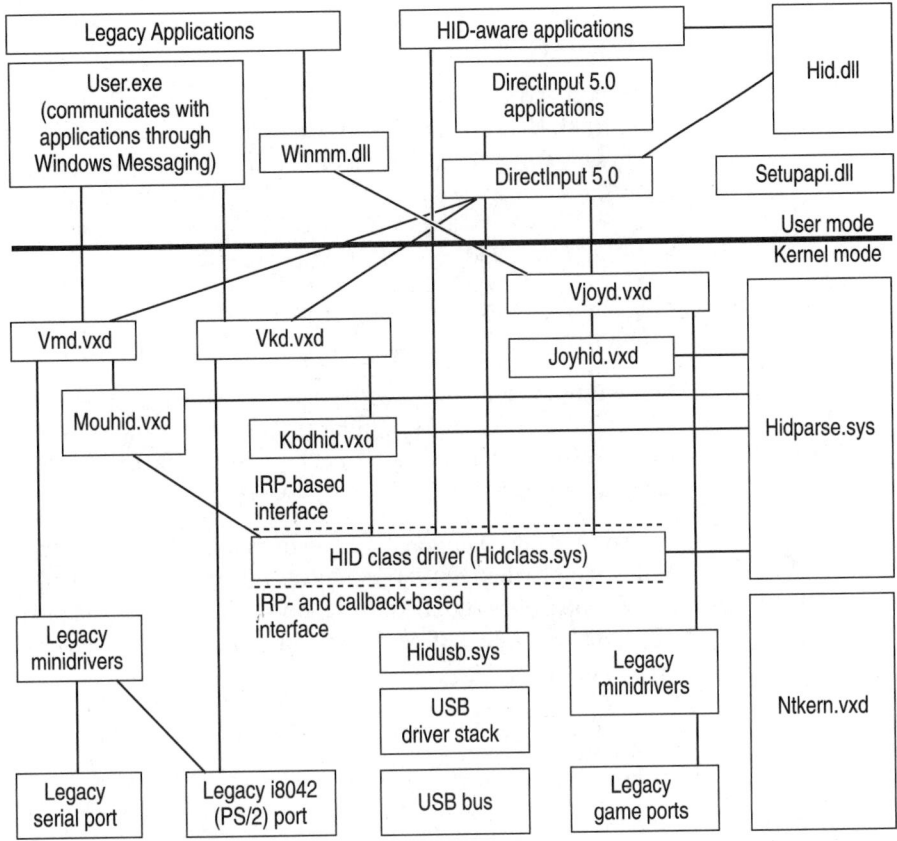

Figure 30.5   HID architecture

The following HID modules are shown in Figure 30.5:

- Hidclass.sys is the bus-independent HID class driver. It sends and receives HID reports to and from its minidrivers. Hidclass.sys also provides input queues that allow multiple clients to have open handles to the same device.

- Hidusb.sys is the USB-specific HID class minidriver. It sends and receives HID reports over the USB bus.

- Hid.dll and Hidparse.sys provide parsing services. Hid.dll is a user-mode parsing service, and Hidparse.sys is a kernel-mode parsing service. These modules aid applications and drivers in parsing HID reports.

- Kbdhid.vxd maps keyboard HID reports into the existing legacy data format expected by Vkd.vxd.

- Mouhid.vxd maps mouse HID reports into the existing legacy data format expected by Vmd.vxd.

- Joyhid.vxd calls Hidparse.sys to find the various elements that might be in a joystick HID report (X, Y, rudder, throttle, hat switch, buttons) and then maps these report values into a data format expected by Vjoyd.vxd.

As in Windows 95, legacy VxD style minidrivers connect Vmd.vxd with the serial and PS/2 ports, and connect Vjoyd.vxd with the game ports.

Plug and Play and power management support for USB/HID devices takes place within the USB driver stack that is part of the new WDM-based architecture.

From an application perspective, any HID device can be accessed either through HID APIs exposed by Hid.dll, or through DirectInput COM methods. DirectInput, which is part of Microsoft's DirectX multimedia architecture, now includes support for HID devices.

Windows 98 also supports HID devices that connect to the system through ports or buses other than those of Hidusb.sys. For example, the IEEE 1394 bus can be developed and supplied by vendors. Vendors can also extend or modify the functionality or data of devices by inserting filter drivers into the USB or HID driver stacks.

For more information about minidriver and filter-driver development, see the WDM DDK.

Using DVD

DVD as an official product name is not an acronym. It is a branded, trademarked name owned by the DVD Consortium. As an acronym, *DVD* has various interpretations, including Digital Versatile Disc and Digital Video Disc, but these letters have come to represent more than just an acronym. As a natural enhancement of CD-ROM, DVD provides the new generation of optical-disc storage technology for a huge array of both consumer electronics and personal computer devices. DVD provides digital data storage that encompasses audio, video, and computer data, and therefore has the potential for replacing current technologies for business data storage, laser disc, audio CD and CD-ROM, VHS videotape, and dedicated game technologies. DVD was designed from the ground up for multimedia applications, with a key goal of being able to store a full-length feature movie.

The DVD Consortium has defined two major compression technologies, MPEG-2 and AC-3, to be used to store over two hours of video and audio on a single DVD disk. In addition, the quality of the stored video and audio is higher than that found on laser disks and CDs, opening up new possibilities for content providers.

Supporting DVD

Windows 98 supports DVD as follows:

DVD movie playback. If the proper decoding hardware or software is present, Windows 98 supports full DVD-Video playback This support is especially important for entertainment computers, but it is also important for any multimedia hardware platform meant to provide good quality support for the playback of movies. This support includes the full range of interactivity and high-quality playback found on a standard DVD-Video player. Because computers are capable of better image quality than television, DVD—on a computer running Windows 98 or Windows NT—can produce a better-quality image than standard DVD-Video player devices connected to a television set.

DVD as a storage device. On most computers that have Microsoft DVD support, DVD can work as a storage device. While most first-generation DVD-ROM drives do not read CD-R disks, all second-generation drives do. DVD-ROM discs and devices provide cost-effective storage for large data files. DVD-RAM drives are currently being shipped to computer dealers. Future plans include writable DVD devices, which will widen the range of options.

Figure 30.6 shows an implementation under the support architecture for existing DVD technologies under Windows 98.

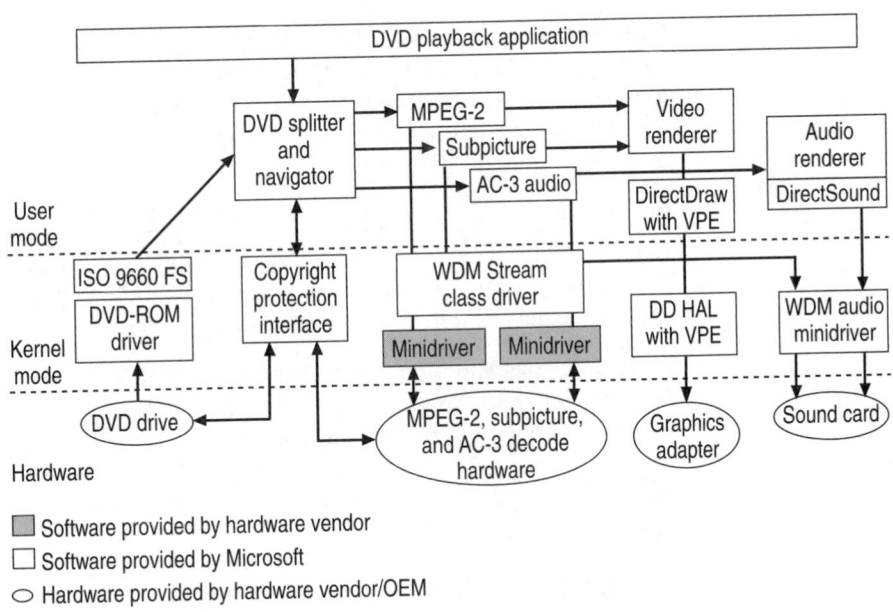

Figure 30.6   Implementation of the DVD support architecture

Advanced features of DVD include multi-angle, multiple audio tracks, and multiple subpicture tracks. For more information about DVD features, see Chapter 12, "Multimedia."

Note Some components in the DVD architecture will change based on advances in other hardware technologies, such as WDM support for the PCI bus under Windows 98. The only components that will always be present are the DVD-ROM driver, the Universal Disk Format (UDF) file system, the WDM Stream class driver, and the DVD Splitter/Navigator.

DVD Movie Playback

The following components comprise support for DVD movie playback under Windows 98:

DVD-ROM class driver. DVD-ROM has its own industry-defined command set, supported through an updated CD-ROM class driver. This driver provides the ability to read data sectors from a DVD-ROM drive.

UDF file system. Support for UDF ensures support for UDF-formatted DVD discs. UDF takes advantage of packet writing and is the industry standard for compact disc storage. As with FAT and FAT32, Windows 98 provides installable file systems for UDF.

WDM Stream class driver. The WDM Stream class driver supports streaming data types, and MPEG-2 and AC-3 hardware decoders. Hardware vendors have to write only a small amount of interface code in a minidriver to ensure that the specific features in their hardware are supported. This allows most DVD decoders to work without user intervention.

DirectShow. Microsoft DirectShow (formerly ActiveMovie) proxy filters and related support include a DVD Navigator/Splitter, proxy filters for video streams, a video mixer, and a video renderer. The proxy filters allow programs written to the DirectShow API to control kernel mode filters.

DirectDraw Hardware Abstraction Layer (HAL) with Video Port Extensions (VPE). Decoded video streams are huge—possibly too large even for the PCI bus on a computer. Manufacturers have solved this problem by creating dedicated buses to transfer decoded video streams from an MPEG-2 decoder to the display card. Microsoft provides software support for these interfaces using the DirectDraw HAL with VPE.

Copyright protection. Copyright protection for DVD is established when key sectors on a disk are encrypted (as with Macrovision), then decrypted before the sectors are decoded. Microsoft provides support for both software and hardware decrypters using a software module that enables authentication between the decoders and the DVD-ROM drives in a computer.

Regionalization. As part of the copyright protection scheme used for DVD, six worldwide regions have been set up by the DVD Consortium. Disks are playable on DVD devices in some or all of the regions according to regional codes set by the content creators. Microsoft provides software that responds to the regionalization codes as required by the DVD Consortium and as part of the decryption licenses.

DVDPlay. Microsoft provides a DVD movie playback application, which can be replaced with another DVD playback application written to DirectShow2.

The DVD-ROM Storage Device

Under Windows 98, DVD-ROM is simply a large storage medium, much like CD-ROM. To enable DVD-ROM as a read-only device, Microsoft provides support for DVD-ROM devices in Windows 98 and support for UDF as an installable file system. Using DVD-ROM device drivers, a DVD-ROM drive is treated as another peripheral, using industry-defined methods to access DVD disks and handle encrypted content.

Understanding DVD and Streaming Data

The *streaming* of data involves loading an application responsible for handling large amounts of data in a constant load, or stream, over time. The application never loads the data completely into memory; the data file is too large, and the operations on the data file are typically sequential. The best example of this for DVD is an MPEG-2 video stream. When a computer plays an MPEG-2 file, a program loads and streams the MPEG-2 data across the computer to be decoded and displayed. The data might enter and exit the host processor and bus of the computer several times during this process. In addition, an MPEG-2 stream starts out at approximately 5 to 10 Mbps. After the stream is decoded, the data transfer rate can easily exceed 100 Mbps. A single data stream this large can saturate and overwhelm a computer's PCI bus; this means an alternate path might be required for the raw, decoded video data.

A single stream demands a potentially large and constant load on a computer, over what could be considered a long time in computer terms. For DVD, the system must be able to independently manage and decode at least four separate streams:

- MPEG-2 video
- AC-3 or MPEG-2 audio
- Subpicture
- Navigation

This must be done so the streams are totally synchronized when they reach their final destinations, with no dropped frames or degraded video. This requires precision in load balancing, synchronization, and processing.

The WDM Stream class driver can deal with these problems because it is optimized to work with any devices that use streamed data. Such devices include those that encode data (for example, video capture devices), and those that decode data (for example, DVD hardware decoders that decode MPEG-2 streams for playing DVD movies). This class driver uses the WDM layered architecture for interconnecting device drivers to optimize data flow within the Windows 98 kernels.

Using Digital Audio

Because Windows 98 supports USB and the IEEE 1394 bus, it can support digital audio. USB and IEEE 1394 have the bandwidth necessary to support digital audio and have mechanisms to provide synchronization between an audio source and an audio sink. Both provide different forms of isochronous and asynchronous services that can be used by distributed audio systems.

Understanding How USB Supports Digital Audio

The following describes the attributes of USB that allow it to accommodate digital-audio devices.

Capacity. With a total transfer rate of 12 Mbps, USB has enough capacity for consumer audio but would be inappropriate for multitrack audio production. Unlike with IEEE 1394, adding nodes to a USB network does not add to the total data-carrying capacity of the network.

Synchronization. Although USB uses a 1-ms master clock for synchronization, the burden of synchronization is placed on the host computer. USB provides three modes of synchronization:

- *Asynchronous* nodes have independent clocks. It is the responsibility of code in the host to add or delete samples to keep a source and sink synchronized.

- *Synchronous* nodes synchronize to the master clock in the host. Two synchronized nodes can talk to each other without host intervention. The host might have to perform sample rate conversions but can assume that clocks on both devices are synchronized relative to one another.

- *Adaptive* nodes derive their clock from the data stream. For example, in an Internet telephone conversation, the nominal data rate might be 8,000 samples per second, but the remote party's sound card might be running at 8,002 samples per second. Every millisecond the computer is expected to send eight samples to the local USB audio device, but because the remote device is sending data faster, the network telephony program can compensate by sending an extra sample every half second. Adaptive nodes can deal with this sort of variance without glitches.

Digital signal processing (DSP) capability. With USB, DSP must take place in the end nodes or in the host. For example, if a DVD drive and a home stereo were connected to a host, and the user wanted to play an AC-3 audio-encoded stream, the AC-3 decoding could take place in either the host or in the stereo set, but not in an intermediate DSP *dongle* (a device, attached to a computer's I/O port, that adds hardware capabilities). The USB requirement for DSP connection is in contrast with the IEEE 1394 bus requirement, in which DSPs can also be connected as interior members of the daisy-chain or tree.

USB device classes. If a device conforms to a defined USB device class, Plug and Play methods can be used to identify the device and load a device driver. This eliminates the need for device manufacturers to ship driver disks with their products.

Intel support. Intel built the USB host controller into the latest Triton chip set, which interfaces the Pentium processor to the PCI bus and motherboard. Because USB is a serial bus, having its controller as part of this chip set adds very few pins and adds negligible cost to the computer motherboard.

Intel also built the 82930 microcontroller into USB. This chip has all the logic necessary to interface with USB and send and receive data. Vendors can combine the standard USB code with code necessary to control their devices. The 82930 microcontroller can provide complete communications and control for consumer or industrial devices.

Appliances as computer peripherals with USB Open Standards. Windows 98 supports OpenHCI and UHCI. Detailed hardware descriptions of the USB interface have been published so that smaller companies can integrate USB into their custom chips without extensive design work.

Not only is USB designed for standard devices, such as joysticks, keyboards, printers, and mouse devices, but because of its low production cost and relatively simple implementation, USB enables a wide class of devices to become computer peripherals. For example, a postage meter containing microcontrollers can have a USB port added for a small increase in cost. Connected to a computer, the meter can become part of a company-wide cost-tracking system. Adding voice output to the postage meter for use by a blind operator requires connecting the postage meter to a computer containing USB audio hardware. A programmer can add audio by using application programming interfaces (APIs) under Windows 98.

If the postage meter conforms to the HID class, Plug and Play support ensures that the device is recognized as soon as it is plugged into the computer. When that occurs, Windows 98 loads in a device driver, configures the device, and makes it available to end-user software. This is particularly useful for telephones. A telephone is both an HID (the keypad) and an audio USB device. It might also include a conventional, ISDN, or high-speed cable modem. If a telephone answering/fax machine has a USB port, the device works fine on its own, but when plugged into a computer, it becomes a modem, a scanner, a printer, and a more intelligent answering machine.

Home entertainment. The home stereo system is another consumer device that already contains a microcontroller and can be easily upgraded to connect to a computer running Windows 98 with USB. Except for the audio data rates, a stereo system is not much different from a telephone with USB. When equipped with a USB interface, a stereo system becomes a USB audio class device and an HID-class device. The microcontroller inside a stereo system is not much different from the microcontroller inside a keyboard; the stereo system microcontroller spends most of its time polling buttons, waiting for the user to change the volume or tone controls.

IEEE 1394 Bus Support for Digital Audio

The following describes the attributes of the IEEE 1394 bus that allow it to accommodate digital-audio devices.

Capacity and synchronization. With the IEEE 1394 bus, it is possible to put a CD drive on one node and a digital-to-analog converter (DAC) on another node. The clocks of both devices can be slaved to the master clock on the bus. Because the IEEE 1394 bus is designed to handle video data (a transfer rate of 400 Mbps), handling multiple tracks of audio is a much simpler task. IEEE 1394 networks can be configured using multiple buses and filtering bridges in a leaf-node configuration so many devices can play in parallel without passing data over the same segment of the bus.

DSP capability. Arbitrary amounts of DSP power can be applied to streams of audio by means of IEEE 1394 dongles. DSPs inside a computer are limited by the total memory of the system and must compete with the CPU for this resource. On the IEEE 1394 bus, signals can be passed between nodes containing DSPs. Each DSP node increases delay to the processing time, but the IEEE 1394 bus can string many DSPs together.

Home entertainment. Microsoft is working with Sony, Yamaha, and Texas Instruments to define standards for home entertainment audio delivery over the IEEE 1394 bus. Microsoft is also working with OEMs and third-party software developers to make Windows 98 the best platform for delivery of multimedia content.

Overview of Multiple Display Support

Aside from continuing support of the conventional display features found in Windows 95, Windows 98 supports a new and important display feature called *Multiple Display Support*. The ability to run multiple applications on the computer has made screen space a precious commodity. It would be convenient to be able to view all your running applications at the same time and not have to keep clicking between windows. The costly solution is to use a very large (35-inch, for example) video monitor; a more economical and flexible solution is to connect two or more smaller monitors to the computer so that each application can be viewed on its own screen, or the entire desktop can be viewed across all the screens. The latter solution is the Multiple Display Support feature.

Multiple Display Support uses the concepts of a primary display and secondary display. For you to be able to use a monitor as a secondary monitor, it must meet certain criteria. It must be a PCI or AGP device, and it must be able to run in GUI mode or without using VGA resources. It must also have a Windows 98 driver that enables it to be a secondary display. For a list of these drivers, see "Technical Notes on Multiple Display," in Chapter 24, Device Management."

The system BIOS picks the primary VGA display based on the PCI slot order, unless the BIOS offers an option for picking which device is to be treated as the VGA device. Also, an important consideration for docking units is that the VGA device cannot be stopped.

As shown in Figure 30.7, Multiple Display Support allows the Windows 98 desktop to cover more than one monitor with no restrictions on size, position, resolution, or refresh rates. You can configure the system to the size and relative position of each monitor and move applications seamlessly from one monitor to another.

Figure 30.7   Example of Multiple Display Support

On a single-monitor system, the actual desktop is the same size and shape as the only monitor on the system. On a Multiple Display Support system, each monitor is actually a view onto the underlying virtual desktop. You can use the Windows 98 Control Panel to set the area that each monitor presents. As shown in Figure 30.8, the primary monitor always has coordinates corresponding to 0,0 for the upper-left corner, and the x and y resolution for the lower-right corner. The actual coordinates viewed on the secondary monitors depend on the layout of the monitors, which you set using Control Panel. The layout of the secondary monitors is usually based on the physical layout of the monitors on the user's desk.

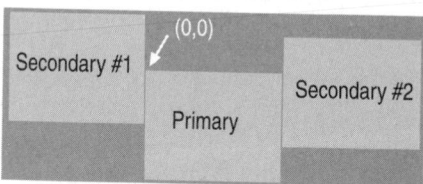

Figure 30.8   A virtual desktop containing three monitors

You can use Control Panel to change the resolution of any of the monitors, but you can change only the coordinates of the secondary monitors. Although both the primary and the secondary monitors use a coordinate system, only the secondary monitors allow their position in the virtual desktop to be changed. The primary monitor's top-left coordinates must remain 0,0 for compatibility. In addition, all the monitors must touch each other on the virtual desktop. This restriction allows the system to maintain the illusion of a single, large desktop that you can seamlessly cross from one monitor to another. At no point do you lose track of the mouse as you move it between monitors.

You can attach up to nine monitors in a multiple display configuration. The coordinates for the second monitor continue from a starting position adjacent to the primary; the coordinates for the third monitor continue from a starting position adjacent to the second monitor, and so on. Since the desktop area that each monitor actually views must be adjacent to another monitor, the virtual desktop is the bounding rectangle of all rectangular areas that can be seen on all attached monitors. For example, if both the primary and secondary monitors have a resolution of 1024 x 768, then a secondary monitor attached to the right of the primary monitor has coordinates from (1024,0) to (2047,767).

If a monitor is not aligned on an axis with its adjacent monitor, or if there are monitors with different resolutions, some of the virtual desktop area might not have a monitor that views that area. For example, the system shown in Figure 30.9 has a 1024 x 768 primary monitor, and an 800 x 600 secondary monitor. The primary monitor has coordinates (0,0) to (1023,767), and the secondary monitor, which is attached to the left of the primary, has coordinates (-800,167) to (-1,767). This results in an area with coordinates from (-800,0) to (-1,167) that is not displayed on either monitor. Windows 98 will not let the user move the mouse into this area, but the area is included in the calculation of the virtual desktop. Therefore the virtual desktop for the example system has coordinates from (-800,0) to (1023,767).

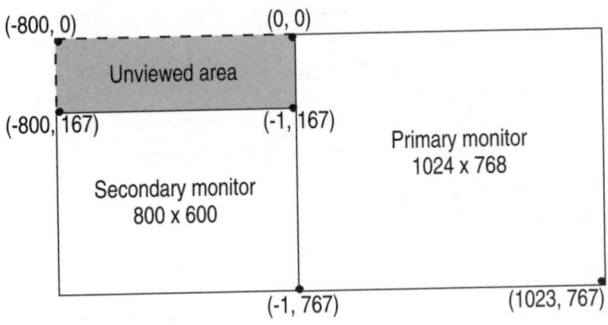

Figure 30.9   Unviewed Virtual Desktop area with monitors of unequal resolution

Supporting Smart Cards

A *smart card* is a small electronic device, approximately the size of a credit card, that contains an embedded integrated circuit. Smart cards are used for such tasks as storing medical records, storing digital cash, and generating network IDs.

The following is a list of system requirements for smart card support:

- Windows 98
- At least 16 MB of RAM
- Up to 3 MB of free disk space
- Windows-compatible smart card reader and device driver
- ISO 7816-compliant smart card

Windows 98 provides the necessary files to enable smart card–aware Windows applications and for service providers to communicate with smart cards through readers attached to Windows-based computers.

The base components on a CD-ROM require a device driver from a smart card reader manufacturer. No device drivers are currently included in Windows 98, but several companies have readers and device drivers available.

You also need a Smart Card Service Provider (SCSP) or Smart Card Cryptographic Provider (SCCP) to expose the services of a smart card to a Windows-based application. The service providers are distributed by the card supplier or issuer and pertain to non-cryptographic and cryptographic services.

Note To develop a device driver or service provider, you must obtain a licensed copy of the Smart Card DDK and Smart Card SDK.

▶ **To install the Microsoft smart card components**

1. From the \scard folder on the Windows 98 compact disk, double-click Setup.exe.
2. Restart your computer.

   Install may replace the Advpack.dll system file.

▶ **To uninstall the Microsoft smart card components**

1. Double-click Add/Remove Programs in the Control Panel.
2. Select **Microsoft Smart Card Base Components**, and then click **Add/Remove**.
3. Restart your computer.

   The Smclib.sys and Smclib.vxd files, used by smart card reader drivers, are not removed during Uninstall, because device drivers that depend on these files to start and run may still be installed on the system. The files may be removed after all smart card reader device drivers have been removed.

   The Msvcrt.dll and Mfc42.dll files are not removed by Uninstall, because they are shared resources.

   The Advpack.dll system file is not removed by Uninstall.

Supporting Still Image Devices

Windows 98 supports *still image* (STI) devices under the WDM architecture. An STI device requires that a minidriver of the WDM STI class be written. Current examples of STI devices are:

- Flatbed scanners, including those with an automatic document feeder, transparency adapter, or other options, such as a start or scan button

- Sheet-fed scanners with paper-inserted detection mechanism
- Hand-held scanners
- STI digital cameras, including those with stored images and associated data (for example, thumbnails and audio)

For more information about writing device drivers for Windows 98, see the Windows 98 DDK.

The STI architecture reduces the software investment made by a hardware vendor. It helps focus the vendor's work on designing device features rather than dealing with system-related tasks. Figure 30.10 illustrates the STI architecture.

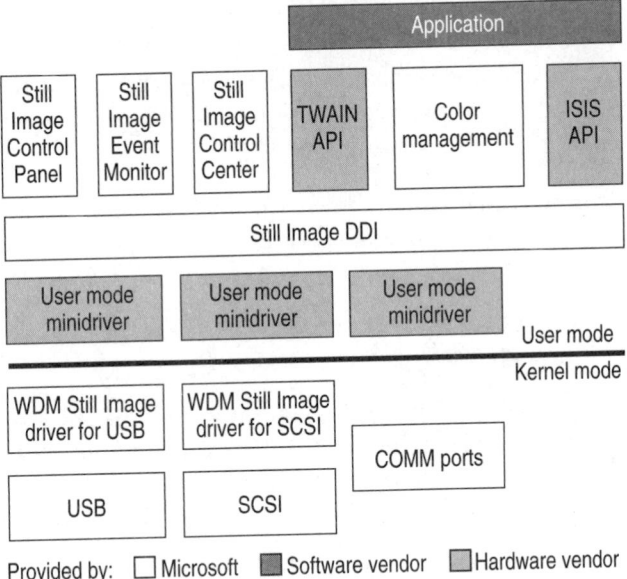

Figure 30.10   STI architecture

The following describes the components shown in Figure 30.10:

Application.   Two primary types of applications use still images. One type is for the editing of image data. Examples of this type are Adobe PhotoShop and Microsoft PictureIt! The other type is for authoring documents that include image data, but that do not focus on editing that image data. Examples of this type are word processing and page layout applications, such as Microsoft Word, or a presentation application, such as Microsoft PowerPoint®.

Still Image APIs.   TWAIN, ISIS, and Adobe Acquire are the common API interfaces in use today. Currently, a hardware vendor has to supply a device-specific component that implements a driver for each supported API.

Color Management. This interface and implementation maintains device color profiles and provides for color-space conversion. All color output from scanners must be defined. To accomplish this, a scanner must either create RGB output or embed the International Color Consortium (ICC) profile for the scanned image into the image file to identify the color-space information for that image.

Still Image Control Panel. In Windows 98, the Control Panel icon Scanners and Cameras gives you access to the following for installed STI devices:

- Listing of the installed STI devices.
- Addition and removal of STI devices that are not Plug and Play.
- Test of the validation of a selected device.
- Vendor-specific configuration or control (by attaching property sheets).
- Control of the association between specific device events and applications to be notified of these events, to be used for the push-model support provided by the Still Image Event Monitor.

The icon appears in Control Panel when Windows 98 detects a Plug and Play STI device, or when you install a non-Plug and Play, STI device through the Add New Hardware Wizard.

For more information about the Add New Hardware Wizard, see Chapter 24, "Device Management."

Still Image Event Monitor. This application (provided by Microsoft) supports push-model behavior by detecting events coming from installed STI devices, and dispatching a set of those events to an application. From Control Panel, you can configure which Still Image-compliant applications are invoked.

Still Image Device Driver Interface (DDI). This DDI (provided by Microsoft) is used to communicate with a particular device. The Still Image APIs, the Control Panel, and the Event Monitor use the Still Image DDI. This DDI uses the color management system as a repository for the color profile supplied for a specific device. The DDI provides interfaces for the following:

- Enumeration
- Device information (primitive capabilities and status)
- Test activation
- Data and command I/O
- Notification for device events, including polling for device activity
- Retrieval of an ICM color profile and other auxiliary information associated with a device

User-Mode minidrivers. These vendor-written modules are small components used to implement device-specific DDI functionality (test, status, and data I/O).

Still Image kernel-mode drivers. These Microsoft-provided modules package a command or data for delivery on a specific bus type. All new kernel-mode drivers provided by Microsoft are WDM-based, although kernel-mode drivers generally need not be. Vendors must supply their own kernel-mode drivers for devices that are not designed to use the standard Microsoft kernel-mode drivers for a specific bus. Currently, kernel mode drivers for SCSI and USB are provided specific to still image devices.

Bus drivers. These Microsoft-provided modules are used to communicate with the STI device. Examples are the USB driver stack, serial-port drivers, and parallel-port drivers.

Supporting Video Capture

Video Capture under Windows 98 is based on the WDM Stream class driver. Windows 98 provides minidrivers for USB and IEEE 1394 cameras, as well as PCI and videoport analog video devices. Support includes DirectShow filters for WDM video-capture interfaces, and for backward compatibility, a Video for Windows (VFW)-to-Stream class mapper. The mapper currently works only with the USB and 1394 digital cameras, and not with the PCI or videoport analog video devices.

Capture applications have been developed using both DirectShow and VFW. Newer capture and conferencing applications are expected to migrate to using the DirectShow interfaces. A sample DirectShow capture application (Amcap.exe) is included in the DirectShow SDK.

Vidcap32.exe is a sample VFW capture application included in the Win32 SDK. It allows you to capture video sequences and images from a VCR, videodisc player, or video camera. Video Capture provides two modes for capturing video sequences:

- Real-time capture
- Step-frame capture

Using Real-Time Capture

Real-time capture processes a video sequence and audio as the events occur naturally or as the video source plays without interruption. A video source for real-time capture (such as a video camera or videodisc) provides an uninterrupted stream of information to the capture hardware. The capture hardware copies each frame of the video sequence (and each portion of audio) and transfers it to the hard disk before the next frame of data enters the capture hardware. A video frame contains one image of the video sequence.

Real-time capture demands a fast computer and hard disk. The computer must process and store each incoming video frame before the next frame is received in the capture board. If the system lags during capture, frames of video data are lost.

Using Step-Frame Capture

Step-frame capture pauses the video source as it collects each frame (image) of data. If audio is also selected, this capture mode rewinds the media in the video source and collects audio data as the video source plays a second time. Step-frame capture collects video frames from a video sequence in a series of steps. Frames are captured one at a time, generally from a paused video device. You can perform step-frame capture manually, advancing the video source using the controls on the video device. Video Capture also provides automatic step-frame capture for video devices that support the Media Control Interface (MCI). With this method, Video Capture issues frame-advance commands to the source device and captures the sequence frame-by-frame. When Video Capture finishes capturing the current frame, it advances the video source to the next capture point.

Step-frame capture provides an alternative for systems that cannot process a video sequence in real time. Because the system can fully process a video frame before contending with the next frame, you can use larger frame sizes and color formats, and you can optionally compress the video sequence during capture. When a step-frame capture is complete, you can capture the audio segment associated with the video frames by playing the source video a second time.

For more information about configuring and using Video Capture, see the Help file Vidcap.hlp included in the Windows 98 SDK.

Supporting Accelerated Graphics Port

Windows 98 supports *Accelerated Graphics Port (AGP)*, a high-performance, component-level interconnect for 3-D graphics applications. Microsoft provides code in Windows 98 that enumerates and initializes devices on the AGP bus. Windows 98 is also responsible for initializing the AGP hardware and managing the mapping from system memory to the video hardware address space. This support is mostly behind the scenes and is not directly accessible to applications programmers. The AGP functionality can be incorporated into applications through the Microsoft DirectDraw API.

Through a hardware-capability bit, DirectDraw allows a graphics driver to indicate that it supports AGP. A DirectDraw driver can specify one or more video memory heaps to DirectDraw that describe how it can address AGP memory. A DirectDraw-based application can specify whether it wants a surface allocated in local video memory, non-local video memory, or system memory. If none of these is specified, DirectDraw chooses the memory class for the surface, and the application can query to find out where the surface was allocated.

AGP allows the graphics processor to see system memory by using the Graphics Address Relocation Table (GART). The GART takes all the virtual pages and makes them look like a contiguous region of memory to the graphics accelerator. The CRTC on the display card does not see the GART.

There are two type of GART memory: Uncached and Write Combined. The data is written straight through to memory for Uncached memory. Multiple writes are combined in a buffer for Write Combined memory. This buffer is controlled by the memory management unit. The advantage of Write Combined is that it is a lot faster to transfer (for example, eight DWORDS at a time as opposed to one DWORD at a time).

In Windows 98, the GART is split evenly between Uncached and Write Combined. The maximum size of the GART is controlled by the BIOS. Some BIOSs allow the AGP aperture (maximum size) to be set. The Graphics Processor can use the GART for texture memory.

Supporting Wireless Connectivity

Windows 98 provides support for *IrDA*, the Infrared Data Association standard for wireless connectivity. IrDA support allows Windows 98 users to connect hardware devices and other computers easily without using connecting cables. This driver set provides infrared-equipped portable or desktop computers with the ability to network, transfer files, and print wirelessly with other IrDA-compatible infrared devices. For example, the user of an IrDA-equipped portable computer can simply walk up to an IrDA-equipped printer, aim the computer at the printer (in the same manner as aiming a TV remote control at a TV), and run the print function. Another example is a user copying a file from one portable computer to another by aiming the first computer at the other and then running the copy function.

Supporting Hardware Profiles

Hardware Profiles are used to set up multiple hardware configurations. This is especially useful for portable computers that have docking stations or workstations with removable storage media.

Hardware Profiles are automatically created for portable computers when the system is docked or undocked. Furthermore, a new hardware profile would be created if the computer is placed in a different docking station.

The following procedures demonstrate how to set up hardware profiles for a portable computer with a docking station that has this configuration:

Configuration	Docked	Undocked
Display driver	S3	VGA
Network	Microsoft Network	None
RNA	No RNA	With RNA

▶ **To set systems properties**

1. Click My Computer.

2. Click **Properties**, and then click the **Hardware Profiles** tab.

3. Verify that two hardware profile options labeled Docked and Undocked exist. If these options are not available, highlight **Original Configuration**, and then click **Rename**. Type **DOCKED** and then click **OK**. Highlight the word **DOCKED** and then click **Copy**. In the **Copy Profile** dialog box type **UNDOCKED**.

▶ **To set up the video driver for docked and undocked configurations**

1. Verify that VGA is installed. If it is not installed, in Control Panel double-click Display. Click the **Settings** tab, and then click **Advanced**. Click the **Adapter** tab, click **Change**, and then install the VGA driver.

2. In Control Panel, double-click System, and then click the **Device Manager** tab.

3. Double-click **Display Adapter**, and then double-click **VGA**.

4. In the **Device Usage** area, make sure Undocked is checked and Docked is unchecked. Click **OK**.

5. In the **Device Manager** tab, double-click **Display Adapter**, and then double-click the **S3** adapter.

6. In the **Device Usage** area, make sure the Docked option is checked and the Undocked option is unchecked. Click **OK**.

▶ **To set up for no network in an undocked state**

1. In Control Panel, double-click System, and then click the **Device Manager** tab.

2. Double-click **Network Adapter**, and then double-click the network card.

3. In the **Device Usage** area of the **General** tab, click the **Disable in this hardware profile** box.

4. Click **OK**.

▶ **To set up for no RNA while docked**

1. In Control Panel, double-click System, and then click **the Device Manager** tab.

2. Double-click **Network Adapters**, and then double-click **Dial-up Adapter**.

3. Click the **Disable in this hardware profile** box.

Tip   Windows 98 scans for floppy drives on each boot, which is helpful for portable computers and other computers where the floppy can be removed. If you are on a desktop with a stationary floppy drive, you can turn this option off to speed up boot time.

1. In Control Panel, click System, and then click the **Performance** tab.

2. Click **File System**, and then click the **Floppy Disk** tab.

3. Uncheck the box next to **Search for new floppy disk drives each time your computer starts**.

4. Click **OK**.

Overview of Power Management

An evolution in computer power management is taking place because of the advent of the *Simply Interactive PC (SIPC)*, a Microsoft initiative to create a computer that never needs to be serviced by the user and is as simple to use as any household appliance. This new computer is instantly available to the user because it uses power management to keep the machine in a low power state when it is not being used rather than turning all the way off (thus avoiding lengthy boot times).

For more information about SIPC, see **http://www.microsoft.com/hwdev/**.

Windows 98 directs power management through the OnNow system. Unlike previous approaches to power management, OnNow manages power for the entire system including all system devices and peripherals. To make this possible, the operating system must direct power to the computer.

With legacy power management architectures, the BIOS controls the power state of system devices. However, OnNow makes it possible for the operating system to coordinate power management activities at all levels and define the power-state transitions for the system.

Computer power management means there is control over how the computer consumes energy and integrates its components. For example, a running application, or mouse, keyboard, or joystick activity, prompts the power management system that the computer is in use. The power management system then allows the computer full power, Otherwise, the power management system drops the computer to a sleep state. Another example is a fax modem, which does not need to use full power all the time. The fax modem can operate in a "standby" state, consuming less energy until it has to receive an incoming fax, at which time it is given full power. This section describes how Windows 98 supports power management.

Understanding How OnNow Works

With OnNow power management, the computer functions as follows:

- The computer is ready for immediate use when the user presses the power button.

- The computer appears to be off when not in use, but can still respond to wakeup events. In other words, the computer seems off according to what users hear and see; they have confidence that the computer is not consuming excess energy, and that data and programs are reliably saved. Wakeup events might be triggered by a device receiving some input, such as a telephone ringing, or by software that requests the computer to wake up at a predetermined time (for example, to download your e-mail so it is ready when you wake up in the morning).

- Software adjusts its behavior when the power state of the computer changes. The operating system and applications work together intelligently to operate the computer, to deliver effective power management according to the user's current needs and expectations. For example, applications do not keep the computer busy unnecessarily; instead, they proactively participate in shutting down the computer to conserve energy and reduce noise.

- All devices participate in the power management scheme, whether originally installed in the computer or added later by the user. Any new device can have its power state changed as system use dictates.

Figure 30.11 shows the components of the OnNow system.

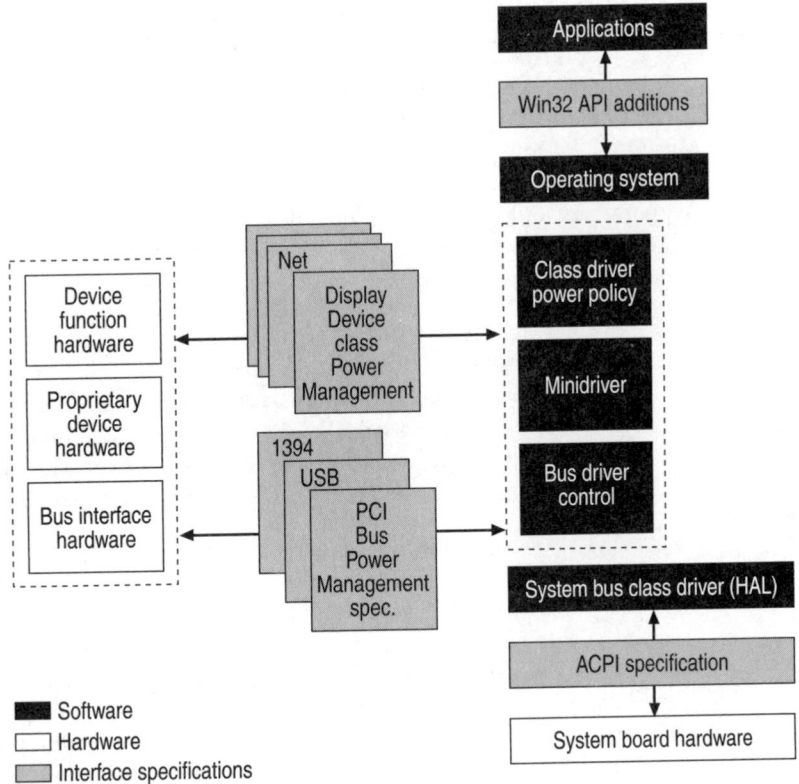

Figure 30.11   OnNow system components

Note Applications developed before the advent of OnNow were designed to assume that the computer is always fully powered while the application is running. Such applications can inadvertently keep the system from entering a lower power state. In addition, these applications can crash when the computer wakes up, either after time has passed or after devices have been removed.

Though Windows 98 performs most of the work for OnNow, applications have to be designed for OnNow power management and Plug and Play to make the entire process seamless.

The goal of the operating system is to conserve energy while the computer is working and to put the computer to sleep when it is not working. The decisions that determine how to save energy and when to go to sleep are referred to as the *power policy*. In OnNow, power policy is based on the end user's preferences, the application requirements, and the system hardware capabilities. The implementation of power policy is distributed throughout the system, with different system components acting as *policy owners* for different aspects. For example, the operating system itself is the policy owner responsible for when the computer should go to sleep, how deep a sleep the computer should go into, and how to operate the processor to obtain energy conservation, and to meet thermal and audible noise goals.

There is also a policy owner for each device class in the computer. The policy owner for a particular device class is the component that knows how the device is used by the end user and the applications. This is generally a high-level component and in most cases a WDM class driver. Each policy owner has to make appropriate power management decisions for its class and work consistently with the operating system's policy for putting the computer to sleep.

Carrying out power policy—actually controlling devices so power consumption or capabilities change—is not the concern of the policy owner. Responsibility for this power control is given to the device drivers for the affected device and is shared among the drivers in the stack. Device-specific drivers or minidrivers are responsible for saving and restoring the device's settings (context) across low-power state transitions. Bus drivers are responsible for giving the actual hardware command to the device to change state. When the policy owner makes the decision to enter a low-power state and communicates it to the device driver through the system, the device driver saves context and then sends the request to the bus driver. This gives the hardware command to the device to enter the low-power state. When the device is to be powered-up, the same sequence occurs in reverse; the bus driver turns on the device, and the device-specific driver restores the saved context.

Understanding Advanced Configuration and Power Interface

For the OnNow system to be successful, Windows 98 must be aware of how power management features integrate throughout the computer. This is done through the OnNow feature known as the *Advanced Configuration and Power Interface (ACPI)*, a system interface that provides a standard way to control power management and Plug and Play functions of the computer hardware. ACPI allows the motherboard to describe its device configuration and power control hardware interface to Windows 98; this allows the operating system to automatically turn on and off standard devices, such as CD-ROMs, network cards, hard disk drives, and printers, as well as consumer devices connected to the computer, such as VCRs, TVs, phones, and stereos.

For a complete OnNow system, the system BIOS must support ACPI. The BIOS plays an important role in the ACPI by working with Windows 98 in performing the necessary initialization processing and handoff during boot and when resuming the working (full power) state.

Figure 30.12 is an overview of the ACPI.

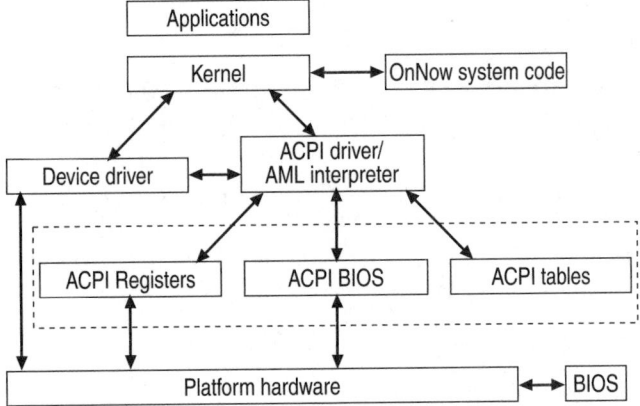

Figure 30.12   Overview of the ACPI

Note With legacy BIOS, the power management features in Windows 98 function, but the legacy BIOS must control power management.

The ACPI specification, currently in version 1.0, has two parts: configuration (Plug and Play), and power management. ACPI gives Windows 98 and the device drivers all power management decision making. The BIOS simply provides Windows 98 with access to the hardware controls for controlling power in the system. Windows 98 and the device drivers, which already know when the system is active, decide when to turn off devices that are not in use and when to put the entire system to sleep.

Since power management is controlled by the operating system, there is a single user interface for managing power that works on all ACPI computers and simplifies the experience for the end user. ACPI provides more detailed knowledge to the operating system about what the system can do and what are the sources of events.

For example, the ACPI computer and operating system can do the following:

- Make sure the screen does not turn off in the middle of a presentation.
- Let the machine wake automatically in the middle of the night to perform some task, yet not turn on the monitor and drives needlessly.
- Let the user choose what the power and sleep buttons do in the system.

During Windows 98 Setup, ACPI is installed only on systems that are listed on the retail compact disc as good ACPI systems. However, if you have had the system BIOS updated to a fully functioning ACPI BIOS, you can have ACPI installed by using the following procedure.

▶ **To install ACPI**

1. Flash the BIOS to the latest rev.

2. Run Regedit.

    Under **HKEY_LOCAL_MACHINE\Software\Microsoft\Windows \CurrentVersion\Detect**, add a String value called **ACPIOption**, and set it to 1.

3. In Control Panel, click Add/Remove Hardware and have it run full detection.

To remove ACPI support, perform steps 1 through 3, but set **ACPIOption** to 2. The settings for **ACPIOption** are as follows:

0 (or not present) – Detect only ACPI BIOSs on good list.

1 – Detect any ACPI BIOS.

2 – Do not detect ACPI BIOSs (remove support if installed).

Alternatively, you can enable ACPI support at setup time using the following command line:

```
setup /p J
```

Understanding Advanced Power Management

In contrast to ACPI, there is the *Advanced Power Management (APM) BIOS* specification, which is currently in version 1.2. Under APM, the BIOS controls system power management. The BIOS has timers that monitor most interrupts, and I/O port reads and writes. When the timer for a device exceeds some value set in the BIOS setup, the BIOS turns off the device. When the system-wide timer exceeds some value set in the BIOS, the BIOS sends a message to Windows 98 to put the computer to sleep. Windows 98 then prepares to suspend the computer and tells the BIOS to do so.

The APM BIOS is also responsible for monitoring the battery status and requesting a suspend if the battery is getting low.

However, the following limitations exist with APM.

Different user interfaces. Each BIOS has its own user interface and its own power management behavior. This means every computer operates differently—users have to be retrained on each computer.

Reasons for suspend are not known. Because of the architecture of the APM BIOS interface, the APM BIOS cannot inform Windows 98 that the request is due to the user pushing a sleep button, the BIOS assuming the system is idle, or the battery running out of power. So Windows 98 must always honor this suspend request and attempt to put the computer to sleep—even if the computer is not idle. It is recommended that users turn off all their BIOS timeout settings.

Devices might be turned off at inappropriate times. By monitoring I/O ports and interrupts, the BIOS is essentially trying to second-guess what the user and the applications are doing. Although this often works, there are many scenarios in which the BIOS can guess incorrectly. For example, the BIOS turns off or slows down a computer in use (such as a screen saver turning on in the middle of a presentation), or the BIOS does not turn off a truly idle computer.

No system capabilities information on APM 1.0 or 1.1 BIOS. With these older versions of the APM BIOS specification, the only way to determine if the computer-supported standby was for the operating system is to try putting it in standby. Not only did some BIOSs not implement standby, but they crashed when the operating system called the BIOS. APM 1.2 provides a way to determine if standby is supported, and the operating system uses standby only if the computer supports it.

The BIOS detects activity only on devices residing on the motherboard. The BIOS cannot detect devices, such as add-in cards, USB devices, and IEEE 1394 devices. As a result, the BIOS might think that the system is not in use even if one or more of these off-motherboard devices is in use.

For more information about how your computer's BIOS supports ACPI and APM, see the MSInfo utility that ships with Windows 98.

Supporting OnNow Through WDM

In addition to providing a common set of I/O services and device drivers for Windows 98 and future versions of Windows NT, WDM includes support of OnNow power management.

WDM drivers can implement power policy and control. Device Driver Interfaces (DDIs) are defined to synchronize power-state changes with other power management activities in the system, and to detect idle devices. I/O request packets (IRPs) set the power state, enable wakeup, and query power status. Power policy decisions generally result in the kernel sending an IRP to a specific system component (often the policy owner itself) to affect a particular power management control.

For more information about WDM, see "Understanding WDM," earlier in this chapter.

Using the OnNow Interface

Windows 98 allows you to monitor OnNow features and set power management options called *Power Schemes* using the Power Management icon in Control Panel.

OnNow includes the following features for Power Management:

The ability to start using the system in just a few seconds by using Standby instead of Off. While on standby, your monitor and hard disks turn off, and your computer uses less power. When you want to use the computer again, it comes out of standby quickly. Standby is particularly useful for conserving battery power in portable computers. ACPI machines have a power/sleep feature that you can access from the front of the computer or from the operating system.

The ability for the system to put itself in standby automatically when not in use.

The ability for the system to automatically wake to handle events, such as running backups, downloading e-mail, and defragmenting your hard disk. This is done through the Task Scheduler. For more information, see Chapter 23, " System and Remote Administration Tools."

A simplified, single-user interface for power management. This includes a new battery meter, low battery alarms, power control panel, Hibernate, and Standby on the shutdown menu.

Enhanced application messaging to allow applications to adjust their behavior appropriately for changes in battery state.

Note To use Power Management, you must have a computer that is set up by the manufacturer to support these features. For more information, see your computer documentation.

Windows 98 provides power schemes that configure the system to go on standby, and the monitor to shut off after predetermined periods of system inactivity.

The following set of power schemes is built into Windows 98:

Home/Office Desk. For desktop machines. This scheme is installed with Typical/Compact/Custom Setup options.

Portable/Laptop. Optimized for portable computers. This scheme includes aggressive settings for running on batteries (the AC settings are the same as desktop), and is installed with Typical/Compact/Custom/Portable Setup options.

Always On.   For use with personal servers. This scheme is similar to Home/Office, but has the standby timer disabled and hard disk timer increased. It is installed when you install a server and is the default for APM desktop computers.

If none of the built-in schemes is appropriate, you can change the properties of a built-in scheme or create an entirely new scheme through the **Power Management Properties** dialog box.

Note   If you want to set up a power scheme that configures automatically on power-up, you need to write a script within Msbatch.inf. See Appendix D, "Msbatch.inf Parameters for Setup Scripts," and Chapter 2, "Setting Up Windows 98."

Using Power Management for the Desktop

Using the Power Management features for the desktop, you can create a power scheme and display the power meter on the taskbar. The power scheme will turn off your monitor after a specified length of time of inactivity. You can choose from three preset Power Management configurations: Home/Office Desk, Portable/Laptop, and Always On.

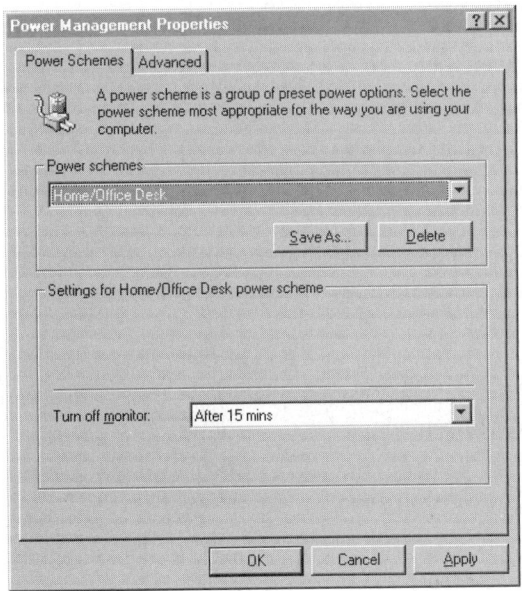

▶ **To change the properties of an existing power scheme**

1. In Control Panel, click Power Management. The **Power Management Properties** dialog box is displayed. Make sure the **Power Schemes** tab is active.

2. Select the power scheme from the **Power Schemes** menu.

3. Select the desired time setting for **Turn off monitor,** and then click **Apply**.

▶ **To create a new power scheme**

1. In Control Panel, click Power Management. The **Power Management Properties** dialog box is displayed. Make sure the **Power Schemes** tab is active.

2. Select the power scheme from the **Power Schemes** menu.

3. Select the desired time setting for **Turn off monitor.**

4. Click **Save As**. When prompted, provide a name for the new power scheme. Click **OK**.

The **Advanced** tab lets you control the System Tray icon. Right-click the taskbar icon to see the status of the power meter, and click the icon to change the power scheme on the fly.

▶ **To add the power meter to the system tray**

1. Click the **Advanced** tab.

2. Select the **Show power meter on taskbar** check box.

3. Click **Apply**.

If your computer supports these options, you can use the **Advanced** tab to make your computer go into Standby or Shutdown mode by pressing the power button or closing the lid.

▶ **To use the Power Management power buttons**

1. Click the **Advanced** tab.

2. Click the **When I press the power button on my computer** list box, and then click **Standby** or **Shutdown**.

3. Click **OK**.

Some ACPI computers support a feature called Hibernate, which saves everything in your computer memory to your hard disk. You would put your computer into Hibernate when you are away from your computer for an extended time or overnight. When you turn your computer back on, all programs and documents that were open when you turned the computer off are quickly restored to the desktop.

Note To use Hibernate, you must have a computer that is set up by the manufacturer to support this option. If the **Hibernate** tab is not displayed in Power Management, your computer does not support this feature.

▶ **To use the Hibernate feature**

1. Click the **Hibernate** tab, select the check box, and then click the **Advanced** tab.

2. Click **When I press the power button on my computer**, and then click **Hibernate**.

3. Click **OK**, and either press the power button.

Using Power Management for Portable Computers

In addition to the tabs provided for the desktop, Power Management for portable computers includes the **Alarms** and **Battery Meter** tabs. A major difference between power management for desktop and portable computers is that you can change settings based on battery use for a portable computer.

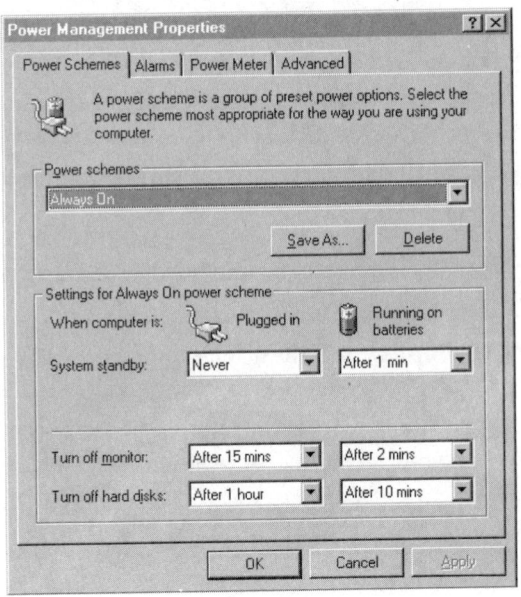

System Standby can reduce the power consumption of your computer. Depending on whether your computer is plugged in or running on batteries, you can choose a different length of time for the computer to go into standby. The time specifies the length of time that your computer is inactive before it going into standby mode.

You can change the properties of an existing power scheme or create a new power scheme using **Power Schemes**. Select a power scheme that works best with the way you use your computer. You can choose from three preset Power Management configurations: Home/Office Desk, Portable/Laptop, and Always On. You can also set suspend time for Energy Start–compliant monitors and the IDE hard drive spin down time.

▶ **To change the properties of an existing power scheme**

1. In Control Panel, click Power Management. The **Power Management Properties** dialog box is displayed. Make sure the **Power Schemes** tab is active.

2. Select the power scheme from the **Power Schemes** menu.

3. Select desired time setting for **System Standby**, **Turn off monitor**, or **Turn off hard disk**, and then click **Apply**.

▶ **To create a new power scheme**

1. In Control Panel, click Power Management. The **Power Management Properties** dialog box is displayed. Make sure the **Power Schemes** tab is active.

2. Select the power scheme from the **Power Schemes** menu.

3. Select the desired time setting for either the **Turn off monitor** option, the **Standby** option, or the **Hard Disk** option. If desired, set other options.

4. Click **Save As**. When prompted, provide a name for the new power scheme. Click **OK**.

▶ **To change the elapsed time before your hard disk automatically turns off**

1. In Control Panel, click Power Management.

2. In **Turn off hard disks**, click the arrows, and then select the times you want.

3. Click **OK**.

▶ **To change the elapsed time before your monitor automatically turns off**

1. In Control Panel, click Power Management.

2. In **Turn off monitor**, click the arrows, and then select the times you want.

3. Click **OK**.

The **Alarms** tab lets you set a low battery alarm and a critical battery alarm. You can set the type of notification—an audible alarm or a displayed message—when your battery drops to the levels you specify. You can also specify whether the computer goes on standby or shuts down when the alarm sounds or a message is displayed.

Note   The critical batter alarm level must be less than the low battery alarm.

▶   **To set the battery alarms**

1. In the **Power Management Properties** dialog box, click the **Alarms** tab.
2. Select the **Set off low batter alarm when power level reaches** check box or the **Set off critical battery alarm when power level reaches** check box.
3. Drag the slider to change the battery level at which a low-battery alarm or message is activated.
4. Click **Alarm Action**, and then click either the **Sound Alarm** or the **Display Message** box, or both.
5. Click the **When the alarm goes off the computer will** box to display the list. You can specify that your computer immediately goes in standby or shuts down when the alarm sounds or a message is displayed.
6. Click the **Force standby or shutdown even if a program stops responding** box if you want the computer to go into standby or shut down even if a program is not responding.
7. Click **OK**, and then click **OK** again.

The **Power Meter** tab shows the current source of power and displays the percentage of power level remaining for all the batteries in your computer.

▶   **To check the power level of the batteries**

1. In **Power Management Properties** dialog box, click the **Power Meter** tab.
2. Click the **Show Details for each battery** box to display the power level for each battery.
3. Click an individual battery icon for more information about each battery.
4. Click **OK**.

You can display the power meter icon on the taskbar using the **Advanced** tab. Right-click the power meter icon on the taskbar to get the status and other details of each battery, and click the icon to change Power Schemes on-the-fly.

▶   **To show the battery meter on the system taskbar**

1. Click the **Advanced** tab.
2. Check the **Show battery meter on taskbar** box.
3. Click **OK**.

You can choose to be prompted for a password when the computer goes out of standby using the **Advanced** tab.

▶ **To be prompted for a password when the computer goes out of standby**

1. Click the **Advanced** tab.

2. Click the **Prompt for password when computer goes off standby** box (the password is the same as the screen saver password).

3. Click **OK**.

If your computer supports these options, you can use the **Advanced** tab to make your computer go into Standby or Shutdown mode by pressing the power button or closing the lid.

▶ **To use the Power Management power buttons**

1. Click the **Advanced** tab.

2. Click the **When I close the lid of my portable computer** list box, and then click **Standby** or **Shutdown**.

3. Click the **When I press the power button on my computer** list box, and then click **Standby** or **Shutdown**.

4. Click **OK**.

Some ACPI computers support a feature called Hibernate, which saves everything in your computer memory to your hard disk. You would put your computer into Hibernate when you are away from your computer for an extended time or overnight. When you turn your computer back on, all programs and documents that were open when you turned the computer off are quickly restored to the desktop.

Note To use Hibernate, you must have a computer that is set up by the manufacturer to support this option. If the **Hibernate** tab is not displayed in Power Management, your computer does not support this feature.

▶ **To use the Hibernate feature**

1. Click the **Hibernate** tab, select the check box, and then click the **Advanced** tab.

2. Click **When I press the power button on my computer**, and then click **Hibernate**.

   – Or –

   Click **When I close the lid of my computer**, and then click **Hibernate**.

3. Click **OK**, and either press the power button or close the lid of the computer, depending on which feature you selected.

Troubleshooting Hardware Management Components

This section contains troubleshooting examples for the Windows 98 hardware management components.

Troubleshooting WDM

Most WDM troubleshooting involves the writing of WDM drivers.

For more information about troubleshooting WDM drivers, see the WDM DDK.

Troubleshooting System Buses

This section contains procedures for troubleshooting the system buses supported by Windows 98.

Troubleshooting USB

Because of the nature of USB devices, no resource settings could cause a USB device to function improperly or fail.

▶ **To resolve problems with USB speakers**

- Most speakers are available in two modes: digital and audio. If you are using USB speakers and not getting any output, make sure the speakers are in digital mode.

▶ **To resolve most other problems involving a USB device**

1. Check the host-controller firmware revision by viewing the host controller's properties in Device Manager. The **General** tab lists the hardware version of the host controller. A version number of 000 indicates that the controller is using the A-1 stepping chip, which is not supported. Contact the original equipment manufacturer (OEM) for an upgraded host controller.

2. If only one device is failing, reconnect that device to another USB port. If the device works, the original port is faulty and should be repaired. If the device does not work when connected to the new port, more than likely the device is faulty and should be repaired or replaced.

3. If the device is bus-powered, it could be drawing too much current to function when connected to a hub port. Connect the device directly to the host controller, bypassing any hubs.

4. If the bus configuration is multi-tiered, make sure the configuration adheres to the following guidelines:

- A bus-powered hub cannot be connected to another bus-powered hub.
- Bus-powered hubs cannot support more than four downstream ports.
- Bus-powered hubs cannot support bus-powered devices that draw more than 100 mA.
- The bus cannot exceed five tiers.

5. Remove the USB host controller from Device Manager and restart the computer. This allows Windows 98 to redetect and reinstall the entire bus.

Troubleshooting the IEEE 1394 Bus

If you are trying to connect two computers together on the IEEE 1394 bus, make sure you use the correct cable. This cable is not supplied with the bus and must be purchased separately.

Troubleshooting Hardware Devices

The following sections describe how to troubleshoot problems when installing hardware device drivers.

Resolving Fatal Exception Errors

If a Fatal Exception error occurs after you install a WDM driver for a hardware device, the device is most likely expecting a specific driver to be installed. To help you correct this error, the device manufacturer usually provides the specific driver on the installation disk.

Determining if a Hardware Device Is Using a WDM Driver

To find out if a hardware device uses a WDM driver, you can use Device Manager or the Microsoft System Information tool (MSInfo).

▶ **To use Device Manager**

1. Right-click My Computer on the Windows 98 desktop and click **Properties**.

   – Or –

   In Control Panel, click System.

2. In the **System Properties** dialog box, click the **Device Manager** tab.

3. Double-click the device name. From the device **Properties** dialog box, click the **Driver** tab.

4. Click **Driver File Details**. The **Driver File Details** box lists the device driver's file name. If the file name has a .sys extension, the driver is a WDM driver.

▶   **To use MSInfo**

1. Use the **Find File** utility to locate and run Msinfo32.exe.

2. In the left pane of the Microsoft Information window, expand **Components** to find the device in question.

3. In the right pane, locate the device driver's file name. If the file name has a .sys extension, the driver is a WDM driver.

For more information about how to use the Windows 98 Device Manager, see Chapter 24, "Device Management."

For more information about MSInfo, see MSInfo Help.

Troubleshooting the OnNow System

Windows 98 troubleshooting techniques are continually being updated. For the latest information, see the Windows 98 Resource Kit Tools Help.

The following shows possible causes of common problems, and ways to resolve them.

Timers are idle.

If **System standby**, **Turn off monitor**, or **Turn off hard disks** is inaccurate or nonfunctional, the causes could be:

- An open application is keeping the computer from going on standby to protect data.
- An open application is performing periodic disk access.
- The BIOS settings are overriding the Windows timers.
- Hard disk spindown timers do not function with SCSI drives.

Try the following:

- Close all applications.
- Press CTRL+ALT+DEL, , and then close all tasks except **Explorer** and **Systray**.
- Check the BIOS settings. If they are greater than the Windows timer settings, try making them less. For example, if the Windows monitor shutdown timer is set to 15 minutes, and the BIOS monitor shutdown timer is set to 2 hours, try changing the BIOS timer to 10 minutes. If the BIOS timer appears to be overriding the Windows timers, contact the hardware vendor for a BIOS update.

The computer is being placed on standby erroneously.

A possible cause is the BIOS settings overriding the Windows timer settings.

Try the following:

- Check the BIOS settings. If they are less than the Windows timer settings, try making them greater. For example, if the Windows standby timer is set to never and the BIOS suspend timer is set to 15 minutes, try changing the BIOS timer to never suspend. If the BIOS timer appears to be overriding the Windows timers, contact the hardware vendor for a BIOS update.

The computer appears to stop responding while in standby mode.

Note To determine whether the problem lies in standby mode, the shutdown of the monitor, or the shutdown of the hard disks, set two of the three options to **Never** and the third to its original setting. Allow the timeout to occur, and determine whether the system appears to have stopped responding. Isolate the failure by trying each of the three combinations, first testing the monitor timer, then the hard disk timer, and then the system standby timer.

The system appears to stop responding after turning off the monitor.

The causes could be:

- The system is responding, but the display is not properly reinitializing.
- The display adapter does not fully support the calls made from Windows to turn off the display.

Try the following:

- While the display is off, move the mouse or press a key on the keyboard to try turning it back on. If this fails, perform the following keystrokes:
  CTRL+ESC
  r
  a:
  ENTER

  If the system is working, but the display is simply not properly initializing, this will cause the system to look for a floppy disk in the a: drive. Check for disk activity in this drive.
- Contact your hardware vendor for more information.

The system appears to stop responding after shutting off the hard disks.

Contact your hardware manufacturer for more information.

The hard disk does not support spindown functionality or is malfunctioning.

Contact your hardware manufacturer for more information.

The system appears to stop responding while in standby mode.

The causes could be:

- The system is responding, but the display is not properly reinitializing.
- An application or driver is allowing the system to go on standby but is causing the system to stop responding.
- The BIOS is causing the system to stop responding.

Try the following:

- See the response to "The system appears to stop responding after turning off the monitor" section earlier in this chapter.
- Close all applications. Press CTRL+ALT+DEL, and end all tasks except **Explorer** and **Systray**. Try uninstalling third-party system management programs, such as crash protectors, memory managers, and performance enhancement utilities.
- Try disabling all devices in Device Manager except the display adapter(s), the mouse, anything under the **USB Devices** category (if you have either a USB keyboard or a USB mouse), and anything under the **System Devices** category. Reboot the computer. If the system goes on standby successfully, re-enable one half of the currently disabled devices. Reboot again. If the system continues to go on standby successfully, re-enable half of the remaining disabled devices. Otherwise, disable the devices you just re-enabled, and re-enable the devices that were disabled. Continue in this manner until the offending device has been pinpointed.

Additional Resources

For more information about	See this resource
For all hardware management issues, including:	**http://www.microsoft.com/hwdev/**
DirectMovie	
Hardware device support details, including HID, DirectX, DirectDraw, digital audio, HAL, STI, AGP, and Multiple Display Support	
Hardware development	
OnNow, SIPC, WDM working with OnNow, ACPI, APM, OnNow device power states, PC 97, PC 98, NDIS, and networking specifications	
HID class, IEEE 1394 bus driver, Port class, STI, USB driver, and WDM Stream class video capture minidriver	Windows 98 Device Driver Kit (DDK) Help

Additional Resources (*continued*)

For more information about	See this resource
Writing WDM class drivers WDM Kernel Troubleshooting WDM DDI and writing device drivers for Windows 98	Win32 Driver Model Device Driver Kit (WDM DDK) and Windows 98 DDK
DirectShow	**http://www.microsoft.com/msdn/sdk/inetsdk/help/**
Configuring and using Video Capture	Windows 98 Software Development Kit Help
IrDA	**http://www.microsoft.com/hwdev/devdes/**
Computer hardware design	*PC97 Hardware Design Guide*, Microsoft Press, 1997
Designing the following for the computer:	
CardBus, IEEE 1394, PC Card, PCI, and USB	
Device drivers in your system	The MSInfo utility
BIOS support for ACPI and APM	
IEEE 1394 standards	**http://www.microsoft.com/hwdev/** **http://www.adaptec.com/firewire/** **http://www.ti.com/**
The latest troubleshooting techniques	Windows 98 Resource Kit compact disc **http://www.microsoft.com/hwtest/** **http://www.microsoft.com/kb/** **http://www.microsoft.com/support/**

C H A P T E R   3 1

Windows 98 Registry

31

This chapter describes how Microsoft Windows 98 components use the *registry*, provides an overview of registry tools, including *Registry Checker*, *Registry Editor*, and *Profile Editor*, and describes how to backup and restore the registry. It provides an overview of the structure of the registry, and describes the registry keys. It also describes how values from Windows 3.*x* INI files are stored in the registry, and includes registry entries for modems, Transmission Control Protocol/Internet Protocol (TCP/IP), and other components.

This chapter is designed for system and network administrators and for "power users." It is not intended for registry programmers (see the *Microsoft Windows 98 Software Development Kit* for that information).

Note This chapter assumes that your Windows 98 files are in the \Windows folder, which is the default folder where Setup copies the system files.

Caution Making a mistake in editing the registry can cause your system to become unstable and/or unusable.

Wherever possible, use the administrative tools, such as Control Panel or System Policy Editor, to make configuration changes, rather than editing the registry. This is to ensure values are stored properly in the registry when changing the configuration.

If you use Registry Editor to change values, you will not be warned if any entry is incorrect. Editing the registry directly by using Registry Editor can cause errors in loading hardware and software, and can prevent users from being able to start the computer.

See Also

- For more information about user profiles, see Chapter 7, "User Profiles."

- For more information about system policies, see Chapter 8, "System Policies."

- For more information about the Windows 98 architecture, see Chapter 28, "Windows 98 Architecture."

- For more information about the registry, see *Inside the Microsoft Windows 98 Registry* by Günter Born.

Overview of the Windows 98 Registry

The structure of the Windows 98 registry has not changed significantly from the Windows 95 registry. What has changed is that the code that handles the registry has become faster and more robust, and the registry now detects when certain problems arise, and automatically fixes them.

The registry is the central storage for all configuration data. The Windows 98 system configuration, the computer hardware configuration, configuration information about Win32-based applications, and user preferences are all stored in the registry. For example, any Windows 98 computer hardware configuration changes that are made with a Plug and Play device are immediately reflected in a configuration change in the registry. Because of these characteristics, the registry serves as the foundation for user, system, and network management in Windows 98.

The registry stores the data in a hierarchical form. Because the registry contains all settings required to configure memory, hardware peripherals, and Windows 98–supplied network components, you will find that it is no longer necessary to configure settings in startup configuration and initialization files. Also, because all settings are stored in a central location, you can provide both local and remote support for system configuration using Windows 98 tools.

To properly manage resources, such as Internet requests (IRQs), I/O addresses, and direct memory accesses (DMAs), Windows 98 uses the registry to track devices and resources allocated for both Plug and Play–compliant devices, ACPI mechanisms, and legacy devices. The registry provides a centralized, dynamic data store for all Windows settings, with a "current configuration" branch that stores information on a per-configuration basis. For example, the Display option in Control Panel stores per-configuration information about display resolution changes and the Print option in Control Panel stores per-configuration information about the default printer.

Device Manager—which is accessed from the System option in Control Panel—provides a graphical representation of devices configured in Windows 98, and allows properties used by these devices to be viewed and changed, as appropriate. Device Manager also shows resources allocated for the configured devices. Through the resource configuration information maintained in the registry, Windows 98 is able to automatically identify and resolve device resource conflicts for Plug and Play–compliant devices. For legacy devices, Device Manager helps users quickly identify and resolve resource conflicts with devices in the system.

The registry is roughly analogous to the INI files used under Windows 3.x, with each key in the registry similar to a bracketed heading in an INI file and with registry values similar to entries under the INI headings. However, registry keys can contain subkeys, while INI files do not support nested headings. Registry values can also consist of binary data, rather than the simple strings used in INI files.

Although Microsoft discourages using INI files in favor of registry entries, some applications (particularly 16-bit, Windows-based applications) still use INI files. Windows 98 supports INI files solely for compatibility with those applications and related tools (such as setup programs). The Autoexec.bat and Config.sys files also still exist for compatibility with real-mode system components and to allow users to change certain default system settings, such as the PATH environment variable. New Win32-based applications can store their initialization information in the registry.

The Windows 98 registry provides the following benefits:

- Registry services use less real-mode memory and less protected-mode memory. This translates to faster startup times and an overall increase in system performance.

- Registry services have much better caching support. This dramatically improves the time used to look up values in the registry. This also translates to an overall increase in system performance.

- Windows 98 automatically detects many sources of corruption. For example, if a computer does not shut down completely due to power failure, Windows 98 detects the improper shutdown and automatically runs Registry Checker to find and fix any registry errors that may have occurred due to improper shutdown.

- Registry Checker is a system maintenance program that finds and fixes registry problems. Each time you start your computer, Registry Checker automatically scans the registry for inconsistent structures, and if no problem is found, Registry Checker backs up the registry once per day. If a problem is found in the registry, Registry Checker can restore the registry from a good backup copy. Registry Checker maintains five compressed backups of the registry that have successfully started the computer. Registry Checker attempts to fix the registry if a backup cannot be found. Registry Checker also removes unused space in the registry, reducing the size of the registry file, and therefore improving performance.

- As with Windows 95, a single source provides data for enumerating and configuring the hardware, applications, device drivers, and operating system control parameters. The configuration information can be recovered easily in the event of system failure.

- As with Windows 95, users and administrators can configure computer options by using standard Control Panel tools and other administrative tools, reducing the likelihood of syntactic errors in configuration information.

- A set of network-independent functions can be used to set and query configuration information, allowing system administrators to examine configuration data on remote networked computers.

- The registry key size limit of approximately 64 KB that existed in Windows 95 has been removed in Windows 98. This allows you to install more applications with shared dynamic link libraries (DLLs) in your computer.

Because user-specific registry information can be maintained on a central network server when user profiles are enabled, users can have access to personal desktop and network access preferences when logging on to any computer, and settings for multiple users can be maintained on a single computer. Also, system policies can be used to enforce certain registry settings for individuals, workgroups, or all users.

For more information about system policies, see Chapter 8, "System Policies."

Overview of the Registry Files

Although the registry is logically one data store, physically it consists of three different files to allow maximum network configuration flexibility. Windows 98 uses the registry to store information in three major categories. Table 31.1 lists the files and describes the categories.

Table 31.1   Registry files

File	Description
User.dat	User-specific information, in the form of user profiles, is contained in the User.dat file. It contains logon names, desktop settings, **Start** menu settings, and so on. During Windows Setup, User.dat is automatically stored as a hidden file in the \Windows directory, but the file does not necessarily remain there. If User Profiles are enabled, users can have their own settings stored in \Windows\Profiles. In a network, this file may be located on a central server.
System.dat	Hardware or computer-specific settings (the hardware profile) are contained in the System.dat file. It contains all the hardware configuration, Plug and Play settings, and application settings. It is always stored as a hidden file on the local machine in the Windows 98 directory.
Policy.pol	System policies are designed to provide an override for any settings contained in the other two registry components. System policies can contain additional data specific to the network or corporate environment, as established by the network administrator. The system policies themselves are contained in the Policy.pol file. Unlike System.dat and User.dat, Policy.pol is not a mandatory component of a Windows 98 installation.

Benefits of the Registry Structure

Breaking the registry into three logical components provides several benefits, which are described in this section.

The registry components can be located in physically different locations. For example, the System.dat component and other Windows 98 system files might be located on the computer's hard disk, and the User.dat component can be stored in one master network directory, and then copied to the hard disk during log on. With this configuration, users can log on to various computers on the network and still have their unique network privileges and desktop configuration, allowing the "roving user" network configuration for Windows 98.

The registry and all of the system files can be installed on the local hard disk. With this configuration, multiple users can share a single computer running Windows 98. Each user has a separate logon user name, separate user profile, separate privileges, and separate desktop configuration.

The network administrator can manage an entire network's user privileges by having a single, global Policy.pol file. Or, the network administer can establish these policies on a server basis or on a per-user basis. In this fashion, a network administrator can centrally enforce a "common desktop configuration" for each user type. For example, a data-entry computer running Windows 98 can be configured so that only two applications (the data entry application and e-mail) can be run. Additionally, the network administrator can specify that data-entry users cannot modify this desktop configuration. In spite of this configuration, the computer running Windows 98 can fully participate in the network and is fully configurable if a different user with more network privileges logs on to the same computer.

Separate privileges can be assigned to users and to a computer. For example, if a user who has sharing privileges logs on to a computer running Windows 98 that has no sharing (no peer services), the user cannot access the computer's resources. This feature is useful if certain computers contain sensitive data that should not be available to everyone on the corporate network.

How Windows 98 Components Use the Registry

The registry contains ordered pairs of keys and their associated values that are manipulated through the Win32 registry application programming interfaces (APIs). For example, the registry might have a Wallpaper key with an associated value of Work.bmp, meaning that the current desktop background is configured to use the Work bitmap.

Additionally, a special category of keys known as *dynamic keys* points to either a memory location or a callback function. Dynamic keys are used by device drivers or Windows 98 subsystems that want to register a dynamic data type, such as a counter, in the registry. In the case of network cards, the dynamic keys represent data, such as data transfer rates, number of framing errors, packets dropped, and so on. In general, dynamic keys are used for reporting data, not for storage in the disk-based registry. Because the dynamic keys exist only in memory, their data can be quickly updated and accessed. The data can be accessed by the system performance tools in Windows 98, which call upon the registry for the data they are monitoring.

Keys and values can be created either programmatically or by using the Registry Editor (REGEDIT) tool. The APIs for programmatically managing the registry are the Win32 registry APIs, which can be remotely invoked by the Microsoft remote procedure call (RPC) (distributed computing environment [DCE]–compliant) support built into Windows 98. Windows 98 includes both the client and server portions of Microsoft RPC, making the registry manageable remotely from another computer running Windows 98. In this scenario, the network administrator's system is the RPC client. It accesses the registry APIs on the target computer running Windows 98 through the RPC server running on the target machine. This RPC access to the registry is secure, and network administrators can limit access to either specified privileged users or a group of network administrators.

With Windows 98, the operating system stores and checks the configuration information in the registry for most configuration settings during system startup. Windows 98 components and applications also use the registry for storing and accessing configuration information:

- Whenever you run Windows 98 Setup, use the Add New Hardware option in Control Panel, or run other setup programs for hardware, the Windows 98 Configuration Manager places hardware configuration data in the registry. This information includes a list of hardware detected in the computer.

- If you install Windows 98 in the same directory as Windows 3.x, your previous desktop settings are moved from INI files to the registry. When you make changes to the desktop configuration, the settings are added to the registry.

- Each time you add or remove a Plug and Play–compliant device on a computer running Windows 98, configuration data is added to the registry. For example, new information is added when you install a PC Card modem.

- Device drivers send and receive load parameters and configuration data from the registry. This data is similar to what you might find on the **device=** lines in the Config.sys file in Windows 3.x. A device driver must report system resources that it uses (such as hardware interrupts and direct memory access channels) so the system can add this information to the registry. Applications and device drivers can access this registry information to provide users with smart installation and configuration programs.

- System policies, user profiles, and administrative tools (such as the Control Panel) can be used to add or modify configuration data in the registry indirectly. Registry Editor can be used to view and occasionally change the system configuration.

Figure 31.1 provides an overview of how Windows 98 components and applications use the registry.

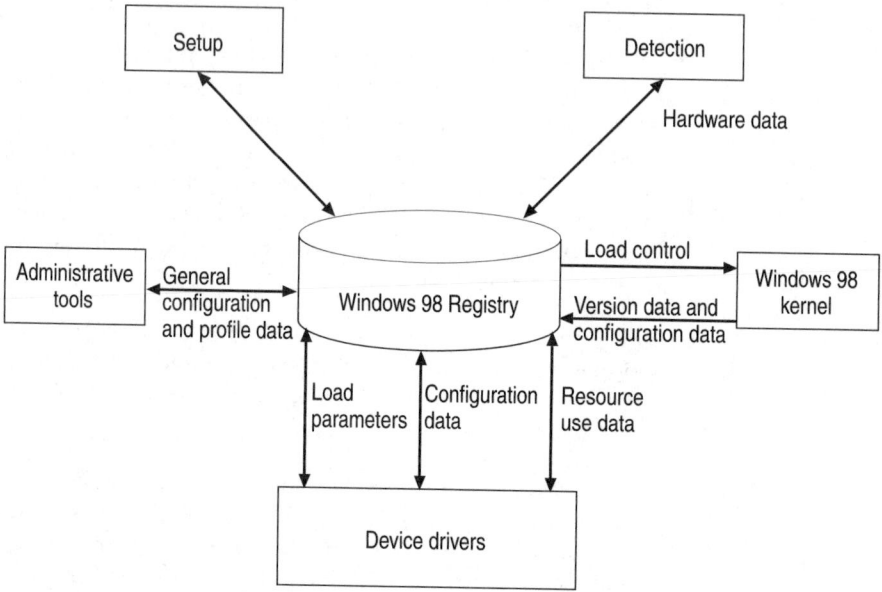

Figure 31.1   Windows 98 registry overview

Windows 98 registry APIs can be used to get information into and out of the registry, and examine system, application, and user information stored in the registry.

A set of registry APIs can make information available through remote procedure calls (RPCs) to Windows 98 management tools from other vendors. This permits administrators to view and modify configuration information remotely for hardware and software components that store information in the registry. Notice that the registry APIs are accessible remotely using named pipes (client-side only), NetBIOS over NetBEUI, Windows Sockets on IPX, and Windows Sockets on Internet Protocol (IP).

Overview of the Main Registry Tools

This section contains a brief overview of tools you can use to modify the registry. The tools are described in more detail later in this chapter.

The simplest and safest way (and the recommended way) to modify the registry is to use the tools listed in Table 31.2.

Table 31.2   Recommended tools to modify the registry

Method	Settings
Control Panel	Most system settings. For example, you use Display properties to modify the appearance of screen elements.
System Policy Editor	User settings, some system settings.
Third-party utilities	Application-specific settings.

You can also modify the registry using Registry Editor, but use it sparingly and carefully. If you use Registry Editor, *always* back up the registry using Registry Checker before changing anything. See "Backing Up and Recovering the Registry" later in this chapter.

Wherever possible, use administrative tools, such as Control Panel or System Policy Editor to make configuration changes, rather than Registry Editor. This is to ensure values are stored properly in the registry when changing the configuration.

Registry Editor

The registry can be edited using the Registry Editor. The registry consists of various parallel "trees." Registry Editor is built on the RPC support and can edit the local Windows 98 registry as well as registries on remote computers running Windows 98. Registry Editor is powerful, yet rudimentary in design, and is intended for use by knowledgeable computer and network support staff, or power users. Most users will never use Registry Editor because registry entries are usually modified through the Control Panel, by applications, or by Plug and Play. Assigning an incorrect value to a registry entry or adding or deleting certain entries can result in a completely disabled operating system.

If you use Registry Editor to change values, you will not be warned if any entry is incorrect. Editing the registry directly by using Registry Editor can cause errors in loading hardware and software, and can prevent users from being able to start the computer.

Windows 98 writes much of its configuration information into two hidden files: System.dat and User.dat. These files are located in the directory specified during Setup that contains the Windows 98 files, which in most cases is C:\Windows. If the system is configured for multiple users, a separate User.dat file is created for each user, and each file is found in the user's custom profiles area (Windows\Profiles*User_Name*\User.dat). You can use the Registry Editor to edit the System.dat and User.dat files. The registry is automatically edited whenever the user makes changes through the Control Panel or from some other Windows 98 applet or application.

Any change made through the Registry Editor takes place immediately, and the new information is written into System.dat or User.dat, as appropriate.

Registry Checker

Registry Checker is a new system maintenance program that finds and fixes registry problems and that regularly backs up the registry. Windows 98 provides an MS-DOS-based program for scanning the registry, backing up, and restoring the registry and system configuration files. It also provides a Windows-based program for scanning and backing up the registry.

Registry Checker backs up the registry at startup, maintaining one backup for each day. It maintains up to five compressed backup copies of the registry. If a serious registry problem is found, Registry Checker restores the most recent registry from a backup copy. If a backup is not available, or if you type **scanreg /fix** at the command prompt, Registry Checker tries to repair the registry (you must exit Windows and run ScanReg from an MS-DOS command prompt).

Registries tend to grow in size, and the bigger the registry, the slower the performance. Registry Checker removes unused space in the registry, reducing the size of the registry file, and thus improving performance. During each boot, Registry Checker determines the amount of free space in the registry files. If there is an excess of free space, it compacts the registry, removing the excess.

Profile Editor

A user profile consists of user-specific information contained in the User.dat file, which is one of the three files in the Windows 98 registry. Optionally, a user profile can also contain special Windows 98 directories. You can enable user profiles after Windows 98 is installed, either locally on a single computer or for multiple computers. You can avoid having to go to each computer to enable user profiles by creating a system policy that can be downloaded automatically when the initial Windows 98 installation is complete. Profile Editor controls these user components of the registry.

System Policy Editor

The System Policy Editor (Poledit.exe) generates the system policies file, Policy.pol. This tool allows network administrators to define specific network policies or user configurations for Windows 98. A global system policy file can centrally enforce a common system configuration for all your users.

System Policy Editor is extensible by third parties; the ADM (administration configuration files) format is a text file that can be extended by network tool vendors or by network administrators as needed. The System Policy Editor works through local file I/O and is not RPC-enabled. Because the system policies file is located centrally on a network server, each server usually needs a copy. All the network administrator needs to do is connect to the network server and edit the system policies file.

Remote Registry Access

Many of the Win32 registry APIs use the remote procedure call (RPC) mechanism in Windows 98 to provide remote access to registry information across a network. As a result, desktop management applications can aid in the management and support of Windows-based computers, and the contents of the registry on a given computer can be queried over a network. Industry management mechanisms, such as Simple Network Management Protocol (SNMP) or DMI, can easily be integrated into Windows 98, simplifying the management and support burden of a management information systems (MIS) organization.

Overview of Other Registry Tools

The following is a description of additional tools for changing registry settings. These are the recommended tools for changing the registry.

Open With Use the **Open With** dialog with the Windows shell to change the registered file types.

File Types Select **Folder Options** from the **View** menu in Windows Explorer to access the **File Types** tab, which lets you inspect and alter registry settings for registered file types.

Control Panel Control Panel contains several icons that, when double-clicked, will open property sheets. Registry settings can be altered with the property sheets.

Property sheets of applications Some applications store their settings in the registry. You can update these settings by modifying the options in the appropriate application property sheet.

Device Manager Use Device Manager to make direct modifications to system hardware and resource settings. Device Manager displays all the hardware on your computer, and gets this information from the registry.

Getting Started with the Registry Tools

This section describes how to get started with the tools that you can use to display, modify, back up, and recover the registry.

Getting Started with Registry Checker

Registry Checker is a system maintenance program that finds and fixes registry problems. Each time you start your computer, Registry Checker automatically scans the registry for inconsistent structures, and if no problem is found, Registry Checker makes one backup for each day. Registry Checker consists of two executable files, Scanreg.exe and Scanregw.exe, which are automatically copied to the \Windows\Command and \Windows folders, respectively, when Windows 98 is installed.

If a problem is found in the registry, Registry Checker can restore the registry from a good backup copy. Registry Checker maintains five compressed backups of the registry that have successfully started the computer. Registry Checker attempts to fix the registry if a backup cannot be found. Registry Checker also removes unused space in the registry, reducing the size of the registry file, and therefore improving performance.

Once per day at startup a new CAB file containing a backup of the registry is created by Registry Checker. The file name is Rb*xxx*.cab (where *xxx* is a unique number assigned when the file is created). The new file replaces the oldest file. These files are located in the \Windows\Sysbckup folder (a hidden folder). Registry Checker always maintains *at least* the last configuration from which the system was successfully booted.

The Registry Checker utility is actually two executable files: Scanreg.exe (*ScanReg*) is a real-mode, MS-DOS executable file and Scanregw.exe (*ScanRegW*) is a protected-mode, Windows executable file. They store copies of the entire registry, both User.dat and System.dat, as well as Win.ini and System.ini, into a compressed file (*filename*.cab).

ScanRegW scans the registry for corruption and determines if it requires optimization, and then backs up the following system configuration files: User.dat, System.dat, Win.ini, and System.ini. This scan occurs automatically when the system is started. On the first successful boot, a CAB file is created and marked as a registry backup that is capable of booting the system. You can run ScanRegW when you want to force a scan and backup of these files. ScanRegW backs up the registry and configuration files using the Rb*xxx*.cab file.

▶ **To run Registry Checker (ScanRegW)**

1. From the **Start** menu, click **Run**.

2. Type **scanregw.exe**, and click **OK**.

ScanReg runs when ScanRegW detects a problem with the registry and it prompts you to restart the computer to fix the problem. ScanReg either restores the registry from a known good backup, or, if no backups are available, it repairs the current registry. If ScanRegW detects that optimization is required, ScanReg optimizes the registry on the next startup. With some severe types of registry damage, Io.sys will detect the problem and the MS-DOS mode configuration menu appears, warning you that a registry corruption has been detected.

For more information about how to run ScanReg, see "Backing up and Restoring the Registry" later in this chapter.

Getting Started with Registry Editor

Registry Editor is a tool for displaying and editing the registry database. Registry Editor (Regedit.exe) is copied to the \Windows directory automatically when Windows 98 is installed.

Caution Making a mistake in editing the registry can cause your system to become unstable and/or unusable.

Wherever possible, use the administrative tools, such as Control Panel or System Policy Editor, to make configuration changes, rather than editing the registry. This is to ensure values are stored properly in the registry when changing the configuration.

If you use Registry Editor to change values, you will not be warned if any entry is incorrect. Editing the registry directly by using Registry Editor can cause errors in loading hardware and software, and can prevent users from being able to start the computer.

▶   **To run Registry Editor**

- On the **Start** menu, click **Run** and type **regedit**. Click **OK**.

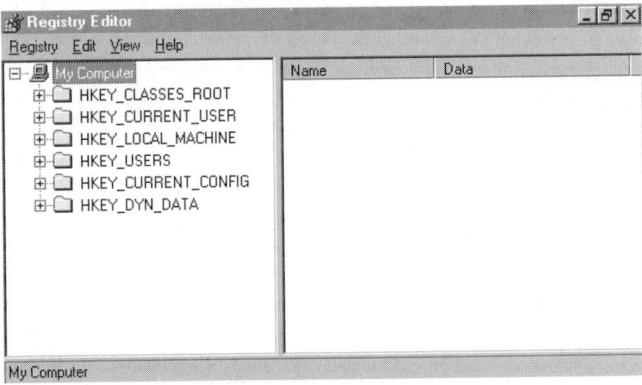

Both mouse and keyboard commands can be used to navigate in Registry Editor.

▶ **To find specific data in the registry**

- In the Registry Editor window, double-click any folder icon for a registry key to display the contents of that key.

  – Or –

  From the **Edit** menu, click **Find**. Then type all or part of the text string you want to find, and click options to specify whether you want to find a key name, a value name, or data.

  After Registry Editor finds the first instance of the text string, you can press F3 to search for the next instance.

Registry Editor can be used to view or modify a registry on a local computer or on another computer over a network. Both the administrator's computer and the remote computer require the Microsoft Remote Registry service to allow remote registry access.

For more information about the Microsoft Remote Registry service, see "Managing Remotely" later in this chapter and Chapter 23, "System and Remote Administration Tools."

Tip The network administrator can restrict users from being able to use Registry Editor to modify the registry by setting a system policy named Disable Registry Editing Tools. However, this policy does not prevent the administrator or another user from modifying the registry by using System Policy Editor.

For more information about this restriction and about using System Policy Editor to modify the registry on individual or multiple computers, see Chapter 7, "User Profiles," and Chapter 8, "System Policies."

The values of the active key appear in the right pane of the Registry Editor window. Each key contains at least one value with the name **Default**. Each additional value for a key must have both a name and a data value.

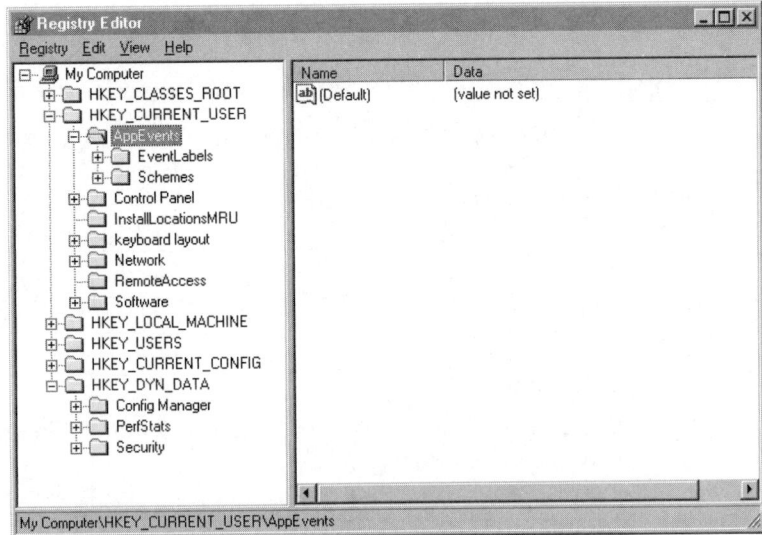

Valid characters to include in a name are A through Z, 0 through 9, blank, and underscore (_). The values appear under Data. In Windows 98, the size of the subkey is unlimited. For better efficiency, use a file to store large amounts of data (subkeys over 64 KB), and then maintain a pointer to this file in the subkey. Individual values within a subkey are restricted to 16 KB of data.

The Registry Editor can handle the data types shown in Table 31.3.

Table 31.3   Windows 98 registry data types

Data type	Description
String	Stored as characters enclosed in quotation marks, it is a variable length, null-terminated set of characters.
Binary	Represented as a sequence of hex bytes (0–9 and A–F), a defined value can be 1 KB–16 KB in size.
DWORD	A binary value that is restricted to 4 bytes, and the value is shown in both hexadecimal and decimal formats: 0x00000000 (0). The first number, 0x00000000, is the hex representation of the value, and the number in parenthesis, (0), contains the decimal representation.

If the Default entry contains no value, the following string is shown:

```
(value not set)
```

The representation and meaning of the value's data depends on the key. A binary sequence can be interpreted as a single byte, a double byte, or a byte sequence. Some numerical values are stored as strings.

Important Before modifying registry values, *always* back up your system. See "Backing Up and Restoring the Registry" later in this chapter.

▶ **To change any value**

1. Click the key in the left pane of the Registry Editor window to display its values in the right pane.

2. Double-click the value. The **Registry Editor** displays one of three types of dialog boxes, depending on the type of value you are changing. Table 31.4 describes the three value types.

Table 31.4   Registry Editor value types

Value type	Description
Text value	The **Edit String** dialog box appears. Type a new value into the **Value Data** box. Text values are automatically displayed in quotation marks ("") and the new value is stored immediately in the registry.
Binary value	The **Edit Binary Value** dialog box appears with the value data in hexadecimal format. Select a value to type a new value. When you click **OK**, the value is stored in the registry.
DWORD	The **Edit DWORD Value** dialog box appears. Select a Base option, and enter the value into the **Value Data** box. A DWORD can never exceed 32 bits.

▶ **To add a new value**

1. Click a key, and then right-click in the right pane of the Registry Editor windows to display the context menu.

2. Select **New** and then select the value type.

   A new entry called **New Key #1** is inserted into the registry. **New Value #1** represents the value type you chose in step two.

▶ **To delete any entry**

- Select the entry, and then select **Delete** from the shortcut menu.

Caution Registry Editor does not have an **Undo** function. All changes are written directly to the disk. If you want to remove an item from the registry, consider renaming it as opposed to deleting it. However, use caution when renaming because this can affect system functionality.

▶ **To rename an entry**

- Select the entry, and then select **Rename** from the shortcut menu.

Getting Started with Profile Editor

Each time a user logs on to a computer, Windows 98 searches the registry under the following key to determine whether the user has a local profile:

HKEY_LOCAL_MACHINE\Software\Microsoft\Windows \CurrentVersion\Profile List

Windows 98 also checks for the user profile in the user's home directory on the server. If the user profile on the server is the most current, Windows 98 copies it to the local computer for use during the current session, and then it loads the settings in this local copy into the registry. If no local user profile exists, Windows 98 copies the server version to the local computer. If no profile is found, Windows 98 creates a new user profile on the local computer using default settings. If the user does not log on, then Windows 98 automatically uses the default user profile.

You can enable user profiles after Windows 98 is installed, either locally on a single computer or for multiple computers. You can avoid having to go to each computer to enable user profiles by creating a system policy that can be downloaded automatically when the initial Windows 98 installation is complete. For more information about enabling user profiles centrally on multiple computers, see Chapter 8, "System Policies."

▶ **To enable user profiles on a local computer after setup**

1. In Control Panel, double-click Passwords, and then click the **User Profiles** tab.

2. Click **Users can customize their preferences and desktop settings**.

3. Select the options you want under **User profile settings**. These options describe what should be included as part of the user profile.

4. Shut down and restart the computer.

Tip If you include desktop icons in your user profile, only the shortcuts (icons that represent links) will be available when you log on to the network from another computer. Actual files on your desktop are part of your local user profile only.

▶ **To disable user profiles on a local computer after setup**

1. In Control Panel, double-click Passwords, and then click the **User Profiles** tab.

2. Click **All users of this computer use the same preferences and desktop settings**.

Note If an application is installed after user profiles are enabled with the option to include the **Start** menu and **Programs** in the profile, only the user who was logged on when the application was installed will have an entry for that application on the **Programs** menu. Other users will have to create shortcuts to the application on their **Programs** menus.

For more information about using user profiles, see Chapter 7, "User Profiles."

Getting Started with System Policy Editor

During Startup, Windows 98 reads the data stored in System.dat and in User.dat, which can be different for each user. System administrators customize user settings in User.dat. For example, they might restrict access to certain desktop components or **Start** menu commands, or change the location of the User.dat file. System policies are a powerful method to manage computers on a network.

The tool for changing these settings is the System Policy Editor, which is shipped on the Windows 98 compact disc.

▶ **To install System Policy Editor**

1. In Control Panel, double-click Add/Remove Programs, click the **Windows Setup** tab, and then click **Have Disk**.

2. In the **Install From Disk** dialog box, click **Browse** and specify the Admin\Apptools\Poledit directory on the Windows 98 compact disc.

3. Click **OK**, and then click **OK** again in response to the dialog boxes.

4. In the **Have Disk** dialog box, select the **System Policy Editor** check box, and then click **Install**.

▶ **To run System Policy Editor**

1. On the **Start** menu, click **Run**.

2. Type **poledit**, and then click **OK**.

The System Policy Editor can be used to directly access the registry to create and edit POL files.

▶ **To access registry settings through System Policy Editor**

1. On the **File** menu, click **Open Registry**.

   The Local User and Local Computer icons appear in the System Policy Editor. Using this local mode changes registry entries on the current machine in use. No POL file is created when you use local mode. If a POL file already exists, local changes may be overwritten during the next log on.

2. Click either **Local Computer** or **Local User**.

If you want to use group policies, you must install that capability on each computer running Windows 98, either when you install Windows 98 using a custom setup script or by using the Add/Remove Programs option in Control Panel.

▶ **To set up capabilities for group policies using Add/Remove Programs**

1. In Control Panel, double-click Add/Remove Programs, click the **Windows Setup** tab, and then click **Have Disk**.

2. In the **Install From Disk** dialog box, click **Browse** and specify the Admin\Apptools\Poledit directory on the Windows 98 compact disc.

3. Click **OK**, and then click **OK** again in response to the dialog boxes.

4. In the **Have Disk** dialog box, select the **Group Policies** check box, and then click **Install**.

Windows 98 Setup places Grouppol.dll in the \Windows\System directory on the client computer, and makes the required registry changes.

For more information about adding the ability to use group policies when installing Windows 98 using custom setup scripts, see Chapter 4, "Automated Installations."

Before you can use individual user profiles, you must enable them in Windows 98.

▶ **To enable user profiles**

1. In the Control Panel, double-click Passwords, and then click the **User Profiles** tab.

2. Click **Users can customize their preferences and desktop settings**.

3. Click **OK**.

For more information about using System Policy Editor, see Chapter 8, "System Policies."

Administrating with the Registry

This section describes tasks and tips for managing the registry, and for using the registry to manage your system.

Managing the Registry

The following tasks help you manage the registry itself.

Finding Information in the Registry

The registry contains thousands of entries, so it can be difficult to find a desired key or value. Scrolling through the hierarchy could take some time. The most efficient approach to find data in the registry is to use Registry Editor.

▶ **To find information in the registry**

1. Start Registry Editor.

2. On the **Edit** menu, click **Find**.

3. Type what you want to look for in the **Find what** field. You can enter a key, a subkey, a value name, or an actual value (text or binary).

4. Click **Find Next**.

Backing Up and Restoring the Registry

The registry is critical to your Windows 98–based computer because Windows 98 and Windows 98–based applications store their configuration information in the registry. Therefore, it is crucial to back up the registry regularly and frequently so that this information can be recovered in the event that the registry is damaged. It is also a good idea to back up the registry before installing a new application or new hardware.

Registry Checker automatically backs up and restores the registry. You can also run it manually at any time using the following procedure.

▶   **To manually back up the registry using Registry Checker**

1. On the **Start** menu, click **Run**.

2. Type **scanregw.exe**, and click **OK**.

First Registry Checker verifies that the registry is structurally sound. If the registry is sound, Registry Checker offers to back it up. Registry Checker will back up the registry and store the compressed CAB file in \Windows\Sysbckup (a hidden directory).

If the registry structure is sound but a content change is keeping the computer from booting, then you need to manually restore from a backup using the following procedure.

▶   **To restore the backup manually**

1. On the **Start** menu, click **Shut Down**.

2. Select **Restart in MS-DOS mode** and click **OK**.

3. At the MS-DOS command prompt, type **scanreg /restore**.

4. Select the latest known good backup.

    Backed up, compressed registry files are listed with the name Rb*xxx*.cab. The files show the time and date of backup. Next to each CAB file are the words **Started** or **Not Started**. **Started** means that the file has successfully started Windows 98, and is a known good file. **Not Started** means that the file has never been used to start Windows 98, so it is not a known good file.

The Registry Checker scan and backup tools can be configured with the Scanreg.ini file. Table 31.5 includes some configurable settings in the Scanreg.ini file.

Table 31.5   Configurable settings in the Scanreg.ini file

Setting	Description
Backup=	Enables and disables Registry Checker. Backup=0 disables backups Backup=1 enables backups
MaxBackupCopies=	Specifies the maximum number of backups to store in the backup folder. MaxBackupCopies=5 is the default.
BackupDirectory=	Changes the location of the backup folder where the CAB files are stored. For example, BackupDirectory=C:\RegBackup.
Files=	Adds system files to be backed up.
Optimize=	Enables and disables automatic registry optimization. Optimize=0 disables optimization Optimize=1 enables optimization

Table 31.6 describes command line options for the ScanReg and ScanRegW utilities of Registry Checker.

Table 31.6   Command line options for Registry Checker

Command line option	Description	Available for
/backup	Backs up the registry with no prompts to the user.	ScanReg and ScanRegW
/restore	Displays a list of backup files available, sorted by date and time of the backup.	ScanReg
"/comment="	Specifies that a comment is attached to the backup, which is displayed with /restore.	ScanReg and ScanRegW
/fix	Repairs the registry files.	ScanReg
/autoscan	Scans the registry files every time it is run, but only backs up once per day.	ScanRegW
/scanonly	Scans the registry files and returns an error level. Does not back up.	ScanRegW

Table 31.7 identifies the error levels returned by ScanReg.

Table 31.7   ScanReg error levels

Error level	Error
2	The registry is bad.
0	No problems found.
-2	Not enough memory; free some memory. In real mode, Registry Checker may require more memory, or high memory (HIMEM) needs to be installed (ScanReg does not work in Safe Mode command prompt only). In protected mode, the Windows drive may be full.
-3	File not found; one or both of the registry files are missing.
-4	Unable to create User.dat or System.dat.
-5	Reading the registry failed.
-6	Writing to the registry failed.
-7	Sharing violation (protect mode only); another application has the registry open.

Caution You may have backed up core configuration files using the Emergency Recovery utility and CfgBack utilities from the Windows 95 compact disc. If these Windows 95 backup registries are restored to the Windows 98 system, the computer will not boot.

For more information about Registry Checker, see Chapter 27, "General Troubleshooting."

Importing and Exporting Registry Data

The registry can be exported, imported, or recreated using the MS-DOS-based version of Registry Editor on either the Windows 98 startup disk or in the \Windows directory. By using the export capabilities of Registry Editor, a specific branch or the entire registry can be saved in text format as a REG file. A branch of or the entire registry can be restored by importing a REG file that was created by exporting the registry.

You can import and export using Registry Editor. All the information required to import the data must be in the imported file and the files need a REG extension. Valid Windows 98 REG files contain only ASCII characters in a predefined format and contain the word REGEDIT4 in the first line. The second line must be blank. The following format is valid for a REG file:

```
REGEDIT4

[HKEY_CLASSES_ROOT\.bmp]
@="Paint.Picture"
"Content Type"="image/bmp"

[HKEY_CLASSES_ROOT\.bmp\ShellNew]
"NullFile"=""
```

All the lines that follow the first blank line can contain entries for registry settings. Each entry starts with the name of the destination key enclosed in square brackets [].The next line or lines are used for the values of a key (which are the values shown later in the right pane of Registry Editor). The value names are included in quotation marks (for example, "NullFile"). Some lines start with @= followed by a value in quotes. The @ character indicates a default value for an entry. These entries are marked as Default in the right pane of the Registry Editor.

Caution The *Microsoft Windows 98 Resource Kit* does not provide sufficient information to guide you through the process of editing a REG file, so it is recommended that you undertake editing a REG file only under the guidance of your product support representative.

Also, use the **regedit /c** option with extreme care, and only when you are sure that the specified REG file contains a complete image of the registry.

▶ **To import with Registry Editor**

1. In **Registry Editor**, click **Import Registry File** on the **Registry** menu.

2. Click a folder, and then click a file name (or enter a file name).

3. Click **Open**.

Tip   You can also just double-click a *filename*.reg file. The extension is associated with Regedit and will be imported automatically.

After a REG file is successfully imported, a message box informs you that the REG file was valid, indicating that it was formatted properly, that it was a valid Windows 98 REG file, and that all information contained in the file and entered into the registry is valid.

▶ **To export a REG file using Registry Editor**

1. In **Registry Editor**, select the branch or subkey that you want to export.

2. On the **Registry** menu, click **Export Registry File**.

3. In the **Export Registry File** dialog box, select the folder in which you want to save the REG file.

4. Enter the new file name.

5. Click **Save**.

The Registry Editor creates a REG file containing the information of the selected branch. This REG file can now be imported as previously described.

By default, the Registry Editor exports only the active branch. You can export the whole registry by selecting **All** in the **Export range** section, but keep the file size in mind.

Accessing the Registry in Real Mode

Registry Editor runs in MS-DOS real mode. If you can boot your computer to MS-DOS mode, you can access Registry Editor. The file Regedit.exe is on the Windows startup disk and in the \Windows folder. For more information about using Regedit, type **Regedit** with no command line options at the command prompt, and a help screen appears advising you how to use this tool.

▶ **To import a registry file into the registry in MS-DOS Registry Editor**

1. On the **Start** menu, click **Shut Down**.

2. Select **Restart in MS-DOS mode** and click **OK**.

3. At the MS-DOS command prompt, type:

   REGEDIT /L:system /R:user filename

   L:system is optional and specifies the location of the System.dat file.

   /R:user is also optional and specifies the location of the User.dat file.

   Filename is the name of the registry file that will be imported.

   For example, the following command will import the contents of Global.reg into User.dat and System.dat:

   REGEDIT /L:C:\Windows\ /R:C:\Windows\Profiles\ A:\Global.reg

Managing Your System with the Registry

This section describes tasks that you can use to manage your system with the registry, including disabling Registry Editor, disabling a user's ability to use any computer but his or her own, and registering file name extensions.

Disabling Registry Editor for a User

You can disable the Registry Editor for a user so that the user cannot change entries that you have set to limit user access.

▶ **To disable Registry Editor for a user**

1. Start **System Policy Editor**, and click **Local User**.
2. Click **System**, and then click **Restrictions**.
3. Select **Disable Registry Editing Tools**.

Note An experienced user can still change registry settings by importing a REG file.

Disabling a User's Ability to Roam

You can keep a user from using any computer but his or her own.

▶ **To disable a user's ability to roam**

1. In **Registry Editor**, create a DWORD value in **HKEY_LOCAL_MACHINE\ Network\Logon**.
2. Enter **UseHomeDirectory** as the value.

Removing Existing User Profiles

You can remove one or all existing user profiles so that all users of the Windows 98–based system will see the same desktop and icons.

▶ **To remove existing user profiles**

1. Start **Registry Editor**.

2. Remove the appropriate *<username>* keys from the following registry key:

    **HKEY_LOCAL_MACHINE\Software\Microsoft\Windows
    \CurrentVersion\Profilelst*<username>***

    – Or –

    To remove all profiles, remove the \ProfileLst subkey.

3. Quit **Registry Editor**.

4. Double-click **My Computer**.

5. On the **View** menu, click **Folder Options**.

6. On the **View** tab, click **Show all files**, and then click **OK**.

7. Remove the appropriate Windows\Profiles*<username>* folder(s).

Registering File Name Extensions

When you select a file name in Windows 98, the file opens in an application associated with that file type. The file is opened with the appropriate application because the file extension is stored in the registry with an association to that application.

File types and their associations to specific applications are stored in the registry during the installation of new software. An application's setup program registers the file extension of the file type and the commands that are applied to this type of file type. All this information is stored in the **HKEY_CLASSES_ROOT** branch of the registry.

Each file type must have two entries in **HKEY_CLASSES_ROOT**. The first entry defines the file extension and a name (name_ID) for this file type. This name is then used in a second entry to define the commands for this file type. In other words, one entry describes its extension and the other contains its properties.

The structure is as follows:

HKEY_CLASSES_ROOT
    .ext = "name_ID"
    name_ID = <"Description">
        shell
            verb = <menu item text>
                command = command string

                ...

Structure and Description for a BAT File

The BAT key defines the file extension (BAT) and the associated value *name_ID*. The associated value name_ID is set to string "batfile," which is the unique name identifier for the second key.

Although the BAT extension is registered by the inclusion of the BAT key, Windows 98 needs additional information about what to do with a BAT file, such as executable commands that enable the user to open the file by clicking it. This is handled by the second key, batfile. The default value that contains the description "MS-DOS Batch File" defines this type of file. The description is what you see in Microsoft Windows Explorer in the **Type** column and the **Registered file types** list on the **File Types** property page of the **Folder Options** dialog box. The **EditFlags** value enables and disables the edit options in the **Edit File Type** dialog box.

The **DefaultIcon** subkey contains the value for the path and file name that contains the associated icon. The **shell** subkey contains information that Windows 98 retrieves about actions associated with the BAT file. The shellex subkey contains information about shell extensions that handle the BAT file.

Registering a new file type lets you manipulate how you access and enable functions, applications, and so on.

The preferred methods to register a file type are listed below:

- The **File Types** tab on the **Folder Options** property sheet from the Windows Explorer **View** menu.
- The **Open With** dialog box, which appears if you have selected a file that is unregistered.

You can also use the Registry Editor to register a file type. Be sure to make a backup copy of the registry before you begin, and be sure to manage every component of the process correctly.

▶ **To register a file type with Registry Editor**

1. Make sure you have a backup copy of the registry.

2. Start the **Registry Editor**, and expand the **HKEY_CLASSES_ROOT** branch.

3. Add a new subkey with the name of the file extension in **HKEY_CLASSES_ROOT** (you must include the dot, as in .bat).

4. Set the default value of this key to the name_ID (this is the name of the second key you need to define the properties).

5. Use the previously defined name_ID to add the second subkey in **HKEY_CLASSES_ROOT**.

6. Add the **shell** subkey, and expand this branch with the verbs for the required commands (**Open**, **Print**, and so on).

7. Add a command key to each verb key.

8. Add the command string (path and name of the executable) in the Default value.

9. Close the **Registry Editor**, and then test the registered file type in Windows Explorer.

Using Per User Settings for User Profiles

Microsoft Internet Explorer 4 browsing software allows multiple users to use a single installation of Internet Explorer 4 browsing software, while retaining unique individual settings for each user.

In general, user settings are put in the **HKEY_CURRENT_USER** key, and machine settings go under **HKEY_LOCAL_MACHINE**. Per machine settings that might change when a portable computer is in its docking station versus when it is undocked go under the **HKEY_CURRENT_CONFIG** key.

When multiple users log on to a workstation, they each get their own profile. A profile is a folder for each user that contains user specific files and configuration information, including their own copy of the **HKEY_CURRENT_USER** registry key (User.dat). A user's profile is in a folder with the user's name, and has a subfolder of \Windows\Profiles.

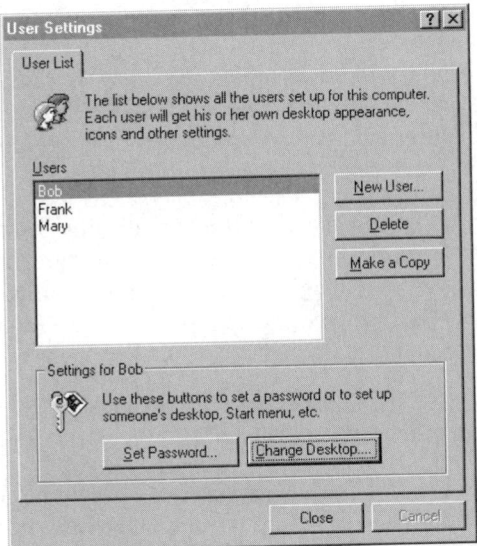

If a network is used, this profile can roam, meaning the user's copy of User.dat is stored on a central server and downloaded to any computer the user logs on to. This way the user can see the same environment no matter which computer he or she is logged on to on the network. It also allows administrators central control over individual user settings.

In addition to containing that user's copy of User.dat, a browsing software profile contains folders for Cookies, Recent, History, Favorites, Desktop, and Application Data.

Setup does not initialize any components in **HKEY_CURRENT_USER** settings during installation. This happens when Internet Explorer browsing software is installed on a machine by a user, and another user (who has never used Internet Explorer browsing software before) logs on at a later time, their profile will have no Internet Explorer browsing software settings.

In addition to simply logging on with a new user name, there is a new way to create a user profile. You will notice a new "Users" icon in Control Panel. This is a new interface and wizard for adding and configuring user profiles. This is simply an alternative user interface for creating a new profile. A reboot is still required.

The first time you click on this icon a wizard will run.

After clicking **Next**, you will be prompted for a new user name and a password for that user. The machine will then reboot. The User Profile Wizard runs only once. After that, the **User List** is displayed when the User icon in Control Panel is clicked, and the correct supervisor password is entered.

The first user that logs on to a machine is automatically the administrator of all consecutive user profiles on that machine. Non-administrators need the administrator's password to change the settings in their profile. The prompt for the supervisor's password is displayed as soon as the User icon in Control Panel is clicked. The supervisor is specified in:

HKEY_LOCAL_MACHINE\SOFTWARE\Microsoft\Windows \CurrentVersion\ProfileList\Supervisor

If the supervisor's password in the PWL file is null, then no supervisor key is created. Registry Editor lets you set up for more than one supervisor.

Managing Initialization Files

Although the registry replaces the basic function of the initialization files used in earlier versions of Windows, the System.ini, Win.ini, and Winfile.ini files still appear in the \Windows directory. These files continue to be used for compatibility with earlier Windows-based applications and device drivers. For example, entries in Win.ini and System.ini created by Win16-based applications are not updated in the registry because such applications do not know how to access the Windows 98 registry.

If you install Windows 98 as an upgrade over Windows 3.x, some INI file settings are copied into the registry, including settings from Control.ini, Program.ini, System.ini, and Win.ini.

Some INI file entries are not moved to the registry, but remain in the INI file for compatibility with Win16-based applications. Most of these entries can be changed without editing the INI files by using the graphical tools provided with Windows 98. However, some INI entries cannot be set using the Windows 98 user interface. These entries are required for some applications to function properly, but should not require manual modification by users.

Win.ini Settings in the registry.   Windows 98 migrates settings from configuration files into the registry during Setup. Table 31.8 shows where Win.ini entries migrated to the registry.

Table 31.8   Registry paths for migrated Win.ini entries

Win.ini entry	Subkey in HKEY_CURRENT_USER
[desktop]	\Control Panel\Desktop
[Windows]	\Control Panel\Desktop
[sounds]	\AppEvents\Schemes\Apps*event*\current

The following lists show entries retained in Win.ini for compatibility with applications written for earlier versions of Windows. These values can be set using Control Panel and other tools in the Windows 98 interface.

Win.ini entries retained and supported in the user interface

[Windows]:

CursorBlinkRate	DoubleClickWidth	MouseSpeed
Device	KeyboardDelay	MouseTrails
DoubleClickHeight	KeyboardSpeed	SwapMouseButtons
DoubleClickSpeed		

[Intl]:

iCountry	iNegCurr	sDecimal
iCurrDigits	iTime	sLanguage
iCurrency	iTLZero	sList
iDate	s1159	sLongDate
iDigits	s2359	sShortDate
iLZero	sCountry	sThousand
iMeasure	sCurrency	sTime

[fonts]: *font-name*

[ports]: *portname*

[PrinterPorts]: *device*

Win.ini entries retained but not supported in the user interface

[embedding]: *object*

[FontSubstitute]: *font-name=font-name*

[Mail]: MAPI

[mci extensions]: *extension*

[Windows]: Load and Run

System.ini settings in the registry.   The following lists show System.ini entries that are migrated to the registry when Windows 98 is installed in the same directory as a previous version of Windows 3.*x*.

Registry paths for migrated System.ini entries

System.ini entry	Subkey in HKEY_LOCAL_MACHINE
[386Enh]:	
Network	System\CurrentControlSet\Services\VxD\Vnetsetup
Transport	Software\CurrentControlSet\Services\VxD*transport entry*
[network]:	
Comment	System\CurrentControlSet\Services\VxD\Vnetsetup
ComputerName	System\CurrentControlSet\Control\ComputerName
EnableSharing	System\CurrentControlSet\Services\VxD\Vnetsetup
LMAnnounce	System\CurrentControlSet\Services\VxD\Vnetsetup
LogonDomain	Network
LogonValidated	Network
MaintainServerList	System\CurrentControlSet\Services\VxD\Vnetsetup
Reshare	System\CurrentControlSet\Network\LanMan*sharename*1
Username	Network\Logon
WorkGroup	System\CurrentControlSet\Services\VxD\Vnetsetup

1 The equivalent of the Reconnect settings is stored in **HKEY_CURRENT_USER\Persistent**.

The following lists show entries that are retained in System.ini for compatibility with applications written for earlier versions of Windows.

System.ini entries retained and supported in the user interface

[386Enh]:

AllEMSLocked	Keyboard	MinUserDiskSpace
AllXMSLocked	KeyPasteCRSkipCount	Mouse
AltKeyDelay	KeyPasteKeyDelay	Paging
AltPasteDelay	KeyPasteTimeout	PasteSkipCount
Display	MaxDMAPGAddress	PagingDrive
DMABufferSize	MaxPagingFileSize	ScrollFrequency
DOSPromptExitInstructions	MinPagingFileSize	

[boot]:

display.drv	mouse.drv	sound.drv
keyboard.drv	network.drv	

[NonWindowsApps]:

CommandEnvSize

System.ini entries retained but not supported in the user interface (*continued*)

[386Enh]:

Device=*filename*	MessageBackColor	NetAsynchFallback
KeybdPasswd	MessageTextColor	NetAsyncTimeout
Local	PagingFile	NetDMASize
Local Reboot		

[boot]:

386grabber=*filename*	fonts.fon=*filename*	shell=*filename*
comm.drv=*filename*	language.dll=*library-name*	system.drv=*filename*
drivers=*filename*	oemfonts.font=*filename*	TaskMan.Exe=*filename*
fixedfon.fon=*filename*		

[drivers]:

alias=*driver-filname*

[mci]:

Entries written by applications

Managing Remotely

Keys and values can be created either programmatically or by using the Registry Editor. The APIs for programmatically managing the registry are the Win32 registry APIs, which can be remotely invoked through the RPC (DCE-compliant) support built into Windows 98.

Windows 98 includes both the client and server portions of Microsoft RPC, making the registry manageable remotely from another computer running Windows 98. In this scenario, the network administrator's system is the RPC client. It accesses the registry APIs on the target computer running Windows 98 through the RPC server running on the target machine. This RPC access to the registry is secure, and network administrators can limit access to specified users.

To access the **Connect Network Registry** command from the Registry Editor, you must install the Remote Registry service on both computers, enable user-level security, and then enable the Remote Administration feature.

▶ **To set up the Remote Registry service from the Windows 98 compact disc**

1. In Control Panel, click Network, and then click **Add** on the **Configuration** property page.

2. Select **Service** in the **Select Network Component Type** dialog box and click **Add**.

3. In the **Select Network** dialog box, click **Have Disk**, and then enter the CD-ROM drive and \Admin\Nettools\Remotreg.

4. Click **OK**. Windows 98 installs the Remote Registry components.

5. When installation is complete, click the **Access Control** tab on the **Network** property sheet.

6. Set the option box to **User-Level access control**, and click **OK**.

7. Open **Registry Editor**, and click **Connect Network Registry** from the **Registry** menu.

8. Enter the name of the remote computer, and then click **OK**.

Understanding the Registry Structure

This section describes the hierarchical organization of the registry and defines the overall structure of keys and value entries.

The primary building blocks for the registry are keys, values, and data. The database for the registry is organized into a hierarchical structure. It is first organized into keys, and each key contains one or more keys or one or more values.

```
Key 1
        Key 1        value
        Key 2        value
        Key 3
        Key 4        value

Key 2
Key 3
```

The Registry Editor displays the contents of the registry database in six root keys. The hierarchical structure that appears in Registry Editor is similar to how Windows Explorer displays hierarchical directory structures. Each of the root key names begins with "**HKEY_**" to indicate that the key is a unique identifier, called a handle.

The HKEYs contain one or more subkeys, and each of the subkeys may contain subkeys. Key and subkey names can contain visible characters, including spaces, underscores, letters, and symbols, but cannot contain backslashes (\). The keys are case-aware, but are not case-sensitive, meaning the keys will recognize upper and lower case, but not require them.

A key's data is contained in the *value*. The data can be in the form of text, binary, or DWORD. Table 31.9 outlines the data types in the registry.

Table 31.9   Data types in the Windows 98 registry

Value	Description
Text	Variable length null-terminated set of characters
Binary	Variable length of hexadecimal digits
DWORD	Single 32-bit value that appears as an 8-digit hexadecimal number (DWORD stands for double word value)

The actual contents or location of a specific registry subkey may differ from what is described here, depending on the services and software installed. However, this description of the general organization will help you understand how to navigate the registry.

The Windows 98 registry structure represents database information specific to the computer and to individual users. The computer-specific information includes setting for hardware and software installed on the computer. The user-specific information includes settings in user profiles, such as desktop settings, preferences for certain software, and personal printer and network settings.

In Windows 98, data is written to the registry when a *flush* occurs—that is, after changed data has aged more than a few seconds, or when an application intentionally flushes the data to the hard disk.

Figure 31.2 shows the registry subtrees.

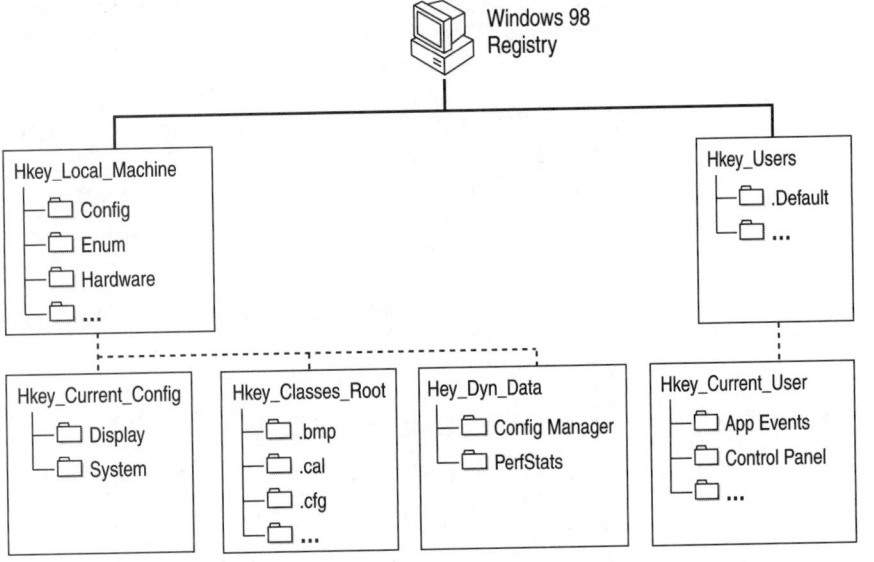

Figure 31.2   Windows 98 registry subtrees

The following briefly describes the registry root keys. Root keys are described in greater detail in "Working with the Registry Keys" later in this chapter.

HKEY_LOCAL_MACHINE This key contains computer-specific information about the type of hardware installed and software settings. This information is used for all users who log on to this system. **HKEY_LOCAL_MACHINE** has several subkeys, described later in this chapter.

HKEY_CURRENT_CONFIG This key handles Plug and Play and contains information about the current configuration of a multiple hardware configuration computer (for example, settings for a docking station). This key is a pointer to one of the configuration keys of **HKEY_LOCAL_MACHINE\Config**—the configuration key (**000***x* for example, **0001**) that contains information about the current configuration of hardware attached to the computer.

HKEY_DYN_DATA Dynamic data (data stored in RAM on the system) is contained in this key. This information may change as devices are added to or removed from the computer. The information for each device includes the related hardware key and the device's current status, including problems. The Device Manager uses this data to show the current hardware configuration, and this data is used to constantly update the System Monitor.

HKEY_CLASSES_ROOT This key points to **HKEY_LOCAL_MACHINE\ Software\Classes**, which describes certain software settings. This key displays essential information about OLE and association mappings to support drag-and-drop operations, Windows 98 shortcuts (which are OLE links), and core aspects of the Windows 98 user interface.

HKEY_USERS This key contains information about all the users who log on to the computer, including both generic and user-specific information. The generic settings are available to all users who log on to the computer. The information is made up of default settings for applications, desktop configurations, and so on. This key contains subkeys for each user that logs on to this computer.

HKEY_CURRENT_USER This key points to a branch of **HKEY_USERS** for the user who is currently logged on.

Interpreting Value Entries in the Registry Keys

Registry Editor displays data in two panes. The value entries in the right pane are associated with the selected key in the left pane.

A value entry has three parts: the data type of the value (which appears as an icon), the name of the value, and the value itself. A value's data cannot be larger than 16 KB. The limit to total registry size depends on available hard disk space and available memory.

Table 31.10 lists the data types currently used by the system.

Table 31.10   Current data types

Data type	Description
[binary icon]	Binary data. Most hardware component information is stored as binary data, and can be displayed in Registry Editor in binary or hexadecimal format. For example, Reboot Flag: 0x00000000.
[text icon]	A sequence of characters representing human-readable text. For example, BitsPerPixel: "8".

Analyzing the Registry Files

The registry is logically one data store, but physically it consists of two different files to allow maximum flexibility for network configurations:

- User-specific information is contained in User.dat. The information in this file is reflected in user profiles.

- Hardware-specific and computer-specific settings are contained in System.dat. This information is reflected in hardware profiles and in the settings displayed in Device Manager.

By default, User.dat and System.dat are stored in the \Windows folder, but these two files can be located in physically different locations. For example, if user profiles are enabled, System.dat can be stored on the local hard disk and User.dat stored in each user's logon directory (\Windows\Profiles*user_name*) or on a server, allowing "roving" users to maintain the same desktop preferences wherever they log on to the network.

For information about how Windows 98 chooses between local and network versions of User.dat when loading a user profile, and how system policies can override settings in DAT files to enforce user-specific and computer-specific information, see Chapter 8, "System Policies."

Working with the Registry Keys

Each branch of the registry contains information that logically belongs together. Each root key reflects a different aspect of the configuration data (that is, the user data and machine-dependent settings). Each of the root key names begins with **"HKEY_"**, which stands for *Key Handle*.

The registry contains keys with values that can change depending on the user and the system. It would be impossible to describe all registry settings, but what follows is a general description of the registry root keys and some of the more significant subkeys.

HKEY_CLASSES_ROOT

This branch of the registry is stored in the System.dat file. This key contains all data used for backward compatibility with Windows 3.*x* OLE and Dynamic Data Exchange (DDE) support. It also contains all the names of registered file types and their properties (icons and commands), and information about Quick Viewers, property sheet handlers, copy hook handlers, and other ActiveX components. An application's setup program registers the file extension of the file type and the commands that are applied to this file type in subkeys of **HKEY_CLASSES_ROOT**.

HKEY_CLASSES_ROOT is a pointer to **HKEY_LOCAL_MACHINE \Software\Classes subkey**, meaning that **HKEY_CLASSES_ROOT** points to all the subkeys in **HKEY_LOCAL_MACHINE\Software\Classes**.

The **Classes** key contains two types of keys:

- *File name extension keys*, which specify the class-definition associated with files that have the selected extension.
- *Class definition keys*, which specify the shell and OLE properties of a class (or type) of document. If an application supports Dynamic Data Exchange (DDE), the **Shell** key can contain **Open** and **Print** keys that define DDE commands for opening and printing files, similar to the OLE and DDE information stored in the registry under earlier versions of Windows. In the following example, **c:\windows\notepad.exe %1** is the open command, and the **%1** parameter stands for the selected file name in Windows Explorer when the command is carried out.

Note It is sometimes necessary to put quotation marks around the **%1**, such as "**%1**", for long file names. This is needed for some programs to work with long file names. For example, with Registry Editor, if quotes are not placed around the file name, you cannot open a REG file that contains a space in the name, such as **Name With A Space.reg**.

File Name Extension Keys

The file name extension keys pertain to the file extensions. For each of those keys, a second file type (batfile, exefile, and so on) exists. Most of these keys are identified by a leading period, followed usually by three characters of a file name extension, such as .bmp. Windows 98 begins a search for any file type by looking in this registry key for a key name that matches the file extension.

Class Definition Keys

The **CLSID** (Class Identifier) key contains ActiveX object properties. This 16-byte value corresponds to a specific ActiveX module. The default value of the key is usually a description of the ActiveX class, such as **General Property Page Object** and identifies the object associated with that CLSID number.

The asterisk (*)key signifies a file extension wild card. The information found here applies to all files regardless of their extensions. You can specify shell extensions, such as context menu items, that apply to all applications with this key.

This key also contains a type of action that can be performed on an object, such as print, open, or edit. This is called a *verb* in the registry. For example, the **Shell** key of **HKEY_CLASSES_ROOT** contains keys that define the actions edit, open, or print, all of which can be performed on a BAT file type. If you right-click a BAT file in Windows Explorer, you find the commands **Edit**, **Open**, and **Print** on the context menu. Also, double-clicking a BAT file in Windows Explorer invokes the open verb.

HKEY_CURRENT_USER

HKEY_CURRENT_USER contains the configuration information of the user profile for the currently logged on user. A user profile ensures that the user interface and operation of Windows 98 will be the same on any computer where that user logs on, if that person's profile is available at that computer.

HKEY_USERS contains the profile configuration information for a default user and the user defined with a user profile that is currently logged on. **HKEY_CURRENT_USER** points to either the default user or the user that is currently logged on.

HKEY_CURRENT_USER contains all the information necessary to set up a particular user environment on the computer, such as application preferences, screen colors, and security access permissions. Many of these settings are the same kind of information that was stored in Win.ini under Windows 3.*x*. **HKEY_CURRENT_USER** has several subkeys, some of which are described in the Table 31.11.

Table 31.11   HKEY_CURRENT_USER subkeys

Subkey	Contents
AppEvents	Contains subkeys holding the path and file name of the system sound files that play when specific system events occur. The **EventLabels** subkey contains the labels for sounds. The **Schemes** subkey contains the wave file for the sounds.

Table 31.11   HKEY_CURRENT_USER subkeys (*continued*)

Subkey	Contents
Control Panel	Contains subkeys for Control Panel settings, including information stored in Win.ini and Control.ini under Windows 3.*x*.
InstallLocations MRU	Contains the locations that applications were most recently installed from (MRU stands for "most recently used").
Keyboard layout	Contains subkeys that contain values defining the current active keyboard layout, which should be set by using the Keyboard option in Control Panel.
Network	Contains subkeys describing persistent and recent network connections.
RemoteAccess	Contains address and profile subkeys for remote network access.
Software	Contains subkeys describing the current user's software settings and containing application-specific information stored in Win.ini or private initialization files under Windows 3.*x*.

HKEY_LOCAL_MACHINE

HKEY_LOCAL_MACHINE contains the configuration data for the local computer. The information in this database is used by applications, device drivers, and Windows 98 to determine configuration data for the local computer, regardless of which user is logged on and what software is in use. The configuration data in this key is stored in the System.dat file.

Hardware devices can place information in the registry automatically using the Plug and Play interface. Software for installing device drivers can place information in the registry by writing to standard APIs. Users can place information about hardware in the registry by using the Add New Hardware option in Control Panel, or by using Device Manager, as described in Chapter 24, "Device Management."

HKEY_LOCAL_MACHINE contains several subkeys, as listed briefly in Table 31.12. The rest of this section provides details about some of these keys.

Table 31.12   HKEY_LOCAL_MACHINE subkeys

Subkey	Contents
Config	A subkey of **Config** is mapped to **HKEY_CURRENT_CONFIG** as the current configuration. A collection of hardware configuration profiles for the local computer. The profiles are found on the **Hardware Profiles** tab in the System option from the Control Panel.
Enum	Contains information about hardware devices connected to the system.
Hardware	Contains information about serial ports and modems used with the HyperTerminal program.

Table 31.12   HKEY_LOCAL_MACHINE subkeys (*continued*)

Subkey	Contents
Network	Network information created when a user logs on to a networked computer, including the user name, primary network provider, whether the logon was validated by a server, and information about the system policies processor.
Security	Contains information about the network security access, provider, and remote administration capabilities.
Software	The computer-specific information about software installed on the local computer, along with miscellaneous configuration data.
System	The database that controls system startup, device driver loading, Windows 98 services, and operating system behavior.

Config Subtree in HKEY_LOCAL_MACHINE

A subkey of **Config** is mapped to **HKEY_CURRENT_CONFIG** as the current configuration. **HKEY_LOCAL_MACHINE\Config** contains information about alternate hardware configurations for the computer. For example, it can contain information about multiple configurations to be used when the computer is connected to a network, when it is undocked from a docking station, and so on. Each alternate configuration is assigned a unique identifier, and this configuration ID has a subkey under the **Config** key. Each configuration appears in the list of hardware profiles in the System option in Control Panel.

When Windows 98 checks the hardware configuration at system startup, one of three things occurs:

- In most situations, the configuration ID is mapped to a unique configuration and Windows 98 selects the appropriate one automatically, and the settings for the related **Config** subkey are used for system configuration.
- If the user is starting the computer for the first time with new hardware components, Windows 98 creates a new configuration for the new configuration ID, and a new **Config** subkey is added to the registry.
- If the configuration ID is mapped to more than one configuration (for example, because Windows 98 cannot distinguish between two configurations), the user is prompted to choose which configuration to use.

Enum Subtree in HKEY_LOCAL_MACHINE

Windows 98 bus enumerators are responsible for building the hardware tree. This includes assigning an identification code to each device on its bus and retrieving the device's configuration information, either directly from the device or from the registry. For more information about the hardware tree and bus enumerators, see Chapter 28, "Windows 98 Architecture."

Bus enumeration information is stored in the **HKEY_LOCAL_MACHINE** **\Enum** subtree. For all types of devices, subkeys contain information, such as device type, assigned drive letter, hardware ID, and device manufacturer, plus driver-related information for network components.

Information about the following types of devices is stored in these subkeys (this is not an inclusive list):

Subkey	Device enumeration
ESDI	Fixed disk devices
FLOP	Floppy disk devices
ISAPNP	Plug and Play devices on an ISA bus
Monitor	Monitor devices
Network	Network protocol, server, and bindings
Root	Legacy devices

Software Subtree in HKEY_LOCAL_MACHINE

The **HKEY_LOCAL_MACHINE\Software** subtree contains configuration information about all installed software that has written its configuration information in the registry. The entries in this key apply for anyone using this particular computer, and include definitions for file associations and OLE information.

The **Software** subkey contains, for example, the information you add when registering an application to use a specific file name extension and information added during installation of Windows-based applications.

The **HKEY_LOCAL_MACHINE\Software** subtree contains several subkeys, including the **Classes** subkey, plus **Description** subkeys for all installed software that has registered itself in the registry, as described in the following sections.

Classes subkey. The **HKEY_LOCAL_MACHINE\Software\Classes** subkey defines types of documents and provides information about OLE and file name extension associations that can be used by applications. **HKEY_CLASSES_ROOT** is an alias for this subkey.

HKEY_CLASSES_ROOT is a pointer to **HKEY_LOCAL_MACHINE** **\Software\Classes**. The sole purpose for **HKEY_CLASSES_ROOT** is to provide compatibility with the Windows 3.*x* registration database.

Description subkeys   The various subkeys of **HKEY_LOCAL_MACHINE\ Software*Description*** contain the names and version numbers of the software installed on the local computer (if that software writes information to the registry as part of its installation process). User-specific information about the configuration of an application is stored at the same relative path under **HKEY_CURRENT_USER**.

Important   The information in each subkey is added by the related application. Do not edit entries in these subkeys unless directed to do so by your application vendor.

During installation, applications record this information in the following form:

HKEY_LOCAL_MACHINE\Software*CompanyName**ProductName**Version*

The key named **HKEY_LOCAL_MACHINE\Software\Microsoft** and its subkey named **Windows\CurrentVersion** are of particular interest. These subkeys contain information about software that supports services built into Windows 98.

The **Setup** subkey under **HKEY_LOCAL_MACHINE\Software\Microsoft \Windows\CurrentVersion** is used internally by Windows 98 for its Setup program.

System Subtree in HKEY_LOCAL_MACHINE

The data in **HKEY_LOCAL_MACHINE\System** is organized into control sets that contain a complete set of parameters for device drivers and services that can be loaded with Windows 98.

All data that controls startup is described in the **CurrentControlSet** subtree under **HKEY_LOCAL_MACHINE\System**. This control set has two parts:

- The **Control** key contains information used to control system startup, including the computer's network name and the subsystems to start.

- The **Services** key contains information to control the loading and configuration of drivers, file systems, and so on. The data in the **Services** key also controls how these services call each other.

Control subkey. The **Control** subkey contains startup parameters for the system, including settings for startup and shutdown, file system performance, keyboard layouts and language support, and so on. Table 31.13 describes some typical **Control** subkeys.

Table 31.13   Typical Control subkeys

Subkey	Contents
ComputerName	The computer name, which should be set using the Network option in Control Panel.
FileSystem	The type and settings of the file system.
IDConfigDB	The identification for the current configuration.
Keyboard layouts	A list of the DLLs for the keyboard language, which should be set using the Keyboard option in Control Panel.
Resources	Descriptions and driver information for multimedia components.
NetworkProvider	Descriptions of the network providers.
Nls	Contains information on national language support, including language and locale preferences, which should be set using the Keyboard option in Control Panel.
PerfStats	Statistics gathered from system components that can be viewed using System Monitor.
Print	Contains information about the current printers and printing environment, contained in several subkeys:
	■ Environments, which can contain subkeys defining drivers and print processors for operating system environments.
	■ Monitors, which can contain subkeys with data for specific network printing monitors.
	■ Printers, which can contain subkeys describing printer parameters for each installed printer.
	■ Providers, which can contain subkeys describing DLLs for network print services.
SessionManager	Global variables that are maintained by the operating system, plus subkeys that list applications that do not run well under Windows 98, DLLs whose version numbers should be checked, and directories and file names for all the Session Manager DLLs.
TimeZoneInformation	Values for time zone settings, which should be set using the Date/Time option in Control Panel.
Update	Value indicating whether Windows 98 was installed over an earlier version of Windows.
VMM32	The file names of VxD files combined into the Vmm32.vxd virtual device driver.

Services subkey for CurrentControlSet. The **Services** subkey in
CurrentControlSet lists the Kernel device drivers, file system drivers, and
Windows 98 service drivers that can be loaded at startup. The **Services** subkey
also contains subkeys with static descriptions of hardware to which drivers can be
attached. Table 31.14 shows some typical **Services** subkeys.

Table 31.14   Typical Services subkeys

Subkey	Contents
Agent_name	Subkeys for each installed system agent, such as Microsoft Network Monitor, SNMP, or network backup agents.
Arbitrators	Subkeys for arbitrators required to manage resources between competing devices, usually including address, DMA, I/O, and IRQ arbitrators.
Class	Subkeys for all classes of devices the operating system supports, such as disk drives, keyboard, display, mouse, and so on.
MSNP32, NWNP32	Subkeys for 32-bit, protected-mode network providers, including logon and security provider information.
VxD	Subkeys for all virtual device drivers, including disk drivers, network components, disk caches, and so on.

Caution Do not change these value entries using Registry Editor. These settings
should be maintained only by the system. Settings for drivers that appear under
the **Services** subkeys can be changed by using Control Panel or system policies.

HKEY_USERS

HKEY_USERS contains all current user information (the **Default** subkey),
plus all previously loaded user profiles for users who have logged on in the
past. The information in the **Default** subkey is used to create the user profile for
a user who logs on without a user profile. The **Default** subkey contains keys for
AppEvents, Control Panel, Keyboard layouts, Network, RunMRU, and Software,
among others.

If the **HKEY_USERS** key shows a **Default** subkey only, then **HKEY_
CURRENT_USER** points to that key in **HKEY_USERS**. If a second key with
a user name exists, then **HKEY_CURRENT_USER** points to that second key.

Whenever similar data exists in **HKEY_LOCAL_MACHINE** and
HKEY_CURRENT_USER, the data in **HKEY_CURRENT_USER** takes
precedence. For example, settings for applications and the desktop defined
by the current user take precedence over default settings.

This subkey includes the same subkeys as **HKEY_CURRENT_USER**.

HKEY_CURRENT_CONFIG

This branch of the registry is stored in the System.dat file. The **HKEY_CURRENT_CONFIG** key points to the current system configuration in the collection of configurations stored in **HKEY_LOCAL_MACHINE \Config\000x**, which contains the current hardware configuration. The number *x* refers to the configuration number. For example, if you have a docked and an undocked mode for your portable computer, you would have a subkey for each configuration: **0001** and **0002**.

The **Display** subkey specifies screen fonts and screen settings, such as resolution. The **Enum** subkey contains subkeys that specify Plug and Play BIOS and the **System** subkey contains subkeys that list available printers.

HKEY_DYN_DATA

Some configuration information in Windows 98 must be stored in RAM because it requires fast modification and retrieval that cannot wait for the registry to flush to the hard disk. All this data can be found under **HKEY_DYN_DATA**. This information under this key is newly created every time Windows 98 starts.

The **Config Manager** subkey, sometimes referred to as the hardware tree, is a record in RAM of the current system configuration. The information is drawn from the devices currently installed and loaded, or that failed loading. The hardware tree is created every time the system starts and updates whenever a change occurs to the system configuration. The information that appears in Registry Editor is provided when this key is displayed, so it is never out of date.

HKEY_DYN_DATA also contains statistics gathered for various network components currently in use on the system. These reside under **HKEY_DYN_DATA\PerfStats**.

VxDs from other vendors can provide dynamic data to this area too. For more information, see the *Win32 Software Development Kit for Windows 98 and Windows NT*.

Plug and Play and the Registry

Plug and Play is both a design approach and a set of personal computer architecture specifications with the goal of making the personal computer, add-in hardware devices, drivers, and the operating system work together automatically without user intervention. In order to achieve this goal, all the components must be Plug and Play. The components of a Plug and Play system include:

- A Plug and Play operating system.
- A Plug and Play basic input/output system (BIOS) or ACPI BIOS.
- Plug and Play hardware devices with drivers.

Depending on whether any of these components are Plug and Play or not, the level of ease-of-use and dynamic operation varies. At the lowest level, where all three components are legacy, or not Plug and Play, the system lacks any dynamic operation and is difficult to use because card jumpers and switches need to be manually set and drivers manually loaded.

At the next level, when a Plug and Play operating system (such as Windows 98) is used with legacy hardware, the system supports dynamic operation of PCMCIA devices and is relatively easy to use.

Hardware setup is made simple by the Device Wizard (which helps to detect, identify, and configure devices), consistent user interface of device property sheets, and availability of device information through the registry and Device Manager. Additional ease-of-use is achieved due to automatic loading of drivers using the Device Installer, and due to smart software that reacts to configuration changes to give dynamic hardware event messages.

At the highest level, where all three components are Plug and Play, installing new devices is as easy as plugging them in and turning on the computer. Hardware setup is completely silent and transparent, and you do not need to modify expansion card jumper settings, or even modify operating system configuration files. Also, the system supports full dynamic operation, including hot docking, Advanced Power Management (APM) 1.1 power management, automatic configuration of boot devices, and programming of motherboard devices.

The registry is the backbone for Plug and Play specifications. It contains hardware-specific information so that when a user plugs a new piece of hardware into the computer, Windows 98 automatically configures the hardware device, or helps the user set it up with a Setup Wizard.

Windows 98 uses the device ID to search the INF files for that device. It then creates an entry in the **HKEY_LOCAL_MACHINE** key and copies information from the INF file into the key. **Enum** keys refer to the Windows 98 enumeration process that checks the hardware device. **HKEY_CURRENT_CONFIG** subkey **Enum** contains various subkeys (**BIOS**, **Root**, and so on) that specify Plug and Play BIOS or other elements. **HKEY_DYN_DATA** subkey **Enum** contains EISA: ISA Plug and Play bus. **HKEY_DYN_DATA\ConfigManager\Enum** defines the allocation of the resource, problems with the device, and configuration information.

The **HKEY_LOCAL_MACHINE\Enum** key contains subkeys for the specific hardware components used by the computer. Windows 98 uses this information to allocate resources, such as IO addresses and interrupts, for the devices. All values in the **\Enum** branch are vendor- and device-specific, so specific information can vary from machine to machine. The following list briefly describes entries in the **\Enum** subkey.

BIOS This subkey contains entries for Plug and Play components of the BIOS (which includes timers, controllers, and direct memory access [DMA] chips). Each **BIOS** subkey starts with the string ***PNP** and is followed by a four-digit number that represents classes by which the components are grouped: ***PNP0000**. Each ***PNP*xxxx*** key contains subkeys (**00, 01**) that contain the data (such as class name, device description string, driver name, and hardware ID) for the device configuration. See Table 31.15 for more details.

ESDI This subkey contains the configuration data of the IDE-controller used for hard disk drives and other devices.

FLOP This subkey contains the configuration data of the floppy disk controllers used in the system.

HTREE This subkey is reserved.

ISAPNP This subkey contains entries for Plug and Play equipment enumerated on an ISA bus.

MF This subkey defines manufacturer-specific information about hardware components.

Monitor This subkey contains information about the monitor used in the system. If setup cannot detect the monitor type, the selection is set by the user.

Network This subkey contains information about the network (for example, redirectors, services, and NetBEUI). The network adapter is specified in the **Root\Net** subkey.

PCI This subkey contains entries for Plug and Play equipment on a peripheral component interconnect (PCI) bus.

Root This subkey contains ***PNP*xxxx*** entries for legacy, non–Plug and Play hardware, such as the CPU, BIOS, network adapters, and printer drivers.

SCSI This subkey contains configuration data for small computer system interface (SCSI) devices.

Table 31.15   \Enum\BIOS values for Plug and Play components

Value	Description
PNP0000–PNP0004	Interrupt controllers
PNP0100–PNP0102	System timers
PNP0200–PNP0202	DMA controllers
PNP0300–PNP0313	Keyboard controllers
PNP0400–PNP0401	Printer ports
PNP0500–PNP0501	Communication ports
PNP0600–PNP0602	Hard disk controllers
PNP0700	Standard floppy disk controller
PNP0800	System speaker
PNP0900–PNP0915 PNP0930–PNP0931 PNP0940–PNP0941	Display adapters
PNP0A00–PNP0A04	Expansion buses
PNP0B00	CMOS real-time clock
PNP0C01	System board extension for Plug and Play BIOS
PNP0C02	Reserved
PNP0C04	Numeric data processor
PNP0E00–PNP0E02	PCMCIA controllers
PNP0F01	Serial Microsoft mouse
PNP0F00–PNP0F13	Mouse ports
PNP8xxx	Network adapters
PNPA030	Mitsumi CD-ROM controller
PNPB0xx	Miscellaneous adapters

Plug and Play codes are grouped in classes according to their four-digit code. You can view and modify the device configuration used on your computer with Device Manager, which is located under the System option in the Control Panel.

Detection and enumeration are the two processes that Windows 98 uses to configure devices. *Detection* is the process Windows 98 uses during its search for legacy or non-Plug and Play devices on a computer. Detection is used during Windows 98 Setup and any time you use the Add New Hardware Wizard to search for new hardware installed in your computer. Detection does not run each time you start Windows 98. During the detection process, Windows 98 creates a log file called Detlog.txt in the root directory of the boot drive. This file is commonly referenced when troubleshooting problems with hardware detection.

Enumeration is the process Windows 98 uses to identify Plug and Play devices in your computer, including those devices on Plug and Play buses, such as ISAPNP, PCI, and PC Card (PCMCIA) devices. Enumeration occurs each time Windows 98 starts and whenever Windows 98 receives notification that a change has occurred in the computer's hardware configuration, such as when you remove a PC Card.

View Preferences and the Registry

This section describes how Windows 98 stores **View** preferences for the desktop and windows that you open. **View** preferences include icon size, position, layout.

Windows 98 stores up to 28 entries containing **View** preferences for the desktop and windows that you open in a most-recently-used (MRU) list. When you close a window, the **View** preferences are written to subkeys with the names **0, 1, 2,** and so on, located in the following registry key:

HKEY_CURRENT_USER\Software\Microsoft\Windows\CurrentVersion \Explorer\Streams

The MRU list in the following registry key defines the order of the 28 entries:

HKEY_CURRENT_USER\Software\Microsoft\Windows\CurrentVersion \Explorer\StreamMRU

When the desktop or one of the windows is no longer included in the MRU list, the desktop or window uses the default settings the next time the desktop or window is redrawn or refreshed.

When you make a change to the desktop or a window, the **View** preferences for the desktop or window are moved to the top of the MRU list. That item remains on the MRU list until it reaches the 28th spot. When an item reaches the 28th spot and another window is closed, the 28th item is removed from the MRU list.

Modem Registry Key Entries

The following section describes information stored in specific modem registry keys that might help advanced users correct problems with the commands that Windows 98 uses to control a modem. To identify modem problems, you can enable Windows 98 to create a Modemlog.txt file (as described in Chapter 21, "Modems and Communications Tools"), which contains responses to and from a modem when a connection was made. The Modemlog.txt file might indicate when Windows 98 is sending an incorrect command string to a modem, or when a response code is not being correctly interpreted. After consulting the documentation for the modem, you might be able to adjust the modem's registry keys to restore proper operation.

Modem registry keys are stored under the following key:

**HKEY_LOCAL_MACHINE\System\CurrentControlSet\Services
\Class*Modem***

For each installed modem, Windows 98 creates one registry key (starting with
\0000); additional subkeys, which contain AT commands that Windows 98 uses to
initialize, dial, and answer the modem; plus other entries that communications and
modem drivers use.

Some of the more important entries that you can use to correct or optimize modem
operation are described in the following sections. The full set of modem registry
keys and the INF file format are documented in the *Microsoft Windows 98 Device
Development Kit.*

Init Key

The multiple, modem-command string entries in the **Init** key initialize the modem
before Windows 98 uses it. The name of each entry is its sequence number,
starting with the number **1**, and its data is the command that is sent to the modem.
Usually, the **Init** key entry **1** is **AT<cr>**, which starts the modem. **Init** entry **2**
usually contains **&F** or a similar command to restore the modem to its default
settings. Subsequent **Init** key entries contain miscellaneous commands to
configure the modem so it is compatible with Windows 98.

Responses Key

The **Responses** key contains strings that the modem might report to Windows 98
in response to a command or during the connection process. The name of each
subkey is the text of a single modem response, and its data is a 10-byte binary
value specifying the meaning of the response to Windows in a coded format. The
first two characters (byte 0) specify the meaning of the response code, using one
of the following values.

Value	Type	Description
00	OK	The modem accepted the previous command.
01	Negotiation Progress	Status information about a new connection is being reported.
02	Connect	A call is connected; the modem is in data mode.
03	Error	The modem rejected the previous command.
04	No Carrier	The call was disconnected.
05	No Dial Tone	No dial tone is present.
06	Busy	The dialed modem is busy.
07	No Answer	The dialed modem did not answer.

Value	Type	Description
08	Ring	There is an incoming call.
1C	Blacklisted	The remote number does not answer as a modem.
ID	Delayed	The user should wait before trying this call again.

The second two characters (byte 1) specify information about a connection that is being made. It is used only for response codes of type Negotiation Progress or Connect, and is one of the following values.

Value	Error control negotiated	Compression negotiated	Cellular protocol negotiated
00	–	–	–
01	–	X	–
02	X	–	–
03	X	X	–
08	–	–	X
09	–	X	X
0A	X	–	X
0B	X	X	X

The next eight characters (bytes 2–5) specify the modem-to-modem line speed negotiated in bits per second (bps). The characters represent a 32-bit integer, doubleword format (byte and word reversed). Common examples for this value include the following.

Bits per second	String
2400	60 09 00 00
9600	80 25 00 00
14400	40 38 00 00
19200	00 4b 00 00
28800	80 70 00 00
33600	40 83 00 00
56000	C0 DA 00 00

The last eight characters (bytes 6–9) indicate that the modem is changing to a different port or Data Terminal Equipment (DTE) speed. Usually, this field is not used, because modems make connections at a "locked" port speed, regardless of the modem-to-modem or Data Communications Equipment (DCE) speed. However, for modems that support only "direct" modes, you can lower the DTE speed by specifying a negotiated DTE speed for a response code, using the same format as the DCE speed described in the preceding table.

Settings Key

The **Settings** key contains commands for configuring various modem settings. After the **Init** key commands are sent, Windows 98 builds a dynamic configuration command string by concatenating various entries shown in Table 31.16. The command string depends on the settings selected in the modem's properties.

Table 31.16   Settings key entries

Subkey	Description	Example
Prefix	Configuration command prefix	AT
Terminator	Configuration command suffix	<cr>
DialPrefix	Dial command prefix	D
Dial_Pulse	Use pulse dialing	P
Dial_Tone	Use tone dialing	T
Blind_Off	Detect dial tone before dialing	X4
Blind_On	Do not detect dial tone before dialing	X3
CallSetupFailTimeout	Specify call setup time-out	S7=<#>
InactivityTimeout	Specify inactivity time-out	S30=<#>
SpeakerVolume_Low	Low speaker volume	L1
SpeakerVolume_Med	Medium speaker volume	L2
SpeakerVolume_High	High speaker volume	L3
SpeakerMode_Off	Speaker always off	M0
SpeakerMode_Dial	Speaker on during dial and negotiation	M1
SpeakerMode_On	Speaker always on	M2
SpeakerMode_Setup	Speaker on only during negotiation	M3
FlowControl_Off	No flow control	&K0
FlowControl_Hard	Hardware flow control	&K1
FlowControl_Soft	Software flow control	&K2
ErrorControl_Off	Error control disabled (normal mode, not direct)	+Q6S36=3S48=128
ErrorControl_On	Error control enabled (auto reliable)	+Q5S36=7S48=7
ErrorControl_Forced	Error control required to connect (reliable)	+Q5S36=4S48=7
ErrorControl_Cellular	Cellular protocol enabled	\N3-K1)M1-Q1*H1
Compression_On	Compression enabled	S46=138
Compression_Off	Compression disabled	S46=136
Modulation_CCITT	Use CCITT modulations for 300 and 1200 bps	B0

Table 31.16   Settings key entries (*continued*)

Subkey	Description	Example
Modulation_Bell	Use Bell modulations for 300 and 1200 bps	B1
SpeedNegotiation_Off	Connect only at default modem speed; do not fall back	N0
SpeedNegotiation_On	Use lower DCE speed to connect, if necessary	N1

Supporting Phone Message Record and Playback

To support the telephone answering machine functions of recording incoming phone messages and playing the messages back through the handset when there is no active call, you must use your modem INF file to put values in the different registry keys outlined in Table 31.17.

Table 31.17   Phone message record and playback registry keys

Registry key	Value
AbortPlay	Command that stops playing audio data immediately (does not play the rest of the audio buffer contents). This command is not used for modems that are not using a serial wave device.
CloseHandset	Command that resets the modem to Class 0.
HandsetSetPlayFormat	Command that sets the modem's handset playback format.
HandsetSetRecordFormat	Command that sets the modem's handset recording format.
LineSetPlayFormat	Command that sets the modem's line playback format.
LineSetRecordFormat	Command that sets the modem's line recording format.
OpenHandset	Command that puts modem in a mode that enables audio to be played back through the handset when there is no active call.
StartPlay	Command that starts playing audio (wave files) out of the modem. If a serial wave driver is being used, a bit in the **VoiceProfile** key controls whether the baud is set prior to the **StartPlay** command or after the **StartPlay** command.
StartRecord	Command that starts recording audio (wave files) from the modem. If a serial wave driver is being used, a bit in the **VoiceProfile** key controls whether the baud is set prior to the **StartRecord** command or after the **StartRecord** command.
StopPlay	Command that can be used to reset the modem's baud after an **AbortPlay** or **TerminatePlay** command. A bit in the **VoiceProfile** key indicates whether **Unimodem/V** has to reset the UART's baud.

Table 31.17   Phone message record and playback registry keys (*continued*)

Registry key	Value
StopRecord	Command that stops recording audio (wave files) from the modem. If a serial wave driver is being used, a bit in the **VoiceProfile** key controls whether the baud is set prior to the **StopRecord** command or after the **StopRecord** command.
TerminateRecord	Command that causes the modem to finish recording its local buffer and stop recording audio data. This command is not used for modems that are not using a serial wave device.
TerminatePlay	Command that causes the modem to finish playing the contents of its local buffer and stop playing audio data after that. This command is not used for modems that are not using a serial wave device.

TCP/IP Registry Key Entries

This section documents the Windows 98 registry entries for TCP/IP.

Configuration settings for Microsoft TCP/IP are stored in the Registry as part of the protocol installation process. If Dynamic Host Configuration Protocol (DHCP) is used on the network, configuration information can also be provided by DHCP client service. DHCP-provided information is stored in the registry in binary format and cannot be altered by editing it. However, static information can be entered in the registry, which overrides DHCP default values.

TCP/IP Registry Entries in the MSTCP Subkey

The value entries are added to the following registry key:

HKEY_LOCAL_MACHINE\System\CurrentControlSet\Services \VxD\MSTCP

Descriptions of the TCP/IP values in the MSTCP are described in Table 31.18 (all data types are DWORD).

Table 31.18   TCP/IP registry entries

Value	Description
BroadcastAddress = broadcast address in hexadecimal	Specifies the address to use for NetBIOS name query broadcasts. The default is based on the Internet Protocol (IP) address and the subnet mask.
BcastNameQueryCount = integer	Specifies the number of times the system will retry NetBIOS name query broadcasts. The default is 3.
BcastQueryTimeout = milliseconds	Specifies the period of time the system will wait before timing out broadcast name queries. The minimum value is 100. The default is 750.

Table 31.18   TCP/IP registry entries (*continued*)

Value	Description
BSDUrgent = 0 or 1	If this value is 1, it specifies that Microsoft TCP/IP is to treat urgent data the way some UNIX systems do (with a maximum of 1 byte of urgent data, for example). If this value is 0, it specifies that the stack is to handle urgent data as specified by RFC 1122. The default is 1.
CacheTimeout = milliseconds	Specifies how long NetBIOS names are cached. The minimum is 60,000 milliseconds (1 minute). The default is 360,000 milliseconds (6 minutes).
DeadGWDetect = 0 or 1	Specifies whether Microsoft TCP/IP will use another gateway if the current default gateway seems to be down. The default is 1.
DefaultRcvWindow = 16-bit number	Specifies the default receive window advertised by TCP. The default is 8192.
DefaultTOS = 8-bit number	Specifies the default type of service (TOS) for IP packets initiated by Microsoft TCP/IP. The default is 0.
DefaultTTL = 8-bit number	Specifies the default time to live (TTL) for IP packets initiated by Microsoft TCP/IP. The default is 128.
DnsServerPort = port	Specifies which DNS server port to send queries to when resolving a name using DNS. The default is 53.
EnableProxy = 0 or 1	If this value is 1, it specifies that this computer is a Windows Internet Naming Service (WINS) proxy agent. The default is 0.
EnableRouting = 0 or 1	Specifies whether to enable static routing. Microsoft TCP/IP does not supply a routing protocol, so all route table entries must be entered using the route command. The default is 0.
IGMPLevel = 0, 1, or 2	Specifies the level of support allowed for IP multicast, corresponding to the levels in RFC 1112. The default is 2.
InitialRefreshT.O. = milliseconds	Specifies the interval over which to contact WINS to refresh the name. The minimum is 16 minutes, and the maximum is approximately 50 days (0xFFFFFFFF). The default is 960,000 milliseconds (16 minutes).
KeepAliveTime = 32-bit number	Specifies the connection idle time in milliseconds before TCP will begin sending keepalives, if keepalives are enabled on a connection. The default is 2 hours (7,200,000 milliseconds).

Table 31.18   TCP/IP registry entries (*continued*)

Value	Description
KeepAliveInterval = 32-bit number	Specifies the time in milliseconds between retransmissions of keepalives, once the KeepAliveTime has expired. Once KeepAliveTime has expired, keepalives are sent every KeepAliveInterval milliseconds until a response is received, up to a maximum of MaxDataRetries before the connection is aborted. The default is 1 second (1000 milliseconds).
LmhostsTimeout = milliseconds	Specifies the period of time the system will wait before timing out when seeking LMHOSTS for name resolution. The minimum value is 1000 milliseconds (1 second). The default is 10,000 milliseconds (10 seconds).
MaxConnections = 32-bit number	Specifies the maximum number of concurrent connections. The default is 100.
MaxConnectRetries = 32-bit number	Specifies the number of times a connection attempt (SYN) will be retransmitted before giving up. The initial retransmission timeout is 3 seconds, and it is doubled each time up to a maximum of 2 minutes. The default is 3.
MaxDataRetries = 32-bit number	Specifies the maximum number of times a segment carrying data or FIN will be retransmitted before the connection is aborted. The retransmission timeout itself is adaptive and will vary according to link conditions. The default is 5.
NameServerPort = port	Specifies the User Datagram Protocol (UDP) port on the name server to which to send name queries or registrations. The default is 137.
NameSrvQueryCount = integer	Specifies the number of times the system will try to contact the WINS server for NetBIOS name resolution. The default is 3.
NameSrvQueryTimeout = milliseconds	Specifies how long the system waits before timing out a name server query. The minimum is 100 milliseconds. The default is 750 milliseconds.
NameTableSize = integer	Specifies the maximum number of names in the NetBIOS name table. The minimum allowable value is 1 and the maximum is 255. The default is 17.
NodeType = 1, 2, 4, or 8	Specifies the mode of NetBIOS name resolution used by NetBIOS over TCP/IP, where 1 = b-node, 2 = p-node, 4 = m-node, and 8 = h-node. This value can be configured using DHCP. The default is 1 (b-node) if no value is specified; if WINS servers are specified and NodeType is not, the default is 8 (h-node).

Table 31.18   TCP/IP registry entries (*continued*)

Value	Description
PMTUBlackHoleDetect = 0 or 1	Specifies whether the stack will attempt to detect Maximum Transmission Unit (MTU) routers that do not send back Internet Control Message Protocol (ICMP) fragmentation-needed messages. Setting this parameter when it is not needed can cause performance degradation. The default is 0.
PMTUDiscovery = 0 or 1	Specifies whether Microsoft TCP/IP will attempt to perform path MTU discovery as specified in RFC 1191. The default is 1.
RandomAdapter = 0 or 1	For a computer with multiple network adapters, specifies whether to respond with an IP address selected randomly from the set of addresses on the computer or whether to return the IP address of the adapter that the request came in upon. The default is 0 (not random; that is, return the address of the adapter that the request came in upon).
RoutingBufSize = 32-bit number	Specifies the total amount of buffer space to allocate for routing packets. This parameter is ignored if EnableRouting=0. The default is 73,216.
RoutingPackets = 32-bit number	Specifies the maximum number of packets that can be routed simultaneously. This parameter is ignored if EnableRouting=0. The default is 50.
SessionKeepAlive = milliseconds	Specifies how often to send session keepalive packets on active sessions. The minimum is 60 seconds. The default is 3,600,000 milliseconds (1 hour).
SessionTableSize = integer	Specifies the maximum number of sessions in the NetBIOS session table. The minimum allowable value is 1 and the maximum is 255. The default is 255.
SingleResponse = 0 or 1	For a computer with multiple network adapters, specifies whether to send all IP addresses on a name query request from WINS. If this value is 1, the system will send one address in a name query response; if 0, it will return all the addresses of its adapters. The default is 0.
Size/Small/Medium/Large = 1, 2, or 3	Specifies how many buffers of various types to pre-allocate and the maximum that can be allocated, where 1 = small, 2 = medium, and 3 = large. The default is 1; the default is 3 if the WINS proxy is enabled.

TCP/IP Registry Entries in the MSTCP\ServiceProvider Subkey

This section describes variables for subkeys that appear in the following registry key:

**HKEY_LOCAL_MACHINE\System\CurrentControlSet\Services\VxD
\MSTCP\ServiceProvider**

The **Class** and **ProviderPath** values are used by the service resolution and registry APIs in Windows Sockets. The **Class** parameter indicates that TCP/IP is a name service provider, and its binary value (8) should not be changed. The **ProviderPath** parameter is a string that defines the location and file name for the 32-bit Windows Sockets DLL (the default is %windir%\system\wsock32.dll).

The following keys describe the order used to resolve host names. A lower number sets a higher priority for name resolution. These settings are used for 16-bit Windows Sockets, which need to rely on the resolvers that are expected to take the least time. The numbers indicate the default values specified in Windows 98.

LocalPriority = 0x1F3 (499)
HostsPriority = 0x1F (500)
DNSPriority = 0x7D0 (2000)
NetbtPriority = 0x7D1 (2001)

TCP/IP Registry Entries in the NetTrans Subkey

The entries in this section must be added to the following registry key, where *n* represents the particular TCP/IP-to-network adapter binding.

**HKEY_LOCAL_MACHINE\System\CurrentControlSet\Services\Class
    \netTrans\ 000n**

Value	Data type	Description
MaxMTU = 16-bit integer	DWORD	Specifies the maximum size datagram IP that can pass to a media driver. Subnetwork Access Protocol (SNAP) and source routing headers (if used on the media) are not included in this value. For example, on an Ethernet network, MaxMTU will default to 1500. The actual value used will be the minimum of the value specified with this parameter and the size reported by the media driver. The default is the size reported by the media driver; an Ethernet network defaults to 1500 bytes and a Point-to-Point (PPP) Protocol dial-up connection defaults to 576 bytes.

Value	Data type	Description
ZeroBroadcast = 0 or 1	String	If this parameter is set to 1, then IP will use zeros-broadcasts (0.0.0.0.) instead of ones-broadcasts (255.255.255.255). Most systems use ones-broadcasts, but some systems derived from BSD implementations use zeros-broadcasts. Interoperation will not work well on the same network for systems that use different broadcasts. Valid Range 0 or 1 (false or true); Default: 0

Changing TCP/IP Node Types

The TCP/IP node type can be manually changed by editing the Windows 98 registry. The location is under the **HKEY_LOCAL_MACHINE** key under the following subkey:

\System\CurrentControlSet\Services\VxD\MSTCP\NodeType

The four TCP/IP node types are defined by number:

Number	Node Type	Description
1	b-node	Broadcast only
2	p-node	WINS only
4	m-node	Broadcast, then WINS
8	h-node	WINS, then broadcast

The default Windows 98 TCP/IP node types are:

- If DHCP=False, and WINS is disabled, then NodeType=1 (b-node)
- If DHCP=False, and WINS is manually set, then NodeType=8 (h-node)
- If DHCP=True, and DHCP sets WINS, then NodeType=4 (m-node)
- If DHCP=True, and WINS is manually set, then NodeType=8 (h-node)
- If DHCP=True, and WINS is disabled, then NodeType=1 (b-node)

Troubleshooting the Registry

This section provides some tips for troubleshooting registry problems, and for troubleshooting your system using the registry.

Understanding Operating System Load and Desktop Initialization

Understanding this phase of the boot process can help when you need to troubleshoot registry and operating system problems.

The Windows 98 operating system load sequence is as follows:

Sequence	Component	Description
1	Registry	Base system information
2	System.ini	Legacy system configuration
3	Kernel32.dll	Main operating system code
4	Gdi.exe and Gdi32.dll	Graphical device interface; graphics engine
5	User.exe and User32.exe	Code for managing the user interface including the window manager
6	Resources and fonts	
7	Win.ini	Legacy system program and user configuration

The Windows 98 desktop initialization sequence is as follows:

1. The Windows shell loads and machine policies are enforced.

2. The desktop components load.

3. If connected to a network, a logon prompt appears. Once the user is logged on, the logon scripts are carried out and policies are enforced for the user.

4. Once the user logs on, the system can process user-specific configuration information and load any user-specific policy files. If the user does not log on, default settings are used to determine user preferences. If network logon is set, the user is logged on to the network during this process.

Troubleshooting Registry Startup Errors

Accessing system registry.

When you start Windows 98, you receive one of the following error messages:

```
Windows encountered an error accessing the system Registry. Windows will
restart and repair the system Registry for you now.
```

Windows 98 will restart your computer and run Registry Checker in MS-DOS mode (Scanreg.exe) to fix the problem.

Not enough memory.

When you start Windows 98, you receive the following error message:

```
Windows was unable to process the registry. This may be fixed by
rebooting to Command Prompt Only and running SCANREG /FIX. Otherwise
there may not be enough conventional memory to properly load the
registry.
```

If you see this message after you run ScanReg /Fix, then you need to free up conventional memory in your computer.

Error When Removing a Program with Add/Remove Programs

When you remove a program using the Add/Remove Programs option in Control Panel, you receive the following error message:

```
An error occurred while trying to remove <Program Name>.
Uninstallation has been canceled.
```

This error can occur if you have manually deleted a program that is listed in the **Install/Uninstall** list in the **Add/Remove Programs Properties** dialog box. To remove a program from the **Install/Uninstall** list, delete the appropriate key under the following registry key:

HKEY_LOCAL_MACHINE\Software\Microsoft\Windows
    \CurrentVersion\Uninstall

Windows 98 Cannot Find a Needed Device File

When you start Windows 98, you receive an error message telling you that Windows 98 cannot find a device file that may be needed to run Windows or a Windows-based application. Sometimes a specific file name is specified.

This error message can occur for either of the following reasons:

- A Windows virtual device driver (VxD) referenced in the System.ini file or registry is missing or damaged.

- One of the StaticVxD values in the registry contains invalid data. For example, the value is blank or contains only spaces. In this case, the missing device driver is not named in the error message.

To resolve this problem, follow each step below until the error no longer occurs:

1. If you recently removed a program or component, reinstall the program or component, then run the uninstall program if one is available. If no uninstall program is available for the program or component, contact the manufacturer to obtain instructions on uninstalling.

2. If the missing device driver has a .386 extension, disable the line referring to this device driver in the System.ini file by placing a semicolon (;) at the beginning of the line.

   For example, if the line referencing the missing device driver reads:

   ```
   device=Example.386
   ```

   change the line to read:

   ```
   ;device=Example.386
   ```

3. If the missing device driver has a .vxd extension, it is a driver designed for use with Windows 98 and is referenced in the registry. In most cases, a program or component with drivers designed for use with Windows 98 will also be listed in the Add/Remove Programs option in Control Panel. Following the instructions in step 1 should correct the problem.

If the error occurs after following the instructions in step 1, you need to locate the value that references the missing device driver in the registry, and delete that registry value.

If a specific device driver is not named in the error message, one of the StaticVxD values in the registry is probably blank or contains only spaces. The StaticVxD values are located in the registry keys below the following key:

HKEY_LOCAL_MACHINE\System\CurrentControlSet\Services\VxD

Use Registry Editor to locate and delete any StaticVxD value in the registry that contains invalid data, is blank, or contains only spaces.

When Windows 98 starts, the System.ini file and the registry are read to obtain a list of device drivers to load. When Windows 98 cannot locate a virtual device driver that it is attempting to load, an error message is generated.

Virtual device drivers are files required by various programs to communicate with your computer's hardware.

The following sample registry key contains a StaticVxD value:

**HKEY_LOCAL_MACHINE\System\CurrentControlSet\Services\VxD
\COMBUFF**

The data for this StaticVxD value is "*COMBUFF" (without the quotation marks; the quotation marks appear in Registry Editor, but are not part of the VxD name). The asterisk (*) preceding the VxD name indicates that the VxD is internal to the Vmm32.vxd file. If the VxD referenced by the StaticVxD value is not internal to the Vmm32.vxd file, its name is not preceded by an asterisk and typically has a .vxd extension.

Additional Resources

For more information about	See this resource
Windows 98 registry	*Inside the Microsoft Windows 98 Registry* by Günter Born
Windows NT registry	*The Microsoft Windows NT Workstation Resource Kit*
	The Microsoft Windows NT Server Resource Kit
Programming the registry	*The Microsoft Windows 98 Software Development Kit*
	Win32 Software Development Kit for Windows 98 and Windows NT

P A R T   7

Appendixes

APPENDIX A

International Windows 98

This appendix summarizes information about local editions and multilanguage support for Microsoft Windows 98, and it provides technical details about defining regional settings in setup scripts.

Overview of Windows 98 Local Editions

Windows 98 is available in several local versions, including:

Arabic	Czech	French	Hungarian	Norwegian	Spanish
Basque	Danish	German	Italian	Polish	Swedish
Catalan	Dutch	Greek	Japanese	Portuguese-Brazilian	Turkish
English	Japanese (NEC PC-9800 Series Version)	Portuguese-Iberian	Slovak	Slovenian	Thai
Chinese S.C.	Finnish	Hebrew	Korean	Russian	Vietnamese
Chinese T.C.					

A single installation of Windows 98 will not support more than one Windows code page. As with earlier versions of Windows, all single-byte international versions of Windows 98 are based on a single Windows code page of 256 code points. The following international versions of Windows 98 are available.

United States. The United States version of Windows 98 is based on the American National Standards Institute (ANSI) Windows code page (1252). This is the code page used for most of the single-byte language versions in North America, South America, Eastern Europe, Western Europe, Scandinavia, South Pacific, Africa, and Asia. This version also forms the base for all other versions.

This version also allows users to select a Windows code page for their particular language needs during setup. Choices include Cyrillic (1251), Central Europe (1250), Turkish (1254), Greek (1253), and Baltic (1257). After it is installed, the Windows code page cannot be changed. The United States release version is available in English, German, Italian, Norwegian, Swedish, Dutch, French, Spanish, Portuguese, Danish, Finnish, Russian, Polish, Hungarian, Greek, Turkish, and other languages.

Far East. Windows 98 is available in Japanese (932), Simplified Chinese (936), Traditional (Taiwan) Chinese (950), and Korean (949). These are the only versions of Windows 98 that support the large character sets and input methods these languages require. They also support a vast array of the unique hardware used in these locales.

Middle East. Windows 98 is available in Arabic (1256) and Hebrew (1255). These are the only versions of Windows 98 that support mixed right-to-left and left-to-right text processing. The Arabic version also includes support for Farsi (Persian).

Thai. Windows 98 is based on the Thai code page (876).

For information about ordering a local edition of Windows 98, contact your software vendor or your local Microsoft office.

The *Win32 Software Development Kit for Windows 98 and Windows NT* and the Microsoft Developer Network provide complete information about the architecture, application programming interfaces (APIs), and other needs for developers who are creating or modifying applications to run on local editions of Windows 98. For information about joining the Microsoft Developer Network, see Appendix I, "Windows 98 Resource Directory."

The *Microsoft Windows 98 Resource Kit* is being made available in at least the following local versions: Bahasa, Simplified and Traditional Chinese, Croatian, French, German, Italian, Japanese, Korean, Portuguese, Slovenian, Spanish, Swedish, and Thai. For information about ordering a local edition of the *Microsoft Windows 98 Resource Kit*, contact your local bookseller or your local Microsoft office.

Developing International Software for Windows 95 and Windows NT, a Microsoft Press book by Nadine Kano, provides details about using the Windows 95 national language support (NLS) API and other information about developing software for use in multiple locales. To order this publication (ISBN 1-55615-840-8), contact your local bookseller. You can also order it directly in the United States by calling (800) 677-7377.

Overview of International Language Support

Windows 98 offers international language support to provide solutions to problems created when using software and exchanging documents among different locales and languages. Windows 98 offers this support at the operating system level for users and at the API level for software developers. This section summarizes this built-in international language support for using Windows 98 throughout the world and the features that Windows 98 provides for enhancing existing or new applications for global use.

Easy-to-use multilanguage fonts and keyboard layouts. With Windows 98, users can easily switch among all available languages and corresponding keyboard layouts configured on the system. This makes it easy for users to integrate information into a multilingual document. By using the Keyboard option in Control Panel, users can easily add and remove keyboard layouts and languages. By using the common **Choose Font** dialog box in applications created for Windows 98, they can choose character-set scripts (such as "Greek") supported by a particular font. For more information, see "Using Multilingual Fonts with Win32-based Applications" and "Using Alternate Keyboards" later in this chapter.

Substitution for unavailable fonts when switching languages. When switching among languages in a document, Windows 98 substitutes matching fonts for the new language if the original font is not available. Users can read and use the text for a similar character set, even if they do not have the font in which the information was originally created.

Preservation of language-specific attributes on the Clipboard. Windows 98 provides additional services for application vendors to easily exchange information between internationally-aware applications, while preserving all language formatting characteristics.

Easy addition of multilanguage support for software developers. Developers can use the Win32 NLS API for loading, selecting, and querying keyboard layouts and languages. NLS services ensure globally-aware information handling by supporting diverse formats for date, time, calendar, number, and currency, and for sorting, character typing, and character mapping. The correct national format for information such as date format or sorting sequence is supplied automatically, based on the settings specified in the Regional Settings option in Control Panel. Win32-based applications can use Windows 98 services to automatically switch between the proper fonts and keyboard layouts as users navigate through a multilingual document. For more information, see "Using Multiple Languages in Windows 98" later in this chapter.

Proper sorting and formatting rules for the current locale. Windows 98 supports diverse rules for interpreting information, such as algorithms for sorting or searching, and formats for time and dates based on the user's locale. Software developers can use the Win32 NLS API to check and use the user's default locale settings or to use a specific locale setting, without using proprietary sorting methods or parsing Win.ini or the registry, and without locale-specific coding. This allows users to easily exchange information internationally, while preserving the integrity of the information. For example, the multilingual support in Windows 98 can be used in applications to account for the following kinds of differences among language rules:

- In French, diacritics are sorted from right to left instead of from left to right as in English.

- In Norwegian, some extended characters follow the *Z* character because they are considered unique characters rather than characters with diacritics.

- In Spanish, *CH* is a unique character between *C* and *D*, and *Ñ* is a unique character between *N* and *O*.

Specifying International Settings

During Windows 98 Setup, the operating system is configured for a default locale, either based on settings that Setup detects from the previous operating system or based on options that the user chooses. Windows 98 Setup also copies most international information for all other supported locales onto the user's hard disk drive, where applications can access them. You can specify international settings during Windows 98 Setup or change the default settings afterward in Control Panel. If a US (1252) locale is desired, you must add any additional language support through the Control Panel after the machine is running.

By selecting a Custom Install, you can choose settings for your specific locale. During Setup, you can customize the following settings in the Computer Settings screen:

- Regional settings, for specifying language and, in turn, the local conventions for other settings such as date, time, and currency formats. This also sets the MS-DOS code page and MS-DOS country settings without changing the operating system (OS) language.

- Keyboard layout, for specifying the default keyboard layout to be used with Windows 98, based on varying local requirements. This also sets the MS-DOS keyboard layout.

- Language support, for selecting one of the following combinations of languages:

  - English/Western European
  - English/Western European and Greek
  - English/Western European and Cyrillic
  - English/Western European and Central European
  - English/Western European and Turkish
  - English/Western European and Baltic

    Windows 98 selects the English/Western European option by default.

After Setup, you can change the following settings in Control Panel:

- Add languages and corresponding keyboard layouts using the Keyboard option, as described in "Using Alternate Keyboards" later in this chapter.

- Modify the local language default for settings such as date, time, and currency using the Regional Settings option.

- Add or remove support for fonts and locales (Greek, Cyrillic, or Central European) in the Add/Remove Programs option.

You can configure each of these settings by defining options in custom setup scripts, as described in the following sections. If user profiles are enabled (as described in Chapter 7, "User Profiles"), the international settings preferences in Windows 98 can be saved in each user's profile. In this case, if a single computer is used by multiple users, each user can select a different default locale.

Changing Regional Settings in Windows 98

To change local conventions after Windows 98 has been installed, use the Regional Settings option in Control Panel. This option sets the default system formats for country, language, date, time, currency, and numbers. You can also customize these formats.

▶ **To change regional settings in Windows 98**

- In the Regional Settings option in Control Panel, click a tab to define settings for that property, as summarized in the following list. When settings are as you want them, click **OK**.

Properties tab	Description
Regional Settings	Specifies the regional settings you want, to automatically define how dates, times, currency, and numbers are displayed and sorted.
Number	Specifies how numbers are displayed (including the decimal character used), how digits are grouped, and how negative numbers are shown; also specifies the measurement system used.
Currency	Specifies how currency is displayed (including the decimal character used), how digits are grouped, and how negative values are shown.
Time	Specifies how time is displayed, including the hour and minute separator; also specifies how morning and afternoon times are designated.
Date	Specifies the calendar type and how short and long dates are displayed; also specifies the character used as the separator between the day, the month, and the year.

Defining International Settings in Custom Setup Scripts

You can specify values in the [System] section of a custom setup script (such as Msbatch.inf) to define regional, keyboard layout, and multilanguage settings other than the defaults.

To specify the regional setting in Msbatch.inf, set **locale=** in [System] to a value listed in the [LocaleList] section of Locale.inf. The following table shows the values for regional settings that are available in certain editions of Windows 98. For some editions of Windows 98, check Locale.inf entries for the proper values associated with the region.

Regional setting	Value	Regional setting	Value
Afrikaans	L0436	French (Luxembourg)	L140C
Basque	L042D	German (Standard)	L0407
Catalan	L0403	German (Swiss)	L0807

Regional setting	Value	Regional setting	Value
Danish	L0406	German (Austrian)	L0C07
Dutch (Standard)	L0413	German (Luxembourg)	L1007
Dutch (Belgian)	L0813	German (Liechtenstein)	L1407
English (United States)	L0409	Icelandic	L040F
English (British)	L0809	Italian (Standard)	L0410
English (Australian)	L0C09	Italian (Swiss)	L0810
English (Canadian)	L1009	Norwegian (Bokmål)	L0414
English (New Zealand)	L1409	Norwegian (Nynorsk)	L0814
English (Ireland)	L1809	Portuguese (Brazilian)	L0416
English (South Africa)	L1C09	Portuguese (Standard)	L0816
Finnish	L040B	Spanish (Traditional Sort)	L040A
French (Standard)	L040C	Spanish (Latin American)	L080A
French (Belgian)	L080C	Spanish (Modern Sort)	L0C0A
French (Canadian)	L0C0C	Swedish	L041D
French (Swiss)	L100C	Spanish (Honduras)	L480A
Spanish (El Salvador)	L440A	Spanish (Puerto Rico)	L500A
Spanish (Nicaragua)	L4C0A	Spanish (Guatemala)	L100A
Spanish (Bolivia)	L400A	Spanish (Panama)	L180A
Spanish (Costa Rica)	L140A	Spanish (Venezuela)	L200A
Spanish (Dominican Republic)	L1C0A	Spanish (Peru)	L280A
Spanish (Colombia)	L240A	Spanish (Chile)	L340A
Spanish (Ecuador)	L300A	Spanish (Argentina)	L2C0A
Spanish (Paraguay)	L3C0A	Spanish (Jamaica)	L2009
Spanish (Uruguay)	L380A	Albanian	L041C
Spanish (Caribbean)	L2409	Bulgarian	L0402
Belorussian	L0423	Czech	L0405
Croatian	L041A	Serbian	L0C1A
Estonian	L0425	Latvian	L0426
Hungarian	L040E	Macedonian (FYROM)	L042F
Lithuanian	L0427	Romanian	L0418
Polish	L0415	Slovenian	L0424
Slovak	L041B	Ukrainian	L0422
Turkish	L041F		

Values listed in the [KeyboardList] section of the Multilng.inf file specify particular keyboards. Use one of the following strings to define the **selectedKeyboard**=*value* in the [System] section of Msbatch.inf (or a similar file).

Keyboard layout	Keyboard value in Multilng.inf
Belgian	KEYBOARD_0000080C,be
Brazilian	KEYBOARD_00000416,br
British	KEYBOARD_00000809,uk
Canadian Multilingual	KEYBOARD_00001009,fc
Danish	KEYBOARD_00000406,da
Dutch	KEYBOARD_00000413,ne
Finnish	KEYBOARD_0000040B,fi
French	KEYBOARD_0000040C,fr
French Canadian	KEYBOARD_00000C0C,ca
German (Standard)	KEYBOARD_00000407,gr
Icelandic	KEYBOARD_0000040F,ic
Italian	KEYBOARD_00000410,it
Latin American	KEYBOARD_0000080A,la
Norwegian	KEYBOARD_00000414,no
Portuguese (Standard)	KEYBOARD_00000816,po
Spanish (Modern)	KEYBOARD_00000C0A,sp
Swedish	KEYBOARD_0000041D,sw
Swiss French	KEYBOARD_0000100C,sf
Swiss German	KEYBOARD_00000807,sg
United States 101	KEYBOARD_00000409,us
United States-Dvorak	KEYBOARD_00020409,dv
United States-Left Dvorak	KEYBOARD_00030409,dv
United States-Right Dvorak	KEYBOARD_00040409,dv
United States-International	KEYBOARD_00010409,usx
Irish	KEYBOARD_00001809,ir
Belgian (Comma)	KEYBOARD_0001080C,bene
Canadian (Standard)	KEYBOARD_00011009,can
German (IBM)	KEYBOARD_00010407,gr1

Keyboard layout	Keyboard value in Multilng.inf
Italian 142	KEYBOARD_00010410,it1
Russian	KEYBOARD_00000419,ru
Bulgarian	KEYBOARD_00000402,bul
Bulgarian (Latin)	KEYBOARD_00000402,bll
Belorussian	KEYBOARD_00000423,BLR
Czech	KEYBOARD_00000405,CZ
Czech (Qwerty)	KEYBOARD_00010405,CZ1
Czech (Programmers)	KEYBOARD_00020405,CZ2
Hungarian	KEYBOARD_0000040E,HU
Hungarian (101 keys)	KEYBOARD_0001040E,HU1
Polish	KEYBOARD_00000415,PL
Polish (Programmers)	KEYBOARD_00010415,PL1
Romanian	KEYBOARD_00000418,RO
Russian (Typewriter)	KEYBOARD_00010419,RU1
Serbian	KEYBOARD_00000C1A,YCC
Serbian (Latin)	KEYBOARD_00000C1A, ycl
Slovak	KEYBOARD_0000041B,SL
Slovak (Qwerty)	KEYBOARD_0001041B,SL1
Slovenian	KEYBOARD_00000424,SLV
Croatian	KEYBOARD_0000041A,CR
Turkish (Q type)	KEYBOARD_0000041F,TUQ
Turkish (F type)	KEYBOARD_0001041F,TUF
Ukrainian	KEYBOARD_00000422,UR
Estonian	KEYBOARD_00000425,ES
Macedonian (FYROM)	KEYBOARD_0000042F,MKD
Latvian	KEYBOARD_00000426,LV
Latvian (Latin)	KEYBOARD_00000427,LT
Italian 142	KEYBOARD_00000426,it1
Albanian	KEYBOARD_0000041C,al
Greek	KEYBOARD_00000408,gk
Greek IBM 220	KEYBOARD_00010408,gk220
Spanish (Traditional)	KEYBOARD_0000040A,sp
Portuguese (Brazilian)	KEYBOARD_00010416,br1
Norwegian (Nynorsk)	KEYBOARD_00000814,no

Keyboard layout	Keyboard value in Multilng.inf
Latin America (El Salvador)	KEYBOARD_0000440A,la
Latin America (Honduras)	KEYBOARD_0000480A,la
Latin America (Nicaragua)	KEYBOARD_00004C0A,la
Latin America (Puerto Rico)	KEYBOARD_0000500A,la
Latin America (Bolivia)	KEYBOARD_0000400A,la
Greek Latin IBM 220	KEYBOARD_00010408,gl220
Greek IBM 319	KEYBOARD_00030408, gk319
Greek Latin IBM 319	KEYBOARD_00040408,gl319
Greek Latin	KEYBOARD_00050408,gkl

Values listed in the [OptionalComponents] section of Mullang.inf specify the optional languages you can add to Windows 98: Greek, Cyrillic (Bulgarian, Belorussian, Russian, Serbian, and Ukrainian), Central European (Albanian, Czech, Croatian, Hungarian, Polish, Romanian, Slovak, and Slovenian), Turkish, and Baltic (Estonian, Latvian, and Lithuanian). Use one of the following strings to define the **multilanguage=**_value_ in the [System] section of Msbatch.inf (or a similar file).

Language	Multilanguage value in Mullang.inf
Baltic	English and Baltic
Central European	English and Central European
Cyrillic	English and Cyrillic
English	English
Greek	English and Greek
Turkish	English and Turkish

For more information about creating custom setup scripts, see Chapter 3, "Custom Installations."

Changing the Code Page

The *code page* is an internal table that the operating system uses to relate the keys on the keyboard to the characters displayed on the screen. Different code pages provide support for the character sets and keyboard layouts used in different countries.

When you install Windows 98, Setup checks the current system configuration to determine the regional settings:

- For Typical Setup, Windows 98 Setup automatically chooses the regional settings for the current system configuration and then automatically installs the related code pages for Windows and MS-DOS based on the current configuration.
- For Custom Setup, you can choose to specify alternate regional settings. Windows 98 Setup automatically installs the standard Windows and MS-DOS code pages for the regional settings selected.

You can use the Regional Settings option in Control Panel to change the locale. This will affect the display in Windows-based applications. However, for MS-DOS-based applications and for the MS-DOS prompt, the code page installed during Setup is always used. Windows 98 does not include any feature that allows you to change the code page used by MS-DOS.

You can, however, use Changecp.exe to change the code page used for console displays (MS-DOS-based applications and the MS-DOS prompt). This application makes all the changes to fonts and other system elements in the registry and other configuration files. CHANGECP is provided with the *Microsoft Windows 98 Resource Kit* utilities.

This application is useful to you if your site uses a character set besides the default code page that Windows 98 Setup uses. You know that you need an alternate code page if, after installing Windows 98, you discover that your MS-DOS-based applications do not display properly—specifically, if the wrong fonts appear or the wrong characters appear as you type.

For example, the default code page installed for French Canadian under Windows 98 is 850, but your site might use code page 863 as a standard. As another example, the United States default is 437, but some companies choose to use code page 850. In these cases, use CHANGECP to install the alternate code page.

▶ **To change the code page used for MS-DOS-based applications**

1. Copy Changecp.exe and any other files in the CHANGECP directory to your local Windows directory using the *Microsoft Windows 98 Resource Kit* utilities.
2. At the command prompt, type **changecp**.
3. Select the code page you want from the list that appears.

   Alternately, you can type **changecp** *code_page_number* if you know the code page that you want.

CHANGECP automatically makes all related system changes. The next time you start Windows 98, the new code page will be used for all MS-DOS sessions.

Important The CHANGECP utility is not designed to be used for changing code pages on a regular basis. Also, frequently switching the MS-DOS code page will confuse users of MS-DOS-based applications.

Using Multiple Languages in Windows 98

Windows 98 provides the keyboard layouts and fonts required to type, edit, view, and print documents containing many different languages. For information about creating a document that contains multilingual text, see "Using Alternate Keyboards" later in this chapter. By default, the version of Windows 98 sold in North America, South America, Western Europe, Scandinavia, Africa, and Australia includes the following keyboard languages and layouts:

Windows 98 languages

Afrikaans	Albanian	Basque	Belorussian
Bulgarian	Catalan	Croatian	Czech
Danish	Dutch (Belgian)	Dutch (Standard)	English (Australian)
English (British)	English (Canadian)	English (Caribbean)	English (Ireland)
English (Jamaica)	English (New Zealand)	English (South Africa)	English (United States)
Estonian	Finnish	French (Belgian)	French (Canadian)
French (Luxembourg)	French (Standard)	French (Swiss)	FYROM
German (Austrian)	German (Liechtenstein)	German (Luxembourg)	German (Standard)
German (Swiss)	Spanish (Modern Sort)	Hungarian	Icelandic
Greek	Indonesian	Polish	Latvian
Italian (Standard)	Italian (Swiss)	Portuguese (Brazilian)	Lithuanian
Norwegian (Bokmål)	Norwegian (Nynorsk)	Spanish (Colombia)	Portuguese (Standard)
Spanish (Argentina)	Spanish (Chile)	Spanish (Guatemala)	Spanish (Costa Rica)
Spanish (Dominican Republic)	Spanish (Ecuador)	Slovak	Russian
Spanish (Mexican)	Spanish (Paraguay)	Spanish (Peru)	Serbian
Spanish (Traditional Sort)	Spanish (Uruguay)	Spanish (Venezuela)	Swedish
Slovenian	Spanish (Panama)	Ukrainian	

Windows 98 keyboard layouts

Czech (Qwerty)	Faeroe Islands	Albanian	Belorussian
Belgian (Comma)	Belgian (Period)	Bulgarian	Belgian (French)
British	Canadian Multilingual	Danish	Dutch
Finnish	French	French Canadian	German
Icelandic	Irish	Italian	German (IBM)
Greek IBM 220	Greek Latin	Greek Latin 319	Hungarian (101 keys)
Irish	Latin American	Latvian (Latin)	Norwegian
Polish (Programmers)	Romanian	Russian (Typewriter)	Serbian (Latin)
Slovak (Qwerty)	Spanish (Modern)	Swedish	Swiss German
Turkish (Q Type)	United States (LH Dvorak)	Romanian	Estonia
Czech (Programmers)	Czech	Croatian	Canadian Standard
Bulgarian (Latin)	Italian	Norwegian	Swiss French
Portuguese (Standard)	Spanish	Swedish	United States (RH Dvorak)
Portuguese (Brazilian Standard)	Portuguese (Brazilian ABNT 2)	United States (Dvorak)	United States (International)
FYROM	Greek	Greek (IBM 319)	Greek Latin IBM 220
Hungarian	Icelandic	Italian 142	Latvian
Lithuanian (IBM)	Polish	United States 101	Russian
Serbian	Slovak	Slovenian	Spanish (Traditional)
Turkish (F Type)	Ukrainian		

For information about adding or removing any of the languages in the preceding list, see Windows 98 Help. To add Central European, Cyrillic, and Greek-based languages, you need to install multilanguage support, as described in the following procedure.

▶ **To install multilingual support**

1. In the Add/Remove Programs option in Control Panel, click the **Windows Setup** tab.

2. In the **Components** list, click **Language Support**, and then click **Details**.

3. Click the languages you want, and then click **OK**.

If two or more keyboard layouts have been installed, an icon on the task bar indicates the active keyboard layout. Users can switch between these layouts by clicking the keyboard icon or by using a key combination specified in the Keyboard option in Control Panel, as described in "Using Alternate Keyboards" later in this chapter.

The Windows 98 compact disc includes TrueType fonts that contain characters for all the Western European and Eastern European languages. After installing multilingual TrueType font support, you can access the complete set of 652 characters in applications that support these fonts, such as WordPad. This allows for proper presentation of fonts for a given language.

An application that uses the common **Font** dialog box can allow users to select from all the character sets and fonts configured in the system. The **Script** box in this common dialog box allows the user to choose the characteristics related to the language of the text being formatted. For example, depending on the character set and the locales available on a particular computer, the **Script** box could allow the user to choose from Western, Greek, Cyrillic, or Turkish characteristics for the selected typeface. Of course, the user must choose the appropriate keyboard for using related text characters.

▶ **To access multilingual TrueType fonts in WordPad**

1. Click the **Format** menu, and then click **Font**.

2. In the **Font** dialog box, select a font characteristic for the language in the **Script** box, and then click **OK**.

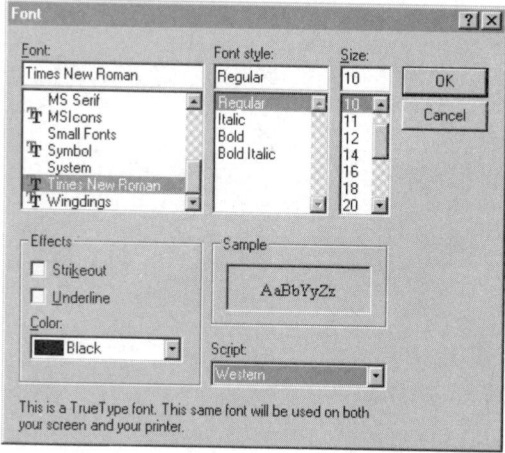

Using Multilingual Fonts with Win32-based Applications

For users who create or edit multilingual content in their documents, a Win32-based application that uses the international services in Windows 98 can automatically activate the correct fonts and corresponding keyboard layouts for editing specific text within a document.

Win32-based applications can indicate the language used in text in a document by tagging the text with a locale identifier. For example, such applications can automatically use spell checking, thesaurus, hyphenation engine, and grammar checking applications associated with the language of the text it is checking, if they are available. They can also format dates according to the language of the text. Applications that use locale identifiers can determine date, time, currency, and number formats, and sorting behavior, and they can use these identifiers to determine which keyboard layout and fonts to use for typing and displaying text in a particular language.

To take advantage of the multilingual font capabilities in Windows 98:

- Make sure your application uses the Win32 NLS API. For information, check the documentation that comes with the application, or contact the software manufacturer.

- Install multilingual support under Windows 98, as described in this section.

- Use the application's dialog boxes for selecting language-related font attributes and for specifying the language attributes of selected information.

Using Alternate Keyboards

If you are using an application that supports tagging text for alternate locales or languages, you can use alternate keyboards to easily create documents that contain more than one language.

▶ **To select the alternate keyboards you want to use in Windows 98**

1. In the Keyboard option in Control Panel, click the **Language** tab.

2. To add another keyboard, click **Add**.

3. In the **Add Language** dialog box, select the alternate keyboard that you want to install, and then click **OK**.

4. If you want to change the default keyboard, select the one you want in the **Language** list, and then click **Set as Default**.

5. If you want to specify a key combination to use to switch between keyboards, click a key combination in the **Switch languages** area.

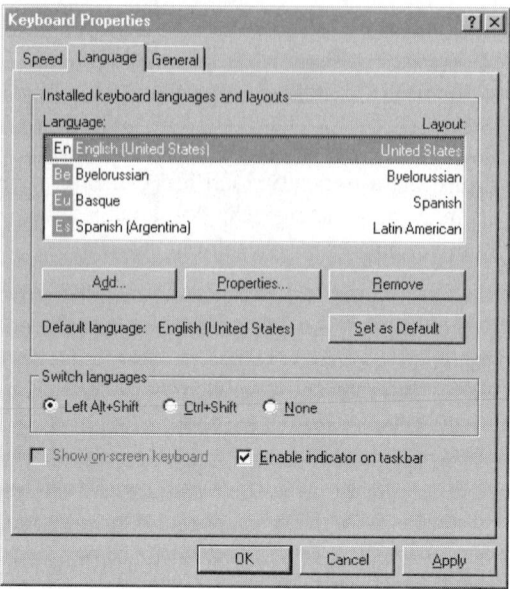

When you want to switch keyboards while working in an application such as WordPad that can take advantage of multilingual support, use the key combination you specified, or use the Windows 98 taskbar.

▶ **To switch to another keyboard using the Windows 98 taskbar**

1. Click the keyboard icon on the taskbar.

2. In the menu that appears, click the language you want to use. Note, in the following illustration, the icon for switching keyboard layouts is at the right end of the taskbar.

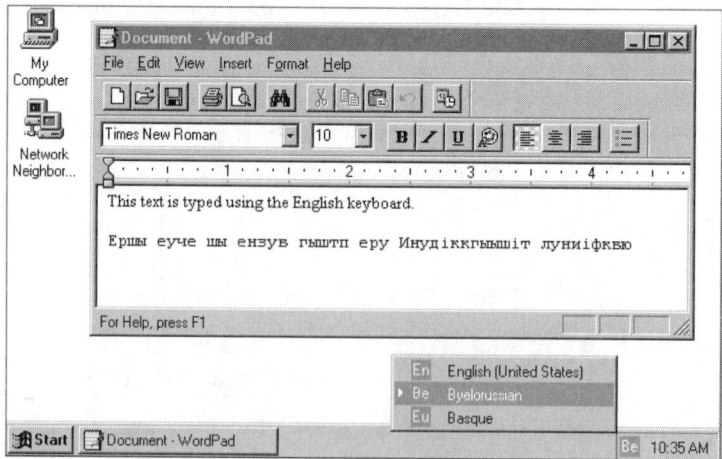

If your application uses the NLS API, you might be able to specify that rules for sorting, searching, spelling, and other actions be used for the portion of text typed using that language. Applications that use the NLS API can distinguish between the default locale the user has set for Windows 98 and the language of text in a document. For example, Microsoft Word for Windows version 6.0 makes language a text property. Just as users can format selected text as bold, italic, or double-spaced, they can format selected text as being in a specific language, as shown in the following illustration of the **Language** dialog box.

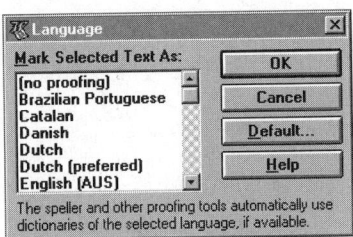

Using Windows 98 Support for Local Conventions

A great deal of linguistic research went into creating the collection of locale information in the Windows 98 registry and the algorithms and tables used by the Win32 NLS API, which includes support for local formats for date, time, calendars, currency, and numbers. The Windows 98 registry contains more than 90 locale-related strings; in addition, the Win32 NLS API allows each application to request information for any locale.

The Windows 98 default date or time formats are the most commonly used formats for each locale, but applications can provide support for other local conventions. Such conventions are ways of formatting information specific to a language, local dialect, or geographic location. Currency symbols, date formats, calendars, numerical separators, and sorting orders can all be affected by these conventions.

Therefore, reformatting a number based on the locale involves more than changing the currency symbol or the decimal separator. A currency symbol can come before the numerical quantity, or it can come after. It might or might not be separated from the number by spaces. The currency symbol can be one, two, or more characters. In addition, if a currency amount is negative, Windows 98 can format it in one of 16 different ways.

As another example of locale differences, some languages such as Finnish, German, Polish, and Russian have several forms for each noun. Windows 98 carries both the nominative and genitive forms of Polish and Russian month names; the form changes depending on the month name's position in the string relative to the day name. For all other languages, Windows 98 carries only one form of each month or day name.

Most locales use the Gregorian calendar, but some editions of Windows 98 also support Hijri (Middle East), Japanese, Korean, Taiwanese, and Thai calendars. (Windows 98 will add support for more calendars in the future as necessary.) Although calendars in the United States list Sunday as the first day of the week, calendars in other countries, such as Germany, list Monday as the first day of the week. Similarly, not all cultures assume that the week containing January 1 is the first week of the year. The calendar type that Windows 98 assigns to each locale accommodates such cultural preferences.

APPENDIX B

Windows 98 System File Details

B

This appendix provides details about the system files supplied with Microsoft Windows 98.

In This Chapter

See Also

- For information on how to create a Windows 98 Startup Disk, see Chapter 2, "Setting Up Windows 98."

- For information on how to use a Windows 98 Startup Disk, see Chapter 5, "Setup Technical Discussion."

Distribution Disk Storage Overview

Windows 98 is stored on the distribution disks as *cabinet (CAB) files*. When the Windows 98 disks are created, files are compressed into folders. The Windows 98 files are read in and written out as a continuous byte-stream. The entire stream is compressed and divided into folders as appropriate. Folders can fill one or more cabinets. The following defines the terms used to describe the distribution files.

Cabinet   A file that contains one or more files, usually compressed.

Folder   A decompression boundary. Large folders enable higher compression, because the compressor can refer back to more data in finding patterns. However, to retrieve a file at the end of a folder, the entire folder must be decompressed.

The Windows 98 distribution disks use distribution media format (DMF), which is a special read-only format for 3.5-inch floppy disks that permits storage of 1.7 MB of data.

Cabinet File Structure

The file structure introduced in Windows 95 has changed slightly in Windows 98. In Windows 95, most of the files were contained in a Win95#.cab structure. The rest of the files were included in the Base#.cab, Catalog.cab, Driver#.cab, Mini.cab, and Precopy#.cab cabinets.

Windows 98 instead groups CAB files by function. The following table summarizes the cabinet files and their contents.

Cabinet file	Quantity	Contents
Base#.cab	2	Files necessary for the first boot.
Catalog3.cab	1	Catalog files necessary for driver certification.
Chl99.cab	1	Offline channel Web pages for the Channel bar.
Driver#.cab	11	Windows 98 drivers. These files are copied to your hard drive only if you need them on first boot. This is the case when the device you are using for the installation media is connected to a sound card.
Edb.cab	1	Various utilities.
Mini.cab	1	Mini Windows, which is used for setting up from MS-DOS.
Net#.cab	5	Network driver-related files. These CAB files are optional and are copied to the hard drive only if you are installing over the network.
Precopy#.cab	2	Setup and INF files.
Win98#.cab	44	Windows 98 files.

The # in the file names uses the following naming convention:

- Base4.cab through Base5.cab
- Driver11.cab through Driver21.cab
- Net6.cab through Net10.cab
- Precopy1.cab through Precopy2.cab
- Win98_22.cab through Win98_69.cab

Organizing the CAB files in this manner allows for easier extraction and a smoother setup. For example, if the computer does not have a network card, the Net#.cab files are not moved to the user's computer during setup.

Viewing and Extracting Cabinet Files Using Explorer

In Windows 98, you can view and extract CAB files using Windows Explorer. In Windows 95, you had to use the command-line Extract program to extract CAB files.

▶ **To view the contents of a CAB file with Windows Explorer**

1. Click the **Start** button, point to **Programs**, and then click **Windows Explorer**.

2. In the left pane, click the letter that represents the drive where the CAB files are located.

3. Navigate to the folder containing the CAB file you want to view.

4. On the right pane, double-click the CAB file you want to view.

   The contents of the CAB file appear in a separate window.

▶ **To extract CAB files with Windows Explorer**

1. Follow the instructions for viewing the contents of a CAB file.

2. In the window displaying the contents of the CAB file, double-click the file you want to extract.

   The **Browse for Folder** dialog box appears.

3. Click a folder in which to save the file you are extracting, and then click **OK**.

You can also extract files by using System File Checker, as described in Chapter 27, "General Troubleshooting." With System File Checker, you do not need to know which CAB file contains the file you need.

Extracting CAB Files Using the Extract Program

The Extract program supports command-line extraction of files from the CAB storage format on disk. Extract does not support any other compression system (that is, it is not backward-compatible with any previous Microsoft disk utilities).

The Extract program (Extract.exe) can be found in the \Windows\Command directory or on the Windows 98 installation media.

Important In general, use the Extract program only if your product support representative indicates that using the Extract program is necessary to retrieve a compressed file from the Windows 98 cabinet files.

Under normal circumstances, you should use the Add/Remove Programs or Network icon in Control Panel to install and uninstall components, applications, and support software from the Windows 98 installation media.

If system files are missing or damaged, run Windows 98 Setup from the Windows 98 installation media, and choose the option to validate and restore files.

Syntax

extract [/y] [/A] [/D | /E] [/L *location*] *cabinet_file* [*file_specification* ...]

–Or–

extract [/y] *compressed_file* [*destination_file*]

–Or–

extract [/y] /C *compressed_file destination_file*

Parameters

/A

Process all files in a cabinet set, starting with the *cabinet_file*. Follow cabinet chain.

/C

Copy source file to destination (to copy from DMF disks).

/D

Display cabinet directory. Do not extract.

/E

Use instead of *.* to extract all files.

/L *location*

Use the directory specified by *location*, instead of the current directory, as the default location to place extracted files.

/Y

Overwrite files in the destination without prompting. The default is to prompt the user if the destination file already exists, and to allow one of the following:

- Overwrite the file.

- Skip the file.

- Overwrite this file and all subsequent files that may already exist.

- Exit.

compressed_file

This is a CAB file that contains a single file (for example, File1.ex_, which contains File1.exe). If *destination_file* is not specified, the file is extracted and given its original name in the current directory.

destination_file

This can be either a relative path (.:, .., C:File1, and so on) or a fully qualified path. It can specify either a file (or files, if wildcards are included) or a directory. If a directory is specified, the file name stored in the cabinet is used. Otherwise, *destination_file* is used as the complete file name for the extracted file.

cabinet_file
> This is a CAB file that contains two or more files. If no *file_specification* parameter is specified, a list is displayed of the files in the cabinet. If one or more *file_specification* parameters are specified, then these are used to select the files to be extracted from the cabinet. Wildcards are allowed to specify multiple cabinets.

file_specification
> This specifies files to be extracted from the cabinets. This can contain the **?** and ***** wildcards. Multiple *file_specification* values can be supplied.

The following table provides some examples.

Command	Behavior
extract *filename.ex_*	Assuming *filename.ex_* contains just the single file Filename.exe, *filename.exe* is extracted and placed in the current directory.
extract *filename.ex_* file2.exe	Assuming *filename.ex_* contains just the single file *filename.exe*, *filename.exe* is extracted and placed in the current directory in the file *file2.exe*.
extract *cabinet.1*	Assuming *cabinet.1* contains multiple files, a list of the files stored in that cabinet is displayed.
extract *cabinet.1 *.exe*	Extracts all EXE files from *cabinet.1* and places them in the current directory.

For more information about the Extract program, see Knowledge Base article Q129605, "How to Extract Original Compressed Windows Files."

Setup Files Overview

The following table describes the key files used for Windows 98 Setup.

File name	Description
Setup.exe	The real-mode Setup component that initializes Windows 98 Setup. If this file is started from MS-DOS, it calls the real-mode stub. If started from within Windows, it is a 16-bit Windows stub.
Suwin.exe	The protected-mode Setup components responsible for calling all other dynamic link libraries (DLLs) used in Setup.
Setupx.dll	The primary DLL used during the Copy Files phase to perform most of the installation procedures. It is responsible for reading INF files, handling disks, and copying files.
Netdi.dll	The module called early in the Setup process to install networking services.
Scanreg.exe	The utility that scans an existing registry for errors.
Scandisk.exe	The utility that checks local hard disks for errors.

Also, the Wininstx.400 directory is created at the beginning of the Windows 98 Setup process. This directory contains a minimal set of files used during setup and requires about 10 to 12 MB of free disk space. This directory is removed upon the successful completion of Windows 98 installation.

Directory File Structure and File Locations

The following figure shows the typical default directory structure created for Windows 98. The bold entries are new entries in Windows 98.

- 📁 Win98
  - 📁 All Users
  - 📁 Application Data
  - 📁 Applog
  - 📁 Catalog
  - 📁 Catroot
  - 📁 Command
  - 📁 Config
  - 📁 Cookies
  - 📁 Cursors
  - 📁 Desktop
  - 📁 **Downloaded Program Files**
  - 📁 Drwatson
  - 📁 Favorites
  - 📁 Fonts
  - 📁 Forms
  - 📁 Help
  - 📁 helpdesk
  - 📁 History
  - 📁 Inf
  - 📁 Java
  - 📁 Media
  - 📁 MsApps
  - 📁 msdownld.tmp
  - 📁 NetHood
  - 📁 ol98logs
  - 📁 Pif
  - 📁 PrintHood
  - 📁 Profiles
  - 📁 Recent
  - 📁 Samples
  - 📁 SendTo
  - 📁 ShellNew
  - 📁 Spool
    - 📁 Printers

```
☐ Start Menu
     ☐ Programs
          ☐ Accessories
          ☐ Internet Explorer
          ☐ Microsoft NetShow
          ☐ Online Services
          ☐ StartUp
☐ Subscriptions
☐ Sysbckup
☐ System
     ☐ Color
     ☐ IE4Setup
     ☐ Iosubsys
     ☐ Macromed
     ☐ Setup
     ☐ Shellext
     ☐ Viewers
     ☐ Vmm32
     ☐ Wbem
☐ System32
     ☐ Drivers
☐ Tasks
☐ Temp
☐ Temporary Internet Files
☐ Tour
☐ Twain_32
☐ Vcm
☐ Vcm.000
☐ Web
```

Location of Key System Files

The following table lists the directories where various types of Windows 98 system files and supporting files are stored.

File type	Directory[1]
Core Windows 98 files	%WinDir%
Shortcuts to applications	%WinDir%\Start Menu\Programs
MS-DOS commands	%WinDir%\Command
Printer drivers	%WinDir%\System
Help files	%WinDir%\Help
Font files	%WinDir%\Fonts
Setup and device installation files	%WinDir%\Inf
PIF files	%WinDir%\Pif
Drivers	%WinDir%\System
VxDs	%WinDir%\System

File type	Directory[1]
I/O Subsystem	%WinDir%\System\Iosubsys
Viewers	%WinDir%\System\Viewers
VxDs added after installation	%WinDir%\System\Vmm32
Java files	%WinDir%\Java\Classes
Internet Explorer browsing history	%WinDir%\History
Shell extensions	%WinDir%\System\Shellext
Active Desktop configuration files	%WinDir%\Web
Internet Explorer file cache	%WinDir%\Temporary Internet Files
Internet Explorer subscription files	%WinDir%\Subscriptions
Dr. Watson troubleshooting utility	%WinDir%\Drwatson

1 "%WinDir%" refers to the directory that is specified during the installation process to contain the Windows 98 files.

The following list shows where key Windows 98 files are stored when Windows 98 is installed on the local hard disk of a computer.

Description	File name	Location
Real-mode operating system and system detection	Io.sys	Root directory of boot drive [1]
Command-line processor	Command.com	Root directory of boot drive
Real-mode stub to start Windows 98	Win.com	Windows
Protected-mode Virtual Machine Manager (VMM)	Vmm32.vxd	Windows\System
Registry	System.dat	Windows [1]
Registry backup files	Rb001.cab through Rb005.cab	Windows\Sysbckup
Registry when first created by Setup	System.new	Root directory of boot drive [2]
User registry	User.dat	Windows [1]
User registry first created by Setup	User.new	Root directory of boot drive [2]
Log of the Setup process	Setuplog.txt	Root directory of boot drive [1]
Hardware detection log	Detlog.txt	Root directory of boot drive [2]
Log of Windows 98 startup process	Bootlog.txt	Root directory of boot drive [2]

Description	File name	Location
Real-mode network configuration	Protocol.ini	Windows
Boot configuration file	Msdos.sys	Root directory of boot drive [1]
Registry created by Setup completion	System.1st	Root directory of boot drive [1]
System initialization file	System.ini	Windows
Customization settings file	Win.ini	Windows
Shell executable file	Explorer.exe	Windows
Compression support file	Drvspace.bin	Root directory of boot drive [2]

[1] This is a hidden file.

[2] This file is visible in the root directory only when the Windows 98 installation has failed. When setup completes, System.new is moved and renamed System.dat. User.new is moved and renamed User.dat.

Location of System Files on Compressed Disks

If you install Windows 98 on a compressed drive, Windows 98 Setup places the following files on the boot drive.

Windows 98 Files on the Boot Drive

Autoexec.bat	Dblspace.bin[1]	Msdos.sys[1]
Autoexec.dos	Detlog.txt[1]	Netlog.txt
Bootlog.prv[1]	Drvspace.bin[1]	Setuplog.txt[1]
Bootlog.txt[1]	Drvspace.ini[1]	Suhdlog.dat[1]
Command.com	Io.dos[1]	System.1st[1]
Command.dos	Io.sys[1]	Wina20.386
Config.dos	Msdos.---[1]	
Config.sys	Msdos.dos[1]	

[1] Indicates a hidden file.

When Windows 98 is installed on an uncompressed drive other than the startup drive, Setup adds the same files (with the exception of Drvspace.ini) to the boot drive, as listed earlier in this section. The only difference is that Win386.swp will be placed on the same drive as the Windows directory. For example, if you have drives C and D, and if you install Windows 98 on D:\Windows, Win386.swp will be on the root of D. Otherwise, it will be placed as described earlier for compressed drives.

The Windows 98 Startup Disk

The Windows 98 Startup Disk has changed significantly for Windows 98. The following functionality has been added:

- Multi-start menu for booting your computer with or without access to the CD-ROM.
- Real-mode IDE CD-ROM support
- Real-mode SCSI CD-ROM support
- Edb.cab file
- RAMdrive
- New extract command (Ext.exe)

For more information on how to make a Startup Disk, how to use it, and its new functionality, see Chapter 2, "Setting Up Windows 98" and Chapter 5, "Setup Technical Discussion."

The Edb.cab File

The Edb.cab file contains several utilities. It is a compressed file whose contents are expanded during the startup process. The following table lists the contents this file.

File	Function
Attrib.exe	Add or remove file attributes.
Chkdsk.exe	Simpler and smaller disk status tool.
Debug.exe	Debug utility.
Edit.com	Real-mode emergency text editor.
Ext.exe	File extract utility.
Format.com	Disk format tool.
Help.bat	Launches the readme.txt for the startup disk.
Help.txt	Text document with information for troubleshooting Windows 98 when it fails to set up correctly, third-party disk partitioning software, and diagnostic tools.
Mscdex.exe	Microsoft CD-ROM file extension for MS-DOS.
Restart.com	Restart your computer.
Scandisk.exe	Disk status tool.
Scandisk.ini	Disk status tool configuration file.
Sys.com	System transfer tool.
Uninstal.exe	Tool for removing Windows 98 from your computer and returning it to its previous state.

Contents of the Windows 98 Startup Disk

The following table lists the contents and describes the function of each file in the Startup Disk.

Note The files contained in the Startup Disk are copied to the \Windows\Command directory only if the user chooses to create a Windows 98 startup disk during Setup. This happens during the first phase of the Startup Disk creation process. If you create a startup disk from Control Panel (From the **Startup Disk** property page in **Add/Remove Programs**) and the startup disk files are not in the \Windows\Command directory, you will prompted for the Windows 98 compact disk. A startup disk will be created but its contents will not be copied locally when you use this method.

File	Function
Aspi2dos.sys	Real-mode Adaptec CD-ROM driver.
Aspi4dos.sys	Real-mode Adaptec CD-ROM driver.
Aspi8dos.sys	Real-mode Adaptec CD-ROM driver.
Aspi8u2dos.sys	Real-mode Adaptec CD-ROM driver.
Aspicd.sys	Real-mode Adaptec CD-ROM driver.
Autoexec.bat	A batch file with a set of instructions that configure your computer when you boot it.
Btcdrom.sys	Mylex/BusLogic CD-ROM driver.
Btdosm.sys	Mylex/BusLogic CD-ROM driver.
Command.com	Command interpreter.
Config.sys	Loads the device drivers.
Drvspace.bin	Microsoft DriveSpace compression driver.
Edb.cab	Cabinet file containing extract utilities.
Ebd.sys	A file that identifies the disk as a Windows 98 startup disk.
Extract	File to expand the Ebd.cab file.
Fdisk.exe	Disk partition tool.
Findramd.exe	Utility to find the RAM drive during startup.
Flashpt.sys	Mylex/BusLogic CD-ROM driver.
Himem.sys	XMS Memory Manager.
Io.sys	System boot file.
Msdos.sys	Boot option information (paths, multiboot, and so on).
Mode.com	Lets you change display parameters such as number columns.

File	Function
Oakcdrom.sys	Generic device driver for ATAPI CD-ROM drives.
Ramdrive.sys	Creates a Ramdrive during startup.
Readme.txt	Readme text document with information about the Windows 98 Startup Disk.
Setramd.bat	Searches for first available drive to be a Ramdrive.
Sys.com	System transfer tool.

Windows 98 INF Files

C

This appendix describes the structure for the information files (INF) used to configure devices and networking components in Microsoft Windows 98.

This information is of particular use if you are creating custom setup scripts. This description of the INF file format will help you read the information in the Windows 98 INF files to find the values provided in Msbatch.inf. The general format is also used for statements in the [*Install*] section of Msbatch.inf.

Windows 98 Device Information Files Overview

Device information files provide information used by Windows 98 to install software that supports a given hardware device. When hardware manufacturers introduce new products, they must create INF files to explicitly define the resources and files required for each class of device.

The format of the INF files is based on Windows 3.*x* INF files:

- Section names are enclosed in brackets ([ ]) and must be unique within an INF file.

- Keys within a section do not have to be unique, but the order of keys within a section is significant.

- Private sections in an INF file are not evaluated by Windows 98.

The operating system detects the unique ID of each device installed. For the device identified, a specific section of the INF file provides information on that class of device; the following describes the information contained in a typical INF file section.

General INF File Format

An INF file is organized in several sections, which define information that Setup and the hardware detection process use to determine the resource needs of the hardware device, and to install software for that device. An INF file is organized by hardware, with each class of device described in its own section. Within each device section, the following general organization applies.

[Version] section
> Contains a simple header that identifies the INF and the class of device this INF supports.

[Manufacturer] and [*Manufacturer Name*] sections
> Lists all the individual manufacturers of the devices identified in this file and lists all the devices built by that manufacturer. These entries are displayed directly to the user and used to generate the appropriate registry entries. There must always be at least one manufacturer section.

[*Install*] section
> Describes the device driver and physical attributes of the hardware device. It also identifies the names of all the [*Install*] sections that contain information and instructions for installing this device.

[ClassInstall] section
> Defines a new class for this device. (Optional.)

[Strings] section
> Defines all localizable strings used in the INF file.

Each section contains one or more entries. The typical entry consists of a key and a value separated by an equal sign. Keys within a section do not have to be unique, but the order of keys may be significant depending on the purpose of the section. An INF file can include comments—any string of text, up to the end of the line, that begin with a semicolon. A comment can start anywhere on a line.

For example:

```
Key=value    ; comment
```

For complete details about the syntax and use of statements in Windows 98 INF files, see the *Microsoft Win32 Software Development Kit for Windows 98 and Windows NT*. For more information about the content structure of Windows 98 INF files, see the *Microsoft Windows 98 Driver Development Kit*.

[Version] Section

Syntax

[Version]
Signature="\$Chicago\$"
LayoutFile=_filename.inf_

The [Version] section defines the standard header for all Windows 98 INF files.

Signature
The signature string is case-insensitive.

filename.inf
Names the INF file that contains the layout information (source disks and files) required for installing this driver software. Typically, for Windows 98 components, this is Layout.inf, Layout1.inf, or Layout2.inf. This line is optional. If not given, the [SourceDisksNames] and [SourceDisksFiles] sections must be given in this INF.

This example shows a typical [Version] section:

```
[Version]
Signature="$Chicago$"
LayoutFile=LAYOUT.INF
```

[Manufacturer] Section

Syntax

[Manufacturer]
manufacturer-name | %strings-key%=manufacturer-name-section

The [Manufacturer] section identifies the manufacturer of the device and specifies the name of the [_Manufacturer Name_] section that contains additional information about the device driver.

manufacturer-name
Name of the manufacturer. This name can be any combination of printable characters, but must uniquely identify the manufacturer and must be enclosed in quotation marks.

strings-key
Name of a string as defined in a [Strings] section.

manufacturer-name-section
Name of the [_Manufacturer Name_] section. This name can be any combination of printable characters, but must uniquely identify the manufacturer name.

The following example shows a typical [Manufacturer] section in which a string key, %M1%, is used to identify the manufacturer. In this example, the *[Manufacturer Name]* section is APEXD.

```
[Manufacturer]
%M1%=APEXD    ; Strings key for this manufacturer
```

[Manufacturer Name] Section

Syntax

[*manufacturer-name*]
device-description=install-section-name, device-id[,compatible-device-id]...

The *[Manufacturer Name]* section gives the device description and identifies the *[Install]* section for this device. The *manufacturer-name* section name must be defined in the [Manufacturer] section.

device-description
  Description of the device to install. This can be any combination of printable characters or a strings key.

install-section-name
  Name of the *[Install]* section for this device.

device-id
  Identifier for this device.

compatible-device-id
  Identifier of a compatible device. More than one compatible-device identifier can be given, but each must be preceded by a comma.

The following example shows a typical *[Manufacturer Name]* section. The name of the *[Install]* section for this device is SuperSCSI. This device-id is *PNPA000 and its compatible device identifier is *PnPA001.

```
[APEXD]
%DevDesc1%  = SuperSCSI, *PNPA000, *PnPA001
```

For each driver installed using this INF file, Setup uses the information in these *[Manufacturer Name]* sections to generate Driver Description, Manufacturer Name, DeviceID, and Compatibility list entries in the registry.

[Install] Section

Syntax

[*install-section-name*]
Copyfiles=*file-list-section[,file-list-section]...*
LogConfig=*log-config-section-name*
Renfiles=*file-list-section[,file-list-section]...*

Delfiles=*file-list-section*[*,file-list-section*]...
UpdateInis=*update-ini-section*[*,update-ini-section*]...
UpdateIniFields=*update-inifields-section*[*,update-inifields-section*]...
AddReg=*add-registry-section*[*,add-registry-section*]...
DelReg=*del-registry-section*[*,del-registry-section*]...
Ini2Reg=*ini-to-registry-section*[*,ini-to-registry-section*]...
UpdateCfgSys=*update-config-section*
UpdateAutoBat=*update-autoexec-section*

The [*Install*] section identifies the additional sections in the INF file that contain descriptions of the device and instructions for installing files and information needed by the device drivers. The *install-section-name* must be defined in a [*Manufacturer Name*] section and consist of printable characters.

Not all entries in this section are needed or required. If an entry is given, it must specify the name of a section. (An exception to this is the **CopyFiles** entry.) More than one name can be given for each entry, but each additional name must be preceded by a comma. The exact format and meaning of the corresponding entry depends on the entry type and is described in later *sections*. Each [*Install*] section should include the creation date of the driver set.

This example shows a typical [*Install*] section:

```
[MyApplication]
Copyfiles=MyAppWinFiles, MyAppSysFiles, @SRSutil.exe
AddReg=MyAppRegEntries
```

Note that by renaming the [MyApplication] section to [DefaultInstall] (in the above example), this Install section would be executed—when the "Install" verb is selected by right-clicking the INF file.

The CopyFiles entry provides a special notation which will allow a single file to be copied directly from the copy line. An individual file can be copied by prefixing the file name with an @ symbol. The destination for any file copied using this notation will be the DefaultDestDir as defined in the DestinationDirs section. The following example shows how to copy individual files:

```
CopyFiles=FileSection1,@myfile.txt,@anotherfile.txt,LastSectionName
```

[*Logical Configuration*] Sections

Syntax

[*log-config-section-name*]
ConfigPriority = *priority-value*
MemConfig = *mem-range-list*
I/OConfig = *io-range-list*
IRQConfig = *irq-list*
DMAConfig = *dma-list*

A [*Logical Configuration*] section defines configuration details, such as IRQs, memory ranges, I/O ports, and DMA channels. An INF file can contain any number of [*Logical Configuration*] sections, as many as are needed to describe the device dependencies. However, each section must contain complete details for installing a device. The *log-config-section-name* must be defined by the **LogConfig** entry in the [*Install*] section.

Not all entries are needed or required. If an entry is given, it must be given appropriate values as described in the subsequent *sections*.

Each entry can specify more than one resource. However, during installation only one resource from an entry is used. If a device needs multiple resources of the same type, multiple entries must be given. For example, to ensure two IRQs for a device, two **IRQConfig** entries must be given. If a device does not require an IRQ, no **IRQConfig** entry should be given. For each entry, Setup builds binary logical configuration records and adds these to the driver section of the registry.

[*Update AutoExec*] Section

Syntax

```
[update-autoexec-section]
CmdDelete=command-name
CmdAdd=command-name[,command-parameters]
UnSet=env-var-name
PreFixPath=ldid[,ldid]
RemOldPath=ldid[,ldid]
TmpDir=ldid[,subdir]
```

The [*Update AutoExec*] section provides commands to manipulate lines in the Autoexec.bat file. The *update-autoexec-section* name must appear in an **UpdateAutoBat** entry in the [*Install*] section.

Not all entries are needed or required. The section can contain as many **CmdAdd**, **CmdDelete**, and **UnSet** entries as needed, but only one entry for **PreFixPath**, **RemOldPath**, and **TmpDir** can be used per file.

Setup processes all **CmdDelete** entries before any **CmdAdd** entries.

For more information about LDID values, see "[*Update INI*] Section" later in this appendix.

[*Update ConfigSys*] Section

Syntax

```
[update-config-section]
Buffers=legal-dos-buffer-value
DelKey=key
DevRename=current-dev-name,new-dev-name
DevDelete=device-driver-name
DevAddDev=driver-name,configkeyword[,flag][,param-string]
```

Files=*legal-dos-files-value*
PrefixPath=ldid[,ldid]...
RemKey=*key*
Stacks=*dos-stacks-value*

The [*Update ConfigSys*] section provides commands to add, delete, or rename commands in Config.sys. The *update-config-section* name must appear in an **UpdateCfgSys** entry in the [*Install*] section.

Not all entries are needed or required. This section may contain as many **DevRename**, **DevDelete**, and **DevAddDev** entries as needed, but the other commands may only be used once per section. When processing this section, Setup processes all **DevRenames** entries first, all **DevDelete** commands second, and all **DevAddDev** commands last.

Not all entries are needed or required. An Update Config.sys section may contain as many DevRename, DevDelete, DevAddDev, DelKey, and RemKey items as needed, but the Buffers, Files, and Stacks items may only be used once in a section. When processing this section, the Installer processes all DevRenames items first, all DevDelete items second, and all DevAddDev items last.

Buffers Item

Buffers=legal-dos-buffer-value

Sets the number of file buffers. As it does with the Stacks item, the Installer compares the existing value with the proposed value and always sets the file buffers to the larger of the two values.

DelKey Item

DelKey=**key** causes the Config.sys command with the specified key to be remarked out in the Config.sys file. For example, the INF file item **DelKey**=**Break** would cause a Break=on command to be remarked out in the Config.sys file. The DelKey item has the same effect as the RemKey item. There can be multiple DelKey and/or RemKey items in a section of the INF file.

The *key* item is the Config.sys command to be remarked out.

DevAddDev Item

DevAddDev=driver-name,configkeyword[,*flag*][,*param-string*]

Adds a device or install command to the Config.sys file.

driver-name
   Name of the driver or executable file to add. The installer validates the file name extension, ensuring that it is .sys or .exe.

configkeyword
> Command name. Can be device or install.

flag
> Optional placement flag. If 0, the command is placed at the bottom of the file. If 1, it is placed at the top. If flag is not given, 0 is used by default.

param-string
> Optional command parameters. Must be valid for the given device driver or executable file.

DevDelete Item

DevDelete=device-driver-name

Deletes any line containing the specified file name from the Config.sys file.

device-driver-name
> Name of a file or device driver. The Installer searches the Config.sys file for the name and deletes any line containing it. Because MS-DOS does not permit implicit file name extensions in Config.sys, each device-driver-name must explicitly specify the file name extension.

This example DevDelete item in an Update Config.sys section deletes lines 1 and 3 but not line 2 of the example Config.sys file:

```
DevDelete=Foo.sys

;; lines in CONFIG.SYS
Device=Foo.sys ;; line #1
Install=foo.exe ;; line #2
Device=Foo.sys /d:b800 /I:3 ;; line #3
```

DevRename Item

DevRename=current-dev-name,new-dev-name

Renames a device driver in the Config.sys file.

current-dev-name
> Name of the device driver or executable file to rename. The installer looks for the name on the right side of a device or install command in the Config.sys.

new-dev-name
> New name for driver or executable file.

Files Item

Files=legal-dos-files-value

Sets the maximum number of open files in the Config.sys file. As it does with the Stacks item, the Installer compares the existing value with the proposed value and always sets the maximum number of open files to the larger of the two values.

legal-dos-files-value
    A legal MS-DOS files value.

PrefixPath Item

PrefixPath=ldid[,ldid]...

Appends the path associated with the given LDID to the path command.

ldid
    Can be any of the predefined LDID values or a new value defined in the INF. For a definition of all the predefined LDID values, see the "Reference" topic about the DestinationDirs section.

RemKey Item

RemKey=**key** causes the Config.sys command with the specified key to be remarked out in the Config.sys file. For example, the INF file item **RemKey**=**Break** would cause a Break=on command to be remarked out in the Config.sys file.

The RemKey item has the same effect as the DelKey item. There can be multiple RemKey and/or DelKey items in a section of the INF file.

key
    The key of the Config.sys command to be remarked out.

Stacks Item

Stacks=dos-stacks-values

Sets the number and size of stacks in the Config.sys file. The Installer compares the existing value with the proposed value and always sets the stacks to the larger of the two values. For example, if Config.sys contains stacks=9,218 and an INF contains stacks=5,256, the installer sets to new value to stacks=9,256.

legal-dos-stacks-value
    A legal MS-DOS stacks value.

[*Update INI*] Section

Syntax

[*update-ini-section-name*]
ini-file, ini-section, [*old-ini-entry*], [*new-ini-entry*], [*flags*]

Replaces, deletes, or adds entries in the given INI file. The *update-ini-sectionname* must appear in an **UpdateInis** entry in the [*Install*] section.

ini-file
> Name of the INI file containing the entry to change. For more information about specifying the INI file name, see the comments below.

ini-section
> Name of the section containing the entry to change.

old-ini-entry
> Usually in the form Key=Value. (Optional.)

new-ini-entry
> Usually in the form Key=Value. (Optional.) Either the key or value may specify replaceable strings. For example, either the key or value specified in the new-ini-entry parameter may be %String1%, where the string that replaces %String1% is defined in the Strings section of the INF file.

The optional action *flags* can be one of these values:

0
> Default. If old-ini-entry key is present in an INI file entry, that entry is replaced with new-ini-entry. Note that only the keys of the old-ini-entry parameter and the INF file entry must match; the value of each entry is ignored.

1
> If both key and value of old-ini-entry exist in an INI file entry, that entry is replaced with new-ini-entry. Note that the old-ini-entry parameter and the INF file entry must match on both key and value for the replacement to be made (this is in contrast to using an action flag value of 0, where only the keys must match for the replacement to be made).

2
> If the key in the old-ini-entry parameter does not exist in the INI file, then no operation is performed on the INI file. If the key in the old-ini-entry parameter exists in an INI file entry and the key in the new-ini-entry parameter exists in an INI file entry, then the INI file entry that matches the key in the new-ini-entry parameter is deleted and the INI file entry that matches the old-ini-entry parameter is operated on in the following way: the key of the INI file entry is replaced with the key in the new-ini-entry parameter. If the key in the old-ini-entry parameter exists in an INI file entry and the key in the new-ini-entry parameter does not exist in an INI file entry, then an entry is added to the INI file made up of the key in the new-ini-entry parameter and the old value. Note that the match of the old-ini-entry parameter and an INI file entry is based on key alone, not key and value.

3
> Same as flag parameter value of 2 described above, except match of the old-ini-entry parameter and an entry in the INF file is based on matching both key and value, not just the key.

To add new-ini-entry to the INI file unconditionally, set old-ini-entry to NULL. To delete old-ini-entry from the INI file unconditionally, set new-ini-entry to NULL. The wildcard character (*) can be used in specifying the Key and Value, and they will be interpreted correctly.

The *ini-file* name can be a string or a strings key. A strings key has the form *%strkey%* where *strkey* is defined in the [Strings] section in the INF file. In either case, the name must be a valid file name.

The name should include the name of the directory containing the file, but the directory name should be given as a logical directory identifier (LDID) rather than an actual name. Setup replaces an LDID with an actual name during installation.

An LDID has the form *%ldid%* where *ldid* is one of the predefined identifiers or an identifier defined in the [DestinationDirs] section. For LDID_BOOT and LDID_BOOTHOST, the backslash is included in the LDID, so %30%boot.ini is the correct way to reference Boot.ini in the root of the boot drive.

The following examples illustrate entries in this section:

```
%11%\sample.ini, Section1,, Value1=2   ; adds new entry
%11%\sample.ini, Section2, Value3=*,   ; deletes old entry
%11%\sample.ini, Section4, Value5=1, Value5=4  ; replaces old entry
```

[*Update IniFields*] Section

Syntax

[*update-inifields-section*]
ini-file, ini-section, profile-name, [*old-field*], [*new-field*]

Replaces, adds, and deletes fields in the value of a given INI entry. Unlike the [*Update INI*] section, this section replaces, adds, or deletes portions of a value in an entry rather than the whole value. The *update-inifields-section* name must appear in an **UpdateIniFields** entry in the [*Install*] section.

Any previous comments in the line are removed because they might not be applicable after changes. When looking in the INI file for fields in the line, spaces, tabs, and commas are used as field delimiters. However, a space is used as the separator when the new field is appended to the line.

[*Add Registry*] Section

Syntax

[*add-registry-section*]
reg-root-string, [*subkey*], [*value-name*], [*Flag*], [*value*]

Adds subkeys or value names to the registry, optionally setting the value. The *add-registry-section* name must appear in an **AddReg** entry in the [*Install*] section.

[*Delete Registry*] Section

Syntax
[*del-registry-section*]
reg-root-string, *subkey*, [*value-name*]

Deletes a subkey or value name from the registry. The *del-registry-section* name must appear in an **DelReg** entry in the [*Install*] section. This section can contain any number of entries. Each entry deletes one subkey or value name from the registry.

[*Ini to Registry*] Section

Syntax
[*ini-to-registry-section*]
ini-file, *ini-section*, [*ini-key*], *reg-root-string*, *subkey*, *flags*

Moves lines or sections from an INI file to the registry, creating or replacing an entry under the given key in the registry. The *ini-to-registry-section* name must appear in an **Ini2Reg** entry in the [*Install*] section.

[DestinationDirs] Section

Syntax
[DestinationDirs]
file-list-section=*ldid*[,*subdir*]
DefaultDestDir=*ldid*[,*subdir*]

The [DestinationDirs] section defines the destination directories for the given [*File-List*] sections and optionally defines the default directory for any [*File-List*] sections that are not explicitly named.

file-list section
Name of a [*File-List*] section. This name must have been defined in a **Copyfiles**, **RenFiles**, or **DelFiles** entry in the [*Install*] section.

Ldid
Windows setup, installation and back-up destination directories.

The following table presents possible names, values, and the use of the directories for LDIDS.

LDID Information

Name of LDID	Value	Directory use
LDID_SRCPATH	1	Source of temporary installation setup directory used by setup, this is only valid during regular install and contains the INF and other binary files. May be read-only location.
LDID_SETUPTEMP	2	Temporary setup directory for install path to uninstall location, this is where we backup files that will be overwritten.
LDID_UNINSTALL	3	Uninstall (backup) directory path for the copy engine.
LDID_BACKUP	4	BUGBUG: backup directory for the copy engine, not used temporary setup directory used by setup, this is only valid during regular install and is guaranteed to be a read/write location for scratch space.
LDID_SETUPSCRATCH	5	Temporary setup directory for scratch space.

Windows destination directories of the installation

LDID_WIN	10	Destination \Windows directory (just user files).
LDID_SYS	11	Destination \Windows System directory.
LDID_IOS	12	Destination \Windows Iosubsys directory.
LDID_CMD	13	Destination \Windows Command (DOS) directory.
LDID_CPL	14	Destination \Windows Control Panel directory.
LDID_PRINT	15	Destination \Windows Printer directory.
LDID_MAIL	16	Destination \Mail directory.
LDID_INF	17	Destination \Windows *INF directory.
LDID_HELP	18	Destination \Windows Help directory.
LDID_FONTS	20	Destination \Windows Font directory.
LDID_VIEWERS	21	Destination \Windows Viewers directory.
LDID_VMM32	22	Destination \Windows VMM32 directory.
LDID_COLOR	23	Destination \Windows Color directory.
LDID_APPS	24	Applications folder location. Shared directories for net install.

Boot and old Windows and DOS directories

LDID	Value	Directory use
LDID_WINBOOT	26	Guaranteed boot device for windows.
LDID_MACHINE	27	Machine specific files.
LDID_HOST_WINBOOT	28	Boot and old \Windows and DOS directories.
LDID_BOOT	30	Root directory of boot drive.
LDID_BOOT_HOST	31	Root directory of boot drive host.
LDID_OLD_WINBOOT	32	Subdirectory off of Root (optional).
LDID_OLD_WIN	33	Old \Windows directory (if it exists).
LDID_OLD_DOS	34	Old \DOS directory (if it exists).
LDID_OLD_NET	35	Old network root directory, only valid during network GenUpgrade.
LDID_MOUSE	36	Path to MOUSE env. variable if set or same as LDID_WIN only valid after mouse class installer.

Variable LDIDs

Variable LDIDs (VarLDIDs) allow for INFs to reliably find the existing Program Files, Accessories, etc., locations.

Directories that have long file names or that may have extended characters in their names may have multiple LDIDs. For example, 28700 and 28701 both point to "Program Files", but 28700 corresponds to the short file name "Progra~1" while 28701 corresponds to the long file name. Likewise, 28700 and 28702 both point to the short name "Progra~1", but 28700 renders this name in the OEM character set whereas 28702 renders it in ANSI characters. Different LDIDs are appropriate for different uses. In general, OEM/SFN LDIDs are uses for file copying, ANSI/LFN are used for strings written to the registry, and ANSI/SFN are used for Setup.ini entries that create start menu shortcuts.

The flag values at the end of the VarLDID.LFN and VarLDID.SFN sections show how the directories are represented internally as strings. The flag values have the following meanings:

0 = OEM/SFN (Default)
1 = ANSI/SFN
2 = OEM/LFN
3 = ANSI/LFN

subdir

Name of the directory, within the directory named by *ldid*, to be the destination directory.

The optional **DefaultDestDir** entry provides a default destination for any **Copyfile** entries that use the direct copy notation (@filename) or any [*File-List*] section not specified in the [DestinationDirs] section. If **DefaultDestDir** is not given, the default directory is set to LDID_WIN.

This example sets the destination directory for the MoveMiniPort section to the \Windows Iosubsys directory, and sets the default directory for other sections to be the \BIN directory on the boot drive:

```
[DestinationDirs]
MoveMiniPort=12
; Destination for MoveMiniPort Section is windows\iosubsys
DefaultDestDirs=30,bin  ; Direct copies go to Boot:\bin
```

[*File-List*] Section

A [*File-List*] section lists the names of files to be copied, renamed, or deleted. Entries in this section have three forms, depending on the type of entry in the [*Install*] section that defines the section name. In addition, the *file-list*-section name must appear in the **CopyFiles** entry.

A [*File-List*] section for a **CopyFiles** entry has this form:

[*file-list*] section
destination-file-name,[source-file-name],[temporary-file-name]

destination-file-name
    Name of the destination file. If no source file name is given, this is also the name of the source file.

source-file-name
    Name of the source file. Required only if the source and destination names are not the same.

temporary-file-name
    Name of the temporary file for the copy. Setup copies the source file, but gives it the temporary file name. The next time Windows 98 starts, it renames the temporary file to the destination file name. This is useful for copying files to a destination that is currently open or in use by Windows.

The following example copies three files:

```
[CopyTheseFilesSec]
file11                   ; copies file11
file21, file22, file23   ; copies file22, temporarily naming it file23
file31,file32            ; copies file32 to file31
```

A [*File-List*] section for a **RenFiles** entry has this form:

[*file-list-section*]
new-file-name,old-file-name

The *file-list-section* name must appear in the **RenFiles** entry.

This example renames the files FILE42, FILE52, and FILE62 to FILE41, FILE51, and FILE61, respectively:

```
[RenameOldFilesSec]
file41,file42
file51,file52
file61,file62
```

A [*File-List*] section for a **DelFiles** entry has this form:

[*file-list*-section]
filename

The *file-list*-section name must appear in the **DelFiles** entry.

This example deletes three files:

```
[DeleteOldFilesSec]
file1
file2
file3
```

In the preceding examples, the given file names are assumed to have been defined in the [SourceDisksFiles] section and the logical disk numbers that appear in this section have been defined in the [SourceDisksNames] section.

[SourceDisksFiles] Section

Syntax   **[SourceDisksFiles]**
filename=disk-number

Names the source files used during installation and identifies the source disks that contain the files. The ordinal of the source disk defined in *disk-number* must be defined in the [SourceDiskNames] section.

This example identifies a single source file, SRS01.386, on the disk having ordinal 1:

```
[SourceDisksFiles]
SRS01.386 = 1
```

[SourceDisksNames] Section

Syntax

SourceDisksNames]
disk-ordinal="*disk-description*"*,disk-label,disk-serial-number*

Identifies and names the disks used for installation of the given device drivers.

This example identifies one source disk and assigns it ordinal 1. The disk description is given as a strings key:

```
[SourceDisksNames]
1 = %ID1%, Instd1, 0000-0000
```

[ClassInstall] Section

Syntax

[ClassInstall]
Copyfiles=*file-list-section*[*,file-list-section*]...
Renfiles=*file-list-section*[*,*file-list-section]...
Delfiles=*file-list-section*[*,file-list-section*]...
UpdateInis=*update-ini-section*[*,update-ini-section*]...
UpdateIniFields=*update-inifields-section*[*,update-inifield-section*]...
AddReg=*add-registry-section*[*,add-registry-section*]...
DelReg=*del-registry-section*[*,del-registry-section*]...

The [ClassInstall] section installs a new class for a device in the [Class] section of the registry. Every device installed in Windows 98 has a class associated with it (even if the class is "UNKNOWN"), and every class has a class installer associated with it. Setup processes this section if one of the devices defined in this INF file is about to be installed and the class is not already defined. Not all entries are needed or required.

The following example specifies the class entry for Setup to create in the registry (AddReg=SampleClassReg), and specifies a normal [*Install*] section in [SampleClassReg]. In this example, the Class description is required, and the relative key (HKR) denotes the class section. This example creates the class Sample and registers the description, installer, and icon for the class:

```
[ClassInstall]
Addreg=SampleClassReg
CopyFiles=@Sample.cpl

[SampleClassReg]
HKR,,,,%SampleClassDesc%
HKR,,Installer,,Sample.cpl
HKR,,Icon,HEX,00,00
```

[Strings] Section

Syntax

[Strings]
strings-key=value

The [Strings] section defines one or more strings keys. A strings key is a name that represents a string of printable characters. Although the [Strings] section is generally the last section in the INF files, a strings key defined in this section may be used anywhere in the INF file that the corresponding string would be used.

Setup expands the strings key to the given string and uses it for further processing. Using a strings key requires that it be enclosed in percent signs (%). The [Strings] section makes localization easier by placing all localizable text in the INF file in a single section. Strings keys should be used whenever possible.

strings-key
A unique name consisting of letters and digits.

value
A string consisting of letters, digits, or other printable characters. It should be enclosed in quotation marks if the corresponding strings key is used in an entry that requires quotation marks.

The following example shows the [Strings] section for a sample INF file.

```
[Strings]
MSFT="Microsoft"
M1="APEX DRIVERS"
DevDesc1=APEX DRIVERS SCSI II Host Adapter
ID1="APEX DRIVERS SuperSCSI Installation disk"
```

Sample INF File

This example assumes a fictitious piece of hardware, a SCSI II Host Adapter built by a company named Apex Drivers. The board requires four I/O ports that can be based at 180H, 190H, 1A0h, or 1B0h. The board requires one exclusive IRQ chosen from 4,5,9,10, or 11. The board can use a DMA channel if one is assigned.

```
;SCSI.INF
;
; Standard comment

[Version]
Signature="$Chicago$"
Provider=%MSFT%
HardwareClass=SCSIAdapter
```

```
[Manufacturer]
%M1%=APEXD   ; Strings key for this manufacturer

[APEXD]
%DevDesc1% = SuperSCSI, *PNPA000, *PnPA001

[SuperSCSI]
; Apex Drivers Model 01 - SuperSCSI+
Log_Config = With_Dma, WithoutDMA
Copyfiles=MoveMiniPort, @SRSutil.exe
AddReg=MOD1

[With_DMA]
; Primary Logical Configuration
ConfigPriority = NORMAL
I/OConfig = 4@180-1B3%fff0(3:0:)
; Allocate 4 ports at base 180,190,1A0 or 1B0, device decodes
; 10bits of I/O address and uses no Aliases.
IRQConfig = 4,5,9,10,11   ; Allocate Exclusive IRQ 4, 5, 9, 10 or 11
DMAConfig = 0,1,2,3   ; Allocate DMA Channel 0, 1 ,2 or 3

[Without_DMA]
; Secondary Logical Configuration
ConfigPriority = SUBOPTIMAL
I/OConfig = 4@180-1B3%fff0(3:0:)
IRQConfig = 4,5,9,10,11

[MOD1]
HKR,,DevLoader,,I/OS
HKR,,Miniport,,SRSmini.386
[DestinationDirs]
MoveMiniPort=12
; Destination for MoveMiniPort Section is windows\iosubsys
DefaultDestDirs=30,bin   ; Direct copies go to Boot:\bin

[SourceDiskSFiles]
SRS01.386 = 1

[SourceDisksNames]
1 = %ID1%, Instd1, 0000-0000

[MoveMiniPort]
SRS01.386

[Strings]
MSFT="Microsoft"
M1="APEX DRIVERS"
DevDesc1=Apex Drivers SCSI II Host Adapter
ID1="Apex Drivers SuperSCSI Installation disk"
```

A P P E N D I X   D

Msbatch.inf Parameters for Setup Scripts

Msbatch.inf defines the format that must be used when creating setup scripts for customizing and automating installations. Customizing and automating installations requires that you create or edit existing setup scripts with the predefined Setup settings you need for your installations.

In This Appendix

Setup Script Parameters   1552

Windows 98 Network Adapter INF Summary   1587

Msbatch.inf Sample File   1592

See Also

- For more information about creating custom setup support to accommodate accessibility needs, see Chapter 3, "Custom Installations."

- For more information about network adapters and protocols, see Chapter 15, "Network Adapters and Protocols."

- For more information about Windows 98 on third-party networks, see Chapter 17, "Windows 98 on Third-Party Networks."

- For more information about logon, browsing, and resource sharing, see Chapter 18, "Logon, Browsing, and Resource Sharing."

Setup Script Parameters

This section summarizes the parameters that can be used in setup scripts.

Setup-related parameters

[Setup] parameters:

ChangeDir	InstallType	PenWinWarning
CleanBoot	NoDirWarn	TimeZone
Devicepath	NoPrompt2Boot	Uninstall (with BackupDir)
EBD	OptionalComponents (with	
Express	InstallType=3)	
InstallDir		

[System] parameters:

Keyboard	Multilanguage	Tablet
Locale	PenWindows	
Mouse	Power	

[NameAndOrg] parameters:

Name	Org	Display

[InstallLocationsMRU] parameters: List of paths

[OptionalComponents] parameters: List of descriptions

[Printers] parameters: Printers to install

Network-related parameters

[Network] parameters:

Clients	IgnoreDetectedNetcards	Services
ComputerName	NetCards	Security
Description	PassThroughAgent	ValidateNetcardResources
DefaultProtocol	Protocols	Workgroup
Display	RemoveBinding	

[*netcard_ID*] parameters: Values from the INF file for the network adapter

[MSTCP] parameters:

DHCP	Gateways	LMHostPath
DNS	Hostname	PrimaryWINS
DNSServers	IPAddress	ScopeID
Domain	IPMask	SecondaryWINS
DomainOrder	LMHosts	WINS

[NWLink] parameters: Frame_Type   NetBIOS

[NWRedir] parameters: FirstNetDrive   ProcessLoginScript
    PreferredServer   SearchMode

[MSTCP] parameters: *(continued)*

[NWRedir4] parameters:	PreferredTree	NameContext
[NWServer] parameters:	BrowseMaster	Use_SAP
[VRedir] parameters:	LogonDomain	ValidatedLogon
[VServer] parameters:	LMAnnounce	MaintainServerList

The setup script parameters are not case-sensitive. They are also not required; if they do not appear in a setup script, Windows 98 Setup just uses default values.

The display of most Setup dialog boxes can be disabled in the setup script so that users cannot change any setting. If the dialog boxes are not disabled, sources of information for parameters are given the following priority:

- Information specified in the setup script
- User input
- Detection information

In this section, the descriptions for an option can contain any of six possible entries, as described in the following table. For an example of the resulting file, see "Msbatch.inf Sample File" later in this appendix.

Entry	Description
Parameter	The name of the parameter as it appears in a setup script.
Values	The values that can be assigned to the parameter and what they mean.
System policy	The name of the corresponding parameter for this entry in System Policy Editor; if no entry appears, there is no system policy.
Default	The built-in value that is used if no other value is provided.

[Setup]

The [Setup] section sets parameters for controlling the Setup process.

Change Installation Directory

This parameter allows you to change the installation directory from the default. For clean installations and upgrades from Windows 3.*x*, the default installation directory is C:\Windows.

Parameter	ChangeDir
Values	0 = Install Windows 98 in the default installation directory.
	1 = Install Windows 98 in a directory other than the default.
Default	0

Clean Installation

This parameter forces a new Windows 98 installation (on a new computer or a computer with a reformatted hard disk) instead of an upgrade from either Windows 95 or Windows 3.1x. For more information on clean installations, see "Running Setup on a New Installation" in Chapter 2, "Setting Up Windows 98."

Parameter	CleanBoot
Values	0 = Do not force a clean installation, perform an upgrade instead. 1 = Force a clean installation.
Default	0

Device Path

This parameter specifies whether Windows 98 should check a source installation path to find INF files, rather than looking only in the Windows INF directory when installing devices. If this parameter is set to 1, network administrators can later add INF files to a single source location to ensure that up-to-date drivers are installed any time a new device is installed on computers running Windows 98. However, set this value to 1 only if the installation source files are in a network directory (not floppy disks or compact disk).

Note that **Devicepath=1** causes the entire INF database to be rebuilt each time a user changes a network component or changes drivers for any device.

Parameter	Devicepath
Values	0 = Do not add a source directory path for INFs. 1 = Add the installation source directory to the path for finding INFs.
Default	0

Windows 98 Startup Disk

This parameter specifies whether to create the emergency Startup Disk during Setup (the command-line override for this is **/ie**). For a setup script intended for hands-free installation, you might want to specify **ebd=0** so that the user is not prompted to insert or remove the floppy disk. If you need to specify **ebd=1**, you can also add a **reboot=0** entry, so that Setup will not attempt to restart the computer while the floppy disk is in the drive.

Parameter	EBD
Values	0 = Do not create an emergency Startup Disk. 1 = Create an emergency Startup Disk.
Default	1

Express

This parameter specifies whether the user can provide input during Setup. If **Express=1**, then Windows 98 Setup uses only the settings specified in Msbatch.inf or built-in defaults and does not ask the user to confirm or enter input. This setting disables most of the user interface for Setup.

Parameter	Express
Values	0 = Allow user input. 1 = Run Setup using only values in Msbatch.inf.
Default	0

Caution If **Express=1**, you cannot add parameters to override safe detection for network adapters, SCSI controllers, or sound cards—which, in some cases, requires installing support after Setup is complete. If you need to force installation of certain hardware when **Express=1**, add specific entries in the [System] section.

Installation Directory

This parameter specifies the directory where Windows 98 is to be installed.

Parameter	InstallDir
Values	Directory name
Default	\Windows directory (if present)

Installation Directory Warning

This parameter allows you to install Windows 98 over an existing Windows installation directory without warning you.

Parameter	NoDirWarn
Values	0 = Warn me before overwriting an existing Windows installation directory. 1 = Overwrite the existing Windows installation directory without warning me.
Default	0

Install Type

This parameter specifies the type of installation for Windows 98 Setup.

Parameter	InstallType
Values	0 = Compact 1 = Typical 2 = Portable 3 = Custom
Default	1

Optional Components

This parameter specifies whether or not to display the **Select Components** dialog box during installation. You must specify **InstallType=3** with this setting.

Parameter	OptionalComponents
Values	0 = Do not display the **Select Components** dialog box.
	1 = Display the **Select Components** dialog box.
Default	1

Pen Windows Warning

This parameter specifies whether to display a warning if an unknown version of Pen Windows is installed.

Parameter	PenWinWarning
Values	0 = Do not display the warning.
	1 = Display the warning.
Default	1

Reboot Prompt

This parameter specifies whether the user should be prompted before rebooting the computer.

Parameter	NoPrompt2Boot
Values	0 = Do not prompt the user before rebooting.
	1 = Prompt the user before rebooting.
Default	1

Time Zone

This parameter specifies the time zone to set on the computer.

Parameter	TimeZone
Values	String enclosed in quotation marks, as described in the following list.
Default	The time zone currently set on the computer.

Time zone strings

Afghanistan	Dateline	Israel	Singapore
Alaskan	E. Australia	Jakarta	South Africa
Arabian	E. Europe	Korea	Sydney
Atlantic	E. South America	Lisbon Warsaw	Taipei
AUS Central	Eastern	Mexico	Tasmania
Azores	Egypt	Mid-Atlantic	Tbilisi
Balkan	Ekaterinburg	Mountain	Tokyo
Bangkok	Fiji	New Zealand	US Eastern
Canada Central	Finland	Newfoundland	US Mountain
Cen. Australia	GT	Pacific	Vladivostok
Central	GFT	Romance	W. Australia
Central Asia	GMT	Russian	W. Europe
Central Europe	Greenwich	SA Eastern	West AsiaWest Pacific
Central Pacific	Hawaiian	SA Pacific	Yakutsk
China	Hanoi	SA Western	
Colombo	India	Samoa	
Czech	Iran	Saudi Arabia	

Uninstall

This parameter is used to specify whether Setup should create a compressed backup version of the existing Windows and MS-DOS directories to be used for automatically uninstalling Windows 98. If you specify **Uninstall=5**, you also must add a value for **BackupDir=***path* that specifies the directory where Setup should place the compressed backup files.

Parameter	Uninstall
Values	0 = Do not allow user to specify Uninstall options, and do not create backup files for uninstalling Windows 98. 1 = Show Uninstall options for user to choose and create backup. 5 = Do not show Uninstall options, but automatically create backup files for uninstalling Windows 98.
Default	1

[System]

This section sets parameters for modifying the system settings.

Tip The correct entries for Msbatch.inf can be copied from similarly named entries in Setuplog.txt for a computer on which Windows 98 has been installed with devices identical to those that you want to install from a setup script.

The following entries are based on INF section names:

Table D.1   [System] parameters based on INF section names

To set this parameter	Use the appropriate section name in the following INF File
Locale	Locale.inf (see also Appendix A, "International Windows 98")
PenWindows	Penwin.inf
Power	Machine.inf
Tablet	Pendrv.inf

The following entries use INF descriptions. The choice must be in the list of compatible devices for that class.

Table D.2   [System] parameters based on INF descriptions

To set this parameter	Use the appropriate description in the following INF File
Display	Msdisp.inf. For example, from the description **%SuperVGA.DriverDesc%=SVGA** for Super VGA, the entry in Msbatch.inf would be **display=svga**.
Keyboard	Keyboard.inf.
Mouse	Mouse.inf or similar file.

Keyboard

This parameter specifies the keyboard layout.

Parameter	SelectedKeyboard
Values	*Value*, where *value* is any of the values listed in the [KeyboardList] section in Multilng.inf.

MultiLanguage

This parameter sets the type of multilanguage support installed for Windows 98.

Parameter	MultiLanguage
Values	English_M = Installs support for English and Western European languages. Greek_M = Adds additional support for Greek. Cyrillic_M = Adds additional support for Cyrillic. CE_M = Adds additional support for Eastern European languages. Baltic_M = Adds additional support for Baltic.
Default	English_M

[NameAndOrg]

This section defines the name and organization for Windows 98 Setup, and specifies whether the user is to be shown the **Name And Organization** dialog box.

Name

This parameter specifies the full user name for this installation.

Parameter	Name
Values	String
Default	None

Organization

This parameter specifies the registered organization for this installation.

Parameter	Org
Values	String
Default	None

Display

This parameter specifies whether the **Name And Organization** dialog box appears during Windows 98 Setup.

Parameter	Display
Values	0 = Do not display name and organization.
	1 = Display name and organization.
Default	1

[InstallLocationsMRU]

This section specifies the paths to add to the list of directories that the user can choose when Windows 98 Setup prompts for a path. For example, this section could appear as follows to specify local and network file locations:

```
[InstallLocationsMRU]
\\server\share\folder=mru1
c:\win98=mru2
\\winserver\source=mru3
```

To force the path for files from which to copy, use **CopyFile=** and related statements in an [Install] section and specify the complete path for the component files.

[OptionalComponents]

This section contains the descriptions that appear in the **Optional Components** dialog box in Windows 98 Setup.

To create entries for this section, type the description enclosed in quotation marks. Each description is followed by 1 (install) or 0 (do not install). The strings that specify the optional components to install are defined in INF files.

Another way to define entries for this section is to copy the [OptionalComponents] section in Setuplog.txt from a computer that already has all the optional components installed that you want defined in the setup script. For an example, the entries to install Briefcase and Net Watcher are as follows:

```
[OptionalComponents]
"Briefcase"=1
"Net Watcher"=1
```

The following tables show the strings for the optional components defined in the Windows 98 standard INF files, grouped by the following component sets:

- Accessibility
- Accessories
- Communications
- Desktop Themes
- Internet Tools
- Microsoft Outlook Express
- Multilanguage Support
- Multimedia
- Online Services
- System Tools
- Web TV for Windows

Additional strings can be defined by other application developers.

Table D.3   Optional component strings

Accessibility
Accessibility Options
Accessibility Tools

Accessories
Briefcase
Calculator
Desktop Wallpaper
Document Templates
Games
Imaging
Mouse Pointers
Paint
Quick View
Screen Savers
    Additional
    Screen Savers
    Flying Windows
    OpenGL Screen Savers
Windows Scripting Host
WordPad

Communications
Dial-Up Networking
Dial-Up Server
Direct Cable Connection
Hyper Terminal
Microsoft Chat 2.1
Microsoft NetMeeting
Phone Dialer
Virtual Private Networking

Desktop Themes
Baseball
Dangerous Creatures
Desktop Themes Support
Inside your Computer
Jungle
Leonardo da Vinci
More Windows
Mystery
Nature
Science
Space
Sports
The 60's USA
The Golden Era
Travel
Underwater
Windows 98

Internet Tools
Microsoft FrontPage Express
Microsoft VRML 2.0 Viewer
Microsoft Wallet
Personal Web Server
Real Audio Player 4.0
Web Publishing Wizard
Web-Based Enterprise Mgmt

Multilanguage Support
Baltic
Central European
Cyrillic
Greek
Turkish

Multimedia
Audio Compression
CD Player
Macromedia Shockwave Director
Macromedia Shockwave Flash
Media Player
Microsoft NetShow Player 2.0
Multimedia Sound Schemes
Sample Sounds
Sound Recorder
Video Compression
Volume Control

Online Services
America Online
AT&T WorldNet Service
CompuServe
Prodigy Internet
The Microsoft Network

System Tools
Backup
Character Map
Clipboard Viewer
Disk compression tools
Drive Converter (FAT32)
Group Policies
Net Watcher
System Monitor
System Resource Meter

Web TV for Windows
Broadcast Data Services
WaveTop Data Broadcasting
WebTV for Windows

Optional Component Dependencies

This optional component	Depends on this component
Direct Cable Connection	Dial-Up Networking
Dial-Up Server	Dial-Up Networking
Virtual Private Networking	Dial-Up Networking

The following table lists optional component strings that are no longer valid in Windows 98. The left column lists the obsolete component; the right column the new string that replaces it.

Obsolete Component Strings

This component	Is replaced by
Extra Cursors	Mouse Pointers
Windows Accessories	Accessories

[Network]

This section specifies the parameters and options for installing networking components. The categories for these parameters include the following:

- Installation parameters
- Computer identification parameters
- Security parameters
- User interface options

Installation Parameters in [Network]

Clients

This parameter specifies the network clients to be installed. It is a list of the device IDs used in the INF files. These IDs are not limited to those in the Windows 98 INF files (Netcli.inf and Netcli3.inf). A site that has an INF file from another vendor can use any device IDs listed in it.

Note If you are installing a network client other than those listed in the INF files provided with Windows 98, you need to obtain an updated Windows 98 INF file from your vendor. You can use INF Installer (Infinst.exe) to add network clients to your Windows 98 installation. For more information on how to use INF Installer, see "Adding Custom Drivers with INF Installer (Infinst.exe)" in Chapter 3, "Custom Installations."

If you are installing multiple clients, the first client in this list will start first whenever the computer is started.

Specify multiple networks in a comma-separated list. If the list contains two network clients, or lists multiple networks with a primary-only network (such as IBM OS/2 LAN Server), Windows 98 Setup presents an error message and displays the Network Configuration properties for changing the selection. The verification process that occurs in Setup still takes place.

Parameter	Clients
Values	Comma-separated list of client device IDs (see the following table)
Default	Defaults in Netdef.inf

The following table shows the device IDs for network clients included with the Windows 98 files (as specified in Netcli.inf and Netcli3.inf).

Device ID	Network
Vredir	Client for Microsoft Networks
Family	Microsoft Family Logon
Netware3	Novell NetWare version 3.x
Netware4	Novell NetWare version 4.x
Nwredir	Microsoft Client for NetWare Networks

The following table shows other valid device IDs for third-party network clients.

Device ID	Network
Novell32	Novell Client for Windows 95/98
Vinesifs	Banyan VINES version 8.02 or later

Network Card Drivers

This parameter specifies the drivers to be installed for network adapters as a list of the device IDs used in the INF files. These IDs are not limited to those included in the Windows 98 INF files. A site that has an INF file from another vendor can use any device IDs listed in that file.

Note In general, it is recommended that you rely on detection in Windows 98 Setup to install the correct driver and define the correct configuration settings.

If you are installing drivers for network adapters other than those listed in the INF files provided with Windows 98, you need to obtain an updated Windows 98 INF file from your vendor. You can use INF Installer (Infinst.exe) to add drivers for network adapters to your Windows 98 installation. For more information on how to use INF Installer, see "Adding Custom Drivers with INF Installer (Infinst.exe)" in Chapter 3, "Custom Installations."

When a network adapter is listed, the usual verification takes place. Windows 98 Setup chooses an NDIS 3.1 or later driver, if available; otherwise, it uses an NDIS 2.*x* driver. Do not specify a Plug and Play or PCI card with the NetCards parameter if that device is enumerated by Windows 98.

Parameter	NetCards
Values	Comma-separated list of network adapter device IDs.
Default	Results of detection.

For example, the following entries would install drivers for Intel EtherExpress 16 or 16TP plus 3Com EtherLink II or IITP:

```
Netcards=*PNP812D,*PNP80F3
```

Caution The virtual private networking (VPN) and Web TV for Windows dial-up adapters should not be specified with the Netcards parameter.

Protocols

This parameter specifies the protocols to be installed as a list of the device IDs used in the INF files. These IDs are not limited to those in the Windows 98 INF files. A site that has an INF file from another vendor can use any device IDs listed in that file.

Note If you are installing network protocols other than those listed in the INF files provided with Windows 98, you need to obtain an updated Windows 98 INF file from your vendor. You can use INF Installer (Infinst.exe) to add network protocols to your Windows 98 installation. For more information on how to use INF Installer, see "Adding Custom Drivers with INF Installer (Infinst.exe)" in Chapter 3, "Custom Installations."

Parameter	Protocols
Values	Comma-separated list of protocol device IDs, as described in the following table.
Default	Defaults in Netdef.inf.

For example, the following entry installs the Microsoft TCP/IP protocol:

```
Protocols=mstcp
```

The following table shows the valid device IDs for network protocols included with the Windows 98 files (as specified in Nettrans.inf).

Device ID	Protocol
Msdlc	Microsoft DLC (real mode)
Mstcp	Microsoft TCP/IP
Ndiswan	Protocol wrapper for virtual private networking adapter
Netbeui	Microsoft NetBEUI
Nwlink	Microsoft IPX/SPX-compatible protocol
Nwnblink	Microsoft NetBIOS support for IPX/SPX-compatible protocol

The following table shows examples of other valid device IDs for third-party network protocols. These are not included with the Windows 98 files.

Device ID	Protocol
Bancom	Banyan VINES protocol for Windows 95
Ipxodi	Novell-supplied IPXODI protocol
Novellipx32	Novell-supplied IPX 32 protocol for Windows 95

Setup verifies these settings, so it is possible to specify only the network clients and let Windows 98 Setup choose the protocols. For example, if you specify **Clients=Novell32**, then Windows 98 Setup adds Novellipx32.

Default Protocol

This parameter sets the default protocol (which is assigned LANA 0), which is the specified protocol bound to the specified network adapter (if the computer has more than one network adapter). If no adapter is specified, the default is the first instance of the specified protocol. Set this value if, for example, the computer will run software that requires a protocol to be bound to LAN adapter (LANA) 0, which can only be defined by setting that protocol as the default protocol. For more information about LAN adapter numbers, see Chapter 15, "Network Adapters and Protocols."

If **netbios=1,** you must set **defaultprotocol=nwnblink** if you want to specify the IPX/SPX-compatible protocol as the default.

Parameter	DefaultProtocol
Values	A protocol device ID as defined in **protocol=** and, optionally, a network adapter device ID, as defined in **netcards=**.
Default	0

The following example sets the default protocol as an instance of NetBEUI bound to a particular adapter:

```
DefaultProtocol=netbeui,*pnp812d
```

Remove Binding

This parameter removes the binding between the two devices. This parameter is used to tune bindings in a setup script.

Parameter	RemoveBinding
Values	Comma-separated list of device IDs
Default	None

Services

This parameter specifies the network services to be installed as a list of the device IDs used in the INF files. These IDs are not limited to those in the Windows 98 INF files. A site that has an INF file from another vendor can use any device IDs listed in that file. When a service is listed in a setup script, the usual verification still takes place.

Note If you are installing network services other than those listed in the INF files provided with Windows 98, you need to obtain an updated Windows 98 INF file from your vendor. You can use INF Installer (Infinst.exe) to add network services to your Windows 98 installation. For more information on how to use INF Installer, see "Adding Custom Drivers with INF Installer (Infinst.exe)" in Chapter 3, "Custom Installations."

The only service installed by default is VSERVER (File and Printer Sharing for Microsoft Networks) if peer sharing services were enabled for Windows for Workgroups.

Parameter	Services
Values	Comma-separated list of service device IDs, as described in the following table.
Default	Windows 98 Setup defaults, depending on the value of **InstallType**.

The following shows the valid device IDs defined in several different INF files.

Device ID	Service	INF file
Nmagent	Microsoft Network Monitor agent	Nmagent.inf
Nwredir4	Microsoft Service for NetWare Directory Services	Ndscli.inf
Nwserver	File and Printer Sharing for NetWare Networks	Netsrvr.inf
Remotereg	Microsoft Remote Registry service	Regsrv.inf
Snmp	Microsoft Simple Network Management Protocol (SNMP) agent	Snmp.inf
Vserver	File and Printer Sharing for Microsoft Networks	Netsrvr.inf

Computer Identification Parameters in [Network]

Computer Name

This parameter sets the computer's network name.

Parameter	ComputerName
Values	String of up to 15 alphanumeric characters and no blank spaces. The name must be unique on the network and can contain the following special characters:

! @ # $ % ^ & ( ) - _ ' { } . ~

If you define a variable in your Msbatch.inf file and then try to use that variable for the ComputerName parameter, Windows 98 assumes that the percent characters % are part of the computer name. For example, if you have an Msbatch.inf file with the following entries:

```
[Network]

ComputerName=%cname%

[Strings]

cname="MyComputerName"
```

Windows 98 will set the computer's network name to **%cname%** and not to **MyComputerName**.

Default	Generated from the first eight characters of the user name.

Description

This parameter is the description for the computer (mainly used by peer servers, such as File and Printer Sharing for Microsoft Networks).

Parameter	Description
Values	String of up to 48 alphanumeric characters. It cannot contain commas, but it can contain any of the following special characters:
	! @ # $ % ^ & ( ) - _ ' { } . ~
Default	User name from licensing information.

Workgroup

This parameter sets the workgroup for the computer.

Parameter	Workgroup
Values	String of up to 15 alphanumeric characters and no blank spaces. The name must be unique on the network and can contain the following special characters:

! @ # $ % ^ & ( ) - _ ' { } . ~

If you define a variable in your Msbatch.inf file and then try to use that variable for the Workgroup parameter, Windows 98 assumes that the percent characters % are part of the workgroup name. For example, if you have an Msbatch.inf file with the following entries:

```
[Network]
Workgroup=%workgrp%
[Strings]
workgrp="WorkgroupName"
```

Windows 98 will set the computer's workgroup name to **%workgrp%** and not to **WorkgroupName**.

Default	Workgroup previously specified; otherwise, a new name is generated from user licensing information by taking the first 15 characters of the organization name. For example, an organization name of "Microsoft Corporation" results in "MicrosoftCorpo" as the default workgroup.

Security Parameters in [Network]

User Security

This parameter specifies the security model to be used and, for user-level security, the type of pass-through agent (that is, server or domain). A client with a security provider must be installed for these values to have an effect.

Parameter	Security
Values	share = share-level security. nwserver = user-level security, validated by a NetWare server. domain = user-level security, validated by a Windows NT domain. msserver = user-level security, validated by a computer running Windows NT Workstation or Windows NT Server as a standalone computer.
Default	share

Pass-Through Agent

This parameter specifies the pass-through agent for user-level security. This value is ignored for share-level security.

Parameter	PassThroughAgent
Values	Server or domain name
Default	No value, or the value of **Workgroup** if **Security=domain**, or the value of **Preferred Server** if **Security=nwserver**. The default is the value of **PreferredServer** if **Security=nwserver**; otherwise, there is no default.

User Interface Options for [Network] Parameters

Display

This parameter controls whether any of the **Network Configuration** dialog boxes appear in Custom Setup.

Parameter	Display
Values	0 = Do not display 1 = Display
Default	1

Validate NetCard Resources

This parameter specifies whether to display a dialog box to resolve resource conflicts if a partial configuration is detected or if there is an IRQ conflict for a network adapter.

Parameter	ValidateNetCardResources
Values	0 = Do not display a wizard page.
	1 = Display a wizard page to resolve resource conflicts.
Default	1

[netcard_ID]

The actual name for this section is the identifier for the network adapter, as defined in the related INF file. This section sets parameters for a specific network adapter, as defined in the [netcard.NDI] sections of the network device INF files provided with Windows 98.

Important In general, it is recommended that you rely on detection in Windows 98 Setup to install the correct driver and define the correct configuration settings.

All entries for a [netcard_ID] section depend on the specific adapter. The actual parameters and settings for a specific network adapter can be found in that adapter's INF file in the Windows INF directory.

To locate settings for a network adapter, check Net.inf for entries, such as the following:

```
CardBrand=brand of network adapter
INFFile=file where these settings can be found
```

In the related INF file for the specific network adapter, search for the adapter's name. For example, you might find the following entry for an Intel EtherExpress 16 network adapter:

```
;*************************************************************
; *PNP812D  Intel Etherexpress 16 or 16TP
;*************************************************************
```

The information in the netcard.INF file is followed by the specific settings, using this format:

```
;netcard model name
[<adapter>.NDI]
actual settings for adapter
```

For example, for the adapter in the previous example, the following entry appears in the Netee16.inf file:

```
[*PNP812D.ndi]
AddReg=*pnp812d.ndi.reg,EXP16.ndi.reg
```

Based on the **AddReg=** entry in this statement, you need to search for the [*pnp812d.ndi.reg] or [EXP16.ndi.reg] sections in the INF file to find the parameters required for a particular adapter. For example, for the related Intel EtherExpress adapter, the following sections appear in Netee16.inf:

```
[*PNP812D.ndi.reg]
.
.
.
HKR,NDI\params\Interrupt,resc,1,04,00,00,00
HKR,NDI\params\IOAddress,resc,1,02,00,00,0
HKR,NDI\params\DMAChannel,ParamDesc,,"DMA Channel"
```

These entries describe the parameters that can be specified for the adapter in a setup script. Furthermore, in this same part of the *netcard*.INF file, the statements also indicate the kinds and ranges of values that can be specified for a particular parameter. For example, in Netee16.inf, the following statements indicate that for **DMAChannel=** you must specify an integer in the range of 1–3, where the default value is 1:

```
HKR,NDI\params\DMAChannel,type,,int
HKR,NDI\params\DMAChannel,default,,1
HKR,NDI\params\DMAChannel,min,,1
HKR,NDI\params\DMAChannel,max,,3
```

The following entry in Netee16.inf indicates that for **Transceiver=** you can specify the values **external** or **onboard** (based on the first string that appears after the **enum** item):

```
HKR,NDI\params\Transceiver,default,,onboard
HKR,NDI\params\Transceiver,type,,enum
HKR,NDI\params\Transceiver,enum,external,,external
HKR,NDI\params\Transceiver,enum,onboard,,onboard
```

Based on the previous examples, the following shows an example of the [*netcard*] section you would add to Msbatch.inf to set parameters for an Intel EtherExpress 16 or 16TP network adapter:

```
[*PNP812D]
Interrupt=
IOAddress=
DMAChannel=2
Transceiver=external
```

Notice that you only need to set values for the parameters where you do not want to use the defaults. For a list of possible parameters for some common network adapters, see "Windows 98 Network Adapter INF Summary" later in this appendix.

[MSTCP]

This section sets parameters for Microsoft TCP/IP. For more information about TCP/IP, see Chapter 15, "Network Adapters and Protocols."

DHCP

This parameter specifies whether TCP/IP is configured to use DHCP for dynamic TCP/IP configuration.

Parameter	DHCP
Values	0 = Do not enable DHCP. 1 = Enable DHCP.
Default	1

DNS

This parameter enables DNS name resolution. You must also set **DNS=1** if you plan to use LMHOSTS for name resolution.

Parameter	DNS
Values	0 = Disable DNS. 1 = Enable DNS.
Default	0

DNS Servers

This parameter is a list of the DNS servers to use in the order to try them.

Parameter	DNSServers
Values	Comma-separated list of DNS server names
Default	None

Domain

This parameter sets the DNS domain that this computer is in.

Parameter	Domain
Values	String
Default	None

Domain Order

This parameter sets a list of DNS domains for host name resolution in the order to try them.

Parameter	DomainOrder
Values	Comma-separated list of DNS domains
Default	None

Gateways

This parameter lists the IP gateways (sometimes called IP routers) in the order they are to be used.

Parameter	Gateways
Values	Comma-separated list of IP addresses
Default	None

Hostname

This parameter sets the DNS hostname for this computer (usually the same value as **ComputerName**).

Parameter	Hostname
Values	String
Default	None

IP Address

This parameter sets the computer's IP address if DHCP is not enabled.

Parameter	IPAddress
Values	Internet Protocol (IP) address (*###.###.###.###*)
Default	None

LMHosts

This parameter enables or disables LMHOSTS for name resolution.

Parameter	LHHosts
Values	0 = Disable LMHosts for name resolution. 1 = Enable LMHosts for name resolution.
Default	1

LMHOST File Path
This parameter sets the path and file name of the LMHOST file.

Parameter	LMHOSTPath
Values	Path
Default	None

Primary WINS Server
This parameter sets the primary WINS name server.

Parameter	PrimaryWINS or WINSServer1
Values	IP address (*###.###.###.###*)
Default	None

Secondary WINS Server
This parameter sets the secondary WINS name server.

Parameter	SecondaryWINS or WINSServer2
Values	IP address (*###.###.###.###*)
Default	None

Additional WINS name servers can be specified using parameters WINSServer3 through WINSServer12.

Scope ID
This parameter sets the scope ID.

Parameter	ScopeID
Values	String
Default	None

Subnet Mask
This parameter sets the IP subnet mask for TCP/IP if DHCP is not enabled.

Parameter	IPMask
Values	IP address (*###.###.###.###*)
Default	None

WINS

This parameter enables WINS for NetBIOS computer name resolution.

Parameter	WINS
Values	N = Disable WINS. Y = Enable WINS resolution. D = Use DHCP instead of WINS.
Default	D

[NWLink]

The parameters in this section specify settings for the IPX/SPX-compatible protocol and are valid only if **protocols=nwlink** is also specified in the setup script. For more information about these parameters as defined using the Network option in Control Panel, see Chapter 15, "Network Adapters and Protocols."

Frame Type

This parameter specifies the default frame type for IPX.

Parameter	Frame_Type	
Values	0 = 802.3 1 = 802.2 2 = Ethernet II	4=Auto 5=Token ring 6=Token ring SNAP
Default	4	

NetBIOS

This parameter specifies whether NetBIOS support for IPX/SPX should be installed.

Parameter	NetBIOS
Values	0 = Do not install NWNBLINK. 1 = Install NWNBLINK.
Default	0

[NWRedir]

This section sets parameters for Microsoft Client for NetWare Networks. For more information about these values, see Chapter 17, "Windows 98 on Third-Party Networks."

First Network Drive

This parameter specifies the first network drive to which to attach in login scripts for Client for NetWare Networks. This parameter overrides the equivalent setting in Net.cfg.

Parameter	FirstNetDrive
Values	Drive letter ("A" or "A:" are equivalent)
Default	F:

Preferred Server

This parameter specifies the NetWare preferred server. This parameter does not override the equivalent setting in Net.cfg.

Parameter	PreferredServer
Values	String
System policy	Preferred Server settings (under policies for Microsoft Client for NetWare Networks)
Default	None

Process Login Script

This parameter specifies whether login script processing is enabled when running Microsoft Client for NetWare Networks.

Parameter	ProcessLoginScript
Values	0 = Disable login script processing. 1 = Enable login script processing.
Default	1

[NWRedir4]

This section sets parameters for Microsoft Service for NetWare Directory Services. For more information about these values, see Chapter 17, "Windows 98 on Third-Party Networks" and Chapter 18, "Logon, Browsing, and Resource Sharing."

Preferred Tree

This parameter specifies the NetWare preferred tree.

Parameter	PreferredTree
Values	String
Default	None

Name Context

This parameter specifies the preferred context for the user to log on to.

Parameter	NameContext
Values	String
Default	None

[NWServer]

This section sets parameters for Microsoft File and Printer Sharing for NetWare Networks. For more information about these values, see Chapter 18, "Logon, Browsing, and Resource Sharing."

Browse Master

This parameter specifies whether a computer configured with File and Printer Sharing for NetWare Networks can be elected browse master.

Parameter	BrowseMaster
Values	0 = This computer cannot be a browse master. 1 = This computer can be a browse master. 2 = This computer is the preferred browse master.
Default	1

SAP Browsing

This parameter specifies whether a computer configured with File and Printer Sharing for NetWare Networks uses Service Advertising Protocol (SAP) browsing. Enabling SAP browsing allows a computer with File and Printer Sharing for NetWare Networks to be seen by any NetWare client, but the computer does not appear in a workgroup in Network Neighborhood.

Parameter	Use_SAP
Values	0 = Disable SAP browsing (use workgroup style browsing). 1 = Use SAP style browsing.
Default	0

[VRedir]

This section sets parameters for Client for Microsoft Networks. For more information about these values, see Chapter 16, "Windows 98 on Microsoft Networks."

Validated Logon

This parameter specifies whether logons are validated on a Windows NT domain. If you set this value to 1, be sure to specify a value for **LogonDomain**.

Parameter	ValidatedLogon
Values	0 = Do not validate logons.
	1 = Validate logon.
Default	0

Logon Domain

This parameter specifies the Windows NT domain to use for logon validation. It can be set even if **ValidatedLogon=0**. If **ValidatedLogon=1**, you must set a correct value for **LogonDomain** to ensure that Windows 98 Setup has access to any required files on a protected network resource, and to ensure that the user can log on successfully when installation is completed.

Parameter	LogonDomain
Values	String
System policy	Log on to Windows NT (under policies for Microsoft Client for Windows Networks)
Default	Value of **Workgroup** in [Network]

[VServer]

This section sets parameters for File and Printer Sharing for Microsoft Networks. For more information about these values, see Chapter 18, "Logon, Browsing, and Resource Sharing."

Announce

This parameter specifies whether the computer configured with File and Printer Sharing for Microsoft Networks announces its presence to LAN Manager computers on the network. Setting this value to 1 increases network traffic but makes browsing faster.

Parameter	LMAnnounce
Values	0 = Do not announce VSERVER to the network.
	1 = Announce VSERVER to network.
Default	1

Browse Master

This parameter specifies how the computer configured with File and Printer Sharing for Microsoft Networks behaves in a browse master election.

Parameter	MaintainServerList
Values	0 = Disabled (this computer cannot be a browse master). 1 = Enabled (this computer is the browse master). 2 = Auto (the computer can be a browse master if required).
Default	2

[Printers]

This section is used to install one or more printers during Setup by specifying a user-defined name for identifying the printer, the model name, and the printer port. Each printer to be installed has a separate entry in this section using the following syntax:

PrinterName=DriverModel,Port

where *Port* can be either a local printer name, such as **LPT1,** or a network path for a network printer, such as **\\printserver1\printA**.

The following restrictions apply:

- The length of the friendly name for the printer name cannot exceed 32 bytes (31 characters plus a NULL character). If the name specified in the custom setup script is too long, Setup will truncate it to fit the requirement.

- The model name must be recognized by Windows 98. You can see the list of supported printer models in the Add Printers wizard or in the printer INF files.

- No commas or quotation marks can be used in any string.

Note If the setup script contains a [Printers] section with no entries, you will not be asked to select a printer the first time that Windows 98 runs. If the [Printers] section exists but it does not have any entries under it, you will not be prompted to select a printer. If the script does not contain a [Printers] section, Setup will ask you to install a printer.

Friendly Name

This parameter specifies the friendly name, model, and port for a printer to be installed. The printer's friendly name is the name that appears in the Printers folder. The model name must be the exact name of a printer driver that is supported under Windows 98; otherwise, Setup skips this entire section.

Parameter   *PrinterName*= any string that does not contain these characters:

\   ,   ;   =

Values   *DriverModel* = The exact driver name for any printer model supported under Windows 98

Port = The port that this printer is attached to (such as LPT1) or a UNC path name to a network print queue

Default   None

The following example installs a local printer and a network printer:

```
[Printers]
My BJC600=Canon Bubble-Jet BJC-600,LPT1
IIIsi Next Door=HP Laserjet IIIsi,\\Server_1\PrtShr_1
```

[Strings]

The [Strings] section defines one or more string keys that Setup expands to the defined string and uses it for further processing. In other sections, a strings key can be used by enclosing it in percent signs (%).

Parameter   *String_Key = Value*

Values   *String_Key* = A unique name made up of letters and digits.

Value = Letters, digits, or other printable characters. It should be enclosed in quotation marks if the corresponding string key is used in an entry that requires double quotation marks.

The following shows three examples of strings keys:

```
[Strings]
KEY_RUNONCE="SOFTWARE\Microsoft\Windows\CurrentVersion\RunOnce"
KEY_INSTALLEDCOMPS="SOFTWARE\Microsoft\Active Setup\Installed
Components\BatchRun"
KEY_IEXPLORERMAIN="Software\Microsoft\Internet Explorer\Main"
KEY_INTERNETSETTINGS="Software\Microsoft\Windows\CurrentVersion\Internet
Settings"
QuickLaunch_Path="Applic~1\Micros~1\Intern~1\QuickL~1"
CurrentVersion="Software\Microsoft\Windows\CurrentVersion"
PrimaryRec="ProfileReconciliation"
SecondaryRec="SecondaryProfileReconciliation"
```

[Install]

The [Install] section sets parameters for copying additional files as part of Windows 98 installation. The format for this section is identical to the format for the [Install] section in general INF files, as defined in Appendix C, "Windows 98 INF Files."

The following sections provide these examples for using the [Install] section for custom installations:

- Installing custom bitmaps and shortcuts.
- Enabling user profiles and remote administration.
- Replacing configuration entries.

[Install] Example: Copying Custom Files

This section describes Msbatch.inf entries for copying custom files while installing Windows 98. In the following example, custom files are copied for a bitmap file containing a corporate logo plus a shortcut to be placed in Network Neighborhood. These custom files must be created by the administrator and placed with the Windows 98 source files on the network.

```
[install]
CopyFiles=newfiles.Copy

[NEWFILES.Copy]
my_corp.bmp      ; bitmap file
my_link.lnk      ; file that contains the shortcut
```

Note that the most flexible means of providing custom links for multiple users is to use system policies. For information about using system policies to create a custom Network Neighborhood or a custom desktop, see Chapter 8, "System Policies."

[Install] Example: Enabling User Profiles and Remote Administration

If you plan to take advantage of user profiles and to allow administration of remote computers, you can enable these capabilities using setup scripts. The following entries are required in Msbatch.inf to enable these features.

```
[Install]
AddReg=User.Profiles, Reg.User.Box.One, User.Box.Two, Remote.Admin

[User.Profiles.Reg]
HKLM,"Network\Logon","UserProfiles",1,1
```

```
[User.Box.One]
HKCU,"%CurrentVersion%\%PrimaryRec%\Desktop",CentralFile,,"Desktop"
HKCU,"%CurrentVersion%\%PrimaryRec%\Desktop",Default,1,01,00,00,00
HKCU,"%CurrentVersion%\%PrimaryRec%\Desktop",DefaultDir,,"%10%\Desktop"
HKCU,"%CurrentVersion%\%PrimaryRec%\Desktop",LocalFile,,"Desktop"
HKCU,"%CurrentVersion%\%PrimaryRec%\Desktop",MustBeRelative,
     1,01,00,00,00
HKCU,"%CurrentVersion%\%PrimaryRec%\Desktop",Name,,"*.lnk,*.pif"
HKCU,"%CurrentVersion%\%PrimaryRec%\Desktop",RegKey,
     ,"%CurrentVersion%\Explorer\User Shell Folders"
HKCU,"%CurrentVersion%\%PrimaryRec%\Desktop",RegValue,,"Desktop"
HKCU,"%CurrentVersion%\%PrimaryRec%\NetHood",CentralFile,,"NetHood"
HKCU,"%CurrentVersion%\%PrimaryRec%\NetHood",Default,1,01,00,00,00
HKCU,"%CurrentVersion%\%PrimaryRec%\NetHood",DefaultDir,,"%10%\NetHood"
HKCU,"%CurrentVersion%\%PrimaryRec%\NetHood",LocalFile,,"NetHood"
HKCU,"%CurrentVersion%\%PrimaryRec%\NetHood",MustBeRelative,
     1,01,00,00,00
HKCU,"%CurrentVersion%\%PrimaryRec%\NetHood",Name,,"*.lnk,*.pif"
HKCU,"%CurrentVersion%\%PrimaryRec%\NetHood",RegKey,
     ,"%CurrentVersion%\Explorer\User Shell Folders"
HKCU,"%CurrentVersion%\%PrimaryRec%\NetHood",RegValue,,"NetHood"
HKCU,"%CurrentVersion%\%PrimaryRec%\Recent",CentralFile,,"Recent"
HKCU,"%CurrentVersion%\%PrimaryRec%\Recent",Default,1,01,00,00,00
HKCU,"%CurrentVersion%\%PrimaryRec%\Recent",DefaultDir,,"%10%\Recent"
HKCU,"%CurrentVersion%\%PrimaryRec%\Recent",LocalFile,,"Recent"
HKCU,"%CurrentVersion%\%PrimaryRec%\Recent",MustBeRelative,1,01,00,00,00
HKCU,"%CurrentVersion%\%PrimaryRec%\Recent",Name,,"*.lnk,*.pif"
HKCU,"%CurrentVersion%\%PrimaryRec%\Recent",RegKey,
     ,"%CurrentVersion%\Explorer\User Shell Folders"
HKCU,"%CurrentVersion%\%PrimaryRec%\Recent",RegValue,
     ,"Recent"


[User.Box.Two]
HKCU,"%CurrentVersion%\%PrimaryRec%\Start Menu",CentralFile,
     ,"Start Menu"
HKCU,"%CurrentVersion%\%PrimaryRec%\Start Menu",Default,1,01,00,00,00
HKCU,"%CurrentVersion%\%PrimaryRec%\Start Menu",DefaultDir,
     ,"%10%\Start Menu"
HKCU,"%CurrentVersion%\%PrimaryRec%\Start Menu",LocalFile,
     ,"Start Menu"
HKCU,"%CurrentVersion%\%PrimaryRec%\Start
Menu",MustBeRelative,1,01,00,00,00
HKCU,"%CurrentVersion%\%PrimaryRec%\Start Menu",Name,,"*.lnk,*.pif"
HKCU,"%CurrentVersion%\%PrimaryRec%\Start Menu",RegKey,
     ,"%CurrentVersion%\Explorer\User Shell Folders"
HKCU,"%CurrentVersion%\%PrimaryRec%\Start Menu",RegValue,,"Start Menu"
HKCU,"%CurrentVersion%\%SecondaryRec%\Programs",CentralFile,,"Programs"
HKCU,"%CurrentVersion%\%SecondaryRec%\Programs",Default,1,01,00,00,00
HKCU,"%CurrentVersion%\%SecondaryRec%\Programs",DefaultDir,
     ,"%10%\Start Menu\Programs"
```

```
HKCU,"%CurrentVersion%\%SecondaryRec%\Programs",LocalFile,
    ,"Start Menu\Programs"
HKCU,"%CurrentVersion%\%SecondaryRec%\Programs",MustBeRelative,
    1,01,00,00,00
HKCU,"%CurrentVersion%\%SecondaryRec%\Programs",Name,,"*.lnk,*.pif"
HKCU,"%CurrentVersion%\%SecondaryRec%\Programs",ParentKey,,"Start Menu"
HKCU,"%CurrentVersion%\%SecondaryRec%\Programs",RegKey,
    ,"%CurrentVersion%\Explorer\User Shell Folders"
HKCU,"%CurrentVersion%\%SecondaryRec%\Programs",RegValue,,"Programs"
HKCU,"%CurrentVersion%\%SecondaryRec%\Startup",CentralFile,,"Startup"
HKCU,"%CurrentVersion%\%SecondaryRec%\Startup",Default,1,01,00,00,00
HKCU,"%CurrentVersion%\%SecondaryRec%\Startup",DefaultDir,
    ,"%10%\Start Menu\Programs\Startup"
HKCU,"%CurrentVersion%\%SecondaryRec%\Startup",LocalFile,
    ,"Start Menu\Programs\Startup"
HKCU,"%CurrentVersion%\%SecondaryRec%\Startup",MustBeRelative,
    1,01,00,00,00
HKCU,"%CurrentVersion%\%SecondaryRec%\Startup",Name,,"*.lnk,*.pif"
HKCU,"%CurrentVersion%\%SecondaryRec%\Startup",ParentKey,,"Start Menu"
HKCU,"%CurrentVersion%\%SecondaryRec%\Startup",RegKey,
    ,"%CurrentVersion%\Explorer\User Shell Folders"
HKCU,"%CurrentVersion%\%SecondaryRec%\Startup",RegValue,,"Startup"

[Remote.Admin]
HKLM,"Security\Access\Admin\Remote",%Server_Domain_Username%,1,ff,00

[Network]
Security=<domain_or_server> ;enables user-level security
PassThroughAgent=<provider_name>
services=remotereg    ;installs the Microsoft Remote Registry agent

[strings]
; specifies the server containing the group or individual account
; to be allowed remote administration capabilities
Server_Domain_Username = "<server_or_domain\account>"
```

▶ **To define the custom values required for enabling remote administration**

1. To enable user-level security, set the appropriate values in the [Network] section for **Security=** and **PassThroughAgent=**.

   For example, on a NetWare network, if the security provider is a server named NWSVR1:

```
Security=server
PassThroughAgent=NWSVR1
```

On a Windows NT network, if the security provider is a domain named NTDOM1:

```
Security=Domain
PassThroughAgent=NTDOM1
```

2. In the [Strings] key, define the value for **%server_domain_username%** to specify the location for the list of user accounts, plus the names of accounts for users who will be allowed remote administration capabilities for this particular computer.

   For example, for a NetWare network, the following specifies the server containing the group or individual account, plus the account name to be given remote administration capabilities:

   ```
   Server_Domain_Username = "NWSVR\HELPDESK"
   ```

   For a Windows NT network, the following specifies the domain containing the account, plus the account name to be given remote administration capabilities:

   ```
   Server_Domain_Username = "NTDOM1\ADMIN"
   ```

Important You must also make sure that the related files supporting Microsoft Remote Registry services are installed with the Windows 98 source files. To do this, use INF Installer, as described in Chapter 3, "Custom Installations."

When you enable remote administration in this way, Setup automatically adds the appropriate Administrators account (including Supervisor and Domain Administrators under Windows NT) to the list of persons or groups allowed to administer the computer remotely, and sets the permissions required for remote administration.

Enabling user profiles in a setup script with Microsoft Batch 98 (**User Profiles** tab in the **General Setup Options** dialog box) is equivalent to using the User Profiles options in Control Panel (**User Profiles** tab in the **Passwords Properties** dialog box).

There are two ways to enable group policies. One way is by adding a line in the [OptionalComponents] section of a setup script, and the other way is by using the **Windows Setup** tab in Add/Remove Programs.

You can also enable group policies for both the Client for Microsoft Networks and Client for NetWare networks.

▶ **To enable group policies by editing a setup script**

- In your setup script, add the following line in the [OptionalComponents] section.

```
Group Policies=1
```

▶ **To enable group policies using Add/Remove Programs in Control Panel**

1. In Control Panel, double-click Add/Remove Programs.
2. Click the **Windows Setup** tab.
3. Select the **System Tools** check box and then click **Details**.
4. Select the **Group Policies** check box and then click **OK**.
5. Click **OK** again in the **Windows Setup** tab.

▶ **To enable group policies for both Client for Microsoft Networks and Client for NetWare networks**

- Add the following entries to Msbatch.inf:

```
[Install]
Addreg=User.Profiles.Reg, Group.Policies.Reg
Copyfiles=Group.Policies.Copy

[User.Profiles.Reg]
HKLM,Network\Logon,UserProfiles,1,1

[Group.Policies.Reg]
HKLM,Network\Logon,PolicyHandler,,"GROUPPOL.DLL,ProcessPolicies"
HKLM,System\CurrentControlSet\Services\MSNP32\NetworkProvider,
    GroupFcn,,"GROUPPOL.DLL,NTGetUserGroups"
HKLM,System\CurrentControlSet\Services\NWNP32\NetworkProvider,
    GroupFcn,,"GROUPPOL.DLL,NWGetUserGroups"

[Group.Policies.Copy]
grouppol.dll

[DestinationDirs]
Group.Policies.Copy = 11
```

For information about user profiles and group policies, see Chapter 8, "System Policies." For information about remote administration of a computer's registry, see Chapter 23, "System and Remote Administration Tools."

[Install] Example: Replacing Configuration Entries

This section presents some sample entries for replacing entries in configuration files as part of Windows 98 Setup.

Depending on the common network configuration at your site, you may determine that you need to remove a line from one or more configuration files as a global procedure before starting Windows 98 Setup. For example, you may want to use a protected-mode protocol, such as Microsoft TCP/IP, instead of the real-mode version of TCP/IP currently being using on the target computers. The following kinds of entries can be used to make these changes during the installation process.

Note If you want to remove TSRs when installing Windows 98 on a NetWare network, you should modify the Netdet.ini file rather than making modifications using Msbatch.inf. For information, see Chapter 17, "Windows 98 on Third-Party Networks."

```
[Install]
UpdateInis=update_prot.Ini
UpdateCfgSys=Update_config.sys
UpdateAutoBat=Update_autoexec.bat

[Update_prot.Ini]
system.ini,386enh,"device=mytcp.386"

[Update_config.sys]

[Update_autoexec.bat]
```

Windows 98 Network Adapter INF Summary

This section presents details about the settings for common network adapters, as defined in the [*netcard*.NDI] sections of the INF files provided with Windows 98. Other adapters are also listed; their settings can be found in the appropriate file in the Windows INF directory. The Net.inf file contains the master information for detecting and configuring network adapters. The specific INF files for network adapters include the following:

Net3com.inf	Netflex.inf	Netnice.inf	Netsmc.inf
Netamd.inf	Netgen.inf	Netnovel.inf	Netsmctr.inf
Netcable.inf	Nethp.inf	Netoli.inf	Nettcc.inf
Netcpq.inf	Netibm.inf	Netppp.inf	Nettulip.inf
Netdec.inf	Netmadge.inf	Netprot.inf	Netub.inf
Netee16.inf	Netncr.inf	Netracal.inf	Netxir.inf

For information about how to find entries for a particular network adapter in an INF file, see "[*netcard_ID*]" earlier in this appendix.

3COM

Cardbrand=3COM
INFFile=Net3com.inf

```
[*PNP80F3]
Interrupt=
IOAddress=
DMAChannel=
MaxTransmits=
DataTransfer=
XmitBufs=
Transceiver=
```

The following adapters also have settings in the file Nec3com.inf:

3Com EtherLink III
3Com EtherLink Plus
NCR Token-Ring 4 Mbps ISA
NCR Token-Ring 16/4 Mbps ISA

NCR StarCard
NCR WaveLAN AT
TokenLink

Digital Equipment Corporation

Cardbrand=Digital Equipment Corp.
INFFile= Netdec.inf

```
;DEC DE201 Etherworks Turbo TP
[*PNP80EB]
Interrupt=
IOAddress=
RamAddress=
MaxMulticasts=
Maxtransmits=
AdapterName=
```

The following adapters also have settings in the file Netdec.inf:

DEC (DE100) Etherworks LC
DEC (DE101) Etherworks LC/TP
DEC (DE102) Etherworks LC/TP_BNC
DEC (DE200) Etherworks Turbo
DEC (DE202) Etherworks Turbo/TP_BNC
DEC (DE210) Etherworks MC

DEC (DE211) Etherworks MC/TP
DEC (DE212) Etherworks MC/TP_BNC
DEC EE101 (Built-In)
DECpc 433 WS (Built-In)
DEC Ethernet (All Types)

IBM
Cardbrand=IBM
INFFile= Netibm.inf

```
;IBM Token Ring
[*PNP80C9]
MaxTransmits=
Primary
Alternate=
RecvBufs=
XmitBufs=
MaxPacketSize=
ProductID=
NetworkAddress=
Iobase=
RecvBufSize=
XmitBufSize=
```

The following adapters also have settings in the file Netibm.inf:

IBM Token Ring 4/16Mbs
IBM Token Ring II/Short
IBM Token Ring (All Types)

Intel
Cardbrand=Intel
INFFile= Netee16.inf

```
;Intel Etherexpress 16 or 16TP
[*PNP812]
IOBaseAddress=
IRQ=
IOAddress=
Transceiver=
IOChrdy=
IOChannelReady=
```

The following adapters also have settings in the file Netee16.inf:

Generic 595
Intel EtherExpress 16 (MCA)
Intel EtherExpress PRO

MADGE

Cardbrand=MADGE
INFFile= Netmadge.inf

```
;Madge Networks Smart 16/4 PC Ringnode
[*PNP81D7]
RxTxSlots=
NetworkAddress=
MaxFrameSize=
RxBufferSize=
TxBufferSize=
MaxTransmits=
Watchdog=
CopyAllData=
AutoOpen=
OpenOptions=
NoMmio=
PromiscuousModeX=

[MadgeISA]
IrqNumber=
IOAddress=
MemBase=
DMAChannel=
```

The following adapters also have settings in the file Netmadge.inf:

Madge Networks Smart 16/4 Ringnode (All ISA Types)
Madge Networks Smart 16/4 AT/P Ringnode
Madge Networks Smart 16/4 AT Ringnode
Madge Networks Smart 16/4 ISA Client Plus Ringnode
Madge Networks Smart 16 Ringnode

Novell

Cardbrand=Novell
INFFile= Netnovel.inf

```
[ne2000]
InterruptNumber=
IOBaseAddress=
Interrupt=
IOBase=
```

The following adapters also have settings in the file Netnovell.inf:

Artisoft AE-1
Artisoft AE-2 or AE-3
Ethernode 16-AT3
National Semiconductor Ethernode *16AT

National Semiconductor AT/LANTIC
NE1000 Compatible
Novell Ne2000 Plus
Zenith Data Systems NE2000 Compatible

Proteon
Cardbrand=Proteon
INFFile=Netprot.inf

```
;Proteon Token Ring (P1392)
[*pnp81eb]
IntLevel=
IOBase=
DMAChannel=
LinkSpeed=
CardSpeed=
Media=
CableType=
DMAClock=
SAEN=
MaxTransmits=
NetworkAddress=
```

The following adapters also have settings in the file Netprot.inf:

Proteon ISA Token Ring (1340)
Proteon ISA Token Ring (1342)
Proteon ISA Token Ring (1346)

Proteon ISA Token Ring (1347)
Proteon Token Ring (P1392+)
Proteon Token Ring (P1390)

Racal
Cardbrand=Racal
INFFile= Netracal.inf

```
; Racal NI6510
[*pnp8113]
IOBase=
MaxReceives=
MaxTransmits=
MaxMulticasts=
```

The Racal NI5210/8 or NI5210/16 adapter also has settings in the file Netracal.inf.

SMC
Cardbrand=SMC
INFFile= Netsmc.inf

```
;SMC9000
[*Smc9000]
Interrupt=
Port_Num=
Xt_Type=
Micro_Channel=
```

The following adapters also have settings in the file Netsmc.inf:

ArcNet Compatible
Pure Data PDI508+ (ArcNet)
Pure Data PDI516+ (ArcNet)
SMC ArcNet adapters

SMC EtherCard adapters
SMC EtherElite adapters
SMC StarCard PLUS adapters
SMC TokenCard Elite

Thomas-Conrad

Cardbrand=Thomas-Conrad
INFFile= Nettcc.inf

```
;Thomas-Conrad (All Arcnet Types)
[*pnp8326]
Interrupt=
IOBase=
MemoryBase=
PacketSize=
```

The following adapters also have settings in the file Nettcc.inf:

TC6045
TC6145
TC6245
Thomas-Conrad TC6042

Thomas-Conrad TC6142
Thomas-Conrad TC6242
Thomas-Conrad TC4035
Thomas-Conrad TC4045

Msbatch.inf Sample File

This section shows a sample setup script.

```
;MSBATCH.INF
;
;Copyright (c) 1995-1998 Microsoft Corporation.
;All rights reserved.
;

[BatchSetup]
Version=3.0 (32-bit)
SaveDate=03/13/98

[Version]
Signature = "$CHICAGO$"

[Setup]
Express=1        ; Allows user input.
InstallDir="C:\Windows"
                 ; Windows 98 installation directory
InstallType=3    ; Custom installation. Refer to the Install Type
                 ; parameter in the [Setup]section earlier in this
                 ; chapter for other installation types.
```

```
EBD=0                    ; Do no create a Windows 98 Startup disk.
ShowEula=0               ; Automatically agree to the terms specified in the
                         ; End User License Agreement and do not display it.
ChangeDir=0              ; Do not change the installation directory
                         ; from the default (C:\Windows is the default
                         ; directory for new installations).
OptionalComponents=1
                         ; Forces Setup to display the Select Components
                         ; dialog box during a batch installation.
                         ; You must set InstallType=3 with this setting.
CleanBoot=0              ; Do not force a new installation. Perform an upgrade
                         ; instead. For more information on running Setup
                         ; on a new computer or a computer with a reformatted
                         ; hard disk, see "Running Setup on a New Installation"
                         ; in Chapter 2 "Setting Up Windows 98."

DevicePath=0
NoDirWarn=1              ; Install Windows 98 over an existing Windows directory
                         ; without warning the user.

TimeZone="Pacific"
Uninstall=0
NoPrompt2Boot=1


[System]
Locale=L0409
SelectedKeyboard=KEYBOARD_00000409


[NameAndOrg]
Name="Pilar"
Org="Widgets"
Display=0


[Network]
ComputerName="Computer1"
Workgroup="Marketing"
Description="Test Computer (Compaq)"
Display=0
PrimaryLogon=VREDIR
                    ; Specifies the primary network logon client.
Clients=VREDIR, NWREDIR
Protocols=NETBEUI, NWLINK, MSTCP
Services=VSERVER, NWREDIR4
Security=DOMAIN
PassThroughAgent="Domain_Name"


[NWLINK]
Frame_Type=4
NetBIOS=0


[MSTCP]
LMHOSTS=1
```

```
            LMHOSTPath="C:\WINDOWS\Lmhosts"
                        ;Specifies the path for the LMHOSTS file.
            DHCP=1
            DNS=0
            WINS=D


            [NWREDIR]
            FirstNetDrive=G:
            PreferredServer=Preferred_Server_Name
            ProcessLoginScript=1


            [VREDIR]
            LogonDomain="Logon_Domain_Name"
            ValidatedLogon=1


            [VSERVER]
            LMAnnounce=0
            MaintainServerList=2


            [NWRedir4]
            PreferredTree=Preferred_Tree_Name
            NameContext=Name_Context-Name


            [OptionalComponents]; 0 means do not install the component.
                                 ; 1 means install it. The default is 0
            "Accessibility Options"=0
            "Accessibility Tools"=0
            "Briefcase"=1
            "Calculator"=1
            "Desktop Wallpaper"=1
            "Document Templates"=1
            "Games"=1
            "Imaging"=1
            "Mouse Pointers"=1
            "Paint"=1
            "Quick View"=1
            "Windows Scripting Host"=1
            "WordPad"=1
            "Dial-Up Networking"=1
            "Dial-Up Server"=1
            "Direct Cable Connection"=1
            "HyperTerminal"=0
            "Microsoft Chat 2.1"=1
            "Microsoft NetMeeting"=1
            "Phone Dialer"=0
            "Virtual Private Networking"=1
            "Baseball"=0
            "Dangerous Creatures"=0
            "Inside your Computer"=0
            "Jungle"=0
```

```
"Leonardo da Vinci"=0
"More Windows"=0
"Mystery"=0
"Nature"=0
"Science"=0
"Space"=0
"Sports"=0
"The 60's USA"=0
"The Golden Era"=0
"Travel"=0
"Underwater"=0
"Windows 95"=0
"Desktop Themes Support"=0
"Microsoft FrontPage Express"=1
"Microsoft VRML 2.0 Viewer"=0
"Microsoft Wallet"=0
"Personal Web Server"=0
"Real Audio Player 4.0"=1
"Web Publishing Wizard"=0
"Web-Based Enterprise Mgmt"=0
"Microsoft Outlook Express"=1
"Baltic"=0
"Central European"=0
"Cyrillic"=0
"Greek"=0
"Turkish"=0
"Audio Compression"=1
"CD Player"=1
"Macromedia Shockwave Director"=1
"Macromedia Shockwave Flash"=1
"Media Player"=1
"Microsoft NetShow Player 2.0"=1
"Multimedia Sound Schemes"=1
"Sample Sounds"=1
"Sound Recorder"=1
"Video Compression"=1
"Volume Control"=1
"America Online"=0
"AT&T WorldNet Service"=0
"CompuServe"=0
"Prodigy Internet"=0
"The Microsoft Network"=0
"Additional Screen Savers"=1
"Flying Windows"=1
"OpenGL Screen Savers"=1
"Backup"=0
"Character Map"=1
"Clipboard Viewer"=1
"Disk compression tools"=0
"Drive Converter (FAT32)"=0
```

```
                "Group policies"=1
                "Net Watcher"=1
                "System Monitor"=1
                "System Resource Meter"=1
                "WinPopup"=1
                "Web TV for Windows"=0

                [Printers]
                HP LaserJet 5Si=HP LaserJet 5Si,\\Print_Server_Name\Share
                HP LaserJet 4Si=HP LaserJet 4Si,LPT1

                [InstallLocationsMRU]    ; Path for Windows 98 installation point.
                "\\Server_Name\Share"

                [Install]
                AddReg=RunOnce.BatchDelay, Run.Installed.Components, Skip.PCMCIA.Wizard,
                User.Profiles.Reg, User.Box.One, User.Box.Two, RegistrySettings

                [RunOnce.BatchDelay]; Adds registry entries to the RunOnce key.
                HKLM,%KEY_RUNONCE%,BatchRun1,,"%25%\rundll.exe
                setupx.dll,InstallHinfSection Delete.MSN.Icon 4 %10%\msbatch.inf"
                HKLM,%KEY_RUNONCE%,BatchRun2,,"%25%\rundll.exe
                setupx.dll,InstallHinfSection Delete.OLS.Icons 4 %10%\msbatch.inf"
                HKLM,%KEY_RUNONCE%,BatchRun3,,"%25%\rundll.exe
                setupx.dll,InstallHinfSection Delete.Welcome 4 %10%\msbatch.inf"
                HKLM,%KEY_RUNONCE%,BatchRun4,,"%25%\rundll.exe
                setupx.dll,InstallHinfSection Delete.Regwiz 4 %10%\msbatch.inf"
                HKLM,%KEY_RUNONCE%,BatchRun5,,"%25%\rundll.exe
                setupx.dll,InstallHinfSection WinUpdate 4 %10%\msbatch.inf"
                HKLM,%KEY_RUNONCE%,WUShortcut,,"wupdmgr.exe -shortcut"

                [Delete.MSN.Icon]    ; Deletes the MSN icon from the Desktop.
                DelReg=MSN.Icon

                [MSN.Icon]              ; Deletes the MSN icon from the Desktop.
                HKLM,SOFTWARE\Microsoft\Windows\CurrentVersion\explorer\Desktop\NameSpac
                e\{4B876A40-4EE8-11D1-811E-00C04FB98EEC},,,

                [Delete.OLS.Icons]   ; Deletes links from OLS desktop folder.
                DelFiles=OLS.Icons
                UpdateInis=OLS.Folder

                [OLS.Icons]            ; Lists the OLS links to be deleted.
                aol.lnk
                at&two~1.lnk
                compus~1.lnk
                prodig~1.lnk
                themic~1.lnk
                aboutt~1.txt
```

```
[OLS.Folder]            ; Deletes the OLS folder after it has been emptied.
wininit.ini,DIRNUL,,"%25%\Desktop\Online~1=1"

[Delete.Welcome]      ; Disables the Welcome to Windows 98 screen
                      ; at startup.
DelReg=Registry.Welcome

[Registry.Welcome]    ; Disables the Welcome to Windows 98 screen
                      ; at startup.
HKLM,Software\Microsoft\Windows\CurrentVersion\Run,Welcome,,

[Delete.Regwiz]       ; Disables the Windows 98 Registration Wizard
                      ; at startup.
AddReg=Registry.Regwiz

[Registry.Regwiz]     ; Disables the Windows 98 Registration Wizard
                      ; at startup.
HKLM,Software\Microsoft\Windows\CurrentVersion\Welcome\Regwiz,@,1,01,00,
00,00
HKLM,Software\Microsoft\Windows\CurrentVersion,RegDone,1,01,00,00,00

[WinUpdate]           ; Disables Start → Settings → Windows Update.
AddReg=Registry.WinUpdate

[Registry.WinUpdate]; Disables Start → Settings → Windows Update.
HKLM,Software\Microsoft\Windows\CurrentVersion\Policies\Explorer,NoDevMg
rUpdate,0x10001,1
HKLM,Software\Microsoft\Windows\CurrentVersion\Policies\Explorer,NoWindo
wsUpdate,0x10001,1

[Run.Installed.Components]
                      ; Sets up the Batch Run for msbatch.inf and
                      ; calls the Installed.Components section.
HKLM,%KEY_INSTALLEDCOMPS%,,,">Batch98"
HKLM,%KEY_INSTALLEDCOMPS%,IsInstalled,1,01,00,00,00
HKLM,%KEY_INSTALLEDCOMPS%,Version,,"1,0,0,0"
HKLM,%KEY_INSTALLEDCOMPS%,StubPath,,"%25%\rundll.exe
setupx.dll,InstallHinfSection Installed.Components 4 %10%\msbatch.inf"

[Installed.Components]
                      ; Prepares additional sections to process.
AddReg=Browser.Settings, Proxy.Settings, Shell.Prep
BitReg=Shell.Settings
DelFiles=QuickLaunch.Icons

[Browser.Settings]   ; Specifies Home, First, Search, Support Pages
                     ; and Support Bar settings.
HKCU,%KEY_IEXPLORERMAIN%,"Start Page",,"http://YourLocalHomePage"
HKCU,%KEY_IEXPLORERMAIN%,"First Home
Page",,"http://www.microsoft.com/windows/memphis/default.asp"
```

```
HKCU,%KEY_IEXPLORERMAIN%,"Search
Page",,"http://home.microsoft.com/access/allinone.asp"
HKLM,%KEY_IEXPLORERMAIN%,"Search
Bar","http://home.microsoft.com/access/allinone.asp"
HKCU, "SOFTWARE\Microsoft\Internet
Explorer\Help_Menu_URLs",Online_Support,,"http://support.microsoft.com/s
upport"""


[Proxy.Settings]    ; Preconfigure proxy gateway settings for IE browser
HKCU,%KEY_INTERNETSETTINGS%,ProxyEnable,1,01,00,00,00
HKCU,%KEY_INTERNETSETTINGS%,ProxyOverride,,";<local>"
HKCU,%KEY_INTERNETSETTINGS%,ProxyServer,,"YourProxyServer:80"


[Shell.Prep]
HKCU,"Software\Microsoft\Internet
Explorer\Desktop\Components\0",Flags,01,00,00,00


[Shell.Settings]
HKCU,"Software\Microsoft\Internet
Explorer\Desktop\Components\0",Flags,0,20,1


[QuickLaunch.Icons] ; List of icons to be removed from Quick Launch
                    ; on the Taskbar.
launch~1.lnk
viewch~1.scf


[Skip.PCMCIA.Wizard]; Skips checking for real-mode PCMCIA drivers.
HKLM,System\CurrentControlSet\Services\Class\PCMCIA,SkipWizardForBatchSe
tup,,1


[User.Profiles.Reg] ; Enable User Profiles.
HKLM,"Network\Logon",UserProfiles,1,1


[User.Box.One]      ; Includes Desktop icons and Network Neighborhood
                    ; in user profile.
HKCU,"%CurrentVersion%\%PrimaryRec%\Desktop",CentralFile,,"Desktop"
HKCU,"%CurrentVersion%\%PrimaryRec%\Desktop",Default,1,01,00,00,00
HKCU,"%CurrentVersion%\%PrimaryRec%\Desktop",DefaultDir,,"%10%\Desktop"
HKCU,"%CurrentVersion%\%PrimaryRec%\Desktop",LocalFile,,"Desktop"
HKCU,"%CurrentVersion%\%PrimaryRec%\Desktop",MustBeRelative,
    1,01,00,00,00
HKCU,"%CurrentVersion%\%PrimaryRec%\Desktop",Name,,"*.lnk,*.pif"
HKCU,"%CurrentVersion%\%PrimaryRec%\Desktop",RegKey,
    ,"%CurrentVersion%\Explorer\User Shell Folders"
HKCU,"%CurrentVersion%\%PrimaryRec%\Desktop",RegValue,,"Desktop"
HKCU,"%CurrentVersion%\%PrimaryRec%\NetHood",CentralFile,,"NetHood"
HKCU,"%CurrentVersion%\%PrimaryRec%\NetHood",Default,1,01,00,00,00
HKCU,"%CurrentVersion%\%PrimaryRec%\NetHood",DefaultDir,,"%10%\NetHood"
HKCU,"%CurrentVersion%\%PrimaryRec%\NetHood",LocalFile,,"NetHood"
```

```
HKCU,"%CurrentVersion%\%PrimaryRec%\NetHood",MustBeRelative,
    1,01,00,00,00
HKCU,"%CurrentVersion%\%PrimaryRec%\NetHood",Name,,"*.lnk,*.pif"
HKCU,"%CurrentVersion%\%PrimaryRec%\NetHood",RegKey,
    ,"%CurrentVersion%\Explorer\User Shell Folders"
HKCU,"%CurrentVersion%\%PrimaryRec%\NetHood",RegValue,,"NetHood"
HKCU,"%CurrentVersion%\%PrimaryRec%\Recent",CentralFile,,"Recent"
HKCU,"%CurrentVersion%\%PrimaryRec%\Recent",Default,1,01,00,00,00
HKCU,"%CurrentVersion%\%PrimaryRec%\Recent",DefaultDir,,"%10%\Recent"
HKCU,"%CurrentVersion%\%PrimaryRec%\Recent",LocalFile,,"Recent"
HKCU,"%CurrentVersion%\%PrimaryRec%\Recent",MustBeRelative,1,01,00,00,00
HKCU,"%CurrentVersion%\%PrimaryRec%\Recent",Name,,"*.lnk,*.pif"
HKCU,"%CurrentVersion%\%PrimaryRec%\Recent",RegKey,
    ,"%CurrentVersion%\Explorer\User Shell Folders"
HKCU,"%CurrentVersion%\%PrimaryRec%\Recent",RegValue,
    ,"Recent"

[User.Box.Two]        ; Includes Start Menu and Program Groups
                      ; in User Profile.
[User.Box.Two]
HKCU,"%CurrentVersion%\%PrimaryRec%\Start Menu",CentralFile,
    ,"Start Menu"
HKCU,"%CurrentVersion%\%PrimaryRec%\Start Menu",Default,1,01,00,00,00
HKCU,"%CurrentVersion%\%PrimaryRec%\Start Menu",DefaultDir,
    ,"%10%\Start Menu"
HKCU,"%CurrentVersion%\%PrimaryRec%\Start Menu",LocalFile,
    ,"Start Menu"
HKCU,"%CurrentVersion%\%PrimaryRec%\Start
Menu",MustBeRelative,1,01,00,00,00
HKCU,"%CurrentVersion%\%PrimaryRec%\Start Menu",Name,,"*.lnk,*.pif"
HKCU,"%CurrentVersion%\%PrimaryRec%\Start Menu",RegKey,
    ,"%CurrentVersion%\Explorer\User Shell Folders"
HKCU,"%CurrentVersion%\%PrimaryRec%\Start Menu",RegValue,,"Start Menu"
HKCU,"%CurrentVersion%\%SecondaryRec%\Programs",CentralFile,,"Programs"
HKCU,"%CurrentVersion%\%SecondaryRec%\Programs",Default,1,01,00,00,00
HKCU,"%CurrentVersion%\%SecondaryRec%\Programs",DefaultDir,
    ,"%10%\Start Menu\Programs"
HKCU,"%CurrentVersion%\%SecondaryRec%\Programs",LocalFile,
    ,"Start Menu\Programs"
HKCU,"%CurrentVersion%\%SecondaryRec%\Programs",MustBeRelative,
    1,01,00,00,00
HKCU,"%CurrentVersion%\%SecondaryRec%\Programs",Name,,"*.lnk,*.pif"
HKCU,"%CurrentVersion%\%SecondaryRec%\Programs",ParentKey,,"Start Menu"
HKCU,"%CurrentVersion%\%SecondaryRec%\Programs",RegKey,
    ,"%CurrentVersion%\Explorer\User Shell Folders"
HKCU,"%CurrentVersion%\%SecondaryRec%\Programs",RegValue,,"Programs"
HKCU,"%CurrentVersion%\%SecondaryRec%\Startup",CentralFile,,"Startup"
HKCU,"%CurrentVersion%\%SecondaryRec%\Startup",Default,1,01,00,00,00
HKCU,"%CurrentVersion%\%SecondaryRec%\Startup",DefaultDir,
    ,"%10%\Start Menu\Programs\Startup"
```

```
          HKCU,"%CurrentVersion%\%SecondaryRec%\Startup",LocalFile,
             ,"Start Menu\Programs\Startup"
          HKCU,"%CurrentVersion%\%SecondaryRec%\Startup",MustBeRelative,
             1,01,00,00,00
          HKCU,"%CurrentVersion%\%SecondaryRec%\Startup",Name,,"*.lnk,*.pif"
          HKCU,"%CurrentVersion%\%SecondaryRec%\Startup",ParentKey,,"Start Menu"
          HKCU,"%CurrentVersion%\%SecondaryRec%\Startup",RegKey,
             ,"%CurrentVersion%\Explorer\User Shell Folders"
          HKCU,"%CurrentVersion%\%SecondaryRec%\Startup",RegValue,,"Startup"


     [RegistrySettings]    ; The registry files must be located in the
                           ; Windows 98 installation directory.
     HKLM,%KEY_RUNONCE%,BatchReg1,
        ,"%25%\regedit.exe /s "%1%\FileName.reg""
     HKLM,%KEY_RUNONCE%,BatchReg2,
        ,"%25%\regedit.exe /s "%1%\FileName.reg""
     HKLM,%KEY_RUNONCE%,BatchReg3,
        ,"%25%\regedit.exe /s "%1%\FileName.reg""
     HKLM,%KEY_RUNONCE%,BatchReg4,
        ,"\\ServerName\Share\Setup.exe"


     [DestinationDirs]
     OLS.Icons=25,Desktop\Online~1
     QuickLaunch.Icons=25,%QuickLaunch_Path%


     [Strings]
     KEY_RUNONCE="SOFTWARE\Microsoft\Windows\CurrentVersion\RunOnce"
     KEY_INSTALLEDCOMPS="SOFTWARE\Microsoft\Active Setup\Installed
     Components\BatchRun"
     KEY_IEXPLORERMAIN="Software\Microsoft\Internet Explorer\Main"
     KEY_INTERNETSETTINGS="Software\Microsoft\Windows\CurrentVersion\Internet
     Settings"
     QuickLaunch_Path="Applic~1\Micros~1\Intern~1\QuickL~1"
     CurrentVersion="Software\Microsoft\Windows\CurrentVersion"
     PrimaryRec="ProfileReconciliation"
     SecondaryRec="SecondaryProfileReconciliation"
```

APPENDIX E

Microsoft Systems Management Server

E

This appendix provides information about Microsoft Systems Management Server (SMS), which can be used to install and maintain Microsoft Windows 98 on networked computers.

For more information about Microsoft SMS, contact your Microsoft sales representative or see the documentation provided with SMS. For information online, connect to the Microsoft World Wide Web site at **http://www.microsoft.com/smsmgmt** and select BackOffice Information and White Papers.

Microsoft Systems Management Server Overview

In a corporate environment where you might have hundreds—or even thousands—of computers, the process of upgrading to Windows 98 can become complex, especially if you want to deploy Windows 98 on all computers at the same time. This appendix discusses how you can use Microsoft Systems Management Server to automate the large-scale deployment of Windows 98, making the upgrade process faster, easier, and less expensive for your organization. It also describes the services offered by SMS for centralized management of computers in an enterprise network, including inventory, software distribution and installation, management of shared applications, remote management and troubleshooting, and network protocol analysis.

SMS organizes computers into a hierarchy of sites. A site is a group of servers and client computers typically located in a single geographical area. A site can consist of one or more domains (that is, a set of servers and clients that are managed as a group) existing on the same local area network (LAN).

SMS uses the terms central, primary, and secondary to identify the capabilities of sites in the hierarchy. A *central site* is a primary site at the top of the hierarchy, from which all sites and computers in the hierarchy can be administered.

A *primary site* has its own Microsoft SQL Server database, which contains all of the hardware and software inventory information for the site and its subsites (sites attached below it in the hierarchy). The primary site can run the SMS Administrator tool for local administration of the site server and all subsites. A primary site must be running Windows NT Server.

A *secondary site* is a site that does not have a SQL Server database or the SMS Administrator tool. This site is administered from any site above it in the hierarchy and has no subsites. A secondary site must be running Windows NT Server.

A primary site can have either secondary sites or other primary sites beneath it in the hierarchy. A secondary site must have a primary site above it and can have no sites below it.

The following figure illustrates a sample SMS hierarchy. The hierarchical site structure is depicted on the administration console, so that you can easily identify a computer based on its location.

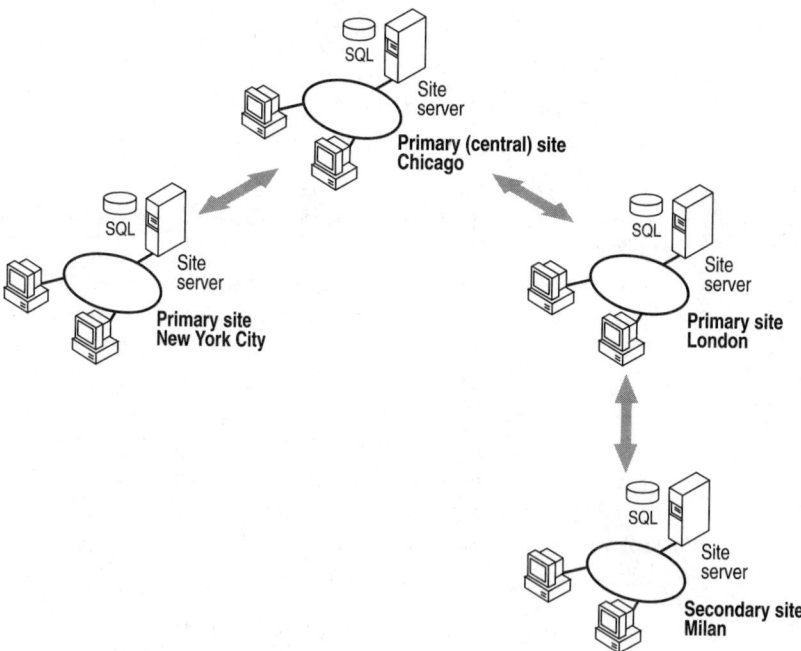

Systems Management Server Requirements

The following lists the basic requirements for using Microsoft Systems Management Server:

- Microsoft Windows NT Server version 3.51 or later.
- Microsoft SQL Server version 4.21 or later.
- A 486/66 MHz or higher processor.
- 32 MB of memory (recommended).
- 100 MB of available hard disk space (on the system disk).
- A CD-ROM drive supported by Windows NT Server.
- A network adapter.
- Microsoft Mouse or compatible pointing device (a mouse is recommended).

Microsoft SMS supports the following connection protocols and clients.

Supported protocols and clients

Connection protocols:

Asynchronous	Remote Access Service (RAS)
IPX/SPX	SNA
ISDN	TCP/IP
NetBEUI	X.25

Clients:

Apple Macintosh System 7	MS-DOS 5.0 or later
Digital Equipment Corporation	Sun Solaris
(DEC) Ultrix	Windows 3.1 or later
DEC VMS	Windows NT 3.1 or later
HP-UX	Windows for Workgroups 3.11 or later
IBM AIX	Windows 95 and Windows 98
IBM OS/2 version 1.x or 2.x	

(Many of the above clients may find their support though third-party add-ons.)

There are a variety of networking architectures that are supported by SMS. The clients that are supported by SMS are dependent on the network architecture as well. For a detailed list and the integration/interoperability capabilities see Appendix B of the *Microsoft Systems Management Server Getting Started Guide*.

The following table lists the typical requirements for sites in an SMS hierarchy, based on an installation of up to 1000 computers. These requirements are grouped according to how each server is used. Notice that all of the servers must be Windows NT Servers running on a Windows NT file system (NTFS) partition.

Systems Management Server servers

Server and processor type	RAM	Disk space	Recommendations
Central site server:			
Intel 486/66 Intel Pentium DEC Alpha	32 MB– 96 MB	1 GB	A high-performance computer is recommended due to the heavy load placed on the central site computer by Microsoft SMS and SQL Server.
Primary or secondary site server:			
Intel 486/66 Intel Pentium DEC Alpha	24 MB	50 MB– 100 MB	28 MB of RAM is required if SQL Server is on the same computer as the primary site server.
SQL Server:			
Intel 486/66 Intel Pentium DEC Alpha	20 MB	Varies	28 MB of RAM is required if SQL Server is on the same computer as the primary site server. Storage requirements depend on the size of the installation.

Systems Management Server Services

This section describes the services provided by SMS to make it easier to manage computers on the network.

Hardware and software inventory. SMS automatically retrieves detailed information about both the hardware and software for every computer within your enterprise, and stores the information in a standard SQL Server database. The inventory properties of the computer can include the microprocessor, the various drives, the network adapter, the memory, the interrupt request (IRQ) table, and a number of other hardware-related components.

Two types of software inventory information are available. The detailed identification inventory looks for a particular set of files (for example, EXE and DLL files) to verify that all of the required files are present and are valid versions. The comprehensive audit inventory checks the files on the computer's disk against a predefined list of applications. SMS can also collect copies of the computer's configuration files and add them to an archive. These inventory features are useful for tracking maintenance and planning upgrades.

Software distribution and installation. SMS makes it easy to automatically distribute commercial or internally developed applications, upgrades or fixes, or virus-checking software to selected personal computers on the local network and at remote sites. SMS distributes and installs software in package form. Packages can be used to install software on client computers. Packages can also install and share software on a network server, or identify existing software on target computers and collect specified files.

Management of shared applications. SMS can control access to shared applications to balance loads and provide fault tolerance and metering. When sharing applications, you can also automatically view a program group tailored to a specific user, no matter which computer the user uses to log on to the network. You determine which network users (or user groups) need access to specific server applications. The server applications database is replicated on all of the logon servers at a site.

Remote control and troubleshooting. SMS provides two remote management features: Help Desk and Diagnostics. *Help Desk* provides direct access to a client (including the ability to carry out commands, transfer files, and restart the computer), allowing you to troubleshoot and support individual remote computers. The *Diagnostics utilities* allow you to view the current hardware and software configuration of a workstation.

Network protocol analysis. The Network Monitor component of SMS is a diagnostic tool that allows you to look at the details of network packets, perform remote captures of packets anywhere on the network, and gather network statistics about a group of personal computers. It enables you to capture and analyze network traffic and detect connection problems or potential network bottlenecks.

The following publications may also provide more information about Systems Management Server:

- *Microsoft Systems Management Server Administrator's Guide*
- *Microsoft Systems Management Server Resource Kit*
- *Microsoft Systems Management Server Evaluation Guide*
- *Microsoft Systems Management Server Deployment Guide*
- *Microsoft Systems Management Server Getting Started Guide*
- *Microsoft Windows NT Server Resource Kit* (for Microsoft Windows NT Server version 4.0) (ISBN 1-57231-343-9)
- *Microsoft SQL Server Resource Kit*

Using Systems Management Server to Deploy Windows 98

Whether you are upgrading ten or ten thousand clients to Windows 98, SMS allows you to perform an automatic upgrade with no intervention from you or the user.

For an overall deployment plan, see the general and detailed discussions provided in Chapter 1, "Deployment Strategy," and Chapter 2, "Setting Up Windows 98." This section provides specific information about how SMS tools help you in planning for and automating the Windows 98 rollout to your company.

The first step in the upgrade process is to determine which of your computers are appropriate for upgrading to Windows 98. Using Systems Management Server, query the SQL Server database to locate all computers that match the upgrade specifications. A predefined query included in SMS examines the CPU, the operating system, the available hard disk space, the installed RAM, and so on. You can use this query as is or modify it to include additional criteria important to your installation.

After identifying the target computers, you are ready to roll out Windows 98 to target computers. The following is an overview of the steps involved in deploying Windows 98 with SMS.

- Create and share a package source directory for the Windows 98 files. This directory can be on any server that can be shared with the network.

- Copy the appropriate files from the Windows 98 compact disc to the new package source directory.

- From the SMS 1.2 SP3 compact disc, copy the following files to the package source directory:

  - Win98.inf from Sms\Logon.Srv\Mstest

  - Dos2w98.exe from Sms\Logon.Srv\Mstest (if you are setting up clients that run MS-DOS)

- Review the INF file for your configuration, and make appropriate changes (such as changing the time zone).

- Create a package containing the Windows 98 source directory.

- To install Windows 98 on one or more clients, create a mandatory job to distribute the package to the clients.

- Send the job to the target computers.

APPENDIX F

HOSTS and LMHOSTS Files for Windows 98

F

This appendix describes how to modify HOSTS and LMHOSTS files to support address-to-name resolution in Microsoft Windows 98 networking.

- The HOSTS file is used as a local Domain Name System (DNS) equivalent to resolve host names to Internet Protocol (IP) addresses.

- The LMHOSTS file is used for name resolution when a Windows Internet Naming Service (WINS) server is not available to resolve NetBIOS computer names to IP addresses.

Each of these files is also known as a *host table*. Sample versions of LMHOSTS (called Lmhosts.sam) and HOSTS files are added to the \Windows directory when you install Windows 98 with Transport Control Protocol/Internet Protocol (TCP/IP) support. These files can be edited using any ASCII editor, such as WordPad or Edit.

Important To use the HOSTS file for name resolution, the Enable DNS option must be selected. To do this, use the DNS Configuration tab in TCP/IP properties in the Network option in Control Panel.

Setting Up HOSTS Files

Microsoft TCP/IP can be configured to search the local host table file, HOSTS, for mappings of remote host names to IP addresses. The HOSTS file format is the same as the format for host tables in the version 4.3 Berkeley Software Distribution (BSD) UNIX */etc/hosts* file. For example, the entry for a computer with an address of 192.102.73.6 and a host name of trey.research.com looks similar to this:

```
192.102.73.6    trey.research.com
```

Edit the sample HOSTS file that is created when you install TCP/IP to include remote host names and their IP addresses for each computer with which you will communicate. This sample file also explains the syntax of the HOSTS file.

Host names are used in virtually all TCP/IP environments. A host name always corresponds to an IP address that is stored in a HOSTS file or on a DNS server and is assigned by an administrator to identify a TCP/IP host or default gateway. A host name can be used in place of an IP address when using **ping** or other TCP/IP utilities.

Host names are not used in the Windows 98 network user interface, such as Network Neighborhood or Net.exe. The only time a host name is used to access a Windows-based computer is when **ping** or **ftp** or another TCP/IP utility is used. In this case, the host name and corresponding IP address must be stored in a HOSTS file.

The HOSTS file is a static file used to map host names to IP addresses. This file provides compatibility with the UNIX HOSTS file. The following describes HOSTS file entries:

- A single entry consists of an IP address corresponding to one or more host names.

- Entries are case-sensitive. Therefore, it is a good idea to assign multiple host names with different cases.

For example, to connect to the UNIX host archive.research.com at the IP address 144.3.56.200, make two entries in the HOSTS file:

```
144.3.56.200 ARCHIVE.RESEARCH.COM
144.3.56.200 archive.research.com
```

This way, a user can connect to ARCHIVE using a utility, whether or not the CAPS LOCK is enabled.

A HOSTS file must reside on each system. By default, the host name **localhost** is an entry in the HOSTS file with the loopback address 127.0.0.1.

The HOSTS file is parsed whenever a host name is referenced. Names are read in a linear fashion. The most commonly used names should be near the beginning of the file. HOSTS file entries do not replace or interact with Windows-based NetBIOS computer names in any way.

The following shows the default HOSTS file provided with Windows 98.

```
# Copyright (c) 1994 Microsoft Corp.
#
# This is a sample HOSTS file used by Microsoft TCP/IP for Windows 98
#
# This file contains the mappings of IP addresses to host names. Each
# entry should be kept on an individual line. The IP address should
# be placed in the first column followed by the corresponding host name.
# The IP address and the host name should be separated by at least one
# space.
#
# Additionally, comments (such as these) may be inserted on individual
# lines or following the computer name denoted by a '#' symbol.
#
# For example:
#
#      102.54.94.97      rhino.acme.com          # source server
#      38.25.63.10       x.acme.com              # x client host
127.0.0.1      localhost
```

Setting Up LMHOSTS Files

When you use Microsoft TCP/IP on a local network with any combination of computers running Windows 98, Windows NT, LAN Manager, or Windows for Workgroups, server names are automatically mapped to their corresponding IP addresses. However, to map server names across remote networks connected by routers (or gateways), you can use the LMHOSTS file if WINS servers are not available on the network. The LMHOSTS file is commonly used to locate remote computers for Microsoft networking file, printer, and remote access services, and for domain services, such as logon, browsing, replication, and so on.

The LMHOSTS file used by Windows 98 contains mappings of IP addresses to Microsoft networking computer names (which are NetBIOS names). Microsoft LAN Manager 2.x TCP/IP LMHOSTS files are compatible with Microsoft TCP/IP.

Microsoft TCP/IP loads the LMHOSTS file into memory when the computer is started. The LMHOSTS file is a text file in the \Windows directory that lists the IP addresses and computer names of remote Windows networking servers that you want to communicate with. The LMHOSTS file should list all the names and IP addresses of the servers you regularly access.

For example, the LMHOSTS table file entry for a computer with an address of 192.45.36.5 and a NetBIOS computer name of Finance1 looks like this:

```
192.45.36.5     finance1
```

The format for the LMHOSTS file is the same as the format for host tables in 4.2 MSD UNIX systems, with the exception that LMHOSTS does not allow a scoped name to be indicated. The computer name is optionally enclosed in quotation marks (this is necessary for computer names that contain spaces).

▶ **To create an LMHOSTS file**

1. Use a text editor to create a file named LMHOSTS, or edit the default file named Lmhosts.sam in the \Windows directory and then save this file as LMHOSTS. This LMHOSTS file will be checked by default as the machine starts.

2. In the LMHOSTS file, type the IP address and the host name of each computer that you want to communicate with. Separate the items with at least one space.

Entries in the LMHOSTS file are not case-sensitive.

You will want to use LMHOSTS for smaller networks or to find hosts on remote networks that are not part of the WINS database (because name query requests are not broadcast beyond the local subnetwork). If WINS servers are in place on an internetwork, users do not have to rely on broadcast queries for name resolution, because WINS is the preferred method for name resolution. Therefore, with WINS servers in place, LMHOSTS may not be necessary.

However, the LMHOSTS file is read when WINS or broadcast name resolution fails, and resolved entries are stored in a system cache for later access. When the computer uses the replicator service and does not use WINS, LMHOSTS entries are required on import and export servers for any computers on different subnetworks participating in the replication.

You can use Notepad or any other text editor to edit the sample Lmhosts.sam file that is automatically installed in the \Windows directory. The following rules apply for entries in LMHOSTS:

- Each entry should be placed on a separate line.

- The IP address should begin in the first column, followed by the corresponding computer name.

- The address and the computer name should be separated by at least one space or tab.

- The # character is usually used to mark the start of a comment. However, it can also designate special keywords, as described in this section.

The keywords listed in the following table can be used in LMHOSTS using Microsoft TCP/IP. Notice, however, that LAN Manager 2.*x* treats these keywords as comments.

Keyword	Meaning
#PRE	Added after an entry to cause that entry to be preloaded into the name cache. #PRE entries in LMHOSTS are looked up and cached prior to WINS lookup. #PRE must be appended for entries that also appear in #INCLUDE statements; otherwise, the entry in #INCLUDE is ignored.
#DOM:*domain*	Added after an entry to associate that entry with the domain specified by *domain*. This keyword affects how the Browser and Logon services behave in routed TCP/IP environments. To preload a #DOM entry, you must also add the #PRE keyword to the line.
#INCLUDE *filename*	Forces the system to seek the specified *filename* and parse it as if it were local. Specifying a universal naming convention (UNC) *filename* allows you to use a centralized LMHOSTS file on a server. You must map the server before its entry in the #INCLUDE section, and also append #PRE to ensure that it is preloaded (otherwise, the #INCLUDE will be ignored).
#BEGIN_ALTERNATE	Used to group multiple #INCLUDE statements. Any single successful #INCLUDE statement causes the group to succeed.
#END_ALTERNATE	Used to mark the end of an #INCLUDE grouping.
\0x*nn*	Support for nonprinting characters in NetBIOS names. Enclose the NetBIOS name in quotation marks and use \0x*nn* hexadecimal notation to specify a hexadecimal value for the character. This allows custom applications that use special names to function properly in routed topologies. However, LAN Manager TCP/IP does not recognize the hexadecimal format, so you surrender backward compatibility if you use this feature. Notice that the hexadecimal notation applies only to one character in the name. The name should be padded with blanks so the special character is last in the string (character 16).

The following example shows how all of these keywords are used:

```
102.54.94.98    localsrv #PRE
102.54.94.97    trey     #PRE #DOM:networking #net group's PDC
102.54.94.102   "appname        \0x14"  #special app server
102.54.94.123   popular  #PRE #source server
```

```
#BEGIN_ALTERNATE
#INCLUDE \\localsrv\public\lmhosts      #adds LMHOSTS from this server
#INCLUDE \\trey\public\lmhosts          #adds LMHOSTS from this server
#END_ALTERNATE
```

In the preceding example:

- The servers named **localsrv** and **trey** are preloaded so they can be used later in an #INCLUDE statement in a centrally maintained LMHOSTS file.

- The server named **"appname   \0x14"** contains a special character after the 15 characters in its name (including blanks), so its name is enclosed in quotation marks.

- The server named **popular** is preloaded, based on the #PRE keyword.

Guidelines for LMHOSTS

When you use a host table file, be sure to keep it up to date and organized. Follow these guidelines:

- Update the LMHOSTS file whenever a computer is changed or removed from the network.

- Use #PRE statements to preload popular entries into the local computer's name cache and to preload servers that are included with #INCLUDE statements.

- Because LMHOSTS files are searched one line at a time from the beginning, you can increase the speed of searches for the entries used most often by placing frequently used servers near the top of the file. Follow these with less frequently used servers, and then remote #INCLUDE statements. The #PRE entries should be at the end of the file, because these are preloaded into the cache at system startup time and are not accessed later. Comment lines add to the parsing time, because each line is processed individually.

APPENDIX G

Shortcuts for Windows 98

G

This appendix summarizes the shortcuts that are built into Microsoft Windows 98 for using the keyboard and mouse to accomplish common actions quickly.

Shortcuts for Objects, Folders, and Windows Explorer

The following brief procedures and tables summarize the standard shortcuts for working with objects in the Windows 98 user interface, including folders on the desktop and Microsoft Windows Explorer.

▶ **To copy a file**
- Press CTRL while you drag the file to a folder.

▶ **To create a shortcut**
- Press CTRL+SHIFT while you drag the file to the desktop or a folder.

▶ **To close the current folder and all of its parent folders**
- Press SHIFT and click the **Close** button on the folder.

▶ **To tab through pages in a properties dialog box**
- Press CTRL+TAB or CTRL+SHIFT+TAB.

▶ **To switch between opening a new window and closing an existing window**

- Press CTRL and double-click a folder.

  If you have more than one window open, this operation closes the active window. If only one window is open, this operation will open a new window.

▶ **To bypass Autorun when inserting a compact disc**

- Press SHIFT while inserting the compact disc.

Common shortcuts for a selected object

Shortcut	Action
CTRL+C	Copy.
CTRL+O	Open.
CTRL+P	Print.
CTRL+S	Save.
CTRL+V	Paste.
CTRL+X	Cut.
CTRL+Z	Undo.
F1	Display contextual Help window.
SHIFT+F1	Activate context-sensitive Help mode (What's This?).
SHIFT+F10	Display pop-up menu.
SPACEBAR	Select (same as 1 click of mouse button).
ESC	Cancel.
ALT	Activate or inactivate menu bar mode.
ALT+TAB	Display next primary window.
ALT+ESC	Display next window.
ALT+SPACEBAR	Display pop-up menu for window.
ALT+HYPHEN	Display pop-up menu for active child window (MDI).
ALT+ENTER	Display properties.
ALT+F4	Close active window.
ALT+F6	Switch to next window within application (between modeless secondary windows and their primary window).
ALT+PRINT SCREEN	Capture focus window to Clipboard.
PRINT SCREEN	Capture desktop image to Clipboard.
CTRL+ESC	Access **Start** button in taskbar.
F2	Rename.
F3	Find.

Common shortcuts for a selected object (*continued*)

Shortcut	Action
DELETE	Delete.
SHIFT+DELETE	Delete file immediately without putting it in Recycle Bin.
ALT+double-click	Display properties.
CTRL+click the right mouse button	Place alternative commands on the pop-up menu (**Open With**).
SHIFT+double-click	Explore an object; if the object does not have an **Explore** command, this starts the default action (usually the **Open** command).
CTRL+F6	Display next child window (MDI).
CTRL+TAB	Display next tabbed page or child window (MDI).
CTRL+ALT+DEL	Reserved for system use.

Shortcuts for managing folders and Windows Explorer

Shortcut	Action
F4	In Windows Explorer, display combo box and move input focus to list.
F5	Refresh display.
F6 (TAB)	In Windows Explorer, move focus between panes.
CTRL+G	In Windows Explorer, choose **Go To** command.
CTRL+Z	Undo.
CTRL+A	Select All.
BACKSPACE	Go to parent folder.

Shortcuts in the Windows Explorer tree

Shortcut	Action
* on numeric keypad	Expand everything under selection.
+ on numeric keypad	Expand selection.
– on numeric keypad	Collapse selection.
RIGHT ARROW	Expand current selection if it is not expanded; otherwise, go to first child.
ALT+RIGHT ARROW	Move forward to a previous view.
LEFT ARROW	Collapse current selection if it is expanded; otherwise, go to parent.
ALT+LEFT ARROW	Move backward to a previous view.
CTRL+ARROW	Scroll without moving selection.
SHIFT+click the **Close** button	Close selected folder and all of its parent folders.

Shortcuts for Internet Explorer

Shortcut	Action
TAB+ENTER	Activate a selected link.
SHIFT+F10	Display a shortcut menu for a link.
CTRL+O	Go to a new location.
ALT+RIGHT ARROW	Go to next page.
ALT+LEFT ARROW	Go to previous page.
SHIFT+CTRL+TAB	Move back between frames.
CTRL+TAB	Move forward between frames.
HOME	Move to beginning of document.
END	Move to end of document.
CTRL+N	Open a new window.
CTRL+P	Print current page or active frame.
F5	Refresh current page.
UP ARROW	Scroll toward beginning of a document.
PAGE UP	Scroll toward beginning of a document in larger increments.
DOWN ARROW	Scroll toward end of a document.
PAGE DOWN	Scroll toward end of a document in larger increments.
ESC	Stop downloading a page.
CTRL+S	Save current page.
CTRL+ARROW	Skip to break and separation characters in URLs (// / . , ? +).
CTRL+END	Skip to the end of the auto-completed URL.

Shortcuts in the common Open and Save dialog boxes

Shortcut	Action
ESC	Cancel current task.
ALT+*underlined letter*	Click corresponding command.
ENTER	Click selected button.
TAB	Move forward through options.
SHIFT+TAB	Move backward through options.
CTRL+TAB	Move forward though tabs.
CTRL+SHIFT+TAB	Move backward though tabs.
SPACEBAR	Click a button if current control is a button; select (clear) check box if current control is a check box; or click option if current control is an option button.
BACKSPACE	Open a folder one level up, if it is selected in **Save As** or **Open** dialog box.

Shortcuts in the common Open and Save dialog boxes (*continued*)

Shortcut	Action
F4	Display **Look In** or **Save In** list within **Save As** or **Open** dialog box.
F5	Refresh view.
BACKSPACE	Go to parent folder if focus is on View window.

General Keyboard-only Commands

The following table shows commands for completing actions from the keyboard.

General keyboard-only commands

Shortcut	Action
ALT+ESC	Display next window.
ALT+SPACE	Display pop-up window for window.
ALT+HYPHEN	Display pop-up window for active child window.
ALT+ENTER	Display properties.
ALT+*underlined letter in menu bar*	Carry out corresponding command on main menu bar, such as **Format** menu bar.
SHIFT+*underlined letter in menu item*	Carry out corresponding command of menu item, such as **Font** command, located in **Format** menu.
ALT+F4	Close application or window.
ALT+F6	Switch to next window in application.
ALT+TAB	Switch to window you last used, or switch to another window by holding down ALT and repeatedly pressing TAB.
ALT+PRINT SCREEN	Copy active window to Clipboard.
PRINT SCREEN	Copy desktop to Clipboard.
CTRL+F4	Close current window in (MDI) programs.
CTRL+F6	Display next child window.
CTRL+ALT+DEL	Task List.
F1	Start Help.
F10	Go to menu mode.
SHIFT+F10	Display context menu for selected item.
CTRL+ESC	Display **Start** menu and move focus to taskbar.
CTRL+ESC, ESC	Move focus on taskbar so you can use TAB and then SHIFT+F10 for context menu, or use TAB and arrow key to change tasks, or use TAB to go to desktop.

General keyboard-only commands (*continued*)

Shortcut	Action
ALT+TAB	Switch to next running application.
ALT+M	When focus is on taskbar or desktop, minimize all windows and move focus to desktop.
ALT+S	When no windows are open and no items are selected on desktop, display **Start** menu; then use arrow keys to select menu commands.

Accessibility Shortcuts

The following table summarizes the Windows 98 shortcuts for Accessibility features. For more information about these features, see Appendix H, "Accessibility."

Accessibility shortcuts

Shortcut	Action
Press SHIFT 5 times	Toggle StickyKeys on and off.
Press RIGHT SHIFT for 8 or more seconds	Toggle FilterKeys (SlowKeys, RepeatKeys, and BounceKeys) on and off.
Press NUM LOCK for 5 seconds	Toggle ToggleKeys on and off.
Press LEFT ALT+LEFT SHIFT+NUM LOCK	Toggle MouseKeys on and off.
Press LEFT ALT+LEFT SHIFT+PRINT SCREEN	Toggle High Contrast mode on and off.

Microsoft Natural Keyboard Keys

The following table summarizes the shortcut keys available on the Microsoft Natural® Keyboard.

Microsoft Natural Keyboard (Windows) keys

Shortcut	Action
Application key or SHIFT+F10	Display pop-up menu for selected object.
Windows logo key	Display **Start** menu.
WIN+F1	Start Help.
WIN+TAB	Cycle through taskbar buttons.
WIN+E	Start Windows Explorer.
WIN+F	Find files or folders.
WIN+CTRL+F	Find computer.

Microsoft Natural Keyboard (Windows) keys (*continued*)

Shortcut	Action
WIN+M	Minimize All.
SHIFT+WIN+M	Undo Minimize All.
WIN+R	Display **Run** dialog box.
WIN+BREAK	Hot key used to display **System Properties** dialog box; reserved for system use.
WIN+*number*	Reserved for manufacturer's use.

APPENDIX H

Accessibility

This appendix describes how to install, configure, and use features in Microsoft Windows 98 that support enhanced accessibility. Network administrators and users with disabilities will find this appendix useful in setting up custom installations. Many accessibility features will also be of interest to users without disabilities such as anyone using Windows 98 without a mouse. This appendix also provides information about Microsoft products and services that make Windows 98 more accessible for people with disabilities.

In This Appendix

See Also

- For information about creating custom setup support to accommodate accessibility needs, see Chapter 3, "Custom Installations."

Overview of Accessibility

Microsoft is committed to making computers easier to use for everyone, including individuals with disabilities. In recent years, Microsoft has established close relationships with users who have disabilities, organizations representing disabled individuals, workers in the rehabilitation field, and software developers who create products for this market. Based on their combined input, Microsoft has defined specific design goals for Windows 98:

- Continue to integrate and improve the Windows 95 features that compensate for difficulties some individuals have in using the keyboard or the mouse.

- Continue to make the visual user interface easier to customize for people with limited vision.

- Provide additional visual feedback for users who are deaf or hard-of-hearing.
- Provide new application programming interfaces (APIs) and "hooks" for independent software vendors (ISVs) developing accessibility aids, including those that allow blind individuals to use Windows.
- Make information on accessibility solutions more widely available, and increase public awareness of these issues.

Windows 98 offers several enhancements designed to meet these accessibility goals. The primary improvements in accessibility for Windows 98 from previous versions of Windows are:

- Scalable user interface elements, including large and extra-large mouse cursors.
- An expanded selection of high-contrast color schemes designed to address various forms of vision impairment.
- Visual cues to tell the user when the application is making sounds.
- Notification to other applications when the user has limited vision, needs additional keyboard support because of difficulty using a mouse, or wants visual captions to be displayed for speech or other sounds.
- Notification to other applications when they should modify behavior to be compatible with accessibility software utilities running in the system.
- Audible prompts during Setup for users who have low vision.

In addition to enhancing the accessibility features available through Control Panel, Windows 98 introduces two new accessibility tools:

- The Accessibility Wizard, which makes it easier for users and administrators to set up accessibility options by selecting from examples instead of having to change numeric values or individual settings in Control Panel.
- The Magnifier, a limited-function screen enlarger that makes Windows easier to see for users with low vision and for users who require occasional screen magnification for such specific tasks as editing art.

Installing Accessibility Options

Windows 98 Setup retains the Accessibility Options that were previously installed automatically when upgrading from earlier versions of Windows. To use a computer that does not have Accessibility Options installed on the hard drive, or to install the Accessibility Tools and the additional color and pointer schemes added to Windows 98, perform the following procedures.

▶ **To install Accessibility Options**

1. Select **Start.**

2. Select **Settings.**

3. Select Control Panel.

4. Select Add/Remove Programs Properties.

5. Select **Windows Setup**.

   The **Windows Setup** tab appears. If all the accessibility components have been installed, the **Accessibility** check box displays a check mark.

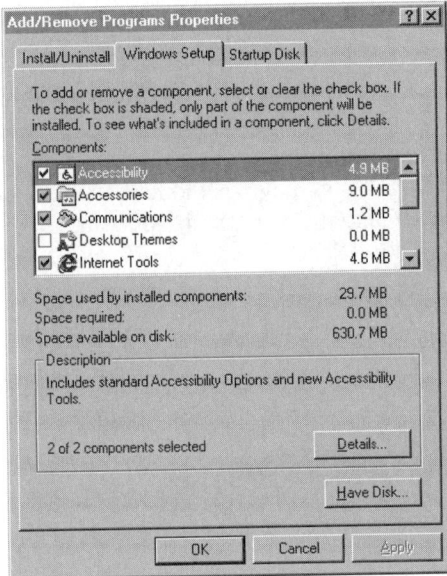
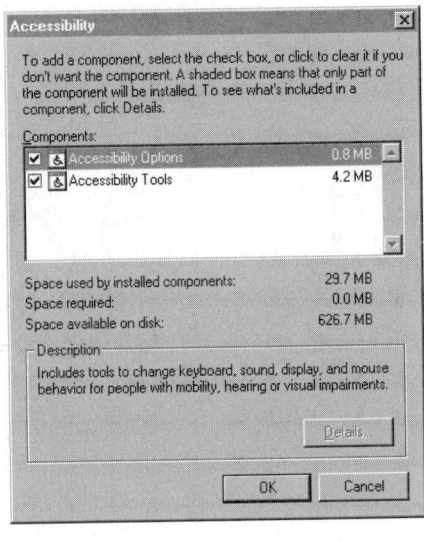

6. In the **Components** list, select **Accessibility.**

7. Select **Details**.

   The **Accessibility** dialog box appears. **Accessibility Options** and **Accessibility Tools** are displayed as two options in the list.

8. Select the **Accessibility Options** check box.

9. Select the **Accessibility Tools** check box.

10. Select **OK.**

11. On the **Add/Remove Programs Properties** page, select **OK.**

Note If you used a compact disc to install Windows, you are prompted to insert it into your computer.

Configuring Accessibility Features Using Control Panel

The Accessibility Options icon in Control Panel controls most of the accessibility features in Windows 98. Users can customize display, keyboard, mouse, and sound operation for their own particular needs. This section presents each feature in detail. Most users will find it easier to configure their settings using the Accessibility Wizard. See "Configuring Accessibility Features with the Accessibility Wizard" later in this chapter.

A few features are available only through Control Panel settings. These include:

- Large fonts.
- Some of the Filter Keys functions.
- All 27 high-contrast custom color schemes (six are available through the Accessibility Wizard, but you may wish to look at the expanded library available through the **Custom** list in the **Display** tab).

Features for Making the Display Easier to See

This section describes the specific accessibility features that Windows 98 provides to make the display easier to see for users with limited vision, including:

- Scalable user interface elements.
- Customizable display for the mouse pointer.
- High-contrast mode.

Scalable User Interface Elements

Users who have limited vision or who suffer eyestrain during normal use of a video display can now adjust the sizes of window titles, scroll bars, borders, menu text, and other standard screen elements.

▶ **To change the color and size of standard screen elements**

1. Select **Start.**
2. Select **Settings.**
3. Select Control Panel.
4. Select Display.
5. Select the **Appearance** tab.

   Use the **Scheme** list to select sample schemes. The selected schemes will be displayed. You can customize item and font choices in the **Item** and **Font** lists after selecting an entry in the **Scheme** list.

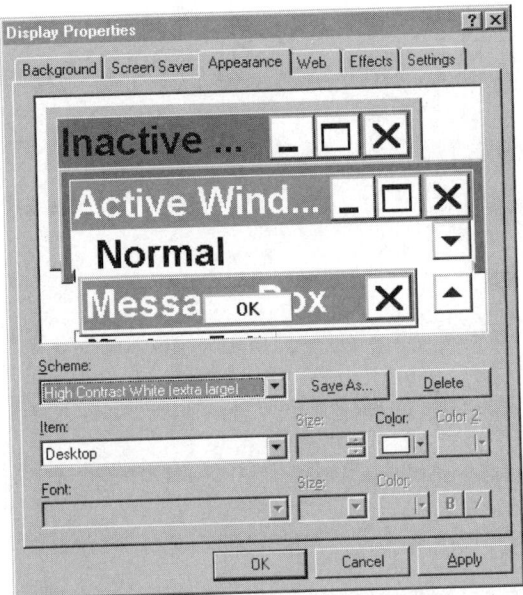

Customizable Display for the Mouse Pointer

Users who have difficulty seeing or following the mouse pointer can now set the following characteristics to improve visibility of the mouse pointer:

- Pointer size
- Pointer color
- Speed of the pointer
- Visible trails of pointer movement
- Animation of the pointer

Customizable mouse pointer display schemes are loaded automatically when you install Windows 98 from the compact disc using the Typical setup. If another setup option was chosen, use the Add/Remove Programs option in Control Panel to install the mouse pointer display schemes from the compact disc. In addition, with the Windows 98 compact disc, the user can install color schemes and select from red, gray, yellow, green, or violet 16-color schemes for the mouse pointer.

▶ **To change the pointer size and color**

1. Select **Start.**
2. Select **Settings**.
3. Select Control Panel.
4. Select Mouse.
5. Select the **Pointers** tab.

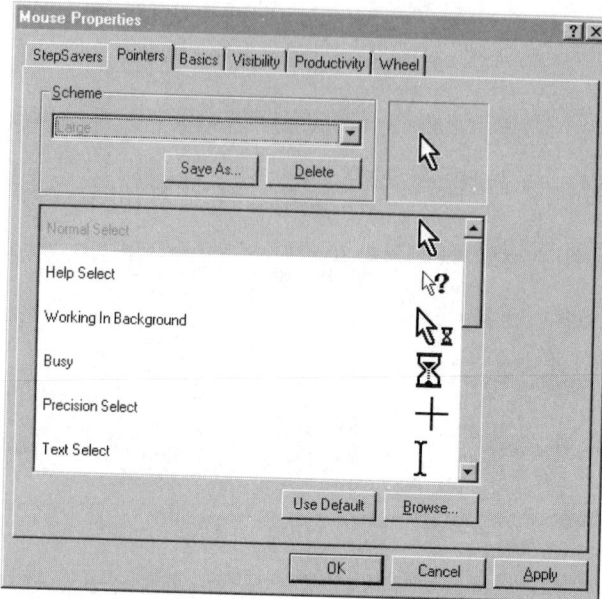

6. Select the scheme you want from the **Scheme** list.

   Sample pointers appear in the lower list.

7. Select **OK**.

▶ **To change pointer speed or add trails**

1. Select **Start**.

2. Select **Settings**.

3. Select Control Panel.

4. Select Mouse.

5. Select the **Visibility** tab.

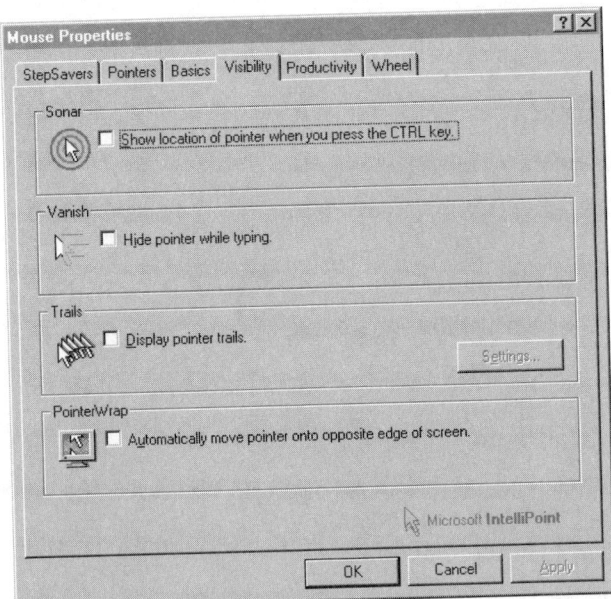

Use the Pointer Speed slider to set the speed of the pointer. Select the **Display pointer trails** check box to display pointer trails, and use the slider to set the length of the pointer trails.

Note Not all displays support mouse pointer color schemes. Windows 98 features an animated hourglass pointer for better viewing.

High-Contrast Mode

Many users with low vision require a high degree of contrast between foreground and background objects to distinguish the objects. For example, some users may not be able to read black text on a gray background, or text drawn over a picture easily. By setting a global flag, users can instruct Windows 98 and applications to display information with a high degree of contrast. Activating high-contrast mode automatically selects the user's preferred color scheme.

Through both Control Panel and the Accessibility Wizard, Windows 98 offers 12 high-contrast screen selections optimized for individuals with low vision.

▶ **To set screen colors in high-contrast mode**

1. Select **Start.**

2. Select **Settings.**

3. Select Control Panel.

4. Select Accessibility Options.

5. Select **Display.**

6. Select **Settings.**

   The **Settings for High Contrast** dialog box appears.

7. Select **Custom.**

8. Select the display you want from the **Custom** list.

9. Select **OK.**

▶ **To set the High Contrast hot key**

1. Select **Start.**

2. Select **Settings.**

3. Select Control Panel.

4. Select Accessibility Options.

5. Select **Display.**

6. Select **Settings.**

   The **Settings for High Contrast** dialog box appears.

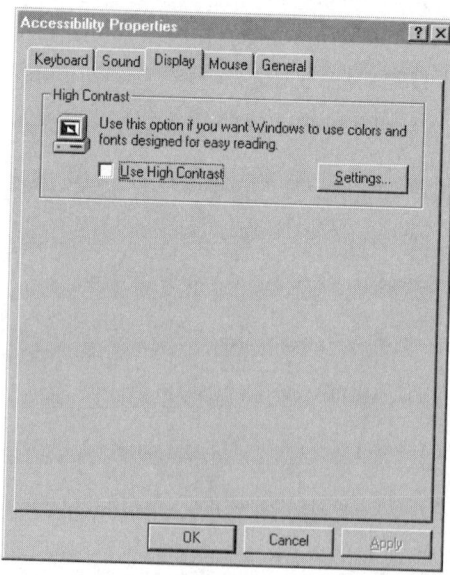
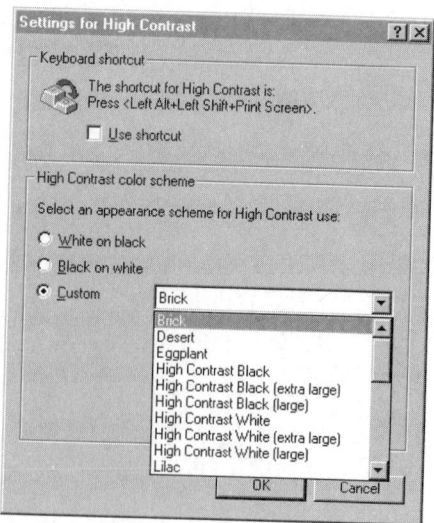

7. Select the **Use shortcut** check box.

   The shortcut key for High Contrast (left ALT+left SHIFT+PRINT SCREEN) is enabled.

8. Select **OK**.

Note You can also activate High Contrast mode using Magnifier.

Features for Making Keyboard and Mouse Input Easier

This section describes accessibility features that assist users who may have difficulty using the keyboard or the mouse. Notice that even without installing accessibility features, you can use the TAB key in dialog boxes to move the focus (that is, the outline that indicates where you are currently working in the dialog box), and you can use the arrow keys to select items in a list. In property sheets that have multiple tabs, you can press CTRL+TAB to select each property sheet in order from left to right. Or you can press the TAB key until the focus is in the tab for the current property sheet, and then press an arrow key to select the next sheet. See "Using Keyboard Navigation" later in this chapter for lists of shortcut keys to use throughout Windows 98.

StickyKeys for One-Finger or Mouthstick Typing

Many software programs require you to press two or three keys at a time. For people who type using a single finger or a mouthstick, that is not possible. *StickyKeys* allows you to press one key at a time and instructs Windows to respond as if the keys had been pressed simultaneously.

When StickyKeys is on, pressing any modifier key (CTRL, ALT, or SHIFT) "latches" that key down until you release the mouse button or press a key that is not a modifier key. Pressing a modifier key twice in a row locks the key down until it is tapped a third time.

▶ **To adjust StickyKeys settings**

1. Select **Start**.

2. Select **Settings**.

3. Select Control Panel.

4. Select Accessibility Options.

5. Select **Keyboard**.

   The **Keyboard** tab appears.

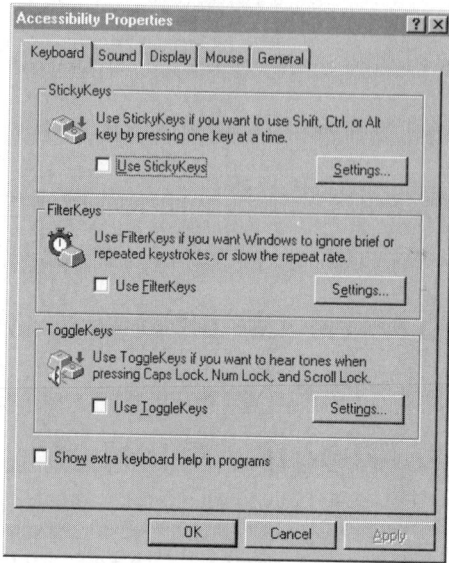
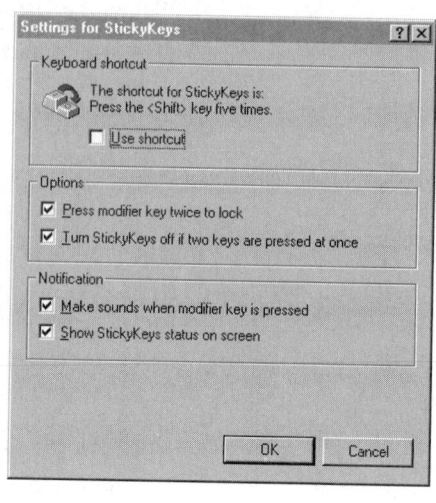

6. To configure StickyKeys, select the related **Settings** button.

   The **Settings for StickyKeys** dialog box appears.

7. Select the options you want from the check boxes.

8. Select **OK**.

▶ **To turn StickyKeys on or off by using an emergency hot key**

- Press the SHIFT key five times.

  If you have the sound features of StickyKeys enabled, you hear a rising siren tone when StickyKeys is turned on or off using the hot key.

StickyKeys operates in two modes: Latched mode and Locked mode:

- Tapping *once* on a modifier key puts it into *Latched mode*. If the StickyKeys sound features are enabled, you hear a short low beep/high beep. When the next non-modifier key is pressed, the modifier key(s) are released.

- Tapping *twice* in succession on a modifier key puts it into *Locked mode*. If the StickyKeys sound features are enabled, you hear a short low beep/high beep after the first tap and a single high beep after the second tap. Once a modifier key is locked, it stays locked until it is pressed a third time.

- Any and all of the modifier keys (SHIFT, CTRL, and ALT) can be latched or locked in combination.

For shared computers, there is an optional feature to keep non-disabled people from being confused when StickyKeys is left on. Whenever other people use the keyboard, they can hold the modifier key down and strike another key simultaneously. If the option **Turn StickyKeys Off When Pressing Two Keys At Once** is enabled, StickyKeys detects that two keys are held down simultaneously and automatically turns the StickyKeys feature off.

Some people do not like to have keyboard sounds, while others find them useful. You can turn feedback sounds on or off in the StickyKeys properties by using the option **Make Sounds When Modifier Key Is Pressed.**

Also, it is possible to disable the Locked mode of StickyKeys by making sure the **Press Modifier Key Twice To Lock** check box is not selected.

FilterKeys for Controlling Keyboard Input

Windows 98 includes features designed to work either separately or in combination to address problems related to keyboard sensitivity. These features are grouped as *FilterKeys* and are known separately as SlowKeys, BounceKeys, and RepeatKeys. These options include the following:

- *SlowKeys* instructs Windows to disregard keystrokes that are not held down for a minimum period of time. This allows you to brush against keys without any effect. When you place a finger on the proper key, you can hold the key down until the character appears on the screen.

- *RepeatKeys* enables you to adjust the repeat rate or disable the key-repeat function on your keyboard. Most keyboards allow you to repeat a key just by holding it down. Although this automatic repeat feature can be convenient for some people, it poses a problem for individuals who cannot lift their fingers off the keyboard quickly.

- *BounceKeys* instructs the computer to ignore keystrokes that are repeated quickly. This is useful for people with tremors whose fingers tend to bounce on the keys when pressing or releasing them.

You can adjust FilterKeys settings by using the Accessibility Options icon in Control Panel, or you can turn a specific FilterKeys feature on or off by using an emergency hot key.

To activate FilterKeys with your default settings, hold down the right SHIFT key for at least eight seconds.

The following sequence of events happens:

1. After four seconds, three short warning beeps sound. This enables you to stop the process if you were turning on FilterKeys accidentally.

2. After four more seconds, a single rising siren indicates that FilterKeys is turned on, using the previously chosen or default settings.

3. After four more seconds, you hear two rising siren sounds, which signal the first level of emergency settings: no key repeats, no acceptance delay, and ignoring repeated keystrokes.

4. After four more seconds (a total of about 16 seconds), you hear three rising sirens, which signal the second level of emergency settings: no key repeats, with an acceptance delay of two seconds.

When you disable FilterKeys (using the same keyboard action), you hear a falling siren.

You can adjust the FilterKeys settings so that unwanted functions have no effect.

▶ **To adjust FilterKeys settings**

1. Select **Start**.

2. Select **Settings**.

3. Select Control Panel.

4. Select Accessibility Options.

5. Select **Keyboard.**

   The **Keyboard** tab appears.

6. Select the **Settings** button related to FilterKeys.

7. Select **Ignore Repeated Keystrokes**, and then select the related **Settings** button.

8. The **Advanced Settings for FilterKeys** dialog box appears.

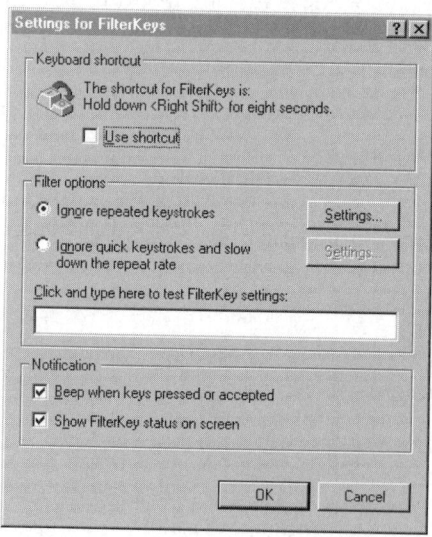
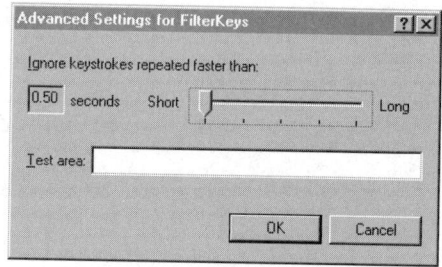

9. Drag the slider to show how much time must elapse after you press a key before subsequent presses of the same key are accepted.

– Or –

Select **Ignore Quick KeyStrokes**, and then select the related **Settings** button. You can then configure settings for RepeatKeys and SlowKeys.

For RepeatKeys, which overrides the settings made using the Keyboard properties in Control Panel:

- First choose whether you want to slow down the repeat rate on the keyboard or disable the repeat altogether.

- If you choose to slow down the repeat rate, drag a slider to set the length of time you must hold a key down before it begins to repeat. If you have trouble releasing a key in time, set this to a long setting. Then drag the second slider to indicate how long to wait between repeated keystrokes for the key that is held down.

- For SlowKeys, define the acceptance delay, which allows you to adjust the amount of time that you must hold a key down before it is accepted by the computer.

Another very useful FilterKeys feature is the option **Beep When A Key Is Pressed**. If this option is on and any FilterKeys functions are active, you hear a beep when you press the key or when the key repeats. For example, if SlowKeys is active, you hear a sound when the key is pressed and when the computer accepts the key. This can be useful when the keyboard is set to respond differently than usual.

ToggleKeys for Audio Cues on the Key's State

People with visual impairments may not be able to see the lights on the keyboard that indicate CAPS LOCK, NUM LOCK, and SCROLL LOCK status. ToggleKeys provides audio cues—high and low beeps—to tell you whether these keys are active or inactive. If ToggleKeys is enabled, when you press one of these keys and it turns on, you hear a high beep. When you press one of these keys and it turns off, you hear a low beep.

▶ **To adjust ToggleKeys settings**

1. Select **Start**.

2. Select **Settings**.

3. Select Control Panel.

4. Select Accessibility Options.

5. Select **Keyboard**.

   The **Keyboard** tab appears.

6. To configure ToggleKeys, select the related **Settings** button.

   The **Settings for ToggleKeys** dialog box appears.

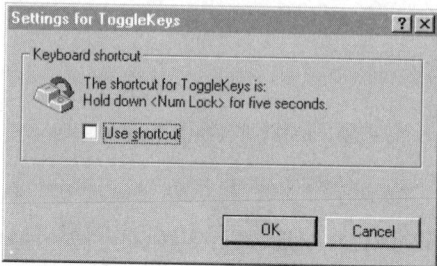

7. In the settings for ToggleKeys, select the **Use shortcut** check box.

8. Select **OK**.

Remember the following points when using ToggleKeys:

- To turn ToggleKeys on or off by using an emergency hot key, hold down the NUM LOCK key for eight seconds.

- When ToggleKeys turns on, you hear a rising siren if sound is turned on.

- ToggleKeys is especially useful for people who accidentally press CAPS LOCK instead of TAB, because it provides immediate feedback when they make such a mistake. ToggleKeys also functions with keyboards that do not have the status indicator lights for the CAPS LOCK, NUM LOCK, and SCROLL LOCK keys. The audible low and high beeps can be very useful for all users with this style of keyboard.

MouseKeys for Keyboard-only Input

MouseKeys lets you control the mouse pointer by using the keyboard. Although Windows 98 is designed to allow you to perform all actions without a mouse, some programs might still require one, and a mouse might be more convenient for some tasks. MouseKeys is also useful for graphic artists and others who need to position the pointer with great accuracy. You do not need to have a mouse to use this feature.

▶ **To adjust MouseKeys settings**

1. Select **Start**.

2. Select **Settings**.

3. Select Control Panel.

4. Select Accessibility Options.

5. Select **Mouse**.

   The **Mouse** tab appears.

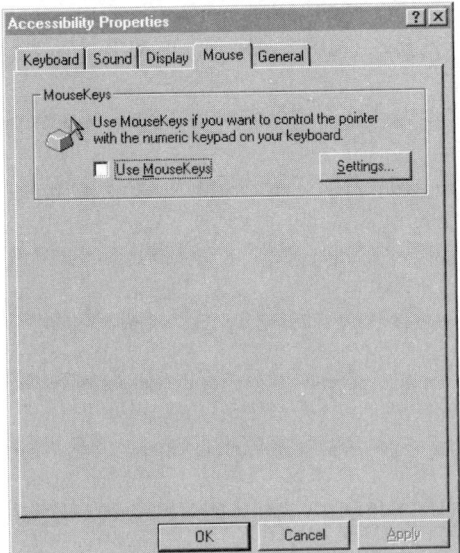
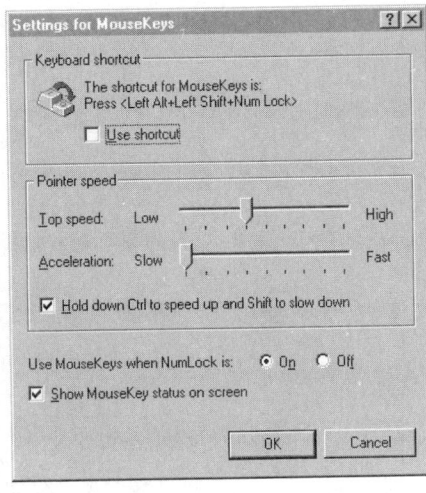

6. To configure MouseKeys, select the related **Settings** button.

   The **Settings for MouseKeys** dialog box appears.

7. In the settings for MouseKeys, use the check boxes and sliders to select the options you want.

8. Select **OK**.

▶ **To turn on MouseKeys from the keyboard**

- Press left ALT+left SHIFT+NUM LOCK.

   When MouseKeys turns on, you hear a rising siren if sounds are turned on.

If you are using only one finger, a mouthstick, or a head-pointer to operate the computer, the easiest way to activate MouseKeys is to first activate StickyKeys by tapping either SHIFT key five times. You can then press the three keys in sequence rather than simultaneously.

Note If SlowKeys is active, all the MouseKeys control keys respond according to the acceptance delay set for SlowKeys.

When MouseKeys is on, use the following keys to move the pointer on the screen:

- On the numeric keypad, press any of the numbered keys immediately surrounding the 5 key (also called the arrow keys) to move the pointer in the direction indicated by their arrows.

- Use the 5 key for a single mouse-button click and the PLUS SIGN (+) for a double-click.

- To drag and release an object, place the pointer on the object, and then press INSERT to begin dragging. Move the object to its new location, and then press DEL to release it.

- To select the left, right, or both mouse buttons for clicking, press the Slash (/) key, the MINUS SIGN (-) key, or the ASTERISK (*) key, respectively.

- To cause the pointer to "jump" across large sections of the screen, hold down CTRL while using the movement keys (any numeric keypad key except 5).

- To move the mouse a single pixel at a time for greater accuracy, hold down SHIFT while using the movement keys (any numeric keypad key except 5).

You can use NUM LOCK to toggle the MouseKeys control pad back to the numeric keypad and vice versa. This is especially useful with a laptop or notebook computer that does not have a separate numeric keypad. On these computer keyboards, the numeric keypad is usually overlaid on top of the standard QWERTY keyboard.

Note If the MouseKeys feature is on but NUM LOCK is toggled to the opposite setting, the MouseKeys icon in the taskbar shows that MouseKeys is disabled.

For example, if you are using the numeric keypad for number entry before starting MouseKeys, when you toggle out of MouseKeys by using NUM LOCK, you can enter numbers with the numeric keypad. If you are using the numeric keypad as a cursor keypad before starting MouseKeys, when you toggle out of MouseKeys by using NUM LOCK, you have a cursor keypad.

It can be useful to combine use of MouseKeys and use of a physical mouse. For example, you can use the standard mouse to move quickly around the screen and then use MouseKeys to move more precisely (unit by unit) to your final destination. Some people cannot use the standard mouse while simultaneously holding down the mouse button, so you can use MouseKeys to lock down the currently active mouse button, move the mouse cursor by using MouseKeys or the real mouse, and then release the mouse button by using MouseKeys.

Features for Replacing Sounds with Visual Cues

ShowSounds is a feature that instructs programs to provide visible feedback, in effect, asking the programs to be "closed-captioned."

SoundSentry tells Windows to send a visual cue, such as a blinking title bar or a screen flash, whenever the computer generates a sound. This enables you to see when the computer is generating sounds, although it cannot help you distinguish between different sounds.

ShowSounds and SoundSentry can be enabled through both the Accessibility Wizard and the **Sounds** tab within Accessibility Options in Control Panel.

You can also assign your own WAV files as custom sounds to any event through Sounds in Control Panel.

For information on using NetMeeting within corporate intranets to communicate real time in text-based chat, see "Conferencing with NetMeeting" in Chapter 20, "Internet Access and Tools."

▶ **To adjust Sound settings**

1. Select **Start**.

2. Select **Settings**.

3. Select Control Panel.

4. Select Accessibility Options.

5. Select **Sound**.

   The **Sound** tab appears.

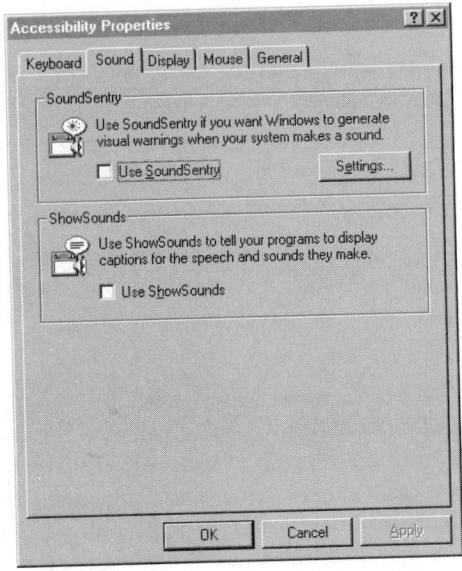
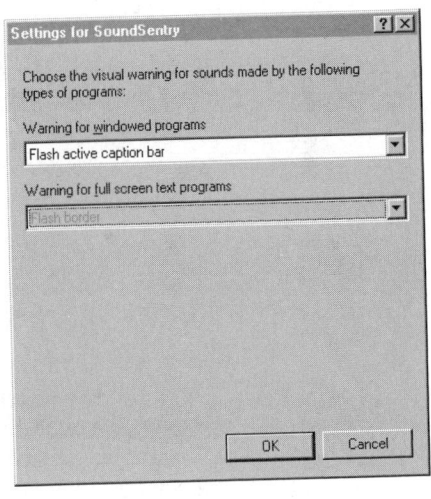

6. To configure SoundSentry, select the related **Settings** button.

   The **Settings for SoundSentry** dialog box appears.

7. Select the options you want from the lists.

8. Select **OK**.

Configuring Accessibility Features with the Accessibility Wizard

You can configure most accessibility features in Windows 98 through both the Accessibility Wizard and Control Panel. The Accessibility Wizard presents examples of accessibility features in one single place, making it easy to customize Windows to each individual's needs. The Accessibility Wizard also provides the option of saving your settings to a disk that can be used on another computer.

▶ **To start the Accessibility Wizard**

1. Select **Start**.

2. Select **Programs**.

3. Select **Accessories**.

4. Select **Accessibility**.

5. Select **Accessibility Wizard**.

    If **Accessibility Wizard** does not appear on the **Programs** menu, you need to install Accessibility Options.

Using the Accessibility Features

Once configured, the accessibility features can be turned on and off at any time using hot keys. Users can also save their accessibility settings as part of their user profiles in Windows 98 so that multiple users can comfortably share the same machine.

Using Accessibility Hot Keys

The accessibility hot keys provide an immediate method of activating accessibility features for people who could not use the computer without first having accessibility features in effect. Also known as shortcuts, *hot keys* allow the user to temporarily turn on a specific feature. Then, after the feature has been turned on, the user can navigate to Control Panel and adjust the feature to the user's own preferences or turn the feature on permanently. The same hot key temporarily turns off the feature if it gets in the way or if another person wants to use the computer without this feature. These keys are shown in the following table.

To	Press
Switch FilterKeys on and off	Right SHIFT for eight seconds
Switch High Contrast on and off	Left ALT+left SHIFT+PRINT SCREEN
Switch MouseKeys on and off	Left ALT+left SHIFT+NUM LOCK
Switch StickyKeys on and off	SHIFT five times
Switch ToggleKeys on and off	NUM LOCK for five seconds

Hot keys are designed to be unique key combinations that should not conflict with keys used by applications. If such a conflict does arise, the hot keys can be disabled, and the user can still use the feature or not, as needed.

As a precaution against accidental use, pressing an accessibility hot key causes special tones to sound (a rising siren tone for on and a falling siren tone for off) and causes a confirmation dialog box to appear, briefly explaining the feature and how it was activated. If the user pressed the hot key unintentionally, the user can cancel the feature's activation at this time. The confirming dialog box also provides a quick path to more detailed help and to the Control Panel settings for the hot key feature, in case the user wants to disable the hot key permanently.

Accessibility Status Indicator

While an accessibility feature is in use, Windows 98 can display an optional visual indicator icon that tells the user which accessibility features are turned on. The icon also provides feedback on the keys and mouse buttons currently being "held down" by the StickyKeys and MouseKeys features. The status indicator icons can appear on the system taskbar or as a free-floating window; users can choose from a range of different sizes.

In the preceding illustration, the three rectangles represent the left SHIFT, CTRL, and ALT keys. As each modifier key is held down by the StickyKeys feature, the corresponding rectangle appears filled.

The mouse in the Accessibility status indicator window may show either the left or the right button shaded, depending on which is selected. Pressing 5, PLUS SIGN (+), or INSERT is equivalent to using that button. If you have selected working with both buttons (equivalent to using the middle button on a three-button mouse), both buttons are shaded. If you lock down one or more mouse buttons using INSERT, the status indicator shows those buttons as being filled, rather than shaded. (To release them, press DEL.)

The stopwatch indicates that the keyboard response is being affected by SlowKeys, BounceKeys, or RepeatKeys features.

Settings for Multiple Users

▶ **To enable multiple users to personalize settings**

1. Select **Start**.

2. Select **Settings**.

3. Select Control Panel.

4. Select Passwords.

   The **Passwords Properties** tabbed pages appear.

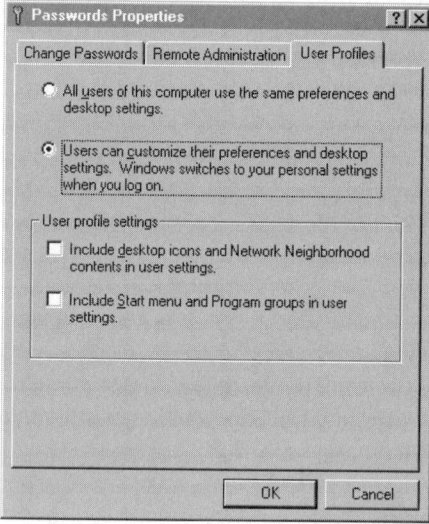

5. Select the **User Profiles** tab.

6. Select the **Users can customize their preferences and desktop settings** radio button.

   Your settings, including all accessibility settings, will be saved for the next time you log on.

7. Select **OK**.

The next person who logs on to Windows can change settings without changing your preferred settings. The next time you log on, your settings will be restored.

Accessibility Time-out

The time-out feature of the **Accessibility properties** dialog box turns off accessibility functionality after the computer has been idle for a certain period of time. It returns the operating system to its default configuration. This feature is useful on computers shared by multiple users.

Using Magnifier

Magnifier enlarges a portion of the display of Windows 98 to make the screen easier to read for people with slight visual impairments or whenever magnifying screen elements may be useful, such as during graphic editing. Magnifier is intended to provide a minimum level of functionality for users with moderate visual impairments. Many users with visual impairments will need a magnification utility program with higher functionality for daily use. For a list of Windows-based magnification utilities, see **http://www.microsoft.com/enable/.**

Using Magnifier, you can:

- Magnify an area of the screen up to nine times the standard display size.
- Follow the mouse cursor, the keyboard focus, the text editing focus, or any combination of these three.
- Invert colors for contrast.
- Toggle High Contrast display for the entire screen.
- Resize and relocate the display area.

When Magnifier is on, the magnified area is merely a display and not itself an active area. The active focus for cursor, keyboard, and other input devices is always in the unmagnified area.

▶ **To start Magnifier**

1. Select **Start.**
2. Select **Programs.**
3. Select **Accessories.**
4. Select **Accessibility.**
5. Select **Magnifier.**

   If **Magnifier** does not appear on the **Programs** menu or one of its submenus, see the procedure "To install Accessibility Options" earlier in this appendix.

You can customize your **Start** bar or create a shortcut to make starting Magnifier easier or to use settings for multiple users.

▶ **To set the magnification level**

1. Start Magnifier.

2. In the **Microsoft Magnifier** dialog box, select an arrow or enter a number in the **Magnification level** box to increase or decrease magnification.

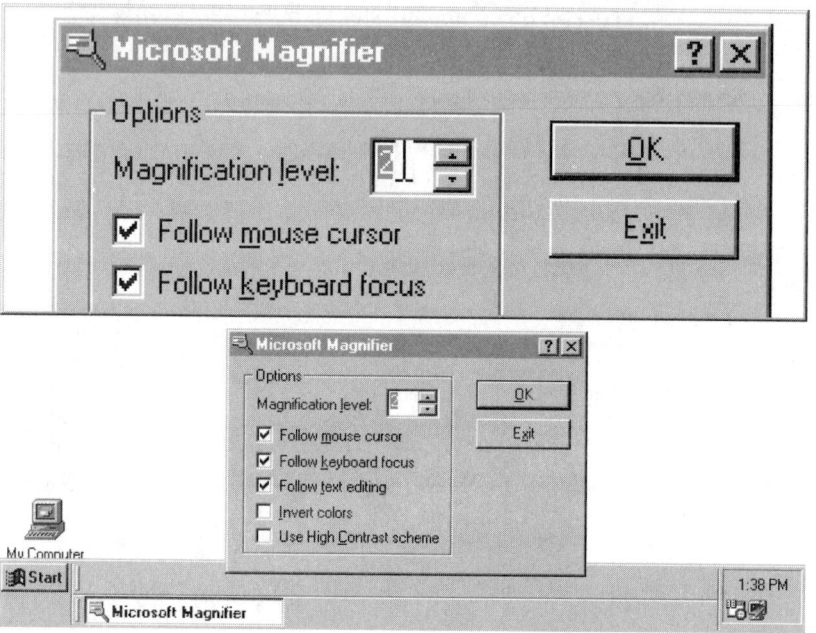

If Magnifier is already running, select its program button on the taskbar to open the dialog box.

You can also change the magnification level from the keyboard by holding down the Windows logo key and pressing the arrow keys. Press the UP ARROW key to increase magnification and the DOWN ARROW key to decrease magnification.

▶ **To set tracking options**

1. Start Magnifier.

2. In the **Microsoft Magnifier** dialog box, select any of the tracking options you want from the following three choices:

- **Follow Mouse cursor**
- **Follow keyboard focus**
- **Follow text editing**

If Magnifier is already running, select its program button on the taskbar to open the dialog box.

You can turn mouse tracking on and off from the keyboard by pressing the Windows logo key + PAGE DOWN.

▶ **To change the size of the magnification window**

1. Move the mouse pointer over the edge of the magnification window. The cursor becomes a double-pointed arrow.

2. Drag the magnification window border to resize the window.

   Keyboard users can use Mousekeys to change the size and position of the Magnifier window.

▶ **To change the position of the magnification window**

1. Place the mouse pointer inside the magnification window.

2. Drag the window to the desired area on your desktop.

   You can dock the magnification window to the top, bottom, or side of your display, or you can position the window anywhere within the desktop area.

▶ **To invert the colors of the magnification window**

1. Start Microsoft Magnifier.

2. In the **Microsoft Magnifier** dialog box, select the **Invert Colors** check box.

   If Microsoft Magnifier is already running, select its program button on the taskbar to open the dialog box.

   You can turn color inversion on and off from the keyboard by pressing the Windows logo key + PAGE UP.

▶ **To copy the contents of the magnifier to the clipboard**

1. Right-click on the area displayed in the magnifier.

   The **copy to clipboard** button appears.

2. Press ENTER.

▶ **To display the screen in High Contrast**

1. Start Magnifier.

2. In the Microsoft Magnifier dialog box, select the Use High Contrast scheme check box.

3. Select **OK**.

   It can take a few seconds for High Contrast Mode to take effect.

▶ **To exit Magnifier**

1. Select the **Microsoft Magnifier** button on the toolbar.

   The **Microsoft Magnifier** dialog box appears.

2. Select the **Exit** button.

Using Keyboard Navigation

Both on the Active Desktop and in Help, you can use the TAB key to rotate through controls such as icons, buttons, list boxes, panes, and links generally in left-to-right and top-to-bottom order. Use SHIFT+TAB to rotate through in reverse order. You can use ENTER to choose icons, choose commands, choose buttons, and activate links.

Many Microsoft products have specific shortcut keys to make keyboard access convenient. Look for the phrases "keyboard shortcuts" or "keystroke shortcuts" in the Help index. Shortcut keys for Windows 98 are listed in Appendix G, "Shortcuts for Windows 98."

Overview of Active Desktop

New features in the Windows 98 Active Desktop include:

- The **Start** menu and menus displayed by Windows Explorer are now custom scrolling menus. This allows you to have more menu commands than fit on the screen at one time, a helpful feature for people who enlarge the menu fonts or customize their menu to have many commands.

- You have several new desktop toolbars to choose from. These include:
  - The Address bar, which functions like the Run command on the **Start** menu.
  - The Links bar, which shows Web sites of general interest.
  - The Desktop bar, which shows the objects on your desktop.
  - The Quick Launch bar, which shows links to commonly used commands.

- You can create your own desktop toolbars with commands you use frequently. See the following procedures.

- You can choose to make your desktop and folder look and act like Web pages, including the ability to activate objects with a single select and to select them simply by hovering the mouse over them. Adjust these and other options by opening any folder and choosing **Folder Options** from the **View** menu.

- You can view any folder as a Web page. Open any folder and choose **as Web Page** from the **View** menu. If you do not like this view, you can switch back to any of the views provided by Windows, including **Large Icons**, **Small Icons**, and **List views**.

For more information on Active Desktop, see Help in Windows 98 and Chapter 6, "Configuring the Active Desktop and Active Channels."

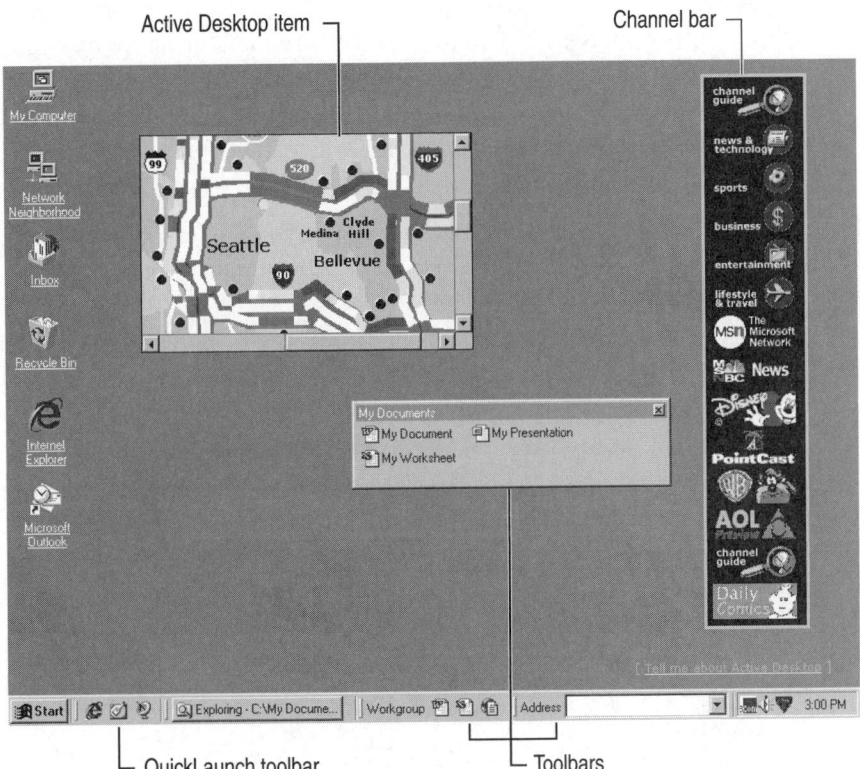

Using Keyboard Navigation in Active Desktop

Press TAB and SHIFT+TAB to move forward and backward between the **Start** button, desktop icons, the QuickLaunch bar, the Taskbar, and the Channel bar. A one-pixel-wide border appears around items so you can see what is selected.

The selection rotates forward through the Active Desktop items in the following order:

1. The **Start** button on the Taskbar

2. The Quick Launch toolbar

   - One of the Quick Launch icons appears selected.

   - You can use the arrow keys to move among the program icons. Once the focus is on an icon, press ENTER to launch the applications, or press SHIFT+F10 to display the shortcut menu for the toolbar. (All the toolbars on the desktop share the same shortcut menu.)

   - The arrow keys wrap; that is, continuing to use the right arrow on the rightmost icon moves you to the leftmost (first) icon.

3. The Taskbar

   - A selection does not appear on the Taskbar, but the focus is in fact there. Press SHIFT+F10 at this point to display the shortcut menu for the toolbar. (All the toolbars on the desktop share the same shortcut menu.)

   - Press the RIGHT ARROW key to select an application. You can press ENTER to display the selected application, or press SHIFT+F10 to display the shortcut menu for that application.

   - Use arrow keys to move among the application buttons.

   - The arrow keys wrap; that is, continuing to use the right arrow on the rightmost icon moves to the leftmost (first) icon.

4. The Desktop icons

   - An icon on the desktop appears selected.

   - Use arrow keys to move between the icons on the desktop. Press ENTER to open the application or document, or press SHIFT+F10 to display the shortcut menu for that icon.

   - Press CTRL+SPACEBAR to select or deselect the current icon; when no icon is selected, you can press SHIFT+F10 to display the shortcut menu for the entire desktop.

   - The arrow keys do not wrap; that is, continuing to use the left arrow on the leftmost selection does not move the focus and does not play an error sound.

5. The Channel bar

   - The topmost button on the Channel bar appears selected.

   - Use arrow keys to move between the icons on the Channel bar. Press ENTER to display a channel using Windows 98.

- The arrow keys do wrap; that is, continuing to use the down arrow on the last selection moves to the top button.
- Note that you can only reach the Channel bar by pressing TAB. The Channel bar is skipped when you navigate in reverse order using SHIFT+TAB.

6. The **Start** button again

If you add other bars, such as the Address bar, Quicklinks bar, Desktop bar, or a New Toolbar, you can also use TAB and SHIFT+TAB to navigate to these bars.

Customizing Desktop Toolbars

You can create your own desktop toolbars with commands you use frequently. This is most useful for people who prefer to use the mouse rather than the keyboard; users who prefer the keyboard usually want to add commands to their **Start** menu instead.

▶ **To create a custom desktop toolbar**

1. Create a folder with the appropriate documents, shortcuts, or programs.

2. Display the shortcut menu for the taskbar by right-selecting on the taskbar, or by pressing CTRL+ESC, ESC, and TAB, then pressing SHIFT+F10.

3. Select the **Toolbar** command, then the **New Toolbar** command.

4. Enter the path to the appropriate folder, or select the folder from the displayed list. You can press the RIGHT ARROW key to display all the folders in a branch.

5. Select **OK**.

   The new toolbar appears on your taskbar.

Overview of Windows 98 Help

Windows 98 includes a new Help facility called HTML Help. Because Help is now displayed as Web pages, most of the accessibility features in the Internet Explorer browsing software are now also available when viewing Help topics. You can override formatting options in Help, display text instead of images, disable animation, and even apply your own style sheet in order to have greater control over how Help is presented. When you adjust these and similar options in the Internet Explorer browsing software and then restart Help, your settings will automatically apply to all help topics you view. For more information on how to customize the display of Web pages and Help through the Internet Explorer browsing software, see that software's Help. Detailed information is also available online at **http://www.microsoft.com/enable/**.

Using Keyboard Navigation in Windows 98 Help

As in previous versions of Help, you can use TAB and SHIFT+TAB to navigate between buttons, links, or panes of Windows 98 Help. Use ENTER to activate links.

When you display a topic in the right-hand pane, it continues to be displayed until replaced with another selection. This can be confusing in navigation, because the topic name currently selected in the left pane may not match the topic shown on the right.

The **Hide** button on the Help toolbar can hide the leftmost pane, which is used for Content, Index, and Search. When this has been done, there is no way to navigate Help or display the leftmost pane with the keyboard.

Using the Keyboard to Display Help Items

You can use keys to display and search for Help topics.

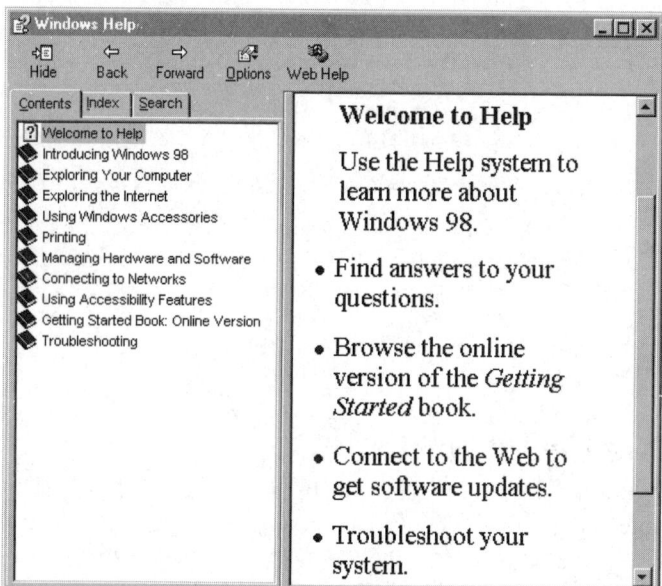

▶ **To display the topics in the Contents page**

1. Press ALT+C to move the focus to the Contents page.

   The highlight indicates the topic in the list being focused on.

2. Use the up and down arrow keys to move the selection in the Contents page.

   ▪ As you select parent topics, they automatically open, as indicated by the open book icon and the expanded list of subtopics.

- As you leave the last subtopic of an opened topic for the next topic, the opened topic closes, collapsing the list and displaying a closed book icon.

- Pressing ENTER also opens and closes topics indicated by book icons.

3. When you have made your selection of an available topic (indicated by a page icon), press ENTER to display the information in the right-hand pane.

- Your topic is displayed in the pane on the right, and the keyboard focus moves to the Help topic. The text you searched for is highlighted wherever it appears in the topic.

- Use the arrow keys to scroll the screen up and down or left and right.

- Press HOME or END to scroll the screen to the beginning or end of the topic.

- Use CRTL+F10 to display the shortcut menu for the topic.

4. To return to the Contents page, press ALT+C.

5. Press ALT+F4 to quit Help.

▶ **To display a topic using the Index list**

1. Press ALT+I to display the Index page.

   The Index page consists of a text field, where you can enter a term, and a list box showing all available index entries.

   The keyboard focus is in the text box. The first time you use this page, the text box is empty.

2. Use the arrow keys to scroll up and down the list of all topics. The selected topics appear in the text box as you scroll.

   – Or –

   Type the topic in the text box. The display scrolls to display matching topics as you type.

3. Press ENTER or ALT+D to display the selected topic.

   Your topic is displayed in the pane on the right, and the keyboard focus moves to the help topic. The text you searched for is highlighted wherever it appears in the topic.

   - Use the arrow keys to scroll the screen up and down or left and right.

   - Press HOME or END to scroll the screen to the beginning or end of the topic.

   - Use CTRL+F10 to display the shortcut menu for the topic.

4 Use ALT+I to choose other topics, or ALT+F4 to close Help.

▶ **To search for a topic by keyword in Windows 98 Help**

1. Press ALT+S.

    The **Search** tabbed page comes to the foreground, and the highlight indicates that the keyboard focus is in the **Keyword** text box.

2. Enter the keyword you want.

3. Press ENTER or ALT+L.

    A list of topics pertaining to your keyword appears in the **Topic** list box.

4. Press ALT+P; and then the DOWN ARROW key to move the keyboard focus to the first item in the **Topic** list box.

    The keyboard focus does not appear in the list box immediately after pressing ALT+P; it appears after using the DOWN ARROW key.

5. Use the UP ARROW and DOWN ARROW keys to select a topic.

6. Press ENTER or ALT+D to display the selected topic.

    Your topic is displayed in the pane on the right, and the keyboard focus moves to the help topic. The text you searched for is highlighted wherever it appears in the topic.

    -   Use the arrow keys to scroll the screen up and down or left and right.
    -   Press HOME or END to scroll the screen to the beginning or end of the topic.
    -   Use CTRL+F10 to display the shortcut menu for the topic.

7. Use SHIFT+TAB to return to the **Topic** list box to choose another topic, or ALT+K to begin another search.

8. Use ALT+F4 to quit Help.

Replacing the Mouse or Keyboard with Other Devices

You can add alternative pointing devices, such as head-pointers or eye-gaze systems, without replacing or disabling the normal mouse.

The Serial Keys feature, in conjunction with a communications aid interface device, allows the user to control the computer using an alternative input device. Such a device needs only to send coded command strings through the computer's serial port to specify keystrokes and mouse events, which are then treated as if they were normal keyboard or mouse input. For more detail on configuring communications aids, see **http://www.microsoft.com/enable/**.

▶ **To replace the mouse or keyboard with other devices**

1. Select **Start**.

2. Select **Settings**.

3. Select **Control Panel**.

4. Select **Accessibility**.

5. Select the **General** tab.

6. Under **SerialKey devices**, select the **Support SerialKey devices** check box.

   To change the serial port and baud rate for your device, select the **General** tab, and then select **Settings**.

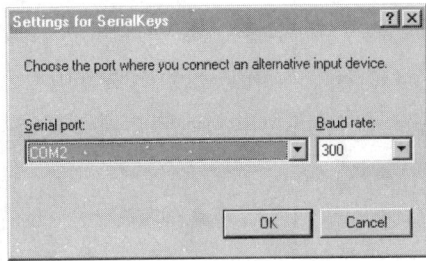

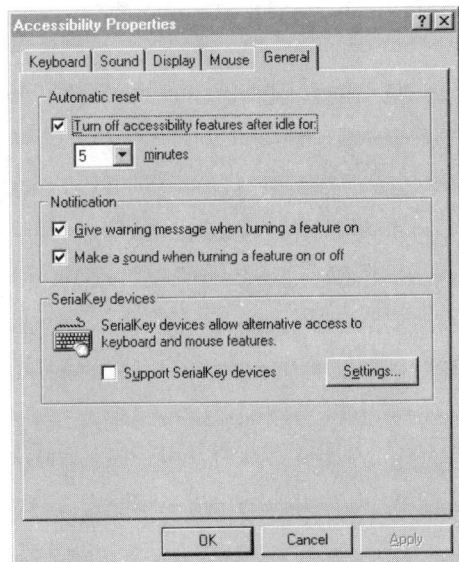

Additional Accessibility Resources

For more information about Microsoft products and accessibility, visit the Microsoft Accessibility Web site at **http://www.microsoft.com/enable/**. This also includes information on how to design accessible Web pages, new PowerToys to make Windows 98 even more accessible, and how to design pages that take advantage of new features in Windows 98.

Microsoft provides a catalog of accessibility aids that can be used with the Windows and Windows NT operating systems. You can obtain this catalog from the Web site or by telephone.

For more information concerning Microsoft products for people with disabilities, contact:

Microsoft Sales Information Center	World Wide Web:	**http://microsoft.com/enable/**
One Microsoft Way	Voice telephone:	(800) 426-9400
Redmond, WA 98052-6393	Text telephone:	(800) 892-5234

Using the Microsoft Text Telephone Service

If you are deaf or hard-of-hearing, complete access to Microsoft product and customer services is available through a text telephone (TTY/TDD) service.

Customer Service

You can contact Microsoft Sales Information Center on a text telephone by dialing (800) 892-5234 between 6:30 A.M. and 5:30 P.M. Pacific time.

Technical Assistance

For technical assistance in the United States, you can contact Microsoft Technical Support on a text telephone at (425) 635-4948 between 6:00 A.M. and 6:00 P.M. Pacific time Monday through Friday, excluding holidays. In Canada, dial (905) 568-9641 between 8:00 A.M. and 8:00 P.M. Eastern time Monday through Friday, excluding holidays. Microsoft support services are subject to the prices, terms, and conditions in place at the time the service is used.

Obtaining Microsoft Documentation in Alternative Formats

In addition to the standard forms of documentation, many Microsoft products are available in other formats to make them more accessible.

Many of the Windows 98 documents are also available as Help, as online user's guides, or on a compact disc that comes with the package.

If you have difficulty reading or handling printed documentation, you can obtain many Microsoft publications from Recording for the Blind & Dyslexic, Inc. Recording for the Blind & Dyslexic distributes these documents to registered, eligible members of their distribution service, either on audiocassettes or on floppy disks. The Recording for the Blind & Dyslexic collection contains more than 80,000 titles, including Microsoft product documentation and books from Microsoft Press. For information about eligibility and availability of Microsoft product documentation and books from Microsoft Press, contact Recording for the Blind & Dyslexic at the following address or telephone numbers:

Recording for the Blind & Dyslexic, Inc.
20 Roszel Road
Princeton, NJ 08540

Telephone: (609) 452-0606
Fax: (609) 987-8116
World Wide Web: **http://www.rfbd.org/**

You can also download many of these books from the Microsoft Web site at
http://microsoft.com/enable/.

Accessibility Guidelines for Software Developers

Windows 98 contains many built-in accessibility features. To make a computer
running Windows 98 truly accessible, application developers must provide
access to their applications' features, taking care to avoid incompatibilities with
accessibility aids.

As part of the *Win32 Software Development Kit for Windows 98 and Windows NT*
and *The Windows Interface Guidelines for Software Design,* Microsoft has
provided developers with documentation that not only outlines these important
concepts but provides technical and design tips to help ISVs produce more
accessible applications. Most of these tips mean very little additional work
to the designer, as long as the person is aware of the issues and incorporates
accessibility into the application design at an early stage. By providing this
information to application developers, Microsoft hopes to increase the general
level of accessibility of all software running on the Windows platform.

Getting More Accessibility Information

In addition to the features and resources available from Microsoft, compatible
products, services, and resources are available from other organizations to users
with disabilities.

Computer Products for People with Disabilities

The Trace R&D Center at the University of Wisconsin-Madison publishes a
database of more than 18,000 products and other information for people with
disabilities. The database is available on their site on the World Wide Web.
The database is also available on a compact disc, *CO-NET CD,* which is issued
twice a year.

The Trace R&D Center also publishes a book, *Trace ResourceBook,* which
provides descriptions and photographs of about 2,000 products.

To obtain these directories, contact:

Trace R&D Center   World Wide Web: **http://trace.wisc.edu/**
University of Wisconsin-Madison   Fax: (608) 262-8848
S-151 Waisman Center
1500 Highland Avenue
Madison, WI 53705-2280

General Information and Referrals for People with Disabilities

Computers and other devices can help people with disabilities overcome a variety of barriers. For general information and recommendations on how computers can help you with your specific needs, you should consult a trained evaluator. For information about locating programs or services in your area that may be able to help you, please contact:

National Information System   Voice/text telephone: (803) 777-1782
University of South Carolina   Fax: (803) 777-9557
Columbia, SC 29208

A P P E N D I X   I

Windows 98 Resource Directory

This appendix provides information on obtaining additional support and information for Microsoft Windows 98. This appendix also discusses the different Microsoft sources for support and assistance.

In This Appendix

Where to Go First

If you encounter a problem using Windows 98, there are a number of easily accessible sources of information available to you:

- Review *Welcome to Windows 98*, which appears automatically when you install Windows 98. You can access *Welcome to Windows 98* in your **Start** menu. Point to **Programs**, **Accessories**, and **System Tools**, and then click **Welcome to Windows**.

- Visit online Help. You can access online **Help** for Windows 98 from the **Start** menu. For assistance solving specific problems, click the **Troubleshooting** option listed in the Help **Contents** tab. Troubleshooters use a step-by-step approach to help you isolate and solve problems.

- Use Microsoft Technical Support Online to gain access to the most up-to-date technical information and resources to answer your support questions. Locate technical articles, programming aids, or commonly asked questions from the Microsoft Knowledge Base. Use this support to connect to available Windows 98 Newsgroups. You can also customize the site to control your search. To begin your search, go to **http://support.microsoft.com/support/**.

- For the latest device drivers and operating system software updates, you can access the Windows Update site by clicking **Windows Update** on the **Start** menu.

- Visit the ResourceLink Web site at **http://mspress.microsoft.com/reslink/**. ResourceLink is a Web site entirely dedicated to the content, tools, and extras of Microsoft Press Resource Kits, including the *Windows 98 Resource Kit*, the *Windows NT Server Resource Kit,* and the *Windows NT Workstation Resource Kit*. This essential extension to the Resource Kits provides easy access to the most up-to-date technical information, tools, and utilities for the support professional.

Getting Answers to Your Technical Questions

You can find late-breaking updates and technical information in the Readme Help files that came with your product disks or compact disc. If you have a technical question about Windows 98 that is not answered in Help, Microsoft offers additional support and services ranging from self-help tools to direct assistance with a Microsoft Technical Support Engineer.

The services and prices listed here are available in the United States and Canada only. Support services may vary outside the United States and Canada. For more information on support in other locations, contact your local Microsoft subsidiary.

Microsoft's support services are subject to Microsoft's then-current prices, terms, and conditions, which are subject to change without notice.

Self Help Resources

- For fast answers to common questions and a library of technical notes delivered by fax or mail, call Microsoft FastTips (800) 936-4200, 24 hours a day, 365 days a year. Microsoft FastTips is an automated system, accessible by touch-tone phone.

- Microsoft Download Service (MSDL) provides direct modem access to Microsoft's electronic technical library, which contains sample programs, device drivers, patches, software updates, and programming aids. The service is available 24 hours a day, 365 days a year. In the United States, dial (425) 936-6735. Connect information: 1200, 2400, 9600, or 14400 baud, no parity, 8 data bits, and 1 stop bit. In Canada, dial (905) 507-3022. Connect information: 1200 to 28800 baud, no parity, 8 data bits, and 1 stop bit.

Direct Assistance

Contact a Microsoft Technical Support Engineer.

Standard No-Charge Support

Microsoft offers 90 days of Standard No-Charge Support for retail versions of Microsoft Windows 98, including questions regarding Personal Web Server, beginning with the first time you contact a technical engineer. Toll charges may apply.

- In the United States, call (425) 635-7222, 6:00 A.M. to 6:00 P.M. Pacific time, Monday through Friday, excluding holidays.
- In Canada, call (905) 568-4494, 8:00 A.M. to 8:00 P.M. eastern time, Monday through Friday, excluding holidays.

If your Microsoft product was preinstalled or distributed with your personal computer, the personal computer manufacturer is responsible for providing your product support. For support, contact the manufacturer or source from which you obtained your Microsoft product.

Pay-Per-Incident Support

If you require support after normal business hours, or if your 90 days of Standard No-Charge Support for Windows 98 and Personal Web Server have expired, you can purchase Pay-Per-Incident Support as follows:

- In the United States, for a fee of $35 (US) per incident, please call (800) 936-5700 or (900) 555-2000, 24 hours a day, 365 days a year.
- In Canada, for a fee of $45 (CDN) plus tax per incident, please call (800) 668-7975, 8:00 A.M. to 8:00 P.M. eastern time, Monday through Friday, excluding holidays.

Support fees for the (800) calls will be billed to your VISA, MasterCard, or American Express card. Support fees for the (900) calls will appear on your telephone bill.

In the United States and Canada, you can also submit your Standard No-Charge Support or Pay-Per-Incident Support questions through the Internet with Web Response. For more details, go to Technical Support Online at **http://support.microsoft.com/support/**.

Microsoft Text Telephone (TT/TDD) services are available for people who are deaf or hard-of-hearing. Using a TT/TDD modem, dial (425) 635-4948, between 6:00 A.M. and 6:00 P.M. Pacific time, Monday through Friday. In Canada, dial (905) 568-9641, 8:00 A.M. to 8:00 P.M. eastern time, Monday through Friday.

For more information about the accessibility of Microsoft products and services for the deaf or hard-of-hearing, see Appendix H, "Accessibility."

Hardware Compatibility Information

Support may be limited if you are running Windows 98 on hardware that is not on the Hardware Compatibility List. To view the most current listing of hardware that works properly with Windows 98, please go to the Microsoft Hardware Compatibility Web site at **http://www.microsoft.com/hwtest/hcl/**.

Windows 98 SDK Information

Developers who are writing applications to run under Windows 98 should obtain the *Microsoft Platform Software Development Kit* (SDK). The SDK is available with a Professional or Universal subscription to the Microsoft Developer Network. It is also available on the Web at **http://www.microsoft.com/msdn/**. For more information, see "Microsoft Developer Network" later in this appendix.

Microsoft TechNet

If you are an information technology (IT) or Help desk professional responsible for administering your corporate network or supporting end users, then you can stay on top of your organization's requirements with TechNet. TechNet is a comprehensive resource for evaluating, implementing, and supporting Microsoft business products. Every month, TechNet delivers two compact discs packed with more than 150,000 pages of the critical information you need to smoothly deploy mission-critical systems and minimize downtime—all while building your technical expertise. To subscribe, see your local authorized retailer, or call (800) 344-2121, 6:30 A.M. to 5:30 P.M. Pacific time, Monday through Friday, excluding holidays.

Microsoft Developer Network

If you develop applications for the Internet or the Windows operating system, or use Microsoft products for any other development purposes, you will enhance your productivity with a Microsoft Developer Network (MSDN) subscription. MSDN is Microsoft's official source for technical programming information, SDKs, DDKs, Windows, BackOffice, Microsoft Office, and Visual Tools for developers. For more information on MSDN subscription levels and benefits, visit MSDN online at: **http://www.microsoft.com/msdn/**. Or call (800) 759-5474, 6:30 A.M. to 5:30 P.M. Pacific time, Monday through Friday, excluding holidays.

Microsoft Certified Solution Providers and Authorized Support Centers

Microsoft Certified Solution Providers and Authorized Support Centers specialize in providing support packages for hardware, network, and software products from both Microsoft and other vendors. For more information or a referral to a Microsoft Certified Solution Provider, call (800) 765-7768 or visit **http://www.microsoft.com/mcsp/**. For more information on Authorized Support Centers, contact your Microsoft account representative, or visit **http://www.microsoft.com/enterprise/asc.htm**.

Obtaining Drivers Electronically

You can obtain current device drivers at the Windows Update World Wide Web site. You can access the Windows Update site by clicking **Windows Update** on the **Start** menu.

Glossary

A

Accelerated Graphics Port (AGP)
A high-performance, component-level interconnect for 3D-graphics applications.

accessibility The extent to which computers are easy to use and available to a wide range of users, including people with one or more physical disabilities.

Active Channel A Web site that automatically delivers content to a user's computer on a regular schedule.

Active Desktop An interface that integrates the Windows desktop with the Internet Explorer browsing software to provide a single metaphor for accessing content or applications.

Active Setup An application that collects information about the user's computer before download of Internet Explorer begins, and then uses this information to manage the download intelligently.

ActiveX An umbrella term for Microsoft technologies that enable developers to create interactive content for the World Wide Web. A set of language-independent interoperability technologies that enable software components written in different languages to work together in networked environments. The core technology elements of ActiveX are COM and DCOM.

address class A basis for differentiating networks of various sizes. The network class can be determined from the first octet of its IP address.

Address Resolution Protocol (ARP)
A protocol for determining a host's Ethernet address from its Internet address.

Advanced Configuration and Power Interface (ACPI) A system interface that provides a standard way to control power management and Plug and Play functions of the computer hardware. ACPI allows the computer motherboard to describe its device configuration and power control hardware interface to Windows 98. This allows the operating system to automatically turn on and off standard devices, such as CD-ROMs, network cards, hard disk drives, and printers, as well as consumer devices connected to the computer, such as VCRs, TVs, phones, and stereos.

Advanced Power Management (APM)
A software interface (defined by Microsoft and Intel) between hardware-specific power management software (such as that located in a system BIOS) and an operating system power management driver.

ANSI American National Standards Institute.

API *See* application programming interface.

applet An HTML-based program built with Java that a browser temporarily downloads to a user's hard disk, from which location it runs when the Web page is open.

application programming interface (API)
A set of routines that an application program uses to request and carry out lower-level services performed by the operating system.

architecture The structure of all or part of a computer system. Also refers to the design of system software.

ASPI Advanced SCSI Programming Interface.

Asynchronous Transfer Mode (ATM)
A communications protocol defined for high-speed data communications.

Authenticode A technology that makes it possible to identify who published a piece of software and verify that it has not been tampered with.

automatic proxy configuration file
A file that dynamically assigns browser proxy settings based on the location of hosts.

B

BIOS Basic I/O system. A set of routines that works closely with the hardware to support the transfer of information between elements of the system, such as memory, disks, and the monitor.

BIOS Parameter Block (BPB) Information located inside the boot sector specific to the logical drive information.

block device A device such as a disk drive that moves information in groups of bytes (blocks) rather than one byte at a time.

boot sector First sector on a logical drive that includes code to boot that drive, specific logical drive information, and error messages.

broadcast In general terms, a transmission sent simultaneously to more than one recipient. In Internet terminology, a transmission sent to a single address to be forwarded to many recipients. In practice, Internet broadcasts function only on local networks, because routers do not forward them.

broadcast client A versatile personal computer that can receive and display broadband digital and analog broadcasts, blending television with new forms of information and entertainment. Broadcast client programming can include television, audio, World Wide Web pages, and computer data content.

broadcast server A computer that sends broadcast programming across a broadcast channel to broadcast clients. The programming sent can include television, audio, World Wide Web pages, and digital data such as stock prices, multimedia magazines, and computer software.

browser A client tool for navigating and accessing information on the Internet or an intranet. A browser interprets hypertext markup language (HTML) and displays information on a computer screen. A popular example is Microsoft Internet Explorer.

bus A set of hardwire lines used for data transfer among the components of a computer system.

bus class driver In Windows 98, a driver that provides an interface between the hardware layer and bus minidrivers.

bus enumerator A driver is responsible for creating the Windows 98 hardware tree.

C

cabinet A file that contains one or more files, usually compressed.

call manager The component that implements the media-specific signaling protocol for virtual circuit (connection) management on connection-oriented networks.

CardBus A 32-bit PC Card.

CD-ROM Compact disc read-only memory. A laser-encoded optical memory storage medium.

CDFS CD-ROM file system, which controls access to the contents of CD-ROM drives.

channel A push technology that allows users to subscribe to a Web site to browse offline, automatically display updated pages on their screen savers, and download or receive notifications when pages in the Web site are modified.

Channel bar An area on the user's Active Desktop that displays all the subscribed channels.

Channel Definition Format (CDF) file A file that specifies the content of an Active Channel and when and how that content should be delivered to the user.

CHAP Challenge Handshake Authentication Protocol.

checksum A calculated value used to test data for the presence of errors that can occur when data is transmitted or when it is written to disk.

chip set A collection of integrated circuits designed to be used together for a specific purpose.

clean boot Booting or starting a computer using the minimum system files in the operating system.

clean installation Installation of an operating system on a new computer or a computer with a reformatted hard disk.

client A process that requests a service provided by another program (called a server). *See* server.

Client for Microsoft Networks A 32-bit, protected-mode file system driver to support all Microsoft networking products that use the SMB file-sharing protocol.

cluster A specified number of sectors grouped together by the FORMAT command. The number is determined by the size of the logical drive. A cluster is the smallest storage unit for storing files.

code page An internal table that the operating system uses to relate the keys on the keyboard to the characters displayed on the screen.

codec Compression/decompression technology for digital video and stereo audio.

cold docking Insertion or removal of a device in the system before which the device must be powered off or restarted.

Compatibility mode A mode protocol defined in IEEE P1284 that provides a byte-wide channel from a computer to a peripheral.

Component Object Model (COM) The object-oriented programming model that defines how objects interact within a single application or between applications. In COM, client software accesses an object through a pointer to an interface—a related set of functions called methods—on the object.

compressed volume file (CVF) A file with read-only, hidden, and system attributes, and that contains a compressed drive.

container applications Applications that maintain compound documents.

cookies A means by which, under the HTTP protocol, a server or a script can maintain state or status information on the client workstation. In other words, a cookie is bits of information about a person's visit to a Web page. A cookie can include such information as the way a Web page was customized or how a visitor shopped on a Web site, or it can be used to track repeat visits.

cooperative multitasking A method by which the operating system requires an application to check the message queue periodically and to relinquish control of the system to other running applications.

D

Data Link Control (DLC) An error-correction protocol in the Systems Network Architecture (SNA) responsible for transmission of data between two nodes over a physical link.

datagram A packet of data and other delivery information that is routed through a packet-switched network or transmitted on a local area network.

DDE Dynamic Data Exchange. An interprocess communication method that allows two or more programs running simultaneously to exchange data and commands.

DDI Device driver interface.

DDK Driver development kit.

default emulated LAN A virtual network that acts like a traditional LAN.

default gateway The gateway used to connect to the rest of the network. *See* gateway.

demand paging A method by which code and data are moved in pages from physical memory to a temporary paging file on disk.

device class driver In Windows 98, a driver that provides an interface between different layers of the WDM architecture.

device node The basic data structure for a given device, built by Configuration Manager; sometimes called devnode. Device nodes are built into memory at system startup for each device and enumerator with information about the device, such as currently assigned resources.

The complete representation of all device nodes is referred to as the hardware tree.

Dial-Up Networking A component of Windows NT and Windows 98 that makes it possible for users to connect to remote networks such as the Internet or a private network.

digital ID An electronic key, obtained from a certificate authority, that provides a means for proving your identity on the Internet. Also called digital certificate or authentication certificate.

DirectShow A multimedia technology designed to play video, audio, and other multimedia streams in a variety of formats that are stored locally or acquired from Internet servers. DirectShow relies on a modular system of pluggable components called filters arranged in a configuration called a filter graph.

DirectX A low-level API that provides user-mode media interfaces for games and other high-performance multimedia applications. DirectX is a thin layer, providing direct access to hardware services, and takes advantage of available hardware accelerators and emulates accelerator services when accelerators are not present.

Distributed Component Object Model (Distributed COM) Additions to the Component Object Model (COM) that facilitate the transparent distribution of objects over networks and over the Internet.

distributed computing Information processing in which computing tasks are divided into two parts, one running on the client computer, the other on the server.

distribution media format (DMF) A special read-only format for 3.5-inch floppy disks that permits storage of 1.7 MB of data.

DIX Digital/Intel/Xerox.

DLL *See* dynamic-link library.

DNS *See* Domain Name System.

dock To insert or remove a device in a computer system.

docking station A base unit into which you can insert portable hardware and that includes drive bays, expansion slots, and additional ports.

Domain Name System (DNS) The naming service used on the Internet to provide standard naming conventions for IP computers.

dotted decimal notation A method of signifying IP addresses in which each set of eight bits is separated from the next eight bits by a period.

Drive Parameter Block (DPB) Identical to the BIOS Parameter Block, except that it is in memory. Applications should access the DPB instead of the boot sector for logical drive information. Proper programming guidelines have always stated that applications should go through the operating system for information instead of going to the hardware itself.

DVD Optical disk storage that encompasses audio, video, and computer data.

Dynamic Host Configuration Protocol (DHCP) An industry-standard (TCP/IP) protocol that assigns Internet Protocol (IP) configurations to computers. The DHCP-server computer makes the assignments, and the client computer calls the server computer to obtain the address.

Dynamic HTML A collection of features that extends the capabilities of traditional HTML, giving Web authors more flexibility, design options, and creative control over the appearance and behavior of Web pages.

dynamic-link library (DLL) An API routine that user-mode applications access through ordinary procedure calls. The code for the API routine is not included in the user's executable image. Instead, the operating system automatically modifies the executable image to point to DLL procedures at run time.

E

emulated LAN A virtual network that acts like a traditional LAN.

encapsulated PostScript (EPS) file
A file that prints at the highest possible resolution for your printer. An EPS file may print faster than other graphical representations.

encryption A way of making data indecipherable to protect it from unauthorized viewing or use.

enhanced metafile (EMF) A device-independent rendering of a print job that is much faster to produce than a device-specific rendering.

enumeration The process by which, during startup, the operating system identifies Plug and Play devices by creating unique device IDs and reporting those IDs to Device Manager.

exception handling An event that occurs as a program runs and that requires software outside the normal flow of control to be run.

explorer (Explorer) bar In Internet Explorer, a way to browse through a list of links while displaying the pages those links open in the right side of the window.

extended capabilities port (ECP) A port that provides high-speed printing.

F

FAQ Frequently Asked Questions. A document containing basic questions and answers.

FAT file system A file system based on a file allocation table, maintained by the operating system, to keep track of the status of various segments of disk space used for file storage.

FAT32 An enhancement of the File Allocation Table file system that supports large drives with improved disk space efficiency.

Fiber distributed data interface (FDDI)
A standard for high-speed fiber-optic LANs.

File Allocation Table (FAT) An area on the disk (floppy or logical drive) set aside to reference file locations on that disk. The table is a chain identifying where each part of a file is located. It acts similarly to a table of contents for a book.

File Control Block (FCB) A small block of memory temporarily assigned by a computer's operating system to hold information about an opened file.

firewall A system or combination of systems that enforces a boundary between two or more networks and keeps hackers out of private networks. Firewalls serve as virtual barriers to passing packets from one network to another.

font mapping Matching screen fonts to printer fonts.

frame In broadcast television, a single screen-sized image that can be displayed in sequence with other slightly different images to animate drawings. For NTSC video, a video frame consists of two interlaced fields of 525 lines; NTSC video runs at 30 frames per second. For PAL or SECAM video, a video frame consists of two interlaced fields of 625 lines; PAL and SECAM video runs at 25 frames per second.

FTP File Transfer Protocol. The Internet standard high-speed protocol for downloading, or transferring, files from one computer to another.

G

gateway A computer connected to multiple physical networks, capable of routing or delivering packets between them.

GIF *See* Graphics Interchange Format.

Gopher An early Internet protocol and software program designed to search for, retrieve, and display documents from remote computers or sites. Gopher clients are used to connect to remote Gopher servers Interaction is typically carried out through a menu hierarchy.

Graphics Device Interface (GDI) The graphical system that manages what appears on the screen and provides graphics support for printers and other output devices. One of three core components in Windows 98.

Graphics Interchange Format (GIF)
A computer graphics file format developed in the mid-1980s by CompuServe for use in photo-quality graphic image display on computer screens. Now commonly used on the Internet.

H

hardware tree The hierarchical representation of all the buses and devices on a computer.

HDLC High-level Data Link Control. A protocol for information transfer in which messages are transmitted in frames.

High Performance File System (HPFS)
An OS/2 file system that allows long file names.

HiPack A file and folder compression format.

home page The central document of a Web site, usually designated as the default document. The starting point for a Web site or section of a Web site is often referred to as the home page.

host ID The portion of the IP address that identifies a particular computer within a particular network ID.

host table The HOSTS or LMHOST file that contains lists of known IP addresses mapped to host names or NetBIOS computer names. Windows 98 uses this for local name resolution if other methods are not available.

hot docking Insertion of a device in the system while the device is running at full power

HTML *See* Hypertext Markup Language.

HTTP *See* Hypertext Transfer Protocol.

Human Interface Device (HID) specification
The device class definition developed by the USB standards group for HIDs. Serves as the basis for the WDM input device support, and unifies input devices by providing flexible data reporting, typeless data, and arrayed and variable input and output.

hyperlink Also called simply a link. A way of jumping to another place on the Internet. Hyperlinks usually appear in a different format from regular text. You initiate the jump by clicking the link.

hypertext Documents with links to other documents. Click a link to display the other document. A hypertext document is a document structured in chunks of text and marked up, usually using HTML, which is connected by links.

Hypertext Markup Language (HTML)
A simple markup language used to create hypertext documents that are portable from one platform to another. HTML files are simple ASCII text files with codes embedded (indicated by markup tags) to indicate formatting and hypertext links. The formatting language used for documents on the World Wide Web.

Hypertext Transfer Protocol (HTTP)
The underlying protocol by which Web clients and servers communicate. HTTP is an application-level protocol for distributed, collaborative, hypermedia information systems. It is a generic, stateless, object-oriented protocol. A feature of HTTP is the typing and negotiation of data representation, allowing systems to be built independently of the data being transferred.

I

ICC International Color Consortium.

ICM Image Color Matching.

IDE Integrated Device Electronics. A type of disk-drive interface where the controller electronics reside on the drive itself, eliminating the need for a separate adapter card.

IE *See* Microsoft Internet Explorer.

IEAK Internet Explorer Administration Kit. A set of tools that make possible the fine-tuning of Internet Explorer browsing software installations.

IEAK Profile Manager A tool that network or workgroup administrators can use to create custom Active Desktop and Active Channel configurations and deploy them to users.

IEEE Institute of Electrical and Electronics Engineers.

impersonation A technique by which one process can take on the security attributes of another process, as when a server process impersonates a client process to complete a task involving objects to which the server does not normally have access.

INF file A file that provides Windows 98 Setup with the information required to set up a device, such as a list of valid logical configurations for the device, the names of driver files associated with the device, and so on. An INF file is typically provided by the device manufacturer on a disk.

Infrared Data Association (IrDA) Publisher of a wireless connectivity standard, which makes it possible to connect computers and hardware devices without using cables.

INI files Initialization files used by Windows-based applications to store per-user information that controls application startup. In Windows 98, such information is stored in the registry, and INI files are supported for backward compatibility.

interactive television Television combined with interactive content and enhancements.

Interlacing A video display technique in which the electron beam refreshes (updates) all odd-numbered scan lines in one sweep of the screen and all even-numbered scan lines in the next. Interlacing takes advantage of both the screen phosphor's ability to maintain an image for a short time before fading and the human eye's tendency to average subtle differences in light intensity. By refreshing alternate lines, interlacing halves the number of lines to update in one screen sweep.

International Organization for Standardization (ISO) An international association of member countries, each represented by its leading standard-setting organization—for example, ANSI (American National Standards Institute) for the United States. The ISO works to establish global standards for communications and information exchange.

Internet A set of dissimilar computer networks joined together by means of gateways that handle data transfer and the conversion of messages from the sending network to the protocols used by the receiving networks. These networks and gateways use the TCP/IP suite of protocols.

Internet Assigned Numbers Authority (IANA) The Internet group that assigns groups of IP addresses to organizations.

Internet Control Message Protocol (ICMP) A network-level Internet protocol that provides error correction and other information relevant to IP packet processing.

Internet Engineering Task Force (IETF) A consortium that introduces procedures for new technology on the Internet. IETF specifications are released in Requests for Comments.

Internet Protocol (IP) The part of TCP/IP that is responsible for addressing and sending TCP packets over the network.

Internet Protocol Control Protocol (IPCP) A protocol used to configure, enable, and disable IP Protocol modules at both ends of the link.

Internet Service Provider (ISP) A public provider of remote connections to the Internet.

interrupt An asynchronous operating condition that disrupts normal execution and transfers control to an interrupt handler. Interrupts are usually initiated by I/O devices requiring service from the processor.

interrupt request (IRQ) A method by which a device can request to be serviced by the device's software driver. The system board uses a programmable interrupt controller to monitor the priority of the requests from all devices.

intranet Use of Internet standards, technologies, and products within an enterprise to function as a collaborative processing infrastructure. The term is generally used to describe the application of Internet technologies on internal corporate networks.

IP Internet Protocol.

IP address Internet Protocol address. A unique address that identifies a host on a network. It identifies a computer as a 32-bit address that is unique across a TCP/IP network.

IPX/SPX Internetwork Packet Exchange /Sequenced Packet Exchange. On Novell NetWare systems, IPX is a network layer protocol used in the file server operating system; SPX is a transport layer protocol built on top of IPX and used in client/server applications.

IRQ *See* interrupt request.

ISA Industry Standard Architecture. An 8-bit (and later, a 16-bit) expansion bus that provides a buffered interface from devices on expansion cards to the PC internal bus.

ISDN (Integrated Services Digital Network) A completely digital telephone /telecommunications network that carries voice, data, and video information over the existing telephone network infrastructure. It is designed to provide a single interface for hooking up a telephone, fax machine, computer, and so on.

J

Java A derivative of the C++ language, SunSoft's distributed programming language, offered as an open standard.

JavaScript A scripting language developed by Netscape Communications and Sun Microsystems, Inc.

Joint Photographic Experts Group (JPEG) A widely accepted international standard for compression of color image files, sometimes used on the Internet.

JPEG *See* Joint Photographic Experts Group.

K

kernel One of three core components in Windows 98. It provides base operating system functionality, including file I/O services, virtual memory management, and task scheduling.

kernel mode The processor mode that allows full, unprotected access to the system. A driver or thread running in kernel mode has access to system memory and hardware.

L

LAN Local area network. A group of computers and other devices dispersed over a relatively limited area and connected by a communications link that enables any device to interact with any other device on the network.

layered architecture An architecture in which each layer isolates portions of the services.

legacy Any feature in the computer system based on older technology for which compatibility continues to be maintained in other system components. In the context of Windows 98, a non–Plug and Play feature.

Link Control Protocol (LCP) A protocol that establishes, configures, and tests the integrity of a data-link connection.

location A set of dialing rules defining a place from which a user makes Dial-Up Networking connection.

logical block addressing (LBA) A method of accessing hard disk drives based on the extensions of INT 13.

logon script A batch file that runs automatically every time the user logs on. It can be used to configure a user's working environment at every logon, and it allows an administrator to control a user's environment without managing all aspects of it.

M

mailslot A mechanism for one-to-one or one-to-many interprocess communications (IPC).

master browse server The computer that maintains the list of servers in a workgroup. Also called browse master.

messaging application program interface (MAPI) An open and comprehensive messaging interface used by programmers to create messaging and workgroup applications—such as electronic mail, scheduling, calendaring, and document management.

Microsoft Internet Explorer browsing software A suite of Internet software that includes several communication and collaboration tools in addition to the Internet client.

Microsoft Management Console (MMC) A general-purpose management display framework for hosting administration tools.

Microsoft Service for NetWare Directory Services A service that enables Microsoft Client for NetWare Networks to log into a Novell Directory Services (NDS) tree.

Microsoft Systems Management Server An application used to install and maintain Microsoft Windows 98 on networked computers.

MIDI Musical Instrument Digital Interface. A serial interface standard that allows for the connection of music synthesizers, musical instruments, and computers. The MIDI standard is based partly on hardware and partly on a description of the way in which music and sounds are encoded and communicated between MIDI devices.

MIDI stream A technology used in advanced sound cards to play very complex MIDI sequences with less CPU use.

MIME Multipurpose Internet Mail Extensions. A standard that extends SMTP to allow the transmission of such data as video, sound, and binary files via Internet e-mail without translating them into ASCII format.

minidriver A hardware-specific DLL that uses a Microsoft-provided class driver to accomplish most actions through function calls and provides only device-specific controls. Under WDM, the minidriver uses the class driver's device object to make system calls.

miniport driver A device-specific kernel-mode driver linked to a Windows NT or WDM port driver, usually implemented as a DLL that provides an interface between the port driver and the system.

mobile computing Computing done by intermittently-connected users who access network resources.

model computer A computer on which all the components needed for other similar computers in your organization have been installed.

MPEG A standard designed by the Motion Pictures Experts Group for video playback of NTSC quality from CD-ROM.

MS-CHAP Microsoft Challenge Handshake Authentication.

Mt. Fuji specification A specific command set used in DVD-ROM drives.

multicasting Transmitting a message to multiple recipients at the same time. A point-to-many networking model in which a packet is sent to a specific address, and only those computers that are set to receive information from this address receive the packet.

multihomed system A computer that is configured with more than one IP address.

Multilink　A protocol that enables a computer to establish a dial-up connection using two modems or ISDN devices.

multipoint data conferencing　A technology that allows two or more people to share information in real time over the Internet or an intranet.

N

name resolution　The process used on the network for resolving a computer address as a computer name, to support the process of finding and connecting to other computers on the network.

named pipe(s)　An interprocess communication (IPC) mechanism that allows one process to communicate with another local or remote process.

NDISWAN　Network driver interface specification wide area network.

NetBEUI　NetBIOS Extended User Interface. A local area network transport protocol provided with Windows 98.

NetBIOS　Network basic input/output system. A software interface for network communication.

NetBIOS Frames Control Protocol (NBFCP)　A protocol used to configure, enable, and disable the NetBEUI protocol modules on both ends of a data link.

netmask　A binary value that defines which portion of the network address must match in order for that route to be used.

network adapter　A hardware card installed in a computer that so it can communicate on a network.

Network Address Translation (NAT)　A process that lets an entire network connect to a PPP server and appear as a single IP address, thus helping to conceal IP addresses from external hackers and to alleviate address space shortage.

Network Device Interface Specification (NDIS)　The interface for network drivers used in Windows and Windows NT operating systems. All transport drivers call the NDIS interface to access network adapters.

network ID　The portion of the IP address that identifies a group of computers and other devices that are all located on the same logical network.

Nibble mode　A mode protocol defined in IEEE P1284 that provides a channel from the peripheral to the host through which data is sent as 4-bit nibbles.

NLS　National language support. Services that ensure globally-aware information handling.

NTFS　Windows NT file system.

O

object application　An application that acts as a server to provide various data objects to be included in a compound document.

OnNow　A design initiative that seeks to create all the components required for a comprehensive, system-wide approach to system and device power control. OnNow is a term for a PC that is always on but appears off and that responds immediately to user or other requests.

Open Datalink Interface (ODI)　A specification defined by Novell and Apple Computer to provide a protocol and API for communicating with network adapter drivers, and to support the use of multiple protocols by a network adapter driver.

Open Group, The　Parent company of a number of standards organizations including The Active Group—now managing the core ActiveX technology, X/Open, and OSF.

OpenType A font specification for Windows 98 that extends the TrueType font standard by adding tables containing information for advanced multilingual typesetting and typographic control.

option ROM Optional read-only memory found on PC bus expansion cards. This ROM usually contains additional firmware required to properly boot the peripheral connected to the expansion card, for instance, a hard drive. Also referred to as an expansion ROM.

OSI Open Systems Interconnection (Reference Model).

P

packet A transmission unit of fixed maximum size that consists of binary information representing both data and a header containing an ID number, source and destination addresses, and error-control data.

PANOSE A font matching system based on a numeric classification of fonts according to visual characteristics.

parse To analyze or separate (for example, input) into more easily processed components.

password A unique string of characters that must be provided before logon or access to a resource or service is authorized.

Password Authentication Protocol (PAP)
A security protocol that uses a two-way handshake for the peer to establish its identity.

password caching Automatically storing a password in a password list (PWL) file so that whenever the user logs on again, the logon password unlocks the PWL file and the resource passwords it contains.

PC Card A trademark of PCMCIA. A removable device that is designed to be plugged into a PC Card slot and used as a memory-related peripheral.

PCI Peripheral Component Interconnect. A high-performance, 32-bit or 64-bit bus designed to be used with devices that have high bandwidth requirements, such as display subsystems.

PCMCIA The Personal Computer Memory Card International Association, which standardizes credit card-sized interface cards used in portables and other small computers.

permission scoping Preventing permissions granted to a trusted component from being misused, either intentionally or inadvertently, by a less trusted component.

permission signing Allowing a signed cabinet file to specify securely not only the identity of the signer but also the set of permissions being requested for the signed classes.

Personal Information Exchange (PFX)
A set of public key-based security technologies that is part of the Microsoft Internet security framework.

Platform for Internet Content Selection (PICS)
A system providing for the voluntary rating of World Wide Web site content by either the publisher of the page or a third-party rating group.

Plug and Play A design philosophy and set of specifications that describe hardware and software changes to the PC and its peripherals, making it possible to add new components without having to perform technical procedures.

Point-to-Point Tunneling Protocol (PPTP)
Protocol that enables a computer to securely connect to the Internet or an intranet by tunneling through an Internet or LAN connection.

PPP Point-to-Point Protocol. An industry standard, a part of Windows 98 Dial-Up Networking, designed to ensure interoperability with remote access software from other vendors. It is used in making point-to-point links, especially with dial-up modem servers.

PPTP *See* Point-to-Point Tunneling Protocol.

preemptive multitasking A method by which the operating system takes control away from or gives control to another running task, depending on the needs of the system.

Private Communication Technology (PCT)
A protocol used to create a secure Internet or intranet channel.

protected mode An operating mode supporting more advanced features than real mode, including multitasking, data security, and virtual memory.

protocol A set of rules and conventions by which two computers pass messages across a network. Networking software usually implements multiple levels of protocols layered one on top of another. Windows 98 includes NetBEUI, TCP/IP, and IPX/SPX-compatible protocols.

protocol rollover Sending ASF files over a default protocol and then trying to send them via an alternative server or protocol if the original attempt fails.

proxy server A server that acts as a go-between, converting information from Web servers into HTML to be delivered to a client computer. It also provides a way to deliver network services to computers on a secure subnet without those computers needing to have direct access to the World Wide Web.

pull model A broadcast model in which information is downloaded as it is requested.

push model A broadcast model in which a server sends information to a large number of clients on its own schedule, without waiting for requests. The clients scan the incoming information, save the parts they have been instructed to save, and discard the rest.

Q

quality of service (QoS) Network characteristics such as desired bandwidth and maximum acceptable delay that an application can request from a network.

R

raster fonts Fonts stored in files as bitmaps and rendered as an array of dots for displaying on the screen and printing on paper. Raster fonts cannot be cleanly scaled or rotated.

real mode The backward-compatible mode of the Intel 80386 family. In real mode, all of the CPU's protection features are disabled, paging is not supported, and program addresses correspond to physical memory addresses. The address space is limited to 1 MB of physical memory and uses a memory segmentation scheme. Real mode is compatible with 8086, the 8088, the 80186, and the real mode of the 80286.

redirector Networking software that accepts I/O requests for remote files, named pipes, or mailslots and then sends (redirects) them to a network service on another computer. Redirectors (also called network clients) are implemented as file system drivers in Windows 98.

registry The database repository for information about a computer's configuration. The registry supersedes use of separate INI files for all system components and applications that know how to store values in the registry.

Registry Checker A system maintenance program that finds and fixes registry problems and backs up the registry.

Registry Editor An application that is used to view and edit entries in the registry.

registry key An identifier for a record or group of records in the registry.

Remote Access Service (RAS) A service that provides remote networking for telecommuters, mobile workers, and system administrators who monitor and manage servers at multiple branch offices.

remote administration Administration of one computer by an administrator located at another computer and connected to the first computer across the network.

remote procedure call (RPC) A message-passing facility that allows a distributed program to call services available on various computers in a network. Used during remote administration of computers, RPC provides a procedural view, rather than a transport-centered view, of networked operations.

Request for Comments (RFC) An official document of the Internet Engineering Task Force (IETF) that specifies the details for protocols included in the TCP/IP family.

resolver Under DNS, a client that queries the name server across the network to gain information about the domain name space.

resource reservation protocol (RSVP) A signaling protocol that is used to establish connections with the QoS requested by an application

RFC *See* Request for Comments.

RIP *See* Routing Information Protocol.

RIP listening A process in which a computer listens in on RIP packets and adds information gleaned from those packets to add entries to the route table. Also called silent RIP.

robot A fast, automated program, such as a search engine, indexing program, or cataloging software, that requests Web pages much faster than humans can.

root directory A specific area set aside to store boot files and directories.

route table A table that is used to determine where a computer routes packets.

Routing Information Protocol (RIP) A protocol that determines the best path for routing traffic over a network.

S

sandboxing The Java security model, which provides control over how Java applets can interact with a computer system.

script A program consisting of a set of instructions to an application or utility program.

scriptlet A reusable Web page in which Dynamic HTML script has been written according to certain conventions.

SCSI Small computer standard interface. An I/O bus designed as a method for connecting several classes of peripherals to a host system without requiring modifications to generic hardware and software.

SDK Software Development Kit. A kit that programmers can use to create new applications.

secure password authentication (SPA) Any authentication in which the actual password is not sent over the network.

Secure Sockets Layer (SSL) A protocol that supplies secure data communication through data encryption and decryption. SSL enables communications privacy over networks through a combination of public key cryptography and bulk data encryption.

security zone In Internet Explorer, a segment of the Internet or intranet assigned a particular level of security.

Serial Line Internet Protocol (SLIP)
A data link protocol that allows transmission of IP data packets over dial-up telephone connections, typically used by UNIX remote access servers.

server For a LAN, a computer running administrative software that controls access to all or part of the network and its resources. A computer acting as a server makes resources available to computers acting as workstations on the network. *See* client.

server message block (SMB) The protocol developed by Microsoft, Intel, and IBM that defines a series of commands used to pass information between network computers. The redirector packages SMB requests into a network control block (NCB) structure that can be sent over the network to a remote device. The network provider listens for SMB messages destined for it and removes the data portion of the SMB request so that it can be processed by a local device.

Service Advertising Protocol (SAP)
The Novell NetWare broadcasting protocol.

setup script A text file that contains predefined settings for all the options specified during setup.

share-level security A security methodology in which passwords are used to restrict access to shared resources on a peer server. The only security level available on peer-to-peer networks.

Simple Mail Transfer Protocol (SMTP)
A protocol used for exchanging mail on the Internet.

Simple Network Management Protocol (SNMP)
The Internet's standard for remote monitoring and management of hosts, routers, and other nodes and devices on a network. A TCP/IP-derived protocol governing network management and monitoring network devices.

smart card A small electronic device, approximately the size of a credit card, that contains an embedded integrated circuit. Used for such tasks as storing medical records, storing digital cash, and generating network IDs.

SNMP *See* Simple Network Management Protocol.

socket A software object used by a client to connect to a server; basic components include the port number and the network address of the local host.

SOCKS A protocol for traversing firewalls in a secure and controlled manner, made publicly available by the Internet Engineering Task Force.

source routing A method of routing data across bridges.

SPI Service provider interface, a single, well-defined set of functions used by Windows 98 to request network services.

step capture A process in which a user captures digital-video data one frame at a time.

Still Image Architecture (STI) A WDM architecture for still image devices. A still image minidriver provides support for still image devices, such as scanners and cameras.

stream A continuous series of bits, bytes, or other small, structurally uniform units.

streaming architecture A model for interconnection of stream-processing components, in which applications dynamically load data as they output it. Dynamic loading means data can be broadcast continuously. *See* WDM streaming.

streaming data Data continuously broadcast to an application. For example, a broadcast client's user might subscribe to continuously broadcast sports scores.

subnet mask A 32-bit value that allows the recipient of IP packets to distinguish the network ID portion of the IP address from the host ID.

subscription Stored information describing how a user will have access to an Active Channel Web site, including frequency and method of access.

swap file A hidden file on the hard drive that Windows uses to hold parts of programs and data files that do not fit in memory.

system policies Settings that allow an administrator to override local registry values for user or computer settings.

System Policy Editor A tool with which one can change many common registry settings for an individual computer.

T

TAPI *See* telephony application program interface.

TCP/IP Transmission Control Protocol/Internet Protocol. A networking protocol that allows computers to communicate across interconnected networks and the Internet. Every computer on the Internet supports TCP/IP.

telephony application program interface (TAPI)
A set of calls that allows applications to control modems and telephones, by routing application function calls to the appropriate "service provider" DLL for a modem.

telnet A protocol used for interactive logon to a remote computer.

thunking A translation process that converts a 16-bit value to its 32-bit equivalent.

TrueType A font specification by which fonts are stored as mathematical models that define the outline of each character.

trust-based security A cross-platform security model that adds intermediate levels of trust to the Java security model.

tunneling The process of sending packets to a computer on a private network by routing them over some other network, such as the Internet.

TWAIN An industry-standard software protocol and API that provides easy integration of image data between input devices, such as scanners and still image digital cameras, and software applications.

TWUNKER A virtual device that allows communications between 32-bit and 16-bit applications.

U

U Interface A 2-wire ISDN circuit, essentially today's standard 1-pair telephone company local loop made of twisted-wire. The U interface is the most common ISDN interface and extends from the central office.

UDF Universal Disk Format. A file system developed by the Optical Storage Technology Association for storage of data on optical media.

UltraPack A file and folder compression format that offers better compression than standard or HiPack compression.

Uniform Resource Locator (URL)
A naming convention that uniquely identifies the location of a computer, directory, or file on the Internet. The URL also specifies the appropriate Internet protocol, such as HTTP or FTP.

Universal naming convention (UNC)
A way to specify a directory on a file server. UNC names are file names or other resource names that begin with the string \\, indicating that they exist on a remote computer.

USB   Universal Serial Bus. A bidirectional, isochronous, dynamically attachable serial interface for adding peripheral devices such as game controllers, serial and parallel ports, and input devices on a single bus.

User   One of three core components in Windows 98. It manages input from input devices, output to the user interface, and interaction with the sound driver, timer, and communications ports.

user profile   User-specific information contained in the file User.dat, which is one of the two files in the Windows 98 registry.

V

VCACHE   A 32-bit, protected-mode cache driver, which replaces the 16-bit, real-mode SMARTDrive disk cache software.

VCOMM   In Windows, a 32-bit protected-mode communications driver.

vector fonts   Fonts rendered from a mathematical model, in which each character is defined as a set of lines drawn between points. Vector fonts can be scaled to any size or aspect ratio.

version table   A file that contains a list of executable files, followed by the version number of MS-DOS with which the applications were designed to run.

Vertical Blanking Interval (VBI)   The time period in which a television signal is not visible on the screen because of the vertical retrace (the repositioning to top of screen to start a new scan). Data services can be transmitted using a portion of this signal.

VFAT   32-Bit File Access using protected-mode code to write to the disk. In Windows 98 the 32-bit virtual File Allocation Table (VFAT) file system is the primary file system.

Video Electronic Standards Association (VESA)
An industry standards organization focusing on IBM-compatible personal computers.

Video Graphics Array (VGA)   A display standard for personal computers.

virtual memory   Memory that appears to an application to be larger and more uniform than it is.

virtual private networking (VPN)   A technology by which one can securely connect to a remote server by tunneling through an intermediary network.

virtualization   The act of managing a system resource so that more than one application can use it at the same time.

VRML   Virtual Reality Modeling Language. A language for coding three-dimensional HTML applications.

VxD   Virtual device driver. The x represents the type of device—for example, a virtual device driver for a display is a VDD and a virtual device driver for a printer is a VPD.

W

WDM   Win32 Driver Model. A 32-bit driver model based on the Windows NT driver model that is designed to provide a common architecture of I/O services for both Windows NT and Windows operating systems for specific classes of drivers.

WDM Streaming (streaming) An extension of the Microsoft DirectShow application programming interface (API) based on the Windows Driver Model (WDM). WDM streaming provides the kernel connection and streaming services used by the WDM streaming class driver and by components of the next major versions of Microsoft Windows NT and Microsoft Windows 98. In these operating systems, WDM streaming provides low-level services in Ring 0 for the lowest latency streaming. DirectShow provides higher-level features and control.

Webcasting The automated delivery of personalized and up-to-date information via the Internet or a corporate intranet.

Win32 Driver Model *See* WDM.

Windows Internet Name Service (WINS) A name resolution service that resolves Windows networking computer names to IP addresses in a routed environment. A WINS server, which is a Windows NT Server computer, handles name registrations, queries, and releases.

Windows NT The portable and secure, 32-bit, preemptive-multitasking member of the Microsoft Windows operating system family. Windows NT Server provides centralized management and security, advanced fault tolerance, and additional connectivity.

Windows NT file system (NTFS) The file system designed for use specifically with the Windows NT operating system. NTFS supports file system recovery and extremely large storage media, in addition to other advantages. It also supports object-oriented applications by treating all files as objects with user-defined and system-defined attributes.

wizard An interactive Help utility within an application that guides the user through each step of a particular task.

Workgroup Advertising A method of implementing browsing for large NetWare networks that include computers running Windows 98 or Windows 95.

World Wide Web (WWW) Also called the Web. The graphical Internet hypertext service that uses the HTTP protocol to retrieve Web pages and other resources from Web servers. Pages on the Web usually contain hyperlinks to other pages, documents, and files.

write-behind caching Temporarily storing data in memory before it is written on disk for permanent storage.

Z

Zero Administration Initiative for Windows An initiative to establish a management infrastructure in Microsoft Windows that will allow managers to automate processes and more effectively exercise centralized management.

Index

Note: An italic page number reference indicates a figure or a table.

Microsoft Press has titles to help everyone— from new users to seasoned developers—

Step by Step Series
Self-paced tutorials for classroom instruction or individualized study

Starts Here™ Series
Interactive instruction on CD-ROM that helps students learn by doing

Field Guide Series
Concise, task-oriented A–Z references for quick, easy answers—anywhere

Official Series
Timely books on a wide variety of Internet topics geared for advanced users

All User Training

All User Reference

Quick Course® Series
Fast, to-the-point instruction for new users

At a Glance Series
Quick visual guides for task-oriented instruction

Select Editions Series
A comprehensive curriculum alternative to standard documentation books

start faster and go farther!

The wide selection of books and CD-ROMs published by Microsoft Press contain something for every level of user and every area of interest, from just-in-time online training tools to development tools for professional programmers. Look for them at your bookstore or computer store today!

Professional Select Editions Series
Advanced titles geared for the system administrator or technical support career path

Microsoft Certified Professional Training
The Microsoft Official Curriculum for certification exams

Best Practices Series
Candid accounts of the new movement in software development

Microsoft Programming Series
The foundations of software development

Professional   Developers

Microsoft Press® Interactive
Integrated multimedia courseware for all levels

Strategic Technology Series
Easy-to-read overviews for decision makers

Microsoft Professional Editions
Technical information straight from the source

Solution Developer Series
Comprehensive titles for intermediate to advanced developers

The *professional's companion* to Microsoft **Internet Explorer 4.**

Microsoft Professional Edition

Covers Microsoft Internet Explorer 4 and Microsoft NetMeeting 2.1

Includes Microsoft NetMeeting 2.1

Microsoft **Internet Explorer ResourceKit**

Comprehensive Resource Guide, Tools, and Utilities for Internet Explorer 4

Microsoft Press

U.S.A.	**$49.99**
U.K.	£46.99 [V.A.T. included]
Canada	$71.99
ISBN 1-57231-842-2	

This exclusive Microsoft® collection provides complete technical information on Microsoft Internet Explorer version 4.0 for the network administrator, the support professional, and the internet service provider. The MICROSOFT INTERNET EXPLORER RESOURCE KIT gives you a technical resource guide packed with authoritative information and an indispensable CD-ROM containing Microsoft Internet Explorer 4, the Microsoft Internet Explorer Administration Kit, valuable utilities, accessory programs, and source code that help you save time and accomplish more—all of which makes it easier for you to deploy and support customized versions of Internet Explorer in your organization.

Microsoft Press

IMPORTANT – READ CAREFULLY BEFORE OPENING SOFTWARE PACKET(S). By opening the sealed packet(s) containing the software, you indicate your acceptance of the following Microsoft License Agreement.

MICROSOFT LICENSE AGREEMENT

(Microsoft Windows 98 Resource Kit Companion CD)

END-USER LICENSE AGREEMENT FOR MICROSOFT SOFTWARE

IMPORTANT—READ CAREFULLY: This Microsoft End-User License Agreement ("EULA") is a legal agreement between you (either an individual or a single entity) and Microsoft Corporation for the Microsoft software product identified above, which includes computer software and may include associated media, printed materials, and "online" or electronic documentation ("SOFTWARE PRODUCT"). The SOFTWARE PRODUCT also includes any updates and supplements to the original SOFT-WARE PRODUCT provided to you by Microsoft. Any software provided along with the SOFTWARE PRODUCT that is associated with a separate end-user license agreement is licensed to you under the terms of that license agreement. By installing, copying, or otherwise using the SOFTWARE PRODUCT, you agree to be bound by the terms of this EULA. If you do not agree to the terms of this EULA, do not install or use the SOFTWARE PRODUCT; you may, however, return it to your place of purchase for a full refund.

SOFTWARE PRODUCT LICENSE

The SOFTWARE PRODUCT is protected by United States copyright laws and international copyright treaties, as well as other intellectual property laws and treaties. The SOFTWARE PRODUCT is licensed, not sold.

1. **GRANT OF LICENSE.** This EULA grants you the following rights:
   - **Installation and Use.** Except as otherwise provided herein, you, as an individual may install and use copies of the SOFT-WARE PRODUCT on an unlimited number of computers, including workstations, terminals or other electronic devices ("Computer(s)") provided that you are the only individual using the SOFTWARE PRODUCT. If you are an entity, you may designate one individual within your organization to have the right to use the SOFTWARE PRODUCT in the manner provided above. The SOFTWARE PRODUCT is in "use" on a Computer when it is loaded into temporary memory (i.e., RAM) or in-stalled into permanent memory (e.g., hard disk, CD-ROM, or other storage device) of that Computer.
   - **Client/Server Software.** The SOFTWARE PRODUCT may contain one or more components which consist of both the fol-lowing types of software: "Server Software" that is installed and provides services on a computer acting as a server ("Server"); and "Client Software" that allows a Computer to access or utilize the services provided by the Server Software. If the compo-nent of the SOFTWARE PRODUCT consists of both Server Software and Client Software which are used together, you may also install and use copies of such Client Software on Computers within your organization and which are connected to your internal network. Such Computers running this Client Software may be used by more than one individual.
   - **Windows Report Tool Component.** *Sample Code.* You may modify the source code portions of the Windows Report Tool Component designated as "Sample Code" in the \diagnose\winrep\sample file to customize the Windows Report Tool feature of Windows 98. You may use such Sample Code only on Computers within your organization and which are connected to your internal network.

2. **DESCRIPTION OF OTHER RIGHTS AND LIMITATIONS.**
   - **Limitations on Reverse Engineering, Decompilation, and Disassembly.** You may not reverse engineer, decompile, or disas-semble the SOFTWARE PRODUCT, except and only to the extent that such activity is expressly permitted by applicable law notwithstanding this limitation.
   - **Rental.** You may not rent, lease or lend the SOFTWARE PRODUCT.
   - **Support Services.** Microsoft may provide you with support services related to the SOFTWARE PRODUCT ("Support Ser-vices"). Use of Support Services is governed by the Microsoft polices and programs described in the user manual, in "online" documentation and/or other Microsoft-provided materials. Any supplemental software code provided to you as part of the Support Services shall be considered part of the SOFTWARE PRODUCT and subject to the terms and conditions of this EULA. With respect to technical information you provide to Microsoft as part of the Support Services, Microsoft may use such infor-mation for its business purposes, including for product support and development. Microsoft will not utilize such technical information in a form that personally identifies you.
   - **Termination.** Without prejudice to any other rights, Microsoft may terminate this EULA if you fail to comply with the terms and conditions of this EULA. In such event, you must destroy all copies of the SOFTWARE PRODUCT and all of its component parts.

3. **COPYRIGHT.**

   All title and copyrights in and to the SOFTWARE PRODUCT (including but not limited to any images, photographs, animations, video, audio, music, text, and "applets" incorporated into the SOFTWARE PRODUCT), the accompanying printed materials, and any copies of the SOFTWARE PRODUCT are owned by Microsoft or its suppliers. The SOFTWARE PRODUCT is protected by United States copyright laws and international treaty provisions. Therefore, you must treat the SOFTWARE PRODUCT like any other copyrighted material **except** that you may either (a) make one copy of the SOFTWARE PRODUCT solely for backup or archi-val purposes or (b) install the SOFTWARE PRODUCT on a single Computer provided you keep the original solely for backup or archival purposes. You may not copy the printed materials accompanying the SOFTWARE PRODUCT.

4. U.S. GOVERNMENT RESTRICTED RIGHTS.

The SOFTWARE PRODUCT and documentation are provided with RESTRICTED RIGHTS. Use, duplication, or disclosure by the Government is subject to restrictions as set forth in subparagraph (c)(1)(ii) of the Rights in Technical Data and Computer Software clause at DFARS 252.227-7013 or subparagraphs (c)(1) and (2) of the Commercial Computer Software—Restricted Rights at 48 CFR 52.227-19, as applicable. Manufacturer is Microsoft Corporation/One Microsoft Way/Redmond, WA 98052-6399.

5. EXPORT RESTRICTIONS.

You agree that you will not export or re-export the SOFTWARE PRODUCT, any part thereof, or any process or service that is the direct product of the SOFTWARE PRODUCT (the foregoing collectively referred to as the "Restricted Components"), to any country, person, entity or end user subject to U.S. export restrictions. You specifically agree not to export or re-export any of the Restricted Components (i) to any country to which the U.S. has embargoed or restricted the export of goods or services, which currently include, but are not necessarily limited to Cuba, Iran, Iraq, Libya, North Korea, Sudan and Syria, or to any national of any such country, wherever located, who intends to transmit or transport the products back to such country; (ii) to any end-user who you know or have reason to know will utilize the Restricted Components in the design, development or production of nuclear, chemical or biological weapons; or (iii) to any end-user who has been prohibited from participating in U.S. export transactions by any federal agency of the U.S. government. You warrant and represent that neither the BXA nor any other U.S. federal agency has suspended, revoked or denied your export privileges.

6. NOTE ON JAVA SUPPORT.

THE SOFTWARE PRODUCT MAY CONTAIN SUPPORT FOR PROGRAMS WRITTEN IN JAVA. JAVA TECHNOLOGY IS NOT FAULT TOLERANT AND IS NOT DESIGNED, MANUFACTURED, OR INTENDED FOR USE OR RESALE AS ONLINE CONTROL EQUIPMENT IN HAZARDOUS ENVIRONMENTS REQUIRING FAIL-SAFE PERFORMANCE, SUCH AS IN THE OPERATION OF NUCLEAR FACILITIES, AIRCRAFT NAVIGATION OR COMMUNICATION SYSTEMS, AIR TRAFFIC CONTROL, DIRECT LIFE SUPPORT MACHINES, OR WEAPONS SYSTEMS, IN WHICH THE FAILURE OF JAVA TECHNOLOGY COULD LEAD DIRECTLY TO DEATH, PERSONAL INJURY, OR SEVERE PHYSICAL OR ENVIRONMENTAL DAMAGE.

MISCELLANEOUS

If you acquired this product in the United States, this EULA is governed by the laws of the State of Washington.

If you acquired this product in Canada, this EULA is governed by the laws of the Province of Ontario, Canada. In such case, each of the parties hereto irrevocably attorns to the jurisdiction of the courts of the Province of Ontario and further agrees to commence any litigation which may arise hereunder in the courts located in the Judicial District of York, Province of Ontario.

If this product was acquired outside the United States, then local law may apply.

Should you have any questions concerning this EULA, or if you desire to contact Microsoft for any reason, please contact the Microsoft subsidiary serving your country, or write: Microsoft Sales Information Center/One Microsoft Way/Redmond, WA 98052-6399.

LIMITED WARRANTY

NO WARRANTIES. Microsoft expressly disclaims any warranty for the Software Product. THE SOFTWARE PRODUCT AND ANY RELATED DOCUMENTATION IS PROVIDED "AS IS" WITHOUT WARRANTY OR CONDITION OF ANY KIND, EITHER EXPRESS OR IMPLIED, INCLUDING, WITHOUT LIMITATION, THE IMPLIED WARRANTIES AND CONDITIONS OF MERCHANTABILITY, FITNESS FOR A PARTICULAR PURPOSE, OR NONINFRINGEMENT. THE ENTIRE RISK ARISING OUT OF USE OR PERFORMANCE OF THE SOFTWARE PRODUCT REMAINS WITH YOU.

NO LIABILITY FOR DAMAGES. In no event shall Microsoft or its suppliers be liable for any damages whatsoever (including, without limitation, damages for loss of business profits, business interruption, loss of business information, or any other pecuniary loss) arising out of the use of or inability to use this Microsoft product, even if Microsoft has been advised of the possibility of such damages. In any case, Microsoft's entire liability under any provision of this EULA shall be limited to the greater of the amount actually paid by you for the Software Product or U.S. $5.00. Because some states/jurisdictions do not allow the exclusion or limitation of liability for consequential or incidental damages, the above limitation may not apply to you.

Si vous avez acquis votre produit Microsoft au CANADA, la garantie limitée suivante vous concerne :

GARANTIE LIMITÉE

EXCLUSION DE GARANTIES.

Microsoft exclut expressément toute garantie relativement au LOGICIEL. Le LOGICIEL et toute documentation s'y rapportant sont fournis « tels quels » sans aucune garantie ou condition quelle qu'elle soit, expresse ou implicite, y compris, mais sans limitation, toute garantie et condition implicite de qualité marchande, d'adaptation à un usage particulier ou d'absence de violation des droits des tiers. Le risque total découlant de l'utilisation ou de la performance du LOGICIEL est entre vos mains.

ABSENCE DE RESPONSABILITÉ POUR LES DOMMAGES.

Microsoft ou ses fournisseurs ne pourront être tenus responsables en aucune circonstance de tout dommage quel qu'il soit (y compris mais sans limitation, les dommages directs ou indirects causés par la perte de bénéfices commerciaux, l'interruption des affaires, la perte d'information commerciale ou toute autre perte pécuniaire) résultant de l'utilisation ou de l'impossibilité d'utiliser ce LOGICIEL, et ce, même Microsoft a été avisée de l'éventualité de tels dommages. La responsabilité de Microsoft en vertu de toute disposition de cette convention ne pourra en aucun temps excéder le plus élevé entre i) le montant réellement payé par vous pour le LOGICIEL ou ii) 5,00 $ US. Parce que certains états/juridictions ne permettent pas l'exclusion ou la limitation de responsabilité relative aux dommages indirects ou accessoires, la limitation ci-dessus peut ne pas s'appliquer à votre égard.

DROITS LIMITÉS DU GOUVERNEMENT AMÉRICAIN

Le LOGICIEL et la documentation sont offerts avec des DROITS LIMITÉS. L'utilisation, la reproduction ou la divulgation par le gouvernement sont sujettes aux restrictions énoncées au sous-alinéa (c)(1)(ii) de The Right in Technical Data and Computer Software, clause au DFARS 252.227-7013 ou aux sous-alinéas (c)(1) et (2) de Commercial Computer Software — Droits limités au 48 CFR 52.227-19, tel qu'applicable. Microsoft Corporation, One Microsoft Way, Redmond, Washington 98052-6399 est le fabricant.

La présente Convention est régie par les lois en vigueur dans la province d'Ontario, Canada. Chacune des parties à la présente reconnaît irrévocablement la compétence des tribunaux de la province d'Ontario et consent à instituer tout litige qui pourrait découler de la présente auprès des tribunaux situés dans le district judiciaire de York, province d'Ontario.

Si vous avez des questions concernant cette licence ou si vous désirez communiquer avec Microsoft pour quelque raison que ce soit, veuillez contacter la succursale Microsoft desservant votre pays, ou écrire à: Microsoft Sales Information Center, One Microsoft Way, Redmond, Washington 98052-6399.

Register Today!

Return this *Microsoft® Windows® 98 Resource Kit* registration card
for a Microsoft Press® catalog. Discover Microsoft Press ResourceLink—the
"essential extension" to Microsoft Press Resource Kits—with fast and easy access
to the most up-to-date content, tools, and utilities directly from the source.
Check it out now at http://mspress.microsoft.com/reslink/

Microsoft®Press

mspress.microsoft.com

OWNER REGISTRATION CARD

1-57231-644-6

Microsoft® Windows® 98
Resource Kit

FIRST NAME   MIDDLE INITIAL   LAST NAME

INSTITUTION OR COMPANY NAME

ADDRESS

CITY   STATE   ZIP

( )

E-MAIL ADDRESS   PHONE NUMBER

For more information about Microsoft Press® products, visit our Web site at

mspress.microsoft.com

Microsoft Press